C0-ALX-789

Nineteenth-Century Literature Criticism

Guide to Gale Literary Criticism Series

When you need to review criticism of literary works, these are the Gale series to use:

If the author's death date is:	You should turn to:
After Dec. 31, 1959 (or author is still living)	***CONTEMPORARY LITERARY CRITICISM*** for example: Jorge Luis Borges, Anthony Burgess, William Faulkner, Mary Gordon, Ernest Hemingway, Iris Murdoch
1900 through 1959	***TWENTIETH-CENTURY LITERARY CRITICISM*** for example: Willa Cather, F. Scott Fitzgerald, Henry James, Mark Twain, Virginia Woolf
1800 through 1899	***NINETEENTH-CENTURY LITERATURE CRITICISM*** for example: Fedor Dostoevski, Nathaniel Hawthorne, George Sand, William Wordsworth
1400 through 1799	***LITERATURE CRITICISM FROM 1400 TO 1800 (excluding Shakespeare)*** for example: Anne Bradstreet, Daniel Defoe, Alexander Pope, François Rabelais, Jonathan Swift, Phillis Wheatley
	SHAKESPEAREAN CRITICISM Shakespeare's plays and poetry
Antiquity through 1399	***CLASSICAL AND MEDIEVAL LITERATURE CRITICISM*** for example: Dante, Homer, Plato, Sophocles, Vergil, the Beowulf Poet

---

Gale also publishes related criticism series:

CHILDREN'S LITERATURE REVIEW

This series covers authors of all eras who write for the preschool through high school audience.

SHORT STORY CRITICISM

This series covers the major short fiction writers of all nationalities and periods of literary history.

ISSN 0732-1864

Volume 21

Nineteenth-Century Literature Criticism

Excerpts from Criticism of the Works of Novelists, Poets, Playwrights, Short Story Writers, Philosophers, and Other Creative Writers Who Died between 1800 and 1899, from the First Published Critical Appraisals to Current Evaluations

Janet Mullane
Robert Thomas Wilson
Editors

Robin DuBlanc
Associate Editor

STAFF

Janet Mullane, Robert Thomas Wilson, *Editors*

Robin DuBlanc, *Associate Editor*

Rachel Carlson, *Senior Assistant Editor*

Grace Jeromski, Ronald S. Nixon, *Assistant Editors*

Cherie D. Abbey, Paula Kepos, Thomas Ligotti, Joann Prosyniuk, Laurie A. Sherman,
Emily B. Tennyson, *Contributing Editors*
Denise Michlewicz Broderick, Melissa Reiff Hug, Jane C. Thacker, Debra A. Wells,
Contributing Assistant Editors

Jeanne A. Gough, *Permissions & Production Manager*
Lizbeth A. Purdy, *Production Supervisor*
athy Beranek, Christine A. Galbraith, David G. Oblender, Suzanne Powers, Linda M. Ro
Kristine E. Tipton, Lee Ann Welsh, *Editorial Assistants*
Linda Marcella Pugliese, *Manuscript Coordinator*
Maureen A. Puhl, *Senior Manuscript Assistant*
Donna Craft, Jennifer E. Gale, *Manuscript Assistants*

Victoria B. Cariappa, *Research Supervisor*
Maureen R. Richards, *Research Coordinator*
Mary D. Wise, *Senior Research Assistant*
Joyce E. Doyle, Rogene M. Fisher, Kevin B. Hillstrom, Karen O. Kaus, Eric Priehs,
Filomena Sgambati, *Research Assistants*

Janice M. Mach, *Text Permissions Supervisor*
Kathy Grell, *Text Permissions Coordinator*
Mabel E. Gurney, *Research Permissions Coordinator*
Josephine M. Keene, *Senior Permissions Assistant*
H. Diane Cooper, Kimberly F. Smilay, *Permissions Assistants*
Melissa A. Brantley, Denise M. Singleton, Lisa M. Wimmer, *Permissions Clerks*

Patricia A. Seefelt, *Picture Permissions Supervisor*
Margaret A. Chamberlain, *Picture Permissions Coordinator*
Pamela A. Hayes, Lillian Quickley, *Permissions Clerks*

The paper used in this publication meets the minimum requirements of American National Standard for Information Sciences—Permanence Paper for Printed Library Materials, ANSI Z39.48-1984. ™

Library of Congress Catalog Card Number 81-6943
ISBN 0-8103-5821-2
ISSN 0732-1864

Printed in the United States of America.

Published simultaneously in the United Kingdom
by Gale Research International Limited
(An affiliated company of Gale Research Inc.)

10 9 8 7 6 5 4 3

Contents

Preface vii

Authors to Be Featured in Upcoming Volumes xi

Additional Authors to Appear in Future Volumes xiii

Acknowledgments 463

Emily Dickinson 1830-1886 1

Fedor Mikhailovich Dostoevski 1821-1881 87

Adam Lindsay Gordon 1833-1870 148

Victor Marie Hugo 1802-1885 189

Fitz-James O'Brien 1828?-1862 233

Sándor Petőfi 1823-1849 256

Lydia Sigourney 1791-1865 288

Henry David Thoreau 1817-1862 317

Ivan Turgenev 1818-1883 374

Preface

The nineteenth century was a time of tremendous growth in human endeavor: in science, in social history, and particularly in literature. The era saw the development of the novel, witnessed radical changes from classicism to romanticism to realism, and fostered intellectual and artistic ideas that continue to inspire authors of our own century. The importance of the writers of the nineteenth century is twofold, for they provide insight into their own time as well as into the universal nature of human experience.

The literary criticism of an era can also give us insight into the moral and intellectual atmosphere of the past because the criteria by which a work of art is judged reflect current philosophical and social attitudes. Literary criticism takes many forms: the traditional essay, the book or play review, even the parodic poem. Criticism can also be of several types: normative, descriptive, interpretive, textual, appreciative, generic. Collectively, the range of critical response helps us to understand a work of art, an author, an era.

Scope of the Series

Nineteenth-Century Literature Criticism (NCLC) is designed to serve as an introduction for the student of nineteenth-century literature to the authors of that period and to the most significant commentators on these authors. Since the analysis of this literature spans almost two hundred years, a vast amount of critical material confronts the student. For that reason, *NCLC* presents significant passages from published criticism to aid students in the location and selection of commentaries on authors who died between 1800 and 1899. The need for *NCLC* was suggested by the usefulness of the Gale series *Twentieth-Century Literary Criticism (TCLC)* and *Contemporary Literary Criticism (CLC),* which excerpt criticism of creative writing of the twentieth century. For further information about *TCLC, CLC,* and Gale's other criticism series, users should consult the Guide to Gale Literary Criticism Series preceding the title page in this volume.

Each volume of *NCLC* is carefully compiled to include authors who represent a variety of genres and nationalities and who are currently regarded as the most important writers of their era. In addition to major authors who have attained worldwide renown, *NCLC* also presents criticism on lesser-known figures, many from non-English-speaking countries, whose significant contributions to literary history are important to the study of nineteenth-century literature. These authors are important artists in their own right and often enjoy such an immense popularity in their original language that English-speaking readers could benefit from a knowledge of their work.

Author entries in *NCLC* are intended to be definitive overviews. In order to devote more attention to each writer, approximately ten to fifteen authors are included in each 600-page volume, compared with about forty authors in a *CLC* volume of similar size. The length of each author entry is intended to reflect the amount of attention the author has received from critics writing in English and from foreign critics in translation. Articles and books that have not been translated into English are excluded. However, since many of the major foreign studies have been translated into English and are excerpted in *NCLC,* author entries reflect the viewpoints of many nationalities. Each author entry represents a historical overview of critical reaction to the author's work: early criticism is presented to indicate initial responses, later selections represent any rise or decline in the author's literary reputation, and current analyses provide students with a modern perspective. In each entry, we have attempted to identify and include excerpts from all seminal essays of criticism.

An author may appear more than once in the series because of the great quantity of critical material available or because of a resurgence of criticism generated by events such as an author's centennial or anniversary celebration, the republication or posthumous publication of an author's works, or the publication of a newly translated work. Usually, one or more author entries in each volume of *NCLC* are devoted to individual works or groups of works by major authors who have appeared previously in the series. Only those works that have been the subjects of extensive criticism and are widely studied in literature courses are selected for this in-depth treatment. Fedor Dostoevski's *Besy (The Possessed),* Victor Hugo's *Notre-Dame de Paris (The Hunchback of Notre-Dame),* and Henry David Thoreau's "Civil Disobedience" are the subjects of such entries in *NCLC,* Volume 21.

Organization of the Book

An author entry consists of the following elements: author heading, biographical and critical introduction, principal works, excerpts of criticism (each preceded by explanatory notes and followed by a bibliographical citation), and an additional bibliography for further reading.

- The *author heading* consists of the author's full name, followed by birth and death dates. The unbracketed portion of the name denotes the form under which the author most commonly wrote. If an author wrote consistently under a pseudonym, the pseudonym will be listed in the author heading and the real name given in parentheses on the first line of the biographical and critical introduction. Also located at the beginning of the introduction are any name variations under which an author wrote, including transliterated forms for authors whose languages use nonroman alphabets. Uncertainty as to a birth or death date is indicated by a question mark.
- A *portrait* of the author is included when available. Many entries also feature illustrations of materials pertinent to an author's career, including manuscript pages, letters, book illustrations, and representations of important people, places, and events in an author's life.
- The *biographical and critical introduction* contains background information that introduces the reader to an author and to the critical debate surrounding his or her work. When applicable, biographical and critical introductions are followed by references to additional entries on the author in other literary reference series published by Gale Research Inc., including *Dictionary of Literary Biography, Children's Literature Review,* and *Something about the Author.*
- The list of *principal works* is chronological by date of first book publication and identifies the genre of each work. In those instances where the first publication was in a language other than English, the title and date of the first English-language edition are given in brackets. Unless otherwise indicated, dramas are dated by the first performance, rather than first publication.
- *Criticism* is arranged chronologically in each author entry to provide a useful perspective on changes in critical evaluation over the years. All titles by the author featured in the critical entry are printed in boldface type to enable the user to ascertain without difficulty the works being discussed. Also for purposes of easier identification, the critic's name and the publication date of the essay are given at the beginning of each piece of criticism. Unsigned criticism is preceded by the title of the journal in which it appeared. When an anonymous essay is later attributed to a critic, the critic's name appears in brackets at the beginning of the excerpt and in the bibliographical citation. Publication information (such as publisher names and book prices) and parenthetical numerical references (such as footnotes or page and line references to specific editions of works) have been deleted at the editor's discretion to provide smoother reading of the text.
- Critical essays are prefaced with *explanatory notes* as an additional aid to students using *NCLC.* The explanatory notes provide several types of useful information, including the reputation of the critic; the importance of a work of criticism; a synopsis of the essay; the specific approach of the critic (biographical, psychoanalytic, structuralist, etc.); and the growth of critical controversy or changes in critical trends regarding an author's work. In some cases, these notes include cross-references to related criticism in the author's entry or in the additional bibliography. Dates in parentheses within the explanatory notes refer to the year of a book publication when they follow a book title and to the date of an excerpt included in the entry when they follow a critic's name.
- A complete *bibliographical citation* designed to facilitate the location of the original essay or book follows each piece of criticism.
- The *additional bibliography* appearing at the end of each author entry suggests further reading on the author. In some cases it includes essays for which the editors could not obtain reprint rights.

An Acknowledgments section lists the copyright holders who have granted permission to reprint material in this volume of *NCLC.* It does not, however, list every book or periodical reprinted or consulted for the volume.

Cumulative Indexes

Each volume of *NCLC* includes a cumulative index listing all the authors who have appeared in *Contemporary Literary Criticism, Twentieth-Century Literary Criticism, Nineteenth-Century Literature Criticism, Literature Criticism from 1400 to 1800, Classical and Medieval Literature Criticism,* and *Short Story Criticism,* along with cross-references to the Gale series *Children's Literature Review, Authors in the News, Contemporary Authors, Contemporary Authors Autobiography Series, Dictionary of Literary Biography, Concise Dictionary of American Literary Biography, Something about the Author, Something about the Author Autobiography Series,* and *Yesterday's Authors of Books for Children.* Readers will welcome this cumulated author index as a useful tool for locating an author within the various series. The index, which lists birth and death dates when available, will be particularly valuable for those authors who are identified with a certain period but whose death dates cause them to be placed in another, or for those authors whose careers span two periods. For example, Fedor Dostoevski is found in *NCLC,* yet Leo Tolstoy, another major nineteenth-century Russian novelist, is found in *TCLC* because he died after 1899.

Each volume of *NCLC* also includes a cumulative nationality index to authors. Authors are listed alphabetically by nationality, followed by the volume numbers in which they appear.

Title Index

An important feature of *NCLC* is a cumulative title index, an alphabetical listing of the literary works discussed in the series since its inception. Each title listing includes the corresponding volume and page numbers where criticism may be located. Foreign language titles may be followed by the titles of English translations of these works or by English-language equivalents of these titles provided by critics. Page numbers following these translation titles refer to all pages on which any form of the title, either foreign language or translation, appears. Titles of novels, dramas, nonfiction books, and poetry, short story, or essay collections are printed in italics, while all individual poems, short stories, and essays are printed in roman type within quotation marks. In cases where the same title is used by different authors, the author's surname is given in parentheses after the title, e.g., *Poems* (Wordsworth) and *Poems* (Coleridge).

Acknowledgments

No work of this scope can be accomplished without the cooperation of many people. The editors especially wish to thank the copyright holders of the excerpted criticism included in this volume, the permissions managers of many book and magazine publishing companies for assisting us in securing reprint rights, and Anthony Bogucki for assistance with copyright research. We are also grateful to the staffs of the Detroit Public Library, the Library of Congress, University of Michigan Library, and Wayne State University Library for making their resources available to us.

Suggestions Are Welcome

In response to various suggestions, several features have been added to *NCLC* since the series began, including: explanatory notes to excerpted criticism that provide important information regarding critics and their work; a cumulative author index listing authors in all Gale literary criticism series; entries devoted to criticism on a single work by a major author; more extensive illustrations; and a cumulative title index listing all the literary works discussed in the series.

The editors welcome additional comments and suggestions for expanding the coverage and enhancing the usefulness of the series.

Authors to Be Featured in Upcoming Volumes

Charles Brockden Brown (American novelist, essayist, short story writer, and pamphleteer)—Considered an important, if minor, American novelist, Brown drew from the Gothic and sentimental literary traditions to create powerful novels of intellectual and psychological exploration. One of the first Americans to gain a significant audience abroad and to support himself by his writing, Brown has often been called the first professional writer in America.

Thomas Carlyle (Scottish philosopher, historian, essayist, and critic)—Carlyle was a central figure of the Victorian age in England and Scotland. Known to his contemporaries as the "sage of Chelsea," he was a satirical and trenchant commentator on the social, spiritual, and political issues of the day. His unique, hard-hitting prose style, which has both infuriated and impressed critics from the nineteenth century to the present, suits the iconoclasm and moralistic fervor of such important and controversial works as *Sartor Resartus, Latter-Day Pamphlets,* and *The French Revolution.*

George Eliot (English novelist, essayist, poet, editor, short story writer, and translator)—*NCLC* will present a critical entry on *Daniel Deronda,* Eliot's final novel. In the interrelated stories of its two principal characters—the self-confident yet unhappy Gwendolen Harleth and the mysterious, compelling Zionist Deronda—the novel reveals the hallmarks of Eliot's fiction: penetrating psychological analysis and insight into human character.

Johann Wolfgang von Goethe (German poet, novelist, dramatist, short story and novella writer, essayist, and critic)— Often judged Germany's greatest writer, Goethe was a shaping force in the major literary movements of the late eighteenth and early nineteenth centuries. His first novel, *The Sorrows of Young Werther,* which recounts the despair and eventual suicide of a young artist in love with another man's wife, epitomizes the *Sturm und Drang* movement. This intensely emotional work created a sensation throughout Europe and will be the subject of an entire entry in *NCLC.*

Nathaniel Hawthorne (American novelist, short story writer, and essayist)—Considered one of the greatest American authors, Hawthorne is known for his exploration of spiritual and moral themes in the milieu of American Puritanism. *NCLC* will devote an entry to criticism of *The Marble Faun,* a novel unusual among Hawthorne's work in its Italian setting, but characteristic in its probing of the mysterious nature of sin and guilt.

William Hazlitt (English critic and essayist)—Hazlitt was one of the most important and influential commentators during the Romantic age in England. In his literary criticism and miscellaneous prose he combined discerning judgment with strongly stated personal opinion, producing essays noted for their discursive style, evocative descriptions, and urbane wit.

Giacomo Leopardi (Italian poet and essayist)—Considered the greatest Italian poet since Dante, Leopardi was influential in formulating Italian Romanticism. His lyric poems, noted for their haunting beauty and intense despair, suggest the illusory nature of human happiness.

George Henry Lewes (English philosopher, critic, journalist, novelist, and dramatist)—The longtime lover of novelist George Eliot and a significant influence on the development of her fiction, Lewes was a prolific and versatile man of letters in his own right. He wrote philosophical works, scientific studies, dramatic and literary criticism, plays, and novels, and served as editor of two influential periodicals, the *Leader* and the *Fortnightly Review.*

Herman Melville (American novelist, novella and short story writer, and poet)—A major figure in American literature, Melville is recognized for his exploration of complex metaphysical and moral themes in his novels and short fiction. *NCLC* will devote an entry to his novella *Billy Budd,* a symbolic inquiry into the nature of good and evil, innocence and guilt.

John Henry Newman (English theologian and writer)—An influential theologian, Newman was a key figure in the Oxford movement, whose adherents advocated the independence of the Church of England from the state and sought to establish a doctrinal basis for Anglicanism in the Church's evolution from Catholicism. Newman's subsequent conversion to Roman Catholicism inspired his best-known work, *Apologia pro vita sua,* an eloquent spiritual autobiography tracing the development of his beliefs.

Thomas Love Peacock (English novelist, poet, and critic)—Peacock is best remembered for his series of novels satirizing intellectual and artistic thought in England during the first half of the nineteenth century. Considered unique in both form and content, Peacock's novels are especially noted for their erudite, classical style, comic characters, and elements of romance.

Stendhal (French novelist, novella writer, autobiographer, and critic)—Stendhal played an important role in the development of the modern psychological novel. In works that combine elements of both realism and romanticism, Stendhal produced subtle analyses of characters alienated from, yet intimately connected with, their society.

William Makepeace Thackeray (English novelist, essayist, short story, fairy tale, and sketch writer)—Best known for his satiric sketches and novels of upper- and middle-class English life, Thackeray is credited with introducing greater realism and a simpler style to the English novel. While *Vanity Fair* is generally accounted his greatest book, many critics consider *The History of Henry Esmond, Esq.*, a historical novel in autobiographical form, Thackeray's most carefully executed and elegantly written work. *NCLC* will devote an entire entry to *Henry Esmond,* described by Edgar T. Harden as "a work of tantalizing complexity."

Additional Authors to Appear in Future Volumes

About, Edmond François 1828-1885
Aguilo I. Fuster, Maria 1825-1897
Aksakov, Konstantin 1817-1860
Aleardi, Aleardo 1812-1878
Alecsandri, Vasile 1821-1890
Alencar, José 1829-1877
Alfieri, Vittorio 1749-1803
Allingham, William 1824-1889
Almquist, Carl Jonas Love 1793-1866
Alorne, Leonor de Almeida 1750-1839
Alsop, Richard 1761-1815
Altimirano, Ignacio Manuel 1834-1893
Alvarenga, Manuel Inacio da Silva 1749-1814
Alvares de Azevedo, Manuel Antonio 1831-1852
Anzengruber, Ludwig 1839-1889
Arany, Janos 1817-1882
Arène, Paul 1843-1896
Aribau, Bonaventura Carlos 1798-1862
Arjona de Cubas, Manuel Maria de 1771-1820
Arnault, Antoine Vincent 1766-1834
Arneth, Alfred von 1819-1897
Arnim, Bettina von 1785-1859
Arriaza y Superviela, Juan Bautista 1770-1837
Asbjörnsen, Peter Christen 1812-1885
Ascasubi, Hilario 1807-1875
Atterbom, Per Daniel Amadeus 1790-1855
Aubanel, Theodore 1829-1886
Auerbach, Berthold 1812-1882
Augier, Guillaume V.E. 1820-1889
Azeglio, Massimo D' 1798-1866
Azevedo, Guilherme de 1839-1882
Bakin (pseud. of Takizawa Okikani) 1767-1848
Bakunin, Mikhail Aleksandrovich 1814-1876
Baratynski, Jewgenij Abramovich 1800-1844
Barnes, William 1801-1886
Batyushkov, Konstantin 1778-1855
Beattie, James 1735-1803
Becquer, Gustavo Adolfo 1836-1870
Bentham, Jeremy 1748-1832
Béranger, Jean-Pierre de 1780-1857
Berchet, Giovanni 1783-1851
Berzsenyi, Daniel 1776-1836
Black, William 1841-1898
Blair, Hugh 1718-1800
Blicher, Steen Steensen 1782-1848
Bocage, Manuel Maria Barbosa du 1765-1805
Boratynsky, Yevgeny 1800-1844
Borel, Petrus 1809-1859
Boreman, Yokutiel 1825-1890
Borne, Ludwig 1786-1837
Botev, Hristo 1778-1842
Brinckman, John 1814-1870
Brown, Charles Brockden 1777-1810
Büchner, Georg 1813-1837
Campbell, James Edwin 1867-1895
Castelo Branco, Camilo 1825-1890
Castro Alves, Antonio de 1847-1871
Chivers, Thomas Holly 1807?-1858
Claudius, Matthias 1740-1815
Clough, Arthur Hugh 1819-1861
Cobbett, William 1762-1835
Colenso, John William 1814-1883
Coleridge, Hartley 1796-1849
Collett, Camilla 1813-1895
Comte, Auguste 1798-1857
Conrad, Robert T. 1810-1858
Conscience, Hendrik 1812-1883
Cooke, Philip Pendleton 1816-1850
Corbière, Edouard 1845-1875
Crabbe, George 1754-1832
Cruz E Sousa, João da 1861-1898
Desbordes-Valmore, Marceline 1786-1859
Deschamps, Emile 1791-1871
Deus, Joao de 1830-1896
Dinis, Julio 1839-1871
Dinsmoor, Robert 1757-1836
Du Maurier, George 1834-1896
Eminescy, Mihai 1850-1889
Engels, Friedrich 1820-1895
Espronceda, José 1808-1842
Ettinger, Solomon 1799-1855
Euchel, Issac 1756-1804
Ferguson, Samuel 1810-1886
Fernández de Lizardi, José Joaquín 1776-1827
Fernández de Moratín, Leandro 1760-1828
Fet, Afanasy 1820-1892
Feuillet, Octave 1821-1890
Fontane, Theodor 1819-1898
Freiligrath, Hermann Ferdinand 1810-1876
Freytag, Gustav 1816-1895
Ganivet, Angel 1865-1898
Garrett, Almeida 1799-1854
Garshin, Vsevolod Mikhaylovich 1855-1888
Gezelle, Guido 1830-1899
Ghalib, Asadullah Khan 1797-1869
Goldschmidt, Meir Aaron 1819-1887
Goncalves Dias, Antonio 1823-1864
Griboyedov, Aleksander Sergeyevich 1795-1829
Grigor'yev, Appolon Aleksandrovich 1822-1864
Groth, Klaus 1819-1899
Grun, Anastasius (pseud. of Anton Alexander Graf von Auersperg) 1806-1876
Guerrazzi, Francesco Domenico 1804-1873
Gutierrez Najera, Manuel 1859-1895
Gutzkow, Karl Ferdinand 1811-1878
Ha-Kohen, Shalom 1772-1845
Halleck, Fitz-Greene 1790-1867
Harris, George Washington 1814-1869
Hayne, Paul Hamilton 1830-1886
Hazlitt, William 1778-1830
Hebbel, Christian Friedrich 1813-1863
Hebel, Johann Peter 1760-1826
Hegel, Georg Wilhelm Friedrich 1770-1831
Heiberg, Johann Ludvig 1813-1863
Herculano, Alexandre 1810-1866
Hertz, Henrik 1798-1870
Herwegh, Georg 1817-1875
Hoffman, Charles Fenno 1806-1884
Hooper, Johnson Jones 1815-1863
Horton, George Moses 1798-1880
Howitt, William 1792-1879
Hughes, Thomas 1822-1896
Imlay, Gilbert 1754?-1828?
Irwin, Thomas Caulfield 1823-1892
Isaacs, Jorge 1837-1895
Jacobsen, Jens Peter 1847-1885
Jippensha, Ikku 1765-1831
Kant, Immanuel 1724-1804
Karr, Jean Baptiste Alphonse 1808-1890
Keble, John 1792-1866
Khomyakov, Alexey S. 1804-1860
Kierkegaard, Soren 1813-1855
Kinglake, Alexander W. 1809-1891
Kingsley, Charles 1819-1875
Kivi, Alexis 1834-1872
Koltsov, Alexey Vasilyevich 1809-1842
Kotzebue, August von 1761-1819
Kraszewski, Josef Ignacy 1812-1887
Kreutzwald, Friedrich Reinhold 1803-1882
Krochmal, Nahman 1785-1840
Krudener, Valeria Barbara Julia de Wietinghoff 1766-1824
Lampman, Archibald 1861-1899
Lebensohn, Micah Joseph 1828-1852

Leconte de Lisle, Charles-Marie-René 1818-1894
Leontyev, Konstantin 1831-1891
Leskov, Nikolai 1831-1895
Lever, Charles James 1806-1872
Levisohn, Solomon 1789-1822
Lewes, George Henry 1817-1878
Leyden, John 1775-1811
Lobensohn, Micah Gregory 1775-1810
Longstreet, Augustus Baldwin 1790-1870
López de Ayola y Herrera, Adelardo 1819-1871
Lover, Samuel 1797-1868
Luzzato, Samuel David 1800-1865
Macedo, Joaquim Manuel de 1820-1882
Macha, Karel Hynek 1810-1836
Mackenzie, Henry 1745-1831
Malmon, Solomon 1754-1800
Mangan, James Clarence 1803-1849
Manzoni, Alessandro 1785-1873
Marii, Jose 1853-1895
Markovic, Svetozar 1846-1875
Martínez de La Rosa, Francisco 1787-1862
Mathews, Cornelius 1817-1889
McCulloch, Thomas 1776-1843
Merriman, Brian 1747-1805
Meyer, Conrad Ferdinand 1825-1898
Montgomery, James 1771-1854
Morton, Sarah Wentworth 1759-1846
Müller, Friedrich 1749-1825
Murger, Henri 1822-1861
Neruda, Jan 1834-1891
Nestroy, Johann 1801-1862
Niccolini, Giambattista 1782-1861
Nievo, Ippolito 1831-1861
Obradovic, Dositej 1742-1811
Oehlenschlager, Adam 1779-1850
O'Neddy, Philothee (pseud. of Theophile Dondey) 1811-1875
O'Shaughnessy, Arthur William Edgar 1844-1881
Ostrovsky, Alexander 1823-1886
Paine, Thomas 1737-1809
Perk, Jacques 1859-1881
Pisemsky, Alexey F. 1820-1881
Pompeia, Raul D'Avila 1863-1895
Popovic, Jovan Sterija 1806-1856
Praed, Winthrop Mackworth 1802-1839
Prati, Giovanni 1814-1884
Preseren, France 1800-1849
Pringle, Thomas 1789-1834
Procter, Adelaide Ann 1825-1864
Procter, Bryan Waller 1787-1874
Pye, Henry James 1745-1813
Quental, Antero Tarquinio de 1842-1891
Quinet, Edgar 1803-1875
Quintana, Manuel José 1772-1857
Radishchev, Aleksander 1749-1802
Raftery, Anthony 1784-1835
Raimund, Ferdinand 1790-1836
Reid, Mayne 1818-1883
Renan, Ernest 1823-1892
Reuter, Fritz 1810-1874
Rogers, Samuel 1763-1855
Ruckert, Friedrich 1788-1866
Runeberg, Johan 1804-1877
Rydberg, Viktor 1828-1895
Saavedra y Ramírez de Boquedano, Angel de 1791-1865
Sacher-Mosoch, Leopold von 1836-1895
Satanov, Isaac 1732-1805
Schiller, Johann Friedrich von 1759-1805
Schlegel, Karl 1772-1829
Senoa, August 1838-1881
Shulman, Kalman 1819-1899
Silva, Jose Asuncion 1865-1896
Slaveykov, Petko 1828-1895
Smith, Richard Penn 1799-1854
Smolenskin, Peretz 1842-1885
Stagnelius, Erik Johan 1793-1823
Staring, Antonie Christiaan Wynand 1767-1840
Stifter, Adalbert 1805-1868
Stone, John Augustus 1801-1834
Taunay, Alfredo d'Ecragnole 1843-1899
Taylor, Bayard 1825-1878
Tennyson, Alfred, Lord 1809-1892
Terry, Lucy (Lucy Terry Prince) 1730-1821
Thompson, Daniel Pierce 1795-1868
Thompson, Samuel 1766-1816
Tiedge, Christoph August 1752-1841
Timrod, Henry 1828-1867
Tommaseo, Nicolo 1802-1874
Tompa, Mihaly 1817-1888
Topelius, Zachris 1818-1898
Tyutchev, Fedor I. 1803-1873
Uhland, Ludvig 1787-1862
Valaoritis, Aristotelis 1824-1879
Valles, Jules 1832-1885
Verde, Cesario 1855-1886
Villaverde, Cirilio 1812-1894
Vinje, Aasmund Olavsson 1818-1870
Vorosmarty, Mihaly 1800-1855
Weisse, Christian Felix 1726-1804
Welhaven, Johan S. 1807-1873
Werner, Zacharius 1768-1823
Wescott, Edward Noyes 1846-1898
Wessely, Nattali Herz 1725-1805
Woolson, Constance Fenimore 1840-1894
Zhukovsky, Vasily 1783-1852

Emily (Elizabeth) Dickinson

1830-1886

American poet.

Dickinson is regarded as one of the greatest American poets. Although almost none of her poems were published during her lifetime and her work drew harsh criticism when it first appeared, many of her short lyrics on the subjects of nature, love, death, and immortality are now considered among the most emotionally and intellectually profound in the English language. Dickinson's forthright examination of her philosophical and religious skepticism, her unorthodox attitude toward her sex and calling, and her distinctive style—characterized by elliptical, compressed expression, striking imagery, and innovative poetic structure—have earned widespread acclaim, and, in addition, her poems have become some of the best loved in American literature. Today, an increasing number of studies from diverse critical viewpoints are devoted to her life and works, thus securing Dickinson's status as a major poet.

Dickinson was born 10 December 1830 in Amherst, Massachusetts, where she lived her entire life. Her father, Edward Dickinson, was a prosperous lawyer who served as treasurer of Amherst College and who also held various political offices. Her mother, Emily Norcross Dickinson, has been described as a quiet and unassuming woman who was frail in health. Dickinson's formal education began in 1835 with four years of primary school. She then attended Amherst Academy from 1840 to 1847 before spending a year at Mount Holyoke Female Seminary. Her studies, including courses in the sciences, literature, history, and philosophy, were largely informed by New England Puritanism, with its doctrines of a sovereign God and the necessity of personal salvation. Dickinson, however, was unable to accept the teachings of the Unitarian church attended by her family, and despite her desire to experience a religious awakening, remained agnostic throughout her life.

Following the completion of her education, Dickinson lived in the family home with her parents and younger sister, Lavinia, while her older brother, Austin, and his wife, Susan, lived next door. Although the details of her life are vague, scholars believe Dickinson first began writing poetry in earnest in the early 1850s. Her otherwise quiet life was punctuated by brief trips to Boston, Washington, D.C., and Philadelphia in the years from 1851 to 1855. Biographers speculate that during one stay in Philadelphia Dickinson fell in love with a married minister, the Reverend Charles Wadsworth, and that her disappointment in love triggered her subsequent withdrawal from society. While this and other suggestions of tragic romantic attachments are largely conjecture, it is known that Dickinson became increasingly reclusive in the following years, spending her time primarily in domestic routine and on long solitary walks with her dog, Carlo.

Biographers generally agree that Dickinson experienced an emotional crisis of an undetermined nature in the early 1860s. Her distressed state of mind is believed to have inspired her to write prolifically: in 1862 alone she is thought to have composed over three hundred poems. In the same year, Dickinson initiated a correspondence with Thomas Wentworth Higginson, the literary editor of the *Atlantic Monthly*. During the course of their lengthy exchange, Dickinson sent nearly one hundred of her poems for his criticism. While Higginson had little influence on her writing, he was important to her as a sympathetic adviser and confidant. Dickinson's reclusiveness intensified following 1869, and her refusal to leave her home or to meet visitors, her gnomic sayings, and her habit of always wearing a white dress earned her a reputation for eccentricity among her neighbors. Her intellectual and social isolation further increased when her father died unexpectedly in 1874 and she was left with the care of her invalid mother. The death of her mother in 1882, followed two years later by the death of Judge Otis P. Lord, a close family friend and Dickinson's most satisfying romantic attachment, contributed to the onset of what Dickinson described as an "attack of nerves." Later, in 1886, she was diagnosed as having Bright's disease, a kidney dysfunction that resulted in her death in May of that year.

Only seven of Dickinson's poems were published during her lifetime, all anonymously and some apparently without her consent. The editors of the periodicals in which her lyrics appeared made significant alterations to them in an attempt to regularize the meter and grammar, thereby discouraging Dickinson from seeking further publication. Subsequently, her poems found only a private audience among her correspondents, family, and old school friends. Her family, however, was unaware of the enormous quantity of verse that she composed. After

Dickinson's death, her sister Lavinia was astounded to discover hundreds of poems among her possessions. Many were copied into "fascicles," booklets formed from sheets of paper stitched together, but a large number appeared to be mere jottings recorded on scraps of paper. Dickinson in many instances abandoned poems in an unfinished state, leaving no indication of her final choice between alternate words or phrases.

Despite the disordered state of the manuscripts, Lavinia Dickinson resolved to publish her sister's poetry and turned to Higginson and Mabel Loomis Todd, a friend of the Dickinson family, for assistance. *Poems by Emily Dickinson* appeared in 1890, and even though most initial reviews were highly unfavorable, the work went through eleven editions in two years. Encouraged by the popular acceptance of *Poems,* Todd edited and published two further collections of Dickinson's poetry in the 1890s as well as a two-volume selection of her letters. Family disputes over possession of manuscripts hindered the publication of further materials, yet over the next fifty years, previously unprinted poems were introduced to the public in new collections. It was not until 1955, with the appearance of Thomas H. Johnson's edition of her verse, that Dickinson's complete poems were collected and published together in an authoritative text.

Nearly eighteen hundred poems by Dickinson are known to exist, all of them in the form of brief lyrics (often of only one or two quatrains), and few of them titled. In her verse, Dickinson explores various subjects: the stern beauty of nature, her fearful attraction towards death, her skepticism regarding immortality, her experience of love and loss, the importance of her poetic vocation, and her feelings toward fame. Drawing on imagery from biblical sources and from the works of William Shakespeare, John Keats, and Robert and Elizabeth Browning, Dickinson developed a highly personal system of symbol and allusion, assigning complex meanings to colors, places, times, and seasons. Her tone in the poems ranges widely, from wry, laconic humor to anguished self-examination, from flirtatious riddling to childlike naiveté. Dickinson's diction is similarly diverse, incorporating New England vernacular, theological and scientific terminology, and archaisms. The meters of her poems are characteristically adapted from the rhythms of English hymns or riddling nursery rhymes. Dickinson's experimentation with half rhyme, slant rhyme, assonance, consonance, and tonal harmony defied the poetic conventions of her day, as did her idiosyncratic capitalization and punctuation, especially her use of dashes for emphasis or in place of commas. The terse, epigrammatic, and elliptical aspects of Dickinson's style further distinguish her poetry from the mainstream of nineteenth-century American verse.

Not surprisingly, most nineteenth-century critics read Dickinson's poetry with a combination of disapproval and bewilderment, objecting to her disregard for conventional meter and rhyme, her unusual imagery, and her apparent errors in grammar and diction. Response to the second and third series of *Poems* repeated the reaction to the first volume—while reviewers berated the oddities of Dickinson's style, the public greeted the poems enthusiastically. In the opening decades of the twentieth century, Dickinson was granted a minor standing in American literature as a regional and primarily sentimental poet whose eccentric life-style and tragic romances warranted more attention than her work. In the 1930s and 1940s interest in Dickinson's life and supposed love affairs continued, but simultaneously, a number of scholars associated with the New Criticism movement focused on the technical merits of her poems, exploring their intrinsic value as literature and ignoring details of biography.

The single most important development in the history of Dickinson scholarship was Johnson's 1955 variorum edition of the complete poems. His work paved the way for subsequent studies, and since the mid-1950s an increasing body of criticism has been devoted to various aspects of Dickinson's achievement. Scholars have undertaken explications and analyses of the poems from numerous perspectives, utilizing linguistic, stylistic, psychological, philosophical, and historical approaches. Studies of Dickinson's language and style often focus on the complex interplay of her diction and imagery with her innovative meter and rhyme; her adept use of images drawn from nature and literature has also been widely examined. Psychological interpretations of her poems and letters have attempted to analyze her motivations for writing poetry, her attitudes toward her femininity, and the underlying meanings of her symbols. Dickinson's unorthodox religious beliefs, her responses to the Romantic and Transcendental movements, and her personal philosophy of skepticism as expressed in the poems have been the focus of other studies, while works undertaken from a historical stance frequently explore the distinctively American qualities of her laconic humor and language as they reflect New England culture. Dickinson has also been the subject of appreciations by creative writers. Although no school of poetry derives directly from her work, American poets as diverse as Hart Crane, Louise Bogan, and Adrienne Rich have cited the influence of her writings. In the 1970s and 1980s studies from a feminist stance have dominated Dickinson scholarship, with notable critics examining, among other issues, the difficulties she faced in reconciling her gender and vocation, the significance of her decision to retire from society, her use of language as a means of rebellion, and her importance to later women writers.

Dickinson is considered in the first rank of American poets. Her work is acclaimed both for its technical originality and for the range and depth of emotional experience she addresses. Moreover, the details of her life and her complex personality continue to intrigue readers. Among the most universally admired and extensively studied figures in English literature, Dickinson has been described by Joyce Carol Oates as "an American artist of words as inexhaustible as Shakespeare, as ingeniously skillful in her craft as Yeats, a poet whom we can set with confidence beside the greatest poets of modern times."

(See also *Something about the Author,* Vol. 29, and *Dictionary of Literary Biography,* Vol. 1: *The American Renaissance in New England.*)

PRINCIPAL WORKS

Poems by Emily Dickinson (poetry) 1890
Poems by Emily Dickinson, second series (poetry) 1891
Letters of Emily Dickinson. 2 vols. (letters) 1894
Poems by Emily Dickinson, third series (poetry) 1896
The Single Hound: Poems of a Lifetime (poetry) 1914
Further Poems of Emily Dickinson (poetry) 1929
Unpublished Poems of Emily Dickinson (poetry) 1935
Bolts of Melody: New Poems of Emily Dickinson (poetry) 1945
The Poems of Emily Dickinson. 3 vols. (poetry) 1955
The Letters of Emily Dickinson. 3 vols. (letters) 1958

EMILY DICKINSON (letter date 1862)

[*Dickinson initiated what was to become a longstanding, important correspondence and friendship with Colonel Thomas Wentworth Higginson, a Unitarian clergyman and lecturer and the editor of the* Atlantic Monthly, *after reading his advice to young writers in "Letter to a Young Contributor," published in the* Atlantic *in 1862. Although Higginson's side of the correspondence was destroyed after Dickinson's death, the poet's letters have proved valuable to scholars, not only for the insight they offer into her poetic practice, but also for the clues they provide to the chronology of her poems. Dickinson's first letter to Higginson, in which she enclosed four poems for his appraisal, is excerpted below.*]

Are you too deeply occupied to say if my Verse is alive?

The Mind is so near itself—it cannot see, distinctly—and I have none to ask—

Should you think it breathed—and had you the leisure to tell me, I should feel quick gratitude—

If I make the mistake—that you dared to tell me—would give me sincerer honor—toward you—

I enclose my name—asking you, if you please—Sir—to tell me what is true?

That you will not betray me—it is needless to ask—since Honor is it's own pawn—

Emily Dickinson, in a letter to T. W. Higginson on April 15, 1862, in The Letters of Emily Dickinson, Vol. II, *edited by Thomas H. Johnson, Cambridge, Mass.: The Belknap Press of Harvard University Press, 1958, p. 403.*

EMILY DICKINSON (letter date 1862)

[*In the following letter, Dickinson responds to Higginson's questions and his evaluation of the poems enclosed in her first letter to him (see letter above).*]

Thank you for the surgery—it was not so painful as I supposed. I bring you others—as you ask—though they might not differ—

While my thought is undressed—I can make the distinction, but when I put them in the Gown—they look alike, and numb.

You asked how old I was? I made no verse—but one or two—until this winter—Sir—

I had a terror since September—I could tell to none—and so I sing, as the Boy does by the Burying Ground—because I am afraid—You inquire my Books—For Poets—I have Keats—and Mr and Mrs Browning. For Prose—Mr Ruskin—Sir Thomas Browne—and the Revelations. I went to school—but in your manner of the phrase—had no education. When a little Girl, I had a friend, who taught me Immortality—but venturing too near, himself—he never returned—Soon after, my Tutor, died—and for several years, my Lexicon—was my only companion—Then I found one more—but he was not contented I be his scholar—so he left the Land.

You ask of my Companions Hills—Sir—and the Sundown—and a Dog—large as myself, that my Father bought me—They are better than Beings—because they know—but do not tell—and the noise in the Pool, at Noon—excels my Piano. I have a Brother and Sister—My Mother does not care for thought—and Father, too busy with his Briefs—to notice what we do—He buys me many Books—but begs me not to read them—because he fears they joggle the Mind. They are religious—except me—and address an Eclipse, every morning—whom they call their "Father." But I fear my story fatigues you—I would like to learn—Could you tell me how to grow—or is it unconveyed—like Melody—or Witchcraft?

You speak of Mr Whitman—I never read his Book—but was told that he was disgraceful—

I read Miss Prescott's "Circumstance," but it followed me, in the Dark—so I avoided her—

Two Editors of Journals came to my Father's House, this winter—and asked me for my Mind—and when I asked them "Why," they said I was penurious—and they, would use it for the World—

I could not weigh myself—Myself—

My size felt small—to me—I read your Chapters in the *Atlantic*—and experienced honor for you—I was sure you would not reject a confiding question—

Is this—Sir—what you asked me to tell you? (pp. 404-05)

Emily Dickinson, in a letter to T. W. Higginson on April 25, 1862, in The Letters of Emily Dickinson, Vol. II, *edited by Thomas H. Johnson, Cambridge, Mass.: The Belknap Press of Harvard University Press, 1958, pp. 404-05.*

EMILY DICKINSON (letter date 1862)

[*Here, Dickinson expresses her feelings regarding publication and fame, defends her practice of poetry, and requests that Higginson serve as her "preceptor."*]

Your letter gave no Drunkenness, because I tasted Rum before—Domingo comes but once—yet I have had few pleasures so deep as your opinion, and if I tried to thank you, my tears would block my tongue—

My dying Tutor told me that he would like to live till I had been a poet, but Death was much of Mob as I could master—then—And when far afterward—a sudden light on Orchards, or a new fashion in the wind troubled my attention—I felt a palsy, here—the Verses just relieve—

Your second letter surprised me, and for a moment, swung—I had not supposed it. Your first—gave no dishonor, because the True—are not ashamed—I thanked you for your justice—but could not drop the Bells whose jingling cooled my Tramp—Perhaps the Balm, seemed better, because you bled me, first.

I smile when you suggest that I delay "to publish"—that being foreign to my thought, as Firmament to Fin—

If fame belonged to me, I could not escape her—if she did not, the longest day would pass me on the chase—and the approbation of my Dog, would forsake me—then—My Barefoot-Rank is better—

You think my gait "spasmodic"—I am in danger—Sir—

You think me "uncontrolled"—I have no Tribunal.

Would you have time to be the "friend" you should think I need? I have a little shape—it would not crowd your Desk—nor make much Racket as the Mouse, that dents your Galleries—

If I might bring you what I do—not so frequent to trouble you—and ask you if I told it clear—'twould be control, to me—

The Sailor cannot see the North—but knows the Needle can—

The "hand you stretch me in the Dark," I put mine in, and turn away—I have no Saxon, now—

As if I asked a common Alms,
And in my wondering hand
A Stranger pressed a Kingdom,
And I, bewildered, stand—
As if I asked the Orient
Had it for me a Morn—
And it should lift it's purple Dikes,
And shatter me with Dawn!

But, will you be my Preceptor, Mr. Higginson? (pp. 408-09)

Emily Dickinson, in a letter to T. W. Higginson on June 7, 1862, in The Letters of Emily Dickinson, Vol. II, *edited by Thomas H. Johnson, Cambridge, Mass.: The Belknap Press of Harvard University Press, 1958, pp. 408-09.*

EMILY DICKINSON (letter date 1862)

[Dickinson responds to Higginson's request for her portrait with a self-description and reiterates her desire that he critique her work.]

Could you believe me—without? I had no portrait, now, but am small, like the Wren, and my Hair is bold, like the Chestnut Bur—and my eyes, like the Sherry in the Glass, that the Guest leaves—Would this do just as well?

It often alarms Father—He says Death might occur, and he has Molds of all the rest—but has no Mold of me, but I noticed the Quick wore off those things, in a few days, and forestall the dishonor—You will think no caprice of me—

You said "Dark." I know the Butterfly—and the Lizard—and the Orchis—

Are not those *your* Countrymen?

I am happy to be your scholar, and will deserve the kindness, I cannot repay.

If you truly consent, I recite, now—

Will you tell me my fault, frankly as to yourself, for I had rather wince, than die. Men do not call the surgeon, to commend—the Bone, but to set it, Sir, and fracture within, is more critical. And for this, Preceptor, I shall bring you—Obedience—the Blossom from my Garden, and every gratitude I know. Perhaps you smile at me. I could not stop for that—My Business is Circumference—An ignorance, not of Customs, but if caught with the Dawn—or the Sunset see me—Myself the only Kangaroo among the Beauty, Sir, if you please, it afflicts me, and I thought that instruction would take it away.

Because you have much business, beside the growth of me—you will appoint, yourself, how often I shall come—without your inconvenience. And if at any time—you regret you received me, or I prove a different fabric to that you supposed—you must banish me—

When I state myself, as the Representative of the Verse—it does not mean—me—but a supposed person. You are true, about the "perfection."

Today, makes Yesterday mean. (pp. 411-12)

Emily Dickinson, in a letter to T. W. Higginson in July, 1862, in The Letters of Emily Dickinson, Vol. II, *edited by Thomas H. Johnson, Cambridge, Mass.: The Belknap Press of Harvard University Press, 1958, pp. 411-12.*

EMILY DICKINSON (letter date 1862)

[In this excerpt, Dickinson responds to Higginson's commentary on her work.]

Are these more orderly? I thank you for the Truth—

I had no Monarch in my life, and cannot rule myself, and when I try to organize—my little Force explodes—and leaves me bare and charred—

I think you called me "Wayward." Will you help me improve?

I suppose the pride that stops the Breath, in the Core of Woods, is not of Ourself—

You say I confess the little mistake, and omit the large—Because I can see Orthography—but the Ignorance out of sight—is my Preceptor's charge—

Of "shunning Men and Women"—they talk of Hallowed things, aloud—and embarrass my Dog—He and I dont object to them, if they'll exist their side. I think Carl[o] would please you—He is dumb, and brave—I think you would like the Chestnut Tree, I met in my walk. It hit my notice suddenly—and I thought the Skies were in Blossom—

Then there's a noiseless noise in the Orchard—that I let persons hear—You told me in one letter, you could not come to see me, "now," and I made no answer, not because I had none, but did not think myself the price that you should come so far—

I do not ask so large a pleasure, lest you might deny me—

You say "Beyond your knowledge." You would not jest with me, because I believe you—but Preceptor—you cannot mean it? All men say "What" to me, but I thought it a fashion—

When much in the Woods as a little Girl, I was told that the Snake would bite me, that I might pick a poisonous flower, or Goblins kidnap me, but I went along and met no one but Angels, who were far shyer of me, than I could be of them, so I hav'nt that confidence in fraud which many exercise.

I shall observe your precept—though I dont understand it, always.

I marked a line in One Verse—because I met it after I made it—and never consciously touch a paint, mixed by another person—

I do not let go it, because it is mine. (pp. 414-15)

Emily Dickinson, in a letter to T. W. Higginson in August, 1862, in The Letters of Emily Dickinson, Vol. II, *edited by Thomas H. Johnson, Cambridge, Mass.: The Belknap Press of Harvard University Press, 1958, pp. 414-15.*

T. W. HIGGINSON (letter date 1869)

[The following excerpt is drawn from one of Higginson's few extant letters to Dickinson. For further commentary by Higginson, see excerpts dated 1870 and 1890.]

Sometimes I take out your letters & verses, dear friend, and when I feel their strange power, it is not strange that I find it hard to write & that long months pass. I have the greatest desire

Thomas Wentworth Higginson, Dickinson's correspondent and adviser.

to see you, always feeling that perhaps if I could once take you by the hand I might be something to you; but till then you only enshroud yourself in this fiery mist & I cannot reach you, but only rejoice in the rare sparkles of light. Every year I think that I will contrive somehow to go to Amherst & see you: but that is hard, for I often am obliged to go away for lecturing, &c & rarely can go for pleasure. I would gladly go to Boston, at any practicable time, to meet you. I am always the same toward you, & never relax my interest in what you send to me. I should like to hear from you very often, but feel always timid lest what I *write* should be badly aimed & miss that fine edge of thought which you bear. It would be so easy, I fear, to miss you. Still, you see, I try. I think if I could once see you & know that you are real, I might fare better. It brought you nearer e[ven] to know that you had an actual[?] uncle, though I can hardly fancy [any?] two beings less alike than yo[u] [&?] him. But I have not seen him [for] several years, though I have seen [a lady] who once knew you, but could [not] tell me much.

It is hard [for me] to understand how you can live s[o alo]ne, with thoughts of such a [quali]ty coming up in you & even the companionship of your dog withdrawn. Yet it isolates one anywhere to think beyond a certain point or have such luminous flashes as come to you—so perhaps the place does not make much difference. (p. 461)

T. W. Higginson, in a letter to Emily Dickinson on May 11, 1869, in The Letters of Emily Dickinson, Vol. II, *edited by Thomas H. Johnson, Cambridge, Mass.: The Belknap Press of Harvard University Press, 1958, pp. 461-62.*

T. W. HIGGINSON (letter date 1870)

[In the following excerpt from a letter to his wife, Higginson describes meeting Dickinson, including a transcription of the poet's conversation. For additional material by Higginson, see excerpts dated 1869 and 1890.]

I shan't sit up tonight to write you all about E.D. dearest but if you had read Mrs. Stoddard's novels you could understand a house where each member runs his or her own selves. Yet I only saw her.

A large county lawyer's house, brown brick, with great trees & a garden—I sent up my card. A parlor dark & cool & stiffish, a few books & engravings & an open piano—Malbone & O D [Out Door] Papers among other books.

A step like a pattering child's in entry & in glided a little plain woman with two smooth bands of reddish hair & a face a little like Belle Dove's; not plainer—with no good feature—in a very plain & exquisitely clean white pique & a blue net worsted shawl. She came to me with two day lilies which she put in a sort of childlike way into my hand & said "These are my introduction" in a soft frightened breathless childlike voice—& added under her breath Forgive me if I am frightened; I never see strangers & hardly know what I say—But she talked soon & thenceforward continuously—& deferentially—sometimes stopping to ask me to talk instead of her—but readily recommencing. Manner between Angie Tilton & Mr. Alcott—but thoroughly ingenuous & simple which they are not & saying many things which you would have thought foolish & I wise—& some things you wd. hv. liked. . . . (p. 473)

"Women talk: men are silent: that is why I dread women."

"My father only reads on Sunday—he reads *lonely* & *rigorous* books."

"If I read a book [and] it makes my whole body so cold no fire ever can warm me I know *that* is poetry. If I feel physically as if the top of my head were taken off, I know *that* is poetry. These are the only way I know it. Is there any other way."

"How do most people live without any thoughts. There are many people in the world (you must have noticed them in the street) How do they live. How do they get strength to put on their clothes in the morning"

"When I lost the use of my Eyes it was a comfort to think there were so few real *books* that I could easily find some one to read me all of them"

"Truth is such a *rare* thing it is delightful to tell it."

"I find ecstasy in living—the mere sense of living is joy enough"

I asked if she never felt want of employment, never going off the place & never seeing any visitor "I never thought of conceiving that I could ever have the slightest approach to such a want in all future time" (& added) "I feel that I have not expressed myself strongly enough."

She makes all the bread for her father only likes hers & says "& people must have puddings" this *very* dreamily, as if they were comets—so she makes them. (pp. 473-74)

She said to me at parting "Gratitude is the only secret that cannot reveal itself." (p. 474)

"Could you tell me what home is"

"I never had a mother. I suppose a mother is one to whom you hurry when you are troubled."

"I never knew how to tell time by the clock till I was 15. My father thought he had taught me but I did not understand & I was afraid to say I did not & afraid to ask any one else lest he should know."

Her father was not severe I should think but remote. He did not wish them to read anything but the Bible. One day her brother brought home Kavanagh hid it under the piano cover & made signs to her & they read it: her father at last found it & was displeased. Perhaps it was before this that a student of his was amazed that they had never heard of Mrs. [Lydia Maria] Child & used to bring them books & hide in a bush by the door. They were then little things in short dresses with their feet on the rungs of the chair. After the first book she thought in ecstasy "This then is a book! And then there are more of them!"

"Is it oblivion or absorption when things pass from our minds?"

Major Hunt interested her more than any man she ever saw. She remembered two things he said—that her great dog "understood gravitation" & when he said he should come again "in a year. If I say a shorter time it will be longer."

When I said I would come again *some time* she said "Say in a long time, that will be nearer. Some time is nothing."

After a long disuse of her eyes she read Shakespeare & thought why is any other book needed.

I never was with any one who drained my nerve power so much. Without touching her, she drew from me. I am glad not to live near her. She often thought me *tired* & seemed very thoughtful of others. (pp. 475-76)

T. W. Higginson, in a letter to his wife in August, 1870, in The Letters of Emily Dickinson, Vol. II, *edited by Thomas H. Johnson, Cambridge, Mass.: The Belknap Press of Harvard University Press, 1958, pp. 473-76.*

MABEL LOOMIS TODD (letter date 1881)

[*The wife of a professor at Amherst College and a friend of the Dickinson family, Todd played an important role in the editing and publication of Dickinson's poetry. In the following excerpt from a letter to her parents written shortly after her arrival in Amherst, Todd describes Dickinson as the "myth of Amherst." For additional commentary by Todd, see excerpts dated 1891 and 1896.*]

I must tell you about the *character* of Amherst. It is a lady whom the people call the *Myth*. She is a sister of Mr. Dickinson, & seems to be the climax of all the family oddity. She has not been outside of her own house in fifteen years, except once to see a new church, when she crept out at night, & viewed it by moonlight. No one who calls upon her mother & sister ever see her, but she allows little children once in a great while, & one at a time, to come in, when she gives them cake or candy, or some nicety, for she is very fond of little ones. But more often she lets down the sweetmeat by a string, out of a window, to them. She dresses wholly in white, & her mind is said to be perfectly wonderful. She writes finely, but no one *ever* sees her. Her sister, who was at Mrs. Dickinson's party, invited me to come & sing to her mother sometime . . . people tell me that the *myth* will hear every note—she will be near, but unseen . . . Isn't that like a book? So interesting.

No one knows the cause of her isolation, but of course there are dozens of reasons assigned.

Mabel Loomis Todd, in a letter to Mr. and Mrs. E. J. Loomis on November 6, 1881, in The Years and Hours of Emily Dickinson, Vol. II *by Jay Leyda, Yale University Press, 1960, p. 357.*

THOMAS WENTWORTH HIGGINSON (essay date 1890)

[*In his preface to the 1890 collection* Poems by Emily Dickinson, *which he edited in conjunction with Mabel Loomis Todd, Higginson defends the originality and beauty of Dickinson's work despite what he views as flaws in form. For further commentary by Higginson, see excerpts dated 1869 and 1870.*]

The verses of Emily Dickinson belong emphatically to what Emerson long since called "the Poetry of the Portfolio,"—something produced absolutely without the thought of publication, and solely by way of expression of the writer's own mind. Such verse must inevitably forfeit whatever advantage lies in the discipline of public criticism and the enforced conformity to accepted ways. On the other hand, it may often gain something through the habit of freedom and the unconventional utterance of daring thoughts. In the case of the present author, there was absolutely no choice in the matter; she must write thus, or not at all. A recluse by temperament and habit, literally spending years without setting her foot beyond the doorstep, and many more years during which her walks were strictly limited to her father's grounds, she habitually concealed her mind, like her person, from all but a very few friends; and it was with great difficulty that she was persuaded to print, during her lifetime, three or four poems. Yet she wrote verses in great abundance; and though curiously indifferent to all conventional rules, had yet a rigorous literary standard of her own, and often altered a word many times to suit an ear which had its own tenacious fastidiousness.

Miss Dickinson was born in Amherst, Mass., Dec.10, 1830, and died there May 15, 1886. Her father, Hon. Edward Dickinson, was the leading lawyer of Amherst, and was treasurer of the well-known college there situated. It was his custom once a year to hold a large reception at his house, attended by all the families connected with the institution and by the leading people of the town. On these occasions his daughter Emily emerged from her wonted retirement and did her part as gracious hostess; nor would anyone have known from her manner, I have been told, that this was not a daily occurrence. The annual occasion once past, she withdrew again into her seclusion, and except for a very few friends was as invisible to the world as if she had dwelt in a nunnery. For myself, although I had corresponded with her for many years, I saw her but twice face to face, and brought away the impression of something as unique and remote as Undine or Mignon or Thekla.

This selection from her poems is published to meet the desire of her personal friends, and especially of her surviving sister. It is believed that the thoughtful reader will find in these pages a quality more suggestive of the poetry of William Blake than of anything to be elsewhere found,—flashes of wholly original and profound insight into nature and life; words and phrases exhibiting an extraordinary vividness of descriptive and imaginative power, yet often set in a seemingly whimsical or even rugged frame. They are here published as they were written, with very few and superficial changes; although it is fair to say that the titles have been assigned, almost invariably, by the editors. In many cases these verses will seem to the reader like poetry torn up by the roots, with rain and dew and earth still clinging to them, giving a freshness and a fragrance not otherwise to be conveyed. In other cases, as in the few poems of shipwreck or of mental conflict, we can only wonder at the gift of vivid imagination by which this recluse woman can delineate, by a few touches, the very crises of physical or mental struggle. And sometimes again we catch glimpses of a lyric strain, sustained perhaps but for a line or two at a time, and making the reader regret its sudden cessation. But the main quality of these poems is that of extraordinary grasp and insight, uttered with an uneven vigor sometimes exasperating, seemingly wayward, but really unsought and inevitable. After all, when a thought takes one's breath away, a lesson on grammar seems an impertinence. As Ruskin wrote in his earlier and better days, "No weight nor mass nor beauty of execution can outweigh one grain or fragment of thought." (pp. 416-17)

Thomas Wentworth Higginson, "Preface to 'Poems by Emily Dickinson', 1890," in Ancestors' Brocades: The Literary Debut of Emily Dickinson *by Millicent Todd Bingham, Harper & Brothers Publishers, 1945, pp. 416-17.*

ARLO BATES (essay date 1890)

[*A prolific journalist, novelist, and poet, Bates was influential in the publication of the first volume of Dickinson's poetry: the Boston firm of Roberts Brothers submitted* Poems by Emily Dickinson *to Bates for appraisal before agreeing to publish the collection. In this excerpt from Bates's review of* Poems *for the 23 November 1890* Boston Courier, *he emphasizes the beauty and originality of her writings while admitting that they are technically flawed.*]

It is seldom that the reviewer is called upon to notice a book so remarkable as the ***Poems*** of Miss Emily Dickinson, which are published posthumously under the editorship of Mrs. Mabel Loomis Todd and Colonel Thomas Wentworth Higginson. The work which it contains has to be treated as so far outside of the ordinary groove, it is so wholly without the pale of conventional criticism, that it is necessary at the start to declare the grounds upon which it is to be judged as if it were a new species of art.

For, in the first place, there is hardly a line in the entire volume, and certainly not a stanza, which cannot be objected to upon the score of technical imperfection. The author was as unlearned in the technical side of art as if she had written when the forms of verse had not yet been invented. She is not so much disdainful of conventions as she seems to be insensible to them. Her ear had certainly not been susceptible of training to the appreciation of form and melody, or it is inconceivable that she should have written as she did. There is on every page ground for the feeling that she was one of those strangely constituted creatures who experience a pleasure from metrical forms, yet who are so insensible to them as to be unable to understand that their own work lacks in that which moves them dimly in the poetry of others. There is evidence that Miss Dickinson was not without some vague feeling for metre and rhythm, yet she was apparently entirely unconscious that her own lines often had neither and constantly violated the canons of both.

There is hardly a line of her work, however, which fails to throw out some gleam of genuine original power, of imagination, and of real emotional thought. There is the real poetic motive here. The high muse has been with her in very truth, passing by to come to her many who have well and painfully learned the secrets of the technique of their art. That the muse was erratic in her choice may be allowed; but it is vain to attempt to deny that it was herself and no other who inspired Miss Dickinson's songs.

There is a certain rude and half barbaric naivete in many of the poems. They show the insight of the civilized adult combined with the simplicity of the savage child. There is a barbaric flavor often discernible, as if this gentle poet had the blood of some gentle and simple Indian ancestress in her veins still in an unadulterated current.

Angels in the early morning
  May be seen the dews among,
Stooping, plucking, smiling, flying:
  Do the buds to them belong?

Is not this the voice of a child?

Some keep the Sabbath going to church;
  I keep it staying at home,
With a bobolink for a chorister,
  And an orchard for a dome.

. . . . .

God preaches—a noted clergyman—
  And the sermon is never long;
So instead of getting to heaven at last,
  I'm going all along!

Could anything be more delightfully pagan, or worse in workmanship?

These two show how near she could come at times to a bit of good workmanship, and how inevitably she spoiled it.

"Autumn"

The morns are meeker than they were,
  The nuts are getting brown;
The berry's cheek is plumper,
  The rose is out of town.

The maple wears a gayer scarf,
  The field a scarlet gown.
Lest I should be old-fashioned,
  I'll put a trinket on.

"Beclouded"

The sky is low, the clouds are mean,
  A traveling flake of snow
Across a barn or through a rut
  Debates if it will go.

A narrow wind complains all day
  How some one treated him;
Nature, like us, is sometimes caught
  Without her diadem.

The touch of humor at the end of the former of these is in a way delightful, but it is not enough to justify the place it holds. The first four verses of the second give a picture with a vividness and grace that could hardly be bettered, but the rest does not please us.

Of the poems dealing with nature this seems to us one of the best.

"The Sea of Sunset"

This is the land the sunset washes,
  These are the banks of the Yellow Sea;
Where it rose, or whither it rushes,
  These are the Western mystery.

Night after night her purple traffic
  Strews the landing with purple bales;
Merchantmen poise upon horizons,
  Dip and vanish with fairy sails.

It is not in her poems dealing with nature, however, that Miss Dickinson seems to us most interesting. These are often marked with much felicity of phrase, and they are apt to be less irregular in form than some of the rest, but there is in her poems upon life and ethical themes far more depth and originality. Take, for example, these two:

The heart asks pleasure first,
  And then, excuse from pain;
And then, those little anodynes
  That deaden suffering;

And then to go to sleep;
  And then, if it should be
The will of its Inquisitor,
  The liberty to die.

"The Mystery of Pain"

Pain has an element of blank;
  It cannot collect
When it began, or if there were
  A day when it was not.

It has no future but itself,
  Its infinite realms contain
Its past, enlightened to perceive
  New periods of pain.

Here is genuine, emotional insight into life, united with no small power of feeling, and, too of expressing. What, too, need be more charming and touching than the spirit of these love songs?

"With a Flower"

I hide myself within my flower,
  That wearing on your breast,
You, unsuspecting, wear me too—
  And angels know the rest.

I hide myself within my flower,
  That fading from your vase,
You, unsuspecting, feel for me
  Almost a loneliness.

"The Outlet"

My river runs to thee;
Blue sea, wilt welcome me?

My river waits reply.
Oh, sea, look graciously!

I'll fetch thee brooks
From spotted nooks,—

Say, sea, take me!

A little rhyme which is eminently characteristic in its breaks and technical faults.

"Transplanted"

As if some little Arctic flower,
Upon the polar hem,
Went wandering down the latitudes,
Until it puzzled came
To continents of summer,
To firmaments of sun,
To strange bright crowds of flowers,
And birds of foreign tongue!
I say, as if this little flower
To Eden wandered in—
What then? Why, nothing, only
Your inference therefrom!

The religious poems are distinguished by a singularly frank fearlessness which is most easily described in Mrs. Browning's phrase as an

—infantine,
Familiar clasp of things divine.

Her spiritual life was evidently so much a part of her existence that it never occurred to her that there was a difference made in the manner of treating one serious feeling because it is a fashion of the conventional world so to treat it. She was always reverent because she could not have been irreverent, but she was reverent toward nature, man and God in the same way. Her theology is of a sort to puzzle metaphysicians, and yet one finds it often most suggestive and stimulating. The strangeness of some of the mixtures which she offers may be seen from this bit:

I reason that in Heaven
Somehow it will be even,
Some new equation given;
  But what of that?

Perhaps there is nothing in the volume which is better than the poem which the editors have called **"Apotheosis,"** and which they have placed among the love poems instead of the religious, perhaps rightly, since Miss Dickinson is more fervid in her expressions concerning love than concerning religion.

"Apotheosis"

Come slowly, Eden!
  Lips unused to thee,
Bashful, sip thy jasmines,
  As the fainting bee,
Reaching late his flower,
  'Round her chamber hums,
Counts his nectars—enters,
  And is lost in balms!

There is little of the imitative in the book. Such a suggestion of Browning as one may find in this last poem or of Emerson in some of the poems to nature there is now and then, but it is not enough to interfere with the feeling of untrammeled freshness with which one reads. We have quoted thus largely because of the charm of this work for us, and because, the poems having never been published before, are sure to be fresh to the reader. It is necessary to lay aside all fondness for technical perfection, and to give one's self up to the spirit, but the being done, the lover of the poetical will find the book a rare delight. There will be those, indeed, who will contend that the book is better for having disregarded technical form, or at least no worse. It is not wholly impossible that in the Editor's Study something looking in this direction will some day see the light. The truth, however, is not so. Had Miss Dickinson possessed the aptitude and the will to learn technical skill, she would have enriched the language with lyrics which would have endured to the end of time, it well might be. As it is, she has put upon paper things which will delight the few, but which will hold their place on suffrance, and as showing what she might have been rather than for what she was. The book gives us keen delight, but it is delight mingled with regret equally keen for what it fails to be. (pp.12-18)

Arlo Bates, "Miss Dickinson's Poems," in The Recognition of Emily Dickinson: Selected Criticism since 1890, *edited by Caesar R. Blake and Carlton F.*

Wells, The University of Michigan Press, 1964, pp. 12-18.

W. D. HOWELLS (essay date 1891)

[Howells was the chief progenitor of American realism and an influential literary critic during the late nineteenth and early twentieth centuries. Although few of his numerous novels are read today, he stands as one of the major literary figures of his era. Having successfully weaned American literature from the sentimental romanticism of its infancy, he became known as "the Dean of American Letters." The excerpt below is drawn from an essay that first appeared in Harper's New Monthly Magazine *in January 1891. Howells's sympathetic reading of Dickinson's* Poems *and high praise for her achievement contributed much to Dickinson's popularity despite the rebuttals of such critics as the reviewer for the* London Daily News *and Andrew Lang (see excerpts dated 1891).]*

The strange ***Poems of Emily Dickinson*** we think will form something like an intrinsic experience with the understanding reader of them. . . . She never intended or allowed anything more [than a few lines] from her pen to be printed in her lifetime; but it was evident that she wished her poetry finally to meet the eyes of that world which she had herself always shrunk from. She could not have made such poetry without knowing its rarity, its singular worth; and no doubt it was a radiant happiness in the twilight of her hidden, silent life.

The editors have discharged their delicate duty toward it with unimpeachable discretion, and Colonel Higginson has said so many apt things of her work in his introduction [see excerpt dated 1890], that one who cannot differ with him must be vexed a little to be left so little to say. He speaks of her 'curious indifference to all conventional rules of verse,' but he adds that 'when a thought takes one's breath away, a lesson on grammar seems an impertinence.' He notes 'the quality suggestive of the poetry of William Blake' in her, but he leaves us the chance to say that it is a Blake who had read Emerson who had read Blake. The fantasy is as often Blakian as the philosophy is Emersonian; but after feeling this again and again, one is ready to declare that the utterance of this most singular and authentic spirit would have been the same if there had never been an Emerson or a Blake in the world. She sometimes suggests Heine as much as either of these; all three in fact are spiritually present in some of the pieces; yet it is hardly probable that she had read Heine, or if she had, would not have abhorred him.

Here is something that seems compact of both Emerson and Blake, with a touch of Heine too:

I taste a liquor never brewed,
From tankards scooped in pearl;
Not all the vats upon the Rhine
Yield such an alcohol!

Inebriate of air am I,
And debauchee of dew,
Reeling, through endless summer days,
From inns of molten blue.

When landlords turn the drunken bee
Out of the foxglove's door,
When butterflies renounce their drams,
I shall but drink the more!

Till seraphs swing their snowy hats,
And saints to windows run,
To see the little tippler
Leaning against the sun!

But we believe it is only seeming; we believe these things are as wholly her own as this:

The bustle in a house
The morning after death
Is solemnest of industries
Enacted upon earth,—

The sweeping up the heart,
And putting love away
We shall not want to use again
Until eternity.

Such things could have come only from a woman's heart to which the experiences in a New England town have brought more knowledge of death than of life. Terribly unsparing many of these strange poems are, but true as the grave and certain as mortality. The associations of house-keeping in the following poem have a force that drags us almost into the presence of the poor, cold, quiet thing:

"Troubled About Many Things"

How many times these low feet staggered,
Only the soldered mouth can tell;
Try! can you stir the awful rivet?
Try! can you lift the hasps of steel?

Stroke the cool forehead, hot so often,
Lift, if you can, the listless hair;
Handle the adamantine fingers
Never a thimble more shall wear.

Buzz the dull flies on the chamber window;
Brave shines the sun through the freckled pane;
Fearless the cobweb swings from the ceiling—
Indolent housewife, in daisies lain!

Then in this, which has no name—how could any phrase nominate its weird witchery aright?—there is the flight of an eerie fancy that leaves all experience behind:

I died for beauty, but was scarce
Adjusted in the tomb,
When one who died for truth was lain
In an adjoining room.

He questioned softly why I failed.
'For beauty,' I replied.
'And I for truth,—the two are one;
We brethren are,' he said.

And so, as kinsmen met a night,
We talked between the rooms,
Until the moss had reached our lips,
And covered up our names.

All that Puritan longing for sincerity, for veracious conduct, which in some good New England women's natures is almost a hysterical shriek, makes its exultant grim assertion in these lines:

"Real"

I like a look of agony,
Because I know it's true;
Men do not sham convulsion,
Nor simulate a throe.

The eyes glaze once, and that is death.
Impossible to feign
The beads upon the forehead
By homely anguish strung.

These mortuary pieces have a fascination above any others in the book; but in the stanzas below there is a still, solemn, rapt movement of the thought and music together that is of exquisite charm:

New feet within my garden go,
New fingers stir the sod;
A troubadour upon the elm
Betrays the solitude.

New children play upon the green,
New weary sleep below;
And still the pensive spring returns,
And still the punctual snow!

This is a song that sings itself; and this is another such, but thrilling with the music of a different passion:

"Suspense"

Elysium is as far as to
The very nearest room,
If in that room a friend await
Felicity or doom.

What fortitude the soul contains,
That it can so endure
The accent of a coming foot,
The opening of a door!

The last poem is from the group which the editors have named 'Love'; the other groups from which we have been quoting are 'Nature,' and 'Time and Eternity'; but the love poems are of the same piercingly introspective cast as those differently named. The same force of imagination is in them; in them, as in the rest, touch often becomes clutch. In them love walks on heights he seldom treads, and it is the heart of full womanhood that speaks in the words of this nun-like New England life.

Few of the poems in the book are long, but none of the short, quick impulses of intense feeling or poignant thought can be called fragments. They are each a compassed whole, a sharply finished point, and there is evidence, circumstantial and direct, that the author spared no pains in the perfect expression of her ideals. Nothing, for example, could be added that would say more than she has said in four lines:

Presentiment is that long shadow on the lawn
Indicative that suns go down;
The notice to the startled grass
That darkness is about to pass.

Occasionally, the outside of the poem, so to speak, is left so rough, so rude, that the art seems to have faltered. But there is apparent to reflection the fact that the artist meant just this harsh exterior to remain, and that no grace of smoothness could have imparted her intention as it does. It is the soul of an abrupt, exalted New England woman that speaks in such brokenness. The range of all the poems is of the loftiest; and sometimes there is a kind of swelling lift, an almost boastful rise of feeling, which is really the spring of faith in them:

I never saw a moor,
I never saw the sea;
Yet know I how the heather looks,
And what a wave must be.

I never spoke with God,
Nor visited in heaven;
Yet certain am I of the spot
As if the chart were given.

There is a noble tenderness, too, in some of the pieces; a quaintness that does not discord with the highest solemnity:

I shall know why, when time is over,
And I have ceased to wonder why;
Christ will explain each separate anguish
In the fair school-room of the sky.

He will tell me what Peter promised,
And I, for wonder at his woe,
I shall forget the drop of anguish
That scalds me now, that scalds me now.

The companionship of human nature with inanimate nature is very close in certain of the poems; and we have never known the invisible and intangible ties binding all creation in one, so nearly touched as in them.

If nothing else had come out of our life but this strange poetry we should feel that in the work of Emily Dickinson America, or New England rather, had made a distinctive addition to the literature of the world, and could not be left out of any record of it; and the interesting and important thing is that this poetry is as characteristic of our life as our business enterprise, our political turmoil, our demagogism, our millionairism. (pp. 189-95)

W. D. Howells, "Emily Dickinson Announced," in his W. D. Howells as Critic, *edited by Edwin H. Cady, Routledge & Kegan Paul, 1973, pp. 189-95.*

***LONDON DAILY NEWS* (essay date 1891)**

[In the following excerpt from a review first published in the London Daily News *on 2 January 1891, the anonymous critic counters W. D. Howells's praise of Dickinson (see excerpt dated 1891) with a negative assessment of her deviations from poetic conventions and standard grammar.]*

"If nothing else had come out of our life but this strange poetry," says Mr. W. D. Howells in *Harper's Magazine,* "we should feel that in the work of Emily Dickinson, America, or New England rather, had made a distinctive addition to the literature of the world." Much more Mr. Howells has to say in favour of the newest poetry and the newest poet. Mr. Howells is a critic not always easy to please, and the world cannot but be interested in hearing what the strains of the Tenth Muse are like. As Mr. Howells justly says, "They will form something like an intrinsic experience with the understanding of the reader of them." This is exactly right. No experience in literature can be more intrinsic than this. The verses remind Mr. Howells of what might be written by "a Blake who had read Emerson who had read Blake," a statement so intrinsic that it quite takes the breath away. What is a Blake who had read Emerson who had read Blake? Is it at all like a Howells who had read Dickinson who had read Howells? Miss Dickinson "sometimes suggest Heine" as much as either Blake or Emerson. To other critics Miss Dickinson's numbers "suggest" a Walt Whitman who had read the Poet Close and attempted to blend with the German Hebrew. For example, here is a piece which Mr. Howells regards as a compound of Emerson, Heine, and Blake. Here it is:

I taste a liquor never brewed
  From tankards scooped in pearl;
Not all the vats upon the Rhine
  Yield such an alcohol.

"Alcohol" does not rhyme to pearl, but Miss Dickinson is not to be regarded as responsible for mere rhymes. Nor for grammar! It is literally impossible to understand whether she means that she tastes a liquor never brewed at all, or a liquor never brewed "from" tankards scooped in pearl. By "from" she may mean "in". Let us give her the benefit of the doubt, and she still writes utter nonsense. It is clearly impossible to scoop a tankard from pearl. The material is inadequate. Now, neither Blake, nor Mr. Emerson, nor Heine was an idiot. Miss Dickinson must bear her own poetic sins; she reminds us of no sane nor educated writer. Indeed, Mr. Howells himself repents and says, "These things are as wholly her own" as another masterpiece which follows. They are, indeed, and we apologize to the poet Close.

Here is another example of the Newest Poetry from New England:

How many times those low feet staggered
Only the soldered mouth can tell.
Try! can you stir the awful rivet?
Try! can you lift the hasps of steel?

We could perhaps if we tried, but we cannot make sense out of balderdash. What are "low feet?" The words are meaningless. This remarkable composition ends thus:

Indolent housewife in daisies lain!

This is no more English than it is Coptic. "In Daisy's lane" might have a meaning. There might be a lane called after a lady whose *petit nom* was Daisy. But the conjectural emendation rests on a belief that the poet was as ignorant of spelling as of sense and grammar. If the poet meant "in daisies laid"—buried in daisies or under daisies—why not say so? "Laid" rhymes to "pane" (and a rhyme was wanted) quite as well as "pearl" rhymes to "alcohol." But Mr. Howells has been captivated by a minstrel who subdues grammar to rhyme, and puts even grammar before sense. "In the stanzas below," says Mr. Howells, "there is a still, solemn, rapt movement of the thought and music together that is of exquisite charm." Here are "the verses below," or a few of them; they are assuredly below contempt:

New feet within my garden go,
New fingers stir the sod,
A troubadour upon an elm
Betrays the solitude.

What in the world has a troubadour to do in New England? And why did he climb a tree? Or was he a bird? And how can solitude be betrayed by a troubadour, somewhere near Boston, in the foliage of an elm? "Touch often becomes clutch" in these poems, exclaims the admiring critic. Touch would be very welcome to become, not only "clutch," but sense, rhyme, and grammar, if it could. Mr. Howells admires

The notice to the startled grass,
That darkness is about to pass.

This is mere maundering. The grass would not be startled in the least, even if it was informed that darkness was not only "about to pass," but about to take high honours. According to the poet, a sacred Person whom we cannot name here

will explain each separate anguish
In the fair school room of the sky.

It were enough if Mr. Howells would explain each separate stanza. Of course the idea occurs that Mr. Howells is only bantering; that he cannot really mean to praise this farrago of illiterate and uneducated sentiment. It is as far below the level of the Poet's Corner in a country newspaper as that is usually below Shakespeare. There are no words that can say how bad poetry may be when it is divorced from meaning, from music, from grammar, from rhyme; in brief, from articulate and intelligible speech. And Mr. Howells solemnly avers that this drivel is characteristic of American life!

The unlucky lady who produced these lines only once printed a poem while she was alive. "She never intended or allowed anything more from her pen to be printed in her lifetime." She did well, and far from regretting her resolution every person of sense will admire it. Many uneducated and incompetent persons get pleasure out of scribbling incoherences. These vaguely correspond to vague sentiments and vague emotions. There is no harm in the exercise, but there is a good deal of harm in publicly praising as excellent and typical poetry, the trash which every editor of a magazine receives in bales. If poetry exists it is by virtue of original, or at least of agreeable thought, musically and magically expressed. Poetry has been defined as "the best thought in the best words." The verses adored by Mr. Howells are conspicuously in the worst possible words, and the thought, as far as any thought can be detected, is usually either commonplace or absurd. The thoughts "take Colonel Higginson's breath away," Colonel Higginson being the editor of the poems. But where is the novelty of thought in

Stroke the cool forehead, hot so often,
Lift, if you can, the listless hair,
Handle the adamantine fingers
Never a thimble more shall wear.

Any reader of Byron's "He who hath bent him o'er the dead" will be familiar enough with such thought as this piece contains, and will be familiar with it in grammar. The pathos of the absence of thimble in mortality is perfectly legitimate, but not so novel as to warrant raptures. It is, in itself, a touching thing that a lady of extremely solitary habits should have solaced herself by writing a kind of verses; but to proclaim that such verses as we have quoted are poetry, and good poetry, is to be guilty of "the pathetic fallacy" in an original manner, and is to encourage many impossible poets. (pp. 24-7)

"The Newest Poet," in The Recognition of Emily Dickinson: Selected Criticism since 1890, *edited by Caesar R. Blake and Carlton F. Wells, The University of Michigan Press, 1964, pp. 24-8.*

SCRIBNER'S MAGAZINE (essay date 1891)

[*In this excerpt from an anonymous review that appeared in* Scribner's Magazine *in March 1891, the critic laments the lack of form in Dickinson's poetry.*]

"When a thought takes your breath away a lesson in grammar is an impertinence," remarks Mr. T. W. Higginson in his sympathetic introduction to the remarkable ***Poems*** of the late Miss Emily Dickinson [see excerpt dated 1890]. . . . This is a happy if rhetorical way of restating the familiar contention that in all departments of art substance is more important than form. By this time anything that may be said *ex parte* on either side of this time-honored discussion is sure to seem a platitude. One thinks of Mill's felicitous tabling of the classics *vs.* the sciences question in education by the query: "Should a tailor make coats or trousers?" Or of the settlement, by a recent authority upon etiquette, of the great problem whether, passing each other in the street, the lady or the gentleman should bow first: "They should bow together," he decides. In irresponsible moments, however—that is to say in most moments—one is apt to have a preference due to the domination of his reflective powers by his temperament. And in the presence of these poems of Miss Dickinson I think a temperament of any sensitiveness must feel even an alternation of preferences—being inclined now to deem them, in virtue of their substance, superior to the ordinary restrictions of form, and now to lament the loss involved in a disregard of the advantages of form. Having one's breath taken away is a very agreeable sensation, but it is not the finest sensation of which we are susceptible; and instead of being grateful for it one is very apt to suffer annoyance at the perversity which is implied in a poet who, though capable of taking one's breath away, nevertheless prefers to do so in arbitrary rather than in artistic fashion. Such a poet, one feels instinctively, should rise above wilfulness, whimsicality, the disposition to challenge and defy.

After all, what do we mean by "importance?" Would it not be fair to say that the term is a relative one to this extent, that as to the importance of any specific thing the contemporary judgment, and that of posterity, are almost sure to be at variance. And is it not true that from the nature of things the contemporary judgment lays most stress on substance, and that the "final" judgment is favorable to form? How many historic things of immense contemporary vogue seem insipid to us, whereas scarcely anything of great formal merit has been allowed to perish. Is there not an element of universality about perfection of form which significance of thought does not possess; or is not perfection more nearly attainable in form than it is in substance? And nothing is so preservative as perfection or any approach to it.

One thing is very certain—neglect of form involves the sacrifice of an element of positive attractiveness as well as offending positively by perverseness and eccentricity. Whether rhyme and rhythm, cadence, purity, flawlessness, melody are essential or not to poetry, the abandonment of the artistic quality which they imply is obviously a loss. "The first indispensable faculty of a singer is ability to sing," exclaims Mr. Swinburne with his usual peremptoriness in his essay on Collins. And all poetry—it may be conceded to him, in spite of the notorious overweighting of his own thought by his musical quality—has at least a lyric element, though, of course, it does not all demand the "lyric cry." Formlessness is the antithesis of art, and so far as poetry is formless it loses that immensely attractive interest which is purely aesthetic. It not merely offends by perversely ignoring the conventionally established though rationally evolved and soundly based rules of the game it purports to play, but in announcing thus, boldly, its independence of any aesthetic, any sensuous, interest, it puts a severe strain on the quality of its own substance—handicaps it in most dangerous fashion instead of giving it that aid and furtherance which the best substance is sure to need. If, as in Miss Dickinson's case, there be occasionally a subtle but essential order in what, superficially, seems chaotic, it may legitimately be maintained that to lay any stress on this is merely to argue against conventionality and not at all in favor of amorphousness. It is simply to assert the elasticity of orchestration and emphasize its range—to exalt the value of new forms over the old. And it is curious to note how prone are all apologists for formlessness, including Mr. Higginson in the present instance, and the admirers of Walt Whitman, *passim*, for example, to insist that what to the convention-steeped sense appears amorphous is in reality the very acme of form. Singularly enough, Mr. Higginson concludes his introduction to these poems by citing a sentence of Mr. Ruskin in favor of "thought" as opposed to "workmanship." Was there ever so striking an example as Mr. Ruskin of what "workmanship" has done even for the most *saugrenu* thought? (pp. 34-6)

"Form and Substance," in The Recognition of Emily Dickinson: Selected Criticism since 1890, *edited by Caesar R. Blake and Carlton F. Wells, The University of Michigan Press, 1964, pp. 34-6.*

ANDREW LANG (essay date 1891)

[Lang was one of England's most powerful men of letters in the closing decades of the nineteenth century. A proponent of the revival of Romantic fiction, Lang championed the works of H. Rider Haggard, Robert Louis Stevenson, and Rudyard Kipling and was harshly critical of the Naturalistic and Realistic techniques of such novelists as Émile Zola and Henry James. A nostalgic vision of the past colored his work as a translator, poet, and revisionist historian. While most of his writings are seldom read today, he is remembered as the editor of the "color fairy book" series, a twelve-volume collection of fairy tales considered a classic in the genre. Lang offers an unsympathetic assessment of Dickinson's poetry in this excerpt from a review published on 7 March 1891 in the Illustrated London News. *His remarks are in part a reaction to W. D. Howells's commentary (see excerpt dated 1891).]*

[***Poems*** by the late Miss Emily Dickinson] is certainly a very curious little book. It has already reached its fourth edition, partly, no doubt, because Mr. Howells praised it very highly. I cannot go nearly so far as Mr. Howells, because, if poetry is to exist at all, it really must have form and grammar, and must rhyme when it professes to rhyme. The wisdom of the ages and the nature of man insist on so much. We may be told that Democracy does not care, any more than the Emperor did, for grammar. But even if Democracy overleaps itself and lands in savagery again, I believe that our savage successors will, though unconsciously, make their poems grammatical. Savages do not use bad grammar in their own conversation or in their artless compositions. That is a fault of defective civilizations. Miss Dickinson, who died lately at the age of fifty-six, was a recluse, dwelling in Amherst, a town of Massachusetts. She did not write for publication. Her friends have produced her work. Sometimes it is as bad as this—

Angels' breathless ballot
Lingers to record thee;
Imps in eager caucus
Raffle for my soul.

This, of course, is mere nonsense. What is a "breathless ballot"? How can a ballot record anything, and how can it "linger" in recording, especially if it is in such a hurry as to be breathless? Indeed, one turns over Miss Dickinson's book with a puzzled feeling that there was poetry in her subconscious, but that it never became explicit. One might as well seek for an air in the notes of a bird as for articulate and sustained poetry here. One piece begins—

This is the land the sunset washes
These are the banks of the Yellow Sea.

And here is rhythm and the large sense of evening air—

Where it rose, or whither it rushes,
These are the Western mystery.

Night after night her purple traffic
Strews the landing with opal bales;
Merchantmen poise upon horizons,
Dip and vanish with fairy sails.

The second verse is not very easy to construe, but there was poetry in the writer. This, again, has the true lyrical note—

I never saw a moor,
I never saw the sea,
Yet know I how the heather looks,
And what a wave must be.

There is not much else that can be quoted without bringing in the fantastic, irresponsible note of a poet who has her own audience, and had constructed her own individual "Ars Poetica." The words of Mr. Aldrich in "The Sister's Tragedy" might have been written about Miss Dickinson—

A twilight poet groping quite alone,
Belated in a sphere where every nest
Is emptied of its music and its wings.

(pp. 37-8)

Andrew Lang, "Some American Poets," in The Recognition of Emily Dickinson: Selected Criticism since 1890, *edited by Caesar R. Blake and Carlton F. Wells, The University of Michigan Press, 1964, pp. 36-8.*

MABEL LOOMIS TODD (essay date 1891)

[*Todd's preface to the 1891* Poems by Emily Dickinson, second series, *which she edited and published in conjunction with Higginson, is excerpted below. For additional commentary by Todd, see excerpts dated 1881 and 1896.*]

The eagerness with which the first volume of Emily Dickinson's poems has been read shows very clearly that all our alleged modern artificiality does not prevent a prompt appreciation of the qualities of directness and simplicity in approaching the greatest themes,—life and love and death. That "irresistible needle-touch," as one of her best critics has called it, piercing at once the very core of a thought, has found a response as wide and sympathetic as it has been unexpected even to those who knew best her compelling power. This second volume, while open to the same criticism as to form with its predecessor, shows also the same shining beauties.

Although Emily Dickinson had been in the habit of sending occasional poems to friends and correspondents, the full extent of her writing was by no means imagined by them. Her friend "H.H." must at least have suspected it, for in a letter dated 5th September, 1884, she wrote:—

My Dear Friend,—What portfolios full of verses you must have. It is a cruel wrong to your "day and generation" that you will not give them light.

If such a thing should happen as that I should outlive you, I wish you would make me your literary legatee and executor. Surely after you are what is called "dead" you will be willing that the poor ghosts you have left behind should be cheered and pleased by your verses, will you not? You ought to be. I do not think we have a right to withhold from the world a word or a thought any more than a *deed* which might help a single soul. . . .

Truly yours,
Helen Jackson

The "portfolios" were found, shortly after Emily Dickinson's death by her sister and only surviving housemate. Most of the poems had been carefully copied on sheets of note-paper, and tied in little fascicules, each of six or eight sheets. While many of them bear evidence of having been thrown off at white heat, still more had received thoughtful revision. There is the frequent addition of rather perplexing foot-notes, affording large choice of words and phrases. And in the copies which she sent to friends, sometimes one form, sometimes another, is found to have been used. (pp. 417-18)

To what further rigorous pruning her verses would have been subjected had she published them herself, we cannot know. They should be regarded in many cases as merely the first strong and suggestive sketches of an artist, intended to be embodied at some time in the finished picture.

Emily Dickinson appears to have written her first poems in the winter of 1862. In a letter to [Thomas Wentworth Higginson (see excerpt dated 25 April 1862)] . . . she says, "I made no verse, but one or two, until this winter."

The handwriting was at first somewhat like the delicate, running Italian hand of our elder gentlewomen; but as she advanced in breadth of thought, it grew bolder and more abrupt, until in her latest years each letter stood distinct and separate from its fellows. In most of her poems, particularly the later ones, everything by way of punctuation was discarded except numerous dashes; and all important words began with capitals. The effect of a page of her more recent manuscript is exceedingly quaint and strong. (p. 418)

The variation of readings, with the fact that she often wrote in pencil and not always clearly, have at times thrown a good deal of responsibility upon her Editors. But all interference not absolutely inevitable has been avoided. The very roughness of her own rendering is part of herself, and not lightly to be touched; for it seems in many cases that she intentionally avoided the smoother and more usual rhymes.

Like impressionist pictures, or Wagner's rugged music, the very absence of conventional form challenges attention. In Emily Dickinson's exacting hands, the especial, intrinsic fitness of a particular order of words might not be sacrificed to anything virtually extrinsic; and her verses all show a strange cadence of inner rhythmical music. Lines are always daringly constructed, and the "thought-rhyme" appears frequently,—appealing, indeed, to an unrecognized sense more elusive than hearing.

Emily Dickinson scrutinized everything with clear-eyed frankness. Every subject was proper ground for legitimate study, even the sombre facts of death and burial, and the unknown life beyond. She touches these themes sometimes lightly, sometimes almost humorously, more often with weird and peculiar power; but she is never by any chance frivolous or trivial. And while, as one critic has said, she may exhibit toward God "an Emersonian self-possession," it was because she looked upon all life with a candor as unprejudiced as it is rare.

She had tried society and the world, and found them lacking. She was not an invalid, and she lived in seclusion from no love-disappointment. Her life was the normal blossoming of a nature introspective to a high degree, whose best thought could not exist in pretence.

Storm, wind, the wild March sky, sunsets and dawns; the birds and bees, butterflies and flowers of her garden, with a few trusted human friends, were sufficient companionship. The coming of the first robin was a jubilee beyond crowning of monarch or birthday of pope; the first red leaf hurrying through "the altered air," an epoch. Immortality was close about her; and while never morbid or melancholy, she lived in its presence. (p. 419)

Mabel Loomis Todd, "Preface to 'Poems, Second Series', 1891," in Ancestors' Brocades: The Literary Debut of Emily Dickinson *by Millicent Todd Bingham, Harper & Brothers Publishers, 1945, pp. 417-19.*

CHICAGO TRIBUNE (essay date 1891)

[*In this excerpt from a largely positive review of* Poems by Emily Dickinson, second series, *the critic comments on the childlike qualities of Dickinson's poetry. This essay was first published in the* Chicago Tribune *on 12 December 1891.*]

[It is the childlike element in Emily Dickinson,] we think, that appeals most strongly to the reader of her poems. One occasionally finds the same difficulty in following the irregular hop-step-and-jump of her thought as in attempting to keep pace with the skipping mental gait of an intelligent child. Her wayward and irresponsible fancy describes every sort of abrupt angle and eccentric curve, but naturally and without effort. This naturalness distinguishes her work from that of Quarles and his fellows, whose far-fetched conceits are so lacking in spontaneity. Of the coquetry and self-consciousness that mar the work of so many poets one never sees a trace; she composes with her eye upon her object and seeks to please herself alone. Her wonderful acuteness and her uncompromising naturalism are not the effect of culture, but a part of her childhood's unforfeited inheritance. She has a child's ignorance of the world, a child's imagination and love of color. One smiles at the significance with which she invests the idea of an Earl; to be "Duke of Exeter"—ah, that is a too, too daring flight! How like a child's fancy is this, which describes the "clear shining after rain":

The boldest stole out of his covert,
  To see if time was there;
Nature was in her beryl apron,
  Mixing fresher air.

One compares her with Emerson, with Scott's "Pet Marjorie," and with Blake, the English painter-poet; but, after all, she is just herself, the solitary example of a floral species as yet unclassified.

Of these characteristics the effect is intensified by the eccentricities of her style. Her verse is often grammatically obscure; she does not hesitate to employ a word in a sense which is foreign to it; the metaphysical quips and fetches in which she indulges are sometimes too fine-spun to be intelligible. Her rhythm, too, is frequently irregular, though never devoid of a certain music; and her numerous false rhymes are unpardonable. Rhymed, unrhymed, and imperfectly rhymed stanzas occur in the same poem, conforming to no rule but that of the writer's caprice. Mrs. Todd speaks of the "thought-rhymes" which appear in her friend's work, "appealing to an unrecognized sense more elusive than hearing" [see excerpt dated 1891]. If we understand the term aright, the "thought-rhyme" is as often absent as present in these irregular stanzas; at any rate, one cannot go jumping from word-rhymes to thought-rhymes and back again, all in the same piece. Mrs. Todd should have taken stronger ground. We are willing to condone these technical offenses because the offender is Emily Dickinson. An Emily who was willing to conform to rules, to suppress her individuality, and to follow the beaten track, would not have been the Emily Dickinson of our admiration. Her faults were merely the defects of her qualities; her originality and her eccentricity were fostered by the same conditions. "When I try to organize," she says of herself, "my little force explodes and leaves me bare and charred" [see excerpt dated August 1862]. Her imperfections, then, are the price of her charm, and a price we are only too ready to pay. (pp. 46-7)

"Second Series of the 'Poems by Emily Dickinson'," in The Recognition of Emily Dickinson: Selected Criticism since 1890, *edited by Caesar R. Blake and Carlton F. Wells, The University of Michigan Press, 1964, pp. 45-50.*

[THOMAS BAILEY ALDRICH] (essay date 1892)

[*Aldrich, an American poet and novelist, succeeded W. D. Howells as editor of the* Atlantic Monthly. *In this excerpt from a negative review of Dickinson's second volume of poetry, Aldrich harshly criticizes the grammar and meter of her works.*]

The English critic who said of Miss Emily Dickinson that she might have become a fifth-rate poet "if she had only mastered the rudiments of grammar and gone into metrical training for about fifteen years,"—the rather candid English critic who said this somewhat overstated his case. He had, however, a fairly good case. If Miss Dickinson had undergone the austere curriculum indicated, she would, I am sure, have become an admirable lyric poet of the second magnitude. In the first volume of her poetical chaos is a little poem which needs only slight revision in the initial stanza in order to make it worthy of ranking with some of the odd swallow flights in Heine's lyrical *intermezzo*. I have ventured to desecrate this stanza by tossing a rhyme into it, as the other stanzas happened to rhyme, and here print the lyric, hoping the reader will not accuse me of overvaluing it:—

I taste a liquor never brewed
In vats upon the Rhine;
No tankard ever held a draught
Of alcohol like mine.

Inebriate of air am I,
And debauchee of dew,
Reeling, through endless summer days,
From inns of molten blue.

When landlords turn the drunken bee
Out of the Foxglove's door,
When butterflies renounce their drams,
I shall but drink the more!

Till seraphs swing their snowy caps
And saints to windows run,
To see the little tippler
Leaning against the sun!

Certainly those inns of molten blue, and that disreputable honey-gatherer who got himself turned out-of-doors at the sign of the Foxglove, are very taking matters. I know of more important things that interest me less. There are three or four bits in this kind in Miss Dickinson's book; but for the most part the ideas totter and toddle, not having learned to walk. In spite of this, several of the quatrains are curiously touching, they have such a pathetic air of yearning to be poems.

It is plain that Miss Dickinson possessed an extremely unconventional and grotesque fancy. She was deeply tinged by the mysticism of Blake, and strongly influenced by the mannerism of Emerson. The very way she tied her bonnet-strings, preparatory to one of her nunlike walks in her claustral garden, must have been Emersonian. She had much fancy of a queer sort, but only, as it appears to me, intermittent flashes of imagination. I fail to detect in her work any of that profound thought which her editor professes to discover in it. The phenomenal insight, I am inclined to believe, exists only in his partiality; for whenever a woman poet is in question Mr. Higginson always puts on his rose-colored spectacles. This is being chivalrous; but the invariable result is not clear vision. That Miss Dickinson's whimsical memoranda have a certain something which, for want of a more precise name, we term *quality* is not to be denied except by the unconvertible heathen who are not worth conversion. But the incoherence and formlessness of her—I don't know how to designate them—versicles are fatal. Sydney Smith, or some other humorist, mentions a person whose bump of veneration was so inadequately developed as to permit him to damn the equator if he wanted to. This certainly established a precedent for independence; but an eccentric, dreamy, half-educated recluse in an out-of-the-way New England village (or anywhere else) cannot with impunity set at defiance the laws of gravitation and grammar. In his charming preface to Miss Dickinson's collection, Mr. Higginson insidiously remarks: "After all, when a thought takes one's breath away, a lesson on grammar seems an impertinence" [see excerpt dated 1890]. But an ungrammatical thought does not, as a general thing, takes one's breath away, except in a sense the reverse of flattering. (pp. 143-44)

If Miss Dickinson's *disjecta membra* are poems, then Shakespeare's prolonged imposition should be exposed without further loss of time, and Lord Tennyson ought to be advised of the error of his ways before it is too late. But I do not hold the situation to be so desperate. Miss Dickinson's versicles have a queerness and a quaintness that have stirred a momentary curiosity in emotional bosoms. Oblivion lingers in the immediate neighborhood. (p. 144)

[Thomas Bailey Aldrich], "The Contributors' Club," in The Atlantic Monthly, *Vol. LXIX, No. 411, January, 1892, pp. 139-44.*

MABEL LOOMIS TODD (essay date 1896)

[The following excerpt is drawn from Todd's preface to the third collection of Dickinson's poetry, which was published in 1896. For further commentary by Todd, see excerpts dated 1881 and 1891.]

The intellectual activity of Emily Dickinson was so great that a large and characteristic choice is still possible among her literary material, and this third volume of her verses [***Poems, third series***] is put forth in response to the repeated wish of the admirers of her peculiar genius.

Much of Emily Dickinson's prose was rhythmic,—even rhymed, though frequently not set apart in lines. . . .

There is internal evidence that many of the poems were simply spontaneous flashes of insight, apparently unrelated to outward circumstance. Others, however, had an obvious personal origin; for example, the verses **"I had a Guinea golden,"** which seem to have been sent to some friend travelling in Europe, as a dainty reminder of letter-writing delinquencies. The surroundings in which any of Emily Dickinson's verses are known to have been written usually serve to explain them clearly; but in general the present volume is full of thoughts needing no interpretation to those who apprehend this scintillating spirit.

Mabel Loomis Todd, "Preface to 'Poems, Third Series', 1896," in Ancestors' Brocades: The Literary Debut of Emily Dickinson *by Millicent Todd Bingham, Harper & Brothers Publishers, 1945, p. 420.*

BLISS CARMAN (essay date 1896)

[Carman was a popular Canadian novelist and journalist. In this excerpt from a survey of Dickinson's poetry first published on 21 November 1896 in the Boston Evening Transcript, *Carman emphasizes the originality and essentially American qualities of her achievement.]*

Pending the coming in of [Kipling's] *The Seven Seas,* it is safe to say that the publication of a new volume of poems by Emily Dickinson is the literary event of the season. Six years ago when her first book was given to the public, it ran through several editions, achieving a larger sale, I believe, than any other first volume ever printed at the University Press, and that is saying a good deal, when one recalls the distinguished works that have issued from that excellent printing shop. Its author's name was entirely unknown, and she herself already passed beyond the confusion of renown; yet so distinctive was her note, so spiritual and intense and absolutely sincere, that she sprang at once into a posthumous fame, unadulterated and almost splendid. It was one more tribute to the New England ideal, the American interest in morality, the bent for transcendentalism inherited from Emerson; and, by the way, it was at the same time another evidence of the alertness of the American reading public, and its sensitiveness to excellent originality. For while there was novelty in the verse of Emily Dickinson, there was nothing sensational, hardly anything strange; no peculiarity on which a cult could batten. Those who admired her verse must admire it for its poetry alone.

I have just said that there is nothing sensational in Emily Dickinson's poetry; and yet there was, in a small way, a genuine sensation in the editorial rooms of one of the oldest journals in New York when our chief, with that tireless and impetuous enthusiasm of his, came rushing in with his bright discovery—like a whirl of October leaves. He is one of the two American editors who have the superfluous faculty of knowing poetry when they see it; he had fallen upon the immortal maid's first book, and the slumbering poet in him was awake. Nothing would suffice but we must share his youthful elation, listen to the strains of this original and accredited singer. The heat of New York, the routine of an office, the jaded mind of a reviewer, the vitiated habit of the professional manuscript-taster—it was not easy to shake off these at once; we were somewhat cold, perhaps, and a little sceptical of the chief's discovery. Still, we must listen. Hear this—

Belshazzar had a letter—
He never had but one;
Belshazzar's correspondent
Concluded and begun
In that immortal copy
The conscience of us all
Can read without its glasses
On revelation's wall.

Why, yes, certainly that is original enough. But can your wonderful prodigy turn off another verse like it?

"Can she? To be sure! Listen again!"

I taste a liquor never brewed.
  From tankards scooped in pearl;
Not all the vats upon the Rhine
  Yield such an alcohol!

Inebriate of air am I,
  And debauchee of dew,
Reeling, through endless summer days,
  From inns of molten blue.

When landlords turn the drunken bee
  Out of the foxglove's door,
When butterflies renounce their drams,
  I shall but drink the more!

Till seraphs swing their snowy hats,
  And saints to windows run,
To see the little tippler
  Leaning against the sun.

Well, we are convinced, indeed. There can be no doubt of the genuineness of this writer. Such work is fresh from the mint; not immediately current without some scrutiny; yet stamped plainly enough with the hall-mark of genius. We could but give unqualified assent; put the new book on the old shelf at once, with its peers, the acknowledged classics of American literature.

Following this first venture, there has been a second collection of poems, two volumes of letters and now this third book of verse. And allowing one's judgment time to cool, I must say the conviction remains that Emily Dickinson's contribution to English poetry (or American poetry, if you prefer to say so) is by far the most important made by any woman west of the Atlantic. It is so by reason of its thought, its piquancy, its untarnished expression. She borrowed from no one; she was never commonplace; always imaginative and stimulating; and finally, the region of her brooding was that sequestered domain where our profoundest convictions have origin, and whence we trace the Puritan strain within us.

For this New England woman was a type of her race. A life-long recluse, musing on the mysteries of life and death, she yet had that stability of character, that strong sanity of mind, which could hold out against the perils of seclusion, unshaken by solitude, undethroned by doubt. The very fibre of New England must have been there, founded of granite, nourished by an exhilarating air. We are permitted, through Colonel Higginson's introduction to the first series of poems, the merest glimpse into the story of her life in that beautiful college town in the lovely valley of the Connecticut [see excerpt dated 1890]. We imagine her in the old-fashioned house with its stately decency, its air of breeding and reserve, set a little back from the street, ambushed behind a generous hedge, and flanked by an ample garden on the side—a garden full of roses and tall elms and the scent of new-mown hay. There among her own, she chose an unaustere and voluntary monasticism for her daily course, far indeed removed from the average life of our towns, yet not so untypical of that strain of Puritan blood which besets us all. It would never, I feel sure, occur to anyone with the least insight into the New England character, or the remotest inheritance of the New England conscience (with its capacity for abstemiousness, its instinct for being always aloof and restrained, rather than social and blithe), to think of Emily Dickinson as peculiar, or her mode of life as queer. Somewhat strange as the record of it may show to foreign eyes, it was natural enough in its own time and place, though sufficiently unusual to claim something of distinction even of itself. Illumined and revealed in her poems, the life and character of this original nature make a fit study for the subtlest criticism—such a criticism, indeed, as I know not where they will receive. And all the while, as we speak of Emily Dickinson's secluded life, and her individual habit of isolation, her parsimony in friendship and human intercourse, I have a conviction that we should guard against the fancy that she was tinged with any shadow of sadness, or any touch of misanthropy or gloom. It seems rather that she must have had the sunniest of dispositions, as she certainly had the most sensitive and exquisite organization. It was not that the persons or fellows seemed to her superfluous or harsh or unnecessary, but rather that in one so finely organized as she must have been, the event of meeting another was too exquisite and portentous to be borne. For there are some natures so shy and quick, so undulled by the life of the senses, that they never quite acquire the easy part of the world. You will hear of them shunning the most delightful acquaintance, turning a corner sharply to avoid an encounter, hesitating at the very threshold of welcome, out of some dim inherited, instinctive dread of casual intercourse. They are like timorous elusive spirits, gone astray, perhaps, and landed on the rough planet Earth by a slight mischance; and when they are compelled by circumstance to share in the world's work, their part in it is likely to be an unhappy one. Theirs is the bent for solitude, the custom of silence. And once that fleeing sense of self-protection arises within them, the chances are they will indulge it to the end. And fortunate, indeed, it is, if that end be not disaster. But in Emily Dickinson's case, the stray health of genius came to the support of this hermit's instinct, and preserved her to the end of life sweet and blithe and contented in that innocent nun-like existence in which she chose to be immured. Her own room served her for native land, and in the painted garden beyond her window-sill was foreign travel enough for her. For that frugal soul, the universe of experience was bounded by the blue hills of a New England valley.

It was, of course, part of the inheritance of such a woman to have the religious sense strongly marked. She came of a race that never was at ease in Zion, yet never was content out of sight of the promised land. It best suited their strenuous and warlike nature always to be looking down on the delectable Canaan from the Pisgah of their own unworthiness. Yet, however severe a face life wore to them, and unlovely as their asperity often was, they were still making, though unwittingly, for the liberation of humanity. They were laying a substructure of honesty and seriousness, on which their intellectual inheritors might build, whether in art or politics. And their occupation with religion, with the affairs of the inward life and all its needs, has left an impress on ourselves, given us a trend from which we swerve in vain. And on every page of Emily Dickinson's poetry this ethical tendency, this awful environment of spirituality, is evident. Meditations of Psyche in the House of Clay; epigrams of an immortal guest, left behind on the chamber wall on the eve of silent departure, these brief lyrics seem:

This world is not conclusion;
  A sequel stands beyond,
Invisible as music,
  But positive as sound.

It beckons and it baffles;
  Philosophies don't know,
And through a riddle, at the last,
  Sagacity must go.

To guess it puzzles scholars;
  To gain it, men have shown
Contempt of generations,
  And crucifixion known.

That is an orphic utterance, no doubt; and such is all of this poet's work. She is, like Emerson, a companion for solitude, a stimulating comrade in the arduous intellectual ways. A symbolist of the symbolists, she is with them a reviver and establisher of the religious sentiment. Full of scepticism and the gentle irony of formal unbelief, putting aside the accepted and narrowing creed, she brings us, as Emerson did, face to face with new objects of worship. In their guidance we come a step nearer the great veil. For it is quite true that he who was hailed as a sceptic and destroyer in his early career, was in reality a prophet and a founder.

And it was inevitable, too, that one so much at home in spiritual matters should be deeply versed in nature—should be on intimate terms of friendship with all Nature's creatures.

Not that her knowledge of them was wide; it could hardly be that. But her sympathy with them was deep. She had ever a word of interpretation for the humblest of the mute dwellers in her garden world, clover or bee or blade. Often in these verses on the natural world there is a touch of whimsical humor that shows her character in very delightful color; as, for instance, in the lines on cobwebs:

The spider as an artist
  Has never been employed,
Though his surpassing merit
  Is freely certified

By every broom and Bridget
  Throughout a Christian land.
Neglected son of genius,
  I take thee by the hand.

There is the touch of intimacy, of fellowship, of kinship with all creation, which is so characteristic of modern poetry, and which is to become characteristic of modern religion. It is the tolerant, gay, debonair note of blameless joy which has been banished so long from the world, coming back to claim its own again.

Did I say that Emily Dickinson's contribution to poetry was more important than that of any other woman in America? Perhaps it is. Yet it has its faults, so hard a thing is perfection in any art, and so perfect the balance of fine qualities necessary to attain it. For while this poet was so eminent in wit, so keen in epigram, so rare and startling in phrase, the extended laborious architecture of an impressive poetic creation was beyond her. So that one has to keep her at hand as a stimulus and refreshment rather than as a solace. She must not be read long at a sitting. She will not bear that sort of treatment any more than Mr. Swinburne will; and for the very opposite reason. In Swinburne there is such a richness of sound, and often such a paucity of thought that one's even mental poise is sadly strained in trying to keep an equilibrium. He is like those garrulous persons, enamored of their own voice, who talk one to death so pleasingly. While in Emily Dickinson there is a lack of sensuousness, just as there was in Emerson. So that, like him, she never could have risen into the first rank of poets. And it was a sure critical instinct that led her never to venture beyond the range where her success was sure.

There is one thing to be remembered in considering her poetry, if we are to allow ourselves the full enjoyment of it; and that is her peculiar rhymes. As Colonel Higginson well remarks, "Though curiously indifferent to all conventional rules, she had a rigorous literary standard of her own, and often altered a word many times to suit an ear which had its own tenacious fastidiousness."

It is usual in verse to call those sounds perfect rhymes in which the final consonants (if there be any) and the final vowels are identical, but the consonants preceding these final vowels, different. So that we call "hand" and "land" perfect rhymes. But this is only a conventional custom among poets. It is consonant with laws of poetry, of course; but it is not in itself a law. It is merely one means at the writer's disposal for marking off his lines for the reader's ear. And when Emily Dickinson chose to use in her own work another slightly different convention, she was at perfect liberty to do so. She violated no law of poetry. The laws of art are as inviolable as the laws of nature.

Who never wanted—maddest joy
  Remains to him unknown;
The banquet of abstemiousness
  Surpasses that of wine.

"Wine" and "unknown" are not perfect rhymes. No more are "ground" and "mind," "done" and "man"; yet they serve to mark her lines for her reader quite well. Why? Because she has made a new rule for herself, and has followed it carefully. It is simply this—that the final vowels need not be identical; only the final consonants need be identical. The vowels may vary. It is wrong to say that she disregarded any law here. The question is rather: Did her new usage tend to beautiful results? For my part I confess that I like that falling rhyme very much. There is a haunting gypsy accent about it, quite in keeping with the tenor of that wilding music. What a strange and gnomelike presence lurks in all her lines! (pp. 61-8)

Bliss Carman, "A Note on Emily Dickinson," in The Recognition of Emily Dickinson: Selected Criticism since 1890, *edited by Caesar R. Blake and Carlton F. Wells, The University of Michigan Press, 1964, pp. 61-8.*

JAMES FULLARTON MUIRHEAD (essay date 1898)

[*Muirhead, a British critic, offers qualified praise for Dickinson's poetry in this excerpt from a discussion of American literature.*]

[Miss Emily Dickinson's] poems are all in lyrical form—if the word form may be applied to her utter disregard of all metrical conventions. Her lines are rugged and her expressions wayward to an extraordinary degree, but "her verses all show a strange cadence of inner rhythmical music," and the "thought-rhymes" which she often substitutes for the more regular assonances appeal "to an unrecognised sense more elusive than hearing" (Mrs. Todd). In this curious divergence from established rules of verse Miss Dickinson may be likened to Walt Whitman, whom she differs from in every other particular, and notably in her pithiness as opposed to his diffuseness; but with her we feel in the strongest way that her mode is natural and unsought, utterly free from affectation, posing, or self-consciousness.

Colonel Higginson rightly finds her nearest analogue in William Blake; but this "nearest" is far from identity. While tenderly feminine in her sympathy for suffering, her love of nature, her loyalty to her friends, she is in expression the most unfeminine of poets. The usual feminine impulsiveness and full expression of emotion is replaced in her by an extraordinary condensation of phrase and feeling. In her letters we find the eternal womanly in her yearning love for her friends, her brooding anxiety and sympathy for the few lives closely intertwined with her own. In her poems, however, one is rather impressed with the deep well of poetic insight and feeling from which she draws, but never unreservedly. In spite of frequent strange exaggeration of phrase one is always conscious of a fund of reserve force. The subjects of her poems are few, but the piercing delicacy and depth of vision with which she turned from death and eternity to nature and to love make us feel the presence of that rare thing, genius. Hers is a wonderful instance of the way in which genius can dispense with experience; she sees more by pure intuition than others distil from the serried facts of an eventful life. Perhaps, in one of her own phrases, she is "too intrinsic for renown," but she has appealed strongly to a surprisingly large band of readers in the United States, and it seems to me will always hold her audience. Those who admit Miss Dickinson's talent, but deny it to be poetry, may be referred to Thoreau's saying that no definition of poetry can be given which the true poet will not somewhere sometime brush aside. It is a new departure, and the writer in the *Nation* (Oct. 10, 1895) is probably right when he says: "So marked a new departure rarely leads to further growth. Neither Whitman nor Miss Dickinson ever stepped beyond the circle they first drew." (pp. 179-81)

[Miss Dickinson's] interest in all the familiar sights and sounds of a village garden is evident through all her verses. Her illustrations are not recondite, literary, or conventional; she finds them at her own door. The robin, the buttercup, the maple, furnish what she needs. The bee, in particular, seems to have had a peculiar fascination for her, and hums through all her poems. She had even a kindly word for that "neglected son of genius," the spider. Her love of children is equally evident, and no one has ever better caught the spirit of

"Saturday Afternoon"

From all the jails the boys and girls
  Ecstatically leap,
Beloved, only afternoon
  That prison doesn't keep.

They storm the earth and stun the air,
  A mob of solid bliss.
Alas! that frowns could like in wait
  For such a foe as this!

The bold extravagance of her diction (which is not, however, *mere* extravagance) and her ultra-American familiarity with the forces of nature may be illustrated by such stanzas as:

What if the poles should frisk about
  And stand upon their heads!
I hope I'm ready for the worst,
  Whatever prank betides.

If I could see you in a year,
  I'd wind the months in balls,
And put them each in separate drawers
  Until their time befalls.

If certain, when this life was out,
  That yours and mine should be,
I'd toss it yonder like a rind,
  And taste eternity.

For her the lightnings "skip like mice," the thunder "crumbles like a stuff." What a critic has called her "Emersonian self-possession" towards God may be seen in the little poem on the last page of her first volume, where she addresses the Deity as "burglar, banker, father." There is, however, no flippancy in this, no conscious irreverence; Miss Dickinson is not "orthodox," but she is genuinely spiritual and religious. Inspired by its truly American and *"actuel"* freedom, her muse does not fear to sing of such modern and mechanical phenomena as the railway train, which she loves to see "lap the miles and lick the valleys up," while she is fascinated by the contrast between its prodigious force and the way in which it stops, "docile and omnipotent, at its own stable door." But even she can hardly bring the smoking locomotive into such pathetic relations with nature as the "little brig," whose "white foot tripped, then dropped from sight," leaving "the ocean's heart too smooth, too blue, to break for you."

Her poems on death and the beyond, on time and eternity, are full of her peculiar note. Death is the "one dignity" that "delays for all;" the meanest brow is so ennobled by the majesty of death that "almost a powdered footman might dare to touch it now," and yet no beggar would accept "the *éclat* of death, had he the power to spurn." "The quiet nonchalance of death" is a resting-place which has no terrors for her; death "abashed" her no more than "the porter of her father's lodge." Death's chariot also holds Immortality. The setting sail for "deep eternity" brings a "divine intoxication" such as the "inland soul" feels on its "first league out from land." Though she "never spoke with God, nor visited in heaven," she is "as certain of the spot as if the chart were given." "In heaven somehow, it will be even, some new equation given." "Christ will explain each separate anguish in the fair schoolroom of the sky."

A death-blow is a life-blow to some
Who, till they died, did not alive become;
Who, had they lived, had died, but when
They died, vitality begun.

The reader . . . will surely own, whether in scoff or praise, the essentially American nature of her muse. Her defects are easily paralleled in the annals of English literature; but only in the liberal atmosphere of the New World, comparatively unshadowed by trammels of authority and standards of taste, could they have co-existed with so much of the highest quality. (pp. 183-86)

James Fullarton Muirhead, "Some Literary Straws," in his The Land of Contrasts: A Briton's View of His American Kin, *Lamson, Wolffe and Company, 1898, pp. 162-89.*

MARTHA HALE SHACKFORD (essay date 1913)

[*Shackford was a noted scholar of medieval, Renaissance, and nineteenth-century literature. In this excerpt, she evaluates Dickinson's significance in American literature, outlining the distinguishing characteristics of her poetry.*]

Emily Dickinson is one of our most original writers, a force destined to endure in American letters.

There is no doubt that critics are justified in complaining that her work is often cryptic in thought and unmelodious in expression. Almost all her poems are written in short measures, in which the effect of curt brevity is increased by her verbal penuriousness. Compression and epigrammatical ambush are her aids; she proceeds, without preparation or apology, by sudden, sharp zigzags. What intelligence a reader has must be exercised in the poetic game of hare-and-hounds, where ellipses, inversions, and unexpected climaxes mislead those who pursue sweet reasonableness. Nothing, for instance, could seem less poetical than this masterpiece of unspeakable sounds and chaotic rhymes:—

"Cocoon"

Drab habitation of whom?
Tabernacle or tomb,
Or dome of worm,
Or porch of gnome,
Or some elf's catacomb.

If all her poems were of this sort there would be nothing more to say; but such poems are exceptions. Because we happen to possess full records of her varying poetic moods, published, not with the purpose of selecting her most artistic work, but with the intention of revealing very significant human documents, we are not justified in singling out a few bizarre poems and subjecting these to skeptical scrutiny. The poems taken in their entirety are a surprising and impressive revelation of poetic attitude and of poetic method in registering spiritual experiences. To the general reader many of the poems seem uninspired, imperfect, crude, while to the student of the psychology of literary art they offer most stimulating material for examination, because they enable one to penetrate into poetic origins, into radical, creative energy. However, it is not with the body of her collected poems but with the selected, representative work that the general reader is concerned. Assuredly we do not judge an artist by his worst, but by his best, productions; we endeavor to find the highest level of his power and thus to discover the typical significance of his work.

To gratify the aesthetic sense was never Emily Dickinson's desire; she despised the poppy and mandragora of felicitous phrases which lull the spirit to apathy and emphasize art for art's sake. Poetry to her was the expression of vital meanings, the transfer of passionate feeling and of deep conviction. Her work is essentially lyric; it lacks the slow, retreating harmonies of epic measures, it does not seek to present leisurely details of any sort; its purpose is to objectify the swiftly-passing moments and to give them poignant expression.

Lyric melody finds many forms in her work. Her repressed and austere verses, inexpansive as they are, have persistent appeal. Slow, serene movement gives enduring beauty to these elegiac stanzas:—

Let down the bars, O Death!
The tired flocks come in
Whose bleating ceases to repeat,
Whose wandering is done.

Thine is the stillest night,
Thine the securest fold;
Too near thou art for seeking thee,
Too tender to be told.

The opposite trait of buoyant alertness is illustrated in the cadences of the often-quoted lines on the hummingbird:—

A route of evanescence
With a revolving wheel;
A resonance of emerald,
A rush of cochineal.

Between these two margins come many wistful, pleading, or triumphant notes. The essential qualities of her music are simplicity and quivering responsiveness to emotional moods. Idea and expression are so indissolubly fused in her work that no analysis of her style and manner can be attempted without realizing that every one of her phrases, her changing rhythms, is a direct reflection of her personality. The objective medium is entirely conformable to the inner life, a life of peculiarly dynamic force which agitates, arouses, spurs the reader.

The secret of Emily Dickinson's wayward power seems to lie in three special characteristics, the first of which is her intensity of spiritual experience. Hers is the record of a soul endowed with unceasing activity in a world not material, but one where concrete facts are the cherished revelation of divine significances. Inquisitive always, alert to the inner truths of life, impatient of the brief destinies of convention, she isolated herself from the petty demands of social amenity. A sort of tireless, probing energy of mental action absorbed her, yet there is little speculation of a purely philosophical sort in her poetry. Her stubborn beliefs, learned in childhood, persisted to the end,—her conviction that life is beauty, that love explains grief, and that immortality endures. The quality of her writing is profoundly stirring, because it betrays, not the intellectual pioneer, but the acutely observant woman, whose capacity for feeling was profound. The still, small voice of tragic revelation one hears in these compressed lines:—

"Parting"

My life closed twice before its close;
  It yet remains to see
If Immortality unveil
  A third event to me,

So huge, so hopeless to conceive,
  As these that twice befell.
Parting is all we know of heaven,
  And all we need of hell.

For sheer, grim, unrelieved expression of emotional truth there are few passages which can surpass the personal experience revealed in the following poem:—

Pain has an element of blank;
It cannot recollect
When it began, or if there were
A day when it was not.

It has no future but itself,
Its infinite realms contain
Its past, enlightened to perceive
New periods of pain.

Her absorption in the world of feeling found some relief in associations with nature; yet although she loved nature and wrote many nature lyrics, her interpretations are always more or less swayed by her own state of being. The colors, the fragrances, the forms of the material world, meant to her a divine symbolism; but the spectacle of nature had in her eyes a more fugitive glory, a lesser consolation, than it had for Wordsworth and other true lovers of the earth.

Brilliant and beautiful transcripts of bird-life and of flower-life appear among her poems, although there is in some cases a childish fancifulness that disappoints the reader. Among the touches of unforgettable vividness there are:—

These are the days when skies put on
The old, old sophistries of June,—
A blue and gold mistake;

and

Nature rarer uses yellow
  Than another hue;
Leaves she all of that for sunsets,—
  Prodigal of blue,

Spending scarlet like a woman,
  Yellow she affords
Only scantly and selectly,
  Like a lover's words.

Never has any poet described the haunting magic of autumnal days with such fine perception of beauty as marks the opening stanzas of **"My Cricket"**:—

Farther in summer than the birds,
Pathetic from the grass,
A minor nation celebrates
Its unobtrusive mass.

No ordinance is seen,
So gradual the grace,
A pensive custom it becomes,
Enlarging loneliness.

Most effective, however, are those poems where she describes not mere external beauty, but, rather, the effect of nature upon a sensitive observer:—

There's a certain slant of light,
On winter afternoons,
That oppresses, like the weight
Of cathedral tunes.

Heavenly hurt it gives us;
We can find no scar,
But internal difference
Where the meanings are.

None may teach it anything,
'T is the seal, despair,—
An imperial affliction
Sent us of the air.

When it comes, the landscape listens,
Shadows hold their breath;
When it goes, 't is like the distance
On the look of death.

It is essentially in the world of spiritual forces that her depth of poetic originality is shown. Others may describe nature, but few can describe life as she does. Human nature, the experiences of the world of souls, was her special study, to which she brought, in addition to that quality of intensity, a second characteristic,—keen sensitiveness to irony and paradox. Nearly all her perceptions are tinged with penetrating sense of the contrasts in human vicissitude. Controlled, alert, expectant, aware of the perpetual compromise between clay and spirit, she accepted the inscrutable truths of life in a fashion which reveals how humor and pathos contend in her. It is this which gives her style those sudden turns and that startling imagery. Humor is not, perhaps, a characteristic associated with pure lyric poetry, and yet Emily Dickinson's transcendental humor is one of the deep sources of her supremacy. Both in thought and in expression she gains her piercing quality, her undeniable spiritual thrust, by this gift, stimulating, mystifying, but forever inspiring her readers to a profound conception of high destinies.

The most apparent instances of this keen, shrewd delight in challenging convention, in the effort to establish, through contrast, reconcilement of the earthly and the eternal, are to be found in her imagery. Although her similes and metaphors may be devoid of languid aesthetic elegance, they are quivering to express living ideas, and so they come surprisingly close to what we are fond of calling the commonplace. She reverses the usual, she hitches her star to a wagon, transfixing homely daily phrases for poetic purposes. Such an audacity has seldom invaded poetry with a desire to tell immortal truths through the medium of a deep sentiment for old habitual things. It is true that we permit this liberty to the greatest poets, Shakespeare, Keats, Wordsworth, and some others; but in America our poets have been sharply charged not to offend in this respect. Here tradition still animates many critics in the belief that real poetry must have exalted phraseology.

The poem already quoted, **"Let down the bars, O Death!"** has its own rustic vividness of association. Even more homely is the domestic suggestion wherewith the poet sets forth an eternally, profoundly significant fact:—

The trying on the utmost,
The morning it is new,
Is terribler than wearing it
A whole existence through.

Surely such a commonplace comparison gives startling vividness to the innate idea. Many are the poetic uses she makes of practical everyday life:—

The soul should always stand ajar;

and

The only secret people keep
Is Immortality;

and

Such dimity convictions,
A horror so refined,
Of freckled human nature,
Of Deity ashamed;

and

And kingdoms, like the orchard,
Flit russetly away;

and

If I could n't thank you,
Being just asleep,
You will know I'm trying
With my granite lip.

More significantly, however, than in these epithets and figures, irony and paradox appear in those analyses of truth where she reveals the deep note of tragic idealism:—

Not one of all the purple host
Who took the flag to-day
Can tell the definition,
So clear, of victory,

As he, defeated, dying,
On whose forbidden ear
The distant strains of triumph
Break, agonized and clear;

and

Essential oils are wrung;
The attar from the rose
Is not expressed by suns alone,
It is the gift of screws.

She took delight in piquing the curiosity, and often her love of mysterious challenging symbolism led her to the borderland of obscurity. No other of her poems has, perhaps, such a union of playfulness and of terrible comment upon the thwarted aspirations of a suffering soul as has this:—

I asked no other thing,
No other was denied.
I offered Being for it;
The mighty merchant smiled.

Brazil? He twirled a button,
Without a glance my way:
'But, madam, is there nothing else
That we can show to-day?'

Since life seemed, to her, seldom to move along wholly simple and direct ways, she delighted to accentuate the fact that out of apparent contradictions and discords are wrought the subtlest harmonies:—

To learn the transport by the pain,
As blind men learn the sun;

and

Sufficient troth that we shall rise—
Deposed, at length, the grave—
To that new marriage, justified
Through Calvaries of Love;

and

The lightning that preceded it
Struck no one but myself,
But I would not exchange the bolt
For all the rest of life.

The expectation of finding in her work some quick, perverse, illuminating comment upon eternal truths certainly keeps a reader's interest from flagging, but passionate intensity and fine irony do not fully explain Emily Dickinson's significance. There is a third characteristic trait, a dauntless courage in accepting life. Existence, to her, was a momentous experience, and she let no promises of a future life deter her from feeling the throbs of this one. No false comfort released her from dismay at present anguish. An energy of pain and joy swept her soul, but did not leave any residue of bitterness or of sharp innuendo against the ways of the Almighty. Grief was a faith, not a disaster. She made no effort to smother the recollections of old companionship by that species of spiritual death to which so many people consent. Her creed was expressed in these stanzas:—

They say that 'time assuages,'—
  Time never did assuage;
An actual suffering strengthens,
  As sinews do, with age.

Time is a test of trouble,
  But not a remedy.
If such it prove, it proves too
  There was no malady.

The willingness to look with clear directness at the spectacle of life is observable everywhere in her work. Passionate fortitude was hers, and this is the greatest contribution her poetry makes to the reading world. It is not expressed precisely in single poems, but rather is present in all, as key and interpretation of her meditative scrutiny. Without elaborate philosophy, yet with irresistible ways of expression, Emily Dickinson's poems have true lyric appeal, because they make abstractions, such as love, hope, loneliness, death, and immortality, seem near and intimate and faithful. She looked at existence with a vision so exalted and secure that the reader is long dominated by that very excess of spiritual conviction. A poet in the deeper mystic qualities of feeling rather than in the external merit of precise rhymes and flawless art, Emily Dickinson's place is among those whose gifts are

Too intrinsic for renown.

(pp. 93-7)

Martha Hale Shackford, "The Poetry of Emily Dickinson," in The Atlantic Monthly, *Vol. III, No. 1, January, 1913, pp. 93-7.*

CONRAD AIKEN (essay date 1924)

[An American man of letters best known for his poetry, Aiken was deeply influenced by the psychological and literary theories of Sigmund Freud, Havelock Ellis, Edgar Allan Poe, and Henri Bergson, among others, and is considered a master of literary stream of consciousness. In the following excerpt from an essay first published in the Dial *in April 1924, Aiken reviews the circumstances of Dickinson's life and the concerns of her poetry for clues to her personality and literary genius.]*

Emily Dickinson was born in Amherst, Massachusetts, on December 10th, 1830. She died there, after a life perfectly devoid of outward event, in 1886. She was thus an exact contemporary of Christina Rossetti, who was born five days earlier than she, and outlived her by eight years. Of her life we know little. Her father, Edward Dickinson, was a lawyer, and the Treasurer of Amherst College; and it is clear that what social or intellectual life was in that bleak era available, was available for her. That she did not choose to avail herself of it, except in very slight degree, is also clear; and that this choice, which was gradually to make of her life an almost inviolable solitude, was made early, is evident from her ***Letters.*** In a letter dated 1853, when she was twenty-three years old, she remarked, "I do not go from home." By the time she was thirty, the habit of sequestration had become distinct, a subject on which she was explicit and emphatic in her letters to T. W. Higginson—editor of the *Atlantic Monthly* at that time. She made it clear that if there was to be any question of a meeting between them, he would have to come to Amherst—she would not go to Boston. Higginson, as a matter of fact, saw her twice, and his record of the encounter is practically the only record we have of her from any "literary" personage of her lifetime [see excerpt dated 1870]. Even this is meager—Higginson saw her superficially, as was inevitable. Brave soldier, courtly gentleman, able editor, he was too much of the old school not to be a little puzzled by her poetry; and if he was fine enough to guess the fineness, he was not quite fine enough wholly to understand it. The brief correspondence between these two is an extraordinary document of unconscious irony—the urbanely academic editor reproaching his wayward pupil for her literary insubordination, her false quantities and reckless liberties with rhyme; the wayward pupil replying with a humility, beautiful and pathetic, but remaining singularly, with unmalleable obstinacy, herself. "I saw her," wrote Higginson, "but twice, face to face, and brought away the impression of something as unique and remote as Undine or Mignon or Thekla." When, thirty years after the acquaintance had begun, and four after Emily Dickinson's death, he was called upon to edit a selection from her poetry, practically none of which had been published during her lifetime, his scruples were less severe, and he spoke of her with generosity and insight [see excerpt dated 1890]. "After all," he then wrote, "when a thought takes one's breath away, a lesson on grammar seems an impertinence." Again, "In many cases these verses will seem to the reader like poetry torn up by the roots." And again, "a quality more suggestive of the poetry of Blake than of anything to be elsewhere found—flashes of wholly original and profound insight into nature and life."

Thus began and ended Emily Dickinson's only important connection with the literary life of her time. She knew, it is true, Helen Hunt Jackson, a poetess, for whose anthology, *A Masque of Poets,* she gave the poem **"Success,"** one of the few poems she allowed publication during her life. And she knew the Bowles family, owners and editors of *The Springfield Republican,* at that time the *Manchester Guardian* of New England—which, as she put it mischievously, was one of "such papers . . . as have nothing carnal in them." But these she seldom saw; and aside from these she had few intimates outside of her family; the circle of her world grew steadily smaller. This is a point of cardinal importance, but unfortunately no light has been thrown upon it. It is apparent that Miss Dickinson became a hermit by deliberate and conscious choice. "A recluse," wrote Higginson, "by temperament and habit, literally spending years without setting her foot beyond the doorstep, and many more years during which her walks were strictly limited to her father's grounds, she habitually concealed her mind, like her person, from all but a very few friends; and it was with great difficulty that she was persuaded to print, during her lifetime, three or four poems." One of the co-editors of ***Poems: Second Series*** assures us that this voluntary hermitage was not due to any "love-disappointment," and that she was "not an invalid." "She had tried society and the world, and had found them lacking [see excerpt by Todd dated 1891]. But this, of course, tells us nothing. Her ***Letters*** show us convincingly that her girlhood was a normally "social" one—she was active, high-spirited, and endowed with a considerable gift for extravagant humor. As a young woman she had, so Mrs. Bianchi, a niece, informs us in the preface to ***The Single Hound,*** several love affairs. But we have no right, without other testimony, to assume here any ground for the singular psychological change that came over her. The only other clue we have, of any sort, is the hint from one of her girlhood friends, that perhaps *"she was longing for poetic sympathy."* Perhaps! But we must hope that her relatives and literary executives will eventually see fit to publish *all* her literary remains, verse and prose, and to give us thus, perhaps, a good deal more light on the nature of her life. Anecdotes relating to her mischievousness her wit, her waywardness, are not enough. It is amusing, if horrifying, to know that once, being anxious to dispose of some kittens, she put them on a shovel, carried them into the cellar, and dropped them into the nearest jar—which, subsequently, on the occasion of the visit of a distinguished judge, turned out to have been the pickle-jar. We like to know too, that even when her solitude was most remote she was in the habit of lowering from her window, by a string, small baskets of fruit or confectionery for children. But there are other things we should like to know much more.

There seems, however, little likelihood of our being told, by her family, anything more; and if we seek for the causes of the psychic injury which so sharply turned her in upon herself, we can only speculate. Her letters, in this regard, give little light, only showing us again and again that the injury was deep. Of the fact that she suffered acutely from intellectual drought there is evidence enough. One sees her vividly here—but one sees her, as it were, perpetually in retreat; always discovering anew, with dismay, the intellectual limitations of her correspondents; she is discreet, pathetic, baffled, a little humbled, and draws in her horns; takes sometimes a perverse pleasure in indulging more than ever, on the occasion of such a disappointment, in her love of a cryptic style—a delicate bombardment of parable and whim which she perfectly knows will stagger; and then again retreats to the safe ground of the superficial. It is perhaps for this reason that the letters give us so remarkably little information about her literary interests. The meagerness of literary allusion is astounding. The Brôntes and the Brownings are referred to—she thought Alexander Smith "not very coherent"—Joaquin Miller she "could not care about." Of her own work she speaks only in the brief unsatisfactory correspondence with Higginson. To him she wrote . . . , "I wrote no verse, but one or two, until this winter" [see excerpt dated 25 April 1862]. Otherwise, no scrap of her own literary history: she appears to have existed in a vacuum. Of the literary events, tremendous for America, which were taking place during her most impressionable years, there is hardly a mention. Emerson was at the height of his career, and living only sixty miles away: his poems came out when she was seventeen. When she was twenty, Hawthorne published *The Scarlet Letter,* and *The House of Seven Gables* the year after. The same year, 1851, brought out Melville's *Moby Dick.* The death of Poe took place in 1849—in 1850 was published the first collected edition of his poems. When she was twenty-four, Thoreau's *Walden* appeared; when she was twenty-five, *Leaves of Grass.* One can say with justice that she came to full "consciousness" at the very moment when American literature came to flower. That she knew this, there cannot be any question; nor that she was stimulated and influenced by it. One must assume that she found in her immediate environment no one of her own stature, with whom she could admit or discuss such things; that she lacked the energy or effrontery to voyage out into the unknown in search of such companionship; and that, lacking this courage, and wanting this help, she became easily a prey to the then current Emersonian doctrine of mystical Individualism. In this connection it is permissible to suggest that her extreme self-seclusion and secrecy was both a protest and a display—a kind of vanity masquerading as modesty. She became increasingly precious, of her person as of her thought. Vanity is in her letters—at the last an unhealthy vanity. She believes that anything she says, however brief, will be of importance; however cryptic, will be deciphered. She enjoys being something of a mystery, and she sometimes deliberately and awkwardly exaggerates it. Even in notes of condolence—for which she had a morbid passion—she is vain enough to indulge in sententiousness: as when she wrote, to a friend whose father had died on her wedding-day, "Few daughters have the immortality of a father for a bridal gift."

When we come to Emily Dickinson's poetry, we find the Emersonian individualism clear enough, but perfectly Miss Dickinson's. Henry James observed of Emerson:

> The doctrine of the supremacy of the individual to himself, of his originality and, as regards his own character, *unique* quality, must have had a great charm for people living in a society in which introspection, thanks to the want of other entertainment, played almost the part of a social resource. . . . There was . . . much relish for the utterances of a writer who would help one to take a picturesque view of one's internal possibilities, and to find in the landscape of the soul all sorts of fine sunrise and moonlight effects.

This sums up admirably the social "case" of Miss Dickinson—it gives us a shrewd picture of the causes of her singular introversion, and it suggests that we are perhaps justified in considering her the most perfect flower of New England Transcendentalism. In her mode of life she carried the doctrine of self-sufficient individualism farther than Thoreau carried it, or the naive zealots of Brook Farm. In her poetry she carried it, with its complement of passionate moral mysticism, farther than Emerson: which is to say that as a poet she had more genius than he. Like Emerson, whose essays must greatly have influenced her, and whose poetry, especially his gnomic poems, only a little less, she was from the outset, and remained all her life, a singular mixture of Puritan and freethinker. The problems of good and evil, of life and death, obsessed her; the nature and destiny of the human soul; and Emerson's theory of compensation. Toward God, as one of her earliest critics is reported to have said, "she exhibited an Emersonian self-possession." Indeed, she did not, and could not, accept the Puritan God at all. She was frankly irreverent, on occasion, a fact which seems to have made her editors a little uneasy—one hopes that it has not resulted in the suppression of any of her work. What she was irreverent to, of course, was the Puritan conception of God, the Puritan attitude toward him.

> Heavenly father, take to thee
> The supreme iniquity,
> Fashioned by thy candid hand
> In a moment contraband.
> Though to trust us seems to us
> More respectful,—we are dust.
> We apologize to thee
> For thine own Duplicity.

This, it must be repeated, is Emily Dickinson's opinion of the traditional and anthropomorphic "God," who was still, in her day, a portentous Victorian gentleman. Her real reverence, the reverence that made her a mystic poet of the finest sort, was reserved for Nature, which seemed to her a more manifest and more beautiful evidence of Divine Will than creeds and churches. This she saw, observed, loved, with a burning simplicity and passion which nevertheless did not exclude her very agile sense of humor. Her Nature poems, however, are not the most secretly revelatory or dramatically compulsive of her poems, nor on the whole, the best. They are often of extraordinary delicacy—nearly always give us, with deft brevity, the exact in terms of the quaint. But, also, they are often superficial, a mere affectionate playing with the smaller things that give her delight; and to see her at her best and most characteristic and most profound, one must turn to the remarkable range of metaphysical speculation and ironic introspection which is displayed in those sections of her posthumous books which her editors have captioned Life, and Time and Eternity. In the former sections are the greater number of her set "meditations" on the nature of things. For some critics they will always appear too bare, bleak, and fragmentary. They have no trappings, only here and there a shred of purple. It is as if Miss Dickinson, who in one of her letters uttered her contempt for the "obtrusive body," had wanted to make them, as nearly as possible, disembodied thought. The thought is there, at all events, hard, bright, and clear; and her symbols, her metaphors, of which she could be prodigal, have an analogous clarity and translucency. What is also there is a downright homeliness which is a perpetual surprise and delight. Emerson's gnomic style she tunes up to the epigrammatic—the epigrammatic she often carries to the point of the cryptic; she becomes what one might call an epigrammatic symbolist.

> Lay this laurel on the one
> Too intrinsic for renown.
> Laurel! veil your deathless tree,—
> Him you chasten, that is he!

This, from ***Poems: Second Series,*** verges perilously on the riddle. And if often happens that her passionate devotion to concise statement in terms of metaphor left for her readers a small rich emblem of which the colors tease, the thought entices, but the meaning escapes. Against this, however, should be set her capacity, when occasion came, for a granite simplicity, any parallel to which one must seek in the seventeenth century. This, for example, called **"Parting."**

> My life closed twice before its close;
> It yet remains to see
> If Immortality unveil
> A third event to me,
> So huge, so hopeless to conceive,
> As these that twice befell.
> Parting is all we know of heaven
> And all we need of hell.

Or this, from ***The Single Hound:***

> Not any sunny tone
> From any fervent zone
> Finds entrance there.
> Better a grave of Balm
> Toward human nature's home,
> And Robins near
> Than a stupendous Tomb
> Proclaiming to the gloom
> How dead we are.

Both these poems, it will be noted, deal with death; and it must be observed that the number of poems by Miss Dickinson on this subject is one of the most remarkable things about her. Death, and the problem of life after death, obsessed her. She seems to have thought of it constantly—she died all her life, she probed death daily. "That bareheaded life under grass worries one like a wasp," she wrote. Ultimately, the obsession became morbid, and her eagerness for details, after the death of a friend—the hungry desire to know *how* she died—became almost vulture-like. But the preoccupation, with its horrible uncertainties—its doubts about immortality, its hatred of the flesh, and its many reversals of both positions—gave us her sharpest work. The theme was inexhaustible for her. If her poetry seldom became "lyrical," seldom departed from the colorless sobriety of its bare iambics and toneless assonance, it did so most of all when the subject was death. Death profoundly and cruelly invited her. It was most of all when she tried "to touch the smile," and dipped her "fingers in the frost," that she took full possession of her genius.

Her genius was, it remains to say, as erratic as it was brilliant. Her disregard for accepted forms or for regularities was incorrigible. Grammar, rhyme, meter—anything went by the board if it stood in the way of thought or freedom of utterance. Sometimes this arrogance was justified; sometimes not. She did not care in the least for variety of effect—of her six hundred-odd poems, practically all are in octosyllabic quatrains or couplets, sometimes with rhyme, sometimes with assonance, sometimes with neither. Everywhere, when one first comes to these poems, one seems to see nothing but a colorless dry monotony. How deceptive a monotony, concealing what reserves of depth and splendor; what subtleties of mood and tone! Once adjust oneself to the spinsterly angularity of the mode, its lack of eloquence or rhetorical speed, its naive and often prosaic directness, one discovers felicities of thought and phrase on every page. The magic is terse and sure. And ultimately one simply sighs at Miss Dickinson's singular perversity, her lapses and tyrannies, and accepts them as an inevitable part of the strange and original genius she was. The lapses and tyrannies become a positive charm—one even suspects they were deliberate. They satisfied her—therefore they satisfy us. This marks, of course, our complete surrender to her highly individual gift, and to the singular sharp beauty, present everywhere, of her personality. The two things cannot be separated; and together, one must suppose, they suffice to put her among the finest poets in the language. (pp. 156-63)

Conrad Aiken, "Emily Dickinson," in his Collected Criticism, *Oxford University Press, 1968, pp. 156-63.*

HART CRANE (poem date 1927)

[Crane was an early twentieth-century American poet and essayist who is best known for his ambitious poem The Bridge *and for his accomplished lyrics. In the following poem addressed to Dick-*

inson and written in 1927, Crane expresses his admiration for her.]

You who desired so much—in vain to ask—
Yet fed your hunger like an endless task,
Dared dignify the labor, bless the quest—
Achieved that stillness ultimately best,

Being, of all, least sought for: Emily, hear!
O sweet, dead Silencer, most suddenly clear
When singing that Eternity possessed
And plundered momently in every breast;

—Truly no flower yet withers in your hand,
The harvest you descried and understand
Needs more than wit to gather, love to bind.
Some reconcilement of remotest mind—

Leaves Ormus rubyless, and Ophir chill.
Else tears heap all within one clay-cold hill.

Hart Crane, "To Emily Dickinson," in Critics on Emily Dickinson, *edited by Richard H. Rupp, University of Miami Press, 1972, p. 13.*

ALLEN TATE (essay date 1928-32)

[*Tate is considered one of the most influential American critics of the twentieth century. His criticism is closely associated with two critical movements, the Agrarians and the New Critics. The Agrarians were concerned with political and social issues as well as literature, and were dedicated to preserving the Southern way of life and traditional Southern values. Although the various New Critics did not subscribe to a single set of principles, all believed that a work of literature had to be examined as an object in itself through a process of close analysis of symbol, image, and metaphor. In the following excerpt, Tate suggests that difficulties in reading Dickinson's poetry arise from the absence of a critical tradition capable of comprehending her work. Tate also considers the impact of the disintegration of New England Puritan culture on her writing. These comments were first published in essays appearing in the* Outlook *(1928) and the* Symposium *(1932).*]

Great poetry needs no special features of difficulty to make it mysterious. When it has them, the reputation of the poet is likely to remain uncertain. This is still true of Donne, and it is true of Emily Dickinson, whose verse appeared in an age unfavorable to the use of intelligence in poetry. Her poetry is not like any other poetry of her time; it is not like any of the innumerable kinds of verse written today. In still another respect it is far removed from us. It is a poetry of ideas, and it demands of the reader a point of view—not an opinion of the New Deal or of the League of Nations, but an ingrained philosophy that is fundamental, a settled attitude that is almost extinct in this eclectic age. Yet it is not the sort of poetry of ideas which, like Pope's, requires a point of view only. It requires also, for the deepest understanding, which must go beneath the verbal excitement of the style, a highly developed sense of the specific quality of poetry—a quality that most persons accept as the accidental feature of something else that the poet thinks he has to say. This is one reason why Miss Dickinson's poetry has not been widely read.

There is another reason, and it is a part of the problem peculiar to a poetry that comes out of fundamental ideas. We lack a tradition of criticism. There were no points of critical reference passed on to us from a preceding generation. I am not upholding here the so-called dead-hand of tradition, but rather a rational insight into the meaning of the present in terms of some imaginable past implicit in our own lives: we need a body of ideas that can bear upon the course of the spirit and yet remain coherent as a rational instrument. We ignore the present, which is momently translated into the past, and derive our standards from imaginative constructions of the future. The hard contingency of fact invariably breaks the standards down, leaving us the intellectual chaos which is the sore distress of American criticism. Marxian criticism has become the latest disguise of this heresy.

Still another difficulty stands between us and Miss Dickinson. It is the failure of the scholars to feel more than biographical curiosity about her. We have scholarship, but that is no substitute for a critical tradition. Miss Dickinson's value to the research scholar, who likes historical difficulty for its own sake, is slight; she is too near to possess the remoteness of literature. Perhaps her appropriate setting would be the age of Cowley or of Donne. Yet in her own historical setting she is, nevertheless, remarkable and special.

Although the intellectual climate into which she was born, in 1830, had, as all times have, the features of a transition, the period was also a major crisis culminating in the war between the States. After that war, in New England as well as in the South, spiritual crises were definitely minor until the First World War.

Yet, a generation before the war of 1861-65, the transformation of New England had begun. When Samuel Slater in 1790 thwarted the British embargo on mill-machinery by committing to memory the whole design of a cotton spinner and bringing it to Massachusetts, he planted the seed of the "Western spirit." By 1825 its growth in the East was rank enough to begin choking out the ideas and habits of living that New England along with Virginia had kept in unconscious allegiance to Europe. To the casual observer, perhaps, the New England character of 1830 was largely an eighteenth-century character. But theocracy was on the decline, and industrialism was rising—as Emerson, in an unusually lucid moment, put it, "Things are in the saddle." The energy that had built the meeting-house ran the factory.

Now the idea that moved the theocratic state is the most interesting historically of all American ideas. It was, of course, powerful in seventeenth-century England, but in America, where the long arm of Laud could not reach, it acquired an unchecked social and political influence. The important thing to remember about the puritan theocracy is that it permeated, as it could never have done in England, a whole society. It gave final, definite meaning to life, the life of pious and impious, of learned and vulgar alike. It gave—and this is its significance for Emily Dickinson, and in only slightly lesser degree for Melville and Hawthorne—it gave an heroic proportion and a tragic mode to the experience of the individual. The history of the New England theocracy, from Apostle Eliot to Cotton Mather, is rich in gigantic intellects that broke down—or so it must appear to an outsider—in a kind of moral decadence and depravity. Socially we may not like the New England idea. Yet it had an immense, incalculable value for literature: it dramatized the human soul.

But by 1850 the great fortunes had been made (in the rum, slave, and milling industries), and New England became a museum. The whatnots groaned under the load of knick-knacks, the fine china dogs and cats, the pieces of Oriental jade, the chips off the leaning tower at Pisa. There were the rare books and the cosmopolitan learning. It was all equally displayed as the evidence of a superior culture. The Gilded Age had already begun. But culture, in the true sense, was disappearing. Where the old order, formidable as it was, had held all this personal experience, this eclectic excitement, in a comprehensible whole, the new order tended to flatten it out in a common experience that was not quite in common; it exalted more and more the personal and the unique in the interior sense. Where the old-fashioned puritans got together on a rigid doctrine, and could thus be individualists in manners, the nineteenth-century New Englander, lacking a genuine religious center, began to be a social conformist. The common idea of the Redemption, for example, was replaced by the conformist idea of respectability among neighbors whose spiritual disorder, not very evident at the surface, was becoming acute. A great idea was breaking up, and society was moving towards external uniformity, which is usually the measure of the spiritual sterility inside.

At this juncture Emerson came upon the scene: the Lucifer of Concord, he had better be called hereafter, for he was the light-bearer who could see nothing but light, and was fearfully blind. He looked around and saw the uniformity of life, and called it the routine of tradition, the tyranny of the theological idea. The death of Priam put an end to the hope of Troy, but it was a slight feat of arms for the doughty Pyrrhus; Priam was an old gentleman and almost dead. So was theocracy; and Emerson killed it. In this way he accelerated a tendency that he disliked. It was a great intellectual mistake. By it Emerson unwittingly became the prophet of a piratical industrialism, a consequence of his own transcendental individualism that he could not foresee. He was hoist with his own petard.

He discredited more than any other man the puritan drama of the soul. The age that followed, from 1865 on, expired in a genteel secularism, a mildly didactic order of feeling whose ornaments were Lowell, Longfellow, and Holmes. "After Emerson had done his work," says Mr. Robert Penn Warren, "any tragic possibilities in that culture were dissipated." Hawthorne alone in his time kept pure, in the primitive terms, the primitive vision; he brings the puritan tragedy to its climax. Man, measured by a great idea outside himself, is found wanting. But for Emerson man is greater than any idea and, being himself the Over-Soul, is innately perfect; there is no struggle because—I state the Emersonian doctrine, which is very slippery, in its extreme terms—because there is no possibility of error. There is no drama in human character because there is no tragic fault. It is not surprising, then, that after Emerson New England literature tastes like a sip of cambric tea. Its center of vision has disappeared. There is Hawthorne looking back, there is Emerson looking not too clearly at anything ahead: Emily Dickinson, who has in her something of both, comes in somewhere between.

With the exception of Poe there is no other American poet whose work so steadily emerges, under pressure of certain disintegrating obsessions, from the framework of moral character. There is none of whom it is truer to say that the poet *is* the poetry. Perhaps this explains the zeal of her admirers for her biography; it explains, in part at least, the gratuitous mystery that Mrs. Bianchi, a niece of the poet and her official biographer, has made of her life. The devoted controversy that Miss Josephine Pollitt and Miss Genevieve Taggard started a few years ago with their excellent books shows the extent to which the critics feel the intimate connection of her life and work. Admiration and affection are pleased to linger over the tokens of a great life; but the solution to the Dickinson enigma is peculiarly superior to fact.

The meaning of the identity—which we merely feel—of character and poetry would be exceedingly obscure, even if we could draw up a kind of Binet correlation between the two sets of "facts." Miss Dickinson was a recluse; but her poetry is rich with a profound and varied experience. Where did she get it? Now some of the biographers, nervous in the presence of this discrepancy, are eager to find her a love affair, and I think this search is due to a modern prejudice: we believe that no virgin can know enough to write poetry. We shall never learn where she got the rich quality of her mind. The moral image that we have of Miss Dickinson stands out in every poem; it is that of a dominating spinster whose very sweetness must have been formidable. Yet her poetry constantly moves within an absolute order of truths that overwhelmed her simply because to her they were unalterably fixed. It is dangerous to assume that her "life," which to the biographers means the thwarted love affair she is supposed to have had, gave to her poetry a decisive direction. It is even more dangerous to suppose that it made her a poet.

Poets are mysterious, but a poet when all is said is not much more mysterious than a banker. The critics remain spellbound by the technical license of her verse and by the puzzle of her personal life. Personality is a legitimate interest because it is an incurable interest, but legitimate as a personal interest only; it will never give up the key to anyone's verse. Used to that end, the interest is false. "It is apparent," writes Mr. Conrad Aiken, "that Miss Dickinson became a hermit by deliberate and conscious choice"—a sensible remark that we cannot repeat too often. If it were necessary to explain her seclusion with disappointment in love, there would remain the discrepancy between what the seclusion produced and the seclusion looked at as a cause. The effect, which is her poetry, would imply the whole complex of anterior fact, which was the social and religious structure of New England.

The problem to be kept in mind is thus the meaning of her "deliberate and conscious" decision to withdraw from life to her upstairs room. This simple fact is not very important. But that it must have been her sole way of acting out her part in the history of her culture, which made, with the variations of circumstance, a single demand upon all its representatives—this is of the greatest consequence. All pity for Miss Dickinson's "starved life" is misdirected. Her life was one of the richest and deepest ever lived on this continent.

When she went upstairs and closed the door, she mastered life by rejecting it. Others in their way had done it before; still others did it later. If we suppose—which is to suppose the improbable—that the love-affair precipitated the seclusion, it was only a pretext; she would have found another. Mastery of the world by rejecting the world was the doctrine, even if it was not always the practice, of Jonathan Edwards and Cotton Mather. It is the meaning of fate in Hawthorne: his people are fated to withdraw from the world and to be destroyed. And it is one of the great themes of Henry James.

There is a moral emphasis that connects Hawthorne, James, and Miss Dickinson, and I think it is instructive. Between Hawthorne and James lies an epoch. The temptation to sin, in Hawthorne, is, in James, transformed into the temptation not to do the "decent thing." A whole world-scheme, a complete cosmic background, has shrunk to the dimensions of the individual conscience. This epoch between Hawthorne and James lies in Emerson. James found himself in the post-Emersonian world, and he could not, without violating the detachment proper to an artist, undo Emerson's work; he had that kind of intelligence which refuses to break its head against history. There was left to him only the value, the historic rôle, of rejection. He could merely escape from the physical presence of that world which, for convenience, we may call Emerson's world: he could only take his Americans to Europe upon the vain quest of something that they had lost at home. His characters, fleeing the wreckage of the puritan culture, preserved only their honor. Honor became a sort of forlorn hope struggling against the forces of "pure fact" that had got loose in the middle of the century. Honor alone is a poor weapon against nature, being too personal, finical, and proud, and James achieved a victory by refusing to engage the whole force of the enemy.

In Emily Dickinson the conflict takes place on a vaster field. The enemy to all those New Englanders was Nature, and Miss Dickinson saw into the character of this enemy more deeply than any of the others. The general symbol of Nature, for her, is Death, and her weapon against Death is the entire powerful dumb-show of the puritan theology led by Redemption and Immortality. Morally speaking, the problem for James and Miss Dickinson is similar. But her advantages were greater than his. The advantages lay in the availability to her of the puritan ideas on the theological plane.

These ideas, in her poetry, are momently assailed by the disintegrating force of Nature (appearing as Death) which, while constantly breaking them down, constantly redefines and strengthens them. The values are purified by the triumphant withdrawal from Nature, by their power to recover from Nature. The poet attains to a mastery over experience by facing its utmost implications. There is the clash of powerful opposites, and in all great poetry—for Emily Dickinson is a great poet—it issues in a tension between abstraction and sensation in which the two elements may be, of course, distinguished logically, but not really. We are shown our roots in Nature by examining our differences with Nature; we are renewed by Nature without being delivered into her hands. When it is possible for a poet to do this for us with the greatest imaginative comprehension, a possibility that the poet cannot himself create, we have the perfect literary situation. Only a few times in the history of English poetry has this situation come about, notably, the period between about 1580 and the Restoration. There was a similar age in New England from which emerged two talents of the first order—Hawthorne and Emily Dickinson.

There is an epoch between James and Miss Dickinson. But between her and Hawthorne there exists a difference of intellectual quality. She lacks almost radically the power to seize upon and understand abstractions for their own sake; she does not separate them from the sensuous illuminations that she is so marvelously adept at; like Donne, she *perceives abstraction* and *thinks sensation*. But Hawthorne was a master of ideas, within a limited range; this narrowness confined him to his own kind of life, his own society, and out of it grew his typical forms of experience, his steady, almost obsessed vision of man; it explains his depth and intensity. Yet he is always conscious of the abstract, doctrinal aspect of his mind, and when his vision of action and emotion is weak, his work becomes didactic. Now Miss Dickinson's poetry often runs into quasi-homiletic forms, but it is never didactic. Her very ignorance, her lack of formal intellectual training, preserved her from the risk that imperiled Hawthorne. She cannot reason at all. She can only *see*. It is impossible to imagine what she might have done with drama or fiction; for, not approaching the puritan temper and through it the puritan myth, through human action, she is able to grasp the terms of the myth directly and by a feat that amounts almost to anthropomorphism, to give them a luminous tension, a kind of drama, among themselves.

One of the perfect poems in English is **"The Chariot,"** and it illustrates better than anything else she wrote the special quality of her mind. I think it will illuminate the tendency of this discussion:

Because I could not stop for death,
He kindly stopped for me;
The carriage held but just ourselves
And immortality.

We slowly drove, he knew no haste,
And I had put away
My labor, and my leisure too,
For his civility.

We passed the school where children played,
Their lessons scarcely done;
We passed the fields of gazing grain,
We passed the setting sun.

We paused before a house that seemed
A swelling of the ground;
The roof was scarcely visible,
The cornice but a mound.

Since then 'tis centuries; but each
Feels shorter than the day
I first surmised the horses' heads
Were toward eternity.

If the word great means anything in poetry, this poem is one of the greatest in the English language. The rhythm charges with movement the pattern of suspended action back of the poem. Every image is precise and, moreover, not merely beautiful, but fused with the central idea. Every image extends and intensifies every other. The third stanza especially shows Miss Dickinson's power to fuse, into a single order of perception, a heterogeneous series: the children, the grain, and the setting sun (time) have the same degree of credibility; the first subtly preparing for the last. The sharp *gazing* before *grain* instills into nature a cold vitality of which the qualitative richness has infinite depth. The content of death in the poem eludes explicit definition. He is a gentleman taking a lady out for a drive. But note the restraint that keeps the poet from carrying this so far that it becomes ludicrous and incredible; and note the subtly interfused erotic motive, which the idea of death has presented to most romantic poets, love being a symbol interchangeable with death. The terror of death is objectified through this figure of the genteel driver, who is made ironically to serve the end of Immortality. This is the heart of the poem: she has presented a typical Christian theme in its final irresolution, without making any final statements about it. There is no solution to the problem; there can be only a presentation of it in the full context of intellect and feeling. A construction of the human will, elaborated with all the abstracting powers of the mind, is put to the concrete test of experience: the idea of immortality is confronted with the fact of physical disintegration. We are not told what to think; we are told to look at the situation.

The framework of the poem is, in fact, the two abstractions, mortality and eternity, which are made to associate in equality with the images: she sees the ideas, and thinks the perceptions. She did, of course, nothing of the sort; but we must use the logical distinctions, even to the extent of paradox, if we are to form any notion of this rare quality of mind. She could not in the proper sense think at all, and unless we prefer the feeble poetry of moral ideas that flourished in New England in the eighties, we must conclude that her intellectual deficiency contributed at least negatively to her great distinction. Miss Dickinson is probably the only Anglo-American poet of her century whose work exhibits the perfect literary situation—in which is possible the fusion of sensibility and thought. Unlike her contemporaries, she never succumbed to her ideas, to easy solutions, to her private desires.

Philosophers must deal with ideas, but the trouble with most nineteenth-century poets is too much philosophy; they are nearer to being philosophers than poets, without being in the true sense either. Tennyson is a good example of this; so is Arnold in his weak moments. There have been poets like Milton and Donne, who were not spoiled for their true business by leaning on a rational system of ideas, who understood the poetic use of ideas. Tennyson tried to mix a little Huxley and a little Broad Church, without understanding either Broad Church or Huxley; the result was fatal, and what is worse, it was shallow. Miss Dickinson's ideas were deeply imbedded in her character, not taken from the latest tract. A conscious cultivation of ideas in poetry is always dangerous, and even Milton escaped ruin only by having an instinct for what in the deepest sense he understood. Even at that there is a remote quality in Milton's approach to his material, in his treatment of it; in the nineteenth century, in an imperfect literary situation where literature was confused with documentation, he might have been a pseudo-philosopher-poet. It is difficult to conceive Emily Dickinson and John Donne succumbing to rumination about "problems"; they would not have written at all.

Neither the feeling nor the style of Miss Dickinson belongs to the seventeenth century; yet between her and Donne there are remarkable ties. Their religious ideas, their abstractions, are momently toppling from the rational plane to the level of perception. The ideas, in fact, are no longer the impersonal religious symbols created anew in the heat of emotion, that we find in poets like Herbert and Vaughan. They have become, for Donne, the terms of personality; they are mingled with the miscellany of sensation. In Miss Dickinson, as in Donne, we may detect a singularly morbid concern, not for religious truth, but for personal revelation. The modern word is self-exploitation. It is egoism grown irresponsible in religion and decadent in morals. In religion it is blasphemy; in society it means usually that culture is not self-contained and sufficient, that the spiritual community is breaking up. This is, along with some other features that do not concern us here, the perfect literary situation.

Personal revelation of the kind that Donne and Miss Dickinson strove for, in the effort to understand their relation to the world, is a feature of all great poetry; it is probably the hidden motive for writing. It is the effort of the individual to live apart from a cultural traditon that no longer sustains him. But this culture, which I now wish to discuss a little, is indispensable: there is a great deal of shallow nonsense in modern criticism which holds that poetry—and this is a half-truth that is worse than false—is essentially revolutionary. It is only indirectly revolutionary: the intellectual and religious background of an age no longer contains the whole spirit, and the poet proceeds to examine that background in terms of immediate experience. But the background is necessary; otherwise all the arts (not only poetry) would have to rise in a vacuum. Poetry does not dispense with tradition; it probes the deficiencies of a tradition. But it must have a tradition to probe. It is too bad that Arnold did not explain his doctrine, that poetry is a criticism of life, from the viewpoint of its background: we should have been spared an era of academic misconception, in which criticism of life meant a diluted pragmatism, the criterion of which was respectability. The poet in the true sense "criticizes" his tradition, either as such, or indirectly by comparing it with something that is about to replace it; he does what the root-meaning of the verb implies—he *discerns* its real elements and thus establishes its value, by putting it to the test of experience.

What is the nature of a poet's culture? Or, to put the question properly, what is the meaning of culture for poetry? All the great poets become the material of what we popularly call culture; we study them to acquire it. It is clear that Addison was more cultivated than Shakespeare; nevertheless Shakespeare is a finer source of culture than Addison. What is the meaning of this? Plainly it is that learning has never had anything to do with culture except instrumentally: the poet must be exactly literate enough to write down fully and precisely what he has to say, but no more. The source of a poet's true culture lies back of the paraphernalia of culture, and not all the historical activity of an enlightened age can create it.

A culture cannot be consciously created. It is an available source of ideas that are imbedded in a complete and homogeneous society. The poet finds himself balanced upon the moment when such a world is about to fall, when it threatens to run out into looser and less self-sufficient impulses. This world order is assimilated, in Miss Dickinson, as medievalism was in Shakespeare, to the poetic vision; it is brought down from abstraction to personal sensibility.

In this connection it may be said that the prior conditions for great poetry, given a great talent, may be reduced to two: the thoroughness of the poet's discipline in an objective system of truth, and his lack of consciousness of such a discipline. For this discipline is a number of fundamental ideas the origin of which the poet does not know; they give form and stability to his fresh perceptions of the world; and he cannot shake them off. This is his culture, and like Tennyson's God it is nearer than hands and feet. With reasonable certainty we unearth the elements of Shakespeare's culture, and yet it is equally certain—so innocent was he of his own resources—that he would not know what our discussion is about. He appeared at the collapse of the medieval system as a rigid pattern of life, but that pattern remained in Shakespeare what Shelley called a "fixed point of reference" for his sensibility. Miss Dickinson, as we have seen, was born into the equilibrium of an old and a new order. Puritanism could not be to her what it had been to the generation of Cotton Mather—a body of absolute truths; it was an unconscious discipline timed to the pulse of her life.

The perfect literary situation: it produces, because it is rare, a special and perhaps the most distinguished kind of poet. I am not trying to invent a new critical category. Such poets are never very much alike on the surface; they show us all the varieties of poetic feeling; and like other poets they resist all classification but that of temporary convenience. But, I believe, Miss Dickinson and John Donne would have this in common: their sense of the natural world is not blunted by a too rigid system of ideas; yet the ideas, the abstractions, their education or their intellectual heritage, are not so weak as to let their immersion in nature, or their purely personal quality, get out of control. The two poles of the mind are not separately visible; we infer them from the lucid tension that may be most readily illustrated by polar activity. There is no thought as such at all; nor is there feeling; there is that unique focus of experience which is at once neither and both.

Like Miss Dickinson, Shakespeare is without opinions; his peculiar merit is also deeply involved in his failure to think about anything; his meaning is not in the content of his expression; it is in the tension of the dramatic relations of his characters. This kind of poetry is at the opposite of intellectualism. (Miss Dickinson is obscure and difficult, but that is not intellectualism.) To T. W. Higginson, the editor of *The Atlantic Monthly,* who tried to advise her, she wrote that she had no education. In any sense that Higginson could understand, it was quite true. His kind of education was the conscious cultivation of abstractions. She did not reason about the world she saw; she merely saw it. The "ideas" implicit in the world within her rose up, concentrated in her immediate perception.

That kind of world at present has for us something of the fascination of a buried city. There is none like it. When such worlds exist, when such cultures flourish, they support not only the poet but all members of society. For, from these, the poet differs only in his gift for exhibiting the structure, the internal lineaments, of his culture by threatening to tear them apart: a process that concentrates the symbolic emotions of society while it seems to attack them. The poet may hate his age; he may be an outcast like Villon; but this world is always there as the background to what he has to say. It is the lens through which he brings nature to focus and control—the clarifying medium that concentrates his personal feeling. It is ready-made; he cannot make it; with it, his poetry has a spontaneity and a certainty of direction that, without it, it would lack. No poet could have invented the ideas of **"The Chariot"**; only a great poet could have found their imaginative equivalents. Miss Dickinson was a deep mind writing from a deep culture, and when she came to poetry, she came infallibly.

Infallibly, at her best; for no poet has ever been perfect, nor is Emily Dickinson. Her precision of statement is due to the directness with which the abstract framework of her thought acts upon its unorganized material. The two elements of her style, considered as point of view, are immortality, or the idea of permanence, and the physical process of death or decay. Her diction has two corresponding features: words of Latin or Greek origin and, sharply opposed to these, the concrete Saxon element. It is this verbal conflict that gives to her verse its high tension; it is not a device deliberately seized upon, but a feeling for language that senses out the two fundamental components of English and their metaphysical relation: the Latin for ideas and the Saxon for perceptions—the peculiar virtue of English as a poetic language.

Like most poets Miss Dickinson often writes out of habit; the style that emerged from some deep exploration of an idea is carried on as verbal habit when she has nothing to say. She indulges herself:

There's something quieter than sleep
Within this inner room!
It wears a sprig upon its breast,
And will not tell its name.

Some touch it and some kiss it,
Some chafe its idle hand;
It has a simple gravity
I do not understand!

While simple hearted neighbors
Chat of the "early dead,"
We, prone to periphrasis,
Remark that birds have fled!

It is only a pert remark; at best a superior kind of punning—one of the worst specimens of her occasional interest in herself. But she never had the slightest interest in the public. Were four poems or five published in her lifetime? She never felt the temptation to round off a poem for public exhibition. Higginson's kindly offer to make her verse "correct" was an invitation to throw her work into the public ring—the ring of Lowell and Longfellow. He could not see that he was tampering with one of the rarest literary integrities of all time. Here was a poet who had no use for the supports of authorship—flattery and fame; she never needed money.

She had all the elements of a culture that has broken up, a culture that on the religious side takes its place in the museum of spiritual antiquities. Puritanism, as a unified version of the world, is dead; only a remnant of it in trade may be said to survive. In the history of puritanism she comes between Hawthorne and Emerson. She has Hawthorne's matter, which a too irresponsible personality tends to dilute into a form like Emerson's; she is often betrayed by words. But she is not the poet of personal sentiment; she has more to say than she can put down in any one poem. Like Hardy and Whitman she must be read entire; like Shakespeare she never gives up her meaning in a single line.

She is therefore a perfect subject for the kind of criticism which is chiefly concerned with general ideas. She exhibits one of the permanent relations between personality and objective truth, and she deserves the special attention of our time, which lacks that kind of truth.

She has Hawthorne's intellectual toughness, a hard, definite sense of the physical world. The highest flights to God, the most extravagant metaphors of the strange and the remote, come back to a point of casuistry, to a moral dilemma of the experienced world. There is, in spite of the homiletic vein of utterance, no abstract speculation, nor is there a message to society; she speaks wholly to the individual experience. She offers to the unimaginative no riot of vicarious sensation; she has no useful maxims for men of action. Up to this point her resemblance to Emerson is slight: poetry is a sufficient form

A portrait of Emily, Austin, and Lavinia Dickinson as children.

of utterance, and her devotion to it is pure. But in Emily Dickinson the puritan world is no longer self-contained; it is no longer complete; her sensibility exceeds its dimensions. She has trimmed down its supernatural proportions; it has become a morality; instead of the tragedy of the spirit there is a commentary upon it. Her poetry is a magnificent personal confession, blasphemous and, in its self-revelation, its honesty, almost obscene. It comes out of an intellectual life towards which it feels no moral responsibility. Cotton Mather would have burnt her for a witch. (pp. 197-213)

Allen Tate, "Emily Dickinson," in his On the Limits of Poetry: Selected Essays, 1928-1948, *The Swallow Press and William Morrow & Company, Publishers, 1948, pp. 197-213.*

AMY LOWELL (essay date 1930)

[Lowell was the leading proponent of Imagism in American poetry. Like the French Symbolists before her, Lowell experimented with free verse forms and, influenced by Ezra Pound, developed a style characterized by clear and precise rhetoric, exact rendering of images, and metrical innovations. Although she was popular in her own time, current evaluations of Lowell accord her more importance as a promoter of new artistic ideas than as a poet in her own right. In the excerpt below, Lowell examines the Imagist qualities of Dickinson's poetry, according her a place as an eminent precursor of the movement.]

I wonder what made Emily Dickinson as she was. She cannot be accounted for by any trick of ancestry or early influence. She was the daughter of a long line of worthy people; her father, who was the leading lawyer of Amherst, Massachusetts, and the treasurer of Amherst College, is typical of the aims and accomplishments of the race. Into this well-ordered, high-minded, average, and rather sombre milieu, swept Emily Dickinson like a beautiful, stray butterfly, 'beating in the void her luminous wings in vain.' She knew no different life; and yet she certainly did not belong to the one in which she found herself. She may have felt this in some obscure fashion; for, little by little, she withdrew from the world about her, and shut herself up in a cocoon of her own spinning. She had no heart to fight; she never knew that a battle was on and that she had been selected for a place in the vanguard; all she could do was to retire, to hide her wounds, to carry out her little skirmishings and advances in byways and side-tracks, slowly winning a territory which the enemy took no trouble to dispute. What she did seemed insignificant and individual, but thirty years after her death the flag under which she fought had become a great banner, the symbol of a militant revolt. It is an odd story, this history of Imagism, and perhaps the oddest and saddest moment in it is comprised in the struggle of this one brave, fearful, and unflinching woman. (pp. 88-9)

The times were out of joint for Emily Dickinson. Her circle loved her, but utterly failed to comprehend. Her daring utterances shocked; her whimsicality dazed. The account of this narrow life is heart-rending. Think of Charles Lamb joking a New England deacon; imagine Keats's letters read aloud to a Dorcas Society; conceive of William Blake sending the *Songs of Experience* to the *Springfield Republican*! Emily Dickinson lived in an atmosphere of sermons, church sociables, and county newspapers. It is ghastly, the terrible, inexorable waste of Nature, but it is a fact. The direct descendant of Blake (although she probably never heard of him) lived in this surrounding. The marvel is that her mind did not give way. It did not; except in so far as her increasing shrinking from society and her preoccupation with death may be considered giving way. She lived on; she never ceased to write; and the torture which she suffered must have been exquisite indeed. (pp. 90-1)

[Mr. Higginson] has told us that this is a poetry of 'flashes,' therefore it must be extremely concentrated; he says that it is wholly original, so it must give free rein to individualistic freedom of idea; he thinks that it exhibits 'an extraordinary vividness of description and imaginative power,' which is merely to restate the third and fourth Imagist canons in other words. His very objection to its rugged character proves that it occupies itself with new rhythms. What else is left? Simplicity and directness of speech, perhaps. For that, we had better seek our answer in the poems themselves. . . . (pp. 95-6)

In ***The Single Hound,*** the fourth and last volume of her work, issued in 1914 by her niece, is this poem. . . .

A prompt, executive Bird is the Jay,
Bold as a Bailiff's hymn,
Brittle and brief in quality—
Warrant in every line;
Sitting a bough like a Brigadier,
Confident and straight,
Much is the mien
Of him in March
As a Magistrate.

I can easily imagine that the language in that poem might have struck Mr. Higginson as 'rugged.' Anything more racy and forthright it would be hard to conceive. The speech of her letters is often sentimental and effeminate; the speech of her poems is almost without exception strong, direct, and almost masculine in its vigour. [**"The butterfly obtains"**], in ***The Single Hound,*** has that acid quality of biting satire which we remarked in Blake's *Songs of Experience*.

The butterfly obtains
But little sympathy,
Though favourably mentioned
In Entomology.
Because he travels freely
And wears a proper coat,
The circumspect are certain
That he is dissolute.
Had he the homely scutcheon of modest Industry,
'Twere fitter certifying for Immortality.

Emily Dickinson had the divine gift of startlingly original expression. Her letters are full of such 'flashes' as:

> I love those little green ones [snakes] that slide around by your shoes in the grass, and make it rustle with their elbows.
>
> The wind blows gay to-day and the jays bark like blue terriers.
>
> The lawn is full of south and the odours tangle, and I hear to-day for the first the river in the tree.
>
> The moon rides like a girl through a topaz town.

And, in a description of a thunderstorm:

The leaves unhooked themselves from trees
And started all abroad;
The dust did scoop itself like hands
And throw away the road.

Her sense of sound was extraordinarily acute, for instance the droning of this:

Like trains of cars on tracks of plush
I hear the level bee:
A jar across the flower goes.

The following might be said to be the inaudible but realized sound of an overwhelming burst of bright light:

. . . mornings blossom into noons
And split their pods of flame.

She has something of Coleridge's feeling for the sound connotations of words, in one place she says:

An awful tempest mashed the air.

Down from Blake through Coleridge, that is Emily Dickinson's line of descent. Here is something of the fantastic quality of "The Ancient Mariner," and the true Coleridge use of colour:

When Etna basks and purrs,
Naples is more afraid
Than when she shows her Garnet Tooth;
Security is loud.

No poet ever revelled more in his own imagination than did this one. She flies her kite with infinite satisfaction to herself and to us. Over poor little Amherst it goes, tipping and veering, and her friends, intrigued but not wholly at ease in the sight, beg her not to let the neighbours see. This poem was sent with a nosegay of brilliant flowers:

I send two Sunsets—
Day and I in competition ran,
I finished two, and several stars,
While He was making one.

His own is ampler—
But, as I was saying to a friend,
Mine is the more convenient
To carry in the hand.

(pp. 96-9)

Religion is an attitude of the spirit, and no one was ever more innately, positively religious than Emily Dickinson. But the cramped religion of orthodox New England repelled her in spite of her training. Her family and friends recognized this dimly, but too dimly not to feel that the point of view needed a kindly cloak. In the Preface to the ***Letters,*** Mrs. Todd explains and explains:

> To her, God was not a far-away and dreary Power to be daily addressed—the great 'Eclipse' of which she wrote—but He was near and familiar and pervasive. Her garden was full of His brightness and glory; the birds sang and the sky glowed because of Him. To shut herself out of the sunshine in a church, dark, chilly, restricted, was rather to shut herself away from Him; almost pathetically she wrote, 'I believe the love of God may be taught not to seem like bears.' In essence, no real irreverence mars her poems or her letters.

Was that necessary? Perhaps it was at the time, although I hardly think so; it certainly is not now. And for that very reason this little volume, ***The Single Hound,*** is worth the other three volumes put together. One cannot help feeling that the editors of the first three series compiled the books with an eye to conciliating criticism. The whole of Emily is not in them, as it is in ***The Single Hound***; in fact, the most interesting part of her genius suffers eclipse at the hands of her timorous interpreters. Yet even in the first collection there are poems which reveal the whole tragedy of her life, poems which must have wounded her survivors if they really understood them, which must have shocked some sensibilities by the sheer brutality of their truth.

I died for beauty, but was scarce
Adjusted in the tomb,
When one who died for truth was lain
In an adjoining room.

He questioned softly why I failed.
'For beauty,' I replied.
'And I for truth,—the two are one;
We brethren are,' he said.

And so, as kinsmen met a night,
We talked between the rooms,
Until the moss had reached our lips,
And covered up our names.

Her whimsicality is very refreshing. It is not only in thought, but in expression:

I bet with every Wind that blew, till Nature in chagrin
Employed a *Fact* to visit me and scuttle my Balloon!

Now notice the next to last line of this poem, and see if it is not complete Imagism:

A little madness in the Spring
Is wholesome even for the King,
But God be with the Clown,
Who ponders this tremendous scene—
This whole experiment of green,
As if it were his own!

'This whole experiment of green!' Why, to read that is to see the little-leaved May world, all broken out in light, jocund verdure, such as happens at no other time of the year!

The exact word, the perfect image, that is what makes these short poems so telling. Take this picture:

Like brooms of steel
The Snow and Wind
Had swept the Winter Street,
The House was booked,
The Sun sent out
Faint Deputies of heat—
Where rode the Bird
The Silence tied
His ample, plodding Steed,
The Apple in the cellar snug
Was all the one that played.

Here is a stanza describing the wriggling forward of a snake. Forget the involutions of the words, and notice only the movement contained in them:

Then, to a rhythm slim
Secreted in his form,
As patterns swim,
Projected him.

If we were to arrange those words in a more usual order, should we get the sinuosity of the snake's advance? I doubt it.

Emily Dickinson is a master in the art of presenting movement. In another poem, she gives all the collateral effects of a snake squirming through grass so poignantly that, as one reads it, one involuntarily looks down at one's feet with a shudder:

The grass divides as with a comb,
A spotted shaft is seen;
And then it closes at your feet
And opens further on.

Those lines illustrate very aptly the 'ruggedness' which so troubled Mr. Higginson. 'Seen' does not rhyme with 'on,' the two words do not even make an assonance; we have only the two *n*'s and the long *e* against the *o* to help the ear to a kind of return. Yet return is here; and that the poet sought for it is quite evident. She would not sacrifice the *exact* word for a rhyme, but she must round her circle somehow.

Emily Dickinson was not one of those poets who rhyme by nature. The necessity for rhyming evidently bothered her. She had no conscious idea of any form of verse not built upon metre. All the poetry with which she was familiar was metrical and rhymed. She tried to tie her genius down to the pattern and signally failed. But she was too much of an artist to cramp herself beyond a certain point. When what she wanted to say clashed with her ability to rhyme, the rhymes went to the wall. In the following poem, she evidently intended to rhyme the second and fourth lines of each stanza, but the words were stubborn, the idea exacting; the result is that there is not a single rhyme throughout, only so many subterfuges, ingenious enough, but a begging of the issue after all.

"The Saints' Rest"

Of tribulation these are they,
Denoted by the white;
The spangled gowns, a lesser rank
Of victors designate.

All these did conquer; but the ones
Who overcame most times,
Wear nothing commoner than snow,
No ornaments but palms.

'Surrender' is a sort unknown
On this superior soil;
'Defeat,' an outgrown anguish,
Remembered as the mile

Our panting ankle barely gained
When night devoured the road;
But we stood whispering in the house,
And all we said was 'Saved!'

I have said that Emily Dickinson had no conscious idea of any form of verse other than the metrical. She does not seem to have known Blake at all, and if she read Matthew Arnold, or Henley, she made no happy discovery of their use of *vers libre*. The poetry she knew was in metre, and she did her best to cram her subtle rhythmic sense into a figure of even feet and lines. But it would not do. Her genius revolted, and again and again carried her over into cadence in spite of herself. Here is a poem, part metre, part cadence:

Peril as a possession
'Tis good to bear,
Danger disintegrates satiety;
There's Basis there
Begets an awe,
That searches Human Nature's creases
As clean as Fire.

The first two lines are perfect metre, the third is cadence, the fourth and fifth again are metre, while cadence returns in the sixth and seventh.

A knowledge of the principles of unitary verse (that is, verse based upon a unit of time instead of a unit of accent) would have liberated Emily Dickinson from the bonds against which she chafed. But she was of too unanalytical a nature to find this for herself, consciously; that she found it subconsciously this poem proves:

Victory comes late,
And is held low to freezing lips
Too rapt with frost
To take it.
How sweet it would have tasted,
Just a drop!
Was God so economical?
His table's spread too high for us
Unless we dine on tip-toe.
Crumbs fit such little mouths,
Cherries suit robins;
The eagle's golden breakfast
Strangles them.
God keeps his oath to sparrows,
Who of little love
Know how to starve!

There is one other way in which Emily Dickinson was a precursor of the Imagists. She, first of all in English I believe, made use of what I have called elsewhere the 'unrelated' method. That is, the describing of a thing by its appearance only, without regard to its entity in any other way. Even to-day, the Imagists are, so far as I know, the only poets to employ this device. Mr. Fletcher constantly uses it in his 'Symphonies,' but they are too long to quote. This little poem, however, will serve as an example of the *genre:*

"The Skaters"

TO A. D. R.

Black swallows swooping or gliding
In a flurry of entangled loops and curves;
The skaters skim over the frozen river.
And the grinding click of their skates as they impinge
upon the surface,
Is like the brushing together of thin wing-tips of silver.

Now hear Emily Dickinson on a humming-bird.

"The Humming-Bird"

A route of evanescence
With a revolving wheel;
A resonance of emerald;
A rush of cochineal;
And every blossom on the bush
Adjusts its tumbled head,—
The mail from Tunis, probably
An easy morning's ride.

'She was not daily-bread,' says her niece, 'she was star-dust.' Do we eat stars more readily than we did, then? I think we do, and if so, it is she who has taught us to appreciate them. (pp. 100-08)

Amy Lowell, "Emily Dickinson," in her Poetry and Poets: Essays, *Houghton Mifflin Company, 1930, pp. 88-108.*

CONSTANCE ROURKE (essay date 1931)

[*Rourke was a pioneer in the field of American cultural history. Her reputation was established by her* American Humor: A Study of the National Character, *which is still widely studied. The work advances Rourke's opposition to such critics as Van Wyck Brooks and T. S. Eliot, who asserted that America had no cultural traditions other than those it had imported from Europe. Rourke theorized that an American cultural tradition indeed exists, and that it is based on humor. The findings presented in* American Humor *and her later* The Roots of American Culture *were a major factor in leading Brooks and other critics to reassess and revise their previously held opinions of America as a cultural wasteland. In this excerpt from* American Humor, *Rourke considers Dickinson's place in the American comic tradition.*]

Emily Dickinson was not only a lyric poet; she was in a profound sense a comic poet in the American tradition. She possessed the sense of scale and caught this within her small compass. A little tippler, she leaned against the sun. The grave for her was a living place whose elements grew large in stone. Purple mountains moved for her; a train, clouds, a pathway through a valley became huge and animate. Much of her poetry is in the ascending movement, full of morning imagery, of supernal mornings: seraphim tossing their snowy hats on high might be taken as her symbol. Her poetry is also comic in the Yankee strain, with its resilience and sudden unprepared ironical lines. Her use of an unstressed irony in a soft blank climax is the old formula grown almost fixed, yet fresh because it was used with a new depth—

Faith is a fine invention
For gentlemen who see;
But microscopes are prudent
In an emergency!

She could cap tragedy with tragi-comedy.

Drowning is not so pitiful
  As the attempt to rise.
Three times, 'tis said, a sinking man
  Comes up to face the skies,
And then declines forever
  To that abhorred abode
Where hope and he part company—
  For he is grasped of God.
The Maker's cordial visage,
  However good to see,
Is shunned, we must admit it,
  Like an adversity.

She was concerned with eternal verities; yet her elastic and irreverent rebellion broke forth again and again—

"Heavenly Father," take to thee
The supreme iniquity,
Fashioned by thy candid hand
In a moment contraband.
Though to trust us seem to us
More respectful—"We are dust."
We apologize to Thee
For thine own Duplicity.

Occasionally her wit turned mordantly upon earthly matters: "Menagerie to me my neighbor be." She saw the small and futile motions in a house to which death had come. And she could double ironically upon herself as well as upon the Deity. In the end—or at least in the composite, for the end is hardly known—she contrived to see a changing universe within that acceptant view which is comic in its profoundest sense, which is part reconciliation, part knowledge of eternal disparity. If she did not achieve the foundation of a divine comedy she was at least aware of its elements; its outlines are scattered through the numberless brief notations of her poems.

Like Poe and Hawthorne and Henry James, though with a simpler intensity than theirs, Emily Dickinson trenched upon those shaded subtleties toward which the American imagination long had turned. "I measure every grief I meet with analytic eyes." Anger, hope, remorse, the weight of the past, the subtle incursions of memory, the quality of despair, and fear, cleavages in the mind, all came under her minute scrutiny—

One need not be a chamber to be haunted,
One need not be a house;
The brain has corridors surpassing
Material place.

Even her glances toward an exterior world at their finest are subjective. Her poetry was indwelling in a final sense; she used that deeply interior speech which is soliloquy, even though it was in brief song.

She never lost a slight air of struggle; this appeared persistently in her sudden flights to new verbal and tonal keys, in her careless assonances which still seemed half intentional, in the sudden muting of her rhymes. She verged toward the dramatic, as others in the tradition had done before her; almost invariably her poems concentrate upon a swift turn of inner drama: yet like the others she sheered away from pure drama. Her language is bold, humorously and defiantly experimental, as if she had absorbed the inconsequence in regard to formal language abroad during her youth in the '50's when Whitman was writing; yet often she achieved only a hasty anarchy in meaning and expression, and created hardly more than a roughly carven shell.

She seemed to emerge afresh as from a chrysalis in each lyric or even in each brief stanza; and the air was one which had been evident before in the sequence of American expression. Emerson had it, as Santayana noted, in everything he wrote. Whitman had it, and was aware of the quality: it was that of improvisation. In one way or another every major American writer had shown its traces, except perhaps Henry James in the broad spaces of his early novels, but he too turned toward experiment in the end. Emily Dickinson was another—perhaps the last—of those primary writers who had slowly charted an elementary American literature; and she possessed both the virtues and the failings of her position. Her poetry has an abounding fresh intensity, a touch of conquering zeal, a true entrance into new provinces of verbal music; but incompletion touches her lyricism. Often—indeed most often—her poems are only poetic flashes, notes, fragments of poetry rather than a final poetry. Yet like the others who had gone before her—Whitman, Hawthorne, Emerson, James—she set a new outpost, even though like them she had no immediate effect upon American literature. It was not until ten years after her death that the early poetry of Edwin Arlington Robinson appeared; and the space widens if the '40's are remembered as formative years for Emily Dickinson, the '80's for Robinson. Nor does he show any perceptible trace of her influence. But if not by her power, then by some profound stress in the American character, the gates were being slowly opened for an ample poetry. (pp. 266-70)

Constance Rourke, "Round Up," in her American Humor: A Study of the National Character, *Harcourt Brace Jovanovich, Inc., 1931, pp. 266-302.*

YVOR WINTERS (essay date 1938)

[*Winters was a twentieth-century American poet and critic. He was associated with the New Criticism movement and gained a reputation as a stringently anti-romantic critic. Maintaining that a critic must be concerned with the moral as well as the aesthetic import of a work of art, he believed that poetry ought to provide rational comment on the human condition, with the poet "seeking to state a true moral judgment." His critical precepts, usually considered extreme, include an emphasis on order, dignity, re-*

straint, and morality. They are embodied in his best-known collection of essays, In Defense of Reason. *In the following excerpt from that work, Winters considers the difficulties inherent in critical evaluation of Dickinson's poetry as he examines several individual lyrics. Winters's commentary was first published in 1938.*]

When the poems of Emily Dickinson first began to appear, in the years shortly following her death, she enjoyed a period of notoriety and of semi-popularity that endured for perhaps ten years; after about ten years of semi-obscurity, her reputation was revived with the publication of ***The Single Hound,*** and has lasted unabated to the present day, though with occasional signs that it may soon commence to diminish. A good many critics have resented her reputation, and it has not been hard for them to justify their resentment; probably no poet of comparable reputation has been guilty of so much unpardonable writing. On the other hand, one cannot shake off the uncomfortable feeling that her popularity has been mainly due to her vices; her worst poems are certainly her most commonly praised, and as a general matter, great lyric poetry is not widely read or admired.

The problem of judging her better poems is much of the time a subtle one. Her meter, at its worst—that is, most of the time—is a kind of stiff sing-song; her diction, at its worst, is a kind of poetic nursery jargon; and there is a remarkable continuity of manner, of a kind nearly indescribable, between her worst and her best poems. The following poem will illustrate the defects in perfection:

I like to see it lap the miles,
And lick the valleys up,
And stop to feed itself at tanks;
And then, prodigious, step

Around a pile of mountains,
And, supercilious, peer
In shanties by the sides of roads;
And then a quarry pare

To fit its sides, and crawl between,
Complaining all the while
In horrid, hooting stanza;
Then chase iself down hill

And neigh like Boanerges;
Then, punctual as a star,
Stop—docile and omnipotent—
At its own stable door.

The poem is abominable; and the quality of silly playfulness which renders it abominable is diffused more or less perceptibly throughout most of her work, and this diffusion is facilitated by the limited range of her metrical schemes.

The difficulty is this: that even in her most nearly perfect poems, even in those poems in which the defects do not intrude momentarily in a crudely obvious form, one is likely to feel a fine trace of her countrified eccentricity; there is nearly always a margin of ambiguity in our final estimate of even her most extraordinary work, and though the margin may appear to diminish or disappear in a given reading of a favorite poem, one feels no certainty that it will not reappear more obviously with the next reading. Her best poems, quite unlike the best poems of Ben Jonson, of George Herbert, or of Thomas Hardy, can never be isolated certainly and defensibly from her defects; yet she is a poetic genius of the highest order, and this ambiguity in one's feeling about her is profoundly disturbing. The following poem is a fairly obvious illustration; we shall later see less obvious:

I started early, took my dog,
And visited the sea;
The mermaids in the basement
Came out to look at me,

And frigates in the upper floor
Extended hempen hands,
Presuming me to be a mouse
Aground, upon the sands.

But no man moved me till the tide
Went past my simple shoe,
And past my apron and my belt,
And past my bodice too,

And made as he would eat me up
As wholly as a dew
Upon a dandelion's sleeve—
And then I started too.

And he—he followed close behind;
I felt his silver heel
Upon my ankle,—then my shoes
Would overflow with pearl.

Until we met the solid town,
No man he seemed to know;
And bowing with a mighty look
At me, the sea withdrew.

The mannerisms are nearly as marked as in the first poem, but whereas the first poem was purely descriptive, this poem is allegorical and contains beneath the more or less mannered surface an ominously serious theme, so that the manner appears in a new light and is somewhat altered in effect. The sea is here the traditional symbol of death; that is, of all the forces and qualities in nature and in human nature which tend toward the dissolution of human character and consciousness. The playful protagonist, the simple village maiden, though she speaks again in the first person, is dramatized, as if seen from without, and her playfulness is somewhat restrained and formalized. Does this formalization, this dramatization, combined with a major symbolism, suffice effectually to transmute in this poem the quality discerned in the first poem, or does that quality linger as a fine defect? The poem is a poem of power; it may even be a great poem; but this is not to answer the question. I have never been able to answer the question.

Her poetic subject matter might be subdivided roughly as follows: natural description; the definition of moral experience, including the definition of difficulties of comprehension; and mystical experience, or the definition of the experience of "immortality," to use a favorite word, or of beatitude. The second subdivision includes a great deal, and her best work falls within it; I shall consider it last. Her descriptive poems contain here and there brilliant strokes, but she had the hard and uncompromising approach to experience of the early New England Calvinists; lacking all subtlety, she displays the heavy hand of one unaccustomed to fragile objects; her efforts at lightness are distressing. Occasionally, instead of endeavoring to treat the small subject in terms appropriate to it, she endeavors to treat it in terms appropriate to her own temperament, and we have what appears a deliberate excursion into obscurity, the subject being inadequate to the rhetoric, as in the last stanza of the poem beginning, **"At half-past three a single bird":**

At half-past seven, element
Nor implement was seen,
And place was where the presence was,
Circumference between.

The stanza probably means, roughly, that bird and song alike have disappeared, but the word "circumference," a resonant and impressive one, is pure nonsense.

This unpredictable boldness in plunging into obscurity, a boldness in part, perhaps, inherited from the earlier New Englanders whose sense of divine guidance was so highly developed, whose humility of spirit was commonly so small; a boldness dramatized by Melville in the character of Ahab; this congenital boldness may have led her, to attempt the rendering of purely theoretic experience, the experience of life after death. There are numerous poems which attempt to express the experience of posthumous beatitude, as if she were already familiar with it; the poetic terms of the expression are terms, either abstract or concrete, of human life, but suddenly fixed, or approaching fixation, as if at the cessation of time in eternity, as if to the dead the living world appeared as immobile as the dead person appears to the living, and the fixation frequently involves an element of horror:

Great streets of silence led away
To neighborhoods of pause;
Here was no notice, no dissent,
No universe, no laws.

By clocks 'twas morning, and for night
The bells at distance called;
But epoch had no basis here,
For period exhaled.

The device here employed is to select a number of terms representing familiar abstractions or perceptions, some of a commonplace nature, some relatively grandiose or metaphysical, and one by one to negate these terms; a number of statements, from a grammatical point of view, have been made, yet actually no concrete image emerges, and the idea of the poem—the idea of the absolute dissidence of the eternal from the temporal—is stated indirectly, and, in spite of the brevity of the poem and the gnomic manner, with extraordinary redundancy. We come painfully close in this poem to the irresponsible playfulness of the poem about the railway train; we have gone beyond the irresponsible obscurity of the poem about the bird.

This is technically a mystical poem: that is, it endeavors to render an experience—the rapt contemplation, eternal and immovable, which Aquinas describes as the condition of beatitude—which is by definition foreign to all human experience, yet to render it in terms of a modified human experience. Yet there is no particular reason to believe that Emily Dickinson was a mystic, or thought she was a mystic. The poems of this variety, and there are many of them, appear rather to be efforts to dramatize an idea of salvation, intensely felt, but as an idea, not as something experienced, and as an idea essentially inexpressible. She deliberately utilizes imagery irrelevant to the state with which she is concerned, because she cannot do otherwise; yet the attitude toward the material, the attitude of rapt contemplation, is the attitude which she presumably expects to achieve toward something that she has never experienced. The poems are invariably forced and somewhat theoretical; they are briskly clever, and lack the obscure but impassioned conviction of the mystical poems of Very; they lack the tragic finality, the haunting sense of human isolation in a foreign universe, to be found in her greatest poems, of which the explicit theme is a denial of this mystical trance, is a statement of the limits of judgment.

There are a few curious and remarkable poems representing a mixed theme, of which the following is perhaps the finest example:

Because I could not stop for Death,
He kindly stopped for me;
The carriage held but just ourselves
And Immortality.

We slowly drove, he knew no haste,
And I had put away
My labor, and my leisure too,
Forr his civility.

We passed the school where children played
At wrestling in a ring;
We passed the fields of gazing grain,
We passed the setting sun.

We paused before a house that seemed
A swelling of the ground;
The roof was scarcely visible,
The cornice but a mound.

Since then 'tis centuries; but each
Feels shorter than the day
I first surmised the horses' heads
Were toward eternity.

In the fourth line we find the familiar device of using a major abstraction in a somewhat loose and indefinable manner; in the last stanza there is the semi-playful pretence of familiarity with the posthumous experience of eternity, so that the poem ends unconvincingly though gracefully, with a formulary gesture very roughly comparable to that of the concluding couplet of many an Elizabethan sonnet of love; for the rest the poem is a remarkably beautiful poem on the subject of the daily realization of the imminence of death—it is a poem of departure from life, an intensely conscious leave-taking. In so far as it concentrates on the life that is being left behind, it is wholly successful; in so far as it attempts to experience the death to come, it is fraudulent, however exquisitely, and in this it falls below her finest achievement. Allen Tate, who appears to be unconcerned with this fraudulent element, praises the poem in the highest terms; he appears almost to praise it for its defects: "The sharp *gazing* before *grain* instils into nature a kind of cold vitality of which the qualitative richness has infinite depth. The content of death in the poem eludes forever any explicit definition . . . she has presented a typical Christian theme in all its final irresolution, without making any final statement about it" [see excerpt dated 1928-32]. The poem ends in irresolution in the sense that it ends in a statement that is not offered seriously; to praise the poem for this is unsound criticism, however. It is possible to solve any problem of insoluble experience by retreating a step and defining the boundary at which comprehension ceases, and by then making the necessary moral adjustments to that boundary; this in itself is an experience both final and serious, and it is the experience on which our author's finest work is based.

Let me illustrate by citation. The following poem defines the subject which the mystical poems endeavor to conceal: the soul is taken to the brink of the incomprehensible, and is left there, for retreat is impossible, and advance is impossible without a transmutation of the soul's very nature. The third and fourth lines display the playful redundancy of her weaker poems, but the intrusion of the quality here is the result of habit, and is a minor defect; there is nothing in the conception of the poem demanding a compromise. There is great power in the phrasing of the remainder of the poem, especially in the middle stanza:

Our journey had advanced;
Our feet were almost come
To that odd fork in Being's road,
Eternity by term.

Our pace took sudden awe,
Our feet reluctant led.
Before were cities, but between
The forest of the dead.

Retreat was out of hope,—
Behind, a sealed route,
Eternity's white flag before,
And God at every gate.

She is constantly defining the absolute cleavage between the living and the dead. In the following poem the definition is made more powerfully, and in other terms:

'Twas warm at first, like us,
Until there crept thereon
A chill, like frost upon a glass,
Till all the scene be gone.

The forehead copied stone,
The fingers grew too cold
To ache, and like a skater's brook
The busy eyes congealed.

It straightened—that was all—
It crowded cold to cold—
It multiplied indifference
As Pride were all it could.

And even when with cords
'Twas lowered like a freight,
It made no signal, nor demurred,
But dropped like adamant.

The stiffness of phrasing, as in the barbarously constructed fourth and twelfth lines, is allied to her habitual carelessness, yet in this poem there is at least no triviality, and the imagery of the third stanza in particular has tremendous power.

The poem beginning, **"The last night that she lived,"** treats the same theme in more personal terms; the observer watches the death of a friend, that is follows the friend to the brink of the comprehensible, sees her pass the brink, and faces the loss. The poem contains a badly mixed figure and at least two major grammatical blunders, in addition to a little awkward inversion of an indefensible variety, yet there is in the poem an immediate seizing of terrible fact, which makes it, at least fragmentarily, very great poetry:

And we, we placed the hair,
And drew the head erect;
And then an awful leisure was,
Our faith to regulate.

Her inability to take Christian mysticism seriously did not, however, drive her to the opposite extreme of the pantheistic mysticism which was seducing her contemporaries. The following lines, though not remarkable poetry, are a clear statement of a position consistently held:

But nature is a stranger yet;
  The ones that cite her most
Have never passed her haunted house,
  Nor simplified her ghost.

To pity those that know her not
  Is helped by the regret
That those who know her, know her less
  The nearer her they get.

Nature as a symbol, as Allen Tate has pointed out in the essay to which I have already referred, remains immitagably the symbol of all the elements which corrupt,dissolve, and destroy human character and consciousness; to approach nature is to depart from the fullness of human life, and to join nature is to leave human life. Nature may thus be a symbol of death, representing much the same idea as the corpse in the poem beginning "'Twas warm at first, like us," but involving a more complex range of association.

In the following poem, we are shown the essential cleavage between man, as represented by the author-reader, and nature, as represented by the insects in the late summer grass; the subject is the plight of man, the willing and freely moving entity, in a universe in which he is by virtue of his essential qualities a foreigner. The intense nostalgia of the poem is the nostalgia of man for the mode of being which he perceives imperfectly and in which he cannot share. The change described in the last two lines is the change in the appearance of nature and in the feeling of the observer which results from a recognition of the cleavage:

Farther in summer than the birds,
Pathetic from the grass,
A minor nation celebrates
Its unobtrusive mass.

No ordinance is seen,
So gradual the grace,
A pensive custom it becomes,
Enlarging loneliness.

Antiquest felt at noon
When August, burning low,
Calls forth this spectral canticle,
Repose to typify.

Remit as yet no grace,
No furrow on the glow,
Yet a druidic difference
Enhances nature now.

The first two lines of the last stanza are written in the author's personal grammatical short-hand; they are no doubt defective in this respect, but the defect is minor. They mean: There is as yet no diminution of beauty, no mark of change on the brightness. The twelfth line employs a meaningless inversion. On the other hand, the false rhymes are employed with unusually fine modulation; the first rhyme is perfect, the second and third represent successive stages of departure, and the last a return to what is roughly the stage of the second. These effects are complicated by the rhyming, both perfect and imperfect, from stanza to stanza. The intense strangeness of this poem could not have been achieved with standard rhyming. The poem, though not quite one of her most nearly perfect, is probably one of her five or six greatest, and is one of the most deeply moving and most unforgettable poems in my own experience; I have the feeling of having lived in its immediate presence for many years.

The three poems which combine her greatest power with her finest execution are strangely on much the same theme, both as regards the idea embodied and as regards the allegorical embodiment. They deal with the inexplicable fact of change, of the absolute cleavage between successive states of being, and it is not unnatural that in two of the poems this theme should be related to the theme of death. In each poem, seasonal change is employed as the concrete symbol of the moral change. This is not the same thing as the so-called pathetic fallacy of the romantics, the imposition of a personal emotion upon a physical object incapable either of feeling such an emotion or of motivating it in a human being. It is rather a legitimate and traditional form of allegory, in which the relationships between the items described resemble exactly the relationships between certain moral ideas or experiences; the identity of relationship evoking simultaneously and identifying with each other the feelings attendant upon both series as they appear separately. Here are the three poems, in the order of the seasons employed, and in the order of increasing complexity both of theme and of technique:

1

A light exists in spring
Not present in the year
At any other period.
When March is scarcely here

A color stands abroad
On solitary hills
That science cannot overtake,
But human nature feels.

It waits upon the lawn;
It shows the furthest tree
Upon the furthest slope we know;
It almost speaks to me.

Then, as horizons step,
Or noons report away,
Without the formula of sound,
It passes, and we stay:

A quality of loss
Affecting our content,
As trade had suddenly encroached
Upon a sacrament.

2

As imperceptibly as grief
The Summer lapsed away,—
Too imperceptible, at last,
To seem like perfidy.

A quietness distilled,
As twilight long begun,
Or Nature, spending with herself
Sequestered afternoon.

The dusk drew earlier in,
The morning foreign shone,—
A courteous, yet harrowing grace,
As guest who would be gone.

And thus, without a wing,
Or service of a keel,
Our summer made her light escape
Into the beautiful.

3

There's a certain slant of light,
On winter afternoons,
That oppresses, like the weight
Of cathedral tunes.

Heavenly hurt it gives us;
We can find no scar,
But internal difference
Where the meanings are.

None may teach it anything,
'Tis the seal, despair,—
An imperial affliction
Sent us of the air.

When it comes, the landscape listens,
Shadows hold their breath;
When it goes, 'tis like the distance
On the look of death.

In the seventh, eighth, and twelfth lines of the first poem, and, it is barely possible, in the seventh and eighth of the third, there is a very slight echo of the brisk facility of her poorer work; the last line of the second poem, perhaps, verges ever so slightly on an easy prettiness of diction, though scarcely of substance. These defects are shadowy, however; had the poems been written by another writer, it is possible that we should not observe them. On the other hand, the directness, dignity, and power with which these major subjects are met, the quality of the phrasing, at once clairvoyant and absolute, raise the poems to the highest level of English lyric poetry.

The meter of these poems is worth careful scrutiny. The basis of all three is the so-called Poulter's Measure, first employed, if I remember aright, by Surrey, and after the time of Sidney in disrepute. It is the measure, however, not only of the great elegy on Sidney commonly attributed to Fulke Greville, but of some of the best poetry between Surrey and Sidney, including the fine poem by Vaux on contentment and the great poem by Gascoigne in praise of a gentlewoman of dark complexion. The English poets commonly though not invariably wrote the poem in two long lines instead of four short ones, and the lines so conceived were the basis of their rhetoric. In the first of the three poems just quoted, the measure is employed without alteration, but the short line is the basis of the rhetoric; an arrangement which permits of more varied adjustment of sentence to line than if the long line were the basis. In the second poem, the first stanza is composed not in the basic measure, but in lines of eight, six, eight, and six syllables; the shift into the normal six, six, eight, and six in the second stanza, as in the second stanza of the poem beginning, "Farther in summer," results in a subtle and beautiful muting both of meter and of tone. This shift she employs elsewhere, but especially in poems of four stanzas, to which it appears to have a natural relationship; it is a brilliant technical invention.

In the third poem she varies her simple base with the ingenuity and mastery of a virtuoso. In the first stanza, the two long lines are reduced to seven syllables each, by the dropping of the initial unaccented syllable; the second short line is reduced to five syllables in the same manner. In the second stanza, the first line, which ought now to be of six syllables, has but five metrical syllables, unless we violate normal usage and count the second and infinitely light syllable of *Heaven,* with an extrametrical syllable at the end, the syllable dropped being again the initial one; the second line, which ought to have six syllables, has likewise lost its initial syllable, but the extrametrical *us* of the preceding line, being unaccented, is in rhythmical effect the first syllable of the second line, so that this syllable serves a double and ambiguous function—it maintains the syllable-count of the first line, in spite of an altered rhythm, and it maintains the rhythm of the second line in spite of the altered syllable-count. The third and fourth lines of the second stanza are shortened to seven and five. In the third stanza the first and second lines are constructed like the third and fourth of the second stanza; the third and fourth lines like the first and second of the second stanza, except that in the third line the initial unaccented syllable is retained; that is, the third stanza repeats the construction of the second, but in reverse order. The final stanza is a triumphant resolution of the three preceding: the first and third lines, like the second and fourth, are metrically identical; the first and third contain seven syllables each, with an additional extrametrical syllable at the end which takes the place of the missing syllable at the beginning of each subsequent short line, at the same time that the extrametrical syllable functions in the line in which it is written as part of a two-syllable rhyme. The elaborate structure of this poem results in the balanced hesitations and rapid resolutions which one hears in reading it. This is metrical artistry at about as high a level as one is likely to find it.

Emily Dickinson was a product of the New England tradition of moral Calvinism; her dissatisfaction with her tradition led to her questioning most of its theology and discarding much of it, and led to her reinterpreting some of it, one would gather, in the direction of a more nearly Catholic Christianity. Her acceptance of Christian moral concepts was unimpaired, and the moral tone of her character remained immitagably Calvinistic in its hard and direct simplicity. As a result of this Calvinistic temper, she lacked the lightness and grace which might have enabled her to master minor themes; she sometimes stepped without hesitation into obscurantism, both verbal and metaphysical. But also as a result of it, her best poetry represents a moral adjustment to certain major problems which are carefully defined; it is curious in the light of this fact, and in the light of the discussion which they have received, that her love poems never equal her highest achievement—her best work is on themes more generalized and inclusive.

Emily Dickinson differed from every other major New England writer of the nineteenth century, and from every major American writer of the century save Melville, of those affected by New England, in this: that her New England heritage, though it made her life a moral drama, did not leave her life in moral confusion. It impoverished her in one respect, however: of all great poets, she is the most lacking in taste; there are innumerable beautiful lines and passages wasted in the desert of her crudities; her defects, more than those of any other great poet that I have read, are constantly at the brink, or pushing beyond the brink, of her best poems. This stylistic character is the natural product of the New England which produced the barren little meeting houses; of the New England founded by the harsh and intrepid pioneers, who in order to attain salvation trampled brutally through a world which they were too proud and too impatient to understand. In this respect, she differs from Melville, whose taste was rich and cultivated. But except by Melville, she is surpassed by no writer that this country has produced; she is one of the greatest lyric poets of all time. (pp. 283-99)

Yvor Winters, "Emily Dickinson and the Limits of Judgment," in his In Defense of Reason, *The Swallow Press Inc., 1947, pp. 283-99.*

THORNTON WILDER (essay date 1952)

[*Wilder was a prominent twentieth-century American author. Contributing to the arts as a playwright, novelist, essayist, and screenwriter, he was three times the recipient of the Pulitzer Prize, winning that award for his novel* The Bridge of San Luis Rey *and for his plays* Our Town *and* The Skin of Our Teeth. *In the following excerpt from an essay originally published in the* Atlantic Monthly *in 1952, Wilder discusses such issues as Dickinson's use of stanzaic forms and her feelings regarding fame and publication.*]

As a poet Emily Dickinson started out with two great disadvantages—an enormous facility for versifying and an infatuation with bad models. Later she was to read absorbedly Shakespeare, Milton, Herbert, and the great English poets of her century, and one is aware of the influence they had upon her language, but one is also aware of how little an effect they had upon the verse forms she employed. Her point of departure was the lyric of the keepsake and the Christmas Annual and the newspaper and the genteel periodical—the avocation of clergymen and of ladies of refinement and sensibility. Even the better poets of the hymnbooks do not seem to have greatly influenced her. Although she was to make some startling innovations within this form, it is no less startling that she made no attempts to depart from the half-dozen stanzaic patterns with which she began. . . . She was extraordinarily bold in what she did within these patterns (she soon *burst their seams*), but the form of the poem and to some extent the kind of poem she admired as a girl continued to be the poem she wrote to the end.

She wrote to Colonel Higginson in April, 1862 (she was then thirty-one years old): "I made no verse, but one or two, until last winter, sir." So far, very few poems have been, with assurance, dated prior to that time; but it seems to me that she here intended the qualification: no verse of the highest conscious intention. There are numbers of poems of about this time, and certainly early (hence, naturally, the darlings of the anthologists), such as **"If I Can Stop One Heart from Breaking"** and **"I Taste a Liquor Never Brewed"** and **"To Fight Aloud Is Very Brave,"** which show evidence of having been preceded by a long experience in versifying. The passage from one stanza to the next is very accomplished indeed, and presupposes an extended practice, in public or in private. It appears certain to me that when, toward 1861, Emily Dickinson collected herself to write verse of the most earnest intention, she had to struggle not only against the pitfalls of a native facility, but against those of a facility already long exercised in a superficial effectiveness—in the easy pathos and in the easy epigram.

Even before she sent the first examples of her work to Colonel Higginson she had won a critical battle over her facility. She had found the courage to write poetry which "insulted the intelligence" of her contemporaries. What shocked Colonel Higginson was not that she occasionally employed "bad" rhymes (such abounded in the poetry of Mrs. Browning); nor that she substituted assonance for rhyme; nor even that she occasionally failed to rhyme at all (that practice he had accepted in Walt Whitman, whose work he recommended to her reading); but that all these irregularities were combined and deeply embedded in the most conventional of all verse forms.

At this distance we can venture to reconstruct her struggles. A new tide had entered her being; she now wished to say with passion what she had been hitherto saying playfully, saying with coquetry. New intensities—particularly in new countries—call for new forms. A childhood fixation, however, prevented her from abandoning the stanzaic patterns of her early reading. She revolted from the regular rhyme, the eternal "my-die" and "God-rod," not because she was too lazy to impose it, but because the regular rhyme seemed the outer expression of an inner conventionality. She called the regular rhyme "prose"—"they shut me up in prose"—and in the same poem she calls it "captivity."

One of her devices shows us how conscious she was of what she was doing. She artfully offers us rhymes of increasing regularity so that our ear will be waiting for another, and then in a concluding verse refuses any rhyme whatever. The poem **"Of Tribulation These Are They"** gives us "white-designate," "times-palms," "soil-mile," "road-*Saved!*" (The italics are hers.) The effect is as of a ceiling being removed from above our heads. The incommensurable invades the poem. In **"I'll Tell Thee All—How Blank It Grew"** she flings all the windows open in closing with the words "outvisions paradise," rhymeless after three stanzas of unusually regular rhymes.

Her "teacher" rebuked her for these audacities, but she persisted in them. She did not stoop to explain or defend them. The Colonel's unwillingness to publish the work showed her that he did not consider her a poet, however much he may have been struck by individual phrases. She continued to enclose an occasional poem in her letters to friends, but they seem not to have asked to see "lots of them." The hope of encouragement and the thought of a contemporary audience grew more and more remote. Yet the possibility of a literary fame, of an ultimate glory, never ceased to trouble her. In poem after poem she derided renown; she compared it to an auction and to the croaking of frogs; but at the same time she hailed it as this consecration of the poet's "vital light." What did she do about it? She took five steps forward and two steps back. It is no inconsiderable advance toward literary pretension to write two thousand poems; yet the condition in which she left them is a no less conspicuous retreat. She called on posterity to witness that she was indifferent to its approval, but she did not destroy her work. She did not even destroy the "sweepings of the studio," the tentative sketches at the margin of the table. Had she left fair copies, the movement would have been five steps forward and one step back; had she directed that the work be burned by others, it would have been three steps back.

I am convinced that she went even further in her wish to appear indifferent to our good opinion; she deliberately marred many a poem; she did not so much insult our intelligence as flout it. As we read the more authentic work we are astonished to find that poem after poem concludes with some lapse into banality, or begins flatly and mounts to splendor. No one would claim that she was free of lapses of judgment and of taste, but the last three words of **"How Many Times These Low Feet Staggered"**. . . or the last verse of **"They Put Us Far Apart"** . . . are, poetically speaking, of an almost insolent cynicism—the first for flatness, the second for cacophony.

That is to say, Emily Dickinson frequently wrote badly *on purpose*. She did not aspire to your praise and mine, if we were the kind of persons who cannot distinguish the incidental from the essential. She had withdrawn a long way from our human, human, human, discriminations and judgments. . . . [She] was singed, if not scorched, in early life by the all-too-human in her family relationships. Thereafter she was abandoned—"betrayed" she called it—by the person (or as I prefer to see it, by the succession of persons) whom most she loved. She withdrew from us: into her house; and even in her house she withdrew—the few old friends who came to call were required to converse with her through a half-open door. She became more and more abstract in her view of people. She did not repudiate us entirely, but she increasingly cherished the thought that we would all be more estimable when we were dead. She was capable of envisaging the fact that there may be no life hereafter: **"Their Height in Heaven Comforts Not"** acknowledges that the whole matter is a "house of supposition . . . that skirts the acres of perhaps." But only such a company, unencumbered with earthly things, would understand what she was saying, and she took ample pains to discourage all others. The poem that begins **"Some work for Immortality, the chiefer part for *Time*,"** is not primarily about books sold in bookstores.

In other words, those who dwell in "immensity" are not finicking literary critics.

It is very difficult to be certain what Emily Dickinson meant by "God," though there are innumerable references to Him. Her relation to Him is marked by alternating advance and retreat. He is occasionally warned not to be presumptuous; that all the gifts He may have to show hereafter (the single work from which she quotes most often is the Book of Revelation) are not likely to exceed certain occasions of bliss she has known on earth. God, a supreme intelligence, was not a stable concept in her mind. On the other hand, she lived constantly close to another world she called Infinity, Immensity, Eternity, and the Absolute. For her these concepts were not merely greater in degree from the dimensions of earth: they were different in kind; they were altogether *other;* they were non-sense. *There* dwelt her audience. If you set yourself to write verses for people down here on earth, in time, you were bound to miss the *tone*—the tone that is current in immensity. Immensity does not niggle at off-rhymes and at untidy verse-endings. Immensity is capable of smiling and probably enjoys those things which insult the intelligence of men. Walt Whitman wrote: "I round and finish little, if anything; and could not, consistently with my scheme. . . ." It would be difficult to assemble five of the maturer poems of Emily Dickinson which one could place before an antagonistic reader and say that they were "finished poems." For those two poets that word "finish" would smack strongly of poems servilely submitted for the approval of judges, princes, and connoisseurs. Art—the work of art—was slow in presenting itself as the project of a continent-conscious American. Hawthorne strove for it, but Hawthorne was not caught up into the realization of the New World's boundlessness; he even averted his face from it, and consciously. Poe's mind knew both the boundlessness and the work of art, and the double knowledge was among the elements that destroyed him. The work of art is the recognition of order, of limits, of shared tacit assumptions and, above all, of agreed-upon conventions. Walt Whitman and Emily Dickinson seemed to be at every moment advancing into new territories in relation to writing; the time for them had not come to consolidate what they had acquired, to establish their limits and to construct their conventions.

I have said before that Americans can find no support for their identity in place, in time, or in community—that they are really in relation only to Everywhere, Always, and Everybody. Emily Dickinson is a signal illustration of this assertion. The imagination of this spinster withdrawn into a few rooms in Amherst was constantly aware that the universe surrounded every detail of life. "I take no less than skies," she wrote, "for earths grow thick as berries, in my native town." Her tireless observation of the animals and plants about her has none of that appropriative feeling that we found in the Concord writers; she knows well that they are living their life engaging in no tender or instructive dialogue with man, and that their life is part of a millennial chain. She "gives them back" to the universe. In this constant recognition of the immensity of dimensions of time and place, she is the least parochial of American poets and exceeds even Walt Whitman in imaginative sweep. She could have rejoined Poe in the preoccupations that lay behind his *Eureka*.

And can we say of her that she wrote for Everybody? Yes; for when one has overcome the "low" desire to write for anybody in particular—the cultivated, the chosen souls, one's closest friends; when one has graduated from all desire to impress the judicious or to appeal to the like-minded—then and only then is one released to write for Everybody—only then released from the notion that literature is a specialized activity, an elegant occupation, or a guild secret. For those who live in "immensity" it is merely (and supremely) the human voice at its purest, and it is accessible to Everybody, not at the literary level, but at the human. It is Everybody's fault, not hers, if Everybody is not ready to recognize it. Perhaps only when Everybody is dead will Everybody be in a condition to understand authentic human speech. "Some work for Immortality, the chiefer part for *Time*." In Emily Dickinson we have reached a very high point in American abstraction. (It is characteristic of her that her thought turned often to the Alps and the Andes.) She was . . . the least confiding of women, the shut-up, the self-concealing; yet if the audience was large enough, if she was certain that Everybody would attend, her lips could unlock to floods of impassioned confession and uninhibited assertion. (pp. 56-62)

Thornton Wilder, "Emily Dickinson," in his American Characteristics and Other Essays, *edited by Donald Gallup, Harper & Row, Publishers, 1979, pp. 48-63.*

THOMAS H. JOHNSON (essay date 1955)

[*Johnson's contributions to Dickinson criticism include his scholarly editions of her poetry and letters and the respected study* Emily Dickinson: An Interpretive Biography, *from which the following excerpt is drawn. Johnson discusses Dickinson's art in the years from 1860 to 1862, examining the poet's use of meters derived from English hymnology, her innovations in rhyme, and her idiosyncratic expression, diction, and punctuation.*]

It seems to have been in 1860 that Emily Dickinson made the discovery of herself as a poet and began to develop a professional interest in poetic techniques. Her thoughts about poetry and the function of the poet can be gleaned from her own poems and from occasional snatches in her letters. Her writing techniques were self-taught. She did not follow traditional theories, but developed her own along highly original lines. Though she could write excellent prose, easy, clear, unmannered, the fact is that she thought in poetry. By 1858, at ease with the way of life she had elected and found congenial, she had begun to let the form of her verse derive from the images and sensations that she wished to realize. Her growth as an artist can be followed by way of her experiments in prosody. She worked steadily at her trade during 1860 and 1861, and by 1862, when she feared that the loss of her muse would overwhelm her, she had mastered her craft.

Although writers of free verse acknowledge a debt to Emily Dickinson, she wrote in fact almost nothing which today would be called *vers libre,* that is, cadenced verse, as distinguished from that which is metrical or rhymed. Her first attempt to do so in 1862, **"Victory comes late,"** seems to have been her last, for it evidently convinced her that such a form was not the medium which best transmitted her mood and ideas. There are a variety of ways to gain controlled liberty. She herself, she felt, needed rhyme and meter. To her contemporaries, and to most critics at the time her poems were first published, her seemingly unpatterned verses appeared to be the work of an original but undisciplined artist. Actually she was creating a new medium of poetic expression.

Basically all her poems employ meters derived from English hymnology. They are usually iambic or trochaic, but occasionally dactylic. They were the metric forms familiar to her from childhood as the measures in which Watts's hymns were composed. Copies of Watts's *Christian Psalmody* or his collection of *The Psalms, Hymns, and Spiritual Songs* were fixtures in every New England household. Both were owned by Edward Dickinson and are inscribed with his name. The latter is bound in brown sheepskin, and bears his name in gold on the cover. Musical notations for proper rendition accompany each song, and the meter is always named. Introductions set forth an explanation of how effects may best be achieved, and discuss the relative advantage of one meter over another for particular occasions. Emily Dickinson's own experimentation went beyond anything envisioned by the formal precisionists who edited Watts's hymns and songs, but the interesting point is that she did not have to step outside her father's library to receive a beginner's lesson in metrics.

The principal iambic meters are these: *Common Meter,* alternately eight and six syllables to the line; *Long Meter,* eight syllables to the line; and *Short Meter,* two lines of six syllables, followed by one of eight, then one of six. Each of these meters has properly four lines to the stanza, so that their syllabic scheme goes thus: *CM,* 8, 6, 8, 6; *LM,* 8, 8, 8, 8; *SM,* 6, 6, 8, 6. Each may also be doubled in length to make eight-line stanzas. Each may also have six lines to the stanza. Thus *Common Particular Meter* has the metric beat 8, 8, 6, 8, 8, 6; and *Short Particular Meter,* 6, 6, 8, 6, 6, 8. Other popular arrangements were *Sevens and Sixes* (7, 6, 7, 6) and *Sixes.* The principal trochaic meters are *Sevens, Eights and Sevens, Eights and Fives, Sevens and Fives, Sixes and Fives,* and *Sixes.* Of the dactyls, which were arranged principally in *Elevens, Elevens and Tens,* and *Tens and Nines,* Emily Dickinson used almost exclusively the last named when she chose it as the meter for an entire poem. But she used the dactyl sparingly and almost always as an adjunct to one of the other meters.

It is significant that every poem she composed before 1861—during the years she was learning her craft—is fashioned in one or another of the hymn meters named above. Her use of Long Meter was sparing, for, as her hymn-book instructions pointed out, it tends to monotony. A very large proportion of her poems are in Common Meter. Next in order are Common Particular, and Sevens and Sixes, in equal proportion. She chose Short Meter for relatively few, but achieved with it some of her best effects. Her trochaics are chiefly Eights and Sevens, and Eights and Fives—a new meter, introduced into hymnody toward the mid-nineteenth century.

The meters so far named by no means exhaust the variations that hymnodists were coming to use, but one need not believe that Emily Dickinson's later combinations of Nines and Sixes, Nines and Fours, or Sixes and Fours derived from a model. By the time she came to use them she was striking out for herself. Indeed her techniques would be of scant interest had she set down her stanzas with the metric regularity of her models, and enforced her rhymes with like exactness. Her great contribution to English prosody was that she perceived how to gain new effects by exploring the possibilities within traditional metric patterns. She then took the final step toward that flexibility within patterns which she sought. She began merging in one poem the various meters themselves so that the forms, which intrinsically carry their own retardment or acceleration, could be made to supply the continuum for the mood and ideas of the language. Thus iambs shift to trochees, trochees to dactyls, and on occasion all three are merged.

At the same time she put into practice her evident belief that verse which limits itself to exact rhyme is denied the possible enrichment that other kinds can bring. Her pioneering is here too in the new order erected on old foundations. She felt no more bound to one kind of rhyme than she did to one meter. She should have realized that she was charting a lonely voyage, and in some degree she did, but her independent nature gave her self-assurance. Her way of poetry was to prove far lonelier than she expected, for it denied her in her own lifetime all public recognition. The metric innovations might have been tolerated, but in her day no critic of English verse would have been willing to accept her rhymes. Milton had proved that English verse could be great with no rhyme at all. No one in 1860, reader or critic, was ready to let it be supple and varied.

Custom decreed exact patterns and exact rhymes in English poetry, with concessions to a spare use of eye rhymes (*come-home*). Her grounding in French and in classical literature, however elementary or imperfect, must have assured her that English custom had no preëmptive sanction. She enormously extended the range of variation within controlled limits by adding to exact and eye rhymes four types that poets writing in English had never learned to use expertly enough to gain for them a general acceptance: identical rhymes (*move-remove*), vowel rhymes (*see-buy*), imperfect rhymes [identical vowels followed by different consonants] (*time-thine*), and suspended rhyme [different vowels followed by identical consonants] (*thing-along*). These rhymes she selected at will, singly or in combination, and she carried her freedom to the utmost limit by feeling no compulsion to use one rhyming pattern in a poem any more than she felt constrained to use a single metric form. Thus in a poem of three quatrains the rhyme in the first stanza may be exact for the second and fourth lines, suspended in the second stanza for lines three and four, and conclude in the third stanza with imperfect rhymes for the first and fourth lines. The wheel horses of her stanzas are always the final lines, whether the poem is written as a series of quatrains or as a combination of stanza patterns.

Within this structure she was seldom wayward, nor did she have to be, for it gave her ample room for variety of mood, speed, and circuit. Examination of the intent of a poem usually reveals a motive for the variations. Sometimes she seems to have felt, as the reader does today, that a poem was unskilfully realized, for she abandoned a great many such efforts in worksheet draft. In the past editors have published her finished poems side by side with texts created from unfinished worksheets. Thus imperfectly realized poems have been given a status which the poet never thought them to have. The level of the poet's achievement is raised when such unfinished labors are not weighed in.

One of the very earliest poems to adopt combinations of patterns is the following, written in 1858.

I never told the buried gold
Upon the hill—that lies—
I saw the sun—his plunder done
Crouch low to guard his prize.

He stood as near
As stood you here—
A pace had been between—
Did but a snake bisect the brake
My life had forfeit been.

That was a wondrous booty—
I hope twas honest gained.
Those were the fairest ingots
That ever kissed the spade!

Whether to keep the secret—
Whether to reveal—
Whether as I ponder
"Kidd" will sudden sail—

Could a shrewd advise me
We might e'en divide—
Should a shrewd betray me—
Atropos decide!

The metric and rhyme shifts are many and seem to be deliberate. The first two stanzas, in Common Meter, are followed by a third in Sevens and Sixes. The fourth, beginning in line two, shifts to trochaic Sixes and Fives, with which the poem concludes in stanza five. The rhymes are exact in the first, second, and last stanzas; imperfect in the third, and suspended in the fourth. There are internal exact rhymes in the first and third lines of stanzas one and two. The poem survives in two fair copies, and in both she has deliberately arranged the second stanza in five lines.

The variations are studied and so elaborate that they distract the reader. She appears to be describing a brilliant sunset, and is undecided whether to share the "secret" or not. The structural form when she narrates the facts of the event is exact in meter and rhyme. Both shift uncertainly as she points out her own indecision. It is not an important poem. The imagery is imprecise and the intent not clearly realized. The poet is still a tyro, but such skill as the poem has—and unmistakably it bears her stamp—lies in the blending of the form with the mood.

The poem below, also written in 1858, is an accomplishment of the first order. The skills she was developing are more easily handled in two quatrains than in five.

I never lost as much but twice,
And that was in the sod.
Twice have I stood a beggar
Before the door of God!

Angels—twice descending
Reimbursed my store—
Burglar! Banker—Father!
I am poor once more!

The first stanza is written in Common Meter with a catalectic third line—that is, it lacks a final syllable. The device was one that she developed with uncanny skill to break the monotony of exact regularity. The second stanza is a trochee in Sixes and Fives. Here the metric irregularity is balanced by exact rhymes. The exactness of the rhymes gives finality to the terseness of the thought. The metrical shift turns the resignation of the first statement into the urgency of the second.

Sometime about 1860 she wrote this:

Just lost, when I was saved!
Just felt the world go by!
Just girt me for the onset with Eternity,
When breath blew back,
And on the other side
I heard recede the disappointed tide!

Therefore, as One returned, I feel,
Odd secrets of the line to tell!
Some Sailor, skirting foreign shores—
Some pale Reporter, from the awful doors
Before the Seal!

Next time, to stay!
Next time, the things to see
By Ear unheard,
Unscrutinized by Eye—

Next time, to tarry,
While the Ages steal—
Slow tramp the Centuries,
And the Cycles wheel!

It is arranged in several metric patterns, altered so rapidly that no single form predominates. The final short stanza alternates iambs with trochees, to give the effect of applying brakes, and thus brings the slow tramp of the centuries to a halt. The final words of each stanza effect a rhyme, and most of the rhymes are exact. In the first stanza the mating rhyme word is in the line preceding, and in the second it is separated by three intervening lines. In the last two stanzas it is at the point normally expected, that is, in the alternating line. There are further rhymes in the first two stanzas, exact, vowel, and suspended. This elaborateness is shaped throughout to the mood the poem intends to convey, a mood of awe in facing the fact that any vision of immortality seen by mortals is a mirage. The structure of the poem allows great latitude in tempo and shading. The poem is one of her best early attempts to create by way of letting the form be shaped by the mood. The method requires a skill which cannot be taught, but must be guided by instinctive taste. She herself did not win through to full success on all occasions. But the universal pleasure this poem has given is some measure of its fulfillment.

A very large number of poems written during 1860 and 1861 experiment with new models. She used much the same technique as that in the poem above when she created **"At last, to be identified,"** evidently with intent likewise to suggest breathlessness. In 1860 she also wrote the expertly realized **"How many times these low feet staggered."** It is the quiet meditation of one who gazes upon the face and form of a dead friend. The metrics are coldly regular. The hovering rhyme of the first stanza becomes exact in the remaining two stanzas. The artistry lies in the vivid concreteness of the detail, set forth with great restraint. On the privacy of this moment no rhetorical extravagance is allowed to obtrude.

The new order of love poems is exemplified by this.

I'm 'wife'—I've finished that—
That other state—
I'm Czar—I'm 'Woman' now—
It's safer so—

How odd the Girl's life looks
Behind this soft Eclipse—
I think that Earth feels so
To folks in Heaven—now—

This being comfort—then
That other kind—was pain—
But why compare?
I'm 'Wife'! Stop there!

Suspended rhymes join each pair of lines except the last, which conclude the poem with exact rhymes. Each stanza has its individual metric form, allied to but not identical with the others. The Sixes and Fours of the first stanza become Sixes in the second. In the third, the Sixes are paired, as are the Fours.

The rhythmic exactness of **"Did the Harebell loose her girdle / To the Lover bee"** is as studied as the irregularity in **"What is 'Heaven,'"** written at the same time. [**"I taste a liquor never brewed"**] is an excellent example of both her concern with and indifference to rhyme and metrical exactness.

I taste a liquor never brewed—
From Tankards scooped in Pearl—
Not all the Frankfort Berries
Yield such an Alcohol!

Inebriate of Air—am I—
And Debauchee of Dew—
Reeling—thro endless summer days—
From inns of Molten Blue—

When "Landlords" turn the drunken Bee
Out of the Foxglove's door—
When Butterflies—renounce their "drams"—
I shall but drink the more!

Till Seraphs swing their snowy Hats—
And Saints—to windows run—
To see the little Tippler
From Manzanilla come!

The poem uses Common Meter, but the regularity is broken in two ways. The third lines of the first and fourth stanzas are both catalectic, and the rhymes of those stanzas are imperfect. These variations unquestionably were deliberate, for they are typical of her modifications of traditional forms. Yet the only surviving manuscript of the poem is a semifinal draft on which she offers alternative readings for two lines. For line three she suggests: "Not all the vats upon the Rhine," and for the final line: "Leaning against the sun." The first alternative, if adopted, would supply the missing half-foot; the second would create an exact rhyme. We cannot infer from the fact that the suggested changes exist that she would have adopted them in a fair copy. She frequently did not do so. There are instances where two fair copies, each sent to a friend, show like indifference to rhyme and metric patterns. One may hazard the opinion that her choice in any event would have been determined by her preference for one image rather than another, not by a desire to create exact meter and rhyme.

She must have been groping too for ways of expression that said things as she individually wished to say them. Certain of her idiosyncrasies in language and grammar become obtrusive when sprinkled too freely, but they are characteristic and often very effective. Her use of what seems to be the subjunctive mood comes first to mind. Yet the fact is that perhaps it is not subjunctive at all in the sense of being grammatically an optative or volitive or potential mood. "Only love assist the wound" may be read as "Only love can assist the wound." But more probably, because more in line with the way her mind worked, she means "Only love does assist the wound." If this is her meaning, then what at first seems to be a subjunctive mood might better be called a continuing or universal present indicative. She recognized her dilemma in the line "Beauty—be not caused—It Is." As a suggested change she offers "is" for "be," as though she were uncertain whether the substantive sense was too unidiomatic to convey her idea clearly. But even the first reading cannot be called subjunctive, for it does not denote a contingency, but expresses an idea as fact. She was trying to universalize her thought to embrace past, present, and future. Such is her intent in the following instances, which could be multiplied greatly, so often does her mind explore universals.

Nature—the Gentlest Mother is . . .
And when the Sun go down—
Her Voice among the Aisles
Incite the timid prayer

The One who could repeat the Summer Day . . .
When Orient have been outgrown—
And Occident—become Unknown—
His Name—remain—

The Robin is the One
That interrupt the Morn

This concept of language is allied to but different from that which prompted her to cultivate elliptical phrases as a way of paring words that complete sentences grammatically but do not communicate. Of course on occasion she cut too deeply into the quick of her thought because she truncated her predication to the point where readers must perpetually grope for meaning. But where her intent is realized, the attar becomes haunting and unforgettable.

She had the precedent of her greatest teacher, Shakespeare, for an occasional reversal of nominatives and objectives: "That Mushroom—it is Him," or "As blemishless as her." She preferred *lain* to *laid* as a past participle. Certain colloquialisms such as *don't* for *doesn't* she used because familiarity with them was natural to her ear and tongue: "It don't sound so terrible—quite—as it did." Others like *heft* for *weight* one suspects she chose because the Anglo-Saxon quality of words always pleased her: "There's a certain Slant of light / . . . That oppresses like the Heft / Of Cathedral Tunes," or "The Brain is just the weight of God— / For—Heft them—Pound for Pound . . ." Learned words irritated her. In the poem in which she says she prefers "star" to "Arcturus" she comments:

I slew a worm the other day—
A "Savan" passing by
Murmured "Resurgam"—"Centipede"!
"Oh Lord—how frail are we"!

Her use of the dash as end-stop punctuation often replaces conventional commas and periods. Within lines it frequently is without grammatical function, but is rather a visual representation of a musical beat. The emotion is thus conveyed in the poem beginning:

Sweet—safe—Houses—
Glad—gay—Houses—

Such dashes become an integral part of the structure of her poetry. Her portmanteau words she took seriously: overtakelessness, repealless, failless. In the lines "Better an ignis fatuus / Than no illume at all" she tries to revive the Elizabethan experimentation in making verbs function as nouns. All of this is a sort of informed waywardness, used with sufficient restraint and affection for language as never to offend even when it does not illuminate. In language as in thought she seems to be asking to take two steps ahead if on occasion she falls back one.

The power of words to evoke a mood is the subject of half a dozen poems. "A Word made Flesh is seldom / And tremblingly partook," she remarks, adding, "A Word that breathes distinctly / Has not the power to die." She knew that the will to select words was not always within her conscious power.

Shall I take thee, the Poet said
To the propounded word?
Be stationed with the Candidates
Till I have finer tried—

But the word came unsummoned. "Not unto nomination / The Cherubim reveal."

Her intent in **"I like a look of agony"** and **"To die takes just a little while"** is to make the reader experience an emotion. She wishes to re-create in words two moments of suffering, yet to stand outside the anguish and by a kind of ironic indifference to deepen the inherent compassion.

I like a look of Agony,
Because I know it's true—
Men do not sham Convulsion,
Nor simulate, a Throe—

The Eyes glaze once—and that is Death—
Impossible to feign
The Beads upon the Forehead
By homely Anguish strung.

The metric pattern is formally exact, relieved from constraint by the use of vowel and suspended rhymes. In the poem **"There's a certain Slant of light"** she reversed the method to gain the same end.

At some period late in 1861, when she came to know of Wadsworth's impending departure, she was evidently panic-stricken. She had become increasingly skillful and productive. Would she ever in fact be able to write again? Public announcement that Wadsworth would soon conclude his duties as pastor of the Arch Street Church was made on 15 March 1862. He remained six weeks longer before the congregation yielded and granted his dismissal, and a week later he and his family were on the high seas. The effect on Emily Dickinson during the early spring seems to have been quite different from what she expected. Her creative abilities, rather than decreasing, enormously multiplied. Yet even as this was happening, she seems to have been deeply apprehensive lest each day's composition be the last. Such an eventuality did not occur, and she was so sure of her achievement that she was willing to write Higginson, enclosing four of her best poems, to ask a professional man of letters to tell her what he thought of them. She was led to seek his guidance for two reasons. She feared that the loss of her muse would prevent further accomplishment and hoped that the inspiration might in some unpredictable way be forthcoming through the new association. Secondly, she was fully aware that her verses deserved an audience. . . . [The] impending departure of Wadsworth [was] closely tied into her compulsion to write Higginson during that April. Her comment to Higginson when she invited him to Amherst seven years later that he had saved her life, and that since then to thank him in person had been one of her few requests, cannot be lightly passed over.

Emily Dickinson's prosodic expertness was fully realized in 1862. The exquisite **"She lay as if at play"** is one of her poems on the theme of death. The brevity of the little life is paralleled by the short trimeter-dimeter lines. The rhymes are delicate interplays of suspended, imperfect, and exact sound arrangements. She marshals her vowels, both in rhymes and within the lines, in such a way as to suffuse with light such a poem as **"I had no time to Hate,"** and especially this below.

"Why do I love" You, Sir?
Because—
The Wind does not require the Grass
To answer—Wherefore when He pass
She cannot keep Her place.

Because He knows—and
Do not You—
And We know not—
Enough for Us
The Wisdom it be so—

The Lightning—never asked an Eye
Wherefore it shut—when He was by—
Because He knows it cannot speak—
And reasons not contained—
—Of Talk—
There be—preferred by Daintier Folk—

The Sunrise—Sir—compelleth Me—
Because He's Sunrise—and I see—
Therefore—Then—
I love Thee—

The shift from iambic to a trochaic beat in the final line is expertly maneuvered. The authority of **"After great pain, a formal feeling comes"** derives from the technical skill with which the language is controlled. As she always does in her best poems, Emily Dickinson makes her first line lock all succeeding lines into position.

After great pain, a formal feeling comes—
The Nerves sit ceremonious, like Tombs—
The stiff Heart questions was it He, that bore,
And Yesterday, or Centuries before?

The Feet, mechanical, go round—
A Wooden way
Of Ground, or Air, or Ought—
Regardless grown,
A Quartz contentment, like a stone—

This is the Hour of Lead—
Remembered, if outlived,
As Freezing persons, recollect the Snow—
First—Chill—then Stupor—then the letting go—

The heaviness of the pain is echoed by *bore, wooden, quartz, stone, lead.* The formal feeling is coldly ceremonious, mechanical, and stiff, leading through chill and stupor to a "letting go." The stately pentameter measure of the first stanza is used, in the second, only in the first line and the last, between which are hastened rhythms. The final two lines of the poem, which bring it to a close, reëstablish the formality of the opening lines. Exact rhymes conclude each of the stanzas.

Emily Dickinson's impulse to let the outer form develop from the inner mood now begins to extend to new freedoms. Among her poems composed basically as quatrains, she does not hesitate to include a three-line stanza, as in **"I rose because he sank,"** or a five-line stanza, as in **"Glee, the great storm is over."** On some occasions, to break the regularity in yet another way or to gain a new kind of emphasis, she splits a line from its stanza, allowing it to stand apart, as in **"Beauty—be not caused—It Is,"** and **"There's been a Death, in the Opposite House."** Sometimes poems beginning with an iambic beat shift in succeeding stanzas to a trochaic, to hasten the tempo, as in **"In falling timbers buried."** It is the year too when she used her dashes lavishly.

This is also the time when she wrote two love poems that employ sexual imagery with unabashed frankness.

Wild Nights—Wild Nights!
Were I with thee
Wild Nights should be
Our luxury!

Futile—the Winds—
To a Heart in port—
Done with the Compass—
Done with the Chart!

Rowing in Eden—
Ah, the Sea!
Might I but moor—Tonight—
In Thee!

When Colonel Higginson and Mrs. Todd were selecting verses for the Second Series of ***Poems,*** in 1891, he wrote her saying: "One poem only I dread a little to print—that wonderful **'Wild Nights,'**—lest the malignant read into it more than that virgin recluse ever dreamed of putting there. Has Miss Lavinia any shrinking about it? You will understand & pardon my solicitude. Yet what a loss to omit it! Indeed it is not to be omitted." The poem was included. The second goes much further in its metric pointedness.

How sick—to wait—in any place—but thine—
I knew last night—when someone tried to twine—
Thinking—perhaps—that I looked tired—or alone—
Or breaking—almost—with unspoken pain—

And I turned—ducal—
That right—was thine—
One port—suffices—for a Brig—like *mine*—

Our's be the tossing—wild though the sea—
Rather than a Mooring—unshared by thee.
Our's be the Cargo—*unladen—here—*
Rather than the "spicy isles—"
And thou—not there—

The water imagery is conspicuous in both poems, but the metrics of the second derives from the mood. The slow regularity of the beginning is speeded up at the end of the second stanza. The third stanza opens with a panting dactyl that slows to a quiet measure, shortened, in the last line, to two feet. The imagery throughout is unmistakably concrete.

This is manifestly erotic poetry. From what experience was she enabled to give these sensations an artistic creation? With what intent did she write the poems? Answers to such questions may be hidden, but their concealment cannot prevent the knowledge that any creation is a true statement of something. She wrote the poems and she transcribed them fair into her packets. When Higginson answered her first letter and commented on the poems she had enclosed, he must have felt that her metric liberties gave her verse some resemblance to that of Walt Whitman, and evidently asked if she had read any of Whitman's poetry, because she replied: "You speak of Mr Whitman—I never read his Book—but was told that he was disgraceful." There is much that one can never know about the human heart. But one dares hazard a guess about one basic difference in the natures of Walt Whitman and Emily Dickinson. Had the shy spinster been confronted with the implications of her artistic achievement, she would have accepted the fact with stoic resignation, whereas Whitman would have expressed pleasure at his success.

The misery occasioned by Wadsworth's departure for California in 1862 did in fact mature her. In that and in succeeding years she wrote with a vision which gives her rank as a philosophical poet. It was much later that she sketched the genre pictures of aspects of life about her. At this point she was exploring within herself, the "undiscovered continent," to determine the relationship between man and both worlds, the seen and the unseen. It is impossible that she could have written earlier such poems as **"The Soul selects her own Society," "She lay as if at play," "I died for Beauty," "We play at**

Paste," and others of like quality. Two written at this time repay a study of their rhyme and their metric organization.

'Twas a long Parting—but the time
For Interview—had Come—
Before the Judgment Seat of God—
The last—and second time

These Fleshless Lovers met—
A Heaven in a Gaze—
A Heaven of Heavens—the Privilege
Of one another's Eyes—

No Lifetime set—on Them—
Appareled as the new
Unborn—except They had beheld—
Born infiniter—now—

Was Bridal—e'er like This?
A Paradise—the Host—
And Cherubim—and Seraphim—
The unobtrusive Guest—

Its theme is supernal love. Parted in life, the lovers meet before the judgment seat for the last "and second" time, and there wed with paradise as host and the angels as guests. The tone is wistful because the poet envisions consummation only after "a long Parting." The first stanza is in Common Meter. The poem gains speed thereafter by employing Short Meter. Suspended rhymes run through all stanzas, and thus the mood of incompletion is echoed in the verse structure. The theme of the second is identical, but the mood is very different.

Of all the Souls that stand create—
I have elected—One—
When Sense from Spirit—files away—
And Subterfuge—is done—
When that which is—and that which was—
Apart—intrinsic—stand—
And this brief Tragedy of Flesh—
Is shifted—like a Sand—
When Figures show their royal Front—
And Mists—are carved away,
Behold the Atom—I preferred—
To all the lists of Clay!

Common Meter is used throughout, and thus the pace is unaltered. The rhymes, in alternate lines, are exact. The mood of the poem is one of jubilant assurance because the election already has been made. Here, as in the first, the prosodic structure helps shape the mood and give it firmer texture.

Emily Dickinson's new-found artistic and spiritual maturity is made strikingly evident by comparing two poems which express attitudes about the problems of daily living. In 1859 she had thought of them in terms of mathematical sums, and had concluded that new problems always seem larger than those with which we have previously dealt.

Low at my problem bending,
Another problem comes—
Larger than mine—Serener—
Involving statelier sums.

I check my busy pencil,
My figures file away.
Wherefore, my baffled fingers
Thy perplexity?

Six years later her perceptions have deepened and the language in which she gives them form has sharpened.

The Missing All—prevented Me
From missing minor things
If nothing larger than a World's
Departure from a Hinge—
Or Sun's extinction, be observed—
'Twas not so large that I
Could lift my Forehead from my work
For Curiosity.

Clearly she had found herself. (pp. 84-102)

Thomas H. Johnson, in his Emily Dickinson: An Interpretive Biography, *1955. Reprint by Atheneum, 1967, 276 p.*

GEORGES POULET (essay date 1956)

[Poulet has been described as an existentialist critic who in his most important work attempts to reconstruct an author's "consciousness," or relation to, and understanding of, time and space, nature, and society. A key element of his early criticism was his belief that every author lives in an isolated world defined by individual consciousness and so cannot be understood in terms of generalizations about an era or period. The task of the critic is to enter this individual consciousness and define it. In his later work, however, Poulet has come to see individual consciousness as united in the all-embracing spirit of an era, and he often discusses authors in terms of the characteristics of an age. Here, he examines how the themes of loss, pain, and suffering unify time in Dickinson's poetry.]

'Tis an instant's play.
'Tis a fond Ambush
Just to make Bliss
Earn her own surprise!

The first moment of the real life of Emily Dickinson has nothing to do with her earlier life as a young girl. It is a moment of absolute surprise that lifts her out of her life, removes her from parents and friends, from customary shores, to fling her out upon the open sea:

Exultation is the going
Of an inland soul to sea,
Past the houses—past the headlands—
Into deep Eternity.

But this moment without past is also without future. Or rather it has for the future its immediate recession, its loss:

Just lost, when I was saved!
Just felt the world go by!

. . . . .

More distant in an instant
Than Dawn in Timbuctoo.

At once for the instant of ecstasy, there is substituted another instant which is that of the disappearance of ecstasy. Nothing is graver in Emily's life than the apparition, in the closest succession, of these two moments, in one of which everything is given, and in the other everything taken away. It matters little that this double experience may be repeated afterwards. What matters is that each time Emily reflects on her existence, she sees it begin with a grand victory immediately followed by a bitter defeat. All her spiritual life and all her poetry are comprehended only in the determination given them by two initial moments, one of which is contradicted by the other, a moment in which one possesses eternity and a moment when one loses it:

The Moments of Dominion
That happen on the Soul
And leave it with a Discontent
Too exquisite—to tell. . . .

In the existence that begins with this loss, what strikes one at first is the persistence of regret, the constant rawness of the wound. It seems that time is composed of a repeated pain and that in each of its moments one is stricken as if for the first time:

It struck me—every Day—
The Lightning was as new
As if the Cloud that instant slit
And let the Fire through.

"Time never did assuage," on the contrary it constantly reinforced regret. And sometimes the pain spreads, and in spreading expands time itself, in such a manner that it seems that "ages coil within the minute Circumference of a single brain"; sometimes, on the contrary, it seems that eternities are suddenly condensed into a single moment of pain:

Pain expands the Time. . . .
Pain contracts the Time
Occupied with Shot
Gamuts of Eternities
Are as they were not.

The more one suffers, the more cruel becomes the contrast between past ecstasy and the present, which is precisely the deprivation of that ecstasy:

Paradise is that old mansion
Many owned before—
Occupied by each an instant
Then reversed the Door. . . .

All duration is made to be the eternal exclusion of an instantaneous eternity. Then one understands how the fullness and intensity of the pains of which existence is composed are exactly the ransom of the lost, unique joy. Time is a pain lived piecemeal, and the sum of the pieces equals a moment of joy:

For each ecstatic instant
We must an anguish pay
In keen and quivering ratio
To the ecstasy.

I took one Draught of Life—
I'll tell you what I paid—
Precisely an existence—
The market price, they said.

Such is Emily's lot: Condemned all her life to unhappiness in order to pay the price of a single instant of happiness. But what is striking is not that she is rebellious and finds her lot unjust. On the contrary, always suffering, she will the sooner repent of remembering too often the single moment which was free of suffering. In her long defeat she will reproach herself for dreaming of her brief triumph. That is what she calls remorse:

Remorse—is Memory—awake—
Her Parties all astir—
A Presence of Departed Acts—
At window—and at Door.

If Emily rejects "remorse," it is because the "presence of Departed Acts" in the mind that contemplates them prevents it from being resigned to their absence. The last sacrifice that seems to be exacted of her is the sacrifice of even the memory of joy. No one is less abandoned than she to the nostalgia for lost happiness and to all the delightful, melancholy, or exasperated feelings that flow from it. A past image should not mask the bitterness of the present nor falsify its meaning and value. It is not enough that happiness is lost; the mind must recognize its loss, loosen its last grip, and explicitly renounce what it no longer possesses. To regret, to remorse, Emily opposes the inverse virtue of renunciation:

Renunciation—is a piercing Virtue—
The letting go
A Presence. . . .

There is no longer a presence, no longer even the feeble link which the mind kept with this presence by memory. To have been once and forever saved would have been too easy. An instantaneous eternity does not suit the human condition. The latter must accommodate itself to time, that is to say to renunciation, to the consciousness of absence and distance, to the patient continuity of pain.

A pain that now is without regret, without past, but also without hope, without temporal future. For it would be as culpable in hoping for a return of ecstasy as it would be in lamenting the ecstasy. The joy had no other reason for being than to make us see that of which we are unworthy. Without once having known happiness, we could not know how ill it suits us, and how well suffering agrees with us. Defeat is our part. Let us be content with defeat. Let us consummate our resignation in despair.

A despair that one must not confuse with the feeling of revolt that often bears the same name. True despair is exactly the lack of hope; or, as Emily herself puts it, "the slow exchange of Hope for something passiver":

The Service without Hope—
Is tenderest, I think. . . .

Without hope, without regret, contracting in both directions, breaking all links with past happiness as with possible happiness, thought no longer has any anteriority or future. It is entirely identified with present grief:

Pain—has an element of Blank—
It cannot recollect
When it began—or if there were
A time when it was not—

It has no Future—but itself—
Its Infinite realms contain
Its Past—enlightened to perceive
New Periods—of Pain.

Thus suffering in Emily Dickinson comes in the end to the same result as the feeling of nothingness in Mallarmé; it unifies the times, it confounds them in the same monotonous continuity, outside of which, it seems, there is nothing that one can see:

The Mind is smooth—no Motion—
Contented as the Eye
Upon the Forehead of a Bust—
That knows—it cannot see. . . .

There is no longer any difference between moments. Everything is made equal by the same pain. And this extent that is perpetually identical to itself, that is found again in every moment and in all moments, is the symbol of an invisible eternity:

Forever—is composed of Nows—
'Tis not a different time. . . .

A time never any different from itself and also equal to space, since in its continuous development it never ceases to be the consciousness of the distance to which the lost object is withdrawn. And this consciousness would continue indefinitely to prolong its monotonous contemplation over this extent, if finally at the end of it, at the extremity of the future, there were not, as at the extremity of the past, a supreme instant which forms the transcendent termination of the level plain. That termination is death.

On the face of someone dying, Emily catches the arrival of that instant which ends and begins all:

'Twas Crisis—All the length had passed
That dull—benumbing time. . . .

. . . . .

The Second poised—debated—shot—
Another had begun—
And simultaneously, a Soul
Escaped the House unseen.

(pp. 345-50)

Georges Poulet, "Emily Dickinson," in his Studies in Human Time, *translated by Elliott Coleman, The Johns Hopkins Press, 1956, pp. 345-50.*

LOUISE BOGAN (lecture date 1959)

[*Bogan was a distinguished American poet whose work is noted for its subtlety and restraint, evidencing her debt to the English metaphysical poets. She served for many years as the poetry critic at the* New Yorker *and is the author of* Achievement in American Poetry: 1900-1950, *a respected volume of criticism. Bogan's comments, first delivered in a lecture on 23 October 1959, center on Dickinson's qualities as a visionary poet.*]

It has been suggested that I develop, on this occasion, a statement I made in 1945, in an article published in that year—that the time had come "to assess Emily Dickinson's powers on the highest level of mystical poetry, where they should be assessed." Since then, the appearance of the ***Collected Poems*** and of the ***Collected Letters,*** superbly edited by Thomas H. Johnson, has made such an assessment less difficult than it formerly had to be. For now, with the existence of these definitive works, the stages of the poet's development are connected and clarified. We are now faced, as we should be, with the career of a writer who—we now realize—throughout her life made the most difficult kind of choices, many directed toward the protection of her sensitive nature and of her remarkable poetic gift. It is the poet Dickinson who has advanced into the full light of literary history and now belongs not only to Amherst, not only to America, but to the world that reads her either in English or in translation.

Now, the term "mystical poetry" is a difficult one to deal with. The words "mystic" and "mysticism" have become rather suspect in modern, materialist society. So it is important to define and place this term, at the outset. Mystics have appeared, it would seem, with fair frequency at many periods, in many cultures; but there is no doubt that when, in the West, we speak of true mysticism, we have in mind the example of the Christian saints. "In Christianity," says Evelyn Underhill, "the 'natural mysticism' . . . which is latent in humanity and at a certain point of development breaks out in every race, came to itself; and attributed for the first time true and distinct personality to its Object"—namely, God. True mystics do not indulge in diffuse pantheism or hold to the aim of "the occult," which wishes to wrench supernal power to human uses. In the words of another commentator: "The aim and content of Christian mysticism is not self or nature, but God."

We can see at once that there is a difference between the character, as well as the aims, of true mystics and of poets; and we know that to come upon the two gifts in one person is extremely rare. But close points of resemblance do exist between the mystic experience, at its purest and best, and the experience of poetic—or indeed, any creative—expression. Poets down the centuries, visited by that power which the ancients call *the Muse,* have described their experience in much the same way as the mystic describes his ecstatic union with Divine Truth. This experience has been rendered at length, and dramatically, by Dante, as well as by St. John of the Cross; and certain poems in the literature of every language attest to moments when, for the poet, "the deep and primal life which he shares with all creation has been roused from its sleep." And both poets and mystics have described with great poignance that sense of deprivation and that shutting away from grace which follows the loss of the vision (or of the inspiring breath), which is called, in the language of mysticism, "the dark night of the soul."

Certainly one of the triumphs brought about by the emergence of the Romantic spirit, in English poetry, at the end of the eighteenth century, was a freeing and an enlargement of poetic vision, and in the nineteenth century we come upon a multiplication of poets whose spiritual perceptions were acute. Beyond Vaughan and Herbert (who, in the seventeenth century, worked from a religious base) we think of Blake, of the young Wordsworth; of Keats and Shelley; of Emily Brontë; of Gerard Manley Hopkins; and we can extend the list into our own day with the names of Yeats and T. S. Eliot. By examining the work of these poets—to whom the imagination, the creative spirit of man, was of utmost importance—we find that the progress of the mystic toward illumination, and of the poet toward the full depth and richness of his insight—are much alike. Both work from the world of reality, toward the realm of Essence; from the microcosm to the macrocosm. Both have an intense and accurate sense of their surroundings; there is nothing vague or floating in their perception of reality; it is indeed as though they saw "through, not with, the eye." And they are filled with love for the beauty they perceive in the world of time—"this remarkable world" as Emily Dickinson called it; and concerning death they are neither fearful nor morbid—how could they be, since they feel immortality behind it? They document life's fearful limitations from which they suffer, but they do not mix self-pity with the account of their suffering (which they describe, like their joy, in close detail). They see the world in a grain of sand and Heaven in a wild flower; and now and again they bring eternity into focus, as it were, in a phrase of the utmost clarity. In the work of Emily Dickinson such moments of still and halted perception are many. The slant of light on a winter day, the still brilliance of a summer noon, the sound of the wind before the rain—she speaks of these, and we share the shock of insight, the slight dislocation of serial events, the sudden shift from the Manifold into the One.

One of the dominant facts concerning Emily Dickinson is her spirit of religious unorthodoxy. Her deeply religious feeling ran outside the bounds of dogma; this individualism was, in fact, an inheritance from her Calvinist forbears, but it was out of place when contrasted to the Evangelicanism to which, in her time, so many Protestants had succumbed. She early set herself against the guilt and gloom inherent in this revivalism. She avoided the constrictions which a narrow insistence on religious rule and law would put upon her. She had read Emerson with delight, but, as Yvor Winters has remarked, it is a mistake to think of her as a Transcendentalist in dimity [see excerpt dated 1938]. Here again she worked through to a standpoint and an interpretation of her own; her attitude toward pain and suffering, toward the shocking facts of existence, was far more realistic than Emerson's. As we examine her chief spiritual preoccupations, we see how closely she relates to the English Romantic poets who, a generation or so before her, fought a difficult and unpopular battle against the eighteenth century's cold logic and mechanical point of view. The names of Blake and Coleridge come to mind; we know that to both these poets the cold theory of Locke represented "a deadly heresy on the nature of existence." It is difficult to look back to this period of early Romantic breakthrough, since so much of that early boldness and originality was later dissipated in excesses of various kinds. But it is important to remember that Blake attached the greatest importance to the human imagination as an aspect of some mystery beyond the human, and to listen to his ringing words: "The world of Imagination is the world of Eternity. . . . The world of Imagination is Infinite and Eternal, whereas the world of generation is Finite and Temporal . . ."—and to remember, as well, that "Blake, Wordsworth, Coleridge, Shelley and Keats shared the belief that the imagination was nothing less than God as he operates in the human soul." C. M. Bowra, writing of the Romantic ethos in general, brings out a fact which has been generally overlooked: that, although Romantic poetry became a European phenomenon, English Romantic poetry "almost alone . . . connected visionary insight with a superior order of being." "There is hardly a trace of this [insight]," Bowra goes on to say, "in Hugo, or Heine or Lermontov. They have their full share of longing, but almost nothing of Romantic vision. . . ." Hölderlin, in Germany tried to share a lost vision of Greece, but on the whole it was the English who accomplished a transformation in thought and emotion "for which there is no parallel in their age." It is surely in the company of these English poets that Emily Dickinson belongs. At its most intense, her vision not only matched, but transcended theirs; she crossed the same boundaries with a like intransigence; and the same vigorous flowers sprang from different seeds, in the spirit of a woman born in 1830, in New England, in America.

The drawing of close parallels between the life and circumstances of poets is often an unrewarding task. But in the case of Emily Dickinson because hers was for so long considered a particularly isolated career, it is interesting to make certain comparisons. It has been pointed out that there is a close resemblance between the lives, temperament and works of Emily Brontë and Emily Dickinson. And one or two resemblances between Emily Dickinson and Blake (Blake taken as a lyric poet rather than as a prophet) can be traced (quite apart from the fairly unimportant fact that Miss Dickinson, in her apprenticeship, closely imitated Blake's form in at least two poems). Both took over the simplest forms of the song and the hymn and turned this simplicity to their own uses. Both seemed to work straight from almost dictated inspiration (Blake, indeed, claimed that his poems were dictated to him intact and entire) but we now know, from an examination of their manuscripts, that both worked over their original drafts with meticulous care. Both had to struggle against hampering circumstances: Blake against poverty and misunderstanding, and Dickinson against a lack of true response in the traditionally stiffened society in which she found herself. To both poets, limitation and boundary finally yielded originality and power; they were sufficiently outside the spirit of their times so that they were comparatively untouched by the vagaries of fashion; they both were able to wring from solitary contemplation sound working principles and just form. T. S. Eliot, in his essay on Blake, speaks of Blake's peculiarity "which can be seen to be the peculiarity of all great poetry. . . . It is merely a peculiar honesty, which, in a world frightened to be honest, is particularly terrifying. It is an honesty against which the whole world conspires, because it is unpleasant. Blake's poetry has the unpleasantness of great poetry. Nothing that can be called abnormal or perverse, none of the things which exemplify the sickness of an epoch or a fashion, have this quality; only those things which, by some extraordinary labor of simplification, exhibit the essential sickness or strength of the human soul." Eliot then remarks that the question about Blake the man "is a question of the circumstances that concurred to permit this honesty in his work. . . . The favoring conditions probably include these two: that, early apprenticed to a manual occupation, he was not compelled to acquire any other education in literature than he wanted, or to acquire it for any other reason than he wanted it; and that, being a humble engraver, he had no journalistic-social career open to him. There was, that is to say, nothing to distract him from his interests or to corrupt these interests—neither . . . the standards of society, nor the temptation of success; nor was he exposed to imitation of himself or anyone else. . . . These circumstances are what make him innocent."

The circumstances which led to Emily Dickinson's very nearly complete seclusion are, of course, different from those which Eliot mentions as applying to Blake. It was physical frailty which put an end to her formal education. But later, as we read the record of her withdrawal, as this record appears in the ***Letters*** (and, of course, the full reasons are not given) we can detect the element of choice working. By the time she wrote to Higginson in 1862 she had made that choice, and only wanted to have it confirmed. She wished to know whether or not her poems were "alive"—if they "breathed." She received a certain confirmation that they were and did; and she kept to her solitude. This solitude was not harsh. Her love for her friends never diminished, nor her delight in their occasional presence; her family ties were strong; her daily round sustained her; and the joy she felt in the natural world—particularly in flowers and in children—continues. Until a series of tragedies (beginning with the death of her father) began to break down her spiritual balance, she held to that balance over a long period of years. Balance, delicacy and force—fed by her exquisite senses and her infinitely lively and inquisitive mind—these are the qualities which reinforce her vision into the heart and spirit of nature, and into her own heart.

An added pleasure is given us, as we read Emily Dickinson's poetry from beginning to end, by the openness and inclusiveness of the work. Every sort of poem has been preserved; no strict process of self-editing has taken place, and we are not faced with periods in which much has been suppressed. The failures and the successes stand side by side; the poems expressing the poet's more childish and undeveloped characteristics and the poems upon which the sentimentality of her time left its mark, are often followed or preceded by poems which define and express the very nearly indefinable and inexpressible. There is no professionalism, in the worst sense, here; and it is interesting to note that, although she sought out Higginson's advice and named herself his "scholar," she never altered a poem of hers according to any suggestion of his. She had, at one time, perhaps been willing to be published, but, later, she could do without print.

We have, then, in Johnson's edition of the poems published in 1955, as complete a record of the development of a lyric talent as exists in literature. Scholars have busied themselves with the record; we know what color she names most frequently (purple) and what books she read (Shakespeare and the Bible well in the lead). We ourselves can discover, in the index to the three volumes, that her favorite subject was not death, as was long supposed; for life, love and the soul are also recurring subjects. But the greatest interest lies in her progress as a writer, and as a person. We see the young poet moving away, by gradual degrees, from her early slight addiction to graveyardism, to an Emersonian belief in the largeness and harmony of nature. Step by step, she advances into the terror and anguish of her destiny; she is frightened, but she holds fast and describes her fright. She is driven to the verge of sanity, but manages to remain, in some fashion, the observer and recorder of her extremity. Nature is no longer a friend, but often an inimical presence. Nature is a haunted house. And—a truth even more terrible—the inmost self can be haunted.

At the highest summit of her art, she resembles no one. She begins to cast forward toward the future: to produce poems in which we recognize, as one French critic has said, both the *voyant* faculty of Rimbaud and Mallarmé's feeling for the mystery and sacredness of the word. This high period begins in the early 1860s, and is not entirely consistent; the power seems to come and go, but it is indubitably there. And when it is present, she can describe with clinical precision the actual emotional event, the supreme moment of anguish, and even her own death itself. And she finds symbols which fit the event—terrible symbols. The experience of suffering is like dying of the cold; or it resembles the approach of a maelstrom, which finally engulfs the victim; one escapes from suffering as from the paws of a fiend, from whose grasp one emerges more dead than alive. One poem, written about 1863, defies analysis: the poem which begins **"My life had stood—a loaded gun."** . . .

My life had stood—a Loaded Gun
In Corners—till a Day
The Owner passed—identified—
And carried Me away—

And now We roam in Sovreign Woods—
And now We hunt the Doe—
And every time I speak for Him—
The Mountains straight reply—

And do I smile, such cordial light
Upon the Valley glow—
It is as a Vesuvian face
Had let its pleasure through—

And when at Night—Our good Day done—
I guard My Master's head—
'Tis better than the Eider-Duck's
Deep Pillow—to have shared—

To foe of His—I'm deadly foe—
None stir the second time—
On whom I lay a Yellow Eye—
Or an emphatic Thumb—

Though I than He—may longer live
He longer must—than I—
For I have but the power to kill,
Without—the power to die—

Is this an allegory, and if so of what? Is it a cry from some psychic deep where good and evil are not to be separated? In any case, it is a poem whose reverberations are infinite, as in great music; and we can only guess with what agony it was written down.

This power to say the unsayable—to hint of the unknowable—is the power of the seer, in this woman equipped with an ironic intelligence and great courage of spirit. The stuff of Emily Dickinson's imagination is of this world; there is nothing macabre about her material (in the manner of Poe) and there is very little of the labored or artificial about her means. If "she mastered life by rejecting it," she mastered that Nature concerning which she had such ambivalent feeling by adding herself to the sum of all things, in a Rilkean habit of praise. "She kept in touch with reality," someone has said of her, "by the clearest and finest of the senses—the sense of sight. Perhaps the great vitality of contact by vision is the essence, in part, of her originality." How exactly she renders the creatures of this earth! She gives them to us, not as symbols of this or that, but as themselves. And her lyrical notation is so precise, so fine and moves so closely in union with her mind, that she is continually striking out aphorisms, from Plotinus to Blake. And as her life goes on, everything becomes whittled down, evanescent. Her handwriting becomes a kind of fluid print; her poems become notations; all seems to be on the point of disappearing. And suddenly all disappears.

"She was a visionary," says Richard Chase, "to whom truth came with exclusive finality [and] like her Puritan forbears she was severe, downright, uncompromising, visionary, factual, sardonic" [see Additional Bibliography].

"My business is to create," said the poet Blake. "My business is circumference," said the poet Dickinson. And we know that the physical center of that circumference was to remain the town of Amherst, which almost exactly one hundred years ago (on December 10th, 1859) Miss Dickinson described with great charm and deep affection, in a letter to Mrs. Samuel Bowles: "It storms in Amherst five days—it snows, and then it rains, and then soft fogs like vails hang on all the houses, and then the days turn Topaz, like a lady's pin . . ."—as delicate a description as a New England town and New England winter weather have ever received. (pp. 27-34)

Louise Bogan, "A Mystical Poet," in Emily Dickinson: Three Views *by Archibald MacLeish, Louise Bogan, and Richard Wilbur, Amherst College Press, 1960, pp. 27-34.*

NORTHROP FRYE (essay date 1962)

[Frye is a twentieth-century Canadian critic best known for his theories of myth criticism, which he employs to explicate a work of literature through an analysis of its archetypal characteristics. In Frye's view, the critic does not make value judgments; the critic's purpose is to classify and describe a work of literature and to examine its relation to other works. In the following excerpt from an essay first published in 1962, Frye discusses such issues as Dickinson's literary reputation, style, and themes.]

There are poets—and they include Shakespeare—who seem to have pursued a policy of keeping their lives away from their readers. Human nature being what it is, it is precisely such poets who are most eagerly read for biographical allusions. We shall find Emily Dickinson most rewarding if we look in her poems for what her imagination has created, not for what event may have suggested it. When, under the spell of Ik Marvel's *Reveries of a Bachelor,* a favorite book of hers, she writes:

Many cross the Rhine
In this cup of mine.
Sip old Frankfort air
From my brown Cigar

it would be a literal-minded reader who would infer that she had actually taken up cigar-smoking, yet this would be no more far-fetched than many other biographical inferences. A poet is entitled to speak in many voices, male, female, or childlike, to express many different moods and to develop an experience in reading or life into an imaginative form that has no resemblance whatever to the original experience. Just as she made the whole of her conception of nature out of the bees and bobolinks and roses of her garden, so she constructed her drama of life, death and immortality, of love and renunciation, ecstasy and suffering, out of tiny incidents in her life. But to read biographical allegory where we ought to be reading poetry is precisely the kind of vulgarity that made her dread publication and describe it as a foul thing. Higginson's comment on her **"Wild Nights!"**, that "the malignant" might "read into it more than that virgin recluse ever dreamed of putting there," indicates that glib speculations about the sexual feelings of virgins are much older than the popularizing of Freud. But whenever they are made they are incompetent as literary criticism.

It would be hard to name another poet in the history of the English language with so little interest in social or political events. The Civil War seemed to her "oblique," outside her orbit, and her only really peevish letter describes her reaction to a woman who told her that she ought to use her gifts for the good of humanity. There are one or two patriotic poems, but they show no freshness of insight. "My business is Circumference," she told Higginson [see excerpt dated July 1862]. She concerned herself only with what she felt she could surround. It is characteristic of lyrical poetry to turn its back on the reader: the lyrical poet regularly pretends to be addressing his mistress or friend or God, or else he is soliloquizing or apostrophizing something in nature. But lyrical poetry also tends to create its own highly selected and intimate audience, like the sonnets and love poems of Shakespeare's day that circulated in manuscript among friends long before they reached print. For Emily Dickinson poetry was a form of private correspondence: "This is my letter to the World," is what she says of her poetry, and she describes the Gospel as "The Savior's . . . Letter he wrote to all mankind." Such a correspondence forms what, for Emily Dickinson, was the only genuine kind of human community, the small body of friends united in love and understanding. "Please to need me," as she wrote to Bowles.

By a flower—By a letter—
By a nimble love—
If I weld the Rivet faster—
Final fast—above—

Never mind my breathless Anvil!
Never mind Repose!
Never mind the sooty faces
Tugging at the Forge!

(pp. 198-99)

• • • • •

The good popular poet is usually one who does well what a great many have tried to do with less success. For the thousands of people, most of them women, who make verse out of a limited range of imaginative experience in life, love, nature, and religion, who live without fame and without much knowledge of literature beyond their schoolbooks, Emily Dickinson is the literary spokesman. She is popular too in her conceptual use of language, for popular expression tends to the proverbial, and the unsophisticated poet is usually one who tries to put prose statements into verse. The Sibyl of Amherst is no Lorelei: she has no Keatsian faery lands forlorn or Tennysonian low-lying Claribels; she does not charm and she seldom sings. Mrs. Todd often spoke of encountering poems in Emily Dickinson that took her breath away [see excerpt dated 1891], but what surprises in her work is almost always some kind of direct statement, sharpened into wit or epigram. When she describes a hummingbird as "A route of evanescence," or says of the bluebird:

Her conscientious Voice will soar unmoved
Above ostensible Vicissitude.

she is using what medieval poets called "aureate diction," big soft bumbling abstract words that absorb images into categories and ideas. She does not—like, for example, D. H. Lawrence—try to get inside the bird's skin and identify herself with it; she identifies the bird with the human consciousness in herself. Many of her poems start out by making some kind of definition of an abstract noun:

Presentiment—is that long Shadow—on the Lawn—

Renunciation—is a piercing Virtue—

Publication—is the Auction
Of the Mind of Man—

and most of her best-loved poems are in one of the oldest and most primitive forms of poetry, the riddle or oblique description of some object. In **"A route of evanescence"** there is no explicit mention of a hummingbird, because the poem tries to catch the essence of the feeling of the bird without mentioning it. Similarly with the snow in **"It sifts from leaden sieves,"** and with the railway train in **"I like to see it lap the miles."**

Such popular features in her work have their own difficulties, and there are others inherent in her peculiar style. She has for the most part no punctuation, except a point represented in the Johnson edition by a dash, which, as the editor points out, is really a rhythmical beat, and is of little use in unraveling the syntax. She also shows a curious preference for an indirect subjunctive form of expression that appears in such phrases as "Beauty be not caused," and she has what seems a most unreasonable dislike of adding the *s* to the third person singular of verbs. The effect of such sidelong grammar is twofold: it increases the sense of epigrammatic wit, and it makes her poetry sound oracular, as though the explicit statements of which her poetry is so largely made up were coming to us shrouded in mystery. As she says:

Tell all the Truth but tell it slant—
Success in Circuit lies

The result is not invariably success: sometimes we may agree with enthusiasm:

How powerful the Stimulus
Of an Hermetic Mind—

at other times we can only say, with the captain in *Pinafore* confronted with a similar type of gnomic utterance: "I don't see at what you're driving, mystic lady":

Endanger it, and the Demand
Of tickets for a sigh
Amazes the Humility
Of Credibility—

Recover it to Nature
And that dejected Fleet
Find Consternation's Carnival
Divested of it's Meat

Every age has its conventional notions of what poetry ought to be like, and the conventional notions of Emily Dickinson's day were that poetry should be close to prose in its grammar and syntax, and that its vocabulary should be more refined than that of ordinary speech. Thus Robert Louis Stevenson was outraged by the word "hatter" in a poem of Whitman's, and asserted that using such a word was not "literary tact." Emily Dickinson deliberately flouts both conventions. Her beat punctuation and offbeat syntax go with an abrupt and colloquial diction. The tang of her local speech comes out in such spellings as "Febuary" and "boquet," in such locutions as "it don't" and "it is him," and in such words as "heft" for "weight." Speaking of heaven, she writes:

Yet certain am I of the spot
As if the Checks were given—

meaning railway checks, the guarantee the conductor gives that one is proceeding to the right destination. Her editors altered this to "chart," which was a more conventionally poetic word, being slightly antique. Emily Dickinson could easily have provided such a word herself, but preferred to form her diction at a humorously twisted angle to the conventional expectations of the reader.

There is little in Emily Dickinson, then, of the feeling that a writer must come to terms with conventional language at all costs. When she meets an inadequacy in the English language she simply walks through it, as a child might do. If the dictionary does not provide an abstract noun for "giant," the poet will coin "gianture"; if the ordinary "diminution" does not give her enough sense of movement, she will substitute "diminuet." Similarly the fact that there is no singular form for "grass" or "hay" does not stop her from speaking of "every Grass," or from writing, to Higginson's horror:

The Grass so little has to do
I wish I were a Hay—

A similar teasing of the conventional reader's ear comes out in her slanting rhymes, which often have the effect of disappointing or letting down one's sense of an expected sound. At the same time even a conventional reader can see that her commonplace stanza forms could hardly achieve any variety of nuance without some irregularities. This is particularly true of the sinewy rhythm that syncopates against her rigid hymnbook meters and keeps them so far out of reach of monotony or doggerel:

Those not live yet
Who doubt to live again—
"Again" is of a twice
But this—is one—
The Ship beneath the Draw
Aground—is he?
Death—so—the Hyphen of the Sea—
Deep is the Schedule
Of the Disk to be—
Costumeless Consciousness—
That is he—

In sophisticated poetry close attention is paid to the sounds of words: vowels and consonants are carefully balanced for assonance and variety, and we feel, when such poetry is successful, that we have the inevitably right words in their inevitably right order. In popular poetry there is a clearly marked rhythm and the words chosen to fill it up give approximately the intended meaning, but there is no sense of any *mot juste* or uniquely appropriate word. In the ballad, for example, we may have a great number of verbal variants of the same poem. Here again Emily Dickinson's practice is the popular, not the sophisticated one. For a great many of her poems she has provided alternative words, phrases, even whole lines, as though the rhythm, like a figured bass in music, allowed the editor or reader to establish his own text. Thus in the last line of one poem, **"To meet so enabled a Man,"** we have "religious," "accomplished," "discerning," "accoutred," "established," and "conclusive" all suggested as alternates for "enabled." Another poem ends:

And Kinsmen as divulgeless
As throngs of Down—

with "Kindred as responsive," "Clans of Down," "And Pageants as impassive As Porcelain"—or, presumably, any combination of these—as possible variants. It is rather more disconcerting to find "New" suggested as an alternate for "Old" in a poem ending with a reference to "Our Old Neighbor—God."

What we find in Emily Dickinson's poetry, then, is a diffused vitality in rhythm and the free play of a lively and exhilarating mind, crackling with wit and sharp perception. These were clearly the qualities that she herself knew were there and especially prized. She asked Higginson simply whether her verse was "alive." As a poet, she is popular in the sense of being able, like Burns or Kipling or the early Wordsworth, to introduce poetry to readers who have had no previous experience of it. She has, on the other hand, a withdrawn consciousness and an intense intellectual energy that makes her almost esoteric, certainly often difficult.

In any case she seems, after her early valentines, to have reached her mature style almost in a single bound. It is otherwise with her prose, no doubt because we have so much more of it from her early years. Her schoolgirl letters, with their engaging mixture of child's prattle and adolescent's self-consciousness, show a Lamb-like gift for fantasy and a detached and humorous shrewdness. She speaks of other girls who "are perfect models of propriety," and remarks: "There 'most always are a few, whom the teachers look up to and regard as their satellites"—which is sharp observation for a fourteen-year-old. After her writing of poetry begins, her prose rhythm moves very close to verse. The first letter to Higginson [see excerpt dated 15 April 1862] is really a free verse poem; some of her earlier poems were originally written as prose, and she often falls into her favorite metrical rhythms, as in the opening of a letter to Bowles: "I am so far from Land—To offer *you* the cup—it might some Sabbath come *my* turn—Of wine how solemn-full!", which is a short meter stanza. Her later letters show a remarkable command of the techniques of discontinuous prose: they were most carefully composed, and the appearance of random jottings is highly deceptive. Continuous or expository prose assumes an equality between writer and reader: the writer is putting all he has in front of us. Discontinuous prose, with gaps in the sense that only intuition can cross, assumes an aloofness on the writer's part, a sense of reserves of connection that we must make special efforts to reach. The aphoristic style of her later letters is, if slightly more frequent in Continental literatures, extremely rare in England or America, yet she seems to have developd it without models or influences.

Her Grace is all she has—
And that, so least displays—
One Art to recognize, must be,
Another Art, to praise.

The most cursory glance at Emily Dickinson will reveal that she is a deeply religious poet, preoccupied, to the verge of obsession, with the themes of death and of immortality—the latter being, as she called it, the "Flood subject." Even in her use of the Bible, her most frequent references are to the passages in Corinthians and Revelation usually read at funeral services; and Paul's remark, that we now see in a riddle, translated as "through a glass darkly," is echoed in her recurrent use of the words "Riddle" and "Disc":

> Further than Guess can gallop
> Further than Riddle ride—
> Oh for a Disc to the Distance
> Between Ourselves and the Dead!

Yet another glance at her letters will also show that in her evangelical surroundings she steadily resisted all revivals, all spiritual exhortations, all the solicitous and charitable heat that, at home, at school and at church, was steadily turned on the uncommitted. Like Huckleberry Finn, whom she resembles in more ways than one, Emily Dickinson had a great respect for orthodox religion and morality, did not question the sincerity of those who practiced it, and even turned to it for help. But she never felt that the path of social conformity and assent to doctrine was her path. Her resistance gave her no feeling of superiority: even her schoolgirl letters are full of a wistful regret that she could not feel what her friends all asserted that they felt. As she recalled later: "When a Child and fleeing from Sacrament I could hear the Clergyman saying 'All who loved the Lord Jesus Christ—were asked to remain—.' My flight kept time to the Words." She belonged in the congregation but not in the Church.

Her elders referred her to the Bible: she read the Bible and took an immediate dislike to the deity that she calls "Burglar! Banker—Father!"—that is, the legal providential God who seems to ratify everything that is meaningless and cruel in life. She remarked to Higginson that her family were all religious except her, "and address an Eclipse, every morning—whom they call their 'Father'" [see excerpt dated 25 April 1862]. She read with distaste the stories of Elisha and the bears ("I believe the love of God may be taught not to seem like bears"), of the sacrifice of Isaac, of the drowning of the world in a divine tantrum and the corresponding threat to burn it later:

> No vacillating God
> Created this Abode
> To put it out.

of Adam who was asserted to be alone responsible for his fall:

> Of Heaven above the firmest proof
> We fundamental know
> Except for it's marauding Hand
> It had been Heaven below.

The whole "punishing" aspect of religious doctrine struck her as "a doubtful solace finding tart response in the lower Mind," and she asks: "Why should we censure Othello, when the Criterion Lover says, 'Thou shalt have no other Gods before Me'?" That is, why blame Othello for being jealous when God tells us that he is himself? She concluded that "I do not respect 'doctrines,'" and added, with a touch of snobbery: "I wish the 'faith of the fathers' didn't wear brogans, and carry blue umbrellas." In short, she took no care to distinguish the Father of Christianity from the cloud-whiskered scarecrow that Blake called Nobodaddy and Bernard Shaw an old man in the sky looking like the headmaster of an inferior public school.

The Son of God for her was also caught in this Father's legal machinery. "When Jesus tells us about his Father, we distrust him." She has a poem in which she compares the doctrine of the revelation of the Father in the Son to the courtship of Miles Standish, and another in which she speaks with contempt of the "some day we'll understand" rationalizings of suffering:

> I shall know why—when Time is over—
> And I have ceased to wonder why—
> Christ will explain each separate anguish
> In the fair schoolroom of the sky—

At other times, she seems to accept Jesus as everything that Christianity says he is. Thus: "That the Divine has been human is at first an unheeded solace, but it shelters without our consent." It seems clear that her relation to the Nonconformist faith in which she was brought up was itself nonconformist, and that it would have violated her conscience ever to have made either a final acceptance or a final rejection of that faith. Her method, the reverse of Tennyson's in *In Memoriam,* was to prove where she could not believe. She did not want to repudiate her faith but to struggle with it. She was fascinated by the story of the "bewildered Gymnast" Jacob, wrestling with and finally defeating an angel who—according to a literal reading of the text which the poet promptly adopted—turned out to be God, and to this story she reverts more than once in her letters. When she compares the Bible unfavorably with Orpheus, whose sermon captivated and did not condemn; when she speaks of Cupid as an authentic deity and asks if God is Love's adversary, she is saying that there is another kind of religious experience that counterbalances, but does not necessarily contradict, the legal and doctrinal Christianity which she had been taught. As she says with a calculated ambivalence: "'We thank thee Oh Father' for these strange Minds, that enamor us against thee."

This other kind of religious experience is a state of heightened consciousness often called "Transport" and associated with the word "Circumference," when the poet feels directly in communion with nature and in a state of "identity"—another frequent term—with it. Nature is then surrounded by the circumference of human consciousness, and such a world is Paradise, the Biblical Eden, a nature with a human shape and meaning, a garden for man. "Home is the definition of God," and home is what is inside the circumference of one's being. In this state the mind feels immortal: "To include, is to be touchless, for Ourself cannot cease." It also enters into a condition of unity or oneness which is partly what the word identity means. "*One* is a dainty sum! One bird, one cage, one flight; one song in those far woods, as yet suspected by faith only!" Similarly the poet can speak, without any violation of grammar, of a "Myriad Daisy" (compare Wordsworth's "tree, of many, one" ["Ode: Intimations of Immortality from Recollections of Early Childhood"]), and, with Emerson, of the single Man who is all men:

> What News will do when every Man
> Shall comprehend as one
> And not in all the Universe
> A thing to tell remain?

Such an experience is based, not on the compelling argument, but on the infinitely suggestive image, or "emblem" as she calls it. "Emblem is immeasurable," she says, and speaks of human beings as the "trembling Emblems" of love. The language of emblems is as rational as the language of doctrine, but its logic is the poetic logic of metaphor, not the abstract logic of syllogism.

Circumference in its turn is the "Bride of Awe," and "Awe" is her most frequent name for the God that is reached by this experience. The human circumference is surrounded by a greater consciousness, to which the poet is related as bride to bridegroom, as sea to moon, as daisy to sun, as brook to ocean—all recurring images. Sometimes the poet uses the word "peninsula" to describe an individual consciousness projecting into experience and attached to an invisible mainland. Invisible, because "No man saw awe," any more than we can see our own backbones. Awe is a lover, incarnate in the bee who loves the rose and the harebell, and a divine lover for whom a feminine poet may make the response of a bacchante or of a vestal virgin with equal appropriateness. Thus Emily Dickinson may say both:

Circumference thou Bride of Awe
Possessing thou shalt be
Possessed by every hallowed Knight
That dares to covet thee

and (where "their" means the world of her bodily impulses):

To their apartment deep
No ribaldry may creep
Untumbled this abode
By any man but God—

Awe is not a dogmatic God, and is tolerant enough to satisfy not only the poet's Christian longings but the paganism that makes her feel that there ought to be a god for every mood of the soul and every department of nature:

If "All is possible with" him
As he besides concedes
He will refund us finally
Our confiscated Gods—

In fact he may even be female, a sheltering mother. "I always ran Home to Awe when a child . . . He was an awful Mother, but I liked him better than none."

In Christian terms, this divine Awe, as she well understood, is the third person of the Trinity, the Holy Spirit, symbolized in the Bible by two of her favorite images, the bird and the wind, the giver of life to nature and of inspiration to humanity, the creative force that makes the poet's verses "breathe," and the "Conscious Ear" that imagination hears with. The conventional Biblical image for the Holy Spirit is the dove, and the poet, picturing herself as Noah sailing the flood of experience, associates the dove who brought him news of land with the fact that the name of another well-known navigator, Christopher Columbus, also means dove:

Thrice to the floating casement
The Patriarch's bird returned,
Courage! My brave Columba!
There may yet be *Land!*

To this person of God, Emily Dickinson continually turned when other things in Christianity puzzled her imagination or were rejected by her reason. She seems to associate him with the power which "stands in the Bible between the Kingdom and the Glory, because it is wilder than either of them." In the detached comment on the Atonement which she superimposes on the famous proverb, "God tempers the wind to the shorn lamb," the "Wind" is the power that escapes from the breakdown of doctrinal machinery:

How ruthless are the gentle—
How cruel are the kind—
God broke his contract to his Lamb
To qualify the Wind—

In a congratulatory message on the occasion of a wedding, the divine power of making one flesh out of two bodies is associated, not with the Father or the Son, but with the wind that bloweth where it listeth:

The Clock strikes one that just struck two—
Some schism in the Sum—
A Vagabond from Genesis
Has wrecked the Pendulum—

The confusion with a female principle, as when she says that "the Little Boy in the Trinity had no Grandmama, only a Holy Ghost," is at least as old as the apocryphal Gospels, where Jesus speaks of the Holy Spirit as his mother. When she says, "The Bible dealt with the Centre, not with the Circumference," she means apparently that the Bible considers man in his ordinary state of isolation, separated from God by a gulf that only God can cross. Such a God is thought of as coming from the outside; but while God is known "By his intrusion," his movement in the human soul is to be compared rather to the tides moving in the sea. "They say that God is everywhere, and yet we always think of Him as somewhat of a recluse." If so, it takes a recluse to find him, and to discover him as the inmost secret of consciousness.

The first fact of Emily Dickinson's experience, then, was that whatever the Bible may mean by Paradise or Eden, the world of lost innocence and happiness symbolized by the unfallen Adam and Eve, it is something that is already given in experience. It is attainable; the poet has attained it; it is not, therefore, a "superhuman site," nor could it survive the extinction of the human mind. Earth is heaven, whether heaven is heaven or not: the supernatural is only the natural disclosed: the charms of the heaven in the bush are superseded by the heaven in the hand—to paraphrase almost at random. To her the essence of the Gospel was the proclamation of the Paradisal vision in such passages as "consider the lilies." But the Bible also speaks of regaining this Paradise and living in it eternally after death. If so, then the experience of Paradise in life is identical with the experience of eternity.

The people we ordinarily call mystics are the people for whom this is true. Eternity to them is not endless time, but a real present, a "now" which absorbs all possible hereafters. Emily Dickinson also often speaks with the mystics of death as a rejoining of heaven, of "Forever" as "composed of Nows," of an eternal state of consciousness symbolized by a continuous summer and noon, of a coming "Aurora," a dawn that will have no night. But in her background there were two powerful antimystical tendencies at work. One was the rationalism of

The Dickinson home.

her generation; the other was the Puritanism in which she had been reared, with its insistence that the divine will was inscrutable, that it made sense only to itself, not to man, and that no human experience could transcend the limits of fallen humanity. For Emily Dickinson, therefore, the identity between the experience of circumference she had had and the post-mortal eternity taught in the Bible remained a matter of "inference." It could be held by faith or hope but not by direct knowledge. This "inference" became the central issue in her struggle with her faith, a fact which she expresses most poignantly when she says: "Consciousness is the only home of which we *now* know. That sunny adverb had been enough, were it not foreclosed."

Paradoxically, the experience of unity with God and nature also produces a sense of division, or "bisection" as the poet often calls it, in the mind. Part of oneself is certainly mortal; part may not be, though even it must also go through death. In a poem beginning **"Conscious am I in my Chamber"** she speaks of the indwelling Spirit as the immortal part of herself; sometimes the distinction is between the poet herself and her soul; sometimes, and more commonly, it is between the soul and the mind or consciousness. "We know that the mind of the Heart must live," she says, and a letter to her seems like immortality because "it is the mind alone without corporeal friend." She also speaks of the body as a "trinket" which is worn but not owned, and in one striking poem the soul is attended by a "single Hound" which is its own identity. But she never seemed to accept the Platonic view that the soul is immortal by nature. If the first fact of her experience is a vision of earth as heaven, the second fact is that this vision is "evanescent," comes and goes unpredictably, and, so far as experience itself goes, ceases entirely at death. It is significant, therefore, that Emily Dickinson should so often symbolize her vision as a temporary and abnormal state of drunkenness:

> Inebriate of Air—am I—
> And Debauchee of Dew—
> Reeling—thro endless summer days—
> From inns of Molten Blue—

The liquor responsible for this state is usually called rum, or some synonym like "Domingo," "Manzanilla," or "Jamaica." When it is the more traditional wine, the word "sacrament," as in the poem **"Exhiliration—is within,"** is seldom far away, for such imaginative drunkenness is a genuine communion. Still, it can lead to hangovers, "With a to-morrow knocking," and, whatever it is or means, it goes and is replaced by ordinary experience.

Ordinary experience is the sacramental or ecstatic experience turned inside out. Here the mind is not a circumference at all, but a center, and the only circumference is an indifferent and unresponsive Nature—"Nature—in Her monstrous House." We may still realize that such "Vastness—is but the Shadow of the Brain which casts it," but in this state the brain cannot cast any other shadow. Where the mind is a center and nature the circumference, there is no place for any divinity: that has vanished somewhere beyond the sky or beyond life. This is the state of "Those Evenings of the Brain," in which the body, so far from being a circumference incorporating its experience, is a "magic Prison," sealed against all intimations of immortality:

> The Rumor's Gate was shut so tight
> Before my Mind was sown,
> Not even a Prognostic's Push
> Could make a Dent thereon—

Like Blake, with whom she has been compared ever since Higginson's preface to the 1890 volume [see excerpt above], Emily Dickinson shows us two contrary states of the human soul, a vision of innocence and a vision of "experience," or ordinary life. One is a vision of "Presence," the other of "Place"; in one the primary fact of life is partnership, in the other it is parting. Thus she may say, depending on the context, both "Were Departure Separation, there would be neither Nature nor Art, for there would be no World" and

> Parting is all we know of heaven,
> And all we need of hell.

But she has nothing of Blake's social vision, and the state that he associates with child labor, Negro slavery, prostitution, and war she associates only with loneliness.

Her two states are often associated with summer and winter, or, less frequently, with day and night. Often, especially in poems addressed to Sue, she speaks of a "Summer-Sister-Seraph!" who inhabits the paradisal world, in contrast to herself as a "dark sister," a "Druid" spirit of winter, frost and the north, waiting for the birds to come back, like Noah's dove, to tell her of a sunnier world beyond. Hence the times of year that have the greatest significance for her are the equinoxes, the March when the birds return and the white dress of winter breaks into color, and the moment in late summer when the invisible presence of autumn enters the year and makes "a Druidic Difference" in nature. The association of this latter period with the moment at which human life faces death makes it particularly the point at which the two lines of her imagination converge:

> God made a little Gentian—
> It tried—to be a Rose—
> And failed—and all the Summer laughed—
> But just before the Snows
>
> There rose a Purple Creature—
> That ravished all the Hill—
> And Summer hid her Forehead—
> And Mockery—was still—
>
> The Frosts were her condition—
> The Tyrian would not come
> Until the North—invoke it—
> Creator—Shall I—bloom?

Emily Dickinson is an impressionist in the sense that she tends to organize her visual experience by color rather than outline, and purple, the color of mourning and of triumph, is the central symbol for her of the junction between life and death. Various synonyms of it such as "Iodine," "Amethyst" and the "Tyrian" above run through her writings.

At times the poet speaks of the paradisal vision as being, not only a "stimulant" given in cases of despair or stupor, but a light by which all the rest of life can be lived, as providing a final answer to the question raised by its passing:

> Why Bliss so scantily disburse—
> Why Paradise defer—
> Why Floods be served to Us—in Bowls—
> I speculate no more—

At other times, in such poems as those beginning **"Why—do they shut Me out of Heaven?"** and **"If I'm lost—now,"** she laments over a lost vision that hints at a still greater loss. Such sudden changes of mood would be inconsistent if she were arguing a thesis, but, being a poet, what she is doing is expressing a variety of possible imaginative reactions to a central unsolved riddle. The fact that her vision is transient sharpens the intensity of her relation to it, for

In Insecurity to lie
Is Joy's insuring quality.

Two recurring words in her poems are "suspense" and "expanse." The former refers to the shadow that falls between an experience and the realization that it has happened, the shadow that adumbrates death; the latter to the possession of the spiritual body which, for us, brings vision but not peace. "These sudden intimacies with Immortality, are expanse—not Peace—as Lightning at our feet, instills a foreign Landscape." She deals mainly with the virtues of faith, hope, and love, but her life had shown her that love, which normally tends to union, may incorporate a great deal of its opposite, which is renunciation. Similarly with faith and hope: "Faith is *Doubt,*" she says, and hope is the thinnest crust of ice over despair:

Could Hope inspect her Basis
Her Craft were done—
Has a fictitious Charter
Or it has none—

Like the Puritans before her, who refused to believe that their own righteousness would necessarily impress God into recognizing them, Emily Dickinson refused to believe that her own vision of Paradise guaranteed the existence of Paradise, even though she had nothing else to go on. And—Puritan to the last—she even faced the possibility that the Spirit of life within her might turn out to be Death, hence the ambiguous tone of such poems as **"Doubt Me! My Dim Companion!"** and **"Struck, was I, nor yet by Lightning."** She told Sue that if Jesus did not recognize her at the last day, "there is a darker spirit will not disown it's child." She means death, not the devil, though her pose recalls the demonic figures in Hawthorne. There are many poems about the physical experience of dying, some tranquil, some agonizing, some dealing with death by execution, by warfare, by drowning—in at least two poems the poet is an Andromeda swallowed by a sea monster. The region of death to be entered, or traversed, is usually a sea, sometimes a forest, or a "Maelstrom—in the Sky," or simply "a wild Night and a new Road," and in **"I never told the buried gold,"** it is an underworld guarded by a dragon.

The world of death is not one that we have to die to explore: it is there all the time, the end and final cause of the vision of the center, just as Awe is the end and final cause of the vision of circumference. "I suppose there are depths in every Consciousness," she says, "from which we cannot rescue ourselves—to which none can go with us—which represent to us Mortally—the Adventure of Death." Some of her psychological poems take us into this buried jungle of the mind. There are a few about ghosts, where the two aspects of the self are treated in the vein of Henry James's *The Jolly Corner*. But Emily Dickinson's sharp inquiring mind has little in common with the ectoplasmic, and these poems impress us as made rather than born. A more genuine fear comes out at the end of this:

Remembrance has a Rear and Front—
'Tis something like a House—
It has a Garret also
For Refuse and the Mouse.

Besides the deepest Cellar
That ever Mason laid—
Look to it by it's Fathoms
Ourselves be not pursued—

This is as near to hell as she ever brings us, as the original version of the last two lines indicates:

Leave me not ever there alone
Oh thou Almighty God!

Yet even such a hell as this has a place and a function. Its presence is in an odd way the basis of vision itself, for "the unknown is the largest need of the intellect," and "could we see all we hope—there would be madness near." Emily Dickinson has a poem about Enoch and Elijah, the two Biblical prophets who were taken directly to heaven, but the figure she identifies herself with is Moses, standing on the mountain top with the wilderness of death on one side and the Promised Land on the other, able to see his Paradise if not to enter it:

Such are the inlets of the mind—
His outlets—would you see
Ascend with me the Table Land
Of immortality—

Many, perhaps most, of Emily Dickinson's readers will simply take their favorite poems from her and leave the rest, with little curiosity about the larger structure of her imagination. For many, too, the whole bent of her mind will seem irresponsible or morbid. It is perhaps as well that this should be so. "It is essential to the sanity of mankind," the poet remarks, "that each one should think the other crazy." There are more serious reasons: a certain perversity, an instinct for looking in the opposite direction from the rest of society, is frequent among creative minds. When the United States was beginning to develop an entrepreneur capitalism on a scale unprecedented in history, Thoreau retired to Walden to discover the meaning of the word "property," and found that it meant only what was proper or essential to unfettered human life. When the Civil War was beginning to force on America the troubled vision of its revolutionary destiny, Emily Dickinson retired to her garden to remain, like Wordsworth's skylark, within the kindred points of heaven and home. She will always have readers who will know what she means when she says: "Each of us gives or takes heaven in corporeal person, for each of us has the skill of life." More restless minds will not relax from taking thought for the morrow to spend much time with her. But even some of them may still admire the energy and humor with which she fought her angel until she had forced out of him the crippling blessing of genius. (pp. 201-17)

Northrop Frye, "Emily Dickinson," in his Fables of Identity: Studies in Poetic Mythology, *Harcourt Brace Jovanovich, 1963, pp. 193-217.*

JOHN WHEATCROFT (essay date 1963)

[Wheatcroft explores the significance of the recurring image of white attire in Dickinson's poetry.]

Dressed to meet You—
See—in White!
["Take Your Heaven further on"]

The poetry of Emily Dickinson is an emanation from New England orthodoxy. In Puritan eschatology the white robe in which the bride of Christ will be garbed is a persistently used figure. It is also one of the most pervasive images in Dickinson's poetry.

The chief Biblical sources of the white robes figure are Matthew xxii. 1-14 and Revelation iii. 5, 18; vi, 11; xix. 8, 14. Transmitted by means of the medieval doctrine of typology and then the visual imagination of Protestant rhetoric, as in Bunyan, the figure was passed to Jonathan Edwards and Isaac Watts. From Edwards' theology and sermons, and from Watts' theology, sermons, and Psalms and Hymns, the image descended to those orthodox nineteenth-century clergymen and teachers whose written and spoken words left their imprint on the mind and feelings of Emily Dickinson—Mary Lyon, Edward Hitchcock, Nathan W. Fiske, Heman Humphrey, and Charles Wadsworth. The poet's imagination fastened upon this figure, to which the richness of centuries had accrued, and exploited it in many ways.

In the process of transforming the commonplace theological metaphor into poetry, Emily Dickinson was enabled to pull together diverse parts of her heritage and of her own sensibility. She also found it possible through poetic manipulation of the figure to resolve intellectual and emotional problems that lay deep within her. And in exploring the white robes metaphor she often ventured into virgin territory of feeling and perceiving. For the thirty years of Emily Dickinson's creative life the private imagination of the poet and the collective imagination of the tradition she inherited consistently interacted. This interaction generated the best part of her poetry. The particular areas of experience that the white robes figure led Dickinson to explore and to order are love and death.

Snow and frost are two of the most commonly used figures for death in the body of Dickinson's poetry. In the poet's imagination these two nature images are closely associated with, indeed at times identified with, the traditional image of white robes. In **"Dying! Dying in the night,"** the poet pleads for someone to bring her light so that she

can see which way to go
Into the everlasting snow[.]

The snow here is overtly a symbol of death and covertly a representation of the white robe the poet hopes to adorn herself with in eternity. In **"Before the ice is in the pools,"** in which the poet is exploring the connection between the coming of the white winter and her own death, she employs the robe figure as a way of comprehending the difference between mortality and immortality: a "Wonder upon wonder," she explains, "Will arive to" her before winter comes. And this wonder she conceives of as a garment in which she will be clothed. At the present time, "on a summer's day," she is able just to "touch the hems" of this wonder, which is, of course, the immortality in which she will be clothed. At the end of the poem the poet wonders whether "the frock" she wept in, that is, her mortal dress, her gown of suffering, will be suitable when she puts on her immortality. The implication is that it will: that what the self is in this world, the way in which she has endured, will be miraculously transformed into the gown that she will fittingly wear in eternity.

In **"Poor little heart"** the white robe, symbolized by the snow in **"Before the ice. . . ,"** has been transformed into a shining transparent garment. The poet insists that even though her "Poor little Heart" is forgotten, forsaken, and broken in the here and now, it will one day be arrayed "Like Morning Glory" by "Wind and Sun." The morning glory, taken literally as the glory of the morning or as the flower (perhaps a pun is intended), symbolizes resurrection; the wind, the breath of the universe, is perhaps a type of the second member of the Trinity; whereas the sun, light that is daily reborn, suggests a type of Christ. In other words, the poet is saying that in the resurrection she will be arrayed in God's robe of immortality. What is especially significant in these early poems is that the poet connects her immortality directly with nature. Indeed, both the color and the texture of the robe of immortality are suggested to her by natural phenomena. (A similar tendency toward a pantheistic resolution of the problem of death can be seen in Edwards.) In such poems under the figure of white robes Dickinson accommodates the orthodox conception of a white-robed resurrection of the body and a nineteenth-century Romantic notion of dying into nature.

The pantheistic is a minor note in Dickinson's poetry, however; the impulse toward a pantheistic resolution of the problem of death is checked by the force of Christian orthodoxy. In a whole series of poems Emily Dickinson expresses a vision she has of death and the dead, not as being in some way absorbed into nature and thus made immortal, but as identities who have passed into another existence. In these poems she sees the dead clothed in white robes, or, we might say, the white robes *enable* her to see the dead. In **"Where I have lost I softer tread"** the poet conceives of those who have died before her and who are able to understand her present suffering as being those who are "dressed in frocks of purest snow." In **"It cant be 'summer',"** in order to contrast the bright red of Indian summer with winter, the time of death, the poet explains that Indian summer "Cant be 'Dying'" because "It's too Rouge," whereas "The Dead shall go in White." The poet conceives of the whole body of the dead as "the shining Fleet" in **"Love can do all but raise the dead."** And in **"Of tribulation these are they,"** which Thomas H. Johnson calls a "paraphrase of Revelations 7," the poet has a Vaughan-like vision of those who have passed through tribulation and have entered into the New Jerusalem. She sees them as being marked off from "The Spangled Gowns," which designate "a lesser Rank / Of Victors," in that they are "Denoted by the White," wearing "nothing commoner than Snow." Here the poet is expressing the orthodox view that there are ranks among the redeemed. Those who have the very highest election the poet envisions in white robes, the bridal gowns of heaven.

By means of the white robe image the poet is able to visualize not only the whole body of the dead but also particular dead. **"She died at play"** certainly seems to be an elegy for a particular woman. The poet tells us that yesterday she saw the woman's ghost strolling "softly o'er the hill" and that today she sees the woman,

Her vestments as the silver fleece—
Her countenance as spray.

The visual image of the white robe has enabled the poet to hold onto in her imagination the picture of a woman who no longer exists as a physical form. **"Bless God he went as soldiers"** seems to be much the same kind of anonymous elegy for a particular man. Here the poet prays that in order to establish her own courage she might have a vision of the brave one who has died like a charging soldier, "In epauletted white." Notice the variety of turns Emily Dickinson is able to give to the traditional figure, the manner in which she is able to adapt the image to each unique poetic situation. In so doing she is not only discovering rich poetic material in Protestant orthodoxy, but she is also enriching the tradition by injecting new life into a figure which in the mouths of clergymen and teachers had become a religious cliche.

The way in which the traditional figure leads the poet to exact perception can be seen even more clearly in **"The event was directly behind him,"** apparently another anonymous elegy. Here the poet is not interested in securing for herself a picture of the dead, but in depicting precisely, clinically, the condition with regard to self-awareness of a particular man as he dies.

For this reason it does not matter that the traditional pictorial and conceptual values that inhere in the metaphor are virtually obliterated; indeed, the traditional image can be barely recognized in the word *robe:*

The event was directly behind Him
Yet He did not guess
Fitted itself to Himself like a Robe
Relished His ignorance[.]

The point of the simile in which the white robes image lies buried is that although the dying man is unaware of his impending death, he fits that destiny so exactly that his lack of knowledge of his fate is a mighty irony.

The white robes image is even less obvious in **"Some arrows slay but whom they strike,"** an elegy on Emily Dickinson's nephew, Gilbert Dickinson, who died at eight years in October 1883. And yet the refined essence of the figure makes for marvelously compressed richness. The elegy is a single quatrain:

Some Arrows slay but whom they strike—
But this slew all *but* him—
Who so appareled his Escape—
Too trackless for a Tomb—

The white robes image has been reduced to the single word *appareled*. The function of the *who* clause in line 3 is to identify the *him,* the one who by dying did not himself die but caused the death of all those whom he left behind. But the identification is made in such a way that within four lines the poet has proved absolutely the truth of her poetic assertion. The noun *escape* carries a good bit of the load here, in that it makes good the point that the *he* did not die. The participle *appareled* works more subtly. In itself the word simply means *dressed* and carries no particularly strong visual suggestion. Yet because of its association—here made clear through the context of an innocent's soul having left the body—with the white robes or shining garments of the resurrected, the word *appareled* contains the picture as well as the idea of the elect's having passed through death—"Too trackless for a Tomb"—into the bliss of eternity. That is to say, the whole weight of the orthodox Christian doctrine of immortality rests beneath this poetic construction. The poem is like an iceberg—most of it rides below the surface. Such a conformation gives tremendous authority to a piece of poetry, for the foundation of the poetic truth, being submerged, can be only *sensed* during the imaginative experience, never *seen*. Only analysis, which is, of course, always after and outside the experiencing of the poem, can discover it. The poet is also able to release great energy from a poem of this sort. The energy bursts from the compression.

The image of white robes also enables Emily Dickinson to form a conception of existence outside of time, a conception of eternity. Not only the dead, who are the inhabitants of the other world, but also superior beings appear within the poet's imagination in white robes. In **"To fight aloud is very brave"** she sees angels marching in plumed procession in "Uniforms of Snow." In **"Why do they shut me out of heaven"** she envisions God as "the Gentleman / In the 'White Robe.'" And in **"Publication is the auction"** she depicts the God whose will is the source of all creative activity, who provides her with her poetic inspiration, as "the White Creator." Here Dickinson employs the color white, coming to her from snow as a death image and from the white robe as a symbol of immortality, to represent the idea of artistic integrity. Rather than auction her mind by publication, the poet prefers to keep herself uncorrupted:

We—would rather
From Our Garret go
White—Unto the White Creator—
Than invest—Our Snow—

In this poem we can see the coming together of diverse themes under the cover of an image from the tradition—the theological doctrine of the Atonement, a tendency to resolve the problem of death by way of a pantheistic idea, the subject of artistic integrity.

By making use of the white robes image Emily Dickinson also finds it possible to foresee her own death and salvation. In a number of poems she employs the metaphor of white robes to signify the recapturing of pre-Fall innocence which, according to orthodox doctrine, the Crucifixion makes possible for the souls of the elect. The poet self-effacingly points out in **"Going to heaven"** that "The smallest 'Robe' will fit" her. In **"Mute thy coronation"** she asks God, or her Lordly lover, to "Fold a tiny courtier" in his ermine, as a symbol of her being received into grace. The poet explains in **"Her little parasol to lift"** that it is her destiny to wear a blemishless summer, a figure in which the pantheistic tendency and the orthodox doctrine of the Atonement are almost perfectly accommodated. Most interesting insofar as the way in which intellectual history reveals itself in poetry is concerned, is **"Taking up the fair Ideal."** This poem is an assertion of faith in an idealism that is not unlike that of Emerson and the Transcendentalists in the face of an Edwards-like recognition of the fact that we live in a fallen world. The accommodation between Idealism and Calvinism is made possible by the use of the white robe image, which here signifies the ultimate transformation of the "fractured" ideal into a "mended" ideal:

Cherishing—our poor Ideal—
Till in purer dress—
We behold her—glorified—
Comforts—search—like this—
Till the broken creatures—
We adored—for whole—
Stains—all washed—
Transfigured—mended—
Meet us—with a smile—

By far the most interesting and most significant use Emily Dickinson makes of the white robes image is her exploitation of the figure to resolve the problem of death in terms of a consummation of love. In **"'Twas a long parting but the time,"** for example, she has a vision of two fleshless lovers standing "Before the Judgment Seat of God" on the occasion of their bridal. The lovers are not clothed in earthly experience—"No Lifetime set—on Them"—but are

Appareled as the new
Unborn—except They had beheld—
Born infiniter—now—

Here the poet is bringing together the image of the white bridal robes, carried in the words *appareled* and *new,* and the notion of the innocence of the child in order to declare the complex state of the lovers who are being united in eternity—complex in that, although they are as innocent as unborn infants, their condition is superior to that of the infant because they have passed through experience. Theirs is a won innocence.

This theme and this vision are persistent in Emily Dickinson's poetry. When dealing with them, the poet typically makes use of the white robes figure. Typically, too, the lover appears in either his earthly or divine form, and at the same time the poet is intent upon exploring the idea of her own death. Indeed, the color white comes to have a dual significance for Emily Dickinson: On the one hand, by virtue of its association with winter, especially in the form of frost and snow, and also by virtue of its being the color of the robes of the dead elect, it is the color of death. On the other hand, because of its conventional use as the color of the gowns of brides in order to denote innocence and because of the eschatological idea of the souls of the elect, appareled in white robes, consummating their love for deity in their marriage with the Lamb in eternity, it is the color of marriage, both earthly and divine. The poet employs the color white and the image of white robes to bring together in a single configuration a complex of themes: death, unfulfilled love for an earthly lover, love consummated with a divine lover.

"Doubt me! My dim companion" is almost certainly addressed to the earthly lover. The poet, realizing the impossibility of consummating her love on earth, asks her lover to

> hallow just the snow
> Intact, in Everlasting flake—
> Oh, Caviler, for you!

Here, surely she is alluding to her own death by way of the white snow and she is also smuggling into the poem an allusion to the white robes that she will be wearing when she is "intact," that is, when she has passed into her elect destiny—union with her lover. This piece is not good poetry, however, for the very reason that Emily Dickinson can be seen consciously to be sublimating her feelings as a historical person. But what seems to be cryptic to the point of meaninglessness is actually quite clear when the reader is aware of the symbolic meaning that "snow" holds for the poet. **"Take your heaven further on," "I am ashamed I hide,"** and **"Fitter to see him I may be"** are similar pieces. Because Dickinson is exploiting metaphor and symbol, that is, using words to effect for herself vicarious pleasure and private satisfaction, these poems seem cryptic. Such poetry is ingenious. It demonstrates the variety of ways in which Emily Dickinson can turn materials from the tradition. But poetry of this sort is too private, too selfish, perhaps, in its intention, to qualify as great literature.

On the other hand, Emily Dickinson can employ traditional materials such as the white robes metaphor to write poetry of genuine consequence. When she proves successful in using the image with its multiple meanings and rich associations, she does not merely exploit her verbal inheritance in order to write out private wish fulfillments, but she allows the image from the tradition to enter into her historical situation, whatever it might be, and enlarge it to a public concern, enrich it with meaning that engages humanity universal, transform it into a construct with value of its own. In **"A solemn thing it was I said,"** for example, the poet is attempting to get perspective on herself, to see the life she finds herself with in terms of its cosmic significance. In the first stanza—which along with the second is the successful part of a mixed piece—she is enabled by means of the white robe image to see herself as elect, a woman with a special destiny. Here, without specifically stating her destiny, she allows her verse to make its own rich implication:

> A solemn thing—it was—I said
> A Woman—white—to be—
> And wear—if God should count me fit—
> Her blameless mystery—

The single word *white,* carrying in itself the idea of divine marriage as subsequent to death, provides most of the force. **"Mine by the right of the white election"** and **"Because I could not stop for death"** are two of Emily Dickinson's finest poems. In both of these she allows the white robes image to appear in a way that seems inevitable. In both, the restraint with which the traditional image is employed releases tremendous poetic energy. The whole Christian doctrine of immortality lies within the single phrase "White Election" in "Mine by the right. . . ." The poet goes on to prove the doctrine experimentally by making a verbal reality of the marriage of the elect soul with deity:

> Mine—by the Right of the White Election!
> Mine—by the Royal Seal!
> Mine—by the Sign in the Scarlet prison—
> Bars—cannot conceal!
>
> Mine—here—in Vision—and in Veto!
> Mine—by the Grave's Repeal—
> Titled—Confirmed—
> Delirious Charter!
> Mine—long as Ages steal!

In the vision of her destiny that the poet wins for herself, the marriage with deity comes as a fulfillment of the life which through suffering has been enlarged to immortal proportions. Standing behind the adjective *white* and dictating it to her are the vision and convictions born out of the suffering and imagination of hundreds of years of the Christian tradition. Here all caprice has gone out of the poetry. The line is a destiny that has been properly met. So thoroughly is Dickinson in control of the imagination with which she stands up to meet that destiny that the reader cannot help feeling the powerful energies that leap out of the single word *white.*

In **"Because I could not stop for death"** the white robes image lies in the fourth stanza, a stanza that was omitted by Mrs. Todd and Higginson in the 1890 edition. As restored by Thomas H. Johnson the poem reads:

> Because I could not stop for Death—
> He kindly stopped for me—
> The Carriage held but just Ourselves—
> And Immortality.
>
> We slowly drove—He knew no haste
> And I had put away
> My labor and my leisure too,
> For his Civility—
>
> We passed the School, where Children strove
> At Recess—in the Ring—
> We passed the Fields of Gazing Grain—
> We passed the Setting Sun—
>
> Or rather—He passed Us—
> The Dews drew quivering and chill—
> For only Gossamer, my Gown—
> My Tippet—only Tulle—
>
> We paused before a House that seemed
> A Swelling of the Ground—
> The Roof was scarcely visible—
> The Cornice—in the Ground—
>
> Since then—'tis centuries—and yet
> Feels shorter than the Day
> I first surmised the Horses Heads
> Were toward Eternity—

Here the traditional white robe of the elect bride of Christ appears in the form of the gossamer gown, a transparent garment made of gauze, and the tulle tippet, a scarf made of thin, fine silk. Nowhere does the poet explain that she and the gentleman driver are on their way to their wedding, that she is the chosen bride of Christ about to consummate her love in a divinely sanctioned marriage. Indeed, she has no need to. Just as the Calvinistic doctrine of election controls the picture and the idea and the language of the first two lines of the poem, the traditional figure of white robes "writes" the last two lines of the fourth stanza for the poet. The fact that she is appareled in her wedding gown makes it perfectly clear that the gentleman driver who in his mercy has elected her to ride off with him in his carriage is nothing less than her full destiny. He is not only personified death, which will remove her from this existence when her ride through the New England landscape takes her into the grave; he is also the bridegroom who presents her with immortality and conducts her into eternity. Dickinson's restraint, which is just the other side of the coin of the inevitability of the imagery, makes this a compelling piece of poetry.

From the orthodox tradition, then, comes the image of white robes into Emily Dickinson's private imagination. Again and again she associates that metaphor with a lover sometimes earthly, sometimes divine. At times the experience covered by the figures remains private, the poet appropriates the image for mere wish fulfillment. But when the traditional figure and the private imagination harmoniously interact, poetry whose significance is cultural emerges.

And, indeed, the color white and the white robe do carry cultural significance in nineteenth-century America. As D. H. Lawrence [in his *Studies in Classic American Literature*] has shown in his assault on the "white females" of Cooper's "White Novels," and the "white-robed females" of Poe and Hawthorne, the color white and the white robe suggest a cultural frigidity, perhaps sterility. They are the protective garment of the American woman who, as she is given identity by the cultural imagination, must remain virgin until eternity. The woman who moves through the body of Emily Dickinson's poetry as the suffering protagonist seems to be such a virgin. There is something running deep inside her that prevents her from fulfilling her desire on earth, from consummating her love in this life. That something is the smell of death. It confronts her at every turn. Whether she directs herself toward a clergyman in Philadelphia or the flowers in her Amherst garden, the smell of death impels her to explore persistently the whiteness that represents for her both consummation and destruction. That compulsive scrutiny of the whiteness of the promised bridal robe and of the whiteness of the frost and snow that shroud the flowers she so deeply and futilely loves yields a richness that constitutes a fulfillment of its own.

What Emily Dickinson is able to discover within the self when it is arrested and alerted by the smell of death is a vision that is itself a metaphor. The consummation of all experience in the marriage of the soul to deity is the crowning symbolic perception of the poet. To put it another way, when explored by the active imagination the robe of frigid innocence is transformed into the garment of experience, the color of sterility and death yields an apprehension of the meaning of death and a vision of symbolic consummation. Out of such a reconciliation of opposites and contradictions the poet is able to construct a hard, sharply defined conception of something which, it would seem, is forever inconceivable to the human mind. By way of metaphor the poet manages to define ultimate human identity: in words she succeeds in apprehending the *sine qua non* of the self. Her conception originates in a picture that is a composite of the whiteness from the tradition and from nature, and it is closed with the realization that being is not mere essence or even value, the realization that to be is to engage.

> 'Tis whiter than an Indian Pipe—
> 'Tis dimmer than a Lace—
> No stature has it, like a Fog
> When you approach the place—
> Nor any voice imply it here
> Or intimate it there
> A spirit—how doth it accost—
> What function hath the Air?
> This limitless Hyperbole
> Each one of us shall be—
> 'Tis Drama—if Hypothesis
> It be not Tragedy—

That Emily Dickinson's view of essential being ends with an insistence upon becoming—"shall be"—, upon engagement—"'Tis Drama"—is a crucial point. For underneath the veil of white virginity is no white-bosomed female epitomizing the frigidity of the imagination of an age. Indeed, the suffering protagonist of Emily Dickinson's poetry is a woman with a "freckled Bosom" [**"Rearrange a 'Wife's' affection"**], with not "a Velvet Cheek / Or one of Ivory," but a "freckled" cheek [**"Themself are all I have"**]. [The critic adds in a footnote: Taken in the theological sense the freckle, of course, represents an impurity, a stain. The recurrence of such words as *freckle, stain, spot* in Emily Dickinson's poetry is an indication of her sense of sin. I must sharply disagree with George F. Whicher on this point: "In her attitude toward sin, for example, she was thoroughly unorthodox. Apparently she hardly ever used the word . . ." [see Additional Bibliography]. In my opinion, Emily Dickinson's attitude toward sin is soundly Calvinistic. Her view of reality insists that both the physical universe and human nature are in a "fallen" condition.] She is the girl who pulled her stockings off and waded in the water for disobedience's sake [**"So I pull my stockings off"**], a "spotted" woman [**"'Unto me?' I do not know you"**], a woman covered with *"stain"* [**"Again his voice is at the door"**]. Rather than symbolizing neurotic frigidity, the white robe of Emily Dickinson is the poet's concession of the fact that the smell of death lurks in every flower and bee, and her recognition that to be is to be unfulfilled. What provides Emily Dickinson's poetry with its energy, with its impulse to explore beyond the limits of ordinary human experience, is an uncontainable desire of imagination that is maintained in the face of an unflinching awareness of the crack in reality, underneath which lies the abyss. The passion of Dickinson the poet ranges all the way from the obvious physical desire of **"Wild nights—wild nights"** to the desire to be ravished ultimately in holiness [**"The thrill came slowly like a boon for"**]. Behind her poetry, even that part of it that seems most "white,"stands a dense cultural and an intense private experience. Emily Dickinson's is an imagination energized by a rich but fragmenting tradition, impelled by a passion for experience. (pp. 135-47)

John Wheatcroft, "Emily Dickinson's White Robes," in Criticism, *Vol. V, No. 2, Winter, 1963, pp. 135-47.*

CLARK GRIFFITH (essay date 1964)

[In this excerpt from his book-length psychoanalytical study of Dickinson's place in the Romantic tradition, Griffith closely considers the theme of dread towards time and mutability in three of her poems.]

Out of her aversion to time and change, there emerge the darkest moments in Emily Dickinson's poetry: her portraits of death, her doubts concerning immortality, her analyses of pain and love and evil, her delineations of the dreaded invasion and of the periodic molestations which the self undergoes. It is the fact of the aversion that needs to be demonstrated first. To that end, let us consider three poems, chosen from among literally dozens of possibilities. The texts obviously share a common attitude toward a single subject, and I shall print them consecutively. But since a certain number of cross-references will be necessary in the ensuing commentary, the designations "A," "B," and "C" will probably prove useful:

[A]

Presentiment—is that long Shadow—on the Lawn—
Indicative that Suns go down—

The notice to the startled Grass
That Darkness—is about to pass—

["Presentiment—is that long Shadow—on the Lawn"]

[B]

Further in Summer than the Birds
Pathetic from the Grass
A minor Nation celebrates
It's unobtrusive Mass.

No Ordinance be seen
So gradual the Grace
A pensive Custom it becomes
Enlarging Loneliness.

Antiquest felt at Noon
When August burning low
Arouse this spectral Canticle
Repose to typify

Remit as yet no Grace
No Furrow on the Glow
Yet a Druidic Difference
Enhances Nature now.

["Further in Summer than the Birds"]

[C]

A Light exists in Spring
Not present on the Year
At any other period—
When March is scarcely here

A Color stands abroad
On Solitary Fields
That Science cannot overtake
But Human Nature feels.

It waits upon the Lawn,
It shows the furthest Tree
Upon the furthest slope you know
It almost speaks to you.

Then as Horizons step
Or Noons report away
Without the Formula of Sound
It passes and we stay—

A quality of loss
Affecting our Content
As Trade had suddenly encroached
Upon a Sacrament.

["A Light exists in Spring"]

Compressing it to a phrase, one might say that the theme of all three poems is that of "the momentous transition." In each case, we are in the midst of change—change which is a product of time's machinations and which, as we watch, is gradually being imposed by time upon the images in the landscape. The overall effect of the poetry is to enlarge beyond the particular shift, until change, and the temporal processes which wrought it, are made to seem a relentless ritual, a kind of slipperiness and evanescence which must be felt as universal qualities. This effect is evident even in "A," the least memorable poem, but one where the specific incident—the particular lapse from light to darkness—clearly possesses the most generalized of implications. In "B" and "C," the intense dramatic impact is largely a result of our perception that the death of the insects and the passing of light are portrayed here merely as symptoms: as small signs of the still larger impermanence which exists always and everywhere and on a cosmic scale. As Yvor Winters has said, in commenting on "B" and "C," both poems present change as inherently terrifying, because mutability is at once "an explicable fact" and yet the basic and essential component of every human experience [see excerpt dated 1938].

It is typical of Winters that while he possesses the greatest possible insight into Emily Dickinson's preoccupations, he nevertheless interprets the time-and-change theme in her work as being primarily "naturalistic" in viewpoint, rather than philosophical. The truth is of course that Winters abhors unresolved metaphysical riddles, which he sees as running counter to his classicism and preference for decorum. Moreover, he holds such riddles to be especially obnoxious in poetry, since, by his own definition, the good poem will automatically banish ambiguity and bring order and resolution to whatever subject it touches. The result is that in Miss Dickinson's time poems, which he deeply admires, Winters declines to find any hint of metaphysical overtones. He orients the texts specifically in *this* world, reads them, indeed, as if they amounted to no more than an orderly description of the disorders in Nature. Thereby, he limits far too severely what the poetry itself conveys.

For the real problem of the momentous transition lies, precisely, in the metaphysical uncertainties which time and change are constantly occasioning. The combination of bafflement and despair that permeates the writing does not spring exclusively from the poet's vision of the changing world as an observable fact, a series of strictly natural phenomena. It derives, mainly, from the way in which this shifting, changing world seems intent on harassing the poet, on blocking her off from understanding, on separating her from any fixed point outside its own mobility. That reading will seem the least warranted probably in the case of poem "A," though even there, as we shall find in a moment, it is bound up with Emily Dickinson's tone and images. In "B" and "C," however, phrase upon important phrase indicates the philosophical drift of the poetry—and suggests that just as the particular movement is made to symbolize movement-in-general, so movement-in-general becomes a horrifying spectacle by epitomizing for the poet everything that is ambiguous and unaccountable in the universe which confronts her.

Note, to begin with, the circumstances recounted in poem "C." Here, as the last word implies, a change on the landscape must be associatd with the speaker's loss of spiritual fulfillment. When the light goes out, the speaker is deprived of a *Sacrament*—is robbed, in other words, of the joy which might have come through some sort of spiritual communion. Not only are time and change seen as being directly responsible for her loss; in the conduct of these two forces, we are made to feel them as deliberately malevolent, as treacherous forces which express, through their every action, a profound contempt for the human observer's needs. The verb *encroach* shows this. Implying trespass or infringement, it points up the extent to which temporal experiences gladly, and even eagerly, impose themselves between the speaker and her quest for communion. When the light is taken away without the *Formula* (that is, without the remedy or the alleviation) *of Sound,* this fact emphasizes, in another way, the cruelties of experience. It draws attention to the intense mystery of time's behavior, and so begets in the speaker a sense of something unfathomably strange in what has happened to her and to her landscape. Taken together, then, the ideas of an *encroachment* and of *silence* get exactly at the attitude toward time which Emily Dickinson will regularly develop. They describe a Power which first robs the human observer of contentment, then goes on to compound the injury by providing her with no clues through which the deprivation might be understood.

This notion that time is a Power—a Power at once ponderous and yet terrifyingly impalpable—is still further magnified by the stress, in all three texts, upon the sheer inexorability of temporal sequence. In poem "A" the arrogance of time is suggested by the lofty *notice* that darkness gives. The same air of relentlessness is introduced into poem "B" through the use of ceremonial words—words like *Custom* and *Mass* and *Druidic*—to convey the facts of change. In poem "C" the steady, inflexible passage of time—the stepping of Horizons or the brisk reporting away of Noons—contributes, once again, to an identical mood. The consequence of this sort of language is one of investing temporality with a distinctively ceremonial guise. Emily Dickinson shows time and change beating down upon the human observer in the form of a grim, remorseless, and overbearing ritual.

In part, no doubt, this was her chief intention. She wished to emphasize the oppressiveness of temporality, to depict it as a process which no act of the human will could curb and against which all human exertions would prove futile. And yet, in poems "B" and "C" at least, one finds an added implication. It is that change could hardly come this ceremoniously or time behave this oppressively, unless a Power existed to direct temporal movements. The very least the ceremonial gestures do is convert Time and Change into monstrous personifications, a pair of forces that have set out intentionally to persecute the human observer. At the very worst, furthermore, the gestures hint that somewhere behind the time ceremony there is its Master, the "approving God" who has invented change as a "Heavenly hurt," and who imposes the hurt on humanity as one mark of His supreme disdain. From the poetry, the final complication to be inferred is this: that the human observer, caught as she is in the midst of the time ritual, can only *suspect* its motions to be meaningful, without having any clear idea of what the meanings really signify. It is her plight, *as* a human observer, to be exposed unwillingly to the dance of time, and to recognize that by the ambiguity of the dance she has been effectively cut off from ever comprehending its source.

Her predicament is poignantly revealed in the emotional point of view which the poetry establishes. As the poet beholds her world in a process of transfigurement, she finds in the spectacle a cause for her most somber feelings. Particularly in poem "B," her reactions extend well beyond the overt circumstances in the text—well beyond a lament for the insects or grief for the dying season—to become identified with a cosmic riddle, of which the overt circumstances supply only a single, concrete instance.

Thus the funeral mass of the insects is a *pensive Custom,* because the poet glimpses, in the alteration before her, a symbol of the saddest and the most solemn engima that humankind must face. Similarly, the feelings aroused by the death of Summer are *Antiquest* feelings, because this specific manifestation of time passing appeals to an old and instinctive dread; it begets a primordial fear, which is the speaker's fear of everything in experience that is ineffable and unknown. The enlarged *Loneliness* which the poet experiences in the presence of change does not come, as Mr. Winters would have it, from a recognition of the "essential cleavage between [herself] . . . and nature." (Actually just the reverse is true: in the perishing of the crickets the poet perceives, with painful clarity, her *kinship* with the natural processes of death and decay.) But *loneliness* is the result of her failure to grasp the reasons for change. It embodies her sense of being, like the cricket, a member of a *minor Nation*—minor not because she is physically small as the cricket is, but because she shares with the insects the plight of being cast adrift in an indifferent and thoroughly unintelligible world.

The tendency of the time poetry is to conceive of time as a veil, one drawn tightly and firmly between the human observer and the stability for which she craves. Where the observer asks for intuitions of Eternity, time and change show her only beginnings and ends. Where she yearns to feel at home in the universe, time poses a problem that leaves her the perpetual outsider, involved in temporal processes but with no understanding of what they mean. The further implication is that a kind of demonic strategy underlies time's behavior, so that time's blotting out of ultimate values is an entirely self-conscious activity. And this implication becomes undeniable when we look, finally, at the two sets of images around which the time poems are habitually organized.

A casual glance at "A," "B," and "C" will suffice to point up the images: images that time bears away on the one hand, and on the other a category of details that time is portrayed as bringing. At one end of the momentous transition, there are such things as *day, light,* and *Summer;* and reading from other time poems, we may add to this group *sun, Spring,* and *flowers.* These are light images that disappear under the pressures of time. For Emily Dickinson, the light images possess a special significance. They are her supreme values, exalting and reassuring her, filling her with momentary ecstasy, adding to her contentment and her spiritual stature. As symbols, they stand for life, for immortality, and for the nearest approach that man can make toward Godhead. If they endured, the poet's faith could easily remain unshaken and unshakeable. But they do not endure. Set off against them are their symbolic counterparts: *night, darkness,* and *Fall,* and from other places *Winter, chill,* and *frost.* These are negative emblems, representing pain and death, bespeaking the malignity or the outright absence of God, suggesting all the limitations on human knowledge. They remind one of one's physical corruptibility. They hold out the threat of a total annihilation after death. They stand, in sum, as Emily Dickinson's thresholds to despair and to the dark night of the soul.

In the time poetry, the movement of the momentous transition is always toward the negative: toward darkness in "A," toward Fall in "B," toward the dissipation of light in "C," toward some similar condition in virtually every time poem that Emily Dickinson ever wrote. Very occasionally, time will appear to have reversed its direction:

> These are the days when Birds come back—
> A very few—a Bird or two—
> To take a backward look.
>
> These are the days when skies resume
> The old—old sophistries of June—
> A blue and gold mistake. . . .

Since this poem is about Indian Summer, however, the reversal is a fraud, and the poet treats it as a cruel and apparently malicious jest on time's part. For, in the main, it seems the business of temporality and mutability to undermine the foundations of human faith. All the human observer must do is raise her eyes to see the impending future swooping down upon her, ready to destroy the light images, to leave in their place some one of the several forms of darkness, and to render her destitute of either hope or belief. (pp. 84-93)

Clark Griffith, in his The Long Shadow: Emily Dickinson's Tragic Poetry, *Princeton University Press, 1964, 308 p.*

ADRIENNE RICH (poem date 1965)

[Rich is regarded as among the best of contemporary American poets. Her early poetry was praised for its stylistic control and restraint of individuality, while her later work is characterized by a thorough shift to personal, political, and feminist themes, and to experimental styles. Rich's poetry, considered by Hayden Carruth to be exemplary of a new aesthetic, is rooted in an existential view of the human condition and of the poet as a self-creator. As a critic, she provides a strongly feminist perspective. Here, Rich offers a poetic tribute to Dickinson. This poem was later published under the title "I Am in Danger—Sir—" in Rich's The Fact of a Doorframe: Poems Selected and New, 1950-1984. *For further commentary by Rich, see excerpt dated 1976.]*

"Half-cracked" to Higginson, living,
afterward famous in garbled versions,
your hoard of dazzling scraps a battlefield,
now your old snood

mothballed at Harvard
and you in your variorum monument
equivocal to the end—
who are you?

Gardening the day-lily,
wiping the wine-glass stems,
your thought pulsed on behind
a forehead battered paper-thin,

you, woman, masculine
in singlemindedness,
for whom the word was more
than a symptom—

a condition of being.
Till the air buzzing with spoiled language
sang in your ears
of Perjury

and in your half-cracked way you chose
silence for entertainment,
chose to have it out at last
on your own premises.

Adrienne Rich, "E.," in Emily Dickinson: The Mind of the Poet *by Albert J. Gelpi, Cambridge, Mass.: Harvard University Press, 1965, p. xiii.*

DAVID T. PORTER (essay date 1966)

[In this excerpt from Porter's study of Dickinson's early poetry, the critic surveys her use of dual perspectives and themes in select poems.]

Emily Dickinson created in the poetry of her formative years a speaker uniquely appropriate to articulate her theme. In concert with the double aspect of her central concern with the aspiring quest—the emotional throes engendered by the search on the one hand and the triumphant exultation at the visionary apprehension of the goal on the other—the speaker appears both in the role of the humble searcher for fulfillment and the successful explorer who finds imaginatively the treasure of the ideal. One speaks from desire, the other from knowledge. In certain individual poems, the speaker is both persons simultaneously.

In those early works which are informed with a strong sense of personality it is apparent that the world of the speaker is closely circumscribed. The subjects are to a large extent grouped about the central idea of fulfillment. These brief poetic discourses in turn determine the character of the speaker, for it is the situations which that person encounters and her reactions to them that combine to give her a discernible personality. Indeed, because of the relatively small area of experience which the speaker confronts, the focus of the poems returns repeatedly to the interior life of the individual, to the close confines of emotional response, and these responses are often devoid of explicitly narrated causal experiences. In this inner drama, within the diminished stage where the senses register experience and react to it, the speaker is both observer and actor. An analytic view of the inner life exists together with implications of the speaker's emotional investment in what she pictures. Emily Dickinson was aware early in her career of this dual approach in her poems, and was aware, too, that the distinction between objective rendering of experience and subjective infusion of personal feeling was not always to be clearly drawn. The recognition is suggested in the declaration in her first letter to Higginson that her "Mind is so near itself—it cannot see, distinctly" [see excerpt dated 15 April 1862].

In the occasional friendship pieces, of course, the effectiveness of the feelings rarely ascends beyond conventional expression of sentiment. In other poems, however, which manifest the integrity of the serious artist, the emotion is intense. More important, a growing incisiveness of self-examination, a heuristic process of self-discovery, is represented. The attitudes which are uncovered embody, in turn, a fundamental duality.

This ambivalence of the speaker structures the poem beginning **"A Mien to move a Queen."** At the center of this personality is a divided attitude: on the one hand the person is searcher and sufferer in a world that inflicts pain; on the other hand the person rises victorious over circumstance, becoming the priestess of truths refined from the anguish of experience. The poet's recognition of this contrary orientation reflects the persistent concern in the early poetry with the problem of self-classification. In the early poetry the speaker repeatedly attempts to locate herself in society, in time, and in the moral scale. In effect, the poems ask whether this person, who is compelled to reveal the innermost drama of the emotions, is a barefoot singer or stately queen, lonely lover or wife, playful sprite or saint, martyr of the emotions or poet. Some of these possibilities appear in **"A Mien to move a Queen."** In the first stanza the character described, like the Maid of Orleans, is both child and heroine:

A Mien to move a Queen—
Half Child—Half Heroine—
An Orleans in the Eye
That puts it's manner by
For humbler Company
When none are near
Even a Tear—
It's frequent Visitor.

The contrasting postures of humility and grandeur are expressed succinctly in the opening line. The ambiguous verb "to move" suggests both the humble manner that would impress the sensibility of a queen and the grander manner which allows the speaker to move *as if she were a queen*. The identification of this person with Joan of Arc ("An Orleans in the Eye") argues the strong purposefulness and triumphant manner which mark the personality in other poems. Lines four and five create that opposite, gentler figure who for "humbler Company" becomes humble herself. The closing three lines of the stanza describe the loneliness and private anguish when the regal manner is put by. The same contrasting qualities recur in the second stanza. The royal mien and the noble mind ("A Bonnet like a Duke") exist simultaneously with the shy wren-like manner and the small hands:

A Bonnet like a Duke—
And yet a Wren's Peruke
Were not so shy
Of Goer by—
And Hands—so slight—
They would elate a Sprite
With Merriment.

The contrary tonalities of this speaker are reasserted in the next stanza. The tone may be soft and enfolding like a snowfall, or it may be as commanding and assured as an empress's:

A Voice that Alters—Low
And on the Ear can go
Like Let of Snow—
Or shift supreme—
As tone of Realm
On Subjects Diadem.

Unable to comprehend such a paradoxical character, other people compromise their disparate reactions and venerate her:

Too small—to fear—
Too distant—to endear—
And so Men Compromise—
And just—revere.

This personality with the contradictory attitudes informs not only many of the early poems, but later ones as well. Consequently, it is a distorting simplification to say, as Archibald MacLeish does [see Additional Bibliography], that a single tone controls the poetic expression. Indeed, as the tone changes from the humble to the playful to the imperious, the reader discerns various relationships which this speaker forms with the world of experience. The relationship is as vital to the understanding of certain poems as any other single element. The poet, in effect, like the painter, makes a faithful record not merely of a visual experience but of his whole response to it.

I do not mean to imply that in Emily Dickinson's poetry the speaker's attitudes are limited to the two depicted in **"A Mien to move a Queen."** At times, indeed, the tone may be burlesque, satirical, or simply narrative. In her first valentine [**"Awake ye muses nine, sing me a strain divine"**], for example, the speaker poses as a court judge pronouncing sentence and reveling in his own rhetorical extravagance. The establishment of this playfully pompous relationship to the subject occurs in the lines in which the speaker declares the purpose of the oration:

Now to the *application*, to the reading of the roll,
To bringing thee to justice, and marshalling thy soul.

In another very early poem, **"'Sic transit gloria mundi',"** similar rhetorical extravagance is apparent; the speaker is a politician, and the tone is gently satirical:

Unto the Legislature
My country bids me go;
I'll take my *india rubbers*,
In case the *wind* should blow!

In contrast to this lighter, satirical tone, more severe criticism is made in **"I've known a Heaven, like a Tent."** The subject of the declaration in this poem is the disappearance of religious faith. To the denigration of orthodox belief, the idea of heaven is embodied not in such conventional metaphors as light or musical harmony but rather in the metaphor of a traveling circus:

I've known a Heaven, like a Tent—
To wrap it's shining Yards—
Pluck up it's stakes, and disappear—
Without the sound of Boards
Or Rip of Nail—Or Carpenter—
But just the miles of Stare—
That signalize a Show's Retreat—
In North America—

No Trace—no Figment of the Thing
That dazzled, Yesterday,
No Ring—no Marvel—

Sharp irony also invades the poem **"One dignity delays for all."** To the extent that the attitude in this poem runs directly counter to the consolatory belief that death brings down even the mighty it may be interpreted as a grave criticism of mortal existence. In effect, the speaker is saying that the specious dignity of a funeral awaits even the simple people who in life enjoy no grandeur. The second and fourth stanzas indicate the ironic tone:

Coach, it insures, and footmen—
Chamber, and state, and throng—
Bells, also, in the village
As we ride grand along!

. . . . .

How pomp surpassing ermine
When simple You, and I,
Present our meek escutscheon
And claim the rank to die!

In addition, the poem contains sharp irony in the implication of the final line that mortals elect death for its accompanying pageant, though of course in the election they necessarily forego the experience.

Similarly, other early poems reflect an attitude that is neither that of the humble quester nor the queen. These works may for convenience be termed narrative poems. In them the speaker is detached, intent principally on creating a character or situation independent of herself. This dramatizing habit of the poet is apparent even in her letters. The daily affairs of the Dickinson family, for example, are rendered in caricature. In a letter to Mrs. Samuel Bowles, dated by Johnson "about August 1861," the poet writes of her sister and mother: "Vinnie would send her love, but she put on a white frock, and went to meet tomorrow—a few minutes ago. Mother would send her love—but she is in the 'Eave spout,' sweeping up a leaf, that blew in, last November." In later correspondence Emily Dickinson often dramatically renders the otherwise homely occurrences in the family. She writes to her cousins about her father's youngest sister Elizabeth: "L[ibbie] goes to Sunderland,

Wednesday, for a minute or two; leaves here at 6½—what a fitting hour—and will breakfast the night before; such a smart atmosphere! The trees stand right up straight when they hear her boots, and will bear crockery wares instead of fruit, I fear. She hasn't starched the geraniums yet, but will have ample time, unless she leaves before April'' (dated 1863). Even the imposing figure of her father did not escape the poet's propensity for caricature: ''Father called to say that our steelyard was fraudulent, exceeding by an ounce the rates of honest men. He had been selling oats. I cannot stop smiling, though it is hours since, that even our steelyard will not tell the truth'' (dated 1865).

In comparable manner, Emily Dickinson creates wry dramatic situations in her early poetry. An example is **''A little East of Jordan''**

A little East of Jordan,
Evangelists record,
A Gymnast and an Angel
Did wrestle long and hard—

Till morning touching mountain—
And Jacob, waxing strong,
The Angel begged permission
To Breakfast—to return—

Not so, said cunning Jacob!
''I will not let thee go
Except thou bless me''—Stranger!
The which acceded to—

Light swung the silver fleeces
''Peniel'' Hills beyond,
And the bewildered Gymnast
Found he had worsted God!

In another exercise of her dramatizing ability, Emily Dickinson creates a brief scene in which two lovers overcome their shyness and effect what can only be described as spiritual union [**''The Rose did caper on her cheek''**]. The artistry, of a low order, is apparent principally in the rhetorical creation of movement through the use of active verbs—''caper,'' ''rose,'' ''fell,'' ''stagger,'' ''fumbled,'' ''danced,'' and ''ticked'':

The Rose did caper on her cheek—
Her Boddice rose and fell—
Her pretty speech—like drunken men—
Did stagger pitiful—

Her fingers fumbled at her work—
Her needle would not go—
What ailed so smart a little Maid—
It puzzled me to know—

Till opposite—I spied a cheek
That bore *another* Rose—
Just opposite—Another speech
That like the Drunkard goes—

A Vest that like her Boddice, danced—
To the immortal tune—
Till those two troubled—little Clocks
Ticked softly into one.

The situation, however trite, is of course an analogue for the poet's central theme of the quest for consummation. The lovers in this drama enact the embarrassment of their separation and the ultimate triumph over it as their hearts merge in ''the immortal tune.''

Another compact drama is created in **''Two swimmers wrestled on the spar.''** The shipwreck metaphor, as we consider it within the thematic matrix outlined in the preceding chapter, suggests that the swimmer who is literally saved by reaching land is also symbolically saved in the religious sense. The other swimmer dies in a gesture of urgent entreaty:

Two swimmers wrestled on the spar—
Until the morning sun—
When One—turned smiling to the land—
Oh God! the Other One!

The stray ships—passing—
Spied a face—
Upon the waters borne—
With eyes in death—still begging raised—
And hands—beseeching—thrown!

The analogue is appropriate to the poet's theme and to the dual aspects of it. One swimmer dies in the anguish of separation, while the other achieves the goal of salvation. Poems in straight narrative are few, however, suggesting that Miss Dickinson knew the most effective treatment of her theme was the lyric, individualized by tone and by the use of novel rhetoric. This individuality enhances the immediacy of the poem as performance. That is, the insistent expression of a particular sensibility makes the person in the poem actively present as speaker. Other devices to create the illusion of spontaneity are analyzed in my later discussion of stylistic techniques.

That orientation of the speaker's attitude that is passive and characterized by humility provides the tonality in a variety of poems. Within them the person is variously searcher, sufferer, meditator on the past and conjuror of the future, and votary in attendance at the ritual of nature. As searcher for consummation, the speaker in **''My wheel is in the dark!''** knows both the loneliness of the quest and the promise of achievement which compels her:

My foot is on the Tide!
An unfrequented road—
Yet have all roads
A clearing at the end.

The persona in **''I never lost as much but twice''** reveals a curiously compounded attitude of supplication and irreverence as she faces a world given as much to deprivation as to fulfillment. The declaration apparently arises from the speaker's third experience of bereavement:

I never lost as much but twice,
And that was in the sod.
Twice have I stood a beggar
Before the door of God!

Angels—twice descending
Reimbursed my store—
Burglar! Banker—Father!
I am poor once more!

A supplicatory attitude unqualified by any rebellious turn of mind appears in the elliptic expression in **''Jesus! thy Crucifix'':**

Jesus! thy Crucifix
Enable thee to guess
The smaller size!

Jesus! thy second face
Mind thee in Paradise
Of our's!

A paraphrase of this austere prayer would read: Jesus! Thy experience of mortality, which ended in the Crucifixion, enables Thee to understand the human predicament. Let the remembrance of that earthly anguish arouse pity in Thee for our present suffering.

The use of the crucifixion metaphor to convey the mortal experience of the speaker who has been denied (or has rejected) earthly honors is present in the middle stanza of **"Unto like Story—Trouble has enticed me."** Here, in addition, the speaker declares her confidence ("I—grown bold") and the strength of her disciplined emotions:

Unto guessed Crests, my moaning fancy, leads me,
Worn fair
By Heads rejected—in the lower country—
Of honors there—

Such spirit makes her perpetual mention,
That I—grown bold—
Step martial—at my Crucifixion—
As Trumpets—rolled.

"Guessed Crests," her metaphor of ultimate achievement, is sufficiently ambiguous to encompass the three goals which the poet's persona may be understood to envision: the consummation of desire in love, of poetic labor in posthumous fame, and of spiritual aspiration in immortality. Whatever the goal (or imaginative fusion of goals), the search is pursued with a profound sense of humility combined with intense commitment.

Emily Dickinson's poetic analyses of suffering include a recognition of the consuming nature of pain. Pain, like the panther, can maim its victim with delicate thoroughness [**"It is easy to work when the soul is at play"**]:

It is easy to work when the soul is at play—
But when the soul is in pain—
The hearing him put his playthings up
Makes work difficult—then—

It is simple, to ache in the Bone, or the Rind—
But Gimblets—among the nerve—
Mangle daintier—terribler—
Like a Panther in the Glove.

Loss may occasion in the speaker a dismay relieved only partially by the pale remembrance of the original joy [**"I held a Jewel in my fingers"**]:

I held a Jewel in my fingers—
And went to sleep—
The day was warm, and winds were prosy—
I said " 'Twill keep"—

I woke—and chid my honest fingers,
The Gem was gone—
And now, an Amethyst remembrance
Is all I own.

The ambiguous jewel metaphor allows no precise identification of the lost object. One knows only that it was precious and that the remembrance of it is a less precious ("Amethyst") possession. Her use of the word "prosy" to suggest the enervating atmosphere which made the speaker careless of her treasure indicates perhaps that the "jewel" was verbal, a particularly good poetic phrase which could not be recovered after sleep had interrupted composition. Typically, Emily Dickinson creates a recognizable emotion in the poem without any clear reference to the fostering experience. Indeed, the striking expression "Amethyst remembrance" may serve as a touchstone for recognizing other examples of her persistent practice of creating emotion independent of experience, the "spectral power in thought that walks alone," as she wrote to Higginson in 1869.

The capacity of the speaker for suffering is infinitely great, as if she could experience the distress of the entire human species [**"A Weight with Needles on the pounds"**]:

A Weight with Needles on the pounds—
To push, and pierce, besides—
That if the Flesh resist the Heft—
The puncture—cool[l]y tries—

That not a pore be overlooked
Of all this Compound Frame—
As manifold for Anguish—
As Species—be—for name—

This voice belongs to one familiar with distress, who knows that grief is all-engrossing, obliterating sensitive response to any other kind of experience. As noted earlier, the speaker recognizes this in **"I felt a Funeral in my Brain."** The declaration occurs also in the closing lines of **"I got so I could hear his name,"** where misery itself, the speaker says, is "too great, for interrupting—more."

The contrary aspect of this ambivalent voice resounds in poems in which the tone is supremely authoritative, declamatory, omnipotent. An adjunctive gnomic quality intrudes in her letters and accounts for such prose fragments as "Honey grows everywhere but iron (valor) on a Seldom Bush." Both the prose and poetry statements have their provenance in an intense inner strength wrought from crucial experiences. In **"I can wade Grief,"** Emily Dickinson employs the metaphor of woven rope to communicate the idea of strength created through deliberate self-control:

Power is only Pain—
Stranded, thro' Discipline,
Till Weights—will hang.

In **"Of Bronze—and Blaze,"** the speaker declares her authoritative manner is derived from viewing the magnificence of nature. The aurora borealis, she says:

Infects my simple spirit
With Taints of Majesty—
Till I take vaster attitudes—
And strut upon my stem—
Disdaining Men, and Oxygen,
For Arrogance of them.

In **"One Year ago—jots what?"** the speaker avows an inner strength unsuspected by her lover. She responds to his assertion that his is the more profound sensibility:

You said it hurt you—most—
Mine—was an Acorn's Breast—
And could not know how fondness grew
In Shaggier Vest—
Perhaps—I could'nt—
But, had you looked in—
A Giant—eye to eye with you, had been—
No Acorn—then.

The attitude of the speaker as victor over the pain of life, the "pale Reporter, from the awful doors" of death [**"Just lost, when I was saved!"**], is the culminating aspect of this side of the speaker's orientation. She has acquired omniscience out of anguish and perception out of pain. The tone of authority is clear in the opening lines of **"I'm 'wife'—I've finished that":**

I'm "wife"—I've finished that—
That other state—
I'm Czar—I'm "Woman" now—
It's safer so.

The attitude is clear from the tone of ecstatic assurance in the familar **"I taste a liquor never brewed."** It reaches one of its most forceful professions in the declaration **"Me, change! Me, alter!"**:

Me, change! Me, alter!
Then I will, when on the Everlasting Hill
A Smaller Purple grows—
At sunset, or a lesser glow
Flickers upon Cordillera—
At Day's superior close!

"The poet's soul," John Crowe Ransom says, ". . . must be severe in proportion as the profuse sensibility . . . tends to dissipate and paralyze its force" [see Additional Bibliography]. The frugal economy of the soul is, of course, apparent in this speaker who possesses enormous strength and emotional discipline. These qualities derive from the experiences of anguish, which the speaker confronts. The anguish can repeatedly be related to the condition of separation from the consummate state of mutual love, of poetic achievement, and of spiritual fulfillment. The authoritative qualities derive, indeed, from her triumph over adversity. Emily Dickinson begins a poem of 1862 [**"The Outer—from the Inner"**] with this quatrain.

The Outer—from the Inner
Derives it's Magnitude—
'Tis Duke, or Dwarf, according
As is the Central Mood—

In specific early poems such as **"A Mien to move a Queen"** and **"Of Bronze—and Blaze,"** both of these qualities of the speaker's character are present. Yet Emily Dickinson's early capabilities are not so confined as this persistent duality suggests, but extended to burlesque, satire, and narrative. The essential duality of her speaker, however, gives us directly and most appropriately the poet's central thematic concern with aspiration. In this quest her speaker both suffers the pain of denial and develops a discipline of the emotions which prevents psychic disintegration. A concomitant of the quest is the visionary achievement of the goal, and in this condition the speaker flaunts her triumphant attitude.

The polarity in both theme and speaker in the early works creates tension which contributes significantly to the effectiveness of the poetry. This effectiveness is artfully enhanced by the poems' characteristic activity as performance, which in turn results from the intimate presence of the speaker. The impact of experience, both real and imagined, on her persona is defined not by the intellect, as in characteristic poetry of the Metaphysicals (with whom Emily Dickinson is somewhat wrongfully compared), but rather by the emotions. Her astonishing control in the early poems over this intense emotional activity is perhaps the most distinguishing mark of her mature artistry in the formative period. (pp. 40-54)

David T. Porter, in his The Art of Emily Dickinson's Early Poetry, *Cambridge, Mass.: Harvard University Press, 1966, 206 p.*

THOMAS W. FORD (essay date 1966)

[In this excerpt from his book-length study of death as a central theme in Dickinson's poetry, Ford suggests that the poet's awareness of death, intensified by the events of the American Civil War, motivated her writing.]

Emily Dickinson's existential awareness of the reality and the "problem" of death had a pervasive influence on the content of the poems she wrote and, indeed, was the principal reason for her turning her energies to poetic composition of any kind. As she put it, in a letter to T. W. Higginson [see excerpt dated 25 April 1862]: "I sing, as the Boy does by the Burying Ground—because I am afraid"—afraid, that is, of death. The remark to her Norcross cousins that she "sang off charnel steps" is a further indication that the poet herself knew that death, and more particularly a fear of it, was a prime motivating force in her creative work. To occupy her mind and to reduce her anxiety over death, she turned to a "study" of the dictionary. She told Higginson that after the death of one of her early "tutors", probably Benjamin Newton, "for several years, my Lexicon—was my only companion" [see excerpt dated 25 April 1862]. This interest in words must have helped give rise to her early efforts to write poetry.

What originally turned Emily Dickinson's attention to death? The religious nature of her environment focused her attention on death and immortality. The town in which she lived was still very definitely attached to its Puritan traditions. Though her father did not join the church until rather late in life, he was from "the old school of Puritanism," and there is no question but that his daughter was reared in an atmosphere of earnest Christian thinking. From all sides she felt a pressure to experience "conversion." Even in the nineteenth century, the heritage of Calvinism was very much alive in Amherst.

Emily Dickinson's inability to experience a personal conversion resulted in doubt and apprehension, especially when she was at the South Hadley Female Seminary (Mount Holyoke). Witnessing the conversion of her classmates, seeing how eagerly they sought the "message," she became increasingly aware that she was among the "lost" and was "one of the lingering bad ones." Would death without conversion close the gates to heaven? She was unsure of heaven, while her contemporaries who had been "saved" claimed to have absolute certainty of its existence. In his *English Notebooks,* Nathaniel Hawthorne said of his friend Herman Melville: "He can neither believe, nor be comfortable in his unbelief; and he is too honest and courageous not to try to do one or the other." Emily Dickinson, too, wavered between doubt and belief all of her life and, like Melville, was too courageous to give up her honest pursuit of truth. She expressed her paradoxical position in the lines:

Of Paradise' existence
All we know
Is the uncertain certainty—
[**"Of Paradise' existence"**]

For a moment she saw a way out of her religious difficulties. If, as Emerson asserted, all men were potentially divine, then there would be no such thing as a membership of the "elect," arbitrarily chosen by God, and she would not be abandoned among the "lost." Furthermore, according to the Transcendentalists, the individual should trust himself rather than tradition. Emily eagerly responded. She would gladly trust her own insight and intuition as against the word of authority. To do so might relieve her from the haunting fear that she was not one of God's chosen.

Puritanism was too much a part of her, however, for the gospel of Transcendentalism to win her total allegiance. Though attracted to the optimistic assertions of Transcendentalism, she continued to see man's position in the universe as an insecure one. Was not death ready to strike at any moment? What if, after all, God *did* receive only the "saved"? Better that one should be constantly alert—better that the door be left slightly ajar to allow God's light, if it should come, to enter. Her lack of total commitment to either view led to spiritual unrest, while her direct observation of death "in action" gave support to neither. And it was this direct, raw, "naive" experience, this personal discovery, that links her attitude with that of existentialism. She was an individual who existed *in time*, intensely aware of the menace of death in every moment. This cold, still, silent thing—the corpse—looked no more like a member of the "elect" than it looked like a self-sufficient private man. Was man infinite or dependent? Should he move with caution or with bold optimism? On these questions Emily Dickinson was unfortunately in the middle, pulled from both directions, throughout her adult life:

Go slow, my soul, to feed thyself
Upon his rare approach—
Go rapid, lest Competing Death
Prevail upon the Coach—
Go timid, lest his final eye
Determine thee amiss—
Go boldly—for thou paid'st his price
Redemption—for a Kiss—

["Go slow, my soul, to feed thyself"]

With the coming of the Civil War, the reality of death prompted her to the fullest use of her poetic talents. She wrote poetry to relieve her anxieties, gazing at death from all sides, testing her vision within the context of her poems, hoping to get close to death, hoping to cope with it artistically. She was not attempting to prove anything; she was not preaching a gospel or trying to present a consistent theory about death. Though she may have hoped that one day her poems might be widely read, she did not write them for this purpose. She wrote them for herself, as a release from emotional stress.

In her poems of death and immortality and in her elegies she gives her ideas free play. They are not consistent. She expresses hope for immortality, then doubt. She pictures this life as merely a test for the next, then as all. She praises God, then condemns Him. She sees man as divine, then as lowly.

In her poems treating the physical aspects of death she makes certain observations from the viewpoint of sensations, finding the most persistent qualities of the dead to be coldness, immobility, weight, and silence.

Her poems personifying death find "him" to have as many contradictions as the universe, and as many complexities. He is timid and bold. He is a lover, a murderer, a brigand, a thoughtful coachman, a democrat, a despot, a comforter, a wild beast. She has no final view of death personified. He remains the great unknown, the great mystery.

Emily Dickinson's poetry also served as a substitute for religion. Very definitely wanting to have a firm religious belief, she could not honestly accept the religion of her time. After their father's death she wrote her Norcross cousins in January, 1863: "Let Emily sing for you because she cannot pray." Here is a distinct indication that she wrote poetry, that she "sang," because she could not pray in the conventional manner to a God whose grace she had not received.

In her best poems Emily Dickinson expressed her fears and oppositions, the conflicts born of Puritan doubts and Transcendental hopes, by images drawn from everyday experience and personal observation. Not an abstract thinker or philosopher, she pulled the abstract down into the world of specific sensation where she could turn, touch, weigh, and handle these concepts.

Death as an awesome force in the universe, thoughts not subject to the test of observation and experience she views existentially through the concrete and homely images of the house: freckled pane, cobweb, buzzing fly, indolent housewife, sweeping, early task, bustle in the house, spools of thread, busy needles, stirring house. In similar fashion she used images familiar to her from her interest in flowers and plants: husk, kernel, pod, sod, crocus, sprig, roses. Observation of nature in her garden led her to associate death with frost and snow—thus, the many *cold* images in connection with death.

Her firsthand observations of deaths in neighboring houses, observations made in the presence of the dying, observations of the gear and ceremonies connected with burials and funerals lent further concrete substance to her poems. The undertaker is the "man of the appalling trade." Death "Dresses each House in Crape, and Icicle." Death takes a friend; those present in the room "placed the Hair and drew the Head erect," and the body now appeared "Too stiff to bended be."

Her attitude toward death influenced Emily Dickinson's technique—the actual combination of words as they appear in the poems. Her basic metrical pattern was that of the hymn books, but with variations. Even here, one can see the influence of her inner conflicts over death and her doubts of immortality. In one sense, at least, her poetry was a great effort to understand death, God, and immortality—a great prayer or hymn for the resolution of her doubts. The external form that she chose, the hymn, reflects her attitude toward her subject matter—a desire to relieve her fear and anxious concern over death and immortality. Unable to join a church, she could offer her own unorthodox "hymns" in an effort to catch God's ear.

While Emily Dickinson's irregularities in rhyme were primarily a device to allow her greater freedom in choice of words, attitude and mood also influenced her use of approximate rhyme. She apparently followed no rule in using approximate rhyme in one place, exact rhyme in another. She did *not* use approximate rhyme only in those poems expressing the fractured nature of the universe. And she did *not* use exact rhyme only in her "light" verse or in poems expressing affirmation or optimistic hope. She did *not* picture the universe, or even the world, as neatly divided into black and white, evil or good, discord or harmony, false rhyme or true rhyme. Here was another point, of course, at which she was at variance with the "saved" and "damned" mentality of Puritanism. To her the world was not this simple. It was a highly intricate and puzzling melange, a mixing of good and evil, of exact rhyme and false rhyme. The very fact that she used a mixture of true rhyme and approximate rhyme reflects her feeling that the universe is an aggregate of elements, arranged—if, indeed, they are arranged—in no simple either-or fashion.

Her attitude toward death influenced certain other characteristics of her verse. The sense of urgency and haste running throughout her poetry reflects her acute awareness of the presence of death, ready at any moment to cut life short. As she told T. W. Higginson, "Shortness to live has made me bold," and she wrote:

Why should we hurry—why indeed
When every way we fly
We are molested equally
By immorality

["Why should we hurry—why indeed"]

Even her use of the dash reflects—and conveys—a feeling of haste and urgency. Impatient with punctuation, afraid to slow down her creative thought, she placed a dash wherever she desired. In similar fashion she omitted auxiliary verbs, brushing them aside boldly to hasten her conclusion. Her fondness for the subjunctive, too, seems to be in keeping with her persistent attitude of doubt.

But her technique involved more than the use of hymn meters, approximate rhyme, eccentricities in the use of the dash, fondness for the subjunctive, and omission of auxiliaries. The heart of her technique, whether planned or instinctive, was her selection and arrangement of words in a poetic structure. An intense interest in words as such was central to her poetics. Her ability to let words mold and shape each other in context, the interplay of the various connotations of her words, their interaction on one another—here is the core of her "style".

Her attitude toward death influenced this last aspect of her technique, for *if* she could use words in unconventional ways, *if* she could unite the like with the unlike by sudden and unexpected juxtapositions, *if* she could consider the complexities and contradictions of words and unite them into an artistic whole in her poem—then perhaps she could accept the incongruities in the universe. If she could join into a meaningful whole seemingly disparate words, then perhaps she could entertain the notion that an apparently disordered universe might in reality be intact, though she would not be admitted to the secret in this life.

Emily Dickinson was ever conscious of "Death's tremendous nearness". The sound of death was rarely beyond hearing distance. Though she never resolved her conflicts, in a sense she triumphed over death by transmuting the uncertainties of her experience into the art of her poetry.

There can be little question that death was her central theme. Clearly it colored all her thinking and gave its tint to the majority of her poems. Even in her lighter verse, death slyly peeks out, largely hidden but none the less there. To call this concern "morbid", as some have done, is to miss the point. For Emily Dickinson, death was the one unmistakable, though undefinable, force in an equivocal universe. Punctual, reliable, dependable, inevitable, absolute—it was the one certainty in a world of uncertainties. A totally independent power, it emerged as the focal point in her thought, her central subject of inquiry. It rose above all else—supreme, omnipresent, and omnipotent. Little wonder that death became, in effect, her "poetic principle". Though not a philosopher, she poetically pursued her interest with Yankee tenacity.

Was the end worth the pursuit? Her poems are the answer. (pp. 176-84)

Thomas W. Ford, in his Heaven Beguiles the Tired: Death in the Poetry of Emily Dickinson, *University of Alabama Press, 1966, 208 p.*

BRITA LINDBERG-SEYERSTED (essay date 1968)

[*In this excerpt from her highly regarded* The Voice of the Poet: Aspects of Style in the Poetry of Emily Dickinson, *Lindberg-Seyersted closely analyzes the style of "Further in Summer than the Birds."*]

A proposed explication of a poem may be regarded as "a hypothesis that is tested by its capacity to account for the greatest quantity of data in the words of the poem" [as Monroe C. Beardsley states in *Aesthetics: Problems in the Philosophy of Criticism*]. The poem I have selected for analysis, **"Further in Summer than the Birds,"** is one that has been widely praised and interpreted. It has been explicated in several different ways, not just regarding deteails of phrasing and imagery, etc., but also as to the more pervasive questions of theme and attitude. I have profited greatly from the profound and acute observations and suggestions of my predecessors in this game. When I produce still another explication, it is in the hope that it will contribute a detail or two to that final hypothesis of the poem's meaning which—if we agree with such a theory of explication—we will in the end regard as superior to other alternative hypotheses.

There are three holographs of this poem, two written early in 1866, and one seventeen years later. (There are also extant two transcripts, both longer than the holographs and poetically inferior.) I reprint—with a few marks of punctuation added—the 1866 copy which Emily Dickinson sent to Colonel Higginson. It is true that in the mid-1860s she used dashes and other marks much less copiously than earlier, but she did not often send off a poem as sparsely punctuated as this one. Since her dashes often suggest how phrases and clauses should be interpreted syntactically and since especially the second stanza of this poem will benefit from such aids, I indicate within parentheses the additional marks of the copy written in 1883. I print alongside the text my analysis of the poem's meter and rhythm:

Further in Summer than the Birds (–)	óo|oó|oȯ|oó	óoˌoóoˌooó
Pathetic from the Grass	oó|oȯ|oó	oóoˌooó
A minor Nation celebrates	oó|oó|oó|oȯ	oóoˌóoˌóooˌ . . .
It's unobtrusive Mass.	oò|oó|oó	oòoóoˌó
No Ordinance be seen (–)	òó|oȯ|oó	òóooˌoó
So gradual the Grace	òó|oȯ|oó	òóooˌoóˌ
A pensive Custom it becomes (–)	oó|oó|oò|oó	oóoˌóoˌòoó
Enlarging Loneliness.	oó|oó|oȯ	oóoˌóooˌ
Antiquest felt at Noon	oó|oó|oó	oóoˌóˌoó
When August burning low	oó|oó|oó	oóoˌóoˌó
Arise this spectral Canticle	oó|oó|oó|oȯ	oóˌoóoˌóoo
Repose to typify (–)	oó|oó|oȯ	oóˌoóoo
Remit as yet no Grace (–)	oó|oó|òó	oóˌoóˌòó
No Furrow on the Glow (–)	òó|oȯ|oó	òóoˌooó
Yet a Druidic Difference	óo|oó|oó|oȯ	óˌooóoˌóooˌ . . .
Enhances Nature now (–)	oó|oó|oó	oóoˌóoˌó

The subject of the poem is the seasonal change from summer to autumn. The poet describes a premonition of this change as something *heard*, not seen. The sounds of warning that reach an attentive ear are those of the crickets chirping away low down in their miniature universe. We are justified in inferring from external evidence that the "minor Nation" is made up of crickets: in a letter accompanying a copy of this poem Emily Dickinson speaks of it as "My Cricket"; she also has other poems on similar themes which name the insects [**"The Crickets sang," "September's Baccalaureate," "'Twas later when the summer went,"** a variant of **"As imperceptibly as Grief,"** and **"The Jay his Castanet has Struck"**]. The speaker, invisible (note the absence of an "I" in this superior version), stands apart from the crickets' sacred ceremony, having no share in their world. No one in particular is addressed. The poem is not a plea, nor an outburst or a question: it is a meditation delivered in a quiet tone. It proceeds from a description of the natural outer world to an intimation of the inner response of the human observer.

For this meditation the poet employs two of her favorite metrical patterns. It opens with a Common Meter stanza which presents actor and action, as well as the time, place, and manner of the action, that is, the crickets' "Mass". The rest of the poem which elaborates on the peculiar character and effect of this mass is framed in the terser Short Meter pattern. The metrical scheme is subtly varied throughout the poem. Initial trochees and frequent variations in degree of stress on the ictus prevent the hymn meter patterns from becoming monotonous. The poem owes its quiet but vital pulsation also—and perhaps more importantly—to the fine tension between meter and rhythm traceable to a fairly great amount of non-coincidence between feet divisions and word and phrase boundaries. Most lines are end-stopped, which lends a certain stability to the verse. The fairly marked pauses at line ends serve to counteract a possible breakdown of order which might have taken place because of a considerable indeterminacy of syntactic structure characterizing some lines—enhanced by the sparseness of punctuation marks.

The rhymes cooperate with the prosodic pattern in establishing a balance between regularity and irregularity. The full rhyme, *Grass-Mass,* appears in the stanza with the greatest number of irregular feet (counting as such other feet than iambs, or iambic feet in which the ictus occurs on a weak syllable, o ȯ). In stanza three there are only two such irregular feet. Counteracting the metrical regularity of this stanza there is the weak sound agreement of a partly unaccented vowel rhyme, *low-typify*. The second and fourth stanzas represent an intermediate state of exactness. The rhyme of stanza two, *Grace-Loneliness,* is fairly "harmonious" (a partly unaccented consonant rhyme with additional similarity between the preceding vowels); in its realization of the metrical scheme this stanza evinces several irregular feet (but fewer than the first stanza). The rhyme of the final stanza, *Glow-now,* is a near-to-perfect sound accord (a vowel rhyme with vowel similarity). The poem is divided into two halves by its rhymes. Stanzas one and two are linked by the final /s/ sounds and the similarity of the preceding vowels. (Note also the alliterative consonant cluster /gr/ and the affinity of the nasals /m/ and /n/ which introduce the rhyming syllables.) The third and fourth stanzas are interrelated by depending on vowels for their sound accord at line ends (*low-Glow-now* forming a close-knit group). The rhymes of this poem do not seem to me to "imitate" the sense of the poem in any notable way. In their blend of exactness and inexactness they contribute to the controlled, but expressive tone that this meditative poem conveys.

Apart from alliteration within lines and across lines and stanzas (*g*radual—*G*race, *G*race—*G*low, *R*epose—*R*emit, etc.), specific sounds lend the verse a sonorousness that—like the mass that the poem speaks of—never becomes obtrusive or excessive. The great amount of nasals: /m/, /n/, and (less) /ng/; and fricatives: /s/ and /z/, create an illusion of crickets buzzing. The poet speaks elsewhere of how the crickets *sang* [**"The Crickets sang"**]; in yet another poem she describes as a *murmuring* the sounds of "some", probably crickets [**"The murmuring of Bees, has ceased"**].

The remarkable unity of this poem is not achieved by a logical order of reasoning; nor do parallelism and repetition form a unifying pattern. The unity is created by diction and imagery. The metaphor of the mass dominates the poem, and the words that make up the complex of this metaphor are closely connected through a subtle chain of associations. These progress from the adverb "pathetic" (used for the more common form "pathetically") which, while describing the manner of the crickets' action, brings in the response of the human observer; they end with a phenomenon which similarly concerns man's response to nature: the "Difference" that enhances the beauty of nature to the observer before the inevitable death of summer.

The poem contains two main vocabularies; one pertaining to nature, its landscape, inmates, and seasons: *Summer—Birds—Grass—Noon—August—Furrow—Glow—Nature*. This is a "native" and quite concrete diction. Religion affords the other set of words: *celebrates—Mass—Ordinance—Grace—Canticle—Repose—Druidic*. "Mass" and "Canticle" are terms used specifically in the Roman Catholic Church; "Ordinance" is principally a Protestant concept; and "Druidic" refers to a Pre-Christian religion. These terms belong to an abstract vocabulary of mixed heritage. The observer's reaction to the mass she is overhearing is first suggested in "pathetic", which to begin with may mean no more than "moving", but which acquires an element of sadness when perceived in the context of the entire poem. The adjective "pensive" strengthens the note of melancholy. The words "unobtrusive", "gradual", and "Custom" are counterpointed to "pathetic" and "pensive" as representing something more neutral and non-emotive; they help to control the expression of the emotion which the crickets' sounds evoke in the listener. Thus we are imperceptibly being prepared for a disclosure of the observer's response to the scene. In spite of this, we are startled by the nakedness and directness of the word "Loneliness" which appears exactly in the middle of the poem—it alone in the second stanza being an Anglo-Saxon noun among naturalized or Latinate words.

The words "gradual" and "Custom" which both relate to time lead up to "antiquest". This Dickinsonian superlative creates a problem for the explicator. What is its antecedent? Mass? Grace? or Loneliness? In the longer version of this poem Emily Dickinson writes "'Tis audibler at dusk"; she is apparently referring to the Mass. Since in the semi-final draft of the shorter version she first wrote "Antiquer", one might reasonably conclude that at least in its original form this word applied to the sounds heard. Elsewhere the poet links crickets to the concept of the ancient: "The Cricket spoke so clear / Presumption was–His Ancestors / Inherited the Floor–" [a variant of **"As imperceptibly as Grief"**]. In the final version of **"Further in Summer than the Birds",** the original reference may have become subsumed in the relation to the more emotionally charged and more immediate word "Loneliness". It is likely that in its vague reference "antiquest"—meaning "most ancient" or what we would call "most archetypal"—ties together the Mass, that is, the *cause* of the observer's thoughts and emotions; the Grace, which is the *influence* on the listener of the sounds overheard; and the Loneliness, which is the *result* of this influence.

"Noon", that is, the height of the day which in Dickinson's imagery stands for glory and fullfillment, contrasts (in what I would call a "slant" contrast) with the other time reference in the third stanza: "August burning low"; she uses the image of the candle or the lamp to indicate the time of year. These opposites crystallize the paradox of that moment when nature's beauty at its peak is about to fall off. Grammatical analysis will clarify the syntax of this stanza and the next. Inversion, ellipsis, and parenthesis obscure the structure and the meaning. The following would be a possible prose version: "It [The Loneliness?] is felt to be most antique at noon when—August burning low [i.e. nearing its end]—this spectral canticle arises, typifying repose. As yet no grace has been remitted [i.e. no wrinkle mars the smoothness and brightness of the face of nature]." ("Grace" is used in its aesthetic sense as a contrast to ugliness and imperfection also in [**"'Tis Opposites–entice"**]: "Deformed Men—ponder Grace—". "Glow" also represents life, as in [**"Praise it–'tis dead"**]: "Praise it–'tis dead– / It cannot glow–".)

In the final lines "Druidic" is the last link in the religious vocabulary. In it ends also the line from "antiquest" as a concept connected to a Pre-Christian period. It echoes the intangible and the mysterious, represented by the statement that "No Ordinance be seen", by the words "gradual Grace", and the adjectives "pensive" and "spectral". "Enhances", finally, looks back to "enlarging" of similar meaning, one referring to the beauty of nature, the other to the emotion that is caused in the human observer by the processes of nature.

The subject of this poem is easily stated; its theme and meaning are more elusive. In fact, its theme seems not one, but rather a complex of ideas. The metaphor of the mass and the references to loneliness have to be closely scrutinized to yield a maximum of meaning. What sort of mass is being celebrated? and why the loneliness? loneliness for what or whom? Richard Chase, who has given us some profound observations on this poem and the complex of ideas it represents [see Additional Bibliography], thinks that the mass is a requiem. I interpret it in a similar way, and I find support for this explication especially in the third stanza. A *canticle* is, according to the dictionary (*Webster*), specifically one of the biblical hymns or songs of praise used in church services. One of these is the *Nunc Dimittis* which begins with the words of Simeon, "Lord, now lettest thou thy servant depart in peace." The connotation of a death mass is reinforced by the following *repose* which means repose in the grave. The canticle *typifies*, that is, foreshadows death. An element of prophesying links the words "Canticle" and "typify" to the epithet "Druidic". It is the Druid as soothsayer that is preeminent in the idea of the "Druidic" change that is imminent. The Pre-Christian religion may also be more closely associated with nature than is Christianity. Elsewhere [**"The murmuring of Bees, has ceased"**] the poet uses the word "prophetic" of some insects which presumably are crickets. In her wisdom, this poem says, nature sends "Appropriate Creatures" to announce her every change; she sends the cricket to prophesy about winter, the death of beauty and life.

Emily Dickinson seems to have been acutely sensitive to nature as something to be enjoyed and as an emblem of life and death. She testifies to this sensitivity in a letter to Higginson (June 7, 1862) [see excerpt above]. She is speaking of her friend Benjamin Newton's death and of how her poetry is a relief to her:

> And when far afterward–a sudden light on Orchards,
> or a new fashion in the wind troubled my attention–
> I felt a palsy, here–the Verses just relieve–

She feels a palsy this time; at another time what she experiences may be a feeling of loneliness. This loneliness is no doubt a sense of isolation: she observes nature, but is not permitted to participate in its processes or commune with it. Nature is indifferent to man: "Summer does not care", she says in another poem [**"Summer–we all have seen"**]. It is also a sense of bereavement through death [**"I hide myself within my flower"** and **"Could that sweet Darkness where they dwell"**]. Paradoxically loneliness may enrich the one who feels it [**"There is another Loneliness"**].

In **"Further in Summer than the Birds"** Emily Dickinson does not commit herself as to the question of immortality. Death is referred to with ambivalence: *grace—antiquest—repose,* these words have no ugly or disagreeable connotations in the context of the poem. Still the new state which is imminent will involve a diminution of beauty, there will be furrows on the glow. The paradox is that the premonition of repose—a desirable state—makes us sorrowful and lonely. God is notably absent in the poem. We are indirectly reminded of His existence through the religious diction and imagery; but the poem's human observer does not commune with Him. Emily Dickinson was evidently aware that her poem expressed no hope of immortality, for in a letter accompanying the 1883 copy she writes: "I bring you a chill Gift–. . ."

There remains to be commented on the word "Grace" as it is used in this poem about the influence of the crickets' song upon the listener. Being part of the metaphor of the mass, it conveys a sense of divine influence acting in man to purify him and make him morally strong. In my reading, this word takes on the meaning of *insight* and *wisdom.* It is an insight into the processes that nature and man undergo; and it discloses to us our plight as being isolated from both nature and God. In the poem **"The Crickets sang",** the speaker recalls that moment of a late-summer evening when the crickets' song revealed to her "A Wisdom, without Face, or Name". In **"Further in Summer than the Birds"** the poet attempts to express an insight won that has no name, that is inexpressible in ordinary terms. But it can be conveyed, indeed it *has* been conveyed to us as imperceptibly as the grace spoken of in the poem. Emily Dickinson has successfully made her raid on the inarticulate. (pp. 261-68)

Brita Lindberg-Seyersted, in her The Voice of the Poet: Aspects of Style in the Poetry of Emily Dickinson, *Cambridge, Mass.: Harvard University Press, 1968, 290 p.*

ADRIENNE RICH (essay date 1976)

[Rich expresses her personal interest in Dickinson's life and poetry and examines "My life had stood—a Loaded Gun." For further commentary by Rich, see poem dated 1965.]

I am travelling at the speed of time, along the Massachusetts Turnpike. For months, for years, for most of my life, I have been hovering like an insect against the screens of an existence which inhabited Amherst, Massachusetts, between 1831 and 1884. The methods, the exclusions, of Emily Dickinson's existence could not have been my own; yet more and more, as a woman poet finding my own methods, I have come to understand her necessities, could have been witness in her defense.

"Home is not where the heart is," she wrote in a letter, "but the house and the adjacent buildings." A statement of New England realism, a directive to be followed. Probably no poet ever lived so much and so purposefully in one house; even, in one room. Her niece Martha told of visiting her in her corner bedroom on the second floor at 280 Main Street, Amherst, and of how Emily Dickinson made as if to lock the door with an imaginary key, turned and said: "Matty: here's freedom."

I am travelling at the speed of time, in the direction of the house and buildings.

Western Massachusetts: the Connecticut Valley: a countryside still full of reverberations: scene of Indian uprisings, religious revivals, spiritual confrontations, the blazing-up of the lunatic fringe of the Puritan coal. How peaceful and how threatened it looks from Route 91, hills gently curled above the plain, the tobacco-barns standing in fields sheltered with white gauze from the sun, and the sudden urban sprawl: ARCO, MacDonald's, shopping plazas. The country that broke the heart of Jonathan Edwards, that enclosed the genius of Emily Dickinson. It lies calmly in the light of May, cloudy skies breaking into warm sunshine, light-green spring softening the hills, dogwood and wild fruit-trees blossoming in the hollows. (p. 50)

For years I have been not so much envisioning Emily Dickinson as trying to visit, to enter her mind, through her poems and letters, and through my own intimations of what it could have meant to be one of the two mid-19th-century American geniuses, and a woman, living in Amherst, Massachusetts. Of the other genius, Walt Whitman, Dickinson wrote that she had heard his poems were "disgraceful." She knew her own were unacceptable by her world's standards of poetic convention, and of what was appropriate, in particular, for a woman poet. Seven were published in her lifetime, all edited by other hands; more than a thousand were laid away in her bedroom chest, to be discovered after her death. When her sister discovered them, there were decades of struggle over the manuscripts, the manner of their presentation to the world, their suitability for publication, the poet's own final intentions. Narrowed-down by her early editors and anthologists, reduced to quaintness or spinsterish oddity by many of her commentators, sentimentalized, fallen-in-love with like some gnomic Garbo, still unread in the breadth and depth of her full range of work, she was, and is, a wonder to me when I try to imagine myself into that mind.

I have a notion that genius knows itself; that Dickinson chose her seclusion, knowing she was exceptional and knowing what she needed. It was, moreover, no hermetic retreat, but a seclusion which included a wide range of people, of reading and correspondence. Her sister Vinnie said, "Emily is always looking for the rewarding person." And she found, at various periods, both women and men: her sister-in-law Susan Gilbert, Amherst visitors and family friends such as Benjamin Newton, Charles Wadsworth, Samuel Bowles, editor of the Springfield *Republican* and his wife; her friends Kate Anthon and Helen Hunt Jackson, the distant but significant figures of Elizabeth Barrett, the Brontës, George Eliot. But she carefully selected her society and controlled the disposal of her time. Not only the "gentlewoman in plush" of Amherst were excluded; Emerson visited next door but she did not go to meet him; she did not travel or receive routine visits; she avoided strangers. Given her vocation, she was neither eccentric nor quaint; she was determined to survive, to use her powers, to practice necessary economies.

Suppose Jonathan Edwards had been born a woman; suppose William James, for that matter, had been born a woman? (The invalid seclusion of his sister Alice is suggestive.) Even from men, New England took its psychic toll; many of its geniuses seemed peculiar in one way or another, particularly along the lines of social intercourse. Hawthorne, until he married, took his meals in his bedroom, apart from the family. Thoreau insisted on the values both of solitude and of geographical restriction, boasting that "I have travelled much in Concord." Emily Dickinson—viewed by her bemused contemporary Thomas Higginson as "partially cracked," by the 20th century as fey or pathological—has increasingly struck me as a practical woman, exercising her gift as she had to, making choices. I have come to imagine her as somehow too strong for her environment, a figure of powerful will, not at all frail or breathless, someone whose personal dimensions would be felt in a household. She was her father's favorite daughter though she professed being afraid of him. Her sister dedicated herself to the everyday domestic labors which would free Dickinson to write. (Dickinson herself baked the bread, made jellies and gingerbread, nursed her mother through a long illness, was a skilled horticulturalist who grew pomegranates, calla-lilies, and other exotica in her New England greenhouse.)

Upstairs at last: I stand in the room which for Emily Dickinson was "freedom." The best bedroom in the house, a corner room, sunny, overlooking the main street of Amherst in front, the way to her brother Austin's house on the side. Here, at a small table with one drawer, she wrote most of her poems. Here she read Elizabeth Barrett's *Aurora Leigh,* a woman poet's narrative poem of a woman poet's life; also George Eliot; Emerson; Carlyle; Shakespeare; Charlotte and Emily Brontë. Here I become, again, an insect, vibrating at the frames of windows, clinging to panes of glass, trying to connect. The scent here is very powerful. Here in this white-curtained, high-ceilinged room, a redhaired woman with hazel eyes and a contralto voice wrote poems about volcanoes, deserts, eternity, suicide, physical passion, wild beasts, rape, power, madness, separation, the daemon, the grave. Here, with a darning-needle, she bound these poems—heavily emended and often in variant versions—into booklets, secured with darning-thread, to be found and read after her death. Here she knew "freedom," listening from above-stairs to a visitor's piano-playing, escaping from the pantry where she was mistress of the household bread and puddings, watching, you feel, watching ceaselessly, the life of sober Main Street below. From this room she glided downstairs, her hand on the polished bannister, to meet the complacent magazine editor, Thomas Higginson, unnerve him while claiming she herself was unnerved. "Your scholar," she signed herself in letters to him. But she was an independent scholar, used his criticism selectively, saw him rarely and always on *her* premises. It was a life deliberately organized on her terms. The terms she had been handed by society—Calvinist Protestantism, Romanticism, the 19th-century corseting of women's bodies, choices, and sexuality—could spell insanity to a woman genius. What this one had to do was retranslate her own unorthodox, subversive, sometimes volcanic propensities into a dialect called metaphor: her native language. "Tell all the Truth—but tell it Slant—." It is always what is under pressure in us, especially under pressure of concealment—that explodes in poetry. (pp. 51-3)

[Who,] if you read through the seventeen hundred and seventy-five poems—who—woman or man—could have passed through that imagination and not come out transmuted? Given the space created by her in that corner room, with its window-light, its potted plants and work-table, given that personality, capable of imposing its terms on a household, on a whole community, what single theory could hope to contain her, when she'd put it all together in that space?

"Matty: here's freedom," I hear her saying as I speed back to Boston along Route 91, as I slip the turnpike ticket into the toll-collector's hand. I am thinking of a confined space in which the genius of the 19th-century female mind in America moved, inventing a language more varied, more compressed, more dense with implications, more complex of syntax, than any American poetic language to date; in the trail of that genius my mind has been moving, and with its language and images my mind still has to reckon, as the mind of a woman poet in America today. (p. 55)

Most of us, unfortunately, have been exposed in the schoolroom to Dickinson's "little-girl" poems, her kittenish tones, as in **"I'm Nobody! Who Are You?"** (a poem whose underlying anger translates itself into archness) or

> I hope the Father in the skies
> Will lift his little girl—
> Old fashioned—naughty—everything—
> Over the stile of "Pearl."
>
> **["'Arcturus' is his other name"]**

or the poems about bees and robins. One critic—Richard Chase—has noted that in the 19th century "one of the careers open to women was perpetual childhood" [see Additional Bibliography]. A strain in Dickinson's letters and some—though by far a minority—of her poems was a self-diminutization, almost as if to offset and deny—or even disguise—her actual dimensions as she must have experienced them. And this emphasis on her own "littleness," along with the deliberate strangeness of her tactics of seclusion, have been, until recently, accepted as the prevailing character of the poet: the fragile poetess in white, sending flowers and poems by messenger to unseen friends, letting down baskets of gingerbread to the neighborhood children from her bedroom window; writing, but somehow naively. John Crowe Ransom, arguing for the editing and standardization of Dickinson's punctuation and typography, calls her "a little home-keeping person" who, "while she had a proper notion of the final destiny of her poems . . . was not one of those poets who had advanced to that later stage of operations where manuscripts are prepared for the printer, and the poet's diction has to make concessions to the publisher's style-book" [see Additional Bibliography]. (In short, Emily Dickinson did not wholly know her trade, and Ransom believes a "publisher's style-book" to have the last word on poetic diction.) He goes on to print several of her poems, altered by him "with all possible forbearance." What might, in a male writer—a Thoreau, let us say, or a Christopher Smart or William Blake—seem a legitimate strangeness, a unique intention, has been in one of our two major poets devalued into a kind of naivêté, girlish ignorance, feminine lack of professionalism, just as the poet herself has been made into a sentimental object. ("Most of us are half in love with this dead girl," confesses Archibald MacLeish [see Additional Bibliography]. Dickinson was fifty-five when she died.)

It is true that more recent critics, including her most recent biographer, have gradually begun to approach the poet in terms of her greatness rather than her littleness, the decisiveness of her choices instead of the surface oddities of her life or the romantic crises of her legend. But unfortunately anthologists continue to plagiarize other anthologies, to reprint her in edited, even bowdlerized versions; the popular image of her and of her work lags behind the changing consciousness of scholars and specialists. There still does not exist a selection from her poems which depicts her in her fullest range. Dickinson's greatness cannot be measured in terms of twenty-five or fifty or even 500 "perfect" lyrics, it has to be seen as the accumulation it is. Poets, even, are not always acquainted with the full dimensions of her work, or the sense one gets, reading in the one-volume complete edition (let alone the three-volume variorum edition) of a mind engaged in a lifetime's musing on essential problems of language, identity, separation, relationship, the integrity of the self; a mind capable of describing psychological states more accurately than any poet except Shakespeare. I have been surprised at how narrowly her work, still, is known by women who are writing poetry, how much her legend has gotten in the way of her being re-possessed, as a source and a foremother.

I know that for me, reading her poems as a child and then as a young girl already seriously writing poetry, she was a problematic figure. I first read her in the selection heavily edited by her niece which appeared in 1937; a later and fuller edition appeared in 1945 when I was sixteen, and the complete, unbowdlerized edition by Johnson did not appear until fifteen years later. The publication of each of these editions was crucial to me in successive decades of my life. More than any other poet, Emily Dickinson seemed to tell me that the intense inner event, the personal and psychological, was inseparable from the universal; that there was a range for psychological poetry beyond mere self-expression. Yet the legend of the life was troubling, because it seemed to whisper that a woman who undertook such explorations must pay with renunciation, isolation, and incorporeality. With the publication of the ***Complete Poems,*** the legend seemed to recede into unimportance beside the unquestionable power and importance of the mind revealed there. But taking possession of Emily Dickinson is still no simple matter. (pp. 58-60)

There is one poem which is the real "onlie begetter" of my thoughts here about Dickinson; a poem I have mused over, repeated to myself, taken into myself over many years. I think it is a poem about possession by the daemon, about the dangers and risks of such possession if you are a woman, about the knowledge that power in a woman can seem destructive, and that you cannot live without the daemon once it has possessed you. The archetype of the daemon as masculine is beginning to change, but it has been real for women up until now. But this woman poet also perceives herself as a lethal weapon:

> My life had stood—a Loaded Gun—
> In Corners—till a Day
> The Owner passed—identified—
> And carried me away—
>
> And now We Roam in Sovereign Woods—
> And now We hunt the Doe—
> And every time I speak for Him—
> The Mountains straight reply—
>
> And do I smile, such cordial light
> Upon the Valley glow—
> It is as a Vesuvian face
> Had let its pleasure through—
>
> And when at Night—our good Day done—
> I guard My Master's Head—
> 'Tis better than the Eider-Duck's
> Deep Pillow—to have shared—
>
> To foe of His—I'm deadly foe—
> None stir the second time—
> On whom I lay a Yellow Eye—
> Or an emphatic Thumb—
>
> Though I than he—may longer live
> He longer must—than I—
> For I have but the power to kill,
> Without—the power to die—
>
> **["My life had stood—a Loaded Gun"]**

Here the poet sees herself as split, not between anything so simple as "masculine" and "feminine" identity but between the hunter, admittedly masculine, but also a human person, an active, willing being, and the gun—an object, condemned to remain inactive until the hunter—the *owner*—takes possession of it. The gun contains an energy capable of rousing echoes in the mountains and lighting up the valleys; it is also deadly,

"Vesuvian;" it is also its owner's defender against the "foe." It is the gun, furthermore, who *speaks for him*. If there is a female consciousness in this poem it is buried deeper than the images: it exists in the ambivalence toward power, which is extreme. Active willing and creation in women are forms of aggression, and aggression is both "the power to kill" and punishable by death. The union of gun with hunter embodies the danger of identifying and taking hold of her forces, not least that in so doing she risks defining herself—and being defined—as aggressive, as unwomanly, ("and now we hunt the Doe") and as potentially lethal. That which she experiences in herself as energy and potency can also be experienced as pure destruction. The final stanza, with its precarious balance of phrasing, seems a desperate attempt to resolve the ambivalence; but, I think, it is no resolution, only a further extension of ambivalence.

> Though I than he—may longer live
> He longer must—than I—
> For I have but the power to kill,
> Without—the power to die—

The poet experiences herself as loaded gun, imperious energy; yet without the Owner, the possessor, she is merely lethal. Should that possession abandon her—but the thought is unthinkable: "He longer *must* than I." The pronoun is masculine; the antecedent is what Keats called "The Genius of Poetry."

I do not pretend to have—I don't even wish to have—explained this poem, accounted for its every image; it will reverberate with new tones long after my words about it have ceased to matter. But I think that for us, at this time, it is a central poem in understanding Emily Dickinson, and ourselves, and the condition of the woman artist, particularly in the 19th century. (pp. 64-6)

Adrienne Rich, "Vesuvius at Home: The Power of Emily Dickinson," in Parnassus: Poetry in Review, *Vol. 5, No. 1, Fall-Winter, 1976, pp. 49-74.*

LOUIS AUCHINCLOSS (essay date 1979)

[An American man of letters, Auchincloss is known primarily as the author of novels of manners in the tradition of Edith Wharton and C. P. Snow. He is also a respected critic who has written major critical studies of such authors as Henry James, Ellen Glasgow, Henry Adams, and Wharton. In this excerpt, Auchincloss discusses Dickinson's attitude toward the publication of her poems, as well as her limited readership and conception of her audience.]

Many aspects of Emily Dickinson's life have fascinated her readers of our era, but none more than her reluctance to publish her poetry. As her fame continues to rise and our own personal reticences to diminish, this reluctance strikes us as more and more curious. In an age when reports of the stools of ill presidents are subject to national scrutiny, when noted public figures discuss their sex lives on television, when it is no shame to admit publicly one's alcoholism or drug addiction, the refusal of a writer to share with us her lyrics on such general subjects as death, immortality, and love seems bizarre, to say the least.

But writers have not always felt it necessary to communicate beyond the limit of those whom they could see or hear. Homer, we may surmise, was satisfied to recite his epics. Shakespeare produced his plays and acted in them, but, so far as we can tell, he was printed in his liftime only in pirated quartos or in order to forestall pirated quartos. John Donne was content to hand copies of his verses to friends. Nearer to our own day, Gerard Manley Hopkins sought only the opinion of a few selected friends as to the merits of his poetry.

Emily Dickinson, contrary to a popular impression, was not content to write verses for herself alone. As soon as she had written a poem that she thought had merit she needed to have it read. She wanted it to be seen by a member of the small appreciative circle of her family and close friends. Several hundred poems were thus transmitted in letters. Her trust was justified by the care with which these were kept. She lived in an age when people kept letters. *That*, to her, was publication enough.

Nonetheless, many critics have believed that she was desperately frustrated, that she was held back from publishing by shyness, fear of failure, dread of exposure, or possibly simply by the negative attitude of Thomas Wentworth Higginson. Yet there is no evidence in her letters of such frustration. Never does she give expression to any violent feeling, any professed horror at the idea of publicity, such as one might expect from a person racked between lust for fame and fear of the limelight. Even when a poem of hers actually appeared in a paper or book, submitted by a friend or correspondent, with or even perhaps without her permission, she did not demonstrate the least distress. Her attitude seems to have been more one of indifference, or even of tranquil disdain. She writes to Louise Norcross in 1872 about a Miss Phelps who begged her to publish:

> She wrote me in October, requesting me to aid the world by my chirrup more. Perhaps she stated it as my duty, I don't distinctly remember, and always burn such letters, so I cannot obtain it now. I replied declining.

Of course, she may not have always felt this way. A decade earlier she had written to her sister-in-law, Sue, to thank her for praising a poem. She added:

> Could I make you and Austin—proud—sometime—
> a great way off—'twould give me taller feet.

This would seem to imply at least a vague prognostication of literary renown, presumably through the press. And not long afterward she wrote her famous letter of April 15, 1862, to Higginson, enclosing four poems and asking him if they "breathed." When he advised her not to be in a hurry to publish, she protested that the idea was as foreign to her thought "as firmament to fin," but one wonders, had he answered more warmly, begging permission to print one or all of the four in the *Atlantic Monthly*, if she would have refused. When an author writes to a famous editor out of the blue, there must be at least a consideration of the possibility of being printed. But even this does not mean that publication was important to Emily Dickinson. It was at the most, I submit, an idea with which she toyed and which Higginson's qualified admiration helped to quash under her more characteristic diffidence. Only a year later her attitude was less equivocal, as expressed in her best known statement on the subject:

> Publication—is the Auction
> Of the Mind of Man—
> Poverty—be justifying
> For so foul a thing.

Some critics have argued that she may have distinguished here between *giving* her poems to the public and selling them, but I see nothing in this. Even if she had given a poem to Higginson, he would still have sold it. What she calls the "disgrace of price" would have equally marked the transaction.

In later years Emily Dickinson became firm enough in her attitude to resist even the strongest appeals to publish of her friend Helen Hunt Jackson. She made only one exception, when she gave Mrs. Jackson **"Success is Counted Sweetest"** for an anthology. But that she was more indifferent to the press than hostile or fearful is borne out by the fact that she did not bother to protest the liberties taken by the editor in the final version of the poem.

Confining her audience to a small group was perfectly consistent with the self-imposed limitations of Emily Dickinson's life. She reacted so intensely to experiences that she could afford few beyond those offered by her immediate environment. She had always to be eliminating persons and places. First, Massachusetts was too big; then Amherst; finally her house and garden were world enough. A handful of friends sufficed for her heart; a handful of readers for her poems. It was not so much that she shrank from life as that a small piece of it provided her perfervid imagination with what it would take a world tour—or a world war—to do for cruder souls.

It was probably difficult for Emily Dickinson even to imagine a reading public. The outside world of men and women had little meaning to her. In the same way it was difficult for her to take in the very existence of the Civil War. "When did the war really begin?" she ends a letter in 1861. She tries to put it out of mind: "I shall have no winter this year on account of the soldiers. Since I cannot weave blankets or boots I thought it best to omit the season." The references to the conflict in the next four years are scanty indeed, and one of them sounds almost callous: "A soldier called a morning ago and asked for a nosegay to take to battle. I suppose he thought we kept an aquarium." But as soon as someone she knew was killed, all the horror of war burst in on her unbearably. She deeply grieved for Frazer Stearns, "his big heart shot away by a minie ball," and sent an anguished appeal to her Norcross cousins: "Let us love better, children, it's most that's left to do."

There was great economy in Emily Dickinson's emotional life. A few deaths could make a war; a few flowers and a robin, a spring. By her own lights, she *did* publish. If her reputation today rested only on the poems sent to the Norcross sisters, Dr. and Mrs. Holland, the Bowleses, Sister Sue, and Higginson, it would still be secure. If her "neighbor" could be her "menagerie," these friends could be her public.

Living in an age of more vulgar satisfactions, I cannot help finding something attractive in Emily Dickinson's contentment with an intimate audience. There is to me an appealing humility in her concept of poetry as the product of two persons: the poet and the reader. As she writes to Louise Norcross,

> It's a great thing to be "great," Loo, and you and I tug for a life, and never accomplish it, but no one can stop our looking on, and you know some cannot sing, but the orchard is full of birds, and we all can listen. What if we learn, ourselves, some day?

Even beyond the idea that poetry exists in communication to a sympathetic listener is the idea that it may exist by itself alone, like the joy that can never be in vain because it "adds to some bright total whose dwelling is unknown." Emily Dickinson, who had said that she must sing because she could not pray, came to compare herself with a bird that was indistinguishable from its own song:

> I found a bird this morning, down—down—on a little bush at the foot of the garden, and wherefore sing, I said, since nobody *hears?* One sob in the throat, one flutter of bosom—"*My* business is to *sing*"—and away she rose! How do I know but cherubim, once, themselves, as patient, listened and applauded her unnoticed hymn?

This mystic sense of her own identification with the universe intensified with age. Living and poetry to her were increasingly intertwined, so that it may not be an exaggeration to say that her life was poetry. Less and less did she need the support of family and friends. She cared more for the dead than the living, more for the absent than for those nearby. Her mother, with whom she had never been close, became a saint in the grave, and she was capable of refusing to see friends when they called and then writing them letters to say how much she missed them.

The letters themselves, indeed, now become bits of poems or introductions to poems. Emily writes to Mrs. Holland, "I must show you a bee that is eating a lilac at the window. There—there—he is gone!" And then she breaks into:

> Bees are Black, with Gilt Surcingles—
> Buccaneers of Buzz.
> Ride abroad in ostentation
> And subsist on Fuzz.

Safe in their Alabaster Chambers -
Untouched by Morning.
And untouched by Noon -
Sleep the meek members of the Resurrection.
Rafter of Satin - and
Roof of Stone -

Grand go the Years
In the Crescent - above them -
Worlds scoop their Arcs.
And Firmaments - row -
Diadems - drop -
And Doges - surrender -
Soundless as Dots,
On a Disc of Snow.

E. Dickinson

A manuscript copy of "Safe in Their Alabaster Chambers," in Dickinson's hand.

Reading these letters, one can feel some of the relief of the artist as she casts off the prose integument and explodes into verse. Here is a prose letter to the Norcrosses which I have arranged in verse lines, adding, in brackets, one article that the rhythm seems to demand:

Affection is like bread,
Unnoticed till we starve.
And then we dream of it
And sing of it
And paint it,
When every urchin in the street
Has more than he can eat.
We turn not older with [the] years
But newer every day.

It was a lonely life in the end, but the compensations must have been considerable. Emily Dickinson became her own oeuvre. (pp. 31-7)

Louis Auchincloss, "Emily Dickinson: The Private Publication," in his Life, Law and Letters: Essays and Sketches, *Houghton Mifflin Company, 1979, pp. 31-7.*

SHARON CAMERON (essay date 1979)

[In this excerpt from the introduction to her highly respected Lyric Time: Dickinson and the Limits of Genre, *Cameron explores Dickinson's conceptions of time and immortality.]*

"There is no first, or last, in Forever—," Emily Dickinson wrote to her sister-in-law, Susan Gilbert Dickinson, in 1864, "It is Centre, there, all the time—," and, in the same year, to the man to whom she was serving such a bizarre literary apprenticeship, Thomas Wentworth Higginson, "The only News I know / Is Bulletins all day / From Immortality." However self-conscious the remarks may be, they effectively draw our attention to a central feature of Dickinson's poetry—its resolute departure from temporal order and its reference to another absent or invisible order that is invoked as "Immortality" or alluded to, in this case, as "Centre." It is hardly surprising that Dickinson's language teases conception, exempting itself as it does from the necessity of acknowledging beginnings and ends and the points that intervene between the two; these are temporal relationships renounced as inferior to the conceptual harmony specified by the permanence of immortality and the promised completion of a center. For underneath words and syntax, at the primary level of thought, we sense Dickinson's belief that to adhere to the exactions of temporal relationship is to relinquish all hope of the immmortality that will replace time itself. Nonetheless it remains a paradox that Dickinson's utterances fragment, word cut from word, stanza from stanza, as a direct consequence of her desire for that temporal completion which will fuse all separations into the healing of a unified whole.

Interestingly enough, she conceives of immortality not as morning but as "noon," and if we investigate the many times the word appears in her poetry, we realize that it implies not only noon, but noon in the middle of summer, not only summer but a summer light whose intensity dazzles to blindness, its glare burning away all but vision of itself. Thus "noon," alchemized into light, comes consistently to stand for the clockless escape from time that would liberate into the longed-for permanence. The pull between time and immortality charges Dickinson's poems. Once she polarized it as follows:

Some—Work for Immortality—
The Chiefer part, for Time—
He—Compensates—immediately—
The former—Checks—on Fame—

Slow Gold—but Everlasting—
The Bullion of Today—
Contrasted with the Currency
Of Immortality—

A Beggar—Here and There—
Is gifted to discern
Beyond the Broker's insight—
One's—Money—One's—the Mine—

In the imperative world of Dickinson's poems, immortality exists because its absence would be intolerable. There is frequently in the poems a time not present that haunts the present as it haunts the speakers' minds, confusing its dominance in memory or dream with a prediction about the future, mistaking itself for prophecy. The present, then, the "time" of Dickinson's poems, is overwhelmed by the promise of another, more satisfactory, order that will destroy time altogether, replace it by "Slow Gold—but Everlasting—," and this belief in that impossible future is strengthened in direct proportion to how deeply a given speaker is mired in the characteristic deprivations of experience. For many of Dickinson's speakers the world is a landslide of lost things, and their imagining of a future, rectifying providence lurks beneath the surface of the speech, as tenacious a conception as it is a wordless one. Silence serves illusion in such instances, for the dream that revenges itself on an inadequate reality by giving to itself what it will never be given conceals the consolation it knows is not true.

The profound confusion of loss and immortality, in which the presence of one signifies the promise of the other, is permitted, even encouraged, by the way in which both are predicated on the transcendence of the body—in the case of loss, as the body is sacrificed to the outlines of memory; in the case of immortality, as the body is carved to the essence that underlies mortal appearance. In the sharing of the substitution (of spirit for body, image for form), temporal deprivation and immortal recompense are bound to each other by the negation at their center. For immortality as Dickinson dreams it into existence is not simply specified as permanence; it is also presence liberated from the mortal encumbrances of both flesh and language. In [**"Conscious am I in my chamber"**], immortality, personified as a bodiless visitor, assumes the prophetic shape of pure essence, and Dickinson's description of it seems to borrow from the central store of a phenomenalist vocabulary she could not possibly have known. "Presence—," she writes, "is his furthest license—." In [**"Of all the Souls that stand create"**], she scripts the presence in more personal terms:

Of all the Souls that stand create—
I have elected—One—
When Sense from Spirit—files away—
And Subterfuge—is done—
When that which is—and that which was—
Apart—intrinsic—stand—
And this brief Drama in the flesh—
Is shifted—like a Sand—
When Figures show their royal Front—
And Mists—are carved away,
Behold the Atom—I preferred—
To all the lists of Clay!

As the dream literalizes itself and takes shape, we see it has no shape at all, that it reduces human form to the essence of an "Atom—" that underlies it; elsewhere the flinging away of the body (in [**"If you were coming in the Fall"**] Dickinson had spoken of tossing it away "like a Rind") is feared as well as desired. After the death of Edward Dickinson, his daughter writes: "I dream about father every night . . . and forget what I am doing daytimes, wondering where he is. Without any body, I keep thinking. What kind can that be?" Yet however it puzzles conception, immortality purified of all but created soul is what Dickinson professes to want, and she sometimes appears to hoard the losses allotted to her, as if through the holes made by time and space immortality might be glimpsed. Implicit in the utterances on loss is the belief that immortality not only will replace an inadequate temporal scheme in the future that is promised by a traditional Christianity (this is the mathematics of recompense about which I just spoke), but also that it does replace temporality in the present, as the body is transcended in the phenomena of loss and immortality alike. It is no wonder that Dickinson retreated to her legendary solitude, for to people her world would have been to forfeit the identification between loss and immortality and to substitute in its stead the palpable forms that negated both. She did not do it. Her poems juxtapose time and immortality with the fervor of a hallucination, and, notwithstanding the simplification of any such statement, the juxtaposition might be said to underlie all the temporal perplexities that aggravate the poems and to create as well the great mirages that transform illusion into something we can only call art, the complex meditations on the terrible grief of dying.

"Tell all the Truth but tell it slant— / Success in Circuit lies," Dickinson writes in [**"Tell all the Truth but tell it slant"**], and the statement turns our attention to the implied synonymy between slantness and circuity, even though one is linear, coming at an angle, and the other curvilinear, working around a circumference. The illogical overlap between obliquity and circuity is a direct consequence of Dickinson's preoccupation with ineffable centerings. For however close the lens of a given poem comes to the subject of attention, to a center, its speaker perceives that subject shift out of the line of direct vision. To see from a perspective is to see at a slant, as the following poem indicates:

> The Angle of a Landscape—
> That every time I wake—
> Between my Curtain and the Wall—
> Upon an ample Crack—
>
> Like a Venetian—waiting—
> Accosts my open eye—
> Is just a Bough of Apples—
> Held slanting, in the Sky—
>
> [**"The Angle of a Landscape"**]

In the "Bough of Apples—" forming its own angle, the subject comes to light readily enough, however deceptively it appears on the wrong side of the horizon, but most poems are not so quick to distinguish the landscape from the linear displacements of the speaker's angle of vision. At a more subtle level of obliquity, entire landscapes can seem like indirect renderings of something larger of which they are a mere part. Landscapes are thus generally symbolic in the poems, bearers of more meaning than a given speaker can interpret (as in **"There's a certain Slant of light"**), or they are deficient of meaning, unable to rise to its occasion (as in **"A Light exists in Spring"**), and this excess or deficit indicates a profound discrepancy between the multitudinous lines of the world and the optics of a central vision that, more often than not, they may be accused of baffling. Thus the horizon, with which a fair number of Dickinson's poems are concerned, is an especially beguiling landscape, because the infinite transformations to which it is subject hint at an ultimate disclosure, the lurking of something behind the visible to which it will shortly give away.

To alter the metaphor, we can distinguish the lines of the characteristic Dickinson angle if we observe that it often brings time and immortality into direct proximity. The angle, then, is a comparative one, but the particular nature of the comparison raises problems: first, because since the immortal world cannot be seen, it must be specified in lieu of any concrete form, discerned in the shape of a formal absence; and second, just because we are at a loss to see the invisible half alluded to, the particularities of the temporal world, when it is invoked, can seem equally inscrutable and, sometimes for lack of any focusing comparative, even arbitrary. Dickinson seems to have the dilemma of an implied but unspecified second world in mind when she writes:

> A Spider sewed at Night
> Without a Light
> Upon an Arc of White.
>
> If Ruff it was of Dame
> Or Shroud of Gnome
> Himself himself inform.
>
> Of Immortality
> His Strategy
> Was Physiognomy.

Here the relationship between what is visible and what is not strains toward formulation in the last stanza, but the polysyllabic abstractions that link appearance, calculated effort, and an intimated other world cohere more as a consequence of verbal patterning (the like sound of words and their arrangement in a sequence suggestive of meaning) than of any demonstrated semantic connection. The poem advances an analogic relationship between "Physiognomy" and "Immortality"; the spider's "Arc of White" (the meaning of which cannot be discerned) is of a piece with the inscrutable web of "Immortality," but the confounding preposition *"Of"* which precedes "Immortality," backs away from the question of how (are the two connected by an identity of elements, by shared origin, or is the spider's unfathomable design a mere characteristic of "Immortality"?). Thus the fact of the relationship overtakes all single explanation of it, and the multiple possibilities hang between the two terms, a web of the poet's making. We might speculate that the form of the web is to the spider's conception of it ("Himself himself inform," as the poem puns) as the web is to immortality, and both the first and last terms of the analogy remain unspecified, for however close Dickinson comes to defining the relationship between the embodied world and the immortal one, she falls short of a satisfactory answer. "Not 'Revelation'—tis—that waits / But our unfurnished eyes—," she had written impatiently, and as if to jar vision from the modesty of its limitations, her poems spin out new attempts at defining the relationship, each time catching it at a different angle.

Sometimes the contrast between the embodied world and the immortal one assumes implicit temporal form, as in the following poem:

> A Bird came down the Walk—
> He did not know I saw—
> He bit an Angleworm in halves
> And ate the fellow, raw,

And then he drank a Dew
From a convenient Grass—
And then hopped sidewise to the Wall
To let a Beetle pass—

He glanced with rapid eyes
That hurried all around—
They looked like frightened Beads, I thought—
He stirred his Velvet Head

Like one in danger, Cautious,
I offered him a Crumb
And he unrolled his feathers
And rowed him softer home—

Than Oars divide the Ocean,
Too silver for a seam—
Or Butterflies, off Banks of Noon
Leap, plashless as they swim.

The discrete movements of the first stanzas, introduced by anaphora and rhythmically imitative of the rapid, uneven motions of the bird glimpsed close-up, give way to the sheer verb of flight, irreducible to singularity or sequence. Riding on the brilliance of Dickinson's similies for it, this latter, seamless movement suggests a further implied contrast between diachronic progression and the synchrony that surpasses it, between the mortal world which can be fathomed and the magical one which evades the understanding as it evades the eye. The second inscrutable world establishes its connection to the immortal one, first, because of the leap meaning takes off the metaphoric "Banks of Noon," which, even were this not Dickinson's temporal indication of immortality, would insist on an interpretation beyond all bounds of the finite, and second, because of the extravagant comparative ushered in by the one simile that does describe a finite reality: "And rowed him softer home— / Than Oars divide the Ocean, / Too silver for a seam—." The grammar makes it ambiguous whether it is the ocean that is seamless or the rowing, and the comparative statement poised between the possibilities insists that Dickinson intended this ambiguity, which imitates the indivisibility it talks about by refusing to allow us to separate the two ideas. In fact the poem exemplifies a typical pattern of development in a good number of Dickinson's utterances, as they linger on concrete, often trivial but entirely comprehensible phenomena, and then alter their focus in a tensile shift of the received lines into a shape that utterly perplexes them. Thus the question raised by **"A spider sewed at Night"** is now posed in the speaker's implicit query of the relationship between sequence and simultaneity, division and seamlessness.

In **"The Soul has Bandaged moments,"** temporal contrast is made explicit, formulated by the soul's transcendence of temporal division:

The soul has moments of Escape—
When bursting all the doors—
She dances like a Bomb, abroad,
And swings upon the Hours,

As do the Bee—delirious borne—
Long Dungeoned from his Rose—
Touch Liberty—then know no more,
But Noon, and Paradise—

and

The Soul's retaken moments—
When, Felon led along,
With shackles on the plumed feet,
And staples, in the Song,

[**"The Soul has Bandaged moments"**]

The contrast between liberty and bondage is measured best by two lines that emphasize its antiphonal strains despite the fact that they are not grammatically parallel: by "And swings upon the Hours," which, borne into motion by the preceding line, eases the speaker from one temporal unit to the next as dexterously as if the hours had become partners in the fluid dance of movement, and by "And staples, in the Song," which continues the metaphor of music by internalizing it as song and, in its most complex achievement, drives together through one word, "staples," the separate ideas of division and pain. Although the poem presents an ostensible contrast between "Dungeoned" moments and "moments of Escape—," it does so partially in order to uncover the underlying dialectic of time and its annihilation (the "deliri[um]" of immortality which is "Noon").

Many of Dickinson's poems are balanced on such a contrast; others lean toward one of its extremes. In the following poem, for example, which envisions a leavetaking of the known temporal world, abstraction invests utterance with the foreignness of the venture:

I saw no Way—The Heavens were stitched—
I felt the Columns close—
The Earth reversed her Hemispheres—
I touched the Universe—

And back it slid—and I alone—
A Speck upon a Ball—
Went out upon Circumference—
Beyond the Dip of Bell—

[**"I saw no Way—The Heavens were stitched"**]

How much language depends upon the conceptual ignorance that underlies it is immediately apparent if we think of the systematic conversion of everything known into a territorial blank. The dead-end of the poem's beginning, which closes the speaker off from heaven and then more dramatically turns the world inside out so that, almost expelled from it, she is left standing upon a mere rim, the "Circumference—" of the last lines, is one of the most drastic metaphors for exile Dickinson ever conceived, and the language is giddy with the speaker's disorientation. When Dickinson's poems go "Beyond the Dip of Bell—," as this one attempts to do, to excavate the territory that lies past the range of all phenomenal sense, they are haunted by the terrible space of the venture, as language is flung out into the reaches of the unknown in the apparent hope that it might civilize what it finds there. At the other extreme, the temporal particularities of the familiar world are observed at close range:

Bees are Black, with Gilt Surcingles—
Buccaneers of Buzz.
Ride abroad on ostentation
And subsist on Fuzz.

Fuzz ordained—not Fuzz contingent—
Marrows of the Hill.
Jugs—a Universe's fracture
Could not jar or spill.

[**"Bees are Black, with Gilt Surcingles"**]

Even here, however, in the last lines, the unexpected "Fuzz ordained—not Fuzz contingent—" rescues the bee from the triviality to which "Buccaneers of Buzz" had almost certainly doomed it. This is not so much metaphor as it is metaphysics when, from another world, the bee is invested with priest-like powers. Inversely, at the end of **"I saw no Way,"** the final image, "Beyond the Dip of Bell—," offers a concrete temporal sound (however it claims a departure "Beyond" it) to which we can anchor the preceding descriptions that might otherwise fail to survive abstraction.

As the contrast between **"I saw no Way—The Heavens were stitched"** and **"Bees are Black, with Gilt Surcingles"** indicates, Dickinson writes best about what she must conceptualize, and Archibald MacLeish states this fact succinctly when he observes that her images are "not always visible . . . nor are they images brought into focus by the muscles of the eye." When we recall some of the most typical Dickinson lines ("Pain—has an Element of Blank—" [**"Pain—has an Element of Blank"**], "A nearness to Tremendousness— / An Agony procures—" [**"A nearness to Tremendousness"**]), we note that these lines strain toward conceptual realization that will replace, as by an effort of mind, what is visible with depictions that more adequately represent the landscape of the mind. Sometimes the angle of a poem is formed by the disparity between the dimensions of the palpable world and those of a less circumscribed interior. So she writes: "Two Lengths has every Day— / Its absolute extent / And Area Superior / By Hope or Horror lent—" [**"Two Lengths has every Day"**]. Sometimes a poem is trained on the divergence of private and public value: "The Voice that stands for Floods to me / Is sterile borne to some—" [**"The Voice that stands for Floods to me"**]. . . . [The] poems that command the most interest are concerned with certain substitutions that relegate the visible world to the second place accorded it by the sharper demands of imagination and desire: the substitution of immortality for temporal progression, the remembered moment for the immediate one, presence for the language it has dispensed with. These poems address themselves to the world of absent things, to what is "Convenient to the longing / But otherwise withheld" [**"Through those old Grounds of memory"**], and as a consequence they often become problematic, for, as I have been asserting, when an absent world is alluded to, especially in a comparative circumstance, the angle of a poem's landscape is frequently difficult to ascertain. (pp. 1-10)

Sharon Cameron, in her Lyric Time: Dickinson and the Limits of Genre, *The Johns Hopkins University Press, 1979, 280 p.*

KARL KELLER (essay date 1983)

[*Keller, a noted Dickinson critic, discusses issues of gender crucial to understanding Dickinson's poetry.*]

Sleeping with Emily Dickinson, you discover a woman who loves words more than she loves *you*.

Emily Dickinson's **"Wild Nights—Wild Nights!"** are just in her head. They are just words in her head. And so the subjunctive:

Were I with thee
Wild Nights should be
Our luxury!

Her subjunctives give her away a great deal. They are a way she camps: discourse that plays with fantasy, that masks a masquerade, that is truthful about her desires but coyly honest that they are mere desires, elaborate pretense that is a convincing act, a lonely but attractive charade, her clowning. The wild nights do exist—*in the poetry*.

The poems on sleeping with someone are instructions, I believe, on how to "take" her. When she writes about wild nights, she is not only describing her ecstasy but also instructing us how to react to her, what to expect, what to get. She thus couples with the critic. She thus holds.

Imaginative penetration is the work of the Dickinson critic. But I think she intended interpenetration. The distinction is critical. Her distinction in this distinction is poetical.

"If anybody / Can the extasy define," Emily Dickinson says about sleeping with a man, it is to her "Half a transport—half a trouble." That's true of sleeping with her, too: "Half a transport—half a trouble." I think she was kidding. She would know the critic is not.

A man trying to write well about Emily Dickinson is an honest case of intellectual drag. The gender doesn't change, the role does. You must come off looking right, you are self-conscious, you dissemble. It is show biz.

Nothing funnier than a man telling how Emily Dickinson influenced him. "When I was a boy, I read Emily Dickinson and she . . ." The rest will trail off into the maudlin or the quaint or will be mildly fortifying. Quite different from seeing in her a sister-spirit, one who experienced what one does or oneself experiencing what she did, the experience crossing the miles and years and genders, creating out of her (knowing oneself) a precursor, or maybe a forerunner making a world in which one could be oneself. That's power.

Criticism, during the whole of Emily Dickinson's lifetime, was a male genre. Poetry also has gender. A woman—and Emily Dickinson is the best instance in American literature—can take liberties with the things of poetry-making. She is free to play, to tease, to violate, to not care, for she is an underdog, an outsider, an excrescence, an irrelevance, an erratic. The critic (male) will scan it for its adherence to regularity, its deviance from the expecter, its eccentricity, its freakishness. If Emily Dickinson "meant" to be the erratic, the freak, the myth, the "Kangaroo among the beauty," then the (male) scansion becomes the irrelevance. How summarily she then turns men into what they had made her! But only—of course—by equivocation; gender distinctions are accomplished only by equivocation. Emily Dickinson, more than most writing women I know before the mid-twentieth century, convinces one that the female is more then a gender, more in fact a separate species. Her anatomy determined her poetics. To know her, a man must perhaps study her nature more than that which nurtured her. Because of that, he can only cross over to her intellectually. He can only *imagine* her species and its aesthetics. She has her own side of the bed.

We are always saved
by judgment of good men

wrote Sappho, who, however, had never heard of such men as T. W. Higginson, Josiah Holland, Samuel Bowles, Thomas Niles, and others who knew Emily Dickinson's poetry and said, lying, that they wanted her. "Two . . . came to my Father's House, this winter—and asked me for my mind," she reported, ". . . [but] they would use it for the World." On the contrary, it was *women* who saved Emily Dickinson: Sue Dickinson, Lavinia Dickinson, Helen Jackson, Mabel Loomis Todd, Martha Bianchi. Women needing women, loving women, giving us women. It is an anomalous rescue, a touching one.

Aaron Copeland set twelve poems of Emily Dickinson's to music. But sopranos must sing them, never a man.

Emily Dickinson's anticipation of a male readership (her critics, not her cult) nears anxiety. She performs; they analyze.

When they perform the poetry, they near anxiety. She then becomes *their* critic.

I'm not sure language always has gender, but it has audience. Emily Dickinson was thoroughly conscious of her audience, but her great disaster was that she chose the wrong one—male critics: Higginson, Bowles, Holland, Newton, Niles, et al. She wanted into the marketplace, such as it was. It is one of her uglier desperations. Her language is so often shaped by what she hoped her audience would be that it can indeed be read by that audience now, an audience of male critics. Underneath all that is, however, somebody else.

Emily Dickinson had the advantage (seldom one for a woman in the 1860s and 1870s) of giving what *she* wanted to give. How simple an advantage!

This woman can tease a man. But though she goes far towards the really crazy, she never loses her inhibitions, for then there would be no imagination necessary, no lure. She pulls a man in.

How was Emily Dickinson to come close to the men she knew or wanted to know? *Poetry was not the way*. She tried it and no one responded. So why should she presume to get close to some of the rest of us? She may leave space for the male critic to come to her, but *he* must make the moves. She may move *for* him but seldom *toward* him.

"I was born bad and I never have recovered. Mine is a disgusting sex," said Alice James. She just said it straight out and she meant it. Emily Dickinson was always saying something like that, too, though not always meaning it. She could say it but it could be with irony that she could say it. Irony gave her two audiences: those who think she means what she says and those who take it facetiously. There is a family of those who are in on her, and there are those who aren't. Is there gender to this split? Are there those genders who get her code, her voice, her pose, and those genders who don't?

Surely she believed her own maxim: "Women talk; men are silent."

Emily Dickinson's is a raised voice. All poetry is hyperbole, of course, but Emily Dickinson deliberately raises her voice: it is what a woman must / can do to get the attention of men.

A case of a man doing Emily Dickinson wrong is William Luce's script for *The Belle of Amherst*. At one point Julie Harris says, plainly and plaintively (though still shouting), noting the teen-age dating in old Amherst: "I know what people say, 'Poor Emily—the only kangaroo among the beauties.'" What she *really* said (it is in a letter to T. W. Higginson in 1862) had to do with her pride in being an eccentric woman: "[I am] Myself the only Kangaroo among the Beauty" [see letter dated July 1862]. She was shouting.

Suortù: a woman defying her fate. Was that Emily Dickinson? I think she was really a heady version of that. I think she thought it was her fate to defy. A woman defying her fate is what a man would expect of a woman. A woman accepting her fate to defy means accepting one's nature, one's humanity, one's gender, one's difference, one's ability, oneself.

Imagining her audience to be male gave Emily Dickinson opportunity to play the deviant. Perhaps she could have played that among women, too, but she would not have had to be as brisk, as nasty, as coy, as teasing, as sure. These postures were created by the men in her mind.

There may have been men in her mind but, except for God, there are hardly any men to speak of in her poetry. Much of her poetry is poetry in which she wishes there were, or she fantasizes about there being, or she documents the absence of. But there are not really very many men. Yet a man can put himself there as reader quite easily. She created the space for someone to understand her, enclose her, love her—quite like all the white space around one of her poems. *She* created that white space, I think we have to believe. She lets one in lovingly.

God was Emily Dickinson's only real male test-case. And I think she knew she had the potency to drive him out, to displace him, to be sufficient. This cannot have been a satisfying position for her, however, unsure as she sometimes was that here was really anybody there to oppose her. She parleyed with this one man in her life. She made an uneasy alliance. She knew that only through a kind of treachery had he delivered up the world into her hands. She sought and found him but her own dark shadow was always larger than his white face. How did she take it: to be greater than the one man you would love? I guess God eventually learned to cling to her, being for her everywhere. He was probably delivered up into her hands. Any other man must be aware of putting himself in the same spot, the same advantage.

Emily Dickinson cannot find a center in (male-made) society, in (male-made) institutions, in her (male-made) home, and not even in the (male-made) universe. Only (perhaps, and then tentatively / tenuously) in herself—and even that isn't reliable. God is, for her, not at the center, not a hold on things, not a focus. Only herself—and she bests Emerson's betterment of the self by showing / doubting its inconsistency. It is not so much that as a woman she is free to be herself as that she is free to doubt herself. But at what a price!

Louise Bogan cutely speaks of Emily Dickinson as a cat trying to speak English. This is almost right. Better: she is a voice trying to hide the fact that she is a real cat. In many ways she is trying to hide the fact that she is a woman. But a *man* can know she is a woman, simply because she may be trying to hide the fact. A man (Proust, Emerson, and Hemingway, for different reasons, are distinct exceptions) would not think it necessary to artfully dissemble and to make the dissembling an art. On a man the genitals do show. A woman may use poetry for stuffing. This is not dishonest, just marketing-necessity. In a man this art would be a hoot. In a woman it is camp.

George Whicher speaks of Emily Dickinson as having eyes that did not focus in the same direction. This may be accurate ophthalmology but it is only a man's trite guess about the diversity in her art. She is shifty, not schizy.

Three large concepts encompass Emily Dickinson: Necessity, Desire, and Expectation. The first two were her own concern; men enter into her life only in the third one. The conformity to (or nodding toward) expectations does not necessarily produce male factors in the poetry but produces factors that men can know fairly well: forms and structures, the communicable vocabulary, common ideas, a philosophy. The erratic in her is something else: that is the female area of her freedom. But is it chauvinist to say so?

Does Emily Dickinson cower before her critics? Is there a lot of sycophancy? I think so. And it is not much fun to watch. She rises above such a (perhaps) necessary act when she falls apart, when she is experimenting, when she is unfinished. The poetry in that state is very much her own. I'm not sure she knew a man could get off on *that* in her.

Why there is so little elegance in Emily Dickinson may perplex a person—perplex a *man,* certainly, since that was, in Emily Dickinson's environment, one of the marks of obeisance a man expected of a woman. Maybe one of the qualities one expects of her now, too. But she will not go there, or not very often, conscious, I believe, of the expectation. Instead, she is deliberately (not carelessly) indecorous. Her determined genre is indecorum; her temptation the indecent. It is not womanly of her to seek this kind of speech, but it is certainly anti-manly—who are forced then to accept her, if they accept her at all, outside the stereotype. The crudeness therefore succeeds, like porn, as art. Elegance is a submission to a set of manners. Emily Dickinson's reference to them is for her quite enough; she did not need always to live them, certainly not when she sat down to make some world of her own in her poetry.

The power of the Tease. I don't think Emily Dickinson knew she had it, or at least didn't know it was a mode of writing, of reaching, of staying, of having without being had. Where in all of literature could she have found it? I think she came by it inadvertently. It was simply natural to her to draw people to what she said but leave them unsure of precisely what she had said. She was always a little cryptic, a little elliptical with people, in manner and in talk, for it gave them room between the brief moments of her awe and her desolation. Her roles—that is, her ploys and playfulness—tease because she makes them very attractive, but they are usually too brief to really *know:* she does not let herself be known well. The brief flirtation lets you know she is there; it doesn't let you know *who* is there. But the teasing is by no means dishonest, it is a defense. You place yourself in a scene (someone else's mind, someone else's life) on your own terms; you delight someone with your terms, by your terms, on your terms, even for your terms; but no one takes over or dares by presumptuousness lay claim or even enter in—unless they are *better*. The tease has to be good enough to make sure they aren't/don't/can't. Emily Dickinson made sure by ellipsis, dodge, a vague daring, an evident superiority of language and idea, staying virtually unknown behind the flash. The lure is alluring and also a little cruel. The tease—spidery—attracts, overwhelms, and then abandons. She wins you and then will not have you even when she needs you. You are on your own, happy victim, with the lovely web, the poem. The lovely web will not fall of your weight, you will try to figure out the intricacy of it, and you will wonder where she went—or did she, dear critic/victim/lover, become the web itself? It's what you have of her, for she has really gone on to flirt elsewhere. The tease won; *you* won. She staged all that. Such a woman!

"The difficulty is my inability to assume the receptive attitude," Alice James wrote to her brother William, "that cardinal virtue in women, the absence of which has always made me so uncharming to & uncharmed by the male sex." No lack of "the receptive attitude," however, in Emily Dickinson. She leaves herself open to men in her poetry, makes herself vulnerable to them, makes a place for them. That no one came to the party—not *really*—was not her fault. A man may come to it now, though, because that space remains there in her poetry. That space, I believe, is always there.

Hard for a man to see, I think, what is erotic about Emily Dickinson's poetry. Having slept with her once, I found it more masturbatory than anything else. Her art, I think, became a kind of orgasm withheld, though lusting still after the concealed and tantalizing, after the incomprehensible, after fantasy. She plays, but she does not climax with you. You thereby become a satisfied voyeur of unfulfilled desire, uncompleted desire.

But who is to say a life of masturbation is not a life? It is private, individual, democratic, undiscussable. A man can never penetrate that in a woman. And no one can know what it is in Emily Dickinson. The critic is totally lost at that. Anyway, wrote Margaret Fuller, "it is a vulgar error that love, *a* love, to Woman is her whole existence."

And so, as I have already said, sleeping with Emily Dickinson, you discover a woman who loves words more than she loves *you*.

"Night's possibility!" Night was often sexual to Emily Dickinson. She could/would sleep with someone.

> Because, Sir, love is sweet!
> . . .
> [I] nearer steal to Thee!
> Enamored. . . .
> **["The Daisy follows soft the Sun"]**

Sleeping with someone—a lover-fantasy! anyone! the reader-critic!—she wants "The peace—the flight—the Amethyst." This is, to her, "Night's possibility." This may be what she gets out of the affair. It is not what one can give her.

There's some sex-talk in Emily Dickinson's lines of verse:

> A transport one cannot contain
> May yet, a transport be—

But there are also a lot of genuinely-meant inhibitions, too:

> Though God forbid it lift the lid—
> Unto it's Extasy!
> **["A transport one cannot contain"]**

That is why you have to worry whether her invitation to bed with her is a tease or not. She may not really want what you have to give. You may take more than she meant to give. That is not real love.

> I let him lead me—Home.
> . . .
> He strove—and I strove—too—
> We didn't do it—tho'!
> **["He was weak, and I was strong—then"]**

"No Man moved Me," she exclaims boastfully at the beginning of one poem [**"I started Early—Took my Dog"**]. When a man "made as He would eat me up" and "followed [her]—close behind," she "started [:was startled?]" and he "bowing—with a Mighty look—. . . withdrew." She frightens off that which she desires. She attracts and then scares off. She teases, we attack, she withdraws, we withdraw. It is all very perplexing.

There are few bodies in Emily Dickinson's lovers in her poems. They are usually "Fleshless Lovers" who

> met—
> A Heaven in a Gaze—
> A Heaven of Heavens—the Privilege
> Of one another's Eyes—
> **["'Twas a long Parting—but the time"]**

Critical work with her is also usually remote, guess-work, unsure. "Watch me, if you want," she says, "but don't touch."

In Emily Dickinson's love poems, people don't sleep together very much. The critic cannot have that for metaphor very often, therefore. But there are other aspects of them that he can have: strong desire, strong memory, advice on luring and teasing, advice on selectivity, the invitation:

How bountiful the Dream—
What Plenty—it would be—
Had all my Life but been Mistake
Just rectified—in Thee

[''I think to Live—may be a Bliss'']

Female bonding is missing in Emily Dickinson's poems because there is a female narrator but no (or very seldom a) female subject. There is a woman speaking (and generally speaking to men, I believe) but no woman loving a woman. ''I tell you these things about myself only to legitimize my voice,'' Grace Strasser-Medina says for apologia in Joan Didion's novel *A Book of Common Prayer*. ''We are uneasy about a story until we know who is telling it.'' It is her voice that is legitimate, not any relationships. *We* supply the relationships. But only on her terms. She may need us, she may not necessarily want us. But Didion has said since then to all this, ''The narrator has got to be telling the story for a reason.'' I cannot find what that reason might have been. I cannot find what *social* reason Emily Dickinson had for writing. Where is the Common Prayer? That is the central difficulty in someone coupling critically with her. And maybe that is *her* central victory.

So what it all comes to is that you sleep with Emily Dickinson, to be sure, but only on her terms, only in her way. You lie there in awe of someone who, on her side of the bed, fantasizes (about all the world; about *you*) so well. Awe is what a male critic learns from her to have towards her if he loves her aright.

''Awe'' has got to be about the vaguest word in Emily Dickinson's language.

populate with awe my solitude—

[''On my volcano grows the Grass'']

We cannot know what she meant by it, if she meant anything at all. She says it when she needs a blank, a space, a perplexity, an upward glance, a sublime shrug, an ''ahhhhhhhh!'' But she sleeps with Awe, a lover:

Ample make this Bed—
Make this Bed with Awe—
In it wait till Judgment break
Excellent and Fair.

[''Ample make this Bed'']

Such vagueness can be shared where explicitness maybe cannot always be. She brings us into an unknown with her and holds our hand there. Or more. Awe is for her the ideal relationship—whatever that means—and the ideal relationship she wants the lover-critic to have with her—whatever that means.

We have laughed for a long time now that people should have thought of Emily Dickinson as ''the myth of Amherst''—that is, the one entertainment to drive to see, the freak of the Valley. But why shouldn't we believe it? *She* created the role; *she* got people to believe it. It was show biz. But more than that, she wanted some awe out of people. One should learn from that how to go to see her: on her terms of awe.

Martha Graham was right to create two Emily Dickinsons in her classic ''Letter to the World'' in 1940, one who steps precisely and stands with dignity and comports herself with strictness, and one who is utterly free in her responses to life and death, ecstasy and fantasy. As the second Emily, she hopped around in multicolors, tied her foot to a scarf and pulled the foot ear-high as she lurched happily as ''the litle tippler leaning against the sun.'' Ned Rorem called her Emily Dickinson one of Martha Graham's ''female monsters,'' her ''female as female,'' her ''more-than-criminal female as Royal Elect.''

How easily the odd becomes awe, the awe becomes attraction, the attraction becomes, well, ''sexual.''

The plate for Emily Dickinson in Judy Chicago's *Dinner Party* is a pink-laced vagina. Of the plate Chicago writes: ''Dickinson felt that her own poetry was dangerous, for it revealed feelings that society had taught women to repress. 'I took my power in my hand, and went out against the world,' she wrote, knowing that her intense creativity was hopelessly at odds with the prevailing ideas of what a woman was supposed to be. . . . Imagining a female creative genius imprisoned in all that lace evolved into my concept of Dickinson's runner and plate. We jiggered a plate with a thick center, which I then carved. Its strength is in stark contrast to the surrounding layers of immobile lace. . . . The soft but fleshy colors suggest a sensuality that nineteenth-century women were not supposed to have. . . . Lace borders over netting with ruffles on the back provide an incongruous setting for a poet whose voice was as powerful as her will.''

A contrast to that. ''Cotton Mather would have burnt her for a witch,'' concludes Allen Tate in what is probably the single most influential essay written on Emily Dickinson, and one of the most blatantly chauvinist pieces of writing about her [see excerpt dated 1928-32]. Emerging at the moment of the breaking up of a culture (''born into the equilibrium of an old and a new order''), she did not have to think about things, only feel them: ''brought down [see where the man puts her!] from abstraction to personal sensibility.''

''She cannot reason at all. . . .''

''She could not in the proper sense think at all. . . .''

''She never succumbed to her ideas, to easy solutions, to her private desires. . . .''

''She did not reason about the world she saw; she merely saw it. . . .''

''She has nothing to say. . . .''

In an effort ''to live apart from a cultural tradition that no longer sustain[ed her],'' she ''withdr[e]w from life to her upstairs room'' and wrote poems for us. Where a man, Hawthorne, faced up to the cultural changes and *thought* about them, a woman, Emily Dickinson, did what any sensible and sensitive woman would do, withdraw and *feel* the change going on, so there would be fine poems of tension for us to read. Again: ''brought *down* from abstraction to personal sensibility.'' She was therefore of service to this ''outsider'' (i.e., this Southern man) who dislikes the things of New England, ''threatening to tear them apart''—the female poet serving the male critic, and because of that service, she is ''a great poet.''

Another contrast. When Steve Allen made his series *Meeting of Minds*, he put Emily Dickinson in the company of Darwin, Galileo, and Attila the Hun. Although he introduces her as ''America's greatest woman poet,'' he has her ''enter[ ], somewhat timidly'' and gives her pathetic, inconsequential lines to speak. She is a squeaker overshadowed by giants. To Attila the Hun she says, ''How dreadful'' and ''Oh, my goodness'' and ''How horrible!'' To Darwin she says, ''Oh, dear'' and ''I was one of those simple people, Dr. Darwin'' and ''Fascinating!'' And to Galileo, she says, ''No!'' and ''That must give you enormous satisfaction'' and ''How infuriating!'' That is, little squeaks to the big ideas and events of history. She reads them some of her poems, to be sure, but about the only thing about herself that they seem to have any interest in is her reclusiveness. They call her "shy," "an enigmatic figure," "curious." Her answer to the charge is: "I felt that I had the right to live and die in obscurity. . . . I've been out with lanterns, looking for myself." Apparently only because pathetic does the woman write well. The men are bold and out conquering the world. The woman, like Milton's puritan, serves sitting/waiting/writing.

Of few poets can it honestly be said that the posture they strike (of necessity? creatively? perversely?) is destructive. Much of Emily Dickinson consoles, but much is unsettling. Much upsets assumptions. Much challenges. Much annoys. She is (often enough to believe it is really her) blatantly disturbing—at least to those who want poets as pillars rather than as bombs.

The soul has moments of Escape—
When bursting all the doors—
She dances like a Bomb, abroad,
And swings upon the Hours. . . .
["The Soul has Bandaged moments"]

This woman, in her more anxious moments, would, I believe, *kill*.

Were words a comfort to this "lonely, isolated woman"? (Who hasn't used the phrase and thought it really meant something?) Was language a compensation, an escape, a consolation, a comfort? Was it a completion, an extension, some kind of dramatic "letter to the [outside, larger, probably unreachable] world"? Well, she hunted down her words so carefully, even if sometimes inaccurately, and placed them so carefully, even if sometimes wrongly, and made such flashes of wit and wisdom out of them, even if sometimes poorly, that it seems askew to think it all such a private matter. Is language ever really private anyway? Her language seems more of an attack upon an imaginary world—loving it, laving it, stirring it, making it smart, stabbing—and so she overwhelms with it. I think she overwhelms. She is almost too much. Maybe *that* fact was comforting to her.

I doubt seriously whether Emily Dickinson was really a "*mad*-woman in the attic" in any serious sense. Her agoraphobia is momentary like most of the roles she played and should not be made out to be a space made for her forever (by men?) nor a place of trial made for her forever (by herself?). She knew how to go mad, to be sure, but she also knew how to get over it. That is the remarkable, and to a man (at least to myself) the interesting, part. Her little madnesses are more attractive than they are pathetic, more drawing than melodramatic, more scenic than serious. She was not determined to go "after great pain." Like everything else she wrote about, it came and went. What is wonderful to witness is her stoicism amid all the transience of things in her life. Three of her loveliest lines (paraphrasing the existentialist of *Ecclesiastes*) are:

How much can come
And much can go,
And yet abide the World!
["There came a Wind like a Bugle"]

The Madwoman of Amherst was awfully sane about it, awfully coherent in telling about the "experience," awfully good at being bad/mad. When she went up into the attic of her "Haunted House," whether that was a haunted life or a haunted art, she went *wild*, not mad. She is up there now, dancing, not screaming. It was, remarkably, a place she could go when she wanted to; she was not locked in. In her own house, it wasn't the attic she went up into anyway; it was a cupola. From which she could see she was superior and into which came many of the things that gave her her Awe and Amplitude. (It is above the bedroom—well above.) If going up there makes one a madwoman, there's a hell of a good universe up there, let's go!

I lie here beside her not believing Emily Dickinson's disclaimer about wanting a large future for herself. "If fame belonged to me," she wrote to Higginson coyly/dishonestly in 1862, "I could not escape her" [see letter dated 7 June 1862]. On the contrary, she very much wanted (from men) fame. "Could I make you and Austin—proud—sometime—a great way off," she confessed to her sister-in-law Sue in 1861, "'twould give me taller feet." She is, in fact, one of the most ambitious writers I know of in the nineteenth century. That she did not know how to fuel (among men) her achievement is neither here nor there. Her many desires have about them the aura of ambition. To be sure, when she slipped into one of her larger views of existence, she belittled all worldly ambition; such was vanity and vexation of spirit. But she was not so nunnish or mad to hold this for long. She held, however vaguely, to a significance to human life and to the superiority of her own. Her touches of renunciation smack piquantly of hypocrisy; ambitious poet may be a contradiction in terms and in very poor taste, but Emily Dickinson did not let her little renunciations make a crippling ambivalence. She has a rather regular naive vulgarity about her hopes for her poetry. She was a go-getter even as she gradually became aware that there was precious little go to get. Her tragic view of much of life—which makes many other things look petty-spirited—she found she could *sell*. Devoted to triumph, she was not constricted by her own dark views of many things, but learned how to make products out of them, her poems. Maybe the world (of men) did not write to her much, as she said, but she did not anathematize the perks of fame it/they could give her. She lied her head off when she wrote to Higginson: "Publication is so far of the mind as firmament from fin." She would have *loved* to have been set among the stars. It has been sheer sexism to make Emily Dickinson one of our saints of failure. Ambition was, after all, one of the ways she defined herself, and one of the ways in which we must.

But I notice she has not noticed me here in bed with her at all. What should I do now? (pp. 67-79)

Karl Keller, "Notes on Sleeping with Emily Dickinson," in Feminist Critics Read Emily Dickinson, *edited by Suzanne Juhasz, Indiana University Press, 1983, pp. 67-79.*

HAROLD BLOOM (essay date 1985)

[Bloom, an American critic and editor, is best known as the formulator of "revisionism," a controversial theory of literary creation based on the concept that all poets are subject to the influence of earlier poets and that, to develop individual voices, they attempt to overcome this influence through a deliberate process of "creative correction," which Bloom calls "misreading." In the following introduction to a selection of critical essays on Dickinson, Bloom discusses the conceptual problems and interpretive obstacles encountered in reading Dickinson's poetry.]

Of all poets writing in English in the nineteenth and twentieth centuries, I judge Emily Dickinson to present us with the most authentic cognitive difficulties. Vast and subtle intellect cannot in itself make a poet; the essential qualities are inventiveness, mastery of trope and craft, and that weird flair for intuiting significance through rhythm to which we can give no proper name. Dickinson has all these, as well as a mind so original and powerful that we scarcely have begun, even now, to catch up with her.

Originality at its strongest—in the Yahwists, Plato, Shakespeare and Freud—usurps immense spaces of consciousness and language, and imposes contingencies upon all who come after. These contingencies work so as to conceal authentic difficulty through a misleading familiarity. Dickinson's strangeness, partly masked, still causes us to wonder at her, as we ought to wonder at Shakespeare or Freud. Like them she has no single, overwhelming precursor whose existence can lessen her wildness for us. Her agon was waged with the whole of tradition, but particularly with the Bible and with romanticism. As an agonist, she takes care to differ from any male model, and places us upon warning:

I cannot dance upon my Toes—
No Man instructed me—
But oftentimes, among my mind,
A Glee possesseth me,

Nor any know I know the Art
I mention—easy—Here
Nor any Placard boast me—
It's full as Opera—

[**"I cannot dance upon my Toes"**]

The mode is hardly Whitmanian in this lyric of 1862, but the vaunting is, and both gleeful arts respond to the Emersonian prophecy of American Self-Reliance. Each responds with a difference, but it is a perpetual trial to be a heretic whose only orthodoxy is Emersonianism, or the exaltation of whim:

If nature will not tell the tale
Jehovah told to her
Can human nature not survive
Without a listener?

[**"The reticent volcano keeps"**]

Emerson should have called his little first book, *Nature*, by its true title of *Man*, but Dickinson in any case would have altered that title also. Alas, that Emerson was not given the chance to read the other Titan that he fostered. We would cherish his charmed reaction to:

A Bomb upon the Ceiling
Is an improving thing—
It keeps the nerves progressive
Conjecture flourishing—

[**"These are the Nights that Beetles love"**]

Dickinson, after all, could have sent her poems to Emerson rather than to the nobly obtuse Higginson. We cannot envision Whitman addressing a copy of the first *Leaves of Grass* to a Higginson. There is little reason to suppose that mere diffidence prevented Miss Dickinson of Amherst from presenting her work to Mr. Emerson of Concord. In 1862, Emerson was still Emerson; his long decline dates from after the conclusion of the War. A private unfolding remained necessary for Dickinson, according to laws of the spirit and of poetic reason that we perpetually quest to surmise. Whereas Whitman masked his delicate, subtle and hermetic art by developing the outward self of the rough Walt, Dickinson set herself free to invest her imaginative exuberance elsewhere. The heraldic drama of her reclusiveness became the cost of her confirmation as a poet more original even than Whitman, indeed more original than any poet of her century after (and except) Wordsworth. Like Wordsworth, she began anew upon a *tabula rasa* of poetry, to appropriate Hazlitt's remark about Wordsworth. Whitman rethought the relation of the poet's self to his own vision, whereas Dickinson rethought the entire content of poetic vision. Wordsworth had done both, and done both more implicitly than these Americans could manage, but then Wordsworth had Coleridge as stimulus, while Whitman and Dickinson had the yet more startling and far wilder Emerson, who was and is the American difference personified. I cannot believe that even Dickinson would have written with so absolutely astonishing an audacity had Emerson not insisted that poets were as liberating gods:

Because that you are going
And never coming back
And I, however absolute,
May overlook your Track—

Because that Death is final,
However first it be,
This instant be suspended
Above Mortality—

Significance that each has lived
The other to detect
Discovery not God himself
Could now annihilate

Eternity, Presumption
The instant I perceive
That you, who were Existence
Yourself forgot to live—

These are the opening quatrains of [a poem] dated by Thomas Johnson as about 1873, but it must be later, if indeed the reference is to the dying either of Samuel Bowles (1878) or of Judge Otis Lord (1884), the two men Richard Sewall, Dickinson's principal biographer, considers to have been her authentic loves, if not in any conventional way her lovers [see Additional Bibliography]. The poem closes with a conditional vision of God refunding to us finally our "confiscated Gods." Reversing the traditional pattern, Dickinson required and achieved male Muses, and her "confiscated Gods" plays darkly against Emerson's "liberating gods." Of Emerson, whose crucial work (*Essays*, *The Conduct of Life*, *Society and Solitude*, the *Poems*) she had mastered, Dickinson spoke with the ambiguity we might expect. When Emerson lectured in Amherst in December 1857, and stayed next door with Dickinson's brother and sister-in-law, he was characterized by the poet: "as if he had come from where dreams are born." Presumably the Transcendental Emerson might have merited this, but it is curious when applied to the exalter of "Fate" and "Power" in *The Conduct of Life*, or to the dialectical pragmatist of "Experience" and "Circles," two essays that I think Dickinson had internalized. Later, writing to Higginson, she observed: "With the Kingdom of Heaven on his knee, could Mr. Emerson hesitate?" The question, whether open or rhetorical, is dangerous and wonderful, and provokes considerable rumination.

Yet her subtle ways with other male precursors are scarcely less provocative. Since Shelley had addressed *Epipsychidion* to Emilia Viviani, under the name of "Emily," Dickinson felt authorized to answer a poet who, like herself, favored the image of volcanoes. Only ten days or so before Judge Lord died, she composed a remarkable quatrain in his honor (and her own):

Circumference thou Bride of Awe
Possessing thou shalt be
Possessed by every hallowed Knight
That dares to covet thee

[**"Circumference thou Bride of Awe"**]

Sewall notes the interplay with some lines in *Epipsychidion:*

Possessing and possessed by all that is
Within that calm circumference of bliss,
And by each other, till to love and live
Be one:—

Shelley's passage goes on to a kind of lovers' apocalypse:

One hope within two wills, one will beneath
Two overshadowing minds, one life, one death,
One heaven, one Hell, one immortality,
And one annihilation . . .

In his essay, "Circles," Emerson had insisted: "There is no outside, no inclosing wall, no circumference to us." The same essay declares: "The only sin is limitation." If that is so, then there remains the cost of confirmation, worked out by Dickinson in an extraordinary short poem that may be her critique of Emerson's denial of an outside:

I saw no Way—The Heavens were stitched—
I felt the Columns close—
The Earth reversed her Hemispheres—
I touched the Universe—

And back it slid—and I alone
A Speck upon a Ball—
Went out upon Circumference—
Beyond the Dip of Bell—

[**"I saw no Way—The Heavens were stitched"**]

"My Business is Circumference—" she famously wrote to Higginson, to whom, not less famously, she described herself as "the only Kangaroo among the Beauty" [see letter dated July 1862]. When she wrote, to another correspondent, that "The Bible dealt with the Centre, not with the Circumference—," she would have been aware that the terms were Emerson's, and that Emerson also dealt only with the Central, in the hope of the Central Man who would come. Clearly, "Circumference" is her trope for the Sublime, as consciousness and as achievement or performance. For Shelley, Circumference was a Spenserian cynosure, a Gardens of Adonis vision, while for Emerson it was no part of us, or only another challenge to be overcome by the Central, by the Self-Reliant Man.

If the Bible's concern is Centre, not Circumference, it cannot be because the Bible does not quest for the Sublime. If Circumference or Dickinson is the bride of Awe or of the authority of Judge Lord, then Awe too somehow had to be detached from the Centre:

No man saw awe, nor to his house
Admitted he a man
Though by his awful residence
Has human nature been.

Not deeming of his dread abode
Till laboring to flee
A grasp on comprehension laid
Detained vitality.

Returning is a different route
The Spirit could not show
For breathing is the only work
To be enacted now.

"Am not consumed," old Moses wrote.
"Yet saw him face to face"—
That very physiognomy
I am convinced was this.

[**"No man saw awe, nor to his house"**]

This might be called an assimilation of Awe to Circumference, where "laboring to flee" and returning via "a different route" cease to be antithetical to one another. "Vitality" here is another trope for Circumference or the Dickinsonian Sublime. If, as I surmise, this undated poem is a kind of proleptic elegy for Judge Lord, then Dickinson identifies herself with "old Moses," and not for the first time in her work. Moses, denied entrance into Canaan, "wasn't fairly used—," she wrote, as though the exclusion were her fate also. In some sense, she chose this fate, and not just by extending her circumference to Bowles and to Lord, unlikely pragmatic choices. The spiritual choice was not to be post-Christian, as with Whitman or Emerson, but to become a sect of one, like Milton or Blake. Perhaps her crucial choice was to refuse the auction of her mind through publication. Character being fate, the Canaan she would not cross to was poetic recognition while she lived.

Of Dickinson's 1,775 poems and fragments, several hundred are authentic, strong works, with scores achieving an absolute aesthetic dignity. To choose one above all the others must reveal more about the critic than he or she could hope to know. But I do not hesitate in my choice, [**"The Tint I cannot take—is best"**], written probably in her very productive year, 1862. What precedents are there for such a poem, a work of unnaming, a profound and shockingly original cognitive act of negation?

The Tint I cannot take—is best—
The Color too remote
That I could show it in Bazaar—
A Guinea at a sight—

The fine—impalpable Array—
That swaggers on the eye
Like Cleopatra's Company—
Repeated—in the sky—

The Moments of Dominion
That happen on the Soul
And leave it with a Discontent
Too exquisite—to tell—

The eager look—on Landscapes—
As if they just repressed
Some Secret—that was pushing
Like Chariots—in the West—

The Pleading of the Summer—
That other Prank—of Snow—
That Cushions Mystery with Tulle,
For fear the Squirrels—know.

Their Graspless manners—mock us—
Until the Cheated Eye
Shuts arrogantly—in the Grave—
Another way—to see—

It is, rugged and complete, a poetics, and a manifesto of Self-Reliance. "The poet did not stop at the color or the form, but read their meaning; neither may he rest in this meaning, but he makes the same objects exponents of his new thought." This Orphic metamorphosis is Emerson's, but is not accomplished in his own poetry, nor is his radical program of unnaming. Dickinson begins by throwing away the lights and the definitions, and by asserting that her jocular procreations are too subtle for the Bazaar of publication. The repetition of colors (an old word, after all, for tropes) remains impalpable and provokes her into her own Sublime, that state of Circumference at once a divine discontent and a series of absolute moments that take dominion everywhere. Better perhaps than any other poet, she knows and indicates that what is worth representing is beyond depiction, what is worth saying cannot be said. What she reads, on landscapes and in seasons, is propulsive force, the recurrence of perspectives that themselves are powers and instrumentalities of the only knowledge ever available.

The final stanza does not attempt to break out of this siege of perspectives, but it hints again that her eye and will are receptive, not plundering, so that her power to un-name is not Emersonian finally, but something different, another way to see. To see feelingly, yes, but beyond the arrogance of the self in its war against process and its stand against other selves. Her interplay of perspectives touches apotheosis not in a Nietzschean or Emersonian exaltation of the will to power, however receptive and reactive, but in suggestions of an alternative mode, less an interpretation than a questioning, or an othering of natural process. The poem, like so much of Dickinson at her strongest, compels us to begin again in rethinking our relation to poems, and to the equally troubling and dynamic relation of poems to our world of appearances. (pp. 1-7)

Harold Bloom, in an introduction to Emily Dickinson, *edited by Harold Bloom, Chelsea House Publishers, 1985, pp. 1-7.*

ADDITIONAL BIBLIOGRAPHY

Anderson, Charles R. *Emily Dickinson's Poetry: Stairway of Surprise*. New York: Holt, Rinehart and Winston, 1960, 334 p.

A respected scholarly explication of selected poems. Anderson discusses Dickinson's views of art, nature, the self, death, and immortality.

Barker, Wendy. *Lunacy of Light: Emily Dickinson and the Experience of Metaphor*. Ad Feminam: Women and Literature, edited by Sandra M. Gilbert. Carbondale: Southern Illinois University Press, 1987, 214 p.

A feminist study of light and dark imagery in Dickinson's poems.

Bennett, Paula. *My Life a Loaded Gun: Female Creativity and Feminist Poetics*. Boston: Beacon Press, 1986, 300 p.

An examination of feminist issues in the lives, thought, and works of Dickinson, Sylvia Plath, and Adrienne Rich.

Bingham, Millicent Todd. *Ancestors' Brocades: The Literary Debut of Emily Dickinson*. New York: Harper & Brothers Publishers, 1945, 464 p.

An account of the editing and publication of Dickinson's poems. Bingham, the daughter of Mabel Loomis Todd, Dickinson's early editor, includes biographical information on the poet and her family.

Blake, Caesar R., and Carlton, F. Wells., eds. *The Recognition of Emily Dickinson: Selected Criticism since 1890*. Ann Arbor: University of Michigan Press, 1964, 314 p.

Reprints significant early reviews and later critical studies.

Bloom, Harold, ed. *Emily Dickinson*. Modern Critical Views. New York: Chelsea House Publishers, 1985, 204 p.

A collection of previously published essays on Dickinson by Charles R. Anderson, Albert Gelpi, David Porter, Robert Weisbuch, Sharon Cameron, Margaret Homans, Joanne Feit Diehl, and Shira Wolosky.

Buckingham, Willis J., ed. *Emily Dickinson, An Annotated Bibliography: Writings, Scholarship, Criticism, and Ana, 1850-1968*. Bloomington: Indiana University Press, 1970, 322 p.

A comprehensive listing of materials relating to Dickinson, complete through 1968.

Budick, E. Miller. *Emily Dickinson and the Life of Language: A Study in Symbolic Poetics*. Baton Rouge: Louisiana State University Press, 1985, 233 p.

Argues that Dickinson's poetry represents the creation of a revolutionary new symbolism "capable of transporting human consciousness beyond the spatial-temporal limitations of the physical world to the universe of divine reality."

Chase, Richard. *Emily Dickinson*. The American Men of Letters Series. New York: William Sloane Associates, 1951, 328 p.

A biographical and critical study emphasizing the impact of Dickinson's cultural environment on her work.

Clendenning, Sheila T. *Emily Dickinson: A Bibliography, 1850-1966*. The Serif Series: Bibliographies and Checklists, edited by William White. Kent, Ohio: Kent State University Press, 1968, 145 p.

A concise, annotated bibliography of works by and about Dickinson published through 1966.

Cody, John. *After Great Pain: The Inner Life of Emily Dickinson*. Cambridge: Harvard University Press, Belknap Press, 1971, 538 p.

A psychoanalytic biography.

Dandurand, Karen. *Dickinson Scholarship: An Annotated Bibliography, 1969-1985*. Garland Reference Library of the Humanities, vol. 636. New York: Garland Publishers, 1988, 203 p.

A bibliography updating the works by Willis J. Buckingham and Sheila T. Clendenning (see entries above).

Dickenson, Donna. *Emily Dickinson*. Berg Women's Series, edited by Miriam Kochan. Leamington Spa, England: Berg Publishers, 1985, 132 p.

A general study that strives to eliminate the popular conception of Dickinson as an eccentric spinster disappointed in love.

Dickinson Studies. Brentwood, Md.: Higginson Press, 1978–

A periodical (formerly the *Emily Dickinson Bulletin*—see entry below) devoted to Dickinson studies, including an annual bibliographical checklist.

Diehl, Joanne Feit. *Dickinson and the Romantic Imagination*. Princeton: Princeton University Press, 1981, 205 p.

Reevaluates Dickinson's works through an exploration of her relationship to the Romantic literary tradition.

Donoghue, Denis. "Emily Dickinson." In his *Connoisseurs of Chaos: Ideas of Order in Modern American Poetry*, pp. 100-28. New York: Macmillan Co., 1965.

Considers Dickinson as a key contributor to American thought.

Duchac, Joseph. *The Poems of Emily Dickinson: An Annotated Guide to Commentary Published in English, 1890-1977*. A Reference Publication in Literature, edited by Jack Salzman. Boston: G. K. Hall & Co., 1979, 658 p.

A guide to English-language commentary on individual poems. Duchac's bibliography covers criticism that was published between 1890 and 1977.

Duncan, Douglas. *Emily Dickinson*. Writers and Critics, edited by A. Norman Jeffares. Edinburgh: Oliver and Boyd, 1965, 110 p.

A critical introduction dealing with Dickinson's life, the publication history of her poetry, and the reception of her work.

Duncan, Joseph E. "The Beginnings of the Revival in America." In his *The Revival of Metaphysical Poetry: The History of a Style, 1800 to the Present*, pp. 69-88. Minneapolis: University of Minnesota Press, 1959.

Includes a discussion of the parallels between Dickinson's poetry and the metaphysical tradition.

Eberwein, Jane Donahue. *Dickinson: Strategies of Limitation*. Amherst: University of Massachusetts Press, 1985, 308 p.

Examines Dickinson's spiritual quest and the symbolic meaning of her reclusive behavior.

Emily Dickinson Bulletin. Charlottesville: Clifton Waller Barrett Library, University of Virginia, 1968-78.

A periodical devoted to studies of the poet and including annual bibliographies. The *Emily Dickinson Bulletin* was superseded by *Dickinson Studies* in 1978 (see entry above).

Ferlazzo, Paul J. *Emily Dickinson*. Twayne's United States Authors Series, no. 280. Boston: Twayne Publishers, 1976, 168 p.

A general introduction to Dickinson's life and poetry.

———, ed. *Critical Essays on Emily Dickinson*. Critical Essays on American Literature, edited by James Nagel. Boston: G. K. Hall & Co., 1984, 243 p.
Reprints criticism by important Dickinson critics.

Frohock, W. M. "Emily Dickinson: God's Little Girl." In his *Strangers to this Ground: Cultural Diversity in Contemporary American Writing*, pp. 98-110. Dallas: Southern Methodist University Press, 1961.
Examines Dickinson's use of a childlike persona in her poems.

Gilbert, Sandra M. "The American Sexual Poetics of Walt Whitman and Emily Dickinson." In *Reconstructing American Literary History*, edited by Sacvan Bercovitch, pp. 123-54. Harvard English Studies, vol. 13. Cambridge: Harvard University Press, 1986.
Compares the gender-defined poetic voices of Whitman and Dickinson.

Homans, Margaret. *Women Writers and Poetic Identity: Dorothy Wordsworth, Emily Brontë, and Emily Dickinson*. Princeton: Princeton University Press, 1980, 260 p.
An acclaimed study of the conflicts between sexual identity and authorship evident in the works of Wordsworth, Brontë, and Dickinson.

Johnson, Greg. *Emily Dickinson: Perception and the Poet's Quest*. University: University of Alabama Press, 1985, 231 p.
Explores Dickinson's dual impulses toward transcendental mysticism and rational skepticism.

Juhasz, Suzanne. *The Undiscovered Continent: Emily Dickinson and the Space of the Mind*. Bloomington: Indiana University Press, 1983, 189 p.
Views Dickinson's reclusive life-style as her means of achieving the freedom necessary to explore her own mind.

———, ed. *Feminist Critics Read Emily Dickinson*. Bloomington: Indiana University Press, 1983, 184 p.
A collection of essays written from feminist perspectives.

Keller, Karl. *The Only Kangaroo among the Beauty: Emily Dickinson and America*. Baltimore: Johns Hopkins University Press, 1979, 340 p.
Surveys Dickinson's affinities with other American authors.

Kher, Inder Nath. *The Landscape of Absence: Emily Dickinson's Poetry*. New Haven: Yale University Press, 1974, 354 p.
An intensive study of Dickinson's ideas that endeavors to interpret the poems as a whole.

Kimpel, Ben. *Emily Dickinson as Philosopher*. Studies in Women and Religion, vol. 6. New York: Edwin Mellen Press, 1981, 308 p.
Identifies parallels between Dickinson's philosophical thought and the ideas of important philosophers.

Leder, Sharon, and Abbot, Andrea. *The Language of Exclusion: The Poetry of Emily Dickinson and Christina Rossetti*. Contributions in Women's Studies, no. 83. New York: Greenwood Press, 1987, 238 p.
A feminist study of Dickinson's and Rossetti's use of language.

Leyda, Jay. *The Years and Hours of Emily Dickinson*. 2 vols. New Haven: Yale University Press, 1960.
A chronological record of Dickinson's life based on letters, the recollections of her family and friends, and public records.

Lilliedahl, Ann. *Emily Dickinson in Europe: Her Literary Reputation in Selected Countries*. Washington, D.C.: University Press of America, 1981, 215 p.
A survey of critical response to Dickinson in Scandinavia, France, Switzerland, and Germany.

Loving, Jerome. *Emily Dickinson: The Poet on the Second Story*. Cambridge Studies in American Literature and Culture, edited by Albert Gelpi. Cambridge: Cambridge University Press, 1986, 128 p.
Studies Dickinson's life and art, seeking to demonstrate that "the seeming dissonance of her words and images is really resonance, if not consonance."

Lubbers, Klaus. *Emily Dickinson: The Critical Revolution*. Ann Arbor: University of Michigan Press, 1968, 335 p.
A detailed review of Dickinson's critical reputation from the first publication of her works through the early 1960s.

Lucas, Dolores Dyer. *Emily Dickinson and Riddle*. DeKalb: Northern Illinois University Press, 1969, 151 p.
Approaches Dickinson's life, letters, and poetry through a study of the history of riddles and her use of them.

MacLeish, Archibald. "The Private World." In *Emily Dickinson: Three Views*, by Archibald MacLeish, Louise Bogan, and Richard Wilbur, pp. 13-26. Amherst: Amherst College Press, 1960.
A discussion of Dickinson's poetic forms.

McNaughton, Ruth Flanders. *The Imagery of Emily Dickinson*. University of Nebraska Studies, n.s. no. 4. Lincoln: University of Nebraska Press, 1949, 66 p.
A study of Dickinson's use of imagery.

McNeil, Helen. *Emily Dickinson*. Virago Pioneers. London: Virago Press, 1986, 208 p.
A thematic exploration of Dickinson's poetry.

Miller, Cristanne. *Emily Dickinson: A Poet's Grammar*. Cambridge: Harvard University Press, 1987, 212 p.
Studies the language of Dickinson's poetry in relation to the poet's conception of the power of words, her cultural background, and her feminine identity.

Miller, Ruth. *The Poetry of Emily Dickinson*. Middletown, Conn.: Wesleyan University Press, 1968, 480 p.
A controversial interpretation of Dickinson's poetry that contradicts the views of most earlier critics and emphasizes the importance of Dickinson's romantic attachments to her work. Miller devotes an extended discussion to the "fascicles," sequences of poems Dickinson copied and stitched together into booklets, stressing the importance of these groupings to a complete understanding of Dickinson's work.

Mossberg, Barbara Antonina Clarke. *Emily Dickinson: When a Writer Is a Daughter*. Bloomington: Indiana University Press, 1982, 214 p.
Examines Dickinson's feminine sensibility and conflicts with her culture, suggesting that an understanding of her role as a daughter is essential to study of her work.

Nathan, Rhoda B., ed. *Nineteenth-Century Women Writers of the English-Speaking World*. Contributions in Women's Studies, no. 69. New York: Greenwood Press, 1986, 275 p.
Includes essays on Dickinson by Peggy Anderson, Tilden G. Edelstein, Vivian R. Pollak, and Anna Mary Wells.

Oates, Joyce Carol. "'Soul *at the White Heat*': The Romance of Emily Dickinson's Poetry." In her *(Woman) Writer: Occasions and Opportunities*, pp. 163-89. A William Abrams Book. New York: E. P. Dutton, 1988.
A consideration of issues important to Dickinson studies covering such topics as paradox in the poet's thought and work; the significance of her secluded life-style; her craftsmanship and distinctive poetic voice; the range of subjects explored in her poetry; and, briefly, her place in American literature.

Patterson, Rebecca. *The Riddle of Emily Dickinson*. Boston: Houghton Mifflin Co., Riverside Press, 1951, 434 p.
A controversial biographical study suggesting that lesbian attachments were an important element in Dickinson's life.

———. *Emily Dickinson's Imagery*. Edited by Margaret H. Freeman. Amherst: University of Massachusetts Press, 1979, 238 p.
Focuses on Dickinson's use of imagery derived from her reading.

Pickard, John B. *Emily Dickinson: An Introduction and Interpretation*. American Authors and Critics Series, edited by John Mahoney. New York: Holt, Rinehart and Winston, 1967, 140 p.
A general introduction to Dickinson's poetry, including explications of several poems.

Porter, David. *Dickinson: The Modern Idiom*. Cambridge: Harvard University Press, 1981, 316 p.
Presents Dickinson as the first practitioner of American modernism.

Power, Sister Mary James, S.S.N.D. *In the Name of the Bee: The Significance of Emily Dickinson*. New York: Sheed & Ward, 1944, 138 p.
Draws parallels between Dickinson's religious attitudes and the teachings of Roman Catholicism.

Ransom, John Crowe. "Emily Dickinson: A Poet Restored." *Perspectives USA*, No. 15 (Spring 1956): 5-20.
A consideration of Dickinson's strengths and limitations in a review heralding the publication of Thomas H. Johnson's definitive edition of her poems.

Rosenbaum, S. P., ed. *A Concordance to the Poems of Emily Dickinson*. The Cornell Concordances. Ithaca: Cornell University Press, 1964, 899 p.
A concordance to Thomas H. Johnson's 1955 edition of Dickinson's poetry.

Rupp, Richard H., ed. *Critics on Emily Dickinson*. Readings in Literary Criticism, vol. 14. Coral Gables, Fla: University of Miami Press, 1972, 128 p.
Reprints a selection of biographical, explicatory, and critical essays.

Salska, Agnieszka. *Walt Whitman and Emily Dickinson: Poetry of the Central Consciousness*. Philadelphia: University of Pennsylvania Press, 1985, 220 p.
Compares Whitman's and Dickinson's artistic visions.

Sewall, Richard B. *The Life of Emily Dickinson*. 2 vols. New York: Farrar, Straus and Giroux, 1974.
A respected biography.

———, ed. *Emily Dickinson: A Collection of Critical Essays*. Twentieth Century Views, edited by Maynard Mack. Englewood Cliffs, N.J.: Prentice-Hall, 1963, 183 p.
A collection of Dickinson criticism reprinted from earlier publications.

Sherwood, William R. *Circumference and Circumstance: Stages in the Mind and Art of Emily Dickinson*. New York: Columbia University Press, 1968, 302 p.
Traces the development of Dickinson's ideology and outlines the chief influences on her thinking.

Thackrey, Donald E. *Emily Dickinson's Approach to Poetry*. University of Nebraska Studies, n.s. no. 13. Lincoln: University of Nebraska Press, 1954, 82 p.
A study of Dickinson's aesthetics concentrating on her interest in language and mysticism.

Ward, Theodora. *The Capsule of the Mind: Chapters in the Life of Emily Dickinson*. Cambridge: Harvard University Press, Belknap Press, 1961, 205 p.
A biographical study focusing on periods of intense emotion in Dickinson's life.

Weisbuch, Robert. *Emily Dickinson's Poetry*. Chicago: University of Chicago Press, 1975, 202 p.
A critical examination of the poet's rhetoric, metaphysical concerns, and complex vision of life.

Wells, Henry W. *Introduction to Emily Dickinson*. Chicago: Packard & Co., 1947, 337 p.
A study of Dickinson's life, surroundings, and works.

Whicher, George Frisbie. *This Was a Poet: A Critical Biography of Emily Dickinson*. New York: Charles Scribner's Sons, 1939, 337 p.
A highly respected early biography of Dickinson.

Wilbur, Richard. "Sumptuous Destitution." In *Emily Dickinson: Three Views*, by Archibald MacLeish, Louise Bogan, and Richard Wilbur, pp. 35-46. Amherst: Amherst College Press, 1960.
A discussion of Dickinson's use of theological and philosophical words redefined to express her personal meaning.

Wolff, Cynthia Griffin. *Emily Dickinson*. New York: Alfred A. Knopf, 1986, 641 p.
A popular biography.

Wolosky, Shira. *Emily Dickinson: A Voice of War*. New Haven: Yale University Press, 1984, 196 p.
Refutes the conception of Dickinson's poetry as limited to personal themes, suggesting that she explores social issues and historical events.

Wylder, Edith. *The Last Face: Emily Dickinson's Manuscripts*. Albuquerque: University of New Mexico Press, 1971, 106 p.
A controversial consideration of Dickinson's idiosyncratic punctuation, capitalization, and notational system.

Fedor Mikhailovich Dostoevski

1821-1881

(Also transliterated as Feodor, Fyodor; also Mikhaylovich; also Dostoyevsky, Dostoievsky, Dostoevskii, Dostoevsky, Dostoïewsky, Dostoiefski) Russian novelist, short story writer, and essayist.

The following entry presents criticism of Dostoevski's novel *Besy* (1873; translated as *The Possessed*, 1913; also translated as *The Devils*, 1953). For a discussion of Dostoevski's complete career, see *NCLC*, Vol. 2; for criticism devoted to his novel *Prestuplenye i nakazanye* (*Crime and Punishment*), see *NCLC*, Vol. 7.

The Possessed is considered one of Dostoevski's four great novels, along with *Crime and Punishment*, *The Idiot*, and *The Brothers Karamazov*. Combining incisive political commentary with Dostoevski's characteristic exploration of the themes of spiritual poverty and redemption, the novel was based in part on the real-life experiences of Sergey Nechaev, a revolutionary who outraged society by advocating violence in his writings and committing a politically motivated murder. Regarded as Dostoevski's finest treatment of political themes, *The Possessed* details the social chaos engendered by radicalism. However, the novel also probes religious, moral, and philosophical issues, as many of its characters represent or embody an ideological stance. Critics have particularly focused on the enigmatic nihilist Nikolay Stavrogin, who is accounted one of the most memorable and mysterious figures in world literature.

Dostoevski wrote *The Possessed* near the end of his long career: he had already published most of his short fiction and journalistic pieces, and of his major novels, only *The Brothers Karamazov* remained to be written. He started work on *The Possessed* during a period of financial difficulties. He and his second wife, Anna, had left Russia in 1867 to escape his creditors. They settled in several different cities in Europe, continually forced to move onward because of Dostoevski's gambling debts. In late 1869, while living in Dresden, Dostoevski began writing *The Possessed* to fulfill an obligation to the journal *Russky vestnik*. His letters and working notebooks show that his design for the work changed greatly while he was writing what was initially planned as a tendentious political pamphlet that would denounce both the liberals who wanted Russia to imitate Western forms of government and the nihilists who rejected all elements of contemporary political society. He was struggling to develop a plan for the work when the Nechaev conspiracy was uncovered.

A disciple of the anarchist Mikhail Bakunin, Nechaev was an active radical at Petersburg University and a leader of the student uprisings there. In 1869 he traveled to Moscow, where he attracted a number of followers, convincing them that he was the leader of an international revolutionary organization called the "Society of National Retribution," which purportedly consisted of a vast network of committees that were each composed of five members. On 21 November 1869, Nechaev and some of his followers murdered one of the members of their group, a student named Ivanov, apparently for disobedience to their cause. The trial of Nechaev's followers (Nechaev himself escaped, but was subsequently captured and imprisoned) took place in St. Petersburg in 1871 just as Dostoevski returned there; he was thus provided with a framework for his political story. Critics agree that he adapted several characters from the Nechaev case, basing Ivan Shatov on Ivanov and Pyotr Verkhovensky on Nechaev; in addition, Dostoevski patterned his groups of radicals after the Society of National Retribution and the murder scene after the description in the official indictment.

While writing *The Possessed*, Dostoevski was working on another project, a series of novels he intended to call *The Life of a Great Sinner*. In this series he planned to contest the radical and violent Nihilist movement and express his fervent desire for the spiritual regeneration of Russia through a return to the roots of Christianity. By late 1870, however, he decided to combine the two projects. Dostoevski experienced great difficulty with the direction and content of the work. After many revisions, he wrote the following in a letter dated 9 October 1870: "I looked at this piece as forced, as contrived, looked down upon it. Then a genuine inspiration visited me—and suddenly I came to love the thing, lay hold of it with both hands, willingly set about cancelling out what had been written. Then in the summer again a change: another new character came forward claiming to be the real *hero of the novel*, so that the former hero (a curious character, but really not deserving the name of hero) was relegated to the second plane. The new hero captivated me to such an extent that I again undertook a revision." Dostoevski's new hero of *The Possessed*, Stavrogin, first appeared in *The Life of a Great Sinner*. With this new emphasis on Stavrogin, who is portrayed as a spiritually tormented soul possessed by the life-denying forces of nihilism, the importance of the political plot diminished, as the philosophical, religious, and artistic elements of the story came to rival it in importance. The circumstances of the work's publication also contributed to its heterogeneity. Because *The Possessed* was originally published serially, the early parts of the novel were already in print before Dostoevski had devised the final plan. This method of publication, together with his frequent revisions, is generally blamed for the novel's complex and confusing plot.

Many critics have approached *The Possessed* through an analysis of its characters, arguing that through them Dostoevski presented his thematic concerns. The novel, which is set in a provincial town in mid-nineteenth-century Russia, focuses on a number of individuals who belong to a political discussion group that is at first led by Stepan Verkhovensky, an aging liberal. Dostoevski details the increasingly violent and anarchic activities of the group as it comes under the influence of Stepan's son, Pyotr. While Pyotr instigates the group's activities, he is under the influence—as are all the others—of Stavrogin. Attractive to some, repellent to others, Stavrogin is fascinating to all, and it is from him that many of his fellows take their creeds. Pyotr, the fanatical, amoral nihilist intent only on destruction and chaos, views him as the messiah of the coming revolution. Alexey Kirilov and Shatov are likewise disciples of Stavrogin, ones to whom he has taught distinct and contradictory creeds. Kirilov bases his life on an extreme atheistic code involving the utter rejection of all save his own will. Ultimately, Kirilov kills himself because, to him, suicide is the supreme expression of self-will. Conversely, Shatov embraces the ideals of Christianity and of Russian nationalism. An anomaly in *The Possessed* in his hopeful belief in the future, Shatov is thought by many scholars to articulate Dostoevski's own religious and political beliefs. It is Shatov who, because he opposes Pyotr's anarchic nihilism and intends to break with the group, is murdered by his fellows. While Stavrogin thus signifies many things to many people, he remains tormented by the emptiness of his soul, and at the close of the novel, he commits suicide.

When *The Possessed* first appeared in *Russky vestnik*, the editor of the journal, Mikhail Katkov, refused to print a section known as "Stavrogin's Confession" that explains Stavrogin's background. In that passage, Stavrogin confesses to the rape of a young girl who subsequently committed suicide. This section was not reinstated during Dostoevski's lifetime; first published in 1922, it is frequently appended to modern editions of the novel. Commentators continue to debate whether Dostoevski himself suppressed "Stavrogin's Confession" in later editions and, if so, why. They also differ in their estimations of its importance to the novel's cohesiveness: while some contend that "Stavrogin's Confession" is essential to the plot and that its omission flaws the novel, others argue that it weakens the design of the story because it provides too much information about the motivation and behavior of Stavrogin. Despite these disparate opinions, critics consistently see Stavrogin as an enigmatic figure who nonetheless holds the key to the novel's meaning. With the addition of this character, commentators note, Dostoevski broadened the theme of *The Possessed*, depicting the internal spiritual disintegration of the individual in the story of Stavrogin and the external political disintegration of the social order in the stories of Stepan and Pyotr.

Together, Pyotr and his father Stepan are Dostoevski's study of the evolution of political ideas in Russia from the effete intellectual liberalism of the 1840s to the dangerous radicalism of the 1860s and 1870s. It is generally agreed that Dostoevski intended these characters as a corrective to what he perceived as Ivan Turgenev's overly sympathetic portrayal of the nihilist Bazarov in his 1862 novel *Ottsy i deti* (*Fathers and Sons*). At the end of *The Possessed*, it is only Stepan, initially depicted as an ineffectual aesthete and naive dreamer, who escapes the cataclysmic denouement of murder and suicide to embark on a voyage of spiritual rediscovery.

Critics have taken a variety of approaches to *The Possessed*. In Russia, the timely publication of the novel during the trial of Nechaev's followers aroused a great deal of controversy, and reviewers at first focused on its political content. Radical critics denounced Dostoevski's depictions of revolutionaries as caricatures and condemned him as an opponent of progress, also reproaching him for reversing his earlier, more liberal beliefs. Conversely, conservatives applauded his rejection of nihilism and endorsement of autocracy, seeing in him a convert to and spokesperson for their position. At the turn of the century, the Russian Symbolists praised the novel for its mysticism, hailing Dostoevski as a prophet. *The Possessed* was briefly acclaimed by Soviet critics after the Russian Revolution for its depiction of social turmoil under czarist rule; within a decade, however, the Soviet government had proscribed all works of literature that failed to explicitly uphold socialist ideals, and the novel was rarely published thereafter.

In the West, critics have addressed a number of topics in the novel. Earlier in this century, many reviewers considered Dostoevski's indictment of the nihilists to be a startling prophecy of Bolshevism and a premonition of the Russian Revolution; this viewpoint characterized much of the reaction to the novel in England around the time of the First World War and in the United States during and after World War II. Discussions of its political basis have also explored the motivation behind Dostoevski's scathing depiction of contemporary Russia. Many commentators have emphasized the spiritual elements of *The Possessed* as well, arguing that Dostoevski's primary intent in composing the novel was to plead for a life of Christian faith. While political, religious, and philosophical issues have dominated many assessments of *The Possessed*, in recent years both Western and Soviet critics have begun to study Dostoevski's technique, focusing on the novel's structure, composition, style, and narrative approach. For not only its philosophical, psychological, and spiritual depth, then, but also for its artistry, *The Possessed* ranks as one of Dostoevski's most important contributions to world literature.

(See also *SSC*, Vol. 2.)

F. DOSTOEVSKY (letter date 1870)

[The following excerpt is drawn from a letter to M. N. Katkov, the editor of the journal Russky vestnik, *in which* The Possessed *was first published. Here, Dostoevski discusses his conception of the novel, outlining the similarities between incidents in contemporary Russia and those in* The Possessed *and describing several*

of its characters. For additional commentary by Dostoevski, see excerpts dated 1873.]

I sent to-day to the office of the *Russky Vestnik* only the first half of Part I of my novel ***The Devils.*** But very soon I shall send you the second half of Part I. There will be three parts altogether, each about ten or twelve folios. There will be no delay now.

If you decide to publish my work next year, then it seems to me necessary to tell you beforehand, if even in a few words, what strictly the novel is about.

One of the biggest events of my novel will be the well-known Moscow murder of Ivanov by Nechayev. I hasten to add: I never knew either Nechayev, or Ivanov, or the circumstances of the murder, nor do I know them now, except from the newspapers. And if I knew I would not copy them. I only take the accomplished fact. My imagination may differ in the highest degree from the actual event, and my Peter Verkhovensky may not at all be like Nechayev; but it seems to me that in my amazed mind there has been created by my imagination the person, the type that corresponds to that murder. Without a doubt it is not useless to exhibit such a person, but in himself he would not have tempted me. In my view, these pitiable monstrosities are not worthy of literature. To my own surprise, that character turns out half comical in my novel. And therefore, notwithstanding the fact that all that event occupies one of the foremost planes of the novel, it is nevertheless only an accessory and setting for the actions of another character, who might indeed be called the chief character of the novel. That other character (Nicolay Stavrogin) is also a sinister one, also a villian. But it seems to me that he is a tragic character, although many people, on reading the novel, are bound to say: "What does it mean?" I sat down to a composition of that character because I had long wished to draw him. In my opinion he is both a Russian and typical character. I shall be very, very sad if I cannot manage him. Sadder still will it be if I hear the verdict that he is a stilted character. I took him from my heart. Certainly, it is a character, rarely appearing in all its typicalness, but it is a Russian character (of a certain stratum of society). But defer your judgment of me until the novel is finished. Something in me tells me that I shall manage that character. I do not explain it now in full: I am afraid of saying the wrong thing. I shall observe this only: that character is described by me in scenes, in action, and not in discussions—therefore there is a hope of his turning out a person.

For a long time I could not manage the opening of the novel. I re-wrote it several times. It is true, with that novel something has happened to me which never happened before: for weeks I would stop working on the opening and would write from the end. Apart from this, I am afraid, the opening could have been livelier. With the five and a half folios (which I send) I have hardly set the plot going. Still the plot, the action, will expand and develop unexpectedly. For the further interest of the novel I answer. It seems to me it is better as it stands.

But not all the characters will be sinister ones. There will also be attractive ones. I am rather afraid that a good deal is beyond my strength. For the first time, for instance, I want to touch on a class of people, still very little touched on in literature. For the ideal of such a character I take Tikhon Zadonsky. Mine is also a bishop living in retirement at a monastery. With him I contrast the hero of my work and bring them together for a time. I am in some trepidation; I have never tried it before, but of that life I know something. (pp. 63-8)

F. Dostoevsky, in a letter to M. N. Katkov on October 8, 1870, in his New Dostoevsky Letters, *translated by S. S. Koteliansky, 1929. Reprint by Haskell House Publishers Ltd., 1974, pp. 63-9.*

FIODOR DOSTOEVSKY (letter date 1873)

[*In the following extract from a letter to the Heir Apparent of Russia, Alexander III, Dostoevski explains his intentions in composing* The Possessed *and details several of its themes. For additional commentary by Dostoevski, see excerpts dated 1870 and 1873.*]

Allow me the honour and happiness of bringing to your notice my work. [***The Devils***] is almost a historical study, whereby I wished to explain how it is that such monstrous phenomena, as the Nechayev movement, are possible in our strange society. My view is that the phenomenon is not accidental, not singular. It is a direct consequence of the great divorcement of the whole Russian education from the native and peculiar mainsprings of Russian life. Even the most talented representatives of our pseudo-European progress had long ago become convinced that it was perfectly criminal for us, Russians, to dream of our distinctiveness. The most terrible thing about it is this, that they are quite right; for, once having *proudly* called ourselves Europeans, we have thereby denied our being Russians. Confused and frightened by the idea that we lag so far behind Europe in our intellectual and scientific progress, we have forgotten that we, in the inmost problems of the Russian spirit, contain in ourselves, as Russians, the capacity perhaps of bringing a new light to the world, on condition of our development being distinctive. In the ecstasy of our humiliation, we have forgotten the most immutable historical law, namely, that without the *presumption* of our own world importance as a nation, we can never be a great nation and leave after us anything distinctive for the good of mankind.

We have forgotten that all great nations have manifested themselves and their great powers just because they were so "presumptous" in their conceit. Just because of that they have benefited the world, and have, each nation, brought into it something if only a single ray of light, just because they have remained themselves, proudly and undauntedly, always and presumptuously independent.

To think like this at the present time in Russia and to express such ideas means to doom oneself to the rôle of a pariah. And yet the principal preachers of our national undistinctiveness would be the first to turn away with horror from the Nechayev creed. Our Belinskies and Granovskies would not believe, if they were told, that they are the direct fathers of the Nechayevists. This kinship and continuity of idea, descending from the fathers to the sons, is what I wished to express in my work. I am far from having succeeded but I have worked conscientiously.

I am flattered and elated by the hope that you, Sire, the heir of one of the greatest thrones in the world, the future leader and ruler of the Russian land, have perhaps paid even the least attention to my weak but conscientious attempt to expose in an imaginative work one of the most dangerous sores of our present day civilisation, a civilisation strangely unnatural and undistinctive, and yet dominating Russian life. (pp. 71-5)

Fiodor Dostoevsky, in a letter to His Imperial Highness, the Heir Apparent, Alexander Alexandrovich in 1873, in his New Dostoevsky Letters, *translated by S. S. Koteliansky, 1929. Reprint by Haskell House Publishers Ltd., 1974, pp. 71-5.*

NIKOLAI MIKHAILOVSKI (essay date 1873)

[One of the early Russian radical critics, Mikhailovski was part of the narodniki, *or populists, a group of intellectuals who anticipated a Socialist revolution led by the peasants. His depiction of Dostoevski and* The Possessed *as reactionary and hostile to the revolutionaries influenced both his contemporaries and later critics, contributing to the tradition of condemning Dostoevski for political rather than literary reasons. His commentary on* The Possessed, *excerpted below, was first published in* Otechestvennye zapiski *in 1873.]*

[Dostoyevski] plays moral and political motifs on the strings of mental illness.

In ***The Devils,*** as well as in ***Crime and Punishment*** and ***The Idiot,*** he organizes whole orchestras of this kind. He does this in two ways. Either he takes a psychological motif, for instance, the feeling of sin and the desire for atonement (a motif which especially interests him), and sets it to work in a character. You see, for instance, that a man has sinned, that his conscience is tormenting him. He finally takes [penance] of some sort upon himself and thereby attains peace of mind. This is one method. It is used by Dostoyevski in ***Crime and Punishment.*** In ***The Devils*** Stavrogin represents an unsuccessful attempt of this kind. The other method consists in putting the solution of some moral problem into the mouth of a man who is tormented by mental illness. In ***The Devils,*** unfortunately, the second method predominates. I say "unfortunately" because this method is obviously not suitable in art. One of the characters in Dostoyevski's last novel [***The Devils***] says: "I did not devour my idea, but my idea devoured me." A great many of Dostoyevski's heroes might say this about themselves. This type is without doubt highly interesting and instructive. But it is one thing to show him as a type, as a living character really being devoured by his idea before the eyes of the reader, and it is another thing to make a man hold forth indefatigably concerning an idea that has been pinned on him. But such is the case with most of the main characters in ***The Devils***. . . . They are devoured by their idea in an entirely different sense. The thing is that Dostoyevski has such a huge store of eccentric ideas that he simply overwhelms his heroes with them. . . . In general, then, instead of characters representing *people who are driven by their own ideas,* in ***The Devils,*** characters are portrayed *who are driven by ideas imposed upon them by the author*. (pp. 35-6)

In every one of [the characters in ***The Devils***] we again see only more deviations. To begin with, people who are psychologically abnormal hardly furnish grounds for drawing a generalization. And since the people in ***The Devils*** are for the most part only props for eccentric ideas, then it becomes even more difficult to take the point of view that they can all be merged into the concept of a herd of possessed swine. The eccentric idea—if the expression may be pardoned—fairly bristles at you all the time. It has nothing in common with noneccentric ideas and other eccentric ideas, and therefore the assemblage of props for eccentric ideas does not permit a synthesis; it is impossible to add them together in one sum. And therefore, no matter how Dostoyevski strove for logic, he did not attain it. (p. 37)

Nikolai Mikhailovski, in an extract from "Criticism Before the Revolution," in Dostoyevski in Russian Literary Criticism: 1846-1956 *by Vladimir Seduro, Columbia University Press, 1957, pp. 35-7.*

F. M. DOSTOIEVSKY (essay date 1873)

[In the following excerpt from his The Diary of a Writer, *Dostoevski defends* The Possessed *against those critics who argued that revolutionaries are, as a whole, fanatical and insane, offering up his own experience as proof. Dostoevski's remarks were written in 1873; for additional commentary by the author, see excerpts dated 1870 and 1873.]*

Some of our critics have observed that in my last novel ***The Possessed*** I have made use of the plot of the notorious Nechaiev case; but they hastened to add that, strictly speaking, there are no portraits in my novel and there is no literal reproduction of that story; that I took a phenomenon and merely sought to explain the possibility of its occurrence in our society as a social phenomenon and not in an anecdotal sense of a mere depiction of a particular Moscow episode.

On my own part, I may say that all this is quite correct. I have not discussed in my novel the notorious Nechaiev and his victim Ivanov. The face of *my* Nechaiev, of course, does not resemble that of the real Nechaiev. I meant to put this question and to answer it as clearly as possible in the form of a novel: how, in our contemporaneous, transitional and peculiar society, are the Nechaievs, not Nechaiev himself, made possible? And how does it happen that these *Nechaievs* eventually manage to enlist followers—the Nechaievtzi.

And recently—true, already about a month ago—I have read in *The Russian World* the following curious lines: ". . . it seems to us that the Nechaiev case could have demonstrated the fact that our student youth does not participate in such follies. An idiotic fanatic of the Nechaiev pattern manages to recruit proselytes only among idlers, defectives—and not at all among the youths attending to their studies."

And further:

". . . all more so as only a few days ago the Minister of Public Education had declared (in Kiev) that after the inspection of the educational institutions in seven districts he could state that *'in recent years the youth has adopted an infinitely more serious attitude toward the problem of learning, and has been studying far more diligently.'* "

These lines, taken by themselves, and judged abstractly, are rather trivial (the author, I hope, will excuse me). But in them there is a twist—an old habitual lie. Their fully developed and fundamental idea is that if, at times, the Nechaievs appear in our midst, they are all necessarily idiots and fanatics, and even if they succeed in recruiting proselytes, these are necessarily found "*only* among the idle defectives and *not at all* among youths attending to their studies."

I do not know exactly what the author of the article in *The Russian World* sought to prove by this twist: did he mean to flatter the college youth? Or did he, on the contrary, by this crafty manœuvre, so to speak, under the guise of flattery, try to cheat them a little, but only with the most honorable motive and for their own benefit? And, to achieve this, did he resort to the well-known device which governesses and nurses apply in the case of little children: "Here, dear children, see how *those* bad, unruly kids are screaming and fighting: they'll surely be spanked because they're so 'undeveloped'; but you are such nice, commendable, sweet little things; here, at your table you sit up straight; you do not swing your little feet under the table, and for this you will surely be given candies."

Or, finally, did the author simply attempt to "shield" our college youth from the government, resorting for this purpose to a device which he, perhaps, considers extraordinary, crafty and refined?

I will say candidly: even though I did raise all these questions, yet the personal motives of the author of the article in *The Russian World* do not interest me in the least. And, in order to make myself fully understood, I will even add that the lie and the old worn-out twist expressed in that thought by *The Russian World,* I am inclined to regard as unintentional and accidental, *i.e.,* that the author of the article fully believed his own words and took them for the truth with that sublime naiveté which, in any other case, would be so laudable—and even touching, by reason of its defenselessness.

However, aside from the fact that a lie mistaken for the truth always assumes a most dangerous appearance (even though it be printed in *The Russian World*), one is struck by the thought that never before had this lie been revealed in so naked, precise and artless a form as in this little article. Verily, make some man pray God—he will smash his forehead. Now, it is interesting to analyze this lie in this particular guise—exposing it, if possible, to the light—because one may be waiting long for another instance of candidness as unskillful as this one.

From time immemorial in our pseudo-liberalism, in our newspaper press it has become a rule to "shield the youth"—from whom? from what?—Often this remains concealed in the gloom of uncertainty, and, therefore, assumes a most absurd and even comic aspect, especially in attacks directed against other periodicals in the sense that "we are more liberal, whereas you are upbraiding the youth and, consequently, you are more retrograde."

I may parenthetically remark that in the same article in *The Russian World* there is an accusation directly pointed against *The Citizen* to the effect that in it there are wholesale charges against our college youth in Petersburg, Moscow and Kharkov. Even leaving aside the fact that the author of the article himself *knows perfectly well* that in *The Citizen* there is nothing, and never has been anything, akin to wholesale and incessant accusations, I shall ask our prosecutor to explain: what does it mean to accuse youth by the wholesale? This I do not understand at all! Of course, this means that, for some reason, one dislikes the youth as a whole—and even not so much the youth, as our young men of a certain age. What twaddle! Who would believe such a charge?—It is clear that both the accusation and the defense were made haphazardly, without giving the matter much thought. Indeed, is it worth while to deliberate upon this: "I have shown that I am liberal; that I praise the youth; that I am scolding those who do not eulogize them—and this suffices as far as subscriptions are concerned, and that's all there is to it!" Precisely, "that's all there is to it," since only the bitterest enemy of our young people would venture to defend them *in this manner* and to bump into such a strange twist as that into which the naïve author of the article in *The Russian World* has bumped (accidentally—of this I am now convinced more than ever).

The real importance of the matter is that this device is the invention not only of *The Russian World*—it is a device common to many periodicals of our pseudo-liberal press, and there, perhaps, it is being used not quite so naïvely. Its essence is: *first*—in wholesale eulogies of the youth, in everything and *quand-même,* and in coarse attacks on all those who occasionally venture to take a critical attitude toward the young people. This device is based upon the ridiculous assumption that they are still so immature and so fond of flattery that they will not understand and will accept everything at its face value. And, in truth, we have reached the point where quite a few among our young men (we are firmly convinced that by no means all of them) actually do grow fond of coarse praise, and do seek to be flattered, and are ready to accuse recklessly all those who do not applaud everything they do, particularly in certain respects. However, here we have as yet a temporary damage: with experience and age the views of our youth are likely to change. But there is another side to the lie which entails direct and material harm.

This other aspect of the device of "shielding our youth from society and from the government" consists of simple *denial of the fact,* at times most impudent and coarse: "There is no fact, there never has been, never could have been; he who says that the fact did take place, calumniates our youth and, therefore, is their enemy!"

Such is the device. I repeat: the bitterest enemy of our young people could not have invented anything more injurious to their direct interests. This I want to prove by all means.

By the denial of a fact quand-même one may achieve amazing results.

Well, gentlemen, what will you prove and in what manner are you going to facilitate the problem, if you start asserting (and God only knows for what purpose) that the "led-astray" youth—that is, those who are capable of being "led astray" (even though by Nechaiev)—must necessarily be composed of none but "idle defectives"—those individuals who do not study at all—in a word, good-for-nothings with the worst propensities?—In this way, by isolating the matter, by withdrawing it from the sphere of those who attend to their studies and by focusing in *quand-même* on none but "idle, defective" individuals, you are thereby condemning in advance these unfortunate young men and definitely forsaking them: "it's their own guilt—they are unruly fellows, idlers, who would not sit still at the table."

By isolating the case and by depriving it of the right to be examined in conjunction with the generic whole (and therein consists the only possible defense of the unfortunate "delusioned" ones), you thereby, as it were, not only seal the final verdict against them, but you even alienate from them mercy itself, because you are directly asserting that their very errors were caused solely by their repulsive qualities and that these youths, who even are guilty of no crime, must arouse contempt and disgust.

On the other hand, what if it should happen that some *case* were to involve by no means "defectives"—not the unruly ones swinging their feet under the table, and not merely idlers—but, on the contrary, diligent, enthusiastic youths precisely attending to their studies, even endowed with good, but only misdirected, hearts? (Please grasp the word: *misdirected.* Where in Europe will you find more vacillation in all sorts of tendencies than in Russia in our day!) And now, according to your theory of "idlers and defectives," these new "unfortunate" ones would prove three times more guilty: "they were well provided; they completed their education; they worked diligently—they have no justifications! They are worthy of mercy three times less than the idle defectives!"—Such is the result directly derived from your theory.

Please, gentlemen (I am speaking generally and not merely to the contributor of *The Russian World*), you are asserting on the strength of "the denial of the fact" that the "Nechaievs" must necessarily be idiots—"idiotic fanatics." Well, is this really so? Is it correct? In this case I am setting aside Nechaiev, and I am referring to the "Nechaievs," in the plural.

Yes, among the Nechaievs there may be very gloomy creatures—disconsolate and distorted ones—with a thirst for intrigue of a most complex origin and for power, with a passionate and pathologically premature urge to reveal their personalities, but why should they be "idiots"?—On the contrary, even real monsters among them may be highly developed, most crafty and even educated people. Or you may think, perhaps, that knowledge, "training," little bits of school information (picked up even in universities) finally mould a youth's soul to the extent that, upon the receipt of his diploma, he immediately acquires an irrevocable talisman enabling him once and forever to learn the truth, to avoid temptations, passions and vices? Thus, according to you, all these graduating youths will at once become something on the order of so many little infallible Popes.

And why do you believe that the Nechaievs must necessarily be fanatics?—Very often they are simply swindlers. "I am a swindler and not a socialist"—says one Nechaiev; true, in my novel ***The Possessed,*** but, I assure you, he could have said it in real life. There are swindlers who are very crafty and who have studied precisely the magnanimous phase of the human, usually youthful, soul so as to be able to play on it as on a musical instrument.

And do you really and truthfully believe that proselytes whom some Nechaiev in our midst could manage to recruit are necessarily good-for-nothings? I do not believe it: not all of them. I am an old "Nechaievetz" myself; I also stood on the scaffold, condemned to death; and I assure you that I stood there in the company of educated people. That whole group had graduated from the highest institutions of learning. Some of them, subsequently, *when everything had passed,* have distinguished themselves by remarkable works in special fields. No, Nechaievtzi are not always recruited from among mere idlers who had learned nothing.

I know that you, no doubt, will say in rebuttal that I am not one of the Nechaievtzi at all, and that I am only a "Petrashevetz." All right—a Petrashevetz. (Although, in my opinion, this is an incorrect name, since a much larger number—compared with those who stood on the scaffold, but quite as we Petrashevtzi—have been left intact and undisturbed. True, they have never known Petrashevsky, but it was not he who was the crux of that long-past story. This is merely what I meant to observe.)

But all right—a Petrashevetz. How do you know that the Petrashevtzi could not have become the Nechaievtzi, *i.e.*, to have chosen the "Nechaiev" path, *would things have turned that way?* Of course, in those days this could not even have been imagined—meaning *that things could have taken such a turn.* Times were altogether different. But permit me to speak about myself only: probably I could never have become a *Nechaiev,* but a Nechaievetz—for this I wouldn't vouch, but maybe I could have become one . . . in the days of my youth.

Now, I have started speaking about myself in order to be entitled to speak about others. Nevertheless, I shall continue to speak only about myself, and if I should mention others it will be only in a general and impersonal sense, quite abstractly.

The Petrashevtzi's *case* is such an old one, belonging to such ancient history that, perhaps, it will be of no harm if I should remind people of it, particularly in such a slippery and abstract sense.

Among us Petrashevtzis (among both those who stood on the scaffold and those who had been left intact—it is the same) there were neither "monsters" nor "swindlers." I do not think anyone would contradict this statement of mine. That among us there were educated people—this, too, as I have remarked, is probably not going to be contradicted. However, undoubtedly, among us there were but few who could have managed to struggle against a certain cycle of ideas and conceptions which had a strong grip upon youthful society. We were contaminated with the ideas of the then prevailing theoretical socialism. In those days political socialism was nonexistent in Europe, and the European ringleaders of the socialists even used to reject it.

Louis Blanc was vainly slapped on his cheeks and pulled by his hair (as if on purpose—his was very thick, long black hair!) by his colleagues—members of the National Assembly, Rightist deputies, from whose hands he was then, on that ill-starred morning in May, 1848, torn by Arago (the astronomer and a member of the government—now dead), when the Chamber was invaded by a mob of impatient and starving workers. Poor Louis Blanc, for a while a member of the provisional government, had in no way incited them: he had merely been reading at the Luxembourg Palace to these pitiful and hungry people about their "right to work"—to people who had lost their jobs, owing to the revolution and the republic.—True, since he was still a member of the government, his lectures on this subject were awfully tactless and, of course ridiculous.

Considérant's journal, as well as Proudhon's articles and pamphlets, were seeking *iner alia* to propagate among these same starving and penniless workers profound disgust for the right of hereditary property. Unquestionably, from all this (*i.e.*, the impatience of hungry people inflamed with theories of future felicity) subsequently there arose political socialism, the substance of which, notwithstanding all aims proclaimed by it, thus far, consists of the desire for universal robbery of all property-owners by the destitute classes, and thereafter "be that as it may." (Since, properly speaking, so far nothing has been decided as to how future society is going to be shaped—and up to date such is the whole formula of political socialism.)

But at that time the affair was conceived in a most rosy and paradisiacally moral light. Verily, socialism in its embryo used to be compared by some of its ringleaders with Christianity and was regarded as a mere corrective to, and improvement of, the latter, in conformity with the tendencies of the age and civilization. All these new ideas of those days carried to us, in Petersburg, a great appeal; they seemed holy in the highest degree and moral, and—most important of all—cosmopolitan, the future law of all mankind in its totality. Even long before the Paris revolution of '48 we fell under the fascinating influence of these ideas. Already in '46 I had been initiated by Bielinsky into the whole *truth* of that future "regenerated world" and into the whole *holiness* of the forthcoming communistic society. All these convictions about the immorality of the very foundations (Christian) of modern society, the immorality of religion, family, right of property; all these ideas about the elimination of nationalities in the name of universal brotherhood of men, about the contempt for one's native country, as an obstacle to universal progress, and so on, and so forth—all these constituted such influences as we were unable to overcome and which, contrarywise, swayed our hearts and minds in the name of some magnanimity. At any rate, the theme seemed lofty and far above the level of the then prevailing conceptions, and precisely this was tempting.

Those among us—that is, not only the Petrashevtzi, but generally all *contaminated* in those days, but who later emphatically renounced this chimerical frenzy, all this gloom and horror which is being prepared for humankind under the guise of regeneration and resurrection—those among us were then ignorant of the causes of their malady and, therefore, they were still unable to struggle against it. And so, why do you think that even murder *à la* Nechaiev would have stopped—of course, not all, but at least, some of us—in those fervid times, in the midst of doctrines fascinating one's soul and the terrible European events which, forgetting altogether our fatherland, we have been watching with feverish tension?

Unquestionably, the monstrous and disgusting Moscow murder of Ivanov was represented by the murderer Nechaiev to his victims—the "Nechaievtzi"—as a political affair, useful to the future "universal and *great* cause." Otherwise, it is impossible to understand how several youths (whoever they may have been) could agree to commit such a saturnine crime.

And in my novel ***The Possessed*** I made the attempt to depict the manifold and heterogeneous motives which may prompt even the purest of heart and the most naïve people to take part in the perpetration of so monstrous a villainy. The horror lies precisely in the fact that in our midst the filthiest and most villainous act may be committed by one who is not a villain at all! This, however, happens not only in our midst but throughout the world; it has been so from time immemorial, during transitional epochs, at times of violent commotion in people's lives—doubts, negations, scepticism and vacillation regarding the fundamental social convictions. But in our midst this is more possible than anywhere else, and precisely in our day; this is the most pathological and saddest trait of our present time—the possibility of considering oneself not as a villain, and sometimes almost not being one, while perpetrating a patent and incontestable villainy—therein is our present-day calamity! (pp. 142-49)

F. M. Dostoievsky, "One of the Contemporaneous Falsehoods," in his The Diary of a Writer, *edited and translated by Boris Brasol, 1949. Reprint by George Braziller, 1954, pp. 142-56.*

K. WALISZEWSKI (essay date 1900)

[*Waliszewski praises Dostoevski's depiction of nihilism in* The Possessed.]

The Possessed is an answer to Tourguéniev's *Fathers and Children,* and that writer, together with Granovski and some other representatives of Occidentalism, is depicted, and turned into ridicule, in its pages. Dostoïevski could not console himself for having been outstripped in the general interpretation of a social phenomenon such as Nihilism, of which Raskolnikov had only been a partial, and a partially comprehended picture. He cannot be said to have entirely succeeded in the retaliation at which he aimed. Stavroguine, the principal hero of his novel, who turns revolutionist out of sheer idleness, is an archaic, and by no means a specifically Russian type. He is enigmatic and confusing, strongly tinged with Romantic features, which the author seems to have borrowed from every quarter—from Byron's *Corsair,* from Victor Hugo's *Hernani,* and from the aristocratic demagogues of George Sand, Eugène Sue, Charles Gutzkow, and Spielhagen. The story is excessively complicated, and its close is extravagantly melodramatic. But Dostoïevski has contrived to see, and bring out, the essential feature which escaped Tourguéniev, I mean the element which has constituted the strength of active Nihilism. By showing that this lies, not in the vague, confused, and ineffective ideas of a handful of ill-balanced brains, nor in the fictious or incoherent organisation of an unstable political party, but in the paroxysmal tension of a band of exasperated wills, he has done real service to the cause of history. (p. 348)

K. Waliszewski, "The Preachers—Dostoïevski and Tolstoï," in his A History of Russian Literature, *William Heinemann, 1900, pp. 330-402.*

VYACHESLAV IVANOV (essay date 1914)

[*Ivanov is recognized as a leading member of the Russian Symbolist movement. This excerpt from his essay on* The Possessed, *which first appeared in* Russkaya mysl *in 1914, is drawn from his important study* Freedom and the Tragic Life: A Study in Dostoevsky. *Here, Ivanov interprets* The Possessed *as an allegory of Christian myth.*]

Dostoevsky conceives of the people as a personality—and not as a personality synthesized by thought, but as independent in essence and as an integral being. It has a peripheral diversity of aspects, and also an inner holiness, that of the one and integral awareness, of the one and integral will.

We must have recourse to the Bible to obtain a clear picture of this. The concept of peoples as personalities and as angels underlies the whole historical philosophy and eschatology of the Scriptures.

In the metaphysical unity of the people two principles may be distinguished. One is feminine and pertaining to the soul; the other is masculine and pertaining to the spirit. The first has its roots in the universal Mother, the living Earth, as a mystical entity; the second . . . may be termed, in Apocalpytic language, the Angel of the people. The free self-determination of the conscious character, the decision to be either for God or against Him—which . . . forms the nucleus of the personal tragedy of the human individual—is the proper function of this spirit; which, within its own sphere of power, is the people's guide. This spirit decides for the whole people, and thereby determines its historical fate.

It must not be forgotten, however, that this decision is taken as an act inherent in the will of the people itself. The spirit of the people can rest upon its own self, it can lock its doors against the Divine Logos; or, on the other hand, it can renounce its selfish Ego and, through the human beings that it has chosen for the task, bring to Earth the tidings that it bears God within itself. Only by bearing God within itself can the people's Ego become universal, the Ego of the whole of mankind.

Lastly, historical evolution can occasion still a third contingency: a kind of estrangement of the Angel from the people, a temporary indecision or impotence of the masculine principle. This is, inevitably, exploited by the Powers of Evil, who thereupon attempt to form a "Legionary" group-soul of human beings inimical to God; and, by means of this, to snatch unto themselves the office of spiritual leadership; to dominate the people's soul and throw it into a blind frenzy.

Dostoevsky belives that the Russian people is a "God-bearing" people. The God-bearing people is, by definition, not the empirical people, though the empirical people constitutes the former's terrestrial body. The God-bearing people is, in its essence, neither an ethnographical nor even a political concept. It is one of the flames of the many-branched candlestick of the mystical Church: a candlestick that sheds its light before the Throne of the Word. Nation and State receive consecration and meaning only in so far as they are vessels of the God-bearing spirit. The outer shell of this spirit may appear sinful; it may be, in fact, sinful, maimed and decaying: but the spirit bloweth where it listeth. The God-bearing people is a living light that shines in the Church, and it is also an Angel of the Lord: yet, until the world comes to an end, the Angel is free in his choice of ways; and, if his loyalty wavers, there comes down upon him the threat of the Apocalypse: "I will remove thy candlestick out of his place, except thou repent." (pp. 57-9)

Dostoevsky, who approaches the idea of God-bearing all-oneness, in ***Crime and Punishment,*** and the idea of the eternally-feminine principle in ***The Idiot*** (as he did previously in **"The Landlady"**), also arrived, through meditation on Russia's possession by the daemons of godlessness and self-will, at a positive perception of the mysterious connections between these two entities. When these perceptions flamed into full brightness, his novel ***The Possessed***—which had previously seemed unhappily conceived and likely to be still-born—suddenly shone before him in a dazzling new light. In his "creative excitement", Dostoevsky set about the rebuilding of the structure upon which he had already started; seeking, and at the same time doubting, whether he could give expression and shape to the whole mighty greatness of the "idea" that he had come to behold.

He had seen with his own eyes, so to speak, how the masculine principle of the people's innermost being—the principle directed towards the ideal of contemplative spirituality—can allow its influence upon the psyche of the people, and upon the external life as a whole, to be supplanted by daemonic "Legion". He had seen, too, how the feminine principle, which is the soul of the Earth of Russia, is filled with torment and with longing for her deliverer, the hero in Christ, the God-bearer. Though, in her bondage and forsakeness, her behaviour may be chaotic, she will always recognize the traitor and usurper who approaches her wearing the mask of Him whom she yearns for and yearningly awaits. She will recognize him, expose him and curse him.

The Myth was born.

In ***The Possessed*** Dostoevsky tried to show how the eternally-feminine principle in the Russian soul has to suffer violence and oppression at the hands of those Daemons who in the people contend against Christ for the mastery of the masculine principle in the people's consciousness. He sought to show how these Daemons, in their attack upon the Russian soul, also wound the Mother of God herself (as shown in the symbolic episode of the desecration of the ikon), although their vilifications cannot reach her invisible depths (compare the symbol of the untouched silver garment of the Virgin Undefiled in the home of the murdered Maria Timofeyevna). Since the basic theme of the novel is the symbolism of the relationship between the Earth's soul, the daring, erring human spirit and the Powers of Evil, it was quite natural that Dostoevsky should be confronted by a presentation of this myth which had already been attempted in the world's literature—although with a different orientation, and without any allusion to the idea of the mission of the Redeemeer: namely, in Goethe's *Faust*.

Maria Timofeyevna took the place of Gretchen; who, after the disclosures in the second part of the tragedy, is identified, as a manifestation of the eternally-feminine, both with Helen and with Mother Earth. Nicolai Stavrogin is the Russian Faust: but in a negative version, since love has been quenched in him, and, with it, the indefatigable striving—erotic, in the Platonic sense—through which Faust is saved.

The rôle of Mephisto is assumed by Peter Verhovensky, who at decisive moments emerges from behind Stavrogin, faithfully imitating the grimaces of his prototype. The relation between Gretchen and the Mater Gloriosa is the same as that between Maria Timofeyevna and the Mother of God. Maria's terror at Stavrogin's appearance in her room is prefigured in Margarete's scene of madness in the prison. Maria's imaginary mourning for a child is almost the same emotion as that which finds expression in Gretchen's hallucinated memories. Maria's song is the song of the Russian soul, a mysterious symbol of the deep life in its inward "cell".

Maria pays for the beloved that he may remain true, not so much to herself, but rather to his destiny as a God-bearer; and she patiently awaits him, fearful and doing penance to earn his deliverance. Similarly, Gretchen turns, in her song, from the old King of the farthest West, of *Ultima Thule,* and from his sun-goblet, to the distant beloved, and touchingly adjures the latter to keep faith—by returning as a new sun.

She who sings the song of love in her inward cell is not only a "medium" of Mother Earth (the late Hellenic scholars who classified ecstasies and trances would have called her "one possessed by Earth" . . .), but also Mother Earth's symbol. In the myth she represents the soul of earth, under the specific aspect of Russian earth. That is why she has her little mirror in her hand: the universal soul is perpetually reflected in Nature. Moreover, it is not accidental that she is the wedded wife of the protagonist of the tragedy, Nicolai Stavrogin. Nor is it accidental that she is not truly his wife, but retains her virginity.

"The Prince of this World" has dominion over the world's soul, but is unable to achieve a real power over it. It just the same way in the Samaritan woman of the Fourth Book of the Gospels is not the wife of him whom she took as her sixth husband.

As though gifted with clairvoyance, Maria Timofeyevna, when she has recovered from her first fright, obstinately addresses Stavrogin as "Prince", opposing him in the same time to another true *him*.

> I must have done *him* some wrong, some very great wrong—only I don't know what it is: that's what will plague me for ever. . . . I pray and pray, and always I think of the great wrong I have done *him*.

This other Prince, the Prince of Light, is the God-bearing hero in whose person Maria, clairvoyante in her Christian simplicity, expects to behold the Prince of Glory.

Even Maria's lameness is a sign of her secret guilt of hostility to God: the guilt of a half-heartedness and disloyalty that perhaps were present in her from the beginning; or, at least, of imperfect loyalty, of a primordial resistance to the bridegroom who deserted her, as Eros deserts Psyche—who, because of an original sin inherent in her mortal being, is sinful in the sight of the Divine love.

> What—aren't you a Prince? I was ready to expect anything from *his* enemies, but such insolence, never! Is he still alive? Have you killed him, or haven't you? Confess. . . . Tell me, you imposter, did you

get a lot for it? Did you ask a big price? A curse upon you. . . .

The "blind owl", the "wretched actor", "Grishka Otrepiev, burdened with the curse of seven Ecclesiastical Councils", "Judas Iscariot", the "Devil" himself, he who has supplanted (and perhaps also destroyed, or, at least, somehow betrayed) the "noble falcon" that "lives somewhere behind the mountains, and soars to gaze at the sun": such are the elements of the "evil dream" that Maria Timofeyevna dreams before the coming of Stavrogin; a dream that returns to her, in her prophetic delirium, when she is in fact awake. With the same clairvoyance Gretchen directly recognizes the nature and aura of Mephisto, which make her loathe the person of her beloved.

But who is Nicolai Stavrogin? Dostoevsky provides a clear token of his great significance: it is not by chance that his name is derived from the Greek word for the Cross. . . . Secret signs foretell for him a sort of royal anointment. In the eyes of beholders he is the legendary prince, Ivan the Tsarevitch: all who come near him feel the strange, superhuman fascination that he exercises. Upon him is shed the grace of a mystical comprehension of the ultimate secrets of the people's soul and its expectation of the God-bearer. He initiates Shatov and Kirillov into the prime mysteries of Russian Messianism. He implants in their souls a deep sense of Christ—together with the most deep doubt of God's existence.

He himself, however, at some decisive moment of his half-hidden and terrible past, has betrayed the holiness that offered itself to him. After his loss of faith in God he gives himself up to practical Satanism, and holds with Satan hallucinated conversations. Accepting no reward, he is not Satan's debtor—as Faust was—but his vassal. He gives Satan his life, which had been promised to Christ, and is thereby condemned to carry a void within himself until, whilst still in his earthly life, he is overtaken by the "other death"; which "other death" manifests itself as an annihilation of the personality within the living body. Spiritually he has died long ago, and all that now remains of him is his fascinatingly beautiful mask.

But the Powers of Evil need him, need his mask—they need him as a vessel of their own will and an executant of their practical purpose: he has already lost his own will. A traitor in the sight of Christ, he is also disloyal to Satan. He must put himself, as a mask, at Satan's disposal, so that this false visage may mislead the world; so that he may play the part of a false Tsarevitch, who will let loose the revolt of the masses: and he finds within himself no will towards this. He becomes unfaithful to the Revolution, and to Russia herself. (Symbols of this: his assumption of a foreign nationality, and especially his wilful abandonment of his wife Maria Timofeyevna.) He becomes unfaithful to everything and everyone, and hangs himself like Judas before he has reached the diabolic cave that he has hollowed out for himself in a dark, precipitous ravine. But his betrayal of Satan does not exempt him from his passive rôle of susceptible intermediary and vehicle for the devilish "Legion" (*St. Mark* V. 9), which gains dominion, around him and by his agency, over the herd of the possessed. They are a herd, and no more, for each of them has in some sort been deprived of his Ego: in each the living Ego is paralysed, and into its place an alien will has entered.

Only two of the people with whom Stavrogin comes into contact have not surrendered their Ego, and are thus separate from the herd: Kirillov and Shatov. How did these two retain command over their Ego? Did these most gifted of Stavrogin's disciples invent for themselves an imaginary homunculus, as Faust's disciple succeeded in doing?

Kirillov, who at nights drinks tea by himself and broods over his own destiny in almost solipsistic self-absorption, asserts his autonomous freedom by a sort of flight from the world. He is, in Nietzsche's phrase, a true "hermit of the spirit", and what he asserts is not so much his outer independence—though he guards this jealousy—as his imaginary metaphysical self-sufficiency, which is what makes him fundamentally an enemy of God. Nevertheless, he keeps a gentle light burning before the image of Christ, which in some fashion of his own he knows and loves.

Since he holds that there is no preter-human reality corresponding to man's conception of God, he considers it logically necessary that man himself should become God: Jesus, he thinks, would have become God even if He had not believed in the Heavenly Father. But man can become God only after he has conquered that "anguish of the fear of death" which he previously called God. To proclaim and seal this conquest, man must perform an act of absolute disobedience. This act can take the form only of suicide—a suicide not caused by misery and affliction, but committed in untrammalled wilfulness and in full acceptance of life. Man must himself mount the empty throne of God, which has been built by man's fear of death.

Such are the views of this atheist-mystic, whose mania anticipates that of Nietzsche, the modern Ixion. Christ alone did not fear death: so Kirillov also will not fear it. Moreover, he must climb the Golgotha of a freely chosen self-pride—he must kill himself, for his own sake. . . .

Thus, in the blindness of arrogance and the wilderness of his spirit, Kirillov sets out to achieve his anti-Christian sacrifice: his anti-Golgotha; a "Man-become-God", as a negative version of God-become-Man; a being that sought to preserve its personality and therefore destroyed itself—that recognized its Sonship, but sought to establish this upon a denial of the Father.

In the terrible end of this dreamer smitten with God-sickness, Dostoevsky wished to show that atheism, in a personality awakened to ontological self-awareness, ends in metaphysical madness. If a man of higher nature persuades himself, as Kirillov did, that "he must believe that he does not believe in God" (Dostoevsky may at this point have had in mind Bakunin's formulation, which was being much discussed at this time, of the incompatibility between faith in God and human freedom), then he feels himself irresistibly driven to self-deification and self-destruction.

Kirillov is by no means an egoistical character. He is noble, compassionate, ready to help others. He has a tender sympathy and love for all living creatures, and with Heraclitean enthusiasm he extols life in all its beauty and self-contradiction. Nay, more, he knows moments of ineffable bliss in the ecstatic contemplation of the harmony of the universe. It is only the fear of death—"the old God"—that, in his view, spoils human existence and turns men into slaves. That is why he vows to perform the act of redemption—the slaying of the old God through his own suicide; and it is also the reason why he divides history into two epochs: the first lasting from the ape to the slaying of God, and the second from the slaying of God to the completely, "even physically", proclaimed transmutation of man into "Man-become-God". Thus, he believes, must the insidious symbol of "God-become-Man" be recast.

This sombre fanatic certainly does not belong to the "herd" of the possessed; nor has it any need of him (it needs leaders of quite another stamp: a Peter Verhovensky, perhaps; or a Shigalov, who, in order to ensure a public welfare based on the principle of equality, seeks to exterminate every germ of higher spirituality, and decrees that all individual heads that in any way rise above the throng must be cut off). Nevertheless, in Dostoevsky's view Kirillov is one of the possessed, since he is diseased with the primitive hatred of God: which Dostoevsky regards as the strongest motive force of the daemonic assault.

Shatov, too, never surrendered his Ego to "Legion". Indeed, he rebelled against the Daemons, and for this was torn in pieces by them. Nevertheless, he, too, is a carrier of the virus. At best he is only a convalescent. When asked whether, amidst all his talk of the God-bearing people, he really believes in God, he stammers in embarrassment: "I want to—I shall believe." He wishes to merge his Ego in the people's Ego, yet at the same time to establish that the people's Ego is the Ego of Christ. He shrank from the Daemons, but began to waver in his belief in the people. [The critic adds in a footnote: The name Shatov is derived from "shatkij"—"wavering".] The falsehood of his attitude towards Christ is shown in the fact that he could not, through Christ, behold the Father. He drew bright revelations from the poisoned well of Stavrongin's soul, and, like his mystagogic master, misapplied them: arriving at the conclusion that the Russian Christ was the people itself, whose mission was to incarnate its spiritual and masculine principle in its coming Messiah, in order through this Messiah (thus, again, through an impostor) to proclaim: "I am the Bridegroom."

It is a mistake to accuse Shatov the mystic of making the Godhead an attribute of the people. On the contrary, he seeks, as he himself says, to elevate the people to Godhead. The blow in the face that he deals Stavrogin is an inevitable act: the heretic punishes the heresiarch for his treachery. Stavrogin refused to become the Russian "Christ", and thus betrayed Shatov's faith and shattered his life.

Nevertheless, this waverer has at least the merit of having wavered away from the herd, and of having, when all is said, found faith in the Earth's soul. This is why Maria Timofeyevna, in her simplicity, feels him to be her friend. Thanks to his love of the true Christ—a love which, false and dim though it be, is rooted in the primitive element of his oneness with the people—"Shatushka" is illumined by the reflected glow of a Grace that has been shed upon him. He appears as a magnanimous, all-forgiving champion and guardian of the feminine soul in its sin and humiliation (as is especially shown in his behaviour towards his wife), and dies a martyr.

From an early age—probably ever since his years of imprisonment—Dostoevsky had pondered over the spiritual mission of the Russian people. Later he speaks of "the independent Russian idea", which his homeland must "bring forth with fearful pangs", and even refers to its "labour-pains" as having already begun.

The riddle propounded in that prophetically inspired work, ***The Possesssed,*** is connected with the nexus of problems contained in this expectation. What is the spiritual meaning of the secret yearning of the Russian Earth for Redemption and the Redeemer? How will the coming of the hero in Christ, her Ivan the Tsarevich—heralded in her prophetic dreams of her God-bearing mission—how will this coming manifest itself? In other words, how can the land of "wise will and wild action", which for ages has been entitled "holy", become indeed "Holy Russia", and the people become the Church? How does a thing, impossible for man, become possible for God? (pp. 59-69)

Vyacheslav Ivanov, in his Freedom and the Tragic Life: A Study in Dostoevsky, *edited by S. Konovalov, translated by Norman Cameron, The Noonday Press, 1952, 166 p.*

J. MIDDLETON MURRY (essay date 1916)

[Murry, an early twentieth-century English critic and editor, is distinguished for the forward-thinking opinions he expressed, both as an editor and contributor to various British journals and in his full-length critical studies. In the following excerpt from his Fyodor Dostoevsky: A Critical Study, *an important early English-language discussion of Dostoevsky as a prophet, Murry comments on the character of Stavrogin and what he represents in the novel; in the unexcerpted portion of the essay, Murry examines several other characters, focusing on their significance to the story and their relationship to Stavrogin. This essay was first published in 1916.]*

Dostoevsky's letters tell us more about ***The Possessed*** than any other of his great books. What they say is little enough, but it is very precious. He had infinite difficulty in writing the book. "None of my works," he writes to Strakhov in 1870, "has given me so much trouble as this one. At the beginning, that is at the end of last year, I thought the novel very 'made' and artificial, and rather scorned it. But later I was seized by real enthusiasm; suddenly I fell in love with my work. . . . Then in the summer came another transformation: up started a new, vital character, who insisted on being the real hero of the book; the original hero (a most interesting figure, but not worthy to be called a hero) fell into the background. The new one so inspired me that I once more began to rewrite the whole. And now when I have already sent the beginning to the office of the *Roussky Viestnik,* I am suddenly possessed with terror—I fear that I am not equal to the theme I have chosen. . . ." Two months later he tells Maikov that he "has undertaken a task to which his powers are not equal." In yet another three months he writes again to thank Maikov for a criticism of the first part—"They are Turgeniev's heroes in their old age"—and explains his letter to Strakhov. "Stepan Trofimovitch is a figure of superficial importance, the novel will not in any real sense deal with him; but his story is so closely connected with the principal events of the book that I was obliged to take him as a basis for the whole. This Stepan Trofimovitch will take his benefit in the fourth part; his destiny is to have a most original climax. I won't answer for anything else; but for that I can answer without limitations. And yet I must say once more: I tremble like a frightened mouse. . . ."

The new hero who rose up suddenly, like a spirit out of the earth, and drove Stepan Trofimovitch Verhovensky from the stage was Nikolay Stavrogin. He, too, descended like his predecessors from out of a mysterious past into life. The narrative tells us that he was Varvara Petrovna's son and Stepan Trofimovitch's pupil; but between that childhood and the manhood in which he appears to us, dark and mysterious years have passed in that strange city of Petersburg, which Dostoevsky reveals to us as like that chasm in the earth, the *mundus* where the old Romans communed with the awful spirits of the dead.

And though they cannot tell why, the inhabitants of the provincial capital which is the scene of the drama, are terrified of Stavrogin. They fear him and they hate him, in a frenzy of fear and hatred, as though he were a portent. He did strange things; he pulled by the nose the harmless Gaganov, who had the innocent habit of saying on occasion that "he couldn't be led by the nose"; he bit the governor's ear, pretending that he would whisper to him. But it was not for these stupid and outrageous acts that he was hated; it was for the manner and the intention with which he did them. By some instinct they knew that he was not mad. "The general outburst of hatred with which everyone fell upon the 'ruffian and duelling bully from the capital' also struck one as curious," says the imaginary eye-witness in whose mouth the narrative is put. "They insisted on seeing an insolent design and deliberate intention to insult our whole society at once." For reasons of which they can give no account to themselves the citizens hate Stavrogin for his *being*, and in spite of their old convictions, it is a relief to them that they can after all ascribe his actions to derangement, when he is seized by a brain-fever while under arrest for the most serious of his outrages.

But they were right before. Stavrogin was not mad. The crafty enthusiast Liputin knew it when he sent his message. And we too now know the nature of the spirit which embodied awakens the unreasoning hatred and fear of society. Stavrogin is one of those who must be taken outside the city walls and stoned until he is dead. Those stupid and outrageous acts were but the trials of his will, for he is Will incarnate. He is utterly alone, having set his individual consciousness against life. He has gone so far on his lonely path that we can see him no more. The far cold distance holds him. In the years that passed between his first descent upon the city and the second, it was rumoured that he had been on an expedition to the icy North. Svidrigailov, too, had talked of such a journey. In the history of both of them this travelling in the cold and silent wastes of the earth was only a symbol, by which Dostoevsky could convey in temporal terms, the lonely and infinite distance to which their spirit had been driven. The chill, still desolation of the timeless world to which Stavrogin has ruthlessly pursued his way, hangs about him, striking terror into the heart of his own mother.

> He remained standing for two minutes in the same position by the table, apparently plunged in thought, but soon a cold and listless smile came on to his lips. He slowly sat down again in the same place on the corner of the sofa, and shut his eyes as though from weariness. . . . Varvara Petrovna knocked at the door gently as before, and again receiving no answer, she opened the door. Seeing that Nikolay Vsyevolodovitch was sitting strangely motionless, she cautiously advanced to the sofa with a throbbing heart. She seemed struck by the fact that he could fall asleep so quickly and that he could sleep sitting like that, so erect and motionless, so that his breathing even was scarcely perceptible. His face was pale and forbidding, but it looked as it were numb and rigid. His brows were somewhat contracted and frowning. He positively had the look of a lifeless wax figure. She stood over him for about three minutes, almost holding her breath, and suddenly she was seized with terror. . . .

The cold horror of that portrait is terrible. Stavrogin is not a man, but a presence. He has looked upon the frozen waste of eternity. We cannot see him; his physical body is only a shell. His spirit is infinitely away. We can follow the road he has gone only by the vision of his dead selves, Kirillov and Shatov and Pyotr Verhovensky. These are the things he has passed beyond, and having passed beyond them, he is lost to sight. To each of these men he has been a leader and a God: each of them, in his supreme moment, cries to Stavrogin in the same words: "Remember how much you have meant in my life!" Even the pitiful Lebyadkin, who had crossed his path in the dark Petersburg days, echoes the words; though of what Stavrogin had taught him, he can express only a remembered, yet significant phrase. "One must really be a great man even to make a stand against common sense." That rang in Lebyadkin's memory; it was the oracle delivered to him by his God. And Lebyadkin had known by sure instinct that Stavrogin had had this greatness. Was it not upon his own sister, the cripple and demented Marya Timofeyevna, that Stavrogin had made trial of it?

"It takes a great man to make a stand even against common sense." It was worth remembering, for even though the message was apportioned to Lebyadkin's understanding, it yet contained all Stavrogin's secret. To have the instinct of common sense in his heart, and to trample upon it just because it was an instinct, and therefore an impediment to the working of his conscious will; to sacrifice all things to his will, all instincts, all impulses, all emotions, all loves, all loyalties; to know himself apart from life and to stamp out the embers of the flame in his soul; to be in all things conscious, since to yield to that which was unconscious was to declare himself a slave to the life which he hated and denied; to will that his own will should be the master absolute of all things—"it takes a great man to make a stand even against common sense." And there were impulses more overwhelming even than common sense.

There is the anger of pride. Nikolay Stavrogin was proud. "You are beautiful and proud as a God," says Pyotr Verhovensky to him. His pride was superhuman, as his will. Yet when his will demanded that his pride should yield, he broke his pride. So when Shatov struck him, he withheld his hand.

> He had scarcely regained his balance after being almost knocked over in this humiliating way, and the horrible as it were sodden thud of the blow in the face had scarcely died away in the room when he seized Shatov by the shoulders with both hands, but at once, almost at the same instant, pulled both hands away and clasped them behind his back. He did not speak, but looked at Shatov, and turned as white as his shirt. But strange to say the light in his eyes seemed to die out. Ten seconds later his eyes looked cold, and I'm sure I'm not lying—calm. Only he was terribly pale. Of course I don't know what was passing within the man, I saw only his exterior. It seems to me that if a man should snatch up a bar of red-hot iron and hold it tight in his hand to test his fortitude, and after struggling for ten seconds with insufferable pain end by overcoming it, such a man I fancy would go through something like what Nikolay Vsyevolodovitch was enduring those ten seconds. . . .

"But, strange to say, the light in his eyes died out." But was it strange? The will of Lucifer had broken Lucifer's pride. Stavrogin had put upon himself the last torment of all and had endured it. Pride was the unconscious form of his triumphant conscious will, and that too he had crushed. Yet not even for that would the light of his eyes have grown dim. He had struck at the inmost of his being, because he willed the omnipotence of his will; and in the very moment of his triumph he knew that it was of no avail. In his soul each succeeding victory could bring only instant desolation, and this was the last desolation of all. When he had killed his pride, he had killed even that which had urged him to kill his pride. The spring of the will itself was broken. There was not only nothing left to will, but of the will itself nothing remained.

That moment was the pinnacle of his assertion of his will. Beneath it were ranged all the other trials which he had imposed upon his unconquerable will. His rumoured debauchery in Petersburg, which was not debauchery but the assertion of his conscious will against the instinct for good whose sovereignty he could not accept; his marriage with the demented cripple, which was the triumph of his will, not over common sense, but over the innate sense of harmonious beauty which resides in all great souls;—these were trials which only his pride could give him strength to sustain. By that he had found in himself the power to pass within his own soul beyond good and evil, beyond beauty and ugliness. There remained one instinct to him, upon which his whole desperate life was built, the instinct of pride. This instinct he had himself created. It was the unconscious counterpart of his conscious will to assertion. It had grown strong with his triumphs. It had borne him beyond good and evil, beyond beauty and ugliness. It bore him now beyond itself, beyond pride and submission; and his spirit died within him. "Only he was terribly pale." The last, the only virtue had gone out of him.

After this moment, Stavrogin in the land of living is dead. He has submitted himself to the last mortification of the flesh. He is now conscious will and nothing more; he is not even incarnate, seeing that the extreme assertion of consciousness itself depends upon supporting instinct. He had killed his last instinct, and by the act he is become a pure spirit. He is will that cannot work its will any more. There is no more contact between him and the physical world which is the vehicle of life.

So Nikolay Stavrogin dies on the day that he makes his first appearance in the body in the story of ***The Possessed.*** For a moment, as it were, in the supreme incandescence of his earthly struggle, he puts on surpassing human beauty. "Now—now, I don't know why," says the narrator, "he impressed me at once as absolutely, incontestably beautiful, so that no one could have said that his face was like a mask. Wasn't it perhaps that he was a little paler, and seemed rather thinner than before? . . ." But Dostoevsky could not tolerate the grossness of his imaginary narrator's vision, and despite himself, he adds: "Or was there perhaps the light of some new idea in his eyes?" And we know what was this new idea. His eyes shone with the joyous expectation of the final battle; he was elate with his own determination to make his pride bow to his will. He had come determined to publish abroad his marriage with the half-witted cripple. To have married her in secret was his victory over his own sense of ugliness; to proclaim his marriage would be the triumph over his pride. But when he entered the room, the occasion had been taken out of his hands. Whether his pride was too great to be thus suddenly overthrown, or whether his mother's instant question diminished from his own will, he was silent. And Shatov, for whom he was a God, felt the *lie* in his silence, and struck him before them all, before Lise, and Darya, his lovers, and before his mother. Shatov struck his God for failing of his Godhead, and this time his God did not fail. Stavrogin held his hand; the final victory was won, and the light of the new idea died down in his eyes. The moment of his absolute beauty passed, and his face became a mask again.

The story of ***The Possessed*** passes between this death of the spirit of Stavrogin and the death of his body. He has no fear of bodily death; then he might kill himself, to conquer the fear. He has no hope in death; he is only afraid that he might deceive himself with such a hope. "I know I ought to kill myself," he writes to Darya Shatov before the end, "to brush myself off the earth like a nasty insect; but I am afraid of suicide, for I am afraid of showing greatness of soul. I know it will be another sham again—the last deception in an endless series of deceptions. What good is there in deceiving one's self? Simply to play at greatness of soul?" And in the brief time of his phantom life, his life in death, which remained to him, he is haunted by the souls that he himself has created, by Kirillov and Shatov and Pyotr Verhovensky. He, the God, has fashioned these men, and given them life, while he himself is dead. They believe in the creeds which he has given them, and believing, they live. But they believe the creeds because they believe in the man. (pp. 157-68)

With Stavrogin's death the last hope of consciousness and conscious will is gone. The most splendid of all the Possessed has rushed down the steep into the sea; rather he has not rushed, but he has gone delicately, like the prince he was, and held himself proof against even the ecstasy of self-destruction. And he is the Prince of this world, for it is not certain proud spirits, but all an age, an epoch of the human consciousness that is possessed. Dostoevsky lavished himself upon the creation of Stavrogin. If Shatov and Kirillov saw in him their God and Pyotr Verhovensky divined in him the prince of the world which should be built up on the ruins of the old, it was not because they were blind, but because he was in very truth the man-God and the prince. Dostoevsky knew that he was the perfect embodiment of an age, superhuman only because he had all the courage of his humanity. Yet he was possessed. Life cannot end in barrenness and destruction, yet it can have no other end. The old life—and it is this old life in which we live to-day—came to its perfect and inhuman flower in Stavrogin; but, because this cannot be the end, a miracle *must* be at hand. It was left to Stepan Verhovensky to read the parable.

> "My friend," said Stepan Trofimovitch in great excitement, "*savez-vous* that wonderful and . . . extraordinary passage has been a stumbling-block to me all my life . . . *dans ce livre* . . . so much so that I remembered those verses from childhood. Now an idea has occurred to me; *une comparaison*. A great number of ideas keep coming into my mind now. You see that's exactly like our Russia, those devils that come out of the sick man and enter into the swine. They are all the sores, all the foul contagions, all the impurities, all the devils great and small that have multiplied in that great invalid, our beloved Russia, in the course of ages and ages. *Qui, cette Russie que j'aimais toujours*. But a great idea and a great Will will encompass it from on high, as with that lunatic possessed of devils . . . and all those devils will come forth, all the impurity, all the rottenness that was putrefying on the surface . . . and they will beg of themselves to enter into swine: and indeed maybe they have entered into them already! They are we, we and those . . . and Petrusha and *les autres avec lui* . . . and I perhaps at the head of them, and we shall cast ourselves down, possessed and raving, from the rocks into the sea, and we shall be drowned—and a good thing too, for that is all we are fit for. But the sick man will be healed and 'will sit at the feet of Jesus,' and all will look upon him with astonishment. . . . My dear, *vous comprendrez après*, but now it excites me very much . . . *Vous comprendrez après. Nous comprendrons ensemble*."

From out of the desolation and sickness must arise a new life of which the man clothed and in his right mind is the symbol. But the sickness is a sickness unto universal death, for it is the human consciousness itself which is the disease. It is a manifestation of life which destroys life. In Stavrogin Dostoevsky had sent forth the greatest of its champions, and he had been vanquished. There remained only the new man, clothed and in his right mind, for a hope. In the new man must be found the new consciousness; in him the assurance of eternal harmony which came to the old man only in the delirium of his sickness, shall be part of his waking knowledge.

It may be that this hope will seem to some a fantastic and unintelligible dream. The logician will say that the destrucion of the present human consciousness and the creation of a new life, wherein spirit shall be no longer divided from body, is no more than empty words which correspond to no thought: the thought in them, they will say, is unthinkable. It is true; yet on the foundation of such unthinkable thoughts Dostoevsky's great work is builded. Those who are not prepared to think them have no business with his books; they will consider his novels to be merely novels, his truth to be merely truth, and his art to be merely art. They should remain within their own garden and enjoy its fruits, which are by no means uncomely; they have the hither to elect upon their side. Even among the Russians they have with them Turgeniev, who saw only a digger of psychological mole-runs or a Marquis de Sade in Dostoevsky, and Tolstoi, who could say that he had no intellect. Turgeniev was a novelist; Tolstoi was a great novelist; Dostoevsky was not a novelist at all. He cannot be measured by the old art or the old logic; he transcended both.

"Transcended" is a hard word, which can be too easily used; yet it contains the truth of Dostoevsky's art and thought. His art was the way of escape from his tormenting doubts, the means of expression for his unthinkable thoughts. The present consciousness he strained to its uttermost limits. Its forms of art and thought he tortured and loaded till they could bear the burden no longer, as his own body could not support the agonised strivings of his spirit. He had somehow to express within these forms visions and ideas which passed beyond them. He deliberately poured a new wine into the old bottles knowing that they would burst; and in himself he felt the incessant ferment of conceptions which it passed even his power to make vocal. The old expressions he charged with a content that was fantastical; his Christianity is not Christianity, his realism is not realism, his novels are not novels, his truth not truth, his art not art. His world is a world of symbols and potentialities which are embodied in unlivable lives; for the art and the creative activity which was the only way of escape from the unendurable torments of his mind, had perforce to be commensurate with the doubts which were the cause of the torments. Therefore his art was metaphysical, which no art can be. He struggled to express conceptions which were truly inexpressible, for which he had need not only of a new art but of a new philosophy. In part he created both these things; he was at least "the prophetic soul of the wide world dreaming on things to come," and he strove to communicate his visions by the instrument of a language and thought that could hardly contain them. . . . In one of his last letters Dostoevsky refers to a sentence of Vladimir Solovyev, the Russian philosopher, who in his youth was surely Dostoevsky's disciple: "I am firmly convinced that mankind *knows much more* than it has hitherto expressed either in philosophy or art." "Just so it is with me," Dostoevsky adds. It was Vladimir Solovyev who used to call Dostoevsky a prophet: and a prophet he was, not in the vulgar sense of one who professes to foretell the incessant changes in the configuration of the material world, but of one who contemplated and sought to penetrate into a new consciousness and a new mode of being which he saw was metaphysically inevitable for mankind. (pp. 196-201)

J. Middleton Murry, in his Fyodor Dostoevsky: A Critical Study, *new edition, Martin Secker, 1923, 263 p.*

V. KOMAROVICH (essay date 1922)

[In this excerpt from an introduction to the first publication of "Stavrogin's Confession," which originally appeared in Russian in 1922, Komarovich explores Dostoevski's intentions regarding the role of the confession in the novel.]

It is not difficult to determine the place which had been intended for that fragments ["Stavrogin's Confession"] in ***The Possessed.*** The manuscript is headed "Chapter IX. At Tikhon's." From the contents it can be seen that the chapter so numbered must be referred to Part Second of the novel. In our fragment the following incidents are supposed to have already taken place: Shatov's box on Stavrogin's ear (the last chapter of Part I.) and Stavrogin's conversaion with Shatov in the night (the first chapter of Part II.). On the other hand Stavrogin's public declaration of his marriage with Maria Timofeevna (Chapter X. Part II.) is only expected and is still being considered by Stavrogin and Tikhon. Thus, our Chapter IX. ought to follow immediately after Chapter VIII. of Part II. ("Ivan the Tsarevich"), where the maddened Peter Verkhovensky confesses in a passionate whisper his incredible love of Stavrogin, and where Stavrogin—in the highest state of tension (as was ever the case with Dostoevsky)—reveals his true self. (Stavrogin as Ivan Tsarevich, the unknown "he" of all Russia, is hiding himself, the "beautiful" and "sun," but through Verkhovensky's wiles is already enslaved by the demon of nihilism.) Yet Stavrogin has two ways and two inclinations which constitute the basis and centre of the novel so far as it affects the religious destinies of Russia. Apart from the temptations of nihilism, he, like the future Aliosha Karamazov, knows also the way to the monastery and to religious obedience. Thus after the embraces of the devil—Verkhovensky (in Chapter VIII.)—there is the confession to Tikhon (in our Chapter IX.).

The question which has to be answered first by the student of this fragment is the question of its relation to the text of the finished novel, ***The Possessed.*** Is this Chapter IX. a part of the artistic whole, which, against the artist's wish, has accidentally been omitted, and which therefore must now be restored to its proper place in that whole? Or is it one of those numerous fragments of Dostoevsky's, which, corresponding to some early but subsequently altered scheme of the novel, have been detached from the finished novel, and have not been included in the final text by the artist, but are now preserved only in Dostoevsky's rough manuscripts as curious examples of the complex origin of his books? As to the first of these suppositions, the words of N. Strakhov, which there is no reason to distrust, speak quite clearly. "The scene from Stavrogin (the rape, etc.) Katkov did not want to publish." Thus the omission of the chapter "At Tikhon's" from the novel did not arise from the artist's decision, but from an external cause, the request of the editor of the *Russkii Vestnik,* where ***The Possessed*** was appearing.

Strakhov's evidence is confirmed by the connection which exists between the omitted Chapter IX. and Dostoevsky's creative activity generally, and also with ***The Possessed*** as an artistic whole.

The motif of a cruelly insulted little girl, developed in "Stavrogin's Confession," is evidently one of Dostoevsky's long-standing and enduring ideas. In the year 1866, at the time of his friendship with the family of the Korvin-Krukovskys, Dostoevsky told this idea of his as "a scene from a novel planned by him in his youth." The hero of the novel one morning goes over all his recollections in memory, and "suddenly in the very heat . . . of pleasant dreams and bygone experiences begins to feel an awkwardness—something like an inner pain, an alarm. . . . It appears to him that he must recollect something, and he makes efforts, strains his memory. . . . And suddenly, he actually called to mind, as vividly and realistically as if it had happened yesterday . . . whereas for all these twenty years it had not worried him at all. He remembered how once, after a night of debauchery and under provocation from his friends, he had raped a little girl of ten."

The connection between this idea and "Stavrogin's Confession" is indisputable. The recollection of a sin after a long forgetfulness leads straight to the closing scene of "Stavrogin's Confession" and to the last "vision."

But there are several connecting links between that idea (which in 1866 he thought of as of long standing and remote) and Chapter IX. of ***The Possessed.*** Putting aside ***Crime and Punishment,*** where Svidrigailov's vision before his death is also an echo of that idea, *The Life of a Great Sinner,* which was conceived by him in the years 1869 and 1870, was without doubt to have developed the theme of the injured girl.

The hero of *The Life* was meant to show by the whole course of his existence the religious consistency of life in general, and the inevitability of the acceptance of God. *The Life* in its first parts was to tell the story of the constant and increasing immersion of man in sin. To the artist this utter absorption of the hero in sin was a necessity. Here Dostoevsky by artistic experiment tested one of his dearest and most secret ideas—his belief that each personality and man's life on earth generally will not desert, nor can desert, the kingdom of the Grace of the Spirit so long as it preserves itself entire; that sin has nothing ontological in itself; that man's soul is by its very nature a "Christian." If the notes of *The Life* are read attentively, one sees how Dostoevsky tries to bring the sin and downfall of his hero to the utmost limits, to the last boundary—and this is in order that Dostoevsky's optimistic belief in the essential illumination of life through Grace should be more strikingly justified, and should prevail in the end of *The Life* where "everything is becoming clear," and the ("great") sinner turns to God and dies confessing his crime.

Sin, the deepest sin, is not innate in, but accidental to, man—this belief of Dostoevsky's dominated *The Life,* and led the artist to contrive situations in which the extremes of sin could be shown. To Dostoevsky the violation of the little girl was an extreme of this sort. This theme was provided by the writer with a view to the religious trials of the hero of *The Life,* for among the notes of the plan there is the following: "He makes an attempt on the lame girl. . . ."

It should be plain that Dostoevsky's interest in this conception had risen not from personal recollections, and was not maintained by them, but by the artist's desire to find some adequate way of expressing in the plot his religious conception of the world.

But it is not only the conception of Chapter IX. that is anticipated by the plan of *The Life.* There is a deeper and closer connection between them.

The note, "he makes an attempt on the lame girl," occurring in the plan, is closely connected as a particular development of the general idea with the other note, "straight into the abyss." But this last is intimately connected with another and quite different note, brief but of great significance in the eyes of Dostoevsky, "The Monastery." The Great Sinner, the violator of the little girl, doing penance to Tikhon in the monastery, was meant to form the second part of *The Life,* and in the plan is sketched out by independent notes.

It is at the same time the artistic skeleton of our Chapter IX. of ***The Possessed.*** The relations between Tikhon and the Great Sinner merely anticipate the dialogue between Stavrogin and Tikhon. "He vowed obedience to the boy" (*i.e.* Tikhon to the Great Sinner); "Friendship with the boy who allowed himself to torture Tikhon by pranks (The devil is in him)." These notes are closely related to those passages of the dialogue of Chapter IX. where Tikhon humbly lowers himself before Stavrogin, asks to be forgiven, confesses his love for Stavrogin, while Stavrogin is haughty and mocking. . . . "The boy has at times a low opinion of Tikhon, he is so funny, he does not know things, he is weak and helpless, comes to me for advice; but at last he realizes that Tikhon is strong in mind, as a babe is pure, and that he cannot have an evil thought."

This note appears already as a simple sketch of the dialogue between Stavrogin and Tikhon, in which the relations of the sinner and the ascetic are depticted in this double way by vacillations between suspicious mockery and adoration.

The close correspondence between "Stavrogin's Confession" and the plan of *The Life* can be explained by the history of the logical construction of ***The Possessed.*** That novel grew from the complicated re-fashioning of the originally simple idea which, as it grew larger and broader, drew into itself fragments of *The Life,* which had been coneived at the same time, but had not yet been executed. Stavrogin's appearance in ***The Possessed*** in the part of the principal hero marks a comparatively late stage in the conception of that novel, which coincides with Dostoevsky's determination not to write *The Life.* Stavrogin's character introduced into the novel the broad religious and artistic problems of *The Life of a Great Sinner.* The Great Sinner's meeting with Tikhon and his confession was an organic part of *The Life,* foreseen by Dostoevsky even in the first moments of inspiration.

In so far as Stavrogin is the Great Sinner, his meeting with Tikhon and confession (*i.e.* our Chapter IX.) are a necessary part of ***The Possessed.*** This conclusion is justified by Dostoevsky's direct evidence. There is no doubt that Dostoevsky had Chapter IX. ("At Tikhon's") in view when he says to Katkov, in his letter of October 8, 1870 [see excerpt above], that in ***The Possessed,*** which was at that time being published in the *Russkii Vestnik,* he "wants for the first time . . . to deal with a certain group of people which has as yet been little dealt with in literature. I take Tikhon Sadonsky to be the ideal of such a character. He too is a priest living in a monastery in retirement. With him I confront the hero of my novel and bring them together for a time." That is, up to the end of writing the novel, Dostoevsky himself considered that Chapter IX. was a necessary, inseparable, and essential part of it. The relationship between *The Life of a Great Sinner* and ***The Possessed*** explains that necessity.

Turning to the completed text of ***The Possessed,*** we find signs of the seemingly accidental disappearance of Chapter IX. Without that chapter certain details of the novel appear to be incomplete. Stavrogin, when he awoke "looking stubbornly and curiously at an object in the corner of the room which had struck him, although there was nothing new or particular there . . ." Shatov, seeing Stavrogin out, says to him: "Listen, go and see Tikhon . . . Tikhon, the late Bishop, who through ill-health lives in retirement in this city, in our Yefimev-Bogorodskii Monastery." The first two details (we could indicate others) are, without Chapter IX., superfluous and have no artistic foundation. And only Stavrogin's confession about the devil who persecutes him, only his meeting and conversation with Tikhon, only Chapter IX., give to these details the sense of that anticipation of motive which Dostoevsky was so fond of using.

Finally, by excluding Chapter IX. from the novel, we violate the characteristic grace of Dostoevsky's construction. We violate Dostovesky's aesthetic principle, according to which the action in its early stages advances by motives concealed from the reader, and only when it approaches the catastrophe is the hidden cause immediately made clear by the hero's lengthy confession. Such a "belated exposition" is Raskolnikov's theory, communicated only after the murder. "The Revolt" and "The Legend of the Great Inquisitor"—Ivan Karamazov's Confession—are communicated to the reader only after he already knows that Ivan has consented in his own mind to patricide ("Voluptuaries"). There is also the case of Versilov's confession to his son—after the absurd letter to Madame Ahmakov and immediately before the catastrophe. Stavrogin's confession before the catastrophe, together with events in the last chapter of the second part and the chapters of the third part, correspond perfectly to this obviously characteristic principle in the construction of Dostoevsky's novels.

Such are the reasons for thinking that Chapter IX. was accidentally excluded and that it is necessary to restore it to its proper place in the novel.

There are, however, reasons leading to an opposite solution of the question, and they are the more convincing.

If we compare the character of Stavrogin, as he appears in the novel, with the new material which our fragment (Chapter IX.) adds to that character, important and deep-seated contradictions are at once apparent. A pale mask concealing behind itself indifference to good and evil—such is Stavrogin as we know him in the novel. Chapter IX. ostensibly brings to life that dead inert force by means of his religious experiences. Here Stavrogin's Confession, however absurdly expressed, is a penance, *i.e.* the act of a live religious will. "You have discovered a great way, an unheard-of way," Tikhon says to Stavrogin, "to punish yourself in the eyes of the whole world by the disgrace which you have deserved; you submitted to the judgment of the whole church, without believing in the church." There is also a true humility in Stavrogin: "You . . . speak to me exactly as to an equal," he says to Tikhon; and Tikhon replies: "Your saying that I speak to you as to an equal, although involuntary, is a splendid saying." And finally, the last verdict of the confessor: "For your unbelief God will forgive you, for you truly respect the Holy Spirit without knowing him." If this "Confession" were included in the novel, then Stavrogin's end, his callous—in a religious sense—suicide, would be perfectly impossible and artistically unprepared for. A man who "truly respects the Holy Spirit" could not have written the letters before his death to Darya Pavlovna; Dostoevsky would have prepared a completely different end from the end of Stavrogin for the elect of the Spirit: "the citizen of the canton of Uri hanged here behind the door, etc." This inconsistency in the principal character of the novel, which arises if Chapter IX. is included, clearly forbids any such inclusion. Besides, there are direct proofs that at the time he finished work on ***The Possessed,*** and also later, Dostoevsky considered that Chapter IX. was excluded from the novel. The words of the Apocalpyse, "And to the Angel of the Laodicean Church," would hardly have been repeated by Dostoevsky at the end of the novel in the last talk of Stepan Trofimovich with the "book-pedlar," if he had not considered that Chapter IX. was finally excluded from the text.

Although ***The Possessed*** was published more than once after 1871, Dostoevsky, though no longer bound by Katkov's censorship, did not include Chapter IX. And finally, the following fact gives us the clearest evidence as to how Dostoevsky regarded the fragment in relation to the text of ***The Possessed:*** a considerable part of "Stavrogin's Confession" was inserted by Dostoevsky almost without alteration in the confession of Versilov (***The Raw Youth***), in 1874. The artist might have used for the new novel the material of the rough draft of the preceding novel, but could not possibly have used a fragment of the authentic text.

Thus, both the completeness of Stavrogin's character and the definitely expressed wish of the author compel us to conclude that Chapter IX. was not accidentally omitted, but did not belong to the novel. It is a variant of the manuscript, but nothing more. How then are we to reconcile this conclusion with the one which tells in favour of the opposite solution? Surely Dostoevsky's letter of October 8, 1870, to Katkov clearly refers to our fragment as a necessary part of the novel.

The date, although it coincides with the beginning of the publication of the novel, does not fix the final moment of the conception of ***The Possessed.*** The autumn of 1870 is the time when the idea of ***The Possessed*** had become closely related in Dostoevsky's mind with the idea of *The Life of a Great Sinner*. Stavrogin is almost identified with the hero of *The Life*. And since the crisis of that Life, as it was planned, was the repentance of the sinner and his conversion to God with Tikhon's help, Dostoevsky had then planned the same conversion for Stavrogin. At that moment (the final moment in the creation of the novel, for the first part was already being published) Dostoevsky might, indeed, have thought that Chapter IX.—the story of the meeting of the sinner with Tikhon and the beginning of his repentance—was necessary.

The second part of the novel was evidently written by Dostoevsky with the determination to show the "great sinner" (Stavrogin) converted. Our Chapter IX. corresponds to the "serene" Stavrogin who does not appear in the novel, and of whom a few hints are preserved in the rough draft which no doubt issue from the idea of *The Life*.

The hesitation and vacillation as to the plan of the novel spread over so long a time that, when he was finishing the second part of the novel (Chapter IX.), Dostoevsky was even nearer to the plan of *The Life of a Great Sinner* than to the form which ***The Possessed*** finally took. He still meant to represent his great sinner, Stavrogin, in the light of Grace. But, as he worked on the last chapter of the novel and approached the catastrophe in the third part, Doestoevsky evidently realized that it was impossible to carry out the religious and artistic objects which he had in view. Dostoevsky did not find himself possessed of the artistic powers needed to convert the Great Sinner, and everything that was leading up to the expected conversion (Chapter IX.) was abandoned. Only an echo of his original intention is left—not in the novel even, but on the first page, in the quotation from the Gospels of the promise to the sinner that he shall find salvation at the feet of Christ. The crimes of the hero appeared to the writer at the end of his work suddenly, and against his expectation, like a stronghold, enduring and self-sufficient.

And in this sketch of the evolution of the significant idea of ***The Possessed*** is shown, I think, the usual course of Dostoevsky's artistic problems and their solution. ***The Idiot, The Raw Youth,*** and ***The Brothers Karamazov*** had all, like ***The Possessed,*** been meant originally to reveal that desire for "universal harmony" cherished by Dostoevsky, the universal Hosannah which Dostoevsky, the thinker, had visualized as the hidden essence of the universe, clouded, but only accidentally, by the phantom of sin. But each time, in the finished work of Dostoevsky, the artist, there triumphed a sterner, but for all that a more religious, conception of the world as a world subject to sin, beyond the Grace of the Spirit, which is granted it as a gift, but not hidden in the substance of nature.

"Stavrogin's Confession," as it echoed Dostoevsky's optimistic view, had inevitably to disappear in his masterpiece. (pp. 121-36)

V. Komarovich, "Introduction to the Unpublished Chapter of 'The Possessed'," in Stavrogin's Confession *by F. M. Dostoevsky, translated by Virginia Woolf and S. S. Koteliansky, Lear Publishers, 1947, pp. 118-36.*

LEONID GROSSMAN (essay date 1925)

[*Grossman was a major Soviet scholar of Dostoevski who wrote both biographical and critical studies of the author, including several discussions of his poetics. In the following excerpt, which was first published in 1925 in* Poetika Dostoevskogo, *Grossman analyzes the style of "Stavrogin's Confession" and identifies what he considers its technical and thematic innovations.*]

"Stavrogin's Confession," which has provoked a whole host of biographical, textual, and psychological questions, is of most interest from a purely artistic point of view. It is one of Dostoevsky's most subtle achievements, given the difficulty of the task he set for himself and his confidence in its accomplishment. It is here that the novelist-innovator succeeded in breaking down [the conventions of] traditional narrative, yet maintaining throughout the constant disfiguration of his material, all of its compositional integrity and artistic economy.

The system of speech patterns and the devices with which he constructs this central chapter of ***The Possessed*** are amazingly original. The protocol-like style, the intentionally incorrect, crudely colloquial speech, the almost bureaucratic carelessness of the writing with its obvious mistakes and inaccuracies—make it seem as if a raw chunk of reality has been torn from the most mundane mass and thrown into the pages of a novel in all its ugly imperfection and repulsive unsightliness.

Dostoevsky tries in every way he can to underscore the artlessness of Stavrogin's confession. He wants to make the reader feel that an unpolished human document lies before him that conveys its horrible admissions through the starkness and harshness of that which was experienced. Here everything is awkward, plain, and humdrumly-terrifying, just like in a real-life crime. It is important for the author to highlight this over-simplified character of Stavrogin's writing and thus to erase from the start any traces of literariness. This is by Dostoevsky's design a formal statement, a judicial or psychopathological account, a note written by a criminal—cold, precise, earnest, and, moreover, full of inaccuracies regarding orthography, syntax, style, and the traditional arrangement of parts [of speech].

"I include this document in my chronicle exactly as it was written,"—thus the author introduces the text of "The Confession." "I have taken the liberty of correcting the spelling mistakes, which are numerous and which even surprised me somewhat . . . however, I have made no corrections in the style, despite the inaccuracies. In any case, it is clear that the author is first and foremost not a man of letters." Stavrogin himself makes this important statement in [his] preliminary remarks: "I am not a man of letters." And he notes further, emphasizing the strictly dry and factual character of his manuscript: "I have eliminated any arguments on my behalf."

And so, with a whole series of reservations and then with the highly contrived narrative system of "The Confession" itself, Dostoevsky strives to eliminate any trace of literariness and to turn it into a bare confession. This is not a page taken from a polished memoir, this is simply the voice of a sinner speaking.

Dostoevsky uses a most subtle compositional device to underscore the unliterary character of this strange psychological concoction. By means of razor-sharp contrasts he exposes the terrible impoverishment of Stavrogin's primitive speech. Standing in marked contrast to the formless mass of Stavrogin's phrasing is the subtle sense of artistic style manifest in the person of his confessor. Opposing the sinner greedy for sensual experience is the contemplative-aesthete, the church hierarch, who has had the age-tested *discipline* of literary *taste*.

Dostoevsky highlights in every way possible the boundless artistic instinct evident in his aging bishop. It is remarkable that this ascetic, who is already close to death, is enveloped in an atmosphere of artistic perceptions, and that he is able to maintain it even in the alien cell of the remote monastery to which he has retreated "for the quiet life." Tikhon's aestheticism is expressed first of all in his surroundings: the exquisitely decorated furniture, the expensive Bokhara rug, the engravings of a secular nature, depicting scenes from mythology, and finally, the carved bookcase where "standing alongside the works of the great dignitaries of the church and the zealots of Christianity, were dramatic works and novels, and perhaps even worse things." Characteristic of Tikhon is his interest in even military-historical works, but only insofar as they are a "most interesting description," a "talented account in a purely literary sense," that is, insofar as they reflect values of a stylistic-compositional order.

Throughout his long life Tikhon has, after all, been a student of the difficult and rich school of verbal art. The age-old traditions of liturgical poetics and the writings of the Holy Fathers have accustomed him to the refined and magnificent vestments of Byzantine style even as reflected in various confessions and other writings of spiritual distress. Because of his familiarity with the brilliant eloquence and the decoratively expressive style of the poet-theologians, who were themselves tempted during their versatile explorations of the erotic theme with its arousing temptations and dark downfalls, this perceptive reader of Isaac Sirin and Vasily the Great is all too aware of Nikolai Stavrogin's verbal impoverishment. The magnificent humility of these Orthodox poets gives way to haughty impoverishment and arrogant sterility! Is it not this deformed word that expresses most fully a ruined and wingless soul? Is it not Stavrogin's stylistics tht provide the most damning evidence against him? This is evidently what his old confessor thought.

The shocking revelations found in the pages of "The Confession" evoke, first of all, a literarily critical response from its first reader.

> Tikhon removed his glasses. . . .
>
> —'Wouldn't it be possible to make some changes in this document?
>
> —Why? Every word I wrote was sincere—answered Stavrogin.
>
> —Perhaps a few changes in style. . . .

But Stavrogin hastens once again to dissociate himself from any literariness—from a verbal preoccupation with rhetorical demands. "You can remark that this is or is not an awkward phrase—think what you please—I certainly am not looking for compliments, etc." He reacts scornfully to this literary gamesmanship and fails to understand the profound approach to his manuscript taken bythe spiritual orator: a master of oral and, most likely, of written speech, a person well-versed in all forms of ecclesiastical and secular literature, who is accustomed to see the word as the organic creation and direct expression of a personal spirit, its most transparent crystallization.

And that is why Stavrogin's fractured stylistics is no less shocking to his confessor than the crime which he committed. In the conversation between them that ensues the basic question of sin and repentance is persistently joined to the problem of artistic form and literary style. The moralist and the spiritual pastor in Tikhon in no way blocks out the connoisseur of verbal treasures. In his discourse he places the unexpected aesthetic question alongside the ethical problem. This has the effect, in places, of turning the conversation between the sinner and the prelate into a dispute between two orators of opposing schools.

Seeming to forget the main issue at hand, they argue continuously about the artistic style, the literary form and the different speech formulae of "The Confession" and finally, even about the elegance or the insufficient prettiness of the crime itself. (pp. 148-51)

And in his own memoirlike fragment—with the exception of the final part—Stavrogin sustains a kind of premeditated tone of complete verbal unadornment and lack of embellishment. He rejects equally the stylistic practices of all his early teachers. The elegant and inspired speech of Stepan Trofimich, luxuriant with witty quotations and French aphorisms is as much forgotten as the academic eloquence of the Gottingen professors with their curious scholarly terms and their lively logical syntheses. Rather, what is recalled is the attention to bare details characteristic of the oral heptameter of Prokhor Malov or of those shoeless clerks with whom Prince Harry once consorted. Perhaps there is also a fleeting echo of the mechanically-verbal impulsiveness of a certain member of that absurd circle, namely, the half-mad engineer Kirillov.

All this could facilitate the immediate exposure of that unprecedented verbal system which reflects so clearly the mechanically intersecting planes of this morbid consciousness.

Let us consider these clumsy, awkwardly constructed phrases that construct the story from beginning to end:

"In one [room] I received *one* woman who loved me. . . . but before that this is what happened. . . . They themselves lived next door [in a room] that was more cramped, so that the door that separated them always stood open—which I especially liked." Or consider too: "I was so base that my heart trembled with joy, I stood firm and waited for her to go out first. . . . I felt a terrible temptation toward a new crime, namely, to commit bigamy, because I was already married, but I ran on the advice of another girl whom I confided in about almost everything, even the fact that I did not love the girl whom I so described and that I could never love anyone."

Such feeble syntax at every step of the way unhinges the sentence structure and seems to abandon it to the arbitrariness of oral intonation, which is the only thing able to smooth over the potholes found in the written sentences.

Such was the artist's task: to convey in its entirety the halting oral speech which springs up in the perverted mind of a criminal. And, of course, it was a very difficult task indeed for a novelist to deform a standard literary story and to use devices which intentionally confuse speech. The breaking down of conventional literary smoothness, the destruction of all normal means of orderly verbal communication, the external break with the generally accepted traditions of the printed word—all this forms part of a most complex stylistic experiment with which Dostoevsky had remarkable success. The stratification of traditionally correct speech, the destruction of syntax and the disruption of "artistic prose" create the completely new sensation that a criminal's consciousness is being exposed.

Corresponding to this within the text of the novel is the letter Stavrogin writes before his death, which is also conveyed "word-for word, without any corrections of even the smallest mistakes in style made by the Russian baron's son *(barič)*, who had not completely mastered Russian grammar. . . ."

Stavrogin's epistolary style is as deformed and impotent as his confessional manner. True, here there are attempts at a certain original lyricism, but due to the isolated quality of such declarations against the general background of official self-analysis, they create a numbing effect. Stravrogin's *love* letter sustains the mute and soulless tone of a formal statement of evidence. It seems either to be responding to an interrogation or to be answering a police questionnaire: "I am going in 2 days. . . . I still have 12,000 rubles. . . . I acknowledge that I am guilty in conscience of the death of my wife. I did not see you after that, and that is why I acknowledge," etc.

Stavrogin's letter to Dasha is in a stylistic sense a continuation of "The Confession." At the end of the novel, before the hero's death, an echo is heard of the most tragic part of his life's journey. It is as if this were to compensate for the fact that the central chapter is not part of the general composition of the novel. Thus Dosteovsky does not miss the opportunity of using the device so important for the author of portraying the hero through his own literary style. Despite the absence of the staggering theme of "The Confession," Stavrogin's last letter creates the same terrible impression with its disintegrating, seemingly decomposed and decayed sentences. Here the syntax and the general manner and tone provide evidence of a moral breakdown, of catastrophic dislocations and internal collapse, and of the state of nonbeing which has already set in. Spiritual decay—that is the hallmark of Stavrogin's stylistics, both in the pages of the underground manuscript printed in foreign typography and in the letter he sends from a remote Russian (railroad) station.

But all this "unliterariness" of "The Confession" is, of course, merely skin deep. The breakup of style that is seen here follows its own laws and is combined with a remarkable faithfulness to the artistic form of the autobiographical confession. Although Dostoevsky destroys the impeccable smoothness of the prescribed narrative form, he, at the same time, follows the inviolable canon of the literary confession. Stavrogin's story is, in this sense, profoundly literary, because it faithfully reflects all the characteristics of the confessional genre as it was established in the mid-nineteenth-century European novel. On the surface, Stavrogin's story seems unfinished and obviously imitative of careless, offhand writing. In actuality, however, it strictly conforms to the artistic rules governing "The Confession" as a literary genre.

Let us look, first of all, at the complex system of aesthetic effects which are achieved in the intentionally disordered and artificially distorted speech. The very fabric of the story is . . . always being torn by strange, incorrect turns of speech. The inaccuracies of the style are flaunted by the author like a prescribed task, and they are painstakingly sustained throughout the entire confession. This device is exploited with remarkable finesse and a feeling for measure: it is barely noticeable as one is reading, but it is somehow imperceptibly perceived nevertheless, and, finally, it is fully revealed only with intense study.

The clumsy, crudely constructed and disjointed phrasing provides, however, a perfect backdrop for the precise, heartfelt, and felicitous formulae. The boldly etched and distinct images stand out in sharp relief against the background of distorted syntax and dull expressions. There is also a striking picturesqueness and almost pathological keenness for sharp details, even in indifferently constructed sentences—as, for example, in the description of the tiny red spider on the geranium leaf. A superb sound-image also comes to mind here: "The windows were open. The people living in the house were all artisans, and all day long, from all the floors came the sound of hammers or songs. . . ."

The stylistics and the thematics of the confession are organically interconnected; wherever the shameful crime predominates, Stavrogin's speech, despite its efforts to maintain a formal official tone, becomes disrupted by unusual, disjointed, and broken-off sentences. This manner falters only at the moment of "catharsis"—when he sees Claude Lorraine's painting (from the Dresden gallery) "Acis and Galatea" transformed into a dream about the Golden Age. This passage, which is subsequently carried over to Versilov's confession, is distinguished by the exceptional grace of its verbal construction, the rhythmic smoothness of its almost verselike structure, and by the airiness and lightness of its harmoniously flowing sentences. The abundance of the la, lo, al, ol combinations creates an undulating and melodically smooth sound picture: "It is a corner of the Greek archipelago; the gentle (light-)blue waves, the islands and cliffs, the flowering coast, the magical panorama, the sunset becoming in the distance—you can't convey this with words. Here is the cradle of European civilization. . . ." The prose of the passage forms a free-style meter:

Here beautiful people lived.
They awakened and they went to sleep
Happy and innocent;
The groves were filled with their joyous songs.
The great abundance of their undepleted powers
Went into love and simple-hearted joy.
The sun flooded with its rays
These islands and (this) sea,
Rejoicing over its beautiful children . . .
A wondrous dream, a lofty delusion!

Here the criminal's formal statement becomes a classical dithyramb, and the wooden officialese used to describe the crime is transformed into the loftiness of a devotional hymn.

All this complex and diverse composition is enframed by raw shreds of bureaucratese. The confession begins and ends with the traditional formulae of official depositions. It is as if the corners of the document with the official stamps intrude upon . . . a criminal's novella. . . . Everything according to form: the name, rank, date, and place of the act committed, the reference to witnesses ("the lower-middle-class [family] may be in Petersburg even now, [and] they will, of course, remember the house. . . ."), the permanent address, the pledge to stay in one place, the signature. It all reeks of the investigator's chambers. The only thing that is missing is the "places for the stamps," and the indecipherability of the design on the official seals.

Such are the naked shreds of an official document in the life of a great sinner. (pp. 151-55)

Such is the extraordinary and subtle compositional system of Stavrogin's "Confession." The sharp self analysis of a criminal consciousness and the merciless recording of all its pettiest bifurcations required even in the very tone of the story of a new principle for the stratification of words and for splitting up pure and fluent speech. Throughout most of the story one feels that the principle of decomposition is working its effects on the orderly narrative style. The killingly analytical theme of the confession of a terrible sinner required such a fractured and continuously disintegrating, as it were, embodiment. The artificially finished, flowing, and balanced speech of a literary description would have been completely unsuited to the chaotically terrifying and anxiously shaky world of a criminal heart. The monstrous ugliness and inexhaustible horror of Stavrogin's reminiscences demanded such a disruption of traditional speech. The nightmarish theme persistently sought out new devices for making the speech distorted and irritating.

"Stavrogin's Confession" is a remarkable stylistic experiment, in which the classic artistic prose of the Russian novel had its first convulsions, and twisted and turned in the direction of as yet unknown future achievements. It is only against the background of the European art of the present time that the criteria can be found to evaluate all the prophetic devices of Stavrogin's disorganized stylistics. (pp. 157-58)

Leonid Grossman, "The Stylistics of 'Stavrogin's Confession': A Study of the New Chapter of 'The Possessed'," translated by Katherine Tiernan O'Connor, in Critical Essays on Dostoevsky, *edited by Robin Feuer Miller, G. K. Hall & Co., 1986, pp. 148-58.*

I. A. RICHARDS (essay date 1927)

[Richards was an English poet and critic who has been called the founder of modern literary criticism. Primarily a theorist, he encouraged the growth of textual analysis and, during the 1920s, formulated many of the principles that later became the basis of New Criticism, one of the most important schools of modern critical thought. In the following excerpt, Richards attempts to depict the essence of Stavrogin and Dostoevski's intentions in creating that character. This essay originally appeared in Forum *in 1927.]*

What is Stavrogin essentially? Several theories have been put forth. According to Mr. Murry [see excerpt dated 1916] he is essentially the Conscious Will which has cut itself completely loose from the life of instinct; he is the limiting point of consciousness and his suicide is the logical outcome of the purely conscious life, the end to which pure consciousness must always come. Stavrogin, by this theory, is purely a Will seeking always more and more extreme tasks to perform. A Will testing its strength to the uttermost. Therefore when this spoilt darling of Saint Petersburg society has exhausted the possibilities of ordinary experience he turns to debauchery, not because it attracts him—nothing attracts him on this theory—but because it doesn't. His debauchery is part of his policy of trying everything. And afterward he turns to exploit the possibilities of the ridiculous. He secretly marries a lame idiot girl, he pulls a pompous clubman's nose, he bites the governor's ear, because these feats are still more arduous tests of his strength. So finally he publicly denies his marriage (knowing that soon he will publicly confess it) and, crowning triumph, he refrains from killing his disciple Shatov when Shatov, because of the lie which Stavrogin has just told, strikes him in the face. This last act of self-conquest is for Mr. Murry the end of Stavrogin. His Will has triumphed over his pride and in so doing it has slain itself. Henceforeward he is only an empty shadow, a dead man already, to whom all things are the same.

This is a very plausible theory. Unfortunately, since Mr. Murry wrote, an additional chapter of ***The Possessed*** has been published. I refer to "Stavrogin's Confession," an addition which throws a flood of light on Stavrogin's psychology and incidentally on Dosteovsky's own. So far from Stavrogin's experiments in the ridiculous being supreme tests of his will power they are seen to have another source. Stavrogin himself is speaking: "Every unusually disgraceful, utterly degrading, dastardly, and, above all, ridiculous situation in which I ever happened to be in my life, always roused in me, side by side with extreme anger, an incredible delight . . . It was not the vileness that I loved (here my mind was perfectly sound) but I enjoyed rapture from the tormenting consciousness of the baseness." With Dostoevsky's other books in mind there is nothing in this that need surprise as Stavrogin's lust for a consciousness of vileness links up with his pride and the two together are the key to his religious dilemma.

According to Shatov (who through his resemblance to Myshkin and Alyosha Karamazov is certainly the character in ***The Possessed*** who has the most authority and the best claim to speak the final word) Stavrogin is "an atheist because he is a snob, a snob of the snobs. He has lost the distinction between good and evil because he has lost touch with the common people." The true Russian is untouched by the difficulties and dilemmas of the intelligentsia because he has his work to do.

"Listen," Shatov says, "Attain to God by work, it all lies in that. Peasants' work, ah, you laugh, you're afraid of some trick."

But Stavrogin was not laughing.

"You suppose that we can attain to God by work," he repeated, "reflecting as though he had really come across something new and serious which was worth considering." Shatov with his belief in Russia, in the new advent, in the Russian Christ (views which Myshkin before and Alyosha afterward also expound and which were Dosteovsky's views also as a publicist) represents a past phase of Stavrogin. A faith which Stavrogin had himself tried in vain to hold. But even Shatov, and here he is speaking for Dosteovsky himself, cannot believe.

When Stavrogin challenges him Shatov can only stammer, "I,—I will believe in God."

Not one muscle moved in Stavrogin's face. Stavrogin too did not believe in God, and as the "Confession" makes clear he had given up trying. What he is trying to do instead is to find a way of forgiving himself. He is tormented by remorse for the crime he confesses to Bishop Tikhov, a crime which Dostoevsky could invent for him to have committed. For Stavrogin at this stage God would have been primarily a means by which he could have been punished and forgiven. But he knows this and such a belief seems to him too easy a way to forgiveness. His self-contempt is so great that, even if Christ could forgive him, he, Stavrogin, cannot. This self-contempt again remarkably resembles pride.

Two years before the crisis of the story Stavrogin had two disciples, Shatov and Kirilov, both men of fine simplicity and innocence. To both Stavrogin had seemed little less than a Messiah. Simultaneously, but without either knowing about the other, he had indoctrinated them with utterly dissimilar creeds, Shatov with a faith in the Russian God and Kirilov with views which in the interval have been worked up into the conviction that it is his duty to kill himself because God does not exist. Since God does not exist he, Kirilov, must be the supreme Will in the universe, and as such he is bound to show self-will and the highest self-will is the destruction of that Will by itself. But Kirilov like Shatov has not lost touch with the common people. His social impulse is still strong. He kills himself in order to prove that man is God, and to make it unnecessary for other men to kill themselves. Once he has proved this, the Man-God will arise, the earthly paradise will come about.

For Stavrogin this strange argument takes a parallel form, but with a difference. Since God does not exist he, Stavrogin, must take on God's functions. He must punish himself in order to forgive himself. In the end he too kills himself. But not to show the way or to inaugurate the reign of the Man-God. He is evil and knows that he is evil, in just the sense in which he himself says that Kirilov is good. Stavrogin has lost his social instincts. They have gone, together with everything else which makes life possible, in the total devastation of his personality. So he "brushes himself off the earth like a nasty insect." But originally Dostoevsky meant to save Stavrogin, to convert him and to restore him to grace. He found in the end that he could not. The decay in Stavrogin had gone too far. The artist in Dostoevsky—something stronger than the prophet, the philosopher, the teacher—intervened. Stavrogin's end was the only one which could be accepted by the whole of Dostoevsky's mind (as opposed to the desperate efforts of a part of his mind, the part which struggled to believe in God).

This is what I [mean] . . . by saying that the clue to Dostoevsky is that he was an artist. All sorts of partial impulses toward edification, toward optimism, toward the preaching of a premature beatitude, toward a simple salvation through faith in the Russian God, were always tugging at him but his sense of life as a great artist, the sense of life as it came to the whole of his mind, not a part only, forced him to take another way. This, incidentally, is why he makes Myshkin, his perfect man, an idiot, a thing that has bewildered many readers. He makes Stavrogin (whom he admired perhaps even more than Myshkin) "brush himself off the earth like a nasty insect" because he felt that there was no possible way of life open to him. His pride, his nostalgia for the ultimate (taking the form of introspection), his lust for self-contempt, had eaten away everything and there was nothing left to be saved.

But to put it this way suggests that Stavrogin is no more than an awful warning of the dangers of disbelief. You can of course make him such a warning if you like, but to do so is to miss the point. Stavrogin is a work of art; we shouldn't look at him as an exhibit in a chamber of horrors or as a specimen in a psychological laboratory. Dostoevsky is not using Stavrogin in order to point a moral. He is doing something much more difficult and much more important than that. Stavrogin is there, not as an object lesson nor as an instance, he is there in order that we may imagine him and, while imagining him, become more completely ourselves.

In so doing we do not necessarily become more like Stavrogin or less like him (though this will depend obviously upon what we were like before). The whole conception that art works by making us copy or shun the examples held up before us can today be rejected as mistaken. What happens is something more difficult to describe. In contemplating Stavrogin, the more fully we realize him and imagine him as Dostoevsky saw him, a change takes place in ourselves. We can express this change by saying that we feel in the presence of beauty. Not that Stavrogin or his suicide or his entanglements in the lives of the other characters are beautiful, far from it; but the whole thing has a combined effect upon the reader, and it is this effect which matters. It was for this that Dostoevsky created him, his history and his fate.

I know that to call this effect the sense of the presence of beauty is misleading. It is only a way of signaling that the effect is valuable in a certain way and if you ask what this way is, I can only say that it makes a fuller and completer life more easy. Impulses in ourselves which make life difficult or narrow it down into an affair of pretenses and evasions become, through such works of art as Stavrogin's story, more manageable. Feelings and impulses for which we have no better names than horror, despair, shame, desolation, pettiness, futility, doubt, and fear get, not pushed out of sight, but somehow reconstituted so as to become parts of a possible way of accepting existence. In other words we find a way of life. This is what God was for Dostoevsky. As Mr. Murry very finely says, "God was for him the possibility of acceptance, the hope of a way of life. He knew that belief in God as a person, the faith of religion as we understand religion, was denied to him forever. He asked no more than a way of life." My own view is that he found it through his work as a creative artist. At the end of his life he wrote in a letter: "There is only one cure, one refuge,—art, creative activity"; and I believe that for those who are less creative the answer is the same.

Yet in this very letter this quest for a way of life is confused once again with the problem of the existence of a Deity. Dostoevsky, never as a thinker in the narrower sense but only as a creative artist, got the two problems separated. He never understood that the way of life which he sought could be its own sanction and that it needs no sanction from a belief in God. The great dilemma which recurs so often in his work—"If God does not exist then all things are lawful"—the dilemma which drove Ivan Karamazov mad, never gave up its secret to him, yet it is really not a dilemma but a riddle, a verbal ambiguity. If there is no God in the sense of no way of life, no scheme of values, then indeed everything is lawful. But a scheme of values, a way of life, is not dependent upon the existence of a Deity, though historically the two questions have been fused together. Our accepted values, which repose finally upon our needs as social human beings, can, of course, gain a powerful support from a belief in a Diety. But this support is inessential and it is one which Dostoevsky himself when he was most fully alive found himself compelled to do without. (pp. 153-58)

I. A. Richards, "The God of Dostoevsky," in his Complementarities: Uncollected Essays, *edited by John Paul Russo, Cambridge, Mass.: Harvard University Press, 1976, pp. 148-58.*

ERNEST J. SIMMONS (essay date 1940)

[*An American biographer and scholar of Russian literature, Simmons wrote* Dostoevski: The Making of a Novelist, *which is considered one of the foremost discussions of his life and writings. In that work, excerpted below, Simmons examines the development of Dostoevski's ideas as reflected in his creative works. Here, he points out the dualism of Dostoevski's political views as shown in* The Possessed.]

When Dostoevski began ***The Possessed*** he had written his niece that he could make of it a book that would be talked of a hundred years hence if only he had the time and means at the disposal of his great rivals in fiction. The artistic imperfections which he worried about have never seriously endangered the immortality of the work, but he could not anticipate then the world events which have made ***The Possessed*** perhaps his most discussed novel today. The socialist revolution in Russia has directed the attention of modern critics to the novel, and they have found it a remarkable prophecy of many recent happenings in that country. Literary critics, journalists, and students of political science have frequently cited it, largely by way of supporting their condemnation of events in Soviet Russia. Often such criticisms reveal a misunderstanding of both Dosteovski's political thinking and its relation to the social history of his age.

History is no doubt an unfailing and obligatory condition of sociological analysis, but it is not easy to interpret Dostoevski's political beliefs in terms of the class struggle and its national surroundings in Russia between 1840 and 1880. Soviet critics have contributed a number of studies of Dostoevski from the Marxian point of view and the results are peculiarly contradictory. Some concepts in his political thinking seemed to have been arrived at by a process of divination, and the panaceas which he offers for Russia's social ills resemble incantations rather than rational cures. Further, the functional role of his creative process is so often a matter of feeling rather than reason that it is difficult to relate it to the practical problems of his times.

It is uncritical to dismiss Dostoevski as a confirmed reactionary, as is so often done, for the temperament of the conservative was essentially foreign to his nature. The dualism reflected in so many of his great characters was simply a projection of the constant struggle that went on in his own mind. In this endless warfare of reason and feeling, the quality of his thought remained dynamic. These characteristics conditioned his political thinking. . . . [The] rebel in him was always just beneath the surface. It could erupt in moments of extreme conservatism. No man suffered more inwardly because of his convictions, for he was constantly undergoing the tortuous process of changing them. In 1876, at a time when he was supposed to be engrossed with reactionary friends and ideas, he wrote in the foreword to the first part of ***The Diary of a Writer:*** 'I reckon myself more liberal than all, although it may be only in this one thing that I do not wish to be lulled.' These facts must be kept in mind in considering his political beliefs as they are reflected in ***The Possessed.*** (pp. 287-88)

Dostoevski's understanding of the theoretical background of the Russian revolutionary movement of his day was most imperfect, and his knowledge of its practical operations extremely limited. This fact, almost as much as his uncompromising hostility, accounts for the mistakes and patent exaggerations of the doctrines and actions of the conspirators in the novel. He admitted that he knew very little about Nechaev, and his information of the actions and personalities of the other conspirators was drawn largely from newspaper reports which, in the circumstances at this time in Russia, were much compressed and by no means unprejudiced. Yet Nechaev inspired the image of Verkhovenski, who represented Dostoevski's idea of the young radical of the age. In his mouth is placed a political programme which Dostoevski apparently believed to be typical of the revolutionists. It will be instructive to examine this programme.

Shigalov is the theoretician of the conspirators in ***The Possessed.*** From the notes to the novel, it appears that his system was suggested by Bakunin's *Catechism of a Revolutionist* which had been introduced into Russia by Nechaev. Any contemporary student of the radical movement knew that there was a world of difference between the popular evolutionary socialism of Herzen and his followers and the destructive peasant anarchism of Bakunin. Whatever may have been the similarity in ends, Bakunin's anarchistic means and totalitarian concepts found little favour among the socialists of this period.

Shigalov declares: 'I am perplexed by my own data: my conclusion is a direct contradiction of the original idea with which I start. Starting from unlimited freedom, I end with unlimited despotism.' His solution of the social question is to divide mankind into two unequal parts. 'One-tenth receives freedom of individuality and unlimited power over the remaining nine-tenths. These must surrender all individuality and become, so to speak, a herd, and, through boundless submission and by a series of regenerations, they will attain a primitive innocence, something like a primeval paradise, although they will have to work.'

Shigalov is prevented from developing his bizarre notions by the many interruptions at the nihilist gathering. He has given a cue to Verkhovenski, however, who also claims to know the full text of Shigalov's system. What he advocates is not Shigalovism or any socialist theory, but the revolutionary tactics of Nechaev, wildly exaggerated in all their reprehensible features. He takes for his slogan freedom, equality, and socialism. For him, these words have special meanings which are not the commonly accepted ones, either as abstract definitions or as descriptions of these terms as they were used in Russian revolutionary theorizing. He explains his meaning to Stavrogin: 'Everyone belongs to all and all to everyone. All are slaves and equal in their slavery. In extreme cases there are slander and murder, but the chief thing is equality. To begin with, the level of education, science, and talents is lowered. A high level of science and talents is suitable only for great intellects, and great intellects are not wanted . . . Slaves are bound to be equal. Without despotism there has never been freedom or equality, but in the herd there is bound to be equality, and that's Shigalovism!'

Verkhovenski's conception of socialism is all of a piece with his notions of freedom and equality. He pictures the millennium for Stavrogin: 'Culture is unnecessary; we've had enough of science! Without science we have material enough for a thousand years, but one must maintain discipline. The only thing that is lacking in the world is discipline. The thirst for culture is an aristocratic search. The moment you have a family or love you get the desire for property. We will destroy that desire: we will make use of drunkenness, slander, spying; we'll make use of incredible corruption; we'll stifle every genius in its infancy. Everything to one common denominator, complete equality.' Then in his effort to induce Stavrogin to be the leader of the projected revolt, Verkhovenski's imagination soars and his language becomes violent. He acts like a man drunk with a sense of power, and one for whom intrigue is an end in itself. In his new State, he tells Stavrogin, a Cicero would have his tongue cut out, a Copernicus would be blinded, and a Shakespeare stoned. Even the Pope will come to terms and help lead the rabble on to victory. Every element of crime and vice will be put to the service of the cause. 'One or two generations of debauchery are essential now,' he continues, 'unparalleled, vulgar debauchery, when man turns into a filthy, cowardly, cruel, selfish reptile. That's what we need! And what's more, a little "fresh blood" that we may get accustomed to it . . . We will proclaim destruction . . . Why, why has this idea such a fascination? But we must have a little excuse; we must. We'll set fires . . . we'll set legends going . . . Every mangy "group" will be of use. From these groups I'll search out for you such fellows who will not shrink from shooting, and will remain grateful for the honour. Well, the upheaval will begin! There's going to be such an overthrow as the world has never seen before . . . Russia will be plunged into darkness. The earth will weep for its old gods.' (pp. 290-93)

Verkhovenski definitely falls into the Self-Willed group of characters, and it is highly significant that Dostoevski should have made such a type the leader and mouthpiece of the radicals. Obviously, Verkhovenski's solution of social problems is bound to be an antisocial solution, for his social feelings are dead, as are those of the other criminal Self-Willed characters, such as Orlov, Petrov, Valkovski, and Svidrigailov. For Verkhovenski, freedom and equality without despotism are unthinkable; they are simply the theoretic expressions of self-will and immoralism. He even admits to Stavrogin that he is not a socialist and that he is a scoundrel. If those prize criminals in ***The House of the Dead,*** Orlov and Petrov, had been able to express their relations to society and their notions of freedom, equality, and socialism, their formulation would have been quite similar to that of Verkhovenski. His ideas on freedom and equality amount to the destruction of society in the name of his own personality. Society becomes an absolute zero in his scheme of things. Verkhovenski, then, is a monster and not a radical, and his social ideology is the criminal creed of the absolutely self-willed man. Dostoevski went completely out of his way to present him in the most unfavourable light possible. His vain, deceitful nature has scarcely a single redeeming feature, and he even stoops to the base treachery of the *agent-provocateur,* for it is hinted at the end that he betrays his own followers to the government.

The social ideology of Verkhovenski is no doubt consistent with this Self-Willed type, but in allowing it to typify the general aims of the Russian revolutionary movement in the 1860's Dostoevski committed a serious error and one that the radicals of the time were quick to condemn. That he was serious in his intention is indicated by a letter to the future Alexander III [see excerpt dated 1873]; in it he says that the novel virtually represents a historical study in which he tries to show that the radical movement resulted largely from the fact that Russian intellectuals were out of touch with the masses and unsympathetic to them.

Dostoevski's error is rooted in the general confusion in his mind concerning the aims of the radical movement and in his indiscriminate mixing of nihilists and revolutionary terrorists. Much of his point of view in understanding the 1860's was hopelessly distorted by the radical experiences of his own youth. He seemed to regard Nechaev as the final violent manifestation of the revolutionary movement that began in the 1840's. In the notes, he calls him the last Russian conspirator, when in reality he was one of the first of the revolutionary-democratic workers in the cause, and one whose extreme tactics were repudiated by his successors. Even Bakunin rejected the tactics of his pupil and eventually broke with him. Yet Nechaev and his followers are often construed in terms of the members of the Petrashevski group, for Dostoevski seemed to think it important to prove that the radical youths of the 1860's had nothing more to offer than the impractical programme of the old liberals of the 1840's. This intention is plainly manifested in the notes where he reminds himself by the observations: 'Nechaev partly Petrashevski' and 'To keep closer to the type of Petrashevski.' Such an approach was probably dictated by his passionate desire to deny any progress in the bourgeois-democratic revolution, which he had come to fear and hate. Nihilism, which had taken on the proportions of a fad in his day, he excoriated in the burlesqued meeting of the conspirators in the novels. Yet he did not understand that nihilism was the result of the despair of all productive action felt by thwarted subjects who possessed absolutely no rights in a state governed by police. The nihilists, however, were crass egoists and had no constructive programme, and there was some justice in Dostoevski's condemnation of them. It was vicious misrepresentation, however, to confuse them with the revolutionary terrorists whose acts had aroused his ire. These radicals were men of lofty ideals, and their definite programme was not designed to create a social system that reduced men to the equality of slaves. Their deeds, however futile, compose one of the greatest stories of selfless, sacrificing activity in the whole history of the Russian revolutionary movement.

Dostoevski either did not know or wilfully maligned the real Russian revolutionists of his time. The underground type of revolutionist who put his faith in the proletariat and ultimately brought about the Revolution of 1917 did not exist in Dostoevski's day. As yet there was no class-conscious proletariat. In actuality the radical movement was made up largely of followers of Herzen whose programme had developed into the widespread Populism of the period. In a sense this amounted to a synthesis of the position of the two old rival camps of Westerners and Slavophiles. The revolutionary theories of the West, when applied to peculiarly Russian peasant conditions, would bring about a social revolution through gradual and non-violent means until finally the communized peasantry would fulfil its universal subversive mission in Europe.

Doestoevski's positive programme, his answer to the social anarchy of the conspirators in ***The Possessed,*** is placed mostly in the mouth of Shatov. The argument was not unfamiliar to his readers. It is simply an elaboration of the statement of Myshkin in ***The Idiot,*** and it derives partly from the Slavophile doctrine. Shatov himself is represented as a Slavophile. The answer has Dostoevski's own peculiar idealistic colouring. Prophecy takes the place of logic, spiritual postulates are substituted for historical analysis. By forsaking Christ, Roman Catholicism has ruined the whole Western world. Out of it has grown socialism, which is predicated on atheism, materialism, and reason. Like the Catholic Church, it strives to achieve equality by despotism. It is only Russian intellectuals, the liberals and radicals, who have been infected by this noxious virus of the West. They must return to the soil, to the masses, and to the Russian Christ. Shatov, a peasant by birth, symbolizes the 'new people' who will not only save Russia, but the world. In the notes there is a bit of dialogue between him and Stavrogin that does not appear in the novel. Yet it pointedly states Dostoevski's formula of salvation for all Russians afflicted by the disease of Western intellectualism, and prophesies the world-mission of the Russian people. (pp. 293-96)

This is too much, even for Stavrogin, and he dismisses it all as 'fanaticism.' The word is not inappropriate. Dostoevski's picture of revolution in ***The Possessed*** has been commended as a startling prophecy of what has happened in Soviet Russia. Parallels have been drawn between Pyotr Verkhovenski's Shigalovism—its freedom and equality through despotism, its atheism, its sacrifice of the dignity of the individual, and its complete justification of any means to achieve the end of purely imaginary socialism—and conditions of life in socialist Russia today. On the other hand, certain elements of Dostoevski's own programme suggest a parallel with the doctrine of Nazism. While Shatov tries desperately to find some spark of the former faith in Stavrogin, he says to him, among other things: 'If a great people does not believe that the truth is to be found in it alone (in itself alone and exclusively in itself), if it does not believe that it alone is fit and destined to raise up and save all by its truth, it at once ceases to be a great nation, and at once turns into ethnographical material and not into a great people. A truly great people can never reconcile itself with a secondary role in humanity or even with the first, but without fail must exclusively play the first role. A nation which loses this belief ceases to be a nation.'

It is only fair to say, however, that Shatov's extreme nationalism, which was Dostoevski's profound conviction, was intimately connected with religious beliefs that verged on mysticism. The truth is God, and Russia is the only 'God-bearing' nation, destined to save the whole world through this symbol of faith. He also associates this truth, by way of refuting the rational truth of socialism as the salvation of nations, with the 'seeking for God,' and the 'spirit of life.' This is the truth that dawns upon Stepan Trofimovich at the end and points the moral of the novel. Just before his death, the evangelical Bible-seller reads him the passage from Luke on the devils that enter into the Gadarene swine—a passage that stands as the epigraph to ***The Possessed.*** He imagines the devils as all the sores, impurities, and foul contagion that will leave the sick body of Russia and enter the swine—the nihilists—and be drowned in the sea. Holy Mother Russia will be healed, and all will 'sit at the feet of Jesus.' Stepan Trofimovich dies, happy in the thought that he has discovered something infinitely great before which he can bow down.

Neither the extremes of Dostoevski's reactionary convictions nor his own brand of socialism—for he had one—are fully revealed in ***The Possessed.*** The novel gives the impression of having been written in anger over a stupid crime that symbolized for him the vicious excesses of the young radical generation. Yet he did not know and hence failed to understand the radical youths of the 1860's who sacrificed all for a futile cause. Like Turgenev, he was incapable of creating a positive revolutionary hero. Nor does the novel reveal any of his profound sympathy for the down-trodden ana oppressed of Russia whose bitter lot these same radicals strove to alleviate. His answer was to idealize their suffering and make out of it a way of life. Instead of practical reforms, he offered them religious and mystical consolation. Yet the ultimate of his solution was the brotherly love and universal happiness of primitive communism, and, like the more enlightened socialists of his own day, he placed his hope for the salvation of Russia in the masses. He would achieve this end, however, by faith in God and in the innate goodness of man, not in revolution and in a planned society. Perhaps more clearly than anything else, the novel reflects the internal contradiction and fear among the mass of bourgeoisie of the time before the spectre of revolt and radical change. (pp. 297-99)

Even before the novel was finished—he worked on it for over three years—there was a shift in his point of view towards the hero and the purpose of the work. At the end of this period, he criticized the novelist Leskov for his unfair treatment of the nihilists in a recently published work. Only a few years later, he took to task a critic who dismissed Nechaev as an idiotic fanatic, supporting his point by mentioning that he himself, in the Petrashevski days of his youth, had been a kind of Nechaev [see excerpt from ***The Diary of a Writer*** dated 1873]. And in the notes to the last part of ***The Possessed,*** there is a brief draft of a foreword which he never used. He wrote: 'In Kirilov is a national idea—to sacrifice oneself immediately for truth . . . to sacrifice oneself and everything for truth—that is a national feature of the generation. May God bless it and bring to it an understanding of the truth. For the whole question consists in what to regard as truth. For this reason the novel was written.' This statement indicates a considerable retreat from the intransigent attitude in which he began the novel. Before he had reached the end, the whole problem had been swept back into the cauldron of his mind—was God the truth, to be achieved by faith, or was truth at the end of man's rational quest? (p. 299)

Ernest J. Simmons, in his Dostoevski: The Making of a Novelist, *Oxford University Press, 1940, 416 p.*

KONSTANTIN MOCHULSKY (essay date 1947)

[Mochulsky, a Russian émigré critic, is a major Dostoevski scholar and the author of Dostoevsky: His Life and Work, *originally published in Russian in 1947 and excerpted below. This wide-ranging study, which is considered a thorough introduction to Dostoevski's novels, combines biographical and critical investigation with insight into the author's philosophical and religious views. Here, Mochulsky explores Dostoevski's poetics as exemplified in* The Possessed. *Arguing that "all the peculiarities of the structure and technique of Dostoevsky's novels are explained by the principle of artistic expressiveness," Mochulsky first defines the concept of expressive art and then demonstrates how the novel's structure and characterization derive from that approach.]*

Dostoevsky was the creator of a new narrative form, the novel-tragedy. In ***Crime and Punishment*** and in ***The Idiot*** it was elaborated and developed, in ***The Devils*** it attained its perfection. ***The Devils*** is one of the greatest artistic works in world literature. In notebook No. 3 [of *The Notebooks for "The Possessed"* (see Additional Bibliography)] the writer himself defines the genre he had created. "I don't describe the city," states the chronicler,

> the setting, mores, people, functions, the relationships and the curious vacillations in these relationships of our provincial capital's strictly private life. . . . I also have no time to be expressly occupied with a *picture* of our little corner. I consider myself a chronicler of one curious, private *event,* that took place among us suddenly, unexpectedly, in recent times, and plunged us all into bewilderment. It goes without saying, since the affair took place not in heaven, but rather among us, that it is just impossible for me not to concern myself sometimes in a purely pictorial fashion with the mores aspect of life in our province; but I caution that I will do this only insofar as it will be required by the most urgent necessity. I will not begin to occupy myself especially with the descriptive part of our contemporary manners.

Dostoevsky's novel is not the description of a city, not a portrayal of manners: the "descriptive part," the conditions of life, do not engage him. He is a chronicler of events that are unexpected, sudden, amazing. His art is contrary to the poetics of Tolstoy, Turgenev, Goncharov: against the *statics* of descriptions and history he advances the *dynamics* of events—movement, action, struggle. He had "no time" to paint with words or to narrate customs in epic style; he was himself seized by a whirlwind and carried along with the rushing current of happenings. In one of his letters to Maikov we find the remarkable sentence: "Being more a *poet* than an *artist,* I have perpetually adopted themes beyond my own powers." The writer was sincerely convinced that his novels lacked sufficient artistry, justified himself by his oppressive working conditions, and humbly acknowledged himself inferior to such artists as Turgenev and Lev Tolstoy. This low opinion of his works is explained by the limitations of his poetics. For Dostoevsky, artistry was identical with *descriptiveness,* "the ability to paint," and he understood that he did not compare in this area with the masters of "the tableau." But he did not guess that his artistry was completely different, not comparable with the former and perhaps superior to it. To the principle of descriptiveness he opposed the principle of *expressiveness* (that which he called poetry); to the epic—the drama, to contemplation—inspiration. Descriptive art reproduces a natural given: it is directed to the sense of measure and harmony, to the Apollonian principle in men; its summit lies in impassioanate, aesthetic contemplation; expressive art tears itself away from nature and creates a myth about man: it calls upon our will and questions our liberty; it is Dionysian and its summit is tragic inspiration. The first is passive and natural, the second active and personal; we admire one, participate in the other. One glorifies necessity, the other affirms freedom; one is *static,* the other *dynamic.*

All the peculiarities of the structure and technique of Dostoevsky's novels are explained by the principle of artistic expressiveness. He knows only man, his world and his fate. The hero's personality appears as the axis of composition; around it the dramatis personae are distributed and the plot is constructed. Raskolnikov stands at the center of ***Crime and Punishment***; at the center of ***The Idiot***—Prince Myshkin. This centralization attains its limit in ***The Devils.*** In the notebook we . . . [find] the notation: *"The prince [Stavrogin] is everything."* And in fact, the whole novel is the fate of Stavrogin alone, everything is about him and everything is for him. The exposition is devoted to the story of Stepan Trofimovich Verkhovensky—the hero's tutor and ideational father; the spiritual roots of the atheist of the sixties are immerged in the "romantic dreaming" of the forties. Therefore, Verkhovensky enters Stavrogin's biography. Next to his father in spirit is set his mother in the flesh—Varvara Petrovna, who is intimately bound by twenty years of friendship to her "hanger-on." Four women are grouped around the hero—Liza Tushina, Dasha, Marya Timofeyevna, and Shatov's wife: all of them, like mirrors, reflect various images of the charming demon. The women are a part of the Russian Don Juan's tragic fate; in them lies his possibility of salvation and the threat of ruin. With repsect to the "eternal feminine" he commits his greatest crime (Matryosha) and his loftiest action (his marriage to the cripple): he awaits resurrection through a woman's love (Liza) and before death comes running to a woman's maternal compassion (Dasha).

The stages of the wanderer Stavrogin's life are marked by women's names; his ideational trials are symbolized by his amorous deceptions. His ruin becomes inevitable when love is finally extinguished in his heart (the farewell with Liza at Skvoreshchniki). Following the first concentric circle—four women—comes a second—four men: Shatov, Kirilov, Pyotr Verkhovensky, and Shigalyov. The image of Don Juan is replaced by the image of Faust—the seeker, eternally dissatisfied and rebellious. Stavrogin is their teacher, their leader, and master. They all live by his life; they are his ideas, which have received independent existence. The hero's complex and contradictory personality generates the Orthodox nationalist Shatov, and the man-god Kirilov, and the revolutionary Pyotr Verkhovensky, and the fanatic Shigalyov. Both the mistresses and the disciples who are in love with their master—all these are only Stavrogin, only his consciousness, dissolving into insurmountable contradictions, struggling with the demon's temptations.

The third concentric circle is composed of secondary personages from Pyotr Verkhovensky's "society": petty devils, let go upon the earth by "the great and terrible spirit of negation": the Virginskys, Liputin, Lebyadkin, Erkel, Lyamshin, and several of the "inhabitants" of the provincial capital. Finally, the governor Von Lembke and the great writer Karamazinov are linked to the main hero through the Drozdov family: Liza Tushina is the daughter of General Drozdov's widow, Karmazinov is her relative. By means of this centralized composition an extraordinary unity of action and proportionality of parts are attained. The radii from all the circles lead to the center; the currents of energy run through the whole organism of the novel, throwing all its parts into action. Shocks and explosions, taking place in the depth of the hero's consciousness, transmit vibrations from one circle to another: the waves dilate and grow, tension seizes a few people at first, then small groups, and finally, the whole city. Stavrogin's inner struggle becomes a general movement, is embodied in conspiracies, revolts, fires, murders, and suicides. Thus ideas are transformed into passions, passions into men, men express themselves in events. The internal and exterior are indivisible. The dissolution of personality, riot in the provincial capital, the spiritual crisis that Russia was experiencing, the world's entry into a catastrophic period of its history—such are the dilating circles of ***The Devils'*** symbolism. Stavrogin's personality is universal to the world and all mankind.

• • • • •

The second particularity of Dostoevsky's expressive art is its *dramatism*. ***The Devils*** is a theatre of tragic and tragi-comic masks. After the exposition—a short account of past events and the characteristics of the main personages (Stepan Trofimovich Verkhovensky, Varvara Petrovna Stavrogina, her son Nikolai Vsevolodovich, her protégée Dasha, the Drozdov and Von Lembke families)—there follows the complication: Stavrogina's plan to marry Stepan Trofimovich to Dasha; it consists of two dramatic dialogues (Stavrogina-Dasha and Stavrogina-Stepan Trofimovich). Old Verkhovensky's forced suit is connected with the mysterious love relations that have arisen abroad among Stavrogin, Liza Tushina, and Dasha. In the following chapters a third love intrigue is noted: Stavrogin-Marya Timofeyevna; Liputin tells the story of the cripple, Liza becomes passionately interested in her, Shatov defends her: Kirilov protects her from the beatings of Captain Lebyadkin. Finally, a fourth love intrigue is referred to in passing: Stavrogin-Shatov's wife. Thus around Stepan Trofimovich's courting the knot of

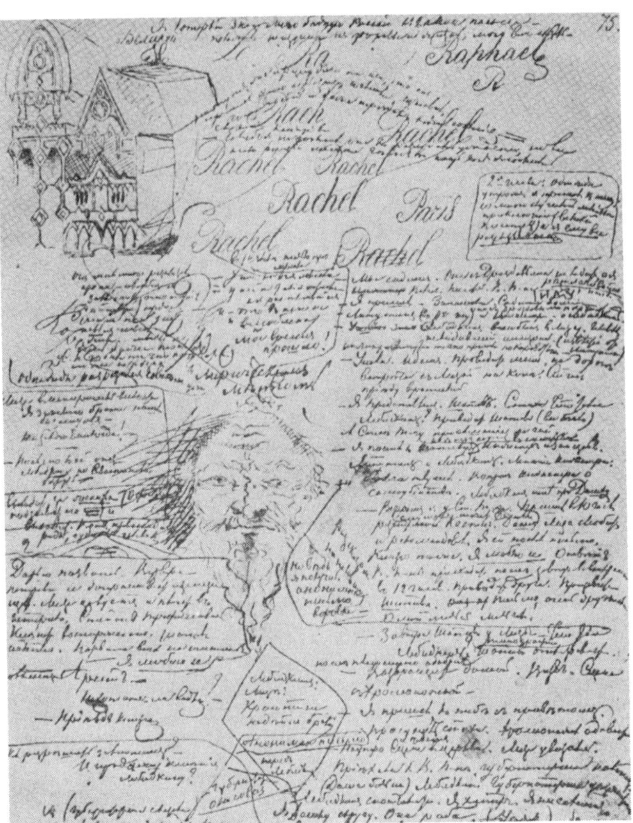

A manuscript page from The Possessed.

the intrigue is complicated and entangled. Four female figures appear about Stavrogin; they are accompanied by new dramatis personae: Dasha is joined with her suitor Stepan Trofimovich and her brother Shatov; Liza Tushina, with her fiancé Mavriky Nikolayevich; Marya Timofeyevna, with her brother Lebyadkin and protectors Shatov and Kirilov; Mariya Shatova, with her husband. Dostoevsky's human world is constructed like a complicated inter-communion and moral pan-unity. The complication leads us to an effective ensemble scene: the "significant day" Sunday arrives. All the leading characters meet "by chance" in Varvara Petrovna's drawing room. Such fatal "chances" are the law in Dostoevsky's world. He transforms this convention of theatrical technique into a psychological necessity. His people are drawn to one another by love-hatred; we follow their approach and have a presentiment of the unavoidability of conflict. The orbits of these planets are calculated beforehand and the points of intersection are determined. With each moment our tension grows, we await the collision, fear it, and hurry it on by our impatience. The author torments us by delaying the tempo before the explosion (retardation) forces us to rise through all the degrees of expectation (gradation), deludes in false denouements (peripeteia), and finally jolts us with the catastrophe. This is the device of his *dynamic composition*. (pp. 433-37)

The novel-tragedy divides into three acts: the complication is given in the form of a "false catastrophe" (the gathering at Varvara Petrovna's, 1st part); the culmination ("At Tikhon's" is prepared by the second ensemble scene ("At Ours," 2nd part), the denouement is introduced by the third mass scene ("The Fête") and falls into a series of separate catastrophes (3rd part). The huge world of the novel, populated by a multitude of people and surcharged with a mass of events, is organized with brilliant art. Every episode is justified, every detail calculated; the disposition and sequence of the scenes are determined by the unity of the design. This world is possessed by a single impulse, animated by a single idea; *it is dynamic, and rushes toward its goal*. (pp. 438-39)

• • • • •

The third characteristic of Dostoevsky's expressive art is its interest. The novel's action must captivate the reader, excite his curiosity. The author draws us into the world of his invention, demands our participation and collaboration. The reader's activity is sustained through the enigmatic, strange, unusual and unexpected nature of the events. The chronicler anticipates and reinforces the impression of his personal evaluations, conjectures, and hints. The complication of the novel (Stepan Trofimovich's courting) is introduced by the narrator's following remark: "Did he have a presentiment that evening of what a *colossal* trial was being prepared for him in the immediate future?" The events abroad in which Stavrogin, Dasha, and Liza took part are surrounded by mystery. Varvara Petrovna endeavors to grasp their significance, but, the chronicler adds: "Something remained there she *did not understand or know*." Nor is this ambiguity explained: the chronicler poses suppositions and loses himself in conjecture; our interest is aroused. Marya Timofeyevna's story is presented in distorted reflections: the malicious gossip Liputin and the drunken scapegrace Lebyadkin give their accounts. The secret's explanation leads to a new involvement; relations between Stavrogin and the cripple are explained by Pyotr Verkhovensky; a fresh lie is imposed onto the former deceptions. The chronicler is perplexed as to why Liza shows such interest in Shatov. "There was in all this," he acknowledges, "an enormous amount that was *unclear*. Here something was understood." Riddles are piled on riddles. The chronicler meets Mlle Lebyadkina; the mysteriousness of the setting astounds him. "Listen, Shatov," he says, "what can I now conclude from all this?" "Eh, conclude what you want," the latter answers. And the narrator enigmatically remarks: "An incredible thought became more and more fixed in my imagination." We are prepared for the improbability of the subsequent revelations. The "significant day," ending in Shatov's slapping Stavrogin, is introduced by such a remark: "This was a day of surprises; a day of the denouement of the past and the complication of what was to come, of shrill explanations and *still worse entanglement*." Stavrogin's respectful, chivalric attitude toward the cripple is incomprehensible, Liza's hysterical excitement is mysterious, Shatov's act remains an enigma. The chronicler underlines this effect by the remark: "But *suddenly* here an incident occurred that *no one could have expected*." In the second part, Pyotr Verkhovensky's whole behavior is confusing in its duplicity and strangeness. He mortally hates Stavrogin and at the same time loves him and kisses his hand. From this dark being a shadow extends at first onto his immediate surroundings, then onto his secret society, and finally over the whole city. The conspiracy spreads, the action of the entire novel is slowly plunged in ominous gloom. Against its background flashes the glow of the fire across the river; the knife of Fedka the convict gleams as he kills Lebyadkin; Pyotr Verkhovensky's shot resounds as it strikes down Shatov.

Enigma is Dostoevsky's favorite device; the explanation of one secret draws after it the appearance of another: the continuous explanations lead to "still worse entanglement." We are involved in a complicated net of events and involuntarily become prosecutors and detectives. In his notebook Dostoevsky writes about the "peculiar tone of the story." "The tone" he remarks in the margins, "lies in *not explaining* Nechayev [Pyotr Verkhovensky] or the prince [Stavrogin]. . . . *Suppress him* (Nechayev) and reveal him only little by little in strong artistic traits." The prince is characterized as an "enigmatic and romantic" personage. On this conscious device is built an effect of contrasting illumination: amidst the precisely outlined and clearly illuminated characters, the main heroes are surrounded by a mysterious shadow; their features are fluid, their contours indistinguishable. And this adds a peculiar, painful expressiveness to the novel's two "demons"; the emptiness of nonbeing shines through their fantastic features. . . . Spirits of negation and destruction—they cannot be ultimately explained or portrayed. Dostoevsky's mastery is in the gradation of shadows, in the light contrasts, and in dual illumination.

• • • • •

The concentration of action around the personality of the main hero, the dramatism of the construction, and the enigma of tone—these are the three properties of "expressive art." The novel-tragedy is saturated with dramatic energy, contains countless potentials of struggle and conflict. Not only is the whole tragic, but also each of its cells. All the dramatis personae, who take part in the common tragedy, simultaneously experience their own personal tragedies. The plots involved in one Dostoevsky novel would be sufficient for ten ordinary "descriptive novels." Let us attempt, out of the counterpoint of ***The Devils***, to distinguish the basic motifs of the "personal tragedies."

Stepan Trofimovich Verkhovensky, with whose history the action of the novel begins and ends, belongs to the writer's greatest creations. The breath and warmth of life is in the image of this pure idealist of the forties. He lives so immediately and naturally on the pages of the novel that he seems independent of the author's own will. Each sentence of his and every act strike us as being inwardly true. With good-natured humor, Dostoevsky pursues the exploits of his "fifty-year-old infant," chaffs at his weaknesses, drolly apes his "gentlemanly" intonations, but decidedly delights in him. The figure of Stepan Trofimovich testifies to the author's extraordinary gift of humor. Verkhovensky was a "most excellent individual," "most intelligent, and gifted." He belonged to a pleiad of celebrated names in the fories; studied in Germany, distinguished himself in a chair at the university, wrote a study on the "causes of the uncommon moral nobility of some certain knights" and a poem resembling the second prt of *Faust*. But his brilliant career was "cut off by a whirlwind of circumstances" and he ended up in the provincial capital, living as a "hanger-on" in the home of his despotic friend and benefactress—Varvara Petrovna Stavrogina. The idealist was reduced to cards and champagne, fell regularly into "civic distress," that is into melancholy, which invariably ended in fits of cholerine. But he was sustained by the "pleasant dream of his beautiful civic attitude." For twenty years he had stood before Russia as an "embodied reproach," and he entered upon the role of one persecuted and exiled. He was married twice: the first time to some "frivolous young girl," by whom he had a son Pyotr. This "fruit of his first, joyful, and still undarkened love" was brought up somewhere in a remote region. His second wife was a German: the marriage appeared, evidently, to be the consequence of his enthusiasm for German idealist philosophy. But the knight-romantic's chief love was his twenty-year-long platonic feeling for Varvara Petrovna, composed of habit, vanity, egoism, and the most lofty and sincere attachment.

The idealist lives by a "higher thought," the idea of eternal beauty; he is a genuine poet; he is familiar with inspiration and a presentiment of world harmony. Dosteovsky entrusts to Verkhovensky his most sacred ideas. But his aestheticism in theory is transformed in practice into unsightly amoralism. Stepan Trofimovich can ecstatically preach the happiness of all mankind and gamble away his serf Fedka at cards. The uprootedness of romantic daydreaming is exposed by the author in biting parody. Verkhovensky writes to Varvara Petrovna from Berlin: "And we have almost Athenian evenings, but only in their delicacy and refinement; everything is noble, a great deal of music, Spanish airs, the dream of all mankind's regeneration, the idea of eternal beauty, the Sistine Madonna, light with interspersions of darkness." There is a discord between dream and reality which sometimes brings the knight of the severe lady to nervous outbursts and he gloomily declares: "*Je suis un* . . . simple parasite, *et rien de plus,*" or: "*Je suis un* . . . man thrust against the wall." This discord is turned into conflict with the arrival of his son Pyotr. Stepan Trofimovich clashes with the nihilists, among whom the first is his *cher* Petrusha. He reads *What's to be Done?* and enters into the battle. Indignation, civil sentiment, and daring kindle in the enervated and weakened aesthete. Verkhovensky boldly states that "shoes are inferior to Pushkin and very much so," and fearlessly comes forward before the unruly audience at the "fête." It is precisely to him, this weak and insignificant character, that Dostoevsky gives the right to unmask the young generation. The author forgives his hero all his falls and sins on account of his chivalrous loyalty to the idea of eternal beauty, for his being imbued with a "higher thought." "Yes, but do you understand," Stepan Trofimovich shouts at his son, "do you understand that if the guillotine is primary for you and that with such enthusiasm, then it is only because the easiest thing is to chop off heads, but having an idea is the most difficult of all. These carts, and how does one say it: 'the rumble of carts, bringing bread to mankind,' are more useful than the Sistine Madonna, or however they say it—is *une bêtise dans ce genre.*" Stepan Trofimovich's words echo Lebedev's prophecy in ***The Idiot*** and prepare for the "temptation of bread's" final exposure in **"The Legend of the Grand Inquisitor."**

At the fête Verkhovensky addresses the nihilists in solemn and inspired words: " 'But I proclaim that Shakespeare and Raphael are superior to the emancipation of the serfs, superior to nationality, superior to socialism, superior to the youthful generation, superior to chemistry, superior to almost all mankind, for they are already the fruit, the real fruit of all mankind, and perhaps the greatest fruit that can possibly exist! A form of beauty has already been attained: were it not attained, I, perhaps, would not consent to live. . . . It is possible for mankind to live without bread; only without beauty is it impossible, for then there will be nothing left to do on earth. The whole secret is here, all of history is here! . . . I will not relent! . . . ,' he cried absurdly in conclusion and banged his fist with all his force upon the table." The "idealist's" tragi-comical speech contains the main idea of the novel and the author's most sacred trust. The former ideal of beauty has become muddled in mankind, and "troubled times" have begun for it. Dostoevsky always held that society is directed by aesthetic principles and that the contemporary crisis was at root a crisis of *aesthetic consciousness*. Stepan Trofimovich's "absurd coming forward" at the fête is his spiritual triumph and practical defeat. The lecturer is hissed and jeered. He puts on his traveling coat, takes his cane, and leaves Varvara Petrovna's house. He will die as he lived, a "Russian wanderer," a homeless spiritual vagabond, a "superfluous man." The tragedy of the uprooted romantic is symbolized by this last journey along the high road. At an inn Verkhovensky meets a book-hawker Sofya Matveyevna and she reads him the Gospel story about the healing of the possessed Gadarene. The somber and terrible novel-pamphlet concludes with a luminous prophecy for Russia. "These devils," pronounces Stepan Trofimovich in great agitation, "these are all the ulcers, all the miasmata, all the impurity, all the devils and imps that had accumulated in our great and dear patient, in our Russia, for ages, for ages. *Oui, cette Russie que j'aimais toujours.* But a great thought and great freedom will overshadow her from on high, all these devils, all this impurity, will go out of her just as with that man possessed. . . . But the patient will be healed and will 'sit down at the feet of Jesus,' and everyone will look with amazement. My dear, *vous comprendrez après,* but now this troubles me very much. . . ." After his prophecy about Russia—the last words of Stepan Trofimovich are devoted to the great idea of immortality. The free-thinker, who had felt himself a pagan, in the likeness of the great Goethe, discovers in death the pledge of eternal life. The aesthetic idea of the novel is crowned by a triumphant, mystical assurance. "My immortality," the dying man says firmly, "is necessary if only because God will not wish to do injustice and completely extinguish the fire of love for Him, once it has been kindled in my heart. And what is more dear than love? *Love is higher than existence,* love is the crown of existence and then how is it possible that existence should not submit to it? If I have come to love Him and rejoiced in my love, is it possible that He should extinguish both me and my joy and turn us into nothingness? If God exists, then I too am immortal! *Voilà ma profession de foi!*" So the *tragedy of the aesthetic consciousness* ends religiously.

A "great, eternal, infinite thought" raises up the old-womanish parasite to the height of mystical contemplation. The idealist of the forties confessed his responsibility for the nihilists of the sixties; he condemned himself to ruin with the devils who had entered into the herd of swine. And by this act of repentance he cleansed himself and shone forth in an immortal idea—in beauty saving the world. Verkhovensky's inner drama is depicted through "sharp artistic traits" with increasing dramatism: the courting of Dasha, the conflict with Varvara Petrovna, the collision and struggle with his son, his final journey and englihtened death at the inn—such are the pathetic acts of this "personal tragedy."

• • • • •

Into the framework of Stepan Trofimovich's story is set the main action of the novel—Nikolai Vsevolodovich Stavrogin's spiritual tragedy. We become acquainted with the hero a few weeks before his suicide, see him in the last critical period of his life. Stavrogin enters the world of the novel, like a living corpse, hoping for resurrection and not believing in its possibility. His tense spiritual life is ascribed to the past and is shown in the refracions of several human consciousnesses: Shatov, Kirilov, Shigalyov embody stages of his religious searchings.

Of all these embodiments *Shatov* is the most vital: the image of the idolized teacher Stavrogin is peculiarly refracted in this disciple's ardent soul. With Shatov ideational duality is transformed into personal tragedy. Dostoevsky makes him the herald of his own religious-national credo and introduces extensive autobiographical material into his story: so, for example, Shatov's joyful excitement at Marie's delivery reproduces exactly the author's experiences at the birth of his first child. Shatov was born Varvara Petrovna's serf, was Stepan Trofimovich's pupil, studied at the university and was expelled after a certain student incident; he married a poor governess, roamed for a long time about Europe; then radically he altered his socialistic convictions and rushed to the opposite extreme. . . . Shatov's ideological conversation with Stavrogin is the highest point of dramatic tension. Dostoevsky knew how to *dramatize thoughts*. In his works ideas are melted in the fire of passion, transformed into powerful energies that live, collide, struggle, explode, destroy, or save. The author characterizes Shatov as "one of those ideal Russian beings who will suddenly be struck by some strong idea and at once will be positively obsessed by it, sometimes forever. They never have the strength to cope with it, but will believe in it passionately and so their whole lives pass afterward as though in the last agonies beneath a stone that has fallen on them and already half-crushed them." Shatov does not reflect, but shrinks under the stone of an idea that has fallen on him; does not philosophize, but screams and groans. The premises lead him not to a logical conlusion, but to a question of life and death. But it is not for Shatov alone that a "strong idea" becomes a personal tragic fate; all Dostoevsky's heroes tempestuously and dramatically *experience* their ideas. Stavrogin says to Kirilov that he *"has felt* a completely new thought." The latter asks him, "You've felt a new thought? That's good." Dostoevsky's people *feel* thoughts. Ideological material served the writer as a potent means of artistic expressiveness. After being slapped, Stavrogin goes to the man who insulted him: the latter has waited for him for an entire week in ague, in fever. He says that he hit him for his "fall," for his "lie"; Stavrogin informs him that he intends in the near future publicly to announce his marriage to the cripple. Shatov asks him to grant him ten minutes. "We are two beings and have met in infinity . . . for the last time in this world. Drop your tone and speak like a human being. . . ." "His ecstasy approached delirium." After Shatov's inspired monologue about the Russian people, the "only God-bearing people," Stavrogin asks coldly: "I wanted simply to know: do you yourself believe in God or not?" "I believe in Russia, I believe in her Orthodoxy. I believe in the body of Christ. . . . I believe that the new Coming will take place in Russia. . . . I believe. . . ." Shatov began to stammer in ecstasy. "But in God? in God?" "I . . . I will believe in God."

This dialogue is the culminating point of Shatov's tragedy: the exponent of the Russian messianic idea does not believe in God! The dichotomy between faith and disbelief destines him to ruin. The somber scene of the murder in the Skvoreshniki park is prepared by a peripeteia—his wife's arrival and the birth of a child. Shatov has not seen Marie for three years: she abandoned him after two weeks of married life in Geneva. But he loves her, as before, with devotion and rapture. She gives birth to a child whose father is Stavrogin. It does not even enter the husband's mind that his wife has betrayed him; the whole night he exerts himself, borrows money, brings a midwife, attends to the patient. A new joyous life begins for him. . . . In the love for his wife and in the mystery of the birth of a new being he finds faith and rises from the dead. At this moment Erkel comes for him and takes him away to the park at Skvoreshniki. There he is killed. The transition from birth to death, from the light of resurrection to the darkness of destruction, is jolting in its mystical terror. The pathetic tension of this scene almost exceeds human strength. Before the story of the murder, Dostoevsky gives a detailed description of the Skvoreshniki park. The *paysage,* introduced in this scene of great tragic depth, becomes a powerful resonator, heightening the dramatic force of the events. With Dostoevsky, the *paysage* appears only in moments of catastrophe, when delaying the tempo reinforces the tension. In ***Crime and Punishment,*** Svidrigailov's final night before his suicide is described; in ***The Idiot,*** we are presented with Rogozhin's house in which the murder of Nastasya Filippovna takes place. Mute nature receives a tongue in moments fatal for man: her symbolic speech accompanies the groans of the dying, the murderers' cries, and the raving of those going out of their minds. In those moments the unity of cosmic life is mysteriously disclosed. (pp. 439-46)

• • • • •

The tragedy of another of Stavrogin's disciples—*Kirilov's*—is parallel and contrasting to the tragedy of Shatov. He is also a man of one idea and contracts beneath the stone which has crushed him; likewise is torn from the soil, blind to real life; is also a fanatic and ascetic whose thought has been transformed into will and passion. His story is related by the author with no less artistic inspiration than the story of his ideological fellow companion and adversary. Kirilov is a young structural engineer. "Well-built and lean, with dark hair, somewhat muddy complexion, and black lusterless eyes, he seemed a little melancholy and confused, spoke disconnectedly and somehow ungrammatically." For four years he remained abroad, in solitude; shut off in his idea, as in an impregnable fortress; completely within himself, in his silence; he has lusterless eyes and impeded speech. Thus "sharp traits" reveal to us the abstractedness of a nature that has fallen out of intercourse with men. Kirilov is a human symbol of *subjective idealism.*

His tragedy lies in his fatal dichotomy of mind and heart. With his mind he arrives at the negation of God and the necessity of suicide; with his heart he passionately loves life and pities people. (p. 447)

Kirilov's idea is summarized by the author in five short overpowering remarks. Kirilov says to Stavrogin: "He who teaches that all are good will end the world." Stavrogin objects: "He who taught it was crucified." *Kirilov:* "He'll come and his name will be the man-god." *Stavrogin:* "The God-man?" *Kirilov:* "The man-god, that's the difference." In fact, the whole astonishing difference is in this transposition. The beginning is placed at the end, and Christ is supplanted by the Antichrist. The paradox in Kirilov's idea is that with iron logic he draws an athetistic deduction from a mystical premise. His consciousness of the divinity of the world leads him to the denial of its Creator. But this denial is only the reverse side of an insatiable love for God. "God has tormented me throughout my entire life," confesses this atheist. His heart cannot live without God, but his mind cannot admit the existence of God. "God is necessary, and therefore *must be,* but I know there is no God and *there cannot be*—it is impossible to live with two such thoughts." His consciousness is thus tragically divided. On one hand there is the murder of God, a declaration of his self-will, the demonic dream of the man-god; on the other—the despair and moral anguish of a believing heart, powerless to overcome the disbelief of reason. Kirilov kills himself not only to destroy the idea of God, but also because without God he cannot live. He says regarding people who have lost their faith: "I've always been amazed that they just go on living."

Pyotr Verkhovensky takes advantage of Kirilov's decision and forces him to assume the responsibility for Shatov's murder. The religious tragedy of the man struggling with God is concluded by the scene of his suicide, almost unbearable in its horror. Kirilov's "man-godhood" is the most ingenious creation of Dostoevsky the philosopher and artist.

Two opposed states of consciousness, which coexisted in Stavrogin, were embodied in his disciples' personalities and were experienced by them as personal tragedies. Shatov and Kirilov are two moments in the dialectic of his spirit. Shatov says to Stavrogin: "At the very time that you planted the idea of God and country in my heart, at the same time, perhaps even on the same days, you were poisoning the heart of this unfortunate, this maniac Kirilov with venom. . . . You filled him with lies and slander and drove his reason to frenzy."

• • • • •

Shatov and Kirilov are Stavrogin's spiritual descendants; *Pyotr Verkhovensky* is his abortion. He remains on a lower plane of existence, sunk in chaotic matter: the former are spirits, he is a petty devil; the first are heroes of a tragedy, he is a personage out of a tragi-comical farce. The author confessed that Verkhovensky turned out a comic character *unexpectedly*. The somber villain's change into a buffoon forced the writer to simplify his characteristics and to transfer his ideological baggage to anoher character—Shigalyov. But, despite this reduction of the revolutionary's image, his spiritual connection with the ideologist Kirilov was nonetheless preserved. Verkhovensky says to Kirilov: "You know that, in your place, I would kill someone else to show my self-will, and not myself. You could have become useful. I'll tell you whom, if you are not frightened. . . . We can come to terms." The latter retorts: "Killing another would be the lowest point of my self-will, and this is just like you. I'm not you: I want the highest point, and will kill myself." If there is no God, man has a terrible freedom. On this the atheists Kirilov and Verkhovensky agree; but they "express self-will" in different ways. Kirilov chooses the higher point—and kills himself; Verkhovensky, the lowest—and kills others. Stavrogin calls Kirilov "magnanimous"; he directs the thrust of his idea against his own breast and perishes in man-godlike grandeur. Verkhovensky translates the notion of self-will into the language of political action. "Everything is permitted" is for him turned into the right to employ falsehood, deceit, crime, and destruction. From the atheistic premise he deduces a theory of political amoralism. For Dostoevsky, socialism and revolution are the natural outcome of atheism. Verkhovensky's traits are described in harsh caricature: he is a "political cheat and intriguer, a scoundrel and false mind," in Kirilov's opinion; Shatov calls him a "bug, an ignoramus, a simpleton, who understands nothing in Russia." (pp. 450-51)

In the course of work on the novel, out of the figure of Pyotr Verkhovensky Dostoevsky formulated his complementary image—*Shigalyov*. Behind the "petty devil," tittering, bustling, and poking about, stands a heavy, clumsy, and sullen demon. Verkhovensky is the giddy Khlestakov of the revolution, Shigalyov is his ponderous Sobakevich. This theoretician of destruction is characterized by his *ears*. "I was struck," says the chronicler, "most of all by his ears, of unnatural size, long, wide, fat, somehow singularly prominent. He produced an inauspicious impression on me." During the session "At Ours" Shigalyov intends to read a notebook filled wih extraordinarily fine writing. He is the creator of a new system of "organizing the world." It is true, the system is still not complete and is contradictory, but nontheless "there can be no other solution to the social formula." His great disclosure concludes with the following sentence: *"Starting out from limitless freedom, I end with limitless despotism."* One-tenth of mankind receives freedom of personality and limitless right over the remaining nine-tenths who are transformed into a herd. Then the earthly paradise will be founded. Shigalyov's system is the logical continuation of Raskolnikov's idea; it will be realized in practice by the "Grand Inquisitor." The "long-eared" theoretician's thought passes as a whole into the legend composed by Ivan Karamazov.

In his "hymn to destruction" Pyotr Verkhovensky is inspired by the theory of Shigalyov, of this "new Fourier." He makes a lyric improvisation out of the scientific treatise. The learned sociologist and the "half-mad" poet complement one another in their worhip of the ideal of satanic beauty.

• • • • •

The tragic motifs of Shatov, Kirilov, Pyotr Verkhovensky and Shigalyov, like rivers flowing into the sea, converge into the main theme of the novel: the tragedy of Stavrogin. The image of the "fascinating demon" is created with inconceivable art. Stavrogin appears at first at a distance, in obscure outline: the chronicler relies on hearsay to narrate his childhood and youth (the distant past); then briefly describes his short stay in the provincial capital three yearas ago (the recent past); and, finally, expounds the events of the last month (the present). A temporal perspective is created: the hero slowly draws near to us, becoming ever more visible and defined. (pp. 453-54)

• • • • •

The omitted chapter ["Stavrogin's Confession"] is the culmination of Stavrogin's tragedy and Dosteovsky's loftiest artistic creation. The struggle of faith with disbelief, which grows through the duration of the whole novel, here attains its most extreme tension. The opposition of the two ideas is embodied in the encounter of two personalities—the atheist Stavrogin and the mystic Tikhon. The enigmatic hero's secret is revealed and the resolution, which we have so long awaited with anxiety and excitement, strikes us in its unexpectedness. Stavrogin irritably and mockingly tells Tikhon about his hallucinations: he, of course, does not believe in the apparitions and realizes that it is a disease. Tikhon answers seriously: "Devils do exist beyond doubt, but the understanding of them can be greatly varied." Then Stavrogin loses his self-possession and betrays himself. With diabolic pride he declares to Tikhon: "I will tell you seriously and insolently: I believe in the devil, I believe *canonically*, in a personal one, not in an allegory, and I have no need to inquire of anyone; this is the whole thing."

Yes, this is the whole thing: Stavrogin canonically believes in the devil, without believing in God; the proud and strong spirit, God-like in his grandeur, has renounced the Creator and closed himself off in selfness. He desired to be by himself—"to express his self-will." "If there is no God, I am God," said Kirilov. Stavrogin has realized this: he is God in his unlimited power and freedom. But in the experience of man-godhood the strong personality finds not triumph, but defeat. His power is purposeless, for there is no point of its application, his freedom is empty since it is the freedom of indifference. Stavrogin is a lie and slave to the "father of lies"—the devil. The god-like personality is split into two countenances; there appears a double—"a nasty, little imp, one of those who have miscarried"; free belief in God is necessarily replaced by faith in the devil. Stavrogin falls into demonic possession, practical satanism. It is his *"credo": "I believe canonically in the devil."* Opposed to it is Tikhon's confession of faith. To the apostate's question whether he believes in God: Tikhon answers, "I believe, . . . And let me not be ashamed of Your Cross, Lord. . . ."

Two forces, the greatest in the world—faith and disbelief, God and the devil—have clashed. This instant of blinding luster has been prepared by the whole action of the novel; for this instant it was also written. (pp. 459-60)

Dostoevsky called Christ the "everlasting ideal of beauty." The man-god, revolting against the God-man, strives to substitute one ideal of beauty with another. Stravrogin is a handsome man, but his beauty recalls a mask. He is a refined gentleman, his fascination is irresistible, his movements and gestures are full of elegance; but in all this there is something repulsive. In the scene with Tikhon his false, deceitful beauty is unmasked: Tikhon is struck not only by the "dreadfulness" of the confession's matter, but also by the disharmony of its style. "But is it not possible to make some corrections in the document?" he asks Stavrogin. "Why?" the latter is perplexed. "I wrote it sincerely." *It might be somewhat in the manner.*" The style of the confession in its verbal slovenliness reflects the spiritual decomposition of its author. The prelate surprises Stavrogin with his remark about the "document." The latter expected horror, confusion, indignation. Tikhon appraises the confession aesthetically: it is not beautiful. He fears that its "ugliness will kill it" and that the proud sinner will not be able to bear his readers' *laughter*. The Antichrist's "beauty" is illusory. Spiritual vision uncovers its unseemliness. Stavrogin's secret is disclosed: he is "a lie and the father of lies." Everything in him is a lie—his beauty, his stength, his yearning for an heroic feat, his grandeur. The "confession" is shameful and unseemly; it contains the disgusting rape of a pitiable young girl.

"Its ugliness will kill it," predicts Tikhon. This takes place quickly. In our eyes Stavrogin is already dead—Tikhon has torn from the pretender the . . . mask of demonic beauty.

After his exposure in the monastery follows the exposure at Skvoreshniki. The man-god proved to be an imp with a cold; the victorious Don Juan an impotent lover and worthy of scorn. Having forebodings of his ruin, he clings to Liza's love; he does not love her and knows this, but nonetheless accepts her sacrifice and draws her after him to death. After the night spent with him at Skvoreshniki, Liza understands, as earlier Marya Timofeyevna did, that her prince is a "pretender." "I must confess to you," she says, "ever since those days in Switzerland—I've been convinced that you have something horrible, filthy and bloody on your conscience, and at the same time, something which casts you *in a terribly ridiculous light*. . . . I will laugh at you for the rest of my life." The devil's fraudulent grandeur provokes laughter. His pretension to an heroic exploit is *comical*. Liza only repeats the words of Tikhon. Then comes . . . the tragedy, the catastrophe. Stavrogin kills himself. "The citizen of the canton of Uri was hanging there behind the door. On the little table lay a scrap of paper with the penciled words: 'Don't accuse anyone, I did it myself. . . .' " The ugliness of his death—suicide—is the last diabolic grimace of the so-called man-god. The "strong personality's" defeat takes place on the plane of life, metaphysics, and aesthetics. Against the "everlasting ideal of Christ" is posed the aesthetic mirage of the Antichrist.

• • • • •

While working on ***The Idiot,*** the author confessed that the whole novel had been written for the sake of the last scene (Nastasya Filippovna's murder). One can generalize this assertion: all Dostoevsky's novels were written for the sake of the catastrophe. This is the law of the new "expressive art" that he created. Only upon arriving at the finale do we understand the composition's perfection and the inexhaustible depth of its design. Reading the novel, we continually move forward, scale a mountain; from the summit of the catastrophe we see the whole *paysage* of the novel spread out as on one's palm. The riddles are explained, the mysteries are disclosed. From Stavrogin's letter before his death we learn the ultimate reality about him. "I have tried my strength everywhere," he writes. "When I tried it for my own sake and for display, it seemed limitless, as it has before throughout my life. . . . But what to apply this strength to—this is what I've never seen, do not see even now. I am still able, as I always was in the past, to desire to do something good, and derive pleasure from this; at the same time, I desire something evil, and also feel pleasure. . . . Only negation has poured out of me, without any generosity and without any strength."

Now, from the heights of the finale, we survey the hero's whole life; his tragedy is the *agony of the superman*. Great gifts were given to Stavrogin. He was destined for a lofty vocation, but he once betrayed his holy-of-holies and renounced God. Spiritual death befell the apostate during life. He knows that a terrible punishment has already begun and that his soul is decomposing. The stench of his spiritual decay forces him to make convulsive efforts to save himself. He assumes "intolerable burden," seeks an heroic exploit, yearns for penance and the people's chastisement. He comes to the provincial capital with a new idea: with the decision to publicize his marriage to the cripple, but upon meeting his wife unexpectedly at his mother's, he solemnly denies her in order not to repulse Liza Tushina. His magnanimous feeling toward Marya Timofeyevna struggles with his sensuous dream of Liza: everything is divided and evil is just as attractive as good. Shatov takes revenge upon the hero for his treason and strikes him in the face. The proud individual suffers the insult—this is his first feat; but even it is equivocal; in his action Stavrogin displays not humility, but excessive strength; not repentance, but a new self-elevation. He goes to Shatov and warns him of his danger; but even this good act is fruitless, since it is motivated by cold arrogance, and not by love. "I am sorry that I can't love you, Shatov," he says to him. And knowing about Pyotr Verkhovensky's plan, he does not prevent him from killing Shatov. Good once more is diverted by evil; moral responsibility for the betrayed disciple's death falls upon his master. His second feat—his intention of announcing his marriage to the cripple—leads to her murder. Marya Timofeyevna curses her betrayer; Stavrogin knows about Fedka the convict's plan and ambiguously encourages him (gives him money). The third exploit—he fired into the air during his duel with Gaganov—is turned into a new and still more cruel affront to his opponent. The fourth—his intention to publish his confession—is exposed by Tikhon as a demonic temptation, and leads to his final abjuration of God (Stavrogin's Antichrist credo). There is no penitence for the demonic superman, he is not capable of humble faith, not fit for a religious feat. Only a miracle can save him. Not believing in a miracle, he grasps at it; but after the night spent with Liza at Skvoreshniki, the "pretender's" final lie is disclosed. Love has long since dried up in his dead heart. Sensuous impulse does not save him and destroys the unfortunate girl. His last attempt at salvation is turned into a new, terrible crime.

The four "exploits"—the four misdeeds—are the four acts of the man-god's tragedy. The fifth act is his suicide. The "living corpse" sunders his illusory existence. The powerful spirit of negation, the metaphysically sterile will, the great strength without application return to nonbeing.

Stavrogin is Dostoevsky's greatest artistic creation. In the family of "strong individuals" (Prince Volkovsky, Raskolnikov, Svidrigailov, Ippolit, Kirilov, Versilov, Ivan Karamazov) he is the strongest; the image of "limitless strength." This is the man of a new aeon, this is the man-god about whom Kirilov dreamed and by comparison with whom Nietzsche's superman seems only a shadow. This is the coming Antichrist, the prince of this world, the terrible prophecy about the cosmic catastrophe drawing near to mankind. Dostoevsky speaks about the ultimate metaphysical mysteries in the language of myths. (pp. 461-64)

Konstantin Mochulsky, in his Dostoevsky: His Life and Work, *translated by Michael A. Minihan, Princeton University Press, 1967, 687 p.*

PHILIP RAHV (essay date 1949)

[*A Russian-born American critic, Rahv was a prominent and influential member of the Marxist movement in American literary criticism. This approach informs his interpretation of* The Possessed; *the essay reflects, in Rahv's words, "my present attitudes toward doctrinal Marxism and the historical experience of the Russian revolution." In this excerpt, Rahv points to the current vitality of* The Possessed *and considers the novel on two levels—as a spiritual and a revolutionary text.*]

The tendency of every age is to bury as many classics as it revives. If unable to discover our own urgent meanings in a creation of the past, we hope to find ample redress in its competitive neighbors. A masterpiece cannot be produced once and for all; it must be constantly reproduced. Its first author is a man. Its later ones—time, social time, history.

To be means to recur. In the struggle for survival among works of art those prove themselves the fittest that recur most often. In order to impress itself on our imagination, a work of art must be capable of bending its wondrous, its immortal head to the yoke of the mortal and finite—that is, the contemporary, which is never more than an emphasis, a one-sided projection of the real. The past retains its vitality in so far as it impersonates the present, either in its aversions or ideals; in the same way a classic work renews itself by impersonating a modern one.

If of all the novels of Dostoevsky it is ***The Possessed*** which now seems closest to us, arousing a curiosity and expectation that belong peculiarly to the age we live in, it is because it deals with problems of radical ideology and behavior that have become familiar to us through our own experience. It is a work at once unique and typically Dostoevskyean. Shaken by the Karamazov fury and full of Dostoevsky's moral and religious obsessions, it is at the same time the one novel in which he explicitly concerned himself with political ideas and with the revolutionary movement.

The fact is that it really contains two novels. It was begun as an openly "tendencious" study of the evolution of ideas from fathers to sons, of the development of the liberal idealism of the thirties and forties of the past century into the nihilism and socialism of the sixties and seventies; but Dostoevsky encountered such difficulties in its writing that he finally incorporated into it many conceptions from *The Life of a Great Sinner*, a projected novel in several volumes which was to be his major effort on the subject of atheism. For that reason ***The Possessed*** might be said to have two sets of characters, one sacred and one profane, one metaphysical and one empirical—the group around Stavrogin, the great sinner, and the group around the Verhovenskys, father and son, who are defined socially and politically. While one set commits sins, the other commits crimes. Externally, in his melodramatic, sinister attractiveness and in the Byronic stress given to his personal relations, Stavrogin derives from early European Romanticism, but in his moral sensuality, in his craving for remorse and martyrdom, he is an authentic member of the Karamazov family. He is doubled within himself as well as through Shatov and Kirillov, his satellites in the story. Shatov represents his Russian, national-messianic side, and Kirillov his "religious atheism"—his experiments with God and eventual destruction of Him to make room for the man-god who kills himself to assert his divinity and prove it.

There can be no doubt that the introduction of Stavrogin into ***The Possessed*** which in its first draft relied exclusively on the Verhovenskys for its interest, gives the novel a psychological depth and moral propulsion that brings it up to the level of Dostoevsky's best work in his later period, the period that opens with the appearance of ***Notes from Underground*** in 1864. For with the introduction of Stavrogin Dostoevsky was able to double the theme of his novel, thus allowing sin and crime, religion and politics, to engage in a mutual criticism of each other. It should be added, however, that the two themes are not fused with entire success. Stavrogin is at times somewhat gratuitously implicated in the younger Verhovensky's political maneuvers; the link between them is often artificial, giving rise to superfluous intricacies of structure and episode. The plot, in part improvised, is insufficiently unified. But this defect is more than made up for—and precisely from the standpoint of plot, always so crucially important in Dostoevsky's creative scheme—by the opportunity provided in Stavrogin's accession to the role of principal hero for the employment of that technique of mystification and suspense, of narrative progression by means of a series of tumultuous scenes and revelations of an agonizing nature, on which the Dostoevskyean novel depends for its essential effects, its atmosphere of scandal and monstrous rumor, is tensions of thought no less than of act and circumstance resolved only when the ultimate catastrophe overwhelms the characters and roll up the plot. Now Stavrogin, whose character is an enigma toward the solution of which everything in the novel converges, is the kind of central figure perfectly suited to this imaginative scheme.

If in the past social critics dismissed ***The Possessed*** as a vicious caricature of the socialist movement, today the emergence of Stalinism compels a revision of that judgment. Its peculiar "timeliness" flows from the fact that the motives, actions, and ideas of the revolutionaries in it are so ambiguous, so imbedded in equivocation, as to suggest those astonishing negations of the socialist ideal which have come into existence in Soviet Russia. Emptied of principle, the Communist movement of our time has converted politics into an art of illusion. Stalin's "socialism" is devoid of all norms; never acting in its own name, it can permit itself every crime and every duplicity. Its first rule is to deny its own identity and to keep itself solvent by drawing on the ideological credit of those revolutionary traditions and heroic struggles for freedom which its brutal totalitarianism repudiates in their very essence. In public the rapacious bureaucrat appears masked as the spokesman of the oppressed and exploited. Marxism, and not the savage doctrine of preserving and extending at all costs the power of the usurpers, is his official philosophy. It is a similar element of counterfeit, of a vertiginous interplay of reality and appearance, which makes Dostoevsky's story so prophetic in the light of what we know of the fate of the Russian revolution.

Thus in its Verhovensky parts the novel reminds us of the most recent political phenomena; and it is not by chance that on the occasion of the Moscow trials the world press unanimously recalled to its readers the name of Dostoevsky, the great nay-sayer to the revolution. This occurred twenty years after Dostoevsky's Russia—that realm of wood and dark furious souls—had been ostensibly demolished and a new harmonious society erected on its ruins. The principles of science and reason had triumphed, we were told. But now the creations of a novelist who considered these same principles to be the spawn of Satan were invoked to explain events which science and reason had apparently found inexplicable. It is not worthwhile, however, to examine ***The Possessed*** in order to appeal to the "Slav soul" for the divulgence of racial or national secrets. The "Slav soul" never explained anything. That swollen concept is the product of the historical romanticism of the Slavophil movement, which substitued brooding about history for making it. Dostoevsky, too, "brooded" in the Slavophil fashion, but that by no means exhausts his contribution to letters. As a supra-historical essence the "Slav soul" is impartial in its testimony, drawing no distinctions between accusers and accused, or between oppressors and oppressed. If you make the unfathomable perversity of the Slav nature your premise, then logically your conclusion cannot exclude any explanation, no matter how wild and incredible. Hence it is futile to look to the author of ***The Possessed*** for revelations about specific historical events, such as the Moscow trials; but much can be learned from a study of the interrelationships between his work and the contending forces that he combined into such extraordinary patterns. Although this analyst of contradictions, who was ever vibrating between faith and heresy, made the revolutionary the object of his venom, there is a real affinity between them.

"In everything and everywhere," he wrote to his friend Maikov in 1867, "I go to the very last limit; all my life long I have gone beyond the limit." Whatever his conscious convictions about orthodoxy, monarchy, and the Russian folk, his temperament and the profoundly dissident if not daemonic force of his imaginative dialectic transformed him into a revolutionary influence in Russian life and culture. And it is precisely this "going beyond the limit" that explains why in spite of himself he became, in his very resistance to the revolution, its herald and prophet. Into his Christianity, too, he injected, as Lunacharsky noted, "the maximum of his revolutionism." Thus Russian orthodoxy found in him a dangerous advocate and protector, for his championship of it took the form of ideas so apocalyptic as to disintegrate its traditional and institutional sanctions. There is no stasis in Dostoevsky's religiosity but rather a dynamism destructive of dogma and seeking fulfilment in the triumph of Christian love and truth in the human world. To be sure, this did not escape the notice of the more subtle partisans of orthodoxy, such as Konstantin Leontiev, an original thinker and religious philosopher who valued in religion its dogma more than its ethics. Leontiev accused Dostoevsky of deviating from Christianity in the spirit of Western humanism and of promoting an "earthly eudaemonism with Christian nuances." He wrote that "in the eyes of a Christian these hopes (of brotherhood and love) contradict the direct and very clear prophecy of the Gospels concerning the worsening of human relations right to the very end of the world. Brotherhood and humanitarianism are of course recommended by the New Testament for the saving of the individual soul; but in the New Testament it nowhere says that through these humanitarian efforts man will ultimately come to peace and love—*Christ did not promise us that . . . that is not true!* . . . Christ told or advised us to love our neighbor *in the name of God;* but on the other hand he prophesied that many will not obey Him. It is in this sense exactly that the new European humanism and the humanism of Christianity are clearly antithetical, and very difficult to reconcile." From the standpoint of orthodoxy Leontiev was doubtless right in his strictures. The truth is that Dostoevsky, despite the commitment of his will to reactionary principles, was at bottom so deeply involved in the spiritual and social radicalism of the Russian intelligentsia that he could not help attempting to break through the inner rigidity of the orthodox tradition toward a dynamic idea of salvation; and in a certain sense what this idea came to is little more than an anarcho-Christian version of that "religion of humanity" which continued to inspire the intelligentsia throughout the nineteenth century and by which Doestoevsky himself was inspired in his youth, when together with Belinsky, Petrashevsky and other social enthusiasts of the 1840's, he took for his guides and mentors such heretical lovers of mankind as Rousseau, Fourier, Saint-Simon, and George Sand.

For if analysed in terms of his social milieu and affiliations, it becomes clear at once that Dostoevsky was the spokesman not of the *narod*—that is the mass of the Russian people, the peasantry—with which he fancied himself to stand in a relation of congenial intimacy, largely of his own imagining, but of the intelligentsia, a class so precariously situated in Russian society, so tightly squeezed between the feudal-artistocratic power above it and the elemental power of the peasant multitude below it, that it had virtually no social space in which to move and grow. It is this stiflingly narrow basis of the Russian intelligentsia which in some ways accounts for its extremes of thought and behavior—the deadly seriousness of its approach to theoretical and ideological issues, its moods of slackness, dreaminess, and passivity alternating with moods of political intransigence and boundless enthusiasm, its fanaticism and tendencies to schism and heresy-hunting combined with tendencies to self-depreciation and self-hatred. In Dostoevsky these characteristics of the Russian intellectuals are summed up to perfection, and that despite his continual quarrels with them, his nagging criticism of them for their alleged estrangement from the people. By his nagging criticism and contempt, which is really self-contempt, he is all the more identified as one of them. In common with many Russian intellectuals he regarded the mysterious power of the *narod* with a fascination that is precisely the negative of their self-contempt and awareness of their own helplessness. Dostoevsky, by idealizing submission, suffering, and the necessity of bowing down before the people, turned this very negativity inside out, endeavoring to convert it into a positive value. But his ambivalent nature did not permit his losing himself in the contemplation of this false though gratifying luster of the positive.

The fact is that it is not in the construction of harmonies but in the uncovering of antinomies that his genius found its deeper expression. His children of light, like Sonia Marmeladov, Myshkin, Alyosha, and Zossima, are passionally and intellectually inferior to his children of darkness, such as Svidrigailov, Raskolnikov, Stavrogin, Kirillov, and Ivan Karamazov. (Myshkin, in whom his author aspired to create the image of a "positively good man," is no doubt the most alive of the children of light, though in saying this one must consider the telling fact that it is primarily from his malaise rather than from his goodness that he gains his vitality as a character.) Ivan

Karamazov, transcending his novelistic framework, is a world-historical creation that overshadows all the saints and pseudo-saints in the Dostoevskyean canon; and one cannot but agree with D. S. Mirsky, who, in discriminating between the lesser and the greater Dostoevsky, notes that his tragedies are "irreducible tragedies that cannot be solved or pacified. . . . His harmonies and solutions are on a shallower level than his conflicts and tragedies. . . . His Christianity . . . did not reach the ultimate depths of his soul." The distinction drawn by Mirsky, and indirectly supported from a theological standpoint by Leontiev, is essential to an accurate understanding of Dostoevsky's relationship to historical Christianity, though nowadays, of course, critics friendly to the new religiosity and aware of the uses to which the example of Dostoevsky may be put in the stuggle against secular ideas, tend to ignore an insight so damaging to the cause of tradition and dogma.

Excluded from the sphere of practical life and confronted by the need of thinking their way out from the historical impasse into which backward and calamitous conditions had driven their nation, the Russian intellectuals lived in and through ideas. This almost predacious feeling for ideas and relatedness to them is actualized in Dostoevsky as in no other Russian novelist. To his characters ideas are a source of suffering. Such people are unknown in countries like America, where social tension is at a relatively low point and where, in consequence, the idea counts for very little and is usually dismissed as "theory." Only in a society whose contradictions are unbridled in temper do ideas become a matter of life and death. Such is the historical secret of that Russian intensity which Western critics find so admirable. Alyosha Karamazov, for example, was convinced "as soon as he reflected seriously, of the existence of God and immortality, and at once he said to himself: 'I want to exist for God, and I will accept no compromise.' " In the same way, adds Dostoevsky, "if he had decided that God and immortality did not exist he would at once have become an atheist and a socialist." As simply as that. And in ***The Possessed,*** Kirillov decides that God "is necessary and must exist," but at the same time he knows that "He doesn't and He can't." "Surely," he says, "you must understand that a man with two such ideas can't go on living." Kirillov shoots himself.

In ***The Possessed*** it is necessary above all to distinguish between its manifest and latent meaning. A counter-revolutionary novel in its manifest intention and content, what it actually depicts in terms of felt experience is the total disintegration of the traditional order and the inevitability of its downfall. The disintegration is of the soul no less than of the social order; and if Stavrogin, with his stupefaction of ennui and loss of the sense of good and evil, represents the decomposed soul, the decomposed society is represented mainly in Verhovensky together with his followers and easy victims. Disintegration is the real theme of the novel, as it is the real theme of ***A Raw Youth, The Brothers Karamazov*** and other major works of Dostoevsky's later period. Thus in ***The Possessed,*** while setting out to report on the moral depravity of the revolution, Dostoevsky was nevertheless objective enough to demonstrate that Russia could not escape it. The hidden ideologue of radicalism and social prophet in him would not be submerged. If it is true, as it has been repeatedly charged, that there was a good slice of the flunkey in his personal psychology, then he was the kind of flunkey, or rather super-flunkey, who even while bowing and scraping says the most outrageous things to your face. This novel, which so delighted the autocratic regime, in reality generalized its breakdown in the political sphere as well as in the sphere of values and moral experience.

In reading this novel one is never quite certain that Pyotr Verhovensky, its chief revolutionary character, is not an agent of the Czar's secret police. Even as he is engaged in preparing an insurrection, this "authorized representative" of an invisible Central Committee, which is located somewhere abroad and turns out to be a myth, describes himself as "a scoundrel of course and not a socialist." He methodically uses blackmail, slander, drunkenness, and spying to achieve his ends. But what in reality are his ends? Give him state power and you get the kind of social type who makes his way to the top in the Soviet secret police. Verhovensky's plan is to organize a network of human knots whose task is to proselytize and ramify endlessly, and "by systematic denunciation to injure the prestige of local authority, to reduce villages to confusion, to spread cynicism and scandals, together with complete disbelief in everything and an eagerness for something better, and finally, by means of fire, a pre-eminently national method, to reduce the country at a given moment, if need be, to desperation." Verhovensky actually carries out this ingenious plan in the town where the scene of the novel is laid—an unnamed town which stands for the whole of Russia. His associate Shigalov—a character who fits Lenin's definition of the petty-bourgeois "gone mad" but who at the same time, in view of the monstrous consistency of his revolutionary-utopian logic, reminds us if not of Lenin personally then surely of Leninism as an historical phenomenon—busies himself with constructing, on paper, a new form of social organization to guarantee complete equality. Starting with the idea of attaining "unlimited freedom" in his Utopia, he soon arrives at the conclusion that what it will actually produce is "unlimited despotism." This throws him into despair, yet he insists that there can be no other solution to the problems of society. Yulia Mihailovna, a well-born and well-to-do lady, wife of the governor of the province, dreams of reconciling the irreconcilable in her own person, of uniting in the adoration of herself "the correct tone of the aristocratic salons and the free-and-easy, almost pothouse manners" of the youthful nihilists, the system of big landed property with free-thinking socialist notions. (In the unsurpassable portrait of this vain woman Dostoevsky created the model of what has since evolved into a ubiquitous social type—the wealthy and thoroughly bourgeois "friend" or "sympathizer" of the Russian revolution who in his befuddlement tries to reconcile his existing status in society with the self-conceit of playing a progressive role and being "in" on the secrets of history.) And what shall one say of Yulia Mihailovna's husband, the governor, who in his snobbish desire to associate himself with the cause of progress, can think of no other objection to the manifestoes urging the people to rebellion except that the ideas expressed in them are "premature." Verhovensky quickly and cruelly turns this objection aside by saying to him: "And how can you be an official of the government after that, when you agree to demolishing churches, and marching on Petersburg with staves, making it all simply a question of date?" Such people are the natural prey of a character like Liputin, an unwashed intriguer, at once a despot and a dreamer, who propounds the theory that there are people on whom clean linen is unseemly. Practicing petty usury, he at the same time holds forth in the language of "the universal republic and harmony of mankind." But the odd thing about him is that he is sincere.

It is exactly through such complex and conflicting motivation that the inevitability of the social breakdown is impressed on the reader's mind. Here the impulse to be rid of a rotting order and to break loose has reached such intensity that it has become objective; penetrating into the innermost, the most differentiated cells of human psychology, it has ceased to be incompatible with degenerte habits and desires. In one scene the writer Karmazinov, a figure through whom the author mercilessly derided Turgenev, describes Russia in terms that approximate the Marxist formula of a revolutionary situation. One must bear in mind that since the intent of the novel is counter-revolutionary, the perception that "Russia as she is has no future" and that "everything here is doomed and awaiting its end" is necessarily put into the mouth of a character, presented as a pompous and conceited coward, at whom we are supposed to laugh. Yet the author makes it plain, even if through indirect means, that Karamazinov is a man of acute intelligence. (pp. 86-95)

If any character in ***The Possessed*** personifies the negation of honor, it is of course Pyotr Verhovensky. But can it be said that he is truly representative of the Russian revolutionary movement? Has it not been pointed out time and again that he is a monster and not a radical? Anyone who has studied Russian history cannot fail to agree that in presenting Verhovensky as typical of radicalism Dostoevsky was oblivious to the innumerable examples of idealistic self-sacrifice which the class struggle in Russia had to show. There can be no doubt of Dostoevsky's spiteful tendenciousness in this respect. Professor Ernest J. Simmons is entirely in the right when he observes, in his book on Dostoevsky, that Verhovensky is no socialist because his ideology is "the criminal creed of the absolutely self-willed man" [see excerpt dated 1940]. But where Professor Simmons is wrong, to my mind, is in contenting himself with this observation, as if that disposed of the matter once and for all.

For if it is true that in a factual sense Verhovensky is altogether untypical of the revolutionary movement of Dostoevsky's time, is it not also true, on the other hand, that this same Verhovensky has since become all too typical—typical, that is, of the men whom the Bolshevik revolution has raised to power and established as Russia's ruling elite. There is an uncanny likeness, after all, between "the criminal creed of the absolutely self-willed man" and the creed, prevailing in practice though for obvious reasons unacknowledged in theory, which is the real motive-force of Russia's self-styled socialist masters. And because this likeness has become an historical fact it is no longer possible to dismiss Verhovensky as a monster and not a radical, as Professor Simmons dismisses him in his book. The revolutionary process as it has taken shape in the new order of Stalinism has indisputably confirmed Dostoevsky's insight that the monstrous in human nature is no more incommensurable with the social revolution than it is incommensurable with institutional Christianity. In point of fact, the totalitarian potential of both is incorporated in the principal symbol of the legend of the Grand Inquisitor—the symbol of the tower of Babel that replaces the temple of Christ.

Thus it can now be seen that as a character-image Verhovensky is symbolically representative of the revolution in its results, if not in its original motives. Of course, Dostoevsky was entirely tendencious when he ignored, in ***The Possessed,*** the role played in the socialist movement by such humanistic and libertarian personalities as Herzen, Chernichevsky, and Mikhailovsky; but here again, unfortunately, his bias is vindicated when it is brought home to us that the revolution, not as it is presented in the Marxist textbooks but as it actually developed, followed the path not of the socialist humanists but of socialist Machiavellians like Tkachev and Nechayev. To be sure, if examined in the light of the struggle for freedom in Czarist Russia, the right to dishonor of which Karmazinov speaks (and you may be sure that in this instance he speaks for his author) seems like a vile imputation. Yet the fact is that it is this right, in essence, that the triumphant revolutionaries arrogated to themselves—and precisely in the fashion of the Dostoevskyean man-gods—when they proclaimed moral standards to be a bourgeois prejudice, proceeding on the assumption that to them all is permitted. It is the tragedy of the Russian people that history has proven Dostoevsky to be a truer prophet than Lenin. Only in speaking out of the depths of negation, however, was Dostoevsky a true prophet. Of his positive prophecies none have been fulfilled. The national-Christian ideology of which Shatov is the mouthpiece in ***The Possessed*** has turned out to be no more than wishful thinking. In the novel Verhovensky murders Shatov, and in real life this crime, endlessly multiplied, has become the foundation of the new Russian state. In this sense Leontiev was again shown to be right against Dostoevsky when he declared that "Russia has only one religious mission, and that is to give birth to anti-Christ." Actually, the anguish of disintegration in Dostoevsky is the creative counterpart of this very idea, an idea strenuously denied in the consolatory and visionary parts of his writings.

But let us look further into Verhovensky's origins in the Russian revolutionary movement of the past century. The biographers of Dostoevsky tell us that the activity of Verhovensky's circle in the novel is an imaginative rendering of the Nechayev episode in the history of Russian radicalism. Now in Nechayevism the revolution suffered its first formidable inroads of Machiavellian deception and double-dealing. Nechayev invented the slogan: "Everything for the revolution—the end justifies the means." He systematically cultivated criminal methods (which are in no way identical with the methods of underground struggle) in the pursuit of his radical ends. Verhovensky's murder of Shatov is patterned on Nechayev's murder of the student Ivanov; and if we know that one section of the *Catechism of a Revolutionary*, composed by Bakunin and Nechayev, calls for "acquaintance with city gossips, prostitutes, and other private sources" for gathering and disseminating information and false rumors, we realize to what an extent, even to the repetition of comic details, the archetype of Nechayev is reproduced in the portrait of Verhovensky. The *Catechism,* moreover, contains something more than formulas of conspiracy and provocation. In that document it is written that "everything which promotes the success of the revolution is moral, everything which hinders it is immoral"—a dictum, at once savage and naive, that Lenin took over in toto, applying it with all the rigor of his political nature and never ceasing to defend it as the only possible ethic consistent with Marxist aims. Lenin's self-will was so inordinate that he always assumed perfect knowledge on his part as to what made for the ultimate success or failure of the revolution. Thus what appeared to him like an objective test of morality rested on nothing whatever except his subjective assumption of perfect knowledge, judgment, and disinterestedness. We can grant him the disinterestedness, but not the knowledge or the judgment. Because of the absolutism of his revolutionary character he failed to look beyond the abstractions of historical materialism to the real interests that lurk behind the ideologies of individuals as well as social groups. He overlooked the inescapable fact that behind every doctrine or program, including his own, there are living men, with immediate and concrete desires, needs, and ambitions, and that this could only mean that Nechayev's dictum would eventually be altered to read that everything is moral which promotes the success, not of the revolution, but of the men who choose to speak in its name, and that everything which hinders them is immoral. Lenin's disregard of the ethics of humanism was implicit in his self-will. The enormity and arrogance of that will is the peculiar sin of Bolshevism, the *hubris* for which Lenin has been paid out by the utter ruin of his revolutionary achievements.

The connection between Nechayevism and the revolution is close indeed. When Bakunin finally repudiated his fanatical disciple he exposed him as one who believed that "in order to create a workable and strong organization one must use as a basis the philosophy of Machiavelli and adopt the motto of the Jesuits: 'Violence for the body; lies for the soul.'" It was not until the Grand Inquisitor himself, the dictator Stalin, gained supreme power that Nechayev's central thought was translated into the terms of real life. Still, the totalitarian virus is no doubt present in Lenin's moral opportunism, an opportunism exalted into a principle of socialist organization and propaganda and thus far more pernicious in its consequences than the casual, unthinking pragmatism and the recourse to expediency that as a rule prevail in political affairs. The revolution is a means and not an end; and the outcome of Lenin's absolutizing of the revolution was that the means so completely usurped the end that it was soon transformed into its exact opposite—into a system reminiscent of Shigalov's thesis rather than of the forecasts of Marx and Engels. What is Shigalov's thesis? That the only way to secure unlimited freedom is through unlimited despotism, or rather that the two concepts are ultimately identical. Therefore he proposes that nine-tenths of mankind be deprived of all freedom and individuality while one-tenth enjoys the unbounded power required for the compulsory organization of happiness. Shigalov's "earthly paradise" is nothing if not a remarkable prevision of Stalin's "workers' paradise." And when one comes to appreciate the fact that Dostoevsky's prognosis of the course of the revolution, however crude in detail, is essentially correct in its main outlines, one cannot but admire his astonishing clairvoyance; and that despite his malicious tendenciousness, which we can now put in the proper perspective without in any way justifying it.

This malice, inherent in Dostoevsky's character, was strengthened by his polemical exertions as a writer. Still, there is no denying that he decided against socialism on a principled metaphysical basis. His antipathy to it had nothing in common with the habitual objections of conservative property-holders, office-holders, and ideologues. He understood that "socialism is founded on the principles of science and reason . . . that it is not merely the labor question, it is before all else the atheistic question, the question of the form taken by atheism today"; and in a variant passage of ***The Possessed*** we find the statement, attributed to Liputin, that "socialism is a substitute for Christianity, it is a new Christianity, which wants to renew the whole world. It is positively the same as Christianity, but without God." Nevertheless he was drawn to it, for he was as much fascinated as repelled by the demonstrations of reason. Like Stavrogin, he never really attained the peace of religious faith, and when he believed he could not actually believe that he believed. He hated socialism because it objectified his lack of belief and both his fear and heretical love of the boundless expansion and change of which the human mind is capable. In his compulsion to test theory by practice he came close to the methods of extreme rationality; and when he subjected Christianity to this rigorous test he found that only a special kind of "idiot" and genius of neuroticism could possibly undertake to lead a Christian life.

His plebianism was another element that tended to subvert his support of the autocracy and the church. On his subjective-psychological side he remained a democrat, regardless of the shifts that took place in his political convictions; and for this reason he could not restrain himself from berating the older generation of Slavophils for their "aristocratic satiety." Like the critic Belinsky and the poet Nekrasov he belonged to the school of commoners, whose inner affinity was with the psychic distortions and the moral agitation and resentment of Gogol rather than with the objective art of Pushkin. In Dostoevsky's work we do not experience that sense of social hierarchies which affects us so strongly in the novels that Tolstoy wrote before his conversion. In modern times the plebian world-feeling is one of the intrinsic conditions of heresy, and the spiritual equality which reigns in Dostoevsky's world seems like a kind of inverted socialism, a commune of the spirit.

In ***The Possessed*** liberal idealism receives the broadest and most perspicacious criticism in the history of political fiction. The comic strokes with which the portrait of the intellectual Stepan Trofimovitch, the elder Verhovensky, is executed, in no way diverts us from its enduring reality and social truth. This characterization has enormous contemporary meanings. It is only now, after fascism and communism have severely penalized Western culture for subjecting itself to the timorous and accommodating counsels of the liberals, that we can fully appreciate Stepan Trofimovitch.

A gentleman scholar and aesthete, he simultaneously abuses and adores the revolution. His standing protest he makes by lying down; he is subtle in his feelings, a self-indulgent humanitarian and a parasite. He is superior to Thomas Mann's Settembrini, whose distant relative he is, for he is understood not argumentatively but through a tangible social milieu. And what a hazardous yet just simplification it was to place him in the position of being the charge of a rich and aristocratic lady, of making an assertive dramatic image out of Varvara Petrovna's support of him. This exchange of cash and culture, however, is not conceived as a simple transaction; on the contrary, it entails mutual distrust, bitterness, and emotional tempests—at one and the same time it involves very real sentiments, even love, and "a mutual exchange of sloppiness."

Stepan Trofimovitch is a typical modern figure, the liberal intellectual with a tender social conscience and a taste for fine feelings and ideas, who, while pluming himself on his advanced position as a champion of the oppressed, is at once thrown into a state of collapse when forced to face the consequences of his own commitments and the cruel exigencies of the historical process. This dilettante of revolution is bound to end up among its first victims. He is unable to cope with his revolutionary son, Pyotr, nor with the nihilists whom the latter trains in his base methods. In *Fathers and Sons*, Turgenev's Bazarov, the prototype of the nihilists in the Russian novel, holds the view that a good chemist is worth twenty poets. But Bazarov's nihilism is only a form of moral empiricism; he is an individualist as yet unaware of the potency of political action. A few decades later, in the 1870's, the nihilistic adversaries of Stepan Trofimovitch had already translated Bazarov's moral empiricism into formulas of political terror and demagoguery. During the Fête—the description of which includes some of the novel's superb scenes—Stepan Trofimovitch defies the political mob by shouting at them: "What is more beautiful, Shakespeare or boots, Raphael or petroleum?" "*Agent provocateur!*" they growl in reply. It is a crushing reply and one that is all too indicative of the manner in which the revolutionaries in power will eventually dispose of the tender-minded intelligentsia. If in his generalizations Dostoevsky recognizes no difference between liberals, nihilists, and socialists, within the living organism of the novel he takes care to distinguish clearly between the elder and younger Verhovensky; paternity in this case is symbolic of a relation of ideas at once positive and negative. The revolutionary doctrine negates liberalism even as it grows out of it. In the historical sense what Pyotr represents is his father's ideas thought out to an outrageously logical conclusion, and for that very reason he becomes his father's worst enemy.

But the vitality of Stepan Trofimovitch's character is by no means confined to the political dimension. He is also a splendidly comical creation, richly illustrating Dostoevsky's gifts as a humorous writer that have been obscured by his accomplishments as psychologist and dialectician. In Stepan Trofimovitch, this "most innocent of fifty-year-old infants" who is capable of the most surprising and subtle insights, Dostoevsky reached the apogee of his comic art—an art that produced such figures as Foma Fomitch of **"The Friend of the Family"** and that entire incredible collection of buffoons, like Lebedev of ***The Idiot*** and Captain Lebyadkin of ***The Possessed***, of whom at least one specimen is invariably to be found in any Dostoevskyean cast of characters. Stepan Trofimovitch does not belong to this species. For all his poltroonery, tormenting vanity, nervous outbreaks, and fondness for French phrases, he is yet invested with a redeeming generosity and openness of feeling that converts him into a figure of heroico-comical proportions. We believe in him as we can never believe in his son Pyotr, in whom there is something cold and amorphous, and whom we can imagine only as a kind of abstract demon all the more terrible in his fury for being doomed to beat his wings in a void. He has no ability to transcend his situation, while his father has this ability above all; and that so endears him to us that in our sympathy we are persuaded that even if he is a bundle of human failings in him the human image is still the goad of love.

There are few scenes in Dostoevsky as marvelous as the scenes of Stepan Trofimovitch's stormy interviews with his capricious patroness, or of his appearance and declamations at the Fête, or of his engagement to Darya Shatova, and, in particular, of his flight and wanderings in the countryside, where he meets the Bible-selling woman, wooing her in his delirium and panic—the flight that ends with his breakdown and the self-confrontation of those last great reconciling speeches in which, as if summing up the rhetoric of a lifetime, he salutes "the Eternal and Infinite Idea" at the same time that he confesses to the lies he has told through all the years, summoning all to forgiveness, for all are guilty, all have wronged one another, in the hope that he too will be forgiven. In those last tremendous pages of the novel we are made to feel as though Stepan Trofimovitch, lying on his deathbed, has departed from his character in order to voice, in unison with his author, a great cry of grief for Holy Russia, a prayer that her sick men be freed of the demons that possess them so that, whole again and much afraid, they may come and sit at the feet of Jesus.

It is significant that the passage from the Gospels, which forms the epigraph to the novel, telling about the sick man cured of his devils and sitting at the feet of Jesus, is made to resound through Stepan Trofimovitch's last speeches, as if to indicate that the author, despite the vindictive spirit of his initial approach to him, is so taken with his creature that he cannot help lending him a modicum of his own faith and outlook. It is a case of sympathy between the creative artist and the created being, in the sense of Keats' notion of "the poetical Character," which forfeits its own identity in taking unto itself the identities formed by the imagination. ("What shocks the virtuous philosopher delights the chameleon poet," said Keats.) Now in Stepan Trofimovitch, modelled on a handsome Moscow professor by the name of Granovsky, a friend of Herzen and Belinsky, the "virtuous philosopher" in Dostoevsky wanted to score off the generation of the 1840's, whose rational humanism he regarded as a source of infection; but Stepan Trofimovitch turned out differently than is anticipated in the original design. Though his function in the novel is to stand as a reproach to the Westernizing intellectuals, he is creatively assimilated to such a degree that in surpassing himself he assumes other roles, not the least of which is to act as a foil to Dostoevsky in his farewell to the Schilleresque period of his own youth, the period of *Schwärmerei* and idealistic grandiloquence, when at one with his contemporaries he shared the exalted feelings inspired by the rational religion of humanity. (pp. 96-104)

Philip Rahv, "Dostoevsky in 'The Possessed'," in his Image and Idea: Fourteen Essays on Literary Themes, *New Directions, 1949, pp. 86-110.*

RICHARD CURLE (essay date 1950)

[In this excerpt from his study of the characters in Dostoevski's four major novels, Curle discusses the revolutionary fervor of Pyotr Verkhovensky; in portions of the essay not included here, Curle also analyzes Nikolay Stavrogin, Varvara Stavrogin, Stepan Verkhovensky, Alexey Kirilov, and Ivan Shatov.]

The sinister figure of Pyotr Stepanovitch, Verhovensky the younger, has become even more sinister in the light of what we now know about communist methods of infiltration and falsity. Without any sort of moral scruple, resolute, crafty and cynical, he understands the technique of disintegration as thoroughly as the most accomplished modern agent from Moscow. His utter indifference to anything but his perverted ideal, his divorce from all normal human contacts and emotions, would, one might suppose, make him detested and avoided by everybody, but on the contrary he is fawned upon and eagerly listened to, partly because he is feared as a herald of unrest who has learnt the art of undermining confidence and breaking old allegiances, but mainly, in the final analysis, because he is strong enough to stand absolutely alone. For his ruthlessness and his cunning would alike be meaningless—that is to say, they would amount to no more than the ruthlessness and cunning of the escaped convict Fedka—were he not, despite his inherent vileness, a genuine fanatic of immense cleverness, of relentless will and of burning, though dreadful, convictions.

In his account of Verhovensky's arrival on the scene Dostoevsky manages to suggest, it seems to me, the feeling that something incalculable and ominous is approaching from the vague outer world. I admit that one cannot appreciate this fully till later, but surely in the initial sentences there is a hint, in the very quality of the words, of a strange, portentous advent:

> And, behold, from the next room—a very large and long apartment—came the sound of swiftly approaching footsteps, little, exceedingly rapid steps; someone seemed to be running, and that someone suddenly flew into the drawing-room, not Nikolay Vsyevolodovitch, but a young man who was a complete stranger to all.

Within a page the narrator goes on to say:

> He talked quickly, hurriedly, but at the same time with assurance, and was never at a loss for a word. In spite of his hurried manner his ideas were in perfect order, distinct and definite—and this was particularly striking. His articulation was wonderfully clear. The words pattered out like smooth, big grains, always well chosen, and at your service. At first this attracted one, but afterwards it became repulsive, just because of this over-distinct articulation, this string of ever ready words. One somehow began to imagine that he must have a tongue of special shape, somehow exceptionally long and thin, extremely red with a very sharp everlastingly active little tip.

This description, following so soon on his arrival that the echo of his steps is still in one's ears, heightens the feeling that we are face to face with a new and formidable type of person. Here again subsequent knowledge lends significance to the account, but my point is that the first sound of the steps coming out of the distance is like a warning signal.

Both naturally and through policy Verhovensky's manner, unless he has some special reason to ingratiate himself, is rough and insolent. It impresses his fellow-conspirators, who regard him as having had special powers conferred upon him by some veiled central committee, it frightens various innocent or selfish people—it even flatters them in a way—and if it infuriates his own father, why, that ony adds to the disorder he wants to create while, at the same time, enabling him to vent his spite and to revenge himself. Being totally unaffected by anyone's opinion of him, save in so far as it serves to bring about that state of chaos out of which another form of society is to arise, having no private life whatsoever—for the more secret life of a revolutionary be, the less private is it—he is able to play his cards with perfect self-assurance and to exhibit at the same moment the contempt he feels for his fellow men. He could only, it is true, have achieved the prestige he did achieve in a society riddled by timid uncertainty and sitting on the volcano of a seething underworld, but unless he had been in himself a very remarkable man, whose personality, however odious, cannot be ignored, he would have proved as ineffectual as most of the people—a highly unpleasant and venomous crew—he has recruited locally to carry out his schemes. Even with Karmazinov, the famous author—it is notorious . . . that Karmazinov was a lampoon of Turgenev—he at once asserts his superiority:

> Pyotr Stepanovitch took his hat and got up from his seat. Karmazinov held out both hands to him at parting.
>
> "And what if all that you are . . . plotting for is destined to come to pass . . ." he piped suddenly in a honeyed voice with a peculiar intonation, still holding his hands in his. "How soon could it come about?"
>
> "How could I tell?" Pyotr Stepanovitch answered rather roughly. They looked intently into each other's eyes.
>
> "At a guess? Approximately?" Karmazinov piped still more sweetly.
>
> "You'll have time to sell your estate and to clear out too" Pyotr Stepanovitch muttered still more roughly. They looked at one another even more intently.
>
> There was a moment of silence.
>
> "It will begin early next May and will be over by October" Pyotr Stepanovitch said suddenly.
>
> "I thank you sincerely" Karmazinov pronounced in a voice saturated with feeling, pressing his hands.
>
> "You will have time to get out of the ship, you rat" Pyotr Stepanovitch was thinking as he went out into the street.

As for his dealings with the Governor Von Lembke and his wife Yulia Mihailovna, a mixture of compliment and brazenness has enabled him to worm his way into their confidence, to put them, as it were, in his power, to such a degree that their capacity to act in a crisis is almost paralysed. In no direction is he more successful, for in the need to nullify their authority he has expended all his infinitely elastic skill. (Both Von Lembke and his wife would well repay further study, but ***The Possessed*** is so rich in characters that it is impossible to enlarge upon them here.)

With the "quintet" and its hangers-on of amateur revolutionists he has formed in the town Verhovensky assumes an air of cool detachment, interspersed by flashes of iron ascendancy, which, as deriving presumably from the centre of everything, hold them suddenly spell-bound in the midst of their bickerings and mutual rudeness. For example, at the meeting he has summoned at the house of the Virginskys he behaves with bored detachment and, while the others are squabbling and theorizing, nonchalantly requests his hostess to lend him a pair of scissors:

> "What do you want scissors for?" she asked, with wide-open eyes.
>
> "I've forgotten to cut my nails; I've been meaning to for the last three days" he observed, scrutinising his long and dirty nails with unruffled composure.
>
> Arina Prohorovna crimsoned, but Miss Virginsky seemed pleased.
>
> "I believe I saw them just now on the window." She got up from the table, went and found the scissors, and at once brought them. Pyotr Stepanovitch did not even look at her, took the scissors, and set to work with them. Arinha Prohorovna grasped that these were realistic manners, and was ashamed of her sensitiveness. People looked at one another in silence. The lame teacher looked vindictively and enviously at Verhovensky.

Having thus demonstrated his scorn of their chatter and in a manner to make them feel small, he suddenly follows it up by baring his teeth—though this, too, is a trick to entangle them—and in a few minutes has each of them exactly where he wants him. A diabolically adroit and masterful schemer!

To understand Verhovensky one must rid one's mind of any lingering idea that a monster cannot be obsessed by passionate beliefs or that repudiation of the "bourgeois" instincts of liberty, kindliness and fair play are necessarily incompatible with an appalling missionary zeal. It is not alone that to the class of being represented by Verhovensky the end justifies the means, but that contorted idealism and criminal tendencies often go hand in hand and bestial ferocity and callousness are frequently the stamp of the selfless fanatic—selfless, that is to say, in denying himself the ordinary amenities of a settled existence, though not at all selfless in other respects. Verhovensky derives pleasure from evil, for he is an evil person, but he also dreams that out of this evil good will come and that the very foundations of life are to be cleansed and redesigned. But these new foundations are themselves planned to make him a despot and to give his savagery full sway to experiment with humanity and to mould it, in the name of progress and socialism, into some ignominous frame of slavery: hatred of men as individuals only spurs on your frenzied zealot to change them into robots over whose destiny he will have ultimate control. As he says to Stavrogin:

> Listen, I've seen a child six years old leading home his drunken mother, whilst she swore at him with foul words. Do you suppose I am glad of that? When it's in our hands, maybe we'll mend things . . . if need be, we'll drive them for forty years into the wilderness. . . . But one or two generations of vice are essential now; monstrous, abject vice by which a man is transformed into a loathsome, cruel, egoistic reptile. That's what we need! And what's more, a little 'fresh blood' that we may get accustomed to it.

There in a nutshell is his philosophy: in the far future hope for mankind, but first of all years and years of scourging and corruption.

The sentences just quoted appear in that thrilling scene . . . in which, like a maniac, he implores Stavrogin to head the new movement, but though it is, indeed, a tremendous scene, dramatic to the last degree, it does not, in my opinion, ring true to his psychology, so convincingly evoked for us throughout the remainder of the book. Men such as Verhovensky do not have the ideas he unrolls before Stavrogin or lose control of themselves in that special way. Listen to this:

> "We shall say that he is 'in hiding'" Verhovensky said softly, in a sort of tender whisper, as though he really were drunk indeed. "Do you know the magic of that phrase 'he is in hiding'? But he will appear, he will appear. We'll set a legend going better than the Skoptsis.' He exists, but no one has seen him. Oh, what a legend one can set going! And the great thing is it will be a new force at work! And we need that; that's what they are crying for. What can Socialism do? it's destroyed the old forces but hasn't brought in any new. But in this we have a force, and what a force! We only need one lever to lift up the earth. Everything will rise up!"

But it is just not credible, and though in reading the chapter one is moved by its power and unexpectedness, afterwards one has the feeling that it is a literary device, extremely telling as such but actually unsound. This bloody-minded man was neither weak enough nor exalted enough to have had such a vision.

No, it is not Verhovensky, the romantic, who holds our attention, it is Verhovensky, the plotter. The first is a figment, whereas the second is only too real. He can drive Kirillov to ecstatic suicide, he can alienate Madame Stavrogin from her friend of over twenty years, he can turn Erkel, the most pure-minded and devoted of his disciples, into a murderer, he can set the whole town throbbing with fever. True, his grand machination crashes about him, but he remains quite unperturbed—it was enough, for the instant, that he had sown unrest—and fades away, leaving his dupes to be captured, while he himself is ready for the next move. As a man, Verhovensky is not particularly interesting, but as a portent he is intensely interesting. He is the voice of chaos and destruction, that voice which, like a syren's song, can lure men to their doom, and he is rampant thoughout Europe to-day. For to rebuild the world, as Verhovensky devised, it must first be pulled down, and then at length, when it *is* rebuilt, men will have lost their souls and their very desire for freedom. (pp. 158-64)

Richard Curle, in his Characters of Dostoevsky: Studies from Four Novels, *1950. Reprint by Russell & Russell, 1966, 224 p.*

DAVID MAGARSHACK (essay date 1953)

[In this excerpt from an introduction to an English translation of The Possessed, *Magarshack describes the circumstances in which Dostoevski composed the novel and the sources of some of its characters and events.]*

It was in Florence that [Dostoyevsky] first thought of a great novel in which he would challenge the progressive movements in Russia and proclaim his faith in the regeneration of his native land (and afterwards the whole of the world) through a return to the tenets of Christianity as held by the Greek Orthodox Church. 'I am thinking of writing a huge novel, to be called *The Atheist,*' he wrote from Florence to his friend the poet Maykov on 23 December 1868, 'but before I sit down to write it I shall have to read almost a whole library of atheists, catholics, and Greek Orthodox theologians. . . . I have the chief character. A Russian of our set, and *middle-aged,* not very educated, but not uneducated, either, a man of a quite good social position, who *suddenly,* at his age, loses faith in God. He has spent all his life in the Civil Service, never leaving the beaten track, and without gaining any distinction, though he was already forty-five years old. . . . His loss of faith in God makes a tremendous impression on him. . . . He pokes his nose among the younger generation, the atheists, the pan-Slavs, the Russian fanatical sects, hermits, and priests; falls, incidentally, under the influence of a Jesuit propagandist, a Pole, and descends to the very depths by joining the sect of the flagellants—and at last comes to Christ and the Russian soil—the Russian Christ and the Russian God. (For goodness sake, don't breathe a word about it to anyone: I shall write this last novel of mine and I shall say everything to the last word, even if it is the last thing I do.)'

The *final* sentence about his saying everything to the last word that he thought about the destiny of Russia and the world occurs twice in his letters to Maykov and Strakhov, his journalist friend, in connexion with the first outline of ***The Devils,*** which, beginning with February 1870, was being serialized in the Moscow conservative monthly *The Russian Messenger*. 'I am working for *The Russian Messenger* now,' he wrote to Maykov from Dresden on 6 April 1870, 'because I owe them money and have put myself in an ambiguous position there. . . . What I am writing now is a tendentious thing. I feel like saying everything as passionately as possible. (Let the nihilists and the Westerners scream that I am a *reactionary*!) To hell with them. I shall say everything to the last word.' And a day earlier he wrote to Strakhov: 'I am relying a great deal on what I am writing for *The Russian Messenger* now, but from the tendentious rather than the artistic point of view. I am anxious to express certain ideas, even if it ruins my novel as a work of art, for I am entirely carried away by the things that have accumulated in my heart and mind. Let it turn out to be only a pamphlet, but I shall say everything to the last word'.

From the notes Dostoyevsky had jotted down in January 1870, it would appear that his first idea was to incorporate the main theme of his proposed novel, *The Atheist,* in ***The Devils,*** whose chief character, however, was not to be an ordinary civil servant but a wealthy prince, 'a most dissipated man and a supercilious aristocrat', whose life was 'storm and disorder', but who in the end 'comes to Christ'. He was to be 'a man with an idea', which absorbs him completely, though not so much intellectually as 'by becoming *embodied* in him and merging with his own nature, always accompanied by suffering and unrest, and having fused with his nature, it demands to be instantly put into action'. The prince is greatly influenced by a well-known

Russian religious writer, who greatly influenced Dostoyevsky himself and who was to have figured in the novel. This writer's main idea Dostoyevsky defined as 'humility and self-possession, and that God and the Kingdom of Heaven are in us, and freedom, too'. But two things made Dostoyevsky give up his original idea of Nicholas Stavrogin, the main character of ***The Devils,*** who in the final draft of the novel no longer appears as a prince, though he is referred to as such in one chapter.

To begin with, his desperate financial position ('I am in a simply frightful position now,' he wrote to Maykov in his letter of 6 April, 'a real Mr Micawber. I haven't got a penny, and yet I must somehow carry on till the autumn') forced him to postpone the writing of his great novel and try to get some money by writing a merely 'tendentious' one. 'What I am writing for *The Russian Messenger* now,' he told Maykov in the same letter, 'I shall finish in about three months, and then, after a month's holiday, I shall sit down to my other novel. It is the same idea I wrote to you about before. It will be my last novel.' And he went on to outline the plot of what was eight years later to become known as ***The Brothers Karamazov.***

While engaged in writing ***The Devils,*** Dostoyevsky returned again and again in his correspondence to the theme of ***The Brothers Karamazov,*** which at one stage he called *The Life of a Great Sinner; and* he made it quite clear that his great idea was to be left to this last novel. What was this 'great idea'? Roughly, it was the idea of the reconciliation of good and evil according to his own peculiar political and religious recipe of a State based on a docile peasant population and run by an autocratic Tsar, who was no longer supported by a landed aristocracy (which Dostoyevsky abominated), but who relied entirely on the Greek Orthodox Church. Dostoyevsky, like Gogol before him, found the solution of the problem of the reconciliation of good and evil, based on so fantastically unrealistic an idea, beyond his strength. In ***The Devils,*** however, he was no longer concerned with so grand a design. All he wanted to do was to settle his own personal accounts with the so-called Westerners, that is, the Russian liberals who dreamt of converting Russia into a constitutional monarchy on the model of a Western European country, and the more revolutionary elements in Russia, who, like himself, refused to have anything to do with the aristocracy or the new class of capitalists, and, unlike himself, with the Tsar or the Church. It was here that quite an unexpected event came to his help. For it was just at this time that, following the murder of a young student in Moscow, a revolutionary conspiracy was discovered, which seemed to fit in with the ideas Dostoyevsky wished to express in ***The Devils.*** The conspiracy was organized by a certain Sergey Nechayev, who was at the time a disciple of Michael Bakunin, the author of *The Catechism of a Revolutionary* and the founder of the anarchist movement.

Nechayev was a Scripture master in one of the Petersburg elementary schools (a *séminariste,* that is, a divinity student, as the contemporary left-wing propagandists were nicknamed by aristocratic writers like Turgenev, because most of them did not belong to the aristocracy and some of the more eminent of them, like the critic Dobrolyubov, came from the priesthood class). Since the autumn of 1868 he had also been an external student of Petersburg University, and took a leading part in organizing the student disturbances in 1868 and 1869. In March 1869 he went abroad with a false passport to Geneva, where he joined Bakunin and the poet Ogaryov, a close friend of Herzen's, and from there they posted revolutionary leaflets to their friends in Russia. He returned to Russia in August of the same year as the self-styled representative of the World Revolutionary Movement at Geneva and organized a 'Society of National Retribution' in Moscow. Dostoyevsky embodied all the facts relating to the organization of this society (the groups of five, etc.) in his novel. On 21 November Nechayev (who was only twenty-two at the time) and four members of the Moscow 'group of five' mudered the fifth member of the group, a young student of the Moscow Agricultural College called Ivanov, for allegedly refusing to carry out the instructions of the Geneva committee. 'Ivanov,' the official act of indictment of Ivanov's murderers stated, 'was enticed to the grotto in the grounds of the Moscow Agricultural College on the pretext of handing over an illegal printing press. There they at first tried to strangle him, but afterwards Nechayev seized the pistol brought by Nicolayev' (another young accomplice) 'and shot Ivanov in the head, after which Ivanov's body was weighted with stones and thrown into the pond.' Dostoyevsky's description of Shatov's murder follows closely the description of Ivanov's murder. After the murder, Nechayev, like Peter Verkhovensky in the novel, escaped first to Petersburg and then abroad. He went back to Geneva, where he rejoined Bakunin and Ogaryov and assisted them in their abortive attempt to revive Herzen's London journal *The Bell.* His ruthlessness in carrying out Bakunin's own principle that the end justifies the means appalled even Bakunin, who soon broke with him. Nechayev then went to London, where he began publishing his terrorist journal *Village Commune,* which was sharply condemned by Engels, the friend and collaborator of Karl Marx. He later returned to Switzerland, where he was arrested by the Swiss police on an extradition order as a criminal and not a political offender and handed over to the Russian police. On 8 January 1873 he was tried for murder by the Moscow District Court and sentenced to twenty years penal servitude. He was not sent to Siberia, however, but incarcerated in the Peter and Paul fortress in Petersburg, where he died one year and ten months after Dostoyevsky, in November 1882.

While Dostoyevsky was writing ***The Devils,*** Nechayev was still at large, and Dostoyevsky, who returned to Petersburg in July 1871, no doubt knew all about his revolutionary activities abroad. The sensational trial of the Nechayev followers in Russia (the police had arrested altogether 152 persons, mostly young boys and girls, of whom seventy-nine were put on trial in Petersburg in July 1871, the rest being released for lack of evidence) furnished Dostoyevsky with more material for his novel, such as, for instance, the political leaflet with the drawing of an axe and the poem 'A Noble Character' found among the leaflets confiscated by the police. An interesting fact that has only recently come to light is that Dostoyevsky even found the prototype of Kirilov in a certain Smirnov, one of the accused in the trial of the Nechayev followers. The following statement was taken by the police from Smirnov and subsequently published in the Russian Press (Smirnov had been banished to the town of Vladimir for his part in the student disturbances): 'In Vladimir I began to suffer from fits of depression and to be more and more obsessed with the idea of suicide; even now I doubt whether I shall be able to get rid of it; as I expect to remain in Vladimir till the end of my term of exile, I decided to kill myself in the spring. This decision is connected with the kind of death I have chosen.'

The discovery of the Nechayev conspiracy, the murder of Ivanov, and the series of sensational developments which finally led to the trial of Nechayev's alleged followers in Petersburg just when Dostoyevsky himself had returned there, forced Dostoyevsky to introduce a great number of vital changes in his novel, although the first part of it had already been published in *The Russian Messenger,* and he only finished it in November 1871. This slipshod method of writing his 'tendentious' novel has made it into one of the most structurally untidy of Dostoyevsky's great novels. Its two chief characters—Nicholas Stavrogin and Peter Verkhovensky—are only pegs on which Dostoyevsky hung his two most violent dislikes: his dislike of the Russian aristocracy and his dislike of the revolutionaries, whom he lumped together in the person of Verkhovensky-Nechayev. Stavrogin himself remains an obscure and enigmatic figure, the mystery surrounding him being mainly due to Dostoyevsky's decision to leave him hanging in the air, as it were, rather than waste 'the great idea' he had decided to keep for his last novel on him. The fact that the editor of *The Russian Messenger* refused to publish a long chapter dealing with Stavrogin's disreputable past must also to a certain extent be held responsible for the obscurity of Stavrogin's characterization. So far as Peter Verkhovensky is concerned, it is only fair to point out that Dostoyevsky himself went out of his way to emphasize the fact that he was not a Socialist, but just a 'rogue'. The other conspirators in the novel, with the exception of Kirilov—the most metaphysicaal character Dostoyevsky created—are quite terrifyingly alive as people, but only caricatures as 'revolutionaries'. The fact is that Dostoyevsky had only a vague idea of the revolutionary movements in Europe and was too apt to distort the ideas behind them. Indeed, his own violent political views precluded a fair and thorough appreciation of any progressive movement. To him even a mild liberal like Stepan Verkhovensky was 'a devil' who could just be 'saved' on his deathbed by a none-too-sincere recantation of his former opinions. It was only in people like Shatov—that is to say, people, who, like Dostoyevsky himself, had turned their back on their liberal past and wholeheartedly embraced a philosophy of life based on autocracy and the Church—that he saw the gleam of salvation for a tortured world. And the tragedy of Shatov was also Dostoyevsky's tragedy: both believed in Christ and both were tormented by their disbelief in God. Both were fanatical adherents of their own new creed because both were at heart uncertain whether it was the right way to the millennium. Shatov toyed with the idea of denouncing his former associates to the police in the same way as Dostoyevsky himself had actually taken steps to denounce Turgenev, the hated aristocrat and atheist, to 'posterity' long before he lampooned him as Karmazinov in ***The Devils.*** (pp. viii-xiii)

[In] spite of its structural and artistic blemishes, [***The Devils***] possesses a tremendous vitality, as well as moments of great tenderness. The novel is best regarded as a political melodrama (the stage at the end of it is literally strewn with corpses). It would be absurd to take Dostoyevsky's political views seriously; but it would be no less absurd to overlook his moments of great inspiration, his amazing insight into the human heart, and his shattering criticism of those aspects of man's character which profoundly affect human thought and behaviour. (p. xvii)

David Magarshack, in an introduction to The Devils (The Possessed) *by Fyodor Dostoyevsky, translated by David Magarshack, Penguin Books, 1953, pp. vii-xvii.*

CHARLES I. GLICKSBERG (essay date 1960)

[Glicksberg discusses depictions of suicide in literature, focusing on Alexey Kirilov and exploring the philosophical justifications for the act used by Dostoevski and later writers.]

Only when the spiritual health of a culture declines does the suicidal obsession, as voiced in its literature, grow strong. A vital culture produces a literature that joyously affirms the will to live; it may create a tragic but never a suicidal art. It is only when energy ebbs, when a society loses its reason for being, that its literature reflects a neurasthenic condition; it becomes enamored of death and dissolution. The will that was once fed by instinctual sources of energy, rooted confidently in the womb of Nature, turns negative and destructive, tired of a life that is not supported by a sure foundation of meaning. What was once Dionysiac ecstasy and intoxication, a creative upsurge of animal faith, a capacity born of immense courage to face the ultimate Ground of Being in all its mysteriousness and terror, degenerates into a morbid preoccupation with the metaphysics of death. (p. 384)

In discussing the literature of suicide, we are not referring to characters who, driven by failure or disease or mutilation or extreme pain, decide to make their exit from the stage of life. There is nothing either heroic or tragic in such an ending. It may, as with Willy Loman in *Death of a Salesman,* communicate a deep sense of the pathos of existence but not the specifically tragic emotion, which is exalted and liberating, springing as it does from a flash of insight that transcends the illusion of time and the world of appearance. The tragic hero who resorts to suicide retains his dignity to the very last. He may reach a point not far removed from madness, but the justification he gives—and there must always be present an imaginatively convincing principle of justification—is never paltry or pitiful. He is imbued with a spirit of greatness as he prepares his own doom. In his decision to die he implicates all of life, God, the whole universe. Because he refuses to compromise, because he is willing to die for the sake of an ideal which he realizes can never be achieved on earth, because he thus passes judgement on life, he enables the living to identify themselves with his fate and thus, strange as it may seem, intensify and enrich their sense of life. For he dies as a rebel, not as a whimpering coward.

Suicides that reach the tragic heights in literature are thus never either psychopathological or purposeless. The suicide of a madman, for example, would lack tragic meaning. Even Kirillov's suicide, in ***The Possessed,*** is not a gratuitous act; it is a defiance of God and a promise of salvation for mankind. (p. 386)

In Gide's fiction, the gratuitous act is a deliberate violation of law and morality. The protagonist murders not for profit but without reason. In Dostoevski's fiction the gratuitous act leads to suicide, only it is blended with a religious motive: the mythic self-crucifixion of the hero as a means of saving mankind from the enslaving illusion of God. It is the man-god who is exalted. What is of signal interest in this strategy of motivation is that the discovery of the absurd culminates in absurdity. The suicidal act is shown, by both Dostoevski and Camus, to be as much a matter of faith as the Pascalian wager or the Kierkegaardian leap. Were it not so, were these sacrificial heroes not actuated in their suicide by some humanly meaningful motive, it is doubtful if they could be fruitfully handled in literature. Characters who die because of grief or financial loss or a psychosis are not of tragic import. They die and are forgotten. The writer who with imaginative power portrays a metaphysical suicide has added a new value to the life of literature. He has brought the gods up for trial, he has passed judgement on life, he has undermined the foundations of faith, he has overcome the tyranny of the flesh, the despotism of instinct.

Our thesis holds that literary suicide is tragic only when it is rooted in a metaphysical or "principled" rejection of life. Not that this needs to be reasoned out in logical terms; logic is not the ruler of life. It is the internal "logic" that counts, the battle the protagonist fights within, the motives that finally prompt him to say no to life. Like Stavrogin in ***The Possessed,*** he finds life not worth having and (after having experimented with all the drugs, all the pleasures, all the perversions) gives it up in disdain, knowing as he does so that even this final gesture is futile.

This is the nihilism that dominates a large part of Existentialist literature. Once God disappears as the creator and controller of the human drama, once existence is infected with the cancer of absurdity, then death, like life, becomes irremediably absurd. The modern hero expects to achieve nothing by his act of suicide. His protest is without consequences; it is useless. That is why Kirillov is fundamentally an unheroic, if fanatical, character. He is obsessed, and yet convinced by his obsession that he is eminently sane in his messianic ambition: he will emancipate humanity from the lie of religion, their craven, infantile dependence on God. By killing himself, he will prove that man is God. His suicide will be the first revolutionary demonstration of godlike freedom, a blow directed against the will of God.

Kirillov is, from the beginning, searching for the underlying reason why men are afraid to kill themselves. Two prejudices, he feels, restrain people from leaping into the vast indifference of death: one is the fear of pain, a small prejudice; the other prejudice stems from the fear of what will happen in the other world. Furthermore, there are two types of suicides: those who kill themselves out of passion, sorrow, or revenge, not deterred by anticipation of pain; the metaphysical suicides belong to the other type, those who kill themselves as the result of reasoning. Kirillov has worked out what he considers a perfectly logical theory of salvation. "There will be full freedom when it will be just the same to live or not to live. That's the goal for all." Once this truth is grasped, then no one will care to live. To the sensible objection that if man fears death it is because he loves life, a powerful instinct implanted by nature, Kirillov, the demented philosopher of death, has his answer ready. That is the very deception he is determined to unmask.

Kirillov declares that he has always been surprised at the fact that everyone goes on living. He has found his faith: "If there is no God, then I am God." If God exists, then He rules with an iron hand and no one can escape from His Will. If not, then Kirillov is free to assert his self-will. That is how he can defeat God. He is resolved to manifest his self-will, and the highest manifestation of self-will is to kill himself, without any cause at all. Here is the Promethean rebel who will be the first in the history of mankind to disprove the existence of God. "What is there to live for?" The laws of Nature, he points out, did not spare Christ, who died for a lie and thus made clear that all of life is a hideous mockery. It is belief in the old God that is responsible for all the suffering of man. Kirillov's religious mania emerges most clearly when he defends the logic of his proposed action:

> I can't understand how an atheist could know that there is no God and not kill himself on the spot. To recognize that there is no God and not to recognize at the same instant that one is God himself is an absurdity, else one would certainly kill himself. If you recognize it you are sovereign and then you won't kill yourself but will live in the greatest glory. But one, the first, must kill himself, for else who will begin and prove it?

By this act of proof he will abolish the fear of death. By asserting his self-will, he is bound "to believe that I don't believe". This is the terrible new age of freedom he is ushering in.

The contradictions in Kirillov's position are all too apparent: he is a religious fanatic, a mad mystic, who has dedicated himself to the task of annihilating God. He is fond of life, even though he has decided to shoot himself. He does not believe in an eternal life after death, only in eternal life here on earth. He believes that the new Saviour will come and his name will be the man-god. Kirillov's suicide is a ritualistic act of sacrifice. The next stage in the evolution of the race will witness the extinction of God, but first someone must act as the assassin of God and reveal the mighty, liberating secret that there is nothing to fear, not even death.

Dostoevski contrasts Kirillov's suicide with that of Stavrogin. The latter suffers from hallucinations—the fate Dostoevski reserves for the nihilistic rebels like Raskolnikov and Ivan. Stavrogin feels homeless on earth, without close ties of any kind, incapable of giving himself in love or in faith. He has tried his strength everywhere and has not learned to know himself. He does not know what to do with his energy, his time, his talent. He derives pleasure from evil though he desires to do good. What troubles him intensely and at last drives him to suicide is the discovery that his desires are too weak to guide him. He is a man without hope. He cannot feel and therefore cannot believe. He cannot share the utopian dreams of the revolutionists. He has lost connection with his country and his roots. He is nothing. From him, as he realizes toward the end, nothing has come but negation, and even this was without greatness, without force. Kirillov could at least be carried away by the passion of an idea and take his life; Kirillov was a great soul because he could lose his reason. Stavrogin declares: "I can never lose my reason, and I can never believe in an idea to such a degree as he did. I can never, never, never shoot myself." This is the punishment he must bear: he blew neither hot nor cold; he could not transcend his analytical, ironic mind. He is afraid of suicide: the supreme act of absurdity in a drama of life that he regarded as inexpressibly absurd. Even the act of killing himself will be, he knows, another sham—"the last deception in an endless series of deceptions". Yet he returns home and hangs himself in the loft. Despair has conquered his titanic pride.

Dostoevski has prophetically anticipated many of the trends of modern fiction. Once the religious sense was banished from fiction, the human being ceased to possess any genuine importance. Nietzsche, in *The Genealogy of Morals,* brilliantly shows how the growth of science resulted in a loss of individuality, the reduction of the human being to atomistic insignificance. If the novelist were to accept this scientific version of human nature, his art would be severely damaged. To escape the trap of determinism, he focuses on dreams, introspection, the unconscious, the inner world of man. (pp. 387-90)

It is Existentialist fiction that projects with intense imaginative pessimism the realization of man's nothingness. Man's existence contains its own negation and is headed inevitably toward death. Man is oppressed by the sense of his finitude, his involvement in death. As he contemplates his own mortality, he achieves the gift of freedom, but out of it springs the feeling of dread: the perception that he hangs precariously over the abyss of nothingness. (p. 391)

Like Kirillov, Camus asks if man is free or is subject to a master. If God exists, then man is not free and God must stand condemned as the originator of evil. If man is free, then he must bear full responsibility for his actions. What kind of freedom, after all, can God confer on man? To have freedom—that means freedom to think and to act. The philosophy of the absurd, while it abolishes the kingdom of eternity, restores freedom to man. But even this is an illusion. The numinous encounter with the absurd destroys all possibility of meaning. Death is not only the sole reality but the supreme absurdity. Nothing in this condition of man can be changed. But without the assurance of eternity, what value can freedom possibly have?

Once the double illusion of freedom and of a high purpose to be fulfilled in life is destroyed, man is truly free, for he has been liberated from the myth of the future. The absurd man finally accepts a universe which is incomprehensible and built on nothingness; he finally accepts a life that is without hope and without consolation. Rejecting the solution offered by suicide, Camus stresses the impotance of being aware of one's life to the utmost, to see clearly, to refuse the temptation of suicide.

Camus therefore concludes that the novelist must keep faith with the absurd and renounce every illusion. He points to ***The Possessed*** as a classic example of the absurd. If life is indeed absurd, then why not condemn Nature and make an end of it all? Logical suicide, however, is an act of revenge. Kirillov takes his life because he is possessed by an idea. His suicide is an act of revolt; he behaves absurdly but his action is dictated by an overweening ambition. If God does not exist, then he is god. But God does not exist; therefore he must demonstrate the truth of this redemptive meaning by killing himself. He illustrates the tragic dilemma of the intellectual who confronts life in a universe that has no God. That is his besetting madness and yet he is not mad. He refuses to serve any master. By slaying God he usurps His power. He kills himself in order to liberate man from the thraldom of hope. Strangely enough, it is out of love for deluded mankind that he takes his life. He is the first Existentialist hero, the personification of the absurd. (pp. 392-93)

Charles I. Glicksberg, "To Be or Not to Be: The Literature of Suicide," in Queen's Quarterly, *Vol. LXVII, Autumn, 1960, pp. 384-95.*

RONALD HINGLEY (essay date 1962)

[In the following excerpt from his critical survey of Dostoevski's fiction, Hingley emphasizes the novelist's humor and skill as a craftsman focusing on the Fête scene.]

The Fête scene [in ***The Possessed***] represents the finest piece of sustained humour and possibly the finest piece of sustained writing in Dostoyevsky's works. . . . (p. 145)

Nowhere in Dostoyevsky's Scandals are the notes of coming doom sounded in more sinister fashion. Many of these go back to points earlier in the narrative, so that by the time the Fête begins almost everyone knows that it will end in a fiasco. The only real interest is—what form will the fiasco take? 'The Fête took place in spite of all confusions'', Dostoyevsky's Narrator explains at the beginning of Part Three, adding that Yuliya Mikhaylovna has by now become so obsessed with her plans that she would not have cancelled them even if her husband had died in the night. Meanwhile, in expectation of crisis, many are 'rubbing their hands in advance' for, as the Narrator explains: 'a Russian takes incredible delight in every kind of scandalous public upheaval.'

As in all transitional periods (the Narrator regards this as a transitional period, adding the typical comment, 'from what or to what our transition was, I do not know') various forms of human scum have floated to the surface. Rumours are in circulation, including one to the effect that Karmazinov (who is among the scheduled speakers) intends to deliver his much-publicized Farewell to his Readers dressed in the costume of a governess of the province. Many people, not knowing that Yuliya Mikhaylovna has decided on an austerity Fête in order to bring in more money for her governesses, have been talking of a free champagne lunch, which seems reasonable in view of the high price of the tickets. The more disreputable section of those who are expecting some sort of 'Belshazzar's Feast' fall into an ugly mood when they find that there is not even to be a bar during the afternoon session.

The celebration is to fall into two parts—a session of literary readings in the afternoon and then, after a long interval, a ball in the evening. Before the afternoon session has even started, things have already begun to go wrong. A tremendous crush develops outside the entrance. Inside the hall a colossal, pock-marked retired Captain 'drunkenly demanded to be directed to the non-existent bar and had to be dragged out'. Unruly shouts come from the public seated in front of the stage on which the reading is to take place: 'Perhaps we don't want any readings. . . . We've paid our money. . . . The public's been taken in. . . . We're the bosses, not the Lembkes.' The Lembkes arrive late and are greeted by an absurd flourish from the orchestra arranged by the nihilist and practical joker Lyamshin, whom Yuliya Mikhaylovna has inadvisedly accepted as master of ceremonies.

Further devices step up the pressure. So much has the Fête captured public imagination that, it transpires, many of the poorest officials have pawned their underclothes, sheets and very nearly their mattresses to 'our Jews', so as to be able to buy tickets and dress their ladies suitably. The magnificent hall which has been lent for the occasion, the silks, velvet and jewellery of the wealthier women, which 'shone and burned on all sides', and the decorations worn by the more reputable menfolk contrast with the guffaws and catcalls of the hooligans who have also gained admission, and ensure that the final calamity shall be on the most spectacular level.

The ceremonies consist of five absurd episodes of uneven length which illustrate many features of Dostoyevsky's comic and satirical genius. Among these are his mastery of the unexpected, the range of his variations on the ridiculous, the breathless, seething atmosphere so splendidly sustained by the style, and above all his ability to go one better, and, at the very moment when one staggering blow has been struck, to strike another and yet more staggering blow.

The first reading is one which had not been on the programme at all. On to the stage—a complete surprise to all except the nihilist conspirators who have put him up to it—staggers the preposterous Captain Lebyadkin, red in the face, wearing a white tie and tailcoat. 'He raised his hand, wiped his forehead with it, shook his shaggy head and with an air of one who has come to a desperate decision took two paces forward and suddenly emitted a short of laughter, laughter not loud, but overflowing, long and happy which made his whole corpulent bulk shake and his little eyes screw up.' Greeted with answering laughs from half the public and claps from the more solid citizens, he is escorted off the stage.

Liputin now appears and explains that Lebyadkin, moved by 'humane and lofty aims', had written an ode in honour of the poor governesses which, in response to shouts from the audience, he proceeds to read aloud. As might have been predicted, Lebyadkin's ode turns out to be in the worst of taste, contrasting the former lot of the governess (who while teaching 'snivelling children' was so desperately keen to get married that she was even ready to 'wink at the sexton') with her present good fortune, now that, equipped with a dowry as a result of the present Fête, she will be able triumphantly to spit in everyone's face—literally 'spit at everything and triumph'.

Liputin's *naglost* in reading this absurd ode is one of the signs, of which more are soon in evidence, that the nihilists have come out into the open and are no longer even bothering to disguise their intention of wrecking the Fête. Into this atmosphere of mounting rowdiness Dostoyevsky injects the victim of his satire whom he treats most savagely of all, Turgenev in the character of Karmazinov.

Karmazinov is greeted respectfully, for Dostoyevsky realizes that the time has now come to decrease the tension momentarily. Ignoring the law whereby even an arch-genius cannot hope to entertain the public unpunished with a literary reading of longer than twenty minutes, Karmazinov proceeds at great length to deliver a piece of mystical, obscure and romantic balderdash, studded with references to obscure plants which have never been heard of outside botanical reference works and dealing, in so far as it can be understood at all, with a love affair of his early youth. It is not easy to take parts of Turgenev seriously again after reading this viciously telling parody. The episode ends with an undignified argument between the 'great writer' and disrespectful nihilist members of the audience, during which the expression on Karmazinov's face seems to say, 'I'm not the sort of person you think. I'm on your side. Only praise me, praise me more, praise me as much as possible. I like it awfully. . . .'

Now that the tradition of public argument with the audience has been established, things go even harder with Dostoyevsky's next victim, Stepan Trofimovich Verkhovensky, who has chosen to treat this as an occasion on which his fate would be decided. He proceeds to challenge nihilism in the name of the aesthetic ideals associated with Russian 'men of the forties', claiming that Shakespeare and Raphael are more important than socialism or chemistry. Various people rush towards the stage and shout insults. Stepan Trofimovich bursts into hysterical tears and a further push is given when one of the interrupters accuses him of having many years before sold the escaped convict Fedka (who now wanders round the town cutting throats) into the army as a recruit in order to pay his card debts. Amid general screams, tears and applause, Stepan Trofimovich raises both hands above his head and curses the audience.

After the disappearance of Stepan Trofimovich, Dostoyevsky has by no means finished. 'Suddenly the final catastrophe burst.' The third reader (a maniac, whom the Narrator has earlier noticed rehearsing his speech off stage to the accompaniment of powerful swings of the fist apparently destined to pulverize some imaginary opponent) rushes on to the stage and delivers an impassioned harangue on the theme 'never has Russia reached such a depth of shame as at the present day'. This is greeted with wild applause. 'That's the stuff! Hurray! This is better than aesthetics!' Dostoyevsky's Narrator comments: 'Russia was being publicly dishonoured, so how could one fail to roar with delight.' Dragged off by a group of officials, the maniac somehow bursts free and rushes back for one final cry of 'But never has Russia sunk . . .' before he is finally removed.

It now remains for a nihilist girl student, another speaker not on the programme, to mount the platform: 'Ladies and gentlemen, I have come to tell you of the sufferings of the unhappy students and to arouse them everywhere in protest.'

These last two episodes are brief, but it is difficult to exaggerate their comic impact, coming as they do at a point when Dostoyevsky seems to have exhausted all the possibilities of comedy. They owe much of their effect to a device which may be called 'loading'. The maniac had been introduced to the reader before the speeches of Karmazinov and Stepan Trofimovich were recounted. His prose style and habit of smashing down his fist are already known, but, having been temporarily forgotten during the excitement which follows, impinge all the more effectively because they are already familiar. Similarly loaded is the girl student's obsession, which has already been conveyed in an earlier chapter, with the fate of the poor students. This device of loading was later to contribute much to the effectiveness of Father Ferapont's outrageous irruption into the vigil over Father Zosima's dead body in ***The Brothers Karamazov.***

The first part of the Fête is now over. The ball which takes place in the evening proceeds in an atmosphere of even greater disorder, but here, despite certain absurd episodes such as the 'literary quadrille', Dostoyevsky has most suitably chosen to tone down the comedy. A more sombre atmosphere is cultivated as the reader observes the tragic derangement of Von Lembke, who in his insanity orders Yuliya Mikhaylovna herself to be arrested. The sequence ends with a dramatic finale entirely free from humour when it is learned that a whole suburb of the town, where many of the guests have their homes, is on fire. The nihilists have done their work. In the remaining section of the novel leading up to and including Shatov's murder, there is no place for the riotous absurdities of the 'literary reading'.

One might searth the whole of fiction in vain for a finer scene than Dostoyevsky's Fête. (pp. 145-49)

Ronald Hingley, in his The Undiscovered Dostoyevsky, *Hamish Hamilton, 1962, 241 p.*

MIKHAIL BAKHTIN (essay date 1963)

[A respected twentieth-century Russian essayist, literary theorist, and philosopher of language, Bakhtin is best known for his influence on the Structuralist and Semiotic literary movements. He was a prominent figure in the Russian intellectual circles of the 1920s, joining in the lively debate about Neo-Kantianism, Phenomenology, and the merits of the Formalists versus the sociological critics. In his pioneering study of Dostoevski's artistry, excerpted below, Bakhtin labeled Dostoevski's novels polyphonic, finding in them "a plurality of independent and unmerged voices and consciousnesses, a genuine polyphony of fully valid voices," none of which necessarily represent the author. Here, he discusses discourse in the section "At Tikhon's," first in the narration of Stavrogin's confession and then in his dialogue with the Bishop. Bakhtin's study was originally published in 1929; this piece is drawn from a translation of a revised edition published in 1963.]

Leonid Grossman [see excerpt dated 1925] took the style of Stavrogin's Confession to be a monological expression of Stavrogin's consciousness; this style, in his opinion, in adequate to the theme, that is, to the crime itself and to Stavrogin's soul. Grossman thus applied to the confession the principles of ordinary stylistics, which takes into account only the direct word, the word that recognizes only itself and its referential object. In actual fact the style of Stavrogin's Confession is determined above all by its internally dialogic orientation vis-à-vis the other person. Precisely this sideward glance at the other person determines the breaks in its style and its whole specific profile. Tikhon had precisely this in mind when he began directly with an "aesthetic critique" of the style of the confession. It is characteristic that Grossman ignores altogether and does not quote in his article what is most important in Tikhon's critique, and deals only with secondary features. Tikhon's critique is very important, for it doubtless expresses the artistic intention of Dostoevsky himself.

What does Tikhon see as the chief shortcoming of the confession?

Tikhon's first words upon reading Stavrogin's notes were:

> "And would it be possible for you to make a few corrections in this document?"
>
> "Why? I wrote it honestly," Stavrogin answered.
>
> "Something in the diction . . ."

Thus the diction (style) and its unattractiveness is what struck Tikhon above all in the confession. We quote an excerpt from their dialogue which reveals the true essence of Stavrogin's style:

> "*It's as if you deliberately want to represent yourself more coarsely than your heart would wish it . . .*" said Tikhon, growing more and more bold. Apparently the "document" had made a strong impression on him.
>
> "Represent? I repeat: I did not 'represent myself' and in particular I did not 'put on airs.'
>
> Tikhon quickly lowered his eyes.
>
> "This document comes straight from the needs of a heart mortally wounded—do I understand you correctly?" he said insistently and with unusual fervor. "Yes, this is penitence and the natural need for it which has overwhelmed you, and you have entered upon a noble path, an unprecedented path. *But you seem to despise and disdain in advance all who will read what is written here, and you are calling them to battle*. You are not ashamed of confessing your crime, *so why are you ashamed of repentance*?"
>
> "Ashamed?"
>
> "You are *ashamed* and *afraid*!"
>
> "Afraid?"
>
> "Mortally. *Let them stare at me, you say; well, but you yourself, how are you going to look at them?* Certain places in your account are even intensified in diction, as if you admire your own psychology and grasp at every trifle in order to astound *the reader* with an insensitivity which you may well not have. *What is this, if not a prideful challenge from a guilty man to a judge?*"

Stavrogin's confession, like the confessions of Ippolit and the Underground Man, is a confession intensely oriented toward another person, without whom the hero could not manage but whom at the same time he despises and whose judgment he does not accept. Stavrogin's confession, therefore, . . . is deprived of any finalizing force and tends toward [the] same vicious circle that marked the speech of the Underground Man. Without recognition, and affirmation by another person Stavrogin is incapable of accepting himself, but at the same time he does not want to accept the other's judgment of him.

> But as far as I am concerned there will remain those who will know everything and who will stare at me, and I at them. I want everyone to stare at me. Whether or not this will make it easier for me I do not know. I resort to it as the last means.

At the same time, however, the style of his confession is dictated by his hatred and nonacceptance of this "everyone."

Stavrogin's attitude toward himself and toward the other person is locked into that same vicious circle which the Underground Man had tread, "paying no attention to his companions" and at the same time stomping his boots so they could not fail to notice that he was paying them no attention. Here it is presented through different material, very far removed from the realm of the comic. But Stavrogin's position is nevertheless comical. "Even in the *form* of this great confession there is something *ridiculous*," Tikhon says.

But if we turn to the Confession itself, we must admit that judged by external indicators of style it differs sharply from ***Notes from Underground.*** No one else's word, no one else's accent forces its way into the fabric. There is not a single reservation, not a single repetition, not a single ellipsis. No external signs of the overwhelming influence of another's word appear to register here at all. Here, indeed, the other's word has penetrated so deeply within, to the very atoms of the construction, the conflicting rejoinders overlap one another so densely that discourse appears on the surface monologic. But nevertheless even the careless ear can catch in it sharp and irreconcilable voices interrupting one another, as was pointed out immediately by Tikhon.

The style is determined above all by a cynical ignoring of the other person, an ignoring that is pointedly deliberate. Sentences are crudely abrupt and cynically precise. This is not soberminded strictness or precision, this is not documentation in the usual sense, because that sort of realistic documentation is oriented toward its referrential object and, for all the dryness of its style, does strive to be adequate to all aspects of the object. Stavrogin attempts to present his word without any evaluative accent, to make it intentionally wooden, to eliminate all human tones in it. He wants everyone to stare at him, but at the same time he repents in an immobile and deathly mask. This is why he rearranges every sentence so that his personal tone does not surface, so that his repentant, or perhaps simply agitated, accent does not slip through. That is why he breaks up his sentences, because a normal sentence is too flexible and subtle in its transmission of the human voice.

We cite a single example:

> I, Nikolai Stavrogin, a retired officer, was living in Petersburg in 186-, indulging in lewdness in which I found no pleasure. For some time I had had three apartments. I myself was living in one of them, in a hotel, with board and maid-service, where at that time Marya Lebyadkin, now my lawful wife, was, too. I rented both my other apartments by the month for love-affairs: in one I received a certain lady who loved me and, in the other, her maid, and for a while I was very much occupied with the effort to bring them both together so that the lady and the girl would meet at my place. Knowing both their characters, I expected some pleasure for myself from this stupid joke.

The sentence breaks off, as it were, at just that point where a living human voice begins. Stavrogin seems to turn away from us as soon as he casts a word our way. It is noteworthy that he even tries to omit the word ''I'' when speaking of himself, where ''I'' is not the simple formal subject of the verb but where it might carry some especially strong and personal accent (for example, in the first and last sentences of the quoted excerpt [where Dostoevsky omitted the first-person singular pronoun]). All those syntactical peculiarities mentioned by Grossman—the broken sentence, the deliberately lackluster or deliberately cynical word, etc.—are in fact proof of Stavrogin's fundamental effort to eliminate, emphatically and aggressively, any living personal accent from his own voice, to speak with his back turned to the listener. (pp. 243-46)

• • • • •

The entire orientation of Stavrogin in [his dialogue with Tikhon] is determined by his dual attitude toward the ''other person'': by the impossibility of managing without his judgment and forgiveness, and at the same time by a hostility toward him and resistance to his judgment and forgiveness. This is what determines all the interruptions in his speech, in his facial expressions and gestures, the abrupt shifts of mood and tone, his ceaseless reservations, his anticipation of Tikhon's replies and abrupt refutation of these imagined replies. It is as if two persons were speaking with Tikhon, merged interruptedly into one. Tikhon is confronted with two voices, into whose internal struggle he is drawn as a participant.

> After the first salutations, unintelligible and uttered for some reason with haste and with obvious, mutual awkwardness, Tikhon took his guest into his study, and, still in apparent haste, sat him down on the sofa in front of the table and settled himself beside him in one of the wicker chairs. At this point Nikolai Vsyevolodovich, to his surprise, lost control of himself completely. It seemed as if he were getting ready, with all his strength, to dare something extraordinary and unquestionable, and at the same time, almost impossible for him. He looked around the study for a moment, obviously not noticing what he had seen; he became lost in thought, but, perhaps, not knowing what he was thinking about. The quiet waked him, and it suddenly seemed to him as if Tikhon were sheepishly lowering his eyes and smiling a completely needless smile. This instantly aroused a feeling of disgust and rebellion in him; he wanted to get up and go out; in his opinion, Tikhon was absolutely drunk. But the latter suddenly raised his eyes and looked at him so strongly and so thoughtfully, and at the same time with such an unexpected and enigmatic expression, that he almost winced, and now it suddenly seemed to him something completely different: that Tikhon already knew what he had come for, that he had been forewarned (although nobody in the whole world could know the reason), and if he was not first to start a conversation, it was because he was sparing him, afraid of humiliating him.

The abrupt changes in Stavrogin's mood and tone determine the entire subsequent dialogue. Sometimes one voice wins out, sometimes the other, but more often Stavrogin's rejoinder is structured as an interruption-prone merging of the two voices.

> These revelations [of Stavrogin's visitation by the devil—M. B.] were wild and confused and really did seem to come from a madman. But at the same time Nikolai Vsyevolodovich spoke with such a strange frankness, unprecedented for him, with such ingenuousness, completely unnatural for him, that it seemed as if his former self had suddenly and unexpectedly vanished. He was in no way ashamed to display that fear with which he talked about his ghost. But all this was instantaneous and vanished as suddenly as it had appeared.
>
> ''This is all nonsense,'' he said quickly and with awkward annoyance, catching himself up. ''I'm going to a doctor.''

And somewhat further on:

> . . . but it's all nonsense. I'm going to a doctor. It's really all nonsense, terrible nonsense. It's me myself in different aspects, and nothing else. Since I added this . . . sentence just now, you almost certainly think that I'm still doubtful and not sure that it's me and not in fact a devil?

In the beginning, one of Stavrogin's voices wins out completely and it seems that ''his former self had suddenly and unexpectedly vanished.'' But then the second voice emerges again, causes an abrupt change of tone and breaks apart his reply. There occurs one of Stavrogin's typical anticipations of Tikhon's reaction, and all the accompanying phenomena already familiar to us.

Before he finally hands Tikhon the pages of his confession, Stavrogin's second voice abruptly interrupts his speech and his intentions, proclaiming its independence from the other, its contempt for the other, thus directly contradicting by its tone the very purpose of the confession.

> ''Listen, I don't like spies and psychologists, at least those who poke into my soul. I don't ask anyone into my soul, I don't need anyone, I can get along by myself. Maybe you think I'm afraid of you.'' He raised his voice and lifted his face up defiantly. ''Maybe you're now completely convinced that I came to tell you some 'terrible' secret and you're waiting for it with all the monkish curiosity of which you're capable? Well, you may be sure that I'm not going to reveal anything to you, no kind of secret, because I can get along perfectly without you . . .''

The structure of this reply and its positioning within the whole dialogue are completely analogous to the phenomena . . . in ***Notes from Underground.*** The tendency toward a vicious circle in one's attitude toward ''the other'' appears here in perhaps even more acute form.

> ''Answer me one question, but sincerely, only to me, or as if to yourself, in the dark of the night,'' Tikhon began in an inspired voice. ''If someone forgave you this (he pointed to the sheets), and not someone you respect or are afraid of, but a stranger, a man you'll never know, reading your terrible confession silently to himself, would the idea of this make it easier for you or would it be all the same? If it might be hard for your self-respect to give an answer, don't say anything but only think it to yourself.''
>
> ''Easier,'' Stavrogin answered in a low voice. ''If you forgave me, it would be much easier for me,'' he added, with downcast eyes.
>
> ''I will, if you forgive me too,'' Tikhon said emphatically.

What emerges here in all its clarity are the functions of the other person in dialogue, the other person as such, deprived of any social or pragmatic real-life concretization. This other person—''a stranger, a man you'll never know''—fulfills his functions in dialogue outside the plot and outside his specificity in any plot, as a pure "man in man," a representative of "all others" for the "I." As a consequence of such a positioning of "the other," communion assumes a special character and becomes independent of all real-life, concrete social forms (the forms of family, social or economic class, life's stories). . . . [In this passage, the] function of "the other" as such, whoever he may be, is revealed with extraordinary clarity. (pp. 262-64)

Mikhail Bakhtin, in his Problems of Dostoevsky's Poetics, *edited and translated by Caryl Emerson, University of Minnesota Press, 1984, 333 p.*

EDWARD WASIOLEK (essay date 1964)

[*A contemporary American scholar of Russian literature, Wasiolek is the author of a noted study,* Dostoevsky: The Major Fiction, *excerpted below. Here, he discusses the circular construction of* The Possessed, *focusing on its characters and scenes.*]

Late in [***The Possessed***] an extraordinary scene takes place between Peter Verkhovensky and Stavrogin. Stavrogin has just left a disorderly meeting of revolutionaries assembled by Peter at Virginsky's when he is overtaken by a breathless Peter at Kirilov's. There Peter delivers a startling confession, the high point of which is the following:

> "Stavrogin, you're beautiful!" Verkhovensky cried out almost in ecstasy. "Do you know that you are beautiful? . . . You are my idol! You're just the sort of man that's needed. I—I especially need a man like you. I don't know anyone but you. You're the leader, the sun, and I am your worm."
>
> He suddenly kissed his hand. A shiver ran down Stavrogin's spine, and he switched his hand away in dismay.

Upon this follows Peter's vision of the new world that will rise on the ashes of the old one. By the ministrations of monstrous vice, people will be reduced to the condition of happy slaves and fearful gratitude before the supreme autocratic will, which will give unity and cohesion to the new society.

There are two centers of gravity in the novel, and the magnetic force that binds them is felt in the trembling adoration Peter expresses for Stavrogin and in his mad vision of a new world. There is the political pamphlet and the metaphysical drama, and they have only the weakest of structural ties. Peter is the center of the political drama, and Stavrogin the center of the metaphysical drama; and most of the characters belong to one or the other. The socialists belong clearly to Peter's plot, and just as clearly Shatov and Kirilov belong to Stavrogin's plot. The two dramas mix only tangentially. Peter may need Kirilov to take the blame for Shatov's death, and Shatov's death to bind his group in fear of blood, but he does not need Kirilov's monstrous dialectic or Shatov's messianic Christianity.

Dostoevsky himself had trouble connecting the two dramas. He began with a political pamphlet, but the metaphysical drama progressively took over. (pp. 110-11)

Peter and Stavrogin bring together the metaphysical and political dramas, but the beginning of both lies in Stepan Trofimovich, the father of Peter and the tutor of Stavrogin. He begins and ends the novel, giving birth to the events and also bringing them to a prophetic conclusion. What ends in chaos, fire, murder, and crime begins with him. (p. 111)

When the novel opens, Stepan Trofimovich has been safely ensconced for a decade in a small provincial town; he lives comfortably under the protection of Varvara Petrovna, the mother of Stavrogin, and is the intellectual leader of the town. About him grows a small circle of the town's "free thinkers"; the townspeople look upon the circle as a hotbed of radicalism. Its members include Liputin, a scandalmonger, family tyrant, and miser; he locks up the scraps of food and the candle ends each night, but dreams nevertheless of Fourieristic phalansteries; Virginsky, who with his wife gets all his ideas from books and who always speaks in a whisper and with deep feeling about the "bright hopes" which he will never abandon; Lyamshin, the post-office clerk who does imitations on the piano of the squeals of pigs, thunderstorms, and the first cry of a baby. Later, Shatov becomes a member of the circle.

At these meetings Stepan Trofimovich orates about love, art, country, and religion to the applause of the members, whose eyes and wits have been dimmed by champagne. And there—as improbable as it may seem—the holocaust that descends upon the small town—the madness of the fête, the murders, the fires, and the moral degeneration of the town—are all prepared. . . . The harmless talk of Stepan Trofimovich includes ideas on three topics dear to Dostoevsky's heart: the peasants, Russian nationalism, and God. According to Stepan Trofimovich, Rachel is worth more than all the peasants of Russia, who for the past hundred years had given Russia only the Kamarinsky dance; Russian nationalism is an outdated opinion and the consequence of sloth and idleness; and the God of the people is something to snicker at. This is the substance of his high liberalism—liberalism without an aim—and of his love for humanity and the fuel for Virginsky's bright hopes. The people are a joke, Russian nationalism is an opinion—and an old and unmerited one at that—and God is a function of the liberal mind. True, it is all innocent chatter, the bloated rhetoric of a comfortable and good-natured buffoon, orated to the approval of the champagne-soaked voices of the circle and the thumpings of Lyamshin on the piano.

The circle is both ideologically and structurally the source of the public events that follow. These events culminate in the murder of Shatov, the suicide of Kirilov, the murders of Liza and the Lebyadkins, the madness of the fête, with its aftermath of fire, murder, and disintegration. What brews in Stepan Trofimovich's circle is brought into being in Julia von Lembke's circle and Peter Verkhovensky's circle. *Dostoevsky uses three circles as structure points of reference in tracing the growth of intellectual and moral degeneration.*

Julia von Lembke, the newly arrived governor's wife, is possessed by ambition. She dreams foolishly and romantically of conquering all the radicals of the province by her wit and kindness and of bringing upon herself the adoration of the radicals and the beneficence of a grateful government. "She dreamed of *giving happiness* and reconciling the irreconcilable, or, rather, of uniting everything and everybody in the adoration of her own person." With her circle a revolution in the town's hierarchy takes place. There is a shift in the intellectual leadership from Stepan Trofimovich to his son, who is the real power behind Julia von Lembke's circle, and in social leadership from Varvara Perovna, the patroness of Stepan Trofimovich, to Julia von Lembke, the patroness of Peter Verkhovensky. The continuity of the change is signaled by the continuing presence of some of the same members, like Lyamshin and Liputin. With the shift in intellectual and social leadership comes a change in the intellectual and social temper. The good-natured, abstract, vague, and harmless "talk" of Stepan Trofimovich's circle becomes cynical, willful, and destructive action in the new circle. Stepan Trofimovich's liberal laughter at God, country, and the people is converted into pranks of an ugly sort. The sacrilege which was only an idea is translated into the blasphemies of putting a mouse behind an ikon and of hiding dirty pictures in the sack of the Bible seller. Stepan Trofimovich's criticism of Christianity for not appreciating women is translated into the liberal raillery of marriage and the kidnapping of a young lieutenant's wife, who is "unliberally" afraid of being punished by her husband for losing money at gambling. In going from Stepan Trofimovich's circle to Julia von Lembke's circle, we move from Stepan Trofimovich's abstract sacrileges to the ugly deeds the talk had implied. Ideas become acts. (pp. 111-14)

Despite the fact that the control over the forces she has gathered about her moves quickly out of her hands, Julia von Lembke is persuaded that the radicals are only boys who will finally be conquered by her high ideals. Her triumph in reconciling everybody to everything will be celebrated at the fête and the ball, which she has ostensibly organized for aid to needy governesses. Despite her plans, the fête unfolds by a logic of its own, devolving quickly into stupidity, crassness, and violence. Instead of a triumphal entrance, Julia is greeted by the wrong music and a drunken Lebyadkin reading a scandalous poem. Then follow the long and self-loving speech of Karmazinov, the impassioned plea of Stepan for the superiority of Pushkin over shoes—this is taken as an insult to liberal thought—and the hysterical approval for the curses that the fist-flailing professor from St. Petersburg hurls at Russia.

The structural significance of the fête is made clear by Stepan Trofimovich and the narrator, both of whom recall Stepan Trofimovich's disastrous trip to St. Petersburg ten years before. Stepan makes his appeal to the superiority of art over shoes as he did then, and he is hooted off the stage in the same manner and by an audience just as liberal and just as crass and stupid. It is as if what had boiled and churned in St. Petersburg ten years previously had reached the provinces. The narrator tells us, in fact, that on the eve of the fête a small army of rabble, itinerants, poets with theses, seminarists, and liberals aggressively concerned with the "woman question" had invaded the small provincial town. The same crude, shrill, and aggressive clamor for human rights and the same hatred for everything Russian that had met and crushed Stepan's "high liberalism" ten years before in St. Petersburg seem to have poured into town. The mad professor from St. Petersburg, who follows Stepan, is an appropriate finale of a revolution in values and temper that had taken place from the high liberalism of Stepan Trofimovich's circle to the radical and vulgar liberalism of Julia von Lembke's circle. What is trampled on now—God, country, and the people—are the same things that Stepan Trofimovich, though more aesthetically, had laughed at. The stupidness, crassness, and destructive elements that lie just beneath the surface of Julia von Lembke's naïveté and self-deception are all openly and liberally nurtured in Peter Verkhovensky's circle.

Peter Verkhovensky's circle of secret revolutionaries is the conspiracy that Julia von Lembke had hoped to uncover and, in uncovering it, to reconcile everyone to everything. In Peter's circle the self-deception of the members is more explicit, the vulgarity more crude, and the hatred of Russia more intense. Our introduction to the members as an organized group is at the Virginsky name day party, where they have been gathered to hear explicitly the instructions Peter has brought from the European centers of revolution. He has convinced them that they are part of a vast network of "committees of five." The meeting is a bitter burlesque of the pretensions of socialists. They have gathered to organize the world, but they cannot even organize a meeting. They have gathered to preach the gospel of social harmony and the universal love of man, and they hate each other intensely and fall into chaotic disharmony over trifles. They are the flower of the town's liberalism, and never has Dostoevsky exposed more ruthlessly the contradiction between the abstract love of humanity men carry in their heads and the reality of their petty wills and vicious actions. The meeting is a chaos of conflicting, mean-minded people, who are filled with hate and contempt for each other. The spirit of the meeting is caught best in the personality and actions of Virginsky's sister, a young nihilist who has just arrived from St. Petersburg. Like a jack-in-the-box with eyes popping out, she keeps leaping to her feet to make some impassioned plea for support for suffering students and for help to arouse them to protest. Dedicated to humanity, she cannot stand the schoolboy who is present, turning on his every remark viciously, meanly, and with undisguised contempt. She calls the uncle she has not seen since childhood a fool and a spiteful person, and the schoolboy a case of arrested development.

The high point of the meeting is the calm, unhurried speech that Shigalyov makes on the necessary nature of the future society. His conclusion—in direct contradiction to the idea he started with—is that nine-tenths of the future state would be composed of happy slaves and one-tenth of masters. His scheme is an affront to those present, for Shigalyov has, with his logic, exposed the deception that lies at the core of the bright hopes of the socialists. As he himself says at the beginning of his speech—and what he says could be said of all those present—"I have come to the conclusion that all the makers of social systems, from the ancient times to our present year, have been dreamers, storytellers, fools, who contradicted themselves and who understood nothing of natural science or that strange animal called man." the meeting itself is a corroboration of this thesis, for those present have demonstrated the contradiction between the fictions men carry in their heads and the natural science of man's nature.

And just as the meeting itself provides an example of the deception that Shigalyov says has plagued all social thinkers, so too it shows us what the cohesive force of society must be. When the meeting is a babble of voices, a chaos of conflicting wills and egos, Peter Verkhovensky yawns, asks for cards, pares his fingernails, and otherwise takes no interest in the efforts of the flower of radicalism to organize itself. But at a certain point, he does bring unity and cohesion to this rabble, and he does it with the only weapon this group or any group of nihilists, socialists, or social planners can have at their command. Peter does it not with an idea, or a bright image, but with *force. For Dostoevsky only force, that is, the human will, remains when one has given up God.* Specifically, Peter asks if the members would inform on a comrade who had performed a political murder, that is, a murder that was necessary for the "cause." They are asked, in other words, to choose between loyalty to socialism and the existing moral order. Collective fear forces them to choose the murder. Later, Peter will attempt to enforce this bond of fear by an actual murder.

Peter provides with his question the hint as to why Shigalyov started with unlimited freedom and ended with unlimited despotism, and he also provides us with the hint as to what is wrong with Shigalyov's system. For despite agreement among critics that Shigalyov's system represents the extremity of Dostoevsky's dire forebodings about socialism, Shigalyov himself has his "bright hope," and only Peter Verkhovensky sees it. As he tells Stavrogin shortly after the meeting, "Shigalyov is an aesthete and a fool like every philanthropist." Shigalyov's bright hope is the 10 per cent of the new order who would live in harmony of unrestricted power and absolute freedom. Peter knows that the dialectic of human psychology is such that the law which results in 10 percent subjugating 90 per cent must necessarily operate in the 10 per cent until there remains only one will.

Peter is supremely without self-deception. Peter knows that 10 per cent free men is just as unreal as 100 per cent free; he knows that 10 per cent free men is a bright hope, and he is a man without bright hopes. Socialists have bright hopes, and he is not a socialist. As he himself says, he is a scoundrel. But this does not mean as the Soviets have bravely tried to interpret his statement, that the socialists are not scoundrels or, as Philip Rahv has tried to interpret it [see excerpt dated 1949], that they must be something other than scoundrels. Rahv's interpretation is not even logical. According to Peter, all men are scoundrels, and there are scoundrels who know they are scoundrels and those who believe they are something else. In other words, there are wise scoundrels and scoundrels who are fools. Socialists are scoundrels—like everybody—and they have bright hopes, but their bright hopes do not make them any less scoundrels. They make them fools as well as scoundrels. Peter is not a socialist because he is not a fool. He knows that the future state will have to be built on the real psychology of men, and not on the fictions of Virginsky, Liputin, or Shigalyov. He knows that reality is the human will, and that historic reality is a deadly and unremitting duel of wills. He sees what Dostoevsky saw and what the Underground Man saw and what all of Dostoevsky's great undeceived heroes were to see. Peter understands that only force will bind the conflicting egos of men into some kind of unity. Will is force, and only a greater force can resolve two conflicting forces. If there is to be harmony, it will haveto be a harmony of force and will. And that will must be superior to all others, Godlike in its power to inspire submission and obedience. That will, for Peter, is Stavrogin's.

Does not Peter Verkhovensky's frantic obeisance to Stavrogin become clear now? He recognizes his spirit's father; and he recognizes the farthest reach of the strong will he is looking for. He knows that the truth of socialism is not the shining ideas of Virginsky or the Fourieristic phalansteries of Liputin's babblings, and he knows that even Shigalyov's stark discussion about the inevitaable course of socialism harbors a self-deception. He knows that the future unity of society can be only a unity of force, and he sees in Stavrogin the supreme self-will that can compel society's unity.

Peter is not alone in clutching Stavrogin's hand and in pleading with him to raise his banner. Shatov and Kirilov do the same with almost the same words. Liza ruins herself for one night with him, and expiates her act with a death indirectly caused by him. Dasha is ready to give up everything for him; Maria Shatov bears his son while cursing him; and Maria Timofyevna, the crippled half-wit, is his wife. Everyone needs him, and Stavrogin needs no one. He is detached, calm, quiet. He is like a dead sun about which the planets he has created continue to move with borrowed light and heat. We learn of him by these fragments of himself, which he has thrown off and which continue to live in the persons of others. Of these, Kirilov and Shatov are the most important.

They are twin creations of Stavrogin. They make a pilgrimage to America—the mecca of liberal ideas—endure its unspeakable humiliations, fall in worship before the ideas of Stavrogin, return to the same town, live together in the same house, and each in a sense causes the other's death. As each reminds him, Stavrogin has given to each the idea that consumes him, and although the ideas are contradictory, given them at about the same time. Kirilov is consumed with the passion to kill God and liberate man, Shatov with the passion of finding God and realizing man. At the core of each is a self-deception, and Stavrogin's liberation from each was a liberation from the self-deception of each. Shatov and Kirilov remind us what Stavrogin was and what he has overcome in himself.

Everything Shatov believes in, Stavrogin himself had declared more than two years before and had since given up. And everything Shatov confesses and Stavrogin had once believed in is what Dostoevsky holds most closely and dearly. According to Shatov, nations are moved by a force other than reason and science. Reason and science have never been able to give ends and indeed have never even been able to define the difference between good and evil. Man is moved rather by an unquenchable and irrational desire to go to the end and to deny the existence of an end. That is, to deny death and affirm life. God is the force that denies death, and he who affirms life carries in him the concrete attribute of God. Try to define that force, and the faith is destroyed. It is a force that is lived, and an unconditional acceptance of it is the condition of its existence. Shatov sees this force as carried in the being of the Russian people, but this is not to reduce God to an attribute of nationality, as Stavrogin cynically suggests and as critics of Dostoevsky have uniformly concluded. It is an attribute of nationality only when the force is *thought* and no longer lived. If it is lived, it will and can be only your force; when it is yours and someone else's, it is no one's. Or, as Shatov puts it, when nations begin to believe in a general God, they no longer believe in God, but the idea of God. Faith in God, in the living affirmation of life, without conditions and particularly without the condition of reason's approval, sanctifies everything Shatov says about God and the Russian people. But Shatov does not have such a faith, as the remorseless questions of Stavrogin reveal. He hopes somehow that faith in the people will lead him to God, but only a faith in God will consecrate his faith in the people. As long as he poses this condition—and hence *thinks* his faith—he cannot *live* his faith in God. Stavrogin had at one point seen clearly his inability to accept God without conditions and had refused to live in the deception of believing in God and refusing to accept him.

Kirilov is one of Dostoevsky's immense creations. All his life he has thought of one thing only—God. "God has tortured me all my life," he confesses, and what we see of him in the novel confirms this. So thoroughly has his "thought" devoured him that he has trouble communicating with those outside him. His language is strangely unsyntactic, and in his discussions, he seldom answers questions that are put to him; he does not seem to notice what the other person is saying. What is the idea that devours him?. . . Kirilov is killing himself out of love of humanity, but this is more than a "pedagogical suicide." He is not only killing God, he is usurping Christ's role. Christ died for man's sins; Kirilov will die for his misunderstandings. As a new man was created by Christ's sacrifice, so too a new man, washed clear of the fear of death and physically transformed, will inherit the earth. . . . [What must be understood] is the dialectical nature of Dostoevsky's world, in which love of humanity (without ceasing to be love), and sacrifice can be self-interest (without ceasing to be sacrifice). Kirilov is imitating Christ; he does sacrifice himself; and he does it out of love of man. But his self-imposed crucifixion is a grotesque imitation of Christ, as his love and sacrifice—despite his intention—are grotesque imitations of true love of man and true sacrifice. Kirilov does not believe in God, and he can—in Dostoevsky's logic—believe only in himself; since he believes only in himself, true love of mankind and true sacrifice are impossible.

Kirilov's logic is impeccable. As he tells Peter: "If God exists, then all is his will, and I can do nothing against his will. If God doesn't exist, then it is my will, and I am bound to express my self-will." If everything is his will, then he cannot be attached to anything, for to be attached is to depend on, and to depend on something is to restrict one's freedom. Kirilov's favorite expression consequently is *vse ravno*—"it doesn't matter." The "free man" must be indifferent to any emotion, value, or obligation. He is not free if he believes in socialism, progress, or in reason. Man's most enduring attachment has been God, and God is therefore his most rooted impediment to liberty. Indeed, all other attachments are derived from a belief in him; once God is dead (as an idea in man's consciousness), then, and only then, will man be free.

Despite his insistence that nothing matters, Kirilov seems to act as if it does. He loves children, feels sympathy for Shatov, loves life, keeps fit by exercising, and feels disgust for Peter. But these are only seeming contradictions. The new man must be indifferent to everything if he is really free, but Kirilov is not yet the new man. Only when he commits suicide and manifests his terrible freedom will he be free, or at least those who believe in his example and have killed the fear of God and afterlife will be free. Kirilov's sympathy for Shatov and his disgust for Peter are not contradictions in his reasoning but only signs that the man himself is not yet free. But there is a deception at the very core of his reasoning, and significantly it is Peter Verkhovensky who sees it and shows it up. Only Peter, with Stavrogin, is totally without deception.

Peter shows up the deceptive core of Kirilov's thinking during their curious meeting on the night Kirilov kills himself. Because he is afraid that Kirilov will lose courage, Peter tries to work himself up to a frenzied excitement—and hopefully suicide—by getting him to talk about why he must kill himself. Peter follows Kirilov's explanations with indifferent curiosity. After Kirilov explains why he will be God when he kills himself, Peter observes irritatedly, "You know what, to show my self-will, I should if I were in your place kill somebody else, and not myself." To which Kirilov answers, "To kill someone else would be the lowest point of my self-will. Such a suggestion could only come from a man with a soul like yours. I am not you; I want the highest point, and I will kill myself." By introducing high and low points of the will, Kirilov brings back the very values his act is supposed to liberate him from. On the one hand, he will prove his total indifference to any value—even that of friendship—by his act; and he must prove his indifference to any value, for otherwise he will be determined by the value he is not indifferent to. Yet he is insisting on the most important part of his will. Peter's casual remark exposed the deception at the core of his thinking, because Peter shows that the low point of his act is just as logical as the high point. To put it another way, Kirilov believes that with the death of God, man will be free to be good; but the logical consequence is that without God, man will be free to do his pleasure, and neither good nor evil will exist. Indeed, the living contradiction to his claim that the "high" part of man's "will" will follow on the killing of God is embodied in Peter. At one point in his irritated conversation with Peter, Kirilov exclaims: "Fool, I'm as big a scoundrel as you, as all, and not a decent fellow. There's never been a decent fellow anywhere." And Peter answers with a truth that is implied by Kirilov's reasoning, but one which he self-deceptively refuses to acknowledge: "So you've got it at last. How could you, Kirilov, with your intelligence, have failed to realize till now that all men are alike, that there aren't any better or worse, but that some men are more intelligent and others more stupid, and that if all are scoundrels (which incidentally is nonsense) there can be no people who are not scoundrels." Kirilov does not understand his "terrible freedom," and he cannot embody it. But one character in the novel understands it and embodies it in all its terrible and attractive aspects: Stavrogin. (pp. 114-24)

Stavrogin represents the totally free will, which in Dostoevsky's logic becomes the despotic will. The very act of "freeing" is an act of "emptying." The will is threatened by every engagement, belief, and emotion. To prove his freedom, Stavrogin must triumph over every attachment to life. As he tells Dasha in his final letter:

> I've tried my strength everywhere. You advised me to do this "that I might learn to know myself." As long as I was experimenting for myself and for others it seemed infinite, as it has all my life. Before your eyes I endured a blow from your brother; I acknowledged my marriage in public. But to what to apply my strength, that is what I've never seen, and do not see now in spite of all your praises in Switzerland, which I believed in. I am still capable, as I always was, of desiring to do something good, and of feeling pleasure from it; at the same time I desire evil and feel pleasure from that too. But both feelings are always too petty, and are never very strong. . . .

Both good and evil are one thing for Stavrogin: pleasure and the particular pleasure of trying his will everywhere. The one time in the novel that his "free" rejection of life breaks down is when he runs off with Liza and spends the night with her. He calls this an "impossible sincerity," for any attachment is a contradiction to his self-willed freedom. The attempt to reattach himself to life is a failure, for he cannot really love Liza. She herself recognizes this.

Stavrogin represents the most complete and consistent embodiment of the principle of freedom without God. The Underground Man is the first step toward Stavrogin, but he is "attached" to life by anger, spite, revenge, and the whole range of negative emotions. Raskolnikov is really on the side of God, although he deceives himself that he wants freedom. Svidrigaylov and Rogozhin are not fully developed, and one is "attached" to sensuality, the other to Nastasya. Only Stavrogin stands undeceived, consistent, terribly and devastatingly free. The price of this freedom is necessarily to cut himself off from humanity. The necessary consequence of the free will without God, for Dostoevsky, is the death of the human being.

Peter asks Stavrogin to raise his banner because he knows that he is on Stavrogin's side, that his banner is Stavrogin's banner, and that his view of the world is Stavrogin's view of the world. He sees in Stavrogin his spirit's father, the inner principle which guides his own feverish activity. Both will later acknowledge this kinship; Peter will call Stavrogin his better half; Stavrogin will call Peter his clown. They are as much one as are spirit and act. The differences between them are aesthetic. Stavrogin is Satan in heroic defiance against God, proud unto damnation: Peter is Mephistopheles, the spirit that propagates the petty actions of evil. What Stavrogin conquers in his soul, Peter turns into practical action. As Stavrogin is the logical, undeceived outcome of the principle Kirilov attempted to reach, Peter is the logical outcome in action, and especially political action, of what is implicit in the views of the socialists.

The free will, Dostoevsky argues, leads to control over oneself and control over others. Stavrogin shows this force over himself, and against life, and Peter shows it against others. There is a correspondence between the inner drama of Stavrogin, and the outer drama of Peter. As Stavrogin kills spiritual life by controlling it, Peter kills physical life by controlling it. Dramatically, the developing inner chaos of Stavrogin is reflected in the developing outer chaos that Peter moves. At the climactic point of self-destruction, the lines meet, and politics and metaphysics complement each other. Peter, Stavrogin's lower half, his devil, converts the movements of Stavrogin's soul into action, and brings to destruction the world that Stavrogin has brought into being. Peter is responsible for Shatov's and Kirilov's death, as Stavrogin had given them ideological life. Peter brings Liza and Stavrogin together, and as a consequence of Mary Lebyadkin's death, which he has arranged, he brings Liza to her death. Stavrogin in his suicide recapitulates in his private drama the death and destruction Peter causes in the public world.

The novel ends like Valhalla with the world that Stavrogin's spirit has brought to life set fire to by his spirit's clown, and Stavrogin himself going up with the flames. His suicide is the triumph of his will over life, even to the soaped cord which will foil any reflexive tricking of the body. Ippolit's suicide had been a fiasco; Kirilov's a deception; Stavrogin's free, conscious, and complete. It is his final triumph over life. The Stavrogin that appears in the expurgated confession chapter is unnecessary, and Dostoevsky wisely did not include it in editions of the novel after he was free of Katkov's objections. There is no inconsistency between this chapter and the Stavrogin that appears in the novel, as some critics have claimed. Those who see a repentant Stavrogin in his visit to Tikhon fail once again to understand the dialectical nature of Dostoevsky's world, for Stavrogin's "confession" is but another test of his strength, another virtue ineluctably corrupted by his strength. The portrait of Stavrogin in the confession chapter is morally consistent, but dramatically inconsistent. Throughout the novel we have a Stavrogin of silence and self-containment, a portrait that accords powerfully with the silent wasteland that his inner strength makes for him. The analytic Stavrogin of the confessional chapter mars this impassive, unattached air. (pp. 130-32)

The Possessed is . . . a finely constructed work of art, and the portrait of Stavrogin is an important advance in the refinement of Dostoevsky's moral dialectic. But ***The Possessed*** is also, as we are often reminded, history. Despite the fact that Dostoevsky took many of his plots from hints he found in newspapers, no other of his novels stems more directly from known events. We know, for instance, that both the central political intrigue and Peter himself are modeled on Nechaev and his own conspiratorial activity, that the fire and madness of the fête were probably provoked by the fires of the French commune, which took place while Dostoevsky was writing ***The Possessed,*** that Stepan Trofimovich is modeled on Granovsky, that Pisarev was in mind when he wrote of the vulgar liberals who insisted that shoes were more important than Pushkin. Some argument has been made that Stavrogin himself was modeled on Bakunin, that the site of the actual murder, *Skvoreshniki,* is closely modeled on the park where the murder took place. Yet as interesting and important as such parallels between novel and public event may be, ***The Possessed*** is not history reflecting itself in art, but art reflecting itself in history. The significance of the events Dostoevsky dramatizes is the significance that he gives them, and not the significance they have in some objective historical sense. It may be interesting to see what Dostoevsky kept unchanged and what he changed, but it is stupid to hold him accountable for literal fact. (pp. 134-35)

[Dostoevsky] insisted that he was representing in ***The Possessed*** "what was possible," and not "what happened." What is possible for Dostoevsky is finally what is possible in human nature. Dostoevsky wanted to show where the roots of an affair of Nechaev's kind lay in the order of things, and he traced them back to a certain naïveté of liberalism, the roots of which, in turn, were to be found in the inclination of the soul. . . .

His imagination has created in ***The Possessed*** the type that corresponds to Nechaev's crime, and indeed through the socialists, Peter, Kirilov, and Stavrogin, the types that correspond to *crime* in general. He shows how the course of public events has its analogue in the soul of Stavrogin, and how in this soul the impulse to crime is paradoxically the impulse to freedom. All events have their roots deep in the soul's soil, where the first tendril of faith in God or self appears. (p. 136)

Edward Wasiolek, in his Dostoevsky: The Major Fiction, *The M.I.T. Press, 1964, 255 p.*

V. A. TUNIMANOV (essay date 1972)

[Tunimanov is a major Soviet Dostoevski scholar. Here, he explores the various forms of narrative technique that Dostoevski used in The Possessed, *addressing the role of Anto Lavrentievich G——v in the novel and his relationship to other characters. Tunimanov's commentary was first published in 1972.]*

In the novel it gradually becomes clear that Anton Lavrentievich G——v is the chronicler-witness of the recent events which took place in his town, and he also recounts this recent past. About himself G——v imparts very scant information: he "accidentally" admits into the chronicle certain remarks by other people, which somewhat reveal his "social" position. We know that he works somewhere, but it is not precisely indicated where. Liputin caustically introduced him to the tipsy Captain Lebyadkin: "'It's Mr. G——v, a young gentleman of classical education and in close touch with the highest society'." G——v is a chronicler, and his personality is in the background and beyond the boundaries of the chronicle, a fact which also creates the necessary conditions for a sort of detached narration that almost completely rules out the "confession" of the narrator himself.

The only part of G——v's personal life that penetrates the chronicle is his short lived and unrequited love for Liza Tushin. The chronicler describes his past feeling for Liza retrospectively and calmly: the story of the origin and dying of the feeling is given in "fragments" in the chronicle. At one time the chronicler runs errands for Liza, carries out her requests, performs services for her. It is true that the emerging function of the chronicler as the faithful servant and knight of the foremost town Amazon somehow dies of its own accord and without any motivation. But in turn, the chronicler's fixed attention, his precise and detailed statement of the heroine's movements, of the slightest changes in her aspect, are motivated: "Liza, I observed, suddenly jumped up from her chair and for some reason as they were going out of the room followed them with a motionless stare to the very door. Then she sat down again in silence, but her face seemed to twitch spasmodically, though she had touched some horrible snake."

In the chronicler's "ideological" biography the main thing he discloses is his sojourn in Stepan Trofimovich Verkhovensky's circle; this is recounted as an idle pastime, from the position of a man who has "matured" and renounced his former "delusions." The chronicler caustically recalls his own personal sojourn in the circle as well. The chronicler's irony is multi-directed, and this is one of the main conditions both of the narrative style and of the general atmosphere and structure of the novel. The irony partly affects the frightened citizens as well, and ridicules their absurd notions:

> At one time they used to say in the town about our circle that it was a hotbed of free-thinking, vice, and atheism; this rumor, by the way, always persisted. And yet all we did in our circle was to indulge in the most innocent, amiable, jolly typically Russian liberal chatter.

Also ridiculed are the groundlessness and abstract character of "political" conversations, the absurdity and irrelevance of the members of the circle:

> We also discussed problems of general concern to mankind, talked severely of the future fate of Europe and the human race, foretold in a doctrinaire fashion that after the fall of the monarchy in France that country would at once be reduced to the position of a secondary power, and we were firmly convinced that that would happen very easily and quite soon. We had long ago prophesied that the Pope would assume the role of a simple archbishop in a united Italy, and had no doubts whatever that this thousand-year-old problem was a trifling matter in our age of humanitarian ideas, industry, and railways.

The chronicler himself is in the past no more than an extra, a claquer in the suite of Stepan, now with regret ("alas") recalling the past impersonal ("we") existence and, from a new position, asking; "But, gentlemen, don't we still hear today, and very often, too, sometimes, the same sort of 'charming,' 'clever,' 'liberal' old Russian nonsense?" To be sure, the derision of the members of the circle and the townspeople also includes self-derision; denial borders on denial of one's own past, censure borders on self-censure.

Participation in Stepan's circle places the chronicler in a special relationship with the head of the town "liberals." G——v is Stepan's confidant. This is a comic feature, and Liza Tushin directly indicates its comic nature to the chronicler: "'I have already formed an amusing idea about you: you're Mr. Verkhovensky's confidant, aren't you?'" In fact, this is actually the chronicler's main occupation, which he carries out with a certain "anguish" and out of "boredom," simultaneously oppressed and amused by the lot that has fallen to him: "Let me observe in passing that I had to put up with a great deal during that unhappy week—never leaving the side of my poor affianced friend, in the capacity of his closest confidant."

The duties of a "closest" confidant remove the question of the chronicler's knowledge of, if not all, then of almost all the circumstances of Stepan's external and inner life, including the most intimate:

> It may be asked how I could possibly come to know so delicate a detail. Well, what if I witnessed it myself? What if Mr. Verkhovesky himself has on more than one occasion sobbed on my shoulder, while describing to me in lurid colours the smallest detail of his talk with Mrs. Stavrogin? (The things he told me on such occasions!)

Such a "short" distance separating the chronicler from Stepan permits G——v to prophesy and guess subtle and forbidden stirrings of the "teacher's" soul, inaccessible to the common view: "It goes without saying that I had long since guessed that great secret of his and seen through it"; "I had only been waiting for that word. Finally this secret word, hidden from me, had been uttered after a whole week of equivocations and grimaces;" "I guessed from the way he looked that he wanted at last to tell me something of the utmost importance, which he must have kept back till that moment."

The confidant "out of boredom" sometimes directly accuses and ridicules Stepan, pursuing, as a rule, high moral aims: "'And such a sordid, such a . . . base thought could occur to you, Stepan Verkhovesky, in your lucid mind, in your good heart and . . . even before Liputin. . .'"; "Being still young, I could not help being indignant at the coarseness of his feelings and the ugly nature of some of his suspicions." The chronicler's penitential little words ("Oh, I was rude and discourteous, and I recall it now with regret") are far from always sincere, and often carry more venom than his direct accusations. The accusations are somewhat "neutralized" and softened not by the belated and frequently insincere repentances, but by the universality of the atmosphere of derision, into which the accuser himself also falls. Here the chronicler speaks extremely sharply about Stepan's estrangement from the world: "Such complete, utter ignorance of everyday reality was both touching and somehow repulsive." The chronicler himself, however, while ridiculing his friend's alienation from fundamentals . . . (the refrain "my poor friend" carries through the novel), has not so very far outstripped him in knowledge of the world, and is capable of the most improbable and stupid suppositions: "A wild and preposterous idea flashed through my mind." Caustically depicting Stepan's latest habits, the chronicler emphasizes that, besides other things, the former still loves "to dip into the champagne." It cannot be denied that this is a debasing trait, and one that produces an undeniably devastating effect in an unexpected context. But here again it does not befit the chronicler to stand in a pose of "high moral standards"; his "poor friend" is terribly communicative and prefers "to dip into the champagne" in company, where the libation may be enlivened by literary and frivolous conversation, or, in its absence, by the unvarying confidant-drinking partner: "As a rule, when we had met before and he had begun complaining to me, a bottle of vodka would almost invariably make its appearance after a little time and everything would become more cheerful"; "Out of sorrow we also drank a little. However, he soon fell into a sweet sleep." Stepan's chatter and verbal nonsense are characterized by one of his most attentive listeners and "pupils." Stepan Trofimovich's speech at the celebration is commented on by the master of ceremonies who absurdly fusses with his rosette, and both these figures are undeniably comical. The sufferings of his panic-stricken friend are described by the frightened chronicler-citizen, stunned by what he has seen: "Mr. Verkhovensky and I, at any rate, at first shut ourselves up and looked on with apprehension from a distance"; "Mr. Verkhovensky and I, not without apprehension about the boldness of our theory, but encouraging each other, at last came to the conclusion. . . ."

The chronicler's "eulogy" for Stepan took shape very early and clearly in the notebooks for the novel (with the exception of only a few nuances, which we omit); the main peculiarity of G——v's tone was also determined: "The chronicler pretends that he feels Christian pity for the darkening of a great character. He excuses [Granovsky (Stepan)], saying that it is all natural. . . ."

This ironic, "pretending" tone begins at the very outset of the novel; after the excessively respectful epithets ("talented" and "much-revered") follows a slow but steady increase in irony. After the allusion to Stepan's constant histrionics, the phrase borrowed from Gogol, "he was a most excellent man," already sounds like a half-concealed sneer.

The simplest device for debasing Stepan's image is the direct contrasting of truth with fabrication, of real and precise facts with the "teacher's" fiction and chatter. The mysterious "whirlwind of concurrent events" is completely dispelled by the chronicler:

> It turned out afterwards that there had been no "whirlwind" and even no "events," at any rate at that particular instant. It was only the other day that I discovered, to my great astonishment, from a highly reliable source, that Mr. Verkhovensky had never lived in our province amongst us as an exile, as we were all led to suppose, and that he had never even been placed under police supervision.

Once again returning to the notorious "whirlwind" that destroyed the career of the freethinker of the forties, the chronicler mercilessly contrasts the fruits of his "sorrowful friend"'s imagination to the truth: "And if the whole truth is to be told, the real cause of the change in his career was the . . . proposal that had been made before and renewed again by Varvara Petrovna . . . to undertake the education and the whole intellectual development of her only son."

The "civic grief" stamped on Stepan's face during the card game prompts the chronicler again to appeal to "truth": "And to tell the truth he was very fond of a game of cards, which, especially in later years, led to frequent and unpleasant squabbles with Mrs. Stavrogin, particularly as he was always losing."

The second device for debasement is also simple: a high-flown and respectful preamble, then a whole system of qualifications, a certain hesitation after them and finally a full negation of what was said at the beginning:

> And yet he was undoubtedly a highly intelligent and talented man, a man who was, as it were, even a scholar, though so far as his scholarship was concerned . . . well, he did not really make any important contribution to scholarship, indeed none at all, I believe.

Here the debasement is consistently carried to its furthest limit, to zero. Precisely here (and this is characteristic of the "eulogy") there follows a partial "rehabilitation" of Stepan: "But, then, that happens again and again in Russia with men of learning."

Still another (and frequent) device for the comic debasement of the "teacher" is the synonymic comparison of extremely heterogeneous and unequal concepts and names. According to the chronicler's description, Stepan ". . . looked almost like a patriarch or, to be more exact, like the portrait of the playwright Kukolnik." Yet another time, Kukolnik falls into a strange synonymic relationship, that destroys the pathetically emotional tone of the chronicler's exclamations:

> This man whom we had looked upon as a prophet for twenty years, our preacher, teacher, patriarch, the Kukolnik who had borne himself so grandly and majestically before us all, whom we regarded with such admiration, thinking it an honor to do so—suddenly this man was sobbing. . . .

The irony here, however, is ambivalent—the worship of "our Kukolnik" is strange and absurd.

The "pretending" G——v often justifies himself by saying that he didn't quite want to say what he just said, since he was recounting it not in the usual sense but in a quite special one. The majority of such stipulations are insincere and produce the reverse impression:

> I used the expression "flung himself into the arms," but don't let anyone jump to any rash and improper conclusions; those arms have to be understood only in the highest possible moral sense. These two remarkable beings were joined forever in a union that was most refined and delicate.

The solemn intonations and grandiloquent words, more than anything else here, promote the appearance of "rash" and "improper" considerations. And the "most refined and delicate union," after the series of anecdotes and details, appears in an utterly ironic light. We can also detect an analogous phenomenon in the chronicler's other justifications and stipulations: "I don't claim for a moment that he had never suffered for his convictions, but I am fully convinced now that he could have gone on lecturing on his Arabs as much as he liked if he had only given the necessary explanations"; "I wish merely to point out that he was a man of a tender conscience (sometimes, that is), and that was why he was so often depressed"; "Mr. Verkhovensky sometimes talked of art, and very well, though a little abstractly. Occasionally he would recall the friends of his youth—all names who had made their mark on the history of Russian progress—he recalled them with emotion and reverence, though not without envy either."

Even such an indisputably major and sincere feature of Stepan as his love for art and refinement cannot avoid the all-penetrating scoffing of his "pupil"-confidant: "So far as books are concerned, I should point out that in later years he seemed to avoid reading. . . . It also frequently happened that he would take De Tocqueville with him into the garden, while he secretly carried a Paul de Kock in his pocket."

The chronicler's statements ("But anyway, these are trifles"; "But that too, of course, is a petty detail") are sly; it is precisely on petty details and trifles that he concentrates his attention, revealing, so to speak, the cherished domestic secrets of "our preacher," showing him in a mire of base details:

> Our friend had certainly acquired not a few bad habits, especially during recent months. He let himself run to seed visibly and rapidly, and it is quite true that he had become slovenly. He drank more, he was more easily moved to tears, and his nerves grew weaker. He had become far too sensitive to everything of artistic value. His face had acquired a strange faculty for changing extraordinarily rapidly, from the most solemn expression, for instance, to the most ridiculous and even stupid.

An accent on petty details is the essential peculiarity of the chronicler's narration in general, and especially when he is speaking of Stepan. The orientation towards "chattering" about trifles, the concentration on petty details, are proclaimed by Dostoevsky in the notebooks for ***The Devils;*** "No matter how superfluous, and idle, and verbose it seems, in essence it is in close connection with the very core of events. It is always this way in reality. An unsuspected thing, a trifling thing, suddenly becomes the main thing, and everything else only revolves around it as something secondary and accessory. (pp. 145-52)

As a character the chronicler is a passive and puppetlike figure, and although he often bustles about, in essence he takes almost no part in the action; what he hears and sees is important, and significantly less important is what he says and does during the events. Part of his function is the collection and systematization of material, and this is the most extensive field of his activity. Finally, part of the chronicler's function is the interpretation of what he has seen, and here he may display exceptional subtlety and depth, or not display it, or simply forego a definite decision. The chronicler's information may also fluctuate from complete knowledge (and here he resembles the omniscient author) to half-knowledge and even incorrect knowledge (and here he is a fallible and mortal man, whose judgments and interpretations are often mistaken). The chronicler may also displace the temporal point of the story: a later, total knowledge is superimposed on his former knowledge; but often G——v "confiscates" this his later understanding of things, transferring the narration entirely into the past. The total point of view (after the catastrophe) is present in the novel in the form of a ramified system of allusions; this projection of results is carried out vaguely (basically regarding details) and unevenly—the story of the chronicler's gradual learning and "enlightenment" form an essential aspect of the dynamism and interest of the novel's development. This story of learning is not emphasized, and in general the chronicler often foregoes explanations; as a result, the characters acquire "independence" and depart from the importunate accompaniment of the chronicler's voice. Narration "from the chronicler" recedes, and scenes without the chronicler's participation at all, or with his minimal participation, come to the fore. The conditionality and, to a certain extent, "outsider's position" of the figure of the chronicler permit the changing of the "scenery" in the narration to take place almost unnoticeably and painlessly for the unity of the chronicle's system; G——v disappears just as easily and unconstrainedly as he appears again. Dostoevsky apparently considered any special notifications to the reader about the change of "scenery" to be superfluous, although, judging by his notebooks, they were planned: "I sat with Gr—— for the third time and listened to his heated conversation with Sh. In general, even if I describe conversations *tête à tête* [*sam drug*]—don't pay any attention: either I have firm data, or, perhaps, I *make it up* myself—but be assured that everything is true. For I have adopted the system of *a chronicle*."

Is it possible to contrast the scenes *"tête-à-tête"* with the scenes that have the chronicler's presence and his "I" narration? Yes and no. The scenes without the chronicler (either based on data received by G——v from others, or made up by him, or, perhaps most frequent of all, representing a combination of fantasy, personal experience and the interpretation of others' opinions) seldom contradict the direct narration of the chronicler, and if they do contradict it, it is in accord with the artistic task. The chamber conversation scenes are an indispensable admission into the chronicle: the chronicler's direct presence in them would, naturally, be very hard to motivate; in some cases it would be "immodest," in others simply impossible. The chronicler must inevitably turn into a storyteller and conjecture substantial *"lacunae"* in the chronicle through his imagination. The crowd scenes, in which the chronicler for a number of reasons does not participate either, are a cross between various sources of information and his imagination. (See in the drafts: "In the discussion of the meetings, make a remark as the chronicler: Perhaps, they had still other meetings—and surely they did—I don't know, but the matter, probably, happened this way. . . .")

In ***The Devils*** there are three basic forms of narrative: (a) narration "from the chronicler," in which the narrator's voice dominates; (b) scenes with the chronicler's participation, in any of which his role may be most different; (c) scenes without the chronicler—intimate, chamber scenes, with the complete or almost complete disappearance of G——v. There is also the combined form of narrative—the crowd scenes.

The establishment of the true proportions among the various forms of narrative, and the methods of linking them, formed Dostoevsky's main "artistic" concern. The vacillations in the process of work on ***The Devils*** were most various, but on the whole one may speak of a gradual intensification of a tendency toward limiting the "explanatory" and "ideological" function of the chronicler. The broadly outlined connection between Stavrogin and the chronicler was especially weakened. In the original outlines, Stavrogin's actions and words were to be more often accompanied by rejoinders and explanations "from the chronicler":

> In the chronicler's voice at the middle or end of his novel: In general Stavrogin had such-and-such an aim; however, that is according to Ush——v's [Shigalyov's] testimony. I don't know what their business there in Switzerland was, but I have correctly defined the essence of their movement, their philosophy, the sense of their actions: I'll vouch for that.

It was also assumed that after Stavrogin's death the chronicler would sum up, give an analysis of the prince's character, in a special ("indispensable") chapter, "Analysis":

> The chronicler, after the prince's death, is to make an analysis of his character (indispensably, a chapter called "Analysis"). Saying that this was a strong, predatory man, who became entangled in convictions and who out of endless pride desired and could only be convinced of that which was completely *clear* . . . etc.

The "Analysis" chapter was never realized, and the story of the chronicler's gradual knowledge of Stavrogin, begun in such promising detail in the first part of the novel, subsequently came to naught; the character passed into other spheres of the narrative, having fallen out of the plane of narration "from the chronicler." G——v avoids personal explanation of Stavrogin's character, leaving that for the prince himself to do in a letter, and for the other characters in the chronicle (Kirillov, Shatov, Khromonozhka [Marya Lebyadkin], Pyotr Verkhovensky, Liza Tushin). Moreover, not only the line from the chronicler to Stavrogin, but also from Shatov to Stavrogin, was curtailed; thus, in the notebooks a whole series of conversations between Stavrogin and Shatov was planned, but in the final text only a single conversation remains, which ends with the prince's assurances that he will not visit Shatov again.

In the first part of the novel, Stavrogin is the object of G——v's intense and unremitting attention; the latter is interested and bewildered by the prince's strange and romantic life, and, like a conscientious chronicler, renders Stavrogin's history, relying on the rumors, opinions, and legends of others, for want of his own information. One of G——v's functions is to interpret and classify opinions. Another, no less important role of the chronicler also comes to the fore here: the keen personal attention of G——v as an observer, who tries to find out the truth, the "essence" of Stavrogin by means of the comparison of a personal, subjective view to the general view. Marya Lebyadkin, Pyotr Verkhovensky, Liza, Shatov, and Kirillov penetrate to the "essence" of Stavrogin, each in his own way and with varying degrees of precision. The chronicler participates especially intensively in the general movement at the beginning. The chronicler's first personal impression is surprise: the legendary Stavrogin of the others' stories turns out to be quite different from the real Stavrogin. For the time being the chronicler's surprise bears only a relatively personal character (he is one of many who are surprised); but neither is it temporary and casual, and it has actual, real roots. It is completely understandable and explicable and does not entirely refute Stavrogin's legendary biography, all the more since that biography is not completely legendary (a statement that has the force of proof, since here also the chronicler superimposes later knowledge on the temporal point of view):

> I was not the only one to be surprised: our whole town was surprised, and our town, of course, knew Mr. Stavrogin's biography, and in such detail that one could hardly imagine where they could have got it from and, what was even more surprising, half of the stories about him were quite true.

The chronicler, joining in the general chorus, is not distinguished from it only at first. He refuses to explain Stavrogin's provocative and strange actions, and this in itself is a marked personal position: G——v has a large choice of interpretations, but he places them all under suspicion, and, what is particularly remarkable, he holds to his previous opinion even "now," that is, after everything that has happened: "For my part, I don't know to this day how to explain it, in spite of the incident which occurred soon afterwards and which apparently explained everything and, it would seem, set everybody's mind at rest." "Everybody"—but not the chronicler.

The scene at Varvara Petrovna's with Stavrogin and the others is the culmination of the first part and the culmination of the narration about Stavrogin "from the chronicler." The chronicler is the "leader" in this scene, the observer and commentator. Stavrogin appears and the chronicler's gaze is immediately riveted to him: alternations, which give rise to questions, are noted:

> But now—now, I don't know why, he looked to me at the first glance as quite incontestably handsome, so much so that it was impossible to say that his face was like a mask. Was it because he was just a little paler than before and had apparently gone thinner? Or was it perhaps because some new idea was now reflected in his eyes?

The chronicler draws attention to Stavrogin's smile, gestures, walk, facial expression (and how it changes), and vocal intonation. He describes them with the precision of a stenographer whose attention the subtlest momentary movements do not escape: "here he exchanged a momentary glance with him," "he spoke with a certain peculiar twist to his face." It is as though the chronicler stops time or stretches an instant into infinity: "So passed five seconds"; ". . . the whole scene did not last more than ten seconds. Still, a great deal happened in those ten seconds." Around a few seconds, which hold so much, the past and present are concentrated. The chronicler's total point of view, achieved as a result of long searching and collecting of facts, is summarized; a long tirade about the heroes of the past (Lunin and Lermontov), similar to Stavrogin in some ways but also different in many others, is introduced; early and late judgments are persistently combined into a single focus:

> I repeat again: I thought him at the time and I still think him (now that everything is over) the sort of man who, if he received a blow in the face or a similar insult, would have killed his adversary on the spot and without challenging him to a duel.

The chronicler's hearing and vision are strained and sharpened to the utmost, his gaze strives to break through the outer shell and penetrate to the inside. Of course the chronicler sees the whole scene "from the outside," but he sees so keenly and penetrates so deeply that his vision achieves supernatural dimensions, approaching in intensity and precision the vision of the infallible and "omniscient" author. The chronicler of course does not simply describe what he saw then: he projects his whole experience, a huge sum of facts, and his final (by the time of the chronicle's creation) knowledge. The chronicler's reticence is, obviously, a proper means for promoting the carrying out of an aim that was essential for Dostoevsky—the interest of the narrative. But this is not all; interest is already achieved by the fact that the chronicler limits himself to an allusion to other facts known to him, which will be communicated subsequently in their own place and their own time. Something else is more important. The reader is informed that the chronicler knows quite a lot about Stavrogin and, despite such an extreme and comprehensive state of information (close to "omniscience"), he cannot explain Stavrogin's conduct with complete assurance. In other words, it is explained at the outset that there will be no final summation, the reader will not receive complete solutions and much will remain obscure at the very end of the novel; by this itself the reader is invited by the author to take whatever personal participation is within his powers in the disentanglement of knots and the guessing of "psychological" rebuses.

Beginning with the second part of ***The Devils,*** perceptible changes in the narration take place; the connection between the chronicler and Stavrogin also undergoes deformation. Even later the chronicler observes Stavrogin, but his vision loses its keenness; he sees little and poorly: "I saw them meeting in the doorway: it seemed to me that both of them stood still for a moment and looked rather strangely at one another. But I may not have seen them properly for the crowd." Even when G——v is presented with an opportunity of demonstrating his talent for penetrating "within," he does not make use of that opportunity. The chronicler also foregoes personal judgments about the hero, with one small exception—the introduction to Stavrogin's letter (in a narrow sense—a stylistic remark; in a broad sense—an accusation): "Here is the letter, word for word, without the correction of a single mistake, in the style of a Russian landed gentleman who has never mastered Russian grammar in spite of his European education."

Stavrogin's letter is a fragment of a hero's never-quite-formulated confession—a confession summing up the failure of a life. The letter contains no discoveries, nothing specifically new; it confirms the opinion of others about Stavrogin, freeing these evaluations of superfluous emotionalism and transience. In the combination of narrative forms chosen for the account of Stavrogin's history, the leading one is objective narration (chamber scenes, conversations *tête-à-tête,* without the presence of the chronicler). The others (narrative by the chronicler and confession) occupy a subordinate, secondary place on the whole, although the proportions are different in the first part of the novel—partly, perhaps, explainable by the vacillations, which concluded in the victory of objective narration by an all-seeing author standing outside the action.

The images of Stavrogin and Pyotr Verkhovensky demanded a different style of narration, different forms, than Stepan:

> "Nechaev and the prince without explanations, but in action, and for St. Tr——ch *always with explanation*"; "The tone consists in not elucidating Nechaev and the prince. Nechaev begins from gossip and commonplaces, and the prince is revealed gradually [by narration] in action and without any explanations"; "The *main thing* is that throughout the novel it never be fully explained why Nechaev came"; "The whole situation and progress of Nechaev must be that the reader sees absolutely nothing but a few buffonish and strange characteristic features. I must not do like other novelists, that is, trumpet from the very beginning that here is an unusual man. On the contrary, I must hide him and only gradually uncover him through artistic features (for example, the difference between his intellect and cunning and his utter ignorance of reality).

Thus, the image of Stepan is revealed by means of narration "from the chronicler," the images of the prince and Pytor Verkhovensky, in dialogue and in action; there are two basic and opposing narrative principles. By the combination of heterogeneous narrative forms, the dynamic flow of the story is achieved, the problem of interest is solved, the functions and boundaries of the chronicler's activity and the variety of distances between chronicler and characters are defined. (pp. 167-75)

V. A. Tunimanov, "The Narrator in 'The Devils'," translated by Susanne Fusso, in Dostoevsky: New Perspectives, *edited by Robert Louis Jackson, Prentice-Hall, Inc., 1984, pp. 145-75.*

MALCOLM V. JONES (essay date 1976)

[*Jones considers* The Possessed *"a novel of travesties," concentrating in the following excerpt on degeneracy and destruction in its depiction of the society as a whole and the individual characters.*]

The story of the writing of the ***The Devils*** and the role in its conception and execution of Dostoyevsky's plans for *The Life of a Great Sinner* (which contributed to his last three novels) and of the Nechayev affair are so well known and so easily accessible that to rehearse them here would be pedantic and tedious. The main facts may be found in almost any book on Dostoyevsky. But one curious aspect of the novel's publication is worth calling to mind. This concerns the fate of the chapter 'At Tikhon's' (containing Stavrogin's Confession), expurgated at the insistence of the editor of *Russkiy vestnick*, where the novel first appeared in serial form. This chapter is now often included in English translations, but Dostoyevsky himself did not reinstate it when the opportunity arose on the publication of the novel in book form.

Arguments about why Dostoyevsky did not put it back in (after Part II, chapter 8, where it was apparently intended to go) and whether it is permissible for the reader to 'reinsert' it contrary to the decision of the author are perfectly natural, but not very fruitful because those on different sides tend to argue from different premises. Perhaps the best intrinsic reason for leaving well alone is that Dostoyevsky was aiming at creating an enigmatic centre to the novel which might be compromised by the relatively clear motivation for Stavrogin's behaviour furnished by his confession and conversation with Tikhon. Having completed the novel without the crucial chapter, it would be understandable if he did not want to disturb the balance of the work by reintroducing a passage which had after all proved expendable.

In his notes for *The Life of a Great Sinner* he had jotted down in 1870:

> But so that the dominant idea of the Life is visible—i.e, though the dominant idea is not wholly explained in words and is always left shrouded in mystery, the reader should always see that the idea is a devout one and that the Life is so important that it had to be started in childhood.

This note has nothing directly to do with Stavrogin, but it indicates that Dostoyevsky was at this time consciously experimenting with ways of rendering the essential while declining to express it explicitly, to strike the right balance between enigma and clarity.

But the missing chapter does nevertheless provide important clues to understanding the novel. It provides that crucial dramatic point at which the hero and the world of fiction are expressed in a common symbol, otherwise missing from the published text. It is to ***The Devils*** what Raskolnikov's dream of the old horse is to ***Crime and Punishment*** and Myshkin's epileptic experience is to ***The Idiot.*** That, when Dostoyevsky decided to project his vision of disintegration and disorder on to a broad social and political plane, he should emphasize this disorder, disintegration and diffuseness by veiling the dominant Idea is by no means surprising, but it does no harm to peep at it since it is available to us. It is, moreover, arguable that, in finally deciding to omit it, Dostoyevsky made an artistic mistake. Camus, who incorporates it in his dramatisation of the novel (*Les Possédés*), seems to have thought so.

Stavrogin complains to Tikhon that he is subject, especially at nights, to a kind of hallucination, that he has sometimes felt the presence of some malicious creature, mocking and 'rational', in all sorts of guises and different characters. These revelations are 'wild and confused' and seem to come from a madman. This horrific experience is akin to that which Ippolit describes in ***The Idiot,*** though Ippolit's experience is not of a rational force. Whatever construction is put upon it, and Tikhon is himself inclined to regard it as a symptom of mental illness, the experience itself is real enough. Stavrogin asks Tikhon: 'Can one believe in the Devil without believing in God?' and Tikhon replies, 'Certainly. You come across it everywhere.'

It is not so much that ***The Devils*** is a novel in which the diabolical in all its forms prevails and the divine in all its forms is banished, though certainly there is no great mystical religious vision of the kind that Myshkin knows. It is rather that the novel depicts travesties of both the diabolical and the divine, the demonic and the ideal. The novel is itself a novel of travesties. It is tempting to add that some have considered it to be a travesty of a novel; but the more one comprehends the former, the less just the latter appears.

Stavrogin is haunted by scrofulous little devils. In the terms of the angel of the Church of Laodicea, he is not hot nor is he cold, he is lukewarm. His devils come to him in various guises, and by his example and by his attempts at indoctrination in the past, he passes them on to others, where they may find more scope for their malice and their 'rationality'. But in spite of their many guises and forms, they all impel mankind toward destruction. This unstoppable process is symbolised in the epigraphs, the one taken from Pushkin, and the other from St Luke. The passage from the New Testament is, of course, the miracle (or acted parable) of the Gadarene swine. Although

Stavrogin's devils are not cast out and he does not regain his sanity, the part of the miracle relating to the fate of the swine is closely paralleled by the fate of 'our town'.

The visit to Tikhon consists not only of Stavrogin's description of his hallucinations. Just as important is his confession of responsibility for the death of Matryosha, details of his affairs in St Petersburg with his decision to marry Marya Timofeyevna and, most important of all for the present discussion, his dream of the Golden Age. . . . Stavrogin calls it:

> A marvellous dream, a sublime illusion! The most improbable of all dreams that ever were, yet it is upon this dream that mankind has, from its very birth, lavished all its powers; it is for this dream that men have sacrificed all, for which they have withered and suffered torment, for which prophets have died on the cross or been murdered, without which nations do not wish to live and cannot die.

Yet this dream has become impotent in Stavrogin, in a large measure owing to his own degeneracy. Before him as he dreams rises the spectre of little Matryosha, standing on the threshold and threatening him with her small fist. And nearly every day he is haunted by his apparition. He claims he could rid himself of it by an act of the will, but for some reason does not want to.

In the novel itself this ideal is distorted and debased: in the theory of Shigalyov (according to which man is to be enslaved for the sake of happiness), in Shatov's vision of the Second Coming, in Kirillov's manic conception of the abolition of pain and fear, in Stepan Trofimovich Verkhovensky's pathetic posturing and preaching. All are alike impotent to stem the tide. The devils, malicious and rational, are victorious.

The strongest reason for reinstating 'At Tikhon's' is therefore not that it furnishes essential details from Stavrogin's past (though it certainly does cast important light upon it) nor that it describes an important episode in the process of Stavrogin's rediscovery of his past (this would also be a valid plea), but that it focuses attention on the spiritual forces which are at war at every level of the novel. Moreover, it also intimates that it is not so much the work of the Devil, as the concerted efforts of a horde of 'petty devils' which overwhelm 'our town', a town which, like Stavrogin, has lost its contact with real values and taken up instead with trivial, frivolous, superstitious, sometimes vicious, always bogus activities and pursuits.

There are three points worth elaborating further. The first is the question of travesty. The whole novel, it was suggested above, focuses on travesties. Stepan Verkhovensky is a travesty of a liberal of the 1840s (Granovsky) Karmazinov is a travesty of the progressive novelist of the older generation with his cultural roots in Western Europe (Turgenev); Stavrogin is a travesty of the Romantic hero (and perhaps also of the Superfluous Man); Ptotr Verkhovesnky is a travesty of a nihilist (Nechayev) and his 'socialism', such as it is, and even more so Shigalyov's, are travesties of socialism. Travesties of Christianity are depicted in the views of Marya Timofeyevna, Shatov, even perhaps Tikhon, certainly Semyon Yakovelevich, though Dostoyevsky probably had ambiguous feelings about them all. The administration of Lembke is a travesty of provincial administration. And so one could go on. Perhaps most important are the travesties of beauty and the ideal as conceived by any and all of the characters in the novel, particularly by Pyotr Verkhovensky. It is his father who declares in a transport of enthusiasm:

> Do you know, do you know that mankind can survive without . . . science, without bread, but without beauty it cannot survive, for there would be absolutely nothing to do in the world! The whole mystery is here, the whole of history is here! Science itself could not endure a minute without beauty. . . .

And he remarks that the new generation has distorted the concept of beauty, and that is the key to understanding it.

Of course, the narrator adopts a tone of restrained, patronising and faintly amused cynicism at the beginning of the novel which helps to create the impression of travesty, but the tone is surely appropriate to the subject-matter. The technique and subject-matter together give rise to the common description of the novel as 'satire' and this is certainly right. The novel is social satire and not only, as Soviet critics in particular point out, satire of socialists and nihilists: it also satirises Tsarist provincial government. One could go further and add that it also satirises eccentric religious views. And if, as is commonly said, Shatov represents some of Dostoyevsky's own personal views, is there not authorial self-satire in the novel too?

The second point concerns a central theme of this novel, taken up again in ***The Brothers Karamazov,*** but less prominent (with the exception of Ippolit) in the earlier novels. This is the theme of Fear and Pain. The conquest by man of pain and fear is, of course, a central point in Kirillov's curious credo. He describes fear as 'the curse of mankind' and declares, 'Life is pain; life is fear'. Stepan Verkhovesnky more than once succumbs to fear. Stavrogin claims that on only one occasion in his life has he really been afraid, just after he has violated little Matryosha. As for pain, the narrator reflects on the occasion when Shatov gives Stavrogin a blow in the face:

> I feel sure that if a man were to grasp, for example, a red-hot iron bar, and clench it in his hand in order to measure his powers of endurance, and try for the next ten seconds to overcome the unendurable pain, and finally overcome it, then this man would, it seems to me, have experienced something very much like Nikolay Vsevolodovich in those ten seconds.

Pain and fear are symbolic of man's trials and tribulations on this hostile planet and they assume an additional importance in the light of Dostoyevsky's personal view that suffering might be spiritually beneficial to man and afford him greater spiritual freedom. But the main characters in ***The Devils*** do not share this insight. They either have no defence or else they try to overcome by willpower. They may, like Kirillov, try to banish pain and fear by a revolution in human consciousness or, like Shigalyov, by the reform of the social order.

The third point which should be developed here is the question of the extent to which the story of the Gadarene swine and Stavrogin's talk of devils are generally applicable to the fictional world of the novel.

Shortly before his death Stepan Verkhovensky hears the passage from St Luke read by Ulitina. He exclaims:

> That's exactly like our Russia. These devils who go out of the sick man and enter into the swine—these are all the sores, all the infections, all the impurities, all the devils and imps that have accumulated in our great and dear invalid, our Russia, over the course of centuries. . . .

For Verkhovensky senior, Russia is the sick man who will be healed when the swine—including himself—have cast themselves into the sea. In the meantime the devils reign in Russia.

But in a fashion which recalls Ippolit, Kirillov gives his account of the Crucifixion, and it leads him to a much more radical view which applies to the universe as a whole:

> Listen to an important idea. There was a day on earth, and in the centre of the earth stood three crosses. One on the cross had such faith that he said to another: "Today thou shalt be with me in Paradise." The day ended, they both died, and they went but found neither paradise nor resurrection. The saying did not come true. Listen, that man was the highest on the whole earth. He was that for which the earth lives. Without that man the whole planet and everything on it is pure madness. Neither before nor since has there been a man like *Him* and never will be, even by a miracle. For that is the miracle, that there has never been and never will be a man like Him. And if that is the case, and the laws of nature did not spare even *Him*, if they did not spare their own miracle, and forced even *Him* to live amongst lies and to die for a lie, then the whole planet is a lie and is founded on a lie and a stupid mockery. Then the laws of the planet are a lie and vaudeville of the devil.

This view of life is a development rather than a repetition of Stavrogin's views, but both express the demoralising thought that the natural order is a mockery of man and his aspirations, based on malice and deceit. Like all such ideas in Dostoyevsky, the fictional world does not altogether give it the lie.

Whether or not Kirillov's vision is true, the novel tells of a period of breakdown and transition in Russian life which extends to every level of provincial society. As the old certainties and patterns break down, denizens of the depths emerge and fringe beliefs and types achieve unwonted prominence. As in all periods of fundamental change and uncertainty, superstition, heresy, chiliastic beliefs, sacrilege, drunkenness come seething to the surface. Groups emerge dedicated to taking the law into their own hands; it is a time for murder, for mob violence; the dregs of society forget their place and their station; standards of decency are challenged and defied; it is a time for grotesque philosophies of life, for usurpers, for a resurgence of the Dionysian principle, for destruction and for incendiarism. It is Raskolnikov's Siberian dream come true. And there is clearly delineated a general quest for a Romantic saviour, a man who will take up the banner (whatever that banner may symbolise) and lead the way to a new life and a new order.

As the novel progresses, the scene of disorder widens from a circle of personal acquaintances to the broader perspective beyond. Fires rage in towns and villages; cholera and cattle plague are rife; there are foolish rumours among the common people; robberies are twice as numerous as usual; there is miscarriage of justice at the top of the administrative hierarchy; criminal negligence on the part of the public health inspectorate; swindling and redundancies in industry. Russians are leaving the country like rats leaving a sinking ship. The scene is apocalyptic.

The breakdown is not just social—that is, collective. It is personal too, and it is aesthetic and ethical as well as religious. Stavrogin admits he has not only lost the sense of distinction between good and evil and beauty and ugliness, but also believes that such distinctions are illusory. The breakdown of personal ideals in the novel is a recurrent motif. In several cases these personal ideals are projected on to one man—Stavrogin—and his indifference causes one disillusionment after another.

Stepan Verkhovensky says of Kirillov, it will be recalled, that he is one of those people who 'supposent la nature et la société humaine autres que Dieu ne les a faites et qu'elles ne sont réellement'. The fact of the matter is that this is true of virtually all the characters in the novel, including Stepan Verkhovensky himself. Whereas the true nature of reality eludes definition, it is clear that most, if not all, the characters must be living in illusory worlds. In some cases this is so obvious that it scarcely requires elaboration. Stavrogin's idealisation of Stepan Trofimovich (of which she is gradually disabused by long experience) or of her son (of which she is disabused in more traumatic fashion); Stepan Verkhovensky's pathetic hopes of cutting a figure among the Petersburg progressives, and of achieving something with his speech at the fête; his general delusions about his own importance; Yuliya Lembke's delusions about Pyotr, which reach such a pitch of absurdity that she ascribes the disasters at the fête to his *absence;* her delusions about her husband's potential and her own influence on the young progressives. This is to say nothing about Kirillov's or Marya Timofeyevna's illusions, or Shigalyov's entirely theoretical utopia. And is Shatov's view of Russia as a God-fearing people (for all Dostoyevsky's approval) any less illusory? It will not escape the reader's attention that Pyotr Verkhovensky's scheming is itself based upon illusions; he play-acts and creates for himself a reputation as a peacemaker; he tells lies and misrepresents reality; above all, his groups of five are largely a fiction, as is his claim that Shatov is a danger to the group. The very structure of the drama is built on the lies and illusions of the characters.

Although ***The Devils*** does not contain a picture of subjective mental confusion to compare with that of Raskolnikov or Myshkin, a confusion of the real world of tangible events and the fantasy world of the mind pervades the fiction. As in ***The Idiot,*** this is underlined by the amount of 'literary work' undertaken by characters. This includes such diverse works as Stavrogin's confession, Karmazinov's 'Merci', Lembke's novel, Stepan Verkhovensky's orations, his scholarly work on the distant past, and his Romantic poem, the theories of Shigalyov and the doggerel of Lebyadkin.

The disjunction between the real world and the world of illusion can be subsumed under the category of the Inappropriate. The question of whether there is such a thing as an appropriate illusion is raised in the novel, but not properly discussed. Shatov reminds Stavrogin that he had once declared that if it were mathematically proved that the truth is outside Christ, he would rather remain with Christ than with the truth.

One sub-category of the Inappropriate which plays a major role in ***The Devils*** is the element of the disproportionate. Myshkin suffered from a lack of proportion. Disproportionate expectations, aspirations and fears rack the world of ***The Devils*** and provide rich soil for the fiasco of the fête. In this world in which the characters see life other than God made it, some seek a new force to bring about a new order. This, at any rate, is the view of Pyotr Verkhovensky.

It is not just that the society of 'our town' is falling apart from old age or natural causes, self-inflicted illusions or degeneracy. All of these create the conditions for the drama. Stavrogin's own past activities have sown seeds which are harvested in the course of the action. There are also, however, those who are actively engaged in wilful destruction and the wreaking of chaos. Pyotr Verkhovensky's declared aim is to undermine the foundations of morality and the state, to bring everything down with a crash by political action, but he has other weapons in his armoury besides his groups of five. One is to insinuate himself into the good graces of the governor's wife and thereby to attain a position of influence in civic affairs and demoralise the governor. From this position of social influence he is able to put other weapons to use. In a conversation with Stavrogin in which he appears literally intoxicated by his ideas, he declares:

> I'm a scoundrel, you know, not a socialist, ha, ha! Listen, I've got them all summed up: the teacher laughing with the children at their God and at their cradle is ours already. The lawyer, defending an educated murderer by saying that he is more developed than his victims and that, in order to obtain money, he could not help killing, is already ours. Schoolboys who kill a peasant for the sake of a thrill are ours. A jury completely vindicating criminals, is ours. A public prosecutor, trembling in court because he is not liberal enough is ours, ours. Administrators, writers, oh, there are many who belong to us, and they don't know it themselves. On the other hand, the obedience of schoolboys and fools has attained the highest degree; the bladders of schoolmasters are full of bile; everywhere vanity reaches inordinate proportions, unheard of, bestial appetites. . . . Do you know how many we shall ensnare by trivial, prefabricated little ideas? When I went away, Littré's theory that crime is insanity was all the rage; when I came home, crime was no longer insanity, but common sense, almost a duty, at the very least a noble protest. "How can an educated man not kill when he needs money?" But this is just loose change. The Russian God has already capitulated to cheap vodka. The peasants are drunk, mothers are drunk, children are drunk, churches are empty. . . .

And much more in the same vein. As to the future, with the aid of Shigalyov, Verkhovensky projects a form of social order which, with the experience of the twentieth century in his mind, the modern reader may see as a travesty of Communism and the idea of the Cultural Revolution:

> Listen, Stavrogin, to level the mountains is a good idea, not a ridiculous one. I am on Stavrogin's side! There's no need for education. We've had enough of science!. . . There's only one thing lacking in the world and that's obedience. The thirst for education is an aristocratic trait. . . . We shall destroy that desire: we shall encourage drunkenness, slander, denunciation; we shall encourage unheard of vice; we shall smother every genius in his cradle. Everything will be reduced to a common denominator, complete equality. . . . But a convulsion is necessary too. We, the rulers, will take care of that. Slaves must have rulers.

Verkhovensky junior talks about the fascination of the idea of destruction, a fascination which seems more powerful than the force of the 'rivers of life' which Shatov describes.

But Verkhovensky's chief weapon in ordinary everyday intercourse with members of provincial society is [buffoonery]. . . . Buffoonery is not a means of establishing self-respect for Pyotr Stepanovich. Like Lebedev, he is a gossip and a rumour-monger, but for Verkhovensky these are potent weapons. They are calculated to help him promote disaster on a wide scale. Verkhovensky understands and exploits buffoonery both in his own behaviour and by employing others, particularly Lebyadkin, with his uninvited, tasteless and inappropriate intrusions into the Stavrogin household and at the fête. Lebyadkin is not the sort of man who can be admitted to a drawing-room, and certainly not the sort of man who can be admitted among the cream of provincial society. Stavrogin says that there is a point at which Pyotr stops being a clown and is transformed into a madman. He is a demonic buffoon, and his clowning is more sinister than that of any of his predecessors or successors in Dostoyevsky's novels. In the person of Pyotr Verkhovensky the type of the buffoon undergoes an important mutation in Dostoyevsky's fictional world. There is a second development of the role of buffoonery in this novel. It may be called collective buffoonery: there had grown up a rather large group of people whose centre was to be found in Yuliya Lembke's drawing room, including several ladies and Pyotr Verkhovensky:

> The young people arranged picnics, parties, sometimes rode through the town in a regular cavalcade, both in carriages and on horseback. They sought out adventures, even concocting them and arranging them themselves. . . . They were called scoffers or mockers because there was nothing much they would balk at.

The activities of this group are not only high-spirited. They are irresponsible, malicious, even sacrilegious and psychologically extremely demoralising. The prank of one of their number in putting a live mouse behind the broken glass of a freshly plundered icon creates such a gloomy impression upon von Lembke that, according to his wife, his depression starts at this time. Finally, they decide that they will take a ride to the abode of the local 'holy fool' Semyon Yakovlevich, and on the way:

> When, after crossing the bridge, the expedition was passing the town inn, someone suddenly announced that a guest had been found shot in one of the rooms of the inn and that they were waiting for the police to arrive. Someone immediately had the idea of taking a look at the suicide. Everyone agreed. Our ladies had never seen a suicide. I remember that one of them said aloud that 'everything had got so boring that they needn't be particular about what kind of entertainment they indulged in, provided it was interesting. . . .' Our entire company looked at him with avid curiosity. There is in general something amusing for a stranger in every misfortune which occurs to his neighbour—whoever he may be. Our ladies looked on in silence, while their companions distinguished themselves by their wit and remarkable presence of mind. . . . Then Lyamshin, who prided himself on his role as a buffoon, gathered a bunch of grapes from the plate; another one, laughing, did the same, and a third was stretching out his hand for the Château d'Yquem, when the Police Commissioner arrived and stopped him, and even asked that the 'room be cleared'.

Decency and fellow-feeling have been banished. How far this is from Sonya Marmeladova or Myshkin, though perhaps not so far from the reactions of the gathered company at Ippolit's abortive suicide attempt. This kind of collective buffoonery, which has as its motive the provision of synthetic thrills, has precisely that effect of undermining all sense of right and wrong, the very foundations of morality, at which Pyotr Verkhovensky is aiming. The introduction of collective buffoonery as one of the psychological circumstances which pave the way for calamity is a stroke of genius by Dostoyevsky. It is not altogether fanciful to see Pyotr Verkhovensky's role vis-à-vis Lembke, his father, Karmazinov and other upholders of conventional values and institutions in the little piano piece composed (or filched) by Lyamshin, on the theme of the Franco-Prussian War:

> It began with the menacing sounds of the Marseillaise:

> *Qu'un sang impur abreuve nos sillons!*
>
> A bombastic challenge was heard, the ecstasy of future victories. But suddenly, together with masterly variations on the rhythm of the national anthem—somewhere to one side, from below, from a corner, but very close, came the miserable strains of *Mein lieber Augustin*. The Marseillaise paid no attention to them; the Marseillaise was at the summit of intoxication with its own grandeur; but Augustin was gaining in strength, it was getting more and more insolent, and suddenly the strains of Augustin began to blend with the strains of the Marseillaise. The latter seemed to be getting angry; at last it noticed Augustin; it tried to shake it off, to chase it away, like some importunate, insignificant fly, but *Mein lieber Augustin* hung on firmly; he was gay and self-confident, joyful and insolent, and the Marseillaise somehow became terribly stupid. It could no longer hide its irritation and hurt dignity; it became a wail of indignation, tears and oaths with arms outstretched to Providence:
>
> *Pas un pouce de notre terrain, pas une de nos fortresses!*
>
> But already it was being forced to sing in time with *Mein lieber Augustin*. Its melody passed in a most stupid way into that of Augustin, it drooped and was extinguished. Only from time to time could there be heard a snatch of *qu'un sang impur* . . . but immediately it passed most offensively into the miserable waltz. It was completely subdued. It was Jules Favre sobbing on Bismarck's bosom and giving away everything, everything. . . . But now it was Augustin's turn to grow fierce: hoarse sounds were heard, one had the sense of endless quantities of beer being consumed, the frenzy of self-glorification, demands for milliards, slender cigars, champagne and hostages; Augustin passed into a frenzied roar. . . . The Franco-Prussian war was at an end.

Ostensibly this is about war; but coming where it does in the novel, in the middle of a series of outrages to good taste and decency, and in view of the fact that the composer is Lyamshin, it is tempting to see it as a musical allegory of the whole process of insinuation and infection conducted by Pyotr Verkhovensky. He already has the young people of the upper set dancing to his wretched tune (the score for which, though not made public, he confides to Stavrogin) and it will not be long before the whole of society is contributing willy-nilly to its success. Common sense forbids a confident assertion that 'un sang impur' is a hint about the circumstances of Pyotr's birth. It is, however, one of those many instances where temptation is placed in the reader's way.

The pranks of this group of young buffoons culminates in the visit to the 'holy fool' Semyon Yakovlevich. Here the serious and the absurd mingle arbitrarily; even religion appears discredited. The group has little or no respect for the holy fool and he appears to deserve none, though the peasants superstitiously interpret his nonsensical pronouncements and deeds as prophecies. Only Drozdov is shocked at the mocking tone of the company. The episode ends in a fittingly unseemly way:

> The lady from our carriage, probably wanting to break the tension, asked Semyon Yakovlevich for the third time in her loud and shrill voice, with an affected smile:
>
> "Well, Semyon Yakovlevich, aren't you going to 'utter' something for me too? And I was counting on you so much."
>
> "*** you, *** you!"
>
> Semyon Yakovlevich, suddenly turning to her, pronounced a quite unprintable word.
>
> The words were uttered fiercely and with frightening clarity. Our ladies screamed and ran headlong outside. The gentlemen burst into homeric laughter. Thus concluded our visit to Semyon Yakovlevich.

This is by no means the only example of collective buffoonery in the novel. The addresses at the fête constitute an instance of unintentional buffoonery; the charades representing well-known newspapers similarly. The most distinguished and respected members of provincial society are beginning to dance in tune with *Mein lieber Augustin* without realising until it is too late. The most cherished ideals are being trodden in the dust and their bearers are, unwittingly at first, cooperating in the exercise. Indeed it is clear that Verkhovensky senior, Karmazinov and Stavrogin are the ideological parents of the young generation and morally responsible for their progeny. Yuliya Lembke nurtures the serpents in her bosom, vainly imagining that by so doing she will draw their poison and reform them. But she too has taken on more than she knows; she too is dancing to Verkhovensky's tune. (pp. 128-39)

Stavrogin is the central character in ***The Devils*** as were Raskolnikov and Myshkin in their respective novels. But something radical has happened to their roles in the plot. Whereas ***Crime and Punishment*** was almost wholly determined by Raskolnikov's drama, ***The Idiot*** has numerous digressions, the main plot is difficult to discern as one reads, and the hero often exercises only a peripheral influence on the events taking place on stage. In ***The Devils*** it becomes impossible to distinguish digression from main plot. In brief it may simply be stated that this is a collective drama; the plot is about 'our town' and its fate. Although this fate is seen in heightened form in the lot of half a dozen or so central characters, these are symbolic of a wider tragedy. The deaths of individual heroes and heroines belong to the falling action. The climax of the novel is the catastrophe of the fête, an occasion which involves scores, perhaps hundreds, of other people. Nothing which contributes to understanding the conditions which permitted this catastrophe to occur can be said to be wholly irrelevant to the main plot and, if anything is, it is surely some of the personal details relating to Stavrogin—his affair with Liza and Dasha in Switzerland, for example, and the largely superfluous Drozdov family.

Stavrogin's contribution to the action of the drama as it passes before the reader's eyes is modest indeed. It consists primarily in his fascination for others, in his ability to shock, to impress, to disconcert and disillusion. It is in the past that he has made his significant contribution, created a reputation and, by his influence on others, set in motion some of the main events of the drama. During the action, it is true, he helps to create an atmosphere which Pyotr Verkhovensky can exploit for his own purposes and he shatters his mother's illusions about him, but it is Pyotr who manipulates events. Stavrogin wanders round the sidelines reaping what he has sown before the action begins. During the action he continues to disconcert by his unpredictability and his power to surprise and shock. He, like Myshkin, though in far different ways, creates an atmosphere of disorder and uncertainty by his constant experiments with himself and with public opinion. He not only flouts public opinion; he presents it with deeds of such perverse eccentricity that society (which must always find an explanation for everything) is thrown into confusion and, when obliged to, accepts the most fantastic explanations of his behaviour. He thus introduces into the atmosphere a fantastic element which makes almost anything seem possible, creating a highly volatile social situation which Pyotr Verkhovensky has little difficulty in turning to his own ends.

There are many in the novel who see in Stavrogin a Romantic hero; not only some of the ladies of the town when he first appears—and the rumours of past deeds add to his Romantic aura—but also Shatov and Verkhovensky seem to think that he could 'raise a banner' and save mankind. He is seen variously as a Prince Harry, a Tsarevich, an Ivan Filippovich (a new religious leader), a mysterious and enigmatic figure, a prince who (like Rodolophe in Sue's *Mystères de Paris*) had visited the slums of the metropolis and mixed with its worst elements. He has led a life of dissipation, run people down with his horses, behaved brutally towards and publicly insulted a young lady of good society. He has fought duels and been court-martialled for it—all very much in the Romantic traditions immortalised in Russian literature by Lermontov in his *A Hero of our Time* and the unfinished *Princess Ligovskaya*. Then, after regaining his commission, he lives with the dregs of Petersburg society, consorts with down-at-heel civil servants, walks about in rags and, as his confession to Tikhon reveals, drives little Matryosha to suicide. On his return to Skvoreshniki the ladies divide into two camps—those who hate him and those who adore him, but both camps are crazy about him.

Later Stavrogin travels all over Europe, even to Egypt, Mount Athos and Jerusalem, and actually visits Iceland on a scientific expedition; he has attended a course of lectures at Göttingen University. He has wandered the surface of the globe like a new version of the Superfluous Man in search of some task commensurate to his energies. Stavrogin never finds this task. Indeed he seems to have destroyed within himself the source of positive values, the sense of what is good and what is evil, what is beautiful and what is ugly. The rule of his life, he proclaims, is that there is neither good nor evil. Kirillov says of him that he has been consumed by an idea: 'If Stavrogin believes, then he does not believe that he believes. And if he does not believe, then he does not believe that he does not believe.' This ironic formulation points to Stavrogin's moral bankruptcy. In his last letter to Dasha, Stavrogin admits that only negation has come from him, and not really even that, that all he has ever done has been petty and lifeless. He has tried his strength everywhere, but to no avail. He is afraid of suicide because he is afraid of showing 'magnanimity'. He continues: '"I know that it will be another delusion, the last in an infinite series of delusions."'

Stavrogin is the Romantic hero reduced to impotence. He can inspire others to various acts of destruction; he has even inspired Shatov's views; but of himself he can achieve nothing. For the time being the day of the Romantic hero has passed, though his aura is still powerful. He is a travesty of a Romantic hero. He narrator writes:

> He would have shot his opponent in a duel, and have hunted a bear it if had been really necessary and would have fought off a robber in the forest as successfully and fearlessly as L-n [a Decembrist], though without any sensation of pleasure, and solely from unpleasant necessity, languidly, listlessly, even with a sense of tedium. The quality of malice was, of course, an advance on L-n, even on Lermontov. Perhaps there was more malice in Nikolay Vsevolodovich than in both of them taken together, but his malice was cold, calm, and if the expression be permitted, *rational*, and therefore the most repugnant and terrifying sort of malice.

For complex psychological reasons Stavrogin may indeed be looking for burdens; he may be trying to test himself; such motives may lie behind his self-control when he is slapped by Shatov and his public announcement of his marriage to Marya Timofeyevna. But the reverberations of such acts reach a very small number of people; it is pathetic to see Stavrogin expending so much energy on them, as pathetic in its way as were the antics of the Underground Man. In the event Stavrogin is not one of Dostoyevsky's great dualistic characters, the battle-ground of two primary opposing psycholgoical principles. The ideal in him has lost its effectiveness; it is cancelled out in his dreams by the haunting figure of little Matryosha, by the image of the spider which is associated with it in his mind. He is drained of outward directed energy, 'his desires are never strong enough'. He is played out, his energies spent. When he has an opportunity to prevent the murder of Shatov and those of his wife and brother-in-law, he seems indifferent. The inner stagnation is expressed in his mask-like face.

Stavrogin nevertheless remains the central figure among the main characters in the fiction, if only because everyone else seems to consider him to be. He is a source of heresies and illusions, a symbol of moral bankruptcy, the focus of crushing personal disillusionment for several characters who have placed their hopes in him, in a world where other transcendent values have lost their power. He is a source of what Dostoyevsky is wont to describe as cannibalism. In his defilement of ideals, he sets the degenerate tone which spreads so swiftly in 'our town'. He is a symbol, above all, of a society at a certain advanced stage of moral degeneration, turning to various forms of excess for diversions or for salvation. it is a society which presents certain parallels with our own. (pp. 140-42)

Malcolm V. Jones, in his Dostoyevsky: The Novel of Discord, *Barnes & Noble Books, 1976, 236 p.*

CZESLAW MILOSZ AND CARL R. PROFFER (conversation date 1983)

[The following comments are drawn from a transcript of a conversation between Proffer, a scholar of Russian literature and one of the founders of Ardis Publishers, the largest publishers of Russian literature outside the Soviet Union, and Milosz, a celebrated Polish poet, essayist, and novelist who was awarded the Nobel Prize in literature in 1980. Their discussion occurred during a visit by Milosz to the University of Michigan, where he conducted public readings, lectures, and classes on Polish poetry and on The Possessed. *In this excerpt from their conversation about Dostoevski, Proffer and Milosz comment on some political elements of* The Possessed, *noting especially its prophetic qualities.]*

PROFFER: There has not been a separate book edition of ***Notes from Underground*** printed in Russian since the Revolution in 1917. It has been published three times in Dostoyevsky's complete collected works in sets of many volumes, but you've never in the entire Soviet history been able to buy a cheap edition of the book, whereas in the United States, at any given time, you'll find half a dozen different translations. Why do you think this is so?

MILOSZ: First of all, it's a book directed against Chernyshevsky. And Chernyshevsky belongs to the progressive line in the nineteenth century. Recall the influence of *What Is To Be Done* on Lenin. A satire like Dostoevsky's on the holy origins of the Soviet system would not be admired in the Kremlin. This is one possibility.

PROFFER: That's true. I was amazed when I was a graduate student, and went to Moscow and looked up on top of the Lenin Library where they have a row of statues of all the great writers of Russia: Tolstoy, Pushkin, Lermontov, Gogol, and Chernyshevsky. But Dostoevsky is not there. Of course that's Stalin era statuary.

MILOSZ: But I have serious doubts whether in spite of the popularity of ***Notes from Undergound*** Dostoevsky is very well understood in the United States. Teaching Dostoevsky, I have had a feeling sometimes of hopeless effort in presenting him as a writer so eminently bound with the history of Russia in the nineteenth century. It's very difficult to convey that to students. My feeling is that Dostoevsky in the United States has been treated primarily as a psychologist. And students are able to analyze the psychology of his characters very well; but when it comes to connections with the history of his style, his concerns with Russia, his political and religious ideas, they are very weak, because they are weak in history in general.

PROFFER: Is this why you picked ***The Possessed*** to concentrate on while you are here?

MILOSZ: Yes, among others, but I wonder how much I was able to convey, because you know very well that if you open ***The Possessed,*** the first chapter is a sort of survey of a few decades of Russian life, and of the Russian intelligentsia. And that's very hard for them to grasp. So I guess there are two Dostoevskys: a Russian Dostoevsky for Russians, and a Dostoevsky for everyone else.

PROFFER: I would go even further. I think there's a Dostoevsky for everybody. Because he's one of those writers who has been adopted by everyone who has an ideological point which they think Dostoevsky proves. I had in my possession for a short while a kit put out by a United States drug company. It consisted of a briefcase, very elegantly designed, and inside there were pockets for 1) a cheap paperback edition of ***Crime and Punishment;*** 2) a cassette recording of a conversation between the head of psychiatry from a southern university, a New York Jewish intellectual, an almost parody Freudian psychologist with an Austrian accent, and someone else I can't remember, discussing ***Crime and Punishment*** from the purely psychological point of view. A booklet came along with this kit featuring topics like "Raskolnikov and his Sister," "The Incest Theme," "Raskolnikov's Psychoses." And what is the purpose of all this? The fourth part of the kit is an advertisement by the company for a variety of drugs which might be appropriate for neuroses or psychoses similar to those in ***Crime and Punishment.***

MILOSZ: Crazy. But it confirms what I said about the fascination with psychology. Certainly Dostoevsky would have been dismayed, because he said, I am not a psychologist, I am a realist.

PROFFER: It has been one of the failings of Russian writers to all believe that they were realists, of course. And not just Russian writers.

MILOSZ: He was concerned with history, above all; Raskolnikov cannot be taken out of the context of the history of the Russian intelligentsia. Remember, Dostoevsky was born in 1821, just at the time the intelligentsia was coming of age, after the defeat of Napoleon. He believed they betrayed the people by choosing violence, as Raskolnikov does, rather than religious or political authority. It begins with the generation of 1848, represented in ***The Possessed*** by Stepan, and ends with the nihilism of elitists like Kirilov, and Shigalyov, and Ivan Karamazov in ***The Brothers Karamazov.*** These are people who hate the Orthodox Church and the people of the Church, the peasantry. Dostoevsky harbored a tremendous fear of the future in Russia. His fear, like Nietzsche's, arose from a sense of apocalyptic presence—that something enormous was about to occur. And the intelligentsia would do nothing to stop it. They would help it come into being by their plots.

PROFFER: Do you think he's a great prophet? Is it that aspect of ***The Possessed*** that draws you to it especially?

MILOSZ: Yes, yes. The prophetic power of ***The Possessed*** was felt by Russians at once, beginning with articles in *Landmarks,* and after the Revolution even the Communists praised ***The Possessed*** as a prophecy—not realizing that they were the devils Dostoevsky was trying to exorcize. (pp. 541-43)

PROFFER: In what way do you think he's a prophet in ***The Possessed***? Are you thinking of Shigalyov, and the psychology of the revolutionary?

MILOSZ: Yes. In Shigalyov we see the gloomy, distraught figure of Nechaev—revolutionary man as free, but homeless and loveless. Dostoevsky believed that man must bow down before something else because he cannot bear himself. This is the burden of Stavrogin, whose name comes from the word "cross" in Greek. He seeks a worthwhile burden but cannot find one. Dostoevsky distrusts intellectuals who claim that "the will of the people" is replacing God, because he sees that those who champion the masses desire only violence, or a reason for committing violence. Dostoevsky feared that Russia would come to resemble America, the incarnation of all evil. (Remember, Shatov and Kirilov spent time in America to observe "the hardest social conditions.") But the novel is not only a gloomy prophecy. Stepan is the father of the devils, but a bit of a buffoon and scoundrel, and a lover of the arts. There is much comedy of manners about him and his sometimes comical revolutionary pupils. American students are disturbed by this. For Americans it is very difficult to concede that a reactionary can write a valid satire.

PROFFER: I think you are probably right. And here we certainly have a case of a reactionary who wrote a very good satire. (pp. 544-45)

PROFFER: Let me conclude by asking you one of my favorite questions. Can a bad man write a good book?

MILOSZ: In my opinion, and to be completely frank, a good man can write a very bad book, but a bad man must have some resources for goodness in order to write a good book, this I believe. Dostoevsky wrote many good works. (p. 551)

Czeslaw Milosz and Carl R. Proffer, "A Conversation About Dostoevsky," in Michigan Quarterly Review, *Vol. XXII, No. 4, Fall, 1983, pp. 541-51.*

ADDITIONAL BIBLIOGRAPHY

Baring, Maurice. "Dostoievsky." In his *Landmarks in Russian Literature*, pp. 80-162. London: Methuen, University Paperbacks, 1960.

Discusses, in an essay first published in 1910, several of Dostoevski's novels and points out the strengths and weaknesses of *The Possessed.*

Beebe, Maurice, and Newton, Christopher. "Dostoevsky in English: A Selected Checklist of Criticism and Translations." *Modern Fiction Studies* IV, No. 3 (Autumn 1958): 271-91.

A bibliography of English-language criticism of Dostoevski through 1958 that includes a section on *The Possessed*.

Berdyaev, Nicholas. *Dostoevsky*. Translated by Donald Attwater. New York: Meridian Books, 1957, 227 p.

Traces Dostoevski's worldview by exploring the spiritual and metaphysical aspects of his philosophy. The book is intended to be more a spiritual biography than a critical analysis, but the insights offered provide background for the works, including *The Possessed*.

Blackmur, R. P. "In the Birdcage: Notes on *The Possessed* of Dostoevsky." *The Hudson Review* I, No. 1 (Spring 1948): 7-28.

An important study of *The Possessed*. Blackmur examines the spiritual novel that evolved out of what Dostoevski originally intended to be a political work.

Buber, Martin. "The Gods of the Nations and God." In his *Israel and the World: Essays in a Time of Crisis*, pp. 197-213. New York: Schocken Books, 1948.

Explicates the theory of the Prince of Nations as originated by the philosophers Nachman Krochmal and Giambattista Vico and demonstrates how Dostoevski modernized that theory in *The Possessed*.

Camus, Albert. *The Possessed: A Play in Three Parts*. Translated by Justin O'Brien. London: Hamilton, 1960, 159 p.

A dramatic adaptation of *The Possessed*. For commentary by Camus on Dostoevski's novel, see *NCLC*, Vol. 2.

Carr, Edward Hallett. *Dostoevsky (1821-1881): A New Biography*. London: George Allen & Unwin, 1931, 331 p.

An account of Dostoevski's life that includes a chapter detailing the biographical background of the novel.

Davison, R. M. "*The Devils:* The Role of Stavrogin." In *New Essays on Dostoyevsky*, edited by Malcolm V. Jones and Garth M. Terry, pp. 95-114. Cambridge: Cambridge University Press, 1983.

Analyzes the role of Stavrogin.

Dolan, Paul J. "Dostoyevsky: The Political Gospel." In his *Of War and War's Alarms: Fiction and Politics in the Modern World*, pp. 36-69. New York: Macmillan Publishing Co., The Free Press, 1976.

Explores the relationship between religion and politics in *The Possessed*.

Dostoevsky, Anna. *Dostoevsky: Reminiscences*. Translated and edited by Beatrice Stillman. New York: Liveright, 1975, 448 p.

A reminiscence of the author by his second wife.

Dostoevsky, Fyodor. *The Notebooks for "The Possessed."* Edited by Edward Wasiolek. Translated by Victor Terras. Chicago: University of Chicago Press, 1968, 431 p.

The complete notebooks Dostoevski kept during the composition of the novel, outlining every element of the story.

Frank, Joseph. *Dostoevsky: The Seeds of Revolt, 1821-1849*. Princeton: Princeton University Press, 1976, 401 p.

———. *Dostoevsky: The Years of Ordeal, 1850-1859*. Princeton: Princeton University Press, 1983, 320 p.

———. *Dostoevsky: The Stir of Liberation, 1860-1865*. Princeton: Princeton University Press, 1986, 395 p.

An ongoing, multivolume critical and historical examination of Dostoevski's life and work that is widely respected by modern scholars.

Gide, André. *Dostoevsky*. Norfolk, Conn.: New Directions Books, 1949, 176 p.

A philosophical study of Dostoevski's work, written in 1923, that includes an analysis of Stavrogin and Kirilov.

Goldstein, David I. "*The Possessed.*" In his *Dostoyevsky and the Jews*, pp. 68-87. Austin: University of Texas Press, 1981.

Examines Dostoevski's attitude toward Judaism, focusing on his portrayal of Lyamshin.

Holquist, Michael. "The Biography of Legion: *The Possessed.*" In his *Dostoevsky and the Novel*, pp. 124-47. Princeton: Princeton University Press, 1977.

A lengthy reading of *The Possessed* that addresses Dostoevski's handling of the question of identity.

Howe, Irving. "Dostoevsky: The Politics of Salvation." In his *Politics and the Novel*, pp. 51-75. New York: Horizon Press, 1957.

Interprets *The Possessed* as a caricature of Russian history.

Katkov, G. "Steerforth and Stavrogin: On the Sources of *The Possessed.*" *The Slavonic and East European Review* XXVII, No. 69 (May 1949): 469-88.

Contends that *The Possessed* is based on Charles Dickens's *David Copperfield*.

Lavrin, Janko. *Dostoevsky: A Study*. New York: Macmillan Company, 1947, 161 p.

A psychological assessment that includes a close examination of Stavrogin.

Livermore, Gordon. "Stepan Verkhovensky and the Shaping Dialectic of Dostoevsky's *Devils.*" In *Dostoevsky: New Perspectives*, edited by Robert Louis Jackson, pp. 176-92. Englewood Cliffs, N.J.: Prentice Hall, 1984.

Considers the role of Stepan Verkhovensky in the novel.

Magarshack, David. *Dostoevsky*. London: Secker & Warburg, 1962, 309 p.

A biography by a prominent translator of Dostoevski's work.

McDowall, Arthur. "*The Possessed* and Bolshevism." *The London Mercury* XVII, No. 97 (November 1927): 52-61.

Points out the revolutionary elements in *The Possessed*, finding in the novel Dostoevski's prophecy of Bolshevism.

Nabokov, Vladimir. "Fyodor Dostoevski: *The Possessed.*" In his *Lectures on Russian Literature*, edited by Fredson Bowers, pp. 128-35. San Diego: Harcourt Brace Jovanovich, 1981.

Identifies, in a lecture written in 1940 or 1941, the dramatic aspects of *The Possessed*.

Peace, Richard. "The Pamphlet Novel: *The Devils*" and "The Great Sinner: *The Devils.*" In his *Dostoyevsky: An Examination of the Major Novels*, pp. 140-78, 179-217. Cambridge: Cambridge at the University Press, 1971.

Contrasts the propagandistic and spiritual elements of the novel, and focuses on its artistic qualities.

Pritchett, V. S. "*Faits Divers.*" In his *In My Good Books*, pp. 72-9. 1942. Reprint. Port Washington, N.Y.: Kennikat Press, 1970.

An impressionistic reading of *The Possessed* that praises Dostoevski's talent as both a comic and political writer.

Seduro, Vladimir. *Dostoevski in Russian Literary Criticism, 1846-1956*. New York: Columbia University Press, 1957, 412 p.

An extensive analysis of Russian critical reaction to Dostoevski through 1956 that also reprints some excerpts of early commentary on *The Possessed*.

———. *Dostoevski's Image in Russia Today*. Belmont, Mass.: Nordland Publishing Co., 1975, 508 p.

An extensive survey of recent Soviet scholarship on Dostoevski.

Tyler, Parker. "Dostoievsky's Personal Devil." In his *Every Artist His Own Scandal: A Study of Real and Fictive Heroes*, pp. 53-69. New York: Horizon Press, 1964.

A character study of Stavrogin.

Wilson, Colin. "The Question of Identity." In his *The Outsider*, pp. 147-77. Boston: Houghton Mifflin Co., Riverside Press, 1956.

Interprets Alexey Kirilov as the quintessential outsider.

Yarmolinsky, Avrahm. *Dostoevsky: His Life and Art*. 2d ed. New Jersey: S. G. Phillips, 1965, 434 p.

A sympathetic critical biography by a noted Dostoevski scholar.

Adam Lindsay Gordon

1833-1870

Australian poet.

Gordon was one of the most important Australian poets of the nineteenth century. Many of his works were based on subjects that were popular in Australia, such as life in the bush country and horse racing, and reflect his experiences as a mounted policeman and steeplechase rider. While Gordon often celebrated an active and robust way of life, he also wrote numerous deeply pessimistic poems in which he portrayed human existence as arduous and without meaning. These apparently conflicting attitudes are combined in Gordon's best works, including "The Sick Stockrider" and "The Rhyme of Joyous Garde," forming a vigorous expression of the stoical and often sardonic temper that has been associated with the frontier environment of nineteenth-century Australia. For the specifically Australian aspects of his verse, notably his often fatalistic outlook and his evocative descriptions of the exotic and desolate landscape of the bush, Gordon was regarded during the late nineteenth and early twentieth centuries as one of the first Australian poets to manifest a sense of national identity. Although many critics have since disputed this claim, citing the English influences on his verse, other commentators have emphasized Gordon's importance to the development of Australian poetry.

Born in Portugal to wealthy Scottish parents, Gordon was raised from the age of seven in Cheltenham, England. In 1848, he was enrolled in the Woolwich Royal Military Academy by his father, who wanted him to obtain a commission in the British army. However, Gordon had little interest in a military career and focused his attention on the study of poetry and on learning to ride in steeplechases. His withdrawal from the school in 1851 without a commission upset his father, and in 1852 their relationship was further strained when Gordon was threatened with arrest after stealing a horse. Many biographers believe that Gordon's parents felt disgraced by this incident and that it was the principal reason his father made arrangements in 1853 to send him to the Australian colonies. Although he was at first unwilling to go, an unrequited love affair prompted Gordon's departure; many biographers maintain that throughout the rest of his life Gordon was troubled by feelings of resentment and depression over leaving England.

Gordon passed his first eleven years in Australia working in the bush, initially as a mounted policeman, then as a traveling horse-breaker and amateur steeplechase rider. He began writing poetry steadily in 1864, incorporating his experiences in the bush country into much of his verse. His first published work, a six ballad sequence entitled *The Feud,* was finished this same year, and three years later he published the verse drama *Ashtaroth* and the poetry collection *Sea Spray and Smoke Drift.* In spite of some favorable reviews of the latter work, none of Gordon's books sold well, and he lost a considerable sum of money financing their printing. Apart from writing poetry, Gordon was gaining renown as a successful and somewhat reckless steeplechase rider. Although the sport was profitable, the income it provided was too small to offset the heavy financial losses he incurred through the publication of his poetry and through a bad investment in a livery stable. By the end of 1868, Gordon was deeply in debt and forced to sell his stable to pay creditors. He then moved to Brighton, near Melbourne, where in 1870 he completed his last collection of verse, *Bush Ballads and Galloping Rhymes.* On the day after the book's publication, even further in debt from printing costs and suffering from long-standing depression, Gordon committed suicide.

Gordon's most popular poems glorify the vigorous life that was characteristic of Australia's colonial period and are especially distinctive for their rollicking cadences and musical rhyme schemes. These qualities are displayed in one of Gordon's best-known poems, "How We Beat the Favourite," which vividly depicts a steeplechase. On the other hand, some of Gordon's other works, including "The Swimmer" and "A Dedication," are brooding and melancholy and express his despair at the meaninglessness of life, an attitude that is reflected in morose and impressionistic descriptions of the desolate Australian wilderness. Gordon's most successful poems, according to critics, are those that combine dramatic adventures with a stoical outlook on life. Such a poem is "The Sick Stockrider," which is considered a pivotal contribution to Australian literature for embodying the spirit of the bushman in verse, anticipating a now-standard form of Australian poetry known as the "bush ballad." A dramatic monologue spoken by a dying cattleman, the poem represents life in the bush as difficult but ultimately fulfilling. Nostalgically recounting the friendships he formed through rugged adventures shared in a harsh environment, the stockrider expresses a philosophy of stoic resignation to a hard life he could not and did not wish to change. This fatalistic view of existence is considered to be Gordon's own and is conveyed in much of his verse, including his most critically acclaimed poem, "The Rhyme of Joyous Garde." An Arthurian narrative, this poem takes an English subject—Lancelot's sorrow over the dissolution of his friendship with King Arthur—but imbues it with a philosophy of life similar to that expressed in "The Sick Stockrider."

For its fatalism and its depiction of the Australian landscape, some early reviewers found in Gordon's verse, in the words of Marcus Clarke, "something very like the beginnings of a national school of Australian poetry." Many commentators have since disputed this viewpoint, contending that his verse epitomizes the sentiments of a displaced Englishman rather than a true Australian. In support of their argument, they note his frequent use of English subjects as well as the dominant influence on his verse of English poets, particularly Lord Byron, Algernon Charles Swinburne, and Robert Browning. While the English influences on Gordon's poetry are apparent, many critics hold that much of it is still fundamentally Australian in spirit. These critics stress that Gordon had a significant impact on subsequent Australian writers because he was one of the first Australian poets to describe the common attitudes and interests of his countrymen.

Few of Gordon's critics consider him a great artist. Even his staunchest admirer, Douglas Sladen, who declared Gordon "the national poet of Australia," observed that "Gordon was not a first rate poet. He had not the broad humanity, the serene power of a Homer, a Chaucer, a Shakespeare, or a Longfellow." However, Gordon's importance to Australian literature is not based on his poetic virtuosity. As Brian Elliot stated, "Gordon's contribution to the literature of his time and the colonial situation, lay in his acceptance of a plain man's plain attitude not only to the surrounding world and to society but to art."

PRINCIPAL WORKS

The Feud (poetry) 1864
Ashtaroth (verse drama) 1867
Sea Spray and Smoke Drift (poetry) 1867
Bush Ballads and Galloping Rhymes (poetry) 1870
Poems of Adam Lindsay Gordon (poetry) 1912
Adam Lindsay Gordon (poetry and letters) 1973

THE MELBOURNE REVIEW (essay date 1876)

[*This anonymous critic generally acclaims Gordon's poetic ability, especially his talent for vividly describing action.*]

[Gordon] was a man possessed of high mental qualifications and an aspiring spirit. A great part of his life was passed in the bush, amid those scenes which he describes so vividly in some of his poems. Himself a bold and fearless rider, he describes incidents connected with hunting and racing in a manner which no mere book-worm could hope to rival. In **"How we beat the favourite,"** the verse seems to sweep along with all the wild impetuosity of the headlong race which he is describing. This poem takes a high rank even among the best English poems of a similar class. **"Britomarte,"** and **"From the Wreck,"** are also vivid delineations of active life, of a very high order of merit. But Gordon did not excel merely in narrative poetry. In the **"Sick Stockrider,"** after dealing as usual with his favourite subjects, bush life and incidents, he concludes with the following pathetic lines:—

I've had my share of pastime, and I've done my share of toil,
  And life is short—the longest life a span.
I care not now to tarry for the corn, or for the oil,
  Or for the wine that maketh glad the heart of man;
For good undone, and gifts misspent, and resolution vain.
  'Tis somewhat late to trouble—this I know,
I should live the same life over if I had to live again,
  And the chances are I go where most men go.
The deep blue skies wax dusky and the tall green trees grow dim,
  The sward beneath me seems to heave and fall,
And sickly, smoky shadows through the sleepy sunlight swim,
  And on the very sun's face weave their pall.
Let me slumber in the hollow where the wattle blossoms wave,
  With never stone or rail to fence my bed;
Should the sturdy station children pull the bush-flowers on my grave,
  I may chance to hear them romping overhead.

The idea contained in the last two lines is singularly beautiful and touching. Gordon, like all our poets, has been largely influenced by contemporary English poetry. Swinburne and Browning seem to have affected his style most. **"The Three Friends"** is a very powerful poem, much in the manner of the latter poet, while in the dedication to ***Bush Ballads,*** a very beautiful piece of writing, he has copied closely the versification and phraseology of Swinburne. The poem will certainly compare very favorably with anything that poet ever wrote. (pp. 224-25)

Of ***Ashtaroth*** we cannot speak very favorably. It is a mysterious production, apparently inspired by a careful study of *Faust* and *Manfred*. There is a Norman baron named Hugo, who is influenced by love, partly for learning, but more strongly for women. The gentleman in black is also present, under the name of Orion. Of course a Corsair and an outlawed count are introduced. Hugo has sold himself to the devil, but, as is usual in such cases, comes out all right in the end. There are the customary paraphernalia to be found in such poems—a convent, a castle, monks, spirits, robbers, &c. To make the resemblance to "Faust" still greater, a kind of "Walpurgis Night" is introduced. Hugo and Orion enter riding, on "black horses," at midnight, in a "mountainous country overlooking a rocky pass." Under these trying circumstances, no wonder Hugo sees strange sights and hears spirits chanting unhallowed songs. The whole poem is a mistake, and is very crudely written. Such lines as the following are quite inexcusable:—

ERIC. Now, I wonder where he is gone!
HUGO. Indeed I had not the slightest idea,
  The man is certainly mad;
He wedded my sister Dorothea,
  And used her cruelly bad.

Even Lord Macaulay's proverbial schoolboy would have been whipped if he had perpetrated such trash as this. There are, however, several fine lyrics scattered through the poem, which atone somewhat for its general barrenness. (pp. 225-26)

"Australian Poetry," in The Melbourne Review, *Vol. I, January-October, 1876, pp. 202-30.*

ARTHUR PATCHETT MARTIN (essay date 1884)

[*Martin praises the lyric qualities of Gordon's poems and finds them worthy of attention by the English reading public, especially for their presentations of Australian themes.*]

Gordon's first literary venture in the way of a volume was entitled ***Sea Spray and Smoke Drift,*** which contains one or two poems now popular throughout the length and breadth of Australia. Among the contents of this volume are several poems which lack polish, and some which are perhaps not worthy of a place; still it contains others which merit more than a mere passing reference, and ***Sea Spray and Smoke Drift,*** despite its deficiencies, is felt to be a valuable addition to the literature of Australia. **"Confiteor"** is a fine poem—in spirit and in story essentially Byronic. It tells of a sin-stained corsair knight, who, having lost "her that he loved best," is too reckless to be shriven, or to listen patiently to priestly admonition, ere setting out on his adventurous voyage. Verse answers to verse, as the priest urges confession, and the knight bitterly retorts until his spiritual adviser himself confesses his own transgressions. (pp. 209-10)

Most of Gordon's poems are singularly sombre in character, and seem to be tinged by the bitter reflections and dark forebodings that led to his own untimely end. They are filled too with a passionate agnosticism, as of one who cannot but hold that there is nothing beyond the grave, and that life itself is a mockery and a delusion, and yet clutches at any evidence of human love or heroism which seems to show that man is more than the beasts of the field. Such are the verses entitled, **"Sunlight on the Sea," "The Song of the Surf," "Wormwood and Night-shade," "Quare Fatigasti";** while in the same volume are two fine ballads so thoroughly antique in spirit that the late Dante Gabriel Rosetti might have enjoyed them. These, with a translation from Horace and one from the Spanish, and, as might be expected from Gordon, a good sprinkling of sporting verses, make up the contents of ***Sea Spray and Smoke Drift.***

Gordon dedicated his second volume of poems, ***Bush Ballads and Galloping Rhymes,*** to the late Major Whyte-Melville, in whom he found a fellow sportsman and brother poet of the turf. These dedicatory verses, though somewhat too Swinburnian in style, are singularly felicitous. It will be seen that he claims for his Muse an Australian habitat, and recognises that the source of his inspiration sprang from the land of his adoption rather than that of his birth.

> They are rhymes rudely strung, with intent less
> Of sound than of words,
> In lands where bright blossoms are scentless,
> And songless bright birds.
> Where with fire and fierce drought on her tresses,
> Insatiable Summer oppresses,
> Sere woodlands, and sad wildernesses,
> And faint flocks and herds.
>
> Where in dreariest days, when all dews end,
> And all winds are warm,
> Wild Winter's large floodgates are loosen'd,
> And floods freed by storm;
> From broken-up fountain-heads, dash on,
> Dry deserts with long pent-up passion—
> Here rhyme was first framed without fashion,
> Song shaped without form.
>
> Whence gathered?—the locusts' glad chirrup
> May furnish a stave,
> The ring of a rowel and stirrup,
> The wash of a wave;
> The chaunt of the marsh-frog in rushes
> That chimes through the pauses and hushes
> Of nightfall; the torrent that gushes;
> The tempests that rave.

In this **"Dedication"** is the bright and vivid verse in which he so beautifully describes the Australian spring-time:

> In the Spring when the wattle-gold trembles,
> 'Twixt shadow and shine,
> When each dew-laden air draught resembles
> A long draught of wine,
> When the sky-line's blue burnisht resistance
> Makes deeper the dreamiest distance,
> Some song in all hearts hath existence,
> Such songs have been mine.

The ***Bush Ballads and Galloping Rhymes,*** as the title indicates, are more purely Australian in subject and character than his first volume. The opening poem, **"The Sick Stock-rider,"** is a true picture drawn from his own experience of station life. Who that has lived at all in the "Bush" but feels the truth of every line in the manly and vigorous reminiscences of the dying stockman!

> 'Twas merry in the glowing morn, among the gleaming grass,
> To wander as we wandered many a mile,
> And blow the cool tobacco cloud and watch the white wreaths pass,
> Sitting loosely in the saddle all the while.
> 'Twas merry 'mid the black woods when we spied the station roofs,
> To wheel the wild scrub cattle at the yard,
> With a running fire of stockwhips, and fiery run of hoofs,
> Oh, the hardest day was never then too hard!

Lying on his bed of illness in enforced idleness how fondly he recalls his rough comrades of the Bush:

> Aye, nearly all our comrades of the old colonial school,
> Our ancient boon companions, Ned, are gone;
> Hard livers for the most part, somewhat reckless as a rule,
> It seems that you and I are left alone.

As I now write I can, in fancy, hear the delighted tones with which one of these "ancient boon companions" used to burst out in the crowded streets of Melbourne, to the astonishment of the passersby, with what he called "Gordon's Epitaph on a Mutual Friend."

> And Carisbrooke the rider at the Horsefall broke his neck,
> *Faith! the wonder was he saved his neck so long.*

The concluding lines of this thoroughly Australian poem are full of genuine feeling, and contain all a bushman's philosophy of life:

> For good undone, and gifts misspent, and resolutions vain,
> 'Tis somewhat late to trouble; this I know—
> I should live the same life over if I had to live again:
> And the chances are I go, where most men go.
> The deep blue skies wax dusky, and the tall green trees grow dim,
> The sward beneath me seems to heave and fall;
> The sickly smoky shadows through the sleepy sunlight swim,
> And on the very sun's face weave their pall.
> Let me slumber in the hollow where the wattle blossoms wave,
> With never stone or rail to fence my bed;
> Should the sturdy station children pull the bush flowers on my grave,
> I may chance to hear them romping overhead.

The **"Sick Stock-rider"** is by no means a highly polished production; but in all the essentials of true poetry, in pathos, intensity and vividness, it surely surpasses the æsthetic outpourings of those young gentlemen whose verses seem to express, not without a certain tricky cleverness, such a high opinion of themselves, and such a poor one of the rest of this universe.

Referring to this poem and others of its class, the poet's sympathetic friend and critic, Mr. Marcus Clarke, observed, "they are very like the beginnings of a National School of Australian poetry" [see Additional Bibliography]. Unfortunately no Australian poet since Gordon has lived a bush life. The youthful versifiers of Melbourne or Sydney know no more than Mr. Oscar Wilde of the mysteries of "branding cattle," or the delights of hunting kangaroos or bushrangers. They go for their inspiration to the spacious public libraries of the city, where they read much the same class of literature as studious young Englishmen do in the British Museum. . . . Adam Lindsay Gordon, on the contrary, had a distinct experience, and lived an unconventional life. He read too; for choice, he read Browning, Tennyson, and Swinburne. But the rough avocations of his daily life, the wild sports and solitary musings of the Bush, always formed the basis, and often furnished the themes of his poetry. The form may have been learned from these great English masters of the Lyre; but the spirit came to him in the weird silences of the Australian forest, and in those profoundly melancholy moments that throw a spell over the minds of cultured men whose lot is cast among rough and oft-times uncongenial comrades.

Of an entirely different character to the **"Sick Stock-rider"** is the remarkable poem which follows it, entitled **"The Swimmer."** The direct influence of Mr. Swinburne is here apparent; but it is no mere slavish imitation of that great master of metre and rhythm. The form and occasionally the trick of expression is identical, but the thoughts are not filched, nor the emotions mimicked. These have surged through the brain of the Australian bushman until, aided doubtless by his study of the English bard, he gives them impassioned utterance in such verses as these:

> I would that with sleepy soft embraces
>   The Sea would fold me—would find me rest
> In luminous shades of her secret places,
>   In depths where her marvels are manifest;
> So the Earth beneath her should not discover
> My hidden couch; nor the heav'n above her.
> As a strong love shielding a weary lover,
>   I would have her shield me with shining breast.

"The Swimmer" is the cry of a strong but baffled soul for rest. He is weary of the stress and strife of this aimless existence; he has found out that life is a delusion, and that blessings are but curses in disguise. He has pondered deeply on life and on death, and can find no consolation save in the sad reflection that,

> Though the gifts of the light in the end are curses,
>   Yet bides the gift of the darkness—sleep.

In this mood he watches the angry waves, and then the old fever of the intrepid horseman seizes on him, and he yearns to bestride the steeds of Neptune, and ride he recks not whither, but haply to some haven of eternal quietude and rest. Surely this apostrophe to the ocean may be read even after Byron's:

> O! brave white horses! you gather and gallop,
>   The storm-sprite loosens the gusty reins,
> Now the stoutest ship were the frailest shallop
>   In your hollow backs or your high-arched manes.
> I would ride you as never a man has ridden,
> In your sleepy swirling surges hidden,
> To gulfs foreshadowed, thro' straits forbidden,
>   Where no light wearies and no love wanes.

The genius of our Bush-bard is essentially lyric. Scattered among these vigorous ballads, and poems of a semi-dramatic character, are songs of a fine pathetic beauty. It is perhaps necessary to quote with some degree of fulness from a poet so completely unknown in England as Gordon, and so I venture to give his brief **"Song of Autumn"** as showing his tender grace as a lyric poet:

> "Where shall we go for our garlands glad
>   At the falling of the year;
> When the burnt-up banks are yellow and sad,
>   When the boughs are yellow and sere?
> Where are the old ones that once we had?
>   And when are the new ones near?
> What shall we do for our garlands glad
>   At the falling of the year?"
>
> "Child! can I tell where the garlands go?
>   Can I say where the lost leaves veer?
> On the brown-burnt banks when the wild winds blow,
>   When they drift through the deadwood drear.
> Girl! when the garlands of next year glow,
>   *You* may gather again, my dear;
> But *I* go when the last year's lost leaves go
>   At the falling of the year."

The ***Bush Ballads*** contains by far the most popular of Australian poems, **"How We Beat the Favourite."** It is not by any means of the same high order of poetry as so much of Gordon's other work, but as a ballad of the turf it is to my mind the best in the language. At all events it is a prime favourite with antipodean reciters at "penny readings," and it may be confidently averred that a "horsey" poem that meets with the approval of an Australian "up-country" audience must be "racy" in more senses than one. Nor in the way of poetic translation do I know of anything to surpass Gordon's **"Three Friends"** from Alfred de Musset. (pp. 211-15)

Gordon's longest and most ambitious effort was ***Ashtaroth, a Dramatic Lyric.*** It cannot be well denied that this drama is in many respects a crude work and that it bears too close a resemblance in its plot and supernatural mechanism to *Faust* and *Manfred*. One would be inclined to condemn it mercilessly, and regret that Gordon wasted so much time in its composition, only that he has scattered here and there throughout ***Ashtaroth*** lyrics as beautiful as any he has written. (p. 216)

It may not unnaturally be thought by the English reader that Adam Lindsay Gordon is ranked too high in these pages, if for no other reason than that he is so unknown to the English literary world. But we should bear in mind the severe handicap in the race for fame involved in mere provincial publication; and intellectually Australia is simply a province of England with the added disadvantage of being separated by a six weeks' voyage from the literary metropolis of the Empire. (p. 217)

Adam Lindsay Gordon, during the period of his poetical activity, instead of living in a Kensington villa or a Fleet Street garret—in an atmosphere of artistic cant or of bohemian gossip—passed his days amongst sheep-shearers and boundary-riders, under the shining splendours of the Southern Cross. Nor was this greatly to his intellectual loss. Burns the Exciseman could not only gauge casks but measure the thoughts and feelings of a Tam o'Shanter, and as a ploughman he learnt to write songs that went straight to the heart of his race. So too it was perhaps well for poor Gordon that his was an unconventional life, even though, like all men of true refinement, he at times felt keenly its isolation.

"Ah! what wouldn't I give to touch a lady's hand again!" he exclaimed. But this phase of feeling was evanescent. Probably his happiest hours were spent in solitude beneath the gum-trees. "The phantasmagoria of that wild dreamland termed the Bush," says Mr. Marcus Clarke in his excellent preface to Gordon's collected poems, "interprets itself, and the Poet of our desolation begins to comprehend why free Esau loved his heritage of desert sand better than all the bountiful richness of Egypt."

On whichever side may have been the balance of pleasure and pain in such a life, we who have the ***Bush Ballads*** are clearly the gainers. Adam Lindsay Gordon is truly the Poet of the Australian Bush, but nevertheless his vigorous verses may have an added charm for those whose days are passed amidst the incessant and unlovely hubbub of London streets or in the peaceful monotony of English rural homes. (pp. 218-19)

Arthur Patchett Martin, "An Australian Poet," in Temple Bar, *Vol. LXX, February, 1884, pp. 208-20.*

FRANCIS ADAMS (essay date 1892)

[*Although Adams feels that Gordon lacks technical accomplishment, he praises his powerful descriptive ability and his expression of life's harsh truths, singling out "The Rhyme of Joyous Garde" as Gordon's best poem.*]

Civilisation had but little real hold on Gordon. A smattering of Horace, backed by promiscuous readings of the more popular poems of Browning, Lord Tennyson, and Mr. Swinburne, constituted a sort of pseudo-intellectuality which was too pitiful an effort to retain what he conceived to be the *fine fleur* of culture to be called an affectation. But in reality he was material absolutely made to the hand of the new conditions under which he found himself. He had little of the true literary sense—less even than Byron. His faults in what Goethe liked to call the ἀρχιτέχνη of his Art are severe. His lyric capacity, too, is distinctly limited. . . . It is now more than twenty years since he died, and he has become something very like the heart and soul of the Australian people. His faults, his limitations escape them, in much the same way as the limitations and faults of Burns escaped the democracy of Scotland. Just as Burns's vilest writing—his inflated, pompous imitations of Dryden and Pope; the tiresome rhodomontade of prose like his derisive love-letters to Mrs. M'Lehose (the Sylvander to Clarinda business)—still seems to simple Scotchmen a triumphant proof of their poet-ploughman's ability to excel in the worldly "grand style," so work like Gordon's appalling imitative parody of *Faust* (***Ashtaroth,*** it is called), together with his stale Latin quotations, bad Latin, worse French, and all the rest of it, seem to the simple Australians the culminating marvel in their poet. But, once more, what does it matter? They are right in the main, far more right, in any case, than the colonial quidnuncs who pester us with their tenth-rate versifiers. For he is the only Australian poet who counts: he is unique and (let me add) he is modern, passably modern, though he was far from aware of it himself.

What I find so remarkable in all this is the fact that such a poet should have won such a place in the heart and mind of any people. For it is Gordon's ideas, no less than Gordon's mere power of describing all forms of sport and violent action, which hold the true Australians, the younger generation of the democracy. No such intellectual spectacle exists anywhere else. His black pessimism, the pessimism of temperament reinforced by reason; his sheer pagan stoicism, proud and contemptuous of all the comforting and consoling religious drugs of the hour; his sombre passion for the truth, however hard, however cruel—what material do such qualities provide for the moulding of a nation? He, it is true, is still touched with doubts and dim hopes concerning these comforts and consolations, but he feels this is weakness and should be cast off, and his young disciples feel that they have cast it off because they have never really known it. The ideal, observe, is embodied in "the fever, the fulness of animal life," which, however, is to mean not only "the allotted work, the deed to do, the death to die," but also the hatred of wrongs and the tenderness for the sufferers in this hell of life. Look you, all the Law and the Prophets, and the Gospels and Epistles too, are there without the alloy of false and superstitious knowledge. To us moderns what makes our "burdens" so "heavy" is that our "natures" are so "weak." This world is a

> world of rapine and wrong,
> Where the weak and the timid seem lawful prey
> For the resolute and the strong.

What, then, shall we do to be saved? Never mind being saved!—

> Question not, but live and labour
> Till yon goal be won,
> Helping every feeble neighbour,
> Seeking help from none.
> Life is mostly froth and bubble,
> Two things stand like stone—
> KINDNESS in another's trouble,
> COURAGE in your own.

("Yon goal" is a symbol of death, of course.) Yet he shirks none of the complicating clauses. He faces everything—disillusionment, disgust, despair.

> Oh! wind that whistles over thorns and thistles
> Of this fruitful earth like a goblin elf;
> Why should he labour to help his neighbour
> Who feels too reckless to help himself?

And then the more spiritual note, but how much sadder and more despairing:—

> The restless throbbings and burnings
> That hope unsatisfied brings,
> The weary longings and yearnings
> For the mystical better things,
> Are the sand in which is reflected
> The pitiless moving lake
> Where the wanderer falls dejected
> By a thirst he never can slake.

No one has sung our modern woe more healthily than Gordon. He has not the poignancy or the delicate grace of Musset, the ghastly cruelty and intensity of Baudelaire. Leopardi has a supreme culture and intelligence utterly beyond him. Heine, with his exquisite lyric and artistic gift, and all the talents of civilization; Arnold, with his Grecian elegiac nobility; even the embryonic Clough has gifts unknown to our rough-riding, dare-devil Australian. But in all of these men there is something sickly and ineffectual which impairs their force, and renders their influence too much like that of a heated room and too little like that of the open air. We have to go to Byron to get the same "keen sense for natural beauty," allied with "a manly admiration for healthy living," that we find in Gordon. Half of the secret of his influence on the Antipodeans lies there. The other half lies surely in the absolute interpretation which they find in him of the philosophy of their land. Wearilessly does he preach his gospel of courage, and in every note. "Mere pluck," he says—

> though not in the least sublime,
> Is wiser than blank dismay.

The death he envies is that of the riders in the Balaclava charge, who perished (in small capitals also), "not in vain, as a type of our chivalry." He forgives everything to Burke (the explorer who perished after crossing Australia), bungling, swagger, ill-temper, the ruin of the expedition, and the death of his comrades, because he himself "died game," lying above ground, pistol in hand.

'Twas well; he toil'd till his task was done,
  Constant and calm in his latest throe;
The storm was weather'd, the battle won,
  When he went, my friends, where we all must go.

God grant that whenever, soon or late,
  Our course is run and our goal is reach'd,
We may meet our fate as steady and straight
  As he whose bones in yon desert bleach'd;
No tears are needed—our cheeks are dry;
  We have none to waste upon living woo;
Shall we sigh for one who has ceased to sigh,
  Having gone, my friends, where we all must go?

We tarry yet, we are toiling still;
  He is gone; he fares the best;
He fought against odds, he struggled up-hill,
  He has fairly earned his season of rest;
No tears are needed, fill up the wine;
  Let the goblets clash and the grape-juice flow.
Ho! pledge me a death-drink, comrade mine,
  To a brave man gone where we all must go!

Nearly all his poems are short, and the one effort he made to win his way into the region of the larger Art was an abject failure. I again refer to ***Ashtaroth.*** But in at least two of his more lengthy and sustained narrative poems he was successful. One of them indeed, **"The Rhyme of Joyous Garde,"** is magnificent. It is the one great poem yet written in Australia. In earlier days of an enthusiastic first acquaintanceship, I committed myself, I remember, to the opinion that it was worth all the *Idylls of the King* put together. I would not put it quite in that way now; but it seems to me that, taken with Mr. William Morris's *Defence of Guinevere,* the **"Rhyme of Joyous Garde"** is assuredly the one product of flesh and blood which has proceeded from the attempt to utilize the Arthurian legend in modern poetry. Gordon's Lancelot has even less historical actuality than Lord Tennyson's, but he is a splendid and puissant personality, a real and glorious creation, as utterly human as heroic. Singularly enough, also, considering the woeful chances in his larger dramatic lyric, Gordon has given us two short extracts from *Unpublished Dramatic Lyrics,* both of which are excellent in their way, despite some confusion and a rather reckless indulgence in Latin and French already alluded to. But in neither of these, good as is the characterization, does he reach to the astonishing height of his portrayal of Lancelot. The whole heart and soul and mind of the great generous, noble, simple, superstitious soldier is there—remorseful for his treachery, yet unable to wish it undone, repentant for his sin yet counting hell torment cheap for that first ecstatic kiss of possession. All the alternations of all the influences of his life—nothing is forgotten. Extracts from the poem cannot be quoted. It should be quoted entire or not at all; for it is all woven together in one inextricable web and woof, forty verses that make a perfect whole, and an achievement as superb as it is unique. I have lamented that Gordon did not, as a worker and artist, stake his all on one single poem, and achieve a masterpiece. Perhaps my lament was needless. Perhaps he knew that in [**"The Rhyme of Joyous Garde"**] he had indeed done this. Certainly it is free, or almost free, from all his technical faults. None of his characteristic weaknesses appear—his slovenliness of thought or phrase, his lapses into inferiority or even vulgarity, his failure to render the impression of an organic whole. No record exists, so far as I am aware, of his opinion that this was, beyond all question, his best—his one perfect piece of work. But, utterly as he was in the dark about himself, far removed as he was from either any comprehensive culture, or any innate faculty for criticism, which might have made this clear to him, it is yet possible that he realized that he had here at last written what none else could have written, and that so long as any genuine appreciation of poetry existed with those who spoke his tongue, his name would be remembered if by this alone. Alas, once more it is only hope which we can entertain of such an idea. Imbeciles everywhere face death confident in their literary immortality. . . . But Gordon? Had he no consolations whatever—slight though even such consolations as a limited perpetuity may grant to the world-weary children of men? As he went out that quiet and sunny morning, silent and alone with his rifle in his hand, resolved to play his final stake for everlasting peace, did no dream pass before him of the hundreds of brave and beautiful boys and girls, of noble and accomplished women and men, who should admire and love him with a whole-hearted passion? Was there nothing before him but the hateful hideousness of life and the "deep-drugged" oblivion of death? It was a superb destiny which awaited him, if he had only known it, and it was as a conqueror, not as a desperate doom-driven failure, that this man should have come forth to

Look around, and choose his ground,
And take his rest!

(pp. 359-65)

Francis Adams, "Two Australian Writers," The Fortnightly Review, *Vol. LII, No. CCCIX, September 1, 1892, pp. 352-65.*

OLIPHANT SMEATON (essay date 1895)

[*Smeaton finds Gordon's poetic abilities limited and his verse inferior to that of other Australian poets, including Henry Kendall and James Brunton Stephens.*]

Viewed absolutely, Gordon exhibits in his work nearly all the qualities that combine to constitute "good poetry," though, when compared with [Alfred Domett, Henry Kendall, James Brunton Stephens], he displays neither the rhythmical strength of the first, the tender grace of the second, nor the superb affluence of the third. In common with Domett, he is the epic poet of the colonies, though, unlike his compeer, epic he wrote none. His potential strength, however, in this line, was shown in his shorter pieces, where he excels as a metrical storyteller. Passionately fond of riding and of sports generally, he seems to have infused into the rhythmic pulse of his verse much of the glorious ecstasy experienced in a swinging gallop on a good horse over the rolling downs, and under the cloudlessly sapphire skies of the great Southern continent. Three-fourths of the verse he wrote is couched in the familiar, impetuous, headlong rhythms he made his own. He writes as one who had been a sharer in the scenes described, not a mere spectator. Hence his abiding popularity with the sport-loving Australasians.

His range, however, is by no means so wide as that of Domett or Stephens. He was not a student of books, but of men and of life in its most stirring, changeful types. His verbal thesaurus, therefore, is in no sense so rich as that of Domett or Stephens. At times he uses the same word over and over again with a wearisome iteration. The crowning virtue, however, is his of delighting in a nervous Saxon idiom—pithy, strong, and sinewy, like his own frame—that appeals at once to the audience for whom he wrote. His poetic imagery, though picturesque and appropriate, minted too in his own brain, is neither so luxuriant, nor drawn from so many natural sources as even that of Kendall. Gordon was less the solitary dreamer of dreams than the latter, and therefore did not love the "bush" so familiarly as his great compeer, the singer of New South Wales. More of the bustling, work-a-day world than of Nature in her lonely, sequestered beauty, does Gordon's imagery savour. He was, like Domett, a careful student of rhythm, and was nearly as successful as the other in his experiments in new and little known combinations. In ***Ashtaroth,*** for example—the one essay he made in dramatic poetry—a poem, too, more epical than dramatic in spirit, despite its form—he has interspersed several lyrics of a weird, unearthly beauty, that cleave to the memory when once read. How suggestive is the final lyric in the drama, for example, of the mournful close of his own life:

Pray that in the doubtful fight,
Man may win through sore distress,
By His goodness infinite,
  And His mercy fathomless.
Pray for one more of the weary
Head bowed down, and bended knee;
Swell the requiem, *Miserere*
  Miserere, Domine
    Bonum, malum, qui fecisti
    Mali imploramus te
    Salve fratrem, causa Christi
    Miserere Domine. *(Miserere.)*

Alike in the qualities of passion and of pathos, Gordon's verse exhibits marked power and individuality, though his passion too often is tinged with cynicism, as in **"Wormwood and Nightshade,"** and his pathos with the shadow of a supreme despair, as in **"Hippodromania," "Gone," "The Roll of the Kettledrum,"** and **"Cui Bono?"** The last-named piece betrays a decided trace of the influence of Charles Baudelaire of the Franco-Sapphic School, while Swinburne is the English poet to whom Gordon bears most affinity, and on whom he most persistently modelled himself. It must be admitted that in some cases he sacrifices sense to sound, as in **"Bellona"** and **"The Song of the Surf,"** and that in poetic strength he was distinctively the inferior of Kendall. This, however, is largely compensated for by his remarkable vividness of epical presentation, his power of portraying a scene in a few words without overlaying it with unnecessary details being singularly great. He was a man who, under circumstances more favourable, might have produced work of worth even more enduring than it is, had Fate, as he said, not thrown the shadow of discontent and incompleteness over all his life. To nothing could he be constant long, so that his life in many respects was a splendid failure. (pp. 489-90)

Oliphant Smeaton, "A Gallery of Australasian Singers," in The Westminster Review, *Vol. CXLIV, No. 5, November, 1895, pp. 488-91.*

DESMOND BYRNE (essay date 1896)

[Byrne suggests that the chief appeal of Gordon's poetry is its depiction of a way of life that is not only exciting, but of "central human interest."]

The strongest note of Adam Lindsay Gordon's poetry is a personal one. When he represents Australia best, he best represents his own striking character. Yet that character had clearly shown itself, as had also his lyric gift, before he saw Australia. He is the favourite poet of the country by a happy fortuity rather than by the merit of special native inspiration. Those tastes of the people which he has expressed in manner and degree so rare as to make a parallel difficult of conception were also his own dominant tastes. From early boyhood they had controlled his life, and in the end they wrecked it.

That any man living an adventurous and precarious life, often in rude associations and without the stimulus of ambition or of intellectual society, should write poetry at all is a matter for some wonder. And when several of the compositions of such a writer are marked by rare vigour and melody, and some few are worthy to rank with the best of their kind produced in the century, it must be held that the gift of the author is genuine and spontaneous. It is impossible to believe that Gordon would have been less a poet had he never lived under the Southern Cross; that he would have cared less for horses and wild riding, for manliness and the exhilaration of danger. Had he become a country gentleman in England, or a soldier, like his father, should we not still have had **"The Rhyme of Joyous Garde," "The Romance of Britomarte," "By Flood and Field,"** and **"How we beat the Favourite."** And do these not form the majority of his best poems? A man apt alike for the risks of the chase or the cavalry charge, with a delicate ear for the music of words, with natural promptings to write, would in any conditions have found time to celebrate the things which his daring and gallant spirit loved. Had he not ridden as well as written the rides related by his **"Sick Stockrider,"** he might have been foremost in that more glorious one so often present to his fiery fancy, and have wielded

The splendid bare sword
Flashing blue, rising red from the blow!

(pp. 159-61)

The deep melancholy in many of Gordon's poems has been attributed to the influence of Australian scenery, and to the loneliness of the earlier years of his life in the colonies. This explanation, if not wholly erroneous, is at least much exaggerated. It ignores the most obvious elements of the poet's temperament. It takes no account of the history of wasted opportunities and regrets, of defeat and discontent, of self-wrought failure and remorse, that may plainly be read in **"To my Sister," "An Exile's Farewell," "Early Adieux," "Whispering in the Wattle Boughs," "Quare Fatigasti," "Wormwood and Nightshade,"** and other poems. The writer, as he himself says, has no reserve in the criticism of his own career.

Let those who will their failings mask,
  To mine I frankly own;
But for their pardon I will ask
  Of none—save Heaven alone.

(p. 164)

It would not be difficult to imagine a more representative poet in the provincial sense than Gordon. His description of the colonies as

Lands where bright blossoms are scentless,
  And songless bright birds,

would be strangely misleading were it not contradicted by other lines from the same hand, showing a delicate appreciation of the rugged features of Australian scenery. But he sees them only in passing, or as a symbol of something he is pondering, or as a contrast to what he has left behind 'on far English ground.' No sight or sound of Australian Nature is a sole subject of any of his poems. His **"Whispering in the Wattle Boughs"** does not express the voices of the forest, but the echoes of a sad youth, the yearnings of an exile; his **"Song of Autumn"** is not a song of autumn, but a forecast of his own death—a forecast that was fulfilled. If he ever felt any enthusiasm for the future nationhood of Australia, he did not express it. And such few native legends as there were, he left to other pens.

In all of his best poems, there is some central human interest, something that tells for courage, honour, manly resignation. When a story does not come readily to his hand in the new world, he seeks one in the old. He fondly turns to the spacious days of the old knighthood, when men drank and loved deeply, when they were ready to put happiness or life itself upon a single hazard. The subjects that Gordon best liked were short dramatic romances, which he found it easier to evolve from literature than from the life and history of his adopted country. Beyond the compositions upon the national sport of horse-racing, the only noteworthy Australian subjects in his three slender volumes are **"The Sick Stockrider's Review of the Excitements and Pleasures of a Careless Bush Life, and his Pathetic Self-satisfaction," "The Story of a Shipwreck," "Wolf and Hound,"** which describes a duel between the hunted-down bushranger and a trooper; and some verses on the death of the explorer Burke. ***Ashtaroth,*** an elaborate attempt at a sustained dramatic lyric in the manner of Goethe's *Faust* and *Manfred,* fills one of the three volumes, and among shorter pieces in the other two are more than a dozen suggested by the poet's reading, by his recollections of English life, and, in a notable instance, by one of the most memorable of modern European wars.

In a dedication prefixed to the ***Bush Ballads,*** Gordon suggests some of the local sources of his inspiration. He obviously overstates his obligations to the country. Some of the best of the poems in this, the most characteristic collection of his work, have no association with it whatever. **"The Sick Stockrider," "From the Wreck,"** and **"Wolf and Hound"** are colonial experiences, finely described. But most of the remaining poems, while they owe something to Tennyson, Browning, and Swinburne, are not in any sense Australian. (pp. 176-79)

But where, save in the retrospect of **"The Sick Stockrider"** and a verse or two of **"From the Wreck,"** shall we find any of the air of the lovely, transient Australian spring? It is rather absurd to place with ***Bush Ballads*** the **"Rhyme of Joyous Garde,"** a recital of the old tragedy of Arthur and Launcelot; the story of seventeenth-century siege and gallantry in the **"Romance of Britomarte;"** the dramatic scenes from the **"Road to Avernus;" ["The Three Friends"]** (a translation from the French); and the psychological musings of **"De Te"** and **"Doubtful Dreams."**

And the galloping rhymes? Yes, there is indeed one galloping rhyme—**"How we beat the Favourite"**—with a ring and a rush, a spirit and swiftness of colour, not approached by the best verse of Egerton Warburton or Whyte-Melville. (pp. 179-80)

Of the longer poems, the two best in artistic quality are **"The Rhyme of Joyous Garde"** and **"The Sick Stockrider."** They afford a complete contrast in subject, tone and treatment. The old Arthurian story is the finer and more finished. There is a nobility in its expression not elsewhere equalled by the author. But the other poem is more direct and simple in its pathos, more easily understood. It tells something of familiar experience in language irresistibly touching and musical. (p. 183)

Gordon's work was introduced to the English public by an article in *Temple Bar* in 1884 [see excerpt dated 1884]. . . . Since then his poems have become known throughout the English-speaking world. Is this because he is called an Australian poet—because people wish to learn something of Australian life from his pages? Do English readers ever ask for the poems of Harpur, or Henry Kendall, or Brunton Stephens? No; Gordon's poems are admired for the human interest in them; for what they tell of tastes and personal qualities dear to the pleasure-loving and fighting Briton in whatever land he may be. It is the sort of admiration that finds fit expression when an English officer and artist makes a present to the publishers of a spirited and valuable set of drawings to illustrate the poem of the Balaclava Charge. No other Australian poet has yet found entrance to the great popular libraries of England. Kendall, who almost deserves to be called the Australian Shelley, tells more of Nature in one of his graceful pages than can be found in a volume of his contemporary. But his thoughts are too remote from the common interests of life; and of his own character he has recorded only what is sad and painful. For the rest, his brief history seems to prove that scarce any service may be less noticed or thanked in Australia than the describing of its natural beauties or the writing of its national odes. (pp. 185-86)

Desmond Byrne, "Adam Lindsay Gordon," in his Australian Writers, *Richard Bentley and Son, 1896, pp. 159-88.*

ALFRED BUCHANAN (essay date 1907)

[Buchanan considers spontaneity, lyricism, and refinement the three qualities that make Gordon a great poet, and he places Gordon's poetry into three classes: action poems, fatalistic lyrics, and works that present a blend of action and fatalism.]

It may be impossible to prove on mathematical lines that Gordon was a great poet. Yet it can be asserted confidently that his verse is marked by three qualities which between them go a long way to make up greatness. These are its spontaneity, its musical quality, and its refinement. Everything else is included under one or other of these three heads.

To take the first of the three—spontaneity, Gordon was above all things a natural singer. This naturalness, this unforced quality, is undoubtedly his first and his finest merit. He hoped for nothing—at least for nothing tangible—from his verses. In one sense, he did not wish to write. He much preferred action. If some one had given him a troop of cavalry and shown him a battery of opposing artillery, he would, in the rush and forgetfulness of one wild, sweeping movement, have experienced more real life, more real pleasure, than he was ever destined to know. Such an experience might have laid once and for ever the ghosts that always haunted him; might have made him feel that he was born to act, as his soldier-fathers had acted, instead of being obliged to sit down in a strange land and listen to memories of action that sang fitfully through his brain. It is for this reason—for the reason that temperament, and heredity, and poetic impulse forced him to find relief in verse whether he wished to or not, whether he was proud of the performance or ashamed of it—that he occupies his unique place. The pen and ink processes are invisible in his best work; it is as though

A wistful, wandering zephyr presses
The strings of some Æolian lyre.

To illustrate the spontaneous manner of Gordon would be to run through a complete list of his published poems. There is no need to go much further than the opening lines of **"The Rhyme of Joyous Garde."** It is instructive to notice how in this, as in others of his poems, the picture seems to create itself:—

> Through the lattice rushes the south wind, dense
> With fumes of the flowery frankincense
> And hawthorn blossoming thickly.

No preparations, no apologies, no preliminary turning and scraping; only the rush of a few lines which sweep the reader, whether he likes it or not, into the enchanted world of dreams. Equally natural, and quite as resistless, is the sentiment of **"Podas Okus."** Here again we feel, so to speak, the pulse-beat of the inevitable; we get again the impression that Gordon could not help the writing; that he himself, and not the Greek, is lying at a tent's entrance; that for him the hues of sunset are blending with the brief glories of an almost vanished life; that it is he, and not Achilles, who murmurs to the golden-haired Briseis:—

> Place your hand in mine, and listen,
> While the strong soul cleaves its way
> Through the death mist hovering o'er me,
> As the strong ship cleaves the wave,
> To my fathers gone before me,
> To the gods who love the brave.

The musical quality of Gordon is a kindred though a distinct merit. A poet may be natural and spontaneous without being particularly musical, just as he may achieve a musical result by what are manifestly artificial means. A lyric poet must, however, aim at musical effect. If he fails to attain this, he is not what he professes to be. . . . The school of self-styled poets founded by *Euphues* made the cardinal mistake of supposing that the form of expression mattered little; that their chief business was to get hold of fresh fancies, and previously unheard-of conceits. We know better than that nowadays. We can put up with the old idea if the treatment is artistic enough and musical enough. In lyric poetry the new or the startling idea creates a kind of metaphysical check, and is not really wanted. In Gordon there is enough of the familiar, enough of the sentimental idea to satisfy every-day requirements, while there is musical quality enough to proclaim the genuine lyric poet. The man had a sensitive ear. It is rarely that he strikes discordant notes. His versification is not flawless; it is not always of the quality of **"The Swimmer"** or of **"Autumn Song,"** but in reading him one feels that Australia has produced a poet in whom there dwelt the rare faculty of music, the genuine gift of melodic form.

The third distinguishing attribute of Gordon is his refinement. . . . When the term is applied to a man or an author in these days, it is necessary to be explicit in order to avoid misunderstanding. One of the merits of Gordon, and one that must tend to make the memory of the man loved, even more than his poetry is admired, is the habit of thought which reflects a fine and clear and elevated temperament; a temperament, that does not lend itself to vice; a temperament, in other words, that is refined. To say that Gordon was so constituted is not to say that he lacked emotional strength or force. He had abundance of either. He had also passion, though it was a passion that ran to self-restraint, to fatalism, and to sombre thought. It never brought him to realism, or even to the verge of it. When he follows a certain impulse and writes:—

> From a long way off to look at your charms
> Made my blood run redder in every vein,
> While he—he has held you long in his arms,
> And kissed you over and over again—

he is going as far as his finer nature will let him go in the painting of pictures dear to the fleshly school. It is almost incredible that a lyric poet who had come under the influence of Shelley and Swinburne should go no further than this. But Gordon's verses are not like most other love verses—they show no indulgence in that more blatant form of sensualism which will insist on its red lips and its soft arms, on its tropic midnights and its reiterated embraces. It is only "from a long way off" that he looks upon the vision splendid; he never vulgarises it by coming too near it; in the better and more enduring sense of the word, he is refined.

To understand Gordon it is necessary to remember that his was a dual personality. First of all he was a man of action. He wrote as a man who loved action, for other men who loved action. . . . But while all his sympathy and all his desires were towards action, his temperament was largely that of the dreamer. It is a rare combination, and one that explains a great deal. When he put his dreams into words—when he set his fancy free in such compositions as **"Doubtful Dreams," "Cui Bono," "A Song of Autumn,"** and others of the kind, it did not occur to him that he was doing anything remarkable. It did not seem to him that fame was to be won in that way. It did not appeal to him that this class of work might call forth rarer qualities, might establish a better claim to gratitude and remembrance, than could the actions of the man who went with a tomahawk into the wilderness, or of the man who led a forlorn hope right up to the cannon's mouth. He wrote not so much to please others as to please himself, and because he was unable to be always silent. He wrote because voices that sang through him would not remain dumb.

There are three classes into which his poetry can be divided. The first and the largest class is that in which the man of action preponderates. These are the verses that tell of deeds of daring, most of them accomplished on horseback. The lines have about them the genuine ring of saddle and sabre. The air seems to be rushing past as one reads them. Almost the whole of what praise or credit came to Gordon in his lifetime was due to what he wrote about men on horseback. Even now he is known to the great majority of his countrymen by such verses as **"How we beat the Favourite," "The Roll of the Kettledrum," "From the Wreck,"** and others of the kind. Poetry of this description may not be the highest possible, but Gordon did it very well. He did it so well that he may be said to have beaten all competitors in this particular line—and that despite his uneven quality, and his occasional lapses into the inartistic and the commonplace. (pp. 120-28)

Of all these poems of action there is none better, perhaps none quite so fine as regards conception and execution, as the **"Romance of Britomarte."** It is a remarkable piece of work. The artistic finish of it does not strike the reader while he is reading. To watch a really fine actor is to forget he is acting; to listen to a tale that is properly told is to forget the teller. It is rarely, indeed, that the mechanical processes do not obtrude themselves. Of genius there has never yet been a satisfactory definition; but the word may surely be reserved for the man or woman who can write a book, or act a piece, or compose a poem, of such quality that the reader or onlooker will forget for the moment everything but that which is placed before him. It is almost impossible to begin reading **"Britomarte"** and to put it down unfinished, or to be conscious of anything but the dramatic interest of the story. The verve and swing of the opening lines

> I'll tell you a story—but pass the jack,
> And let us make merry to-night, my men—

carry the reader on a rushing wave from beginning to close. It is a tale of great and successful daring, purporting to be told by the chief actor himself; but no crudeness, or bad taste, or braggadocio mars the effect. Thinking of such a piece one forgets to be sorry for the author. Irrespective of fame, or the lack of fame, he must have known that the work was good; he must have known that criticism could neither help it, nor harm it; he must have experienced the joy of creation, which comes only to certain natures, and not often to them.

On the second class of his poetry, which may be described as fatalism set to music, opinions are likely to differ widely. The majority of people prefer **"How we Beat the Favourite"** to **"Doubtful Dreams,"** but then the majority of people have from time immemorial been the worst judges of poetry. These verses that belong to the second class—the class not of action, but of brooding fancy—are well represented by the piece entitled **"The Swimmer."** All the philosophy in them is contained in the four lines:—

A little season of light and laughter,
Of love and leisure, and pleasure and pain,
And a horror of outer darkness after,
And dust returneth to dust again.

All the music of them is exemplified in the same piece, for example in the lines commencing:—

I would that with sleepy, soft embraces
The sea would fold me, would find me rest
In luminous depths of her secret places
In gulfs where her marvels are manifest.

They are melancholy and mystic, and not hopefully inspiring, these verses in which the writer seeks to link the unsatisfactory present with the unknown beyond. Yet they have a sweetness of their own. The strings that throbbed in Gordon to the touch of his mother, the Night, have, indeed, a siren quality, akin to the lute of Orpheus when heard on the eve of everlasting sleep in the garden of Prosperinë. Preferable sometimes to the utterance of a noisy and blatant optimism—finer than the blare of brass instruments or the shouting of crowds—is the voice of the reed shaken by the wind.

As a final word something may be said of Gordon's third and highest class of achievement, namely his blending in verse of the active *with* the melancholic temper. He could do two things: he could write of action, and he could write of sadness. Now and again he combines in one poem all that is best and most distinctive in these two sides of his nature. There are times when he devotes his verse to enterprises of some kind, to feats on horseback, or to feats in war. There are other times when he discards action, and lets the sombre mood of the moment envelop him. The hour of his greatest and rarest inspiration is when he mixes the action with the sentiment; when he unites the warrior with the poet; when he fuses in the same fire the contrasted (but not necessarily antagonistic) temperaments of a Bayard and a Byron, of a Lancelot and a Lamartine.

It is undeniable that **"The Rhyme of Joyous Garde"** represents the summit of Gordon's poetic achievement. And the reason is that it brings together in complete harmony the two spirits which alternately strove for mastery in the life of the man. The movements in **"The Rhyme of Joyous Garde"** are varied, but they fit into each other, and grow out of each other, as do the movements in a Beethoven symphony. First of all there is the atmosphere of pure idealism, of pure romance. There is the breath of the south wind, rich with the glory of the hawthorn and the frankincense. It is the man of action, who is also a poet, that is speaking. The setting is that of Arthurian England. Every line of the opening verse is flooded with the sentiment of a romantic country—a country in which brave men lived, and in which great deeds were done.

Against this rich, warm-tinted background is outlined a battle picture. Here begins the second movement. First the country itself, with its sunny fields and blossoming hedges; then the memory springing to life of great daring and heroic achievement:—

Pardie! I nearly had won that crown
Which endureth more than a knight's renown,
When the pagan giant had got me down,
Sore spent in the deadly grapple.

In a couple of resonant verses he explains why. The third movement begins when the woman enters. It is romance again, but romance of a more intense, more personal, more richly emotional kind. It forms the dominant note of this varied theme:—

The brown thrush sang through the briar and bower,
All flushed or frosted with forest flower,
In the warm sun's wanton glances;
And I grew deaf to the song-bird—blind
To blossom that sweetened the sweet spring wind,
I saw her only—a girl reclined
In her girlhood's indolent trances.

The realism of the picture is carried no further. With fine artistic sensibility Gordon recognises that he has said enough. The woman has entered; the man has grown blind to the blossom and deaf to the songbird; the eternal tragedy, which is not altogether a tragedy, has begun.

For the rest, the poem plays upon two strings. Alternately there are echoes from the fields of undying renown, and again voices of sad and hopeless and unending regret. The well-known lines beginning:—

Then a steel-shod rush, and a glittering ring,
And a crash of the spear staves splintering

are a memorable piece of versification. They arrest and perpetuate the fighting Arthurian spirit, they convey in words the actual clash of arms, and they bring back the forgotten mood of the man of personal valour as possibly no other verses have yet done. Such a word picture might be expected to leave weak and tame anything that followed; but with equal conviction, and with equal command of tone and touch, Gordon strikes again the chord of intense spiritual shame and sorrow, gradually merging it into one of religious appeal and exhortation. On this latter note the poem closes.

The man who had done this great thing surely deserved something in this existence, or in some other existence, in return for what he had given to the people among whom he lived. Surely, one likes to think, there must be, somewhere, at some time or another, a compensation, a recompense, for the tragedy of a life that merited so much success and vanished, or *seemed* to vanish, in such utter dark. (pp. 129-36)

Alfred Buchanan, "Adam Lindsay Gordon," in his The Real Australia, *T. F. Unwin, 1907, pp. 113-36.*

DOUGLAS SLADEN (essay date 1912)

[An English novelist, critic, and the originator of the first Who's Who, *Sladen was a devoted admirer of Gordon, whose placement in the Poets' Corner of Westminster Abbey was partly due to Sladen's efforts. In the following excerpt, Sladen examines Gor-*

don's poetry, noting its appeal to readers of all backgrounds, and declares him the "national poet of Australia."]

Beyond dispute Gordon is the national poet of Australia. In Victoria and South Australia nearly every family owns Gordon's poems, and they are better known than any English poet's are known in England. And rightly, because Gordon is the voice of Australia. But for him Australian literature would be less loyal than it is to the Old Country. For all Australians respect a man who was so much after their own heart, who would stand up to anybody with his fists, or put a horse at anything; who loved the bush like a home and extorted the admiration of all bushmen; who founded Australia's school of grim fatalism; who voiced Australia's code of honour.

Adam Lindsay Gordon was the national poet of Australia not only because he was a real poet, and wrote living poetry about the romantic old colonial days when Australia was in the making, but because he was a typical example of the fine strain which gave the Australian people its greatest qualities. (p. 254)

When . . . Gordon was writing of the wild life of the old colonial days he was writing of a subject which no one knew better than himself. The author of the **"Sick Stockrider"** had spent long years in the society of stockriders, when he was a horse-breaker, going from station to station; most authorities except Mr. F. Vaughan are agreed that he did the ride from the Wreck to fetch assistance himself; there are people yet who believe that he killed his bushranger in a cave before he wrote **"Wolf and Hound"**; the author of **"How we Beat the Favourite"** was the most famous steeplechase-rider in Australia. (pp. 257-58)

The fact stands out that these poems which are so redolent of the bush were written in the bush by one who made the bush his life. Their background is full of the broad effects which would have been his atmosphere to a short-sighted man who spent his life in the bush. (p. 260)

Gordon made his bush effects with bushmen—he used little else except sounds, light and darkness, heat and shade.

And this method has great advantages, because it makes his poems truly *dramatic lyrics*—not musings about still life, scenery or natural history, like so many forest poems, even Kendall's. The Kendall method produces the better poetry, and more good writers, but the world at large will always be more interested in dramatic lyrics, and personally I think that Gordon, with his literary offspring Rudyard Kipling, stand at the very top of the tree in this form of writing. I do not of course claim for them the technical finish of the great masters of poetic style, but Browning achieved his fame without any respect for perfection of metre and vocabulary. And both Gordon (who could recite Browning by the page) and Mr. Kipling have a splendid and haunting swing, and have swept into the net of poetry a miraculous draught of expressions and experiences of common life. Gordon gave the bushman and the jockey his halo of poetry, Mr. Kipling laid it on the head of Tommy Atkins (the descendant of the archers of Crecy and Poictiers), the engineer, the merchant seaman, and the flotsam of Empire. These two have put the theories of Walt Whitman into a more articulate form. They have sung in ringing ballads the struggles of the men who lead hard and dangerous lives in their everyday round. Their song is always of battle, though their battles are not always those of knights in mail, or clashing armies. They are the poets of action.

A portrait of Gordon when he was a mounted policeman.

The curious feature in the matter is that Gordon, much the more classical of the two in language and subject, led a wild bush life, while Mr. Kipling has always written as an observer, not drawing on his own experiences. It is his genius which has enabled him to put himself inside the minds of his heroes. It is on him that the mantle of Gordon, the laureate of the brave, has fallen, rather than on the writers of bush ballads, who are spoken of as the School of Gordon. (pp. 260-61)

I have found plenty of beautiful writing in the works of those whom we call the school of Gordon, but I have found nothing to equal Kendall in his moments of inspired simplicity like

"After many years" or Gordon in **"The Sick Stockrider,"** which is the best poem of its kind in the language. It is very beautiful, its choice of metre is instinctively just; it is terse, presenting a great picture with few superfluous details; and the genius of Australia sits brooding over every line, for it is the Bushman's Requiem. All through it we hear the voice of manhood which has borne the burden and heat of a warrior's day, and now, sorely stricken, is waiting for death with the dignity of the Dying Gladiator of the Capitol. It is a wonderful piece of painting; no poem that was ever written could more truly be called a picture. And, above all, it has the qualities of Sir Arthur Sullivan's "The Lost Chord." That song is simple and popular in its materials, but no matter how large or how varied the assemblage which is listening when it is played, every heart in the assemblage is lifted up and filled with a flood of feeling not far from tears. If Gordon had only written **"The Sick Stockrider"** he would have been secure of immortality. (pp. 262-63)

"The Sick Stockrider" is Australia's "Scholar Gipsy," not so purely poetical as Matthew Arnold's, not perhaps a greater poem, but secure of reaching a hundred hearts where the Oxford poem reached one.

The concluding lines of **"The Sick Stockrider"** read as if Gordon had written them as an epitaph for himself; indeed, many would like to see them engraved on the broken column with a laurel wreath which marks his resting place amid the wild flowers which make the North Brighton Cemetery (near Melbourne) an exquisite *rus in urbe*.

I am ready to acknowledge that **"The Sick Stockrider"** stands far above Gordon's other work in the same line—**"The Ride from the Wreck,"** and **"Wolf and Hound"**—his only other typically bush poems, though **"Gone,"** the Dedication to Whyte Melville, and a few others deal with the subject. (pp. 264-65)

[**"From the Wreck"**] was of course inspired by Browning's "How They brought the News to Ghent," published ten or twenty years earlier, but in every way is far superior to Browning's manufactured article. For in Gordon's poem we have the description not from an observer but from the man who did the ride, or other such rides, while Browning did not write like a man at arms any more than he looked like a man at arms. Gordon's poem was also truer poetry. Still **"From the Wreck"** is inferior as poetry to **"The Sick Stockrider"** because it was written consciously after a model instead of being a swan-song from the heart.

> The wild swan's death hymn took the soul
> Of that lone place with joy,

wrote one of the greatest of England's poets—almost a prophecy of Gordon's Sick Stockrider.

"Wolf and Hound" has little poetical merit though it is a vigorous and life-like description of an exciting episode, and full of bush colour. The only other poem of Gordon's in which there is any great deal of bush colour is his dedication of ***Bush Ballads and Galloping Rhymes*** to the novelist Whyte Melville, which is directly inspired by Kendall, and in truth reads more like Kendall than Gordon. This again is not Gordon at his best, though the picture is a brilliant one. The last poem in this group is **"Gone,"** written about the lost explorers Burke and Wills. But its local colour has no great value.

There are touches of Australian colour here and there in poems like **"De Te,"** but the Australian racing poems contain hardly any local colour except the names of the horses and their humans. Apart from **"The Sick Stockrider"** and **"From the Wreck,"** Gordon's fame rests chiefly on his English horse poems, of which **"How we Beat the Favourite"** is the best, though not the most poetical. His best poems, tested only as poetry, are his poems of regret like **"Doubtful Dreams," "De Te,"** and **"A Song of Autumn,"** and their setting is Australian.

In these without achieving Swinburne's mastery of rhythm and vocabulary he is more interesting, because Gordon writes not of lovers but of strong men fighting fate. Struggle is Gordon's favourite theme. (pp. 267-68)

But most readers . . . will be interested in Gordon chiefly as the Laureate of Sport—and his fame as a laureate of sport rests not so much on the sporting tips in verse which he wrote for *Bell's Life in Victoria* and the *Australasian*, as on the sporting poems which he wrote in Australia. . . . They are the poems which furnish most of the quotations which have passed into proverbs in Australia. **"How we beat the Favourite"** was one of them. This poem is by universal consent the best racing poem in the language. It was necessary that a poet should combine perfect knowledge of steeplechasing and the ability to write an unconventional poem with a certain stateliness as well as verve, in swinging metres, before **"How we Beat the Favourite"** . . . could be written. It presents a perfect moving picture of a race: it is matchless. If you read the verses aloud you get the galloping of the horses in sound as well as in meaning.

With **"How we Beat the Favourite"** may be grouped the poems in **"Ye Wearie Wayfarer"**—**"By Wood and Wold"** (a preamble); **"By Flood and Field"** (a legend of the Cottiswold); **"Zu der Edlen Jagd"** (a treatise on trees—vine-tree v. saddle-tree); **"In Utrumque Paratus"** (a logical discussion); **"Lex Talionis"** (a moral discourse); **"Potters' Clay"** (an allegorical interlude); **"Cito Pede Preterit Ætas"** (a philosophical dissertation); **"Finis Exoptatus"** (a metaphysical song); and **"The Roll of the Kettledrum"** and the poems in **"Hippodromania,"** though these last deal with riding in Australia. And undoubtedly this group had much to do with the fact that in Australia Gordon is more of a household word than Shakespeare. It is in them that most of his sayings which have become proverbs like—

> No game was ever yet worth a rap
> For a rational man to play
> Into which no accident, no mishap
> Could possibly find its way,

occur. (pp. 270-71)

"The Last Leap" ought perhaps to be mentioned here. It is not written in the vernacular like his other horse-poems. Its brevity, its nearer approach to classical English would almost fit it for inclusion in serious anthologies were it not too much a reflex in its most pathetic touch of Black Auster in Macaulay's Lays.

But Gordon was not only a horse-poet. He was the Laureate *par excellence* of the over-intrepid and over-generous, we might perhaps say "the Laureate of wild oats." The cavalier poets—most of them heroes—of the great Rebellion, would have hailed him as their bright particular star. That kind of bravery, that kind of generosity, which illuminate a life with flashes of lightning instead of an even brilliance, found in him their most eloquent advocate. (p. 274)

There is an echo of despair in nearly all Gordon's poems, but it is not the kind of despair which apathetically lets things go by default, nor does his poetry breathe much suggestion of the last terrible refuge which he did actually seek; it is more the despair of a "forlorn hope," the courage of despair.

Some lines in **"Finis Exoptatus"** give us the Gordonian philosophy at its noblest—

Question not, but live and labour
  Till yon goal be won,
Helping every feeble neighbour,
  Seeking help from none.

Life is mostly froth and bubble,
  Two things stand like stone—
Kindness in another's trouble,
  Courage in your own.

Courage, comrades! This is certain—
  All is for the best;
There are lights behind the curtain;
  Gentles, let us rest.

The eight Fyttes of **"Ye Wearie Wayfarer"** have probably won Gordon as many friends as any of his poems. They are so full of his bushman's philosophy, which has become the Gospel of Australia, so full of his sayings which have become proverbs in Australia. (pp. 274-75)

They are ringing in metre, picturesque in expression, full of striking allusions; they show us Gordon before the fearlessness and sturdiness of his youth were broken by constant injuries to his head in steeplechasing, and pecuniary disillusions.

The five pieces of **"Hippodromania"—"Visions in the Smoke," "The Fields of Coleraine," "Credat Judaeus Apella," "Banker's Dream"** and **"Ex Fumo dare Lucem,"** with the exception of the first, are not at all equal to the eight pieces in **"Ye Wearie Wayfarer"** as poetry. In fact, they are not poetry at all. They are merely excellent racing rhymes. In the same way the **"Romance of Britomarte"** is not a poem, but a metrical story, whose chief illumination is its knowledge of horsecraft. Like ***Ashtaroth*** it is full of immaturities.

The best of the poems written directly under the influence of Swinburne, whose rhythms Gordon loved more than any other poet's, are **"Podas Okus,"** which describes the death of Achilles, **"The Rhyme of Joyous Gard"** (as Arthurian scholars spell it), and **"The Swimmer."**

"Podas Okus" and the **"Rhyme of Joyous Gard"** are very much under the influence of Swinburne, but they are strengthened with Gordon's own warrior touch, and contain some very fine lines and passages. (pp. 276-77)

The **"Rhyme of Joyous Gard"** is supposed to be written by Sir Launcelot of the Lake, in the monastery whither he had retired as a penitent, over the death of Queen Guinevere, who had also retired to a convent at Amesbury. In form it may be too beholden to Swinburne, and Gordon had but a slight acquaintance with the legend compared to Tennyson, but he has earned his right to handle the subject by the personality, his own personality, which he has infused into Launcelot. (p. 278)

This is a ringing poem which carries the reader right along.

Gordon was not so successful in the imitations of the old Scottish Border ballads which he attempted. Most of his poems have some merit, except ***Ashtaroth*** and the **"Road to Avernus"** and the **"Old Leaven,"** but poems like **"Fauconshawe"** and **"Rippling Water"** and **"Unshriven,"** have not enough *raison d'être*. They suggest to me the immature author who had written ***The Feud*** . . . feeling his way towards the vigorous gift of poetic expression which was to give him a permanent place in the literature, not only of Australia, but of England.

Gordon wrote a few poems of very high merit which do not depend on local colour (except in the case of the last one), or his own personality for their interest: **"The Song of the Surf," "From Lightning and Tempest," "A Song of Autumn"** and **"The Swimmer."** (p. 279)

[**"The Swimmer"**] has passages of supreme beauty, and is of the highest interest in a biography of Gordon because the sea had such an extraordinary fascination for him. Regardless of the savage blue sharks which infest the coasts of Australia, he would swim half a mile out to sea, and once taxed himself so severely that he only just had the strength to get back again. When he was living near Cape Northumberland he would lie for hours on the edge of the cliff gazing at the sea, and he seems to have liked it best in its fiercest moods, though he makes no allusions to boating on it. It took a man who revelled in swimming to write this verse—

I would that with sleepy soft embraces
  The sea would fold me—would find me rest
In luminous shades of her secret places,
  In depths where marvels are manifest;
So the earth beneath her should not discover
  My hidden couch—nor the heaven above her—
As a strong love shielding a weary lover,
  I would have her shield me with shining breast.

Of the poems Swinburnian in form and pessimism, but full of the personality of Gordon, the best is **"Doubtful Dreams,"** . . . though there are also splendid lines in **"De Te," "Quare Fatigasti,"** and **"Wormwood and Nightshade."** (pp. 280-81)

"Laudamus" falls into the same group, but it is inspired by Alfred de Musset more than by Swinburne. It is a poem with striking beauties, and contains four of Gordon's most famous lines—

Let us thank the Lord for His bounties all,
  For the brave old days of pleasure and pain,
When the world for both of us seem'd too small—
  Though the love was void and the hate was vain—

In connection with **"Laudamus"** it is natural to mention **"Cui Bono,"** a poem not at all of the same rank, because it is made up entirely of aphorisms, some of them rather cheap aphorisms, without the backbone of romance which adds so much to the other. The sayings in it are much quoted by the people who "spout" Gordon. And with **"Cui Bono"** must be mentioned poems like **"Sunlight on the Sea,"** which contains the famous anachronism, *Tonight with Plato we shall sup;* and **"Ars longa, Vita brevis."**

One other class of poem remains to be noticed, the autobiographical. Chief among them come **"Whisperings in Wattle-boughs," "To my Sister"** and **"I am Weary, Let me Go."** (pp. 281-82)

The often-quoted poem **"To my Sister"** is chiefly valuable biographically. It shows that it was not want of sensibility and natural good feeling which made Gordon so wild as a boy. His wildness was due to the fact that he was born strong, brave and adventurous and was allowed to run wild. The world would have applauded his escapades as fine and spirited if he had been born a little higher in the scale of rank.

This poem, written three days before he sailed for Australia, when Gordon was about twenty, is, of course, immature compared with his best work, though it contains some typically Gordonian lines, such as—

> On earth there's little worth a sigh,
> And nothing worth a tear.
>
> (p. 282)

"I am Weary, Let me Go" is a Nunc Dimittis poem, written glibly but with strong internal evidence of not being Gordon's work, though it is stated on the good authority of the *Australasian* to be his.

"Whispering in Wattle-boughs" is on the same theme as **"To my Sister,"** but Gordon has grown up poetically in the interval. Here is a really fine lyric, written with the ease and strength of rhythm which furnished a great factor in Gordon's popularity.

It is uncertain whether **"No Name"** should be included in this group, or in the group which contains **"Doubtful Dreams"** and the beautiful translation from De Musset's **"Three Friends."** It is however, sometimes believed to be autobiographical and, in that case, belongs here. (p. 283)

Personally, I am not of the opinion that this poem refers to any event in his own life, I think I can trace its origin in Browning.

The sources of Gordon's popularity as a poet are personality, subject and style. Chief among them is the intense personality which vibrates through them. Gordon is never a Wordsworth, filling his hives steadily from all the suitable flowers round him. He never writes poems as intellectual exercises—as essays in rhyme and rhythm on phases supplied by Nature or domestic incidents. His poems well up from his heart like strong springs and sweep the reader along with them. In other words he is a *vates,* the word which the Romans applied to a great poet, in all senses of the word—not only as a maker of verses but as a prophet and a preacher, who has a message to deliver. He was one of those curious vessels chosen by the Lord to stop the passer-by, and force him to take an interest in the enigma of life. That wonderful personality, so arrestive, so splendid, so tragic, must have been given him for the purpose.

Subject, of course, counted for an immense deal in Gordon's popularity. But it was not till his last days that Gordon wrote of sport consciously because people were interested in sport, and the verses he wrote under that influence, except **"Visions in the Smoke,"** which may have been written already and merely served as the sample which secured him the order for the others, are, but for their knowledge of horses and their metrical merits, among the least valuable of Gordon's poems. Up to this he had written of sport because sport was the matter that lay nearest to his hand. Like Walt Whitman, he had said nothing is unsuitable for poetry which can be made a vehicle for feeling and creation.

But his magnificent **"How we Beat the Favourite"** and the ringing, manful, breezy, picturesque poetical proverbs of **"Ye Wearie Wayfarer"** belong to a very different order. Gordon wrote those because he felt Australia in his veins. (pp. 283-84)

The third element in the popularity of Gordon was the charm of the style he evolved. Gordon was familiar with the sporting verses which had been written by hunting men in England, but, unlike most sporting men, he also loved all good poetry—Latin and Greek and French as well as English. So he was able to improve his models. What made him better than all other sporting poets was that he was a much better poet than any of them, and that he had exactly the ear for devising and executing the ringing metres which his subjects demanded. There is no other volume of sporting poetry so dashing as Gordon's, dashing in subject, style and metre. Gordon was a genius. (p. 285)

But Gordon was not a poet of the first order. He had not the broad humanity, the serene power of a Homer, a Chaucer, a Shakespeare, or a Longfellow. Within his narrow range, he was strong, but his range was somewhat narrow. He was, however, a true poet, as is shown by his universal and growing popularity in his own land. A poet who appeals to the lettered and the unlettered alike, who is popular with the student and popular with the stable-boy, must be a true poet. A man may appeal to a class as the mouthpiece of that class; he cannot appeal to all classes alike if he be not genuine.

The **"Sick Stockrider"** is the essence of the man. It displays, in a marked degree, his eloquence, his ringing rhythm, his knowledge of the bush, and it is the child of his history, the genuine outcome of his wild heart. Had he never written another piece his fame would have been assured. Like **"Doubtful Dreams"** it rings with the manly melancholy of Gordon. (p. 286)

Douglas Sladen, "An Introduction to Gordon as a Poet," in Adam Lindsay Gordon and His Friends in England and Australia, *by Edith Humphris and Douglas Sladen, Constable & Company Ltd., 1912, pp. 254-86.*

FRANK MALDON ROBB (essay date 1912)

[Robb examines the influence on Gordon of nineteenth-century English poets.]

The sources of Gordon's poetry have for the most part been dismissed by the critics with few words, yet we can scarcely understand the 'making' of Gordon without taking account of these—so true is it that, as one critic has written, 'he owed more to Byron and Browning, Tennyson and Swinburne, than to Australia or to anything Australian.' It is therefore to these four poets that we must look, if we would discover 'the reddened sources' from which he drew his inspiration. To these four, however, Marcus Clarke, in a well-known sentence in his famous Preface, [see Additional Bibliography], rather fancifully and baselessly, as we think, adds a fifth. Speaking of Gordon's South Australian experiences he writes, 'He lost his capital, and, owning nothing but a love of horsemanship and a head full of Browning and *Shelley,* plunged into the varied life which gold-mining, "over landing", and cattle-driving affords.'

I. SHELLEY.—Let us take these five, then, as representing the main external influences exerted over the Australian poet, and first examine this least substantial debt to Shelley. At first sight Shelley and Gordon seem to have but little in common; the former—'nourished upon starbeams and the stuff of rainbows, and the tempest, and the foam,' as William Watson says,—with his unsurpassed and unsurpassable mastery of metrical resource, stands unassailable as a lyric poet. He has achieved such *tours de force* with metres and rhymes and rhythms that they constitute a standard to themselves. Perhaps other poets have had as deep a 'sense of the mystery of words and their lightest variation in the skein of poetry', but none have had the spontaneous ease of Shelley, or his variety of complex melody. 'His eye,' it has been well said, 'was a prism to all the radiant colouring of verbal imagery.' He, whose lyric poetry stands preeminent in our literature, and the entrancing 'nocturnal ether' of whose verse is to other poetry what that poetry is to cold prose, so that we wonder sometimes if he was really a man or a mermaiden, 'an Undine in human form who might one day return to the elements,' stands unapproachable, on the one hand; and on the other, Gordon, who has given us no real lyric poetry at all—though undoubtedly possessed of the true lyrical faculty—with his often crude, unpolished, and jingling, but withal gallant, energetic, and racy verse. He has no reliable sense of rhythm—not much of rhyme; one can never be sure, even in his most careful, conscientious, and ambitious work, that his ear and taste will not play him false. He is apt to drop straight from the stars into the puddles. His exceedingly limited and narrow range of metres means a correspondingly narrow range of thought and emotion, and technically his verse is full of unpardonable and mortal weaknesses.

To draw any parallel between him and Shelley, or to trace any direct debt to that consummate master of poetic expression, would tax even the most ingenious casuist, and a master of fanciful rhetoric such as Marcus Clarke himself. It is true that Shelley may have fired a train of idealism in the Australian poet, as he has done in the case of so many others—and notably in Browning—without its being easy to trace his influence in detail. None of the records of Gordon's library or of the books to which he had access, either in South Australia or in Brighton, contains special reference to the poems of Shelley; but, as we shall show when we come to deal with his debt to Browning, it may be that it is only in so far as the latter drank in the Shelleyan influence, that Gordon, who certainly in turn was largely moulded by Browning, owes him any debt at all. Of Shelley's influence in the making of the youthful Browning there is no question, and we venture to think in turn that of all the formative influences on the poetry of Gordon, that of Browning is the strongest. It is, therefore, at most, a Shelley filtered through Browning that left his impress on the Australian poet.

II. Byron.—Turning now to Byron, his debt is much more easily traced. There is in Gordon not a little of that 'carelessness and negligent ease' which Sir Walter Scott detected in Byron, and something too of that rapidity, energy, and lyrical resonance which marks the work of the greater poet. It is deficient in subtlety, and often written loosely, and almost at random. Men read Byron—and Gordon in his degree—not for fine phrases, but for the directness of some cry, and above all for the breadth and effectiveness of any utterance of theirs taken as a whole. It is easy to see the kinship in temperament and temper between Gordon and the author of *The Corsair*. After all, Byron's chief appeal will always be in the relief he brings to circumscribed lives. It is not by the prosperous and successful that his power is most felt. It was true in 1814, as it is true to-day, that men and women who were accessible to no other poetry were accessible to his, and especially to the straitened does he come with his breezy and large horizons, his love of the illimitable and of freedom, and of that in man which dares even to the uttermost. And it is these very qualities which endear Gordon to the Australian bushman in the oppression and isolation and monotony of his life, induced as these qualities are by the spaciousness of the plains, the loneliness of the mountains, and the sense of desolation and melancholy, which, in spite of all that arm-chair critics of him have written, Marcus Clarke was right in affirming to be 'the dominant note of Australian scenery'—not of course in its city-parks, not even in the more or less humanized and accessible and domesticated belt of verdure and habitation that rings our continent, but in its weird, barren, drought-stricken, trackless heart, which the true bushman, and he alone, knows. Into his life, mentally and socially circumscribed, cut off from his kind, Gordon comes with an irresistible appeal, just as Byron came to the slum-bound and the *revoltés* of great cities a century ago. 'It is all very well for the happy and well-to-do to talk scornfully of poetic sentimentality'—in a word, of Byromania. 'Those to whom a natural outlet for their affection'—and social and mental intercourse with their fellows—'is denied know better.' And it is true of Gordon, as Matthew Arnold said it was of Byron, that

> He taught us little, but our soul
> Had *felt* him,

and it is just that 'feeling' that makes the difference between a poet whose technique we admire, and a poet whose verses we love.

It is easy, too, to trace in Gordon something of Byron's diseased egoism, his cynicism and morbidity, though self-scorn for his weakness rather than boasting is the key-note of Gordon's personal confessions. Certainly he was not guilty of Byron's theatricality or bombast; nor was he *le fanfaron de vices qu'il n'avait pas*, [''the braggart of vices that he did not possess''], which Byron's most charitable critic declares the latter to have been. Still, believing as we do that Gordon's early life had in it something that warped and stained his outlook in all the after years, some bitterness of his own heart with which a stranger might not intermeddle, some secret which it required all that a man had of courage and endurance to bear and hide, we may find parallelisms between his work and Byron's not a few, points of resemblance which only prove that in Byron, Gordon found an expression, and a method of expression, 'fit and fair and simple and sufficient' for some of his own needs; but it is more than arguable whether, even at moments when he was haunted by the unforgettable past, Gordon consciously drew from Byron the sombre colouring with which he depicted or hinted at these early experiences—whatever they were—that gloomed and embittered him. He is too sincere and unaffected for that. Gordon certainly had a secret painful memory which he kept in a secret place in his life, and as far as the present writer can learn he never—not even to the friendly insistence of Marcus Clarke—lifted the shutter that would have revealed what that secret was. Gordon's attitude to those who would penetrate the mystery of his early years was,

> A peep through my window, if folk prefer;
> But, please you, no foot over threshold of mine!

and if at times the peeper saw or heard glimpses or sounds of that which Gordon so valiantly strove to keep hidden within, it was rather *against* than *with* the poet's will.

The sign-manual of the Byronic influence is not only seen in that mysterious production of the poet's called ***Ashtaroth***, although that was apparently inspired not only by a careful study of *Faust*, but also of Byron's *Manfred*. The Norman Baron of the poem, Hugo by name, is swayed by love, partly for learning but more strongly for women. The gentleman in black is also present, under the name of Orion; naturally also a Corsair and an outlaw Count are introduced. Hugo has sold himself to the devil, but, as is usual in such cases, comes out all right in the end. There are the customary paraphernalia to be found in such poems—a convent, a castle, monks, spirits, robbers *et hoc genus omne*. What makes the resemblance to *Faust* still greater is the introduction of a kind of ''Walpurgis Night''. Hugo and Orion enter riding on 'black horses' at midnight in a 'mountainous country overlooking a rocky pass'. It is little wonder under such trying circumstances that Hugo sees strange visions and hears spirits chanting unhallowed songs. The whole poem is a mistake, and is very crudely written. Even Byron, with all his vices of impromptu work, was never guilty of lines such as the following:

ERIC. Now, I wonder where he has gone!
HUGO. Indeed, I have not the least idea;
The man is certainly mad.
He wedded my sister, Dorothea,
And used her cruelly bad.

Gordon, moreover, made no secret of the fact that Byron had been a formative influence in his poetic career. (pp. lxxxii-lxxxvii)

Gordon too had certainly, even as Byron, 'the damning inevitable sign of a man born to wear the golden tassel,'—for he was an aristocrat at heart—viz. the vice of impromptu work which, like Byron, Gordon steadily refused to polish, to file, or to furbish. Byron said in this connexion, 'I am like the tiger; if I miss the first spring I go growling back to my jungle. There is no second. I can't correct and I won't.' It was after this fashion that Gordon wrote. [Mr. William Trainor, a close friend of Gordon's,] tells how, one night as he fell asleep, he saw the poet still fully dressed reaching out for a pencil and some scraps of paper which, when he himself woke the next morning, the poet had just completed his task of filling with the lines of the well-known poem **"From the Wreck"**, and it was never afterwards altered or touched by Gordon, except for the omission of the last four lines. . . . Readers of ***Sea Spray and Smoke Drift,*** however, will not need anyone to point out how closely at times Gordon followed his 'model' in these earlier poems. But here, as in all these estimates of his obligation to other poets, we would not have it understood that Gordon plagiarized from Byron or anyone else. There are points of contact in the poet and the poems, but such plagiarism always vindicates itself. The truth is, that not once nor twice, nor here nor there, is an idea or a figure borrowed, but that Gordon in his youth passed, as many poets have done, so under the spell of Byron's vital, vigorous, flowing verse and picturesque personality that it became impossible not to reproduce him.

III. SWINBURNE.—The influence of Swinburne on Gordon must be bracketed with that of Byron, and on the whole the position may be summed up by saying, that the influence of both was a baneful and unhealthy one for such a temperament as that to which Gordon was heir. . . . [The] observant reader will find in Gordon very much of the manner of Swinburne, especially in that powerful poem, **"The Three Friends,"** which is a translation from the French of Alfred de Musset almost entirely in the Swinburnian style. This poem could scarcely be excelled in the original, and it seems to us to surpass in power and terseness even the best of Swinburne's erotic poems. Also in the **"Dedication"** to the ***Bush Ballads,*** one of Gordon's most beautiful pieces of writing, he has copied very closely the versification and phraseology of Swinburne. That poem will certainly compare very favourably with anything the poet ever wrote.

In the magnificent poem, too, entitled **"The Swimmer"**, where we are held spellbound by the melancholy beauty of the verses, . . . the influence of that master of alliteration and assonance is clearly visible. In that poem Gordon gives fresh utterance to the soul-hungry prayer of the Psalmist—'Oh that I had wings like a dove and could flee away and be at rest'. From Swinburne, Gordon learned that love of the sea, which makes the former one of the greatest, if not the greatest, sea-poet in our English speech. Gordon loved all sport based on fighting, and every splendid contest, whether of men fighting or of horses racing, and equally, the 'bloodshot swordblade' of the dying sun, and the 'brave white horses' of the sea, seemed to thrill his heart's heart. It is strange to notice how his melancholy musings and his desire to be at rest are at times broken in upon by this unappeasable love for movement and conflict. Like the Brahmin, he wished to attain Nirvana, but to gain it he would make one last terrific struggle, and that struggle to him would be no less a joy than the rest it brought. He is indeed almost truculent at times in his sense of the infinite value of struggle and contest. In this, however, Gordon is more closely akin to Browning than to Swinburne. The poem ends with that splendid apostrophe to the sea, mouthed in the grand old Berserker spirit and with the strong yearning of the Viking, who longed to end his days on the stormy element where he had lived and fought:

Oh! brave white horses! you gather and gallop,
The storm sprite loosens the gusty reins;
Now the stoutest ship were the frailest shallop,
In your hollow backs, or your high arch'd manes.
I would ride as never a man has ridden,
In your sleepy, swirling surges hidden,
To gulfs foreshadow'd through straits forbidden
Where no light wearies and no love wanes.

Gordon uses alliteration, too, even more than Swinburne does—which is saying much. Such lines, for instance, as

Flickers, flutters, flags, and falters,
Feebly, like a waning lamp,

from **"Podas Okus":** or

Weary and wasted, and worn and wan,
Feeble and faint, and languid and low,

from the poem called **"Gone"**, are two of the many illustrations that rise to one's mind, though not behind these is

Rapine and ruin and rape lie around thee,

from **"Bellona".**

IV. TENNYSON.—From what has been already said it might be anticipated that Gordon would have much sympathy with the old knightly times, such as existed in the days of the Round Table, when adventurous spirits went forth they knew not whither and encountered they cared not what—such times as Tennyson has made his own in the *Idylls of the King*. Such poems as **"The Rhyme of Joyous Garde"** and **"The Romance of Britomarte"** testify to this, though in the former the influence of Swinburne, and in the latter of Macaulay and the "Border-Ballads", which Gordon knew almost by heart, are also visible. They are full of life, and the poet's heart beats in harmony with their stirring stories. (pp. lxxxix-xcii)

Gordon's rough and ready verse, 'the verse being as the mood it paints', has not much in common with the consummate artistry of Tennyson. Yet here and there in Gordon the artistic finish of which the late Laureate was such a past-master is not lacking. In the last line of the first quatrain of **"The Sick Stockrider"**, there is an illustration of the pictorial effect of alliteration and assonance,—in a word, of onomatopoeia,—which Tennyson himself need not have been ashamed to have wrought:

All through the hot, slow, sleepy, silent ride—

where you get a very artful and effective idea of slowness, heat, exhaustion and thirst. There is also a very palpable use of the metre of *Locksley Hall* in **"The Road to Avernus"**.

V. Browning.—It is, however, when we come to deal with the poet's debt to Browning that we strike the deepest note in Gordon's verse. To the influence of Browning, Australia—which loves the jingling rhymes, the living pictures, the rough-hewn language of Gordon, while its predilection for Browning is to say the least somewhat masked—owes more than it thinks. The very forms in which Gordon expresses himself—forms that make his words sing themselves in one's head for days—are forms of a school of poetry which without Browning would not have been. Gordon too has learned not only the forms of the master, but he has learned and appropriated and popularized in some degree the deeper power of Browning, which, at one period in their careers at least, makes Browning's admirers Browning's slaves. No one who has read even a little of both these poets can question for one moment the resemblance between them. There are lines in Gordon which simply startle the lover of Browning. (pp. xciii-xciv)

There are three entire poems in which the most striking correspondence between the poets makes itself felt. The first and best known of these is that between Gordon's ride **"From the Wreck"** and Browning's "How we brought the Good News from Ghent to Aix", but there are two others equally striking—those between **"Wolf and Hound"** and "Childe Roland to the Dark Tower came", on the one hand, and between **"Laudamus"** and "Evelyn Hope" on the other. In all these three poems there is at once manifest a striking contrast as well as evident agreement. The likenesses between the first twin-pair of these are too patent to need exposition.

"Childe Roland" is the story of a soul,—'my soul, your soul, any one's soul', as Browning put it,—marching on its lone way through an awful, shabby and hungry land—the eerie, half-starved aspect of the earth in the poem with what Mr. Chesterton calls 'the sense of scrubbiness' in Nature, making it one of the most ghastly and most powerful things of its kind in modern literature—to its goal, 'the dark Tower'. The poem is vague, as befits a spiritual allegory of the soul's quest and achievement, so vague that Browning said of it 'It means for each man what each man finds in it'. Gordon has translated this parable of the soul's aspiration and conquest into the story of a hunt after a bush-ranger. His intention that the reader should not miss the resemblance to Browning is conclusively proven by his setting of two of the lines of Browning's poem at the head of his own verse:

> The hills, like giants at a hunting, lay,
> Chin upon hand, to see the game at bay.

But the whole language of Gordon bears the impress of his 'model'. Instead of Browning's 'hoary cripple with malicious eye' we have the picture of the 'splitters who would swear through a ten-inch board'. The natural scenery—'the dry swamps', the 'low grey rocks girt round', 'the blood-red sunset', the peaks to the westward 'dyed black on a curtain of crimson cloth', the men 'caged like beasts for a fight'—is practically common to the two poems. 'Childe Roland' is afraid that the 'ghastly something close to the water's edge' may be a dead man's cheek; Gordon's hunters find that the horrible 'something' is the print of a 'horse's shoe and a rider's boot' which 'had left clean prints on the clay'. (pp. xcvi-xcvii)

The fact is that Gordon has so assimilated the Browningesque spirit and atmosphere that without conscious plagiarism he has 'learned his great language, caught his clear accents and made him his pattern' not only in form but in substance.

The *titles* of Gordon's poems are, for example, singularly Browningesque. If we set them out in parallel columns their close resemblance becomes at once manifest, thus:

Browning	Gordon
"Tertium Quid"	**"Quare Fatigasti"**
"Now"	**"Gone"**
"Summum Bonum"	**"Cui Bono"**
"Saul"	**"Delilah"**
"Memorabilia"	**"Hippodromania"**
"De Gustibus"	**"De Te"**
"Instans Tyrannus"	**"Ars Longa"**
"Dis Aliter Visum"	**"In Utrumque Paratus"**
"Prospice"	**"Laudamus"** *or* **"Confiteor"**
"Too Late"	**"No Name"**
"The Death in the Desert"	**"A Song of the Surf"**
"Time's Revenges"	**"Borrowed Plumes"**
"Arcades Ambo"	**"Vae Victis"**

(p. xcviii)

But in Gordon's *language* the resemblance is still more noteworthy. He uses alliteration, as we have seen, as much as Swinburne, and even more constantly than Browning, and his whole play of words is suggestive of Browning in its lack of conventionality. In their mode and power of rhyming the two stand almost alone. Both of them have a marvellous facility in the art, and can make rhymes in spite of the limitations of English speech. The thought of each poet sweeps on, and it is a sorry day for both if it has to be deflected for the purpose of a musical ending, for both can bend impossible combinations into rhyme to suit their purposes. Both can rhyme, and do rhyme continually, in two and even three syllables. Nothing could be more like Browning than the jingle of Gordon's 'double-bank us' to rhyme with 'Plancus', or 'rail am' to rhyme with 'Balaam', or 'wide on' to rhyme with 'Sidon'; and if Browning has shocked the ears of some of his superfine critics by making 'Manchester' rhyme with 'haunches stir', or 'explosive' with 'O sieve', or 'promise' with 'from mice', Gordon has also severely shocked one of his editors by rhyming 'nor shun' with 'caution', 'sweet sure' with 'creature', and, perhaps we may add even more oddly, 'Lady Mary' to rhyme with 'military', and 'ship shun' to rhyme with 'Egyptian'. Both poets—Browning in "The Grammarian's Funeral", and Gordon in the **"Dedication"** to ***Bush Ballads***—have lit upon the same rhyme (with a difference) for 'loosened'; Browning being hilariously thankful to think of 'dew send', while Gordon with equal gratitude haps on 'dews end'.

Neither poet is in the least circumscribed by the fact that the English language provides no rhyme. The manner in which Latin phrases, and sometimes French ones, take their places in the swing of the stanzas of both is, as Gordon might have put it, 'a caution to see.' Thus Gordon, momentarily troubled by the fact that the word 'result' is clamouring for a rhyme to complete his verse, is quite happy when he sees ahead of him such a Latin phrase as 'quem perdere vult', or 'prius' to rhyme with 'nigh us', or 'fremuerunt' with 'inherent'. Similar instances will occur to the minds of all readers of Browning. Sometimes, in this passion for rhyme, words are broken off in the middle. Sometimes they are made to rhyme with English; sometimes they are translated; sometimes laughed at; sometimes unwarrantable liberty taken with their pronunciation. Of course it is not to be expected that Gordon has either the vast vocabulary or the erudition of Browning—that most catholic-minded poet of our language, with his colossal knowledge of the byways and dark ends and unfrequented alleys of history, and, as Walter Savage Landor pointed out, with 'tongue so varied in discourse', as to make Chaucer alone comparable with him. But many lines in Gordon betray their paternity in unmistakable fashion; they are sealed of the tribe of Browning. A line like

> Mere guesswork and blank enigma

might have strayed from almost any part of *The Ring and the Book*.

Gordon's language, too, is terse and packed like Browning's. The accusation made against Browning by John Sterling, when *Paracelsus* first appeared, was that he was guilty of 'verbosity', and it seems to have been one of the few criticisms that left its impress on Browning; the consequence was that in his desire to avoid an overplus of words he often does not put in enough words to make his meaning clear, and in this Gordon is sometimes not far behind him. Both poets revel in antithesis and apposition; both are fearlessly vivid; in both we have 'learned dictionary words giving a hand to street-slang'; in both at times something of the 'wind-in-the-orchard style, that tumbled down here and there an appreciable fruit with uncouth bluster'. Both coin words in German fashion to suit their ideas; both make free use of dashes, and Gordon even betrays sometimes the Browningesque propensity which

> Loves to dock the smaller parts of speech,
> As we curtail the already curtailed cur.

Nouns, adjectives, and verbs pile themselves into sentences in both not always easy to analyse. An apostrophe like 'God we have sinned!' in Gordon's **"From Lightning and Tempest"** reminds one of the similar absence of interjection in Browning's 'Christ God who savest man!' from "Count Gismond", and who else—unless it were either Browning or Charles Stuart Calverley parodying him—would have begun a poem with

> Am I waking? Was I sleeping?
> Dearest, are you watching yet?

"Christmas Eve" need only be set side by side with almost any poem that Gordon has written to test the accuracy of the above comparisons. Both poets often light on the one right word, and their language is apt and expressive enough, but neither of them is the least afraid of language; each sometimes catches sight of a thought far ahead of him or a fancy breaking through language to escape, and straightway, forgetting all else, they plunge forward to lay hands on it, regardless of grammar and punctuation and consecution of words left all in wrack behind them.

But there is between the two a much stronger bond than that of mere language. The *subjects* of which they love best to write prove them still more akin than any external resemblances of speech could do. Of course Browning's range is much more extensive than Gordon's. The marvellous width of Browning's thought, with its limitless horizons, is one of his chief characteristics. No subject comes amiss to him; he is the child of the nineteenth century culture; the heir of all the ages that have preceded him; and as far as out-of-the-way and recondite knowledge is concerned stands without peer in English literature. (pp. xcix-cii)

For any trace of [Browning's] passion for music and painting, of his minute and accurate knowledge of all things imaginable, of his tastes for politics and history—especially the history of unknown men and the politics of little-studied countries—we shall, of course, look vainly in the small books of the Australian poet. It could not be otherwise. Browning lived beyond the allotted span of human life, and for three-quarters of a century was student and artist; Gordon died at thirty-seven, a bushman. Browning is steeped in the literary and artistic atmosphere of Italy—his poems breathe the classic air of the most classic lands in the world; Gordon, 'sitting loosely in the saddle all the while,' rode along the tracks of a land with no past, composing his verses as he rode along with his leg thrown over his saddle-pommel to make a desk; writing his songs in an Australia that had no literary or artistic atmosphere, and 'by the long wash of Australasian seas' that had never before been sung. Yet the favourite subjects of Gordon's muse are all especial favourites of Browning.

Nothing, for example, is more thoroughly a part of Gordon than his love of horsemanship. . . . Now that love of horsemanship is so thoroughly characteristic of Browning, that one may well imagine it formed the earliest, if not the strongest, point of contact between Gordon and the English poet. The author of "How we brought the Good News", "The Last Ride Together", and "Through the Metidja to Abd-el-kadr", could not but attract the author of **"Hippodromania", "How we beat the Favourite"**, and **"From the Wreck"**. The motto of **"Hippodromania"** might have been Browning's 'Sing, riding's a joy! For me, I ride.' Such a point needs no elaboration. There is prominent in both the keen love of riding for its own sake, and the sense of sympathy between man and horse which only true horsemen know. . . . The sense of movement, and the sound expressing the sense of movement in an almost cinematographic fashion, as far as riding is concerned, perhaps find their highest level in Browning's and Gordon's equine poems. That power and artistry, which Browning employs in "Ivan Ivanovitch" to express the onrush of the wolves after the sledge, are paralleled by the fierce joy of the breathless pace of Gordon's rider in **"How we beat the Favourite"**.

Again both poets love, above all sky scenes at least, the sunset. Attention has already been drawn to the similarity between the 'curtain of crimson cloth' in **"Wolf and Hound"**, and the lurid glow of the setting sun in "Childe Roland"; but this is only one of many illustrations that might be adduced of their common love of that natural phenomenon. The sunset in *Sordello,*

> A last remains of sunset dimly burned
> O'er the far forests, like a torch-flame turned
> By the wind back upon its bearer's hand
> In one long flare of crimson; as a brand,
> The woods beneath lay black; . . .

and a dozen others will readily suggest scenes in the Australian poet, and notably that great description of the sun sinking behind the sea from **"Visions in the Smoke"**:

> But the red sun sank to his evening shroud,
> Where the western billows are roll'd,
> Behind a curtain of sable cloud,
> With a fringe of scarlet and gold;
> There's a misty glare in the yellow moon,
> And the drift is scudding fast,
> There'll be storm, and rattle, and tempest soon,
> When the heavens are overcast.
> The neutral tint of the sullen sea
> Is fleck'd with the snowy foam,
> And the distant gale sighs drearilie,
> As the wanderer sighs for his home.

There are four times as many sunsets in Gordon as there are pictures of dawn or daybreak. Both poets also are in love with the sea, especially with its changes of storm and calm, its dread secrets, its unintelligible roar and moan. Gordon lived in South Australia beside the Southern Ocean, and many an hour he spent in solitary meditation by the seashore, and who shall tell the 'long, long thoughts' of the poet as he looked out on the 'unplumb'd, salt, estranging sea' that separated him from the old home and the old life? Gordon certainly owes much to Swinburne in this respect, but with Gordon as with Browning, the sea and the sunset are something more than subjects of admiration. Each of them feels a living sympathy existing between Nature in these aspects and himself.

Greek, and even Hebrew, literature has a prominent place in the writings of each of the poets. The part that Greek literature played in Browning's songs and stories and dramas is one of the most considerable factors in his writings. Gordon's **"Podas Okus"**, his projected poem dealing with 'Penthesilea', Queen of the Amazons, his many references to Greek history and mythology, and his Homeric epithets, show how this same attraction for Hellenic literature laid hold of him. But still more striking is the Hebrew element in both poets. Browning's "Jochanan Hakkadosh", and "Rabbi Ben Ezra", and "Solomon and Balkis", are paralleled by Gordon's **"Potter's Clay"** and **"Delilah"**—the latter poem, by the way, like Browning's "Guardian Angel", suggested by a picture. The fascination of Old Testament history in both poets is seen, in that Gordon introduces Job and David, Balaam and Gideon, as easily and often as Browning introduces Moses and Aaron, Saul and Abner, while Mother Eve is a favourite with both. In their discussion of matters theological there are evidences of agreement, and Gordon's friend 'Ephraim' and 'Puritan elder', who is of opinion that

> Thou mayest seek
> Recreation singing a psalm,

irresistibly remind us of some of the personages in the 'little Zion Chapel' on the heath in "Christmas Eve". They have many other common subjects, perhaps the most outstanding of which is the frequent allusions in both to the pleasures of feasting and wine, and if Browning does not lay quite so much stress as Gordon on the 'cool tobacco cloud', or share his enthusiasm for the 'ancient clay', he at least speaks kindly of 'this piece of broken pipe, a shipman's solace erst'. Both poets, too, undoubtedly have that love of action, of movement and of fighting, that

> Riot of chargers, revel of blows,
> And fierce flush'd faces of fighting foes,

of which Gordon writes so well and bravely in **"The Rhyme of Joyous Garde"**, and which are so prominent in others of his poems.

But the real affinity between them lies much deeper than either their common language or their common choice of subjects. Gordon has derived from Browning habits of thought, tastes, tendencies, moral and spiritual outlooks, which have left their indelible and revealing marks on all his verse. The freedom of Browning in his poetry is found in some degree in Gordon. The verse of neither disdains the commonest and most insignificant of objects. In this, of course, both Browning and Gordon are more or less typical of the nineteenth century, for the characteristic of that century is, that it is more than any other distinguished by its apotheosis of the insignificant and the common. There is nothing in the universe which may not generate the poetic spark and bring about the instant of incandescence. Even when the introduction of these things is positively comical, or grotesque, they do not scruple to introduce them. Neither poet deals much with abstractions; neither ever forgets the little concrete details, which, to a man who really lives, are more important than any generalizations, however comprehensive, and may suddenly send an arrow through his heart. Both poets take the liberty of introducing their own personalities into their verse, and even pause for a laugh from the reader at their own expense. If Browning could stop to say, 'Why I deliver this horrible verse,' or

> That bard's a Browning; he neglects the form,
> But ah! the sense, ye gods, the weighty sense!

or

> And, Robert Browning, you writer of plays,
> Here's a subject made to your hand!

Gordon is no whit behind him, when he pauses with quizzical eye to speak of 'the duffer who writes this lay', or to interject, 'this writing bad verses is very fatiguing!' Both poets quote from, and criticize, other poets as well as themselves, and in keeping with the suggestion above—that nothing is too small or too slight for their observation—it is noteworthy how the ears, eyes, and nostrils of their horses are drawn with faultless strokes. . . . Certainly Gordon, in his description of the clash of stirrups, the foam-flecks on the bull's face as he fronts the toreador, proves himself not unpossessed of the same close powers of scrutiny and love and observation of Nature, which is visible in the author of "Saul" and "Karshish". Both poets, too, in common with another characteristic of the nineteenth century, are under the spell of the *macabre* and the ghastly—a characteristic which culminated in the ghoulish and intensive horror of the weird tales of Edgar Allan Poe. Blood flows and clots, wounds gape, the nostrils and lungs of the drowning man, as in **"The Song of the Surf"**, are water-filled, quite in Browning's style. The details of death—the cere-cloth, the winding-sheet, the work of the worms in the grave, and the weird realism of such things—can be found in both poets. The concluding lines of Gordon's **"The Sick Stockrider"**, where the dead stockman may chance to hear the 'sturdy station children' romping overhead, have their counterpart in Browning's 'prattle of the birds' which

> Amuse the dead awhile,
> If couched they hear beneath the matted camomile.

and who could write more like Browning, without actually copying him, than Gordon in those splendid original lines:

> One gleam like a bloodshot sword-blade swims on
> The sky-line, staining the green gulf crimson,
> A death stroke fiercely dealt by a dim sun,
> That strikes through his stormy winding sheet?

Both poets are exquisitely pure, and yet both have the intense feeling and boldness of description of virile men in dealing with the sensuous. Both, that is to say, have the purity of fire rather than the purity of snow. There is in each a vivid realism, a passionate appreciation, almost intoxicating in its intensity, of sense. The red glow of a woman's lips, as in Gordon's **"No Name"**, the exquisite whiteness of brow, the curve of arms and neck, and the love of gold hair, are equally felt by both poets. Browning, who could write of the passionate kiss of Ottima in *Pippa Passes* and speak of the 'neck's warmth' in the scarf given to Naddo by Adelaide in *Sordello*, would have loved the 'shoulder's snowy tip' and the 'rose-red lips', which caught and held Gordon's desire; and the latter's description in **"Fauconshawe"** of Mabel's ivory white fingers among her raven hair, may be set alongside Browning's 'face like a silver wedge mid the yellow wealth', to show how real such impressions were to them both; and Gordon, no less than the author of "A Story of Pornic", dwells with particulr affection on

> The golden sunset gleaming
> On your golden gleaming hair.

Both poets, too, show a strong love of colour. This indeed is one of the chief characteristics of Browning. . . . [He sees] the poppies crimson to blackness; the red fans of the butterfly falling on the rock like a drop of fire from a brandished torch; the starfish rose-jacinth to the finger tips; and a hundred other passionate seizures of colour. . . . His use of 'reds and blues that artist never dreamed of' is paralleled by Gordon's use of the 'blue and the green' in **"Wormwood and Nightshade",** and finds another counterpart in the Australian's descriptions of the races, where the 'silks' are so finely and so constantly painted. Gordon, like Browning, can be searched—and it repays the reader to search them both—for colour impressions. In one of the most typical examples, Browning flings in the black horse at the end much as Gordon does in the **"Dedication"** to ***Bush Ballads,*** and just exactly in the way an artist would do it who loved a flash of black life in the midst of a dead expanse of gold and green, one of those spots of blackness in creation that makes the colours felt:

> Fancy the Pampas' sheen!
> Miles and miles of gold and green
> Where the sunflowers blow
> In a solid glow,
> And—to break now and then the screen—
> Black neck and eyeballs keen,
> Up a wild horse leaps between! . . .

[As Mr. Stopford Brooke observes], Browning 'lost a great deal of the colour of which he was once so lavish' as he grew older; therefore it is the Browning that Gordon knew who has this trait in so marked a fashion. Browning indeed at this period reminds one of the pictures of Tintoret with his madness of colour, black and gold and sombre purple, white mist and barred clouds, and the thunder roar in his skies. Gordon's picture of the salmon, 'lilac, shot through with a silver ray,' might have come from the greater poet, while Gordon's lines from **"The Swimmer"**:

> The blue sea over the bright sand roll'd;
> Babble and prattle, and ripple and murmur,
> Sheen of silver and glamour of gold—
> And the sunset bath'd in the gulf to lend her
> A garland of pinks and of purples tender,
> A tinge of the sun-god's rosy splendour,
> A tithe of his glories manifold. . . .

remind one of the sunbath'd sea in "Fifine at the Fair". Of course, both Browning and Gordon are visibly in Shelley's debt at moments like these.

But the greatest lesson that Gordon learned from Browning, by far the most formative influence in his thought and in the expression of his thought in verse, is the art of what has been called 'Psychological Drama'. The Dramatic Monologue is Browning's most typical contribution to the *form* of literature. (pp. cii-cxii)

Gordon learned it early. In his dramatic poems—and that means almost everything that he has written—the drama is that of processes going on in the soul itself, not in its environment or deeds merely. His **"Road to Avernus",** with its striking duel-scene, is like Browning's twin poems "Before" and "After", a portrayal of antagonistic *souls*. . . . Or we may compare Browning's "The Worst of It" with Gordon's **"The Rhyme of Joyous Garde",** because they each display the same fiery action and reaction of thought. Both poets, too, know the power of physical terror or panic to make 'the spirit's true endowments stand out plainly from its false ones', to drag out the masked truth from beneath the falsity of the outward seeming; this is delineated in Gordon's **"Lightning and Tempest",** much as it is in Browning's "Caliban", and in "Adam, Lilith, and Eve". In fact it is not too much to say that Gordon believes as firmly as Browning in what Mr. Chesterton finely calls 'the Doctrine of the Great Hour', in which

> Just this or that poor impulse,
> Which for once had play unstifled,
> Seems the sole work of a life-time
> That away the rest have trifled.

Especially do both poets apply this doctrine to the power of a great sin, a great hate, but above all a great love, to test and try the essential man or woman beneath the outward show. . . . It enters, of course, into far more poems of Browning than it does of Gordon; it is the great moral of *The Ring and the Book,* and is, as Mr. Chesterton says, 'the mainspring of a great part of his poetry taken as a whole.' It is the central idea of "The Statue and the Bust", where a crime frustrated by cowardice brings the touchstone to two lives. Even where the poets part company,—Browning voicing 'the utterances of so many imaginary souls—not mine', Gordon delivering over with mournful iteration the sad tale of his own heart,—Gordon carries the master's 'great lesson' with him. The keen psychological analysis and construction, which marks the 'Men and Women' of Browning's books, and makes them live their lives, and love their loves, and hate their hates as real men and women do, is visible no less in Gordon, though it is *himself* that he analyses so relentlessly and often, and which makes his own life-tragedy, which culminated at Brighton Beach, the unforgettable memory which his book leaves with us.

It is just at this point that they part irrevocably. The one takes the 'high road' to the hills of hope, where the sunlight falls and the breezes play, and the other takes the 'low road' that ends in disillusionment and despair. Had Gordon learned but one more lesson from the great Teacher at whose feet he had so often sat, there would have been no suicide at Brighton Beach; and the whole tone of the immediately succeeding generation of Australian poets might have been different. As it is, Gordon, who has left his impress so deeply on men like A. B. Paterson, Henry Lawson, John Farrell, Edward Dyson, Barcroft Boake, and others of what are known in Australia as the *Bulletin* bards, seems to have begun a wail of pessimism, cynicism, and hopelessness whose echoes have not yet ceased to vibrate. In Gordon's impatience of restraint, and that settled melancholy of his, he has close affinity with Edgar Allan Poe, for whom life seems too to have had no passive side, but was only the 'fever called living'; but the melancholy of Gordon was more obtrusive and less subdued than that of Poe. Gordon, least of all poets, succeeds in burying his identity. This characteristic melancholy is seldom absent, and, where it appears, it gives a tone to the whole poem. Often it deepens into a fierce despair, and an utter recklessness that seems to overcome his better nature:

> And where there's little left to hope,
> There's little left to dread.

And again:

> Why should he labour to help his neighbour,
> Who feels too reckless to help himself?

And the often quoted lines:

I should live the same life over, if I had to live again;
And the chances are I go where most men go.

Both Browning and Gordon have much in common even of character. The brave spirit that 'held we fall to rise, are baffled to fight better, sleep to wake', who wrote "Pippa's Song" and "Prospice", was not braver than he who wrote **"Gone"** and **"Thick-headed Thoughts"**; but Browning believed in the good of life, and Gordon doubted. The very 'heart's heart' of the faith of Browning is that 'all we have willed or hoped or dreamed of good shall exist; not its semblance but itself'; and though

On earth the broken arcs; in the heaven, a perfect round.

Now and then amid the din and heart-break of his life-struggle, the Australian poet comes face to face with Browning's optimism, and at times he almost believes it:

Yet if all things change to the glory of One
Who for all ill-doers gave His own sweet Son,
To His goodness so shall he change ill,
When the world as a wither'd leaf shall be,
And the sky like a shrivell'd scroll shall flee,
And the souls shall be summon'd from land and sea,
At the blast of His bright archangel.

as in **"The Rhyme of Joyous Garde".** But doubt presses hard on the heels of hope. No poet has ever portrayed more fearlessly the workings of fate and the force of evil than Browning has done, but he always believes that there is a path from the deepest depth to the highest height; and when he has looked life's worst and ugliest facts in the face as in the ghastly realism of the first scene of *Pippa Passes,* he still comes back to the strong conviction of a goodness that must be triumphant in the end, for

God's in his heaven—
All's right with the world!

Gordon tries to follow him, but it is with faltering feet and uncertain purpose, and sometimes with blank misgivings. Kismet and Circumstances are his final philosophy of life.

Things were to have been, and therefore
They were, and they are to be,

is Gordon's reading of "The Potter and the Clay"; Browning's is

Look not thou down but up!
To uses of a cup.

The last thing that Gordon has to say is,—

We have had our share of strife,
Tumblers in the mask of life,
In the pantomime of noon
Clown and pantaloon.

Let it not be quite our last quotation. Let us, however artistically inadmissible it may be to breathe, no matter how faintly, through the silver clarions of hope in an essay on Gordon, end rather with the closing prayer of his own **"Road to Avernus"**:

The unclean has follow'd the undefiled,
And the ill *may* regain the good,
And the man *may* be even as the little child!
We are children lost in the wood—
Lord! lead us out of this tangled wild,
Where the wise and the prudent have been beguil'd,
And only the babes have stood.

(pp. cxiii-cxviii)

Frank Maldon Robb, "The Making of Gordon," in Poems of Adam Lindsay Gordon, *edited by Frank Maldon Robb, Oxford University Press, London, 1912, pp. lxxxii-cxxiv.*

A. G. STEPHENS (essay date 1933?)

[*A journalist and editor, Stephens was a prominent Australian literary critic of the late nineteenth and early twentieth centuries. He finds Gordon's poetry stylistically imitative and intellectually commonplace but successful in its depiction of subjects derived from Gordon's personal experience. In the absence of evidence to indicate when Stephens's remarks were written, this essay has been dated 1933, the year of his death.*]

Gordon's character is best learned by considering him not as an Australian, not as an Englishman, but as a Scottish Highlander; that is to say, as a Celt, whatever the circumstantial difference. Born without full physical health and steady balance of mind, his Celtic qualities and defects seemed excessive. Typically he was a chieftain of Celts: he had power of leadership and everywhere strove to lead. In the current of existence he was prevented from realizing his ideal of himself; living thwarted, he died baffled. His poetry shows his rare passages of success, his abiding sense of failure.

On the high path, Gordon's poetry is not poetical. Perhaps it holds only one stanza that should move a fit reader to tears—a stanza of **"Argemone,"** his last, most passionate reiteration of brooding grief. Poetical blood he had, the high heart and bounding pulse of youth, and a romantic brain like Byron's—another Gordon—yet not a poetical brain. His emotion was so self-centred that he could rarely generalize intensely.

Australian popularity of Gordon is naturally accounted. He adapts Scott and Aytoun and Lockhart, Byron and Macaulay, Swinburne and Tennyson, Whyte-Melville and the Brownings—with doubtless other writers of his epoch—and weaves their ideas, their measures, and sometimes their phrases, altered by his own mind and coloured by his experience, into poetry for people who have never known the sources of his poetry. From the adored Byron of his boyhood to the beloved Swinburne of his manhood, Gordon's work is imitative. So he becomes a translated classic of the Bush.

His poetry is intellectually obvious. Often crossed with a personal warp, commonplace wisdom is its typical woof. Everybody's wisdom makes Everyman's prophet. The world and the Bush hold many defeated people; Gordon preserves the reflective sorrow of his own defeat in Everyman's verses.

He has strong, melodious rhythms, and manages them well. The alliteration may be cloying; the beat is often monotonous; but primitive ears are greedy of linguistic sweets, primitive minds lean on a regular stress, love a succession of monotonous stanzas. For melody, Gordon's habit of remembering gave him models; and the Cheltenham clergyman's school left him with a marked sense of time, an appreciation of the caesura. For writing verses he was indeed well equipped; and, allowing for monotony, for excess, the sonority of some of his stanzas is captivating. Of free utterance, large harmony, he has little; but for melody we can say that he became a good pupil of Swinburne.

Then we reckon with Gordon himself, with his dash and his pluck, his sincerity, simplicity, his pride and modesty, his manliness and gentlemanliness, his sympathy with nature. These, past the grave, have built his memorial in literature. He wrote, as he rode, 'straight.' Mind and body he was a steeplechaser, reaching through obstacles the lofty image aspiring, the white post seen afar.

His small harvest of verses was gathered in three years preceding his death. Fitly enough, he wrote little during his period of Australian prosperity. Instead of rhyming, he hunts; instead of brooding, he enters Parliament. Only when ill fortune clouds his blue sky does he take his black pen. As his troubles increase, so his verses; and just when his talent seems developing to a rich fruitage he feels himself driven to suicide.

In the end we love him for transfusing life: his poetry is a man's heart beating. (pp. 45-7)

A. G. Stephens, "Writers and Their Work: Adam Lindsay Gordon," in his A. G. Stephens: His Life and Work, *edited by Vance Palmer, Robertson & Mullens Ltd., 1941, pp. 45-7.*

ARCHIE JAMES COOMBES (essay date 1938)

[*In the following excerpt, Coombes finds that while Australia inspired Gordon's imagination, it also hindered his intellectual development.*]

A certain English critic of the early nineties, moved by sundry fulsome panegyrics of Gordon's literary achievements, declared with some show of impatience that Gordon was "a third-rate English poet spoiled by residence in Australia." At the time this dictum fell like heresy upon devoted ears. Nevertheless, the judgment reveals a truth of critical insight. As a poet Gordon is far more frequently the Englishman in exile than the Australian. He is not inaccurately placed, in the world's standard, as a third-rate poet, even though he possessed and displayed some of the qualities which might have entitled him to rank more highly. His residence in Australia cannot be said to have rendered him wholly happy or successful. It gave him contact with spaciousness, freedom from convention, and scope for adventure of a kind; but in what might have proved more fruitful for his genius, it remained a desert. Culture, whether of books or of congenial intellectual companionship or of social intercourse, it was unable to provide. The public spirit of the times in which he lived was too engrossed with those material things inseparable from pioneering days in young colonies to react with any sympathy upon a poet's dreams. Life itself was a succession of makeshifts, in which beauty had no status. Cast into such conditions at the age of twenty, and remaining steeped in them till his death at thirty-seven, Gordon may be said to have been made and marred as a poet by residence in Australia.

It is idle to speculate upon what he might have produced had he never left England; but it seems reasonable to maintain that the impulse toward poetic expression, if not generated, was at least made urgent by his life in the colonies. As it had been with a score of others, so it was with him, that poetry was a sanctuary for his soul against the loneliness and the monotony of intellectual littleness in the existence he was compelled to lead. Australia thus drove him to exercise his fine natural endowment by denying him opportunities for adequate self-expression in other directions. But the tyranny of primitive conditions, while demanding bricks, withheld the straw. Australia in the sixties, particularly South Australia, could not nourish a poet of Gordon's temperament. He was starved of food for thought. Australia could aid him in few ways either in modes of thought or in objects upon which to think, and those are the missing rungs in Gordon's poetic ladder.

More than any other Australian poet Gordon endeavoured to make poetry the application of ideas to life. He exhibits insistent urge toward thought, but his mind lacks the discipline that a richer acquaintance with books and the influence of an intellectual atmosphere might have imparted. His theories end nowhere. There is endless interrogation about matters which in the end he decides are all for the best. His more serious mental exercises often become a pendulum-like swing between pairs of contrasted ideas which carry him in no way forward in a scheme of reasoning. His intensity could avail him little in his processes of thought; and his imagination, which was powerful enough to lend high value to ideas, could not achieve much with a dearth of inspiring ideas to work upon. The disparity between his imaginative power and his ability to reason was responsible to some extent for the sense of failure and despair everywhere in his verse. He felt as if he were shut in by a blank wall. He met it wherever he turned. He called it the enigma of life; but it was in the main the private and particular enigma of his own intellectual limitations. The sense of oppression from which he suffered was inwrought with the pangs of intellectual malnutrition. Australia made him a poet, but starved him of a poet's fare. His thoughts found nothing to sustain them in objective experience; and since imaginative reason was denied the endeavour "to raise a mortal to the skies," he fell back upon sentimentalisms "to draw an angel down." (pp. 56-8)

Archie James Coombes, "Adam Lindsay Gordon," in his Some Australian Poets, *1938. Reprint by Books for Libraries Press, 1970, pp. 40-58.*

P. I. O'LEARY (essay date 1944?)

[*O'Leary questions Gordon's reputation as the national poet of Australia while praising his descriptive ability and noting his influence on later Australian poets. In the absence of exact information regarding the date of O'Leary's commentary, this essay has been dated 1944, the year of his death.*]

There was a time when Adam Lindsay Gordon was regarded as being almost the very voice of Australian life, certainly of that part of Australian life more closely associated with the bush. In that voice, it was claimed, were notes expressive of a certain robust sense of freedom, of an air of recklessness and adventure, of a devil-may-care element not without either exhilaration or a formative influence on national characteristics. There has come a questioning of that voice, a doubt of its genuineness, for which we did not have to wait until today. It is said its ring is not metal-true.

It seems to me that in a certain haste to disown Gordon there is a likelihood of his being as greatly undermerited as he may be said to have been overmerited. But it may confidently be declared that Gordon never was the voice or even a voice of Australia. That he was so regarded may be laid to the charge of such uncritical, if industrious, masters of the zealous mistake as Douglas Sladen [see excerpt dated 1912], and others.

The fact is Gordon was the first, as he is the greatest, of the New Chums in Australian literature. He was, for all his love of the horse and the open, always an alien in these southern baronies of the sun. He took part in the life about him, either in town or bush, in the street as well as on the station, but he was not part of it. He was a figure removed even externally, and in much greater measure in thought and disposition.

The careful reader may find evidence of this in almost every poem written by Gordon in which there is more than a surface occupation with subjects that may justly be termed Australian. In no work of Gordon's may we more clearly see this than in **"The Sick Stockrider,"** which, fine ballad though it unquestionably is, is as sentimental a piece of theatrical poetics as Australian literature possesses.

Gordon did not know the stockrider of his day. He might ride with him, wheel the wild scrub-cattle with him, talk with him, but he never shared his outlook, his practical if direct philosophy, or the things of his heart; and, moving among such booted and spurred cattlemen, he lacked that imaginative sympathy that would have enabled him to know them better even than they knew themselves.

But, if Gordon gives us a picture sentimentalised and too Little-Nellish of his stockrider, how exact, admirable and truly poetical he is in his treatment of the scene and the surroundings in which Ned and his emotional mate passed their active days. That wonderful phrase-picture, so full of the beauty, the tang, the health and glow of an Australian forenoon, beginning

'Twas merry in the glowing morn, among the gleaming grass,

is as fine an achievement with pen and words as ever Lambert or Streeton have accomplished with brush and paint.

The best passages in Gordon's poetry are descriptive passages. This descriptive or pictorial quality, a great sense of movement and delight in action, and an obvious manliness are the three marks of that poetry—these, and a morbid, pessimistic strain springing from a fixed fatalism, not without pathological interest and constitutional in the poet whose self-destruction may be traced immediately to it.

Take that descriptive quality. How exquisite its expression is at its best in Gordon:

In the Spring, when the wattle-gold trembles
'Twixt shadow and shine,
And each dew-laden air-draught resembles
A long draught of wine.

Such a beautiful verse as that, and this, evoking memories in all who have had experience of the sound of cattle bells in the bush, are to be prized:

Hark! the bells on distant cattle
Waft across the range,
Through the golden-tufted wattle,
Music low and strange.

There can be no denial of the beauty and poetical effectiveness of those lines. No repetition of quotation can dull their loveliness. Even the false rhymes in the last verse quoted do not take from the charm of it.

And that sense of movement! What could be finer than this?:

Hard behind them in the timber, harder still across the heath,
Close beside them through the tea-tree scrub we dash'd;
And the golden-tinted fern leaves, how they rustled underneath
And the honeysuckle osiers, how they crash'd!

It may not be in such country as this flora indicates that the cattleman rides today. But the cattlemen whom Gordon knew rode across such country. The picture is true in every way.

It is here that we find the source of Gordon's popularity—a popularity that is still a considerable thing, though with some abatement. The subjects of which Gordon wrote in such poems as **"The Sick Stockrider," "How We Beat the Favourite," "From the Wreck,"** and many others, are precisely of that order of verse that makes an appeal to the greatest number. Reflective and highly imaginative poetry will never have many readers, comparatively. Its enjoyment and understanding are reserved for the few. The average reader of verse is attracted, and held, by such numbers as are easily understood. That reader will always prefer, says Moore to Mangan, not that the latter is so hard to understand, and Longfellow to Browning.

Gordon's poetry is almost as full of this direct and rousing appeal as is the poetry of Scott. In poetry of the order of which he wrote, it is a high, and, what is of more importance, a necessary virtue.

On the presence of this in Gordon's poetry was founded that primacy of popularity that he among Australian poets certainly had conceded to him in other years, if not today. The very titles ***Sea Spray and Smoke Drift, Bush Ballads and Galloping Rhymes*** ring with the meanings, the atmosphere, the stir and colour to be found in Gordon's poetry. These titles explain its popularity.

Not only did Gordon, in his ringing lines, in which hoof-beats and surf-wash may be heard by the inner ear, cast a potent spell for the reader who likes poetry strong and definite in outline and obvious in detail, but he was the inspirer and forerunner of those poets who, coming later, were to celebrate the horse in long lines and poetical gallopades, and to write our bush-ballads.

When we are in a mood to under-rate Gordon let us remember that his influence on Lawson and Paterson, to speak of no other writers, is a real and active leaven. The horses that rush past the reader in **"How We Beat the Favourite,"** gallop in many later rhymes by other poets, and strong and astonishingly fine pieces of scenically descriptive verse that we read in Gordon gave hints to succeeding writers in whose poems the unsuspecting reader would expect them least to show. (pp. 28-31)

There is much in Gordon's poetry that is unworthy of remembrance. There is a good deal of slap-dash writing which is only doggerel, of verse fabric which is downright fustian. But there are splendid lines and beautiful passages in his finest work. In his greatest single piece, **"Rhyme of Joyous Garde,"** he asserts his claim to be numbered among the poets. It is a claim that must be allowed.

Gordon is still regarded abroad, especially in England, as Australia's chief poet. He is not Australia's chief poet. In England he is also regarded by many as breathing the very spirit of our land. That is because Australian writers, their works if not their pomps, are as little known in England as in the land in which they lived and wrote—and write—their works.

The Laureate of the Centaurs, as Gordon has been called, has appealed to the Australian imagination, less because of the considerable body of true poetry to be extracted from his writings, than because of a certain romantic-tragic air that surrounds his name, and makes it something resembling a legend, and because of the place the horse has in his verses. (p. 32)

P. I. O'Leary, "Adam Lindsay Gordon," in his Bard in Bondage: Essays of P. I. O'Leary, *edited by Joseph O'Dwyer, The Hawthorn Press, 1954, pp. 28-32.*

JUDITH WRIGHT (essay date 1965)

[*Wright argues that the uncritical acceptance of Gordon's poetry has allowed its pervasive melancholy to "poison" the work of later Australian poets.*]

Gordon, though not much noticed in his lifetime, became phenomenally well known after his death, and that among all kinds of readers. This seldom happens to poets, whose audience is generally select and predictable; and certainly as a poet Gordon was no more than mediocre. For quality of writing, even minor versifiers like the later Roderic Quinn could equal and surpass him. Why did Gordon attract so mixed and enthusiastic an audience?

To begin with, like that of Byron (on whom he so much modelled himself) his fame was at least partly due to his personal characteristics. In England, he would scarcely have attracted much notice as a poet; in Australia, the fact that he was 'one of the Gordons', had been, in a manner never since clarified, a wild young man, had come to Australia and made himself a certain fame as a steeplechase rider (and a good rider could command the hearts of most men), and chose for poetic subjects not only classical and English themes, but Australian themes as well, went very far. His appeal was dual—with the 'backblockers' to whom both horses and ballads were dear, and with the snob element of the exiled English middle class groups who 'dearly loved a lord' or anyone with aristocratic connexions. (pp. 57-8)

It was, in fact, Gordon's bestriding of the two sides of the 'split' in Australian consciousness, between Australianism and Europeanism, that ensured his success. He became a kind of secondhand Byron, with modern overtones, a legend rather than a poet; but by glorifying the kind of life lived by the drover and stockrider, and by using the material with which his Australian period provided him, he did more to catch the atmosphere of a kind of life then at its zenith than had been done by any other Australian poet. (p. 58)

Just how 'original' was Gordon in his Australian verses? The most characteristically 'Australian' of them is probably **"The Sick Stockrider".** It is interesting to compare this with a bush song which appeared in *The Queenslanders' Colonial Camp Fire Song Book,* published in 1865, five years before the appearance of ***Bush Ballads and Galloping Rhymes*** (in which **"The Sick Stockrider"** was printed).

"The Sick Stockrider" is written in a Swinburnian metre of a trochaic eight-foot line followed by a five-foot; the ballad, "The Stockman's Last Bed" has a four-beat anapaestic line in a four-line verse, with a chorus of two similar lines. But for all the difference of their metres, the Gordon poem being in a then fashionable form (Browning used this kind of metre in "A Toccata of Galuppi's" and—though with divided lines—in "Soliloquy of the Spanish Cloister") and the ballad in a more traditional metre, there are certain elements common to both.

The first line in Gordon's poem:

> Hold hard, Ned! Lift me down once more, and lay me in the
> shade

may be compared with the chorus of the ballad:

> For we laid him where wattles their sweet fragrance shed
> And the tall gum-trees shadow the stockman's last bed,

and with its last two lines,

> Ride softly the creek-bed where trees make a shade,
> For perhaps it's the spot where poor Jack's bones are laid.

These lines, again, may be compared with the last verse of Gordon's poem:

> Let me slumber in the hollow where the wattle-blossoms wave
> With never stone or rail to fence my bed. . . .

There is also a possible comparison between Gordon's line

> With a running fire of stockwhips and a fiery run of hoofs

and the ballad's line

> The crack of his stockwhip, his steed's lively trot. . . .

All this may be no more than coincidence; but the mention of 'wattles' near both graves is perhaps more significant than it may seem. For neither balladists nor, on the whole, more academic early poets (with the exception of Barron Field) often mention Australian trees or wildflowers by name; the wattle occurs in scarcely any other ballads or poems written before the early 'sixties.

Even if the resemblances between the ballad and the poem are entirely accidental, each forms an interesting critique on the other. For though it is crude and simple enough, the ballad is (for once) not sentimental; it has a note of sincerity and mourning, and even in certain respects the tone of one of the early English ballads. Here is the first verse of one of the Robin Hood ballads ("A Little Geste for Robin Hood"):

> Lithe and listen, Gentlemen
> That be of free-born blood;
> I shall you tell of a good yeoman,
> His name was Robin Hood.

And the first verse of "The Stockman's Last Bed":

> Be ye stockman or no, to my story give ear,
> Alas for poor Jack, no more shall we hear
> The crack of his stockwhip, his steed's lively trot,
> His clear 'Go a-head, boys', his jingling quartpot.

In each there is the same direct and economical approach to the audience.

Gordon's poem is in the first person, making it more artificial in tone. The lengthy reminiscences of the 'sick stockrider' which follow are vivid enough, and there is even a legendary quality about some of the verses:

> In these hours when life is ebbing, how those days when life
> was young
> Come back to us; how clearly I recall
> Even the yarns Jack Hall invented, and the songs Jem Roper
> sung;
> And where are now Jem Roper and Jack Hall?

But when the poem leaves these direct reminiscences for the moralizing of the last few verses, the tone is one of sentimental cliché:

> I've had my share of pastime, and I've done my share of toil,
> And life is short—the longest life a span. . .

This is popular moralizing (the next verse is a well-known album-piece), and by the time the stockrider is directing the patient Ned on the location of his grave ('Let me slumber in the hollow where the wattle-blossoms wave') the temporary reality given by the reminiscences has evaporated. The poem has become a sentimental piece for recitation.

Poor Jack of the earlier ballad (who 'while drafting one day was horned by a cow, "Alas", cried poor Jack, "it's all up with me now"') is a figure with far more immediate reality, if less theatrical romance.

Indeed, Gordon wrote little that was truly original and stamped with reality; and sometimes he did some outrageously imitative verses. **"From the Wreck"**, for instance, is so close to its Browning original that it is practically an infringement of copyright.

But Gordon will always be forgiven his poetic sins for the sake of the legend of his life and for his place in the uncertain growth of Australian writing. Without his recognition of the kind of life that was lived in the outback, and the stamp of approval that was given it by his using it in his verse, it might have taken many years longer than in fact it did to establish certain facets of life here as potentially poetic material. After Gordon came the deluge of '*Bulletin* bards', as well as a renewed activity among lesser writers. Australia had begun to recognize itself.

One legacy, however, he left to Australian versifying which did it no good—a certain tendency to a negative despair. Gordon had, basically, brought his problems from England with him; they were bound up with his own life and temperament, and Australian conditions did nothing to help him solve them. The Byronic brooding, the melancholy, the rejection of the world that mark his verse are sentimental and shallowly based, perhaps, but they found a certain echo in the temperament of Australians. Moreover they led to certain effects on Australian writing, if not on the Australian psyche, whose sources need to be recognized. (pp. 58-61)

The story of Gordon's life and death is well known, and that it should have been elevated into the realms of romance is easy enough to understand. But the story is not essentially or typically Australian, just as Gordon is not a typically Australian writer. The poems with an Australian background are few, and there is reason to think that Gordon did not consider them his best; he did not think highly of **"The Sick Stockrider"** for instance. He may have had a higher opinion of his "fashionable" themes, and of the poems written under the influence of Byron and of Swinburne, such as ***Ashtaroth*** and **"Bellona"**; but his weaknesses and crudities of sense and thought show up more clearly in these than in the less ambitious action-and-narrative poems that have made his reputation.

Action, in fact, was a necessity for Gordon. Left to brood and philosophize, he sank into self-pity and a kind of cynicism that sprang more from personal frustration and bitterness than from any depth of thought or feeling. It is hard to tell, at times, how much this cynicism owed to Gordon's habit of striking attitudes and how much to his own personality. At any rate, it is of quite a different nature from the irony of the 'backblockers' and the bush singers, his predecessors in the bush ballad. More realistic and direct, the sardonic note of the bush singers derives more from circumstances than from the mood of the singer; its conditions are particular, not generalized. It has been loosely called cynicism; but cynicism is darker and emptier than this. Cynicism is rather to be found in verses like these of Gordon:

> Though our future lot is a sable blot,
> Though the wise ones of earth will blame us,
> Though our saddles will rot and our rides be forgot,
>   DUM VIVIMUS, VIVAMUS!

(p. 62)

This kind of swaggering emptiness—the emptiness that precedes insanity or suicide—represented in Australia the kind of moral impasse that was then facing the consciousness of Europe, in the person of Nietzsche. It was not different in kind, but it was very different in degree. Gordon had not arrived at it through an intellectual awareness of the 'death of God', as Nietzsche had; but it nevertheless permeated his being, and left its poison in his verse. The voice was the voice of Gordon, but the words were the words of Europe's own despair.

And Gordon's restless need for action and physical occupation, which is also reflected in his poetry, was symptomatic of the same disease. Kipling, with his idolization of violence and authority, machines and armies, his barrack room ballads and his invocation of the God of Battles, is fundamentally as empty of faith as Gordon, but his despair was translated into a worship of violence. Gordon, less capable of self-deceit and more lacking in resources, turned the violence on himself.

But the fundamental hollowness of his outlook and the darkness at the core of his verse found a certain echo in later Australian writing. . . . Gordon's 'sickness was his soul' (to quote the words of another English pessimist) and when he 'played the man' and ended himself, it meant more than that he had merely been unable to pay his financial debts. He had also been unable to pay spiritual debts that were far more pressing. The sting of this he left behind him, poisoning his verse; and traces of the same poison can be found in the work of some writers who admired and followed him, in his own generation and the next. (pp. 62-3)

[Most] of the backblock balladists who admired and recited Gordon's verses were too realistic—and too hard-worked—to take his point of view on life very seriously. But there was, nevertheless, a kind of Gordon cult here and there, among the lonely and semi-educated young men of the outback; a cult of hopelessness and a certain Gordonian melodrama and self-pity. His swinging rhythms, his fake-masculine recklessness and flamboyance that lapsed into mournful sentimentality, appealed to young men leading a lonely and deprived life in the bush, as did the cult of horsemanship and action in which Gordon was an obvious leader.

So there was a price to pay for uncritical devotion to Gordon. (p. 63)

Judith Wright, "Adam Lindsay Gordon and Barcroft Boake," in her Preoccupations in Australian Poetry, *Oxford University Press, Melbourne, 1965, pp. 57-67.*

C. F. MacRAE (essay date 1968)

[MacRae traces the expression of love, sorrow, and joy throughout Gordon's poetry.]

Romantic love played a relatively small part in the life of Adam Lindsay Gordon. The one powerful attachment of his early days came to nothing. Then he went to Australia, where he flirted occasionally and married once. The flirtations, with one possible exception, were not serious, and the marriage was not passionate. One would expect, therefore, little love-poetry in the ordinary sense. That is, one would expect little of the kind of love-poetry that seems to arise out of the writer's own deeply felt experience, such as Arnold's "Marguerite" poems are generally judged to be. Three poems make up Gordon's whole tale, and one of those is doubtful to the last degree.

The one clear example is in the poem **"To My Sister,"** written just before he sailed from England. Three stanzas, twenty-four lines, are devoted to his lost love. They begin:

I loved a girl not long ago,
And, till my suit was told,
I thought her breast as fair as snow,
'Twas very near as cold;

and they end:

But absent friends are soon forgot,
And in a year or less
'Twill doubtless be another's lot
Those very lips to press!

The whole passage is a straightforward statement of what had happened in his last interview with Jane Bridges, in smooth and competent verse, but it is not highly poetical. The passage includes a declaration that "Those words I never spoke before, / Nor ever shall again." This is the conventional feeling of the newly rebuffed lover, seldom to be taken seriously. Gordon meant them more seriously than most, as it turned out. When he came to marry, years later, he disclaimed all "romantic nonsense."

"Whisperings in Wattle-Boughs," published in ***Sea Spray and Smoke Drift,*** contains a stanza (the fifth) which looks like an oblique reference to his early love. The second, third, and fourth stanzas are addressed respectively to "father mine," "sister dear," and "ancient friend." The fifth follows:

Oh, whisper buried love, is there rest and peace above?—
There is little hope or comfort here below;—
On your sweet face lies the mould, and your bed is strait
and cold—
Near the harbour where the sea-tides ebb and flow.

The image is false to the fact, since Jane Bridges outlived Gordon, but in view of its placing in the pattern of the poem we are led to assume that it is derived from the memory of his early, unlucky love. The important consideration is the change in mood which the change in fact reveals. The cold, rejecting "belle dame sans merci" is replaced by the sympathetic pathos of the dead sweetheart.

The third and dubious instance is **"Thora's Song"** from ***Ashtaroth,*** reprinted separately in ***Bush Ballads and Galloping Rhymes.*** Ostensibly, this has nothing to do with Jane, or with Gordon either. It is dramatic, and entirely within the story. It is the lament of a woman, not of a man. The opening line, "We severed in autumn early" may be mere coincidence; and anyway Gordon's farewell interview with Jane was about the beginning of August, which is hardly in the autumn. Despite all this, we may justly think that the roots of the poem are in the emotions of Gordon's past, with its experience of separation and of coming "not back again."

One other poem has to do with love, directly, but love significantly takes a second place in it. The opening piece of ***Sea Spray and Smoke Drift*** is **"Podas Okus,"** a monologue spoken by Achilles on his deathbed, to Briseis. The opening is "Am I waking? Was I sleeping? / Dearest, are you watching yet?" But it is quickly clear that Achilles is not thinking much about Briseis, but about his former comrades-in-arms, about his glory, about how "None can baffle Jove's decree," and about the multiform "doom" that brought about and surrounded the Trojan war. The ending of the poem suggests the balance of Achilles' emotions:

Lightly lay your red lips, kissing,
On this cold mouth, while your thumbs
Lie on these cold eyelids pressing—
Pallas
thus thy soldier comes.

At the climax, it is not Briseis that fills Achilles' mind and his emotions, but Pallas and his own soldiership. It hardly needs to be added that this was characteristic of Gordon's own makeup.

Apart from these lyric, or semi-lyric, expressions of romantic love, the theme finds little place in Gordon's verse. What there is, is almost entirely conventional, if not commonplace. Hugo, in ***Ashtaroth,*** is torn for a time by an illicit passion for Agatha, but that passion (which also comes to nothing) is a minor theme. ***The Feud,*** earlier, contains love as well as avarice and fighting, but the story is drawn from a well-known source and Gordon adds little to it except for some small expansion of detail. In **"The Rhyme of Joyous Garde"** the thoughts of the aging Lancelot are as much with Arthur and Arthur's enemies as they are with Guinevere. Moreover, it was not Gordon's love-poetry that his earliest public responded to. It was quite other emotions and other experiences which, wedded to verse probably not quite immortal, won Gordon his unique following among Australian readers, and those overseas.

It is not the joy of love, but the sorrow of love that Gordon expresses. The joy of love he seems not to have experienced, and he made no attempt to deal with it. He had experienced the loss of love, though in an adolescent fashion, and that was what he kept to.

When we come to the second form of love, which might be called, for short, "fraternal love," the case is different. We would not expect much love for his family to appear in the poetry. He left home before he was twenty; he never returned, and, so far as is now known, was never in effective communication with his family again. He felt that he had disgraced them, and that they had fallen short in their sympathy with him. Of these two feelings, the first appears to have been the stronger. Whatever he may have felt, he did not show resentment, except by one hint, in **"Early Adieux":**

My mother is a stately dame,
Who oft would chide with me;
She saith my riot bringeth shame,
And stains my pedigree.

There seems to be a touch of irony in these lines, but nothing more.

Family feeling does come to light in several places. These have mainly to do with his father, and reflect darkly happy memories. The Third Fytte of **"Ye Wearie Wayfarer"** opens with a memory of "some words my father said." The clear expression of this feeling is in the second stanza of **"Whisperings in Wattle-Boughs":**

Oh, tell me, father mine, ere the good ship cross'd the brine,
On the gangway one mute hand-grip we exchang'd,
Do you, past the grave, employ, for your stubborn, reckless
boy,
Those petitions that in life were ne'er estrang'd?

These lines reveal, at the least, how Gordon came to regard his father in later years, when time had mellowed his memories. It is to be noted, too, that in the three poems of exile, **"To My Sister," "An Exile's Farewell,"** and **"Early Adieux"** (two of them certainly and the third presumably early verses written at the time of his migration), Gordon's father is not mentioned at all—except as he is included by the word "parents." Interpretation here is altogether conjectural, but the soundest guess would seem to be that Gordon's memory of his father was, at this time, sharp and painful. His mother had disapproved of him, but he had not minded that much. She had shut herself out of his world, and if she was grieved by his behavior, that was her problem. But he did feel differently about his father, and the sense of having let his father down was one which he could not then bear to think about. It was only years later that he was able to let his feeling for his father come to light, and find an expression in his poetry.

It was neither his family nor his sweetheart(s) that aroused the expressions of human love to be found in his best-remembered poetry. It was the friend and the co-worker for whom these expressions were reserved. The most significant document here is not **"The Sick Stockrider,"** but **"The Rhyme of Joyous Garde."** The story behind the poem is the familiar Arthurian legend of illicit passion, which brought to an end the fair, best hope of the Arthurian kingdom. In *The Idylls of the King*, this is where Tennyson places the emphasis. The affair, the scandal, is a slow staining spreading outward, creating cynicism, puzzlement, and finally indifference and contempt toward knightly vows. William Morris puts the emphasis on love, interpreted as real love between Lancelot and Guinevere—a love tragically rendered illegitimate by the accident of a loveless marriage. Gordon's emphasis is different from either.

"The Rhyme of Joyous Garde" begins with two stanzas of descriptive introduction. Then, following a transitional stanza beginning "For the days recall what the nights efface," the fourth stanza reads:

> Would God I had died the death that day
> When the bishop blessed us before the fray
> At the shrine of the Saviour's Mother;
> We buckled the spur, we braced the belt,
> Arthur and I—together we knelt,
> And the grasp of his kingly hand I felt
> As the grasp of an only brother.

This is the governing mood of the poem. The sense of guilt is strong, and is emphasized by the climax of the last six stanzas. But the main tenor of the poem is not that of sin against God or of sin against society, but of the sin against Arthur. It is a sin against friendship. He had loved Arthur, and he had betrayed him. This is established in the fourth stanza. It does not need to be reiterated, and it is not. A few touches, scattered through the poem, give it all the emphasis it needs. Two lines in the twenty-sixth stanza will serve as an example: "And the once loved knight, was he there to save / That knightly king who that knighthood gave?" The point of these lines, when they are read in the context of the whole poem, is not the hierarchical relationship of king to knight, but the relationship of knight to knight, one of them being the king.

The emotion of the poem is a sorrowful one, of love betrayed. But the love is not that of man and woman; it is the love of man and man. It is the love of two men engaged together in a common life, with common aims, who had shared experiences of life-and-death struggles. And this emotion is achieved without undervaluing the other. The passion of Lancelot's love for Guinevere is included.

> When I well-nigh swoon'd in the deep drawn bliss,
> Of that first long, sweet, slow, stolen kiss,
> I would gladly have given for less than this
> Myself, with my soul's salvation.

What is more, theoretic love is not pictured as mere physical passion.

> I would languish thus in some loathsome den,
> As a thing of naught in the eyes of men,
> In the mouths of men as a by-word,
> Through years of pain, and when God saw fit,
> Singing His praises my soul should flit
> To the darkest depth of the nethermost pit,
> If *hers* could be wafted skyward.

The love for Guinevere was real love, the love which seeks the welfare of the beloved at any cost. But in the full context of the poem, Lancelot's love for Guinevere seems an incident—not a trivial incident (quite the contrary) but essentially an incident nonetheless. It is the relationship between Lancelot and Arthur that strikes home to us.

"The Sick Stockrider" shows one similarity to **"The Rhyme of Joyous Garde."** The same emotion of friendship is established at the opening of the poem, and is maintained only by oblique hints through the rest of it. The apostrophe of the first four lines,

> Hold hard, Ned! Lift me down once more, and lay me in the shade.
> Old man, you've had your work cut out to guide
> Both horses, and to hold me in the saddle when I sway'd,
> All through the hot, slow, sleepy, silent ride.

sets an emotional pattern. It is made implicitly clear at the beginning, and it becomes explicit a little later in the poem, that "Ned" is no chance Good Samaritan. He has had a close, long-standing relationship with the speaker. In fact, this is "mate-ship," but that is another matter. Ned and the speaker have, like Arthur and Lancelot, been through much together. The "we" that appears and reappears ("We led the hunt throughout, Ned," for example) tells us that, and suggests even more than it tells. Ned has been engaged in an office of friendship, trying to get his sick friend home. At least, we suppose he is trying to get him home; the destination of the ride is artistically left to the imagination, but the lines "Five miles we used to call it from our homestead to the place / Where the big tree spans the roadway like an arch;" give us a sufficient hint.

There are two opposed but complementary emotions in the poem. One is the remembered joy of old accomplishment and old friendship. All this belongs to the past, but it is heart-lifting to remember. The emotion of sorrow, it is important to note, also belongs to the past. The stockrider is not feeling sorry for himself, except in the fact that almost all his old friends are gone. It is the death of other men, not his own, that affects him. The two feelings, of joy and of sorrow, come together in the lines:

> In these hours when life is ebbing, how those days when life was young
> Come back to us; how clearly I recall
> Even the yarns Jack Hall invented, and the songs Jem Roper sung;
> And where are now Jem Roper and Jack Hall?

When the poem is seen in this light, the final sixteen lines appear as a coda. The four lines beginning "I've had my share of pastime, and I've done my share of toil" make a transition, and a skillful transition. Then follows the conclusion, with its acceptance of both life and death, ending in the funerary instructions and the memorable image of the grave.

Another poem with the double image of the joys and the sorrows of friendship, and with the sorrow more than ever predominating, is **"Sunlight on the Sea,"** subtitled "The Philosophy of a Feast." It begins in a joyful mood: "Make merry, comrades, eat and drink / (The sunlight flickers on the sea)." The end of the first stanza sums up the positive aspect of the scene.

> I see you feasting round me still,
> All gay of heart and strong of limb;
> Make merry, friends, your glasses fill,
> The lights are growing dim.

The very next line brings in the mournful side, with "I miss the voice of one I've heard." From here on there is maintained the contrast between the pleasure of the feast, and the thought of those who are absent or dead. The whole poem is a polarity of joy and sorrow, but the joy is slightly artificial. The reality of fellowship is in its loss, and the final line of each stanza is "The lights are growing dim." This line is a refrain, and its sense changes as the poem goes on. At the end of the first stanza it seems to mean: the toil and danger of the day are now over and as the light wanes we can relax and enjoy our ease. In the intervening stanzas it takes an increasingly darker meaning. The dimming lights are a symbol of death, and of the number of the dead (or absent) which increases as time goes on. At the close, it has a cosmic significance. Death closes all, for every man and even, perhaps, for the world itself.

The important feature of **"Sunlight on the Sea"** is the essential nobility of the poem. What it says is not "eat, drink, and be merry, for tomorrow we die," but rather "eat, drink, and be merry, although tomorrow we may die." It is the spirit of Stevenson's *Aes Triplex,* though in a more limited form. This is underlined by the sixth stanza, with its image of the Spartan soldiers feasting undismayed before Thermopylae.

An entirely different poem is the one called **"Laudamus,"** the final piece in ***Bush Ballads and Galloping Rhymes*** as it first appeared. This is a poem of hate, rather than of love, although it is hate that is ending and in the process of turning into reconciliation. Two men have loved one woman. The speaker addresses his rival as "Brother," which may mean one of two things. Either the rivals were brothers by blood, or they were former friends whose friendship was broken and turned to hatred by their rivalry for the woman. In any case, the woman has died, the reason for their hatred is gone. The sense of the title is clarified in the fourth stanza:

> Let us thank the Lord for His bounties all,
> For the brave old days of pleasure and pain,
> When the world for both of us seem'd too small—
> Though the love was void and the hate was vain—

The "pleasure and pain" duality is made explicit, and here for once the joy, at least potentially, over-crowds the sorrow. The reconciliation which the poem implies is felt as permanent. It will go even beyond the grave. The poem ends:

> We shall meet my friends, in the spirit land—
> Will our strife renew? Nay, I dare not trust,
> For the grim, great gulf that cannot be spann'd
> Will divide us from her. The Lord is just,
> She shall not be thrust where our spirits stand.

For the most part, though, Gordon accepts the proposition that love of our fellowmen (as distinguished from love of our fellowman) entails more of sadness than of joy. The joy is temporary and the sorrow is inevitable. Friendships, no matter how warm, are made to be broken, either by betrayal as in **"The Rhyme of Joyous Garde"** or by death as in **"The Sick Stockrider."** And yet, Gordon succeeds very nearly in keeping a balance between the two emotions of joy and sorrow. The love and fellowship of man with other men is not only a real joy while it lasts, but when it has ended it does not cease to exist. The past, because it is the past, is unchangeable. It is real and it remains. This is the point, or one of the points, of the sick stockrider's reminiscences. The joys of the past adventures which the two men have shared are a part of the pattern of their lives, which is permanent. Death completes the pattern, and by adding to it alters it, but it does not destroy the good things that have already been woven into it.

The third species of love is the love of external nature, of landscape and of trees and flowers. It is peculiarly prominent in the poetry of the "colonies" during the nineteenth century, and especially so in Canada, where is produced the "Maple Leaf School" in the 1880's and 1890's. Gordon's treatment, or lack of treatment, of nature is one of the counts made against him in the indictment for not being sufficiently "Australian." He aroused indignation by writing in **"A Dedication"** to ***Bush Ballads and Galloping Rhymes*** of "lands where bright blossoms are scentless, / And songless bright birds." Yet one supposes that the lines are literally true. The writer cannot answer for the bright flowers, being somewhat deficient in the sense of smell. Nor has he any skill as a bird-watcher, or bird-listener. But he does feel sure that the kookaburra (though perhaps not bright enough to qualify as evidence) has not much of a song. The fact remains, nevertheless, that there has existed a feeling that Gordon did not do right by the landscape of his adopted country.

There are several reasons for this. The first is that Gordon was not a landscape poet, in any sense. He was a poet of human activity and human thoughts and feelings. The landscape was never anything but setting and background, where needed, to a scene or story of activity. Such primarily descriptive passages as Harpur or Kendall wrote (or, in Canada, Lampman or Roberts or Campbell) were simply not among his interests. Secondly, much of his material was drawn unashamedly from England and from the past. Even **"How We Beat the Favourite,"** one of his most popular poems among Australians, is set in the English Cotswolds. And the stories that he drew from a distant past, such as **"The Romance of Britomarte,"** necessitated a setting far from Australia. Australia, in that sense, had no past. Thirdly, he was extremely nearsighted, and could not possibly be aware of the landscape except in a general, and blurred, fashion. Last, and least, it is true that to some extent landscape is landscape all over the world. It is a matter of experience that the Canadian who travels to England will see many scenes which, although they have the flavor of England, remind him also of some stretch of country which he has seen in his own homeland. (pp. 83-92)

It is true that in Gordon's poetry there are no wallabies and not much wattle. We are not bombarded with dingoes, wombats, saltbush, malee scrub, nor even gum-trees. If he regarded the kangaroo as the "spirit of Australia" he gives no sign of it. This does not matter much. These are details such as any tourist might put into a travelogue.

No; the real charge against Gordon in this regard is that he does not render the tone, the "feel," of the Australian landscape. That tone is fundamentally different from the landscape of England. The color is different. Even Gordon's limited vision might be presumed to be aware of that. The Australian trees, especially when seen in a mass, are nearer to blue-gray than to the bright green of England. And there is the loneliness of the countryside. Even today, the visitor from North America is struck by the comparative isolation of the Australian stations, different from the farm-lined roads of Ontario or New England. To a man coming from England more than a century ago the contrast should have been even more striking. The distances from one center of population to another, and the roughness of the country between, ought to have been noticeable, if not awe-inspiring, to one who had been used to the tidy, cosy humanity of the countryside in the English shires. There is almost no recognition of this in Gordon, except for a touch of it, but an obscure touch, in **"The Sick Stockrider."**

One further explanation stands out. Of all the various aspects and forms of nature, the one which most attracted Gordon, at least in his maturer years, was the sea—and the sea is pretty much the same everywhere, especially when we remember that he never saw the beaches of New South Wales or Queensland.

But what difference does all this make? The fact is that he took relatively little interest in landscape. It was not his *métier*. And who is to say that it ought to have been? We do not blame a dentist for not removing tonsils, nor a surgeon for not filling teeth.

Though there was little of the Romantic love of natural scenery in Gordon, it was not entirely absent. It was in his life, and in his poetry, though subordinate and subdued. He seems to have had a strong affection for the rural setting of the cottage at Dingley Dell, even though, as it turned out, he did not live there for long. In his poetry, he opens the **"Dedication"** to ***Bush Ballads and Galloping Rhymes*** with forty-eight lines of which forty-seven are on this theme.

Whence gather'd?—The locust's glad chirrup
  May furnish a stave;
The ring of a rowel and stirrup,
  The wash of a wave,
The chaunt of the marsh frog in rushes,
That chimes through the pauses and hushes
Of nightfall, the torrent that gushes,
  The tempests that rave.

The third line of this stanza is the only break in the catalogue of natural beauty. The culmination is in the sixth stanza, one of the oftenest quoted of his verses.

In the Spring, when the wattle gold trembles
  'Twixt shadow and shine,
When each dew-laden air draught resembles
  A long draught of wine;
When the sky-line's blue burnish'd resistance
Makes deeper the dreamiest distance,
Some song in all hearts hath existence,—
  Such songs have been mine.

The stanza just cited calls for two comments. The first is that in the passage which it concludes Gordon does come unusually close to giving us the feel of the Australian landscape. Besides the "wattle gold" and the "dreamiest distance," and setting aside the songless birds and the scentless flowers, we have "Insatiable Summer," "sere woodlands," "sad wildernesses," "faint flocks and herds," "dry deserts," and "trunks Eucalyptian." It is a respectable catalogue. The second comment is that if Gordon had ended the poem at the end of the sixth stanza, it would have been misleading. The reader would have been entitled to object, and to retort, "Such songs have *not* been yours." The next poem in the volume was **"The Sick Stockrider,"** in which natural scenery plays a part, but a different part and a subordinate part. Then, following **"The Swimmer,"** which is in part a nature-poem, we have **"From the Wreck,"** which contains but hardly features the landscape, **"No Name," "Wolf and Hound," "De Te,"** and **"How We Beat the Favourite,"** which last is not Australian at all, except in spirit. Of the remaining poems in the book not one has to do with Australian scenery, with the possible and insignificant exception of **"A Song of Autumn."** Indeed, **"Doubtful Dreams"** begins "Aye, snows are rife in December, / And sheaves are in August yet." Not in Australia they aren't!

Now a distinction has to be made. Gordon was an outdoor man and his poetry is outdoor poetry. But there is a difference between an outdoor man and an outdoor poet. The outdoor poet, in this sense of the term, loves the countryside in a way which impels him to observe it closely and describe it attentively, often in photographic detail. Gordon, in his poetry at all events, did not love the countryside in that way. He loved *being* in the countryside; he loved the experience of the open air. The difference is subtle but important.

There is one exception. The sea did come to exercise a power over him, which appears in his poetry, especially in **"The Song of the Surf."** The first two stanzas, beginning:

White steeds of ocean, that leap with a hollow and wearisome roar
On the bar of ironstone steep, not a fathom's length from the shore

is true landscape—or, rather, seascape—poetry. The remaining two stanzas introduce the image of a drowned corpse, and a rebuke to foolish mortals:

Think'st thou the wave that shatters questioneth His decree?
Little to us it matters, and naught it matters to thee.

"The Swimmer" is in the same category. It begins with three stanzas of descriptive matter, which ends:

And the sunset bath'd in the gulf to lend her
A garland of pinks and of purples tender,
A tingle of the sun-god's rosy splendour,
  A tithe of his glories manifold.

The fourth stanza begins:

Man's works are graven, cunning, and skilful
  On earth, where his tabernacles are;
But the sea is wanton, the sea is wilful,
  And who shall mend her and who shall mar?

It continues in this vein through eight stanzas, and closes with two stanzas of pure description, returning at the close to the mood in which it began.

Undeniably Gordon both felt and communicated an emotional response to nature. But it was a qualified response and a balanced response. There was joy in it, and also something corresponding to sorrow. That is, there was the recognition that nature was not all sunshine and gladness. He had none of that trust in nature that the early Wordsworth had before his brother was drowned at sea. Gordon is nearer to Byron.

One further point remains. There was an aspect of nature toward which his response was singleminded. He loved horses, though, but since the horses were sooner or later trained and domesticated by man, they were not wholly a part of nature. Horses were his great love throughout his life:

Yet if man, of all the Creator plann'd,
  His noblest work is reckoned,
Of the works of His hand, by sea or by land,
  The horse may at least rank second.

So he wrote in the First Part of **"Hippodromania."** This emotion was one which never left him. It is reflected throughout the racing poems, but finds its most striking expression in **"The Roll of the Kettledrum; or, The Lay of the Last Charger."** In this poem it is the horse who is the speaker. He recalls to mind the part he played in the Charge of the Light Brigade. Then his mind is engaged by the figure of the old Colonel, who is lonely, so lonely that as he finally turns away his last words are, "Would to God I had died with your master, old man!" Gordon attributes to the horse a lively sympathy with man and man's sorrows, and rationalizes the attribution:

The wide gulf that parts us may yet be no wider
  Than that which parts you from some being more blest;
And there may be more links 'twixt the horse and his rider
  That ever your shallow philosophy guess'd.

Emotion is also attached, sometimes, to abstract ideas and ideals. Patriotism is the most common of these, and it is absent from Gordon's poetry. Australians in his day and for a good while thereafter were not particularly patriotic. (pp. 92-6)

[Gordon's] patriotism was concrete, not abstract. The reference in Fytte VIII of **"Ye Wearie Wayfarer"** to "the chimes of sweet St. Mary's / On far English ground" gives us a rare look into feelings for his early homeland which he normally concealed or seldom allowed himself to feel. The feelings were for the sights and sounds of the country, not for its flag or its political arrangements.

Nor did he show any enthusiasm for such concepts as liberty or equality. He had all the liberty he needed, and as a policeman his concern had been for law and order. He had enough sense to realize that liberty is impossible without law and order, but he made no point of it. (p. 97)

The ideals of courage and kindliness aroused a response in his poetry, even as abstractions, but poetry cannot be made out of abstractions. When he said that "kindness" and "courage" are things that "stand like stone," he had gone as far as the abstractions would take him.

The concrete images of courage that went into his poetry were a different matter. They were a part of his main emotional response, what we have called the "love of life." It was really a love of one side of life only, the muscular side which belonged to the out-of-doors and "God's glorious oxygen." Like the other positive emotions, it involves both joy and sorrow—joy when the emotion brings fulfillment and sorrow when it is faced with loss or frustration.

Both sides are present in **"The Roll of the Kettledrum."** The poem is a highly charged emotional presentation of contrasting themes of life and death. The emotion of life, the thrill of being alive, is heightened by the presence of death, which is heightened in turn in two ways. The death that threatens is dramatic. It is not mere death, but death by violence; it is not mere death by violence, but death in battle. The battle is the most dramatic kind of battle. It is a cavalry charge, for one thing, and for another, to the reader who recognizes the connotations of the story, it is a charge against hopeless odds. These are fighters who, like Cyrano de Bergerac, do not fight always to win. It is the spice of danger that gives life its value.

The last line of the twenty-first stanza, which ends the first half of the poem, is the significant one: "He was never more happy in life than in death." This is the opinion of the "last charger," but there is no doubt that Gordon meant this, and meant us to feel that his hero was happy in his death because he had been happy in life, that he had taken all his risks gladly, and that he had "died game" and therefore died well.

The line is glossed by a passage near the end of Fytte II of **"Ye Wearie Wayfarer":**

I remember the laugh that all the while
  On his quiet features played:—
So he rode to his death, with that careless smile,
  In the van of the "Light Brigade;"

So stricken by Russian grape, the cheer
  Rang out, while he toppled back,
From the shattered lungs as merry and clear
  As it did when it roused the pack.

The negative side of this emotion makes the theme of the second half of the poem. The old colonel envies the early death of Nolan. The colonel also has loved life in all its aspects, and has lost it through the passage of time. Age has enfeebled his body and has robbed him of his family by death or disgrace. Taking the poem as a whole, we have to admit that the emphasis is on this negative side, for three reasons. First, the second half of the poem is longer than the first, by twenty-nine stanzas to twenty-one. Secondly, the final climax of the poem is the colonel's regret for not having died young. Thirdly, the title of the poem refers to the poem's ending rather than to the battle scene; the roll of the kettledrum in the last stanza is an accompaniment to the colonel's final speech.

This duality, and this balance, of emotion runs right through Gordon's poetry, with one apparent exception. The joy of life goes along with the acceptance of death and the risk of death. When death crowns life with honor, it is to be embraced. When life goes on too long, the joy of living is replaced by the sorrow of outliving what has made life worthwhile. The exception is **"The Sick Stockrider,"** who, unlike the colonel in **"The Roll of the Kettledrum,"** is able to rejoice in the thought of the activities and friendships of the past. Elsewhere, the emotional pattern is adjusted to this proposition: life is to be rejoiced in while it is bold and free and active, but unless it is crowned by early death the joy will turn to sorrow, and to the conclusion which Browning uncharacteristically stated in his depression after the death of Miss Egerton Smith, "Sorrow did, and joy did nowise—life well weighed—preponderate." (pp. 97-9)

C. F. MacRae, in his Adam Lindsay Gordon, *Twayne Publishers, Inc., 1968, 157 p.*

BRIAN ELLIOTT (essay date 1973)

[Elliott examines Gordon's poetry, contending that many twentieth-century Australian critics have treated Gordon unjustly, being biased by a nationalistic tendency to reject colonial writers.]

In order to understand Adam Lindsay Gordon and make sense of his work, the modern Australian reader must appreciate an odd literary and historical phenomenon. He must somehow digest the fact that the writer who, fifty years ago, was regarded as without dispute the most vital and representative of Australian poets, has become for contemporary criticism almost a dead weight. It is literary and academic rather than popular opinion which has rejected Gordon, though popular opinion does not lag far behind the academic lead. Of course, the vividness of Gordon's colonial impact has faded for the general reader, and a falling-off is not unexpected. But in more responsible critical opinion, the effect seems extraordinary. Gordon seems to embarrass, or somehow nonplus sophisticated contemporary Australian writers. (p. 1)

A painting of Gordon on the steeplechaser Viking.

What actually happened to account for the disposition of so many later readers to close their eyes and shut their ears to Adam Lindsay Gordon? One need not claim he was a second Homer, or even a Swinburne *manqué,* to recognize that an injustice has been done. But no doubt the reason is simple. There is a strong cleavage between the colonial and the post-colonial spirit. Precision is impossible but if an arbitrary date is helpful, one might put the division at about 1920. Politically, of course, colonialism ended with the federation of the States. But it took the First World War to bring home the full realization of the nation's new status, and perhaps it is not too much to suggest that it took a second world war to confirm the conviction finally. The whole period 1914-45 was one of vital, eager, but in some ways ruthless reorientation. As, at such a period of growth and change, people are always much more certain about what they want to discard than about what they want to replace it with, Gordon was quick to go. With the colonial attitude of mind went the poetry which, more effectively than any other, symbolized and summed it up. 'Colonial' became an indecent word and most colonial literature and art was voted below contempt. (p. 2)

Gordon's poetry *is* poetry, but a good deal of misunderstanding may be overcome if we first come to a decision about what *kind* of poetry it is. Some part of the enjoyment of poetry lies in the psychological 'placing' or identification of the experience recaptured; some of it lies in the auditory pleasure of the verse itself. No obligation rests upon poets to be continually in a lofty mood. Gordon's contribution to the literature of his time and the colonial situation, lay in his acceptance of a plain man's plain attitude not only to the surrounding world and to society but to art. He wrote comparatively little 'poetical' poetry. He addressed himself—perfectly sincerely—to people like himself. He assumes only a background of experience of common life under colonial conditions. If (as I think he may largely have done) he learned his metres from Edgar Allan Poe, or at times from Shelley, possibly on occasion Swinburne—or from Browning, an influence specially patent in **"From the Wreck"**—it was to technique that these literary influences were limited. Everything in his work that is most memorable possesses a plain, unvarnished, straightforward energy. One must make a fair effort to look at what he wrote from a contemporary colonial point of view: if one does, one can see that his appeal lay in his capacity to come to grips with colonial life and to see and describe it without distortion. (pp. 18-19)

It is true that his code gave scope to some romantic posturing that a modern reader may wish away, as well as to a good deal of moralising that to a modern taste is a severe bore. But there can be more than one way of looking at these. A sympathetic interest will arise a good deal more easily in the mind of a reader who knows and understands the colonial outlook, than will come to one who has never taken the trouble to see the period in perspective. Something the same may be said of Gordon's general subject matter, especially his preoccupation with horses. Indeed, horses may provide the key, in a sense. . . .

To Gordon and the men of his age, horses were much more than a barbershop excitement. They were indispensable necessities of life. Anyone who doubts Gordon's soundness in regard to the importance of horses may turn to the essays included in *The Laureate of the Centaurs:* **"Racing Ethics", "The Ring and the Books", "The Arab Horse"**. These are declarations of his detestation of several distasteful aspects of racing practice, but at the same time affirmations of the need for encouraging and supporting the breeding of good horses, upon whose stamina society was heavily dependent. It was a poetical accident, and a fortunate one, as Gordon saw the position, that horses were beautiful as well as useful animals; but their necessity came before that beauty. The place horses occupied in his mind was thus not exaggerated. (pp. 19-20)

There can be no sound criticism of Gordon that does not appreciate that he was never a mere rhyming jockey. Nobody thought so in colonial times; not even the most prejudiced reader who studies him now can continue to think so for long. It is unfortunate that circumstances do favour such a first impression, since a number of poems in the first of his two collections (***Sea Spray and Smoke Drift***) were in fact written for the sporting pages and could be considered as merely a kind of versified turf gossip. In a few instances his lines become the vehicle of some lively rhyming tips. But these pieces were written only for the occasion and for money; taken plainly for what they are, they are worth regarding as bits of vivid local and historical colour, but they are not poetry, have never been claimed to be poetry, and Gordon least of all would wish to have them regarded seriously in a poetical light. They were simple journalism, good of their kind. Looked at in this way, they take on an interest they could never otherwise have. Gordon was not ashamed of them and had no need to be. He chose to preserve them in book form; we may properly be grateful for the result without calling it literature. Journalism of this leisurely sportive quality is something we now seldom see. Even these turf pieces of his are full of erudite Latin tags. (So were his speeches in parliament.) It will not be hard to find errors in his Latin, but no one can doubt his respect for the classics. His allusions are usually very apt. One need not call him a scholar or exaggerate his learning; most of it was ordinary schoolboy reading. But he had an ear for cadence in words, and seemingly learned to appreciate the quality of verbal rhythm in Latin long before he ever discovered any aptitude of his own for English verse. He is said to have had an excellent memory for lines of poetry, almost photographic; though a most unmusical voice and a dull style in recitation, with an excessive amount of 'sing-song'. By the same token he had virtually no ear for vocal or instrumental melody. Verse was his signal compensation for this lack, a not uncommon shortcoming in poets. The peculiar quality of Gordon's characteristic rhythm in verse—not exactly quantitative, and yet more heavily emphatic, syllable-to-syllable, than English stress-rhythm need be—is perfectly compatible with the training in classical metres he had at school. His classical foundations are to be seen as clearly in his published 'turf gossip' sequences as anywhere. **"Ye Wearie Wayfarer"** contains an extraordinarily high proportion of 'learned' allusions. But Gordon was not in his day exceptional. He was in fact merely talking the language of his class. He addressed himself to colonial 'gentlemen' who were the products (in most cases) of a very similar education to his own, whether obtained 'at home' or 'colonially'.

"Ye Wearie Wayfarer" is, then, flimsy as 'literary' material, but highly interesting when approached from other points of view, personal or historical. Its treatment of the sporting themes (Gordon's attention is not confined to racing, though horses always interested him deeply) reminds us that the colonial gentleman was still a reflex image of the English country gentleman, who was often a reader as well as a hunter and rider.

Gordon's verses are almost all cast in one or another formal pattern of ballad metre, and this is no accident; he was an eager admirer of English ballad poetry, whether modern or traditional. Each one of the eight 'fyttes' of the **"Wayfarer"**, except the last, has a brief verse epigraph; in six of the seven cases, the quoted poems are ballads. (pp. 21-3)

[The **"Wayfarer"** pieces in ***Sea Spray and Smoke Drift***] are capable of illustrating several more of [Gordon's] qualities. With their colonial-gentleman style goes a conversational, relaxed manner: not a bar-room, but a clubroom sociability. There is a good deal of 'I remember'—

> I remember the lowering wintry morn
> And the mist on the Cotswold hills. . .
>
> I remember how merry a start we got
> When the red fox broke from the hill. . .

And no little advice of a prudential kind:

> And the maxim holds good, *'Quem perdere vult Deus, dementat prius* ["Whom God would destroy, He first makes mad"].

The disposition of colonial society to moralize was well marked; Gordon was not the only poet to give it voice. Nor were these moral exhortations the part of his work least valued by his colonial admirers. As well as 'Kindness in another's trouble, Courage in your own', they respected him for a whole repertoire of simple pioneering wisdom. One is tempted to refer to it especially as a 'bush' ethic, but no doubt 'colonial' is adequate. It is naive and belongs to the frontier, but usually has a bottom of sense. In its day, and in its immediate situation, there was value in it. The effect of the colonial environment was to strip away subtlety from most matters, and moral precept, to be effective, could always best be reduced to a plain and simple formula. Especially courage, tenacity, persistence and stoic cheerfulness were important, and were all stressed in the code of the pioneer. . . . Through much of **"Ye Wearie Wayfarer"** Gordon is thinking about England . . . , but the best of his poetry—the part of it which most indubitably *is* poetry—relates to his experience of the life and landscape about him. There is enough of this in the horsey pieces to show his imagination at work, and to exhibit him as the true *poet* of colonial Australia.

The opening of **"Ye Wearie Wayfarer"**, Fytte I, runs:

> Lightly the breath of the spring wind blows
> Though laden with faint perfume,
> 'Tis the fragrance rare that the bushman knows,
> The scent of the wattle-bloom.
> Two-thirds of our journey at least are done,
> Old horse! Let us take a spell
> In the shade from the glare of the noon-day sun. . . .

Here the setting is actual, the local colour true. Again the passage about the wattle blossom and the bells, already referred to, has something very sympathetically moving in it, with a double nostalgia that is eloquent in both keys at the same time:

> Hark! the bells on distant cattle
> Waft across the range,
> Through the golden-tufted wattle,
> Music low and strange;

Like the marriage peal of fairies
Comes the tinkling sound,
Or like chimes of sweet St. Mary's
On far English ground.
How my courser champs the snaffle,
And with nostril spread,
Snorts and scarcely seems to ruffle
Fern leaves with his tread;
Cool and pleasant on his haunches
Blows the evening breeze,
Through the overhanging branches
Of the wattle trees.

Incidentally, that Gordon (like a colonial Yeats or a Mangan) could still care for fairies, is not so very surprising when one bears in mind his familiarity with the old ballads. That he should retain a yearning to hear the old church bells in Cheltenham is, of course, not surprising at all. But that he could effectively combine these interests with an image of the wattle was, in colonial terms, a minor miracle. Once again what one wishes to stress is that Gordon's poetry—the essence of it—is always to be discovered in images of facts. The wattle, the cattle bells, the old church so far away, the horse that champs the snaffle . . . all are present and real. Gordon, it is true, at times displays an impulsive pleasure in sunset lights and a few such conventional clichés. But the instances are beautiful and he is sincere. Sophisticated criteria are neither here nor there with such a poet, but truth to fact is vital. And even his moralism, naive as it may be, makes plain and simple sense in its context:

Courage, comrades, this is certain
All is for the best—
There are lights behind the curtain—
Gentles let us rest.
As the smoke-rack veers to seaward
From the 'ancient clay'
With its moral drifting leeward,
Ends the wanderer's lay.

I have spent so much argument upon **"Ye Wearie Wayfarer"** in order to defend Gordon rather than to defend those particular verses. The fact is, the main characteristics are there and in strength—the horsey pieces often have a vitality that is less easily seen in poetry more ambitious. It is so perhaps because the horsey poems are immediately and directly in touch with plain experience; perhaps also because of their simple and limited but always plain nearness to nature (both the earth itself and human nature). Again, perhaps because they are free of complication or subtlety, they always have Gordon's true and basic quality in them. He can and does write better poetry, but here are the simple foundations. If we pass from **"Ye Wearie Wayfarer"** to **"Hippodromania"** in the same volume we see a more carefully managed control over both verse and discourse. These are still bits of turf gossip and club humour, lighthearted racecourse prognostications, etc., as are the others; but the first and the last pieces in the group contain landscape material that has more weight than the wattle-blossom lyrical parts of the **"Wayfarer"**, and seems more deliberately and seriously meant to relate to the poet's own personal situation. The first 'part' (he no longer calls the divisions 'fyttes'), **"Visions in the Smoke"**, is a colonial tobacco idyll. It recalls a quiet, thoughtful occasion near Port Macdonnell, where the poet was living, at Dingley Dell, in 1865. He liked to lie on the cliff and gaze out over the sea, smoking his pipe:

With the anodyne cloud on my listless eyes,
With its spell on my dreamy brain,
As I watch the circling vapours rise
From the brown bowl up to the sullen skies,
My vision becomes more plain,
Till a dim kaleidoscope succeeds
Through the smoke-rack drifting and veering,
Like ghostly riders on phantom steeds
To a shadowy goal careering.

The passage is more difficult to interpret than it might be, because no one yet has given a satisfactory account of what Gordon's physical vision actually was. All the evidence suggests that he was painfully myopic, but some details are puzzling. G. G. McCrae, who knew him well, said that he had never known him to wear spectacles [see Additional Bibliography]. Certainly in all his landscape impressions a certain dimness or diffused quality in the outlines seems important. Yet one also has the impression that everything he wishes to single out is clearly and brilliantly seen. Once again a seascape closes the **"Hippodromania"** sequence, with images of sunset and the suggestion of an approaching storm. The imagery by itself, detached from the argument, is beautiful, meaningful and exact, yet at moments seems to dissolve away in light or fade into the receding distance. The first two lines of the following passage seem very distinct as a description of the restlessness of the sea:

Already green hillocks are swelling,
And combing white locks on the bar,
Where a dull, droning murmur is telling
Of winds that have gather'd afar. . .

But in the second two, we see the stress has moved from sight to sound; in the four which then follow it becomes merely moral. The next (and final) strophe begins again with visible effects. These, however, do not demand a particularly sharp focus of the eye: emphasis falls on brilliance and colour, and the beauty of the light is broadly suffused, without articulate outlines. When Gordon spoke of starlight, which he loved, we cannot be entirely sure he was even capable of distinguishing individual stars. Yet for all that he responded powerfully to whatever he did see in sunset and evening lights:

Yet the skies are still tranquil and starlit,
The sun 'twixt the wave and the west
Dies in purple, and crimson, and scarlet
And gold. . .

The remaining verses are prosaic—intentionally so.

The spirit of the **"Wayfarer"** is whimsically discursive. That of **"Hippodromania"** is more orderly, systematically witty. The wit is sometimes breezy, sometimes nonchalant, sometimes ironical. One may make what one can of

Yet if man, of all the Creator plann'd,
His noblest work is reckoned,
Of the work of His hand, by sea or by land,
The horse may at least rank second.

In light vein:

Our common descent we may each recall
To a lady of old caught tripping,
The fair one in fig leaves, who d—d us all
For a bite at a golden pippin.

Park IV of **"Hippodromania"**, **"Banker's Dream"**, is a light and amusing, and very well put together ballad of a race, related for once *by the horse*. Part III, **"Credat Judaeus Apella"**, a reply to the editor's request for a rhymed racing tip when Gordon had no opinion to offer, is very brightly written in the best horsey manner. (pp. 26-32)

I turn to the other writings in ***Sea Spray and Smoke Drift,*** which, however, for the most part interest me less than the horsey pieces.

The first poem, **"Podas Okus"** is a ballad on a Homeric subject, seriously and romantically treated, and already highly coloured with a kind of poetic despair that was apparently part of Gordon's personal as well as his literary character:

I am ready, I am willing,
To resign my stormy life;
Weary of this long blood-spilling,
Sated with this ceaseless strife.

The moral of Troy is for Gordon no different from the moral of the bush: courage in the face of adversity, stoicism in the prospect of death. A better piece, perhaps, is **"Gone",** a ballad on the death of Robert O'Hara Burke, whose pathetic story had a profound effect upon colonial society, although some later commentators have regarded him as an incompetent leader and his death, therefore, as more stupid than tragic. His competence is not in question here, however. Burke and Wills both perished in the desert after a dramatically ironical failure to make contact with their supporting force at Cooper's Creek; they became vivid and potent symbols, not only of the bravery of all explorers, but also of the malevolence of the inland landscape. . . . Gordon's attitude to life showed increasingly a kind of grim fortitude:

What matters the sand or the whitening chalk,
The blighted herbage, the black'ning log,
The crooked beak of the eagle-hawk
Or the hot red tongue of the native dog?

. . . . .

No tears are needed—fill out the wine,
Let the goblets clash, let the grape-juice flow;
Ho! pledge me a death-drink, comrade mine
To a brave man gone where we all must go.

There are a number of deliberately literary poems in the ***Sea Spray*** volume, including a spirited translation from Horace (**"Pastor Cum"**, Hor. Odes I.15), but the style invariably drifts towards a ballad mood. **"Fauconshawe"** might well earn inclusion in a collection of Victorian ballads; so also might **"Rippling Water",** with its intelligent, and musical, use of a double refrain ('The rippling water murmurs on'). **"Bellona"** is not of particular interest, except for its transparent debt to Edgar Allan Poe. **"Whisperings in Wattle-Boughs"** is an odd piece, perhaps worth more regard than I feel disposed to give it: it is full of allusions to the poet's father, sister, friend and loved one, and may be intimately autobiographical, but the pattern is not distinguished and the poem as a whole somehow sounds uncharacteristically hysterical. The ballad **"Wormwood and Nightshade"** is a longer and better poem; it contains references to a romantic love affair, also probably autobiographical, but again the clues are obscure and it is not profitable to follow them. **"Ars Longa"** is a cheerful ballad of moral commonplaces. Gordon (for any significant reason?) alters the refrain, at its last appearance, to *'Mors grata, vita brevis'*. **"The Last Leap",** a short ballad about the shooting of an injured horse, shows Gordon at his best in the early style, compassionate yet stoic:

With the flash that ends thy pain
Respite and oblivion blest
Come to greet thee. I in vain
Fall: I rise to fall again:
Thou hast fallen to thy rest—
And thy fall is best!

The last poem in the volume, **"The Roll of the Kettledrum",** had in its day a great success. It is a long ballad concerned with the same military heroics and glories of defeat as Tennyson celebrated in "The Charge of the Light Brigade". Had the Victorian taste for those stirring excitements persisted, no doubt the reputation of this piece would have survived longer. But alas! their splendour has long since faded. Nor does Gordon's poem gain anything from his repetition here of the device which in the comic **"Banker's Dream"** succeeded very wittily—once again the story is told from the point of view, not of the rider, but the horse.

Sea Spray and Smoke Drift is a volume of colonial verse that has a good deal of historical and some poetical force; it is pungently redolent both of bush and a few sharp stable aromas, and should not be forgotten. But it does not, after all, contain the best of Gordon. Four or five poems in the later volume, ***Bush Ballads and Galloping Rhymes,*** are, as literature, worth all the rest of his writings.

Gordon is sometimes given credit for having developed, if not for having invented, a native Australian kind of ballad. . . . This is not an altogether deserved reputation. . . . Gordon's rhymes are ballads in design and style, but they look to English and literary rather than to local and popular models; whatever their subject matter, they owe little to Australian influences. **"How We Beat the Favourite"** is an example that is interesting in this connection. Its one-time wide popularity in Australia might, in most readers' logic, entitle it to be called an Australian poem. Nor does anything in its content assert an impediment. There is no absolute reason why an Australian ballad may not treat of any subject it pleases. A rhyme about an English hunting incident might still be acceptable if it fits the requirements in other respects. But this piece stands half-way between a native-colonial and a sentimental-exile point of view. The action is lively, the wit sharp, the energy abundant, and the subject horsey—but most Australian readers will consider it horsey in an English and literary way. The excitement is full of an English (horsey) gentleman's nostalgia, and this nostalgia is what governs the rhythms. It is more like Whyte-Melville than Paterson, certainly. So it may be judged a vigorous ballad, but not convincingly an Australian one; and therefore it is easy to understand why its former strong hold on Australian readers has now fallen slack. Once it was recited with verve beside every campfire; now, when even **"The Sick Stockrider",** is seldom heard, there would seem to be little prospect of reviving **"How We Beat the Favourite".**

But **"The Sick Stockrider"** is a different matter. Much as it has lost by the attrition of time, it remains an Australian institution. If any of Gordon's poems could be claimed as a prototypical Australian ballad, this one comes nearest. It can hardly be said to come right into the category. It is presented too seriously, its style is too conscious and deliberate, too literary. . . . But campfire reciters were once passionately fond of it. If it has now fallen out of the repertoire, it will be for reasons different from those that drove **"How We Beat the Favourite"** into eclipse. It faded because the whole colonial mythology has suffered a collapse. But no established mythology ever disappears entirely—it only sinks in deep and invisibly.

The bushman who dies in the saddle is a colonial archetype. Gordon did not invent him. A ballad called "The Stockman's Last Bed" appeared in *The Queensland Colonial Camp Fire Song Book* in 1865, several years before **"The Sick Stockrider",** and it is certain the theme was then widely distributed.

Gordon's poem was transparently a literary treatment or application of it, a dramatic monologue somewhat in the style of Browning. It was a deliberately noble (or heroic and elegiac) exploitation of a current colonial theme. It is true that Gordon himself professed not to regard the poem particularly highly, and he seems to have been very easily persuaded by Marcus Clarke, when he published it in his *Colonial Monthly Magazine,* to cut off the final strophe. Admittedly it was a prosaic one. Yet Clarke was probably wrong. Gordon's characteristic lapses into the commonplace are very natural and as a rule occur only when he brings his poetical and his prosaic imagination together. After the lines which speak of the bushman hearing the 'sturdy station children' romping on his grave, the deleted lines continue:

> I don't suppose I shall, though, for I feel I like sleeping
> sound. . . .

Then follows a typically Gordonesque reflection:

> That sleep they say is doubtful. True; but yet
> At least it makes no difference to the dead man underground
> What the living men remember or forget. . . .

The rest is trite, but still in his vein. Whether or not Clarke omitted it, the conclusion should be restored.

In making a fresh attempt to arrive at a judgement of **"The Sick Stockrider"** one must decide what its quality is without being too ready to condemn those who have rejected it. For it is, after all, very much a period piece. We are not yet far enough away from the colonial frame of mind to set it properly in proportion; we have been eagerly concerned to discover our latest realities, and this seems impossible without a little hostility towards the old ones, once adequate, now outdated. Gordon, and particularly **"The Sick Stockrider",** suffer by this change. Nevertheless such a ruthless repudiation of the old colonial spirit is a fault. It will correct itself as maturity advances. Let us in the meantime try to take the poem simply as it is, sentiment, philosophy, morals and all. Whether or not we now feel its historical interest dominates its poetic, it is certainly an item of colonial Victoriana we can ill afford to neglect.

The poem is not really dependent upon its narrative, which is not even particularly vivid or connected. The Stockrider is apparently dying, or at least aware of death as near. The drift is mostly a nostalgic looking back over a hard, not unromantic, active past life. There is a summing up and an acceptance: whatever he has sacrificed, whatever he has missed out on, the bushman will die at peace. There is a stoic, genuine, and on the whole a sweet resignation. Here is manifestly the bushman's ideal image of the man of natural sensibility—which, in these terms, is not so very different from reason, for Gordon's code is essentially one of practical good sense. Religion is elementary and fundamentally moral:

> Enigmas that perplex us in the world's unequal strife,
> The future may ignore or may reveal.
> Yet some, as weak as water, Ned! to make the best of life,
> Have been, to face the worst, as true as steel.

Though trite, this was the poet's own belief.

One remembers principally from **"The Sick Stockrider"** its stoicism and its emphasis on bush companionship, hence upon bush loneliness, with all the complex nostalgias of its remoteness. In two factors Gordon's achievement is superb: the colour, mood and brilliance of his landscape impressions, and the representation of colonial character in action. His personal involvement emerges through both of these last:

> 'Twas here we ran the dingo down that gave us such a chase
> Eight years ago—or was it nine?—last March.

The fox whose image lies behind the dingo's is not objectified here; but the colonial hunt, different as was its quarry, subtly and poignantly recalls other days, other places, other excitements.

There are a good many landscapes either implied or denoted in the poem. Strangely enough, the setting is left more or less indeterminate. . . . The events and landscapes which count for the Stockrider are all remembered ones; after the first four lines of dramatic monologue it is no longer necessary to relate the contents to the actual setting or the literal occasion. A credible actuality is implied in the Stockrider's 'Hold hard, Ned! Lift me down . . .' and the impression of the 'hot, slow, sleepy, silent ride' carries visual conviction. But then we are presented with a series of enchanted vistas. These very plausibly could, since some of the names are actual, refer to verifiable localities. But in effect they amount only to a sequence of dream-like memories: the dawn at 'Moorabinda' (Moorabinta?), Arbuthnot's boundary fence, the Limestone cattle camp (Limestone Wells?—a staging place on the old road to Mount Gambier), the creek at Carricksford, and other station landscapes glimpsed in the light of dawn—'Katâwa' with its 'sandpeaks all ablaze', Glen Lomond with its 'flushed fields'. These images, to be seen complete, must be reconstructed from hints and phrases, yet they come surprisingly clear:

> Now westward winds the bridle path that leads to Lindisfarm,
> And yonder looms the double-headed bluff;
> From the far side of the first hill, when the skies are clear and
> calm
> You can see Sylvester's woolshed fair enough. . . .

Almost every item of description in the piece is bright and vivid, however fragmentary. A little can suggest a great deal:

> 'Twas merry in the glowing morn, among the gleaming grass,
> To wander as we've wandered many a mile,
> And blow the cool tobacco cloud, and watch the white wreaths
> pass,
> Sitting loosely in the saddle all the while.

Scenes of action and colour are recalled with the same vividness:

> . . . To wheel the wild scrub cattle at the yard,
> With a running fire of stockwhips and a fiery run of hoofs:
> Oh! the hardest day was never then too hard!

Recollections of riding and pursuit follow—a chase after the bushrangers, 'Starlight and his gang'—and then, in melancholy, piquant contrast, a passage calling back, in bushman's terms, the vanished human past:

> In these hours when life is ebbing, how those days when life
> was young
> Come back to us! How clearly I recall
> Even the yarns Jack Hall invented, and the songs Jem Roper
> sung;
> And where are now Jem Roper and Jack Hall?

(pp. 33-41)

Revaluing his life, the Stockrider concludes that it has been, by and large, a good one. Undoubtedly here Gordon spoke for his colonial contemporaries, whatever complex personal feelings may have underlain the sentiment:

> This I know—
> I should live the same life over, if I had to live again. . .

Something better than mere colonial defeat that prompts the thought,

. . . And the chances are I go where most men go.

Gordon is at his most eloquent and lyrically impassioned when he describes dim effects of light, accompanied by strong contrasts of colour and emotion:

The deep blue skies wax dusky, and the tall green leaves grow dim,
The sward beneath me seems to heave and fall;
And sickly, smoky shadows through the sleepy sunlight swim,
And on the very sun's light weave their pall.

The suggestion of the station children pulling the flowers and romping on his grave is thoroughly cheerful. The conclusion is, of course, as has already been pointed out, moral. But **"The Sick Stockrider"** is essentially neither a preaching nor a melancholy poem: the impression with which it leaves one is of a life roughly yet powerfully fulfilled. It is a stoic fulfillment; in the colonial context, a good and acceptable one.

This extended analysis of the **"Stockrider"** must serve as a key to the rest of ***Bush Ballads and Galloping Rhymes,*** except for one other poem to be looked at more closely presently, and just a few general remarks.

"The Swimmer" is a personal piece, and has some splendid phrases and lines in it; but it has, perhaps, more autobiographical than literary interest. One might wish to single out one line in particular, the first:

With short, sharp, violent lights made vivid. . .

—because it epitomizes Gordon's style, in his landscapes and in his impressionism generally. **"From the Wreck"** has been the subject of a good deal of speculative discussion as to whether the incident it refers to was an actual one—the wreck of the *Admella* near Cape Northumberland in 1859. But the probability is that the story is related to no particular disaster. . . . A more identifiable influence was a purely literary one: Browning's "How They Brought the Good News from Ghent to Aix," whose movement and metre it emulates. This is a good, lively, imaginative ballad of action, which, once again, gains strength from its horsey subject matter. Towards the end there is a recognizable glimpse of local scenery, though the mountain (Mount Gambier or Mount Schanck) is not expressly named. **"Wolf and Hound"** is another poem of action, perhaps a magnification of the part in the **"Stockrider"** which refers to the pursuit of the bushrangers. The idea seems to have fascinated him. . . . In **"De Te"** we have a characteristic line and a characteristic landscape:

A burning glass of burnish'd brass,
The calm sea caught the noontide rays,
And sunny slopes of golden grass
And wastes of weed-flower seem to blaze.
Beyond the shining silver-greys,
Beyond the shades of denser bloom,
The sky-line girt with glowing haze,
The farthest faintest forest gloom,
And the everlasting hills that loom.

"Doubtful Dreams" is a strange poem and one which a biographer must certainly study. Here it suffices to mention that it seems to have been written in response to someone's urging Gordon to return to England. But in 1868, when this was written, he had little real thought of returning:

Aye, snows are rife in December,
And sheaves are in August yet,
And you would have me remember
And I would rather forget. . .

The allusion is obscure but probably refers to the old affair with Jane Bridges. It is bitter.

It is perhaps a pity that Gordon's ambitious contribution to the Victorian Arthurian legend, **"The Rhyme of Joyous Garde"** is not better known. As something between a formal ballad and a heroic narrative, it has some good qualities and is always full of energy, if not of much subtlety. Having once established his style, Gordon assuredly could never have been weaned from his rough rhythms, harsh rhymes and clashing, trumpet-like harmonies. These were his birthright as a poet; for good or ill they mark everything he wrote, and in fairness should not be begrudged him. But it is doubtful whether such tactics, excellent in the bush, can be made to suit an Arthurian subject. If one judges by Malory rather than Tennyson, however, the discrepancies do not seem quite so indecorous. **"The Rhyme of Joyous Garde"** could be described as Malory rendered in the tones of Macaulay and the mood and spirit of Jorrocks, an odd enough conjunction; yet its hearty excess of vigour, though it makes the poem awkward, never absolutely spoils it. A colonial-style moral of course carries the day, finding expression in very simple—dare one suggest, bushmanlike?—terms. Near the end Lancelot offers this stalwart prayer for Guinevere:

If ever I smote as a man should smite,
If I struck one stroke that seem'd good in Thy sight,
By Thy loving mercy prevailing,
Lord! Let her stand in the light of Thy face,
Cloth'd with Thy love and crown'd with Thy grace,
When I gnash my teeth in the terrible place
That is fill'd with weeping and wailing.

It is not, after all, a poem that can now be taken too seriously; yet it is not ignominious. It is minor poetry of a certain stature; by no means despicable.

I would claim rather more, perhaps, for **"The Romance of Britomarte."** But this ballad was certainly an easier one to write. Even taking into account Gordon's nostalgic yearning towards the historical past, its subject was more naturally congenial. It is another horsey piece. In **"Joyous Garde"** and **"Britomarte"** Gordon consummated the promise of ***The Feud.*** Both hark back to the old-time ballad, both celebrate tales of action in historical (or rather, 'period') settings, and both appeal rather to a literary than a traditional or popular judgement. The name Britomarte hints (misleadingly) at a reading of Spenser. . . . Britomarte herself—perhaps not altogether surprisingly—turns out not to be a Spenserian character after all, but a mare with a literary name. The main incident is a desperate ride which achieves a grand and noble purpose but costs the horse its life. In this style **"Britomarte"** is assuredly Gordon's best work. **"From the Wreck"**, with a similar ride, beside it seems a brilliant bit of colonial virtuosity. This is much more—a considered and reasoned poetical composition. It is hardly satisfactory to detach samples but this stanza illustrates something of the brightness and pace of the style:

Brown Britomarte lay dead in her straw
Next morn—we buried her—brave old girl—
John Kerr, we tried him by martial law,
And we twisted some hemp for the trait'rous churl;
And she—I met her alone—said she,

'You have risked your life, you have lost your mare,
And what can I give in return, Ralph Leigh?'
I replied, 'One braid of that bright brown hair.'
And with that she bowed her beautiful head,
'You can take as much as you choose,' she said.

Now only one poem remains for close scrutiny. (pp. 41-6)

I have delayed my remarks upon one poem, because it is one which demands—or at any rate bravely supports—a detailed examination. At the head of Gordon's last volume, ***Bush Ballads and Galloping Rhymes,*** stand the verses reprinted in many anthologies—entitled **"A Dedication".** They were addressed to an author Gordon respected and whose approval he valued. I think of it also as his own statement of affirmation. It expressed not only the dedication of his one talent to the art which in his rough way he loved and served, but also that of his half-reluctant heart to the only landscape which, in the end, he could accept as his. It was thus his *apologia,* and, dominating the last and best of his books, summed up and epitomized his poetical existence. Placed first, it was written (I plausibly believe) last. On the day after the book appeared, overwhelmed with depression and despair, troubled with a burden of unrepayable debt, Gordon took his own life.

The lines are formally addressed 'To the author of Holmby House'—that is, G. J. Whyte-Melville. *Holmby House* (published in 1860) is a spirited novel, a crisp and lively story about Cavaliers and Roundheads. (p. 51)

The poem opens abruptly, 'They are rhymes . . . ' The headword is meaningless unless the reader relates it to the title of the volume. Such an opening reinforces an impression that Gordon wrote the lines rapidly in response to an unpremeditated impulse. The tone is brave and lively. What it covers up, of course, may be another affair, but there is no hint here of impending suicide though the poem may well be the last he wrote. Its very impetuousness suggests that it could have been composed in haste within a few days of its actual printing, and therefore very shortly before his death. If this supposition is correct, it is worthwhile noticing how the spontaneity of the language is marked by an unusually excited condition of both poetical and critical sensibility. **"A Dedication"** is a rational expression of Gordon's genuine attachment to Australia and seems poetically a positive, even a happy assessment.

There is an impression that his attachment is so strong, the pressure of it so urgent, he cannot stop even to make his rhetoric clear. 'They are rhymes rudely strung . . .' He means all his rhymes, but these 'bush ballads' and 'galloping' pieces in particular. These were the rhymes ('rude' though they might be) which defined his personal relationship to the world he accepted as his.

I propose now to take up the text, and to quote and comment as I go.

They are rhymes rudely strung with intent less
Of sound than of words . . .

At the outset Gordon's expression is hasty—not necessarily a defect, since the mood of urgency, even impatience, is an important ingredient in his thought; but the effect is less than perfectly lucid. He means that the poems have been strung together in a responsive and receptive state of mind, but with regard less for prosody or literary finesse, than for the spirit which prompts them. Both 'sound' and 'words' are inadequate precisely to convey this thought, though we understand his intention.

In lands where bright blossoms are scentless,
And songless bright birds;

The cliché embodied in these lines is a very hoary one and not even Australian in origin. The question is rather one of context: why is it dragged in, and what is Gordon really referring to? The drift so far is: 'This is verse roughly but honestly made, in a country which at first sight seems to offer no natural inducements to poetry'. To analyze the implications of songless birds and scentless flowers would be to embrace the scope of all European (or English) prejudice against unfamiliar birds, flowers and landscape phenomena generally, considered as the supporting framework of a poetical tradition. The standing view was that a new environment which could not re-affirm the ancient formulas of poetical convention (according to which flowers and their sweet perfumes, birds with their singing voices, have always a fixed value) were incapable of inspiring the poetic imagination at all. It is important to see that here only the conventional aesthetic impact of nature was in question. The simple contention seems to have been that where the phenomena were anomalous—and all variations from familiar expectation are anomalies—poetry based upon them must necessarily be unsound. Where birds were brilliant but voiceless, and flowers bright but without perfume, the lyrical impulse itself could not be sustained. Such a notion never asked what either landscape or poetry amounted to in themselves. It only looked at the conventional precedents. Then, when it could find no trilling nightingales in the woods, concluded there could be no music of any kind: no melody, whether of birdsong or rhyme. When, furthermore, it was considered that among Australian birds the parrot tribe predominated—birds known to be both bright in colour and noisy, discordant screechers—the preconditioned mind was put to a further quandary about colours. It was not—it never was—a question of facts or verifiable truth. Poetry stood outside of, or superior to the phenomena, depending upon understood relationships. European writers who celebrated the fragrance of the violet did not then, nor need they now, explain that this is a poetical generalization. By far the greater number of wild violets are scentless. This is known in Europe. To Australian readers, on the other hand, whose knowledge of violets is limited to the literary tradition reinforced from some experience of cultivated garden varieties, it comes as a surprise, even a shock, to be told so. A wide scope for misunderstanding arises when the preconceptions of one culture-area are imported into another. In the older tradition of poetry certainly—including the Romantic and Victorian—facts, once observed, tended to transmute themselves to symbols. Where the symbols no longer stood for the same values, nature itself seemed committed to chaos. It is no wonder if Gordon's birds and flowers, though unlikely to have caused a ripple in the English reader's mind, provoked indignant controversy in Australia.

It appears now a storm in the critical teacup. But it is still worth asking, Did Gordon mean literally what he said, or what was his motive in saying it? Was he merely repeating the cliché mechanically, even a little wearily—it had been said so often before!—or did he in any sense believe it? He was well aware that parrots were not nightingales. So was he aware that wattle blossom (whose exhilarating effect, however, he says in this same poem, resembles a long draught of wine) was not the same as violets or roses. The point, I believe, is really a simple one. In speaking to Whyte-Melville, Gordon was merely, and for the moment only, using the language he understood. The poem as a whole was concerned—passionately, more passionately than in any other utterance of Gordon's—to explain what the Australian symbols were and how they worked. He could afford therefore to make the concession. It is even a patient one, as though he were saying: 'You are an Englishman, you think like an Englishman, you can't possibly know how nature affects us here in Australia. Very well, our birds aren't like English birds and our flowers aren't like English flowers: parrots are bright and noisy, the bush flowers lack familiar fragrance, there are no nightingales. So far, the nature-symbols are still unresolved, one's expectations are upset, the new experiences are a little chaotic. But let me tell you that there *is* room here for nature—a rather different nature—to have its effect on poetry, and this poem is intended to show it.' Or to put the approach a little differently: 'You expect certain things to be wrong here. I won't contradict you, but instead point out some things that are fresh, new and right.'

Hence the fervour with which this **"Dedication"** is animated. Gordon cannot wait to lead in gently to his subject: he attacks it almost brutally. After only four lines, brushing past the 'rudeness' of the materials that are at hand—crude metres, unprofitable birds, unresponsive flowers—he rushes at once into one of the broadest and most sweeping nature-symbols of the Australian system, a cliché of clichés, yet a valid observation of nature in her most typical opulence, according, at least, to the colonial way of seeing her. This is what Bernard Smith meant by 'typical' landscape [in his *European Vision and the South Pacific*]:

> Where, with fire and fierce drought on her tresses,
> Insatiable summer oppresses
> Sere woodlands and sad wildernesses,
> And faint flocks and herds.

But emphasis upon this 'typical' image was still novel in Gordon. Drought, fire, heat, thirst and faintness created so effective an impression that later poets repeated the pattern tiresomely. In Gordon's generation it represented a new act of perception. The heat, the brightness, the languor, all brought vivid advances in the *poetical* comprehension and assimilation of the landscape. (pp. 53-7)

The second strophe suggests a mood of the landscape which can be verified in every Australian reader's experience:

> Where in dreariest days, when all dews end,
> And all winds are warm,
> Wild Winter's large floodgates are loosen'd,
> And floods, freed by storm,
> From broken-up fountain heads, dash on
> Dry deserts with long pent-up passion—

Here Gordon does not describe winter, but refers picturesquely to those sudden storms which follow after heat and drought. Hot February or March weather sometimes brings in a violent type of storm that ends with floods, sometimes with disaster. 'When all dews end, And all winds are warm'—the lines describe many a summer night. His 'fountain heads' are of course the huge black cloud masses which build up at such times.

> Here rhyme was first framed without fashion,
> Song shaped without form.

The message is now plain: 'Poetry is possible here.' 'Without fashion' signifies, I think, directly, responsively, impulsively, even compulsively. 'Without form' carries on the suggestion. Gordon is claiming for his own 'rhyme' that it is spontaneous and natural poetry, though it may lack the grace of sophisticated verse.

> Whence gather'd?—The Locust's glad chirrup
> May furnish a stave;

His inspiration in this heightened mood comes *directly,* be it noted, from nature, not by transmission from traditions and symbols. This was poetry of a new, vigorous inspiration. By 'locust' he probably meant cicada, the creature with whose monotonous but insistent music the bush is so vividly alive on hot days. The other stimuli were just as actual; they owed nothing or next to nothing to preconceived, poetical suggestion. All were unpremeditated, natural landscape-impressions.

> The ring of a rowel and stirrup,
> The wash of a wave.
> The chaunt of the marsh frog in rushes,
> That chimes through the pauses and hushes
> Of nightfall, the torrent that gushes,
> The tempests that rave.

Though his song is said to be shaped 'without form', there is more planning here than meets the eye. This last strophe is constructed entirely out of sounds; even in introducing the rhythm of riding, Gordon thinks of the audible 'ring of a rowel and stirrup'. In the next, by contrast, the stress is upon colour and visible forms.

> In the deepening of dawn, when it dapples
> The dusk of the sky,
> With streaks like the redd'ning of apples,
> The ripening of rye,
> To eastward, when cluster by cluster,
> Dim stars and dull planets that muster,
> Wax wan in a world of white lustre
> That spreads far and high:

There is a similar sky-image in the poem **"Argemone",** but it was plainly a preliminary run for this passage: here the impression strengthens by the addition of a rusty-coloured light, suggested by ripening rye, and by the clear colour of sunrise in 'redd'ning'. The stars—'mustered' in the sky as though they were a flock or a herd—have a misty dimness that prompts us to ask once again, just how distinctly did the short-sighted Gordon see them? But that he was powerfully aware of their intense 'white lustre' we accept without question.

There follow other 'typical' images of sunset, which merge into equally 'typical' images of bushfire—not actual but suggested—

> In the gathering of night gloom o'erhead, in
> The still silent change,
> All fire-flush'd when forest trees redden
> On slopes of the range.

Sunset in rocky and rangy bush country in summer is a time of strange lights; Gordon never failed to respond to light. Here the strangeness is captured in the odd rhymes and the suggestions of an apparently alien time and place:

> When the gnarl'd, knotted trunks Eucalyptian
> Seem carved, like weird columns Egyptian,
> With curious device, quaint inscription,
> And hieroglyph strange.

Perhaps 'Eucalyptian' is an inexcusable barbarism—at first one even wonders if the poet was quite serious in inventing it—yet as the passage grows familiar it takes on a kind of rough rightness; for better or worse, Gordon engraved the word on steel of his own tempering. The capital 'E' seems deliberate, and fitting. As for the allusion to Egypt, outlandish as it seems, it is by no means unique. Egypt is often brought in by early writers, when describing the bush landscape, as an archetype of changeless antiquity.

We have had one strophe concerned with sounds, one with light and colour, and then one with a complex of oppressive sensations: heat, flame, grotesque shapes, all leading to suggestions of inscrutable mystery ('hieroglyph strange'). Now comes a modulation to a gentler key:

In the Spring, when the wattle-gold trembles
'Twixt shadow and shine,
When each dew-laden air draught resembles
A long draught of wine;

With the return of the dews comes also a restoration of freshness and fragrance to the bush (which calls for no explanation—it is not of the English kind) and the intoxication of the poet's mood (vaguely Keatsian) now seems both true to the sensations of Australian spring and fully characteristic of himself. But in the next line we have something that looks mildly like a stumbling block:

When the sky-line's blue burnish'd resistance
Makes deeper the dreamiest distance. . .

What are we to make of this 'resistance'? We should beware of interpreting 'burnish'd' to mean merely *brassy:* it means rather *clear,* untroubled by clouds, and, though warm, not oppressively hot. The 'resistance' of the skyline is therefore connected with its brightness and clarity. But the word is odd. One's impulse is to suppose it was dictated by the need of a rhyme to 'distance' and 'existence'. This objection does not really stand. Either because of the plangency of Gordon's music or because it really is right, the word defies substitution, just as, in its place, does 'Eucalyptian'. Again, Gordon's faulty eyesight may be involved. 'Resistance' implies a difficulty. Is it one of physical focus? *Something* resists the viewer's grasp. For Gordon the struggle seems to enhance the intensity of the experience. For us the expression may possibly work in another way, hinting at a vision beyond the vista we see, something inherent in the blue, but resistant to easy understanding. And if that is a super-subtle reading, we have become accustomed to the word anyway. No one would now wish it away:

When the sky-line's blue burnish'd resistance
Makes deeper the dreamiest distance,
Some song in all hearts hath existence,—
Such songs have been mine.

Not all Gordon's 'songs', of course, were derived, as he claims these were, directly from nature. But it is interesting to see that, in this most explicitly personal of all his writings, he appears to value his landscape-inspirations above everything else. At best his descriptions are fragmentary; yet landscape is the core of his poetic substance.

The last three strophes have all begun with 'In'—they are answers to the question, 'Whence gather'd?'. Now he closes this part of the **"Dedication"** and moves on to interests more closely connected with the person to whom it is addressed. 'They' now refers to his local 'songs', or more specifically to the landscape-impulses which motivated them.

They came in all guises, some vivid
To clasp and to keep;
Some sudden and swift as the livid
Blue thunder-flame's leap.

This swept through the first breath of clover
With memories renewed to the rover—
That flash'd while the black horse turn'd over
Before the long sleep.

The allusions to the rover (himself, the exile) and to the black horse (an image which seems to refer to the shooting of an injured horse in an earlier poem, **"The Last Leap"**), though they appear to lead away from his first intention, actually amount to a quite skilful epistolary modulation. The next strophe following is addressed directly to Whyte-Melville as a brother writer and equestrian, who has urged him to escape from exile. Here is Gordon's tribute to *Holmby House*; and once again he finds an opportunity, now in more prosaic style, to repeat that his own work is necessarily crude and colonial. He launches into a passage of praise of *Holmby House,* drawing particularly upon an incident in the novel where Humphrey Bosville, riding to escape from a troop of pursuing Roundheads, pauses, after leaping the brook called Northern Water, in order to look back and wave an ironical farewell. This ill-considered gesture gives the troopers time to fire at him while he rashly presents a broadside; the horse, a sorrel, is killed, and Bosville's capture follows. Given this allusion, there is no more need to interrupt the run of the verse here:

To you (having cunning to colour
A page with your pen,
That through dull days, and nights even duller,
Long years ago ten
Fair pictures in fever afforded)—
I send these rude staves, roughly worded
By one in whose brain stands recorded
As clear now as then,

"The great rush of grey 'Northern Water',
The green ridge of bank,
The 'sorrel' with curved sweep of quarter
Curl'd close to clean flank,
The Royalist saddlefast squarely,
And, where the bright uplands stretch fairly,
Behind, beyond pistol-shot barely,
The Roundheaded rank.

"A long launch, with clinging of muscles,
And clenching of teeth!
The loose doublet ripples and rustles!
The swirl shoots beneath!"

From one writer to another, this lively reminiscence was a fine and even a charming compliment; moreover, what may so far have seemed largely a private literary rhapsody has now become quite clearly a letter. But enough is enough, and so the main topic returns: the poet's exile. Gordon knows he can now never return to England and the mood of the poetry once again changes abruptly back from action to reflection, from excitement to melancholy.

Enough. In return for your garland—
In lieu of the flowers from your far land—
Take wild growth of dreamland and starland,
Take weeds for your wreath.

How well—if we accept 'wild growth' and 'weeds' on sight—do 'dreamland and starland' express Gordon's offering? The phrase shows how he thought about his poetry. It seems to apply only to certain parts and passages. But clearly the poetry he cherished most was the part of his work which interpreted his *landscape* in terms of *light.*

The rest of the poem is more than merely nostalgic—it opens a wound.

Yet rhyme had not failed me for reason,
Nor reason for rhyme,
Sweet Song! had I sought you in season,
And found you in time.
You beckon in your bright beauty yonder,
And I, growing fainter yet fonder,
Now weary too much when I wander—
Now fall when I climb.

This passage is a little obscure. If there is anywhere in the poem a touch of strained emotion, it may be here; but it is not a point to insist upon. The meaning of 'reason' is elusive, but I take it he is saying that, had he known early enough how poetry would eventually be able to sustain his mind, he might never have been led as a youth into idle courses or felt the need to seek distraction from them by emigration to Australia. The sense of 'Now fall when I climb' is harder to interpret, because its import may depend upon one's knowing how close he was to the abyss which finally engulfed him.

It is noteworthy that in this poem which, with whatever haste it may have been written, is assuredly Gordon's most thoughtful personal statement, there is very little of his habitual moralizing strain. This **"Dedication"** was too near to both heart and conscience for mere glib verse-making. However the last strophe has a touch of it. It is the weakest spot; yet perhaps the poem could not have been his at all without any. What his bush philosophy meant by 'go westward' (? towards death, the setting sun), by 'best' and 'worst' and 'worthless', we need not trouble to push to definition. The writer himself emerges through the fog and the poem finds its end:

It matters but little in the long run,
The weak have some right—
Some share in the race that the strong run,
The fight the strong fight.
If words that are worthless go westward,
Yet the worst word shall be as the best word,
In the day when all riot sweeps restward,
In darkness or light.

"A Dedication" sums up all that Gordon felt and could express about his own poetry. It is clearly, in the end, a very imperfect manifesto: the utterance of a part-blind poet pitched by circumstance into a strange, part-articulate colonial community, and troubled moreover by doubts and uncertainties inherent not merely in his own or the general colonial situation, but in the mental climate of the age. (pp. 57-65)

Brian Elliott, in an introduction to Adam Lindsay Gordon *by Adam Lindsay Gordon, Sun Books, 1973, pp. 1-70.*

H. M. GREEN (essay date 1984)

[*An Australian poet and critic, Green is the author of the comprehensive critical study* A History of Australian Literature: Pure and Applied *(1961), which was revised after his death by his widow, Dorothy M. Green. In the following excerpt from this work, Green discusses Gordon's significance as an Australian poet.*]

Gordon has a real importance for Australian poetry. He was the first Australian poet to be read by the ordinary man, even if what the ordinary man valued in him was not the best that Gordon had to offer; and, what is much more important, his riding rhymes, whatever their spirit and origin, were an important factor in the creation of the Australian ballad by Paterson and others. But to accept Gordon as, in the words of his biographer, Sladen, "one of the standard poets of the English language", or to regard him as "the great Australian poet" would be absurd. In the best of his work his emotions are sincere and intense, but they are limited in kind and quality and do not lead the mind outward; he writes also in a rush of emotion that is sometimes not deeply felt and may even be second-hand, so that the result is wordy and lacking in precision, creating no more than a vague emotional atmosphere. Yet sometimes he reaches a much higher level, as in **"The Sick Stockrider"**, whose line about the "hot, slow, sleepy, silent ride" embodies the very spirit of the outback horseman in the vast Australian noon; in the succeeding verses the ore is spread, as is natural, thinner in the rifts, but here again there is the same characteristic atmosphere, conveyed in words that are, if not so inevitable, hard to forget:

'Twas merry in the glowing morn, among the gleaming grass,
To wander as we've wandered many a mile,
And blow the cool tobacco cloud, and watch the white wreaths pass,
Sitting loosely in the saddle all the while.
'Twas merry 'mid the blackwoods, when we spied the station roofs,
To wheel the wild scrub cattle at the yard,
With a running fire of stockwhips and a fiery run of hoofs;
Oh, the hardest day was never then too hard!

No poem so humanly Australian had appeared hitherto, and very few had struck so individual a note. **"A Dedication"** to ***Bush Ballads and Galloping Rhymes*** contains several groups, each of several lines, that are again individual and impressive, notably those in which

. . . with fire and fierce drought on her tresses,
Insatiable Summer oppresses
Sere woodlands and sad wildernesses,
And faint flocks and herds,

and there are groups of a similar sort, though in tone Swinburnian, in **"The Swimmer"**, and more in **"Joyous Garde"**. Sometimes a line of Gordon's will produce a strikingly dramatic effect in virtue of its contrast with the textual and emotional context: of this there are several examples in **"The Road to Avernus"**, in one of which, upon the man's passionate outburst the girl's reply falls like a shock of cold water:

"Yonder are Brian and Basil watching us fools from the porch"!;

there is another example, as cynical but full of pity, at the conclusion of **"From the Wreck"**, where the rider is looking at the body of the little mare that he has had to ride to death:

How much for her hide? She had never worn shoes.

But we read Gordon, as has been finely said "not for fine phrases, but for the directness of some cry, and above all for the breadth and effectiveness of any utterance . . . taken as a whole" [see excerpt by Frank Maldon Robb dated 1912]. And we read him because even if we ourselves are not hunters, sportsmen, soldiers, adventurers, he uncovers some underlying stratum of such men in us, opening up to us the road of adventure and blowing over it the wind of romance. Gordon's appeal therefore is wider than it may at first sight seem. It is directed neither to the artist nor to the intellectual, as such, for in Gordon's verses the first may be offended at much that he finds and the second at much that he does not find; yet as men, both types may be drawn to Gordon: it is directed neither to the taste nor to the intellect but to the blood. Gordon is very human and full of enthusiasm, and it is by reason of these qualities in him, as much as of his spring and vividness and resonance, that we are drawn into the rhythm of his speed and feel that we are galloping with him along some track of romance or by-path of romanticized history that might not at all appeal to us in real life. Except **"From Lightning and Tempest"** all Gordon's best work appears in ***Bush Ballads and Galloping Rhymes:*** this poem is a fine piece of moral eloquence, in which statement and symbol are closely matched; it may owe something to the Old Testament. **"The Road to Avernus"** is Byronically melodramatic; there is a touch of *Manfred* about it and to modern taste it is rather naïve, though with touches of crude power. Of **"How We Beat the Favourite"** it may be said that it is almost first-rate of a third-rate kind; the virtues of **"Wolf and Hound"** are purely popular virtues; in it "Childe Roland" has been vulgarized; **"From the Wreck"** is fine vigorous stuff, but as a riding rhyme it is not to be compared with **"Britomarte"**, which of its kind could scarcely be bettered. There remains the splendid **"Swimmer"**, whose best verses Swinburne might have been glad to sign: but it *is* Swinburne; the influence of the greater poet has not been resolved to such an extent that the product becomes Gordon's. And there is **"A Song of Autumn"**, with its beautiful introductory lines,

> Where shall we go for our garlands glad
> At the falling of the year?,

whose impression remains, in spite of their old-fashioned phrasing. Finally, what is by far the best of Gordon's poems, and what is certainly among the best that have come out of Australia, if it may be taken to have come out of Australia: **"The Rhyme of Joyous Garde"**. Whatever this poem may owe to Swinburne or Tennyson, it is Gordon's own: beside such verses as the following the "Idylls" seem anaemic and "The Defence of Guenevere" sickly; it is hard to find anything to compare with them until we come to Grenfell's "Into Battle"; indeed it is probably the finest poem of its kind in English, though we have had about enough of this sort of thing after two world wars:

> We were glad together in gladsome meads,
> When they shook to the strokes of our snorting steeds;
> We were joyful in joyous lustre
> When it flush'd the coppice or fill'd the glade,
> When the horn of the Dane or the Saxon bray'd,
> And we saw the heathen banner display'd,
> And the heathen lances cluster.
>
> Then a steel-shod rush and a steel-clad ring,
> And a crash of the spear staves splintering,
> And the billowy battle blended.
> Riot of chargers, revel of blows,
> And fierce flush'd faces of fighting foes,
> From croup to bridle, that reel'd and rose,
> In a sparkle of sword-play splendid.
>
> And the long, lithe sword in the hand became
> As a leaping light, as a falling flame,
> As a fire through the flax that hasted;
> Slender, and shining, and beautiful,
> How it shore through shivering casque and skull,
> And never a stroke was void and null,
> And never a thrust was wasted.

The question of Gordon's standing, as distinct from his influence, in Australian poetry, seems to depend finally on whether this particular poem may reasonably be regarded as Australian. On the whole there seems no good reason why it should not; there would have been no doubt about it if its author had been Australian-born, and very little if he had identified himself thoroughly with Australia. There must be now and then in a daughter literature, even after those early stages in which the new growth can scarcely be distinguished from the parent tree, works that belong equally to the parent and to the daughter country: perhaps this is one. If we assume that Australia has a claim to his finest poem, then, taking into account also such other fine poems and passages as have been here referred to, Gordon must be accounted among notable Australian poets, though very far from the first of them. (pp. 177-80)

H. M. Green, "Kendall and Gordon," in his A History of Australian Literature: Pure and Applied, 1789-1923, Vol. I, *revised edition, Angus & Robertson Publishers, 1984, pp. 156-80.*

ADDITIONAL BIBLIOGRAPHY

Clarke, Marcus. "Adam Lindsay Gordon." In *Australian Essays,* edited by George H. Cowling and Furnley Maurice, pp. 45-9. Melbourne: Melbourne University Press in association with Oxford University Press, 1935.

A general commentary by an Australian novelist and friend of Gordon. The essay is often referred to by later critics, primarily for Clarke's statement that Gordon's poetry is "something very like the beginnings of a national school of Australian poetry" and for his observations on the effects of the Australian landscape on that country's writers.

Hutton, Geoffrey. *Adam Lindsay Gordon: The Man and the Myth.* London: Faber and Faber, 1978, 217 p.

A biographical study with a brief exposition of Gordon's *Bush Ballads and Galloping Rhymes.*

Jordan, Richard Douglas. "Adam Lindsay Gordon: The Australian Poet." *Westerly* 30, No. 2 (June 1985): 45-56.

Analyzes Gordon's poetry and its critical reception, defending his importance to Australian literature.

Kendall, Henry. "The Late Mr A. L. Gordon: In Memoriam." In his *Selected Poems of Henry Kendall,* edited by T. Inglis Moore, pp. 67-8. Sidney: Angus and Robertson, 1957.

A poetic tribute by an acquaintance.

Kramer, Leonie. "The Literary Reputation of Adam Lindsay Gordon." *Australian Literary Studies* 1, No. 1 (June 1963): 42-56.

An outline of Gordon's critical reputation and assessment of his position in Australian literature.

Martin, Arthur Patchett. "The Poet of the Australian Bush." *Murray's Magazine* X, No. LV (July 1891): 93-102.

A biographical sketch.

McCrae, George Gordon. "Adam Lindsay Gordon." *Southerly* 5, No. 1 (1944): 26-8.

Personal reminiscences of Gordon.

Perkins, Elizabeth. "Towards Seeing Minor Poets Steadily and Whole." In *Bards, Bohemians, and Bookmen: Essays in Australian Literature,* edited by Leon Cantrell, pp. 39-55. Queensland, Australia: University of Queensland Press, 1976.

A critical examination of three colonial poets: Charles Harpur, Henry Kendall, and Gordon.

Slessor, Kenneth. "Kendall and Gordon." In his *Bread and Wine: Selected Prose,* pp. 74-91. Melbourne: Angus and Robertson, 1970.

A negative critical commentary arguing for the relegation of Gordon's stature in Australian literature, noting such flaws in his poetry as faulty scansion, poor rhymes, and trite phrasing.

Victor Marie Hugo

1802-1885

French novelist, poet, dramatist, and critic.

The following entry presents criticism of Hugo's novel *Notre-Dame de Paris* (1831); translated as *The Hunchback of Notre-Dame* (1833). For a discussion of Hugo's complete career, see *NCLC,* Vol. 3; for criticism devoted to his novel *Les misérables,* see *NCLC,* Vol. 10.

Hugo's first major novel, *Notre-Dame de Paris,* is considered one of the most significant historical romances in French literature. Important in the context of Hugo's career as a statement of his developing aesthetic and social ideals, *Notre-Dame de Paris* is also recognized as an intellectually and emotionally powerful romantic tragedy. Critics have especially praised the novel for its masterful depiction of medieval Paris, its intricately ordered narrative, and its memorable portraits of such stock romantic characters as the gentle monster, the evil cleric, and the beautiful, orphaned heroine. Already an acclaimed poet and dramatist at the time of its publication, Hugo gained a still greater audience with *Notre-Dame de Paris,* becoming one of the few authors to achieve comparable success in three significant genres.

In the decade prior to composing *Notre-Dame de Paris,* Hugo had achieved a remarkable following as one of the commanding figures in French Romantic literature. His fame was further increased in 1830 with the production of his sensational drama *Hernani,* which drew large audiences who vigorously debated the literary merits of the work. Groups of Romantic writers and artists attended performances to demonstrate support for Hugo's revolutionary use of language and innovative dramatic techniques; traditionalists attended in order to denounce Hugo's disregard of the classic precepts of drama, including unity of time, place, and action. Hoping to benefit from the publicity surrounding *Hernani,* his publisher pressed him for a novel, adding a clause to their agreement requiring Hugo to pay a considerable fine for each week the manuscript was overdue. Determined to meet his contractual responsibilities, Hugo returned to a novel he had begun researching in the late 1820s about Parisian life during the Middle Ages. He worked furiously, completing the book in January 1831; it was published as *Notre-Dame de Paris* the following March.

Notre-Dame de Paris is essentially a romantic tragedy. The story concerns the lust of the evil archdeacon Claude Frollo for Esmeralda, an innocent gypsy dancing girl, who, through a simple but kind action, has gained the love of Quasimodo, the hunchbacked bell ringer of Notre-Dame cathedral. Spurned by Esmeralda, who is herself in love with Phoebus de Châteaupers, a handsome scoundrel, Frollo conspires to have her arrested and convicted as a witch. As her execution approaches, Quasimodo rescues the girl, giving her refuge in the cathedral tower. In a scene often praised for its great dramatic power, a crowd of Parisian commoners attacks the cathedral in an attempt to liberate Esmeralda from Quasimodo, whose noble motives are unknown to the throng. Frollo intercedes, delivering Esmeralda to the civil authorities, and the novel ends tragically with a description of Esmeralda and Quasimodo embracing in death.

In researching *Notre-Dame de Paris,* Hugo studied several chronicles of medieval life, borrowing historical details and names for his characters from annals of the period. Hoping to render the atmosphere of medieval Paris naturally and artistically rather than produce a dispassionate historical report, Hugo incorporated various devices intended to enhance the historical atmosphere of the novel, including archaic diction and grammar and frequent description of Gothic art and architecture. The vibrancy and acuity of his portrait have elicited frequent praise from reviewers, one of whom wrote: "It seems as if we were but listening to [Hugo's] reminiscences of the time of Louis XI. To put old Paris before our eyes appears to be rather an act of memory than an act of study, and he sets it forth with a freshness which sparkles in the fancy."

While composing *Notre-Dame de Paris,* Hugo followed the Romantic precepts he had defined in 1827 in the preface to his historical verse drama *Cromwell,* and commentators often refer to that preface in their discussions of the novel. One of the most important principles put forth in that essay concerns the necessity of portraying the grotesque as well as the beautiful. Hugo viewed the grotesque as the complement of the sublime, and considered fidelity to the multifarious nature of creation to be one of the underlying tenets of literary composition. His comments on the place of the grotesque in literature are often recalled in discussions of *Notre-Dame de Paris* that emphasize his tragic portrait of the hunchback, Quasimodo. However, many critics contend that the translation title by which the work is best known to English-speaking readers, *The Hunchback of Notre-Dame,* and the popular film version of the novel have focused unwarranted attention on Quasimodo. Citing the novel's original title, they have maintained that the cathedral itself occupies the central position in the work and that its hybrid architecture—a combination of Gothic and Romanesque elements—serves as a model of the composite nature of the novel. According to Ilinca M. Zarifopol-Johnston: "What is Gothic in the cathedral is dramatic in the novel; what is Romanesque in the cathedral is epic in the novel." Such a fusion accords with the aesthetic theory developed by Hugo in the preface to *Cromwell;* rejecting classical models, which demand purity of construction, Hugo considered a mixture of themes and styles necessary to achieve literary completeness.

According to Hugo, the composition of the novel was in part the result of his discovery of the Greek word *anankè* carved into a wall in Notre-Dame cathedral. Variously translated as "fate," "fatality," "destiny," "necessity," and "doom," *anankè* is recognized by critics as a guiding force in the novel, and Hugo himself announced in his preface that "C'est sur ce mot qu'on a fait ce livre" ("It is on this word that I made this book"). Throughout *Notre-Dame de Paris,* elaborate images demonstrate Hugo's belief that the pursuit of such intangible goals as knowledge, love, and truth is invariably obstructed by the forces of destiny. A second theoretical concern in the novel is Hugo's concept of the relationship between architecture and literature. He maintained that before the invention of the printing press, the architecture of a society served as its literature, embodying everything important and particular to that society, including its ideal of beauty, understanding of the universe, and greatest ideas. The advent of printing transformed "literature," in Hugo's view, from a destructible to an indestructible art: buildings were usually one-of-a-kind structures that could be easily destroyed; printed materials, however, were produced in great quantities and widely disseminated. In *Notre-Dame de Paris* Hugo used this argument in an effort to convince his contemporaries to preserve architectural works as the literature of past ages, rather than destroy them through neglect or clumsy restoration.

Conceived during a turbulent period in French history and completed in the months immediately following the tumultuous July Revolution of 1830, *Notre-Dame de Paris* also embodies Hugo's views on numerous social and political issues, most notably on the development of the common people as a significant political force. The character Jacques Coppenole, a Flemish visitor to the court of Louis XI, serves as a representative of the common people and an exponent of Hugo's democratic ideals in the novel. In an important scene in the Bastille with the king, for example, Coppenole hears the sounds of the crowd gathering to attack the cathedral and prophetically warns the king that while the hour of the people has not yet arrived, it will come. As in his previous novel *Le dernier jour d'un condamné* (*The Last Day of a Condemned*), Hugo also expressed in *Notre-Dame de Paris* his abhorrence of capital punishment and his belief that even in a society professing equality under the law, the poor remain oppressed.

Contemporary French reviewers were generally unimpressed by the novel when it was published. Researcher Max Bach has attributed this unenthusiastic response to the partisan concerns of various groups of critics, including those who objected to the absence of religion in the novel and those who believed that Hugo had slighted the bourgeoisie. Nevertheless *Notre-Dame de Paris* gained a wide audience among the novel-buying public and followers of the Romantic movement. In England, many early critics praised Hugo's vivid portrayal of Parisian life in the Middle Ages and the artfulness with which he forged the melodramatic, tragic plot, but expressed concern over the violence and unpleasantness in the novel. As social and moral interpretations of the novel gave way in the following century to more sophisticated analyses detailing its elaborate construction and complex philosophical basis, *Notre-Dame de Paris* gained a critical reputation as the first great historical romance in French literature. At the same time, the novel became a worldwide popular success, inspiring translations into more than twenty languages. In the words of Frank T. Marzials, *Notre-Dame de Paris* is a "great book, a magnificent book most unquestionably, a book before which the critic may fitly throw down all his small artillery of carpings and quibblings, and stand disarmed and reverent."

(See also *Something About the Author,* Vol. 47.)

VICTOR HUGO (essay date 1831)

[*In the following preface to the first edition of* Notre-Dame de Paris, *Hugo cites his inspiration for the novel.*]

Some years ago, when visiting, or, more properly speaking, thoroughly exploring the Cathedral of Notre-Dame, the writer came upon the word

'ANÁΓKH
["fate," "destiny"]

graven on the wall in a dim corner of one of the towers.

In the outline and slope of these Greek capitals, black with age and deeply scored into the stone, there were certain peculiarities characteristic of Gothic calligraphy which at once betrayed the hand of the mediæval scribe.

But most of all, the writer was struck by the dark and fateful significance of the word; and he pondered long and deeply over the identity of that anguished soul that would not quit the world without imprinting this stigma of crime or misfortune on the brow of the ancient edifice.

Since then the wall has been plastered over or scraped—I forget which—and the inscription has disappeared. For thus, during the past two hundred years, have the marvellous churches of the Middle Ages been treated. Defacement and mutilation have been their portion—both from within and from without. The priest plasters them over, the architect scrapes them; finally the people come and demolish them altogether.

Hence, save only the perishable memento dedicated to it here by the author of this book, nothing remains of the mysterious word graven on the sombre tower of Notre-Dame, nothing of the unknown destiny it so mournfully recorded. The man who inscribed that word passed centuries ago from among men; the word, in its turn, has been effaced from the wall of the Cathedral; soon, perhaps, the Cathedral itself will have vanished from the face of the earth.

This word, then, the writer has taken for the text of his book. (pp. xxxiii-xxxiv)

Victor Hugo, in a preface to his Notre Dame de Paris, *translated by Jessie Haynes, P. F. Collier & Son, 1902? pp. xxiii-xxxiv.*

VICTOR HUGO (essay date 1832)

[In the following essay, originally published as the author's preface to the 1832 edition of Notre-Dame de Paris, *Hugo explains the addition of three new chapters to the novel.]*

The announcement that this edition was furnished with several *fresh* chapters was incorrect; they should have been described as hitherto *unpublished*. For, if by *fresh* one understands *newly written*, then the chapters added to this edition are not fresh ones. They were written at the same time as the rest of the work; they date from the same period, were engendered by the same thought, and from the first formed part of the manuscript of ***Notre-Dame de Paris.*** Moreover, the author cannot imagine adding new developments to a work of this nature, the thing being once finished and done with. That cannot be done at will. To his idea, a novel is, in a sense, necessarily born with all its chapters complete, a drama with all its scenes. Do not let us think there is anything arbitrary in the particular number of parts which go to make up that whole—that mysterious microcosm which we call a novel or a drama. Neither joins nor patches are ever effectual in such a work, which ought to be fashioned in a single piece, and so be left, as best may be. The thing once done, listen to no second thoughts; attempt no touchings up of the book once given to the world, its sex, virile or otherwise, once recognised and acknowledged; the child, having once uttered its first cry, is born, is fashioned in that way and no other; father or mother are powerless to alter it, it belongs to the air and the sun; let it live or die as it is. Is your book a failure? *Tant pis,* but do not add chapters to those which have already failed. Is it defective?—it should have been completed before birth. Your tree is gnarled? You will not straighten it out. Your novel phthisical, not viable? You will never give it the life that is lacking to it. Your drama is born lame? Believe me, it is futile to supply it with a wooden leg.

The author is therefore particularly anxious that the public should know that the interpolated chapters were not written expressly for this new edition. They were not included in the previous editions for a very simple reason. When ***Notre-Dame de Paris*** was being printed the first time, the packet of manuscript containing these chapters went astray, so that they would either have had to be rewritten or omitted. The author considered that the only chapters of real import were the two dealing specially with art and history, but that their omission would in no way disturb the course of the drama; and that the public being unconscious of their absence, he alone would be in the secret of this hiatus. He decided then for the omission, not only for the above reason, but because, it must be confessed, his indolence shrank affrighted from the task of rewriting the lost chapters. Rather would he have written a new book altogether.

Meanwhile, these chapters have reappeared, and the author seizes the first opportunity to restore them to their proper place, thus presenting his work complete—such as he imagined it, well or ill, lasting or perishable; but in the form he desired it to have. (pp. xxxi-xxxii)

Victor Hugo, in a preface to his Notre Dame de Paris, *translated by Jessie Haynes, P. F. Collier & Son, 1902? pp. xxxi-xxxii.*

THE EXAMINER **(essay date 1833)**

[In the following excerpt, an anonymous critic praises the "vigour, ambition, and familiarity with the age" exhibited in Notre-Dame de Paris. *The critic also attacks a review of the novel published in the* Edinburgh Review *in July 1833, charging its writer with misreading an important passage of the story and, thus, inaccurately judging Hugo's intentions and achievement. For an excerpt from the* Edinburgh Review *essay, see* NCLC, *Vol. 3.]*

The ***Notre-Dame*** of Victor Hugo must take rank with the best romances by the Author of *Waverley*. If it fall short in copiousness and variety of incident and adventure, it transcends on the other hand in vigour, animation, familiarity with the age. The reader of this book will never stop to admire the antiquarian lore of the author; it seems as if we were but listening to his reminiscences of the time of Louis XI. To put old Paris before our eyes appears to be rather an act of memory than an act of study, and he sets it forth with a freshness which sparkles in the fancy. 'Tis centuries since, but the scene has the vividness of the present sunshine. ***Notre-Dame*** abounds with characters any one of which would have served to carry on the interest of a modern novel. La Esmeralda, a gipsy dancing girl, will remind the reader of the Fenella of Scott, but there is the difference between them of a being of warm blood, and the plastered gew-gaw figure on the top of a Twelfth cake. La Esmeralda has all the reality that Fenella wants. Quasimodo, a monster of strength and ugliness, whose frightful aspect has made him an object of disgust to the world, which he repays with hatred to all but two beings, Frollo, who has reared him from his deserted childhood, and La Esmeralda, who has succoured him in suffering and ignominy, is a character not original, but managed with admirable power. Upon Frollo all the mischief turns. He is a monk whose pent passions, long subdued and late excited, overbear his reason, and turn him to a fiend. As his case exemplifies the curb to nature, so his brother's (a spendthrift abandoned to debauchery) exemplifies the spur, but the passions of the first boil over in injury to others, and the profligate is mischievous only to himself. La Esmeralda is the unfortunate object of the monk's desires; he is hateful to her and rejected; and Frollo, resolved that no other shall enjoy what is denied to him, ultimately betrays her up to summary execution under a sentence of witchcraft. This incident occurs in the Place de Grève at the break of day, and the priest, certain of the instant execution of the victim with no more ceremony than goes to the hanging of a dog, hurries up to one of the towers of Notre-Dame to witness the event. The night has been one of tumult, outrage, blood, and terror; the morning is all calm and loveliness, and just as the sun pours his glories on the scene—with the opening of a day such as she loved to live for—La Esmeralda tastes the bitterness of death. . . . [We] think, in power, in horror, and the skilful use of circumstances, [this terrible scene] stands out unrivalled. (p. 533)

Now for a specimen of critical accuracy. The *Edinburgh Review* refers to

> That awful scene where the archdeacon, gazing down from the tower of Notre-Dame upon the execution of his victim in the square beneath, is seized by Quasimodo—who has now relapsed into the savage, since the destruction of the only being to whom his heart had opened—and hurled from a height of two hundred feet "plumb down" upon the pavement below. This description is terrible beyond conception. Every motion, every struggle of the wretched priest, every clutch of his nails, every heave of the breast, as he clings to the projecting spout which has arrested

> his fall; then the gradual bending of the spout itself beneath his weight; the crowd shouting beneath, the monster above him—weeping;—(for he had loved the priest, and only the fury of disappointed attachment had urged him to this crime;)—the victim balancing himself over the gulf, his last convulsive effort ere he resigns his hold, even the revolutions of his body as he descends, his striking on the roof, from which he glides off like a tile detached by the wind, and then the final crash and rebound upon the pavement—all are portrayed with the most horrible minuteness and reality.

First, Quasimodo has not hurled the monk from a height of two hundred feet "plumb down" upon the pavement below; he has hurled him over the balustrade, but his fall has been stopped within a few feet of the summit. The horror of the scene is in the suspension and not in the sheer descent—in the protracted and hopeless, nerveless, giddy struggle, and not in a sudden pitch to destruction, and the reviewer mars the effect by placing the final catastrophe before the lingering circumstances that comprehend a world of agony.

The reviewer, in running over the circumstances of horror, says, "the crowd shouting beneath." So the reviewer would have conceived it very likely, but Victor Hugo has another method of raising the horror of a scene. He says, "down in the Parvis (the open space at the foot of the cathedral) there were some groups of worthy starers, *quietly* striving to guess what madman it could be that was *amusing himself* after so strange a fashion. The priest could hear them saying—for *their voices mounted up to him clear and shrill*—Why, he'll surely break his neck."

It is this careless indifferent speculation which strikes worse than mockery clearly and shrilly upon the monk's ear while in his agony for self-preservation and throes of mortal dread. There is no where concern for his terrible peril. Before him are the stones grinning in fantastic effigies; below him people coolly conjecturing that he will break his neck; above him the grim face of Quasimodo weeping: and here is another notable blunder of the reviewer, who observes upon his weeping that he had loved the priest, as if Quasimodo was weeping for the priest! No such thing; Quasimodo is weeping for the sufferings of La Esmeralda wavering and writhing on the gibbet, and not for the priest. He sees not the priest; another object fills his eyes; and it is the misery of the priest to be struggling within arm's length of one who *could* save him, but who is so absorbed in the sufferings of another, that he is not even conscious of his hideous jeopardy. The author says, "Quasimodo would only have to stretch out his hand to him to draw him from the gulf; but he did not so much as look at him— he was looking on the Grève—he was looking on the gibbet—he was looking on the gipsy girl;" and the exact critic describes him as relentingly weeping for the priest's helpless and horrible posture of peril. Reading with this misunderstanding the reviewer could not comprehend half the effect of the scene which he pretends to estimate. The repeated reference to Quasimodo weeping, in describing the monk's agony, is to heighten the misery by the presence of the means of safety within arm's length of the tortures of terror and despair; but Quasimodo, who could save by stretching out a hand, is insensible to the hideous struggle that is going on under his very feet. He is deaf: had the clinging monk a breath to spare in the voice of a hundred men, the ear of him who had the helping hand would be insensible to it. . . .

Before the execution of La Esmeralda there is a very fine tragic scene, full of nature, in the discovery of her mother. The parent recovers her child (stolen by gipsies in her infancy) just at the moment that the pursuers are on her track. The mother's pleadings are beyond words pathetic.

Another very grand scene, but not of the same high order, is an attack on Notre Dame by the Truands, or mendicants and vagabonds of Paris, then a formidable body.

The fault of the book is the opening, which tires by its grotesqueness before the purpose is developed. The reader must not be deterred by this heavy introduction, for he will be no sooner clear of it than he will feel the interest of the story, which steadily increases to the catastrophe, where it makes the heart leap as it rushes boiling on, not without eddying, round incidents that stay the imagination without diverting the main tide of the curiosity. (p. 534)

A review of "Notre-Dame: A Tale of the Ancien Régime," in The Examiner, *No. 1334, August 25, 1833, pp. 533-34.*

JULES JANIN (essay date 1837)

[In the following excerpt, Janin offers a favorable appraisal of Notre-Dame de Paris, *considering the role of "necessity" in the plot of the novel and examining Hugo's presentation of medieval society.]*

It is not in his contributions to the theatre that we must look for M. Victor Hugo in his power and freedom. To find him in his strength, read those of his verses which are the result of his better and purer inspiration; read ***Le dernier jour d'un condamné***; and, above all, read his great master-piece, ***Notre-Dame de Paris***—that enthralling resurrection of the old times, old manners, and old passions of our history. It is especially in ***Notre-Dame de Paris***—a terrible and powerful narrative, which haunts the memory with the horrible distinctness of a nightmare—that M. Victor Hugo displays, in all their strength, at once the enthusiasm and self-possession, the boldness and flexibility of his genius. What varieties of suffering are heaped together in these melancholy pages—what ruins built up—what terrible passions put in action—what strange incidents produced! All the foulness and all the superstitions of the middle ages are melted, and stirred, and mixed together with a trowel of mingled gold and iron. The poet has breathed upon all those ruins of the past; and, at his will, they have taken their old forms and risen up again, to their true stature, upon that Parisian soil which toiled and groaned, of yore, beneath their hideous weight, like the earth under Etna. Behold those narrow streets, those swarming squares, those cut-throat alleys, those soldiers, merchants, and churches; look upon that host of passions circulating through the whole—all breathing, and burning, and armed! Each of those passions is clothed in its own appropriate garb—the robe of the priest and that of the woman—the helmet and the bonnet—or goes naked in the beggar's rags, and raging like the passion of the wild beast. Behold, too, how all that multitude *obeys* without a murmur; how *authority*—that now disfranchised thing—weighs, with its leaden hand, on all those heads, on all those consciences, and on all those wills! How well has he exhibited that people of the sixteenth century, who were born to submission—submission to the king—submission to the priest—submission to all the powers of the earth! *Necessity! Necessity!* That Greek word, which forms the text of his book, M. Hugo has done more than write upon the old towers of Notre Dame—he has stamped it into every page of his poem. *Necessity* it is which compels Claude Frollo to love the Bohemian dancing-girl; *necessity* which orders the dance of Esmeralda, and sends her fluttering through the sunshine,—Esmeralda, that oriental pearl, broken to pieces by her contact with the wandering maniac. *Necessity,* in this book, is Louis XI.—the all-powerful king—who looks over all things, from the height of his authority, entrenched within his own will—the will of Louis XI., that iron rampart within whose shelter France was so strong. Thus, throughout the whole of this extraordinary work, M. Hugo has followed his double vocation of poet and of architect, of historian and romancer. He has fed it, at once, from the fountains of memory and of invention. He has set all the bells of that great city ringing, and all its hearts beating—save only the hearts of Louis and his gossip Tristan, who had no hearts. Such is this book—a brilliant page torn out of our history—the living image of a stirring society which glances in the sun, like the scales of a serpent when it changes its skin—a splendid epopée, beginning with poetry, and ending with blasphemy—a long human strife, over which for ever hang, as in a banner displayed, the old stone towers of Notre Dame de Paris. It is this great and inexhaustible book which will contribute its most brilliant ray to the literary fame of the author; and which, in a wiser head than his, must, at once, have decided his vocation.

At the same time, need I point out . . . the lamentable disposition of M. Victor Hugo, continually to deliver himself up to the horrible—to undertake the defence of all deformities, moral and physical? What is ***Notre-Dame de Paris,*** but an elaborate restoration of *the ugly,* in the domain of literature? Quasimodo is a creature even more deformed than Triboulet. The author has exhausted his powers of imagination and description, to twist that dorsal spine, to die those yellow teeth, to distort that horrible mouth, to cover that hideous face with warts and pustules. Quasimodo is, beyond dispute, the most abominable of all the creations of *ugliness.* Never came forth toad more horribly gifted with its poisonous foam, than Quasimodo, the bell-ringer, has come forth from the head of M. Victor Hugo. As for the beautiful Esmeralda,—that *dancing song*—that aerial vision—who stands out, all dazzling with whiteness and purity, from amid the filth of the drama—what is that bright creation, in spite of all, other than the *fille de joie,* softened down to its simplest condition of innocence? Here, once more, breaks out, in all its frankness, and clearly displayed, the poetical passion of M. Hugo for that *enfant perdue* of our corrupted civilisation which is called the *fille de joie.* (p. 504)

Jules Janin, "Literature of the Nineteenth Century: France," in The Athenaeum, *No. 506, July 8, 1837, pp. 466, 499-506.*

FRANK T. MARZIALS (essay date 1888)

[In the following excerpt from his Life of Victor Hugo, *Marzials praises the artistry of* Notre-Dame de Paris *and contrasts the background of human evil and suffering in the novel with the pleasant atmosphere of Sir Walter Scott's* Quentin Durward.]

[***Notre-Dame de Paris*** is a] great book, a magnificent book most unquestionably, a book before which the critic may fitly throw down all his small artillery of carpings and quibblings, and stand disarmed and reverent. That Victor Hugo had realised his ambition of crowning with poetry the prose of Sir Walter Scott, I shall not affirm. But then it scarcely seems as if any such crowning were needed, or possible; for the good Sir Walter's faults lay neither in lack of imagination, nor lack of fervour, nor an absence of elevation of tone, nor, in short, in a deficiency of aught that goes to the making of poetry. *Quentin Durward* deals with the same period as ***Nôtre-Dame de Paris,*** and if one places the two books side by side in one's thoughts, such differences as there are will hardly seem to be differences in degree of poetical inspiration. Our own great novelist's work is fresher, healthier perhaps, more of the open air. A spirit of hopefulness and youth and high courage seems to circulate through his pages—a sort of pervading trust that the good things of this world come to those who deserve them, that merit has its prizes, and unworthiness its punishments. There is blood enough and to spare in the book, and a good deal of hanging and much villainy. But our feelings are not greatly harrowed thereby. We need not weep unless so minded. If a good tall fellow is lopped down here and there,—like the worthy Gascon whom Dunios strikes through the unvisored face—the tragedy comes before we have known the man long enough to grow greatly interested in him. We are only affected as by the death of a very casual acquaintance. And such sufferers as the Wild Boar of the Ardennes deserve their fate too thoroughly to cause us the most passing pang. So does Scott, in his genial kindliness, temper for us the horrors of the Middle Ages. He does not blink them, as M. Taine erroneously seems to hold. He presents them, with consummate art, so that they shall not cause unnecessary pain. Victor Hugo, in ***Nôtre-Dame,*** was animated by a quite other spirit. After the manner of his nation—for French fiction tolerates an amount of unmerited misery to which the English reader would never submit—he looks upon life far more gloomily. Claude Frollo may perhaps deserve even the apalling agony of those eternal moments during which he hangs suspended from the leaden gutter at the top of the tower of Nôtre Dame, and has a hideous foretaste of his imminent death. Quasimodo is at best but an animal with a turn for bell-ringing, and, apart from his deformity and deafness, not entitled to much sympathy. But Esmeralda, poor Esmeralda, who through the deep mire of her surroundings has kept a soul so maidenly and pure, who is full of tender pity for all suffering, and possesses a heart that beats with such true woman's love—what had she done that Victor Hugo should bestow the treasure of that love upon the worthless archer-coxcomb, Phœbus de Chateaupers, that he should make her frail harmless pretty life, a life of torture, and cause her to die literally in the hangman's grasp? Was it worth while that Esmeralda's mother, Paquerette la Chantefleurie, should find her child again, after long years of anguish, only to relinquish her, after one brief moment of rapture, for that terrible end? Quentin's courage and practical sagacity are crowned with success: he saves the woman he loves. But by what irony of fate does it happen that Quasimodo's heroic efforts to defend Esmeralda have for only result to injure those who are trying to save her, and the hastening of her doom?

Gloom, gloom, a horror of darkness and evil deeds, of human ineptitude and wrong, such is the background of ***Nôtre-Dame.*** If Scott gives us a poetry of sunshine and high emprise, Victor Hugo gives us, and here with a moe than equal puissance, the poetry of cloud—wrack and ungovernable passion. There is no piece of character-painting in *Quentin Durward* that, for tragic lurid power and insight, can be placed beside the portrait of Claude Frollo. Lucid and animated as are such scenes as the sacking of the bishop's palace, and the attack on Liège, they are not executed with such striking effects of light and shade as the companion scene in ***Nôtre-Dame,*** the attack of the beggars on the cathedral. Scott's landscape is bright, pleasant, the reflection of a world seen by a healthy imagination and clear in the sunlight of a particularly sane nature. Victor Hugo's world in ***Nôtre-Dame*** is as a world seen in fever-vision, or suddenly illumined by great flashes of lightning. The mediæval city is before us in all its picturesque huddle of irregular buildings. We are in it; we see it: the narrow streets with their glooms and gleams, their Rembrandt effects of shadow and light; the quaint overhanging houses each of which seems to have a face of its own; the churches and convents flinging up to the sky their towers and spires; and high above all, the city's very soul, the majestic cathedral. And what a motley medley of human creatures throng the place! Here is the great guild of beggar-thieves even more tatterdemalion and shamelessly grotesque than when Callot painted them for us two centuries later. Here is Gringoire, the out-at-elbows unsuccessful rhymer of the time. Anon Esmeralda passes accompanied by her goat. She lays down her little mat, and dances lightly, gracefully to her tambourine. See how the gossips whisper of witchcraft as the goat plays its pretty tricks. And who is that grave priest, lean from the long vigils of study, who stands watching the girl's every motion with an eye of sombre flame? Close behind, in attendance on the priest, is a figure scarcely human, deformed, hideous, having but one Cyclops eye—also fastened on the girl. Among the bystanders may be seen the priest's brother, Jehan, the Paris student of the town-sparrow type that has existed from the days of Villon even until now. Before the dancer has collected her spare harvest of small coins, a soldier troop rides roughly by, hustling the crowd, and in the captain the poor child recognises the man who has saved her from violence some days before—the man to whom, alas, she has given her heart. In such a group as this what elements of tragedy lie lurking and ready to out-leap? That priest in his guilty passion will foreswear his priestly vows, stab the soldier, and, failing to compass his guilty ends, give over the poor child-dancer to torture and death. The deformed Cyclops, seeing the priest's fiendish laughter as they both stand on the top of Nôtre Dame tower, watching the girl's execution, will guess that *he* is the cause of her doom, and hurl him over the parapet. And the student too will be entangled in the tragic chains by which these human creatures are bound together. His shattered carcase will lie hanging from one of the sculptured ornaments on the front of the Cathedral.

Living, living,—yes, the book is unmistakably palpitatingly alive. It does not live, perhaps, with the life of prose and every-day experience. But it lives the better life of imagination. The novelist, by force of genius, compels our acceptance of the world he has created. Esmeralda, like Oliver Twist, and even more than Oliver Twist, is an improbable, almost impossible being. No one, we conceive, writing nowadays, with Darwinism in the air, would venture to disregard the laws of inherited tendency so far as to evoke such a character from the cloud-land of fancy. If he did, Mr. Francis Galton would laugh him to scorn. The girl's mother—one does not want to press heavily upon the poor creature, and it must therefore suffice to say that she was far from being a model to her sex. The father was anybody you like. From such parentage of vice and chance what superior virtue was to be expected? And, failing birth-gifts, had there been anything in education or surroundings to account for so dainty a product? Far from it. The girl from her infancy had been dragged through the ditches that lie along the broad highway of life, and is dwelling, when we came across her, in one of the foulest dens of the foul old city. She is almost as impossible as Eugène Sue's *Fleur de Marie* in the *Mysteries of Paris*. And yet, impossible as she may be, we still believe in her. She is a real person in a real world. That Paris of gloom and gleam may never have existed in history exactly as Victor Hugo paints it for us. It exists for all time notwithstanding. And Claude Frollo exists too, and Jehan, and Gringoire, and Coppenole, the jolly Flemish burgher, and Phœbus, and the beggars,—all the personages of this old-world drama. I should myself as soon think of doubting the truth of the pitiful story told by Damoiselle Mahiette, of how poor Paquerette loved and lost her little child, as I should think of doubting that Portia did, in actual fact, visit Venice, disguised as a learned judge from Padua, and, after escaping her husband's recognition, confound Shylock by her superior interpretation of the law.

In the ***Orientales*** and ***Hernani***, Victor Hugo had shown himself a magnificent artist in verse. In ***Nôtre-Dame de Paris***, he showed himself a magnificent artist in prose. The writing throughout is superb. Scene after scene is depicted with a graphic force of language, a power, as it were, of concentrating and flashing light, that are beyond promise. Some of the word-pictures are indelibly bitten into the memory as when an etcher has bitten into copper with his acid. Henceforward there could be no question as to the place which the author of the three works just named was entitled to take in the world of literature. Byron was dead, and Scott dying. Chateaubriand had ceased to be a living producing force. Goethe's long day of life was drawing to its serene close. Failing these, Victor Hugo stepped into the first place in European literature, and that place he occupied till his death.

And what light did Olympian Goethe, the star that was setting, throw upon ***Nôtre-Dame de Paris***? A light not altogether benignant, nor, if one may venture to say so in all humility and reverence, altogether just.

> "Victor Hugo has a fine talent," he said in one of his conversations with Eckermann, "but he is imbued with the disastrous romantic tendencies of his time. This is why he is led astray, and places beside what is beautiful that which is most unbearable and hideous. I have been reading ***Nôtre-Dame de Paris*** these last few days, and it required no small dose of patience to endure the torments which that perusal cost me. It is the most detestable book ever written. . . . What shall we think of a time that not only produces such books, but enjoys them?"

Whereupon one sighs to think that even the gods sitting on Olympus are in some slight sort subject to the infirmities of age, and lose the power of looking with an equally large equity upon the present and future, as well as upon the past. (pp. 108-14)

Frank T. Marzials, in his Life of Victor Hugo, *Walter Scott, 1888, 253 p.*

ANDREW LANG (essay date 1902?)

[*Lang was one of England's most influential men of letters in the closing decades of the nineteenth century. A proponent of the revival of Romantic fiction, Lang championed the works of H. Rider Haggard, Robert Louis Stevenson, and Rudyard Kipling, and was harshly critical of the Naturalistic and Realistic techniques of such novelists as Émile Zola and Henry James. In the following excerpt, Lang discusses strengths and weaknesses of* Notre-Dame de Paris, *also arguing that the second edition of the novel is a less powerful narrative than the first edition because it is disrupted by additional digressive chapters. Lang's remarks were most likely first published in 1902.*]

After the Lilies were driven from France in the days of July, 1830, Hugo wrote, at a great pace, his first famous novel, ***Notre-Dame de Paris.*** There was need of hurry, owing to an imprudent covenant to deliver the "copy" by a given date. For some five months the author was a recluse, working all day. Possibly he had to "read up his subject" as well as to write. The traces of "reading up" historical and antiquarian details for his purpose are, I think, apparent. (p. ix)

Hugo began ***Notre-Dame,*** in the circumstances naturally, with dogged and gloomy desire to finish a task. This it may be which renders the initial chapters, the vast descriptions of people, crowds, street scenes, ambassadors, the Cardinal, and the rest, rather prolix. But when once Esmeralda, Claude Frollo, and Quasimodo appear, the story races on. Gringoire, the typical poet, concentrated in the fiasco of his own play, while every other person is more than indifferent, has humour and is sympathetic. But Gringoire following Esmeralda and her goat; Quasimodo divinized in burlesque, a Pope of Unreason, yet tickled, for once, in his vanity; Esmeralda, a pearl on the dunghill, dancing and singing; the empty, easily conquering Phœbus; the mad and cruel love of the priest, Claude Frollo—when these are reached, the story lives, burns, and rushes to its awful portentous close. "Rushes," I said, but the current is broken, and dammed into long pools, mirrors of a motionless past, in all editions except the first. Hugo, as he tells us, lost three of his chapters, and published the first edition without them. Two of them were the studies of mediæval architecture, which interfere with the action. However excellent in themselves (intended, as they are, to raise a vision of the Paris of Louis XI), these chapters, introduced just where the author has warmed to his work and the tale is accumulating impetus, are possibly out of place. We grumble at Scott's *longueurs:* the first chapter of *Quentin Durward* is an historical essay. But Hugo certainly had not mastered the art of selection and conciseness. His excursus on architecture is admirable, but imprudent. (pp. x-xi)

The interest, before the architectural interruption, lay in the chase of Esmeralda by Gringoire; in the beggar-world, with its king and gibbet, like the Alsatia of the *Fortunes of Nigel* vastly magnified. The underworld of Paris, that for centuries has risen as the foam on the wave of revolution, fascinated Hugo. The hideous and terrible aspect of these grotesques he could scarcely exaggerate. It is urged that Esmeralda, a finer Fenella—a success, not a failure—could not have been bred and blossomed in her loathsome environment. The daughter of a woman utterly lost, till redeemed by the maternal passion, Esmeralda must have gone the way of her world. But it is Hugo's method to place a marvellous flower of beauty, grace, and goodness on his *fumier*. The method is not realism; it is a sacrifice to the love of contrast. In short, this is the "probable impossible" which Aristotle preferred to the "improbable impossible"; and the reader who yields himself to the author has no difficulty in accepting Esmeralda and the heart-breaking story of her mother. Claude Frollo demands and receives the same acceptance, with his fraternal affection, his disbelief in all but the incredible promises of alchemy, his furious passion, and fury of resistance to his passion. Whether Esmeralda is made more credible by her love of Phœbus, which proves her bane, is a question. That love strikes one as a touch of realism, an idea that Thackeray might have conceived, perhaps relenting, and rejecting the profanation. Whether the motive clashes or not with the romanticism of Esmeralda's part, we may excuse it by the ruling and creative word of the romance—'ΑΝΑΓΚΗ—Doom.

On one essential point Hugo certainly does not exaggerate. The trial of Esmeralda is merely the common procedure in cases of witchcraft. With the evidence of the goat, the withered leaf, and the apparition of the mysterious monk against her, there was no escape. Thousands were doomed to a horrible death . . . on evidence less damning. The torture applied to Esmeralda is that with which Jeanne d'Arc was threatened, escaping only by her courage and presence of mind. For the rest, the Maid endured more, and worse, and longer than Esmeralda, from the pedantic and cowardly cruelty of the French clergy of the age. One point might be perhaps urged against the conduct of the story. The Inquisition spared the life of the penitent sorceress, in Catholic countries, though Presbyterian judges were less merciful than the Inquisition. Esmeralda, who confessed to witcheries, under torture, would as readily have recanted her errors. It does not appear why she was hanged. If executed for witchcraft, it would have been by fire; and obviously she had not murdered Phœbus, who led the archers at the rescue of the Cathedral from the beggars. That scene is one of the most characteristic in the book, lit by flame and darkened by smoke. The ingenuity by which the mother of Esmeralda is made to help in causing her destruction, blinded as she is by 'ΑΝΑΓΚΗ, is one of Hugo's cruel strokes of stage-craft. The figure of such a mother, bankrupt of everything in life but the maternal passion, haunted Hugo, and recurs in Fantine. The most famous scene of all, vivid as with the vividness of a despairing dream, is the agony of the accursed priest as he swings from the leaden pipe on the roof of Notre-Dame. Once read the retribution is never forgotten—the picture of the mad lover and murderer swaying in air; death below; above, the one flaming eye of the monstrous Quasimodo.

The portrait of Louis XI, as compared with Scott's of the same King, has been likened to a Velasquez as vastly superior to a Vandyke. To myself, Scott's Louis appears rather to resemble a Holbein; Hugo's to be comparable to a miser by Rembrandt. But such comparisons and parallels are little better than fanciful. I find myself, as regards the whole book, sometimes rather in agreement with the extravagantly hostile verdict of Goethe—never, indeed, persuaded that ***Notre-Dame*** is "the most odious book ever written," but feeling that the agonies are too many, too prolonged, and too excruciating, the contrasts too violent. (pp. x-xiii)

Andrew Lang, in an introduction to Notre Dame de Paris *by Victor Hugo, translated by Jessie Haynes, P. F. Collier & Son, 1902? pp. v-xxv.*

MADAME DUCLAUX (essay date 1921)

[In the following excerpt from her biography of Hugo, Duclaux discusses Notre-Dame de Paris *in the context of Hugo's career, praising his graceful prose and recognizing the prominent role the cathedral serves in the novel.]*

Notre-Dame de Paris is unlike any other novel of Victor Hugo's. It has an extraordinary grace, and, if I dare say so of our Titan and his works, a prettiness, a delicacy of its own. It is without the fluidity and the sublime tenderness of ***Les misérables*** or ***Les travailleurs,*** or ***Quatrevingttreize***; and it possesses so much more beauty than his earlier books that we cannot compare them, or we might find a certain resemblance to ***Han d'Islande,*** romantic and fantastic as it is. But it is Victor Hugo's drawings that best compare with the complex and innumerable outlines, the play of light and shade, the picturesqueness, the mediaeval quality of ***Notre-Dame.*** The story attempts to portray the life of the fifteenth century in Paris in all its heights and depths, its fairness and foulness, from the thieves' den to the Cathedral belfry, from the laughing young women of the world in the noble's palace to the torture-chamber in the crypt. . . . And every detail is original and finished with the same loving exquisiteness—just as the trefoils and gargoyles far out of sight on the towers of the Cathedral are no less carefully chiselled than the faces of the saints in the Portals; every symbol is elaborated with an ardour of feeling that masks a hidden irony. And, in fact, if we strip the story of all this wealth of detail, often so beautiful that we lose sight of the plan beneath, the fable of ***Notre-Dame de Paris*** is sad—sad, and as simple, and as epic as a story from the ***Légende des siècles.*** It is the tale of a young girl who flits through the multitudinous and complicated ways of life, as extraneous to its regulations, as natural, as pure, and as capricious as a wind-sown wild flower. This is Esmeralda, the foundling gipsy, with her goat. And they symbolize Caprice, Imagination, Beauty, the Eternal Feminine (as Goethe would say), drawing all hearts, acknowledging no law. Four men love Esmeralda, follow her, attempt to win her: there is Frollo, the cleric, who is Science and Passion; there is Gringoire, the poet, a friendly creature, of all the most akin to the young girl, being himself irresponsible, harmless, seeing in the world nothing but Beauty; there is Quasimodo, the dwarf, the man of the people, with his great heart and his dog-like devotion; and there is Phébus de Châteaupers, a gallant young officer with nothin particular inside his handsome pate. And of course Esmeralda chooses him—just as Life chooses him. For, with the exception of Gringoire, every other character in the book comes to a tragic end—who can forget Esmeralda hanging from the gibbet like a broken flower, or the anguish of the hermit mother, the dizzy fall of Frollo from the height of his tower, or Quasimodo, in the vault with the dead girl, enjoying his death in the darkness? It is true that Hugo tells us that Phébus also "fit une fin tragique"—his tragic end, however, was merely matrimony:

S'il me plaît de cacher l'amour et la douleur
Dans le coin d'un roman ironique et railleur,

writes the poet in his ***Feuilles d'automne.*** For if he has nothing but irony and raillery for human beings, those trivial puppets of destiny, if for them he has neither love nor hope nor faith, nor any gospel save the word ΑΝΑΓΚΗ—Necessity—yet his heart is dilated with all the theological virtues when he turns from them to that which will outlast them—the beauty of the Cathedral. "There is," says Sainte-Beuve in his not very interesting criticism of the book, "something architectural in Victor Hugo's imagination—something picturesque, angular, *vertical,* and fantastic." (pp. 103-05)

The real heroine of ***Notre-Dame*** is the Cathedral, which Victor Hugo knew inch small, which he had visited perhaps a thousand times in his eight-and-twenty years, which he loved and, above all, in which he recognized the expression of his own genius. Victor Hugo was of the same race as the mediaeval masons who had transposed into stone the immense variety of Nature. Here was an example to show that Beauty can exist outside the limits of Measure, Unity, Order; that there can be a grace and a grandeur independent of the laws of classic perfection; a Beauty that draws its elements from the abundance and the complexity of the elements that it associates, in a harmony as elastic as that of the trees in a forest or the leaves on a bough. Everything in Gothic art is calculated, but nothing is exact, no angle true, no line straight, and it is this supple and, as it were, spontaneous asymmetry, these almost imperceptible curves and irregularities, which give their look of growth and life to these immense Cathedrals. . . . Contrast was the very law of [Hugo's] art. He saw the moral world as we see objects in strong sunshine, each cut out in sharp relief and doubled by the depth of its shadow. He could not imagine Beauty without evoking the image of Deformity, nor dream of ambition without the sense of a possible collapse, nor enjoy Love without remembering Death, nor turn to Faith without feeling on his shoulder the cold touch of Doubt. But also, and more and more as time went on, he could not look on a fallen woman without seeing in her a possible angel, nor see deformity and not believe it to conceal a beautiful soul, nor suffer defeat but his heart would beat high for the coming triumph, nor endure bereavement without the dim instinctive sense of a life beyond. (pp. 105-07)

Madame Duclaux, in her Victor Hugo, *Henry Holt and Company, 1921, 268 p.*

MATTHEW JOSEPHSON (essay date 1942)

[*An American poet, biographer, editor, and critic, Josephson is best remembered for championing the Dadaist movement in the early 1920s. In the following excerpt from his biography of Hugo, Josephson assesses* Notre-Dame de Paris *as the first great historical romance novel in French literature.*]

The idea of ***Notre-Dame de Paris*** went back to [Hugo's] youth, his enthusiasm for Gothic art, and his association with Charles Nodier, who had charge of all the old armour in the ancient Arsenal. Climbing all over the ancient cathedral of Notre-Dame, investigating its structure, inspecting its stone carvings, and studying the ancient books in the adjacent cloister library, he conceived the framework of his rather satanic tale. Like Matthew Lewis, English author of *The Monk,* a "horror novel" much read in France, like Luther, and like Dante, Victor Hugo became deeply absorbed in Lucifer during his readings in medievalism. A long period of war, like that of 1792-1815, has almost invariably been followed by one which turns to contemplate not only God and His mysteries, but, by antithesis, Satan, as well, and his dark works.

Hugo's accuracy and scholarship have been brought into question. Yet the old books he read on fifteenth-century Paris, by Comynes, Jean de Troyes, and the later Sauval, with their exact contemporary chronicles, were the best he might have chosen in the 1820's. Ernest Feydau, the distinguished French archaeologist, has declared that, compared with the work of the antiquarian Sauval, which he borrowed from, or any other chronicler, Hugo's romance pictured the life and atmosphere of the late fifteenth century with remarkable clarity and fullness. From the old chronicles he drew French names of ancient flavor: Lewis's "monk" must certainly have suggested the satanic alchemist, Archdeacon Claude Frollo; the hunchback, Quasimodo, the cathedral bell ringer, he drew from his own boyhood memories of Spain where there was a deaf-mute hunchback porter in the seminary he attended; the gipsy girl, Esmeralda, her goat, and the cavalier, Phébus de Chateaupers, were not difficult to invent. The character of the cathedral he absorbed, as he studied it stone by stone—carvings, statuary, and gargoyles—sometimes in the company of Deveria and the sculptor David d'Angers.

His larger purpose, aside from writing a diverting romance, was, as he explained in the **"Preface to *Cromwell,*"** to picture—in contrast with the seventeenth- or eighteenth-century classicists, who wrote of pagan times—the little understood Christian eras, with their saints and martyrs, their sorcerers and necromancers, their cathedrals and gargoyles, their heroism, their faith, their torture. In effect, Victor Hugo clung to this plan for fifty years, for he returned to it in the epic ***Légende des siècles,*** written in the autumn of his life.

Notre-Dame de Paris became the first great historical romance in French literature. Before this, others had written garbled historical narrations: his friend Vigny had done one of Richelieu in *Cinq Mars* (1826), and Prosper Mérimée had done something in 1829 on Charles IX. But no one reads these any more, whereas Hugo's romance, despite its intellectual limitations, is so inherently dramatic—in this sense an advance technically over previous works in the field—it is so colorful and atmospheric in its descriptions, and even in its digressions, that it is still read in twenty languages, and, thanks to its crude representation some years ago in motion-picture form, has assumed almost a legendary character. (pp. 169-71)

[The novel's] fairly tall tale serves but as a frame within which Hugo hangs his immense, teeming, strongly-colored canvas of old Paris in the time of François Villon, with its thieves' dens, nobles, guilds, masques, holidays, and witch trials. Hugo is "an eye," and appears most effective in his large descriptions; the word painting of the city scene, viewed from the cathedral belfry in all its labyrinthine detail, makes up one of the book's many digressions—this, of nearly a hundred pages, like a smaller picture within a larger one—and is done with such intensity of feeling, such verve and abandon, that it seems today more interesting than his two-dimensional characters and their destinies. These are for the most part silhouettes rather than full portraits, save for the grotesque hunchback Quasimodo and the briefly-glimpsed, ill-favored King Louis XI. In his early period, Victor Hugo, like the other romantics, failed in the realization of character in detail. The characters in ***Notre-Dame de Paris*** he evidently regarded as symbols of Beauty or Evil; the cathedral was as a symbol of the age and its faith that broods over the whole drama.

The account of the nocturnal attack on the cathedral by the army of thieves, as a high point, has rightly been judged one of the great passages in the literature of the picturesque. He is eloquent also in achieving, by the use of technical detail (more or less accurate), effects of the grotesque and the satanic. His searching study of Quasimodo in all his ugliness and suffering and the coolness with which he dwells upon scenes of flagellation or torture also suggest a somewhat sadistic strain in him. Hugo's critics promptly remarked that his book was in no sense the work of a pious Christian writer. The social-minded Liberals as well as the literary Conservatives of the period reproached him for his apparent absorption in the merely picturesque and supernatural. Yet the book had a certain objective power, a sustained dramatic force, that created enchantment in its time and even today, by an overturn of taste, causes it to be greatly favored again, by the literary surrealistes. (pp. 171-72)

Matthew Josephson, in his Victor Hugo: A Realistic Biography of the Great Romantic, *Doubleday, Doran & Co., Inc., 1942, 514 p.*

RICHARD B. GRANT (essay date 1968)

[*Grant is an American educator and critic who specializes in nineteenth-century French literature. In the following excerpt from his study of image, myth, and prophecy in Hugo's narrative works, he analyzes the recurring image of the spider and fly as the metaphor by which Hugo expressed the concept of fatality central to* Notre-Dame de Paris. *Grant also links this metaphor to Hugo's portrayal of an impenetrable "double barrier" existing between humans and their transcendent ideals.*]

Our point of departure [in a discussion of ***Notre-Dame de Paris***] must be the prologue to the work, for it sets as central the theme of fatality that had become visible in ***Cromwell*** and that is also at the heart of ***Marion de Lorme*** and ***Hernani.*** Imagining that some unknown medieval hand (fatality is in a sense anonymous) has carved the word Anankè on the wall of one of the towers, Hugo speaks of this word as having a "sens lugubre et fatal," and he uses the word "renfermer" not only to refer to "sens" but . . . also to the "lugubre et fatal" prisons that dominate the landscape and whose role is to enclose various characters. Hugo himself concluded the preface on Anankè or Fatality with the words: "C'est sur ce mot qu'on a fait ce livre." This theme hardly needs any examination here, for it is by now a platitude of Hugo criticism. But the form that Hugo gave it, the many elaborations of the "sens lugubre et fatal" enclosed within it, needs more careful treatment. Two passages from Book VII merit extensive quotation. The scene is Claude Frollo's monastic cell in one of the towers of Notre-Dame. . . . Here Frollo is seen observing the spider's web.

> Dom Claude, abîmé en lui-même, ne l'écoutait plus. Charmolue, en suivant la direction de son regard, vit qu'il s'était fixé machinalement à la grande toile d'araignée qui tapissait la lucarne. En ce moment, une mouche étourdie qui cherchait le soleil de mars vint se jeter à travers ce filet et s'y englua. A l'ébranlement de sa toile, l'énorme araignée fit un mouvement brusque hors de sa cellule centrale, puis d'un bond elle se précipita sur la mouche, qu'elle plia en deux avec ses antennes de devant, tandis que la trompe hideuse lui fouillait la tête.—Pauvre mouche! dit le procureur du roi en cour d'église, et il leva la main pour la sauver. L'archidiacre, comme réveillé en sursaut, lui retint le bras avec une violence convulsive.
>
> —Maître Jacques, cria-t-il, laissez faire la fatalité!
>
> Le procureur se retourna effaré. Il lui semblait qu'une pince de fer lui avait pris le bras. L'œil du prêtre était fixe, hagard, flamboyant, et restait attaché au petit groupe horrible de la mouche et de l'araignée.

The intensity of the above passage more than suggests its importance, but in order to make the meaning absolutely clear, Frollo goes on to say: "Voilá un symbole de tout." He then proceeds, as he speaks of the fly, to suggest to the reader the heroine, Esmeralda:

> Elle vole, elle est joyeuse, elle vient de naître; elle cherche le printemps, le grand air, la liberté; oh! oui, mais qu'elle se heurte à la rosace fatale, l'araignée en sort, l'araignée hideuse! Pauvre danseuse! pauvre mouche prédestinée! Maître Jacques, laissez faire! c'est la fatalité! Hélas! Claude, tu es araignée, tu es la mouche aussi! Tu volais à la science, à la lumière, au soleil . . . au grand jour de la vérité éternelle, en te précipitant vers la lucarne éblouissante qui donne sur l'autre monde . . . tu n'as pas vu cette toile d'araignée tendue par le destin.

Now, gripped by a wild and hopeless passion for the gypsy girl, he struggles helplessly in the grasp of the "antennes de fer" of fate.

Victor Brombert has noted that "les nombreuses araignées et leurs hideuses toiles où se débattent les mouches effarées" are the "prétexte" for innumerable metaphors, and it has long been observed that the image of the spider is an important one in Hugo. . . . But the image needs to be examined in its function in the pattern of narrative, rather than merely being referred to as a symbol of fate. First, however, one might well pause to ask the question: Where did this spider come from? . . . [The theme of fatality developed] little by little until it became an important one. But spiders? If we search Hugo's earlier efforts in prose and verse, if we check through ***Han d'Islande*** and ***Bug-Jargal,*** there seems to be nothing but an occasional bit of local color that has no symbolic function. There is a mention in ***Han*** that the monster seizes his victim with a "bras de fer," and in ***Bug-Jargal*** Habibrah is described in arachnoid terms, but the yield is slim indeed. One cannot refrain from wondering why this image developed in Hugo and why it developed at this time. The question seems to be important, for Hugo's subsequent literary career shows a continuation and evolution of this image. . . . (pp. 49-51)

[Perhaps] the question is unanswerable and perhaps too it is unimportant, after all, that it be answered. It suffices to say that we have the image and that it is the basis for the whole fabric of the novel. By means of the image, the concept of fatality is added to the earlier idea that the way up is the way to destruction. But as image it is not as yet complete, for Claude Frollo continues:

> Et quand tu l'aurais pu rompre, cette toile redoutable, avec les ailes de moucheron, tu crois que tu aurais pu atteindre à la lumière! Hélas! cette vitre qui est plus loin, cet obstacle transparent, cette muraille de cristal plus dur que l'airain qui sépare toutes les philosophies de la vérité, comment l'aurais-tu franchie? O vanité de la science! que de sages viennent de bien loin en voletant s'y briser le front! que de systèmes pêle-mêle se heurtent en bourdonnant à cette vitre éternelle!

In short, the original pattern of the rise to destruction has been amplified to include not only the spider but a *double* barrier between man and his ideal, this latter obstacle as impenetrable as it is invisible.

The image may be summarized as follows: A person (fly) in a dark recess, flying up toward the light (knowledge, truth, love, or any transcendent ideal), is caught in a spider web of fatality and devoured. But beyond this web which might possibly be broken through lies the invisible pane of glass that blocks all human efforts. The web and spider are within the realm of the finite, but the second barrier seems infinite. (p. 52)

[We] said earlier that the whole novel is an intricate working out of the image of spider and fly, thematically and formally. We saw that Claude Frollo associated himself both with killer and victim, and Esmeralda with the fly. But there is much more. Let us start with the heroine who, as Frollo had said of her, "vole, elle est joyeuse, elle cherche le grand air, la liberté." Her dark recess is in a sense a sociological one. She lives with that vast army of *truands* in the *cour des miracles,* but she is not of it nor is she contaminated by its evils, either in appearance, speech, or morals. She is a prisoner, having been kidnapped in infancy. Her chance for escape comes, she thinks, when she sees the vulgar military officer, Captain Phœbus de Châteaupers, whom she loves at first sight and toward whom she goes. It is certainly no coincidence that his name is Phœbus, the sun. That he is thoroughly unworthy of her adoration changes none of the patterns of action. The irony merely reinforces the bitterness of fatality. Her first sight of him occurs when he rescues her from Quasimodo in the dark labyrinthine streets of Paris, and with the memory of his heroic action in her mind, she is willing to leave the *parvis* of Notre-Dame, where she is performing for a crowd, and climb (the upward image) to the apartment where Phœbus and some aristocratic girls have invited her to perform with her pet goat. She seems to be escaping from the milieu of the *truands* to a finer life, but her amorous rendezvous with Phœbus in a house of assignation brings out the truth of the matter. Frollo, the spider, had accosted the impecunious Phœbus in the street. The priest is described in terms that suggest the lurking predator: "une espèce d'ombre qui rampait derriére lui," and who clutched the captain by the arm. The text refers to "la tenaille qui l'avait saisi," a suggestion both of the *antenne de fer* of the spider and the grip of fate. Frollo offers Phœbus money with which to pay the proprietress of the house so that Frollo can watch from a hidden recess. When the captain arrives there, the sun image finds an ironic reprise, as he "se hâta de *faire dans un écu reluire le soleil.*" All the elements of the image are now assembled: the dark recess, the fly, the watching spider, and the sun. . . . Up in the room Esmeralda learns that Phœbus has no intention whatever of marrying her, and then, accepting this cruel fact in humility, lets Phœbus make love to her. At this moment the spider comes out of his hiding place and, like an arachnid, pounces on his victim. Frollo stabs the sun-god Phœbus, Esmeralda faints and, almost unconscious, she feels "un baiser plus brûlant que le fer rouge du bourreau." Frollo manages to make his escape from this hovel with its "toiles d'araignées à tous les coins." Shortly afterward, she is arrested and tried for the attempted murder of the soldier.

With her trial the imagery is transferred from the erotic to a social context, befitting the experience. The hall of justice is now the dark recess "vaste et sombre," night is falling and the windows "ne laissaient plus pénétrer qu'un pâle rayon qui s'éteignait," as if once in the grip of that fatality, Justice, the sun itself disappears from view. Here Esmeralda pleads innocent to the muder of Phœbus but is not believed. Taken below to a torture chamber, she finds herself in a room with no opening onto the transcendent: "Pas de fenêtre à ce caveau." The illumination is provided by a hellish glow from the coals heating the instruments of torture. Here we find "des tenailles, des pinces"—which recall the spider's legs and Claude Frollo's grip. Esmeralda is trussed gently upon a table, like a fly in a web, and strapped down. . . . After brief torture, she confesses to whatever they wish, and "elle retomba sur le lit de cuir . . . pliée en deux, se laissant pendre à la courroie bouelée sur sa poitrine." Hanging by the leather strap, she is like a fly in a web, even bent in half like the fly cited in the original statement of the image.

After her conviction, she is incarcerated in a black dungeon cell which is located, apparently, beneath the torture chambers. This double level of the cave somehow reflects in a descending order the double barrier of web and window of the ascending imagery of the episode in Frollo's cell. Above are the "lumière" and the "cloches," symbols of a glorious ideal; here below, on the other hand, are "zones où s'échelonnent les nuances de Phorreur." In this medieval setting, Hugo calls upon Dante for his chapter title: "Lasciate ogni speranza." The way up to the sun of Phœbus has indeed led to disaster. (pp. 53-5)

But Esmeralda's experience with fatality is not yet completed. Saved from execution at the last moment by Quasimodo, she finds asylum in Notre-Dame, only to be removed from sanctuary in the cathedral by Gringoire the poet and Frollo during the attack by the *truands,* who have come to save her. As she is dragged off to the gallows by the mad priest, we are told that the ominous clouds above are "noirs, lourds, déchirés, crevassés, pendaient comme des hamacs de crêpe sous le cintre étoilé de la nuit. On eût dit les toiles d'araignées de la voûte du ciel.'' Fatality has been projected into nature. Arriving at the gibbet, Frollo announces to her, ''Choisis entre nous deux,'' as he holds her in his powerful grip.

Her response to this command is to wrench herself from his grasp and fall at the foot of the gibbet, ''en embrassant cet appui funèbre.'' Is she not in this act repeating the original image? She breaks through the grasp of the spider only to find herself before death itself, the ultimate barrier. As a matter of fact, even the gallows with its ''bras décharné'' recreates the black arm of the spider. When she later dies at dawn on these gallows, ''la corde fit plusieurs tours sur elle-même'' (the wrapping image again) and ''Claude contemplait ce groupe épouvantable . . . l'araignée et la mouche.'' This final touch had been prepared when the executioner climbed the ladder to the noose with the body of the unconscious girl who hangs over his arm ''gracieusement pliée en deux.''

But her death is to be postponed for a few moments, in the best tradition of the novel of suspense. In order to be free to seek the watch, Claude for a moment hands Esmeralda over to a religious recluse, Sœur Gudule, who inhabits near the gibbet a cell called the Trou aux rats, and who has sworn vengeance on all gypsies who years ago had kidnapped her infant child. By this device Hugo introduces the theme of fatality in the context of the family, for although at first neither realizes the fact, Gudule is Esmeralda's long-lost mother. (pp. 55-6)

The recognition scene (managed by a slipper) between mother and daughter seems to save the heroine. The mother breaks down the bars of the window by sheer strength born of love and drags the girl inside the cell as the watch approaches. This act of destroying the bars certainly fits the basic image announced by Claude: ''Et quand tu l'aurais pu rompre, cette toile redoutable . . . tu crois que tu aurais pu atteindre à la lumière?'' At first it looks as if this gloomy prediction will not come true. The watch disappears to seek Esmeralda elsewhere. But just when all is saved, the silly girl hears Captain Phœbus' voice and rushes toward the opening in the cell crying: ''Phœbus! à moi, mon Phœbus!'' Alas, ''Phœbus n'y était plus.'' The web had been broken and the fly had escaped, but she had been stopped by a second barrier. The watch hears her voice, returns, and seizes her, and she dies soon afterward. Here the meaning of the second barrier seems to anticipate what Hugo would state in his preface to ***Les travailleurs de la mer***: that beyond the fatalities of dogma, laws, and things, there is the ''anankè suprême, le coeur humain.'' At any rate, her reaching out to the sun of her life destroys her.

We have seen that Esmeralda encounters spiders in the form of Claude Frollo, Justice, and Sœur Gudule, although in the latter case the spider becomes beneficent. But there is yet another: Quasimodo. First his lair, the cathedral itself. One immediately calls to mind the large central *rosace* of Notre-Dame and the fact that in the central image the spider's web was called a ''rosace fatale,'' thus providing an admirable link with the Gothic architecture of fifteenth-century Paris. The main *rosace* lets light into the cathedral just as the light from the outside streams through the web in Frollo's cell. The lacy quality of the architecture is captured in an early description in which Hugo likens a *rosace* to ''une étoile de dentelle,'' and this latter word appeared in the original image. To make the comparison explicit, we need only to turn to the first appearance of Quasimodo at the Fête des fous. During the celebration, a pane of glass in a *rosace* is broken and the competitors for the ugliest face put their heads through the hole. The malformed Quasimodo wins, his countenance ''rayonnait'' in the aperture, exactly where a spider would be positioned. When Hugo describes him physically, he suggests something resembling a spider: ''Une grosse tête hérissée de cheveux roux; entre les deux épaules une bosse énorme dont le contrecoup se faisait sentir par devant; un système de enisses et de jambes si étrangement fourvoyées qu'elles . . . ressemblaient à deux croissants de faucilles qui se rejoignent par la poignée; de larges pieds, des mains monstrueuses; et, avec toute cette difformité, je ne sais quelle allure redoutable de vigueur, d'agilité et de courage.'' The bell-ringer rarely leaves the cathedral, just as a spider is imagined rarely to leave its web. To be sure, the imagery that Hugo uses to describe the hunchback is multiple, for he is a ''reptile,'' a ''lézard,'' and particularly a snail living in its shell, the cathedral. Thus, the building itself becomes something of a Quasimodo in stone, for Hugo insists on its architectural irregularity and composite nature. Quasimodo even resembles the church in other ways: he is stone deaf and his one eye repeats the one central *rosace* of Notre-Dame. Hugo speaks of the deafness architecturally, for his ability to hear is ''la scule porte que la nature lui eût laissée toute grande ouverte'' and it is now ''brusquement fermée.'' Now Hugo shifts back to the image of the eye: ''En se fermant, elle intercepta l'unique rayon de joie et de lumière qui pénétrât encore dans l'âme de Quasimodo.'' His soul is now in a ''nuit profonde'' and he is ''séparé à jamais du monde par *la double fatalité* de la naissance inconnue et de sa nature difforme, emprisonné dès l'enfance dans ce double cercle infranchissable.'' The double barrier of fatality has appeared again.

The picture presented here is that of a soul that is prisoner inside a body, just as the body is prisoner inside the cathedral. With this preparation accomplished, Hugo can then show us this soul as if he were taking us on a guided tour through Notre-Dame:

> Si maintenant nous essayions de pénétrer jusqu'à l'âme de Quasimodo à travers cette écorce épaisse et dure; si nous pouvions sonder les profondeurs de cette organisation mal faite; s'il nous était donné de regarder avec un flambeau derrière ces organes sans transparence, d'explorer l'intérieur ténébraux de cette créature opaque, d'en élucider les recoins obscurs, les culs-de-sac absurdes, et de jeter tout à coup une vive lumière sur la psyché enchaînée au fond de cet antre, nous trouverions sans doute la malheureuse dans quelque attitude pauvre, rabougrie et rachitique comme ces prisonniers des plombs de Venise qui vieillissaient ployés en deux dans une boîte de pierre trop basse et trop courte.

The language is significant. The psyche is in chains, ''ployé en deux.'' One cannot doubt that we have here yet another—more subtle—elaboration of the spider-fly fatality image transferred to a psychological plane.

The relationship between Quasimodo and the cathedral has sexual overtones, curiously enough. The bell-ringer's favorite *cloche* is called Marie, and their contact is erotic: ''Tout à coup la frénésie de la cloche le gagnait; son regard devint extraordinaire; il attendait le bourdon au passage, comme l'araignée attend la mouche, et se jetait brusquement sur lui à corps perdu.'' This passage becomes frankly sexual with the addition of the phrases: ''la cloche monstrueuse hennissait toute haletante sous lui'' and ''elle était possédée et remplie de Quasimodo.'' Finally, ''donner la grosse cloche en mariage à Quasimodo, e'était donner Juliette à Roméo.'' Hugo rarely leaves one in doubt.

With this concept of Quasimodo as spider established, it is easy to see that like Claude Frollo he pounces on his prey. When Esmeralda first encountered the hunchback in the darkened labyrinth of Paris (the web image), he carried her off "ployée sur un de ses bras." But if he is acting out the role of an evil spider at this moment under Frollo's direction, Hugo assures us that "la méchanceté n'était peut-être pas innée en lui," for he had, because of his deformities, been ostracized by society. Like Sœur Gudule who has changed from hating to loving, he also is changed. When much later he finds himself strapped to a pillory to be scourged, now a fly in society's web, he cries out "A boire!" in a wild fusion of Gargantua and Christ. Esmeralda offers him water, and, almost as if baptized, he dies to evil and is reborn to good. Henceforth, although he continues to be a spider, he is now a beneficent one. Although there is occasionally imagery derived from other animals, the key scenes show the center of Hugo's vision. When Esmeralda finishes her "amende honorable" on the steps of Notre-Dame, Quasimodo slides down a rope from the balcony, seizes her, and bounds into the church crying out "Asile." There is here something of the spider lowering itself by a dragline. The heroine is of course unaware of his transformation. Conditioned by a series of disasters and confused by the total experience, she shows fright the next morning when the hunchback appears at her cell in Notre-Dame. The image is—eternally—the same: "Un joyeux rayon du soleil levant entrait par sa lucarne [= rosace] et venait leui frapper le visage. En même temps que le soleil, elle vit à cette lucarne un objet qui l'effraya, la malheureuse figure de Quasimodo." She expects the evil spider to pounce, only to hear him say gently: "N'ayez pas peur." He even agrees to stay out of her sight because of his ugly appearance. It is not the least of the bitter ironies of this book, incidentally, that given his moral beauty, all his efforts to help her lead to her death. His only consolation will come with her death. His skeleton is found wrapped around hers in the charnel house. The beneficent spider could achieve no more. Fatality willed in his case that the heroine would prefer the false Phœbus, whom Hugo describes as cracked crystal, to the humble sandstone of the hunchback.

Esmeralda is not the only fly. Claude Frollo had cried out: "Claude, tu es la mouche aussi," and the central image fits the priest as well as it does the gypsy. Claude's dark recess is the very cell in which the spider image was first explicitly elaborated. He too tries to fly toward the sun. For him, the light is—ostensibly—that of pure philosophical truth. He is not only a priest but an alchemist seeking to make gold, not for earthly gain, but because "L'or, c'est le soleil, faire de l'or, c'est être Dieu." But for the priest, the pure light of the sun is corrupted. Speculating on how to extract gold from fire, he quotes the alchemists of the past: "Magistri affirme qu'il y a certains noms de femme d'un charme si doux et si mystérieux qu'il suffit de les prononcer." And one Manou says: "Où les femmes sont honorées, les divinités sont réjouies. . . . La bouche d'une femme est constamment pure; c'est une eau courante, c'est un rayon de soleil." The transformation from the purity of light to evil sexuality is completed as Frollo murmurs: "Maria, Sophia, La Esmeral . . .—Damnation! toujours cette pensée." One might observe the transition of the feminine names from the divine, through the more secular but still abstract Wisdom (or knowledge) to sexuality. Esmeralda replaces God, or the Virgin, and becomes Claude's "soleil." Ironically, she is in fact a sort of patron saint of the *truands* of the Cour des miracles: "toute sa tribu . . . la tient en vénération singulière, comme une Notre-Dame." . . . And indeed, she is virtue incarnate, as we see from her humane rescue of the poet Pierre Gringoire about to die on the beggars' gallows, as well as from her giving Quasimodo a drink on the pillory. (pp. 56-60)

But for Claude Frollo, she cannot be a true sun, for he is a priest and she is both a gypsy (a non-Christian group) and a desirable woman. He knows that it is blasphemy to cry as he does that Esmeralda is "une créature si belle que Dieu l'eût préférée à la Vierge." Claude's resolution of his intolerable tension is at least logical. She can come only "du ciel ou de l'enfer." But precisely because she is a desirable gypsy girl, he must conclude: "C'était un ange! mais de ténèbres, mais de flamme et non de lumière." Of course, his logical conclusion is incorrect. She is not a true gypsy but a stolen Christian. Her true name, Agnès, is more reminiscent of the paschal lamb than of a sorceress. Yet for the priest she is "sombre, funèbre, ténébreuse comme le cercle noir qui poursuit longtemps la vue de l'imprudent quii a regardé fixement le soleil." Hugo's imagery has here anticipated Nerval's *Desdichado*. Frollo is explicit in his interpretation when he said . . . that "Tu volais à la science, à la lumière, au soleil," but the shining sun was really a dark one, and as a result he says of himself "tu te débats, la tête brisóe et les ailes arrachées entre les antennes de fer de la fatalité!" If he is a fly, then Esmeralda must be the spider for him. Here the imagery becomes obscured, for it is hardly possible to portray the lovely girl directly as a grotesque predatory insect. The only hints that we have are first, that in his mind she is transformed from a luminous to a black sun, whose dark rays would form something of a black body and legs. . . . The other hint is her ability to torture Claude Frollo by repeating to him: "c'est Phœbus que j'aime, . . . c'est Phœbus qui est beau." Just as Esmeralda had felt the priest's burning kisses on her, "il poussa un cri violent, comme le misérable auquel on applique un fer rouge," and we remember the arachnoid images of the torture instruments used on her. Beyond these tiny hints, Hugo apparently was unwilling to go. Here again, fatality is ironic, because Esmeralda, whose name signifies "emerald," the precious stone which in medieval lore was effective in calming lust, does not calm Claude Frollo's passion, but on the contrary inspires it and unwittingly brings about his destruction.

Claude, with his fly's gossamer wings of virtue stripped off, resolves—boldly—to go in the other direction, toward the black arts, toward Hell. Immediately the imagery adjusts itself to fit the changes. Because of his baldness and his flapping sleeves, he is referred to as a *chauve-souris* (one recalls *Mus*dœmon). He also appears at times as a specter; his eyes are glowing coals, etc. He becomes a demonic character from melodrama in the tradition of Lewis' Monk. This change in Frollo's direction from up to the light to downward, forces us to face up to a seeming contradiction. . . . [In the previous works of Hugo] the way down was the way to salvation, and yet Frollo is not saved by his descent, falling, like Habibrah or Musdœmon, with a cry of "Damnation" from the balcony of Notre-Dame. Yet there is no question of the descent. He describes his own progress in these terms: "Je n'ai pas rampé si longtemps à plat ventre et les ongles dans la terre à travers les innombrables embranchements de la caverne sans apercevoir, au loin devant moi, au bout de l'obscure galerie, une lumière, une flamme, quelque chose . . . où les patients et les sages ont surpris Dieu." To this he adds, "je rampe encore; je m'écorche la face et les genoux aux cailloux de la voie souterraine. J'entrevois, je ne contemple pas." Why does he not succeed, why is he destroyed if avoiding direct ascent preserves one from destruction?

The answer must lie in the moral qualities of the "hero." In contradistinction to Ordener or to Léopold d'Auverney, Claude is anything but a virtuous man. His own obsessions with sex keep him, like Lancelot, from finding any Grail. Further, his goal is blasphemous. "Faire de l'or, c'est être Dieu" and "saisir Dieu" show a demonic mode of thought, and in 1831 Hugo was not ready to take the next step and redeem the totally wicked, as he would many years later in the analogous situation of ***La fin de Satan.*** If we must seek an explanation for Hugo's attitude, it is likely that in 1832 the *faune,* if he was, as Guillemin claims, already guilty of marital infidelity, was not ready to forgive himself as he would later. . . . To conclude: When the priest tries to ascend to the pure light, he is blocked first by the web of lust and even if he were to break through it, he would know "la vanité de la science." In desperation trying the demonic arts, he feels somehow that he can seize God, or the Ultimate. Like Lucifer, his fall is as prodigious as his pride. Unlike Hugo's Lucifer, it is permanent. To succeed in reaching God requires unselfishness or humility.

Esmeralda and Frollo are not the only victims of the dazzling light of the absolute. Even Sœur Gudule, the recluse, is a fly as well as a spider. She lives in a dark recess, from which she is separated by the barred window of her cell. Her "sun" is her daughter whom she hopes to find. If she can locate her, she plans that the two will leave Paris and go off to Rheims, which she idealizes as a Paradise. She does break through the web of the barred window to save her daughter, but she cannot do anything about the ultimate fatality, the "anankè suprême" of the human heart. Esmeralda will die for Phœbus rather than live for her mother. In this case, the web was a self-imposed claustration, but it was there nonetheless. (pp. 61-3)

The individual fates of the separate characters are all expressed with the same images interlocked in intricate patterns. But the novel (or romance) is not only personal; it has political overtones which continue the note first sounded in ***Han,*** then in ***Bug-Jargal*** and in ***Cromwell,*** where rebellious miners, slaves in revolt, and grumbling populace (the last act of ***Cromwell*** is called *Les Ouvriers*) provide a disturbing backdrop to the actions of the protagonists. In ***Notre-Dame,*** the *peuple* is presented in the fifteenth century as a future political force that will some day destroy the monarchy. The early pages of the tale are built around a series of antitheses: classic against romantic, old against young, rectors against students, aristocracy against the people, who are in turn symbolized by the artisan Jacques Coppenole.

In 1830, Hugo's attitude toward the masses had already arrived at the point where he sided with them, provided that they fitted his social (and Romantic) concept of a noble working class. As he was to define it a few years later in ***Le Rhin,*** there is the *peuple* (noble, worthy) and the *populace* (the rabble). Both positive and negative aspects of the lower class are captured in ***Notre-Dame*** by the image of the sea, which makes an early appearance here in Hugo's fiction. The ocean can be calm, beautiful, and co-operative at one moment, and uncontrollably violent the next. Hugo uses the image for both groups. He calls the vile beggars "populace" and a "flot irrésistible" which is "hurlant, benglant, glapissant, . . . se ruant." The more sedate crowd that has come to see Gringoire's play is called the *peuple* having "l'aspect d'une mer, dans laquelle cinq ou six rues, comme d'autant d'embouchures de fleuves dégorgeaient à chaque instant de nouveaux flots de têtes." Hugo adds to this maritime imagery words like *ondes, courant, vagues.* This is the lower class for which Coppenole speaks. "Ajoutons que Coppenole était du peuple, et que ce public qui l'entourait était du peuple. . . . L'altière algarade du chaussetier flamand, en humiliant les gens de cour, avait remué dans toutes les âmes plébéiennes je ne sais quel sentiment de dignité encore vague et indistinct au quinzième siècle." Strong in his class consciousness, Coppenole later announces in his conversation in the Bastille with no less a personage than Louis XI, that in 1482 "l'heure du peuple n'est pas venue," and then in an obvious anachronism predicts the fall of the Bastille. . . . Is the change of political structure inevitable? Hugo seems to think so, generalizing: "Toute civilisation commence par la théocratie et finit par la démocratic," and Hugo explores the problem further through imagery as Louis XI visits the prison cells of the Bastille.

The monarch is spending the night in his *chambrette* in this fortress, which we may safely take as a symbol of pre-Revolutionary France. From here he leaves to inspect his cages, special cells in which political prisoners hope in vain for liberation. Their cages are barred: "Il y avait aux parois deux ou trois petites fenêtres, si drument treillissées d'épais barreaux de fer qu'on n'en voyait pas la vitre." One prisoner, who has been inside a cell for fourteen years, pleads for mercy. The King pretends not to hear his desperate plea for clemency, and as he moves away, "le misérable prisonnier, à l'éloignement des flambeaux et du bruit, jugea que le roi s'en allait. Sire! sire! cria-t-il avec désespoir. La porte se referma." The image is clarified shortly afterwards as Pierre Gringoire gives a lesson in statesmanship to his monarch. "Sire," he cries, "vous êtes le soleil," and "la clémence est las seule lumière qui puisse éclairer l'intérieur d'une grande âme. La clémence porte le flambeau devant toutes les autres vertus. Sans elle, ce sont des aveugles qui cherchent Dieu à tâtons." Thus, to shift to the prisoner's point of view, the average citizen is in a cage, blocked from the light by the cage with its spider web of bars. This recess is the creation of Louis' political caprice, we are led to understand, but even if he could break out of the dark cage, he would still not be free, for he would find himself still inside the Bastille, symbol of France of the *ancien régime.* Again we see the double barrier, the second more formidable than the first. And by walking off with his light, the King abdicates his central position as sun, leaving mankind in darkness. In the essay "Ceci tuera cela," which forms an integral part of the whole work, Hugo intervenes to explain that royalty is medieval and passé. The imagery used here is important: "le soleil du moyen âge est tout à fait couché," and with the invention of the printing press after the "dark" Middle Ages, "des nouveautés vont se faire jour." If the monarchy is a setting sun, what will be the new center of light? If we remember Hugo's idea that all civilizations begin as theocracies and end as democracies, the new light can only by the *peuple* itself. (pp. 64-6)

This transference of light to the people creates, on the political plane, a radical transformation of the image. The fly and the sun are no longer opposite. The fly (*peuple*) becomes the sun (also *peuple*), with the result that if the imprisoned masses can only break through their bonds, they have, in a sense, but to fly toward themselves! In short, the luminous ideal is no longer unattainable in political terms. . . .

Up to this point, we have viewed ***Notre-Dame*** as an artistic entity whose center is not a hero, nor even as some critics have suggested, the cathedral itself, but an image that unites the novel and permits one to counter Guyard's complaint that Hugo couldn't choose between the historical, ideological, and poetic novel. The historical evocation of the Middle Ages permits the development of the cathedral-recess with its *rosace* as spider web and its monolithic architecture symbolic of feudalism. These forms are linked to Hugo's themes: preoccupation with architecture as such, liberalism as manifested by the democratizing possiblities of the printing press and the hope of future revolution, the plea for a better judicial system. the themes are in turn linked via the imagery to the characters in the grip of various passions. As Hugo himself said in ***Notre-Dame***: "L'idée mère, le verbe, [était] dans la forme." (p. 68)

Richard B. Grant, in his The Perilous Quest: Image, Myth, and Prophecy in the Narratives of Victor Hugo, *Duke University Press, 1968, 253 p.*

PATRICIA A. WARD (essay date 1975)

[*In the following excerpt from her study* The Medievalism of Victor Hugo, *Ward assesses themes of social injustice and political change in* Notre-Dame de Paris. *She also examines Hugo's narrative technique with reference to the novel's historical atmosphere, characterization, setting, and plot.*]

The trio of main characters [in ***Notre-Dame de Paris***] might appear initially to be simply three "types" who reappear constantly within the *oeuvre* of Hugo: the doomed *proscrit,* the monster figure, and idealized feminine beauty. Frollo, Quasimodo, and Esmeralda are not *vraisemblables* when judged according to the canons of realism. Relying on sources such as Collin de Plancy, Du Breul, and Sauval, Hugo surrounds these three characters with an aura of the fantastic. But the Parisians within the novel create a myth for the three figures, and it is clear that popular belief accepted the fantastic as part of the normal course of events. (p. 40)

[In his descriptions of Claude Frollo, Phoebus, and Esmeralda], Hugo intensifies the element of the grotesque which he first portrayed as an active part of the medieval imagination in **"La préface de *Cromwell*,"** and he underscores the difference between the mature mind of the modern reader and the mental attitudes of the medieval populace.

The pathetic dimension of the people becomes a dominating theme of the novel. Unenlightened humanity suffers, and it glimpses only now and then the possibility of freedom. The two sources of power which cause this suffering are the Church and the Throne. Hugo accentuates the lack of civil justice and the acceptance of this injustice. Both Louis XI and his magistrates are indicted indirectly for the sufferings of Quasimodo and Esmeralda, representatives of the oppressed people. Robert d'Estouteville, provost of Paris, becomes the object of much irony in the chapter entitled "Coup d'oeil impartial sur l'ancienne magistrature." He has literally hung on to his position and become one with it despite the penchant of Louis XI to keep changing his counselors. (pp. 40-1)

Similarly, Claude Frollo represents all the learned superstition of the age which, in Hugo's eyes, existed within the Church. His belief in fatality, 'ἀνάγκη, a non-Christian concept, denies liberty to the individual. Like a possessed man, he sees the trapping of a fly by a spider as symbolic of the human situation. . . . Claude sees himself as both fly and spider, victim of fate and agent of its designs. A representative of the Church, he has protected Quasimodo, harboring him in the cathedral but, at the same time, taking away his freedom. Quasimodo is the dog, says Hugo, Frollo, the master.

The monsterlike Quasimodo physically represents the misery of a society filled with the ugly. In the popular mind, Esmeralda's and Quasimodo's presence in the cathedral represents injustice, even though the hunchback has rescued and protected the gypsy in his one act of freedom. When the crowd attacks Notre-Dame near the end of the novel, it wishes only to destroy the symbols of ecclesiastical power. (p. 41)

The architectural setting of the novel, particularly that of the cathedral, has received considerable attention from scholars and critics. It has been called the principal character or a magnet controlling the human characters. . . . Literary historians have praised Hugo's poetic translation of his antiquarian interest into word pictures of the church and the city, and his personal "guerre aux démolisseurs" has been interpreted as "la pensée d'esthétique et de philosophie" which Hugo claimed to have hidden in the book. The architectural setting is also linked to the same historical, political, and social concerns that caused Hugo to develop the theme of the people and their future triumph in the novel.

From the attention devoted to gothic architecture in the 1826 preface to the ***Odes et ballades*** and the 1829 introduction to the ***Orientales,*** it is clear that the gothic for Hugo meant the flamboyant—light, airy, and rich in detail. Although the grotesque was also central to his vision of medieval art, he invariably portrays the gothic style in this fixed way. When he turned to fifteenth-century Paris, however, he chose Notre-Dame cathedral, "une oeuvre de transition," to represent this society marked by flux and change. In the chapter devoted to the architecture of the church, Hugo says that it is not a definite, complete monument open to classification; it is situated between the romanesque and gothic. "Notre-Dame de Paris n'a point . . . la majestueuse simplicité des édifices qui ont le plein cintre pour générateur. Elle n'est pas, comme la cathédrale de Bourges, le produit magnifique, léger, multiforme, touffu, hérissé, efflorescent de l'ogive."

The discussion of gothic architecture continues but in different terms; it is called the second transformation, which terminated with William the Conqueror. For the first time, Hugo places the gothic in a political context by speaking of the family of churches in that style: "communales, et bourgeoises comme symboles politiques libres, capricieuses, effrénées, comme oeuvre d'art; seconde transformation de l'architecture, non plus hiéroglyphique, immuable et sacerdotale, mais artiste, progressive et populaire, qui commence au retour des croisades et finit à Louis XI." Gothic architecture is seen as the free expression of a popular, progressive effort so that Hugo now has extended his more liberal stance into his interpretation of the gothic, politicizing it, in effect. Paradoxically, he portrays medieval society as something less than free, though the progressive freeing of architecture parallels the slow movement of the populace toward freedom. As a result, in this novel, Notre-Dame cathedral . . . embodies, in part, the spirit of the late Middle Ages. It inspires both admiration and terror. The somber aspects are linked to Quasimodo, that other embodiment of the suffering people, so that the two are seen as outgrowths of the injustices in medieval history. Of Quasimodo's relationship to the cathedral, Hugo writes that "la cathédrale ne lui était pas seulement la société, mais encore l'univers, mais encore toute la nature." The richness of the gothic cathedral becomes the richness of nature and replaces the outside world for Quasimodo. (pp. 42-3)

In viewing the city of Paris in the 1400s, Hugo was most impressed by the homogeneity and unity of its architecture. . . . Throughout the novel, however, this architectural unity is juxtaposed with the theme of historical change. Hugo the antiquarian who wished to preserve the monuments of the past may have admired the unity of the Paris of Louis XI, but he knew that the winds of social change were already leading to the Renaissance; a never-ending series of architectural changes would follow, and Hugo viewed with horror any attempts to destroy the last vestiges of these past architectural eras. Paris was perhaps more beautiful, though less harmonious, fifty years later when renaissance architecture added "le luxe éblouissant de ses fantaisies et de ses systémes" to the Paris of 1482. (p. 43)

Hugo's sensitivity to historical change is most evident in the important chapter "Ceci tuera cela." Implicit in the development of his thought is the idea that humanity collectively expresses itself in some art form and that, from generation to generation, this mode of expression changes. Architecture had been the book of mankind up through the fifteenth century—"le grand livre de l'humanité, l'expression principale de l'homme à ses divers états de développement soit comme force, soit comme intelligence." Like writing, architecture evolved from alphabet to hieroglyphic to symbol until "l'idée mère, le verbe, n'était pas seulement au fond de tous ces édifices, mais encore dans la forme." Hugo repeats his interpretation of the gothic as the expression of the people, and links the romanesque style to the hierarchical world of the Christian Middle Ages. The "style roman" reflects authority, unity, impenetrability, and the absolute, "partout la caste, jamais le peuple. Mais les croisades arrivent. C'est un grand mouvement populaire; et tout grand mouvement populaire, quels qu'en soient la cause et le but, dégage toujours de son dernier précipité l'esprit de liberté." The ogive, made possible by the liberating spirit of the crusades, is consequently the expression of freedom in architectural form, and it prefigures the inevitable movement toward popular freedom in politics and society. Everything begins to change and architecture is dethroned in the fifteenth century with Gutenberg's invention of printing; the book will kill the edifice. "L'invention de l'imprimerie est le plus grand événement de l'histoire. C'est la révolution mère. C'est le mode d'expression de l'humanité qui se renouvelle totalement." The sixteenth century thus becomes the age in which thought is emancipated, and this emancipation leads directly to Luther. Religious unity is broken, but printing makes reform possible. The tragedy of this inevitable historical development is that architecture as a collective expression disappears and a period of "décadence magnifique" ensues. "L'architecture ne sera plus l'art social, l'art collectif."

It is easy to see why Hugo continually juxtaposed the fifteenth and sixteenth centuries and why his attitude toward the late Middle Ages was ambivalent. He regretted that the individual was destined to replace the collective in artistic expression, for art would never again have the liberating force for a society that the gothic cathedral had for the medieval spirit. The stirrings of the masses and the disappearance of the feudal system, on the other hand, pave the way for the revolution of ideas in the sixteenth century. Although Hugo sees progress in history as inevitable, in ***Notre-Dame*** he does not advocate revolution per se. Rather, his belief in the power of the word as the embodiment of the ideal lies behind his admiration for the revolution within civilization during the Renaissance. This position represents Hugo's moderate liberalism of the 1830s, and it parallels his interpretation of the Revolution of 1789 in his essay on Mirabeau. There Hugo admires Mirabeau the orator because of his power with words and ideas, and he sees the revolution less in terms of politics than in terms of ideas. It lay the groundwork for all future progress so that Hugo conceives of his own century as the heir to the new ideas of that revolution. In his introductory essay to ***Littérature et philosophie mêlées,*** he says that progress in art is a corollary of social progress. But elsewhere, he again indicates that the goal toward which history is moving will be reached slowly but inevitably. (pp. 43-5)

Hugo's fascination with the historical process and with the recreation of the social and architectural milieu of medieval Paris has caused a number of critics to comment negatively about the organization of the novel. Hugo has been accused of trying for spectacular effects and of inaccuracy in his painting of the architecture of Notre-Dame and the vivid activities of the Cour des Miracles. (p. 45)

Understanding how Hugo attempted to give form to history and fictional narrative in ***Notre-Dame de Paris*** is useful in reaching a judgment about the aesthetic worth of the book. ***Notre-Dame*** defies classification, but Hugo did have definite ideas about the "historical novel" as a genre. His early statements about history and the novel were made in connection with Walter Scott; in the *Conservateur littéraire,* he praises Scott's fidelity to historical detail and coloring. This opinion is repeated in the well-known article on *Quentin Durward* in the *Muse française*. . . . In the conclusion to the article, Hugo calls for a new novel which will be both dramatic and epic; picturesque, but poetic; real, but ideal; true, but large in scope. Since Scott was a genius who could guess and reconstruct the past, Hugo probably thought of historical fidelity more as "reconstitution of atmosphere" than as accuracy of detail. For this reason, the passage on local color from **"La préface de *Cromwell,*"** cited earlier, is extremely important. Since local color had to permeate the literary work, it was much more than the picturesque. The poetic imagination transformed such detail into a unifying atmosphere for an entire work, in this case the novel. In describing his own method in ***Notre-Dame,*** Hugo says that he *painted* Paris during the fifteenth century—he evoked it through imaginative insights.

> C'est une peinture de Paris au XVe siècle et du quinzième siècle à propos de Paris. . . . Le livre n'a aucune prétention historique, si ce n'est dépeindre peut-être avec quelque science et quelque conscience, mais uniquement par aperçus et par échappées, l'état des moeurs, des croyances, des lois, des arts, de la civilisation enfin du XVe siècle. Au reste, ce n'est pas là ce qui importe dans le livre. S'il a un mérite, c'est d'être oeuvre d'imagination, de caprice et de fantaisie.

Hugo does not always couple the narrative of the novel with the historical atmosphere. The principal characters are his own creations. In fact, much later in his career, he claimed never to have written a historical drama or novel. "Ma manière est de peindre des chose vraies par des personnages d'invention." Further, the unifying principle is not found in a strict narrative sequence, but in contrast and scope (drama and epic). This aspect of Hugo's creativity in prose is often misunderstood, but it is simply an extension of his "unlimited lyricism," to use Thibaudet's phrase. The twentieth-century reader is left, then, with a melodramatic plot apparently derived from "gothic horror" as it existed both on the stage and in fiction. It appears to have relatively little to do with the historical atmosphere that provides a record in poetic form of how the nineteenth century perceived the Middle Ages. Historical atmosphere and plot do merge on occasion, however, when the narrator interrupts the story line or when the trio of main characters assumes a symbolic function within the fifteenth-century milieu.

Hugo the narrator is supremely conscious of his role in reconstituting the medieval past, and his intrusions into the narrative sequence reinforce the reader's sense of historical distance between his own era and that of the novel. In fact, the work begins with a hyperbole that emphasizes this passing of time. "Il y a aujourd'hui trois cent quarante-huit ans six mois et dix-neuf jours que les parisiens s'éveillèrent au bruit de toutes les cloches sonnant à grande volée dans la triple enceinte de la Cité, de l'Université et de la Ville: Ce n'est cependant pas un jour dont l'histoire ait gardé souvenir que le 6 janvier 1482." Hugo will make the day memorable for the nineteenth century, and thereafter he intervenes for many different reasons as he contrasts the two eras. From time to time, he underlines the stated purpose of the novel, to combat the destruction of the monuments of the Middle Ages, by recreating verbally a site which has already disappeared. (pp. 46-7)

At other times, Hugo emphasizes that the spirit which once animated the architecture of Paris has disappeared so that what remains is only a monument. The relationship between Quasimodo and Notre-Dame in the chapter "Immanis pecoris custos, immanior ipse" indicates that the animating spirit of the hunchback gives the cathedral its "fantastic, supernatural and horrible" aspect. Quasimodo is the "soul" of the cathedral. "A tel point que pour ceux qui savent que Quasimodo a existé, Notre-Dame est aujourd'hui déserte, inanimée, morte. On sent qu'il y a quelque chose de disparu. Ce corps immense est vide; c'est un squelette; l'esprit l'a quitté, on en voit la place, et voilà tout."

The narrator also interprets and judges the Middle Ages, and in these interpretations there is usually an implied comparison with the nineteenth century. Thus, when Louis XI comes in disguise with his doctor to visit Claude Frollo and a prologue of mutual flattery between the two "learned" men ensues, Hugo comments that the custom is still in existence as it was then. . . . Other examples could be cited, ranging from Hugo's explanation of why there were no police in the Paris of Louis XI to what constituted a place of asylum in the Middle Ages. The most striking example of historical distance to create irony is the treatment of the poet-philosopher Gringoire. Even though Gringoire is the author of the ill-fated mystery play and the object of abuse by the *truands*, he is treated with a tone of detachment so that he serves only a comic purpose. He seems to be a nineteenth-century character wearing medieval costume. For instance, when Gringoire decides to follow Esmeralda after the procession for the *fête des fous*, Hugo says that Gringoire acts from a vague desire to follow the train of events. "Si Gringoire vivait de nos jours, quel beau milieu il tiendrait entre le classique et le romantique!"

Most intrusions into the narration are direct addresses to the reader. (pp. 47-8)

[These] intrusions into the narrative indicate two concepts of time in ***Notre-Dame.*** On one hand, time is the Past, a vital period in history, recaptured, suspended in motion through aesthetic form; on the other hand, time is the actual measurable period of the events of the plot, a chronology unimportant to Hugo. The novel opens on the sixth of January 1482, a day he hopes to make memorable because the events occur that trigger the sequence of happenings comprising the "actual" time of the plot. But for five of the eleven books of the novel, Hugo has reduced the movement of the narrative sequence to slow motion; the date remains 6 January. In book six, actual time is speeded up; it is now 7 January. By book seven, March 1482, the sequence is further accelerated; book eight brings us to April, and thereafter events follow rapidly to a conclusion. Because of this division of the "actual" time, the reader's attention needs direction; the author's fascination with recapturing the vitality of an epoch overshadows the plot. These two concepts of time may pose problems if the reader looks for one "actual" narrative time. (p. 48)

By breaking the thread of narration, Hugo establishes the historical atmosphere of the Past in books one through five of ***Notre-Dame.*** [Michel Butor] has indicated that the "parenthesis" is one of the major ways the plot is interrupted. It is a pause for historical or poetical consideration which appears to be perpendicular to the anecdotal narration but is intimately connected with it. The parenthesis enlarges the context of the anecdotal narrative and is typified by the chapter "Ceci tuera cela." Here, Hugo takes Claude Frollo's belief in fatality, removes it from the plane of his passion for Esmeralda, and transforms it in the theme of the inevitable changes under way in fifteenth-century society and art. The chapters "Notre-Dame" and "Paris à vol d'oiseau" are also outside the narrative sequence, but they enlarge the reader's understanding of the physical milieu. These two chapters in the first half of the novel follow the initial events and precede the fourth book, which contains a flashback to the previous history of Claude Frollo and Quasimodo; this ensures that the symbolic aspects of the cathedral are connected by the reader to the priest and the bell-ringer. Emphasis on unified architecture provides a contrast with the prophecy of change in the chapter "Ceci tuera cela" which follows the history of Frollo and Quasimodo.

Books one and two illustrate aspects of Hugo's technique that enhance the historical atmosphere and obscure the "actual" narrative time—even though the purpose of these chapters is to trigger the plot sequence. The novel begins with the presentation of Gringoire's mystery play before a huge crowd in the Palais de Justice; Quasimodo is the king to the fools, and Esmeralda makes her first appearance. The second book continues with Esmeralda's dance at the Place de Grève, Gringoire's attempt to follow Esmeralda, the aborted kidnaping of the gypsy, and the "marriage" of Esmerald and Gringoire. In both sections, Hugo's dramatic-lyric bent dominates, and the crowd scenes with their raucousness and lively repartee overshadow the action of the main plot.

In some of Hugo's attempts to reconstitute a scene through words, his verbal creation seems to take over the page; the resulting aesthetic of expansive verbal dynamism matches the vitality of the popular age Hugo describes. The crowd that is waiting for the beginning of the mystery play is compared with the movement of rising water, an image that is developed and expanded. . . . After completing the description of the crowd, Hugo proceeds with several pages of brilliant repartee that amplifies the medieval student milieu. A similar technique is used when he enumerates in detail each section of the parade of "underworld" figures during the *fête*.

The physical environment is also vitalized by Hugo's amplifications. In one paragraph, he calls the Cour des Miracles a "cercle magique," "cité des voleurs, hideuse verrue à la face de Paris," "égout," "ruche monstrueuse," "hôpital menteur," and "immense vestiaire.". . . . The description continues, but the narrator's theme is clear: "tout semblait être en commun parmi ce peuple." All elements of human suffering and the consequent evils blend into one monstrous whole in the Cour des Miracles; and there is an interaction between the people and the Paris in which they are enclosed—when Paris becomes a seething mass of humanity, there is a superb union of style and theme.

Hugo's treatment of history and narrative indicates that he was not primarily concerned with presenting a chronicle of past events. A single "historical" occurrence, the arrival of a delegation in Paris to negotiate the marriage of Margaret of Flanders and the Dauphin, is a stage for the opening scenes of the novel. As in *Quentin Durward,* the characters with a basis in history, primarily Louis XI, are on the periphery of the plot. Claude Frollo may have been modeled on a historical archdeacon, but the character is closer to Ambrosio in Lewis's *The Monk*. Hugo does *use* history, however, and the architectural thesis that medieval monuments must be saved marks his book as propaganda, though it is more than that. Hugo's evocation of the collective sufferings of the people and of their self-expression in art interprets social and intellectual history in terms of his own political sympathies and marks a step toward his tendency after exile to use the Middle Ages overtly for political ends.

The central plot remains a tale of melodramatic horror, anchored here and there to the historical milieu and enhanced by "parentheses." The main characters of this plot rarely derive motivation for their actions from their milieu, nor are there frequent attempts to see why they act as they do; for these reasons there is a basic unevenness in Hugo's handling of history and narrative in ***Notre-Dame de Paris.*** Often he relies on the use of animal imagery to describe a character instead of analyzing his or her inner thoughts and feelings. Throughout the novel, for instance, Esmeralda is referred to as a bird or small, helpless creature. Such images are numerous at the beginning of the book where she is introduced as a wasp, a nightingale, a cicada, and a warbler. Like Hugo's other female figures, she becomes a fixed, fragile, and idealized type. Later, when she is threatened, she bcomes the fly caught in the spider's web of fate. Quasimodo cannot be compared easily with anything of the animal realm, for he is half monster himself—a Polyphemus or a Cyclops. When the two creatures are in the cathedral, Quasimodo refuses at first to enter Esmeralda's room, sensing that she recoils before his ugliness. . . . Then he gives an uncharacteristic statement of his own feelings about his ugliness; this is one of the few times we see into his character: "—Moi, je suis quelque chose d'affreux, ni homme, ni animal, un je ne sais quoi plus dur, plus foulé aux pieds et plus difforme qu'un caillou!"

The omnisicent narrator, so knowledgeable in most things, often disavows any insight into the inner thoughts and emotions of his characters. When Quasimodo rings the bells of Notre-Dame and feels the "monsters of bronze" vibrate, he is called "un étrange centaure moitié homme, moitié cloche." But the narrator refuses to analyze Quasimodo's emotions; he indicates that he is unable to explore "this opaque creature."

The same technique is applied to Claud Frollo in the chapter "Utilité des fenêtres qui donnent sur la rivière" in which we find the priest hidden behind a door as Phoebus and Esmeralda are about to arrive for their assignation. The narrator gives all his attention to the priest at the beginning of the chapter, only to tell the reader that he is unable to analyze the priest's emotions and thoughts. . . . When the two lovers enter the room, we immediately abandon Claude to follow the sensational scene between Phoebus and Esmeralda. We return behind the door when the narrator presents us with the image of the tormented face of the lascivious priest. "Qui eût pu voir en ce moment la figure du malheureux collée aux barreaux vermoulus eût cru voir une face de tigre regardant du fond d'une cage quelque chacal qui dévore une gazelle." After the narrator comes back to the seduction scene, he gives one final view of the priest from the point of view of Esmeralda as she glimpses the livid face of Claude behind Phoebus. "La jeune fille resta immobile, glacée, muette sous l'épouvantable apparition, comme une colombe qui lèverait la tête au moment où l'orfraie regarde dans son nid avec ses yeux ronds."

With this one-dimensional characterizations, events happen to Quasimodo, Esmeralda, and Claude Frollo, but there is no effect on their fixed personalities; symbolic functions are spelled out directly as parallels between these figures and their historical milieu. Quasimodo and Esmeralda may stand for the extremes of misery in nature and society, but the connection between the fatal passion of Frollo for Esmeralda and the sufferings of the masses within the inevitable movement of history seems tenuous. Still, ***Notre-Dame*** marks an improvement over ***Han d'Islande*** where the exotic setting was a picturesque décor and no attempt was made to join this setting to the narrative sequence involving Ethel and Ordener. In the later novels, when Hugo has shed the last vestiges of the *roman noir,* there is a more complete union of history and narrative. (pp. 49-52)

Patricia A. Ward, in her The Medievalism of Victor Hugo, *The Pennsylvania State University Press, 1975, 134 p.*

KATHRYN E. WILDGEN (essay date 1976)

[In the following excerpt, Wildgen explicates elements of traditional romance and myth in Notre-Dame de Paris.]

The first and most obvious method of studying ***Notre-Dame*** is as a romance rather than as a novel. As source book for the characteristics of the romance, I will use Northrop Frye's essays on literary criticism. The characters most essential to a romance are a hero, a heroine, and a villain who are, respectively, courageous, beautiful, and opposed to the courageous and beautiful. The plot consists of adventure, either a long one, or a series of short, less complicated ones. As Mr. Frye puts it, "The complete form of the romance is clearly the successful quest, and such a completed form has three main stages: the stage of the perilous journey and the preliminary minor adventures; the crucial struggle, usually some kind of battle in which either the hero or his foe, or both, must die; and the exaltation of the hero." The job of the hero is essentially that of deliverer, come from a world superior both physically and metaphorically to that of the villain. In conjunction with the quest, which is the hero's central concern, is the task of defending the innocent from the wicked. The hero and the villain are physical and moral opposites. "The enemy is associated with winter, darkness, confusion, sterility, moribund life, and old age, and the hero with spring, dawn, order, fertility, vigor, and youth." The birth of the hero is usually associated with a flood and is of quite mysterious origin. The hero often must pay the price of physical handicap in order to possess the superior power or wisdom necessary for him to fulfill his task. There are sometimes ladies of pleasure in the path of the hero who distract him from the task of deliverer of the heroine from whatever threatens her. The hero is often separated from the heroine by a sexual barrier of some sort, usually a river that must be crossed, symbolizing the fact that union with the heroine is one aspect, and an important one, of the successful quest. At the end of the adventure, the hero and his prize in the form of a beautiful woman retire to a lonely spot and pass from active to contemplative pursuits.

I would suggest that ***Notre-Dame*** follows closely the pattern of romance as delineated by Northrop Frye and that the romance has indeed a hero, albeit an unusual one, in the person of Quasimodo; a villain, Claude Frollo; and a heroine, Esmeralda. First, let us examine each of these characters as romantic archetypes and then the plot scheme as romantic plot.

Quasimodo's birth is of such mysterious origin that we have no inkling of the circumstances surrounding it. Chronologically speaking, we see him first when he is four years old, deposited in Esmeralda's place at the lodging of Paquette. This event does take place in the spring of the year. At this time he is adopted by Claude Frollo, which fact accounts for his name, the first words of the Introit of the Mass for the first Sunday after Easter. As he grows older, he develops a prodigious strength, perhaps, as Frye suggests, as compensation for his deformity. Viewed in this way, his deformity would be an indirect cause of the force he needs to accomplish successfully his task. This fact takes him out of the realm of the ordinary hero. . . . Because of his deformity, Quasimodo has never been able to demonstrate the fertility usually associated with the hero of romance. However, at one point in the narrative, he is described in metaphorical terms as extremely potent sexually. I am referring to the erotic episode with his favorite among the harem of belles, the figurative ladies of dalliance that traditionally interfere with the hero's accomplishment of the will of the heroine. His favorite Marie "était possédée et remplie de Quasimodo comme d'un génie familier." It is interesting to note that once he is under the spell of Esmeralda's beauty he abandons his belles as a former debauchee abandons public women for his true love. Ever since the moment when Esmeralda brought him water at the *pilori,* "les voisins de Notre-Dame avaient cru remarquer que l'ardeur carillonneuse de Quasimodo s'était fort refroidie. . . . Etait-ce que Marie avait une rivale dans le coeur du sonneur de Notre-Dame, et que la grosse cloche et ses quatorze soeurs étaient négligées pour quelque chose de plus aimable et de plus beau?"

At one moment in the narrative, Quasimodo is even represented as beautiful. The transformation occurs at the moment when he embraces Esmeralda after having rescued her from hanging and bears her triumphantly into Notre Dame: "la foule trépignait d'enthousiasme, car en ce moment-là Quasimodo avait vraiment sa beauté. Il était beau, . . . cet orphelin, . . . il se sentait auguste et fort." If ***Notre-Dame*** were a fairy-tale, Quasimodo would have been transformed into a handsome prince when Esmeralda brought him water to ease the pain of his torture, as do the heroes of "The Frog Prince" and "Beauty and the Beast." But this is not a fairy-tale and the bringing of the water is not love's first kiss. Esmeralda's heart already belongs to another. However, union with his female is the goal of the romantic quester, and, at this moment, even though Esmeralda is unconscious, Quasimodo finds his beauty in union with the beautiful because this is the premature fulfillment of his dream. He usually finds his own ugliness reflected in the eyes of the gypsy. He is beautiful in this moment because he is close to her and she does not shudder at the very sight of him. This episode prefigures the only possible union for the pair, union in death, in the unconscious. However, this union is premature because it is necessarily temporary. Esmeralda will not remain so disposed and the sinister evil that separates them still exists.

Charles Laughton appearing in the title role of the 1939 film version of The Hunchback of Notre Dame.

A romantic hero is defined in his relations with other people. He must be surrounded by and involved with other romantic characters, the most important of which is the villain, the moral and physical opposite of the hero. Quasimodo finds his match in Claude Frollo, the satanic priest whose goal is the destruction of Esmeralda in order that she not belong to any other man. His name, not as explicitly symbolic as that of Quasimodo, has unpleasant connotations—Claudius the traitor comes to mind as does the thought of claustration, an activity he engages in himself. He is a dark character. Consider his black cassock, the black cloak that covers his missions of evil, his black eyes, the darkness that surrounds his attempted murder of Phoebus, his first attempt to kidnap Esmeralda, his visit to her in the dungeon, his visit to her when she is in asylum in Notre Dame, and his final attempt to get her to escape with him, and the darkness that covers the work he does in his *cellule* to which he retires only after sunset.

His sterility is manifested in the state of virginity in which he has chosen to live and in his attempt to replace flesh and blood with Science as mistress. . . . His sparse and iron-grey hair is in notable contrast with the lush red overgrowth that sprouts on the head of his *carillonneur*. Although he is only thirty-six years old, he is presented as an old, old man. Hugo underlines this fact on several occasions: "il était chauve; à peine avait-il aux tempes quelques touffes de cheveux rares et déjà gris; son front large et haut commençait à se creuser de rides"; "en 1482, Quasimodo avait environ vingt ans, Claude Frollo environ trente-six ans: l'un avait grandi, l'autre avait vieilli."

Frollo prefers the old languages, Latin and especially Greek, as vehicles for the inscriptions that cover the walls of his cell. Even as a child he was like an old man, sad and serious. In contrast with Quasimodo, who undertakes apparently simple tasks and fulfills them, Claude is confounded at every turn of the road. His life is a series of *échecs,* from his attempt to instill into his brother a sense of responsiblity to his attempt to force Esmeralda's love.

Esmeralda is the lady to be delivered from the obnoxious advances of the old man. She is young, beautiful, and, most important, she is a virgin. She is also a queen among her people. Just before her mystic marriage to Quasimodo, they are separated by the Seine, which her hero will have to cross before they can retire to the cave of Montfaucon.

Hence, in ***Notre-Dame de Paris*** one finds the three principal characters of romance involved in the archetypal romantic plot of the perilous journey that Quasimodo embarks on at the moment of his appearance in the *rosace* and his coronation as *Pape des Fous,* and the numerous minor adventures that dot his history until the crucial struggle with Claude Frollo at the summit of the cathedral of Paris. It is not possible to call the marriage of Quasimodo an exaltation of him when one considers the work only as romance. But there is more to ***Notre-Dame*** than these romantic aspects. The story repeats a basic, perhaps the most basic, myth. Of course, the myth is displaced. Quasimodo is not a god. But since "myth and romance both belong in the general category of mythopoeic literature" (Frye), the transition from one to the other is easily accomplished and the two exist side by side in, I dare say, all romances. However, I would suggest that the mythic qualities of ***Notre-Dame*** outnumber greatly the elements of romance, and that the characters of the drama are more mythic than romantic.

[According to Joseph Campbell in his *Hero with a Thousand Faces*], "We have come two stages: first, from the immediate emanations of the Uncreated Creating to the fluid yet timeless personages of the mythological age; second, from these Created Creating Ones to the sphere of human history. The emanations have condensed, the field of consciousness constricted. Where formerly causal bodies were visible, now only their secondary effects come to focus in the little hard-fact pupil of the human eye. The cosmogonic cycle is now to be carried forward, therefore, not by the gods, who have become invisible, but by the heroes, more or less human in character, through whom the world destiny is realized." In this discussion of ***Notre-Dame*** it is simplest to begin with the smallest cosmos, that of Quasimodo, and then to examine the rest of the work to see if the action is repeated on a larger scale in a larger context.

The cathedral is referred to on at least two different occasions as the world of Quasimodo: "la cathédrale ne lui était pas seulement la société, mais encore l'univers, mais encore toute la nature"; "Notre-Dame avait été successivement pour lui . . . l'oeuf, le nid, la maison, la patrie, l'univers." These statements refer to the cathedral only in relation to Quasimodo. But the church considered apart and in itself is a strikingly complete cosmos. Perhaps the first attribute that comes to mind when one sees Notre Dame, espcially for the first time, is the gigantic size of the edifice. The church is a mountain of stone situated on an island and the mountain in the midst of water is a very important symbol of the cosmos among some religions. It represents order drawn from chaos, symbolized by the formless water: "the mountain in the midst of the sea symbolized the Isles of the Blessed, a sort of Paradise . . . a world apart, a world in miniature . . . the perfect place, combining completeness (mountain and water) with solitude, and thus perfect because at once the world in miniature and Pardise." [Mircea Eliade] has further comments on the Sacred Mountain and its characteristics:

1. The Sacred Mountain—where heaven and earth meet—is situated at the center of the world.

2. Every temple or palace . . . is a Sacred Mountain, thus becoming a Center.

3. Being an axis mundi, the sacred city or temple is regarded as the meeting point of heaven, earth, and hell.

Notre Dame is a temple by nature, a mountain in appearance, and is quite obviously a meeting point of heaven, earth, and hell. Quasimodo dwells in heaven, the bell-tower that rises into the sky, that "vrille de pierre qui perce le ciel." Earth is the body of the church that is eternally peopled with statues of kings and saints, a society that was sufficient for the *bossu,* one that he preferred to that of real men. Claude Frollo inhabits hell: "Voilà l'archidiacre qui souffle, l'enfer pétille là-haut."

There is another important aspect to Notre Dame: the church is the place from which Quasimodo emerges to embark on the journey that will eventually lead to his struggle with Claude Frollo and to his death. The cathedral has been a place of exile for him; his deformity has caused him to shun the company of men and hide in a tower where very few dare to go. Whenever he does go out he is not recognized as anything but an object of derision—his exile is complete until it is time for it to be broken. The theme of return from exile is important; this return marks a beginning of a new mode of life for the hero. "The folk tales commonly support or supplant this theme of the exile with that of the despised one, or the handicapped: the abused . . . the orphan, stepchild, ugly duckling, or the squire of low degree" (Campbell). The exile could be likened to a period of retreat in order to gain moral or physical strength.

That period of Quasimodo's life when he seldom ventured from his bell-tower came to an abrupt end on 6 January 1482 when he appeared to the multitude in the *rosace* of the Palace of Justice and was acclaimed Pope of Fools. . . . The cyclic passing of the old and the regeneration of the new as one of the principal themes of ***Notre-Dame*** is announced in the preface of the book. The word ΑΝΑΓΚΗ scratched on the wall both expresses the inexorability of change and itself embodies a series of disappearances: the person who scratched the word on the wall; the word itself; the wall which bore the word. The last word of the preface, *terre,* is resumed in the last word of the book, *poussière,* that to which all must turn and whence all will come.

It is therefore most appropriate that Quasimodo should come forth on this day of chaos. His arrival is surrounded by popular prophecies, enacted rather than spoken. Church, State, and University are the butt of every jeer. In Pierre Gringoire's ill-fated *moralité,* Merchandise and Labor are fighting with Clergy and Nobility. "Jupiter" is roundedly put down by Clopin Trouillefou. The cardinal is tolerated because he is lax and deficient in his office. Jacques Coppenole demands to be announced as *chaussetier*. There are several quotations from the *Aeneid,* the saga of the founding of a new race, a new nation. Everything about the feast suggests a desire of change for the new.

The old established order is personified in Claude Frollo, who combines in his character the three aspects of the monster that must be killed before the cosmos can be established. He is father, a magician, and powerful. Joseph Campbell considers the father as the archetypal enemy because he is the first to intrude upon the world of the infant and its mother. Despite his clerical celibacy, Claude Frollo is a father figure, and there are at least two who depend on him as sons, Quasimodo and Jehan Frollo. His care for these two began as an act of charity and his love for his younger brother is described in edifying terms. His reasons for accepting the *bossu* are not very clear, but we may safely assume that they were at least partially charitable. As Claude Frollo grows old before his time, his paternity sours with him, and especially for Quasimodo, he becomes the tyrant-father.

Sir James Frazer sees the tyrant of the old order best personified in the magician who managed to achieve the highest position of authority over his fellow men. Claude Frollo was doubly a magician. To those sceptical souls who were not Roman Catholics in 1482, the hocus-pocus of the Mass was sheer magic, part of the hold of popish idolatry. To medieval believers, it was a short step from religion to magic, and Claude was commonly considered to be a warlock of some sort: "ce jeune clerc monsieur Claude Frollo est un sorcier"; "sa réputation de savant avait été au peuple, où elle avait un peu tourné . . . au renom de sorcier."

Joseph Campbell, I believe, most completely describes the nature of the ogre from whose grasp freedom must be wrenched: "the dragon to be slain by him [the hero] is precisely the monster of the status quo: Holdfast, the keeper of the past. From obscurity the hero emerges, but the enemy is great and conspicuous in the seat of power; he is enemy, dragon, tyrant, because he turns to his own advantage the authority of his position." "Stated in direct terms: the work of the hero is to slay the tenacious aspect of the father . . . and release from its ban the vital energies that will feed the universe." Claude, as a clergyman, stands to gain as much as Louis XI stands to gain from maintaining the status quo. Louis is the embodiment of nobility, and Claude is the representative of both clergy and nobility, since he is either of the *haute bourgeoisie* or the *petite noblesse*. He, more than anyone, uses his rank and prestige for his own purposes which are the intimidation and seduction of Esmeralda. His iron grasp, described often and vividly, is the physical manifestation of his desire for gold and the power it brings.

A word remains to be said concerning the heroine of ***Notre-Dame,*** Esmeralda the gypsy. If the totality of the hero's task is to slay Holdfast, then Esmeralda acts as a mere catalyst, precipitating the action and subordinating herself to the accomplishment of Quasimodo's destiny. But her role is more extensive than that, for fruitful union is the necessary sequel to the killing of the tyrant. "The hegemony wrested from the enemy . . . the life energy released from the toils of the tyrant Holdfast—is symbolized as a woman. She is . . . the virgin rescued from the unholy lover. . . . She is the image of his destiny which he is to release from the prison of enveloping circumstances" (Campbell).

Esmeralda is presented as Quasimodo's opposite, hence complement, in various ways. When Esmeralda is near, water is usually to be found nearby. Pierre Gringoire winds up in the water in the street at the time of his unsuccessful attempt to rescue her from Quasimodo. The little song she sings to her disappointed husband is about water. She is the giver of water to Quasimodo. The chief discomfort of her dungeon is its dampness and the only sound there is the drip, drip of water. Quasimodo, on the other hand, is usually followed, preceded or accompanied by fire. He is first seen as *Pape des Fous* by the light of the bonfire lit to celebrate his feast. He uses fire to destroy the attackers of Notre Dame. At the moment when he sees Esmeralda being led to the noose, "toutes les pointes de Paris . . . prenaient feu à la fois."

Esmeralda is a creature of the night—the moon seems to accompany her. She arrives at dusk in the Place de Grève. In the house of assignation with Phoebus, the moon shines through the window and the shoulder that Frollo glimpses is "ronde et brune, comme la lune qui se lève dans la brume." Her trial for Phoebus' murder is at seven in the evening. Quasimodo functions best in the daytime when the sun is shining. At night he is deprived of his most powerful weapon, his ugliness, and his two nocturnal essays both fail. (He fails to capture Esmeralda for Claude, and he cannot make Phoebus come to Esmeralda when she is living in Notre Dame.) It is approximately noon when he receives the crown of *Pape des Fous,* when he is scourged publicly, and when he rescues Esmeralda from hanging. His red hair, and his red and purple *surtout* are reminiscent of the colors of the sun. When he visits Esmeralda in her room in the cathedral, she sees his face at the same moment that she sees the sun. Simultaneous with the accomplishment of his heroic task, the morning sun appears.

Esmeralda dwells on earth. Her body and hair are dark like the earth and her name suggests the deep green of the emerald, the color of the grass that covers the earth. She visits heaven, Quasimodo's dwelling, and hell, the dungeon prescribed by Claude, only extraordinarily. Quasimodo's home is heaven; he descends to earth only to complete his task. Quasimodo, not Phoebus, is the true sun. But his mate's eyes are blinded by the sun; she can see only when her eyes are closed in death. Joseph Campbell explains that the heroine's refusal of the hero does not vitiate the mythical pattern. "When the hero-quest has been accomplished . . . the adventurer still must return with his life-transmuting trophy. . . . But the responsibility has frequently been refused. . . . Numerous indeed are the heroes fabled to have taken up residence forever in the blessed isle of the unaging Goddess of Immortal Being."

I suggested earlier in this discussion that Quasimodo's cosmos was the smaller of two cosmoi, that of Notre Dame and that of the city of Paris itself. The theme of overturn of entrenched power is not limited to the drama of Quasimodo and Claude Frollo; it is suggested in those sections of the book in which the People, the King and Notre Dame fill the roles of Quasimodo, Claude Frollo and Esmeralda, respectively. The period of history before the invention of printing could be considered as the exile of the People, the appearance of the press as the summons to adventure. The People are usually described as the downtrodden of the city, those in blind submission to authority as Quasimodo was, although he could have destroyed his oppressor with a single blow. Notre Dame's fate is similar to that of Esmeralda because the church is liberated from the powerful by the People. Louis XI is compared to Jupiter, whose ears are to be found in his feet—thereby imposing the necessity of groveling on anyone who wishes a favor. Pierre Gringoire, while speaking with the King, assumes the same attitude as Quasimodo dealing with Claude. Louis considers Notre Dame as his woman; he is furious when the People try to take her away from him.

However, the People were not to triumph for several centuries. Notre Dame would remain the exclusive mistress of the clergy, who would remain under the power of the nobility. But the

People's triumph was prefigured and encouraged by the success of the bell-ringer of Notre Dame. (pp. 319-27)

> *Kathryn E. Wildgen, ''Romance and Myth in 'Notre-Dame de Paris',''* in The French Review, *Vol. XLIX, No. 3, February, 1976, pp. 319-27.*

W. WOLFGANG HOLDHEIM (essay date 1976)

[Holdheim interprets the theories of art and history presented in Notre-Dame de Paris *through a close examination of Hugo's conceptions of time, architecture, literature, and epic narrative.]*

> Sans doute ces chapitres retrouvés aurent peu de valeur aux yeux des personnes, d'ailleurs fort judicieuses, qui n'ont cherché dans ***Notre-Dame de Paris*** que le drame, que le roman. Mais il est peut-être d'autres lecteurs qui n'ont pas trouvé inutile d'étudier la pensée d'esthétique et de philosophie cachée dans ce livre, qui ont bien voulu, en lisant ***Notre-Dame de Paris,*** se plaire à démêler sous le roman autre chose que le roman, et à suivre, qu'on nous passe ces expressions un peu ambitieuses, le systéme de l'historien et le but de l'artiste à travers la création telle quelle du poète.

This passage from Hugo's ''Note ajouté à l'édition définitive (1832)'' of ***Notre-Dame de Paris*** [see excerpt dated 1832] refers to an amusing episode in the publication of the book. The second edition contained three sections that were missing in the original one (of the preceding year): the unimportant last chapter of Book IV (''Impopularité'') and, more significantly, the two chapters making up Book V. In the ''Note,'' Hugo heatedly protests against the accusation that these additions were indeed written later: a poetic creation is a ''mystérieux microcosme'' that springs ''d'un seul jet'' from the poet's imagination and cannot be arbitrarily retouched. What, then, is his explanation? The file had simply been mislaid, but had turned up again by 1832. The improbability of this assertion has given rise to certain suspicions. Did Hugo, impelled by financial motives, perchance play hide-and-seek with the publisher and the public? As late as our century, Emile Henriot [in his essay ''Hugo et *Notre-Dame de Paris,*'' 1930] has felt the need to defend the poet's moral integrity on that score.

Henriot unfortunately fails to deal with the much more important aesthetic implications of the matter. Hugo's indignant defensiveness may very well be directed against the unspeakable blasphemy of questioning the indivisible spontaneousness of his inspiration. But for post-romantics such as ourselves, a work is no longer a mysterious entity whose intactness will inevitably be destroyed by a two-stage creation. Yet there is no denying that unity really seems to be lacking in this case. In fact the ''Note'' itself explains that Hugo felt free in 1831 to omit the ''mislaid'' sections because their absence would remain unnoticed: they ''n'entamaient en rien le fond du drame et du roman.'' The first chapter of Book V (''*Abbas beati Martini*'') is but the feeblest attempt to relate the historical and aesthetic disquisitions of the second chapter (''Ceci tuera cela'') with the action. Indeed it is customary to discuss those important disquisitions in their own right, without reference to the story; there are even editions which simply leave them out. However, this also goes for the two chapters of Book III (''Notre-Dame'' and ''Paris à vol d'oiseau''). The theorizing of the Fifth Book merely supplements and extends that of the Third, which was contained in the edition of 1831. The problem of the unity is exacerbated, but not created by the additions. The apologia is significant because it draws our attention to a structural duality which characterizes the original conception and is consciously reinforced in 1832.

This should give pause to any critic who might be tempted to leave matters at that, without further investigation. Hugo's remarks cited at the beginning tend to minimize ''le drame,'' ''le roman,'' ''la création telle quelle du poète'' (i.e., the plot, the story)—a judgment, incidentally, which the discerning reader can hardly contest. Literary scholarship has always given equal (or even greater) importance to the ''système de l'historien,'' which is traditionally studied in the context of French romanticism, rather than in that of ''le roman.'' And here, precisely, Hugo's commentary becomes slightly puzzling. It refers to ''la pensée d'esthétique et de philosophie *cachée* dans ce livre.'' Just what is ''hidden'' about it? The author's philosophical views seem, rather, to have been driven home with a sledge hammer. And yet he invites us to ''démêler *sous* le roman autre chose que le roman'' and to pursue the historical thought ''*à travers* la création . . . du poète.'' Under and through (not in addition to) the story. Moreover, the ''création telle quelle du poète'' is said to conceal not only ''le système de l'historien,'' but also ''le but de l'artiste.'' Do we owe this third point exclusively to the author's love for triadic formulation? This, to be sure, would be nothing unusual for Hugo. ''Artiste'' would then be simply another word for ''art historian.'' On the other hand, an artist's ''*but*'' is different in kind from an historian's ''système.'' Perhaps it behooves us to assume, at least heuristically, that Hugo has really pursued—in and through his poetic creation—an artistic purpose which is somehow connected with his historical thinking. This means that we should examine that philosophy of history, which is so brash and yet supposedly so mysterious, from the point of view of its functionality in the text. True, it markedly interrupts the action on two occasions; but there may exist more subtle filiations, less palpable forms of integration, which fall outside the easy limits of a plot.

An historian's conception of time is, of course, a matter of crucial interest. In the case of a romanticist like Hugo, we are prone to assume that he perceives temporality in a positive way, especially if he writes an historical novel which is to represent one transitory historical moment (1482): ''Aussi le Paris gothique ne fut-il complet qu'un moment.'' Indeed we find that the very first chapter of Hugo's theoretical disquisitions is dominated by the concept of time. He there expresses his indignation about ''les dégradations, les mutilations sans nombre que simultanément le temps et les hommes ont fait subir au vénérable monument [Notre-Dame].'' Characteristically, the dualistic formulation (''le temps et les hommes'') is almost immediately replaced by a triadic one: time, revolutions, and fashions. This change, however, does little to modify the basic polemical opposition which pits time against human meddling; the revolutions, which have a certain grandeur, merely bring out the abject pettiness of the fashions. But the duality is not absolute, both of its poles are viewed in a negative light. The destruction wrought by ''time'' is not a value, just a less pronounced disvalue. The savng grace is that time ''a répandu sur la façade [of the Cathedral] cette sombre couleur des siècles qui fait de la vieillesse des monuments l'âge de leur beauté.'' Hugo's philosophical statements, then, do not contain a positive view on temporal development. Time is sympathetically perceived only in the limited framework of an aestheticizing cult of the past.

This limitation might be ascribed to Hugo's particular context and purpose: he is polemically concerned with the artistic perfection of one particular monument of the past. But his formulations have a puzzling aspect which goes far beyond such an *ad hoc* evaluation and casts light on his view of time itself. If we look closely, after all, the polarity of "time" and "man" is almost shocking. Does it not confine "time" to natural change, excluding the component of human duration—i.e., of historicity? Are "les hommes" perchance not agents of temporal developments? The second (pseudo-triadic) version does nothing to avoid this implication. Fashions, it appears, are not temporal, and historical events such as revolutions are not considered as workings of "le temps."

It might be objected that we should not take Hugo too seriously. For all his philosophizing, he is really a poet and a rhetorician from whom we can expect no logical and terminological rigor. Perhaps his sense of time should be sought in his poetic eloquence rather than in his conceptual acrobatics. And here indeed, matters do look different at first sight. The "marée montante" of time is described in sentences which truly catch the flavor of its creative dynamism. The grand edifices evolve through the ages; "chaque flot du temps superpose son alluvion, chaque race dépose sa couche sur le monument"; and this growth takes place "sans trouble, sans effort, sans réaction"—"suivant une loi naturelle et tranquille." The chapter on "Paris à vol d'oiseau" irresistibly breaks through all confinements. And when Hugo presents the mutations of the Christian churches as eternal variations on the permanent basis of the Roman basilic, he grasps that essential dialectic of unity and multiplicity, Being and Becoming, which Goethe has called "Dauer im Wechsel."

There is altogether something Goethean in the sense of time which emerges from Book III of ***Notre-Dame.*** Hugo as well gives preference to the gradual, oceanic variety of change; the volcanic-revolutionary transformations with their "voies de fait, brutalités, contusions, fractures" remain destructive, they seem to have no creative function in the historical process. This means that Hugo's lyrical evocation of temporal becoming sharpens (rather than cancels) the opposition between "time" and "man." Let us note the extra-human, aquatic symbolism which dominates Hugo's account of meaningful development. Time is a *mounting flood* whose *waves* deposit *layers* and *alluvions,* in a constant process of growth that is devoid of efforts and contortions. The law of "time" is natural, not subject to man's intentionality; creative time is not human duration. But would this not mean that it works its way outside of history, which (as we tend to think) is the realm of the human spirit, not of nature? The implications would be odd for one who writes an historical novel. We should ask how the matter presents itself in the narrative practice of ***Notre-Dame de Paris.***

The bulk of the work, of course, remains an account of human action, but Hugo himself comes close to admitting the weakness of this "création telle quelle." "Le drame, le roman" is a cliché-ridden plot of more than ordinary thinness and has only the barest historical significance. The progression, above all, is unpersuasive and devoid of narrative cohesiveness. A number of tableaux, visually external and pointedly static, are loosely connected and superficially dynamized by means of a simplistic dialectic of mechanical antitheses. The resulting rhythm of "development" is haltingly discontinuous, melodramatically inorganic; it constitutes not more than a jolting pseudo-movement, a histrionic degeneration of time. This pale orgy of fragmentation could (at best and not without effort!) be considered a diminished version of the spasmodic transformations which Hugo the theorist ascribes to revolutions; to his ideal of creative time it is diametrically opposed.

There are parts, however, in which this ideal struggles for narrative expression—a fact which seems to have escaped most critics of the book. They are easily recognizable by their aquatic symbolism. Thus when the beggars prepare to attack the Cathedral, their advancing horde appears to Quasimodo as a moving river which gradually becomes identifiable as a torrent of human beings. Such passages usually occur in the mass scenes, which are artistically the best sections of the book. This context has an evident inner logic. Mass scenes can present man in a form which is not irreconcilable with Hugo's preference for oceanic movement. The crowd is a monumental and (as it were) dehumanized version of the human; its instinctive irresistible flux seems to replace intentionality by a dynamism that is paradoxically passive, thus despiritualizing historical duration and turning it into natural becoming. The depiction of turbulent collectivity can effect a seeming "naturalization" of human time.

The best example is the entry of the Parisians into the Palais de Justice, one of the stylistic high points of the book. . . . (pp. 58-63)

The crowd is palpably in motion as a totality, not as an accumulation of individual subjects. In fact the relationship between subject and object is somewhat odd. Who are the grammatical "subjects" of this "action"? They range from reifications of collective images and emotions (the waves of humanity; "les cris, les rires, le trépignement") to downright objects ("la place du Palais," the streets, the staircase). There is an attempt to transform the passive into the active, the object into the *agens,* which once becomes jarringly evident in a passive construction which is artificial in French: "le grand escalier" is being "remonté et descendu." The important thing, however, is that the staircase appears as a flowing continuum. Thanks to the varied imagery of the water, the trend towards the object never takes the form of abstract objectality.

Many of the objects are architectonic, thus introducing one of the principal themes of the book. The streets, the Palace and its staircase already point towards that super-Object which determines the very title of the novel. But is not the Cathedral made by human hands? It is, but (as we are pointedly informed) in the same anonymous, collective, non-intentional manner as mass movements. And in this way, Notre-Dame ultimately turns out to be less a work of man than an "ouvrage des siècles," a creation of natural time: "Le temps est l'architecte, le peuple est le maçon." But how can time continue to dominate such a product? Closed in itself, stately and majestic, the Cathedral must seem to transcend the flowing movement of the seasons. The monumentality of collective dynamism has here coagulated into the towering Monument, creating a new problem for the author. The "naturalization" of time is superseded by a monumentalization of time.

Let us look at Hugo's art-historical considerations with references to the Cathedral of Notre-Dame. That monument is by no means "complet, défini, classé"; it forms no unity of style, is no longer quite Romanesque but not yet Gothic—it is an "édifice de la transition." Notre-Dame, then, is presented as nothing less than an embodiment of Becoming, a petrified version (indeed a monumentalization) of time.

The matter, however, is more complex. The synthesis of rigidity and motion becomes even more evident, and takes on added implications, when we consider the nature of its two stylistic components. Hugo sums it up in a famous formula: "La greffe de l'ogive sur le plein cintre." The Romanesque arch is the hieroglyphic and theocratic Church in which everything tends towards an ideal of lifeless fixity; in its ornamentation, geometric forms are more important than flowers and flowers more significant than animals, while man plays almost no role at all. The Gothic pointed arch, on the other hand, is free, popular, progressive and capricious. The meaning of this opposition is driven home in Book V, added in 1832. We there learn that the two styles express a fundamental contrast that recurs in history time and again. Romanesque architecture, caught in a stagnant immobility that lasts for centuries, is "l'unité,. . . l'immobilité, l'horreur du progrès . . ."; it represents the rigidity of dogma which fortifies the stone "comme une seconde pétrification." Gothic architecture, a product of the unsettling Crusades, is constantly in rapid development; it is a creation of caprice, imagination, even "fantaisie," whose essence is "la variété, le progrès, l'originalité, l'opulence, le mouvement perpétuel." The earlier style embodies the timelessly absolute, the hieratically universal; the later one: the particular, the temporally dynamic. There are good reasons, then, why Hugo's heroine should be the Cathedral of Notre-Dame. Merging these two conceptions of reality, it is "puissante et féconde comme la création divine dont elle semble avoir dérobé le double caractère: variété, éternité." The monument synthesizes hieratic rigidity and human vitality, staticity and dynamism, Being and Becoming, eternity and time.

Already in Book III, the stones of the Cathedral are compared to the pages of a history of France, and Paris as a whole is referred to as a "chronique de pierre." Book V develops these analogies into a systematic theory, thus giving an unsuspected (and a hitherto unheeded) meaning to the literary image of Notre-Dame. Architecture, so we read, is nothing else than the literature of ancient times. The stones are letters, hieroglyphs, which combine to form syllables, words and sentences, and to grow into chronicles of stone. The monument comprises the totality of an epoch, "l'architecture est le grand livre de l'humanité." Served by the other arts, it is the *Gesamtkunst* of the Middle Ages; literature as well, "pour être quelque chose," must "venir s'encadrer dans l'édifice sous la forme d'hymne ou de *prose*." The symbolism of an entire era is thus fixed into "une forme éternelle, visible, palpable": thought seeks eternal durability, and the stone is "solide, durable et résistant." The essential foundation of architecture, therefore, is eternity, fixity, rigidity. But within those welcome limits set by its medium, architecture has been able to accommodate the principle of dynamism: the heterogeneous and grotesque, the particular—in a word: Gothic art, representing a "liberté de l'architecture" which foreshadows our modern freedom of the press.

This means that architecture itself, in principle, harbored the germ of a total transformation. Yet in Hugo's view, the arabesque-like play of Becoming on a secure foundation of Being could probably have lasted for an indefinite time. It was a mechanical invention (that of printing) which finally brought about a revolutionary change. True, the desire for eternity was paramount in that development as well: a printed book is ultimately more durable than a building. The paper, however, is not "solide" but on the contrary "vivace," not "palpable" but "insaisissable": the new eternity is paradoxically defined by "ubiquité" and continual movement. Eloquently, though with his familiar schematic generalization, Hugo describes how architecture was displaced by literature. As Frollo puts it: "le livre tuera l'édifice." The architectonic *Gesamtkunstwerk* dissolves and each art goes its separate way, but it is primarily the printed book which destroys the building, gradually acquiring the vigor of its victim. Michelangelo's St. Peter is the last desperate triumph of architecture; thereafter, the paper ruthlessly swallows up the stone. As early as the 17th century, the printing press gives us a great literary epoch. Then, "au moment où le dixhuitième siècle s'achève, elle a tout détruit. Au dix-neuvième, elle va reconstruire."

The promise, therefore, lies with Hugo's century. How is that promise going to be kept? We learn that the paper edifice is colossal. It comprises that "cathédrale de Shakespeare" as well as the "mosquée de Byron," the "bas-relief en marbre blanc d'Homère" together with the seven heads of the polyglot Bible. But there is more than the great works of *belles lettres*. The 18th-century "Encyclopédie" and the revolutionary "Moniteur" as well are parts of a huge building, a veritable second Tower of Babel. This "immense construction," then, is not one single work. It contains the totality of everything that is being printed, is an "édifice" with a thousand floors—ever open and continually growing, for the gigantic machine of the press "vomit incessamment de nouveaux matériaux pour son oeuvre." The Babel of modern times is "toujours inachevé."

There is something dissatisfying, indeed anticlimactic in this vision of the present and the future. The triumph of literature seems unable to escape from its mechanical beginnings. Can we truly believe that the author of ***Notre-Dame de Paris*** views his creation as a mere wave in the paper torrent of modern printing? Moreover, after a genuinely speculative reflection, this conclusion of Hugo's theoretical disquisitions falls back into a purely rhetorical use of metaphors. Perhaps, under the guidance of Hugo's own theories, we should speculate in our turn. We cannot help noticing, for example, that the rhetorical metaphors which strikingly emerge at the end of Book V are architectonic. Could this perchance reflect a nostalgia for a synthesis of literature and architecture, in which the solidity of stone once more (somehow) gets its due?

An affirmative answer to that question is in fact implicit in the parallelism between writing and building, posited by Hugo. Taken seriously and extended to the modern era, that theory will suggest a precise relationship between Hugo's modern book and the ancient "book" of Paris, between the Cathedral of paper and that of stone. The monument in the Ile de la Cité is the architectural monolith that has assimilated the literary principle of temporal movement. The modern author strives for a similar synthesis, but in reverse. The basis is now the temporal dynamism of the word instead of the staticity of the stone. In the Middle Ages, language had to seek integration in the building; now it is (on the contrary) the edifice which must be merged into the novel. Yet in this subordinating integration it plays an altogether crucial role: the monumentalization of time which it represents becomes a monumentalization of the book. It makes ***Notre-Dame de Paris*** the dynamic book which recaptures the silent majesty of the stone—a symbol of Time which appropriates monolithic Timelessness. Hugo's work is not meant to be just one example of writing among others, but an absolute Book in an almost Mallarméen sense—a *livre de pierre* (not *de fer*) *vêtu*.

Hugo's theorizing in ***Notre-Dame*** makes another point which adds scope to our interpretative perspective. In Book III, the Cathedral is declared to be a sister of the Iliads and the Romanceros, and again the added Fifth Book emphasizes and extends what would otherwise be no more than a remark in passing: on the one hand, the Iliads of the Middle Ages took the form of Cathedrals; on the other hand, the poems of that epoch "ressemblent aux monuments." The architectural era after all has its major poetic genre: the epic, a collective creation like the building, and in every way its literary analogue.

This near-identification of the architectural and the epic casts yet a new light on the experiment of ***Notre-Dame de Paris.*** There can be little doubt that the Cathedral is also to be viewed as a petrification of epic monumentality—grandeur and monumentality being always the prime characteristics of epicity in Hugo's view. Could it be that the work of 1832 presents itself as a synthesis not only of literature and architecture, but concomitantly of the novel and the epic? (pp. 63-8)

In his nostalgia for the epic, Hugo is very much a child of his era. To find out how he views it, we can turn to a passage in the **"Préface de *Cromwell*"**:

> Une sorte de gravité solennelle s'est empreinte partout, dans les moeurs domestiques comme dans les moeurs publiques. Les peuples n'ent conservé de la vie errante que le respect de l'étranger et du voyageur. La famille a une patrie; tout l'y attache; il y a le culte du foyer, le culte du tombeau.

Epicity, we note, is more than a literary genre: it is a state of being that characterizes an entire era—to use Hegel's term: a veritable "epischer Weltzustand." The stationery imagery ("foyer," "patrie," even "tombeau," "attacher") indicates the foundation of this epic state of being: it is one of solidity, rest, and fixity—just as in the creations of the concomitant architectonic age. The "vie errante" survives only as a memory. Yet movement cannot be completely expelled from human existence; therefore, it takes place in the mode of "gravité solennelle."—of a measured *gravitas* which corresponds to the weighty monumentality of both epic and edifice. This ritual dignity strips time of all spasmodic (dramatic) suddenness. It is a stylized motion that tends towards immobility—Becoming intercepted by Being, a veritable taming of Time.

In our tumultuous age, however, Time can no longer be so effortlessly tamed. Becoming reigns supreme and has to reconquer and integrate Being; Literature must regenerate and assimilate the solidity of Architecture; the new Epic is bound to be a construction in which the modern Novel somehow incorporates the monolithic grandeur of the architectonic Epicity of old. And this, I believe, is the "but de l'artiste" which we are invited to discover "à travers la création telle quelle" of 1832. There is "le drame, le roman," and there is the epic majesty of the Cathedral. One must admit that their synthesis is not carried off too well. The staircase of the Palais de Justice may seem to come to life for a moment, but such an optical illusion cannot be sustained throughout an entire novel for the weighty Cathedral of Notre-Dame. Hugo goes to great lengths of stylistic ingenuity to mobilize the Monument, but its frozen statelines proves restive to his lyrical efforts. And the building's art-historical content, with its symbolic fusion of dynamism and stasis, remains narratively ineffective: that monumentalization of time in its turn requires a temporalization of monumentality which is never consummated. When the beggars at last attack the Church in force, it is very much as if the despairing author ended up by trying to storm his own creation!

The heroine of stone, then, remains an irreducible block of Being in a universe of Becoming. But it would be facile to attribute this duality exclusively to the novelistic clumsiness of Hugo. It is hard to believe that he was artistically quite incapable of filling his building with continual life and clamor, of merging it more integrally with the plot. Perhaps such a technical success would merely have concealed a more essential duality, perhaps there is a deeper meaning in the author's failure. How indeed can we expect a homogenization of Being and Becoming in an era where men are (in Baudelaire's words) "les esclaves martyrisés du Temps"? The graduality of solemn *gravitas* would be an unpersuasive compromise; the two poles are too sharply defined, too exclusive, to be reconciled. And thus Becoming, in ***Notre-Dame de Paris,*** relapses into the perverted and stereotype temporality of melodrama; other novelists will truly shape it into a positive principle for the renewal of the novel. And Being, in ***Notre-Dame,*** contracts into that abstract monolithic objectality which will, in various forms, increasingly make its appearance in the novel—for the last time, provisionally, in the not entirely unprecedented experimentation of the *nouveau roman*. (pp. 69-70)

W. Wolfgang Holdheim, "The History of Art in Victor Hugo's 'Notre-Dame de Paris'," in Nineteenth-Century French Studies, *Vol. V, Nos. 1 & 2, Fall, 1976 & Winter, 1977, pp. 58-70.*

STIRLING HAIG (essay date 1979)

[Haig discusses stone as the principal image in Notre-Dame de Paris *and the cathedral as the novel's centralizing locus. According to Haig, Frollo's assertion that "the book will destroy the edifice" is the controlling philosophical concept of* Notre-Dame de Paris.*]*

Recent interpretations of Hugo's novel have sought to suggest that the work's interest and unity are to be found in the concept of myth or romance, and that the action of ***Notre-Dame*** turns about a central character, identified now as Claude Frollo, now as Quasimodo. While such readings unquestionably lay open new dimensions and critical perspectives, they cannot entirely replace more traditional, or perhaps "orthodox" views, which put the cathedral itself squarely in the center of the work's historical and dramatic interest. Indeed, the cathedral's very mass, the sheer temporal and geographical space that it occupies in the novel would be difficult to ignore or to displace. The text speaks for it—in the title, in the introduction, in the whole *Livre Troisième*, in the dénouement, in the elusive theme of *anankè*—and throughout the cathedral is figured in the ubiquitous *signifiant* of ***Notre-Dame de Paris,*** the stone.

The stone is the petrification of the medieval world and its characteristic theocracy; it is its fate, its death. To the ethereal heights of the church, Victor Hugo could have apposed the magic lightness of La Esmeralda's dance, which suggests heights and the flight of the magic carpet: "Elle dansait, elle tournait, elle tourbillonnait sur un vieux tapis de Perse, jeté négligemment sous ses pieds. . . ." For La Esmeralda's domain *is* height, and escape from gravity. The curious literally seize ladders the better to observe her dancing ("Et pourquoi a-t-il pris cette échelle?—Pour aller voir la Esmeralda . . .); after her "mariage au pot cassé" with Gringoire, Hugo will designate her as an "être aérien," and for weeks she will find asylum in the perches of Notre-Dame itself. But Hugo's purpose is, in the end, to prepare a particularly dramatic, brutal reversal of these ascensional motifs, and this *péripétie* is associated with the stone from which both church and gibbet are made. For La Esmeralda, "l'asile était une prison comme une autre" and she will last be seen dancing at the end of a rope, hanging from one of fifteenth-century Paris's numerous stone gibbets, and bearing all the grisly weight of the executioner pressing down upon her delicate neck:

> Quasimodo qui ne respirait plus depuis quelques instants vit se balancer au bout de la corde, à deux toises au-dessus du pavé, la malheureuse enfant *avec l'homme accroupi les pieds sur ses épaules*. La corde fit plusieurs tours sur elle-même, et Quasimodo vit courir d'horribles convulsions le long du corps de l'égyptienne. (my italics)

We witness this scene through the anguished observation of Claude Frollo and Quasimodo standing on the towers of Notre-Dame and looking down, across the Seine, to the place de Grève: from afar and above. Descent, fall, and stone are replicated in Frollo's death. Pushed by Quasimodo, his weight will bend the lead gutter (the tombal metal), and plunge him into the realm of stone-death: "Tout était pierre autour de lui: devant ses yeux, les monstres béants; au-dessous, tout au fond, dans la place, le pavé; au-dessus de sa tête, Quasimodo qui pleurait." Frollo does not fall straight down, but hits first the slate roof of a nearby house, where he becomes as a stone ("tuile") that falls on stone: "Il glissa rapidement sur le toit comme une tuile qui se détache, et alla rebondir sur le pavé. Là, il ne remua plus." In the course of his fall, Claude Frollo is not so much crushed as he is petrified.

Quasimodo's tears, in this final scene of the living, humanize him in extremis, but he too undergoes an analogous death: having descended into the cave of a vast stone ossuary to embrace the dead Esmeralda, he turns into a calcified skeleton that "falls into dust" at first touch.

Thus the cathedral—centralizing locus of the novel's action—and its stones determine the register of the characters' *anankè*. The word itself is engraved into the walls of Notre-Dame. If it has disappeared from the walls through scraping or cleaning, it has nevertheless been preserved by the very element that succeeds stone and "kills" it, the book—the book, that is, being written by Victor Hugo: "Ainsi, hormis le fragile souvenir que lui consacre l'auteur de ce livre, il ne reste plus rien aujourd'hui du mot mystérieux gravé dans la sombre tour de Notre-Dame. . . ." The writer of the hand-graven word—*manuscript*—has been "effaced," as has the word *anankè* itself, as may be effaced one day the church itself. But the book subsists: "C'est sur ce mot qu'on a fait ce livre."

That this world is dead, and removed from living concerns is perhaps at the basis of Hugo's constant interventions into his *récit*, ruptures that continually remind us that the world of Quasimodo, La Esmeralda, and Claude Frollo is firmly in the past. Hugo's technique, on this point, is precisely the opposite of the traditional historical novelist's, who strives to make us forget the temporal abyss. Hugo's interventions underscore that chasm, as they refer us exclusively to present or recent history. The comparisons emphasize, in other words, the presence of the gap, rather than its absence: "Si Gringoire vivait de nos jours, quel beau milieu il tiendrait entre le classique et le romantique!"; "Si nous n'étions pas au quinzième siècle, nous dirions que Gringoire était descendu de Michel-Ange à Callot"; "ce qui procura à Gringoire . . . une sensation à peu près pareille à celle qu'éprouverait Micromégas . . ."; "Qu'on arrange ces choses comme on pourra. Je ne suis qu'historien"; "J'ADORE CORALIE. 1823, SIGNÉ UGÈNE. *Signé* est dans le texte"; "un escalier aussi roide qu'un alexandrin classique."

Hugo's idée-force, which he wished to place in the very center of ***Notre-Dame de Paris,*** is in the cathedral and in the second chapter of Livre Cinquième, entitled "CECI TUERA CELA." First spoken by Claude Frollo in the preceding chapter, this banal phrase, composed of prosaic and hardly fatidic demonstratives, is tersely parsed in the following manner: *"Ceci tuera cela. Le livre tuera l'édifice."* The thought is two-sided, according to Hugo.

The regret and chagrin that accompany Frollo's fateful utterance are the stunned fear of the priest whose sacerdotal functions and investiture are menaced by the book. The printed word is likened to the angel Legion and, anticipating Mallarmé's *siècle épouvantá de n'avoir pas connu / Que la mort triomphait dans cette voix!* it is the voice of doom whose six million wings will muffle the voice of the pulpit and the non-printed word: "C'était la voix du prophète qui entend déjà bruire et fourmiller l'humanité émancipée, qui voit dans l'avenir l'intelligence saper la foi, l'opinion détrôner la croyance, le monde secouer Rome."

The corollary of the thought concerns not the priest but rather—still according to Hugo—the *savant* and the *artiste*. To the change of form in expression corresponds something deeper, which he likens to new articulations of humanity. Hugo first explains this in a somewhat simplistic way: "le livre de pierre . . . allait faire place au livre de papier. . . . L'imprimerie tuera l'architecture." In the beginning was the Word, yet for a secularizing Hugo it was not made flesh, but stony, granitic syllables: "Le dolmen et le cromlech celtes, le tumulus étrusque, le galgal hébreu sont des mots"; Karnac is a whole sentence. And the stones change, they are not solely capable of raising the Temple and the Law. If romanesque architecture is a theocratic masonry exuding "l'autorité, l'unité, l'impénétrable, l'absolu, Grégoire VII," the gothic brings the odor of the masses, and issues in the era "des Jacqueries, des Pragueries, et des Ligues." The gothic brings a new discourse; it embodies still the sacerdotal mysteries, but it also writes or carves its own subversion—liberty, democracy. "Toute civilisation commence par la théologie et finit par la démocratie." The next text blows revolutionary; Hugo's thoughts here anticipate Bakhtin's concept of *dialogism:* beside the code of the established order, the polyphonic revolutionary text makes a second discourse heard, and this one contests the order it expresses. And so, for Hugo, the poet of the gothic era makes himself an architect—the dogmatic edifice has fallen into his domain. So long as the priest has his basilica and his altar, "l'artiste la bâtit à sa guise. Adieu le mystère, le mythe, la loi. Voici la fantaisie et le caprice." And here, too, we shall say, is where the much maligned character of Pierre Gringoire comes in. Yet his day has not entirely come. An older order must first die. We are in the fifteenth century, and the printed word's epoch will not arrive until the sixteenth: Luther and the Reformation are inconceivable without their precursor, Gutenberg.

"CECI TUERA CELA" sends us back to reread the great descriptive and historical chapter on Notre Dame itself (Livre Troisième, Chap. 1). There Hugo had emphasized to a surprising degree, the *mixed* character of the edifice. The cathedral was neither entirely romanesque, nor entirely gothic. It was a hybrid, an unfinished work—*pendent opera interrupta*—an "édifice de la transition." "Ce n'est plus une église romane, ce n'est pas encore une église gothique. Cet édifice n'est pas un type"; "Cette église centrale et génératrice est parmi les vieilles églises de Paris une sorte de chimère; elle a la tête de l'une, les membres de celle-là, la croupe de l'autre; quelque chose de toutes."

Hugo thus stresses that the dying world of Claude Frollo—of the stone-writ book, that is, the cathedral itself—is the principal manifestation of the struggle against *anankè* in the novel. (In the preface to ***Les travailleurs de la mer,*** Hugo cites triple *anankès,* and ***Notre-Dame de Paris*** as representing "l'anankè des dogmes.") Notre Dame *shows* liberty succeeding dogmatism; it is a visualization of fatality and obstacle. That Hugo should view both cathedral and book as successive embodiments of man's tongues, voices, messages, is underscored by the repetition of the Babelic analogy. In the chapter "Notre-Dame," architecture is figured as the beehive: "Le grand symbole de l'architecture, Babel, est une ruche." The link with "CECI TUERA CELA" is emphasized by the return of the same image, this time with the printed word as the second term of the analogy. After a long architectural-literary passage evoking "la cathédrale de Shakespeare . . . la mosquée de Byron" in which the notion of the literary edifice is paramount, Hugo ends his chapter with the new mention of Babel:

> Certes, c'est là aussi une construction qui grandit et s'amoncelle en spirales sans fin; là aussil il y a confusion de langues, activité incessante, labeur infatigable, concours acharné de l'humanité tout entière, refuge promis à l'intelligence contre un nouveau déluge, contre une submersion de barbares. C'est la seconde tour de Babel du genre humain.

Claude Frollo and Quasimodo, and Esmeralda too, are lives whose destinies are linked to Notre Dame's, the stone cathedral of death. Its destiny weighs upon them, and crushes them. Their deaths do not signal the end of witchcraft, alchemy, or monsterdom. But at least two of them are the tutelary gods of the cathedral whose "book" is dying. The legacy of this old, moribund world, this book, falls into the possession of an unworthy heir: Pierre Gringoire.

Who else do we perceive in transports of rapturous contemplation before the *esthetic* beauties of architectural monuments than Gringoire, whose artistic endeavors suggest the uncertain, unpredictable infancy of the printed word? Gringoire is an *incunabulum,* he frets in the cradle of art. In the scene just alluded to (Livre Dixième, Chap. 1: "Gringoire a plusieurs bonnes idées de suite rue des Bernardins"), Gringoire is busy applying himself to the composition of a commentary of a work not insignificantly entitled *De cupa petrarum,* and is seen "reading" a richly sculpted chapel near Saint-Germain-l'Auxerrois: "il y a un lien intime entre l'hermétique et la maçonnerie. Gringoire avait passé de l'amour d'une idée à l'amour de la forme de cette idée." And when asked by Claude Frollo if he is happy, he responds: "En honneur, oui! J'ai d'abord aimé des femmes, puis des bêtes. Maintenant j'aime des pierres."

Gringoire is thus part of the transformation or the transition of the meaning of stone; embodying the succession that Hugo had assigned to the meaning of architecture in "CECI TUERA CELA," he can escape the stone-death of the dogmatic, dying world. He is the novel's projection toward the printed word through his profession as "philosopher," that is, scribbler. His association with the printed word established the import of his escape from the clutches of the spider king. His escape is no mean feat, and he is alone in extricating himself from the web of death that ensnares the other characters. In the presence of Louis XI, who initially sees "no objections" to Gringoire's being hanged, our "philosopher" will improvise a brilliant speech that saves his neck. His performance, he would agree, far outranks his early, abortive attempts to stage his mystery play in the novel's opening scene. His plea is buffoonish in appearance—its ostensible purpose and effect are to so demean its author as to make him an unworthy object of the monarch's wrath: "La grande foudre de Dieu ne bombarde pas une laitue." Yet his admixture of self-abasement and flattery do not entirely mask a Bakhtinian dialogic slant. When Gringoire begs pity on a "pauvre homme honnête, et qui serait plus empêché d'attiser une révolte qu'un glaçon de donner une étincelle!" we remember that ice can burn, that the printed words of a monk (another "philosopher"?) will soon plunge Europe into turmoil, that the "clownish" character of Gringoire, who here proclaims himself a maker of tragedies and a poet ("Je fais des tragédies . . . Je suis poète . . . je suis un lettré"), is very close to his Olympian creator writing a novel on the symbiosis of printed word and democracy soon after the revolutionary days of July 1830.

June 1830 is the date Hugo gives to "Ce siècle avait deux ans" of ***Les feuilles d'automne,*** the poem in which Hugo gives his famous self-definition of "écho sonore." The same collection bears witness to his increasing preoccupation with the "people's hour": **"Rêverie d'un passant," "Pour les pauvres,"** and particularly the parting verses of the closing poem, "Amis, un dernier mot!"

> Oh! la muse se doit aux peuples sans défense.
> J'oublie alors l'amour, la famille, l'enfance.
> Et les molles chansons, et le loisir serein,
> Et j'ajoute à ma lyre une corde d'airain!

These verses mark an important transition—they look forward to the realization of "la Muse Indignation," that is, the invective of ***Châtiments,*** and they constitute an important step away from the role of passive consoler assigned to the artist in **"Le poëte dans les révolutions"** (***Odes et Ballades***).

But this far surpasses the possibilities open to Pierre Gringoire. Nevertheless, other artists will inherit a legacy from him. For a Hugo imbued with a passionate commitment to humanitarian reform, the old order must first die, and take death away with it: "J'aime la cathédrale et non le moyen âge" (***Les quatre vents de l'esprit***). All Hugo's passion, his scorn and contumely, are poured into the following, remarkable passage denouncing execution and flowing in one long and uninterrupted sentence:

> C'est une idée consolante, disons-le en passant, de songer que la peine de mort, quil, il y a trois cents ans, encombrait encore de ses roues de fer, de ses gibets de pierre, de tout son attirail de supplices permanent et scellé dans le pavé, la Grève, les Halles, la place Dauphine, la Croix-du-Trahoir, le Marché-aux-Pourceaux, ce hideux Montfaucon, la barrière des Sergents, la Place-aux-Chats, la Porte Saint-Denis, Champeaux, la Porte Baudets, la Porte Saint-Jacques, sans compter les innombrables échelles des prévôts, de l'évêque, des chapitres, des abbés, des prieurs ayant justice; sans compter les noyades juridiques en rivière de Sene; il est consolant qu'aujourd'hui, après avoir perdu successivement toutes les pièces de son armure, son luxe de supplice, sa pénalité d'imagination et de fantaisie, sa torture à laquelle elle refaisait tous les cinq ans un lit de cuir au Grand-Châtelet, cette vieille suzeraine de la société féodale, presque mise hors de nos lois et de nos villes, traquée de code en code, chassée de place en place, n'ait plus dans notre immense Paris qu'un coin déshonoré de la Grève, qu'une misérable guillotine, furtive, inquiète, honteuse, qui semble toujours craindre d'être prise en flagrant délit, tant elle disparaît vite après avoir fait son coup!

The voice that denounces capital punishment—and *Le Dernier Jour d'un condamné* dates from 1829—also announces, however timidly, the entrance of the artist in the arena. Gringoire can preserve life only for himself and for Djali, the artist's talisman that he takes from Esmeralda, but then even Hugo has not quite chased death from the place de Grève. Far from being the insubstantial character that critics since Ballanche have made him out to be, Pierre Gringoire stands at the center of the novel's emphasis on transition. He is Victor Hugo's whimsical portrait; his literary progeny, like the printed word, is legion; and ***Notre-Dame de Paris*** is Hugo's portrait of writing as a young art. (pp. 343-50)

Stirling Haig, "From Cathedral to Book, from Stone to Press: Hugo's Portrait of the Artist in 'Notre-Dame de Paris'," in Stanford French Review, *Vol. III, No. 3, Winter, 1979, pp. 343-50.*

SUZANNE NASH (essay date 1983)

[*In the following commentary on* Notre-Dame de Paris, *Nash explores the apparent conflict between Hugo's iconoclastic and conservative ideas regarding art and society.*]

Throughout his work, wherever questions of great art or revolutionary action are concerned, Hugo's glorification of the iconoclastic forces of change is rendered ambiguous by a nostalgia, felt on the level of both theme and imagery, for the permanence of an essential order. Nowhere else is this conflict more evident than in ***Notre-Dame de Paris,*** where revolutionary change is explicitly linked to architectural and scriptural forms of "modern" art and where the story told seems strangely at odds with the values underlying its most powerful narrative techniques.

I will explore this ambiguity by examining the contradictory treatment of the various "Notre-Dame de Paris," that is, the historical stone-and-mortar cathedral to which the authorial voice refers, the structure of Hugo's written narrative entitled ***Notre-Dame de Paris,*** and the Notre-Dame of Paris which is projected as symbolic space within that structure.

Although Hugo insists repeatedly upon the doomed nature of the historic building because of the destructibility of stone, beginning his novel under the sign of its effacement, he never allows his reader to forget the existence of this referent and the genesis of his book in time. There are three major interventions by the authorial voice which bring that referent sharply into focus. The first is in the Introduction: "Il y a quelques années qu'en visitant, ou, pour mieux dire, en furetant Notre-Dame, l'auteur de ce livre trouva, dans un recoin obscur. . . ." The second is in Book III, with its two chapters, "Notre-Dame" and "Paris à vol d'oiseau"; and the third occurs midway through the novel in Book V, "Ceci tuera cela."

In the first chapter of Book III, "Notre-Dame," written shortly after the July Revolution, in October of 1830, the conflict between conservatism and radicalism to which I have already referred is the most apparent. Some 100 pages into the text the narrator arrests his story to describe the monument which inspired his work. The authorial voice is clearly nostalgic about the loss of the old order, which he identifies with the cathedral as it appeared during the thirteenth century. He laments the loss of the structure's original integrity, choosing an organic image to do so. The cathedral is depicted as an old woman whose once beautiful face and robes have been scarred and deformed by the passage of time and by the carelessness of man, especially of artists. He then proceeds for several pages, through preterition, to restore the church as she used to be, replacing all of the beautiful structures which are missing or defaced. He lingers lovingly on the one-splendid façade depicting the glory and authority of the theocratic era: ". . . les trois portails creusés en ogive, le cordon brodé et dentelé des vingt huit niches royales, l'immense rosace centrale flanquée de ses deux fenêtres latérales comme le prêtre du diacre et du sous diacre. . . ." The adjectives which he uses to characterize this queen stress her harmony and her unity in diversity: ". . . tranquille grandeur de l'ensemble, vaste symphonie en pierre . . . une et complexe, . . . puissante et féconde comme la création divine. . . ." With the loss of all that, with the intrusion of new styles, he says the spectator "croirait que le lieu saint est devenu infâme, et s'enfuirait." Then, abruptly, without transition, there is a shift in perspective and in the judgment brought to bear on these culprits of history. Notre-Dame, we are informed, was never, after all, a pure form: "Notre Dame de Paris n'est point du reste ce qu'on peut appeler un monument complet, défini, classé. Ce n'est plus une église romane, ce n'est pas encore une église gothique. . . . C'est un édifice de la transition." She began as a Romanesque structure, and, with the return of the crusaders, the Gothic arch was grafted onto the original base. There was no organic relationship between the two: "C'est la greffe de l'ogive sur le plein cintre." He has recourse to pre-Christian allusions to describe the phantasm that she was and finally ends with the Biblical reference to the Tower of Babel, giving, through the sheer accumulation of images, this traditionally negative figure a strangely positive connotation: "Cette église centrale et génératrice est parmi les vieilles églises de Paris une sorte de chimère; elle a la tête de l'une, les membres de celle-là, la croupe de l'ature; quelque chose de toutes." She is of the "vestiges cyclopéens, les pyramides d'Egypte, les gigantesques pagodes hindoues. . . . Chaque flot du temps superpose son alluvion, chaque race dépose sa couche sur le monument. . . . Le grand symbole de l'architecture, Babel, est une ruche." Yet, by caping his symbol ("Babel") of the generative potential of absolute relativism with another organic image ("ruche"), he transforms that potential into inner necessity. Finally, after a description which seems to revel in the fertility of the human imagination for change, he returns to his original position at the very end of the chapter to say that all of this is only superficial ornamentation, that the basic design of the church is still Christian and can never be disturbed by these changes; in other words, that the Christian message is always there to be deciphered and believed: "Du reste, toutes ces nuances, toutes ces différences n'affectent que la surface des édifices. . . . La constitution même de l'église chrétienne n'en est pas attaquée." Thus, Chapter I of Book III begins and ends on a note of conservative idealism, interrupted in the middle by a brief glorification of the monstrous deformity of an edifice in the process of becoming and whose basic design is no longer discernible.

The third authorial intervention in Book V, the chapter entitled "Ceci tuera cela," which was written about a month later than "Notre-Dame," but withheld by Hugo from the 1831 edition, along with Chapter II of Book III, "Paris à vol d'oiseau," and Chapter I of Book V, *"Abbas Beati Martini,"* seems, on the other hand, to represent a point of view which transforms the conflict of views apparent in "Notre-Dame" into a rationalized, revolutionary poetics. Here Hugo interrupts his story to make certain we understand the nature of the objectification of Human Thought into its various scriptural forms. The "ceci" to which Frollo had dolefully referred in an earlier chapter is the book or printing, and the "cela" is the stone edifice in which he presides as priest and chief interpretant; but unlike Frollo (who could be said to be representative of the conservative voice beginning and ending "Notre Dame"), what the authorial voice stresses is the similarity between "ceci" and "cela," that is, the effacement of specific referent, rather than the replacement of one by another. For the narrator there is no essential difference between architecture and books; the latter are simply less destructible than the former because books can be printed in millions of copies and there is only one of each cathedral, just as there was only one of each handwritten parchment before printing was invented. Both architecture and books are forms of writing; it is history which changed the nature of that writing and in precisely the same way for each type of expression. Indeed, Hugo's post-revolutionary novel begun at the end of the Restoration and finished under the July Monarchy has more in common with the Notre-Dame of the fifteenth century, that period of political and social transition, than with any transparently symbolic morality play of the twelfth or thirteenth century. The event which, according to the narrator, caused the radical change in the *nature* of writing—whether that writing be in stone or in ink—was the discovery by the bourgeoisie and the people of the *concept* of freedom, that is, of the advent of democracy and the overthrow of the old monarchical, theocratic structure. The very earliest architectural forms, those which existed before the concept of freedom, Hugo tells us, were like the letters of the alphabet, each letter representing an idea, a kind of hieroglyphics: "On plantait une pierre debout, et c'était une lettre, et chaque lettre était un hiéroglyphe, et sur chaque hiéroglyphe reposait un groupe d'idees comme le chapiteau sur la colonne." In the next stage the structures represented words, and sometimes, as in the case of Karnac, when there was enough stone and enough space, an entire sentence. Finally, the temples represented books: "Tous ces symboles, auxquels l'humanite avait foi, allaient croissant, se multipliant, se croisant, se compliquant de plus en plus; les premiers monuments ne suffisaient plus à les contenir." But what characterized all of these early edifices, according to Hugo, despite their growing complexity, was the unity of message and form. All were modes of what he calls "symbolic" writing, that is, writing that could be deciphered according to one key, of which the priest was the guardian: "L'idée mère, le verbe, n'etait pas seulement au fond de tous ces édifices, mais encore dans la forme. . . . Sur chacune de ses enceintes concentriques les prêtres pouvaient lire le verbe traduit et manifesté aux yeux. . . . Ainsi le verbe était enfermé dans l'édifice, mais son image était sur son enveloppe *comme la figure humaine sur le cercueil d'une momie*" (my emphasis). One is struck by Hugo's chilling analogy. This kind of monologistic writing had become, in his view, a form of petrification. Later on in the passage he expatiates on this theme: "Les caractères généraux de toute architecture théocratique sont l'immutabilité, l'horreur du progrès, la conservation des lignes traditionnelles . . . le pli constant de toutes les formes de l'homme et de la nature aux caprices incompréhensibles du symbole." Symbolic writing was dead, ungenerative writing. He adds wistfully that every form of deformity even had an inviolable meaning. In Western civilization the Romanesque represented this kind of unified vision. It was, according to Hugo, the crusades which dealt the liberating blow to such an authoritarian structure: "C'est un grand mouvement populaire; et tout grand mouvement populaire, quels qu'en soient la cause et le but, dégage toujours . . . l'esprit de liberté. . . . L'autorité s'ébranle, l'unite se bilurque." Doubleness, rift, ambiguity rather than unity and a decipherable language characterize this new form of writing; seditious pages appear on the storied doors of the cathedrals, pages hostile to the Holy Scripture. The Gothic cathedral and its complex dialectic of relationships replaces the Romanesque—the Gothic, then, is associated in Hugo's mind with revolution and the rise of democracy. Writing is now fundamentally different from what it was: "L'hiéroglyphe déserte la cathédrale et s'en va blasonner le donjon pour faire un prestige à la féodalité. . . . Le livre architectural n'appartient plus au sacerdoce, à la religion, à Rome; il est à l'imagination, à la poésie, au peuple." Form and message, he goes on to say, are once and for all severed; indeed, message has virtually disappeared, and it is form which constitutes the vitality of the structure. The word as truth has been effaced from the wall, and the endless process of questioning and change begins. It is difficult to miss the analogy with Hugo's own neo-gothic novel as it is described in the Introduction of March 1831, written after the novel was completed. Only a few years ago, the author tells us, he saw a word, ANANKE (Fatalité), inscribed on the cathedral wall. That word, already a subversion of the Christian Word (Providence), has now been effaced, and it is on this *missing* word that Hugo will construct his new edifice: "C'est sur ce mot qu'on a fait ce livre." Thus, the sentence ending the introduction and beginning the novel is an ironic distortion of Christ's words, "On this rock I will build my church." In the course of the cathedral's writing, Frollo, the evil priest still caught in the old order and in an obsessive search for the alchemist's Truth of truths, will rewrite the subversive word on Hugo's fictional walls to inspire the series of ironic substitutions which constitute the novel's structure.

It would seem, then, that it was not until he had finished writing ***Notre-Dame de Paris,*** or, perhaps more significantly, it was in the process of that writing, with the drafting in November 1830 of Book V, that Hugo came to believe in the value of a text which eludes the "truth" and, in so doing, escapes imprisonment by the message (Fatalité) it projects. The intensity of Hugo's struggle with the conflicting values reflected in his explicit commentaries on the stone-and-mortar referent in Books III and V can be better assessed if we look at the realization of that structure as written narrative and at the Notre-Dame de Paris as it appears thematized within the text.

As I pointed out above, attention to the cathedral as such is deferred for a long while, and, when reference is made, it is in another code—in the historical present, outside of the context of the story. Everything in the first two Books suggests the fragmentation, dislocation, indeed destruction, of any form of unifying composition. The main characters are introduced in a series of dramatic and profane spectacles which occur outside the church doors, outside the celestial city. The story begins with a series of negatives, first situating the events in a specific historical moment—the sixth of January, 1482—and then questioning the reliability of any such moment: "Ce n'est cependant pas un jour dont l'histoire ait gardé souvenir que le 6 janvier 1482." We enter the narrative at a carnivalesque time, an anti-day celebrating two festivities each of whose symbolic significance places the other into question: *La Fête des fous* and *Le Jour des rois*. A turbulent Parisian populace has gathered in the streets and is distracted by three events which interrupt each other and stand in contradiction to each other. The first event, honoring *Le Jour des rois,* is the presentation of a mystery play in the great room of the Palais de Justice. The play is late in getting started in this profane theater: it features Jupiter and Venus and is presented to a crowd which pays no attention except to deride it. In fact, the play never gets beyond the Prologue because it is interrupted by cries of "Noël," "Noël": the king of fools has been elected. The prize is awarded to the person who can make the ugliest grimace, and Quasimodo is the winner. But, as Hugo succinctly puts it, for this Romantic figure of the grotesque, "La grimace était son visage." This is not the vitalistic, topsy-turvy world of the Renaissance, but, to use Bakhtin's formulation, a world of permanent dislocation. Quasimodo's body assures anything but his earth-consciousness. He is condemned to chastity and solitude, cut off even from the populace—Hugo's "new man," whom at times he seems to incarnate. It is not the other side of the healthy body—a buttocks or a fertile belly—which is presented for the crowd's delight, but an outrageously botched head complete with a wart over one eye, wild red hair, broken teeth, and a gaping mouth; and this misleadingly demonic appearance is framed in the broken opening of the rose window of the Palace chapel. Shards of the spiritual world suggested by the novel's title thus constitute the décor of the opening scene. Quasimodo, this "à peu près" who will be our hero, is even described in terms which suggest a building fallen into ruins and put back together again badly, with no notion on the part of the maker as to what the basic design should be. Like the cathedral described at the center of Book III, the bellringer who exists as an incrustation within its walls is a grotesque structure, one part having been grafted onto another with no organic rapport. As the crowd shouts "Noël" and Pierre Gringoire, the disappointed author of the ridiculous mystery play, realizes that he will not be able to bring the Holy Virgin on stage because his musicians have left to lead Quasimodo's triumphal parade through the streets of Paris, the third diversion occurs—"La Esmeralda" is dancing in another quarter. We later discover that this is the gypsy dancer of whom the Faustian priest of Notre-Dame will blasphemously say: "Une créature si belle que Dieu l'eût préférée à la Vierge, et l'eût choisie pour sa mère, et eût voulu naitre d'elle si elle eût existé quand il se fit homme"; of whom the narrator will say: "elle était d'une beauté si rare qu'au moment où elle parut à l'entrée de l'appartement il sembla qu'elle y répandait une sorte de lumière qui lui était propre." There are numerous other references throughout the novel which suggest that Esmeralda represents a secularized figure for the Virgin, yet another Notre-Dame de Paris, a street version, so to speak. It is, for example, she who intercedes on behalf of Quasimodo by bringing him water when he is pilloried, an act which transforms the figure of bodily deformity into a loving, spiritual being. But when we first meet Esmeralda she is surrounded by hellish, rather than heavenly, attributes. She is dancing across the river from Notre-Dame in the Place de Grève, theater for the pillory and the gibet; it is dusk rather than dawn (the time associated with the Virgin in Christian iconography); Esmeralda and the faces of the spectators are bathed in scarlet light from the reflection of the fires burning at the approach of night; and the male characters watching her are caught in a kind of thralldom which suggests lust rather than worship. Indeed, every time she dances her twirling circular dance throughout the novel, it is for an audience of hidden voyeurs—Frollo and Quasimodo from the battlements of Notre-Dame, Phoebus from the balcony of his fiancée, Gringoire in the midst of the crowd below; all are sexually aroused, all diverted by her from their various pursuits. She becomes an idolatrous obsession rather than a source of faith and peace. Indeed, Quasimodo stops ringing the bells of the cathedral, stops making the Church speak to the city, after he discovers Esmeralda.

Thus we enter a form of writing which is characterized, as far as narrative technique, theme and characterization are concerned, by fragmentation, discontinuity and disfiguration, the very signs of destruction which the narrator sees scarring the beauty of the original Notre-Dame de Paris in Book III. On the other hand, these same characteristics lend the introductory pages their extraordinary energy; they give us the impression that anything may happen as we watch the popular version of traditional romance disappear—the beautiful virgin, pursued by the monster and saved by the handsome knight—and we revel in the piling up of the new tower of Babel rising out of the ruins of the beautiful old cathedral.

It seems that one must be prepared to give it all up, in fact, judging from the violence and savagery with which Hugo destroys our hopes for a redemptive reading. The cathedral as poeticized symbolic space is presented as a gaping, tomb-like void, empty of the faithful, inhabited only by a priest turned alchemist and a monstrously deformed bell-ringer who does not so much dwell in the cathedral as he belongs to it. Every relationship in which we invest our hope for some lasting value is destroyed. Esmeralda is blindly in love with a false god, Phoebus, a hopelessly vapid fop—she never sees beyond his material form. After years of self-martyrdom, Esmeralda's mother, La Sachette, recovers her lost child, only to be rewarded by having her hanged in the Place de Grève in a blaze of ironic light—at dawn, the time of the Holy Virgin, who *never* intervenes for anyone's prayers. All the major characters die a horrible death, except the failed poet Gringoire, who abandons Esmeralda to Frollo and runs away with her goat into the darkness of the city to live out his life writing bad plays for a corrupt officialdom. Deafness or voyeurism relegate every subject to a state of irremediable solitude, and the crowd, that hope for democracy and freedom, turns vicious in the end, forgets its goal to save Esmeralda from the hangman's noose and batters in the great storied portals of the cathedral in which she has sought asylum in order to pillage the wealth of jewels and gold which it holds.

The full measure of the loss of sacred value has been encoded into the text by the way its various narrative strands negate so dramatically the stories of mercy and salvation depicted on the great doors of the stone building that are destroyed by the crowd. Although the narrator mentions the portals more often than any other structural part of the cathedral—nearly every critical event takes place in front of them, and Frollo is constantly examining them in an effort to decipher their meaning—he never tells us precisely what they represent. To know, the reader must look at the restored cathedral still standing today. The narrator does not say, for example, that four of the six doors which open the way to the celestial city inside hold images from the life of the Virgin: her birth with Saint Anne, her marriage, her death, resurrection and crowning by her Son in heaven. We meet only La Sachette, the prostitute mother of Esmeralda, who so idolatrized her baby that one day she lost her to the gypsies while idly vaunting her beauty to a neighbor. Instead of the Virgin's marriage, death and resurrection, we watch the senseless martyrdom of Esmeralda, hanged on a gibet, twisting like a snake on the rope before being thrown into the ossuary, where Quasimodo joins her as a grotesque bridegroom. The narrator does not say that on the Porte Rouge one can see Saint Louis being crowned by an angel and blessed by Christ. We read only of the cruel Louis XI holding court in the Bastille, from which he betrays his Church by ordering that the victim to whom she has granted asylum be taken prisoner and hanged. And, finally, he does not say that on the Porte du Cloître—the door Frollo always enters to reach his alchemist's tower—is depicted the miracle of Theophile, the learned critic who sold his soul to the Devil for the gift of philosophical knowledge, but who is forgiven and redeemed through the intercession of the Virgin, shown standing with him, holding the sword which slays Satan. We hear Frollo vainly beg for Esmeralda's mercy, and we follow his transformation from that of a suffering, visionary imagination into the symbol of Satan himself as he falls from the towers of

Notre-Dame, pushed by the orphaned monster to whom he had once granted asylum.

In the violence of its satire and the savagery of its ironies, this early novel seems to represent for Hugo a kind of terrible expurgation of his lingering nostalgia for the old order so eloquently described as an aging and majestic queen in Book III, an expurgation which nevertheless generates a radically new style and vision. The old design had to be let go in order to allow the forces of freedom and democracy represented by the people to flood beyond the containing walls of the medieval city. For the novelist in October of 1830 that force has a brutal, even demonic nature, symbolized by the underworld characters of the Cour des Miracles. It is the crowd which gathers eagerly to witness the martyrdom of her own orphaned children, Esmeralda and Quasimodo, when they are tormented or brought to death by the crowd's own oppressors. But it is also the crowd whose hilarity unmasks the dessicated figures of officialdom present at all of these gatherings, and somehow its cruelty is more acceptable than the death-grip of the old order represented so grimly in the Bastille by the torture instruments rationally created to maintain its institutionalized control.

One character, Jacques Coppenole, who appears at the beginning and at the end of the novel, seems to represent all of the most positive attributes of what that people may become. He arrives for the mystery play with the delegation from Holland and immediately wins the crowd's sympathy by refusing to be announced under any fancy title, but simply as "chaussetier." He is a member of the "peuple," the narrator tells us, the new class of bourgeois which is rising out of the lower stratum and penetrating the ruling class. . . . He is a long-time friend of the King of the Truands, disguised here as a beggar covered with rags, and he chooses to sit with the beggar rather than with the officialdom to which he has gained access. At the sight of this defiant self-confidence a revolutionary ripple of delight seems to run through the crowd. It is he who interrupts the Prologue to the mystery play, denouncing the vapidity of its inflated rhetoric, and proposes to the crowd a different sort of spectacle, the election of the *Pape des fous*, with all its subversive implications. Jacques Coppenole appears in one other important scene in this long novel, at the end, the scene in the Bastille, where Louis XI decides to use the rage of the populace to achieve his own nefarious ends. The Flemish delegation is there as the sounds of revolt begin to rise from the streets. It is the same crowd which, like the revolutionary vandals of 1787 and 1789, will batter in the portals of Notre-Dame, and Jacques Coppenole calmly announces, in the presence of the King, his pleasure in hearing such sounds. The King allows him to speak, fascinated by his honesty and his unruffled self-assurance, but not before he has insisted that the revolt is not serious and that he can stop it with a mere furrow of his brow. Coppenhole answers, prophetically for post-revolutionary France: "Cela se peut, sire. En ce cas, c'est que l'heure du peuple n'est pas encore venue. . . . Quand le beffroi bourdonnera, quand les canons gronderont, quand le donjon croulera à grand bruit, quand bourgeois et soldats hurleront et s'entre-tueront, c'est l'heure qui sonnera." Coppenole disappears from the novel, the truands take over, and the dreadful dénouement where both Esmeralda and Quasimodo die moves irremediably forward. But an optimistic note has nevertheless been sounded, and if we leave the novel with a dreadful sense of loss, we leave it marveling at the inventiveness and energy through which this loss has occurred. (pp. 122-31)

Suzanne Nash, "Writing a Building: Hugo's 'Notre-Dame de Paris'," in French Forum, *Vol. 8, No. 2, May, 1983, pp. 122-33.*

KATHRYN M. GROSSMAN (essay date 1983)

[In the following excerpt, Grossman discusses the heterogeneity of the cathedral's architecture as it is reflected in the themes and structure of Notre-Dame de Paris.*]*

At the end of "Paris à vol d'oiseau" [in Volume III of ***Notre-Dame de Paris***], where fifteenth-century Paris is evoked from atop Notre-Dame in one of Hugo's great digressive *tours de force*, the reader finds himself listening to a symphony of bells pealing throughout the city:

> D'abord la vibration de chaque cloche monte droite, pure, et pour ainsi dire isolée des autres dans le ciel splendide du matin. Puis, peu à peu, en grossissant elles se fondent, elles se mêlent, elles s'effacent l'une dans l'autre, elles s'amalgament dans un magnifique concert. Ce n'est plus qu'une masse de vibrations sonores qui se dégage sans cesse des innombrables clochers, qui flotte, ondule, bondit, tourbillonne sur la ville, et prolonge bien au-delà de l'horizon le cercle assourdissant de ses oscillations. Cependant cette mer d'harmonie n'est point un chaos.

In this way, Hugo crowns his revelation of the "plan géométral" underlying the apparently chaotic disposition of the city's streets with the creation of yet another heterogeneous, but deeply harmonious, order. After unravelling the spatial labyrinth of Paris, he combines its many voices in the thunderous temporal articulation of a monumental "opéra."

This triumph of harmony over cacophony, of congruity over disorder, teases the reader with echoes of several patterns already established in the novel. For instance, the deafening noise of the bells, along with their uncoordinated ringing and the jumbled aspect of the city around them, reminds us of Quasimodo, whereas their lively dance and inarticulate song are the unmistakable hallmarks of la Esmeralda. By the same token, this symphony for a thousand voices has occurred previously, in the minor, comic mode, when Pierre Gringoire, "tout assourdi par la fatale vibration des mille sonnettes du mannequin," manages to orchestrate his own "redoubtable carillon" in the Cour des Miracles. And a static but equally magnificent version of this concert has just received extended treatment in the chapter on "Notre-Dame," the cathedral itself appearing as a "vaste symphonie en pierre." Like both Paris and the orchestra of bells, the cathedral gives an overall impression of harmony, despite its mixed origins: beneath "la prodigieuse variété extérieure de ces édifices . . . réside tant d'ordre et d'unité." Its mystery of the triune God, equally incongruous at first approach, adumbrates that of the symbiotic relationship between the "trois grandes divisions de Paris" developed at length in "Paris à vol d'oiseau." It seems evident, then, that a number of important structures and themes in the novel converge at the end of the third book. (pp. 205-06)

We shall start with the cathedral itself, backdrop for much of the main action of the novel. In "Notre-Dame," Hugo insists on its composite, transitional nature: "Notre-Dame de Paris n'est pas du reste ce qu'on peut appeler un monument complete, défini, classé. Ce n'est plus une église romane, ce n'est pas encore une église gothique. Cet édifice n'est pas un type." Such "constructions hybrides" defy convention because they can never be fully contained or explained by one set of rules. In fact, according to the author, convention has been the most ruthless enemy of the cathedral: in the guise of fashion it has done more to damage its majestic beauty than time and revolution combined.

Since the hybrid building cannot be subsumed by a higher aesthetic order, it must then be considered a law unto itself. But this does not necessarily imply disorder. In "Ceci tuera cela," Hugo is careful to show that "la fantaisie et le caprice" of Notre-Dame are firmly enrooted in its essentially lawful foundation: "on y sent partout l'autorité, l'unité, l'impénétrable, l'absolu. . . ." The Gothic springs forth from the Romanesque, the cathedral's "loi de poésie" is indissociable from its 'loi de géométrie." Thus, whereas arbitrary rules imposed from without can only have a harmful effect, the grounding of the building in a certain "roideur du dogme" assures its basic solidity. It is the combination of this rigidity with the radical liberty of Gothic architecture that gives Notre-Dame its sublimely harmonious originality. (p. 206)

Hugo's reading of Notre-Dame, itself hardly conventional, also invites a radical exegesis of such major characters in the novel as Quasimodo, la Esmeralda, Pierre Gringoire, and Claude Frollo. The cathedral's specifically architectural mixed alliance presents, for example, an obvious parallel with that of the hunchback and gypsy dancer. Certainly the tragedy of their heterogenous and fruitless "mariage" in death at the close of the novel repeats that of the union *sui generis* of disparate elements in the cathedral. Moreover, Notre-Dame can be viewed as representing all the magnificent edifices of its age, doomed to die out by the advent of the printing press.

To begin with, one might attempt to derive a dualistic system whereby a grotesquely limited Quasimodo was juxtaposed to a purely free and sublime Esmeralda. Unfortunately, the book develops far too many parallels, rather than just contrasts, between these two personages to justify such a simplistic arrangement. The gypsy's characteristic "moue" is as much a "grimace" as the cripple's face, itself a "grimace sublime." Both are orphaned and adopted children, both subsist outside society, both transcend their situations to act spontaneously and generously toward each other. Quasimodo is, in fact, neither la Esmeralda's opposite nor her complement, as [Kathryn E. Wildgren] maintains [see excerpt dated 1976], but her reverse image. According to Jeffrey Mehlman, the two characters, substituted for each other as children and bearing la Esmeralda's sobriquet of "Similar" (="à peu près"= "Quasimodo") names, are to be considered equivalent: "The novel thus elaborates a surprising interchangeability between the epitomes of the sublime and the grotesque." Phoebus, who rechristens both outcasts with much the same irreverence and inattention, witnesses their tendency to displace one another the night of la Esmeralda's attempted abduction by Quasimodo at the behest of Claude Frollo. Like the girl's mother before him, he is left to complain: "Vous m'avez laissé en votre lieu, ma belle, . . . un assez rechigné drôle, borne et bossu. . . ." The parity that has proven so tragic for la Chantefleurie thus becomes, in the indifferent eye of Phoebus, a matter for flirtatious banter.

This fundamental identity, portrayed by their final union, is in part due to the nature of the aesthetic principles they embody. Recent efforts at defining the grotesque, for instance, tend to agree that, in and of itself, it fuses several incongruous elements—the ridiculous and the horrible—which never quite achieve resolution. At the same time, the sublime has been deemed to surpass the merely beautiful by overcoming a sense of awe and fear before the seemingly limitless powers of the universe. The two experiences are thus, from the outset, equally impure in that they elicit responses from the ethical and aesthetic faculties alike. Their frequent interplay in melodrama, an important post-Revolutionary genre, stems from their simultaneous emergence in the modern consciousness as modes for dealing with the desacralized, and therefore potentially absurd and ambiguous, world around it.

The resemblance between Quasimodo and la Esmeralda thus contains ethical/political, as well as aesthetic, overtones. In this perspective, the chaste and compassionate relationship of these two "siblings" can be seen to foreshadow the notion of human confraternity embraced later on by the French Revolution. But this very synonymity—within the family or before the law—of highly disparate "equals" constitutes in turn a kind of metaphor, perhaps the greatest of all, namely that all men are brothers. The fact that the novel's most apparently dissimilar personages end by enduring quite analogous fates vigorously underscores the truly senseless ethos of their own era. For, as the *surdus* who is reduced to reading the world in terms of its explicit signs, the hunchback becomes the victim of an equally deaf judge. Likewise, la Esmeralda finds herself bound over to the same insouciant magistrate that her pet goat has learned to imitate. In other words, Jacques Charmolue's officiation at the trial of la Esmeralda is no less a parody of justice than his caricature as performed by Djali, or than the *dialogue de sourds* between Florian Barbedienne and Quasimodo, or than Pierre Gringoire's "trial" in the Cour es Miracles. This failure of the medieval legal structure to accommodate those who appear to be outlaws reveals its deepest flaws. It is, literally, *absurdus*, a grotesque system of justice, treating men with equal inequity. In order to be rectified, this methodical and paternalistic distribution of nonsense must await the Revolution, which inaugurates an entirely different vision of brotherhood. The higher order of resolution that will ultimately result from such political chaos is signaled by the very concert of bells, "cette symphonie qui fait le bruit d'une tempête," that Hugo seems so gratuitously to deploy in the midst of his novel.

As far as Gringoire and Frollo are concerned, they too can be read as a series of patterns which overflow their superficial psychological pretexts. An "esprit essentiellement mixte, indécis et complexe, tenant le bout de tous les extrêmes, incessament suspendu entre toutes les propensions humaines et les neutralisant l'une par l'autre," Gringoire remains all his life a completely sterile hybrid, one whose lukewarm "équilibre" is rarely disturbed. That he is perpetually threatened with hanging only reinforces this disengaged, tepid, amoral, "suspended" side of his temperament. His ridiculous survival to write wretched epics and tragedies, while ignoring the suffering around him, serves to stress the truly dynamic tensions and relationships that comprise the drama in which the other characters are involved. As the writer's alter ego, Gringoire appears then as a "parodie de lien entre des irreconciliables," suggesting through the very emptiness of his eclecticism the qualities of the real artist. We come to recognize the features of that missing other through his inverted image Gringoire, just as turning Quasimodo inside out consistently reveals la Esmeralda. The absent, but sublime, author suddenly eclipses his negatively present counterpart.

Frollo, too, stands in opposition to the couple la Esmeralda/Quasimodo. As one whose outwardly ordered existence belies a terrible inner strife, he contrasts boldly with the crippled bell-ringer and errant gypsy, who reach superior orders of being through both their art and their compassion. In a way, he closely approximates Hugo's conception of the Romanesque: his rigidity, his adherence to "la théocratie, la caste, l'unité, le dogme, le mythe, Dieu," and his basic incorrigibility all associate the archdeacon with the dogmatic foundations of his cathedral. Since he is literally overthrown by Quasimodo at the book's end, this may well signal the hunchback's corresponding identity with Gothic architecture. Such a designation would take into account not only Quasimodo's grotesque appearance and intellectual aberrations, but also his capacity for free moral and aesthetic expression. Moreover, it would explain his fervent adoration of the only mother he has ever known, Notre-Dame de Paris: "il y avait une sorte d'harmonie mystérieuse et préexistante entre cette créture et cet édifice." The oedipal overtones of Frollo's upset by his adopted "son" must thus infuse the Gothic triumph over Romaneque architecture as well. This modern example of "une architecture de peuple succédant à une architecture de caste" merely announces, however, that the people (Quasimodo) are destined eventually to supplant their king (Frollo).

Yet this is not the final reversal of authority. Relations already observed among the main protagonists and within the architectural world of the novel can be found on several other levels too. For Hugo's discussion of the Gothic in "Ceci tuera cela" is just part of a lengthy development by the author on the genealogy of the printed word itself. In this account, Gothic architecture assumes a striking resemblance to la Esmeralda's dance: "Les caractères généraux des maçonneries populaires . . . sont la variété, le progrès, l'originalité, l'opulence, le mouvement perpétuel." Notre-Dame's transitional nature may perhaps reemerge, albeit in a different form, in the homeless but profoundly principled gypsy. Certainly, she makes her ephemeral appearance on the eve of the revolution which inaugurates the supremacy of printing, a "révolution mère" that overturns architecture as ineluctably as the French Revolution will overturn the monarchy: "le livre de pierre . . . allait faire place au livre de papier. . . . Un art allait détrôner un autre art." Moreover, this aesthetic revolution seems to be linked to la Esmeralda's song. Printed thought, for Hugo, is "volatile, insaisissable, indestructible. Elle se mêle à l'air." The beauty and order beneath the wildness of la Esmeralda's singing and dancing, like that underlying the "prodigieuse variété extérieure" of the cathedral, point the way to "la seconde tour de Babel du genre humain": "Là chaque oeuvre individuelle, si capricieuse et si isolée qu'elle semble, a sa place et sa saillie. L'harmonie résulte du tout." Thus does the lost child end by bridging the gap between these two monumental artistic forms. Through the love that she inspires, she succeeds in permanently dissociating the Gothic bellringer from his Romanesque servitude and in orienting him toward the future.

This future contains, of course, one further major upheaval. Besides falling to both printing and the republic, it is also inherited by the Romantic movement, that other great French Revolution which Hugo, even as a young "ultra," was already associating with the literary efforts of his age as early as 1823. That is when he first mentions the "singulier phénomène littéraire né d'un autre phénomène politique, la révolution française. Il y a aujourd'hui en France combat entre une opinion littéraire encore trop puissante et le génie de ce siècle." Given this fundamental relationship between a politic and an aesthetic of freedom in Hugo, must we not review the function of the illegitimate—i.e., the unlawful, the unsanctioned—characters of ***Notre-Dame de Paris***? Victor Brombert's assertion [in *The Romantic Prison: The French Tradition*] that the "restrictive rules of neo-classical tragedy (negative value)" are related to "monastic rules or values" is highly suggestive in this context. In other words, Claude Frollo may represent far more than just the Romanesque in Hugo's novel. When the author states that the "caractères généraux de toute architecture théocratique sont l'immutabilité, l'horreur du progrès, la conservation des lignes traditionnelles," he is indicting the weaknesses of Classicism itself. His praise, then, of Gothic buildings as "des édifices pénétrables à toute âme, à toute intelligence, à toute imagination, symboliques encore, mais faciles à comprendre comme la nature" would therefore announce the triumph of Romantic popularism over the *hermétisme* of Neo-classical art.

Such a hypothesis seems to conform to the results of our study thus far. Frollo's alliance with the forces of inflexible rule-giving marks him as a symbol of the worst traits of French Classicism. . . . By the same token, the apparently chaotic, but ultimately ordered existence of Quasimodo and la Esmeralda invests them with the positive values of Romantic literature. The very incongruity of their relationship only adds to this link with Hugo's own aesthetics, Romanticism being above all a willed contamination, a *mélange des genres* which transcends dissonance to achieve a superior harmony. Finally, the discovery of the absent author through comparing Gringoire to this sublime/grotesque pair can be considered a paradigm for the parallel between the Romanesque/Gothic on the one hand and architecture/printing, then the more occulted monarchy/republic, and eventually Classicism/Romanticism on the other.

If we choose to read this seemingly universal history of supplanting, dethroning, and succeeding as analogous to the triumph of the son over the father, then the violence of such "progress" becomes rather disturbing. Hugo's assertion that: "Le livre imprimé, ce ver rongeur de l'édifice, la suce et la dévore" plainly depicts the new generation as a kind of parasite or vampire deriving strength from the old. Nevertheless, this repeating pattern need not be viewed in a purely negative manner. Reference to Hugo's treatment of Notre-Dame permits an entirely different perspective by providing one additional parallel between that edifice and the author's conception of Romanticism. For, just as the cathedral's "poetic" side is grounded in its "geometry," so is Romantic freedom firmly founded on Classical lawfulness. The higher realm to which the one belongs comprehends (=understands and includes) the other. Once again we are dealing, not with a dualistic system, but with a more complex relationship between presumed opposites. Instead of being destroyed by the child, the parent is actually subsumed and perpetuated in an even more glorious form. In this context, Romanticism appears as the rightful heir of Classicism, rather than its mere usurper. When the young Hugo writes that "l'abbé d'Aubignac se bornait à *suivre* les règles; Racine *à ne pas les enfriendre,*" he is establishing his own aesthetic genealogy, one which will be further explored several years later in ***Notre-Dame de Paris.*** The presence of guiding principles in post-Revolutionary literature—as well as politics—assures its divergence from pure anarchy and, therefore, its legal birthright. After the degenerative and destructive activities of the eighteenth century, the printed word, "au dix-neuvième siècle, va reconstruire."

The novel itself supports this claim of an underlying unifying structure quite clearly. Its higher law, like that of the Gothic cathedral, is, of course, that of nature: "Les grands édifices, comme les grandes montagnes, sont l'ouvrage des siècles. . . . La chose s'accomplit sans trouble, sans effort, sans réaction, suivant une loi naturelle et tranquille. C'est une greffe qui survient, une sève qui circule, une végétation qui reprend." This analogy, already noted by Jean Gaudon, nevertheless leaves open the question of the book's "loi de géométrie," the "original well-disciplined and designed arrangement" that John Ruskin declares to exist at the center of every Gothic sculptor's elaboration of the Romanesque. This skeletal framework turns out to consist of an intricate but closely woven system of triads: the cathedral houses and expresses a triune God; Paris is composed of three basic neighborhoods, "la Cité, l'Université, et la Ville"; three suitors, the one grotesque, the other demonic, the third a dreamer (the famous "tres para una") pursue la Esmeralda; the plot unfolds on the three public "stages" of the Palais de Justice, the Place de la Grève, and the Parvis de Notre-Dame. In each case we find ourselves confronted by the essential mystery of *communication,* be it in the use of architectural symbol, in the network of streets such that "ces trois fragments de cité formaient un seul corps," in the mediation through one woman of the fates of three widely dissimilar men, or in the presence of connecting ropes or ladders between audience and participants at the three principal "theatres" where the narrative unfolds.

The pervasiveness of this structure, even down to the frequent tertiary rhythm of the sentences, suggests the existence of the same point of reference outside each of these particular cases. In fact, we need only reexamine both Hugo's own well-known statement defining the new novel as being "à la fois drame et épopée, pittoresque, mais poétique, réel, mais idéal, vrai, mais grand, qui enchâssera Walter Scott dans Homère" and his hints in the novel's preface about "la pensée d'esthétique et de philosophie cachée dans ce livre" to discover this triadic archetype—***Notre-Dame de Paris*** itself. By harmoniously combing the three genres of drama, epic, and essay, Hugo's work aspires to the fundamental order and unity it continually claims for the cathedral whose name it bears.

That this cathedral serves as the nucleus of the glorious symphony previously referred to can be no accident, for it is there that the drama of communication (consonance) and non-communication (discord) between its various characters takes place. While edifice and novel alike may well play on the Pythagorean notion that nature and art can be reduced to a numerical order, they also insist on the Augustinean conception of harmony as emerging from an apparently discordant diversity. Notre-Dame orchestrates a great concert, despite the several kinds of dissonant relationships both within and around it. The poetic voice of ***Notre-Dame de Paris*** too is situated at its centre, "c'est-à-dire au lieu même d'une dialectique de la totalité," whereby it is attuned to the entire universe.

Notre-Dame, then, serves not so much as the book's main character, but as its very prototype. So that when, by an opposite movement, the literary work seems to incorporate and perpetuate the monument threatened by extinction, we must learn to read through such a superposition to the structure beneath. In 1825, Hugo's statement in **"Sur la destruction des monuments en France"** that: "Il faut qu'un cri universel appelle enfin la nouvelle France au secours de l'ancienne" may possibly refer to just architecture. However, given his respect for such "monumental" Classicists as Corneille and Racine, the figure of the cathedral definitely assumes still another dimension in 1831. The "old" France succored here by the "new" is the legacy of the Classical era, the challenge of creativity under law.

Thus do we begin to seize the dynamics of the genealogy of Hugo's novel. At once playing on its virgin birth by "Notre-Dame" and avowing the paternal influence of Classicism, ***Notre-Dame de Paris*** constitutes a search for origins and originality alike. La Esmeralda finds her mother and, despite the absence of the father, finally achieves legitimacy. Quasimodo abandons his mother / sweetheart, Notre-Dame, and his malevolent father, Claude Frollo, when he falls in love with the gypsy dancer. Unlike Hugo, neither succeeds in discovering the "good" father, the *deus absconditus* of the post-Sacred world. On the other hand, the union of these two characters at the novel's close reminds us that it is essentially their interaction which has engendered the book's dramatic movement and its most spectacular moments, much as the cathedral has supplied its basic formal pattern. The axis of interchangeability or brotherhood—that is, of metaphor—complements therefore at a fundamental level of the novel that of extension or paternity—that is, of metonymy. The intersection of both modes of substitution constitutes, in fact, the mainspring of Hugo's book, itself the replacement *and* the perpetuator of the celebrated cathedral.

In this way, the unique but theoretically infertile heterogeneity of Notre-Dame de Paris, reflected in that of the couple la Esmeralda / Quasimodo, does produce that one miraculous offspring which Hugo designates as his book. Even more wonderful, however, is the ultimate fate of his work as he predicts it. The last of one line, it will be the first of another, assuring thereby its continuity as well as its originality. Such is the heritage of an alliance between the "loi de géométrie" and the "loi de poésie" from which it springs. Its potential sterility will thus yield to a future of fruitfulness: "Un poète ne sera jamais réputé grand parce qu'il se sera contenté d'écrire suivant les règles. La morale ne résulte pas des lois, mais de la religion et de la vertu. La littérature ne vit pas seulement par le goût; il faut qu'elle soit vivifiée par la poésie et fécondée par le génie." Allied to both genius and the printing press, the creative function of Romantic art will, for Hugo, be marvelously (re)productive. (pp. 206-13)

Kathryn M. Grossman, "Hugo's Poetics of Harmony: Transcending Dissonance in 'Notre-Dame de Paris'," in Nineteenth-Century French Studies, *Vol. XI, Nos. 3 & 4, Spring & Summer, 1983, pp. 205-15.*

VICTOR BROMBERT (essay date 1984)

[Brombert is an American critic who has written extensively on modern French literature, including an important examination of the works of Gustave Flaubert. In the following excerpt from his study Victor Hugo and the Visionary Novel, *Brombert offers an extended analysis of* Notre-Dame de Paris *focusing on stone as the central image of the novel.]*

There are subjects enough for several novels packed into ***Notre-Dame de Paris.*** Beyond the cathedral itself, the title points to the city that was to haunt Hugo's imagination for the rest of his life. Notre-Dame, the edifice, stands symbolically at its topographic and historical center. The melodramatic plots develop a number of individual dramas, all linked in some way to the architecture of the cathedral and to the labyrinth of the city: the gargoyle-like hunchback, whose soul is confined in the double prison of deformity and deafness; the passion-ridden priest, victim of his own evil, who seems to come straight out of a Gothic tale; the persecuted virgin-orphan, who succumbs to the love she feels and inspires. And around these central characters a variety of marginal figures evolve, occasionally usurping the center of attention: the mischievous, riot-prone student; the leaders of the mob; the ironic writer-beggar; the bereaved mother driven to ascetic reclusion and to madness; the cunning old king whose terminal illness announces historical change.

The wealth of themes is even more impressive than the variety of human dramas: the encounter of the Beauty and the Beast; the symbolic political rivalry of the lovers (the sinister Priest, the frivolous Soldier, the coarse People); the dawn of the modern world under the sign of the recently invented printing press; knowledge and the will to power; the politically explosive anger of the underworld; a nostalgic glorification of ancient monuments; an implicit theory of the grotesque that challenges all forms of conservatism. And above all this hovers the notion of *anankē,* announcing destruction and death.

Notre-Dame de Paris is indeed a novel about death; and *anankē,* the Greek word for fate, which the author claims to have seen engraved inside one of the cathedral towers, is according to him the foundation of the book: "C'est sur ce mot qu'on a fait ce livre." Hugo, however, translates this abstract notion into a vivid and disturbing symbol. For *anankē* is close in sound to *arachnē,* the Greek word for spider; and the recurrent image of a fly caught and destroyed in a spider's fateful web becomes one of the unifying metaphors of the novel.

Perhaps more important still is the central image of stone, present both concretely and metaphorically in the title. The houses and the monuments of the city are a creation in stone—a "rêve de pierre," as Baudelaire was to put it. Walls, statues, paving blocks, gargoyles, gables, towers, and buttresses invade the setting. The metaphorical presence of stone is even more pervasive. Frollo, the somber archdeacon, is repeatedly represented as a man of stone, vaguely recalling the Commendatore of the Don Juan legend. When he falls to his death, he rebounds like a tile on the pavement. Quasimodo, the hunchback, is not only stone deaf, but his "psyche" is described as imprisoned within stone walls. ***Notre-Dame de Paris*** can be read as an elaborate series of variations on the themes of oppression and incarceration.

The stone metaphor extends even to ideas, to abstractions. There is petrification through fear, but there is also the more frightening petrification through dogma. The symbolic range of the image includes political violence and the dynamics of history. ***Notre-Dame de Paris*** was written in the immediate aftermath of the July Revolution of 1830. Hugo repeatedly alludes to the function of the paving blocks during the insurrection. His personal notes, as he considers his novel, are filled with stone images: "Depuis Juillet, le trône est sur le pavé"; "Le plus excellent symbole du peuple, c'est le pavé." More significant still is the conviction that the Parisian street is the revolutionary setting par excellence: "le mot terrible de la révolution de 1830, c'était *le pavé.*" These partly disquieting, partly hope-filled revolutionary associations become more meaningful in terms of the larger symbolism of the novel, if one keeps in mind that Hugo came to view Paris not only as the capital of the nineteenth century but as the civilizing center of the world, the city of ideas and ideals, whose steady change and growth and whose forest-like "vegetation of framework and stone" suggest live roots and *living stones,* in an almost religious sense.

Hugo's Paris, that "chronicle of stone," is thus the city of fixity as well as of change. The narrator is at once the antiquarian crusading to preserve and the historian concerned with mobility, progress, and transitional situations. The notions of permanence and transformation seem to intermingle, as they do in the preface to ***Les feuilles d'automne,*** written only a few months later, in which the poet tersely states that revolutions transform everything except the human heart. It is hardly surprising that side by side with stones and stone metaphors, ***Notre-Dame de Paris*** insistently proposes hybrid forms and figures, suggesting mixture, incompleteness, and processes of becoming.

Architecture itself is affected by hybridity. The Place de Grêve, the setting of many dramatic scenes, offers a simultaneous display of architectural evolution, blending in the same field of vision the semicircular Roman arch, the Gothic ogive, and the square window of the emerging new style. Centrally located stands a "hybrid construction" symbolically carring three different names. But it is not only the sinister Place de Grêve, the traditional site of public executions, that appears as one of those weird "intermediary beings" Hugo spoke of in his preface to ***Cromwell.*** The cathedral, too, looms as an extraordinary composite in time and space. Unlike other constructions, which correspond to a moment in history or represent a perfect type, Notre-Dame, in which several styles exist and commingle, is no longer a Romanesque and not yet a Gothic structure. It is an edifice in transition, the product of a grafting process.

The stress on hybrid forms appropriately extends to the writing of the novel itself. A historical novel is by definition a problematic mixture of "fiction" and "fact," raising moreover the subtler question of history as fiction. The generic blendings, as well as the need to reconcile the artist's and the historian's concerns, are explicitly mentioned by Hugo in a prefatory note. The reader is asked to unravel that which belongs to the realm of the historian from that which is part of the artist's aim. (pp. 49-52)

It is not surprising that in ***Notre-Dame de Paris*** hybridism extends to the characters themselves. Gringoire, the parodistic alter ego of the poet-dramatist, is an "esprit essentiellement mixte," an indecisive, complex composite of all human passions and propensities. There is more than a hint of incompleteness in Frollo's observation that this half-sage, half-madman is but a rough sketch of something or other—a "vaine ébauche de quelque chose." Incompleteness and approximation are, of course, inherent in the name of Quasimodo the hunchback. The first two syllables (meaning "in part" or "almost") are made explicit in the remark that this deformed being is but an *"à peu près."* Quasimodo's hybrid nature is what makes him a monstrous creature; he is neither a beast nor a complete human being. He refers to himself as distressingly indeterminate, a "je ne sais quoi." Popular superstition sees him as the "bastard" progeny of the archdeacon and the devil. The hilarity he provokes is more than a manifestation of heartlessness; it betrays a fear of the unknown. He has come to be associated with the Mardi Gras, the occasion of all travesties and of coarse farces and grimaces. He cohabits with monsters of stone, and at a distance he could be mistaken for the gargoyles that serve as mouths through which the gutters of the cathedral disgorge themselves. He is the animate brother of the grisly, laughing gargoyles, the yelping gorgons, the fire-breathing salamanders, the sneezing griffins—to all the stone monsters that occasionally awaken from their sleep of stone and appear to come to life.

This life of the stones cannot be dismissed as a simple matter of "grotesque" sensationalism. The name Quasimodo harks back to the First Epistle of Peter, whom Christ compared to a rock ("Tu es Petrus . . ."), and who, in his Epistle, compares those he addresses to newborn babes in search of the "living stone" of God. "Quasimodo geniti infantes . . ." is the introit of the Sunday Mass following Easter. "Quasimodo" is thus at once the linguistic signal of a figure of speech (comparison, metaphor) and a triple reference to innocence, petrification, and spiritual renewal.

Hugo's notion of the grotesque cannot, in any case, be reduced to facile picturesqueness. The famous preface to ***Cromwell*** developed a theory of the grotesque involving broad issues: the stages of civilization, the imitation of nature (mimesis), the relation between ugliness and the sublime, the anguish of modern man. If, in ***Notre-Dame de Paris,*** the Cyclopean eye of Quasimodo corresponds to the Cyclopean rose window of the cathedral, if animals look like men and human beings like animals, it is because all limits, all boundaries, seem to be erased in what Hugo conceives as the pandemonium of a total vision. For such a vision necessarily implies transgression. What are ultimately transgressed, beyond the sterile canons of "good taste," are the conventional lines of demarcation between ugliness and beauty, between evil and good. Transgression, in Hugo's view, serves to span the widening rift that in modern man separates body from soul. That is why, in the preface to ***Cromwell,*** Hugo called for a new poetic vision, capable of bringing about a "fertile union" of opposites. "Tout se tient," he proclaimed. But if all is related, and ultimately connected, this also means that the writer must help break down all rigid systems, while maintaining and even glorifying a sense of mystery and incompleteness. (pp. 53-4)

In ***Notre-Dame de Paris,*** the affinities between hybrid constructs and incompleteness characterize in particular one form of architecture: writing. The edifice of literature, according to Hugo, always remains unfinished. All the ages of mankind are busily at work in his synoptic vision. Each word and each text, like every stone brought to a building, means not just an addition but a transformation. Typically, the graffiti on the cathedral wall—the Gothic, Hebrew, Greek, and Roman scripts—blend by effacing one another. Hugo's preoccupation with language and literature as a composite effort at endless becoming helps explain the powerful presence of the Tower of Babel imagery, here and elsewhere in his work. The chapter about the relentless labor of writing concludes with the image of the "seconde tour de Babel du genre humain." Hugo had only recently written his visionary poem **"La pente de la rêverie,"** in which the tower of the many languages occupies an enigmatic central position. ***Notre-Dame de Paris*** relates architecture to scripture, no less than vision to history. The emblem for architecture as well as for writing is Babel. It is both a disturbing and exhilarating emblem, if only because neither edifice nor text is ever complete. They are works of transition: "Pendent opera interrupta." To describe the cathedral, Hugo significantly refers to a literary monument, Virgil's *Aeneid.*

The transition motif also affects the text of history. The choice of 1482 as the historical setting for the novel is highly significant. Louis XI, whose shrewd reign helped dismantle the feudal edifice, is about to die, and the Middle Ages appear to be coming to an end. The late fifteenth century is thus a pivotal point, a transitional moment in the larger drama of history, whose sequential progression also seems to be subject to the fateful rule of *anankē*. Centuries, explains Hugo, are the inscrutable and often self-contradictory sentences in a much larger text that tells of a steady progression. Along this linear time scale of history, each moment is both a transition and an effacement. Political systems and power structures replace one another. This very special concern for historical mutation, this transitional perspective on both past and future, explains the cultural anachronisms that stud the novel (references to Montaigne and to Régnier, for example), as well as the number of political allusions to the far-distant fall of the Bastille.

The year 1789 looms both as a projected future in relation to the narrated time (1482) and as a relevant past for the author and his reader from the perspective of the writing time (1830). The French Revolution, which is not the overt subject of ***Notre-Dame de Paris,*** is nonetheless its mythical time: it lies both behind and ahead. But if the mythical time is 1789, the actual or psychological and political time is 1830—the year Hugo wrote the novel, a year that was itself perceived as a period of transition. The July Revolution marks a historic interruption; it signals the end of the Bourbon Restoration and the beginning of Louis-Philippe's constitutional monarchy. There is little doubt that Hugo, like many of his contemporaries, viewed the events of July 1830 as an articulation in a deeper change. It represented a gap, an ellipsis. The many topical allusions to contemporary events (the July street violence, the riots of December and of the following February, the sack of Saint-Germain l'Auxerrois, the National Revolution of Belgium, the debates on the death penalty) all stress the transitional and hybrid nature of the times. Together with his generation, Hugo is haunted by the revolution of 1789. The discontinuities of 1830 are understood to correspond to the larger discontinuities of the Restoration. Thus Hugo maintains from the outset that the "hybrid royalty" of Louis-Philippe is but a "useful transition": the time for the Republic is not ripe—but it will come. In the meantime, the revolution of July 1830 is an aborted revolution; just as in the novel, the underworld's assault on the cathedral is a failure. The populace is not ready; it is not yet aware of its historical mission. Symbolically, Quasimodo does not understand who his natural allies are. Hunchback and vagabonds engage in a fratricidal struggle. (pp. 54-6)

Two characters in the novel live out their destiny in intimate contact with the stones of the cathedral: the hunchback foundling, Quasimodo, and his adoptive father and master, the archdeacon Frollo. Quasimodo's association with the edifice goes beyond intimacy; it is symbiotic, even incestuous. He not only speaks with the stone figures, but lives in a "mysterious and preexistent harmony" with the cathedral. This harmony takes the form of "cohabitation"; Hugo even uses the sexually more suggestive word *accouplement*—mating. The strong sexual charge of this love relation is nowhere more apparent than in the elaborate description of Quasimodo's ecstasy as he rings the bells. The choice and the sequence of verbs *(flatter, commencer, s'ébranler, palpiter, frissonner, déchaîner, saisir, étreindre, éperonner, hennir)* unmistakably suggest an orgasmic crescendo. Fifteen bronze bells make up Quasimodo's "seraglio"; but his favorite concubine is the big bell called Marie. The incestuous intimacy is brought into even sharper relief when Hugo explains that the bells are what Quasimodo loves most in the "maternal edifice." The womb becomes the figure of the world. As the foundling has grown up, the cathedral has successively been "his egg, his nest, his home, his country, the universe." Yet this maternal space is also "possessed" and "filled" by Quasimodo.

The symbiotic process is, of course, also a process of identification. Just as Quasimodo's grimace *is* his face, so he becomes a "living chimera," threatening—according to popular superstition—to change other human beings into stone. Hugo's metaphor for Quasimodo's monstrous shape is that of a grotesque stone building: his deformed back has the shape of a dome, his bandy legs are like spiraled columns. Ultimately, his entire body is viewed as a prison—a "boîte de pierre"—confining his atrophied yet yearning psyche.

Petrification, in ***Notre-Dame de Paris,*** is always related to the dialectics of a spiritual absence-presence. Quasimodo communicates life to the stones of the cathedral precisely because his deafness allows him to hear with his eyes; his somber figure radiates a strange light. The misbegotten reality of his being is converted into a poetic force. It is because his deafness separates him from ordinary language that the Beast finds the mediating symbolic language of poetry and flowers with which to address Beauty. His contemplative disposition—the precondition of the poet's vision, according to Hugo—is bought at the heavy price of a mutilating imprisonment in the self. But the most important spiritual signal associated with the hunchback is that of his name, which not only recalls the living stones of Saint Peter's Epistle ("Quasimodo geniti infantes . . .") but links his mortal destiny to a hope for resurrection. The foundling infant, left near the church door, was discovered by Frollo on so-called Quasimodo Sunday, the Sunday after Easter, and his name is thus quite literally patterned on the words ("quasi modo") with which the introit of that special Sunday Mass begins.

In the case of Frollo, the symbolism of the living stone is more ironic and more disturbing. Whether motionless or agitatedly wandering through the streets of Paris, he is repeatedly described as a living statue. He himself feels that he is changed to stone, petrified by the horror of his own being, by his complicity with death. The image of the walking statue unavoidably brings to mind Don Juan's avenger-antagonist, the marble statue of the Commendatore. As Hugo himself was quick to point out in another context, Don Juan's damnation complements the damnation of Faust. There is no doubt that the legend of Faust, as well as the Don Juan—Commendatore motif, informs ***Notre-Dame de Paris*** thematically. Power as eros and eros as power—each is the obverse of the other; they are interchangeable conceptual forces at work. Frollo, in his study cell, is devoured first by "an appetite for science," by a libidinous desire for knowledge, and next by a fever of the senses, a boundless and frustrated appetite of the flesh: the two appetites feed each other. The image of Faust is equidistant from that of the Commendatore; this is made perfectly clear by a reference to an engraving attributed to Rembrandt, depicting Doctor Faustus in a dark cell exactly like Frollo's.

The irony of such allusions and references is that they tend at the same time to amplify and to reduce Frollo, who belongs to the demonic tradition of the Gothic novel; he is a sibling of Matthew G. Lewis's and E.T.A. Hoffmann's accursed monks. (pp. 60-2)

Guilt and spiritual emptiness characterize Frollo's more lucid moments. Fire and ice, the traditional extremes of hell, alternately symbolize the priest's state of mind. Self-diagnosis amounts to a lament over loss of faith. In the chapter carrying the Dantesque title "Lasciate ogni speranza" ("Abandon All Hope"), Frollo laments that he carries the prison chill of despair within him: "J'ai la nuit dans l'âme."

This darkness in the soul, this spiritual emptiness that extends to the cathedral itself, seems to subvert and negate the symbolism of the living stone. Religion in ***Notre-Dame de Paris*** is at the same time a negative force and an absent faith. All stones tend to form walls; all walls suggest prisons; and prisons, while confining, also generate the age-old dream to "go beyond," to achieve transcendence. There are indeed many places of confinement in ***Notre-Dame de Paris:*** the Trou aux Rats where Sister Gudule, the recluse, has buried herself alive in an anticipated tomb; the dungeon where Esmeralda languishes after being tortured; the penal cave in the Bastille where the bishop of Verdun has been shivering for fourteen years in one of the iron cages contrived by Louis XI; Frollo's cell; and the cathedral itself, which in this novel functions more as a fortress than as a place of worship. The peculiarity of these carceral spaces is that their transcendental potential is minimized. Walls, even church walls, seem at best only to recall the memory of an absent yearning.

Put into other terms, the many religious signals in the novel (the "Saint Peter" or *petrus* motif; the link established throughout between the gallows and the Cross; the name of Quasimodo; his public flagellation, including the crowd's laughter and the soiled sponge thrown in his face), precisely because they point to a spiritual void, function in a negative and negatory manner. Quasimodo's deafness symbolically keeps him in the dark. As for Frollo, it is not so much the melodramatic elements—his alchemical activities, his attempt at rape, his satanic laughter, which echoes the rasping laughter of Sister Gudule—that suggest the absence of God, but his poetic and tragic vision. Looking at the sky reflected in the waters of the Seine, he has the "terrible vision" of the reflected abyss. He tries to flee, in vain. The vision of the abyss is inside him.

The tragic counterpart to this vision is Frollo's symbol for fate: the fly caught in the transparent web. Fly and spider become a metaphysical emblem, a "symbole de tout," not because the fly is caught and destroyed but because it is caught and destroyed while trying to reach light and freedom. The spider's web is compared to a glass window, and more specifically to the rose window of the cathedral ("rosace fatale"), which interposes between the light beyond and the fly the cruel obstacle of a transparent wall. Even the religious Gothic construct is thus seen in a nonreligious and even antireligious perspective, confirming the priest's conclusion about the vanity of religion, the "inutilité de Dieu."

This sense of spiritual vacuity spreads to the entire novel, affecting the various characters and, from all the evidence, the young author himself. Did he not confess as much in a contemporaneous poem, **"La prière pour tous,"** addressed to his daughter, in which he refers to his soul as empty of faith—"vide de foi"? (pp. 63-4)

The emptiness in question is not, however, a conceptual flaw. As the narrator himself observes, it is precisely intellectual activity that undermines faith. Yet the cathedral, a stronghold of religion, seems an empty shell. It is almost everything: an architectural landmark, an observation tower, a fortress, a place of refuge. But it is not a place of worship. Quasimodo seems to be its only true life-spirit. With him gone, the cathedral will stand deserted, inanimate, like a gigantic skeleton. But even while he fills the immense edifice with his Cyclopean presence, its function seems to be that of a monstrous carapace. The dark and deserted nave, where hardly anyone ever seems to move about, is a place of mourning. Notre-Dame is a church without candles and without human voices—"sans cierges et sans voix." Even worse, it is a prayerless church. The only religious service described in the novel has to do with the grim punitive ceremony in which Esmeralda, stripped to her shift, barefoot, and with a rope about her neck, does public penance before mounting the gallows. Prayer, later so important in Hugo's understanding of religion, seems altogether absent or undermined by irony. The old king even prays to the Virgin Mary to justify having Esmeralda put to death.

The religious edifice is not merely empty; it is downright threatening. Through the open portal, the length of the church looks like a cavern or the dark entrails of a mythological monster.

The rose window, at once Cyclops' eye and fateful spider, seems to cast an evil spell both outside and inside the cavernous space. A sepulchral light communicates to everything the complexion of death. It is as though the entire edifice were given over to evil practices. Frollo's hallucinatory vision transmutes the livid arches into mitres of damned bishops. But even the supposedly "objective" narrator describes the cathedral as a harmful construct whose great portal "devours" the populace under the relentless eye of the rose window. (p. 65)

To serve the cause of profound transformations and to help give birth to the future became eventually, for Hugo, the chief functions of the poet. For the time being, he only dimly perceived the full thrust of his own ideas. ***Le dernier jour d'un condamné*** had ideological implications that reached beyond apparent intentions. A sense of historical and political necessity, it seemed, was at work beneath the controlled literary surface. This deeper sense of an ideological drive, of an emerging yet still largely repressed commitment, may explain Hugo's fascination with the notion of *anankē* around 1830. The preface to ***Les feuilles d'automne*** does speak of the hidden work of revolutionary ideas still buried in potentially explosive "underground passages." The metaphor suggests a revolutionary undermining of tired and corrupt societies, as well as the sense of a fated subconscious elaboration.

A curious feature of Hugo's work is that his tropes and literary imagination tend to act out sedition and to subvert the established order long before these tendencies are conceptualized and translated into political terms. In later years, Hugo was to insist, somewhat anachronistically, that his early literary efforts had had a revolutionary motivation. . . . But the anachronism is only on the surface, and the ideological thrust of his early texts reaches far beyond mutinous syntax and versification, or flamboyant imagery. It is moreover significant that, in Hugo's own view, literary insurrection should have given the signal. For such a view of his own political evolution casts an even brighter light on the narrator's comment, in ***Notre-Dame de Paris,*** that the invention of the printing press is the matrix of revolutions.

Revolution appears thematically as a constant prophecy in ***Notre-Dame de Paris.*** An ineluctable forward movement of history seems to carry from Louis XI's dismantling of the feudal edifice to Mirabeau's work in favor of the people, and, beyond 1789, to the still unattained goal of revolution at the time Hugo is writing. The "hour of the People" will come, prophesies the Flemish delegate Coppenole; it will come, he ominously tells the king during their interview in the Bastille, when the tower of the king's fortress falls.

These somewhat facile prophecies are made more meaningful, in the context, by constant references to repressive social, judiciary, and political conditions. Justice, in the form of the presiding magistrate during Quasimodo's trial, is quite literally deaf. Penal inhumanities—floggings, the pillory, torture, public executions—pervade the text. Even the gentle aristocratic ladies derive cruel pleasure from humiliating a gypsy. As they torment Esmeralda, they are compared to young Roman ladies, amusing themselves by having gold pins thrust into the breast of a beautiful slave. But it is the king's despotic bent, his tyrannical sense of decorum (he has the pavement speedily washed after the massacre), and above all his hubris in trusting his own strength and the strength of the Bastille that underscore the prerevolutionary motifs of the novel.

The iconography and legend of the fall of the Bastille are at the heart of ***Notre-Dame de Paris***—both as a memory and as a projection. The old fortress can be seen at a distance, as a sinister counterstructure to the cathedral; its gloomy bell can be heard far away. The king uses it as his residence, preferring its austere walls to those of the Louvre. It is the stronghold of monarchy. And the most dramatic action in the novel is mob action, when the Truands—the hordes of the Parisian underworld—arm themselves and assault that other symbolic fortress, the cathedral. The collective event is like a general rehearsal for July 14, complete with pillage of weapons, mob anger, a procession of frightening physiognomies, and chaotic exploits, while the tocsin lends the event a fierce solemnity.

The account of this assault upon a symbol of authority has mythical grandeur. The advancing mob of *argotiers* is seen as an awesome procession of dark and silent figures, a "river" of humanity, a frightful herd of men and women in rags, armed with scythes, pikes, and halberds. In the torchlight, the black pitchforks project like horns over the hideous faces. The huge beam serving as a battering ram is transformed into a hundred-legged mythological beast butting against a giant of stone.

This figuration of joint action and communal assault derives directly from the iconography of the French Revolution. The epic grandeur of the event is further enhanced by references to the *Iliad* and to Homeric epithets. But the combination of myth and historicity proposes a bidirectional perspective: the event still to happen has already occurred. The French Revolution, by the same token, is a matter of the past, yet remains to be accomplished in the future—depending on whether one looks at history from the standpoint of 1830 or of 1482. This ambivalence clearly bespeaks a political dilemma. On the same page, the reader is told that the hour of the people is not yet ripe ("l'heure du peuple n'est pas venue") and that this hour will come ("Vous l'entendrez sonner"). The two sentences have a different ring, depending on whether they are read from the fictional point of view of 1482, or from the writer-reader point of view, after the unfinished business of the July Revolution of 1830.

The narrator's attitude toward the *peuple*—one of the most highly charged words, politically and emotionally, of the nineteenth century—is even more ambivalent. The mystique of the idealized lower classes is inscribed in the revolutionary tradition. "Le Chant du départ," one of the best-known revolutionary marching songs, proclaims the regal dignity and irresistible force of the new sovereign—the People. "Le peuple souverain s'avance." In the context of ***Notre-Dame de Paris,*** the people's sense of dignity is still a "vague" and "indistinct" potential. Their forward march is, however, overwhelming. Recurrent water images—river, ocean, tides—suggest relentless flux and ineluctable historical processes. The opening pages describe the crowd in front of the Palais de Justice in terms of sea, waves, swells, and currents that ceaselessly assault the "promontories" of the houses. This human flood tide knows no ebbing. Its force is a constant threat of violence. Hugo speaks of the "flot irrésistible" of the crowd, of its providing a spectacle of "terror."

The threat is in the flood's destructive power. A poem dated May 1830 warns the king to pay heed to the oceanic high tide of popular forces ("la haute marée / Qui monte incessamment") if he wants to survive in this century of violent change. What complicates and enriches the image of these oceanic forces is the association of Paris with the ocean. Quasimodo, we are told, dreams of no other ocean than Paris, which roars at the feet of the cathedral's colossal towers. (pp. 68-71)

It is revealing that the *peuple* so intimately associated by Hugo with the oceanic and volcanic city imagery should be presented, and magnified, in a grotesque perspective. Quasimodo becomes horribly beautiful as he challenges the society that made him an outcast. In the act of saving Esmeralda from the hand of "justice," the Beast becomes the Beauty. Later, during the seige of the cathedral, in the weird nocturnal light, the deformed bell-ringer looks like a hoary old king out of some legend. Hugo's ideology of the grotesque and the dialectics of ugliness and the sublime, which he discussed in the preface to ***Cromwell,*** were to him obviously not a simple matter of picturesqueness and artistic license. In offering the view that the grotesque was a predominantly modern manifestation, corresponding to the increasing rift between the physical and the spiritual, Hugo had in mind renewed possibilities of a *total* vision. He thus anticipated Mikhail Bakhtin, an attentive reader of Hugo, who proposed that the grotesque and the *carnavalesque* are elements of a collective ritual, a liberation from the established order. The Mardi Gras, with its roots in folklore, stands at the center of this carnival atmosphere. It is significant that Phoebus, having forgotten Quasimodo's name, remembers only that it is the name of some religious holiday, something like Mardi Gras, the merrymaking day before Lent.

Riotous heterogeneity characterizes the grotesque and the *carnavalesque*—two notions overtly linked in Hugo's text. The spectacle of aggressive variety begins in the early pages of ***Notre-Dame de Paris,*** during the election of the Pope of Fools. All possible shapes and forms, all possible human expressions, are displayed in this competition of ugliness. In setting up his "théâtre des grimaces," Hugo deliberately refers to the notion of the grotesque ("grotesque échantillon des deux sexes"). And he associates this grimacing parade with the masks of the Venice carnival, as well as with the grimaces of the sculpted *mascarons,* the grotesque stone heads of the Pont Neuf. Stones remain at the center of the novel. There is something of the petrified nightmare in Hugo's theater of grimaces.

Theatricality and the awareness of the theater are significant features of ***Notre-Dame de Paris.*** They no doubt reflect some of Hugo's preoccupations and stage battles of 1830. But they also go beyond such professional concerns. The novel begins with a spectacle. The opening chapter describes a crowd in the great hall of the Palais de Justice, before and during a performance of an allegorical mystery play. The spectacle is multiple: the mystery play, the crowd of spectators, and the dignitaries on their platform are all jarring actors in a vast performance. The narrator himself refers to a "spectacle of spectators." And the "spectacle" of the dignitaries—the Cardinal de Bourbon, the Flemish delegation—has political implications. So does the allegory of Gringoire's mystery play: Nobility, Clergy, Trade, and Labor are interlocked in an apparently endless drama. These political-theatrical signals prepare a whole network of thematic and symbolic associations. History, politics, social injustice, and the dialectics of the grotesque all have in common a theatricalization that intensifies the ideological complexity of the novel. The Palais de Justice, where Gringoire's unsuccessful mystery play is performed, is the same place where Esmeralda, after emerging from the torture chamber, is condemned to death before an impatient crowd that is compared to an audience in a theater. The "theater of grimaces" disturbingly blends expressions of savage mockery and pain.

Problematic laughter echoes throughout the book. . . . Some of the laughter in ***Notre-Dame de Paris*** is light-hearted, joyful, teasingly irreverent, boisterously contagious: the laughter of the students, and the impish *fou rire* of Jehan, Frollo's dissipated younger brother. But *fou rire,* in Hugo's work, is never innocent. The *fou rire* of the rabble comes in cruel response to the naked horror of Quasimodo's body on the pillory. This kind of laughter is at the same time cruel and obscene. "Chanson obscène" and "gros rire" are wedded in the same sentence. Cruelty and sinister moods are in fact almost automatically signaled by fits of laughter—a carry-over from the Gothic novel and from melodrama: the "rire sinistre" that greets Gringoire in the Cour des Miracles, the "rire lugubre" of Sister Gudule, obsessed by the idea of revenge, the collective laughter of the mob as the tormented Quasimodo begs for water, the "bestial" laughter of the hangman, the "abominable" and even "demonic" laughter of the fallen priest. With Hugo, however, laughter has ideological implications, and Bakhtin was surely wrong when he stated that for Hugo laughter was mostly a "negation," a degrading and destroying principle. Hugo's laughing rabble in ***Notre-Dame de Paris,*** although not yet the dignified *peuple,* is compared to Homer's laughing gods on Olympus. The hierarchical inversions proclaiming the majesty of the buffoon, which were to receive their most elaborate mythopoetic expression in the great poem **"Le Satyre,"** are founded on the dissolving, subversive, but also affirmative laughter from below. This, no doubt, is the full meaning of the bond established between the grotesque and the sublime—a bond that involves a radical inversion of values. (pp. 71-4)

In this perspective, it is significant that the only *peuple* to be represented in ***Notre-Dame de Paris*** is the Parisian underworld: the tribe of beggars, vagabonds, and criminals crowding the slums of the Cour des Miracles—a terrifying and alienated city within the city, with its own laws of lawlessness. This Kingdom of Slang is an urban figuration of hell, a labyrinth inhabited by what Hugo himself defines as the "lowest stratum" of the population. But this throng of outlaws is potentially prerevolutionary in its vindictiveness toward the social order. Trouillefou, the king of this grotesque realm of argot, explains that the cruel laws of society—in particular, capital punishment—must be turned against society itself.

These pages on the underworld, in which the real and the fantastic intersect, are among the most striking in the novel. Their power was much admired by Flaubert. Their grossly realistic yet nightmarish and visionary quality brings to mind a fusion of Breughel, Franz Hals, Callot, and Goya. Hugo himself repeatedly mentions names of painters. The prosaic and brutal realities of the tavern are accompanied by a reference to Callot, and the horrors of prison suggest "l'oeuvre extraordinaire de Goya." The poetry of hell—a human hell—is perceived as a form of hallucination, a "rêve horrible,"as Gringoire penetrates into the Truands' violent and parasitic world.

This asocial and essentially apolitical (or prepolitical) proletarian mass may have its strange appeal: vitality, love of excess, black humor, verbal inventiveness. . . . But no matter what its virtues, the "lowest stratum" represented by the Truands is seen in a negative, pathological perspective. These ruffians follow their worst instincts. Lazy, debauched, and cruel, they are collectively depicted as a lower form of animal life (swine, snails in the mire, crabs, insects, spiders) or as a huge wart on the city. Hugo compares the entire Cour des Miracles to a vast sewer. These living masses of real and false afflictions, these limping, shuffling wretches—lame, one-armed, one-eyed, covered with festering sores—are like sinister actors forever preparing to play their part in the comedy of theft, prostitution, and murder that is enacted day and night on the streets of Paris. (The theatrical metaphor extends even to crime.) The picture is certainly not flattering to the lower classes. Hugo is quite outspoken: the "good people of Paris" (the "bon populaire parisien") are hardly less cruel and bestial than this horde of beggars and criminals.

The point seems to be that if the "hour of the people" has not come yet, it is because the *peuple*, except as a utopian notion, does not yet exist. (pp. 74-5)

Victor Brombert, in his Victor Hugo and the Visionary Novel, *Cambridge, Mass.: Harvard University Press, 1984, 286 p.*

ILINCA M. ZARIFOPOL-JOHNSTON (essay date 1985)

[In the following excerpt, Zarifopol-Johnston studies the structure and philosophical principles of Notre-Dame de Paris *in an attempt to demonstrate that Hugo synthesized elements from a variety of literary traditions into a complex and artistic whole.]*

Although universally acknowledged as a thrilling melodrama, Hugo's ***Notre-Dame de Paris*** is often treated by critics as a literary and artistic failure, either because its plot seems to be weak, disconnected, and full of Romantic cliches, or because of insufficient connection between its plot and Hugo's ambitious "art-historical" context. In a prefatory Note added to his final edition of 1832 [see excerpt dated 1832], Hugo seems to have foreseen his novel's divided audience, and also the two main foci of its controversial reputation: those interested mainly in its plot, and those attracted by its larger historico-aesthetic context.

> Mais il est peut-être d'autres lecteurs qui n'ont pas trouvé inutile d'étudier la pensée d'esthétique et de philosophie cachée dans ce livre, qui ont bien voulu, en lisant ***Notre-Dame de Paris,*** se plaire à démêler sous le roman autre chose que le roman, et à suivre, qu'on me passe ces expressions un peu ambitieuses, le système de l'historien et le but de l'artiste à travers la création telle quelle du poète.

Whether they have been used to attack or defend the novel, these two critical approaches have remained largely separate; attempts to establish a more unified view of the plot and the novel's informative art-historical essays have so far proved largely unsatisfactory. However, I believe it is possible to bring the two together, and thus to provide a basis on which to integrate the novel's popular and aesthetic reputations.

Hugo's Note, if taken literally, seems to underplay the importance of plot even more than certain critics' view of it. Indeed, his comment seems to encourage the idea that the plot, without its supporting cultural perspective, is just a collection of cliches from popular melodrama, whose collective title might be "Esmeralda, the Gypsy Virgin," "The Wicked Monk," or, as indeed it is known by almost all English readers, ***The Hunchback of Notre-Dame.*** Hugo's Note seems to beg for a more sophisticated reading of his novel. Sympathetic critics have responded mainly by making the cathedral their focus of attention, implicitly rescuing the novel from its popular ***Hunchback*** reputation by reconstituting it as the impressive ***Notre-Dame.*** For critics interested mainly in the plot, the cathedral becomes either one of the book's central characters, or a unitary setting for its action, or "the center and dynamic element of the action." For critics interested mainly in the thought of the novel, the cathedral functions as Hugo's standard of artistic achievement—which, in the opinion of critics who have tried to combine both approaches, the plot cannot match.

But if Hugo emphasized the importance of the book's philosophical thought in his Note, he is also reported to have said of it, "S'il a un mérite, c'est d'être oeuvre d'imagination, de caprice et de fantaisie." What the Note in fact stresses is not so much that there is in the book a "pensée d'esthétique et de philosophie," as that these philosophical thoughts are "cachée dans ce livre," and therefore of some consequence for the reading of the novel. Critics looking single-mindedly for the book's "thoughts" have found them in such explicit form (in chapters like "Notre Dame," "Paris à vol d'oiseau," and "Ceci tuera cela") that they have ignored Hugo's clue that his thoughts were "hidden," or been outraged by it: "Just what is 'hidden' about it? The author's philosophical views seem, rather, to have been driven home with a sledge hammer."—[W. Wolfgang Holdheim; see excerpt dated 1976]. There would be truth in this objection if such chapters were taken as cultural generalizations only superficially related to the fiction. But if Hugo's words are taken to mean what they say, then one could advance the hypothesis that there is indeed "à démêler sous le roman autre chose que le roman." In this view, the three chapters just cited provide something other than the novel itself which is nonetheless contained within it, another work of art which is also another text, the cathedral of Notre Dame. These three chapters are an intrinsic part of the book containing its code of interpretation. By describing something other than the book, they reveal the hidden anatomy of the novel, the abstract ideas which govern its organization: Hugo's historico-philosophical concept of the tension between necessity *(Anankè)* and freedom (with a prefiguration of its resolution in the victory of democracy) and, parallel to it, Hugo's special aesthetic concept of the "epic" as a graft between the traditional epic and the drama. As Hugo says in his Note, the events of the plot signify very little in themselves, they are only signs to be interpreted, just as the figures on the cathedral are "hieroglyphs" to be deciphered. The three essay chapters give readers an instrument or code by which they can read and interpret the events of the plot correctly. Instead of disrupting the novel, the chapters spell out its essential features, but only for those who know how to read them. They too are like the hierogylphic figures inscribed on the cathedral, since *literacy* in overcoming fate is required of both the poet and the expert reader. Awareness of Hugo's use of the "mise en abîme" technique, or more precisely, *ecphrasis* shows that ***Notre-Dame de Paris*** is a text with only a partially hidden meaning, since it carries its own gloss embedded within itself. As in the votive icon paintings of Eastern Orthodox Christianity, where the family donating the new church is represented with a miniature replica of it in their hands, ***Notre-Dame de Paris*** contains the image of a work of art which is at one and the same time "autre chose" than the novel itself, yet plainly to be identified with the book which contains it. One of the main themes of the novel is hermeneutical—what is the proper or scientific way to read signs or texts?—and the key to reading the text, ***Notre-Dame de Paris,*** is to read accurately the other text inscribed in it, Notre-Dame de Paris, the cathedral.

Seen in this light, Hugo's statement that the novel is a work of "imagination, caprice and fantasy" is not incompatible with his statement that it contains "an aesthetic and philosophical thought." A work of "imagination, caprice, and fantasy" does not signify what critics have generally taken it to mean (namely, a work presenting an arbitrary string of events), but rather a work highly motivated by the presence of an abstract scheme of interpretation, the "aesthetic and philosophical thought" which cuts across it as an organizing principle. By calling his novel a work of "imagination, caprice and fantasy," Hugo resembles E. M. Forster's "fantasist" writer for whom the novel is "something that could not occur. I must ask you first to accept my book as a whole, and secondly to accept certain things in my book." Ideas in ***Notre-Dame de Paris*** count more than events. As a work of "fantasy" it has a logic of "ideological causality" as opposed to "phenomenal causality."... The governing structural principle of ***Notre-Dame de Paris*** is its own heterogeneity, a graft or mixture of themes, genres, styles. It is embodied by the image of Notre-Dame, the cathedral. Understanding the book-cathedral relationship leads to a more profound reading of the book. By establishing this relationship, Hugo implicitly raised his novel above, and achieved a literary criticism of, the common adventure novel popular in the early nineteenth century, whose master was Walter Scott.

Hugo provides plenty of justification for this kind of reading. He establishes a general identity between literature and architecture in the chapters "Abbas Beati Martini" and "Ceci tuera cela." "L'architecture est le grand livre de l'humanité."

> —Pasquedieu! qu'est-ce que c'est donc que vos livres?
> —En voici un, dit l'archidiacre,
> Et ouvrant la fenêtre de la cellule, il désigna du doigt l'immense église de Notre-Dame. . . .

These general identifications are reduced to a very specific and pointed one in the book's title: ***Notre-Dame de Paris*** is to be identified with Notre-Dame de Paris, a famous but also very peculiar specimen of Gothic architecture. Thus the minute descriptions of the cathedral, the general considerations about architecture and literature which they engender, and the overall descriptions of fifteenth century Paris are essential to the novel because they provide Hugo a mode of self-reflection, i.e., an interpretive mirror within the text. Hugo took great care to spell out his reasons for choosing Notre-Dame de Paris and not any other Gothic cathedral as his book's central figure:

> Notre-Dame de Paris n'est pas de pure race romaine comme les premières, ni de pure race arabe comme les secondes. C'est un édifice de la transition. . . . D'ailleurs, ces édifices de la transition du roman au gothique ne sont pas moins précieux à étudier que les types purs. Ils experiment une nuance de l'art qui serait perdue sans eux. C'est la greffe de l'ogive sur le plein cintre.
>
> Notre-Dame de Paris est en particulier un curieux échantillon de cette variété . . . Cette église centrale et génératrice est parmi les vieilles églises de Paris une sorte de chimère; elle a la tête de l'une, les membres de celle-là, la croupe de l'autre; quelque chose de toutes.

The cathedral is interesting, in Hugo's conception, because it is not of "pure race." It is an "edifice of transition," combining the main stylistic characteristics of all the other old churches in Paris, and thus being a complex and "complete" work of art. Its "completeness" derives from its double nature, that subtle "nuance of the art" which only works of *mixed* character possess.

"Completeness" is the highest artistic value for Hugo, inseparably linked to the idea of mixture. The **"Preface to *Cromwell*"** attempts to demolish the classical theory of the purity of genres and styles, and to establish instead a theory of "impurity" as a condition of perfection. According to this theory, any heterogeneous work of art stands a greater chance of being complete, and thus closer to perfection, than a pure one. Any work of art "complete" in this way Hugo calls an "epic." Thus the cathedral of Notre-Dame, not being of "pure race," is called an "epic" by the same token that the works of Dante and Shakespeare are "epic," whereas Homer's works are less than "epic" because they lack the mixed quality of, for example, the Divine Comedy. . . . Homer's epics, not being sufficiently "epic," would need to be "completed" in order to rise to the perfection of Dante's epic; they require drama.

Hugo suggests how this could be done in a novel in his essay on Walter Scott:

> Après le roman pittoresque, mais prosaïque, de Walter Scott, il restera un roman à créer, plus beau et plus complète encore selon nous. C'est le roman, à la fois drame et épopée, pittoresque, mais poétique, réel, mais idéal, vrai, mais grand, qui enchâssera Walter Scott dans Homère.

A novel that combines the characteristics of Scott with those of Homer can equal in artistic value a play by Shakespeare of Dante's *Comedy*; it would be "epic" by virtue of its completeness. A Scott novel possesses the essence of drama in its picturesqueness, its lifelike combination of the sublime and the grotesque, and its portrayal of particulars, all of which make it "réel" and "vrai." As such, however, its significance would be limited; it would not be complete. It needs to be incorporated into the epic mode, so that its particular scenes would acquire general meaning within a recursive epic structure, which does not grow but unfolds invariably, repeatedly illustrating a pre-established divine scheme. Homer, the Old Testament, Dante, and the medieval quests are alike in this respect: they all possess this structure which transforms each individual episode into an exemplification of one meaning, the "poétique," "idéal," "grand," or, in a word, the divine. But this epic mode by itself, if not filled with vivid dramatic pictures of particular sublimities or grotesqueries, is in turn insufficient. Hugo would thus improve simultaneously upon Homer and Scott by putting them together, grafting one on the other. The resulting novel would be "epic," a mixture of themes, genres, and styles of representation.

Notre-Dame de Paris contains within itself the image of an "epic" cathedral. Insofar as this image is a mirror of the novel itself, the novel is equally "epic," as defined by Hugo: "à la fois drame et épopée." The cathedral's most characteristic mark is its heterogeneity, "la greffe de l'ogive sur le plein cintre," the graft between Gothic and Romanesque styles. This graft reflects a similar one in the novel: what is Gothic in the cathedral is dramatic in the novel; what is Romanesque in the cathedral is epic in the novel.

Romanesque churches are characterized by "la grave et massive carrure, la ronde et large voûte, la nudité glaciale, la majesteuse simplicité." They are "sombres, mystérieuses, basses . . . toutes hiéroglyphiques, toutes sacerdotales, toutes symboliques" every one of their architectural details being an expression of the dogma that has inspired it. Thus they are repetitious and heavily immobile in structure, each element signifying what all the others signify: "Du reste, toute forme, toute difformité même y a un sens qui la fait inviolable. . . . Dans ces architectures, il semble que la roideur du dogme se soit répandue sur la pierre comme une seconde pétrification."

The main features of Romanesque churches, also possessed by the cathedral of Notre-Dame, resemble Hugo's definition of Homeric epic: "L'épopée solennise l'histoire," and is characterized by "la simplicité." History is enlarged and simplified in the epic, given a unique and unified interpretation, because of the dogma underlying it, as in the Romanesque cathedral. In the cathedral of Notre Dame, Romanesque gravity and massiveness subdue Gothic lightness and height; the all-pervading spirit of a monolithic dogma somehow restrains a great variety of decorative design. Similarly, in ***Notre-Dame de Paris***, the epic provides a controlling framework for the dramatic. At the same time, in this cathedral the Gothic style, though still tame, had for almost the first time affirmed its full personality. The cathedral of Paris is as much the "magnifique, léger, multiforme, touffu, hérissé, efflorescent" product of the Gothic arch as it is of the Romanesque; as "communale et bourgeoise, capricieuse et effrénée" as it is sacerdotal and dogmatic. Within the framework of a single dogma, it manages to express, like all Gothic cathedrals, the complexity of life and nature: "la variété, le progrès, l'originalité, l'opulence, le mouvement perpétuel." Similarly, in the novel the epic framework is filled with the drama of life and nature in all its incidental, accidental, particular, and individual forms. Like Gothic architecture, the dramatic style of representation depicts life ("le drame peint la vie") and its main attribute ("la vérité") is the individual, not the general or dogmatic truth.

These close resemblances between definitions of styles belonging to two different arts, though according to Lessing so dissimilar (one spatial, the other temporal), based on the analogy of the *graft*, are persuasive enough to pursue further in an interpretation of ***Notre-Dame de Paris***.

There is in ***Notre-Dame de Paris***, on the one hand, a historical period represented comprehensively in its totality, but formalized and simplified by a conceptual framework: *Anankè*, or Fatality, Necessity. On the other hand, this historical period is also represented in detail, selectively and specifically, with circumstantial events brightly and dramatically spotlighted. The episodes of ***Notre-Dame de Paris*** are like variations on a theme: *Anankè*, "C'est sur ce mot qu'on a fait ce livre." Richard Grant has convincingly shown that the novel is unified by a recurrent pattern of spider web imagery which expresses its theme of fatality in a wide variety of contexts: sexual (the triangle of Esmeralda-Frollo-Phoebus), social (the unjust tribunals which examine Esmeralda and Quasimodo), familial (the sub-plot of the recluse), political (king vs. People), and religious (the Church as pervasively beneficent or demonic). [see excerpt dated 1968]. Recognition of a unity at the semantic and metaphorical level implies also a structural unity. Yet critics have traditionally denied this to ***Notre-Dame de Paris***, making it infamous rather for structural laxity and a haphazard, composite character. Grant's demonstration of the novel's unity-in-diversity is striking not only because it identifies *Anankè* as a structural principle, but even more because it helps to reveal that this novel is organized on the level of ideas rather than of events, that it has "ideological" rather than "phenomenal" causality.

But though it seems at first glance that the dogma of *Anankè* is the only principle of structural interpretation for ***Notre-Dame de Paris***, we must remember that "l'inscription a disparu," and *Anankè* in the novel is only a memory, not a living force: "Ainsi, hormis le fragil souvenir que lui consacre ici l'auteur de ce livre, il ne reste plus rein aujourd'hui du mot mysterieux gravé dans la sombre tour de Notre-Dame." From Hugo's perspective, at the time he was writing, *Anankè* had already been superseded by the principle of freedom, which he evokes in the novel as conflicting with *Anankè*. The narrative is indeed organized at the level of interpretation rather than of events, but its semantics are not simply those of *Anankè*, but of the tension between *Anankè* and freedom, progress, and history. Consequently, its structure is not one of unity-in-diversity but of willed diversity, of mixture, of a graft. The book is not dedicated to *Anankè* but to the tension which ultimately subdued it. The book's episodes are like variations on a theme, but they are not subservient to that theme. The theme of *Anankè* organizes them in a repetitive structure, giving them equal moral significance, yet they have such strong individuality and drama that they constantly pull against the superimposed epic structure and claim a life of their own. Hugo achieves a peculiar structural mixture of epic and dramatic by rendering the individual epic episodes dramatically (focus on individually characteristic features, heightened tempo, climax, and resolution); in this he resembles both Dante and the Old Testament. A dynamic relationship exists between epic and dramatic structures in the book, the former constantly trying to drag the latter back into its web. *Anankè* wins out in the end, and thus may be said to govern the book, but Hugo's reminder that the inscription was effaced and his historical essays make clear that *Anankè* is only one pole of the tension, one half of the graft. The governing concept of the graft confers upon ***Notre-Dame de Paris*** an epico-dramatic status which justifies Hugo's claim that it is more than it appears to be; as a genuine, organic graft between the epic and the drama it achieves a generic status far greater than that of a melodramatic adventure novel, even one unified by a theme such as *Anankè*.

As an example of how the scenes of ***Notre-Dame de Paris*** partake of both epic and dramatic without one ever taking the upper hand over the other, I shall analyse two scenes which could potentially have been the climactic turning points of the action, had they occurred in a conventional adventure novel: the attack of the beggars on the cathedral of Notre-Dame and the recognition scene between Esmeralda and the recluse of La Tour Roland. Both of them enact a climax where there cannot be one. They give the illusion of a climax because of their drama, but they do not effect any revolution in the course of the action because they are contained in an epic framework.

Had ***Notre-Dame de Paris*** been like Scott's *Ivanhoe* and not something more complex (or more complete," in Hugo's sense), the attack on the cathedral could have constituted its climax, exactly as the attack of Robin Hood's band on the Norman castle of Front de Boeuf is the real climax and turning point of *Ivanhoe*. The various disparate plots of *Ivanhoe* (Normans vs. Saxons, outlaws vs. society, legitimate vs. illegitimate kings) are all set in direct confrontation during the attack. The outcome of the attack, victory for the Saxon/outlaw/Richard party, marks the turning point for all subsidiary conflicts as well. Similarly, in ***Notre-Dame de Paris***, the attack on the cathedral brings together the novel's private and public lines of events. A major confrontation takes place between the power of the king and the power of the people, between the outlaws of society and its socially most sanctified institution, the Church, but the outcome of this conflict is of no consequence to the subsidiary conflicts. The efficacy of the outcome in changing fate is blunted by the fact that it is itself but another manifestation of fate, another instance in which prediction is fulfilled. In itself, the episode is very dramatic to be sure, marked by uniquely unusual turns of event. The beggars storm the cathedral like a fortress, using clever tactics and strategies, but are astonished to see the cathedral apparently able to defend itself, as Quasimodo (unbeknownst to them) hurls stones and timbers from the roof as if from heaven. After the bizarre spectacle of Jehan Frollo's desperate death, the scene becomes still more passionate, as the beggars throw themselves upon the cathedral in a frenzy of determination which indeed results in a brief moment of triumph:

> La ville semblait s'être émue. Des tocsins éloignés se plaignaient. Les truands hurlaient, haletaient, juraient, montaient, et Quasimodo impuissant contre tant d'ennemis . . . voyant les faces furieuses se rapprocher de plus en plus de sa galerie, demandait un miracle au ciel. . . .

Notre-Dame de Paris is not a book in which saving miracles happen, yet paradoxically here the miracle does happen: the king's men arrive, disperse the beggar army, and save the cathedral from sacrilege. However, the sudden apparition of Phoebus and the knights is an irony, and has only the appearance of a "deus ex machina." The hand of destiny has disguised itself as its very opposite, saving grace. Its effect is to speed up the fulfillment of the individual characters' fate rather than to change it, and only to delay the fulfillment of a historical prediction, that the power of the kings of France is doomed. The presence of Jaques Coppenole and the "populist" Flemish delegation in the opening chapters stands for that prediction, which is actually proferred by Coppenole at the moment of the battle of Notre-Dame:

> —Écoutez, sire! Il y a ici un donjon, un beffroi, des canons, des bourgeois, des soldats Quand le beffroi bourdonnera, quand les canons gronderont, quand le donjon croulera à grand bruit, quand bourgeois et soldats hurleront et s'entretueront, c'est l'heure qui sonnera.

King Louis' moment of victory is brief and illusory, in historical perspective; he is the higher instrument of fate in the "story" of ***Notre-Dame de Paris***, but as representative of the Ancien Regime he, like Frollo, is doomed to fall, doomed to lose before the democratic march of history.

In similar fashion, the recognition scene between Esmeralda and her mother precipitates the end but does not change the course of the action, quite in contrast to the function of recognition scenes in normative tragedy or drama, where they precipitate the end *by* changing the course of the action. In ***Notre-Dame de Paris,*** the meaning of the recognition scene is conferred by another structure, not the dramatic but the epic. The scene itself is of course achieved by dramatic means: spotlighting technique and great suspense. Esmeralda is left by Claude Frollo in the hands of the terrifying recluse of the Place de la Grève. She is more dead than alive with fear, bewilderment, and horror, while the old woman is exuberant with revenge. The gray light of dawn ilumines only these two figures in the ominous gibbet. The rest of the setting is buried in darkness, filled with indistinct noises and the imminence of threat and danger. The recognition between mother and daughter takes place in this setting of increasing suspense, heightening the drama still further. Their comparison of the two little shoes, their leisurely, mutual expressions of common happiness in the midst of approaching danger, and above all their forgetfulness of that danger, even as the reader becomes increasingly aware of it and of the need to act quickly—all these contribute to the suspense of the scene. The reader is finally totally discomfited and anguished when the girl, instead of running away with her mother, climbs into the tower and thus constitutes herself a prisoner all over again.

However, suspenseful as this scene is, it is usually viewed as part of a somewhat superfluous sub-plot of the recluse, and is often cut from cinema versions of the novel. Yet to view the scene as superfluous results from a misconception of ***Notre-Dame de Paris*** as being entirely dramatic; in this conception, such scenes seem cumbersome, melodramatic exaggerations of suspense (rather than legitimately dramatic ones), contributing to the book's artistic failure and, perhaps even worse, its easy popular success.

But if ***Notre-Dame de Paris*** is viewed as a *dramatic epic,* it does not really matter whether there are ten or twenty such scenes, for none of them can be superfluous in the way some of them would be in a drama. In the *Odyssey,* for example, Ulysses's recognition by Penelope is rendered as a last success in a long series of trials, all equally successful. It is Ulysses's fate to be a successful trickster. All the episodes in the *Odyssey* anticipate this last episode; they all prefigure that which is preordained to occur, illustrations of an underlying conceptual scheme—the "dogma" of fate—by which every episode is uniformly interpretable. Esmeralda's fate, though the reverse of Ulysses's, resembles his in form. His trials are always crowned with success; hers, with failure—all attempts to prevent her from meeting her predestined death are abortive. The form of their destiny is epic, recursive and circular, not dramatic, incremental and progressive. The epico-dramatic character of ***Notre-Dame de Paris,*** consisting of the simultaneous presence of two conflicting structures, affects in an essential way its suspense, an element characteristic of drama, but not of epic. Suspense is present in ***Notre-Dame de Paris,*** but deflated, devalued. The underlying pattern of fatality renders it inappropriate. The reader knows that, as Albouy puts it, "la loi d'airain de l'Anankè rend impossible les recommencements, les rehabilitations." He knows that what will happen will be like what has already happened. Such a pattern transforms the adventures of the characters into "ritual ordeals" whose outcome can be predicted in explicit forms. The novel contains several such explicit predictions: the recluse's curse, the parable of the spider and the fly. In virtually all the episodes, the end is prefigured from the very beginning. One episode in particular, formed by the chapters "Trois cœurs d'homme faits différemment," and "Fièvre," foretells the novel's denouement in terms almost identical to those in which it is described when it actually occurs. In this episode, Esmeralda's execution is postponed because Quasimodo, himself a "graft," a monster, who seeks to go beyond "fatality," cuts the fatal knot. Yet the execution is nevertheless enacted in Frollo's sick and feverish mind, who sees in fantasy what he will actually see in reality from the roof of the cathedral at the end, thus foreseeing his own fall to death and "Damnation!"

With ends thus prefigured and suspense at the level of the overall structure annulled, Hugo can satisfy his desire to portray background naturally and leisurely. His technique, reminiscent of Homer is that of retarding or delaying the action and foregrounding the background, bringing everything out into the clear by means of what often seems to be digression. But he does not want to abandon suspense altogether since it is an essential element of the other half of his graft. He resolves this apparent contradiction by placing the preponderance of the major digressive elements in one block, near the beginning of the book, whereas in the Homeric epics the digressive, delaying element goes along with the episodes it amplifies and illumines. The recognition episode in the *Odyssey* is interrupted by a description of a past action, the hunt in which Ulysses acquired the scar by which he is recognized. As Auerbach points out, the inserted story relaxes the suspense of the scene, but also fulfills the need for complete explanation characteristic of the Homeric style. The recognition scene in ***Notre-Dame de Paris*** does not have a built-in digressive element, so it is much more suspenseful and dramatic. But the need to explicate fully is also important to Hugo, and so the digressive and explanatory elements, though absent from the scene proper, are not absent from the book. The recluse's story of her stolen baby, to which she briefly alludes in her moving speech to the soldiers, constitutes the recognition scene's missing explanatory element and is located near the beginning: Book VI, Chapters 3 and 5, "Histoire d'une galette au levain de maïs" and "Fin de l'histoire de la galette." Other scenes from the beginning of the novel can be interpreted similarly. Book II, Chapter 6 ("La cruche cassée") explains Gringoire's obligation to save Esmeralda from death, while the historical and political considerations that make King Louis intervene at the end of the book are spelled out in dramatic form in the scenes at the Palais de Justice in Book I. Book VI, Chapter 4 ("Une larme pour une goutte d'eau"), rather than simply increasing the book's melodramatic aspect, is a scene which explains Quasimodo's reason for saving Esmeralda in Book VIII, Chapter 6 ("Trois cœurs d'homme faits différemment"). These scenes have a discontinuous relation with the scenes upon which they nevertheless have a direct bearing; this discontinuity allows the scenes to be dramatic yet at the same time does not rob them of a broad explanatory context. All of the first six books of ***Notre-Dame de Paris*** serve the function of bringing forth the background and projecting the outcome, retarding the action proper until Book VII. All of them stand, although in various ways, in the same relationship to the drama of the novel, that of meaning to event. Most of them externalize the workings of the plot, ensuring that nothing is left unexplained. Some of them, like the chapters on the cathedral, on Paris, and on architecture, also serve to externalize the hidden anatomy of the novel itself.

Hugo, true to his conception of the value of a mixed structure and style, the "graft," seems to draw upon both of the major Western traditions of representing reality as defined by Auerbach, the Homeric and the Biblical. According to Auerbach, Homer tends to make everything explicit, his meanings are open, already systematically interpreted, whereas the Biblical tradition never gives any more background or explanation than is absolutely necessary for the dramatic development of scenes, its meanings remaining closed, cryptic, and in need of interpretation. ***Notre-Dame de Paris*** partakes of both traditions insofar as its meaning is neither totally open nor totally hidden. It has what the Bible does not have, its own gloss embedded in the text. But it is displaced, missing from where it "naturally" belongs, and therefore obscured. Interpretation and explanation do not accompany each episode, the meaning-episode relationship is not linear. Similarly, the interpretive key to a proper reading of the whole book as a "graft" is, though wide open to view, also veiled, presented as a digression, when it is in fact an *ecphrasis*. The key to Hugo's technique is "hidden" only to the extent that it could not be more obviously revealed, as it is figured in the structure which gives title and entry to his entire conception, the Gothic-Romanesque cathedral in the dramatic-epic book, Notre-Dame de Paris in ***Notre-Dame de Paris***. (pp. 22-34)

Ilinca M. Zarifopol-Johnston, "Notre-Dame de Paris: The Cathedral in the Book," in Nineteenth-Century French Studies, *Vol. XIII, Nos. 2 & 3, Winter & Spring, 1985, pp. 22-35.*

ADDITIONAL BIBLIOGRAPHY

Bach, Max. "First Reactions to Victor Hugo's *Notre-Dame de Paris.*" *Kentucky Foreign Language Quarterly* III, No. 2 (Spring 1956): 59-66.

Recalls critical opinions of the novel expressed by Hugo's contemporaries. According to Bach: "The bourgeois critics felt hurt at the little importance given in *Notre-Dame* to their class; the democrats' judgment was determined by the book's lack of social significance; the catholics' objectivity was impaired by the absence of religion; the irreductible survivors of Classicism, usually liberal bourgeois, seemed convinced that Hugo's masterpiece was to be relegated to the same class as the terrible *Han d'Islande.*"

Barrett, Elizabeth. "Wimpole Street." In her *Elizabeth Barrett to Miss Mitford: The Unpublished Letters of Elizabeth Barrett Barrett to Mary Russell Mitford,* edited by Betty Miller, pp. 87-276. London: John Murray, 1954.

Includes several comments on Hugo and his work, most notably a statement of 27 November 1842: "[I] do consider *Notre-Dame* to be the greatness, par excellence, of its . . . *poet.* Now answer me as if you were in the confessional. Is not *Notre-Dame* a more wonderful work, a more sublime *poem,* than anything which our Scott ever performed or imagined, or saw in a dream when he rested from his *Ivanhoe*? Can you hesitate—can you *not* say *Yes*?"

Bowley, Victor E. A. "*Notre-Dame* and *Les Misérables* on the English Stage." *The French Quarterly* XI, No. 4 (December 1929): 210-21.

Discusses English dramatic adaptations of Hugo's two most significant novels.

Chesterton, G. K. "Victor Hugo." In his *A Handful of Authors: Essays on Books and Writers,* edited by Dorothy Collins, pp. 36-44. New York: Sheed and Ward, 1953.

An essay originally published in *Pall Mall Magazine* in 1902 discussing Hugo as a representative of two nineteenth-century movements—Romanticism and democracy. Chesterton writes, "In *Notre-Dame de Paris* he revealed to the modern world all the beauties and terrors of the old medieval order, and showed how pitilessly the individual was sacrificed to such an order."

Flaubert, Gustave. Letter to Louise Colet. In his *The Letters of Gustave Flaubert: 1830-1857,* edited and translated by Francis Steegmuller, pp. 193-94. Cambridge, Mass.: Harvard University Press, Belknap Press, 1980.

A letter dated 15 July 1853 praising *Notre-Dame de Paris.* According to Flaubert: "What a beautiful thing *Notre-Dame* is! I lately reread three chapters in it, including the sack of the church by the beggars. That's the sort of thing that's *strong!*"

Grant, Elliott M. "Romantic Victory." In his *The Career of Victor Hugo,* pp. 44-64. Cambridge: Harvard University Press, 1946.

Sees *Notre-Dame de Paris* as a work of imagination, poetry, and romance, but concludes: "In spite of these undeniably splendid qualities, *Notre-Dame de Paris* cannot be considered a first-rate historical novel, for the characters are not genuinely representative [of the era depicted]. . . . Like *Hernani, Notre-Dame de Paris* belongs to serious literature only because of Hugo's extraordinary poetic talent."

Hooker, Kenneth Ward. "The Foundation of Hugo's English Reputation: *Notre-Dame de Paris* (1831-1836)." In his *The Fortunes of Victor Hugo in England,* pp. 27-42. New York: Columbia University Press, 1938.

Recounts the initial critical debate in England over the novel and its first translations into English.

Houston, John Porter. "Pure Poetry and Inspiration from Art." In his *Victor Hugo,* pp. 23-41. New York: Twayne Publishers, 1974.

Contains a section on *Notre-Dame de Paris* in which Houston discusses prominent themes and motifs in the novel, including Gothic architecture, fate, and images of the spider and the fly.

Levi, Moritz. "Victor Hugo, the Novelist." *The Forum* XXXIII, No. 4 (June 1902): 499-504.

Includes references to *Notre-Dame de Paris* in a general discussion of Hugo as a novelist.

Maurois, André. "Anankè." In his *Victor Hugo*, translated by Gerard Hopkins, pp. 166-75. London: Jonathan Cape, 1956.

A biographical and critical sketch associating people and events in Hugo's life with the novel and examining Hugo's conviction that *anankè* is a controlling force in the world.

Maxwell, Richard. "City Life and the Novel: Hugo, Ainsworth, Dickens." *Comparative Literature* XXX, No. 2 (Spring 1978): 157-71.

Examines the influence of *Notre-Dame de Paris* on representations of London in the novels of William Harrison Ainsworth and Charles Dickens.

Mehlman, Jeffrey. "Literature." In his *Revolution and Repetition: Marx, Hugo, Balzac*, pp. 42-125. Berkeley and Los Angeles: University of California Press, 1977.

Includes a textual analysis of *Notre-Dame de Paris* in a larger discussion of depictions of French political revolutions in literature, notably in Hugo's *Quatre-vingt treize*.

Moore, Olin H. "How Victor Hugo Created the Characters of *Notre-Dame de Paris*." *PMLA* LVII (March 1942): 255-74.

Traces the evolution of the principal characters of the novel through an examination of Hugo's notes and manuscripts.

Reinhard, Joakim. "Victor Hugo's Novels." *The Sewanee Review* VII (1899): 29-47.

Contends that, with *Notre-Dame de Paris*, Hugo became "one of the first writers of fiction to reveal a perception of the artistic possibilities inherent in the preservation of the unity of place or, rather, of atmosphere, in a novel."

Richardson, Joanna. "The Man." In her *Victor Hugo*, pp. 1-114. New York: St. Martin's Press, 1976.

Considers *Notre-Dame de Paris* and contemporary nineteenth-century responses to it within a discussion of Hugo's career.

Smith, G. Barnett. "*Notre-Dame de Paris*." In his *Victor Hugo: His Life and Work*, pp. 65-76. London: Ward and Downey, 1885.

A biographical and critical sketch concluding that "in eloquence, in vigour, in animation, and in all the masterly pageantry of a bygone age, [*Notre-Dame de Paris*] will continue to hold a unique position amongst symbolical and historical romances."

Ullmann, Stephen. "Some Romantic Experiments in Local Colour." In his *Style in the French Novel*, pp. 40-93. New York: Barnes & Noble, 1964.

Examines Hugo's use of archaic diction and grammar to achieve local color in *Notre-Dame de Paris*.

Fitz-James O'Brien

1828?-1862

Irish-born American short story writer, poet, dramatist, and essayist.

O'Brien was a versatile contributor to the popular magazines of his time, but he is today remembered exclusively for his fantastic stories, two of which, "The Diamond Lens" and "What Was It?", are considered classics of the form. O'Brien's tales of the fantastic, which also include "The Lost Room" and "The Wondersmith," are esteemed for their highly inventive plots. In addition, critics often note O'Brien's pseudoscientific presentation of the fantastic and his use of eccentric, if not insane, narrators, techniques that link his works with those of Edgar Allan Poe; however, while Poe's tales are generally indefinite in setting and laden with Gothic atmosphere, those of O'Brien feature recognizable contemporary backgrounds and display an overall realism that distinguishes them from earlier works of fantastic literature. For these qualities of his stories, O'Brien is credited with anticipating the methods of subsequent authors of fantasy and science fiction.

Biographers know little about O'Brien's early life. He was born in Cork, Ireland, to James and Eliza O'Brien. Following his father's death, his mother remarried and moved with her then fifteen-year-old son to Limerick. During O'Brien's six years there, some of his poems were published in Irish newspapers, the earliest one appearing in a Dublin weekly when he was sixteen. In 1849, after receiving an inheritance of about 8,000 pounds, O'Brien moved to London and began pursuing a literary career in earnest, regularly contributing essays and poems to periodicals. In 1851, his first story, "An Arabian Night-Mare," was published in Charles Dickens's *Household Words*, and also during this year he edited the *Parlour Magazine of the Literature of All Nations,* a temporary publication devoted to the Great Exhibition held in London. During the two-and-a-half years that he was in England, O'Brien lived extravagantly and spent most of his inheritance. When he moved to New York City in 1852, he continued to live lavishly. He soon became a favorite member of the bohemian literary circle that met at Pfaff's Cellar on Broadway and often passed long evenings of writing, dining, and drinking in their company. His first writings published in America appeared in the comic magazine the *Lantern,* and he contributed to this periodical throughout 1852. Early the next year, O'Brien began his most important literary association when one of his essays appeared in *Harper's New Monthly Magazine*; over the next nine years, he steadily contributed numerous stories, poems, and articles to this periodical. Two other magazines that figured prominently in his career were *Putnam's Monthly* and the *Atlantic Monthly,* the latter of which published his best-known story, "The Diamond Lens." Soon after the outbreak of the American Civil War in 1861, O'Brien enlisted in the Union army. He was fatally wounded the following year.

As a contributor to the mass-circulation periodicals of his day, O'Brien wrote for a general audience, and his short fiction assumes such forms as the sentimental romance, the Dickensian Christmas story, and the fantastic tale. It is in this last category, according to critics, that his best works may be found. These stories, particularly "The Diamond Lens" and "What Was It?", have been praised for their depiction of extraordinary events made plausible by realistic and contemporary settings, a formula that did not become common in fantastic literature until later in the nineteenth century. Both works provided a model for realism in fantasy fiction. While "The Diamond Lens" takes place in a second story apartment on New York's Fourth Avenue, "What Was It?" is set in a New York boarding house, where two friends are beset by an invisible being of unknown nature and origin. The latter story preceded a number of influential works with similar plots, including Ambrose Bierce's "The Damned Thing" and Guy de Maupassant's "The Horla." Critics often note the dominant influence of Poe on O'Brien. Both authors shared a fascination with abnormal mental states and frequently used eccentric narrators who relate bizarre and horrific incidents. Like Poe, O'Brien also imbued his stories with an air of abstruse or pseudo-scientific learning to lend credibility to otherwise preposterous occurrences. These features are best exemplified by "The Diamond Lens," which portrays the mental deterioration of a scientist who constructs a powerful microscope and becomes obsessed with a beautiful microscopic woman. Athough O'Brien is considered among the distinguished followers of Poe, commentators agree that he did not reach his predecessor's level of artistry: O'Brien's narrative technique is often faulted as carelessly discursive and his dialogue as stilted and unconvincing. Nevertheless, O'Brien remains notable for his pioneering use of a realistic framework for his fantastic stories. While his other writings are forgotten, he continues to be regarded as an important innovator in the science fiction and fantasy genres. As Sam Moskowitz has stated: "Only when he turned to science fiction or fantasy did he begin to display the full force of his truly outstanding talents. . . . Though his output of such work was small, the quality is truly remarkable and its influence is still visible in today's science fiction and fantasy."

(See also *Dictionary of Literary Biography*, Vol. 74: *American Short-Story Writers before 1880*.)

*PRINCIPAL WORKS

A Gentleman from Ireland (drama) 1854
"The Diamond Lens" (short story) 1858; published in periodical *The Atlantic Monthly*
"What Was It?" (short story) 1859; published in periodical *Harper's New Monthly Magazine*
"The Wondersmith" (short story) 1859; published in periodical *The Atlantic Monthly*
The Poems and Stories of Fitz-James O'Brien (poetry and short stories) 1881
Collected Stories (short stories) 1925
The Fantastic Tales of Fitz-James O'Brien (short stories) 1977

*Most of O'Brien's poems and short stories were originally published in periodicals.

R. H. STODDARD (essay date 1881)

[*Stoddard unfavorably appraises O'Brien's poems and stories.*]

O'Brien is not a poet. He was an exceedingly clever versifier, but I do not feel that he was a true poet. There is no sincerity in his work, which is as bright and thin as ice. He failed most, I think, when he was most ambitious; in other words, when he was trying hardest to be sincere. **"Sir Brasil's Falcon"** is a pretty fable, but it is not above the average of Willis's blank verse; and **"Kane,"** in which he groans for power, like Tennyson's organ, reads like the first draft of one of Taylor's labored and least happy Odes. . . .

O'Brien's stories . . . are rather remarkable than excellent. **"The Diamond Lens,"** which has been most widely praised, fails, as many of Poe's stories do, in non-recognition of that dread Power which the ancients embodied in Nemesis. They are informed with creative fancy, but are without conscience. If they have any prototypes, they should be sought among the fantasies of Hoffman, which are given over to the same imaginative lawlessness. Haste is evident in all that he wrote—impatient carelessness, and violated taste. (p. 44)

R. H. Stoddard, "The Best of the Bohemians," in The Critic, *New York, Vol. 1, No. 4, February 26, 1881, pp. 44-5.*

SCRIBNER'S MONTHLY (essay date 1881)

[*This anonymous critic views O'Brien's work as inconsistent in quality.*]

It was well for Fitz-James O'Brien, one of the cleverest of all the Bohemians, that he died a brave death in the second year of our civil war. A rebel shot ended an unhappy and ill-ordered life; and the world was willing to look generously on the brilliant promise of his early career as a writer—a promise which his riper years might not have been able to redeem with adequate performance. This is the impression left after a careful study of [***The Poems and Stories of Fitz-James O'Brien***]. . . . The startling cleverness of his work at its best, taken in connection with its commonplace feebleness at its worst, at first bewilders the reader, and then invites him to critical analysis. And when O'Brien's literary art is reduced to its primary elements, we cannot but be convinced of its unsoundness and—in a fair sense of the word—of its insincerity. Here is a man who, at times, has written so well that his achievements seem, at first sight, to surpass the models of their class; and who, on other occasions, has shown absolute shallowness of thought and poverty of expression. This cannot be called simply "unequal" work—that is, work of one kind, varying in degree of excellence. It is not homogeneous; it is of two kinds; and by the utmost stretch of courtesy or amiability in criticism, we cannot accept the inferior kind as the false product, because a man with a mind fine enough to appreciate a higher type of literature would never seek to do less worthy work. If he did it, it must have been because he could not help himself. Therefore, we suspect O'Brien's strong literary effects, and when we get behind their dazzle and brilliancy, we soon find the secret—which was once another man's.

It is not that O'Brien was in any way a plagiarist. He was not. But he had a strange power of absorption,—or rather of assimilation, to express an elusive idea in a slovenly manner. He saw what some earlier author had done; saw it was good; and at once set about doing better in the same line. When the moment of factitious inspiration was over, he dropped to the level of an honest mediocrity. This peculiarity is to be seen in all his charming yet disappointing short stories. He probably begins a tale as well as any master of the art; but the tale always ends, like a burnt-out Catharine-wheel, in a weak whirl and sputter that destroy the illusion and make us forget the fire. **"The Diamond Lens"** is his only story where the strength is sustained throughout, and this is largely because the construction is dramatic—in that the movement is steadily toward the final climax. When we read the opening pages of **"The Lost Room,"** we say: Poe never had a weirder dream, nor told one in language so rich and graceful. **"Tommatoo"** and **"The Wondersmith"** commence with descriptive passages that suggest a new Dickens, with a chastened English style. The first part of **"My Wife's Tempter"** is scarcely unworthy of Hawthorne. Yet before the end of any one of these stories we come to the real author, Fitz-James O'Brien, a good writer, who gives us fair weight of fiction for our money; but upon whom we look with some ill-will because we thought him a great genius, and he was not. (p. 471)

In his poems we see most of O'Brien himself. **"The Sewing-Bird,"** and **"The Finishing School"** are, perhaps, echoes of William Allen Butler's now almost forgotten success, "Nothing to Wear," or of some earlier prototype; but in his shorter lyrics we recognize the Celtic poet, simple, enthusiastic, healthily sentimental, writing verse of real singing quality, with odd Irish rhymes, technically false, true in assonance. The three stanzas of **"The Wharf-Rat"** make a wildly colored picture, hint at a story, and the one line that rings in the memory—

> "And a girl in the Gallipagos isles is the burden of his song"—

has something of the sea-swing in it that vibrates through Longfellow's poem of which the refrain is:

"A boy's will is the wind's will,
And the thoughts of youth are long, long thoughts."

The whole poem is worth quoting, and no other in the book gives a fairer idea of what O'Brien could do—at times. (pp. 471-72)

"Three New York Poets," in Scribner's Monthly, *Vol. XXII, No. 3, July, 1881, pp. 469-72.*

HENRY SEIDEL CANBY (essay date 1909)

[Canby was a professor of English at Yale and one of the founders of the Saturday Review of Literature, *where he served as editor in chief from 1924 to 1936. He was the author of many books, including* The Short Story in English, *a history of that genre which was long considered the standard text for college students. In the following excerpt from that work, Canby characterizes O'Brien as an unrefined but remarkable storyteller who achieved success through understanding and utilizing the methods of Poe.]*

[O'Brien] wrote numerous stories, in this fecundity anticipating the later short-story writers, perhaps because, like them, he was armed with the right technique for the purpose. [The volume ***The Poems and Stories of Fitz-James O'Brien***] . . . contains but a selection, but yet enough to form a fair estimate of quality. Some are love stories; others tales of remarkable or horrible incident; but the best and the most characteristic are narratives in which the supernatural is employed in an ingenious fashion to gain the effect desired. **"What Was It?"** (1859), **"The Diamond Lens,"** (1858), and **"The Wondersmith"** (1859), are the striking examples of this craft.

Although O'Brien's stories are contemporary with the tales of Mrs. Gaskell, they have a modern ring to them; except for a touch now and then of mid-century sentiment, they are scarcely old-fashioned. If we seek for the reason, we shall find it not so much in any external trait of style as in the skilful adaptiveness of the author. All his stories are somewhat suggestive of earlier masters. There is Dickens clearly in **"Milly Dove"**; Hawthorne in the same story; Lamb or De Quincey in **"The Dragon Fang"**; but reminiscences of the new-fashioned Poe lurk in every one. O'Brien was the first author to imitate successfully in English the methods of Poe. Viewed in its external aspects, this memory of his predecessor appears in such idiosyncrasies of tale-telling as the use of an abnormal hero who lives in an abnormal abode and is most irregular in his habits. Both authors, to be sure, were fair models for their own heroes, but Poe, possibly with Byron's aid, began the practice. Far more weighty, however, is another debt owed by O'Brien to the tales of the grotesque, a debt for structure. In spite of wayside palaverings, the best of his stories aim, in every part, straight to the end. The first paragraph implies the last. The mystery ends in a climax as vivid as it is impugnable. **"What Was It?"** is an account of an invisible man-monster who grapples with an opium-smoker in a New York boarding-house, and is caught. Poe might have been glad to conceive it. **"The Diamond Lens,"** through which a somewhat diluted Poe hero sees adorable Animula disporting in a drop of water, then loves her, and goes mad when, as the drop evaporates, his beloved dies literally beneath his eye—this story Poe would have approved, would have built up far better, and probably spoiled by an attempt at humor. As it stands, O'Brien is daring and original in the conception; the machinery which makes a story possible is all from Poe. In brief, O'Brien did what no one else in English had done before, really learned the Poe technique. If he was a little too slavish in his use of it, yet his ideas were sufficiently original to strike a balance, and the result is this, that his stories are still readable where less dependent tales have lost their savor.

But we have done scant justice to one of our pioneers in the short story if we leave him here. He died young; his best stories were written before he was much over thirty; their imitativeness might have been a prelude to an achievement like Bret Harte's, the exploitation of such characters as Dickens saw, by the new short-story method. As it is, although so fond of the *macabre,* O'Brien studies life as the novelists of his day were studying it, even when he looks through the glasses of Poe. Consider the pathetic love-affair of the cripple and the gypsy's daughter in **"The Wondersmith,"** the homely familiarity of the Twenty-sixth Street boarding-house in which the invisible monster is found, the definite New York which is the setting for so many of his stories. This is the manner, not of Poe's fancies, hot from the romantic movement, but of our own imaginings. O'Brien, it is true, succeeded only when he worked up his local color and his contemporary portraits under the stress of a sensationally grim plot, which fused all into one definite impression. But at least, in some measure, he was applying the impressionistic story, hitherto used consciously only in pursuit of the terror of the soul, to reasonably familiar life. Of **"The Diamond Lens"** and **"The Wondersmith,"** Mr. Winter says [see Additional Bibliography], "They electrified magazine literature, and they set up a model of excellence which, in this department, has made it better than it ever had been, in this country, before those tales were printed." Now Poe's technique had certainly been more original and more perfect, and Hawthorne's stories more fully charged with matter and with meaning. Surely, electrification could only have come from the example of a new story-telling used in tales which, for all their extravagance, had more of the common clay of life than was to be found in earlier examples of the impressionistic short story.

O'Brien's imagination might have carried him far, and did place him unquestionably among the ranks of remarkable narrators. The idea of **"The Diamond Lens"** is at least unique; the invisible man-monster of **"What Was It?"** is one of those conceptions which insure a story; but the plot of **"The Wondersmith"** is still more indicative of power. Mannikin toys are inspired by evil souls and empowered to flesh their tiny swords in the children who loved them. The imagination which conceived and moved this tale without absurdity did much, even in this very unequal narrative. There is nothing else quite like **"The Wondersmith"** in American literature. Hood might have done it, had he known how to tell a good short story; Hawthorne might have hit upon the fancy, and made the tale far more serious, more gloomy, more sententious, but scarcely so pleasing; neither could have blended so much life, imagination, extravagance in one reasonably coherent whole, and contrived to leave a very definite impression of the heart of the story. O'Brien, with all his journalistic carelessness, accomplished just that because, in his amateur fashion, he really understood Poe's technique for the short story. (pp. 282-85)

Henry Seidel Canby, "The Mid-Century in America," in his The Short Story in English, *Henry Holt and Company, 1909, pp. 280-98.*

FRED LEWIS PATTEE (essay date 1923)

[An American literary historian, critic, poet, and novelist, Pattee was a pioneer in the study of American literature. In the following

excerpt, Pattee comments upon a large selection of O'Brien's tales, marking their place in the development of the American short story.]

[The] spirit and the method of each [of O'Brien's tales] is such as to suggest instantly some other work. **"The Bohemian,"** for instance, recalls "The Gold Bug"; **"Baby Bloom"** and **"Belladonna"** read like travesties of the feminine romance so fashionable during the period; **"Baby Bertie's Christmas"** and **"A Screw Loose"** and **"The Child that Loved a Grave"** are after the Dickens Christmas-story manner; the first part of **"The Wondersmith"** is also redolent of Dickens, but the rest of it reads like a translation of a Hoffman tale of "The Sand Man" variety or "Nutcracker and the King of the Mice"; **"A Drawing Room Drama"** and **"Uncle and Nephew"** are manifestly French; just as **"A Nest of Nightingales"** is an Irish extravaganza, and **"The Dragon Fang"** an echo of the Chinese manner of narration. In **"Sister Anne"** he has his fling at the Fanny Fern school of fiction. Sister Anne, a romantic country girl, runs away to New York to be a poetess, but is advised by a gentleman whom she meets to turn to prose. "Write some pretty country sketches," he tells her. "You can call them 'Dried Leaves' or some other vegetable title, and they will be sure to succeed." Accordingly, Sister Anne creates a sensation with a series of sketches entitled "Lichens," under the signature of "Matilda Moss," is invited to Miss Ransack's literary *soirées*, prepares to publish books, and finally marries the great literary genius, Stephen Basque, who turns out to be the gentleman who had first offered her advice.

Too often has O'Brien's name been coupled with Poe's. The two men undoubtedly were alike in one thing: both wrote tales with journalistic intent, striving always for newness and variety and telling effect upon readers, and both were quick to make use of new discoveries and new scientific theories as literary material, pressing them to their logical ends. O'Brien clearly used the methods of Poe in such scientific fantasies as **"The Diamond Lens," "How I Overcame My Gravity,"** and **"Seeing the World."** Further, however, one may not go. Poe was an artist: O'Brien an amateur, groping toward art; Poe worked by deliberate intention—thinking, and analyzing, and seeing the end from the beginning: O'Brien improvised and wrought with flashes of intuition. Like all Irishmen, he could tell a moving ghost story, but his work even in this field is clumsy when compared with Poe's creations. Poe never gave the impression of hasty work, and seldom did he descend to melodrama.

Few have missed success by so narrow a margin as did O'Brien. Especially was he gifted with invention. **"The Crystal Bell,"** had its theme been carefully wrought out, would have been a story of power; **"The Diamond Lens"** is a conception as original as anything of Hoffman's. The device of the ferocious manikins in his **"The Wondersmith,"** the use made of hypnotism in **"The Bohemian,"** the gruesome episode of **"The Lost Room,"** and the invisible monster in **"What Was It?"**—a theme afterward used by Maupassant in his "Le Horla," and by Bierce in "The Damned Thing"—are all decidedly ingenious, but in each there is lacking something that holds forever the tale from the domain of masterpieces. In **"What Was It?"** for instance, the final cast made of the thing and the statement that this cast might be viewed in the museum is a fatal defect. Neither Maupassant nor Bierce would have made such an ending. Always is it the last touch that discloses the artist.

The best tales of O'Brien from the standpoint of modern technique are his **"A Drawing Room Drama,"** the one bit of his art that its reader does not finish with the last sentence, since it leaves him after the last sentence with a terrible and a strange surmise concerning the woman who has not been charged with guilt; **"A Terrible Night,"** with its unusual surprise ending; **"Uncle and Nephew,"** which is French in its lightness and vivacity of style; **"The Bohemian"** and **"The Diamond Lens."** Of this last and **"The Wondersmith,"** published in the early numbers of *The Atlantic*, William Winter remarked that "They electrified magazine literature, and they set up a model of excellence which in this department has made it better than it ever had been, in this country, before the tales were printed" [see Additional Bibliography]. The statement is too strong, yet it cannot be denied that O'Brien's tales in the mid-'fifties, with their lightness and freshness and brilliancy of style, were a marked contrast to the lumbering and moralized fiction then all too current. There was about them an exotic atmosphere, a newness as from strange importations from over the sea, a vivacity and lightness that is only described by the adjective "French." Undoubtedly in America their influence did far more than did the influence of Poe to take from the short story its heavy tread and its clumsy art.

And yet O'Brien is not a large figure in the history of the short story. He was an influence in a feeble decade and he brought elements that were greatly needed, but his reign was brief. He was an improviser, too headlong and excited to do work of permanence. He lacked sincerity, he lacked poise, and he lacked real taste, and taste is basically a moral quality. (pp. 157-59)

Fred Lewis Pattee, "The Decade after Poe," in his The Development of the American Short Story: An Historical Survey, *Harper & Brothers Publishers, 1923, pp. 145-65.*

EDWARD J. O'BRIEN (essay date 1925)

[*O'Brien was an American poet and critic who also edited numerous collections of short stories, including the well-known annual* The Best Short Stories *(1914-1940). Here, he remarks upon the merits of O'Brien's short stories, favorably comparing them with the works of Poe.*]

A young man who came to New York in the early fifties of the last century to make his literary fortune would have had one great immediate ambition, especially if he were a writer of short stories. He would have blushed with pleasure if he had been introduced to Fitz-James O'Brien, just as a young man who came to New York for the first time fifty years later would have written home with pride that Richard Harding Davis had shaken hands with him or that O. Henry had bought him a drink. Davis and O. Henry are not yet forgotten, but how many people to-day could tell you what stories Fitz-James O'Brien has written? And yet O'Brien seems to me rather more significant in our literary history than either Davis or O. Henry, and to his contemporaries he was little short of a god.

Good work, however, is always sure of a resurrection. Have we not witnessed in these days the acclamation as great writers of Herman Melville and Emily Dickinson and Stephen Crane? America has been led by Van Wyck Brooks, Waldo Frank, and others to seek for a usable past. In these writers, it finds at least part of what it is seeking, and while we are in a duly chastened mood, the time seems fitting to add to the roll the name of the most distinguished American story-teller between Edgar Allan Poe and Bret Harte. (pp. vii-viii)

[Fitz-James O'Brien's] literary life was exceedingly irregular and very productive. He had the energy, when he cared to use it, of a Dumas or a Balzac. His best is superb, and his worst shockingly bad. He thought he was a poet, and so did his contemporaries, but a charitable posterity will leave his poems decently buried. He was a tolerably successful hack-playwright, no better and no worse than the authors of most contemporary Broadway successes. He was a temperamental critic, excellent in general principles, wilful in their particular application. I think we need not exhume any of his criticism. His judgments on his contemporaries are as shocking as those of Poe. But what important contemporaries were living for either Poe or O'Brien to criticise? But the best of his short stories call for no apologies, except our own for neglecting them so long. His own public was more intelligent. (pp. x-xi)

Like Melville, like Poe, and perhaps like Hawthorne, his mobile face had a daemon in it, that haunted daemon of unfulfilled expression so common in the history of American literary life. These men are not only daemonic, but they have a preoccupation with the scientific. The Goncourts writing fifty years ago noted the existence of this mathematical daemon and forecast from it the present machine age of America, seeing such an unfulfilled abstract literature as a portent, and knowing its power. What the Goncourts found in Poe, this "science hallucinée," is present to an even greater degree in O'Brien. . . . You may call **"The Diamond Lens"** or **"The Wondersmith"** or **"The Lost Room"** as rococo as you please. They are rococo, and so are Poe's stories and Poe's poems. But we are beginning to perceive that there is something to be said for the Rococo. T. S. Eliot and Conrad Aiken and the Sitwells are now admired, and rumors of the Magnasco Society have begun to cross the Atlantic. Perhaps we shall have a Rococo Society of our own.

Well, be that as it may. What qualities of interest do we find in Fitz-James O'Brien's best short stories to justify us in reading them to-day? I should reply that they are the creative result of a very powerful intellect playing with considerable intensity upon an interior life of great depth and terror, and not only registering with precision its own reactions to its discoveries, but formulating a philosophy as daring as Poe's, if less outspoken. The daemonic quality in O'Brien sprang from as potentially powerful an energy as that of Poe or Melville, but it is less direct because less concentrated. Nevertheless, neither man has forecast the machine soul more powerfully than O'Brien did in **"The Wondersmith"** when he spoke of that artificial eye with "a fearful speculative light in its iris." His puppet life of evil full of unreality and phantasmagoria reflects the fear that is in so many writers who followed him in all countries, and his jaunty air of improvisation with all its freshness and fertility of imagination suggests the assumed ease of a thoughtful whistler exorcising doom. Like Poe, his stories have the same passionate love of phantom women, the same madly rational motive of crime, the same artificial defences against any revelation of the writer's personality. (pp. xi-xiii)

Edward J. O'Brien, in an introduction to Collected Stories, *by Fitz-James O'Brien, edited by Edward J. O'Brien, Albert & Charles Boni, 1925, pp. vii-xiii.*

PAUL FATOUT (essay date 1931)

[Fatout contends that O'Brien's potential for literary greatness was undermined by his hasty writing methods and fondness for socializing.]

[Fitz-James O'Brien] wrote as he lived—erratically, sometimes at a sticky table surrounded by the din of clattering beer mugs and the roar of cameraderie. . . . Latent within him was a constant fund of creative energy which he tapped at will. But he burned with no gem-like flame; the talent he undoubtedly owned was inhibited by his love for sociability. His muse was no jealous mistress but a complacent companion to whom good fellowship and libations were fit substitutes for literary endeavor. (p. 54)

His methods were those of the newspaper man who hammers out copy against time while a copy boy waits at his elbow to snatch each sheet the moment it is finished. . . . Perhaps, had he been weaned from these methods; perhaps, had he taken his writing more seriously; perhaps—but it is useless to conjecture what might have happened. He was brilliant and slapdash; an aristocrat and a Bohemian; a *bon vivant* torn between the demands of literature and of life; and he was a better teller of tales than any about him.

Like Poe and Hoffman, whom he had met in his early reading, he had an active imagination which led him into the fantastic, the bizarre, the pseudo-scientific. He filled his stories with horrible and insane elements. Thus, **"The Diamond Lens"** tells of the inventor of a super microscope who falls in love with a microscopic woman whom he finds in a drop of water. To gain possession of a valuable lens he murders its owner as cold-bloodedly as Montresor walled up Fortunato. Then, when the drop evaporates and his atomic inamorata died, he goes mad. . . . **"The Bohemian,"** like "The Gold Bug," revolves about buried treasure, adds mesmerism, and drives the heroine to death. **"The Lost Room"** with its somber setting, ghostly visitants, and weird music is reminiscent of "The Fall of the House of Usher."

Following these paths of disorder, the same paths that led Poe into case books, the reader wonders why O'Brien, apparently a citizen of the real and not the shadow world, a man with an excess of animal spirits, should make excursion after excursion into the territory of the morbid and the supernatural. Such travels are grist for the mills of literary alienists. Joseph Wood Krutch, the man who gave Poe a virulent inferiority complex, has suggested that O'Brien was abnormally sensitive, a little deranged nervously, and possibly neurotic. (pp. 55-6)

At its best O'Brien's writing ripples along in succinct, crisp sentences. The style is clipped. Compression is evident. Thus, **"My Son, Sir!"** dashes off with precipitate speed:

> He had come up, years upon years ago, to the metropolis a poor friendless boy. Ran off errands in a wholesale store for a couple of years. Got promoted to a clerkship. Scraped money together, and then set up for himself in some extraordinary business or other—making elastic insertions for ladies' boots, I think it was—and when his hair began to turn, had, by dint of boldness, perseverance and good luck, made about half a million of dollars.

"The Diamond Lens" concludes tersely:

> They now say that I am mad; but they are mistaken. I am poor for I have neither the heart nor the will to work; all my money is spent, and I live on charity. Young men's associations that love a joke invite me to lecture on Optics before them, for which they pay me, and laugh at me while I lecture. "Linley, the mad microscopist," is the name I go by.

"The Lost Room" begins with admirable short strokes that effectively brush in a background of suspense and expectancy:

> It was oppressively warm. The sun had long disappeared, but seemed to have left its vital spirit of heat behind it. The air rested, the leaves of the acacia-

> trees that shrouded my windows hung plume-like on their delicate stalks. The smoke of my cigar scarce rose above my head, but hung about me in a pale blue cloud, which I had to dissipate with languid waves of my hand.

But the shadows of importunate landladies fall intermittently athwart his lines and disconcert him. He blunders into paragraphs of stilted conversation, he stops his story to introduce irrelevant love motifs, he becomes fatuously sentimental, he ends with a moralizing flourish. Artist enough to know that these were imperfections, he yet did not prune them out because he did not have to. He himself realized the prostitution of his talent by the uncritical enthusiasm of editors for his work and by interfering circumstances of social obligations, circumstances he was too fond of to combat. **"The Enchanted Titan,"** published in *Harpers* in February, 1861, may well be a cry of distress, the ages-old cry of a frustrated sensitive man:

> Curse you! O, a hundred thousand curses
> Weigh upon your soul, you black enchanter!
> Could I pour them like the coin from purses,
> I would utter such a pile instanter
> As would crush you to a bloody pulp.
> But my rage I fain am forced to gulp;
> Anathemas are vain against cold iron,
> Nor can I swear this magic box asunder,
> Where I've been stifling since the days of Chiron,
> Fretting on tempered bolts, and hurling muffled thunder.

(pp. 57-8)

Paul Fatout, "An Enchanted Titan," in South Atlantic Quarterly, *Vol. XXX, No. 1, January, 1931, pp. 51-9.*

ANITA MOFFETT (essay date 1932)

[Moffett compares the works of O'Brien with those of Poe, focusing on the authors' mutual interest in fear.]

It is one of the mysteries of literature that one writer should survive to a later generation while another, as well or better known in his own time, is neglected or forgotten. No less strange is the way in which the revolving wheel of chance brings back to renewed favor one who has been temporarily in eclipse.

Fitz-James O'Brien is an example of this inconstancy of fortune. . . .

"The Diamond Lens" and **"The Wonder-smith"** perhaps exhibit best the quality of O'Brien's imagination. . . .

In [both of these stories] there is a strange blend of outmoded phraseology and idea, with thoughts genuinely and daringly penetrating. The fantasy at its highest point balances perilously on the edge of the ridiculous, yet somehow always maintains its equilibrium. The reader is always struck by the prodigality of the author's imaginative invention. Ideas and fancies bubble upward continuously from an apparently inexhaustible source. Each might be the nucleus of a full story by an author more parsimonious with his material.

The comparison of O'Brien with Poe, so often made, suggests analogies and differencs. Both explored psychological territory that in their time was all but unknown. It is interesting to consider how a modern writer might recast one of the stories in this volume, **"The Golden Ingot,"** as a psychological study without changing an incident in its plot. Both men were preoccupied with the fascination of fear. "I feel my capacity," says one of O'Brien's characters, "to experience a terror greater than anything yet conceived by the human mind—something combining in fearful and unnatural amalgamation hitherto supposed incompatible elements." Whether the tale that follows, **"What Was It?"** retains its full force today must be left to the reader. For every one there is some individual source of terror. Poe found it in the idea of burial alive. In O'Brien's own work some readers may find their strongest impression of the sinister in the slaughter of the birds by the manikins, when "the feathery rustlings became fewer and fainter, and the little pipings of despair died away."

More sound in health than Poe, and in touch with the more pleasurable experiences in life, O'Brien perhaps did not depict the opposite extreme of horror with Poe's appalling intensity of conviction. Nor did he show (or, perhaps, trouble to show) the same capacity for following a train of purely abstract reasoning to its end. In their philosophy the approach of both was the poetic one; both relied on the validity of intuition in the attempt to grasp ideas which lie (in Poe's phrase) "out of the brain of man." Poe, in "Eureka," explained in detail the cosmic system he had worked out; among superseded theories and mistaken deductions he successfully seized upon ideas regarded as valid today—the conception, among others, that "matter is motion, and motion is matter."

O'Brien makes no such attempt to chart the regions into which, at times, his imagination penetrates. What he sees there he shows in the form of parables, not to be pinned down too closely to any formula of explanation. The reader catches glimpses of an unearthly radiance, and, again, of sinister elements. He sees human mind and human ingenuity employed in inventing devices which become the instruments of their makers' evil will; worlds beyond worlds whose inhabitants undergo the equivalent of human suffering.

Anita Moffett, "A Forgotten Master of the Fantastic," in The New York Times Book Review, *September 11, 1932, p. 2.*

JOSEPH J. REILLY (essay date 1932)

[Reilly argues that although O'Brien's imagination rivaled that of Poe, his early death prevented him from fully developing his artistic abilities.]

One day in April, 1862, a young Irish lieutenant of thirty-four, attached to McClellan's army, wrote the following letter from Virginia, where he lay dying, to a friend in New York:

> The surgeons removed my shoulder bone and a portion of my upper arm. I nearly died. My breath ceased, heart ceased to beat, pulse stopped. However, I got through. I am not yet out of danger from the operation, but a worse disease has set in. I have got tetanus, or lock jaw. There is a chance of my getting out of it,—that's all. In case I don't, good bye, old fellow, with all my love. I don't want to make any legal document, but I desire that you and Frank Wood should be my literary executors,—because after I'm dead I may turn out a bigger man than when living.

That final pathetic sentence, half wish, half prophecy, was destined to come true, for the fame of Fitz-James O'Brien has survived the revenge of time's whirligig and steadily greatened until he is now known as author of some of the most remarkable tales in American literature. (pp. 214-15)

Like most men capable of original work, O'Brien was not ashamed to study the productions of other writers and to imitate their method and style when the humor seized him. He knew his Hawthorne and his Poe, and caught some of the latter's tricks with surprisingly good effect. He did not stop there but followed Poe back to E.T.W. Hoffmann to whom his obligations in **"The Wondersmith"** are unmistakable. Here his theme is of the kind one plans for children before an open fire, creating an atmosphere wherein marvels can happen because time and place are not. . . . The story made a sensation when published in the *Atlantic Monthly* but the reason is hard to find. It has neither Celtic witchery nor German glamour and lacks that touch of inevitable magic which gives soul to every authentic tale of ghost and fairy. Perhaps it was but a *jeu d'esprit* written after an evening with the "Serapionsbrüder" of Hoffmann, but in any event the conception is handled with no Celtic lightness and is as out of place in O'Brien's genius as a leprechaun in Wilhelmstrasse.

O'Brien treats a variety of themes, but they are markedly unequal in value. **"Tommatoo"** presents well-worn elements: a benevolent old Italian father, his beautiful daughter, and two suitors, one good, the other villainous, with virtue not compelled to be its own reward. **"Milly Dove"** is a sentimental tale in which King Cophetua, in the person of the great Alexander Winthrop, falls in love with a beggar maid in the person of Milly Dove who, pretty and scarcely out of her teens, is clerk in the candy shop of a New England village. **"The Golden Ingot"** is a tale of alchemy, whose possibilities one might suppose to have been exhausted generations before had not Balzac employed it in one of his greatest novels. In **"The Pot of Tulips,"** O'Brien turns to the ghost story; in **"My Wife's Tempter"** to the diabolical influences of Mormon propaganda, a subject more intriguing in his day than in ours. In **"The Lost Room"** he invades the realm of visions and beholds men and women in the garb of earlier centuries holding high revelry, only to see them melt away again into thin air. Perhaps O'Brien had delved into the "Gesta Romanorum" and found a romantic appeal in the story which William Morris was later to tell as "The Writing on the Image."

In **"The Bohemian,"** a more distinguished story than these others, the theme is mesmerism, a tempting morsel for every delver into the weird, which in treatment is under obvious obligations to Hawthorne's "The Birthmark." Philip Brann (the Bohemian) possesses mesmeric power and finds a susceptible subject in Annie Deane, the fiancée of Henry Cranston. When hypnotized the girl makes revelations regarding a lonely spot in which treasure has been concealed for years. The cupidity of Brann and Cranston is satisfied when their expedition in quest of the booty is successful but the price is tragically high; for Miss Deane, whose nervous energies are depleted by the trance, fails to rally and dies in her repentant lover's arms.

The ethical undercurrent of the story is evident in Annie's appeal to her lover to forego the quest. One recalls "The Birthmark," the trepidation of Georgiana at her husband's desire to remove the crimson stain from her cheek; his insistence and her loving acquiescence; the seeming success at first and the tragic dénouement. Cranston on the one hand and Aylmer on the other risk the lives of the women they love, the one to gain wealth, the other to gratify his ideal of beauty, and the selfishness of each incurs a swift and terrible punishment.

In **"Mother of Pearl,"** O'Brien owes nothing to either Hoffmann or Hawthorne but much to Poe. The story recounts the marriage of the narrator with a beautiful American girl, Minnie, whom he meets while traveling in the East. When Pearl is born both love the child with equal passion. On their return to America all is well for a time but gradually an unaccountable languor succeeds Minnie's exuberant vitality and arouses the apprehensions of her husband. A holiday is planned to New York, where they attend the theater and see Matilda Heron (an actress whose wild genius O'Brien admired) in a performance of "Medea." Minnie is profoundly affected; her eyes never wander from the stage, her face is tense and her body sways with emotion. . . . That night the husband unaccountably awakens to find his wife bending over him with a dagger in her hand. He has barely time to draw his body aside and escape the plunging weapon. To his upbraiding his wife responds with stoical indifference, while he, bewildered, feels his love turn to loathing. He hastens home with her and lays her case before a physician, who takes up his residence with the hapless couple and devotes himself to a study of Minnie while the husband finds some measure of consolation in Pearl. . . . One night the two men sit talking late. Outside the mournful autumn winds stir the dead leaves and "chilly draughts come from unseen crevices, blowing on back and cheek till one feels as if some invisible lips were close behind, pouring malignant breaths on face and shoulder." Suddenly they hear a sound which fills them with vague terror. Springing to their feet they fling open the door and behold the figure of Minnie approaching, tall and white, a candle in her hand, her gown spotted with blood. She has murdered Pearl. She makes her awful confession calmly, smoothing her hair with her blood-stained fingers. While residing in India she contracted the hasheesh habit which gradually bound her as with chains of steel; the greenish paste became her very existence. It was while under its influence that she attended the performance of "Medea" with her husband in New York, and

> from that instant, murder became glorified in her sight. . . . Her soul became rapt in the contemplation of the spilling of blood. I was to have been her first victim, Pearl her second. She ended by saying, with an ineffable smile, that the delight of the taking away of life was beyond imagination.

The tale concludes with a paragraph technically superfluous, but interesting because so clearly reminiscent of De Quincey's celebrated apostrophe to opium in his "Confessions."

Throughout this tale, we have numerous proofs that O'Brien had studied Poe to advantage. Minnie is of the type so common in Poe, slender, beautiful, high strung, with large dark gray eyes, transparent skin, and mobile features. Her sinuous body possesses a strange and subtle grace; her voice is low, sweet, and musical. Quite in the manner of Poe, O'Brien pictures the gradual change by which her buoyant joyousness fades into lassitude which, in turn, lapses into a brooding melancholy. He achieves an atmosphere (again like Poe) surcharged with impending disaster and in the effective concluding tableau O'Brien has in his eye "The Fall of the House of Usher." In each case there are two men (a brother with Poe, a husband with O'Brien) with nerves wrought to the breaking point; the time is the fateful hour of midnight; the autumn winds sigh mournfully outside; a sound is heard which chills the listeners' hearts, and the door, flung wide, reveals the apparition of a woman whose white garments are stained with blood.

It is a pity that O'Brien did not follow his model in rigidly excluding all non-essentials. Poe would have foregone the incident in which the infant Pearl is rescued from a shark by a Malay diver and have resisted the temptation to discuss histrionic art at the performance of "Medea." Had O'Brien's exuberant genius been schooled to a stricter literary abstinence **"Mother of Pearl"** might have ranked as one of the best tales of its type in American literature. But O'Brien was his own man after all and it was not of his genius in his ebullient twenties to accept restraints, even artistic ones, with resignation.

To judge the brilliant young Irishman adequately, we should consider his two best tales, **"What Was It?"** and **"The Diamond Lens."** It is these which won him fame during life and on which rests his chief claim to an abiding place in the history of the American short-story. **"What Was It?"** was written at odd moments in the lodgings of his friend Thomas Bailey Aldrich and like **"Mother of Pearl"** shows clearly the influence of Poe.

The teller of the tale, when about to fall asleep one night, feels something drop as if from the ceiling upon his chest and two bony hands encircle his throat. The suddennness of the attack for a moment disconcerts him, but he regains his self-possession and struggles desperately in the darkness, until at last the murderous visitant is over-powered and pinioned on the bed. The victor, gasping, gets to his feet and turns on the light only to feel his brain reel as he beholds—nothing.

> I had one arm firmly clasped around a breathing, panting, corporeal shape; my other hand gripped with all its strength a throat as warm, and apparently fleshy as my own, and all in the bright glare of a large jet of gas, I beheld absolutely nothing!. . . Imagination in vain tries to compass the awful paradox.

The creature is bound with cords which rise and fall with its breathing while the clothes shake with its convulsive efforts to escape. The next day the strange thing is anaesthetized and a mold made which discloses its form.

> It was shaped like a man,—distorted, uncouth, and horrible—but still a man. It was small, not over four feet and some inches in height, and its limbs revealed a muscular development that was unparalleled. Its face surpassed in hideousness anything I had ever seen. . . . It was the physiognomy of what I should fancy a ghoul might be. It looked as if it was capable of feeding on human flesh. . . .

As the days pass pathos is added to horror for there is no way of feeding the strange creature whose struggles for life grow hourly weaker. At last it dies and is hastily buried, still a thing of mystery, sinister and invisible.

There is a fascination about this tale which still remains, and it is worth noting that Ambrose Bierce, the inheritor of Poe's mantle in our generation, has not hesitated to follow O'Brien's lead in at least two of his stories, "The Damned Thing" and "Stanley Fleming's Hallucination."

What O'Brien's story might have become in Poe's hands one may easily conjecture. That the Irishman had the American in mind as he wrote is obvious in more instances than one. It was in the manner of Poe to make the narrator and his friend Dr. Hammond opium addicts, and it was in the manner of Poe (and reminiscent of De Quincey) to picture the two hedonists winning from the drug the secret of its ultimate and most exquisite delights. Like Poe also are O'Brien's occasional affectations, his pretenses of excursions into the recondite. O'Brien has his raconteur, lying on his bed, courting sleep, read a "History of Monsters,"—"a curious French work which I had lately imported from Paris."

One smiles, perhaps approvingly, at O'Brien's cleverness in imitating the American's tricks. It was unfortunate that he failed to master his artistry! Never would the crafty Poe have permitted a plaster cast to be made of The Thing (he made no mistakes after "Berenice") any more than he revealed the ghastly secrets of the Pit or secured a daguerreotype of the reincarnated Ligeia!

A portrayal of a scene from "What Was It?"

It was in *The Atlantic Monthly* for January, 1858, that O'Brien published his masterpiece, **"The Diamond Lens."** Here his imagination, if not more daring than in **"What Was It?"** took a longer flight and deserves the conspicuous place universally granted it for originality of conception, sustained interest, and poetic fancy.

"The Diamond Lens" is the story of a man whose interest in optics has become a very passion until he dreams of a lens so perfect as to defy all obstacles and to penetrate the wonders of a life whose infinite minutiae have thus far escaped the investigations of science. He consults a medium (a vulgarism, alas, of which the fastidious Poe would never have been guilty) and under the spur of her disclosures seeks out the Jewish Simon, owner of a perfect diamond. Though put on his guard by his visitor's questions, Simon is not immune to the vintage of '48, and finally produces his treasured stone, which shimmers under the lamp as if "all the glories of light, ever imagined or described, were pulsating in its crystalline chambers." The half-drunken Simon is stabbed to death and the murderer makes off with the gem.

During the following months he devotes night and day to transforming his diamond into a lens, and with infinite skill finally achieves it. Trembling with excitement he places it on its platform and adjusts it above a single drop of clear water. At first he beholds only a vast luminous abyss. Depressing the lens with infinite care "on every side I beheld beautiful inorganic forms, of unknown texture, and colored with the most enchanting hues," like clouds of the highest rarity which

> undulated and broke into vegetable formations, and were tinged with splendors compared with which the gilding of our autumn woodlands is as dross compared with gold. Far away into the illimitable distance stretched long avenues of these gaseous forests, dimly transparent, and painted with prismatic hues of unimaginable brilliancy. The pendent branches waved along the fluid glades until every vista seemed to break through half lucent ranks of many colored drooping silken pennons. What seemed to be either fruits or flowers, pied with a thousand hues, lustrous and ever varying, bubbled from the crowns of this fairy foliage. No hills, no lakes, no rivers, no forms animate or inanimate, were to be seen, save those vast auroral copses that floated serenely in the luminous stillness, with leaves and fruits and flowers gleaming with unknown fires, unrealizable by mere imagination.

Surely such a scene were fit abode for animate beauty; and as if in answer to the thought there suddenly emerged from out the silken vista a creature of ineffable loveliness.

> I cannot, I dare not [how often Poe "could not and dared not" but *did!*] attempt to inventory the charm of this divine revelation of perfect beauty. Those eyes of mystic violet, dewy and serene, evade my words. Her long lustrous hair following her glorious head in a golden wake, like the track sown in heaven by a falling star, seems to quench my most burning phrases with its splendors. . . . Her motions were those of some graceful naiad, cleaving, by a mere effort of her will, the clear, unruffled waters that filled the chambers of the sea.

Bewildered by this vision he steps back from his lens and his eye falls upon the tiny drop of water below it. What a harrowing thought possesses him! "Animula" (for so he names this radiant divinity) dwells worlds apart from him, in a sphere which only his magnified vision can invade, imprisoned in a drop of water. . . . Through the hours that follow his eyes scarcely leave the lens; rapture thrills him as he beholds her floating like a beam of light through the glimmering avenues of her dwelling.

He becomes oblivious of time; his life is absorbed in vain adoration. As well reach for the stars at night as for this tiny creature disporting in that luminous world at once so near and so infinitely far. He must break himself of this mad fancy before it destroys his reason. He tears himself away, seeks the world outside, and attends the theater only to leave in disgust and return to his lens—and Animula. But during his brief absence she has undergone a tragic transformation. Her face is now thin and haggard; her limbs trail heavily; the luster of her golden hair has faded. To him hers is a world forbid and the thought of his impotence drives him to distraction. The last throes come. He faints, to recover hours later amid the wreck of his instrument, shattered in mind and body. They call him madman now, but he insists that they are mistaken. He lives in poverty, but his memory dwells in that world apart where Animula had her brief but radiant existence.

The daring imagination which conceived this story reveals O'Brien at his best. From the moment when the diamond comes into the hands of the insane optician, the tale never falters or loses its poetic fire. For these virtues Poe might have been proud to claim it. But in structure it is weak—an indictment always true of O'Brien, never of Poe. How relentlessly the American, like a surgeon with his scalpel, would have cut away the visit to Madame Volpes, the medium, and pruned down the incident of Simon to a single paragraph! That done, he would have abstained, recognizing in many a touch a skilful student of his own methods. There is the preliminary self-disclosure in which the scientist declares that his fancy soars beyond the limitations of his microscopes and that, lying awake at night, he has dreamed of a lens so powerful as to pierce through all the envelopes of matter down to its component atoms. There is the marshaling of the names of great scientists to whom the homage of a devotee is paid; the discussion of references to scientific discoveries thrown off with the nonchalance of the savant; the confession early in the tale that the narrator "supposes he is mad; for every great genius is mad upon the subject in which he is greatest." In the murder episode moreover, Poe would have beheld a student of his "Cask of Amontillado." For here is the same cold-blooded determination to compass a murder, the same success in plying the victim with wine, the same skilful innuendoes, the same torment of soul deliberately inflicted on the victim, the same moral blindness on the part of the destroyer, and finally, the same diabolical minuteness in recounting the catastrophe, colored by exultation in the one case over the triumph of vengeance and in the other over the attainment of the coveted gem. In the description of Animula and her gorgeous dwelling Poe would have found a choice of diction and a poetic fervor worthy of his own genius, and yet vitally different; for here was no pensive melancholy such as darkened the soul of Poe, but an ardor by which O'Brien (and the universal Celt) claims kinship with the stars. (pp. 218-34)

With Poe melancholy was a habit of mind; his insistence that the finest poetry must be tinged with sadness was typical. O'Brien's melancholy was a phase of his Celtic temperament which, in the ardor of the moment, soars through the empyrean, only to plunge on the chill morrow into the slough of despond. We dwell, after all, in a world of brick and stone and mortar, of trials and sufferings and evil chance, and it is not written that the Celt should everlastingly forget the din of the market place and dwell with garlanded head among the fields of asphodel.

All of which must not be thought to imply that O'Brien was a mere dreamer of dreams. Even a poet may die for his vision and the brilliant Irish lad who offered his sword to the Government at the outbreak of the Civil War had, within a year, repaid with his ardent young life for the generous adoption of America. Scarcely more than a boy, he was dead in his early thirties before he had fully learned how important is form in literature and how rigid are the bounds which Art prescribes to the imagination even in its highest flights. What he might have accomplished had years been granted him, we can only conjecture. Perhaps he might have achieved a place beside the greatest of American short-story masters, sharing unchallenged honors with Irving, Poe, Hawthorne, and Bret Harte. (pp. 235-36)

Joseph J. Reilly, "A Celtic Poe," in his Dear Prue's Husband and Other People, *The Macmillan Company, 1932, pp. 214-36.*

HORACE GREGORY (essay date 1933)

[Gregory comments on O'Brien's strengths and weaknesses as a short story writer.]

[Fitz-James O'Brien's] stories show an inability to sustain an original intention, as though O'Brien, writing at top speed, had found himself too slow for the onrush of his imagination and had become impatient and bored before he reached the final paragraph. There is much of the actor's eloquence in O'Brien, the love of tinsel for tinsel's sake, and always the desire to bring his brief performance to a close by an unmotivated sword thrust of melodrama. O'Brien's rhetoric is completely justified in such stories as **"The Golden Ingot," "What Was It?"** and the group of sketches in which the Chinese conjurer, Piou-Lu, is the protagonist. In these his imagination fits in with the florid style of his day—Walt Whitman's editorials, the speeches of Daniel Webster, and the familiar idiom heard across the footlights of romantic drama, the popular diet of the nineteenth-century New Yorker. He could do much in the opening paragraph of a short story, perhaps more than any who have followed his craft, but once his atmosphere was created, he tired of the game. His characters—they are more like lay figures than human beings—are less substantial than Poe's. Often they are young gentlemen of leisure looking for excitement, which is found by looking down the lens of a microscope or purchasing a haunted house. The bare dramatic incident is presented, and from then onward the story is left to shift for itself. In his horror tales O'Brien remains skeptical throughout, but the very fact that he alone is unconvinced by the testimony of his characters carries conviction to the reader. In the semi-humorous fantasies of Piou-Lu, O'Brien's rhetoric is a delight, and the sketches have the same charm that is revealed in Victorian bric-a-brac.

Horace Gregory, "O'Brien's Tales of Horror," in The Nation, *New York, Vol. CXXXVI, No. 3525, January 25, 1933, p. 100.*

FRANCIS WOLLE (essay date 1944)

[Wolle provides a year-by-year survey of O'Brien's stories and a discussion of his poetry. For further commentary by Wolle, see excerpt dated 1945.]

With the appearance of **"The Two Skulls"** in the February [1853] number of *Harper's New Monthly Magazine* [Fitz-James O'Brien] began a series of writings for the Harper Brothers which continued, with what was for O'Brien a surprising regularity, until the time of his death nine years later. (p. 53)

The obituary notice in *Harper's Weekly* in 1862 does not mention **"The Two Skulls,"** but its author . . . says instead that the earliest of O'Brien's contributions which he "can now identify appeared in November, 1853. From that time until the month before his death, with a few short intermissions, almost every number contained something from his pen." (p. 55)

In the issue for November, 1853, only **"A Dead Secret"** exemplifies any one of the various styles in which O'Brien was accustomed to write, and it alone deals with the sort of material which later became a source of his strength. The first of O'Brien's mystery stories, this early example does not exhibit the finish of **"What Was It?,"** nor the power of **"The Diamond Lens,"** nor does it so definitely localize the setting as does **"Tommatoo," "The Pot of Tulips,"** or **"The Wondersmith"**; but it does, following the example of Poe, revel in the weird and gruesome, create a mystery which it does not solve, place its hero in an abnormal situation or an abnormal state of mind, and let him tell his story in the first person. **"A Dead Secret"**—one of those half-punning titles of which O'Brien is fond—refers to the secret of a dead man, a character in the story, with whose suicide the answer to the secret is lost. It also seems to apply to another dead man, a man who has been recently hanged, the man who is telling the story. This man, or man's spirit, or whatever one may call the yarn-spinning remains of a hanged man, describes the implacable pursuit and fiendish persecution to which he was subjected because his identity was mistaken for that of the man who had committed suicide. Although the story is too long and too melodramatic, the struggles of the hero to free himself from the relentless and ever-tightening coils of an inexplicable dilemma create suspense and sustain it to the end.

"The Two Skulls" is a very much less interesting production and serves as a far from promising introduction to the series of many distinctive pieces which it inaugurates. It tells of how skulls are measured by pouring shot into them, and then launches into a disquisition on the greatness of man, considering chiefly why a great man is disappointing to meet personally. (pp. 55-6)

[A poem that O'Brien wrote in] 1853 appeared in the September issue of the *United States Magazine and Democratic Review*. "**'Sir Brasil's Falcon'** By Fitz-James O'Brien" is the superscription which introduces a lengthy poem in blank verse, telling the story of a knight, who, when hot and thirsty at the end of a hunt, painfully filled his drinking horn at an almost dried-up stream. As he raised it to his lips, his falcon with its wing dashed the horn from his hand and spilled the drink. When this occurred for a third time, the knight angrily killed the falcon, and found out too late that the faithful bird had saved his life by preventing his drinking the poisonous slaver from the jaws of a dragon. The poem contains much ornate description, the interest of the author being largely in style. It is reminiscent of the romantic school as seen in Spenser, or Keats, or in the descriptive parts of the poetical romances of Sir Walter Scott. The method for a time interests, but the ornamentations are not in themselves of sufficient beauty to hold the attention through a too slowly moving story. (pp. 63-4)

"Belladonna," the first authenticated short story for [1854], appeared in the June *Harper's*. Oddly mixing many styles and moods, it is in spots delicately sentimental; in spots, slyly, lightly gay; and in many places, charming with the lovely smooth rhythms of a Poe's "Eleanora" (1842). As a whole however, it is far from deserving praise—the moods are too many, the touches not sure.

For the opening O'Brien used a method which grew to be more or less characteristic of him. He gives an initial setting definitely localized, realistic, and acceptable to the reader. From this he leads to places and incidents less acceptable and less familiar, carrying the reader with him by the confidence he has already established. In his best stories this is done with great skill; in **"Belladonna"** only an artificial and conventional example of it is seen. A guest visits his friend in his home, made happy by a lovely and loving wife. The host relates to his guest how he met and won her, and by so doing carries the reader from his familiar home to the scene of his penniless wanderings in France. This he follows with the story of his romantic courtship. Another point of O'Brien's technique, later many times repeated but first made use of here, is to have a proud but poor man as the hero. Although this is a conventional subject of the time, the details of poverty and the makeshifts to conceal it are often so circumstantially vivid that the reader, who knows of the author's easygoing shiftlessness and impecuniosity, is constantly tempted to give such details an autobiographical interpretation.

F. L. Pattee in *The Development of the American Short Story* makes the comment that **"Belladonna"** reads like a travesty "of the feminine romance so fashionable during the period" [see excerpt dated 1923]; and his suggestion receives striking support from references to the Fannie Fern school made by O'Brien over a year and a half later in the story **"Sister Anne."** The heroine, Anne Plymott, begins her literary career by writing verses over the name Filbert; later she writes a "series of sketches entitled 'Lichens,' under the signature of 'Matilda Moss'." Finally, she is advised to "write some pretty country sketches. You can call them 'Dried Leaves,' or some other vegetable title, and they will be sure to succeed." **"Belladonna"** and **"Sister Anne"** bear many points of resemblance to Fannie Fern and Fanny Forrester, especially in their oversweet sentiment and in the ridiculously forced and petty melodrama necessary to assure soft romantic endings; and, after the words of the author himself which have just been quoted, one would be justified in assuming that these stories are indeed satirical of their own style and method were it not that the same offenses of overdrawn sentiment and melodrama are repeated with perfect seriousness in other stories which are unrelieved by the humor that makes this one suspected. **"Tommatoo," "My Wife's Tempter," "Dora Dee," "Mary Burnie of the Mill,"** and **"Baby Bloom"** prove that where the question of melodrama is concerned, O'Brien sins as woefully and with as sincerely solemn a face as the worst offenders either of the 1850's or of the present decade. Besides, O'Brien was writing to make a living; and, as tenderly sentimental stories were certain of a market, he turned them out frequently, relying on his strongly marked imitative faculty to equal the most tearful of the women scribblers.

Largely sentimental also is O'Brien's next sketch, **"The Fiddler."** It is so obviously didactic that the autobiographical interest of the introductory paragraphs, depicting a young writer much cut up by an unfavorable review of one of his poems, is soon destroyed. (pp. 82-3)

[O'Brien's last story for 1854, **"Mrs. Macsimum's Bill,"**] is the first of a series of stories which deal, in what is usually a neatly concentrated form, with phases of life in fashionable New York society; and four more of them—**"My Son, Sir," "The Beauty," "A Drawing-Room Drama,"** and **"The Duel"**—appeared in *Harper's* during the next year. The plot of **"Mrs. Macsimum's Bill"** is a comparatively obvious one, dealing with the extravagance of the society woman, to meet whose expenditures the husband is forced to give out promissory notes and to contract unwise debts. Of course, there is the lover willing to destroy the note against the husband if the wife will pay the price he most desires. The triteness of the devices used to secure the happy ending—the husband overhears the lover's proposals and almost at the same moment receives news which retrieves his credit—would seem unconditionally to damn the story; but the artificial mould in which the whole thing is cast, together with the neatness with which each minor artificiality fits into and helps build up the total effects, is, in its kind, thoroughly admirable. It has the close-knit quality of a Scribe farce, and is French in the fine finish it applies to an inconsequential trifle. (pp. 83-4)

[In 1855, *Harper's Monthly* printed ten of O'Brien's stories]: four of which use New York society life as a background—**"My Son, Sir," "The Beauty," "A Drawing-Room Drama,"** and **"The Duel"**; four of which are sentimentally melodramatic—**"Baby Bloom," "Duke Humphrey's Dinner," "Milly Dove,"** and **"Sister Anne"** (the titles indicate the sentimentality); and two of which deal with the occult. These are **"The Bohemian"** . . . and **"The Pot of Tulips."**

"My Son, Sir" and **"The Beauty"** are companion stories, as are **"A Drawing-Room Drama"** and **"The Duel."** Although O'Brien had frequently written social satire both in prose and verse earlier than this, such satirical thrusts had been mocking and gay, directed for the most part against the foibles of social usage. This type of writing is perennial, and in the eighteen-fifties it was practiced with animated skill not only by O'Brien but by George William Curtis, Edmund Clarence Stedman, and other clever young men of the New York group. In **"My Son, Sir"** and **"The Beauty,"** however, he develops his satire not in a spirit of playful thrusting but with a cutting edge which seeks to accomplish the reform of dangerous customs sanctioned by the artificial conventions of the wealthy class. Such satirical attacks at false standards, at superficial codes of conduct, at the brutal selfishness of moneyed interests, and at effeminacy in the wrong places continued for the rest of O'Brien's life to be part of his product in both prose and verse. These first two stories, though sharply condemnatory in idea, are comparatively mild in method of presentation; for they are told by Mr. Troy, an old bachelor, who wishes to warn parents as to what will be the sad fate of their children if brought up in the midst of luxurious indulgence and educated in the most fashionable schools. In both cases the father fails in business and the child comes to a tragic end. The son of the first story becomes a drunkard and a gambler and is finally stabbed in a drunken brawl on the East Side. The daughter of the second story, having received the proper finishing at Madame Cancan's, has learned to do nothing useful. So when her father's swindling schemes fail, she becomes a beggar and a brandy sot and dies of delirium tremens. Both stories are interesting in their Thackeraylike pictures of the hollow mockery behind Fifth Avenue society, and in their tragic climaxes; but both are spoiled by the obvious moralizing of Mr. Troy in the final paragraphs.

The second pair of stories deal with dueling. **"A Drawing-Room Drama"** is brief and pointed, and though the material is that of melodrama, it is handled with such conciseness as not to force the note. Montaigne, jealous of the attentions of a reigning beauty to another man, challenges and kills him, only to learn that the slain man was, in secret, her husband. **"The Duel,"** which vividly describes an evening gathering at the Chrysanthemum Club in Broadway, builds up its interest step by step to the tragic outcome. Two companions are rivals in love. Drinking leads to tactlessness, tactlessness to insult, insult to giving the lie; the lie is followed by the blow, and the blow by the duel. Pistols unloaded by friends proving ineffective, they resort to swords. One friend kills the other and escapes to Europe. Up to this point the story commands the reader's attention; but when a paragraph is added telling how the victor dies of a broken heart for having killed his friend, the moral is overemphasized and the unity destroyed. Because it stops without moralizing, **"A Drawing-Room Drama"** shows the better technique. F. L. Pattee says that it is the one bit of O'Brien's art "that its reader does not finish with the last sentence, since it leaves him after the last sentence with a terrible and a strange surmise concerning the woman who has not been charged with guilt."

As a contrast to these stories dealing with the rich and dissipated society of a great city, the three sentimental stories deal with poor but worthy lovers of nature. Of these **"Milly Dove"** has the most delicate finish of style. In reading it one becomes conscious of other literary voices of the time—it is a Dickenslike idyll in its sentimental tenderness worked out by melodrama; it has the soft, finished cadences of one of Hawthorne's *Mosses from an Old Manse* (1846); it suggests Thackeray in its frequent intrusions of the somewhat genial author; and it contains details of flowers, of music, of panorama mechanisms, of philosophy—all to give an impression of much learning, in the manner of Poe. It is, as Joseph J. Reilly points out, a "sentimental tale of the 'Duchess' variety in which King Cophetua, in the person of the great Alexander Winthrop, falls in love with the beggar maid in the person of Milly Dove" [see excerpt dated 1932]. Of course, this pointing out such a wide variety of borrowings from sources so dissimilar is in reality calling attention to a type of constructive ability which was O'Brien's.

"Baby Bloom," which came earlier in the year, and **"Duke Humphrey's Dinner"** and **"Sister Anne,"** which followed, frequently depart from a strict adherence to the sentimental mood. **"Duke Humphrey's Dinner,"** in fact, contains just as much humor as it does sentiment and pathos; and in a contemporary notice is called, strangely enough, "a racy narrative of fashionable life." It seeks to arouse the reader's sympathy and pity for the young husband and wife, hungry and cold in their garret tenement, who have been used to better things; it would make the reader laugh at their jokes and at the airs they give themselves over the imaginary banquet they consume, while at the same time it would have him become teary at the bravery with which each beguiles his starving senses for the sake of keeping up courage in the other; it asks him to share Richard's glee when he procures two dollars with which to buy himself and wife bread and sausages; and it would have him tearfully rejoice when the long-lost friend unexpectedly appears to repay old debts and supply the young couple with a real dinner. The human sympathy demanded is merely superficial, and, though possible, the coincidence which brings about the denouement is melodramatically forced. The reviewer for *The Critic*, however, considers **"Duke Humphrey's Dinner"** "the one simple, natural, possible story" in [the 1881 collection ***The Poems and Stories of Fitz-James O'Brien***], preferring it to **"Mother of Pearl," "The Golden Ingot,"** and **"The Diamond Lens."** "This is full of a brightness and pathos which show, if not the burning of genius, at least the warmth of human feeling." (pp. 102-05)

Both the other stories, **"Baby Bloom"** and **"Sister Anne,"** have been suspected of being travesties "of the feminine romance so fashionable during the period." In the case of **"Sister Anne"** this has already been shown to be almost certainly true; but that **"Baby Bloom"** is travesty seems most unlikely. Sentimental melodrama was fashionable, and Fitz-James O'Brien was a facile complier with fashion. A rural Harlem village is the scene where lives Baby Bloom with her German parents—her father the taciturn harness maker, who spends much time over his pipe and his beer, and her fat mother, who busies herself raising chickens (a touch of the sly humor of Irving here). Baby's chief occupation is to be pastorally beautiful, picking flowers, until the carpenter's apprentice has an opportunity to see and fall in love with her. Baby then has an adventure with a maniac ornithologist, who drives her to seek refuge in the woods and pursues her in the most uncanny and terrifying way; and, when she is just about to succumb panic-stricken to his maniacal persecutions, she is rescued by the timely arrival of her loving apprentice.

The part played by the insane ornithologist, the suspense created by the abnormal pursuit, and the terror of uncertainty with which it is followed connect **"Baby Bloom"** with the occultism of **"The Bohemian"** and with the supernaturalism of **"The Pot of Tulips."** Not one of the three characters of **"The Bohemian"** is normal—the hero who tells the story is money-mad, the heroine is psychically hypersensitive, "a *clairvoyante* of the first water," while the extraordinary Bohemian is a mesmerist and mind reader. In addition to these elements of the uncanny, the story has the adventure interest of the search for buried treasure, and unusualness of atmosphere is suggested by direct references to Poe's "The Gold Bug." These things make the story interesting; but it is almost spoiled by a too early and too patent suggestion of the catastrophe and by such an obvious pointing of the moral at the end as "Below stairs, in the valise, lay the treasure I had gained. Here, in her grave-clothes, lay the treasure I had lost!" In its ethical undercurrent [according to Reilly] "it is under obvious obligations to Hawthorne's "The Birthmark"; as it is in the girl's initial hesitation, in her later acquiescence in risking her life at the instance of the man she loves, and in her sudden death as a punishment for his selfishness.

That O'Brien was familiar with both the prose and verse of Edgar Allan Poe, at least as early as his first year in America, was demonstrated by his imitation of Poe's poetic technique in **"Oinea"** and by his reference in the discussion thereof to "The Pit and the Pendulum." Though at first O'Brien seems to have been influenced by the weirdness and highly colored romance in the sensational Irish novels of Joseph Sheridan Lefanu, from the time he wrote **"The Bohemian"** and **"The Pot of Tulips"** the methods and moods of Poe became more and more unmistakable in his work.

"The Pot of Tulips" is among the best half dozen of O'Brien's stories. It is a ghost story, smoothly written and convincingly told. It assumes the pose of having been written solely for the purpose of scientific or psychic elucidation; and, by contrast, the terrifying effects are all the more potent. The settings are definitely localized and are entirely acceptable, although a Dutch villa on the Hudson could hardly fail to suggest Sleepy Hollow and Rip Van Winkle. The first element of the unusual is the fanatical jealousy of Mr. Van Koeren, the grandfather. This is followed by the tragic story of his son Alain, by the description of the queerly carved mantelpiece, by the arrangements for the night, and by the appearance of the ghost. The ghost is accompanied by a cold wind, a luminous cloud, and an odor of corpses, and carries in its hands a pot of tulips. The tulips are, of course, the clue to the family mystery, and the working out of the clue forms the last part of the story. The author sticks to his point with extraordinary singleness of purpose, introducing almost nothing to distract the reader's attention. Harry Escott, the narrator, is thoroughly plausible in his mediocrity, and at the end of the story he adds a postscript to the effect that any person "who wishes to investigate this subject, will find an opportunity by addressing a note to Mr. Harry Escott, care of the publishers of this Magazine." That the tale and its postscript were convincing is borne out by the following statement from *Harper's Weekly:* "Scores of letters, and not a few personal applications, were received, asking for means of communicating with Mr. Escott. I remember one young man, who called so often, and was so firmly convinced that in this narrative lay the germs of some great revelation, that I was compelled to tell him that the whole was a pure effort of the imagination. Unfortunately he would not believe me." (pp. 105-07)

It might have been supposed that with his apprentice work done . . . Fitz-James O'Brien would in the year which was to follow (1856) go on and produce some of his best work. Such, however, was not the case. He did not immediately follow up his early successes, and not for two years did he write anything of real importance or show any advance in his art. And yet by the end of 1855 he had written social satire, satirical invective in both prose and verse, literary criticism, plays, and short stories of both the supernatural and sentimental varieties. (p. 110)

Two of the stories [O'Brien wrote in 1856], **"How Nellie Lee Was Pawned"** and **"Mary Burnie of the Mill,"** are sentimental ones. The first of these is told in the first person, and begins with numerous circumstantial details about the prosaic life of the author. This method of introduction O'Brien had used before—in the preceding year in **"The Bohemian," "The Duel,"** and **"The Pot of Tulips"**—and with it he was to achieve some of his best effects—in **"The Diamond Lens," "Mother of Pearl," "The Lost Room," "The Golden Ingot," "My Wife's Tempter,"** and **"What Was It?"** In this way the reader is beguiled by a series of minor details and by the commonplaceness of the author and the setting to an unconscious acceptance of the later uncanny, bizarre, or supernatural incidents which form the nucleus of the story. A century and a half earlier the method had been perfected by Daniel Defoe, notably in "The Apparition of Mrs. Veal" (1705), but with the reintroduction of the supernatural into fiction with *The Castle of Otranto* (1764) and *The Mysteries of Udolpho* (1794) the practice had been to assume tacitly and immediately the reader's belief in the miraculous and the superhuman. This assumption continued to affect the writing of the romantic period of the early nineteenth century, as seen in the poetry of Coleridge and the horrors of "Monk" Lewis (1795) and Charles Robert Maturin (1820), until it reached a culmination of artistic handling in "The Masque of the Red Death" (1842), "The Tell-Tale Heart" (1843), and others of the grotesque tales of Poe. Fitz-James O'Brien, trying his hand at the story of weird and grotesque atmosphere at a time when the impulse of the romantic movement was on the wane, could not improve on Poe; and so, while imitating many of Poe's technical devices, he rediscovered and added what may be regarded as the modern touch of the commonplace setting. Thus he forms an important connecting link between the tale of terror and the methods of modern realism.

In the two stories at present under discussion, however, this method is made to subserve the purpose of sentimentalism rather than that of the macabre. For **"How Nellie Lee Was Pawned"** it is almost as necessary an introduction as it is for the weirdness of **"The Lost Room"** (1858); for the circumstance of the girl who was pawned by her artist father in order that he might raise money to buy canvas is as difficult of acceptance as is the tale of the man who, in his own house, one night extraordinarily finds his way into a mysterious room which he can never discover again. [**"How Nellie Lee Was Pawned"**], therefore, begins with details of the author's many dealings with the pawnbrokers of Chicory Street. As he is on his way to the shop of Lazarus Levi to see what he can raise on a chessboard, he tells incidents of his former life in London and in Paris and of having at one time written an article for *Blackwood's Magazine*. This time the author calls himself not Harry Escott but M. Papillote; and M. Papillote, neatly finished though his story is, is revealed as not nearly so skilled a raconteur as Escott, who was responsible for the uncanny relation of the mysteries of **"The Pot of Tulips"** and is used again as the narrator of **"What Was It?"**

"Mary Burnie of the Mill" also bears but little scrutiny in comparison with other O'Brien stories, though if compared with those of most of his contemporaries it stands high. Contrary to his usual practice in the sentimental type, O'Brien ended this story tragically; but, in accord with his practice, he definitely localized the idyllic setting and placed the mill on the Passaic River, New Jersey, thirty miles below its source. Here, at the overheard suggestion of Nellie Bryce, Mary Burnie, her rival, drowns herself in the milldam, so that she will not be a drag upon the man she loves. The moral at the end is as offensive as usual—Nellie (like the heroine of **"The Beauty,"** a product of Madame Cancan's finishing school) is revealed as essentially a murderess, and when her hero is butchered in one of the Central American wars, she comes to a realization of the justice of heaven.

Not only in prose, but also in verse—though here even less adequately—O'Brien was, in compliance with a constant demand of the magazine readers of the eighteen-fifties, working out the sentimental vein. In **"When We Husked the Corn"** the husband on his silver jubilee recalls the days of his wooing. It was corn-husking time, and the climax comes as follows:

Away you fled, and I pursued,
Till all too faint you were to warn;
And—know you not how well I wooed
A husking of the corn?

"How It Happened" is also a reminiscence of early love (probably they all hark back to "John Anderson, My Jo" and the older songs that suggested it, and will remain perennially popular, as the songs "When You and I Were Young, Maggie" and "Silver Threads among the Gold" would seem to indicate). It is neither good nor bad, simply typical, and ends on the same key as the above:

And now the white snow, come again,
Once more peeps through our window-pane,
And Ben and I sit side by side,
Nor has the flame we burned with died.

Such obvious, flat conclusions to such pallidly sentimental verses make one thankful that O'Brien indulged in so few tender poems; and it is a relief to turn to even such a trifle as **"The Crystal Bell,"** a story in which magic and oddity supply the keynote for a short dream. The author finds himself in possession of a bell which tinkles when anyone tells him an untruth. With it he tests the girl he loves; the bell tinkles. He denounces her; she smashes the bell; he wakes up; and the story ends, "I never told Annie Gray that I had ever doubted her even in a dream, until we had been a month married." (pp. 118-20)

[The poems **"What Befell"** and **"By the Alders"**] are two of the three macabre pieces that O'Brien wrote during the year 1856, all three, seemingly, having been written about the same time and probably from the same place, his New Jersey retreat. **"A Terrible Night,"** a story published in the October *Harper's*, is the third treatment of the gruesome and supernatural.

The nine stanzas of **"What Befell"** tell of a ghost or demon that snatched an eloping bride from the seat behind her lover as he spurred his horse "hard by the terrible gallows-tree." It is technically correct, but it fails to convey the horrible impression that was intended. **"By the Alders"** is weirdly and uncannily suggestive of evil impulses and of crime. A woman led her lover (who tells the story) to the riverside where she flung her babe into the water. For a moment he hid his head in agony, but when he looked up to cry, "Still loved, a pardon!" she was not there.

But I saw a dint in the weedy bed,
And I felt a ghost in the troubled air!

If the reader can safely get over the third line,

> She gripped my arm, she clutched my hair,

without ridicule, the gruesome atmosphere of the poem will establish itself.

The pity of it is that O'Brien's verse so often contains lines of just this sort; his sense of humor when he was writing poetry often failed him. His prose is always more successful, and **"A Terrible Night"** is no exception. It is a ghastly tale of lonesomeness and fear in the woods of northern New York, done with tremendous effect. The tension of suspense is most powerfully worked up and culminates in the horror of a most startling and awful surprise ending—an ending worthy of Frank R. Stockton, O. Henry, or any other of our most skillful technicians of the short story. In its dream horror it is the best of O'Brien's tales up to the time of its appearance in October; but it was followed in November by such a weak piece of sentimentalism as **"Mary Burnie of the Mill,"** and in December by such an inconsequential treatment of dreams as **"The Crystal Bell."** That O'Brien resorted so constantly to the flippantly satirical or the flabbily sentimental when he could be so vivid in the macabre was due to the unreliability of his taste and to his lack of self-discipline and unsteadiness of application, even in the field where he excelled. Also, as he was a free lance in the journalistic field, and as a certain volume of production with selling qualities was necessary to keep him alive, he turned out what came easiest to him and what would have the readiest and widest market. In the decade of the eighteen-fifties this was romantic sentimentalism; so for a time O'Brien joined the ranks of Donald Grant Mitchell and Thomas Bailey Aldrich (the best of the sentimentalists) and turned out "sob stuff," until, with the publication of **"The Diamond Lens"** (1858) and **"What Was It?"** (1859), his unique gift in the macabre was recognized. (pp. 121-23)

O'Brien contributed to the Harper publications during [1857] nine poems and five stories. **"Dora Dee,"** the first of the stories, is a melodramatic incident in three parts. Dora Dee, found in an ash barrel and adopted by a sexton, becomes the beautiful rival of the woman with whom she has a position as companion. Dora, driven out into the snow and the bitter cold, gets lost near Washington Square and succumbs near some stables on Fifth Avenue. Her lover follows her tracks through the snow, finds her, carries her home, and marries her the next morning. Totally forced and unreal, yet interesting as to plot, it is a horrible example of what was the popular literature of that day—or for that matter of the present. (p. 144)

This is matched in badness, and in a rhyming title—**"Helen Lee"**—by the worst poem of the year. It is so servilely imitative of Longfellow—of *Hiawatha* (1855) and *Evangeline* (1847)—that it becomes unbearable.

> Oh, the pleasant, pleasant autumn!
> How it seemed like spring-time to them!
> How the flowers budded, blossomed
> In their hearts afresh each day!
> Oh, the walks they had together
> From the singing schools and parties,
> In the white and frosty moonlight,
> In the starlight cold and gray!

So it goes on—with the description of the cornhusking and the country scenes like Whittier, and the use of similes pure Longfellow. If atmosphere is for a moment created, it is ruined almost immediately after by false, flat notes.

> When she sought her little chamber,
> Long she could not sleep for thinking
> Of his looks, his voice, his language,
> For the youth had turned her head.

The next to the last stanza leaves the bride smiling at her teasing husband Richard. Then, to end, Farmer Lee weeps and attitudinizes:

> "For I have not lost a daughter,
> But a worthy son have found!"

Up to this final moment there had been no idea that he had lost or would lose her. Why bring it up now?

With **"Dora Dee"** and **"Helen Lee"** the writing of Fitz-James O'Brien reaches its lowest point, which, it may be noted, coincides almost exactly with the halfway mark in his career of authorship in America. After this there is nothing so poorly done; everything shows a little improvement; and some of the things show marked power and become intrinsically valuable.

Of the other eight poems of the year all preceded **"Helen Lee"** except one. This one, **"Bacchus,"** in which the all-powerful god of drink extols the use of alcohol, is a parody of Emerson's recently printed "Brahma." The other seven are a miscellaneous assortment: **"What Santa Claus Brought Me"** tells a sentimental love story; sentimental too is **"The Little Maid I Lost Long Ago,"** an elegy written smoothly and delicately, and containing a touch of mysticism; **"My Valentine,"** has the clever turns of the half-sentimental, half-humorous *vers de société;* while similar in type is **"By the Passaic,"** a trivial, graceful, attractive *jeu d'esprit,* written in slyly elaborate verse.

The poem which on its appearance received the largest amount of contemporary comment is a memorial to Elisha Kent Kane. This arctic explorer died on February 16, 1857 "at Havana, Cuba, whither he had gone in the hope of regaining a health shattered by his sufferings in the north." On March 14 **"Kane,"** a poem in his memory, appeared in *Harper's Weekly*. This ode *The New York Times* calls "a piece of poetry full of dignity and beauty, and which strikes the highest note of all that O'Brien produced." Parts of it are unquestionably done with stately power, notably the third stanza and the vivid descriptions of the arctic trials in the sixth. The simile of the fourth stanza, however, likening Kane to an iceberg melting away in a southern sea, is too farfetched in its conceit to sustain the mood. The whole poem is sufficiently rhetorical to gain greatly when its periods are subjected to oral delivery. (pp. 144-46)

"A Summer Idyl" tells a love story with a certain frank sensuousness of expression very different from what was the habit of the New England group of poets. With the age-old combination of a mild night, the moon, a stream, and a girl, O'Brien makes an attractive setting, beginning

> It was a moonlit summer night;
> The heavens were drenched with silver rain;
> And frowning rose Katahdin's height,
> Above the murmuring woods of Maine.

Then follow the suggestions of the passionate situation so foreign to the Longfellow method of treatment; yet with what a delight of relief the subscribers to *Harper's* must have read in the details of the poem, reflections of their own—the eternal—love-making:

> Her stooping face, no longer wan,
> Flushed in the harvest-time of love,

and

> I drew her down upon my breast.

Already some of the readers were no doubt too much shocked to continue; but the rest finished it with:

And in the vague electric spark,
Felt ony when cheek touches cheek,
I knew through all the shadows dark
The promise that she did not speak.

Then, fortunately, O'Brien knew enough to stop, with only a repeated variation on the first stanza.

On the Fourth of July *Harper's Weekly* printed a patriotic poem which has since become well known under another title, through its inclusion in many school readers. It appeared originally under the caption,

HOW THE BELL RANG.
July 4th, 1776.

But since as early as 1883 it has always been entitled **"Independence Bell—July 4th, 1776,"** and it has from its first appearance continued to be printed anonymously. Fitz-James O'Brien, however, is the author. . . . The story of the boy who waits to notify his grandfather when the Continental Congress shall have signed the Declaration of Independence, and of the old bellman who rings forth the glorious news is so familiar as to need no retelling. Suspense is well sustained, and the subject is handled with such a vivid sense of the dramatic as to give a patriotic thrill. (pp. 147-48)

Of the short stories, **"Uncle and Nephew"** appeared a month after **"Dora Dee."** It is an interesting story, dealing with cases of monomania in the two chief characters, an uncle and his nephew. The abnormal states of mind are treated in Dr. Auvray's sanatorium, the setting being given with much circumstantial detail as to time, place, and character. First the nephew is insane and ties up his uncle; then the conscience-stricken uncle becomes insane, and the nephew is cured. The style is clever—"manifestly French," says Pattee—and the effect of short, seemingly irrelevant sentences is telling. The ways of insanity and the cures for it are, in the Poe way, written up with a great show of authority and learning.

Poesque, also, is the fantastic story of **"Seeing the World."** (p. 149)

The next story, **"A Screw Loose,"** in style, background, and names used is closer to the manner of "The Man about Town" [the column O'Brien wrote for *Harper's* in 1857] than to the startling extravagances of **"Uncle and Nephew"** and **"Seeing the World."**. . . [The] story, though depending on coincidence, is tolerably well told—"after the Dickens Christmas-story manner," as Pattee says. It is not so neat and compact, however, as the stories of two years earlier—**"My Son, Sir," "The Beauty," "A Drawing-Room Drama,"** and **"The Duel"**; and it is therefore with a feeling of progressive accomplishment that one returns to the weirdness of atmosphere which is uppermost in the last story of the year.

The interest in **"My Wife's Tempter"** depends on the fear of the unknown, the curiosity about the unsolved, which was growing to be typical of O'Brien. In this story it is secured by the use of the Mormons, whose proselyting activities, because of general ignorance as to their methods and their religion, inspired great fear in the popular mind. A Mormon ruins the happiness of a man's home, secretly converts the man's wife, and tempts her to run away with him. The story is too long, but the weird atmosphere is a worthy precursor to that of **"The Diamond Lens,"** which followed close on its heels as the first of O'Brien's output for 1858. (p. 150)

[**"The Diamond Lens"**] shows very plainly the use that O'Brien made of the Poe technique—what he learned from Poe and made use of, what he added, and in what points he was incapable of following Poe's example.

The plot of **"The Diamond Lens"** immediately takes advantage of the interest in scientific discovery and scientific speculation which characterized the mid-nineteenth century, and in its pseudoscientific way suggests the possibility and the far-reaching results of the finding of a perfect lens. It invents as its principal, almost its sole, character a man to whom such a search becomes a monomania, which stifles all other ideas and purposes in life and which blunts his moral sense. Under such stimulus he commits a cold-blooded, carefully carried-out murder. Through this crime he secures and creates the perfect lens, with the result that by its means he is able to see in a drop of water, moving there and having her being, the ideal of feminine beauty, the perfection of women. He calls her Animula and falls in love with her; but with ironic retribution, though he can watch her free, beautiful life as she moves within the water drop, he cannot communicate with her. Animula must remain for him a wholly unattainable ideal, and when, in spite of all that he can do, the drop of water begins to evaporate, he is forced to witness her gradual fading away. So brooding upon his frustration and consumed with longing for her, he becomes mad.

This is almost pure Poe. Un-Poelike, however, is the way in which O'Brien creates his mood of queerness, of unreality. Poe, by his use of suggestive, colorful, atmospheric words, in the first paragraph, in the first sentence even, secures the feeling of brooding horror, of impending doom. O'Brien, on the other hand, starts with a paragraph or two of details that set before the reader what, though perhaps not entirely usual, are nevertheless elements belonging to a perfectly acceptable and almost normal situation. The germs of the ensuing abnormalities are, of course, present, but it is only after beguiling the reader into a confident acceptance of his initial premise that O'Brien makes his transitions into the realm of the weird and supernatural. In **"The Diamond Lens,"** which is told in six parts, the entire first part is devoted to this purpose of inspiring faith in the storyteller and belief in the subject of his narrative. It deals with the curiosity and natural enthusiasm of a boy for a pet hobby, admits his egotism, selfishness, and colossal ignorance, and tells of his desire to get away from unsympathetic parents at home and of his accomplishing this by being sent to study medicine in New York. It should perhaps be stated that part of the apparatus for securing the "suspension of disbelief" is to have the hero tell his own story, to have the narration made in the first person—another particular in which O'Brien is imitating Poe. For that matter, nothing of the method just described is original with O'Brien; Defoe had shown the possibilities long before. But to O'Brien must be given the credit for showing how the Defoe elements could be successfully combined with the type of grotesque tale that Poe so highly developed.

Section two continues the story of Linley's settlement in a New York lodginghouse and of his development as a microscopist. All this is continued in a matter-of-fact way, but a few details, and more hints, are introduced which suggest that all is not quite normal. Finally, in the third section, in which is described a spiritualistic séance, the borders of the acceptable and natural are broken through; but any reader who has continued thus far will not balk at the supernatural spirit-rappings for which he has been well but subtly prepared by constant suggestions of the abnormal. Then follows the murder, and at last in section five the revelation of the radiant being, the infinitesimally tiny Animula. By this time there is absolutely no question of either acceptance or repudiation on the part of the reader. He is following the story for what it will give him, his curiosity is caught, he shares the emotions of the hero, and is as curious as is the latter in the discoveries to be revealed by the wonderful diamond. The sixth section gives the scientifically probable, tragic results of the discovery, returns to everyday life in telling of the hero's present situation, and ends with "They say now that I am mad; but they are mistaken."

The foregoing analysis has already indicated wherein lies what is perhaps the chief limitation which has prevented O'Brien from rivaling the power of suggestive horror and the artistic perfection of Poe. He lacks Poe's concentration; his stories are always just a trifle too long. Whereas Poe makes every word, every sentence, count in building up and producing a single unified effect, O'Brien by his very attempt to carry over from the acceptable to the impossible has to work in at least two moods. This makes for discursiveness, and though the variety of effect obtained may in itself be good and interesting, it never possesses quite the compelling intensity of the best of Poe's horror stories.

With all these reservations in favor of Poe, it is nevertheless certain that **"The Diamond Lens"** remains what its contemporaries thought it, an excellently executed and absorbingly interesting short story. (pp. 152-53)

"From Hand to Mouth" [written shortly after **"The Diamond Lens"**] begins with a definite setting, "The evening of the 8th of March, in the present year," and describes a heavy snowstorm and the opera—the first performance of Meyerbeer's *The Huguenots*—which he, the author, attended that night. From this setting the author, telling his story in the first person, makes a very skillful transition to the super-fantastic setting of the Hotel de Coup d'oeil. Here, surrounded by thousands of disembodied eyes, ears, hands, and mouths, which though stationary function like normal organs, a most unheard-of set of complications takes place. Unlike Animula of **"The Diamond Lens,"** the impossibilities of this story never become convincing, but instead the whole is suffused with an atmosphere of fantastic queerness, which invites not sympathy or belief but which stimulates the curiosity and wonder of the reader as to what even passably plausible conclusion the author can invent for such outlandish premises. In Chapter XII the hero describes himself and, as usual, O'Brien uses this opportunity to describe his own features. (pp. 158-59)

In August [of 1858] *The Knickerbocker Magazine* printed both a poem and a story by O'Brien. The poem, **"The Boatman of Whitehall,"** is an obvious melodramatic ballad telling of Ben's success in love through the defeat of his rival in a rowing match. The story is much better. Powerfully melodramatic, **"The Golden Ingot,"** tells of a girl sacrificing herself in order to save the life of her father, who believes he is an alchemist. The doctor, who tells the story, does it with earnestness, sympathy, and conviction. And when, finally, he and the daughter, Marian, undeceive the father in regard to the secret he thinks he has discovered and the ability he thinks he possesses to transmute baser stuff into gold, the father dies from the shock. Once more, certain elements of the O'Brien-Poe formula are present—the monomania, the local setting (Seventh Avenue above Twenty-third Street), and the pseudoscience aired with the seeming casualness of great learning. One example of the display of learning, a sentence spoken by the old alchemist, is "That which Nicholas Flamel did in 1382, that which George Ripley did at Rhodes in 1460, that which Alexander Sethon and Michael Scudivogius did in the seventeenth century, I did in 1856."

An especially interesting point of technique is the way in which O'Brien makes triple use of one of his favorite devices. As has been said, the doctor is the chief narrator, but when he makes his professional visit to the old man, that character at some length tells his own story to the doctor, and later the daughter in justifying herself indulges in another personal narrative. The story is, then, a sort of elaborate monologue containing within itself two other fairly developed monologues. It sticks much more closely to the point than do most of O'Brien's stories—there are practically no digressions—and its only flaw seems to be a slight stiltedness of expression in the conversation between the doctor and Marian.

The chief interest of **"The Golden Ingot"** is not in ingenuity of device as it is in **"From Hand to Mouth,"** nor in power of the imagination as in **"The Diamond Lens,"** nor in morbidity of conception as in **"What Was It?"** or **"The Lost Room,"** but lies rather in the sympathy evoked by the great suffering which can result from following a delusive obsession. (pp. 161-62)

Far less concentrated than **"The Golden Ingot," "The Lost Room"** works through a discursive introduction of the familiar-essay type into an atmosphere which wins acceptance for the gruesome supernaturalism of the climax. The story, though not so divided, consists of three parts. In part one the storyteller sits in the oppressive heat of the gathering twilight and makes an inventory of the various objects in his room, dwelling upon the personal associations with which each object is surrounded. In one instance he mentions an ancestor on his maternal side, "Sir Florence O'Driscoll by name," and gives the history of his piracies, of his affair with Queen Elizabeth, and of his being dispossessed. Like the description of his own appearance in **"From Hand to Mouth,"** . . . this is only another example of the use O'Brien makes of his personal background for literary material; and the difficulty for the investigator is to know how to separate such authentic details from the highly imaginative ones with which they are frequently intermixed. Part two emphasizes the growing sultriness of the night, describes the peculiar, lonely atmosphere of the house with its endless corridors and its gibbering ghoullike servant, and tells of the author's extraordinary encounter in the blackness of the cypress-shrouded garden. The story reaches its culmination in the third part, with the author's rapid return to his room, to find it completely transformed—brilliantly illuminated, set with Renaissance furnishings, and occupied by people of a corresponding era. Yet in all the objects, transformed as they are, he recognizes the basis of his familiar possessions. Refusing to eat of the horrible banquet of these sensual ghouls, he is ousted from the apartment, which during the moment of his ejection returns to its original form. Then the door closes; he turns; a blank wall faces him; and he never finds a trace of his room or possessions again.

The descriptive passages of **"The Lost Room,"** with their touches of wit, of sentiment, of weirdness, and of awful suggestion, are especially well done; and the part dealing with the familiar so transformed as to be only eerily suggestive of itself, inextricably entangled in the manner of a bad dream, is vivid and convincing. The cause of this gruesome experience is never positively stated, but the suggestion made is clear enough and is even more uncanny than the happening itself. (pp. 165-66)

The outstanding production of the year 1859 was **"What Was It? A Mystery,"** the startling success of which almost if not quite duplicated the sensation made by **"The Diamond Lens."** With the exception of the latter this story far excels any other of O'Brien's stories. It tells of an encounter with a monster which can be felt and heard, but not seen. It is weird and uncanny, and suggestive of terror beyond anything else O'Brien wrote. The mystery of the inexplicable, the fear of the unseen, permeate the atmosphere. The reader is held fearfully wondering what is to be the next dreadful revelation. If imitation is a sign of admiration, **"What Was It?"** has been most flatteringly admired; for Guy de Maupassant a few years later in "La Horla" (1886) repeated with powerful effectiveness the terror and horror of the invisible ghost. Still later Ambrose Bierce in "The Damned Thing" (1898) and H. G. Wells in "The Invisible Man" (1897) took advantage of the same device.

In contrast with **"The Lost Room"** this story is direct and to the point, containing no digressions. Even the introduction is shorter than usual, and most of it necessary and purposeful giving the story local place and time and relating circumstantial details about the first-person author. Such a technical device had by this time become a distinctive mark of O'Brien's short-story writing; and the signature of "Harry Escott" at the end definitely connects **"What Was It?"** with the earlier **"A Pot of Tulips,"** the narrator of ghostly mystery seeming in both cases to vouch for the truth of the tale by affixing his name. (p. 171)

One other story of interesting supernatural invention, though without the undefined horror of **"What Was It?,"** also marks the year 1859. **"The Wondersmith,"** the second and last of O'Brien's stories to be contributed to *The Atlantic Monthly*, deals with evil people, who through evil impulses produce instruments of evil and who, being caught in their own toils, perish by the means they had produced. The gypsy wondersmith, maker of wicked mannikins; the fortuneteller, with her black bottle full of the evil souls which animate them; the French artisan in artificial eyes, with the huge glass eye placed outside the door to warn against interruption of their evil rites; and Oaksmith, the English gypsy, make a rare quartet of criminals. Through their uncanny skill at their respective crafts they become the wielders of supernatural agencies. Yet their machinations are frustrated, not through outside aid as the introduction of Solon, the humpback, and Furbelow, the monkey, would seem to predict; but through their own evil, in its premature triumph, overreaching itself. Worse than futile are their schemes as they perish in the tortures of the frightful poison and, together with the mannikins, are burnt out of existence in the flaming house.

The powerful impression of this plot is somewhat diluted by the introduction of Zonéla, the stolen child of the wondersmith, whose love episode with Solon, though it adds a sentimental touch to the story, affects the conduct of its development not at all. One other weakness in the plot is the elaboration of detail with which Kerplonne's great glass eye is introduced. Its supernatural properties make one expect that at some crucial moment it will by its weird warning aid evil and thwart good; but it does absolutely nothing.

In spite of these strictures, which point out minor irritations rather than major defects, **"The Wondersmith"** remains a marvelously interesting story. The main episode of the diabolical, murderous toys, of the pigmy slaughter in the birdshop, and of the toys' final attack on their vengeful creators is told with real skill and imaginative intensity. As the hero in **"What Was It?,"** abnormal from the use of opium, lives in a perfectly believable boardinghouse on Twenty-sixth Street between Seventh and Eighth Avenues, so the chief character in **"The Wondersmith,"** abnormal from his fierce hatred of humanity, especially of Christians and children, inhabits a shop in a vividly described slum district of New York, on a street the authenticity of whose details is unquestionable. The sordidness of the squalid street is so accurately described that when the supernatural is introduced it seems perfectly plausible.

In addition to its inherent interest, **"The Wondersmith"** sounds many echoes of other work. As Fred Lewis Pattee says, the first part is "redolent of Dickens, but the rest of it reads like a translation of a Hoffman tale of 'The Sand Man' variety or 'Nutcracker and the King of the Mice'." Almost identical is the statement by Joseph J. Reilly that O'Brien "imitated Poe in studying Hoffman, to whom his obligations in **"The Wondersmith"** are unmistakable." (pp. 173-74)

With the publication of **"The Wondersmith"** Fitz-James O'Brien had completed the writing of his best stories. During the two and a half years of life remaining to him he did not again equal the performance of **"The Diamond Lens," "What Was It?"** and **"The Wondersmith."** It is, therefore, chiefly upon these that his claim to a place in the development of the short story in America must rest. (p. 174)

Francis Wolle, in his Fitz-James O'Brien: A Literary Bohemian of the Eighteen-Fifties, *University of Colorado Studies, 1944, 309 p.*

FRANCIS WOLLE (essay date 1945)

[Wolle describes some typical traits of O'Brien's writing style as exemplified by his unfinished story, "Violina." For additional commentary by Wolle, see excerpt dated 1944.]

"Violina" . . . exhibits a number of qualities characteristic of O'Brien's method and subject matter. It is merely a fragment, consisting of five and a half neatly written folio pages and ending with the first paragraph of section two. But in this short space some of his habits as a storyteller are clearly evident.

O'Brien begins the story with a contrast between present poverty and former affluence, an autobiographical situation which he frequently exploits. . . . When his money was spent Fitz-James was reduced to all sorts of makeshifts to keep alive—he was often without a clean shirt, and had to borrow money for food, wheedle irate landladies into extending credit for room rent, and dodge duns who haunted him for unpaid bills on clothes. This seamy side of life is frequently described in O'Brien's writings from almost the beginning of his life in America until its end. As examples one might mention **"The Poet"** in the comic weekly *The Lantern* as early as July 31, 1852; **"Hard Up"** in *Putnam's Monthly Magazine* for July, 1854; many sharp details in "The Man About Town," the popular column run by the new periodical *Harper's Weekly* during its first year, 1857; and the first paragraph of the second unfinished story, **"On a Rock."** Two stories of an early date which emphasize the continuance of gentlemanly behavior even under the most adverse circumstances are **"Elegant Tom Dillar"** (*Putnam's*, May, 1853) and **"The Fiddler"** (*Harper's New Monthly Magazine*, September, 1854). The social satires, in which the difference between real gentility and flamboyant pretension is always implicit, are too numerous to mention; but they began with **"The Ballad of Sir Brown"** in *The Lantern* as early as March 13, 1852, and were still gaining marked attention as late as May, 1858, with **"The Finishing School"** in *Harper's*. In fact, in the second paragraph of **"Violina"** O'Brien mentions two of the names he had used in earlier sketches to designate superficially showy society men—Bleeker Lounge and Croton Poole.

This fragmentary story typically exemplifies O'Brien's narrative technique, however, at the beginning of the third paragraph, in which he places the two old-fashioned houses definitely "in the upper end of Lexington Avenue" and mentions "deep roads cut away on three sides of the gardens." Such localization of setting by placing it in a specific part of New York city, even naming the street, is done for the sake of plausibility, for leading the reader into acceptance of the later extraordinary or supernatural incidents. In connection with this he piles up many familiarly acceptable details and so establishes his verisimilitude before launching forth into the uncanny episodes which are the reason for the existence of the stories. The device had, of course, been handled successfully in fiction at least as early as Defoe; but it is O'Brien's contribution to the development of the short story to have made use of this technique by applying it to the type of supernatural and horror story of which Edgar Allan Poe was master. O'Brien was a great admirer of Poe and an imitator of many of his devices, such as the narration in the first person, the use of pseudoscience, the air of precise and abstruse learning; and for subject matter he was fond of the same weird, gruesome, uncanny, and supernatural occurrences as Poe and of the hero in an abnormal state of mind; but instead of Poe's vague settings "out of place, out of time," O'Brien worked into his unearthly episodes through an initial setting laid in a locality both familiar and commonplace. O'Brien's success in the use of this technique was so marked that it was imitated by later writers, and various critics have pointed out its influence in the almost direct imitation of de Maupassant's "La Horla," in F. Marion Crawford's "The Upper Berth," in H. G. Wells's "The Invisible Man," in Ambrose Bierce's "The Damned Thing," in Henry James's "The Turn of the Screw," and in Kipling's "They."

In **"The Diamond Lens"** the hero makes his fantastic, microscopic discovery in a small second-floor apartment on Fourth Avenue; the grotesque, invisible monster of **"What Was It?"** haunts an attractive Twenty-sixth Street boardinghouse between Seventh and Eighth Avenues; the lethal, animated toys of **"The Wondersmith"** destroy a house in the squalid lane which branches off Chatham Street near the East River; and similarly the luminous, odoriferous ghost of **"The Pot of Tulips,"** the sinister ghouls of **"The Lost Room,"** and the disembodied hands, mouths, eyes, and ears of **"From Hand to Mouth,"** all come into action in settings so usual and commonplace as to be unquestioned.

O'Brien's general method is seen throughout the third and fourth paragraphs of **"Violina"**—though more briefly here than is usual. There is the enumeration of physical details to give a picture of the state of dilapidation of the houses and gardens; while at the same time the atmosphere of gloomy isolation which pervades them prepares the reader for almost any untoward occurrence. In fact, the "cruel rusty knife" of the last sentence, "with strange stains upon its handle" and the possibility of finding in the shrubbery "the skeleton of a hand or some other awful memorial of murder" definitely foreshadow future evil.

The eccentricity of the inhabitants of these houses gives further cause for speculation and continues to be in line with O'Brien's customary method. In the case of John Brent, the old gunmaker, O'Brien is seen imitating Poe's use of pseudoscience, for Brent claimed to be on the point of rediscovering "the Greek fire which Archimedes invented, and the secret of which was supposed to be forever lost." Certainly some extraordinary manifestation—at the least an explosion, perhaps a supernatural appearance—will result from Brent's experiments. Mrs. Marrabin's "subterranean existence" is also provocative of unusual possibilities and makes one wonder whether her husband had really been drowned or whether he may not appear again either in the flesh or in some ectoplasmic projection. The odd appearance of both Mr. and Mrs. Brent is interpolated with the humorous emphasis on certain isolated physical qualities, in line with the method used so successfully by Dickens; but O'Brien returns to his own use of the unusual with the coincidence of the two young men, rival violinists of exactly the same age living in such peculiar surroundings next door to each other and each a great musician in his own way. Louis Brent's sudden access to fame through his concert at the Astor Place opera house—another bit of localization—and the consequent eclipse of his brilliant young neighbor, Theodore Bernmann, together with the fact that Mrs. Marrabin's pretty and romantic daughter Amy is on the premises ready to supply the love interest, are circumstances which build up in the reader the expectation of an excitingly complicated plot. Amy is almost sure to be enraptured by Louis and his music on the beautiful summer evening with which the second chapter begins.

The analytical differentiation of the playing of the two young men in the story reveals another major interest of O'Brien—music and the theatre. He had as his close friends the most prominent actors of the day, he wrote a number of plays—one of which, ***A Gentleman from Ireland,*** met with great success—he was a dramatic critic, he became press agent for Matilda Heron on her Boston tour, he loved music, and he haunted the opera. A number of his stories and sketches introduced characters of the musical and theatrical world, and in **"The Fiddler"** of 1854 he had shown the effect of musical genius on the listener, though without trying to analyze it, as he does in **"Violina."** (pp. 329-32)

Francis Wolle, "'Violina' by Fitz-James O'Brien: A Manuscript Typical of His Technique," in Elizabethan Studies and Other Essays in Honor of George F. Reynolds *by Francis Wolle and others, University of Colorado Studies, 1945, pp. 328-36.*

SAM MOSKOWITZ (essay date 1963)

[*Moskowitz extols O'Brien as a pioneer in the fields of science fiction and fantasy, viewing his works as a significant influence on later authors.*]

Any serious student of American letters asked to name the half-dozen writers of the nineteenth century who exerted the greatest influence upon the development of the American short story would be most unlikely to omit Fitz-James O'Brien. And he would have to admit that O'Brien's high standing as a practitioner of the short story was earned primarily on the basis of the science fiction he wrote, secondarily on his works of fantasy and horror; and on his other works, not at all.

His most famous story, **"The Diamond Lens,"** became the literary sensation of the year, when it appeared in the *Atlantic Monthly* for January 1858. The story deals with a young microbiologist, who, in his thirst for knowledge, is frustrated by the limitations of his glass. To find a way of constructing a superior one, he consults, through a medium, the spirit of

Leeuwenhoek, the father of microscopy. Informed that he needs a diamond of 140 carats in order to construct a finer instrument, he obtains such a stone by killing a close friend who owns one.

Through a special lens ground from the diamond, he views in a drop of water a microscopic world of surpassing beauty. In that tiny cosmos, his attention is drawn to a humanlike female creature he names Animula. He falls hopelessly, despairingly in love with the small unattainable woman, whose grace and delicacy make the most accomplished women dancers of the ballet appear gross and clumsy by comparison.

Though the drop of water containing the fantastic, minute world was coated with oil of turpentine to insure its protection, it gradually evaporates. Helpless to do anything about it, the young scientist watches his beloved Animula shrivel and die.

Shattered by the experience, he loses the will to work and spends the rest of his life on charity. Occasionally he is invited to lecture at optical societies, where his theories are always regarded as good for a laugh.

The tale carries the reader along with such verve, displays such a richness of imagination, and engenders so high an interest that it is little wonder that the editor of *Atlantic* felt that he could claim sole credit for publishing an original work of fiction which was destined to change the entire direction of American short-story writing.

An illustration of the microscopic woman from "The Diamond Lens."

This claim was not completely without substance, for though O'Brien did not write with the brilliant economy of means and accomplished style of Edgar Allan Poe, he did add an effective note of credibility to his stories by placing them in the familiar setting of the New York City of his day. The result was the beginning of a trend which the famous critic, Arthur Hobson Quinn, in his book *American Fiction* termed "the transition to realism." That O'Brien was able to contribute to and profoundly influence a trend toward realism with stories of scientific extrapolation is impressive evidence of his originality and literary skill. (pp. 62-4)

While **"The Diamond Lens"** derived much of its form from Poe and Hawthorne, **"The Wondersmith,"** another highly admired short story, which first appeared in the *Atlantic Monthly* for October 1859, was patterned after the style of E.T.A. Hoffmann. The tale is a superbly atmospheric blend of science and fantasy, so individualistic that it remains unique of its type in American literature.

The use of wooden manikins which can perform many of the actions of a human being makes this tale historically important as one of the earliest robot stories. What no one has mentioned until now is the debt A. Merritt's classic horror fantasy *Burn Witch Burn!* owes to this story. Not only the basic plot, but the devices in Merritt's novel—the fiendish, soulless devil dolls; the evil mover behind the scenes; the tiny, needlelike weapons dipped in poison employed by the dolls; the malevolent eyes of the manikins—are all so similar to those in **"The Wondersmith"** as to make coincidence unlikely.

In **"The Wondersmith,"** there is a truly memorable scene of a battle between the "Lilliputian assassins" and two caged, talking Mino birds. During a battle, in which the Mino birds have inflicted heavy casualties on their murderous adversaries, they are outflanked:

> Quick as lightning the Mino turned to repel this assault, but all too late; two slender quivering threads of steel crossed in his poor body, and he staggered into a corner of the cage. His white eyes closed, then opened; a shiver passed over his body, beginning at his shoulder-tips and dying off in the extreme tips of the wings; he gasped as if for air, and then, with a convulsive shudder, which ruffled all his feathers, croaked out feebly his little speech. "What'll you take?" Instantly from the opposite corner came the old response, still feebler than the question—a mere gurgle, as it were, "Brandy and water." Then all was silent. The Mino birds were dead.

Earlier the same year, the March issue of *Harper's New Monthly Magazine* had carried O'Brien's story **"What Was It? A Mystery,"** which is a well-conceived, almost documentary account of a man who is attacked by an invisible creature and who, after a terrific battle, subdues it. A plaster cast is made of the mysterious thing, which reveals a humanlike form with a hideous face. The creature refuses to eat any food set before it and starves to death, carrying its mystery to the grave with it.

Chronologically, this story precedes Guy de Maupassant's "The Horla" and Ambrose Bierce's "The Damned Thing," both with very similar plots. There is strong internal evidence that Bierce drew heavily upon the idea and techniques of presentation of **"What Was It?"** in composing his own story. Since there is no bibliographical record of O'Brien's story being translated into French, it is doubtful that de Maupassant was actually influenced by O'Brien. (pp. 65-6)

Probably the least known of all of O'Brien's science fiction stories is **"How I Overcame My Gravity."...**

While it is marred by the use of a dream ending, a plot technique virtually taboo in modern science fiction, the skillfully written story has historical importance in suggesting the gyroscopic principle as a possible antigravity method and in advancing the theory that a weightless object hurled hard enough by a catapult might travel away from the earth forever.

Had O'Brien dared go just a little further in this line of reasoning, he might have preceded Edward Everett Hale by a few years as the first human being to suggest, in either factual writing or fiction, the concept of an artificial earth satellite. As it was, O'Brien might very well have sparked Hale's thinking along such lines, since both were contributors to the same periodicals during the same period and it is more than likely that Hale read most of O'Brien's output. (p. 67)

"The Golden Ingot" by Fitz-James O'Brien may ring familiarly to some, since it was adapted to television only a few years back. It tells of an old scientist who is searching for a way to turn baser metals into gold and believes he has succeeded when one morning he finds a gold ingot in his crucible. He dies of a stroke upon learning that his daughter, in order to make him happy, has saved her money and secretly purchased a gold ingot. While almost a bit too direct and bare, and containing a note of the overmelodramatic, the story is nevertheless an effective one.

Among the better-known fantasies of Fitz-James O'Brien is **"The Lost Room,"** which tells of a man who leaves his room on an errand, then returns to find it filled with strangers, and the furniture changed. Unable to prove it is his room, he tosses dice for it and loses. He is ejected. When he tries to regain entrance there is only a blank wall and he never again finds his room. This story has inspired the writing of dozens of similar others on the theme. Despite some not-too-convincing dialogue on the part of the lead character, the overall effect of an evil and usurping power is powerful and memorable.

One of O'Brien's most charming and delightful fantasies is **"The Dragon Fang Possessed by the Conjurer Piou-Lu."** In modern times, only Frank Owen among Western writers has come as close to capturing the complete essence and mood of Chinese storytelling. This tale of a Chinese conjurer is strikingly successful and truly outstanding.

If there was any factor that characterized O'Brien's talent, it was his professional versatility. This is aptly displayed by his mastery of the standard ghost story gambit in **"The Pot of Tulips."** In that story the ghost of a man who hid evidence of his wealth, so that a child he thought was not his own would fail to inherit his property, returns from the grave to remedy his error by pointing out the hiding place of his legacy. It is a good story of its kind, strongly reminiscent of another great Irish fantast, Sheridan Le Fanu. (pp. 69-70)

O'Brien wrote a remarkable surrealistic fantasy in **"From Hand to Mouth,"** originally serialized in *The New York Picayune* during 1858. Disembodied eyes, ears, hands, and mouths fill a hotel room in this story, which, though skillfully composed, loses the reader with situations so complex that not even the author could figure them out, for he never finished the last installment. The publisher of the weekly, Frank H. Bellew, finally completed the story himself.... Despite its faults, the writing of **"From Hand to Mouth"** is sheer delight and the light handling of surrealistic nightmarish imagination compares favorably with Lewis Carroll.

Other stories by Fitz-James O'Brien, worth mentioning for their elements of the supernatural or horror, are **"The Bohemian,"** which employs hypnotism to induce extrasensory perception. Though the devices of the story are dated, a number of passages are sheer poetry. **"Jubal, the Ringer"** concerns a bell ringer who employs a flock of bats to loosen the plaster binding the stones of his belfry, then utilizes the acoustical vibrations of his bell to bring the stones crashing down into the church, killing himself and the woman he loves (who is marrying another), together with the marriage procession. **"A Terrible Night"** is a suspense story in which a man kills his best friend as a result of a fear-induced nightmare. The wife in **"Mother of Pearl"** kills her child and attempts to kill her husband while under the influence of narcotics.

Many American critics agree that Fitz-James O'Brien made a signal contribution to the art of short-story writing by "the addition of a Defoe-like verisimilitude to the Poe-like tale of terror." Among them are Henry Seidel Canby, who in his excellent critical work *The Short Story in English* lists the three most important influences of the 1850s and '60s in the short story as Fitz-James O'Brien, Edward Everett Hale, and Bret Harte; and Edward J. O'Brien, late editor of the famed O'Brien's best short-story collections of the year, who stated: "Fitz-James O'Brien was the most distinguished short story teller between Edgar Allan Poe and Bret Harte" [see excerpt dated 1925].

O'Brien's failing, in the long-term literary view, was that he was *too* talented, too versatile, and too conscious of what the market of his period preferred. O'Brien was a true professional—whether in story, essay, poem, song, play, or critique, he could usually strike the mood of the times and give the editors and the public just what they wanted. Making a sale was not his problem. As a result, if O'Brien's standing among American authors depended upon his general fiction and verse, anything more than a footnote in a general history of literature would have been an act of courtesy.

Only when he turned to science fiction or fantasy did he begin to display the full force of his truly outstanding talents. At such times his interest in the subject matter compelled him to write with his mind on the story instead of on the editor or the public. Though his output of such work was small, the quality is truly remarkable and its influence is still visible in today's science fiction and fantasy. (pp.70-2)

Sam Moskowitz, "The Fabulous Fantast—Fitz-James O'Brien," in his Explorers of the Infinite: Shapers of Science Fiction, *World Publishing Co., 1963, pp. 62-72.*

H. BRUCE FRANKLIN (essay date 1978)

[Franklin discusses O'Brien's short stories, paying particular attention to "The Diamond Lens," which he praises for its originality and for its depiction of the psychological implications of scientific discovery.]

If he had not written a handful of brilliantly original short stories, O'Brien would long since have been forgotten. Even in such derivative tales as **"The Bohemian"** (1855), where the narrator's passionate love for gold fatally induces him to have his fiancée mesmerized to reveal the whereabouts of a treasure, O'Brien contributes something relatively new to science fiction, a realistic setting bringing mid-century New York City to life. **"From Hand to Mouth"** (1858) is a remarkable surrealistic fantasy in which a man sits in the Hotel de Coup d'oeil surrounded by disembodied but functioning eyes, ears, mouths, and hands. In **"The Lost Room"** (1858), a strange house whose intricate "corridors and passages, like mathematical lines, seemed capable of indefinite expansion," becomes the scene of an orgy by six male and female "enchanters" who apparently succeed in kidnapping the narrator's room into some other world or dimension. In **"The Wondersmith"** (1859), a band of gypsies manufactures an army of toy soldiers, equips them with poisoned weapons, brings them to life, and almost succeeds in having them kill all the Christian children at Christmas; this story is notable in the history of science fiction, despite its fantastic framework, for its extended descriptions of the army of miniature automata. Three of his science-fiction stories are of special significance.

"How I Overcame My Gravity," published in *Harper's Monthly* two years after O'Brien's death, is an interesting but rather slight tale undercut by the use of dream to explain away its action, if that is what really happens. The mad-inventor narrator, who believes he has already solved "the problem of aerial locomotion" by enunciating his "grand principle of progression by means of atmospheric inclined planes," now tells of his first meeting with the toy gyroscope, which he describes, in great detail, as a wondrous and strange invention. He immediately sets about to construct a gyroscopic vehicle, which, launched by a catapulting mechanism, will carry him vast distances by suborbital flight. A group of friends watch him launch his extremely rapidly spinning gyroscopic capsule (the setup for his innerspace travel strikingly resembles the initial setup for the time travel in Wells's *The Time Machine*). After launching, the narrator realizes that he had not made the capsule strong enough to withstand the centrifugal forces he is employing, the capsule disintegrates at apogee, and he awakes to find himself clutching his wife's silver tea-urn. The story has two interesting aspects. First, it contains a detailed, reasonably accurate, and significant technological speculation; the principle of gyroscopic stability at extremely high speeds is of course the basis for modern inertial guidance systems in both airplanes and rockets. Secondly, and more significantly for science fiction if not for science, the dream device may possibly be much more functional than it would at first appear, for if the technological adventure is a dream, there is no way of determining when the dream began. That is, because the beginning of the dream cannot be distinguished from the rest of the narrator's life, one is not at all sure that at the end he has awakened into a less dream-like reality. This is not then the kind of dream device which makes the science fiction a mere dream (as in Mary Griffith's *Three Hundred Years Hence* or Edward Page Mitchell's "The Tachypomp"); it is more like those fictional dreams which suggest anything may be a dream (as in Hawthorne's "Young Goodman Brown," Poe's *Narrative of Arthur Gordon Pym*, and Twain's *The Great Dark*).

"What Was It? A Mystery" (*Harper's Monthly*, 1859) tells of an encounter with an invisible being whose nature remains an enigma, although a plaster cast, made while the creature is chloroformed, reveals it to be a hideous diminutive humanoid. It is the prototype for the science fiction of the inexplainable alien being who can be cataloged neither as ghost, freak, nor visitor from another planet or dimension. The essential characteristic of this kind of being is that he represents a mystery, violating at least one of our habitual ways of perceiving phenomena. O'Brien gives only a speculation to account for him:

> Here is a solid body which we touch, but which we cannot see. The fact is so unusual that it strikes us with terror. Is there no parallel, though, for such a phenomenon? Take a piece of pure glass. It is tangible and transparent. A certain chemical coarseness is all that prevents its being so entirely transparent as to be totally invisible. It is not *theoretically impossible*, mind you, to make a glass which shall not reflect a single ray of light,—a glass so pure and homogeneous in its atoms that the rays from the sun will pass through it as they do through the air, refracted but not reflected. We do not see the air, and yet we feel it.

"What Was It?" may have influenced de Maupassant's "The Horla" (1887) and almost certainly influenced Bierce's "The Damned Thing" (*ante* 1896) and H. P. Lovecraft's "The Color Out of Space" (1927).

"The Diamond Lens," published in the *Atlantic* the year before, is far and away O'Brien's most original, most influential, and best work. In this story O'Brien opened up to fiction all of the dimensions of the microscopic worlds. The microscope may have suggested the Lilliputians of *Gulliver's Travels*, but they are certainly not microscopic beings. Perhaps before **"The Diamond Lens"** there were fictional plunges into the microscopic worlds, but they have not as yet come to light. "Microcosmus," a slightly earlier work by O'Brien's friend William North, has long since been lost. When **"The Diamond Lens"** appeared, O'Brien was accused of having stolen it from "Microcosmus"; his denial, printed in the New York *Evening Post*, January 20, 1858, seems convincing—and is interesting for other reasons:

> In the composition of **"The Diamond Lens"** I derived considerable aid from Doctor J. D. Whelpley of this city, himself an accomplished writer and practical microscopist. To him I am indebted for some valuable suggestions connected with the scientific mechanism of the plot, and he was a witness of the gradual development of the story under my hands.

This statement suggests the extent to which O'Brien was concerned with the scientific veracity of his story, and it also points to the existence of an early team approach to the writing of science fiction, something which has recently become common. And J. D. Whelpley's "The Atoms of Chladni" appeared just two years after **"The Diamond Lens."**

Scientific veracity in **"The Diamond Lens"** comes from O'Brien's skillful use of the history and principles of microscopes. In fact, a diamond lens had actually been used for microscopic investigations, as described in 1827 in *The Quarterly Journal of Science* and *The Franklin Journal*. Of course O'Brien could hardly be expected to give a scientific explanation for Animula. This would have to wait for the settlers who were to come behind **"The Diamond Lens"**—such as Theodore Sturgeon's "Microcosmic God" (1941), in which the scientist breeds and develops an advanced society of humanoid microbes, and James Blish's *The Seedling Stars* (1957), in which manipulated human genes produce a microscopic race of men (some of whom discover an Animula-like figure of their own size). Before genetic manipulation came along, the followers of **"The Diamond Lens"** tried all kinds of fantastic ways to break through into the microscopic worlds, from Twain's *The Great Dark*. . . , which uses dream to make the microscopic world become the real world, to Henry Hasse's "He Who Shrank" (1936), which uses an unexplained chemical to propel the ever-shrinking protagonist through microscopic worlds within worlds within worlds without end.

Much praised, much imitated, **"The Diamond Lens"** has yet to be explicated. Perhaps the best place to begin is in the fantasy of childhood:

> I had a little husband, no bigger than my thumb;
> I put him in a pint-pot, and there I bid him drum.
> I gave him some garters, to garter up his hose,
> And a little pocket handkerchief to wipe his pretty nose.
>
> Mother Goose

Or, as Humbert Humbert puts it in *Lolita*, "What I had madly possessed was not she, but my own creation, another fanciful Lolita." O'Brien's real importance lies not just in opening up to fiction the microscopic dimensions of existence but in opening up to fiction the psychological dimensions of what we can perceive in the microscopic dimensions.

The hallucinatory nature of the objective world was certainly a common subject of fiction before **"The Diamond Lens,"** but O'Brien may have been the first to dramatize what happens when the scientific vision becomes more and more microscopically precise until it approaches perfection. On one hand then lies the Scylla of the psyche, unconsciously projecting one's own image into objects. On the other hand lies the Charybdis of the self, ultimately finding one's own image in objects, as described in Sir Arthur Eddington's summary of modern physics:

> . . . we have found that where science has progressed the farthest, the mind has but regained from nature that which the mind has put into nature.
>
> We have found a strange foot-print on the shores of the unknown. We have devised profound theories, one after another, to account for its origin. At last, we have succeeded in reconstructing the creature that made the foot-print. And Lo! it is our own.
>
> *Space, Time and Gravitation* (1959 ed.)

The question, as O'Brien so brilliantly perceived, is how to keep the infinitude of external dimensions from absorbing or being absorbed by the infinitude of internal dimensions. Or, as the narrator of **"The Diamond Lens"** puts it in his opening sentence: "From a very early period of my life the entire bent of my inclinations had been towards microscopic investigations." The conventional interpretation of the story has it as the drama of a man who falls in love with the beautiful girl he finds living in a droplet of water. This interpretation overlooks the most significant dimensions of this microscopic discovery, for O'Brien is dealing as much with the world of the mind as with the world on the slide. What the narrator sees as he peers into the minute hole in his diamond lens and perceives a refracted image of beauty is the heart of all ambiguities inherent in the relations between the subjective and objective worlds.

The narrator, one immediately learns, typifies the isolated, asexual, introverted, dehumanized, peeper-in at life, toying with objects in a narcissistic frenzy. He is much like Owen Warland of "The Artist of the Beautiful," who "would turn the sun out of its orbit and derange the whole course of time, if . . . his ingenuity could grasp anything bigger than a child's toy,'" and who finds a real woman too gross. He is also much like Aylmer, who is revolted by the most beautiful woman in the world because he is fatally fascinated with an image of ideal feminity projected from his own mind. After falling in love with his microscopic image of feminine perfection, the narrator of **"The Diamond Lens"** sees in the *danseuse* reputed to be "the most beautiful and graceful woman in the world" nothing but "muscular limbs," "thick ankles," "cavernous eyes," "crudely painted cheeks," and "gross, discordant movements." With an exclamation of disgust that drew every eye" upon him, he feels in the middle of her *pas-de-fascination* to return "home to feast my eyes once more on the lovely form of my sylph."

O'Brien uses two myths to define the relation between the narrator and his Animula, and, by so doing, redefines these myths in terms of his science fiction. The first is the myth of Eden. Before the appearance of Animula in his microscopic world, the narrator is a willfully isolated kind of Adam: "I was like one who, having discovered the ancient Eden still existing in all its primitive glory, should resolve to enjoy it in solitude. . . ." But as Eve was made out of Adam, so the narrator begins the process:

> Like all active microscopists, I gave my imagination full play. Indeed, it is a common complaint against many such, that they supply the defects of their instruments with the creations of their brains. I imagined depths beyond depths in Nature. . . .

Finally, after letting himself become possessed by a pair of fiends, a fiendish vision, and a fiendish suggestion, he finds a mate in his Eden:

> It was a female human shape. When I say "human," I mean it possessed the outlines of humanity,—but there the analogy ends. Its adorable beauty lifted it illimitable heights beyond the loveliest daughter of Adam.

The loveliest daughter of Adam did not come from the normal procreative process; the first female human shape was a piece of himself.

The Eden myth describes the cleavage of man into man and woman. The other myth O'Brien employs dramatizes the reverse, the joining of a woman and a man into one being—the archetypal hermaphrodite. O'Brien is quite explicit about relating Animula to Salmacis, the narrator to Hermaphroditus: "She lay at full length in the transparent medium, in which she supported herself with ease, and gambolled with the enchanting grace that the nymph Salmacis might have exhibited when she sought to conquer the modest Hermaphroditus." The source of this myth is Ovid's *Metamorphoses*, Book IV, lines 285-389, which is well worth examining in relation to **"The Diamond Lens,"** for it provides much of the basic structure of the story and displays in a naked form many of its central concerns.

The myth is the explanation of why the waters of a particular fountain make men weak, feeble, and effeminate. Hermaphroditus leaves his native home to seek out unknown places. He comes upon a lovely pool inhabited by a beautiful nymph who burns with desire for him. She lures him into the pool by hiding from his sight, then strips, swims to him, and wraps her naked body around his. He struggles to escape, but she implores the gods never to let them be separated; then:

> Their mingled bodies become a single form,
> As the grafted twig and bark join themselves,
> Growing together into maturity.
> So they, embraced, their limbs entwined, become
> Not two, but a double form, not a girl
> Nor a boy, but neither and yet either.

The notion that this myth was a variant of the creation of Eve from Adam dates back at least to 1632, to George Sandys's commentary in his translation of the *Metamorphoses*. Sandys also pointed out the resemblance of both stories to Plato's myth that man was first created hermaphroditic, then split into male and female, and ever since has yearned to return to the original unity. By the time of **"The Diamond Lens,"** some mythographers were explaining all these myths in terms of a primeval belief in a hermaphroditic god who created the universe out of itself. Under "Hermaphroditus," Charles Anthon's *Classical Dictionary*, a standard mid-nineteenth-century reference work, summarizes the leading authorities on the myth:

> The doctrine of androgynous divinities lies at the very foundation of the earliest pagan worship. The union of the two sexes was regarded by the earliest priesthoods as a symbol of the generation of the universe. . . . [they taught that] before the creation, the productive power existed alone in the immensity of space. When the process of creation commenced, this power divided itself into two portions, and discharged the functions of an active and a passive being, a male and a female. . . . the priests changed their ordinary vestments, and assumed those of the other sex in the ceremonies instituted in honour of these gods, for the purpose of expressing their double nature.

The narrator, absorbed by his "newly discovered world," does not know "how long this worship of my strange divinity went on." **"The Diamond Lens"** ends by subsuming both myths to which it refers—Adam and Eve, Hermaphroditus and Salmacis—and possibly their common mythic sources, under the fantasies of the primitive time of individual life. The narrator, exposed to his vision and exposed by it, reverts first to childhood ("I sobbed myself to sleep like a child"), then to infancy ("I determined to make some effort to wean myself"), and finally to virtual pre-existence:

> When I awoke out of a trance of many hours, I found myself lying amid the wreck of my instrument, myself as shattered in mind and body as it. I crawled feebly to my bed, from which I did not rise for months.

The great strength of O'Brien's science fiction is its inventiveness, which also became its great weakness whenever he allowed ingenuity to dominate. **"The Diamond Lens"** remains a masterpiece because here O'Brien subordinated his brilliant invention to a profound exploration of the diseased psychology of one of the main figures of his age, the would-be lone genius of scientific creation. (pp. 319-27)

H. Bruce Franklin, "Fitz-James O'Brien and Science Fiction," in his Future Perfect: American Science Fiction of the Nineteenth Century, *revised edition, Oxford University Press, 1978, pp. 319-27.*

ADDITIONAL BIBLIOGRAPHY

Clareson, Thomas D. "Fitz-James O'Brien: 1828-1862." In *Supernatural Fiction Writers: Fantasy and Horror*. Vol. 2, *A. E. Coppard to Roger Zelazny*, edited by E. F. Bleiler, pp. 717-22. New York: Charles Scribner's Sons, 1985.

A biographical and critical essay.

Hayes, Michael. Introduction to *The Fantastic Tales of Fitz-James O'Brien*, by Fitz-James O'Brien, edited by Michael Hayes, pp. 9-11. London: John Calder, 1977.

A sketch of O'Brien's life with brief critical comments.

Parry, Albert. "Death of the First Bohemia." In his *Garrets and Pretenders: A History of Bohemianism in America*, pp. 49-61. New York: Covichi-Friede Publishers, 1933.

Discusses O'Brien's association with the bohemian literary circle that met at Pfaff's Cellar in New York City.

Seldes, Gilbert. Introduction to *The Diamond Lens and Other Stories*, by Fitz-James O'Brien, pp. 9-17. 1932. Reprint. New York: AMS Press, 1969.

A biographical overview with commentary on O'Brien's occasional speculative insights into the future of science.

Winter, William. "Sketch of O'Brien." In *The Poems and Stories of Fitz-James O'Brien*, by Fitz-James O'Brien, pp. xv-xxviii. 1881. Reprint. New York: Garrett Press, 1969.

A biographical sketch by an acquaintance of O'Brien. This collection also contains recollections by six other contemporaries of O'Brien.

———. "Bohemian Days" and "Vagrant Comrades." In his *Old Friends: Being Literary Recollections of Other Days*, pp. 52-78, pp. 79-106. New York: Moffat, Yard and Co., 1909.

Recollections by an intimate of the literary circle to which O'Brien belonged.

Sándor Petőfi

1823-1849

(Born Sándor Petrovics) Hungarian poet, dramatist, novelist, and short story writer.

Petőfi is regarded as the greatest Hungarian lyric poet of the nineteenth century. During his brief but prolific career, Petőfi revitalized the mannered and ornamental Hungarian lyric poem by taking a fresh approach to the form based on the content, rhythm, and meter of Hungarian folk songs. The result, poems more direct in diction, style, and construction, reflected his belief that poetry should not be an academic exercise, but instead should serve as a voice of the people. Disregarding literary tradition, Petőfi introduced realistic details of peasant and country life into poems ranging from highly personal and emotional statements to those advocating social reform. Although Petőfi also wrote short stories, plays, and a novel, these have generally been of interest to scholars only as indications of his literary development. Critical commentary continues to focus on his lyrics and epic and narrative poems; today, he is best remembered for "Nemzeti dal—Talpra magyar" ("National Song"), considered by many the anthem of the Hungarian Revolution of 1848, and for the folk epic *János vitéz (Childe John)*.

Petőfi was born in the Great Plains region of Hungary, the landscape and culture of which figure prominently in many of his poems. Although his father was a well-to-do Serbian of noble heritage, Petőfi, in adherence to his republican ideals, seldom alluded to his aristocratic background in later years; in fact, when he became a writer he changed the form of his name from the Serbian Petrovics to the more Hungarian Petőfi. As a youth, Petőfi was sent to a variety of boarding schools, where he gained proficiency in English, French, and German and also exhibited an interest in literature, writing his first poem at the age of fifteen. Petőfi's studies were interrupted in 1839 when he ran away from school to pursue an acting career after a political dispute with one of his teachers. Petőfi soon realized that he could not support himself as an actor, and he enlisted in the army, but was discharged because of poor health. Afterwards, he attended classes at the Academy in Pápa, where he frequented literary gatherings. With the publication in 1842 of his poem "A borozó" in the *Athenaeum*, an influential Pest literary journal, Petőfi began to look upon poetry as a calling. During the next two years he continued to write, but was unable to earn a living. In desperation, he collected the poems he had written and presented them to Mihály Vőrősmarty, a well-known poet and editor of the *Athenaeum*, who recognized Petőfi's talent. With Vőrősmarty's aid, the collection *Versek: 1842-1844* was published in 1844 to widespread acclaim. Petőfi's reputation grew with the publication of the narrative poems *A helység kalapácsa* and *Childe John*, and he became a notable celebrity in Pest, exercising increasing cultural and political influence.

While Petőfi's literary activities increased during 1845-46, disappointments in love, monetary concerns, the adverse reaction of critics to some of his work, and the political situation in Hungary combined to produce a deep depression that manifested itself in his poetry and that appears to have lasted until the summer of 1846. Later that year on a journey into eastern Hungary, Petőfi met Júlia Szendrey, a wealthy, aristocratic young woman whom he came to idolize. His love for her inspired many poems before and after they were married in 1847 and became a major influence on his later poetry.

Petőfi's republican idealism increased in the months following his marriage as he became more involved in the volatile politics of Pest. The city had become a center for groups of radicals pressing for political and social reforms from the Austrian Hapsburg regime, which had ruled Hungary since the seventeenth century. As the acknowledged leader of the radical poets, Petőfi held political gatherings in his home for those supporting such reforms as freedom from censorship and the removal of foreign troops from the country. In March of 1848, Petőfi wrote his best-known poem, "National Song," a patriotic appeal for political independence. He and his companions succeeded in having this and their "Twelve Points," a statement delineating their political demands, published without censorship on 15 March, and they also gained some measure of support from the government. Peaceful reform eluded them, however, despite these victories, and by the end of 1848, Hungary's relationship with Austria had disintegrated to the point of armed conflict. In October of that year, Petőfi accepted a commission as captain in the Hungarian army, just one month before the birth of his only child. He participated in the battle of Segesvár on 31 July 1849, and although uncertainty exists regarding the circumstances of his death, most researchers have concluded that he was killed in the battle and subsequently buried in a mass grave.

Although the main themes of Petőfi's poetry—love and patriotism—remained constant, his literary career can be divided into two periods. In the works dating from the first period, which lasted roughly until the early part of 1845, commentators note the gradual emergence of Petőfi's unique use of folk song elements. During this period, he eventually abandoned the archaic diction and conventional sentiment typical of most eighteenth-century poetry in favor of simpler word choice, musical rhythms, and the expression of deeply felt emotions. The lyrics of this time are characterized by playful or dramatic qualities, striking imagery, and realistic details of everyday life. The content and settings of Petőfi's lyric poems also reflect his interest in the folk song: his narrators, especially in the love poems, are often peasant lads, and the works frequently describe life in small villages or in the Hungarian Plains region. Two of Petőfi's most well-known narrative poems date from this period and exhibit the folk song elements and lyricism characteristic of his shorter works. *A helység kalapácsa,* a mock-heroic epic about the love of two men for the same woman, satirizes the romantic epics written by earlier Hungarian writers. *Childe John,* also published during this time, is a lengthy folk epic describing the adventures of a peasant who leaves his village to make his fortune. This poem, in which Petőfi combined details of village life, descriptions of warlike conquests, and fairytale elements, was critically acclaimed from the moment of its publication and remains his best-known work.

Petőfi's later period began with his bout of depression during 1845-46. In general, the works Petőfi produced during these months of personal crisis are more experimental and less optimistic in tone than his earlier verses. According to some scholars, Petőfi's depression ultimately resulted in changes in both his style and subject matter: he began writing more forcefully and although he continued to write love poems—it is estimated that he wrote some 120 poems to his wife both before and after their marriage—he increasingly concentrated on political themes. It is generally agreed that the poems from Petőfi's second period are his most mature offerings in their command of language, style, and theme. Critics note, for example, that Petőfi's poems dealing with Hungary's struggle for independence display a greater sureness of purpose. Unlike such previous patriotic verses as "Egri hangok" and "Honfidal," which glorified the past and were written for the upper classes in sentimental, refined language, Petőfi's later political poems, including "National Song," were addressed to the common people and called for a positive program of economic and social reform. Significantly, in many of the poems of this period, Petőfi's narrator has developed from a peasant lad into a poet-philosopher who emphasizes the importance of national liberty. This feature is united with the themes of love and politics in Petőfi's final narrative poem, *Az apostol (The Apostle).* Its hero, Szilvester, is faced with a choice between compromising his political ideals for the survival of his family or fighting for freedom at their expense. He chooses the latter and, after a life of tragedy, is put to death for fighting oppression.

Most of Petőfi's poetic works were favorably received by the Hungarian people, yet contemporary critical response was not always positive. Some of his innovations met with skepticism, with many Hungarian critics faulting his "coarseness" and the irregular meter of his poems. His reputation grew steadily, however, especially with the publication of *Childe John* and later, with "National Song." Petőfi's death in battle made him a national hero, and rumors that he was still alive further fueled interest in his life and writings. While Petőfi's popularity in Hungary has continued undiminished to the present day, he has not achieved the same stature in English-speaking countries: the value of his poetry has been acknowledged, but the difficulty of translating his works has kept them relatively unknown. In Hungary, Petőfi has been widely imitated by generations of writers, who have been inspired by his realism, his emphasis on the spoken language, and use of verse forms based on Hungarian folk songs. Cited as a significant influence on such later Hungarian writers as Endre Ady, Petőfi is today recognized as nineteenth-century Hungary's preeminent lyric poet.

***PRINCIPAL WORKS**

"A borozó" (poetry) 1842; published in periodical *Athenaeum*
A helység kalapácsa: Hósköltemény négy énekben (poetry) 1844
Versek: 1842-1844 (poetry) 1844
Czipruslombok Etelke sírjáról (poetry) 1845
[*Cypress Leaves from the Grave of Dear Ethel* published in *Alexander Petőfi,* 1912]
János vitéz (poetry) 1845
[*Childe John* published in *Tales and Traditions of Hungary,* 1851; also published as *John the Hero* in *Translations from Alexander Petőfi, the Magyar Poet,* 1866]
Szerelem gyöngyei (poetry) 1845
Versek: 1844-1845 (poetry) 1845
Felhők (poetry) 1846
A hóhér kötele (novel) 1846
Összes költeményei (poetry) 1847
Tigris és hiéna [first publication] (drama) 1847
***Az apostol: Elbeszélő költemény* (poetry) 1848
[*The Apostle* published in *Alexander Petőfi,* 1912]
"Nemzeti dal—Talpra magyar" (poetry) 1848
["National Song" published in *The Magyar Muse: An Anthology of Hungarian Poetry, 1400-1932,* 1933; also published as "National Ode" in *Sixty Poems by Alexander Petőfi,* 1948]
Újabb költeményei: 1847-1849 (poetry) 1851
Translations from Alexander Petőfi, the Magyar Poet (poetry) 1866
Selections from the Poems of Alexander Petőfi (poetry) 1885
Összes művek. 6 vols. (poetry, drama, travel sketches, and prose) 1892-96
Evadne, and Other Poems (poetry) 1894
Levelei (letters) 1910
Alexander Petőfi: The Apostle. Childe John. Simple Steve. Cypress Leaves from the Grave of Dear Ethel. Selected Lyrics (poetry) 1912
Sixty Poems by Alexander Petőfi (1823-1849) (poetry) 1948
Összes müvei. 7 vols. (poetry, drama, travel sketches, letters, and notes) 1951-64
Útirajzok, úti jegyzetek (1845), úti levelek (travel sketches, notes, and letters) 1962
Összes költeményei (poetry) 1972

*Many of Petőfi's poems first appeared in Hungarian periodicals, including *Athenaeum, Pesti Divatlap,* and *Eletképek.*

**This work is chronologized by date of composition; original publication information is not available.

THE ATHENAEUM (essay date 1851)

[*This critic reviews a German translation of* Childe John, *calling the poem "a mere string of absurd adventures."*]

The poem of ***The Hero János*** is said to be the production most proper to convey to readers in Western Europe an idea of the quality of "one of the chief, or at all events the most popular, among the hundred poets of modern Hungary." [Petőfi], says his German translator [Kertbeny], is the favourite writer of the people. ***The Hero János*** their favourite of all his poems; "because it is quite in the manner of the storytellerrs who recite their legends in the lonely tavern or by the watch-fire:"—to which, after reading the poem, we must add,—to hearers in mental condition little above the wanderers who find the like amusement in a Tartar bivouac. For this "favourite tale" is a mere string of absurd adventures. It begins, indeed, on the real ground of a Magyar peasant's life; but soon shoots off into rambling expeditions in aid of inconceivable kings, dragon flights through the air, and encounters with stupid giants,—concluding in fairy land:—and in all these differs from children's books only by a want of the fancy that renders most of them in some degree poetic. This bastard kind of fiction can be pleasing only to very dull and ignorant minds in our day. All others will detect the absence of that *quasi* truth which pervades the wildest of such tales as were really born of the love of the marvellous and dazzling among a rude and poor people. Those will always interest intelligent readers, as the first lispings of poetry on untutored lips. They often attest the purity of their origin by traits of energy or pathos striking and moving in themselves, however strangely accompanied. But the modern who attempts the like inventions without any faith in the wonders which he relates or part in the life they belong to, may indeed caricature the poverty and unreason of early fables, but will seldom imitate their proper beauties; while, should he try to trick them out with ornaments in a more advanced style, he is pretty sure to spoil the effect of both. This, at all events, is the result in the poem of ***The Hero János***. (p. 16)

The hero of the "favourite poem" is a foundling; herds sheep for a farmer, whose wife has brought him up,—is turned away for losing half his flock while making love to Iluska, his pretty neighbour,—and sets out to make his way in the world. He first falls into robbers' hands: is admitted, for his courage in defying their threats, as one of the gang; but takes occasion the same night, when all are buried in drunken sleep (no watch being kept), to kill every man,—and wanders on. After roaming "seventy and seven times" up and down the kingdom, he meets with a troop of hussars, bound on an expedition to succour the French against the Turks,—is admitted as one of them, and rides away with the rest. From this point all regard for nature and probability ceases. The journey takes the most unaccountable direction: through the Tartar kingdom,—into Italy, "where it is always winter,"—thence, by Poland, into India. Here the king of the French is found, hard pressed. His daughter has been carried off by the Turks:—her hand is promised to whoever shall rescue her. Next day, the handful of Magyar hussars defeat quite easily the countless army of Turks. János snatches the lady from the arms of a chief who is flying from the lost battle: but refuses her hand for Iluska's sake, accepting instead a treasure of gold. With this, he turns homeward, intending to marry his beloved. The ship which he sails in is lost, with all his gold, in a storm. He reaches the shore by "clinging with both his hands to the clouds,"—finds a griffin, mounts him, and by dint of vigorous spurring completes the rest of his journey. But Iluska has died in his absence. He plucks a rose from her grave, conceals it in his bosom, and goes forth once more on his travels, hoping for death. On this expedition he finds giants and other monstrosities; all of which he attacks and subdues,—until he reaches Fairyland. There he approaches a lake, into which, in an excess of poignant regret for Iluska, he throws the rose gathered on her grave, intending to plunge after it, and so end his sorrows. But the pool turns out to be the "Water of Life":—the rose is changed to Iluska, and János lives with her in endless joy as King of the Fairies. Such is a bare outline of the tale:—which belongs to no time,—in which the realities of place are treated as we have seen,—in which the only motive of any poetical worth is the incident of the rose. All else is a confusion of aimless marvels, strung together without skill, and not even exciting by any show of apparent difficulty. In all dangers the brave Magyar is so easily victorious, that nobody after the first encounter can feel the least anxiety for his fate. The whole piece is of the rudest composition; and the verses (unrhymed Trochaics), if we may credit the German translation with the literal truth of version and character which it professes, are often no less rough and prosaic than is the treatment of the subject. The ornaments meant for picturesque figures and imagery have little of the rustic but spontaneous grace of true popular song,—but are rather borrowings from worn-out poetical finery of modern times. (pp. 16-17)

To exhibit the barren places or extravagances of the story would give no pleasure and produce but small profit. It must suffice to say, that the former take up two-thirds of the whole,—and that in the latter the improbabilities, however absurd, are not in the least amusing.

Those who have read Bowring's specimens of the genuine vulgar song of the Magyars, will remember that in these poetic elements do not much abound. That collection, indeed—supposing the instances fairly chosen—may be said to show the barest stock, perhaps, in all finer qualities of national poetry of any that have been formed of popular lays and ditties indigenous in other parts of Europe. But writers who now compose in this vein—natural only when the poet shares with his audience the impressions of a very rude stage of culture—are less likely to reach whatever excellence the species may have had, just in proportion as they belong in any given degree to a more advanced station and age. This we have felt in reading [Petőfi]. He cannot properly be ranked with the unsophisticated bards of a quite uncivilized race,—while he falls very far short indeed of the stature which modern cultivation demands from the poet who would live in our own day. . . . (p. 17)

A review of "The Hero János: A Peasant Tale," in The Athenaeum, *No. 1210, January 4, 1851, pp. 16-17.*

THE LONDON REVIEW OF POLITICS, SOCIETY, LITERATURE, ART, AND SCIENCE (essay date 1866)

[*This critic reviews the collection* Translations from Alexander Petőfi, the Magyar Poet, *which included some of the first English translations of Petőfi's poems.*]

Alexander Petöfi was the Burns of Hungary, and, although born in a most humble station and leading a vagabond life, which one would think little likely to cultivate the mind, he succeeded in producing rustic songs which Henry Heine has said "are sweeter than the nightingale," and which have certainly placed him at the head of all Hungarian poets. His poems have often been well translated into German and into other languages also, but not so well. The poems of Petöfi are characterized by great simplicity, feeling, and passion; and although he led such a vagabond life, and was at one time a strolling player, his effusions are not in a single instance disgraced by the impurities which disfigure the productions of many of his compeers, and in particular those of Burns. As the number of persons who are acquainted with the Magyar language is very small, the English poetic public will doubtless be obliged to so eminent a linguist as Sir John Bowring for giving them an opportunity, by means of the translation before us [***Translations from Alexander Petöfi, the Magyar Poet***], of gaining some idea of Petöfi's works; although, without wishing to disparage Sir John, we must say they will only see them "through a glass darkly." The German translations of Petöfi's poems are certainly better than Sir John's; but to persons who have not read either the Magyar originals or the German translations, the present English versions, which are the best we have as yet seen, will afford some pleasure. Some of Petőfi's shorter poems are exquisite gems, full of most strikingly original and beautiful ideas, the brilliancy of which, albeit dimmed by translation in the book before us, is something marvellous. . . .

We cannot speak highly of the longer poem, called ***Janòs the Hero,*** which in the original is most outrageously extravagant in its plot, and which, when very roughly translated by Sir John into very rugged alternate prose and verse—for this part of the book is much less carefully rendered than the rest,—becomes extremely barbarous and even ludicrous. We are of opinion that all attempts at *translating* poetry into poetry in the strict sense of the word must be failures. The right thing is for a man who is poetically inclined, and who has the power of versifying, to borrow the ideas of a foreign poet and entirely refashion them; and this Sir John Bowring has not succeeded in doing—he has simply produced half-metrical translations, with few exceptions, not poems. How differently the ideas of foreign poets may be reset in English, we having a striking example of in Longfellow. Should ever the complete works of Petöfi or the best of them be given to us in English by a true poet, they would be a fresh treasure added to our language. Sir John Bowring has not been very felicitous in the selections he has made from the productions of the prolific writer whom he undertook to present to English readers, and we really do not think he has done him anything like justice. Sir John's little book only gives the reader a slight glimpse of the "poetic" jewels which he might have bestowed on our language had he possessed the requisite art to reset them.

"Petöfi, the Hungarian Poet," in The London Review of Politics, Society, Literature, Art, and Science, *Vol. XIII, No. 332, November 10, 1866, p. 528.*

FREDERICK RIEDL (essay date 1906)

[Riedl assesses Petőfi's place in Hungarian literature and describes the elements of his lyric poetry.]

Petőfi's place in Hungarian poetry is easily defined. He is the greatest Hungarian lyric poet. Song was the natural and spontaneous expression of his personality. Feelings were ever welling up in his soul and finding an outlet in song. He was an "impressionist" in the highest sense of the word. All his feelings—patriotism, friendship, love, anger, political sympathy—quickly rose to passion. "My heart," he once said, "is like the echoing forest, to one call it responds with a hundred cries." He never endeavoured to moderate his feelings or to suppress them. He followed the first impulse and unrestrainedly gave himself up to the impression of the moment. He enjoyed the gladness of his heart, and suffered from its sorrow, in a measure quite unknown to other men. "Though the earth were covered with snow, if I could but sow in it the seeds of my joyful spirit, a forest of roses would lighten the winter's gloom."

His great capacity of feeling naturally made him extremely sensitive and excitable. Sanguine by nature, and full of youthful fervour, he was easily impelled to rash deeds, but never to any course which deviated from the path of honour. He was content with no compromise, could endure no compulsion, and wished to enjoy freedom in all its fulness and perfection. In the intercourse of everyday life there was a repelling restlessness in him, some stiff pride, and occasionally a certain superficiality, but in the service of freedom he was thorough and faithful to the end. For freedom he was ready to give all, even life itself.

Petőfi, like his great contemporary and fellow-worker, Arany, based his poetry upon popular traditions and feelings. He embodies many of them in his verses, but always uses them with the conscious art of a cultured poet. It was as if he had grafted the cultivated rose of true poetry upon the wild rose of the popular imagination. The former gave the beauty, and the latter the sap and strength.

Both Petőfi and Arany were pupils of the people. Arany learnt from them his graphic language, the plastic simplicity of his sentences and his epic construction. Petőfi used the features of the popular songs, though altered in accordance with his own individuality.

The essential characteristics of the popular Hungarian songs may be discerned in his poetry. We feel while reading his verses that we are standing on Hungarian soil. Nowhere can we find the qualities of the people and the character of their daily life better portrayed. The characters that he introduces are typically Hungarian, and the sober self-consciousness of the people, their quiet dignity and their well-known discreet reserve, are as faithfully depicted in his poetry as their warm feelings are reflected in himself. In the mature poetry of Petőfi we see love as the Hungarians conceive it, full of strength and warmth, and without any touch of French frivolity or German sentimentalism. Petőfi's writings give us a glimpse of Hungarian life and the Hungarian soul, lighted up by the flame of poetical exaltation.

He often borrowed the subjects and the rhythmical beauty of the popular songs. Those songs, born of the people, never treat the feelings in an abstract way, never merely mention that in the soul of the singer this or that sentiment is present, for one reason or another, but place the whole situation before us in a little scene. They scarcely ever contain a general expression of joy or grief; it is nearly always the joy or grief of a clearly outlined individual in certain well-defined surroundings. Hence the great plasticity of the scene. This dramatic power is one of Petőfi's most striking characteristics. Nearly all his songs make us the witnesses of some little drama. Another poet might say "Sweet maid, I loved thee at first sight. Our eyes just met and thy glance set my heart on fire." But Petőfi writes a charming little peasant song, **"Into the Kitchen door I strolled."**

The cottage door stood open wide.
To light my pipe I stepped inside,
But, oh! behold, my pipe was lit,
There was indeed a glow in it.

But since my pipe was all aglow
With other thoughts inside I go,
A gentle winning maiden fair
That I perchance saw sitting there,

Upon her wonted task intent
To stir the fire aflame, she bent;
But oh! dear heart, her eyes so bright
Were radiant with more brilliant light.

She looked at me as in I passed
Some spell she must have o'er me cast.
My burning pipe went out, but oh!
My sleeping heart was all aglow.

Petőfi's lyrics possess a genuine freshness, which is found in such perfection in no poetry outside the popular songs. It cannot be acquired; the more the poet strives after it, the farther does he drift away from it. The songs of the people, on the other hand, are invariably full of it. Those nameless singers composed their songs under the overpowering impulse of strong feeling and were impelled by no other motive. And if a popular song is not full of life, if it is not simple and genuine, it quickly perishes and fails to win the ear of all men. Poets by profession achieve the triumph of perfect sincerity and freshness much more rarely than the unknown authors of the songs of the people. But Petőfi's verses were very different from the oratorical compositions of his contemporaries. All he says is simple, and expressed with fervour and the instinctive sincerity of a just mind. Deep, strong feelings, put into the simplest possible words—that is the typical Petőfi poem.

Related to his freshness is his sincerity. He shows himself to us as he is. For him poetry is not a means of enabling him to assume this character or that, but an opportunity to lay bare his inmost soul. His poetry is an open confession. All the incidents of his life, the news he hears, and the books he reads, profoundly impress his heart and his whole being. It never occurs to him to pander with the truth, and he pours his whole soul into his poems.

Other poets reveal themselves most frequently in carefully chosen moods. Not so Petőfi. He pours forth like a torrent all he thinks and feels and suffers. He tells us that he has been hungry, and cold and penniless, or that his father struck him, or that he was a strolling player, and that his coat was ragged. Who would have dared to speak like this before him? The poets would have been ashamed to appear in such sorry garb before the public. They thought a holiday mood needful to their singing, and that a gala dress must commend their poetry.

The classical Berzsenyi, by the way, actually used to put on a Roman *toga* when he wished to feel in the proper mood for writing odes. With some poets we feel as if a barrier existed between them and us. Petőfi never makes us feel like that. He is not afraid of standing near us, that we may feel in close touch with him. He does not disdain to speak of subjects commonly thought trivial, and he allows us to see into the depths of his soul. How did he dare to do this? Because he knew that the depths of his soul could only reveal his absolute sincerity. He could venture to speak of trivial, every-day matters, because his personality turned even the grayest and dullest incident to gold. His imitators endeavoured to copy his sincerity, and tried to speak in his daring way. Apollo might appear unclad,yet not every naked Greek youth carrying a lyre was an Apollo. The mantle of Petőfi did not descend on his imitators. (pp. 204-07)

Petőfi was the first who dared to see, as the poet ought to see, and his observation is always sincere. He sees everything around him, and speaks of it, but he sees it with the poet's eye. He was the first whose eye discovered the beauty of the Hungarian Lowlands. Hundreds of poets may have passed through the Lowlands and have seen their plains and farms, their roadside inns, horse-herds and highwaymen, but no one detected the element of poetry in them. Petőfi discovered the Lowlands for poetry. He seems to have thought: "Why speak about the snow-capped peaks of Helvetia, or the 'melodious bowers of Arcadia,' or the sources of Tiber, when the Hortobágy is here? Learn to *see,* and you may find poetry in the homely scenes around you." But it was not only that he looked at the Lowlands with other eyes. He differed from other poets in his attitude to Nature. Nowhere has Nature been reflected with more youthful freshness and dewy beauty, than in his poems. She was no mere spectacle for him, but the extension so to speak of his own mental self. The clouds were his brothers. The Lowlands were the symbol of freedom. On an autumn day he says to his wife: "When thou kissest me, touch my lips lightly, that we may not disturb the beginning of Nature's Slumber." In his songs, Nature is spiritualised and endowed with feeling. Hills and valleys find voice in his verses, but not to teach some moral lesson, as in fables, but to express their own joys and sorrows.

Petőfi not only feels Nature but describes her. His descriptions of scenery are remarkably clear and plastic. An artist could paint them or an engineer draw them on a map. And even these poems are not merely descriptive, but lyrical as well, because they are penetrated by the poet's strong individual feeling. When he describes a dingy, neglected roadside inn, in his **"Kutyakaparó,"** he not only draws a graphic picture of the scene, but he conveys that feeling of leaden dulness and tediousness which benumbs the traveller as he enters the house. We not only see a rickety, weather-beaten house, neglected rooms, and a morose inn-keeper, but we become a prey to the very feeling which overpowered the author. Another happy feature of his descriptions is that he does not depict an object as an isolated existence in space and time, but introduces it to us as the scene of a series of incidents.

He probes deeply into the mysteries of human existence, and displays an inclination to muse on the transient nature of things. For him, the present hour is filled with thoughts of the future. His poem **"At the End of September,"** reveals not only the happiness of the moment, his rapturous love for his wife, and the beauty of the castle garden around them, but also contains forebodings of the future, his early death and his widow's quick forgetfulness. Lyrics have three themes recurring: Love, Nature and Death. The three eternal motives are united by a melancholy presentiment in **"At the End of September."** He commences by musing on Nature, then dwells on the idea of Death, and finally arrives at the third motive, Love.

The lindens are scattering their fragrance like clover,
While the gay flowers bloom in the garden below;
A fawn-coloured mist spreads its canopy over
The earth, and the mountains are covered with snow.

On the bosom of youth summer's brightness is glowing,
And the buds and the blossoms abundantly spread;
But the dews and the darkness my path are o'erflowing,
And the dead leaves of autumn are dropt on my head.

For so our lives fade, like the bud and the blossom;
But come to me sweet one! in gentleness come!
And lay thy dear head on my welcoming bosom,
That head which to-morrow may bend o'er my tomb.

If I die, wilt thou shed tears of sorrow above me,
When my eyes shall be closed in the dark silent grave?
Ah! May not the words of some youth who will love thee
Make thee willing to part with the name which I gave?

Then take thou the veil of the widow and bind it,
A dark-waving flag, to the cross o'er my tomb;
I shall rise from the death-world, beloved, to find it
A kerchief for tears in that far land of gloom.

But thought of oblivion shall never, oh never
Weigh low on my spirit, or cause me to grieve,
For my love will be with thee for ever and ever,
And live while eternity's cycles shall live.

Even in his epic poems, Petőfi was above all a lyric poet. He was too subjective to become an impartial narrator of events. Whenever the characters in his epics speak, it is from the heart of Petőfi that the words rise to their lips. His most popular epic poem is ***János Vitéz.*** Petőfi wrote it at the age of twenty-one, in a fortnight, in a mean, dingy little back room. ***János Vitéz*** is the most truly Hungarian fabulous story ever told. What other poets tried to accomplish when their talents had attained their fullest development, that is, to write an epic poem thoroughly popular and national in its spirit, Petőfi did with playful ease at the very commencement of his career. There is no imitation, in his work, of the poets of any other country. The characters are all drawn from the fountainhead of Hungarian life. The hero himself, a young peasant lad, a shepherd who becomes a soldier, is a typical Hungarian. The form of the verse and the language of the poem are in entire harmony with the popular songs. The way he relates an event is precisely the way a tale is told among the people. The miraculous element in the poem is also borrowed from the popular imagination. Petőfi did not, like Vörösmarty, laboriously explore the ancient Hungarian mythology to find his subjects, but with the good fortune of genius, grasped the treasures which lay stored up and ready to hand in the popular fairy tales. The poem is exactly like a fable told by the people, but with the superior and conscious art of a good story-teller. (pp. 208-11)

Petőfi's last great epic poem, ***The Apostle,*** is a series of boldly drawn but exaggerated events and feelings. The hero is a man of the people, full of lofty ideas, which, however, cannot be realised in actual life. He ends his life as the murderer of the king. In the story of his love there are some of the features of Petőfi's love-story, but chiefly the sadder ones, such as the obstacles to his marriage. The account of the hero's cheerless childhood reminds the reader of Dickens's novels, which were so much admired by Petőfi. The bird which cheers the imprisoned apostle seems to have flown to his cell from that of the prisoner of Chillon. It is certainly reminiscent of Byron. In the pathos of the hero there is a resemblance to the *Girondins* of Lamartine, while his bold defiant attitude recalls the manner of *Coriolanus*. (p. 214)

Petőfi once called himself "the wild flower of Nature." But it would be a mistake to think that he did not study poetry. Certainly, he was always true to himself, but his talents were not altogether uncultivated. In his selection of themes he was influenced by Lenau. His humour reminds us of Csokonai, his irony and his descriptions, of Heine. His boldly expressed love of freedom has much in common with the temper of Shelley and Byron, while some of his *genre* poems resemble those of Béranger. His thrilling oratory shows that he admired Shakespeare, and his dramatic style, full of striking antitheses, recalls that of Victor Hugo. In some of his patriotic poems we seem to recognise the melancholy of Vörösmarty, and certain of his popular romances reveal clearly the influence of Arany. Many a river and brook flowed into that vast and deep ocean, the soul of Petőfi, and yet its most striking and characteristic features, and its peculiar colours, are all his own, and his are the pearls, too, which formed in its depths. (p. 215)

Frederick Riedl, "Alexander Petőfi," in his A History of Hungarian Literature, *translated by Charles Arthur Ginever and Ilona de Gjöry Ginever, 1906. Reprint by Gale Research Company, 1968, pp. 190-216.*

JOSEPH REMÉNYI (essay date 1953)

[*Reményi was a Hungarian-born American man of letters who was widely regarded as the literary spokesperson for America's Hungarian community during the first half of the twentieth century. His novels, short stories, and poetry often depict Hungarian-American life, and his numerous translations and critical essays have been instrumental in introducing modern Hungarian literature to American readers. In the following excerpt, which was first published in* Sándor Petőfi: Hungarian Poet *(1953), he provides a survey of Petőfi's works.*]

As there is unequal distribution of economic wealth and political power in the world, there is disproportion in the linguistic horizon and influence of a nation. Consequently, when a poet shows a measure of talent in English or French, he may gain reputation by a casual reading of his work; but if a poet writes in an isolated, albeit supple and forceful language, such as the Magyar language, he must have exceptional qualities in order to reach the public outside his national boundaries. Sándor Petőfi, who is acclaimed as the first Hungarian lyricist of world-wide fame, and who knew the true bent of his creative ability, is apt to be judged abroad as a minor Shelley or Burns, which is unjust to the English or Scottish poet, as well as to the Hungarian poet. Petőfi's poems, as a rule, written with unerring sense of composition and with freshness, require congenial translators; and even if the translations should not be technically faulty or if the occasionally loose meters of the Hungarian poet (loose, but not slovenly, and without detriment to rhythmical vitality) should reveal corresponding characteristics in translation, one misses the real Petőfi.

If the value of art lies "in its uniqueness," Petőfi's poetry, charged with feeling and imagination, is a splendid example of such uniqueness. The crux of the matter seems to be that the understanding of Petőfi's originality, which is really the individualization of the typical with a Hungarian rhythm, necessitates a thorough knowledge of the Magyar language. His simplicity, which seems unexcelled or has few equals, except in folk songs, is bound to hinder translators and non-Hungarian readers who are disoriented in the "exotic realm" of this Hungarian poet's directness and spontaneity.

There are, however, translations in which Petőfi's voice is not entirely lost, although it would be difficult to discover a foreigner's reaction to his poetry with the intensity with which Flaubert reacted to Shakespeare when he said: "When I read Shakespeare I become greater, more intelligent and pure." There is no intention of comparing the Hungarian poet with the English bard. The point I try to make is that despite the enthusiasm of foreign men of letters, such as Heine, Uhland, Béranger, Coppée, and despite their admission that Petőfi's influence had been marked ever since his appearance on the

An 1848 portrait of Petőfi's wife by Miklós Barabás.

Hungarian literary scene, the very fact that he wrote in Hungarian barred a complete sharing of his work with foreign readers. In Hungary his books do not gather dust in libraries. Petőfi presents a vivid contrast not merely to most of his Hungarian contemporaries but to the lyric and epic poets of Western Europe. As a pure lyricist he surpassed his Hungarian predecessors and as an epic poet, with Mihály Vörösmarty and János Arany, he must be considered superb in this field of creativeness. Western European lyric poets, such as Wordsworth, Shelley, Burns, Byron, Lamartine, Béranger, Hugo, Matthisson, Lenau, Heine, Körner, who had very little or no regard for outward conformity, whose writings were prompted by an inner urge, and who represented what Francesco De Sanctis, the Italian critic and literary historian, defined as "living form," that is to say, form not separable from content, possess traits similar to those of Petőfi and indicate a kindred spirit; for example, their poetry suggests a released force of emotions, a romantic temperament, and at times a realistic reverence for human dignity. Petőfi lacked the somnambulism of some of these poets, their world weariness, or their orgy of self-pity. But metrical and topical similarities do not say that the unsparing criticism with which he assailed and castigated vested interests, the mobility and vigor of his spirit, the simplicity of his feelings, were externally imposed features of his creative personality. His most fragile poems or verbal snapshots must be identified with his genius. Except some of his early verses, in which one notices a faint echo of foreign and Hungarian poets and some obsolete words—an echo of "almanac" poetry, as it is sometimes called—Petőfi's poems show that no unintegrated experience ever affected the manner and matter of his work. The alternation of the obvious and the unexpected in his poems, their revolutionary, patriotic, humanitarian, idyllic, buoyant, or mocking tone, the concreteness of his visual and auditory images, the honesty of his feelings, which was antithetical to mellifluous sentimentalism, the freshness of his heart and mind, the impeccable character of a man whose youth was in contrast to his poetic maturity—all these qualities served values of lasting significance which no "modern trend" of creative or critical writing could dim. (pp. 84-5)

The name Sándor Petőfi immediately calls to mind the Hungarian Puszta (the Great Plains). There are two reasons for this. One is that the poet was born in that region of the country and the other is that he did not sever his spiritual and poetic contact with his native surroundings, even when away from there. One who never set foot on Hungarian soil can feel its reality in Petőfi's poetry. . . . While Petőfi expressed with identical power his manifold experiences, and all his expressions sprang from his belief that there is no human dignity without personal freedom, social duty, national loyalty, and universal outlook, his turn of mind and emotional directives—in spite of the wide scope of his poetry—compelled him to return in spirit from time to time and in fact to his childhood home. In his poem, **"Az alföld" ("The Lowland")**, he sings thus:

> What, O ye wild Carpathians, to me
> Are your romantic eyries, bold with pine?
> Ye win my admiration, not my love;
> Your lofty valleys lure no dreams of mine.
>
> Down where the prairies billow like the sea,
> Here is my world, my home, my heart's true fane.
> My eagle spirit soars, from chains released,
> When I behold the unhorizoned plain.

This is not provincialism; this is not regionalism; this is a poet's peculiar ability to delve into a world of his own which is at once real and unreal. In the outpouring of his soul and affection for his native soil Petőfi responded with equal fervor to its barren indifference and to its benevolent warmth; he seemed like one standing upright while the sun was beating down mercilessly from a cloudless sky, and—despite its intense heat—he knew that the sun is also a blessing to the earth. Regardless of whether he sang in a plaintive "private" voice or seemed the expression of the *vox populi,* regardless of whether he emphasized with pensive or sanguine temperament his lonely lot, much of his poetry sounds like a call that reaches out from his native heath. There is no muddled thinking in these poems, no rhetorical or rattling language. In their brevity and length they reveal the poet's sure grasp of his material. It is evident that his early years left a deep imprint on him, and even in his mixed emotions regarding his childhood and adolescence one senses that he nurtured a profound love for his early environment. . . . [One] could say that Petőfi's poetic fondness for his early environment was an instinctual gratitude for the folk songs and fables he heard from his parents and their friends. Like Pushkin, who never ceased to praise his nurse for the fairy tales she told him, Petőfi seemed to have felt that the imagination of the Magyar people and the immense vista of the Lowland lay a claim on him which he could not ignore, nor forget. His spirit remained in tune with his past when in later years he almost starved and there was no indication that he was destined to become the greatest lyric poet of nineteenth-century Hungary. It never left him, not even when he faced the seeming hopelessness of his future; and it remained faithful to him when he was at last recognized. Petőfi maintained that without roots there was no reliable creative rhythm. In order to render an appropriate critical appraisal of his work, this postulate of his poetry must be considered in the right perspective.

The first half of the nineteenth century was one of the most successful epochs of Hungarian culture. In a relatively short time, notwithstanding political, social and economic obstacles, the nation enriched the world with the works of unusually talented writers and poets. Ferenc Kazinczy, Dániel Berzsenyi, József Katona, the two Kisfaludy brothers, Ferenc Kölcsey, Baron József Eötvös, Mór Jókai, Mihály Tompa, Mihály Vörösmarty, János Arany, and others, while playing on various strings of the creative spirit, added breadth and diversity to Hungarian culture as poets, writers, critics, and translators. In the realm of public life evolutionary and radical reforms hastened the nation's path away from feudalism. Petőfi's lyricism, courageous optimism, valiant and defiant confidence in the nation's future, seemed to justify and clarify this striving for a better, nobler, happier Hungary and mankind.

No wonder that Gyula Illyés, the twentieth-century Hungarian poet, wrote this in the introduction to his biography of Petőfi: "I rejoice in being able to write about him" [see Additional Bibliography]. Petőfi's life and work reveal the ethos of a much misunderstood and maligned nation, the character and sentiment of a people, and the genius of an individual. There is no chip-on-the-shoulder resentment, no inferiority complex in his work, because he was writing in a language unknown outside the borders of Hungary; there is unity in his life and his creative attainment. In a shock-hardened and disastrous world—certainly in need of spiritual and social sanitation as is ours of today—this Hungarian poet, who lived and wrote with consistent honesty, whose many poems became folk songs, in whom there was nothing insipid or aggravatingly plebeian, whose "common sense" made sense, provides inspiration, stimulation, and consolation for those whose dormant belief in human values requires the magic of an awakening spirit. Neither the Pickwickian characters of a petty bourgeois "good will" nor the demagogical or autocratic expansionists of "social justice" will find in Petőfi's works real satisfaction, but those who are awake to the need for a full and just life and are unwilling to be duped by high-sounding phrases or flippant slogans should look upon this poet, who rose above the deplorable pettiness of a mere existence, as an inspirational expression of man's strength in his battle with fate for the sake of human faith. Besides his *écrasez l'infâme* attitude, which was that of one who served progress in a truly enlightened fashion, there was Petőfi the pure poet, the singer of love and nature, family ties and other homely subjects of great poets. As to the basic nature of his poetry it is imperative to see him primarily in the light of his creative spirit. It was this creative spirit which enabled him to be a realist with a romantic temperament, to be universal within the frame of Hungarian life, to be what he essentially was: a brave human being who upheld as a man and as a poet the principle of free speech, an artist of the word, an intuitively sagacious person, a tribute to the social and imaginative resourcefulness of his own nation, the personification of integrity which neither flattery nor persecution could stay in the pursuit of its goal. (pp. 87-9)

[Petőfi's] love poems . . . , his patriotic, political, and meditative verses, his elegies, drinking songs, family poems, and descriptive verses show him to be the pure singer that he was. Instead of conversing with nature in an Emersonian sense, he was a part of nature. He could draw a precise verbal picture of sharp contours or create a mood of soft or vibrant color. The majority of his poems reveal harmony between inspiration and technique. This spiritually and emotionally unfettered poet was instinctively an artistic disciplinarian. The impression of extemporaneousness that many of his poems give, even their minor discords, do not harm their artistic authenticity. There was no glibness in his manner of writing, although he wrote with ease. The choice of subject matter seemed always instinctual. This holds true of his longer poems as well as of the short ones. His poems are clean in the best sense of the word; he never uses offensive language. Even in his antireactionary expressions, abundant in blunt and blistering terms, he remains a poet. He did not write for the "learned" reader, but the learned reader could learn a great deal from him. There is a beautiful blending of musical vowels and suggestive consonants in his poems; his language illustrates the wealth of the Hungarian people's idiom. Except in his early verses, where some archaic or contrived terms are noticeable, in their essence and perspective his words correspond with the living vocabulary of the common people. His extensive use of simple words, his rhyme schemes, his stressed and unstressed syllables, are as fresh today as they were a hundred years ago. His images make the intangible tangible; they are concise in manner, vivid in presentation, impressive in their effect.

Petőfi's narrative poetry, with a strong lyrical undertone, makes of him as much a celebrated poet as does his lyric work. His narrative poems are products of a fertile imagination or have an ironic purpose; in some the theme is remote from our present-day problems. The frankness that characterized his lyric poems also characterized his narrative poetry. How pertinent are his remarks regarding hypocrisy: "It is an easy craft, every villain can practice it; but to speak openly, from the depth of the soul, is what only a noble heart can and dares." The literary classicism ("classicism" here means mature creative expression independent of the writer's romantic or realistic bent) which developed in Hungary in the second half of the nineteenth century, found aesthetic support in Petőfi's poetry and prose. His prose, like his poetic language, was free of mannerisms; lucidity was its chief feature. It was distinctly his own, and it served his analytical judgment as well as his wit and his intuitive approach to people, things, events, and incidents. His short stories with a rural background have artistic quality, although they are primarily didactic, but he failed as novelist and playwright. His only novel is an echo of gruesome Western romanticism, and his so-called historical play shows similar defects. He wrote another play which he destroyed after refusal for production. Neither in content nor in method do these words do justice to Petőfi's greatness. They perhaps explain his admiration for Dumas *père*. But as the translator of *Coriolanus* he was quite distinguished. Critics agree that the value of the translation is fundamentally poetic. As Mihály Babits, the noted Hungarian poet and critic, aptly states, "in his Shakespeare translation, Petőfi was guided not by theories but by his poetic instinct."

It is difficult to single out the "best lyrics" of Petőfi, as many of them are "the best." Many are short pieces; many are set to music and are now folk songs. As a matter of fact, in rhythm and sentiment they seem to spring from the oral tradition of Hungarian folk melodies. There is a lyrical tone in his descriptive poems which, however, does not weaken the quality of their lively movement. They show some consistency with the principle of the Horatian *ut pictura poesis*, although Petőfi was the voice of nature rather than the imitation of nature. In other words, it is not the Renaissance application of the Horatian maxim that one observes in his descriptive poetry, but nature reflecting her own image without the artful stratagem of verbal embellishment. (pp. 94-5)

Petőfi's social and political poems, such as **"A magyar nemes"** (**"The Hungarian Nobleman"**), **"Pató Pál úr"** (**"Mr. Paul Pató"**), **"A kutyák dala"** (**"The Song of the Dogs"**), **"A farkasok dala"** (**"The Song of the Wolves"**), **"A XIX. század költői"** (**"Nineteenth-Century Poets"**), **"Európa csendes, újra csendes"** (**"Europe Is Still, Still Again"**), and many other poems show that his interests were focused on a view which resented the *panem et circenses* solution of public issues and stressed a need for a drastic social and political change. He could be terse, firm, satirical, and sing with frenzy. Didacticism is noticeable in his epic poems; some of his views stemmed from a kind of Rousseauesque fervor of social and political justice. Within the range of his world, to which Petőfi's medium of expression was well adapted and which in its atmospherical qualities was in perfect accord with the metrical patterns he used, one is always conscious of the immediate and the intimate; that is to say, the experience seems real because the image is so concrete. His peasants, shepherds, soldiers, gypsies, Hungarian Robin Hoods, braggadocio characters, indolent gentry, hospitable folk, old and young people, and lovers—one may say Hungarian types—are as true to life through their artistic and not photographic presentation as his genre pictures of orchards, gardens, woods, pastures, weeping willows, rivers, and dusty village roads. **"A négy ökrös szekér"** (**"The Four Ox-cart"**) is one of his typical poems:

> The event I tell of happened not in Pest:
> Romance is there a thing at which men scoff.
> The members of our noble company
> Mounted the cart, and then they started off.
> They went upon a cart, an old ox-cart;
> Two pairs of bullocks were their team bizarre.
> Drawing the cart along the highway white,
> The four great oxen plodded on afar.
>
> The night was luminous, the moon was high;
> Pale in the midst of clouds it wandered there
> As when a widow in a cemetery
> Seeks for her husband's grave in wan despair.
> The wind—a merchant from the nearby fields,—
> Had bought their sweetest scent for his bazaar.
> Drawing the cart along the highway white,
> The four great oxen plodded on afar.
>
> I, too, was one of that glad company;
> By little Erzsébet I sat that night.
> While all the other members of our band
> Chatted aloud and sang in their delight.
> I dreamed in silence—then said suddenly
> To my sweet neighbor: "Shall we choose a star?"
> Drawing the cart along the highway white,
> The four great oxen plodded on afar.
>
> "If we should choose a star," I whispered on
> To little Erzsébet, "the star some day,
> If destiny should separate us two,
> Will serve to lead us back, where'er we stray,
> To a remembrance of the happiest time."
> And she was willing, and we chose a star.
> Drawing the cart along the highway white,
> The four great oxen plodded on afar.

The reliable rhythmic structure that characterizes his lyrical, political and social poetry is observable also in his epic poetry. His epic poems hold one's attention because of their imaginative wealth and ingenious treatment. **"Bolond Istók"** (**"Silly Steve"**) relates the experiences of a young man whom the world judged to be a fool, who, however, proved to be very sane indeed. He found shelter in the home of an old couple. His meeting their lovely granddaughter, their love, marriage, and his ability to reorganize and manage a farm, is told with pleasing narrative inventiveness. The poem, optimistic in its theme and its resolution, has the charm of a folk tale; it voices Petőfi's healthy spirit. János Arany, too, wrote a poem based on the subject, but his poem remained a fragment. **"Szécsi Mária"** (**"Mária Szécsi"**), a poetic narrative, was inspired by the heroism of a Hungarian noblewoman; István Gyöngyösi, a seventeenth-century poet, had been the first to write of her. The theme was used by János Arany and Mihály Tompa in epic poems, and others used it in plays and stories. ***Az apostol*** (***The Apostle***) expressed Petőfi's revolutionary spirit. **"Szerelem átka"** (**"The Curse of Love"**), **"Tündérálom"** (**"Fairy-Tale Dream"**), and his historical epics, **"A király esküje"** (**"The King's Vow"**), **"Kun László krónikája"** (**"The Chronicle of Ladislas Kun"**), **"Kont és társai"** (**"Kont and His Brothers-in-arms"**), are valuable documents of Petőfi's epic qualities. Petőfi was conscious of his vatic mission. **"Dalaim"** (**"My Songs"**), **"Jövendölés"** (**"Prophecy"**), and other poems clearly show to what extent he believed in his poetic fate. **"Az őrült"** (**"The Madman"**) is probably his most rhapsodic work. This poem, as if written in a trance, is a mingling of lyric and narrative elements; it seems different from his other works. **"Az ember"** (**"Man"**) reveals his philosophical temperament; **"Homer és Osszián"** (**"Homer and Ossian"**) is a beautiful ode, inspired by Greek and Celtic poetic history.

But of all his epic poems the longest, ***János vitéz*** (***Childe John***), is the most delightful and the most powerful. It consists of twenty-seven cantos, written in the metrical structure (rhyming lines) of Count Miklós Zrínyi, the seventeenth-century Hungarian epic poet, whom János Arany compared with Torquato Tasso. ***János vitéz*** is a charming and lusty tale of Kukoricza Jancsi (Johnny Corncob), a sheepherder, and his love for Iluska (Helen), "a sweet, blonde, blue-eyed maiden." The farmer fired Jancsi because he was careless in tending the herd. In his sadness the boy roams over hill and dale, and in his wanderings he visits France, Italy, and the Land of the Tatars, Poland, and India. The poet disregards geographical authenticity, which is frequently the empirical logic of fairy tales. Wherever Jancsi finds himself, he never stops thinking of Iluska. Then the king rewards him with a sackful of gold and his blessing. On the wings of a griffon and upon the clouds he flies home, but arrives too late, as Iluska, abused by her stepmother, is dead. He leaves home again, wanders into the Land of the Giants, where he slays their king and becomes their leader. He then wanders into the Land of Darkness, where dwell the witches. With his magic flute he summons the giants, who kill all the witches, including Iluska's stepmother. After this he reaches Fairyland, the land of "eternal spring." Passing a lake he tosses into its waters a rose he had plucked from Iluska's grave. The lake is "the water of life." The rose becomes Iluska. The fairies elect him their ruler, and Jancsi and Iluska live happily ever after.

Even this brief synopsis of ***János vitéz*** should indicate how richly Petőfi fused his own imagination with folklore. In the twentieth century a libretto was made of this epic by Károly Bakonyi and Jenő Heltai, and set to music by Pongrác Kacsóh; as an "operetta" it was played innumerable times in Budapest and in the provinces. In ***János vitéz*** Petőfi's idealistic purport is transparent. The correlation of animate and inanimate things, the real, the plausible, the possible and the impossible, and faith in ultimate justice typify Hungarian folk tales. Petőfi was true to this pattern. (pp. 96-9)

The Hungarian poet should not be classed as a minor Shelley or Burns, but as a first-rate lyric poet in his own right. Like every real poet he could transform reality, thus creating a singular relationship between the actual and the imaginary. There are no strained images in his poems, no preciosity, no versifying hullabaloo, regardless of whether he writes about love, weddings, dancing, spinning, taverns, horses, cattle, storks, or whether he gives a graphic description of the countryside, of harvest in full swing, or of foliage turned red. Recalling Oscar Wilde's aphorism about nature's imitating art, one may say that in this sense Petőfi added color and depth to the Hungarian landscape. His poetry [according to Mihály Babits] "has the authenticity of lyrical realism. Petőfi had his Byronesque period, but as he himself remarked he 'had ample reason' to be embittered. He had a wholesome spirit and was one of those who were sad only then when there was reason for sadness." Even his martial songs are not bombastic or stereotyped; one hears the voice of the genuine lyricist. The element of surprise, which according to T. S. Eliot's acute observation is so essential in poetry, is evidenced in many of his poems.

In his epic poetry Petőfi knew how to weave his wistful smiles into a story, his selflessness, the natural order of things, the spirit of the common people. In spite of his youth he was conscious of the fact that tragedy is an inevitable part of human life; some of his reflective poems prove this. It is interesting to note that while he was a contemporary of Leconte de Lisle, the leader of the French Parnassians who stressed *impassibilité,* Petőfi shows no "emotionless objectivity" in either his epic or his lyric poems. There was no art for art's sake formalism in his work, but there was a respect for form; no moral precepts, but the morality of the creative spirit which by its very nature was concerned with truth. He was organically so constituted that he could not be merely an observer; he had to participate in life. It is practically impossible to try to extract passages from his writings in which one could not see the man himself. His sense of awareness, combined with his imagination, was such that he could not be indifferent to anything.

Some objections were raised to the "too simple" means by which he achieved his effect. Many of his poems exemplify the validity of art which consists in concealing art. He was accused of naïveté. This is a stupid condemnation. "Even a short poem that gives words to a mood discovers and reveals a structure, at once simple and very complex" [as Scott Buchanan remarked]. The "simplest" poem is likely to be a combination of symbols, images, ideas, feelings, and concise language. There were no literary salons in Hungary where he could have been acclaimed for "lofty" or "sophisticated" reasons. Petőfi accepted his own place as poet and citizen, and wrote and lived thus. He was young, and youth bestowed upon him the dangerous gift of candor. He lacked the cunning of the hardheaded merchant or the shrewdness of the peasant; he also lacked the stoic dullness of the defeated intellectual and the speculative mind of the systematic philosopher. Without complete formal education, but endowed with a linguistic intelligence which, for example, enabled him to acquire a working knowledge of French, English, and German, and with an irrepressible imagination, his achievements must be considered extraordinary indeed. (pp. 103-04)

[Petőfi's] place as the foremost nineteenth-century Hungarian lyricist has never been challenged. His poetry has stood the test of time. Petőfi is the beloved poet of the Hungarian nation. It is to be hoped that the time will come when not only discriminating critics but the general public of the world will read and appreciate his poetry for its true merit. (p. 105)

Joseph Reményi, "Sándor Petőfi, Lyric Poet (1823-1849)," in his Hungarian Writers and Literature: Modern Novelists, Critics, and Poets, *edited by August J. Molnar, Rutgers University Press, 1964, pp. 84-105.*

D. MERVYN JONES (essay date 1966)

[The following discussion of Petőfi's narrative poetry is drawn from a chronological survey of the author's works. Jones's essay is regarded as an important English-language study of the poet.]

[The year 1844] saw the appearance of Petőfi's first longer narrative poem—an epic in four cantos entitled ***The Hammer of the Village*** (***A helység kalapácsa***) (August). The hero is the village blacksmith Fejenagy, for whom 'the hammer of the village' was a description, in the best epic tradition, given him 'poetically, by the richly imaginative people'. In the first canto we see him alone in the village church, left behind after the service.

> Ah, but what terrible noise, what sudden din disturbs the sepulchral calm of the church? Thunder? Or porridge boiling in a pot? No! There a man is snoring. It is so! this is a human form. In a corner, leaning on his two clenched fists, he sleeps . . . but lo! he is awake, when he has had his fill of snoring. He yawns . . . he rubs his eyes and looks round. He sees and suspects . . . heathen are his suspicions. He goes to the door; he shakes the handle, and he shook it in vain. With his keen mind he saw at once the position, and said: 'I am shut in.' And yet again he said: 'I am shut in.' Then, as befits a man, he called thee to his aid, Presence of Mind. And he asked thee not to desert him. And thou didst not desert him.

So he climbs into the belfry and escapes through the belfry window, letting himself down on the bell-rope. He makes for the village inn, where the landlady, 'chaste Erzsók', has the 'leasehold in perpetuity of the workshop of his heart,' but arrives just when the 'tender-hearted local cantor' was himself declaring his love to Erzsók, on his knees, begging her 'virgin lips' to say 'at once whether the green garland of hope shall wreathe my brow, or the club of despair batter me to death'.

'"I will batter you to death . . . I am Despair!" said . . . no! thundered a voice, the voice of broad-handed Fejenagy: and with his broad hands he seized the collar of the tender-hearted cantor, and raised him from his knees, so that not even his heels touched the ground: then dropped him, so that his nose did touch the ground.' 'His howls were the cause of tumult among the merrymakers'; the dancers stood still, the gypsy trio forgot to make the heavenly music of their instruments any more.' The cantor told how the 'scheming-souled sexton' had 'inflamed the fires' of his love, and plotted to lock the blacksmith up in the church; so 'the hammer of the village' set upon the sexton and punched his nose, to which the sexton replied by seizing the blacksmith's hair and pulling it like the bell-rope. 'This horrible sight gripped the tender nerves of chaste Erzsók, and the poor dear fell into the whirlpool of unconsciousness.' Another of the company placed her tenderly on her bed—and went off to tell the judge that 'war has broken out, and rages; the pub of chaste Erzsók has become a battlefield . . . men are dropping down like flies in autumn.' So the 'hammer of the village' ended up in the stocks, while the cantor was hauled off by his formidable wife, 'Márta of the Amazon stature'.

Even without the title to tell us that this is a 'heroic poem' it would be clear that it is primarily a parody of epic; clear from the style, from the use of descriptive formulae peculiar to epic, from the similes. It is written not in hexameters but in fragments of hexameters; for (like Mozart's *Musical Joke,* to which it is in many respects parallel) it makes fun of inept execution as well as of inane conception—not only in the language, the attempts at sublimity mingled with the grossest bathos, but also in the helplessness of construction and the endless retardations of the action caused by the fatuous apostrophes, descriptions, and digressions. Well may the poet exclaim 'And . . . but whither hast thou transported me, swift wheelbarrow of ardour?'

The Hammer of the Village was prompted by a current literary debate on whether epic was obsolete, though it cannot have been intended as a positive contribution to the discussion. The parody is firmly rooted in epic, but has also wider implications as a more general satire on the false sublime and incongruity between style and matter—implications with meaning for some of Petőfi's minor contemporaries. It certainly cannot be interpreted as an attack on Vörösmarty, who had long ago abandoned epic and for whom Petőfi felt an admiration as a writer fully equal to his gratitude to and affection for the man. (pp. 240-42)

[In] November and December [1844], when he wrote his masterpiece of narrative poetry, . . . ***János vitéz,*** Petőfi drew inspiration from several of Vörösmarty's works, especially *The Valley of the Fairies,* and Vörösmarty was one of the delighted company to whom he read his new poem.

[***János vitéz***] cannot be better described than by quoting the words of F. L. Lucas about the *Odyssey:* it is 'not merely a tale of changes and chances in perilous seas; it is a tale of loyalties that all those changes and chances failed, in the end, to break.' It is the story of a foundling shepherd-boy, named Kukorica Jancsi (Johnny Maize) because he was discovered in a field of maize as a baby. He has fallen in love with Iluska, a lovely fair-haired girl, who like him is an orphan, and whose stepmother is as cruel to her as Jancsi's foster-father is to him. At the opening of the poem they meet by a brook where Iluska is washing clothes; then in protecting her against the fury of her stepmother at the delay in completing the washing, he fails to notice that his flock has strayed and that many of the sheep have been lost. For this negligence his enraged foster-father drives him out of the house. Jancsi bids a pathetic farewell to his beloved and sets forth into the world.

> He trudged on, trudged on in the dim night, only his heavy cloak rustled about his neck. Poor Jancsi thought his cloak was heavy, but the weight was in his heart.

But he keeps going, and at length sees what he believes to be an inn, and enters. The house, however, is occupied by bandits, and their leader replies to Jancsi's greeting in threatening words which are also full of poignant dramatic irony:

> 'Man of misfortune, who are you, that you dare to set foot on this threshold? Have you parents? have you a wife? Whatever you have, they will never see you again.'

Jancsi replies to these threats with an indifference and bravery which win over the bandit chief, who shows him a barrel of silver and another of gold, and invites him to join them. Jancsi accepts (though 'with feigned good humour'), his mind filled with thoughts of how happy he will make Iluska with this treasure; but soon he pulls himself up sharply, and instead of joining the bandits, sets fire to their house the same night. It is as dramatically effective as it is unexpected that Jancsi's first adventure should be not an obstacle but a temptation, and the effect is the greater because the poet resists the temptation to moralize. And nothing could show more vividly the depth of Jancsi's love for Iluska than his rejection of the short cut. Nor are the bandits sympathetic characters, even in their fate; Petőfi intentionally calls them 'bandits' (zsiványok), using a word which is purely pejorative, with none of the glamour attaching to the 'betyár'.

Jancsi now meets, and joins, a force of hussars who are on their way to defend France against the Turkish invader. They make the journey to France by way of the land of the Tartars, Italy, Poland, and India; when battle is joined Jancsi kills the Turkish general who has abducted the King's beautiful daughter. In gratitude the princess offers him her hand in marriage, whereupon 'a violent struggle arose in his heart, but he quelled that struggle, remembering his Iluska' who has not been mentioned since Jancsi set out for France with the hussars.

The opening canto of the poem, where Jancsi meets Iluska as she is washing clothes in the brook, already suggests a parallel with the meeting of Lysseus and Nausicaa in the *Odyssey;* but it is the fair French princess who is the Nausicaa of [***János vitéz***]. The whole passage in fact closely resembles the Phaeacian episode of the *Odyssey,* not least in the superbly delicate touch with which Petőfi handles it.

> Thus he [Jancsi] spoke gently to the fair princess: 'Let us go, my rose, first to your father. There we will consider the matter more closely.'

So Jancsi tells the King his story, of his love for Iluska which needed no oath to seal it. The Princess herself is moved to tears of 'sorrow and pity,' and her father, rejecting at once any idea of forcing Jancsi into marriage, knights him (so that from now on he is no longer Jancsi (= Johnny) but János vitéz (= Sir John)) and sends him on his way in a ship laden with treasure.

When Odysseus leaves Alcinous's island, his contests with superhuman forces are over; but those of János are now about to begin. His mind full of the words with which he will greet Iluska on his return, he sets sail; the migrant storks, too, remind him of his home, but

> The next day, just as the horizon had prophesied, a wind arose—and no feeble one: the tossing waves of the sea sobbed under the lash of the roaring storm.

The ship is struck by lightning and destroyed, but

> The water carried him away on high, on high, so that the fringe of the cloud touched its crest; then Sir John swiftly seized the cloud with both hands.

This same wave transports the reader into Fairyland; János clings to the cloud till it brings him to a rock where a gryphon has its nest. On the bird's back he rides to his home village. 'I bring no gold, I bring no treasures,' he thinks, 'but I bring the same faithful heart.' However, he finds Iluska's house inhabited by strangers, and learns that she is dead. Plucking a rose from her graveside, he sets out again into the world, with two companions, his grief and his sword.

In the depths of a forest he meets a potter whose wagon is stuck in the mud. To extricate it is child's play for the knight; nor can the potter deter him from the road which leads to the land of the giants, a road by which none have returned—for János intends to 'wander to the end of the world, till the day of my death for which I long.' Yet it is not really death which

Petőfi as portrayed by Gyula Benczúr in 1909.

the knight is seeking; when the giants' frontier-guard comes to crush the intruder beneath his feet, János defends himself, holding his sword above his head. The giant treads on the blade, and his prostrate body serves as a bridge over which János crosses the brook into Giant-land.

Boldly entering the royal palace he finds the giant king and his sons eating rocks for lunch; the King tears off a piece as a 'dumpling' (galuska) for János, who hurls it straight back, striking the King a fatal blow on the forehead. The giants beg the knight to show mercy and accept their allegiance; he agrees to acknowledge them as his vassals, but only on condition that he instal a vice-regent and continue his travels. The giants are not told, and we do not need to be told, why he makes this condition.

János's new subjects give him a whistle, with which he can summon them at will. The first task for which he thus invokes their aid is the destruction of the witches, whose land he has entered. The last surviving witch turns out to be Iluska's stepmother (who had been described in the opening scene of the poem as a 'furious witch', though only incidentally), and her end marks a turning-point in the story.

> My knight János wandered on, his heart was now quite cured of grief, for when he looked at the rose on his breast, what he felt was grief no more.

When János reaches the coast, the sea too (which, it need hardly be said, Petőfi had never seen) takes on a different aspect:

> The sea stirred not, but now and then brightly coloured little fish sported on its smooth surface, and when a ray of sunlight caught their scaly bodies, it quivered like the light of a flashing diamond.

But this sea is the Ocean (Óperenciás tenger), and the old fisherman whom János meets cannot convey him across it; the lord of the giants must again summon his faithful vassals. A giant comes and carries him over the waters, with mighty strides, 'at terrible speed'. Even so it is three weeks before land appears, and then the land they reach is 'only an island', as the giant says, not the further shore of the Ocean which János hails. But this island is Fairyland, and János is curious to see it, though first he must kill the monsters which guard its gates. When he is victorious, and enters, the blissful happiness which he alone cannot share brings back his despair—but only for a moment; seeking guidance from his rose he throws it into the lake situated at the centre of Fairyland. The flower is transformed into Iluska.

> I could tell all splendidly, only not what the knight János felt then.

The fairies are enraptured by Iluska's beauty, and the lovers are hailed as King and Queen of Fairyland.

[***János vitéz***] is essentially a folk-tale, and Petőfi establishes the same friendly relationship with his readers as does the teller of a folktale with his audience, by the same informal, improvisatory style:

> I'm not telling fibs, but the gate [of the fortress of the giant king] was so big that, that . . . well, I really don't know how big it was, but you can imagine; the giant king doesn't have his building done on a small scale.

As so often in folk-tales, the action is divided between a natural and a supernatural world, but this is the least important fact about the poem, because Petőfi ignores the distinction; he has instinctively grasped that calculated transitions would kill the story stone dead. Above all, the poem succeeds because the story, and the verse, move swiftly; and the poet completed its 370 stanzas in about a month. It achieves artistic unity, too, from the constancy of János's love for Iluska, and also from the consistency with which he moves towards his final triumph by overcoming ever greater difficulties, not only extraneous obstacles but the grief and death-wish in his own heart. However, the assurance of ultimate victory, though unobtrusive, was there from the start; the despair of János's thoughts was never translated into action. When he first sets out on his travels, as he 'trudges along, with the dark shadows and dark thoughts in his mind', 'when the sun reached the highest point of heaven, it occurred to him that he ought to have a bite'. And he remains the same, till the destruction of the witches finally 'heals his heart'. (pp. 243-47)

Of the 160 poems Petőfi wrote in 1847, two are extended narratives. **"Szécsi Mária"** (August) is an accomplished piece of work—faint praise for Petőfi; the problem presented by the undeniable treachery of the heroine's surrender is solved by showing her as realizing that war is not for women, that a woman can only act the part of a gallant warrior. But **"Mad Istók"** (**"Bolond Istók"**) (November-December), a story of a favourite figure of Hungarian folk-lore, is another matter.

It opens with a dramatic monologue by someone in terror at the approach of his enemy. Only in stanza 6 do we learn that the enemy is a rainstorm, only in stanza 13 do we learn that the unfortunate traveller is a philosopher:

> The rain can soak all my clothes and strip me; but one thing it cannot strip off, philosophy.

In stanza 24 we learn this philosopher's name, Mad Istók; but he is not so mad, he tells us, as to sleep out in the open on a night like this. 'There is a farm, I will go in. . . . The chimney is smoking, *ergo,* there is a fire in the kitchen, *ergo,* I shall warm myself, indeed I may get some dinner. What fortune, what bliss, that I learnt logic . . . long live schools!'

The owner of the house receives him hospitably, and a splendid dinner is produced; but Istók's attempts to flavour it with the 'salt of conversation' meet with no response. 'When the tree of your life is beginning to fall,' replies his host, 'and you cannot even say that the bird of happiness once rested on its branches, or sang one song, but torments hang there like men on a gallows, then say what the world is like'. Not only has his loved one died 'pelted by the mud of slander', but of his three sons he has lost two and is estranged from the third. With much hesitation, Istók rebukes him: despair is the greatest of sins, 'the darkest atheism'. The old man drank in the philosopher's discourse 'as a child drinks its mother's milk', and on the following morning, when Istók bade his last farewell, his host asked him to stay on, indefinitely. Istók had just before predicted happiness for the old man, and his prophecy is immediately fulfilled by the arrival of a girl who announces herself as the old man's granddaughter, and begs him to protect her from her father who is forcing her to marry against her will. So when the father comes to fetch his daughter (whom he had forbidden to visit her grandfather) the old man bars his way 'like a column of ice in the Arctic Sea'. Now, and again later, Istók takes his leave, but eventually 'he was not so mad as to leave the place where he was so much loved'; at the close of the poem

> The young wife spins and sings: her grandfather and husband play with the two boys.—Outside, the winter storm howls . . . there indoors, the spinning-wheel whirls round and the song gaily rings out. . . .

"Mad Istók" glows with the poet's own happiness, and he effortlessly escapes the dangers latent in his story—he avoids being pretentious, by writing in a popular style: avoids being sententious, by making his philosopher a figure of fun, in exactly the right measure, at the outset: also avoids being monotonous, by the irregularity and variety of his verse-forms. If parts of the poem now seem sentimental, that is just the difference between the nineteenth century and the twentieth. (pp. 275-77)

'Dark is the city, night lies on it', begins [***(Az apostol) The Apostle*** (June-September, 1848), Petőfi's last and longest narrative poem]; then we are taken to a garret where the father of a starving family, when his loved ones have gone to bed, stays up and resolves to serve the whole of humanity: 'he who before belonged to his family, now belongs to the world'.

The poet now shows us the earlier life of his hero. As a baby he was left by his mother in a cab and discovered by a lord and lady, who passed him on to the coachman with the words: 'Here is your tip, in your cab, a lovely little baby'. 'Why were you not born a dog?' continues Petőfi, addressing his hero. 'Then you would have been brought up in this lady's lap, . . . but because you were a man and not a dog, God knows what fate will be yours'. The coachman deposits the foundling on the doorstep of an inn, and he is adopted first by a drunken thief who brings him up to steal, then (when this foster-father has been hanged) by an old beggar-woman who brings him up to beg; then by a 'surly lord'. The boy's name, given him by his first foster-father, is Szilveszter.

Szilveszter's position in the household of the lord is that of a servant, and he has to endure all the bullying inflicted on him by his young master, the lord's son; only the prospect of receiving an education, not the good food and clothing, restrains him from following his instinctive desire for freedom and leaving. In ability he far surpasses his young master, and their tutor often puts the lord's son to shame by unfavourable comparisons with the foundling, which only aggravates the bullying. This treatment combines with his education to awaken Szilveszter's democratic consciousness—' "Did God create one man another's superior? . . . I will endure it no more" '—and he leaves the lord's castle, regardless of the consequences. His tutor goes after him with a parting gift of money, and urges him to continue his studies: ' "you were not born for yourself, but for the country, for the world" '. 'This was the first time he [Szilveszter] had ever met with affection'. He was then sixteen.

So Szilveszter goes out into the world, rejoicing in his newfound freedom. The desire to serve his fellow men grows on him, as he is struck by the contrast between the beauty of Nature and human misery; he reads world history, and becomes convinced that he is 'a ray which helps the earth to ripen'. His conspicuous moral and intellectual stature brings him many attractive offers of posts from lords; but he rejects them all, choosing instead to follow the poor men who invite him to become their village notary. He is loved in every home in the village—except the lord's castle and the vicarage; but the lord's daughter falls in love with him so deeply that when the lord and the priest turn the villagers against him and he leaves for the capital, she follows him and they live together as man and wife.

But the ease with which the villagers were incited to hatred against him has not affected his sense of his mission: ' "It will be different; the people is still a child, easily to be deluded; but it will grow to maturity, will reach man's estate. Just because it is a child, it must be tended" '. Szilveszter writes a book, but when he submits it for publication to an editor, the latter replies ' "You are a great man, and also a great fool! . . . Have you never heard of the censorship?" ' Szilveszter will not abandon his principles, even now; but he must live, so he 'copies out the thoughts of others', as Petőfi had done at Pozsony in 1843. In due course two children are born to him; it is at this point in his life that we saw him at the opening of the poem. But he cannot support his family, and his younger child dies of starvation in infancy.

Discovering a clandestine press, he has his works printed there; they 'cannot die in his head'. 'What was in these works? That priests are not men, but devils, and kings are not gods, but only men; that every man is equally a man, and that it is not only man's right but his duty to his Creator to be free; for he who esteems not God's fairest gift, esteems not God Himself!' 'The thirsty world greedily swallowed this pure, soothing drink . . . but power grew pale' with anger, and the author was arrested, his tearful pleas to be allowed to bid farewell to his family brutally rejected, and imprisoned for ten years. On his release he returns home, to learn that his wife has died of a broken heart—as he had dreamt in prison—and he cannot even trace her grave; his son has left home; he himself is remembered by the old woman whom he questions as a 'godless criminal'. Then comes the worst blow of all; he finds that while he has been in prison 'human dignity has daily shrunk like a dwarf, tyranny waxed like a giant' not only in his country, but in the whole world. He tries to assassinate the king, unsuccessfully, and ends his life on the gallows.

Like **"Mad Istók,"** ***The Apostle*** accurately reflects Petőfi's state of mind at the time of its composition. Now, however, we have an idealism whose ultimate nobility is almost totally obscured by the bitterness and uncontrolled vehemence with which it is expressed. The vehemence shows itself in a concern to omit no harrowing detail—in which the poet indeed sometimes overreaches himself; the lack of control, in a desire to infuse the maximum of emotional content into individual episodes, sometimes with little regard for the whole. Not only is the opening in some respects inconsistent with the corresponding part of the main narrative; Petőfi is unable to idealize Szilveszter's dedication to his mission without compromising the attempt to idealize also his devotion to his family.

The poem is not primarily autobiographical, though several passages are unmistakably autobiographical in origin, and the choice of the name Szilveszter, suggested to the foundling's foster-parents in the poem by the fact that they discovered him on New Year's Eve, was doubtless suggested to the poet by the fact that his own birthday was 1 January. In addition, the lord of the village where Szilveszter served as notary, and the lord's daughter, owe their existence to Szendrey and Julia, just as the villagers are recognizably the hostile electorate in Petőfi's constituency. In other respects, however, the Apostle is the Socialist Táncsics rather than Petőfi. In the village-notary episode he owes something to Tengelyi—for literature as well as life has contributed to his portrait, and foreign literature as well as Hungarian; the account of Szilveszter's early life clearly shows the influence of *Oliver Twist,* and the description of his imprisonment is inspired by *The Prisoner of Chillon,* particularly the bird whose song cheers the prisoner:

> Sing, sing, my little bird, sing! . . . From your song I see that I once lived, that even now I live; from your song come thoughts of my youth, the youth that has long, long ago flown past, this fair spring, and the flower of this spring, fair love! Your song arouses my sufferings, but at the same time it comforts me, and pain comforted is perhaps even sweeter than joy itself. Sing, sing, my little bird, sing!

The Apostle is international; the village may be unmistakably Hungarian, but we are nowhere told in which country the action takes place. World Freedom was Petőfi's ideal. (pp. 280-83)

D. Mervyn Jones, "Petőfi (1823-1849): Lyric," in his Five Hungarian Writers, *Oxford at the Clarendon Press, 1966, pp. 229-89.*

ISTVÁN SŐTÉR (essay date 1973)

[Sőtér considers the relationship between Petőfi's early folk poetry and his later political beliefs and writings.]

During the first half of the nineteenth century Hungarian literature underwent a process of development from which it emerged a truly modern, truly national literature. The new European forms, the lyric and the novel, as well as the various achievements in the drama, assumed a national, more Hungarian complexion. This development was made possible by a turning on the part of contemporary literature toward folk poetry, a movement in which a large part was played by a sense of social responsibility. The greatest poets of the period made a deliberate attempt to change "non-folk" poetry, a product chiefly of the educated, into something more national, by using the forms in which the thoughts and feelings of folk poetry were expressed. This trend toward popularism in Hungarian literature during the last century is unparalleled in the literature of the world. Hungarian folk poetry surpassed its origins and became capable of expressing universally human and, in the broadest sense, national sentiments. The movement bore fruit chiefly in the lyric and the verse epic: in the novel and the drama the forms of romanticism continued to survive. In the case of Sándor Petőfi, folk poetry exerted the same fertilizing influence as folk music, a century later, exercised on the music of Bartók and Kodály.

The development of impulses already present in folk poetry, and his use of popular literary forms in the expression of universally human and, in the broadest sense, national sentiments, make Sándor Petőfi the greatest Hungarian poet.

Petőfi's first poems, based as they were on the lyricism of the folk song, surprised his contemporaries with their ease and lightness. Themselves like lyrical folk songs, the poems gave voice to a type of experience and gusto which the nation, as it rushed toward the 1848 revolution, felt to be peculiarly, exclusively its own. There was a kind of mutinous plebeian rebellion in Petőfi's whole poetic attitude, and at the same time a new sensitivity that brought a new world into the Hungarian lyric, enriching the whole of Hungarian poetry with the warmth, depth and perspective of folk poetry.

In his lyrics Petőfi discovered the Hungarian countryside, whose ambience he transmitted through his own feelings. The types and characters of his folksongs are this countryside's inhabitants: villagers, horsemen, shepherds, the guests in country inns, bandits, deserters, itinerant journeymen and the craftsmen from the small towns.

The poems are genre portraits, but the poet has identified with them so strongly that he seems to be painting scenes from his own life. But then, he was doing that as well. Until him, the world which Petőfi discovered had had no poetic witness.

It is a friendly, intimate world, and because in order for people to come closer together, the narrow family circle is needed, somehow in these poems of Petőfi we are always surrounded by the village in winter. Outside a snowstorm rages, paths are covered, wolves wander down out of the mountains onto the Great Plain: inside, however, is life, a warm stove and a table surrounded by good, simple folk celebrating a nameday or the killing of a pig—the simple, customary, and unpretentious joys of human society.

After so much cheerfulness, such innocent pleasures, friendship and intimacy, it may come as a surprise that a few years later, this same poet should hurl his lance at the throne of royal authority, and make of his poetry a herald of revolution. Had Petőfi's mind changed, his cheerfulness deserted him? Rather, he was living in two different, opposing worlds. The one, which he hated, would not suffer the other, in which he felt comfortable and which was his true home. For the sake of this second world, Petőfi desired revolution. The poet of innocent joys, then, of necessity became a revolutionary, but he did not turn his back on the real pleasures of life. Petőfi's attitude toward pleasure is not epicurean. There is something humble and unassuming in those poems where he depicts the ordinary man, his celebrations and everyday life: whether they speak of pain or happiness, desire or deception, they are always radiant, certain of their power, testimonies of free men. Petőfi was incapable of adapting to the mean and commonplace: however often he raised his voice in support of the downtrodden and oppressed, he never confused their broken voices with his own.

His poetry is folk poetry but more perfect, on a higher level, the level which the folk song may, at one time, have reached. It is folk poetry, but of the kind which easily becomes the poetry of an entire nation. Petőfi's shepherd song, for example, became a song for the entire nation's youth.

It is difficult to tell when Petőfi's folk songs remain simply genre portraits, and when, though they remain folk songs, they throw off their folk costume to become lyrical poetry of the highest rank. The most beautiful belong to the gallery of folk portraits and to the poet himself, in equal measure. Hearing them, one seems to be in some golden age of the folk: the country is filled with strong, free men, an ideal people in an ideal nation.

How ideal was it, really? Only a poet of Petőfi's rank could have made it so. His background is mere pain and suffering: of all his contemporaries, the poets and politicians of "Young Hungary," no-one suffered or did more without than he. The joy of life which his work preserves had to be defended against a merciless world. And yet, glancing over the first three years of his poetic career, generally called the folk song period, we see nothing but radiance, unselfconscious harmony, gentleness and playfulness. The poetry is glad to be alive, even when it sings of pain. Was there any real reason for joy? There was: first and foremost in Petőfi himself, who at this time was still in harmony with his world.

It is astounding how soon Petőfi discovered what sorts of experience were to be treasured most. But then he discovered himself, and his vocation, early. Poetry, which is brimming with life; life, which is filled with poetry: such things are not won easily, nor freely given. But until he began his fight and to pay dearly for this poet's life, the charm and naturalness surrounding him promised, like a summer morning, eternity.

It is, in fact, a Hungarian idyll: a perfect and unassuming world, which requires nothing but a particular condition of the spirit. Such a condition is rare, but for Petőfi, at that time, the exception was the rule. Life was as smooth as the gentle rocking of a cart as it travelled off into the warm, clear night—not far, only to the nearest village—yet somehow, it seemed, into eternity.

During these three years, he was the sort of poet who can only be pampered or envied. If Petőfi had remained only a poet of enchanting charm and humour, who sang of love, the family and the countryside, he would remain one of Hungary's greatest poets, a daring innovator in the Hungarian lyric. But he became the poet not of the heights alone, but of the depths of life as well. He went through serious crises, great trials of character, and through them all he stuck to his own way with unswerving resolution and sovereign determination, never compromising, accepting every sacrifice, taking every risk. He heeded no man's advice, ignored all summonses, exhortations and admonitions, and in the end proved to be right. No-one knew his vocation better than he, and possessing that knowledge he could not back down before any man.

The first three of his seven creative years were illuminated by the brightness which his first poems, with their surprising newness, created around him. However, the world soon hastened to take its blessings back. In 1846 Petőfi's sky began to darken, and out of the raging storm about and within him, he was reborn, a revolutionary.

The turn in his poetic career was marked by a narrative poem called ***John the Hero,*** which summarized all that had gone before.

The miraculous adventures of John the Hero are joined by the poet like scenes from a puppet show: almost, one might say, a comic puppet show. The most playful aspect, however, is the surprising ease and naturalness with which the miracles occur. John Barleycorn, the shepherd, becomes John the Hero in one continued advance, so that finally he becomes king not only of the giants, but of the whole of Fairyland. Petőfi's miracles in this poem are not miraculous at all: the more incredible, the more comprehensible they seem. It is astounding how easily and quickly John attains victory, how lightly he brushes each obstacle aside; as though Petőfi wanted to show that every conclusion is foregone, if only we embark upon the enterprise with bold resolution. That, certainly, is what he himself did. In the land of great adventures, all roads lie open to the brave.

Tale though it is, the poem also expresses a deep truth. No-one ever dreamed a more down-to-earth fairyland than Petőfi. Perhaps the dreams of romanticism are refuted best not by sober reality, but by a sober fairy tale.

The man, John, must conquer death: in this the poem touches ancient poetic myths throughout the world. Behind the cheerful story and the light, humorous telling, is the recognition from which Petőfi's revolutionary perspective soon must arise: that John Barleycorn, within the framework of his former life, cannot be content; nor *will* he be content so long as he has not performed the great work awaiting him—the conquest of the tyrant, death.

The basic thought is serious, but the story on whose wings this weight is borne is light, perky, simple, exactly like John's return home, first hanging from a cloud, then on a griffin's back.

The idyll of ***John the Hero*** is bound up with tragedy, and the love of life therein intertwines closely with the awareness of death: the final happiness follows only after death is defeated. Petőfi is not exaggerating: not for himself, not for anyone else. In order to preserve his world he must endure trials and suffering, and he knows that history, though in the far distant future it helps John to conquer, for him, no doubt, is preparing tragedy. But in this way life becomes complete, through pain as well as joy. All his struggles, each shock he endures, are a search, until at last he encounters his own tragedy in the revolution. (pp. 54-7)

Petőfi would be neither a true revolutionary nor a great poet if his poetry did not, even now, continue to express the complete fullness of life. His poems on youth, spring, the eternal freshness of love, are now juxtaposed against the revolutionary verses, and thus acquire new meaning. In Petőfi the joys and struggles of life are never separated: rather, they lead into and become absorbed in one another. (p. 58)

On the brink of catastrophe, Petőfi's poetry once again becomes optimistic, and the brilliance and force which had enchanted his readers from the start, returns. It is heart-rending to read his avowals of absolute faith, the conviction of invincibility with which, a few months before his death, he went off to battle.

But another thing is also true: he never lived to be broken by the revolution's failure, the subsequent terror, the absolutism and the terrible humiliation which awaited his contemporaries. He steps triumphantly beyond them, invincible, free as light, like the clouds and the birds.

Petőfi took poetry, revolutionized it, then committed it to the service of revolution. In his time, in all of Europe there is no one else who devoted his life so unequivocally to poetry, and poetry to the ideals of progress, revolution and humanity. He remained the people's poet until the end, and was able thereby to become not only the nation's poet, but one of the greatest poets of mankind as well. The joy he took in living, his love of freedom, his nobility and constancy to revolution, his cheerfulness, anger, happiness and tragedy, bestow on him such an extraordinarily high place, it is as though he were not the conqueror, but rather a constant denizen of John the Hero's Fairyland: a bird of passage, elusive as a cloud, which descended for a short time to live among the people of his beloved countryside. He is the one Hungarian poet in whom every prophecy was fulfilled—at times, indeed, more completely than even he had hoped. (p. 59)

István Sőtér, "Sándor Petőfi: Folk Poet and Revolutionary," in The New Hungarian Quarterly, *Vol. XIV, No. 49, Spring, 1973, pp. 54-9.*

LÓRÁNT CZIGÁNY (essay date 1973)

[In this structural analysis of Childe John, *Czigány focuses on the realistic and supernatural elements of the poem.]*

Although the initial publication of ***János vitéz*** was soon followed by a second edition, showing that it met with the approval of the readers, critics nevertheless were at a loss to make up their minds about it. It was understood at face value, for Hungarian critics were familiar with the background; thus, they did not ascribe the poet's geographical inconsistencies in the story to ignorance, or as an attempt to fool the reader, as the *Athenaeum* did [see excerpt dated 1851]; the coasts of Bohemia were explained away in Shakespeare, but a contemporary poet in England could not get away with making out that India and France have a common border!

The question perplexing the Hungarian critics' minds was a difficult one: what was the *genre* of the poem exactly? Was it a fairy-tale? Then what to do with all those geographical references linking the poem to reality? But it could not be a realistic narrative, for it contained too many supernatural elements. As an epic on the classic scale, it was too short and the rules of composition were not observed. It was thought to be too vulgar; and, with the exception of Pulszky who attempted to analyse the poem when reviewing it, most of the critics agreed with their contemporary, F. Császár, who declared ***János vitéz*** to be "a pretty, but boring folk-tale."

It was pretty indeed. The poem was written in the traditional form of narrative poetry, the Hungarian form of the alexandrine, with a very simple rhyming device, the couplet; it was characterized by an ease of versification, so that even the most rigorous philologists could find only a few constructions or word orders in the whole poem that were unusual according to standard spoken Hungarian. Similarly, the rhyming was executed effortlessly, as if in the speech of the narrator rhymes would occur naturally. Apart from about half a dozen words that became obsolete, but by no means unintelligible to modern readers, the poem still radiates its original freshness. It is as if it were narrated by a talented peasant story-teller, whom one would not be surprised to meet in a village community today. The overall effect of the poem, when contrasted with Petőfi's contemporaries, is astonishing: the sophisticated poetic language of Vörösmarty, for example, contains peculiarities characteristic of the Romantic movement only, and certainly does not create a timeless effect.

It is the general view, now, that after Gyulai's penetrating analysis of Petőfi's poetry in 1854, the novelty of the poet's style and subject-matter was finally accepted, and his poetry was considered the greatest peak in Hungarian poetry. Gyulai analysed no more than the general features of Petőfi's poetry, outlining only its chief characteristics. Later Petőfi philology repeatedly examined ***János vitéz*** along the guidelines proposed in Gyulai's essay. If Petőfi's source of inspiration was the folk-tale and folk-poetry, the philologists reasoned, the basic elements of ***János vitéz*** must originate in those sources. Such Petőfi philology thus was at great pains to derive the various motifs from Hungarian folk-lore, in spite of the fact that some of the motifs could not have originated in folk-tales. Giants don't eat rock for dinner; heroes of folk-tales don't attempt suicide, at least not in Hungarian folk-tales. Furthermore, folk-tales contain no descriptions of scenery, a distinct feature of ***János vitéz.*** General works on Petőfi and histories of Hungarian literature have stressed the "Hungarianness" of ***János vitéz,*** as if Petőfi had been about to create a Hungarian universe.

Modern Marxist philology treated the poems essentially as symbolic: the fate of ***János vitéz*** symbolized the fate of the Hungarian people; their hopes and expectations were fulfilled by János who eventually arrived at happiness, having marched victoriously over ever-increasing obstacles. It is not very difficult to see that this interpretation had in mind the march of the Hungarian peasantry from feudalism to socialism. The Marxist interpretation, when fully explained, is not so crude as described here, at least not in the context of ***János vitéz.*** But when referring to Petőfi's poetic and political heritage, it makes it crystal-clear that the establishment of the People's Republic met the requirements Petőfi would have set for the progress of the people.

Textual analysis, however, may reveal the existence of a different and more complex structure, and provide answers to questions not yet satisfactorily answered by scholarship. It is evident that the characteristics of the language and style—i.e. unaffected speech and simplicity of form—result in a singular focussing on the hero of the tale even today.

The hero is a foundling shepherd-boy, named Jancsi Kukoricza (Johnny Maize) because he was discovered in a field of maize as a baby by the late, kind-hearted wife of his foster-father (*Canto* XIV). Johnny is in love with Iluska, a beautiful fair-haired girl, who like him is an orphan and whose stepmother is as cruel to her as Johnny's foster-father to him.

At the opening of the poem, they meet by a brook where Iluska is washing clothes and Johnny is grazing the sheep entrusted to him by his foster-father. In the beautiful summer afternoon, they forget about their respective duties and enjoy their secret meeting; this is interrupted by the sudden appearance of Iluska's stepmother, anxious to find out the reason why Iluska is late in returning with the linen. The wicked creature wildly abuses and humiliates the girl for making love instead of working:

Woe is you Helen, poor little orphan girl!
The furious old hag is already behind you.
Her big mouth opens, her lungs expand,
And so she rouses you from your dream of love:

'You miserable wretch, you shameless bitch,
Is this the way you disgrace yourself before the world?
Idling in the sun and in this unholy manner?
Look at yourself! May the devil . . .'

Johnny attempts to protect his lover, but in vain; then, in addition, the shepherd boy discovers that his flock has gone. For this negligence, the enraged foster-father drives him out of the house. After a pathetic farewell to his beloved, Jancsi sets forth into the world:

He trudged on, trudged on in the soft night
Only his heavy cloak rustled about his neck
Poor Jancsi thought his cloak was heavy
But the weight was in his heart.

Next day, about midnight, he arrives at what he thinks is an inn in a thick desolate forest. He enters in hope of a good night's rest, only to find that it is a robbers' hideout. Their leader replies to Jancsi's greetings in threatening words which are also full of poignant dramatic irony:

'Man of misfortune, who are you?
That you dare to set foot on this threshold?
Have you parents? have you a wife?
Whomever you have, they will never see you again.'

The twelve robbers are dumbfounded, on seeing how little effect their speech has made on the tired, desperate Jancsi; they interpret this as a sign of outstanding bravery and invite him to join them. Jancsi is tempted by the silver and gold the robbers show him; he could "make good," and make a new start with Iluska. When the robbers get drunk and fall asleep, he is about to fill his bag with gold-coins; but he pulls himself up sharply, and instead of robbing the bandits sets fire to their house:

The roof became a single flame in a minute
The red tongue of the flame rose to the sky
The clear blue sky blackened
And the shining full moon became pale.

As the unusual light spread
It wakened the owls and bats
The swishing of their outstretched wings
Disturbed the rest of the trees.

The first rays of the rising sun
Touched the smouldering ruins of the house
And looked inside the house through the wrecked window
Seeing the corpses of the robbers.

This is the first unit of the poem, consisting of *Cantos* I-VI. The narrative is strictly realistic up to this point; the events could have happened to any poor peasant lad and his lass. This simple story of a village tragedy, nevertheless, has one difference. Usually the fugitive peasant boys, most of whom invariably became robbers or else perished and who peopled the woods of nineteenth-century Hungary, were admired and idolized by the people. But Petőfi's bandits are not sympathetic characters; they are not even called *betyárs*—a term confined to the Robin Hood type of glamorous highwayman both in Romantic literature and in folk-tales—they are called *zsivány,* a rather pejorative term.

It is both effective and unexpected that Johnny's first adventure is not an obstacle, as is usual in both folk and fairy-tales, but a temptation. By overcoming temptation, Jancsi is established as a hero of moral stature, not just another vagabond who was bound to be a helpless victim of circumstance no matter what his original cause or intentions were. Johnny's love for Iluska emerges as a profound emotion that cannot be mixed with anything so base as the blood-stained gold of the bandits. While the point is driven home, Petőfi also surmounts *his* first hazard: avoiding the temptation to moralize.

The realism of the first unit is accentuated by the strict account of time. Jancsi and Iluska meet in the early afternoon of the first day; the farewell takes place the same evening; driven by despair Jancsi walks during the night and the morning of the next day. In the afternoon he is overcome by sleep; later in the day he is awakened from his happy dream about Iluska by a storm and forced to go on. He arrives around midnight at the robbers' hideout completely exhausted, hence his indifference to the danger he is walking into. After having some food and drink with the robbers, an almost euphoric experience sharpens his dulled senses: it is then that he realizes the impossibility of his "making good" with stolen money. He leaves the burnt-out house on the morning of the third day; but from now on, as we shall see, the time-factor becomes irrelevant.

In the second unit (*Cantos* VII-XVII), the great adventure takes place. If a village boy wanted to leave his community, and to stay on the right side of the law, his only chance was to join the army. In the world of the folk-tales, the hero, usually the youngest of three brothers, goes out into the world to try his fortune. *Világgá megy* is the expression. The same subconscious force operates in children after some minor misdeed: to run away, to make good, to prove themselves. The realization of wishful thinking is easy in the folk-tale.

Jancsi, however, is still walking on firm ground, though getting further and further away from his village. Eventually he meets a unit of hussars who are on their way to defend France against the Turkish invaders. Because he considers himself an aimless fugitive, he does not care that the hussars are on their way to kill and be killed. He joins them, and they make their long journey via the land of the dog-faced Tartars, where they obtain a free pass only with the assistance of the visiting king of the Negroes who happens to remember the hospitality extended by Hungarians when he had travelled among them. The hussars' itinerary is somewhat confusing: from Tartary they go to Italy where they suffer terribly in the eternal winter which characterizes the climate of that country, but

The hardened nature of the Hungarians
Withstood the bitter cold
And in any case, if they were too cold
They got off their horses and took them round about their necks!

After having crossed Poland, next they find themselves in India where:

It should be known the army sweated here
They threw off dolmans and collars
For God's sake! The sun above their heads
Was about an hour's distance!

India, luckily, borders on France, and the hussars get what they really deserve—a good night's rest. As the King of France and his country are in a pitiful state, early next morning they duly set about their duty: they route the invaders in a truly magnificent battle. Jancsi is the hero of the day: he not only kills the Turkish General, but sets free the beautiful daughter of the King of France kidnapped by the General's son. In gratitude, the fair Princess offers her hand in marriage. This is the second temptation of Jancsi. Iluska's memory, however, is still vivid in his mind; his loyalty is unshaken, and politely he declines the Princess' offer. Declining the hand of the fair Princess is described with a delicate psychological touch, for Jancsi suggests he speak first with the girl's father as would be obligatory in his village.

Thus he spoke gently to the fair Princess:
'Let us go, my rose, first to your father.
There we will consider the matter more closely.'

The opportunity to avoid giving a flat refusal arises when, in the course of celebration of the victory by the hussars, the King requests the brave stranger to relate his life story. After listening to Jancsi's singularly unhappy fate and of his love for Iluska, the Princess is not offended at all but is moved to tears of compassion. The French King also realizes that the marriage would be a burden to the stranger, not a special favour; to reward the services rendered by Jancsi, he knights him; no longer will he be called Jancsi Kukoricza (Johnny Maize), but *János vitéz,* Sir John, and he is sent on his way with a ship laden with treasure.

The poem could end here. Jancsi has "made good." After the adventures, he could return to his village and live there with his Iluska happily ever after. The story, however, does not end with János vitéz's return; the ship is caught in a storm, is struck by lightning and destroyed. This event marks the beginning of the third unit: János vitéz's struggle with superhuman forces (*Cantos* XVII-XXVII). In the middle of the storm:

> The water carried him high up, high up,
> So that its crest touched the fringe of clouds.
> Then Sir John swiftly
> Seized the cloud with both hands.

The very same wave transports the reader to a make-believe world densely populated by supernatural beings. Sir John clings to the cloud, till it brings him to a rock where a gryphon nests. On the bird's back he rides home to his village. He has lost his treasure, but he is compensated for his loss by the anticipation of seeing Iluska. Iluska's house is, however, inhabited by strangers who tell the story of how Iluska died as a victim of her stepmother's cruelty. Plucking a rose from her graveside Sir John sets out again into the world, without aim, but with two companions: his grief and his sword.

> 'Little orphan rose who grew out of her dust,
> Be my faithful companion in my wanderings;
> I wander, I wander to the end of the world,
> Until the desired day of my death arrives.'

In the depth of a dense forest, he meets a potter whose cart is stuck in the mud. It takes only a second for the knight to pull the cart out; in exchange for this service, the potter tells János that the road he has taken leads to the Land of the Giants. It is a road by which nobody has ever returned. He is not deterred, since he is seeking his own death. But when he is accosted by the frontier guard of the Giants, he defends himself by holding his sword above his head. The giant treads on the blade, and falls. The prostrate body serves as a bridge for János into the Land of Giants. Entering the Royal Palace he sees the King and his court, dining upon rocks; they invite him to share their food, else they will use his crushed body as spice for their dry food. Finding no excuse to decline the deadly invitation, János cunningly asks for a smaller piece of rock, a "dumpling." This he hurls back, hitting the King fatally on the forehead. The bewildered giants beg him to accept them as his vassals. Sir John complies with their request, on these conditions: that a vice-regent be elected, and that the giants be liable to serve whenever he summons them with a blow on the whistle presented to him by the giants expressly for this purpose.

The first task of the giants is to destroy the witches in the Land of Darkness. The last witch turns out to be Iluska's stepmother:

> 'But I'll beat the hell out of this one!'
> And János took the witch from the hands of the giants.
> Alas she slipped from his grip,
> She picks up her heels and runs, and is already far away.

> 'Damn it! Go and fetch her!'
> Shouted János to one of the giants,
> Who took him at his word and seized the old hag
> And hurled her high up into the air.
>
> The last witch was found dead
> In the vicinity of Sir John's village;
> And as she was hated by everybody and loathed,
> Not even a crow cawed after her.

The acting out of Johnny's vengeance is incomplete, even in the realm of fantasy: he is unable to revenge Iluska's death with his own hand. The end of Iluska's stepmother still marks an important turning point in the story: for János' grief is cured by killing her.

The reader is full of expectation from now on, because there is a notion somewhere deep in the human mind to the effect that, if János has failed in the real world, he must find at least a substitute, but no less gratifying, happiness in the world of expectations.

His seemingly aimless wandering brings János to the coast of the Ocean. This is the *Óperenciás* ocean, the boundless main which separates us from the fulfilment of our dreams. The ageless fisherman, upon whom János chances there, cannot assist him; a giant has to be summoned to provide transport over the immense water at a suitable speed. "What could be on the other side?"—János asks in midflight. "The end of the universe, where the *Óperenciás* merges into the spaceless void"—answers his faithful vassal, the giant. Before approaching this spaceless void János perceives land, an island: so he instructs the giant to change course and to land on this island in the middle of nowhere. The giant tells his master: it is Fairyland, difficult to enter because it is guarded by monsters.

János has to overcome the final obstacles by himself. The first gate is guarded by three fierce bears, the second by three terrible lions, the third by a giant dragon-monster. The cunning Sir John tackles the obstacles one by one and enters Fairyland:

> In Fairyland winter is not known
> They live in the splendour of eternal spring
> There is no sunrise and sunset
> The soft scarlet of eternal dawn plays in the sky.
>
> Fairy-boys and fairy-girls live there
> For happiness only, not knowing death
> They need neither food nor drink
> They can live by the sweet kisses of love alone.

It makes János desperate, for he cannot share the friendly fairies' happiness, because his Iluska is dead—

> 'Here, where love has its own realm
> Should I spend my life alone?
> Wherever I glance it should point only
> To the lack of happiness in my heart.'

In sudden despair he throws the rose plucked from Iluska's grave into the lake he finds in the middle of Fairyland. He is about to follow the rose, when the flower is suddenly transformed into Iluska, because the lake is nothing less than the source of life: "the water of life." Because the rose grew out of Iluska's remains, the water can call her back to life. The fairies are enraptured by Iluska's beauty, and the lovers—united after so many changes and chances—are hailed as King and Queen of Fairyland.

It is essential to consider the structure of ***János vitéz*** in terms of the three units described above; these units do not represent any sort of artificial division, for the story naturally falls into three parts.

As to the first unit, this might refer to some vague autobiographical episode: most probably it is the projection of some childhood love. It is interesting, in any case, that the poet and the hero are about the same age.

The intense realism of the first incident was possibly responsible for accusations by contemporary Victorian-minded critics alleging the vulgarity of the poem. Although Petőfi does not explicitly say so, he leaves little doubt that Jancsi and Iluska were caught making love. Hence the humiliation and the intense embarrassment in Jancsi's reply to the abuse of the stepmother, toned down only by the use of euphemisms, but unequivocally showing a rage hardly fitting the standards of what could be allowed in the refined poetry of the 1840's. Petőfi follows a different set of norms altogether, those of village society. When attacked by his infuriated stepfather, Jancsi runs away—not out of fear:

> Johnny Maize ran away away, but
> By no means was he afraid of him,
> He was a strong lad, worth twenty in a fight,
> Although he had not seen winter twenty times.

He ran because, according to the strict village morals, it is the gravest of sins to raise a hand against one's parents or the person who provides for him. The sorrow of village people is also different from what is customary for Romantic heroes. No matter how great Jancsi's grief was for leaving Iluska:

> When the sun reached the highest point of heaven
> It occurred to him that he ought to have a bite.

The crucial point of the first unit is the episode with the robbers. Many fugitive peasant lads joined them, and the desperate Jancsi's decision to do likewise would be small wonder. By leaving his community, he places himself outside the jurisdiction of the unwritten laws of his community; but he is not yet a criminal. The temptation is great: if you run away, you have to make good. Even a superficial knowledge of the Hungarian folk-tales proves that this is an expectation deeply seated in the subconscious. If Jancsi joins the robbers he might become rich; but he can no longer return to his village; he forfeits his right to marry Iluska with honour. He would become taboo in the village, a non-person. According to this mentality no other life could exist for him; so it is not moralizing on the part of Petőfi that makes Jancsi reject the treasure, but realistic choice.

What choice is there for Jancsi to make good? Petőfi again chooses the only way open to a peasant boy. Living in poverty and not knowing the world outside his own village, a peasant lad had the chance to see the world and leave his narrow sphere only if he joined the army. To become a soldier, especially a hussar, was the height of ambition for any able-bodied village youngster. The splendour of hussar life, the glittering uniform, the larger-than-life adventures filled the mind; this sunk into the subconscious of village people, next to timeless cravings and desires surfacing only in folktales, very often in symbolic forms. The hussar army formed by King Mátyás in the late fifteenth century, giving the name to light cavalry in many other European countries, was maintained by the Habsburg rulers, a living link with the past. The tradition and anecdotes of hussar life were kept alive by generations of veterans, who returned sometimes after twenty years of service. They told countless stories in the village inns, mixing fragments of historical and geographical facts in freely with their own inventions. The uneducated village lad who fought in the hussar army saw the world within the frame of his village.

If Petőfi was to retain realism he had to present his second unit, the adventures of the hussars, within the frame of these references. This accounts for such geographical inaccuracies as having India bordering upon France; since both are far away, the direction does not really matter. The mountains rise so high that the heat is intolerable. (From time immemorial, at least since Daedelus and Icarus, it has always been hot up there!) The King of France is more like an old, well-to-do Hungarian farmer than the ruler of that country. When, after the victory of the hussars, he invites them to a banquet, the description is rather like that of a village wedding feast. What is important, no matter how incredible the adventures may seem, is that there are no supernatural elements in the second unit. For example, even the country of the dog-faced Tartars goes back to the thirteenth-century travellers' tales, together with collective memories of the Mongol invasion of Hungary in 1241.

Petőfi knows we are not accepting everything as the literal truth. He presents the tall stories in such a way—quite a *tour de force*—that even an uneducated village reader would get suspicious. When the hussars, on their way to France, obtain water in the sky-high mountains by squeezing the clouds, it may sound credible to a peasant living in the Hungarian Lowland who has never seen a mountain. The same credulous person, nevertheless, would not swallow another incident: when the hussars travelling in Italy, the country of "eternal winter," protect themselves against the cold by taking their horses round about their necks as living cloaks, and also for the sake of the exercise. It is these types of incidents that establish the so-called "naive realism" of the second unit.

The story of the second unit is built up very strictly to culminate in the possibility of Jancsi "making good." Returning to the village—as Sir John was to, with the treasure that was so truly deserved by his bravery and deeds—would be the proper way to reappear before the villagers, not to speak of Iluska and his foster-father. In exceptional cases, it *could* happen to a village boy; but no such incident existed in the collective memory of the villagers. There are, on the other hand, numerous examples of the returned veteran, who brought back nothing more than a bunch of tales—how he made good, and how he lost his fortune in an unfortunate incident that would have made him the richest man in the village—but as it is, he has to be contented with relating wonderful stories for a couple of drinks to a grateful but credulous audience.

This type of folk-hero had already entered Hungarian literature in the figure of János Háry, the hero of J. Garay's *Az obsitos* (*The Veteran*), published in 1843. The figure is still alive today, thanks to the composer Zoltán Kodály who set him to music. János Háry is a boasting old soldier, depicted sometimes ironically but always humorously. By contrast, Petőfi's ***János vitéz*** is a tragedy.

If Sir John marries the French King's daughter, realism maintained carefully by employing devices of "naive realism" suffers a mortal blow. For to have him lose his affection for Iluska would make the story lose its *raison d'être*. But even more, Jancsi would not be here to tell the story. The story, however, could end only with János' return to the village and his living happily ever after. Yet being very sensitive to social injustices, Petőfi knows that the lot of the peasants is hard work, relieved only by day-dreaming about success and happiness in a substitute world, the world of folk-tales and folk-songs. Thus, a happy ending in the second unit would make no more social relevance than any other "success story"—like those of the poor but honest working girl who eventually marries the firm's boss, a theme with many variations in the golden years of Hollywood. Along these lines, it may be noted, one of the Hungarian film versions of ***János vitéz*** ends with János' returning to the village to become a model citizen.

Paradoxically, in order to stick closer to reality, the story has to be transferred into a make-believe world. For who would think seriously that a foundling boy and an orphan girl, both of them belonging to the poverty-stricken masses of peasants, could break the social barriers that exist between the "haves" and the "have-nots." Jancsi can kill a giant easily, but he cannot compete with a rich peasant, let alone a landowner who lives in a world beyond even Fairyland. The road to social and poetical justice leads to Fairyland.

Therefore, in the third unit, János can find happiness only in a world where the rules of realism are no longer valid. It is the only way to reconcile realism and poetic justice. The story advances on lines similar to Hungarian folk-tales; the reader knows that János will overcome any and all obstacles, and this unobtrusive assurance of ultimate victory is more gratifying than any Romantic answer to Jancsi's plight.

Petőfi does not use elements of Hungarian folk-tales only. The rock-eating giants may remind the reader of the giants of Northern mythology; the second adventure, Jancsi's struggle with the witches, is one of a quite medieval kind. Fairyland, located in the middle of nowhere, echoes the ageless tradition of the Venus Mountain. It is a recurrent feature in medieval poems, rooted in Grecian fantasy—the island shining in the distant land to the West beyond the pillars of Hercules. It might have something to do with the lost world of Atlantis, or the island of Leuke to which Thetis leads her son Achilles on sea-horses, accompanied by Tritons and Nereids, to wed him to the beautiful Helen of Troy. All are variations on a theme, which still finds its echo in ***János vitéz.*** For the idea of a place where life is free from all troubles, one spent solely in enjoyment, has excited the imagination of all ages and peoples.

It is also a recurrent feature in Hungarian Romantic literature, the two best variations on the theme having been written by Vörösmarty. His *Valley of the Fairies* (*Tündérvölgy*, 1826) is usually regarded as a predecessor of ***János vitéz,*** although it represents Romantic imagination let loose without the more strict ordering of Petőfi's work. The approach of Vörösmarty's other epic, *Csongor and Tünde* (*Csongor és Tünde*, 1831), is basically different: Csongor sets forth in search of happiness which he finds neither in wealth nor in power but in the true love of Tünde from whom he had been separated. Csongor is the bearer of a philosophical question: where can happiness be found? János has never questioned that his happiness is to be found with Iluska, but he has lost it within the reality of the world (where the symbolic figure of Csongor never set foot). As a peasant boy, the victim of his circumstances, János has little chance to regain it.

It is not easy even in the third unit for János to achieve happiness. Although Petőfi provides him, besides his exceptional strength, with bravery and cunning on an epic scale—qualities not usually found in simple shepherd boys—Jancsi still needs the assistance of the giants. It is with their help that he can revenge Iluska's death upon her stepmother in the Land of Darkness (*Canto* XXI), and the very same giants help him on his way to Fairyland. By acting out his fantasy of revenge he has regained peace of mind; still, he is on the verge of suicide in Fairyland. For not even Fairyland seems to contain enough happiness to compensate János for his loss in the real world. To achieve catharsis, the reader needs a miracle even in Fairyland: it is the Water of Life that resurrects Iluska.

Although Fairyland is beyond the boundless sea of *Óperenciás*, Petőfi brings it within the reach of everybody,

> And the world seen in the dreams of the fairies
> Fairyland is only a shadow of this world
> When a human being has known a girl for the first time
> He is overcome by the joy of this dream.

The story has come full circle; we are back on earth. It is a triumph for realism.

What gives Petőfi's masterpiece artistic unity? It cannot be better characterized than by quoting the words of F. L. Lucas on the *Odyssey*. For it is "not merely a tale of changes and chances in perilous seas, it is a tale of loyalties that all those changes and chances failed, in the end, to break."

The loyalty of the young Johnny Maize does not flag in the heart of Sir John after all those adventures so many years later. He is still faithful to the memory of the dead Iluska in Fairyland, where the fairies are friendly to the stranger. But the chief test of his loyalty is the French Princess, the Nausicaa of Sir John (*Canto* XIV). It is this unfaltering devotion to Iluska which lends artistic unity and epic dimensions to this peasant tale. It is the main-spring of John's actions, by which he overcomes temptations and obstacles—not only obstacles in the outside world, but his own grief and his death wish. And it is on account of this quality in our hero's character that Petőfi renders him poetic justice in the final *Canto*. It is also by way of compensation for the harsh realities of life for the reader, the reader to whom Petőfi addressed himself—that is, the "people" who had very little chance within the existing social order.

Fulfilling the desire of the "people" for a better life, yet without leading them into a cheap escapist world, was a very difficult task to accomplish. By describing Fairyland in the way he did, Petőfi came to the conclusion that the only kind of human happiness which is available to mankind is love. By love, he means the embrace of two earthly beings. It is in their embrace that they can get "a glimpse of Fairyland." This is a simple and democratic message, based on a simple truth—for no racial, religious or social injustice can prevent human beings from getting that "glimpse." (pp. 74-86)

Lóránt Czigány, "'János Vitéz': The 'People's Epic'," in Mosaic, *Vol. VI, No. 4, Summer, 1973, pp. 69-87.*

G. F. CUSHING (essay date 1974)

[*Cushing discusses Petőfi's works in terms of the Hungarian literary tradition, focusing on the poet's "irreverence in the literary field and its effects."*]

Petőfi represents one of the peaks in the literary history of Hungary. It is customary to talk of him in superlatives and to consider him as a unique phenomenon. His brief life, political activity, romantic marriage and mysterious death all serve to heighten his fascination for generations of Hungarians, while, through the medium of translations, others have been able to catch something of the vivid power of his poetry and the freshness of his equally effective prose. When he is seen as part of the whole literary scene in Hungary he stands out even more vividly, first as an outsider with a personality forceful enough to break into a well-established tradition, and then as a leading figure in the new tradition he himself created. Outsiders are never welcome to supporters of a committed cause, and the commitment of literature to the national cause was taken for granted in Hungary by the time that Petőfi began to write; indeed, he himself had been educated in this tradition. The present study is concerned with his irreverence in the literary field and its effects. This irreverence is not to be equated with iconoclasm, for Petőfi was not a destroyer, nor does it imply mere rudeness, of which there are many examples in his private life, varying from adolescent impishness to the studied insult. His irreverence is the reaction of a highly-articulate, well-educated, sensitive and flamboyant personality to what he considers to be a dead tradition. (p. 159)

Apprenticeship in the Hungarian literary tradition could be very lengthy. The poems of Dániel Berzsenyi, one of [Ferenc] Kazinczy's protégés, appeared after careful selection and editing in 1813, though some of them had been written before the turn of the century. Vörösmarty had a briefer introduction for, like many later authors, he found encouragement among his friends at the university and entered the circle of writers through them. The success in literary circles of his epic *Zalán futása* (*The Flight of Zalán*) and the recognition of his talent by Károly Kisfaludy set the seal on his career as a writer. Bajza had a similar introduction, as did Toldy. In each case there was encouragement, criticism and discussion, all of which helped to mould the aspiring young writer in the tradition of the age. This also implies a willingness on the part of each newcomer to accept the tradition and enter into it, but since it was linked with the idea of national progress and this was the time of reform, there were no obstacles to overcome. Literature was seen to have a leading role in the political progress of Hungary, and without the tight organisation at its head it is doubtful whether it would ever have inspired so much effective political action in later years. Moreover, Hungarian literature flourished as never before; there were fierce controversies fought out in literary journals, short stories on contemporary themes and above all a great variety of verse, from epic to epigram, from the purest classical to the most sentimental romantic strain. A poetic language, avoiding the worst excesses of the language-reformers and containing a mixture of older words and forms, gradually became accepted, though the complications of Hungarian prosody had still to be explored.

This was the established tradition that Petőfi sought to enter by the only possible door—by sending specimens of his verse to two editors. The first, János Garay, apparently did not consider them worth publishing or the nineteen-year-old author worthy of a reply. The second, to whom Petőfi wrote a brief formal note, was Bajza; he not only selected **"A borozó"** for publication, but offered his friendship and advice. Bajza undoubtedly chose the most individual of the four poems he received: drinking-songs were fashionable, and the publication of this one doubtless encouraged Petőfi to continue his efforts in this line, which savoured more of the highly individual lyrics of Csokonai (1773-1805) than those of the keepers of the established romantic tradition. Petőfi had strong ideas of his own, as can be seen from his subsequent letter to Bajza, in which he asked him not to publish two poems he had sent, since he had 'evoked a great antipathy to them'. He also declared that he would trust Bajza's judgment, but not that of his rival Lázár Horváth, editor of *Honderű*. In brief, Petőfi at the very beginning of his literary career displayed a pronounced individuality which did not decrease as the years passed. Yet for the time being he seems to have been willing to accept advice. His next letter to Bajza contains the passage:

> Once again I enclose some poems and repeat my request; please treat them with the utmost severity, even if there is only one good one among them, or not even that. At least let me be assured that I have not produced bad work in the public eye. I have followed your good advice to write folk songs in quantitative metre in **"Távolból"**—without much success.

Here Petőfi is beginning to rebel against the contemporary tradition of writing 'artistic' folk poems. The lyric poets of the romantic age had come to the conclusion that such poetry should not appear as if written by a peasant; the poet should select whatever elements in folk poetry were of artistic value and write them into his verse. This Petőfi had attempted but in doing so had failed to satisfy his own sense of poetry. Of Bajza's advice there is no record, but the issue was a live one. Although folk poetry had been collected for some decades, it was only now organised by the Kisfaludy Society. Petőfi's rejection of the advice is interesting; it was polite enough, but it demonstrates the difference between two generations. The older poets had propounded theories and discussed the acceptance of folk poetry into the national literature; they had then written suitable examples, but in every case after they had developed their own lyric style and read what had happened in the same field abroad. To them such writing was largely experimental, or at most an interesting exercise. It is to their credit that they tried to imitate the spirit and not merely the external trappings of folk song, but they did not write from the heart. The best examples, such as those of Kölcsey and Vörösmarty, are artistic imitations by poets well-versed in the vocabulary and technique of romantic verse. As for Petőfi, he had an innate feeling for verse, but no long experience of the craft of writing, and he found in folk song his natural medium. It is no surprise that he felt constricted by the advice he received and, very wisely, did not pursue it further. The poem in question bears little resemblance to a folk poem: it is a lyric verse whose typically romantic vocabulary and expression heighten its pathos; it also demonstrates that the young Petőfi could write very well to order, even though his heart was not in it.

It was in the following year, 1844, that Petőfi published his first independent work, ***A helység kalapácsa*** (***The Hammer of the Village***). It is a prime example of sheer irreverence on his part. Subtitled 'A Heroic Poem in Four Cantos', it is a deliberate, brilliant and devastating parody of the heroic epic so carefully cultivated during the previous thirty years. The romantics always bemoaned the lack of a national epic in Hungary, and it had become almost a patriotic duty for poets to try their hand at this genre. Since most of them possessed lyric rather than epic proclivities, their attempts were at best noble failures and at worst disastrous. From Endre Pázmándi Horváth's *Zirc emlékezete* (*Memoir of Zirc*) of 1814 onwards there were continual efforts to master the art of the epic. The young Vörösmarty made a brave attempt in 1824 with his *Zalán futása*, whose purple passages are a delight but which fails to sustain epic interest throughout its length. Other lesser poets made valiant efforts, but for the most part produced rolling hexameters of intense gravity and pathos; the total effect was one of unrelieved lifelessness, with more bombast than inspiration. It is small wonder that Toldy deplored the lack of an Hungarian *Iliad* as late as 1843, and two years later Erdélyi declared that the national epic had yet to be written. It was in these circumstances that Petőfi's parody appeared.

Written at the instigation of Imre Vahot, the editor of *Pesti Divatlap*, but in the event rejected and passed to another publisher, ***A helység kalapácsa*** tells the tale of a brawl at a village inn. It was sparked off by the local blacksmith, the 'hammer of the village' from whom the poem takes its title, and the parish clerk, who are both desperately in love with the widowed landlady of the inn. It is a singularly unheroic theme and has an equally unheroic ending, with the blacksmith in the stocks and the parish clerk dragged off by his amazon of a wife. Petőfi clothes the tale in all the trappings of heroic epic. It has snatches of hexameters, deliberately bathetic Homeric epithets ('the bashful Erzsók with her fifty-five-year-old charms') and introduces most of the tricks of language used by previous poets to obtain nobility of style—but here they only heighten the comic effect. In short, Petőfi parodies everything that can be parodied—theme, structure, style and language—and the result is a superbly comic poem which ought to have been appreciated in its day but instead left both critics and public aghast. Literature, after all, was something to be taken seriously; it had a national and therefore ennobling aim. Moreover, on the title-page itself ***A helység kalapácsa*** was stated to be a heroic poem, and when readers realised that it was not, they felt that they had been misled and therefore regarded it as tasteless, if not offensive. Jenő Poór declared poetry to be debased by such writing and pitied readers who were misled into thinking that they were going to read something of the standard of Endre Horváth's *Arpád* or Vörösmarty's *Zalán futása*. Dardanus, alias János Pompéry, inveighed against the use of swearwords in poetry, and Lajos Nádaskay asked whether the poem had any moral aim, whether it could amuse the educated reader or raise the cultural level of the ordinary folk. He could find nothing but negative answers to his queries, and concluded that literature gained nothing from such a work. Much later, when Petőfi had become a legendary figure, there were critics who still felt it necessary to explain away this poem. Pál Gyulai, whose study of the poet's contribution to Hungarian lyric verse did much to establish his reputation, declared in his lectures during the academic year 1877-8 that ***A helység kalapácsa*** had been written against the spate of bad novels and short stories of its age, since at that time epic was not being written. This view has often been repeated since. But Petőfi was a superb writer of prose, as his ***Uti levelek*** (***Travel Letters***) and ***Uti jegyzetek*** (***Notes on a Journey***) demonstrate, and it would have been much simpler and more to the point for him to have parodied bad prose style in prose of his own. Though parody was certainly not new in Hungarian literature—it had played its part in the battle between Kazinczy and the critics of his reforms, for example—it was an innovation for it to be used on such a large scale and to attack such a sacred tradition as the creation of national epic. Comic epic, on the other hand, had existed before the romantics thrust it aside: Csokonai's *Békaegérharc* (*Battle of Frogs and Mice*) (1791) and *Dorottya* (1799) are good examples, and Petőfi's favourite poet of that period, the 'good old Gvadányi', had written his well-loved *Falusi nótárius* (*Village Notary*) in 1788. It is only fair to recall that Gvadányi had intended his poem to be taken seriously, and that his village notary had become a figure of fun to later generations, particularly since Gaál had put him on the stage in his version of 1838. It is also worth noting that Petőfi's affection for Gvadányi did not prevent him from parodying his verse effectively in **"A régi jó Gvadányi"** (**"Good old Gvadányi"**), written in the same year as *A helység kalapácsa.*

Petőfi's real target was a whole literary genre and the poets who pursued it. These included Vörösmarty, one of his mentors and indeed the prime mover in the publication of his first collection of lyric poetry, which was published immediately after the appearance of his parody. True, Vörösmarty had long given up writing epic, but he can scarcely have failed to notice the use of some of his favourite devices. It is also true that Petőfi had a high regard for both Vörösmarty and his verse; in his ***Uti jegyzetek*** he refers to the Danube 'flowing as majestically as Vörösmarty's hexameters', and two years later he attributes his whole life and poetic career to his aid. In matters of art, however, Petőfi did not allow his judgment to be overridden by personal considerations, and it was this which made his action seem astounding to his contemporaries. Taken in isolation, ***A helység kalapácsa*** appears to display extreme irreverence for tradition and a lack of sensitivity towards those well-meaning poets who maintained it. Whatever its reception, it certainly killed this tradition stone-dead. But Petőfi was not an iconoclast, as already stated; having killed one tradition, he immediately established a new one with his ***János vitéz*** . . . of 1845. The two poems should be viewed together as the end of one line and the beginning of a newer, healthier one—and it required a genius to do this. (pp. 161-65)

Such a sudden eruption of critical parody, allied with a formidable display of poetic talent took Hungarian literature completely by surprise. Since most contemporary critics, as we have seen, were so concerned with the aesthetic effect of the poem—and many later critics echoed them—they failed to realise that it was also a brilliant comic poem in its own right. The characters, all village folk, act and speak naturally, and the effect is far more realistic and natural than many efforts of that and later ages to portray peasants in literature. Thus, while Petőfi was irreverent to literary tradition, he wrote with inside knowledge of his characters; after all, even at the age of twenty-one, he had travelled more widely in Hungary than many older men, and had certainly seen more of real rustic life than most of his literary elders. This is why ***A helység kalapácsa*** is more than a mere parody and can be enjoyed by those who have no knowledge of the literary situation in Hungary or of the writers whom Petőfi was attacking.

This irreverent act, and even more the sequel, ***János vitéz,*** paved the way for new literary activity in Hungary. Arany, for example, wrote his *Az elveszett alkotmány* (*The Lost Constitution*) in 1845; this was a political satire which undoubtedly owed much to Byron, but also included elements reminiscent of Petőfi. Without ***János vitéz*** to break new ground, it is doubtful whether Arany's remarkable *Toldi* would ever have been written. Petőfi himself retained his fondness for the mixture of criticism, comedy and mild parody, particularly in poems where he was describing the Hungarian scene. In 1847, for example, he wrote the splendid miniature **"Kutyakaparó"** (**"Dogscratcher"**), with its vivid picture of the solitary, neglected wayside inn:

Inside and out, the Dogscratcher's
A miserable inn;
The unsuspecting traveller
Will find nothing within.
He won't get food, and if he looks
Just once upon the wine,
He'll curse old Noah, that he took
Into his ark a vine.

And in the same year he used a similar mixture in his uncompleted long poem **"A táblabíro"** (**"The Magistrate"**). The introduction and four cantos that have survived give an all too realistic picture of the typical fat, lazy county magistrate:

It's a good thing I'm writing about him and not drawing
a picture of him—my paper would be far too small for that.
The most important part of Mr Tamás Fegyveres is that
whose purpose is to digest food. Who has seen the Gellért
Hill in real life? That hill is this stomach—in
miniature.

He lives in a tumbledown house at the end of the village. It has a clock-tower which shows the time on only three of its four faces: the magistrate has removed the hands on the west side so that his deadly enemy, who lives in that direction, cannot tell the time. The description of the magistrate waking late in the morning is again a parody of the classical epic style. Tamás Fegyveres is fast asleep:

So fast asleep, indeed, that all the neighbours know,
And children hear his snores, while in the street they play:
'Is that a trumpet? P'raps the army's on its way!'
But now he gives a start. The nasal music's died
As if around his neck a rope were tightly tied;
His eyebrows, like a pair of hostile bears, attack
Each other with a rush, but halt upon their track.

It is one of the tragedies of Hungarian literature that this poem was never finished. Yet in its incomplete form it shows that Petőfi did not give up the strain of irreverence first found in ***A helység kalapácsa.*** (pp. 167-68)

To the previous generation, and in particular to critics, Petőfi could be as irreverent as any adolescent who believes that his elders have taken the wrong path. Vörösmarty persuaded the National Circle, a group of literary-minded individuals, to undertake the publication of Petőfi's first collection of lyric poems. Naturally this was scrutinised by a selection committee, which promptly rejected some fifteen drinking-songs—of the type which had won Bajza's approval, and which were fashionable at the time. Petőfi reacted in an irritable little poem, **"Irtóztató csalódás"** (**"A terrible disappointment"**), in which he ranged himself alongside other famous writers of this genre: Anacreon, Csokonai and Béranger. Nevertheless, he could not afford to castigate his benefactors too thoroughly, and the verse ends in a jesting promise not to pursue the type further. He was always oversensitive to criticism, as he admits in the unpublished Foreword of 1847; his somewhat adolescent annoyance and irreverence appear most vividly in his constant war with critics, whom he rates as dull and unpoetic individuals. In his **"A termés zet vadvirága (" Wild Flower of Nature")**, he proclaims himself a wild flower of nature, and tells his critics to stop barking and snapping at him, or he will choke them with a tough bone; let them 'hack away at the stunted shoots from hothouses'. They need not cite rules at him, for poetry was never beaten into him with a stick at school. In any case, he is not blooming for the 'squeamish dolts' of critics, but for folk of real taste. He concludes:

So please leave me in peace
Once and for all.
In any case, it's not very profitable
To shout at deaf ears.
And if you ever feel like teasing me,
Just take a grab at me:
I am a wild flower of unbounded nature—
With prickles.

The theme is continued in **"Rosz verseimről"** (**"On my bad poems"**), where he concedes that critics may possibly even be human, and in **"Gyalázatos világ"** (**"Monstrous World"**), both written in 1845. In this latter he calls them a serpents' brood and threatens to trample them underfoot. From the general he goes to the particular. He attacked *Honderű* in a verse addressed to that journal, and one of his critics by name in **"Császár Ferenc őnagyságához,"** a poem whose complete text came to light only in 1940. His mood never varies: in **"Mi lárma ez megént?"** (**"What's this uproar again?"**), he concludes:

Know that I treat you roughly—
It's no use, that's my style.
If men insult me, I shall reply with the sword,
But dogs I merely whip.

His prose is equally full of attacks on critics, from the jocular reference in ***Uti jegyzetek*** where he declares that he hates them even more than horseradish sauce to the more substantial charges in his ***Uti levelek.***

Here again he was attacking tradition, for literary criticism played a very important part in moulding the literature of the age. (pp. 171-72)

Petőfi's critics often attacked his verse for its 'unpoetic' language. His reply is to be found in the unpublished Foreword:

I dare to state boldly before the judgment-seat of my own conscience that I know of no man nobler in thought and feeling than I, and I have always written and still write what I have thought and felt, . . . If occasionally I am somewhat freer than others in certain expressions and subjects, this is because in my view poetry is not an aristocratic salon . . .

Petőfi, as sculpted by Béni Ferenczy in 1948.

Bajza had already declared that literature was a republic; now Petőfi declared that the language of poetry itself was democratic, and in this he broke through the tradition of his immediate predecessors, who had evolved a verse-style and vocabulary appropriate to the romantic spirit. One of the astonishing features of Hungarian literary development in the early 19th century is the swiftness with which Hungarian poets discovered how to use the resources offered by the reformed language. It is a far cry from the well-meaning pedantic exercises of the period 1800-20 to the variety and perfection of Vörösmarty scarcely a decade later. The romantics set extremely high standards. To readers versed in such poetry, Petőfi's direct, colloquial and sometimes prosaic language seemed almost obscene and certainly irreverent in its scorn for tradition. But what many critics failed to observe—or perhaps were too appalled by the language to note—is that Petőfi himself is the centre of his lyric verse; he deliberately casts himself in the roles he portrays and uses suitable language, whether it is 'poetic' or not. When he describes an outlaw, he plays that part; he could play the drunkard, the student, the soldier, the lover—indeed any character, and provide the language and style most natural to it. He had, after all, served his apprenticeship on the stage, and there was a great deal of the actor in him. Others had written lyrics *about* various characters; none had penetrated them so thoroughly or realistically.

Coupled with this ability to use language naturally was an innate sense of style and form. Who else could have obscured hexameters so neatly as in **"Játszik öreg földünk"** (**"Our old earth is playing"**)? His parodies have already been noted. His range was formidable, from macaronic verse (**"Deákpályám"** (**"My school career"**)) to the solemnity of **"A nemzetgyüléshez"** (**"To the National Assembly"**). This technical ability and the apparent ease with which he wrote again made him suspect to his fellow-writers. He was also suspected of pandering to the masses instead of attempting to raise their standards. He was not ashamed to use their language, and his success in adopting their style can be gauged by the immediate acceptance of his verse by them. While educated Hungarians read his poetry, the folk sang it and transmitted it orally, often modifying it, as Gyula Illyés notes in his biography [see Additional Bibliography]. To his critics Petőfi has the answer in his Foreword:

> These gentlemen have not the least idea of Hungarian rhyme and rhythm. They search for Latin metres and German cadence in Hungarian poetry, and these do not exist in my verse, it is true, but it was not my intention anyway to keep strictly to them. Hungarian rhythm and rhyme have not yet been defined; they will develop later, if at all, and gain definition, so I have no knowledge of them either—but I do have some inkling of them . . . I am led by my instinct, and where I am accused of the greatest negligence in rhyme and metre is perhaps the very place where I come closest to the perfect, the true Hungarian verse-form.

Here Petőfi puts his case admirably. Latin metres and German forms had indeed dominated the early 19th century, and Petőfi himself uses them frequently enough. The study of 'Hungarian' verse-forms began well after Petőfi's death and is still a controversial matter. How right Petőfi was to trust his own judgment can be demonstrated by a comparison of his folk poetry with that of his countless imitators.

His simplicity was also frequently criticised. He made poetry look too easy and walked the tightrope between simplicity and banality with remarkable good sense. (It is here that his translators have often failed him.) He comments:

> I cannot comprehend how even among exceptional folk there are those who either don't know or don't realise that simplicity is the first and supreme rule, and that a man who has no simplicity has nothing at all. And let them not protest that their thoughts are too lofty to be expressed in common language.

Some of Petőfi's most effective poems are also the simplest: **"Szabadság, szerelem"** (**"Liberty and Love"**) is a good example:

> Liberty and love,
> These two I must have.
> For my love I'll sacrifice
> My life.
> For liberty I'll sacrifice
> My love.

This does not imply, however, that the thoughts contained in such poems are necessarily simple or light-hearted, as can be seen in **"A bánat? Egy nagy óceán."** It is easy to forget, as his critics also apparently did, that he could write in as lofty a style as the most confirmed romantic. Apart from the obvious and not very good poems in his sentimental outburst ***Cipruslombok Etelke sírjáról*** (***Cypress Leaves from the Grave of Etelke***), which delighted so many female readers, **"Tündèrálom"** (**"Fairy Dream"**) is a superb example of his romantic style, with its long lines, strict rhymes and solemnly picturesque language:

> No shore, no pathway is there yet before me,
> I'm tossed for ever as the waves roll by;
> Still more I'm tossed upon the mighty current . . .
> I cannot anchor and I cannot die.
>
> Then evening came. In golden clouds the sun
> Sank down behind the hills of violet hue
> And all the plain, that arid ocean wide,
> Began to fill with pallid, misty dew.
> The rock whereon we stood, in the last rays
> Glowed purple as the cushions on a throne—
> But then it was a throne, and on it we
> The young king and queen of happiness unknown.

No other Hungarian poet of the 19th century used the resources of the vocabulary so fully, from the delicacy of

> Nyom nélkül jártak, oly könnyűk valának,
> Könnyebbek, mint a szellő, mint a lég.

to expressions like 'léha söpredek' and 'óbégattatok rútul'. It is quite unjust to accuse him of writing nothing but 'unpoetic' verse. His sheer range confounds his critics.

If Petőfi's attitude to critics was consistently irreverent, he had other targets too. He had no love for clerics, and said so more than once. But in one sphere his irreverence appeared to go beyond the bounds of good taste: his attitude to Hungary and the Hungarians seemed almost treasonable to many. When the relatively lenient censor Reseta read his collected works before publication he refused permission for **"A magyar nemzet"** (**"The Hungarian Nation"**) to appear, saying, 'My dear boy, I can't permit you to slander my nation!' The refrain of this powerful poem declares that the Hungarian nation does not deserve to live, since it is selfish, ungrateful and degenerate (and Petőfi makes no distinction here between 'nation' and 'people'). This is no isolated example. He castigates his country in phrases which have become familiar enough now, but in their day had the power to shock. It was the fact that a poet used such language that made Petőfi's irreverence the more inexcusable. Since the days of Széchenyi's *Hitel* (*Credit*), reformers and writers had constantly tried to rouse the Hungarians to action, and they did not mince their words. Petőfi had a sense of vocation at least as strong as that of Széchenyi. He could poke fun at such characters as the country magistrate, but when his emotions were roused he expressed himself with a ruthlessness and ferocity that took both friends and critics aback. . . . No reformer had become as exasperated as this. Nor did any of them proclaim 'I am Hungarian. And my face blazes with shame; I must be ashamed to be Hungarian.' As the critical year 1848 approached his impatience grew, as can be seen in **"A magyar ifjakhoz" ("To the Hungarian Youth")** and **"A szájhősök" ("The Braggarts")**, both written in 1847; they demand action, not empty words. And he pours out his scorn in **"Okatootáia,"** the country which wishes to have nothing to do with civilisation: 'Flourish, noble country, great nation, and may civilisation not trouble you for ages!' In 1848 his sheer desperation at the inactivity and lassitude around him calls forth such poems as **"A nemzethez" ("To the Nation")**. By now, however, his irreverent voice was not alone in chastising the Hungarians: even among the older generation there was a change of mood, as Vörösmarty's "Országháza" ("House of Parliament") demonstrates. Yet most of these wrote in more measured tones; comparison between Petőfi's impetuous tirades and Bajza's "Ébresztő" ("Alarm") or Garay's "Kelet népéhez" ("To the People of the East") and "Szabadsági dal" ("Freedom Song") shows how far the well-established writers were bound to past tradition. Their emotions, however strong, are clothed in deliberately 'poetic' language and lack the brutal urgency of Petőfi. There is no doubt that Petőfi enjoyed shocking his readers as much as he enjoyed battling with his literary rivals. If he was branded as an irreverent young puppy, then he would play that part and live up to his reputation, some indication of which appears in his ***Uti levelek***:

> When we emerged on the plains of Heves, the clergyman began to abuse the flat lands, whereupon I deemed it my duty to speak up in their defence, and what's more, in true Petőfi style—that's to say with appropriate churlishness. I can't help it. Let no one abuse in my hearing my beloved, the French, cream cheese and noodles, and the plains. From this time onwards I had a continuous dispute with the reverend gentleman.

Petőfi found it necessary to defend himself for his irreverence on several occasions. His argument each time is that he was given frankness at birth and could never escape from it. The idea that frankness is a licence to be rude is an adolescent view, but he clung to it. (pp. 174-78)

The question must now be asked: was Petőfi's irreverence merely a personal phenomenon that stirred Hungarian literary life briefly, or did it have a lasting effect? The answer is that Hungarian literature was never quite the same again. His influence during his brief life was remarkable, and his irreverence, like his literary innovations, left its effect. Yet the collapse of the revolution of 1848-9, and with it the destruction of all that the national literature had been advocating, meant that there was little immediate room for outsiders; Hungarian literature had to reorganise itself and find a new national aim. Petőfi was a dangerous example, though far too vivid and recent a figure to ignore completely. True, he had many imitators, which led the critic Pál Gyulai to end his definitive study *Petőfi Sándor és lyrai költészetünk* (*Sándor Petőfi and our lyric poetry*) with an apt comment on the state of literature only five years after his death:

> In recent verse there is little to cheer us. Neither in form nor in content has it produced excellence or novelty. We read works written with more or less success, but the sounds of well-known strains come from them. We hear Petőfi in a thousand variations. Unconsciously or deliberately they dig up his emotions and ideas, they appropriate his words and his tone, and the result is poetry which has some claim to originality but enriches neither literature nor the heart with new treasures.

(pp. 179-80)

G. F. Cushing, "The Irreverence of Petőfi," in The Slavonic and East European Review, *Vol. LII, No. 127, April, 1974, pp. 159-81.*

ENIKŐ MOLNÁR BASA (essay date 1980)

[In this excerpt from her full-length study of Petőfi's life and works, Basa discusses Petőfi's narrative poem The Apostle.*]*

Petőfi's comments on the role and purpose of poetry clearly showed his belief in the mission of the poet. Even in the objective lyrics, he had a higher purpose than just the delineation of a scene or a picturesque way of life; he saw these works as political statements because they gave the common people a place in literature, to paraphrase his own comment to Arany. But there is a group of poems, supplemented by some prose works, letters, and diary entries, that give explicit evidence of his political and philosophical concerns. The critical comments on society in ***Úti jegyzetek,*** though couched in a light vein, already showed this involvement. His ***Úti levelek,*** more personal in tone since they record his courtship and marriage, also revealed his interest in the Reform movement. He was closely involved with the campaign to bring new ideas into the rigid processes of local elections, and he was generally accepted as one of the leaders of the Revolution. This role emerges clearly in his diary, a record of his ideas and activities between March 15 and April 29, 1848.

In the summer of 1848, following the establishment of a parliamentary form of government and the extension of the franchise, both Petőfi and Arany ran for office. Though both were defeated in their home districts by the conservative candidates, Petőfi's campaign speeches and his comments on the victory of old-style politics showed that he was willing to work for reforms within the legal framework. As yet, he was not a revolutionary, only a reformer. He was, however, beginning to see that the lack of idealism and dedication among the leaders might lead to the distortion of the ideals that had unified the nation on March 15 [when, inspired by the publication of Petőfi's **"Nemzeti Dal—Talpra magyar"** and a twelve-point manifesto of political reform, the youth of Pest united peacefully and gained nominal acceptance of their demands from authorities]. He sought the remedy in writing, hoping to educate the electorate to their responsibilities and to remind the elected officials of the important trust they held. On April 22, 1848, he urged Arany to accept the editorship of a new periodical in order to insure its retaining a populist national slant. Arany, who shared Petőfi's hopes for the role of poets in shaping a new social consciousness, was willing. He hoped that he could "speak to the people . . . because it is not such a secondary task to uplift the people slowly through literature that it would not deserve attention in the present times. I would like to be effective here; this would be my element."

Petőfi, living in the capital and involved in the debates between the conservatives and the liberals, was full of hope at first. On July 1, 1848, he wrote: "How beautiful that future will be, my friend, how beautiful! You cannot imagine it; only I can know that for I see it as clearly as I see your portrait on the wall." By August 16, however, he began to have doubts that this future could be realized without "a revolution which turns everything upside down but which also saves everything." He felt the nation to be on the eve of this great revolution; if it should fail to happen, however, he believed the "nation would be lost, and lost so shamefully as no nation had yet been lost." It is in the same letter that he announced the completion of his long narrative poem, ***Az Apostol (The Apostle)***. (pp. 111-12)

During the summer of 1848, while compromises were sought with the Habsburgs, the new laws were slowly and not always perfectly implemented. To Petőfi it seemed that the promise of March had been betrayed. Even among his companions he sensed an emerging conservatism. His defeat in the elections for the Kiskún district, and especially the virulent personal campaign against him, added to his disappointment. The poetic result of these months was . . . ***Az Apostol.*** Though written in the summer of 1848, it contained ideas found in much of his earlier poetry. Here, however, these were concentrated in the heroic and tragic figure of Szilveszter who embodied much of Petőfi as he saw himself.

First, the poem affirms that resistance, even when futile, is noble. Still, it is an extremely pessimistic poem, because the victory of right is projected into the future, indicating that Petőfi had quite given up on reforms in his own time. The hero suffers and dies for his ideals, but instead of being honored, he is despised even by those whom he sought to help.

The poem, of over 3,600 lines, is divided into twenty chapters of irregular length. For the vehicle of his chagrin and disappointment, Petőfi chose a flexible style which allowed him to move easily from narrative to lyrical passages. The basic iambic rhythm and the varied line lengths suggest free verse, giving it both variety and naturalness. Almost never do two consecutive lines have an equal number of syllables, and this planned irregularity extends to the rhyme also: it is occasional and used for emphasis or to increase the lyricism of a passage. Thus, some speeches and descriptions seem to be songs set into the poem while others suggest meditative odes.

Into this poem Petőfi poured the thoughts of many years. Gyula Illyés called it "the dictionary of his principles" in which the meanings he ascribed to words like "happiness, liberty, God, priest, rebellion, tyranny, king" are revealed [see Additional Bibliography]. Within limits, this statement is true, but it must be remembered that the poem found its form in a very dark period of the author's life, and consequently only the dark side is shown.

The poem opens in the middle of the hero's career at a time when he is almost destroyed by anxieties over the future of his country. The opening scene, chosen for its emotional impact and thematic importance, shows the hero in the moment of decision: should he choose his ideals and bring death upon his loved ones, or choose survival, and compromise his dedication to liberty and humanity. By putting his learning at the service of the establishment, he would assure a comfortable future for himself and his family, but he would be untrue to himself and betray all of their former sufferings. While Szilveszter ponders this decision, the poet sketches the poverty of the little household in suggestive and realistic terms: a flickering candle reveals a damp garret room furnished only with a rough table and bed, some chairs and straw sacks. Here, the mother attempts to nurse her starving child while the older boy sleeps. The father, sitting at the table, is lost in thought, but when he has given the last piece of bread to the child and all the rest are asleep, his thoughts soar: he has made his decision, and he accepts his destiny: he will work to free his fellowmen and prays to God for strength. The reward he seeks is the happiness of others. With this, the scene closes and Szilveszter, too, sleeps.

In the next stanzas, Petőfi contrasted the gloom of the opening lines with the promise of dawn. There, the moonless and starless dark night made "the world as black / as a rented conscience." Here, the rising sun seems to crown the sleeping man "with a golden crown that is like / A bright, warm kiss from God's lips." The setting and the shift from hopelessness to the promise of a glorious future, as well as the apotheosis suggested by the sunlight streaming on the sleeping man, is an appropriate introduction to the survey of his life. The biographical flashback introduced by the question, "Who is this man, so haunted by fate yet seemingly blessed by God?" is answered in the following chapters.

Szilveszter, abandoned as infant, is found by a thief on December 31—thus his name. He can hardly walk when his foster father begins his training in the trade, but when the child is only four, the thief is caught and hung. He would most likely starve, but a sham beggar, an old hag, takes him in to beg for her. In a few years' time, he is saved from a life of crime by a well-to-do gentleman who decides to take him home as a servant and whipping boy for his own son. Though in better physical circumstances, Szilveszter finds the young man's tyranny hard to bear. His only consolation is that now he has a chance to study; he therefore submits to the abuse heaped on him until his sixteenth year. At this time, a particularly unjust attack by the "young master" triggers a rebellion that can not be stifled, as he declares:

> . . . ha a lázadás az,
> Midőn az ember érzi és kimondja,
> Hogy ő is ember, mint akárki más,
> Ugy büszkén mondom: lázadó vagyok.

> If it be rebellion / When a man feels and says / That he, too, is human like anyone else, / Then I'll proudly say: I am a rebel.

Though again without food or resources, Szilveszter's prospects are still not hopeless: the tutor, who had long sympathized with the bright boy, gives him money to complete his studies.

As he reflects on how best to invest the money so generously given him, Szilveszter decides to dedicate his life to bettering the lot of other men. Liberty, he knows, is the means of happiness for the world, and so he vows to serve this ideal with his knowledge. The long monologue in which this resolution is born begins with a homely metaphor: a grape, though a small fruit, needs a full summer and many, many rays of sunlight to mature, so the world, a much larger fruit, must need millions of years—but it, too, will eventually mature. The rays that nurture it, however, are great men's souls, and these are not born often. He is such a ray, he realizes, and so he must set to work:

> Mi célja a világnak?
> Boldogság! s erre eszköz? a szabadság!
> Szabadságért kell küzdenem,
> Mint küzdtek érte oly sokan,
> És hogyha kell, elvérzenem,

Mint elvérzettek oly sokan!
Fogadjatok, ti szabadság-vitézek,
Fogadjatok szent sorotok közé
Zászlótokhoz hűségct esküszön. . . .
Alszol, kicsiny
Kis magzatom;
Mit álmodol? . . .
Hisz még nem a föld
Ölében alszol,
Anyád ringat még,
Anyád ölel.—
Aludj, aludj,
Szép gyermekem. . . .

What is the goal of the world? / Happiness! And the means to this end? Liberty! / I must strive for Liberty, / As so many others have done, / And if I must, I'll bleed to death / As so many others have done! / Accept me, you heroes of Liberty / Accept me among your ranks: / I swear allegiance to your banner. . . .

This dedication is first tested when Szilveszter refuses a lucrative post in a grand man's retinue to serve as a notary for an unimportant village. But, because he teaches the people his ideas of liberty, he is driven away. What is hardest to bear is that the very men he had sought to help now turn against him. The only friend who remains true is the lord's daughter: she follows him and chooses to share his life.

New disappointments, however, follow. The great work he had been working on is not accepted by any publisher, since it cannot get the censor's approval. Thus, in order to earn something and provide for his family, he takes a copyist's job. As the years pass, the family increases to four and his great work still remains without a patron. This, then, is the state of affairs on that dark night when the hero contemplates his future.

The section concludes with the same lines that had served to introduce it: the rising sun brings the promise of better times. Ironically, events become even darker. The lines, however, link the various sections stylistically and indicate quite clearly that these eleven chapters form a separate unit within the poem.

The morning fails to live up to its promise. The infant dies at its mother's breast and Szilveszter must bear one more burden. However, instead of violent grief and recriminations, the poem strikes a minor key. The mother's sorrow is expressed in a tender lullaby. Death brings no real separation, she asserts in her gentle words:

Do you sleep / My little child; / What do you dream? / . . . Not yet do you sleep / In the earth's bosom, / Your mother rocks you still, / Your mother hugs you; / Sleep, sleep, / My beautiful child. . . .

Even when she contemplates the little grave, all the mother can think of is the time they will spend together as she speaks to the child. The effect of the whole scene is a relief from suffering: the dead child is almost envied by the others.

After this sentimental interlude, Szilveszter seems to be at last on the verge of success: an underground press publishes his work. But the moral victory he savors is brief: the authorities soon move against him. Before he is silenced, however, he delivers a denunciation of the "criminal king." He curses the king in words that evoke the violence of the French Revolution. Instead of support, however, he only gains hatred, even among the masses in whose name he speaks. He is most enraged, however by the lack of decency shown by man to man: he would go to prison meekly if only he were allowed to say farewell to his wife and child; he would consider his chains ornaments if only he would not be leaving behind him a helpless family. In prison, Szilveszter first rages against injustice, but with time he sinks into a stupor. The only thing that rouses him is a vision of his wife come to bid him farewell after her death. In a fit of anger, he seeks to commit suicide, but then settles into his old lethargy.

Ten years pass during which he loses all interest in life until one day a bird sings on the window of his cell. In a lyrical outburst, hope is reborn:

". . . Dalolj, dalolj, kis madaram, dalolj,
Eszembe jut dalodról,
Hogy egykor éltem, hogy még most is élek,
Eszembe jut dalodrul ifjuságom,
A régen régen elszállt ifjuság,
E szép tavasz, s ezen tavasznak
Virága, a szép szerelem!
Dalod fölkelti szenvedésimet,
De egyszersmind meg is vigasztal,
S a megvigasztalt fajdalom talán
Még édesebb, mint maga az öröm,
Dalolj, dalolj, kis madaram, dalolj!" . . .

"Sing, sing my little bird, sing / Your song reminds me / That once I lived, and even now am alive, / Your song brings back my youth, / The long, long ago lost vigor, / This lovely spring, and the spring's / Flower, beautiful love! / Your song rouses my griefs / But at the same time consoles them, / And pain consoled is perhaps / Even sweeter than joy itself, / Sing, sing my little bird, sing."

Such alternation between scenes of deep despair, rage, and hopeless stupor with the images of hope and renewal was characteristic of Petőfi. Here, however, he used the technique more consistently and more skillfully than he had done in the briefer lyrics. The device adds to the success of the narrative: it provides the relief needed in any tragedy. Appropriately, into what seems the most hopeless period of Szilveszter's life, a promise of better things is introduced. Szilveszter believes that the bird, the free creature of free skies, is a messenger of hope and freedom, and he rallies. After all, he concludes, the world must grow weary of its chains and shame will eventually rebel. Fittingly, the bird does prove to be an omen, and Szilveszter is soon set free.

Upon his release, he seeks his old home, but no one there can tell him where his wife lies buried or what has become of his son. Worse still, the nation is not free, but has sunk even deeper into servitude. Yet, he still hopes:

Was such suffering then in vain, / In vain such sacrifice / Which nobler hearts have brought / For mankind? Useless / All effort, all struggle? / That is impossible, a hundred times impossible!

Out of desperation, he formulates a plan: he will kill the king, and thus eliminate the source of all oppression.

This final resolution taken, he mingles with the festive crowds that cheer the king, shouts, "Let the king die," and fires his weapon. The apostle of freedom, however, is reviled by the masses who gladly see him executed in a few days' time. Unsuccessful in his own time, Szilveszter regrets he had paid such a high price for human blindness that *will* not see.

In the concluding chapter, Petőfi presented the future: later generations, better than their fathers, do gain the freedom Szilveszter had sought, and glorify these martyrs of the cause.

Petőfi left the time and scene of this poem vague. While it is clear that the narrative is set in a time close to the poet's own, little else is specified. The relative modernity of the poem is seen in the liberal and revolutionary sentiments worked into the romantic tale, but more importantly in the emphasis on an urban setting, the constant mention of the press, and the threat of censorship. The locale, left similarly undetermined, could be any country where the evils Szilveszter combats were found: censorship, the privileges of birth and wealth, the oppression of new ideas.

However, the poem is not vague, and in the details that lend realism to the story it is clear that Petőfi is writing about a composite picture of the Austrian monarchy he seems to have evolved. This is based on the knowledge of poverty and hardship that he himself had faced in his wanderings, and his often unnecessary conflicts with authority of almost every kind. Quick to take offense himself, he was supersensitive to what he imagined to be the misuse and abuse of power. Thus, he exaggerated what he knew and created a poem against a personified Tyranny, not against oppression in any one country or at any one time. The theme of the poem is not one man's struggle against evil, but rather the search for an answer to the question of how this evil (tyranny, oppression, injustice) can be resisted. Is a futile fight worth the effort? Is it justified? Petőfi had to face these questions in the summer of 1848, but they are questions that had been valid earlier and have continued to be valid. Thus, the poem does touch on universal themes, and the vagueness of the setting is appropriate. (pp. 127-34)

Enikő Molnár Basa, in her Sándor Petőfi, *Twayne Publishers, 1980, 190 p.*

BÉLA G. NÉMETH (essay date 1983)

[*In this chronological study tracing Petőfi's development as a poet, Németh identifies different stages in his writing career.*]

His Life and Personality

Petőfi is still the Hungarian poet best known abroad. He was the beloved of the gods, lavishly endowed with everything a great poet needs: talent, the right historical situation, a manifest destiny. He lived twenty-six years in all, and left behind a body of work which in both quality and volume cannot be ignored in any assessment of world literature. At the same time it constituted the turning-point of an era in the literature of his nation. And he was given what was only given to Byron: a death which made of him a symbol and a myth. This poet of love, liberty and faith in life died on the battlefield as a volunteer in the cause of freedom. In Hungary, his name is synonymous with the very word "poet". It is not that he had no forerunners: Csokonai and Kölcsey, as well as such Romantics as Vörösmarty, contributed a great deal towards the foundations of the populist movement. But all the hopes and endeavours of the *népies* period, still regarded as one of the peaks of Hungarian literature, found their consummation in Petőfi. (p. 222)

The Poet of the People

His early poems were imitations of folksongs, genre scenes and autobiographical outpourings. He rejected the high-flown stateliness, rhetoric and ornamentation of Romanticism for the natural ease and directness of folk song and its structural simplicity. He preferred the Hungarian metre based on stress to one based on the length of syllable. He wrote on the joys and sorrows of love, the sadness engendered by the lack of love: **"I Turned into the Kitchen"** (**"Befordúltam a konyhára"**), **"All Along the Village Street"** (**"A faluban utcahosszat"**), **"To Blazes! . . ."** (**"Lánggal égo"**), **"Love, Love"** (**"A szerelem, a szerelem"**), **"There are Thousands"** (**"Ezrivel terem"**), etc. He was particularly attracted to village scenes and characters which were also popular with the Romantics. But Petőfi's genre scenes are not the "interesting" figures depicted by the Romantic poets but the ordinary people he met on his wanderings—the shepherd, the innkeeper, the strolling player, the schoolboy, the field-guard. His humour does not derive, as it so often did with the Romantics, from the exposure of an inferior character to a superior point of view. He identifies himself with his characters in understanding and sympathy; he is not laughing at their expense, they are both comic and likeable as in **"Csokonai,"** **"The Inkpot"** (**"A tintásüveg"**), **"Master Pinty"** (**"Pinty úrfi"**), and the **"Meditation of a Thirsty Man"** (**"Szomjas ember tűnődése"**). His characters are dramatic characters; they speak in the first person, he enjoys throwing himself into the personality of the tippler, the happy-go-lucky fellow with no heed for the morrow. But some honest, revealing personal poems are already beginning to appear. The poems in which he reveals his inner self, as well as his village pictures and songs, clearly show how an element of Romanticism broadens and develops into a new quality in his poetry. The Romantics also sought out what was natural and genuine, and they also expressed it in terms of characters and people. But their characters and people were idealized and stylized and their concern for them was more a matter of nostalgia for an ideal past and lack of faith in the present; it was an expression of their hopes rather than their knowledge and assurance. For Petőfi the natural and the right of his subjects to be seen as they were, unclothed by romantic fancy, was a matter of everyday fact. In his poetry things are what they are, he did not feel as the Romantics did any inability to understand the world around him.

The Development of a Populist Programme

Quite characteristically, he expressed his conscious revolt against the Romantic attitude with an excellent parody of the heroic poem. This marks the beginning of his second period, when he consciously adopted populism. The two epic poems which are the most typical examples of this period are his parody ***The Hammer of the Village*** (***A helység kalapácsa,*** 1844) and a narrative poem, ***John the Hero*** (***János vitéz,*** 1844). The first is laid in the village pub where two village gallants "Big-handed Fejenagy", the blacksmith and the "tender-hearted local cantor" vie for the favour [of] the "chaste Erzsók". The whole village appears in this poem, and the rivals, of course, end up with a fight. This is not just a straightforward parody of the Romantic epic as a genre. The real parody lies in the down-to-earth story and the down-to-earth characters dealt with in a high-flown Romantic style. ***John the Hero*** is just the opposite. The tale, the trappings are stock Romantic; the treatment, the picture projected, is anything but Romantic. The hero, John, is a foundling, brought up by his cruel shepherd stepfather. He falls in love with the orphan Iluska who is equally badly treated by [her] stepmother. One day, while dallying with Iluska, John's flock strays and the sheep are lost; he is driven out of the house and sets out to seek his fortune. Iluska dies of grief. After a number of adventures, typical of folk-tales, János arrives in Fairyland where he becomes the prince of the country and is reunited with Iluska. This poem not only symbolizes the victory of the poor and defenceless; it is not only an example of the new "epic", written in the language of common speech and the form of versification used by the common people, it also reveals the changes which had taken place in the relationship and outlook of man to the world and to life in general. In Romanticism, realistic themes generally took on a mysterious irrational meaning; with Petőfi, even the unrealistic subjects were treated rationally and realistically. The poems breathe out a faith in man as he is, an emotional and "intellectual" faith typical of populism in general and Petőfi in particular. Romanticism was impregnated with uncertainty and mistrust towards man and the world; Petőfi was assured and confident that the world could be understood and ordered aright.

Personal and Poetic Crisis

Petőfi never lost the faith and certainty so characteristic of revolutionaries in revolutionary ages; but there were times in his life when they weakened and on occasion seemed to fail completely. The worst of these periods followed the completion of ***John the Hero*** and is known as the "Clouds" period. The progressive political movements, to which Petőfi had by now given his whole-hearted support, ran into difficulties, he lost some of his friends and felt painfully lonely. In his cycle of poems ***Clouds*** (***Felhők,*** 1846), his rejection of the world, his profound pessimism and his anarchic rebellion can be seen in the fragmented, aphoristic style and in the hyperbolic images and phrases. To find an appropriate form for such feelings he turned to the novel. ***The Hangman's Rope*** (***A hóhér kötele,*** 1846), and to drama: ***Tiger and Hyena*** (***Tigris és hiéna,*** 1845). In action, situation and characters both these works conform to the pattern of French Romanticism, but they are pervaded by the same sense of suffering as the poems of the ***Clouds*** cycle, and it is this lyric element that gives them certain value. They are important more for the stages in his development they reveal than for their intrinsic merit. The need to face the contradictions of the society in which he lived, helped the poet to work out an intellectual and political foundation for his hitherto spontaneous faith in life, which brought him into line with contemporary revolutionary thinking. His style, which up to that time had been developed to express personal feelings and emotions, broadened to take on a more philosophical and reflective colour.

By dealing successfully with this crisis in his life, his work, and the popular style he had adopted, benefited in three different ways: he integrated poetry and politics; his love poetry became more subtle, structured on several levels, and his narrative poetry acquired a philosophical character.

His Political Poetry

Although he had written political poems all along from the beginning of his career, they had been written spontaneously and, as it were, by the way. From this period onwards, his political poetry was consciously, directly conceived, influencing his images and descriptions. The sinking sun was compared to the bloody despot expelled from his country:

> Like a king banished to the border of his land,
> the sun looks back over the rim of the world,
> he gives one last glance
> from his angry face,
> and as soon as his eye reaches the further horizon
> the kingly head loses its bloody crown.
> (**"The Puszta, in Winter"—"A puszta, télen"**)

the clink of wine glasses to the clanking handcuffs of captive nations (**"My Songs"—"Dalaim"**). By this time he was known and appreciated by the radical public, and had won a devoted friend of equal poetic stature, János Arany. He made several attempts to form literary circles in support of his political ideas (The Society of the Ten and the circle connected with the journal *Életképek*). He had won a number of friends (amongst them the novelist Jókai) and he regarded Arany's epic poem *Toldi* as another token of the persuasive success of their literary and political work. The letters the two poets exchanged preserve the memories of a warm friendship and trace the formation of the policy and programme of the new movement: "When the people rule in poetry, they will be near to ruling in politics as well, and this is the task of this century," was how Petőfi expressed it.

He was one of the greatest poets of world literature with a deliberate political mission. Even Goethe would not have applied his derogatory *garstiges Lied*—squalid song—to Petőfi, so personal, so deeply subjective, so truly lyrical was Petőfi's political poetry. This was true from the beginning of his career and it was not at the battle of Segesvár, where he died, that his famous lines gained credit:

> Love and Liberty
> Are all the world for me!
> For love I'd sacrifice
> My life on every day,
> For freedom I would give
> My very love away! . . .

In politics he moved from the centre left of national liberalism to the extreme left of the revolutionary movement.

He was politically widely read and very well-informed, familiar not only with the figures and events of the Great French Revolution but also with the complete spectrum of its ideas. His revolutionary and democratic beliefs led him to give the general ideas of progressive Romanticism a definite and specific significance. The Romantics, for instance, believed that one of the criteria of the True Man was the love of one's native land. Petőfi shared the feelings expressed in the Romantic question of Sir Walter Scott: "Breathes there a man, with soul so dead, / Who never to himself hath said, / 'This is my own, my native land!'" But he believed that one's native land could only be loved if it gave freedom, life and equality to its sons. Romanticism continued to glorify the "People" and demanded a place for them at the centre of national culture. It was Petőfi's belief that the "People" should also have a place at the centre of the nation's political life. Nor was it for his own nation alone that he desired freedom. He answered the great vexed question of Hungarian politics, the "national minorities" question, by demanding freedom for all nations and nationalities. In a great poem, **"One Thought Keeps Tormenting Me . . ." ("Egy gondolat bánt engemet,"** 1846), comparable in its power to the greatest Romantic-Symbolist visions, he dies exaltedly in the final battle for world freedom.

> Let it be there they take up my scattered bones
> when the great day of mass burial comes,
> and with measured, solemn music of the dead
> and black-draped banners lifted up ahead
> the heroes are given to their common grave.
> Sacred world-freedom, it is you who must grieve! . . .

He admired Béranger, in common with many others in Europe at that time, but in reality he was closer to Shelley and Schiller's white-hot love of freedom than to Béranger's mediocre versification.

It was also politics which led him to abandon the Romantics' idealization of the past. Unlike Vörösmarty and his disciples, he saw little beauty in the past, the time when the people, he believed, lived in permanent degradation. Like Michelet, he despised the history of kings, priests and nobles. He advised

Arany never to write about even the best of kings, yet nonetheless a king. He regarded revolutionaries as alone worthy subjects for celebration in verse. He looked towards the future with whole-hearted ardour, and even welcomed technological progress as the inseparable counterpart of capitalist development. The redeeming and reformist attitude of Romanticism acquired a concrete meaning in his work, and merging with his patriotic feelings, intensified into a Messianic fervour. The national consciousness of the Romantics was nourished on the great deeds of the past; Petőfi was inspired by the belief that he stood in the front line in the battle for national freedom.

The Romantics had chosen Hamlet as a symbol of their doubts and indecisions; Petőfi saw the solution of human problems in the useful social deed and not in brooding meditation: "Whether it will be useful or not? / That is the question of questions. / Not 'to be or not to be'." (**"Light!"—"Világosságot!"**) This utilitarian and hardly poetic principle, so much like Goethe's *"wahr ist, was fördernd ist"*, brought him, of all his contemporaries, closest to Heine and the Russian revolutionary democrats. The main dilemma of Romanticism centred on the relationship between social man and the independent individual; Petőfi found the answer to the contradiction in social action.

His Love Poetry

After the early cycles (***Cypress-leaves—Cipruslombok,*** 1845 and ***The Pearls of Love—Szerelem gyöngyei,*** 1845) his most beautiful love poems were those written to his wife, Júlia Szendrey. These poems have been the subject of criticism in later times. His critics have reproached him for continuing to write love poems to his wife, and to her alone. These poems are, they claim, chastely conventional productions, "average", "normal". There is some truth in this, especially if considered from a psychoanalytical point of view. But it is a matter of approach. In one of his best-known love poems (**"September's End"—"Szeptember végén"**), in autumn melancholy the young husband asks the wife bending over him:

> Tell me, if I die first, will you shed tears
> and cover up my body with a shroud?
> Or could another man bear out my fears
> and second love then blot my name quite out? . . .

His critics remonstrated that in his poetry the "game of love and death" was set in a framework of ordinary life, treated melodramatically, almost bordering on banality. His love poetry is none the less very powerful poetry, for he accepted and lived the "game of love and death" as an unadorned everyday fact of normal life.

It is in fact this very aspect of his love poetry which was new. This is what love is like in the lives of the common people: it is one of the facets, parts of a whole life. Love was worthy of consideration as such, and the "man in love" remained his own essential self. One seeks in vain the myth or mystery of love in Petőfi's poetry. It is untainted by the decadent morbidity of contemporary poetry, the demoniac elements of Romanticism and, as a general rule, by eroticism erected into a myth. Yet his love poems were not written purely for their own sake: explicitly or implicitly, there was always the desire to communicate. It was inspired by the love of family and common human existence and the desire for a constructive life. Not only being in love, but also appreciating the woman as a partner in life. For Petőfi, a well-balanced person, love was not a refuge from life, but at once a concentration and a dispersion of all his life-force. His most famous love poems are: **"What Shall I Call You"** (**"Minek nevezzelek"**), **"The Sad Wind of Autumn Speaks to the Trees . . ."** (**"Beszél a fákkal . . ."**), **"The Bush Trembles"** (**"Reszket a bokor . . ."**), **"Answer to the Letter from My Beloved"** (**"Válasz kedvesem levelére"**), **"I Love You, My Sweet"** (**"Szeretlek, kedvesem"**), etc.

Descriptive Poetry

Petőfi's descriptive poetry appeared in epic and lyric form, in genre poetry, and in his own disguised self-revelations, and runs through reminiscences, meditations, anecdote and many other poetic forms. Yet the main characteristic of his descriptive poetry is that the subject-matter is always taken from ordinary landscapes or figures and events of common life. His is the world of the common people, a world ordinary but never vulgar or uninteresting. He succeeded in giving intensity and substance to moments and objects of daily existence. The Romantics were tormented by the emptiness of life. For Petőfi everything was infused with an emotional fullness, a mood of intimacy: a winter evening at his parents', sunset over the snow-covered Puszta, the noises of animals in the half-dark of the warm stable, the distant soughing of the windmill in a hay-scented field, the trouble-racked life of his father and his comic old man's grumbles, the revels of the village lads, the delicious midday meal of the shepherds, a bonfire at night on the bank of a flooding river, his mother's faithful old dog and her only hen, the deserted inn, a funeral procession in a village, a village wedding, the market, and countless similar scenes, as in **"The Plains"** (**"Az Alföld"**), **"The Ruined Inn"** (**"A csárda romjai"**), **"The Puszta, in Winter"** (**"A puszta, télen"**), **"Kutyakaparó,"** **"Old Sári"** (**"Sári néni"**), **"Panni Panyó,"** **"The Tisza."** The Romantics, it is true, were also attracted to such objects and settings. But the Romantics, such as Stifter and Wordsworth, Lamartine and Brentano, Coleridge and Eichendorff, used them as means of escaping from their own lives. Here, again, Petőfi began as one of the Romantics, only to develop and transcend them. It was a natural consequence of his political and intellectual evolution that he should exalt ordinary landscapes and the speech of the common people. Neither his sketches nor his intimate genre poetry ever lapsed into escapist idylls, nor his style into mannerist simplicity. Just as his political attitudes were founded on a realistic appraisal of the common people, his development as an artist was based on a realistic understanding of their ways; he recognized that their virtue lay in their essential being and not in their outward peculiarities, and that what would provide opportunities for renewal and further development was not the forms in which it was couched at present, but the possibilities offered them.

Whatever he touched was impregnated with his youthful confidence. The landscape of his poetry, the salt Plains between the river Danube and the river Tisza, which had up to that time been considered the least poetic of Hungarian landscapes, under the magic of his pen became the conventionally "beautiful Hungarian landscape" for a century to come. The Romantics sought a characteristic national landscape. Petőfi created it. But it was not, as his imitators believed, the "characteristic", "exotic", "eastern" Hungarian quality which shines through his poems, but the faith and confidence which brightened the landscape. There too is the implication that life can be made beautiful and meaningful, thus fulfilling the aspirations of the Romantics: he treated the landscape as existing in its own right for man to make of it what he will: the "home of life". Lenau, who was the only important precursor of Petőfi in his description of landscape, was wont to describe this world as the fairyland of a much-desired simplicity and naturalness. It was this part of his poetry which most clearly revealed his keen sense of humour. Humour is a rare gift in a young revolutionary poet, especially one in the main stream of Romanticism. The Romantics displayed cruel satire and bitter irony, but little humour. Petőfi indeed could also write searing satire, but it is his humour which his readers remember. He writes, indeed, of the injuries inflicted by the reactionary noble, and some of his poems at least were composed in an outburst of rage. But his nobleman, Pál Pató, a listless bachelor leading a shabby existence, whose answer to every suggestion—a new roof for his house, a better crop in his field, a young wife in his home, is "Oh, we've plenty of time for that" in time became a proverbial figure. So did another "Hungarian noble" boasting that he cannot read or write, and expecting his privileged position to get him into Heaven. Petőfi transmuted into literature the sometimes coarse, sometimes tender humour of the world of his youth, the peasants, strolling players, craftsmen and students, very much as Burns did in Scotland.

His Poetic Language

By the time he had written ***John the Hero*** Petőfi had developed a use of language and an individual style peculiarly his own. After 1846 it slowly grew into a language and style capable of embracing the whole variety of life, and we can therefore justifiably call it a "democratism of style". It was not the "language of the people" nor the "language of folklore", not even the language of folk poetry. He used the common speech of everyday—purified, refined and enriched. Everyone understood it, everyone felt that were he to write he would write in the same way. And his language gave his readers a sense that their lives too were the subject of poetry. He established a democracy of words, sentence construction, poetic imagery and objects, in which every thought and feeling was expressed by a word, image or gesture which subconsciously called up immediate and spontaneous associations in the great mass of the people. The Romantics sought a direct and natural approach; Petőfi found it. The Romantics suffered from the gap between life and poetry, between the poet and common man, Petőfi filled it. Yet, the perfection of his form was as extraordinary as his knowledge of literature and his cultural equipment. He was well-read in German, French and English; he translated Shakespeare. One dazzling piece of bravura followed another; he moved effortlessly from one type of poetry to another, adopting new metres and styles as he wished, and solved the most difficult problems of technique with grace and ease. Were he not so ardently a man of the people, so impatient a revolutionary, so motivated by such strong political beliefs, he might be called Mozartian. For over a century his successors and imitators were enchanted and misled by this very ease. Believing it was enough to sing "as it comes", they claimed that Petőfi sang "as a bird sings".

The Revolutionary

At the time of the 1848 Revolution, Petőfi embraced the extremes of radical Jacobinism and advocated republican views of total equality in society. Apart from shorter poems, such as **"Judgement"** (**"Az ítélet"**), **"A Sea Has Wakened Up"** (**"Föltámadott a tenger"**), **"Life or Death"** (**"Elet vagy halál"**), **"National Song"** (**"Nemzeti dal"**), **"I Dream of Bloody Days"** (**"Véres napokról álmodom"**), **"Italy"** (**"Olaszország"**), etc., the main evidence of his growing radicalism is to be found in the Romantic epic, ***The Apostle*** (***Az apostol,*** 1848). Its hero is a foundling by the name of Sylvester. Brought up by a beggarwoman and an old thief, he struggled to obtain an education and became inspired by great ideas. He worked as a tutor in a rich family, and later as a village clerk, always ready to defend and teach the peasants. Driven out by the lord and the local priest, he lived in misery in the city with his wife and child, and was imprisoned as a propagator of dangerous ideas. But he retained his faith that his ideals would finally triumph, even if he himself died in the struggle. Petőfi was successful in portraying social and political contradictions hitherto beyond the grasp of even the radical politicians of Hungary. The ideological significance of this work lies in the extent to which his conclusions reached out beyond those of all his contemporaries, while at the same time, some of Sylvester's monologues attain philosophical heights unprecedented—except for a few poems by Kölcsey—in Hungarian poetry.

That the common people may still be misled, should not dishearten those who fight on their behalf, nor will it lessen the historical value of revolutionary ideas, was the way Petőfi summed up his failure as a candidate in the parliamentary elections, where he lost to his rival, a local landlord. In the lull in the revolution he wrote a few beautiful poems, full of quiet memories and longings for his family, and also a small number of reflective poems (**"The Skylark Sings"—"Pacsirtaszót hallok megint"**; **"At the End of the Year"—"Az év végén"**; **"On the Death of My Parents"—"Szüleim halálára"**), but most of his work at this time was written as a call to battle (**"Battle-song"—"Csatadal"**; **"Onward to the Holy War"—"Föl a szentháborúra"**; **"Respublica"**; **"Europe is Silent"—"Európa csendes, újra csendes"**). In the summer of 1849, Petőfi hurried to join Bem in Transylvania; and the poet of the people died in battle and was probably buried in an unknown grave of the fallen. The political ideas he personified sank underground for a long time, but the new literature he brought into being remained the dominant trend of the whole period. (pp. 223-32)

Béla G. Németh, "Sándor Petőfi (1823-1849)," in A History of Hungarian Literature *by István Nemeskürty and others, edited by Tibor Klaniczay, Corvina, 1983 pp. 222-32.*

ADDITIONAL BIBLIOGRAPHY

Bátori, Joseph A. "The Lyrical Poetry of Sándor Petőfi." *The Canadian-American Review of Hungarian Studies* III, No. 1 (Spring 1976): 29-34.

An overview of the characteristics of Petőfi's poetry.

Czigány, Lóránt. "Comet of the Revolution: Petőfi." In his *The Oxford History of Hungarian Literature from the Earliest Times to the Present*, pp. 179-97. Oxford: Clarendon Press, 1986.

A critical survey of Petőfi's poetry within a biographical framework.

Edwards, Tudor. "Vienna: The Biedermeier Age and the Revolutionary Aftermath." *History Today* X, No. 10 (October 1960): 668-77.

An examination of the political climate of Europe in the mid-nineteenth century. Petőfi's role in the Hungarian Revolution of 1848 is placed in historical perspective.

Gáldi, László. "Petőfi and Eminescu." *The American Slavic and East European Review* 7, No. 2 (1948): 171-79.

Compares the literary, intellectual, and political sources of Petőfi's inspiration with those of Mihail Eminescu, a Rumanian poet and political activist.

Hegedüs, Sandor von. "Alexander Petőfi." *Royal Society of Literature of the United Kingdom*, n.s. XVII (1938): 125-36.

A biographical and critical sketch.

Hevesi, Alexander. "Two Great Hungarian Poets." *The Slavonic and East European Review* IX, No. 25 (June 1930): 94-106.

A biographical and critical study of Petőfi and his contemporary, the Hungarian poet János Arany.

Illyés, Gyula. *Petőfi*. Translated by G. F. Cushing. Budapest: Corvina, 1973, 590 p.

A major biography of Petőfi with analyses of many of his poems.

Köpeczi, Béla. Foreword to *Rebel or Revolutionary? Sándor Petőfi as Revealed by His Diary, Letters, Notes, Pamphlets and Poems*, edited by Béla Köpeczi, translated by Edwin Morgan, G. F. Cushing, and others, pp. 11-25. Budapest: Corvina Press, 1974.

A biographical essay focusing on Petőfi's political ideology.

Radó, György. "Petőfi Abroad." *New Hungarian Quarterly* XIV, No. 49 (Spring 1973): 60-71.

Discusses the history of the translation of Petőfi's works.

Reményi, Joseph. "Alexander Petőfi." In *Sixty Poems by Alexander Petőfi (1823-1849)*, translated by Eugénie Bayard Pierce and Emil Delmár, pp. 5-8. Budapest: Petőfi Society, 1948.

An introductory essay on Petőfi and his works.

Tezla, Albert. "Sándor Petőfi." In his *Hungarian Authors: A Bibliographical Handbook*, pp. 463-80. Cambridge, Mass.: Harvard University Press, Belknap Press, 1970.

A bibliography of works in English and Hungarian by and about Petőfi.

Yolland, Arthur B. *Alexander Petőfi, Poet of the Hungarian War of Independence: A Literary Study (1823-49)*. Budapest: Printing Office of the Franklin-Society, 1906, 62 p.

A primarily biographical examination of Petőfi that demonstrates, through a study of representative poems, the close connection between his life and works.

Lydia (Howard Huntley) Sigourney

1791-1865

American poet, sketch writer, essayist, and novelist.

Often called the "sweet singer of Hartford," Sigourney was one of the most popular poets in America during the first half of the nineteenth century. Her celebration of religious and patriotic values, talent for writing commemorative poetry, and reputation for moral integrity strongly appealed to the American public of her time. A prolific author, Sigourney contributed widely to magazines and published numerous volumes of her work, becoming one of the first women in the United States to establish a successful and remunerative career as a writer. Although beloved by her enthusiastic readers, Sigourney's works were not always highly regarded by contemporary reviewers, and subsequent critics have reacted similarly.

Sigourney was born in Norwich, Connecticut, the only daughter of Zerviah Wentworth Huntley and Ezekiel Huntley, a gardener in the employ of a wealthy matron, Mrs. Daniel Lathrop. Encouraged by both her mother and Mrs. Lathrop to read and write at an early age, Sigourney received her primary education from the Lathrop library and local schools. She later paid tribute to the influential guidance of her father's employer in her fictional *Sketch of Connecticut, Forty Years Since* and in her autobiography, *Letters of Life*. Determined to become a teacher and aid her parents financially, Sigourney went on to supplement her early education by studying at a Hartford school; subsequently, she opened schools for young ladies in Norwich and Hartford. In 1815, she published her first book, *Moral Pieces, in Prose and Verse,* to critical acclaim. Encouraged by this positive reception, Sigourney continued to write. However, when in 1819 she married Charles Sigourney, a Hartford hardware merchant who disapproved of the public nature of her writing career, she modified her literary aspirations by adopting an anonymous mode of publication. During the early years of their marriage, she not only published books, but also contributed poems and prose pieces to over twenty periodicals, using the proceeds to aid her parents and support charities. In 1833, Sigourney published *Letters to Young Ladies,* one of her most popular works; prompted by its success and an increasing need for money, Sigourney, despite her husband's objections, allowed her name to be placed on later editions of the book. The popularity of this volume created a new demand for her work and, by 1839, she was able to support her household by writings published under her own name.

A prolific contributor to periodicals, as well as to annuals and gift books, Sigourney became familiar to a broad range of the reading public. An astute businesswoman, she reissued much of her magazine verse in the form of various collections and editions, thereby profiting from her writings and keeping her name before the public. By the early 1840s, her popularity was so great that magazine editors vied for her contributions. In 1841, Edgar Allan Poe, then editor of *Graham's Magazine,* requested material for the journal, and the editor of the competing *Godey's Lady's Book* paid her for exclusive use of her name on the title page. Her prestige as a writer was established, and on a trip to England she met William Wordsworth, Thomas Carlyle, and Maria Edgeworth, later recounting her travels in *Pleasant Memories of Pleasant Lands*. Sigourney reached the height of her popularity in the late 1840s with the publication of *Illustrated Poems,* a lavish edition issued in a series that included the works of William Cullen Bryant and Henry Wadsworth Longfellow. A national figure, she was often courted by dignitaries and literary celebrities, and her works were anthologized in many collections of American prose and poetry. During the last years of her life, Sigourney composed little that was new, often reissuing retitled versions of earlier volumes. She died at her Hartford home in 1865, after having prepared her autobiography, which was published the following year.

Sigourney produced a large variety of works in both prose and poetry, yet the whole of her literary output attests to her overriding moral concerns. Her prose works include history, biography, a novel, sketches, essays, and her autobiography. While these writings were widely read by her contemporaries, Sigourney was primarily known for her poetry. The subjects of her verse—death, religion, and history—were first formulated in *Moral Pieces, in Prose and Verse* and, according to critics, never changed. Her verses commemorating the deaths of both famous and unknown persons were perhaps her best-loved works. Such eulogistic poems as "'Twas but a Babe" and "The Faithful Editor" were admired for their sentimentality, moral concerns, and elaborate, euphemistic language describing the spiritual aspects of death.

Despite Sigourney's initial popularity, critical reception of her works has often been unfavorable. During her lifetime, reviewers acknowledged her skill with blank verse and language, but found little original thought in her writing. Poe labelled her work imitative in theme and form, while other critics accused her of producing too much unpolished material. Contemporary criticism was never completely derogatory, however, since few magazine editors competing for her poetry and prose wished to offend her. In addition, the irreproachable morality of her works and her upstanding character were highly respected. Subsequent commentators have devoted less attention to her moral purpose, and several recent reexaminations of her works have focused on their literary qualities. For the most part, however, current interest in Sigourney's writings remains largely historical, and they are seldom anthologized today. The characteristics of her works that captured nineteenth-century audiences—sentimentality and didacticism—fail to appeal to modern readers. Thus, although her writings are little read, Sigourney is recognized as one of the first successful female writers in the United States.

(See also *Dictionary of Literary Biography,* Vol. 1: *The American Renaissance in New England;* Vol. 42: *American Writers for Children before 1900;* and Vol. 73: *American Magazine Journalists, 1741-1850.*)

PRINCIPAL WORKS

Moral Pieces, in Prose and Verse (poetry and essays) 1815
Traits of the Aborigines of America (poetry) 1822
Sketch of Connecticut, Forty Years Since (sketch) 1824
Poems (poetry) 1827
Female Biography: Containing Sketches of the Life and Character of Twelve American Women (sketches) 1829
Evening Readings in History: Comprising Portions of the History of Assyria, Egypt, Tyre, Syria, Persia, and the Sacred Scriptures (history) 1833
Letters to Young Ladies (letters) 1833
Poems (poetry) 1834; also published as *Selected Poems,* 1838
Poetry for Children (poetry) 1834
Sketches (sketches) 1834
Zinzendorff, and Other Poems (poetry) 1835
History of Marcus Aurelius, Emperor of Rome (biography) 1836
Pocahontas, and Other Poems (poetry) 1841
Pleasant Memories of Pleasant Lands (sketches) 1842
Poetry for Seamen (poetry) 1845
Myrtis, with Other Etchings and Sketchings (sketches) 1846
Illustrated Poems (poetry) 1849
The Faded Hope (memoir) 1853
Lucy Howard's Journal (novel) 1858
The Man of Uz, and Other Poems (poetry) 1862
Letters of Life (autobiography) 1866

THE NORTH AMERICAN REVIEW AND MISCELLANEOUS JOURNAL (essay date 1815)

[*In an excerpt from a review of Sigourney's first published work,* Moral Pieces, in Prose and Verse, *this critic praises her poetry.*]

[***Moral Pieces, in Prose and Verse***] contains a mixture of prose and poetry, of which, the latter we think the best. Many of the pieces are given as compositions, addressed to young girls under the writer's charge, and are well adapted for that purpose, though they do not appear to much advantage in this collection. Miss Huntley, we have been informed, is a most deserving and interesting young woman, who, in the most adverse circumstances, has educated herself; and, by constant exertion, providing for the support of some relatives, as well as for her own, has emancipated herself from the humblest penury, and still found leisure at a very early age, to compose this volume. Worth of this kind would have been a strong motive for subscribing to the book, but not sufficient to have noticed it here, if the verses themselves had not possessed very considerable merit. (pp. 111-12)

One great negative merit of these poems is, that they are almost wholly free from any false taste, from any thing either in thought or style, that is turgid or vulgar. There is much freedom and facility in the manner, a correctness and harmony in the features, though generally tinged with melancholy; that make us strongly wish, that the writer would devote herself to some work of greater scope and higher character than any of these occasional verses. We think there are one or two passages in the poem **"On the Dove's Leaving the Ark,"** which partake of the sublime. The description of the deluge,

> And slowly as its axle turn'd
> The wat'ry planet mov'd and mourn'd,

the whole of the passage ending with these two lines,

> Nor slightest breath her bosom cheer'd
> Her own soft wings along she heard,

If not sublime, which we think it to be, will at least be allowed by all, to be exquisitely beautiful and pathetick.

After considering the indications of genius, afforded by these disconnected poems, the variety and facility of versification they discover, joined to what we have heard of the fair author's solid acquirements, and her power and habit of severe application, we should, if our advice were a little more imposing, earnestly counsel her to devote her mind to some more considerable undertaking. (pp. 119-20)

"Miss Huntley's Poems," in The North American Review and Miscellaneous Journal, *Vol. I, No. I, May, 1815, pp. 111-21.*

AMERICAN QUARTERLY REVIEW (essay date 1835)

[*This critic evaluates the literary merit of Sigourney's* Sketches.]

Mrs. Sigourney is doubtless one of those whose "reputation is a part of the reputation of the country itself." Her poetical genius, in particular, has given her a high rank among American authors, and her countrymen have justly appreciated her merits. This, however, as it has before been said, renders it only the more necessary, that when arraigned at the critics' bar, she should be judged with strict impartiality. It should be remembered that *her* writings, with all their excellence, are not the standard of genius; and though many of them may have come fully up to the real standard, the possibility of partial and temporary, or even of entire and continued failure, is not thereby precluded. It may be thought from such an exordium, that we intend to express ourselves in terms of unmeasured severity and censure in regard to [Mrs. Sigourney's ***Sketches***]. But we hasten to correct such an anticipation. Were we thus to express ourselves, *we* should feel, as many others undoubtedly would, that impartiality at least could not be our boast, though we had avoided that indulgent flattery, which we have before so much deprecated. There are certainly many things in this volume which do credit to the lady; but still, as a whole, we must think it unworthy of her former reputation; and though singly, it may have little effect upon her literary character, a few such publications must give the impression, not that Mrs. Sigourney is devoid of genius (for the contrary has been already satisfactorily established,) but that she manifests great inequality of genius. Our chief objection to this book is, that it ever was a book. A sweeping objection truly. But we proceed to explain ourselves. We certainly do not mean to say, that the tales of which it is composed should never have been made public. They would have suited very well the ephemeral pages of a newspaper, or of a miscellaneous magazine, where they would have made a less pretending appearance, would have been examined less critically, and would sooner have been forgotten. Here they might have pleased; and if high expectations had not been excited by the name of the authoress, might have been read without disappointment. But when they assume the more permanent, we may add, the more imposing form of a separate volume, with the name of a favourite writer emblazoned upon its title, "Sosiorum pumice mundus," greater pretensions to merit are always supposed, and greater disappointment is the consequence of failure to excite interest. (pp. 347-48)

But to proceed; these "Sketches" are six in number. The first is entitled **"The Father,"** and its object is to portray paternal affection, "the love of a father for a daughter." The subject of this tale is uninteresting, because it is common-place, and there is not enough incident to feed the reader's imagination. The authoress seems here to have aimed rather at beauty of style, than at a pleasingly invented narrative; and, indeed, taking this piece as a whole, more attention has apparently been paid to the mere composition, than in any of those which follow. In one respect, it may be said, that Mrs. Sigourney has succeeded; for certainly much of the sketch is beautiful as regards style simply. That it is so, we may show by a [quotation] . . . from the short introduction to the piece:

> But my present purpose is to delineate a single and simple principle of our nature—the most deeply rooted and holy—*the love of a father for a daughter*. My province has led me to analyze mankind; and in doing this, I have sometimes thrown their affections into the crucible. And the one of which I speak has come forth most pure, most free from drossy admixture. Even the earth that combines with it, is not like other earth. It is what the foot of a seraph might rest upon, and contract no pollution. With the love of our sons, ambition mixes its spirit, till it becomes a fiery essence. We anticipate great things for them—we covet honours—we goad them on in the race of glory; if they are victors, we too proudly exult—if vanquished, we are prostrate and in bitterness. Perhaps we detect in them the same latent perverseness, with which we have waged warfare in our own breasts, or some imbecility of purpose with which we have no affinity; and then, from the very nature of our love, an impatience is generated, which they have no power to sooth or we to control. A father loves his son as he loves himself—and in all selfishness there is a bias to disorder and pain. But his love for his daughter is different and more disinterested; possibly he believes that it is called forth by a being of a higher and better order. It is based on the integral and immutable principles of his nature.
>
> (pp. 348-49)

But notwithstanding the beauty of the style, Mrs. Sigourney has undoubtedly failed to give a deep absorbing interest to her tale; which, we think, may be attributed to the fact, that mere beauty of composition, unless that beauty be of the highest order, cannot compensate for poverty of invention, and the want of an interesting subject. And, after all, her's is often rather a beauty of words and figures, than of originality and thought. Such at least is the impression which we have received; and we think that any one, after rising from the perusal of this story, will agree with us in saying, that it is destitute of the power to interest the feelings, (that is, in any high degree,) to excite the imagination, or even to rivet the attention. It will be remembered, that all our remarks apply to this work only, not to any of her former or subsequent productions. (pp. 349-50)

The **"Legend of Oxford,"** the next sketch in order, is written in a much more simple, and apparently unlaboured style, than the former; which is, indeed, an almost necessary consequence of its being more historical, or narrative in its character. Oxford, a small town in Massachusetts,—"originally," as the authoress tells us, "a colony of French Protestants," who were driven from France by the persecutions attendant on the revocation of the edict of Nantes,—is the scene of the narrative, which comprises the relation of three distinct occurrences in the history of this town. It commences with its first settlement, and carries on the reader, through a period of a few years, to the time when the Huguenots were obliged, on account of savage cruelties, to desert it, and take refuge in the neighbouring colony of Boston. (p. 353)

We may remark, generally, in regard to this tale or legend, that it is much more interesting than the preceding: but still it has only a negative excellence—a freedom from great faults, rather than any positive recommendations. In short, we think it has few, if any, of those qualities which would evidence superiority of talent in the authoress. (pp. 354-55)

We have said that the **"Legend of Oxford"** is much more interesting than the sketch which precedes it; and the next, entitled the **"Family Portraits,"** is, in most respects, a manifest improvement upon both. We have heard it called a "foolish love story;" but be this as it may, there are few, we imagine, who would not join with us in saying, that it possesses greater literary merit, and is more entertaining, than any other part of the volume. This opinion, to be sure, is merely relative; and after what has already been said in regard to the preceding pieces, may not be considered as, of itself, a very flattering recommendation; nor do we intend it as such. It has already been remarked, that, in our view, Mrs. Sigourney has not done justice to herself in this volume, and the same may be said in regard to each tale, considered as a whole; though in the one now before us, while there are great faults, there are also some good qualities, and these more worthy of attention than any we have yet noticed. (p. 356)

Of the remaining three tales we shall speak very briefly. They are less interesting than those which we have particularly examined. **"Oriana,"** it is true, presents some beauties of style, and some originality of subject; but more than this can scarcely be said in commendation. As to **"The Intemperate,"** and **"The Patriarch,"** we cannot account for their publication in this place, unless the object were to add a few more pages to the volume; they are certainly altogether unworthy of the authoress. We observe, in conclusion of these remarks, that the opinion which we have given in regard to the work under consideration, is at least candid, though some may be disposed to think it severe. If we are not mistaken, this book has already passed through three editions, for which fact, we must confess, we are unable to account, unless Mrs. Sigourney's name, on the outside of the volume, has tended to strengthen the impression produced by the contents. (p. 358)

"Sigourney's 'Sketches'," in American Quarterly Review, *Vol. XVII, No. 34, June, 1835, pp. 341-58.*

THE NORTH AMERICAN REVIEW **(essay date 1835)**

[*This critic enthusiastically reviews Sigourney's 1834 collection* Poems.]

About twenty years ago, at the very outset of our critical labors, the earliest publication of Mrs. Sigourney, then Miss Huntley was reviewed in this journal [see excerpt dated 1815]. It was considered as evincing much real merit and still greater promise, and derived an additional claim to attention from the circumstances under which it was prepared; circumstances reflecting so much credit on the author, that a slight allusion to them here will not be thought indelicate. She was indebted for her education to her own exertions; in early life she had none of the advantages, which affluence and leisure can bestow; yet, under the pressure of various inconveniences, she cultivated with success the art to which she owes her fame. It remained to be seen, whether, under other and more favorable circumstances, she would retain the same inclination, and go on improving in the way to which her youthful tastes inclined her. This was by no means certain; many are the ladylike accomplishments, which, like the burden of the pilgrim, are thrown aside with infinite satisfaction, at certain eventful stages in life's journey; but the reputation she has since acquired has been so general, that we need hardly say how our hopes have been fulfilled. Without devoting her attention exclusively to poetry, or engaging in the composition of any extensive work, Mrs. Sigourney has continued from time to time to give to the public, principally through the medium of the magazines and annuals, a variety of productions, by which she has acquired a high rank as a popular and useful writer.

The volume before us [***Poems***] is a collection of the poetical productions, which the author has thought proper to publish in a more permanent form. Some of its contents were written at a very early age; others, as she herself assures us, were composed at later periods, amidst domestic occupations or maternal cares; and the greater portion of them were suggested by passing circumstances, and may be regarded as extemporary in their nature. She describes them "as the wild flowers which have sprung up in the dells, or among the clefs of the rock;" but we feel ourselves entitled to assure her, that they will neither bloom like the wild flowers in solitude, nor fade as soon; they will be more likely to be numbered among the lasting favorites of the garden. Such writings do not ask nor admit of the display of some of the very highest attributes of poetry, and to these Mrs. Sigourney presents no claim. The excellence of all her poems is quiet and unassuming. They are full of the sweet images and bright associations of domestic life; its unobtrusive happiness, its unchanging affections, and its cares and sorrows; of the feelings naturally inspired by life's vicissitudes from the cradle to the death-bed; of the hopes that burn, like the unquenched altar fire, in that chosen dwelling place of virtue and religion. The light of a pure and unostentatious faith shines around them, blending with her thoughts and giving a tender coloring to her contemplations, like the melancholy beauty of our own autumnal scenery. Sometimes she watches the gorgeous array of the clouds at sunset, but her eye looks beyond them to the habitation of the disembodied spirit; sometimes she muses at the eventide, and the forms of the loved and lost are present to her view; presently she carries us to the domestic fireside, and while dwelling on its blessings, points to the great Source from which they flow; again, we see the mother at the bedside of her dying boy, or herself extended on the bed of death,—and the lofty aspirations of the Christian faith invest the verse with a dignity appropriate to their own sublimity. Mrs. Sigourney's habitual tone of thought is pensive, but not melancholy; serious, but not severe; and her views of life, without being joyous, are not shaded by repulsive gloom. Every subject she touches is made the fountain of calm reflection, which is often striking, and always pure. If she does not often excite the reader to enthusiastic admiration, she generally leaves a strong impression of her power, and never fails to inspire respect for the qualities of her mind and heart.

Mrs. Sigourney's versification is, in general, correct and sweet; although, in this respect there are occasional instances of want of care. The effect of short pieces, like the greater part of her's, very much depends upon the delicacy and perfection of their finish; in those of greater magnitude, the attention is withdrawn from minute defects, or they are lost in a comprehensive survey of the general portions; as an imperfection, which would pass unheeded in a panorama, is at once detected in a cabinet picture. Her writings in blank verse are, however, remarkable for the music of their flow. In their style of thought and expression, they remind us of those passages of Cowper, where the movement of the verse is in perfect keeping with the gravity and tenderness of the subject. Like him, she is attracted only by Nature's soothing and gentle aspects; her spirit holds no communion with the elements in their wrath; she takes no delight in witnessing the whirlwind and the storm; she looks on all the seasons, as they change, not to people them with images of gloom, but to draw from them whatever of happiness and instruction they can give. A voice of praise is uttered in her Winter Hymn; the beautiful drapery of the woods in autumn reminds her less of approaching decay, than of the newness of life which is to follow. We could not desire that the moral influence of her writings should be other than it is; while she pleases the fancy, she elevates the heart.

Great as Mrs. Sigourney's merit certainly is, she has not yet displayed it with so much effect as she may and will do, if she shall be inclined to render poetry a more exclusive object of pursuit. Thus far, it has evidently been little more than the amusement of her leisure hours; with less divided attention, she has the power of accomplishing higher and better things. The productions before us are ornaments, wrought without much effort by taste and ingenuity; they resemble the lighter works, with which the scientific inventor occupies the time that he can spare from his severer labors. Whenever, instead of limiting her range to that portion of the atmosphere which can be traversed with a light and careless wing, she shall prepare herself for an adventurous flight, she cannot fail to gain a permanent place in the public favor. (pp. 446-48)

"Mrs. Sigourney and Miss Gould," in The North American Review, *Vol. LXXXIX, October, 1835, pp. 430-53.*

THE QUARTERLY CHRISTIAN SPECTATOR **(essay date 1835)**

[*An anonymous reviewer compares Sigourney's poetry to that of Mrs. Felicia Hemans, an English poet known for her lyric verse, and discusses Sigourney's* Zinzendorff, and Other Poems.]

Mrs. Sigourney's name is already enrolled among the first of our female writers. With a slow but sure progress she has been gaining upon the hearts of her fellow-citizens, and has secured the meed of deserved praise, even from the not easily pleased critics of Britain. To those who know her, and the happy influence which she exerts in favor of religion and benevolence, not a word of commendation is needful. [***Zinzendorff, and Other Poems***] is mostly composed of small pieces which have already appeared in the papers of the day. They are of course various in their subject, and unequal in their execution. Yet no one of them is below mediocrity; all of them betoken an easy, graceful mind, and are marked by a smooth and polished diction. Her poetry belongs to the class of the placid and attractive, sprinkled with pensive thought and descriptive pathos, rather than to the startling, spirit-stirring kind. She has been called the American Hemans; and yet these two writers are, in our view, quite dissimilar. Mrs. Sigourney, we think, in her poetry, does not possess to so great a degree, the element of passion and feeling, as Mrs. Hemans. We question whether she could have wrote the "Siege of Valencia," "Vespers of Palermo," or "Forest Sanctuary," and others of similar cast, which have come from Mrs. Hemans' pen. Yet, with less of feeling or passion, there is in her productions an equal if not a superior exhibition of poetic taste; the arrangement of words, the striking epithets, at one glance placing the object before the eye, indicate poetic talent of a high description. There may be sometimes, perhaps, a little too much of the artificial or studied character in her style. We perceive this fault more in her prose than in her poetry, and we attribute it to an unusual attention to correctness and euphony. If we mistake not, it is, to a certain degree, perceptible in all our most polished writers. First thoughts, as they come glowing from the heart, are often best; if we trim them down with rhetorical precision, the life and freshness which they breathe upon the page are gone. Poetry like this before us, is incapable of at once arousing the deep and hidden elements of the soul into a feverish excitement and unhealthy action; but in its dew-like, subduing character, it may reach to the inmost recesses of the spirit, allay its troubled risings, and beget a more abiding and happier influence. No one could read it and be worse for it; few, we think, but would become better by its perusal.

The crowning excellence of Mrs. Sigourney's poetry, however, is its *evangelical* character. Here we consider her as taking rank far above Mrs. Hemans, and more gifted ones of the other sex. Mrs. Hemans seems indeed to favor religion, but there is nothing distinctive in her views. Mrs. Sigourney is not afraid openly to confess the Savior. "Jesus crucified," the "Spirit of God," and kindred phrases, may be found in her pages. It is too common a fault even with evangelical writers, by a kind of poetic license, to array their virtuous personages in an immaculate purity, and a sort of sinless innocency, which we fear is no where to be found on this earth. They mean, indeed, to be understood as speaking comparatively; but their language, probably, to the unthinking reader, conveys a false impression. Mrs. Sigourney avoids this evil more than is usual; and we attribute it to the fact, that she sets out with the intention never to sink the christian in the poet. Her poetry is the poetry of home-life; the affections clustering around the manifold objects of the domestic circle, and exhibiting in the varied scenes of man's changeful trial, the necessity and beneficial influence of virtuous feelings, and the piety of the gospel. Seldom does she look out on the wide and warring world, in its dark and troubled heavings. Those themes which delight the muse of Gray, and other lyric bards, seem to have no attraction for her gentler spirit. This is as it should be. Woman is ever most at home in the peaceful circle, and among the less glaring topics. We have had lauding enough of military glory and the feats of reckless ambition. Already they live too lasting in the praises of gifted minds, without their being invested with new haloes of attraction by the admiration of the softer sex. Still less does Mrs. Sigourney incline to the merely romantic fancies of genius. Her delight is in graver and more sober thoughts. She portrays life, but it is not the ideal life of many; it is life with its sweet and endearing charities, its sad and painful trials, just as we see them daily exhibited. Love, as it reigns in the breast of the betrothed, the bosom friend, the mother, the son or daughter, and all its other relative shades, is depicted; but love, as it dazzles in the lines of by far the greater portion of writers, is nowhere to be met in her pages. The dreamy raptures, and the fulsome adulation of those who seem to know nothing of, or care for, a permanent and rational attachment, whose verse is full of "angels," and "bright eyes," and the hues and drapery by which is expressed the idolatry of high-wrought, short-lived and bewildering passion,—they will here be sought in vain. But the deeper and holier fount of christian affection, the sweet inspiration of confiding hearts blent in the strictest union, and sympathizing together in the mutations of life,—such love is here, wreathed with the choicest garlands of hope, or lending its alleviation to sooth the anguish of the desolate and sorrow-stricken heart. She seems aware, that some may think the volume is dimmed by the sombre shades of adverse incident, oftener than they could wish; for in her preface she says: "Should it be objected, that too great a portion of them are elegiac, the required apology would fain clothe itself in the language of the gifted Lord Bacon: 'If we listen to David's harp, we shall find as many hearse-like harmonies as carols; and the pen of inspiration has more labored to describe the afflictions of Job, than the felicities of Solomon.'" This reminds us of another remark which we were about to make. Mrs. Sigourney's poetry is the poetry of one who evinces a familiarity with the sacred volume; and from its rich and holy pages she draws many of her finest thoughts, and the imagery in which she has clothed them. (pp. 670-72)

We have already said enough to show, that we do not view Mrs. Sigourney's poetry of the highest grade, considered as the exhibition of genius and mental power. But, utilitarians as we profess ourselves, we do not hesitate to call it *good* poetry, tending to promote the highest welfare of man; and her's will be the satisfaction, to a degree that many a more eminent writer can never possess, of having written no line which at death she might wish to blot. Thus privileged, she may well be content to leave to others the more sparkling treasures of the imagination, while she gathers up and garners for hearts that prize them, the choicer and more durable riches.

The principal poem, from which the volume borrows its title, is of no great length, and of course affords but a small opportunity for a wide range of characters and incidents. Its object is to describe the early labors of Zinzendorff, the Moravian leader, among the Indians in the interior of Pennsylvania. It opens with this line:

T'was summer in Wyoming.

Then follows a picture of the "fair vale," the Susquehannah, with its varying streams, the towering hills, and the numerous beauties of the landscape. Leaving these, we are brought at once into the "wilder scene," the abode of the "rude native tribes." In a few sentences she places before us the characteristics of these now exiled sons of the forest. Zinzendorff, "the white-browed stranger," is, as it were, dropped among them. They can scarce credit his purpose announced:

> That from a happy home, o'er ocean's wave,
> He thus should come, to teach a race unknown,
> Of joys beyond the tomb.

All, however, are not so incredulous. Kindness wins its way to the heart, and none are more keen to detect the hypocrite, than the eagle-eyed but seemingly careless Indian:

> Yet some there were
> Who listen'd spell-bound to his charmed words;
> The sick man drew them as the breath of heaven
> Into his fever'd bosom, while the hymn
> That swell'd melodious o'er the open grave,
> Soothe'd the sad mourner 'mid his heathen woe.
> Young children gather'd at his beaming smile,
> And learn'd the name of Jesus,—pressing close
> To touch his garments, or to feel his hand
> Resting upon their heads. Such power hath love
> O'er sweet simplicity, ere sin hath taught
> Suspicion's lesson.

We notice here, what appears to us a defect in this part of the poem. The intervening time is not marked with sufficient distinctness. It was summer at Zinzendorff's arrival; yet how soon success attended him, through what period of effort he had to pass, is not clearly described. (pp. 673-74)

As "time sped his wing," Zinzendorff's labors are crowned with success, a colony is founded among the sheltered valleys,—the place now known by the name of Bethlehem, and celebrated for its Moravian schools.

> But now the hour
> That took the shepherd from his simple flock,
> Drew swiftly on.

The recollections of home, of the amiable woman whom the missionary had left behind him, still dwelt within his heart, and prompted his return. His mission being accomplished,—a church planted in the wilderness, and converts brought within its folds, he bids them farewell, and embarks for "his own baronial shades." The Indians crowd together to witness the departure of their true friend, and watch the fast-receding vessel which bears him forever from their eyes. Here properly closes the action of the poem. The remaining lines are an eulogy upon the self-denying efforts and success of the sect to which Zinzendorff belonged, and of which he may be considered the founder.

From the description which we have given of the poem, it will be seen, that there is little opportunity afforded for a wide range of character or development of incident. Still, we think more might have been done in this way. Mrs. Sigourney's purpose, however, seems not to have been to write a lengthened poem, but to furnish a few pages designed as a tribute to the meek devotion and self-denying benevolence of the Moravians. Of course she has kept herself within narrow bounds. (p. 676)

Most of the *smaller* pieces in this volume have already been published in the various religious papers of the day. Embracing so many and yet so very dissimilar subjects it could hardly be expected, that they should possess equal merit. The judgment of readers will be different respecting them, according to the difference of their tastes. The lines on Niagara, and Napoleon's Epitaph, have been generally admired as among the best in the present collection. We might easily mention others. The allegorical piece called **"The Friends of Man," "The Funeral at Sea," "The Departure of Hannah More from Barley Wood, at the age of eighty-three," "Nature's Beauty," "Child left in a Storm,"** all have struck us as containing many fine thoughts, and beautifully expressed. (p. 677)

Much of the imagery in these smaller pieces, though drawn from objects common to poetry in general, and not unfrequently to be met with on the lyric page, yet in the hands of Mrs. Sigourney seem to have acquired an originality, and come upon us with a freshness and power, that is very pleasing. (p. 678)

Many of these shorter pieces are in blank verse. Mrs. Sigourney's blank verse has an easy and polished flow. It is most wanting in force and energy; yet it is by no means destitute of these qualities. It would be unfair perhaps to judge of her capabilities by what she has written; since her poetry for the greatest part seems to have been thrown off without effort, and is evidently not the best specimen which by more careful attention and endeavour she might produce. Yet there is enough in this and former volumes to assure us, that, were she so inclined, she might do still better. (pp. 679-80)

A review of "Zinzendorff, and Other Poems," in The Quarterly Christian Spectator, *n.s. Vol. VII, No. IV, December, 1835, pp. 670-80.*

[EDGAR ALLAN POE] (essay date 1836)

[Considered one of America's most outstanding men of letters, Poe was a distinguished poet, novelist, essayist, journalist, short story writer, editor, and critic. Poe stressed an analytical, rather than emotive, approach to literature, emphasizing the technical details of a work, instead of its ideological statement. Although Poe and his literary criticism were subject to controversy in his own lifetime, he is now valued for his literary theories. In this review of Zinzendorff, and Other Poems, *Poe examines the reasons for Sigourney's popularity and accuses her of imitating the poetry of Mrs. Felicia Hemans.]*

Mrs. Sigourney has been long known as an author. Her earliest publication was reviewed about twenty years ago, in the *North American* [see excerpt dated 1815]. She was then Miss Huntley. The fame which she has since acquired is extensive; and we, who so much admire her virtues and her talents, and who have so frequently expressed our admiration of both in this Journal—we, of all persons—are the least inclined to call in question the justice or the accuracy of the public opinion, by which has been adjudged to her so high a station among the *literati* of our land. Some things, however, we cannot pass over in silence. There are two kinds of popular reputation,—or rather there are two roads by which such reputation may be attained: and it appears to us an idiosyncrasy which distinguishes mere fame from most, or perhaps from *all* other human ends, that, in regarding the intrinsic value of the object, we must not fail to introduce, as a portion of our estimate, the means by which the object is acquired. To speak less abstractedly. Let us suppose two writers having a reputation apparently equal—that is to say, their names *being equally in the mouths of the people*—for we take this to be the most practicable test of what we choose to term *apparent popular reputation*. Their names then are equally in the mouths of the people. The one has written a great work—let it be either an Epic of high rank, or something which, although of seeming littleness in itself, is yet, like the "Christabel" of Coleridge, entitled to be called *great* from its power of creating intense emotion in the minds of great men. And let us imagine that, by this single effort, the author has attained a certain quantum of reputation. We know it to be possible that another writer of very moderate powers may build up for himself, little by little, a reputation equally great—and this, too, merely by keeping continually in the eye, or by appealing continually with little things, to the ear, of that great, overgrown, and majestical gander, the critical and bibliographical rabble.

It would be an easy, although perhaps a somewhat disagreeable task, to point out several of the most popular writers in America—popular in the above mentioned sense—who have manufactured for themselves a celebrity by the very questionable means, and in the very questionable manner, to which we have alluded. But it must not be thought that we wish to include Mrs. Sigourney in the number. By no means. She has trod, however, upon the confines of their circle. She does not *owe* her reputation to the chicanery we mention, but it cannot be denied that it has been thereby greatly assisted. In a word—no single piece which she has written, and not even her collected works as we behold them in the present volume, and in the one published some years ago, would fairly entitle her to that exalted rank which she actually enjoys as the authoress, *time after time,* of her numerous, and, in most instances, very creditable compositions. The validity of our objections to this adventitious notoriety we must be allowed to consider unshaken, until it can be proved that any multiplication of zeros will eventuate in the production of a unit.

We have watched, too, with a species of anxiety and vexation brought about altogether by the sincere interest we take in Mrs. Sigourney, the progressive steps by which she has at length acquired the title of the "American Hemans." Mrs. S. cannot conceal from her own discernment that she has acquired this title *solely by imitation*. The very phrase "American Hemans" speaks loudly in accusation: and we are grieved that what by the over-zealous has been intended as complimentary should fall with so ill-omened a sound into the ears of the judicious. We will briefly point out those particulars in which Mrs. Sigourney stands palpably convicted of that sin which in poetry is not to be forgiven.

Philadelphia Nov. 10 1841.

Dear Madam,

Since my connexion, as editor, with Graham's Magazine, of this city, I have been sadly disappointed to find that you deem us unworthy your correspondence. Month after month elapses and, although our list numbers "good names", we still miss that of Mrs Sigourney. Is there no mode of tempting you to send us an occasional contribution? Mr Graham desires me to say that he would be very especially obliged if you could furnish him with a poem, however brief, for the January number. His compensation — for the days of gratuitous contributions are luckily gone by — will be at least as liberal as that of any publisher in America. May I hope to hear from you in reply? Excuse, dear Madam, this villanous steel pen, and believe me with high respect

Yr. Mo. Obt.

Edgar A Poe

Mrs L. H. Sigourney.

A letter to Sigourney from Edgar Allan Poe requesting material for Graham's Magazine.

And first, in the *character of her subjects*. Every unprejudiced observer must be aware of the almost identity between the subjects of Mrs. Hemans and the subjects of Mrs. Sigourney. The themes of the former lady are the unobtrusive happiness, the sweet images, the cares, the sorrows, the gentle affections, of the domestic hearth—these too are the themes of the latter. The Englishwoman has dwelt upon all the "tender and true" chivalries of passion—and the American has dwelt as unequivocally upon the same. Mrs. Hemans has delighted in the radiance of a pure and humble faith—she has looked upon nature with a speculative attention—she has "watched the golden array of sunset clouds, with an eye looking beyond them to the habitations of the disembodied spirit"—she has poured all over her verses the most glorious and lofty aspirations of a redeeming Christianity, and in all this she is herself glorious and lofty. And all this too has Mrs. Sigourney not only attempted, but accomplished—yet in all this she is but, alas!—an imitator.

And secondly—in points more directly tangible than the one just mentioned, and therefore more easily appreciated by the generality of readers, is Mrs. Sigourney again open to the charge we have adduced. We mean in the structure of her versification—in the peculiar turns of her phraseology—in certain habitual expressions (principally interjectional,) such as *yea! alas!* and many others, so frequent upon the lips of Mrs. Hemans as to give an almost ludicrous air of similitude to all articles of her composition—in an invincible inclination to apostrophize every object, in both moral and physical existence—and more particularly in those mottos or quotations, sometimes of considerable extent, prefixed to nearly every poem, not as a text for discussion, nor even as an intimation of what is to follow, but as the actual subject matter itself, and of which the verses ensuing are, in most instances, merely a paraphrase. These were all, in Mrs. Hemans, mannerisms of a gross and inartificial nature; but, in Mrs. Sigourney, they are mannerisms of the most inadmissible kind—the mannerisms of imitation.

In respect to the use of the quotations, we cannot conceive how the fine taste of Mrs. Hemans could have admitted the practice, or how the good sense of Mrs. Sigourney could have thought it for a single moment worthy of her own adoption. In poems of magnitude the mind of the reader is not, at all times, enabled to include in one comprehensive survey the proportions and proper adjustment of the whole. He is pleased—if at all—with particular passages; and the sum of his pleasure is compounded of the sums of the pleasurable sensations inspired by these individual passages during the progress of perusal. But in pieces of less extent—like the poems of Mrs. Sigourney—the pleasure is *unique,* in the proper acceptation of that term—the understanding is employed, without difficulty, in the contemplation of the picture *as a whole*—and thus its effect will depend, in a very great degree, upon the perfection of its finish, upon the nice adaptation of its constituent parts, and especially upon what is rightly termed by Schlegel, the *unity or totality of interest*. Now it will readily be seen, that the practice we have mentioned as habitual with Mrs. Hemans and Mrs. Sigourney is utterly at variance with this unity. By the initial motto—often a very long one—we are either put in possession of the subject of the poem; or some hint, historic fact, or suggestion is thereby afforded, not included in the body of the article, which, without the suggestion, would be utterly incomprehensible. In the latter case, while perusing the poem, the reader must revert, in mind at least, to the motto for the necessary explanation. In the former, the poem being a mere paraphrase of the motto, the interest is divided between the motto and the paraphrase. In either instance the *totality* of effect is annihilated.

Having expressed ourselves thus far in terms of nearly unmitigated censure, it may appear in us somewhat equivocal to say that, as Americans, we are proud—very proud of the talents of Mrs. Sigourney. Yet such is the fact. The faults which we have already pointed out . . . are but dust in the balance, when weighted against her very many and distinguishing excellences. Among those high qualities which give her, beyond doubt, a title to the sacred name of the poet are an acute sensibility to natural loveliness—a quick and perfectly just conception of the moral and physical sublime—a calm and unostentatious vigor of thought—a mingled delicacy and strength of expression—and above all, a mind nobly and exquisitely attuned to all the gentle charities and lofty pieties of life. (pp. 112-13)

We now bid adieu to Mrs. Sigourney—yet we trust only for a time. We shall behold her again. When that period arrives, having thrown aside the petty shackles which hitherto enchained her, she will assume, at once, that highest station among the poets of our land which her noble talents so well qualify her for attaining. (p. 115)

[Edgar Allan Poe], in a review of "Zinzendorff, and Other Poems," in The Southern Literary Messenger, *Vol. II, No. 12, January, 1836, pp. 112-17.*

THE SOUTHERN LITERARY MESSENGER (essay date 1836)

[This excerpt from a laudatory review of Letters to Young Ladies *stresses its moral correctness.]*

We have to apologize for not sooner calling the attention of our readers to these excellent [***Letters to Young Ladies***] of Mrs. Sigourney—which only to-day we have had an opportunity of reading with sufficient care to form an opinion of their merits. Our delay, however, is a matter of the less importance, when we consider the universal notice and approbation of the public at large. In this approbation we cordially agree. The book is, in every respect, worthy of Mrs. Sigourney—and it would be difficult to say more.

The letters (embraced in a duodecimo of two hundred and twelve pages,) are twelve in number. Their subjects are, Improvement of Time—Domestic Employments—Health and Dress—Manners and Accomplishments—Books—Friendship — Cheerfulness — Conversation — Benevolence — Self-Government—Utility—and Motives to Perseverance. Little has been said on any one of these subjects more forcibly or more beautifully than now by Mrs. Sigourney—and, collectively, as a code of morals and *manner* for the gentler sex, we have seen nothing whatever which we would more confidently place in the hands of any young female friend, than this unassuming little volume, so redolent of the pious, the graceful, the lofty, and the poetical mind from which it issues.

The prose of Mrs. Sigourney should not be compared, in its higher qualities, with her poetry—but appears to us essentially superior in its *minutiæ*. It would be difficult to find fault with the construction of more than a very few passages in the [***Letters to Young Ladies***]—and the general correctness and vigor of the whole would render any such fault-finding a matter of hyper-criticism. We are not prepared to say whether this correctness be the result of labor or not—there are certainly no traces of labor. The most remarkable feature of the volume is its unusually extensive circle of illustration, in the way of brief anecdote, and multiplied reference to authorities—illustration which, while apparently no more than sufficient for the present purpose of the writer, gives evidence, to any critical eye, of a far wider general erudition than that possessed by any of our female writers, and which we were not at all prepared to meet with in one, only known hitherto as the inspired poetess of Natural and Moral Beauty. (p. 505)

"Sigourney's Letters," in The Southern Literary Messenger, *Vol. II, No. 8, July, 1836, pp. 505-06.*

THE AMERICAN BIBLICAL REPOSITORY (essay date 1837)

[In this excerpt from a review of an enlarged edition of Letters to Young Ladies, *the critic commends its value to women.]*

One of the first things observable in the perusal of [***Letters to Young Ladies***], is the accurate estimate which the author forms of the true excellencies of the female character. With a kind of intuitive precision, she perceives and delineates all the delicate shades which go collectively to constitute the real loveliness of woman. She treats woman, not as the gay insect of the hour, to be admired and followed after for some brief space of time; but as a rational, immortal, accountable being. She seeks to exalt the standard of her mental and moral attainments; to make her useful and happy here, and prepare her for the companionship of angels hereafter. The book contains no sentiment or thought, which a dying christian mother would not wish to have engraved deeply on the heart of her daughter.

Such is the character of the sentiments inculcated. The mode of inculcating them, is so bland, so meek, so full of the milk of human kindness, and christian love, that it would seem impossible that the author should plead in vain with the youth of her sex. There is no monitorial dictation or stoical formality. It is the going forth of the heart to meet hearts; it is the communion of an elder sister with beloved younger sisters, portraying the loveliness of knowledge and of virtue, and fondly alluring them to follow her own foot-steps in the onward, upward course.

The work is replete with classical and historical illustrations, evincing that the mind of the author is "rich with the spoils of time." The style is a fine specimen of good writing. Though buoyant with the spirit of poesy, it is nevertheless remarkable for its simplicity and precision. While it assimilates to the gracefulness of Goldsmith and the simple elegance of Addison, it presents a point and strength of diction, which we were not prepared to expect from the female pen. (pp. 302-03)

In its present enlarged and matured form, the work reflects great credit on the literary character of our country. It forms a gem in her cabinet of letters. We wish to see its circulation co-extensive with our vast empire. Every daughter of our land should read and study it. (p. 318)

"Mrs. Sigourney's Letters," in The American Biblical Repository, *Vol. IX, No. 26, April, 1837, pp. 301-18.*

THE ATHENAEUM **(essay date 1839)**

[This anonymous critic for a British periodical contends that Sigourney's works, like those of many of her American countrywomen, lack discipline and polish.]

In Mrs. Hale's volume [*The Ladies' Wreath: A Selection from the Female Poetic Writers of England and America*] we have specimens of twelve [American] poetesses, (we say nothing of the other twelve, selected from our own countrywomen,) and first among them is Mrs. Sigourney. This, the post of honour, seems by common consent to be awarded to this lady, who is frequently called the American Hemans, which, considering the great popularity of the latter in the United States, indicates a very high estimate of her power—too high we think. That Mrs. Sigourney has considerable poetical talent we do not deny, but there are other female writers,—and we might refer even to the volumes before us in proof,—hardly, if at all, her inferior. The question, however, cannot be hastily decided, for Mrs. Sigourney has rarely, if ever, done herself justice; but then this remark is equally applicable to all these American poets. We infer from the accompanying 'Notices,' that Mrs. Hale is herself perfectly aware that her countrywomen mistake the matter sadly, when they persuade themselves that poetry is a mere gift of Providence, like a bird's voice, and requiring no more effort or practice;—quite as much so as when they fall into the opposite theory, of its being a mere work of labour and culture, independent of genius. Mrs. Sigourney may not have fallen into either error, but she is certainly, for whatever reason, wanting in many qualities which her sobriquet leads us to look for. The *English* Hemans, let what will be said of her mannerism, was not merely a woman of great and rich poetical genius, but of a most severe and scrupulous, though self-imposed poetical training. She had also a native taste, which was too easily offended to allow even a trifle to go from her pen less perfect than she was able to make it. This, in certain moods, might require little labour; but whatever labour it did require was bestowed. Hence, some of her "trifles" are among the most perfect of her poems, and will immortalize her name, as like trifles have preserved the names of Gray and Collins, and others, who have condensed whole lives of *culture,* as it were, into some few stanzas,—have had the genius, let us say, as well as the judgment to do so. Now, Mrs. Sigourney is not without spirit. She can be eloquent at times. There is a fine flow of both thought and music in her **"Coral Insect."**. . . But this same piece is a proof in point for our argument. Short as it is, it is neither finished, nor sustained in spirit to the end: indeed, we do not remember one of Mrs. Sigourney's poems that is so, though many of them contain fine vigorous passages. Many, on the other hand, are but respectable prose from beginning to end. Some, whose titles excite most expectation, such as those relating to Washington and his mother, most disappoint us. The thoughts are generally dignified in themselves—nothing more; while the effort which seems to have been conscientiously made to do them a sort of poetical justice in expression, is so manifest as to take off the attraction which they would have in mere prose. The lines on **"Niagara,"** though the least unsatisfactory of this class of poems, contain but an elaborate display of well got up sentiments. We should say that Mrs. Sigourney writes a great deal too much, even for one who had had a more severe disciplining in all the not inconsiderable matters subservient to a true and complete poetical education. If she would give us a page yearly instead of a volume, and take the time for writing it when she feels most in the mood, and devote the rest of her leisure to such a process as Mrs. Hemans went through for many years, we should then see what art and labour would enable her to accomplish. As it is, her best things, in our opinion, are those of which she herself thinks least. They are the pieces that were struck out whole—clean-coined—from the mint of a full mind, warmed by external excitement, and taken by surprise. In most of this American poetry there is a want of naturalness,—of the quiet ease which only thorough preparation and great practice can bestow. The writers think too lightly of poetry; they do not appreciate the *art* and science of it enough. Instinct, and genius, and spirit, are all very well; the more of them the better. But they must be managed, and made the most of. Some of Mrs. Sigourney's prose, too, let us not forget, is very good. This is her element after all. The *spirit* of her writings, be it observed, is universally good. (pp. 24-5)

A review of "The Ladies's Wreath: A Selection from the Female Poetic Writers of England and America," in The Athenaeum, *No. 585, January 12, 1839, pp. 24-5.*

***THE MONTHLY REVIEW,* LONDON** **(essay date 1843)**

[This critic assesses Sigourney's collection of travel sketches, Pleasant Memories of Pleasant Lands.*]*

Mrs. Sigourney's work [***Pleasant Memories of Pleasant Lands***] is the result of the travels of an American lady and poetess through England, Scotland, and part of France. It is no regular account of a journey, but a series of separate notices, partly prose, partly in verse, of various places and persons of more than common interest, mingled with such reflections and remarks as might naturally suggest themselves to the fair traveller's mind. The production, therefore, is of no very laboured character; but that does not prevent it from being very entertaining, and by no means uninstructive. The prose is generally very good,—some of the poetry excellent; and the whole,—free from any shade of querulousness or its frequent cause, national prejudice,—makes a delightful volume. These [***Pleasant Memories of Pleasant Lands***], we are pretty sure, will be found by numerous readers as pleasant as (by her application of the epithet) we hope their authoress found the tour during which they were compiled. We care not how many works of the sort, conceived in the same right spirit, spring up interchangeably, from alternate visitors, between England and America. Their obvious and desirable tendency is to promote between the two countries that good feeling which the true friends of either would never wish to see interrupted; and, consequently, however feeble the attempt, some praise and thanks are always due for the intention. In this instance . . . we should be no true critics did we not find some fault in the work even of a lady; and we must take leave to say, that we should not have regretted the omission of the greater number of the poems in blank verse. It is not that it is *bad,* it is *not good;* and that, from the days of Horace, has been held a fatal fault in poetry. Why will people try to write blank verse? It is a hopeless task. Take away Milton, Shakespeare, Thomson's *Seasons,* and one or two more, and we have hardly a line of it worth reading in the language. Why, then, attempt what, ordinarily speaking, none can hope to accomplish? Mrs. Sigourney, however, has only failed where success would have been almost superhuman: that she can and does write elegant and graceful poetry is easily shown. (p. 486)

A review of "Pleasant Memories of Pleasant Lands," in The Monthly Review, *London, Vol. I, No. 4, April, 1843, pp. 486-92.*

THE AMERICAN LITERARY MAGAZINE (essay date 1849)

[*This critic praises Sigourney for confining her poetic inspiration "within woman's proper domain."*]

No name could be chosen, more appropriate than [that of Mrs. Sigourney], to commence a series of notices of our female writers. She is one, above all whom we know, who neither loses the woman in the writer nor the writer in the woman. She illustrates what a female author ought to be. No trait, exhibited in her works, is more vividly clear than her perfect womanliness. Nor do we owe this impression to our knowledge of her personal character, which is as free from the masculine manners or *bas bleuism,* often generated in a lady by contact with the public through the press, as is that of the most delicate of her sex; but from the universal and pervading tone and spirit of her publications. She never forgets her sex or its claims. She indulges in no bravura; she indites no love-song. Her writings exhale the purity of feminine delicacy, as well as that of the truest morality and the peacefullest religion. It is wonderful that she always lets her fancy play within woman's proper domain, and we therefore repeat that we could have made no fitter selection for a great name among the records of female genius, than hers.

She is the most distinguished of the literary ladies of America. Her fame is of longer standing and has held its own better, perhaps, than that of any of her female contemporaries. She has not been a victim of literary fashion, to be put on and put off according to caprice. There is a solidity in her reputation, most enviable. Her name is more a household word than that of others of her sex. Having appeared before the public as a poet, essayist, writer of fiction, author of treatises on elementary ethics for the young, and having succeeded in all departments, she has taken a broad and comprehensive hold on popularity. Now we do not in these remarks intend to institute a comparison between her and her female contemporaries in the matter of merit. We should scout so envious a task. Our design is simply to assign to her the true place she holds in the esteem of the public—to tell what she *is* rather than what we, as critics, think she may be—to dwell not on her intrinsic superiority of merit, but on what Cicero ascribes to Pompey, as the crowning virtue of all his character—her *felicitas,* her good fortune or success. We are talking merely of the *vox populi*—the virtue of popularity.

It may here be suggested, that the fact that she was one of the first to impress the sign of womanly genius on American literature has given her a sort of precedence. We render due honor to the sagacity of this suggestion and acknowledge its correctness. But we are at the same time sure, that it will not be claimed that accident has placed her where she is. If any one doubts to what her fame is due, let him ask the *hearts* of her readers.

We are proud to make the allusion. It is a vindication of the righteous sentiment of our race, to know that a woman's heart, as expressed in her writings, has given her an empire over masses of mankind, to which no ambition need blush to aspire. It is a vindication of woman's true position in the field of literature. It shows that, to be sure of fame, she must be true to a woman's nature,—weave around genius the drooping and delicate graces of a gentle heart and appeal to the best sentiments rather than to the strong passions or stern intellectual tastes of mankind.

The richness, evenness and propriety, which distinguish Mrs. Sigourney's style, have been of less advantage to her than her consistent adherence to her great principle,—of writing for an object and for a good object. It is always to commend what is beautiful,—to honor religion,—to inculcate morality,—to elevate the character of her sex,—to administer comfort to bleeding hearts,—to discourage false views of life,—to promote social harmony,—to honor the affections,—to express gratitude,—to excite veneration for things, present or past, that deserve veneration—to paint natural sorrows or pure joys,—to fill the atmosphere around her with hopes "that make not ashamed," and desires that need no chastening,—that Mrs. Sigourney writes. The rule is without exception. Her fancy never plays for the sake of its own sparkle. There always seems to be a sympathy beneath, that prompts the flow of thought. This is . . . the touchstone of Mrs. Sigourney's success and secures for her writings the honors of classics. It is not to be wondered at, that her poems find so easily a place among the recently-published boudoir editions,—so splendidly printed and illustrated,—of our American bards, such as Bryant, Longfellow and Halleck. (pp. 390-92)

"Lydia Huntley Sigourney," in The American Literary Magazine, *Vol. IV, No. 1, January, 1849, pp. 387-400.*

THE NORTH AMERICAN REVIEW (essay date 1849)

[*In this excerpt from a review of Sigourney's* Illustrated Poems, *the critic examines the merits and limitations of her poetry.*]

[***Illustrated Poems***] contains about a hundred poems. They are on a variety of subjects, and in a variety of forms, but they all bear unmistakable marks of one mind, looking at nature and human life from one position. Their leading peculiarity is devotional sensibility, and their leading charm the extreme, the translucent purity of thought and feeling displayed in the expression of the religious and domestic affections. As is the case with most female poets, Mrs. Sigourney's powers act with intensity only on those subjects which have fallen within her own experience, or which spontaneously fasten on her womanly sympathies. She does not evince that masculine imagination, by which the mind passes out of its own individual relations of sex and person, and animates numerous and widely different modes of being. Her poems not only declare her at once to be a woman, but a woman who, as far as regards composition, has disciplined her mind into one or two moods, and persists in seeing every thing under their conditions. Though there is no lack of freedom in expression, the reader still feels certain that there will be no inconsistency of emotion and purpose, however various may be the topics of her poems,—that the passions will ever be represented in their due relations to an exacting religious sentiment, and that the rush of sensibility, by which, in a sensitive mind, the feeling of the moment, whether joyous or despairing, colors every thing with its gloomy or glittering hues, will be resolutely checked by a predominating sense of moral obligation. Her mind, therefore, is not flexible and impassioned, but didactic; and fancy, feeling, understanding, and imagination all obey rules,—obey them, it is true, without strain or struggle, and almost with the quickness of instinct, but still in this obedience manifesting subjection, not sovereignty.

It is evident that a religious mind, thus subject to the higher powers, and at the same time confined within its own realm of thought and emotion, would perceive nature and human life always in their relations to God, but would have the range of its perceptions narrowed by the limitations of its own personality. We have, therefore, to make one or two more distinctions in considering Mrs. Sigourney as a poet of the religious and domestic affections, before we can reach the source of her merits or defects.

The truth of the all-pervading presence of a conscious Deity in nature, and of a Providence in the sorrows and joys of mankind, seems to have been fixed in her mind as a doctrine before it was felt as an overpowering conception or emotion; and, consequently, she rather goes to nature and life prepared to look and search for the signs of divine presence, than to be amazed by having the overwhelming truth suddenly flashed into her mind from without, through the vital processes of imagination. Accordingly, though she has a deep and thoughtful feeling of holy things, her hymns rarely rise to the raptures of holy passion, in which the soul, by a divine disinterestedness, seems to dissolve its whole individual being into one ecstatic song of adoration. This last mood of mind, the highest and grandest exercise of imagination, and the perfection at once of what is purely religious and purely poetical, it is no disparagement to Mrs. Sigourney to say she does not possess; for it is the loftiest and finest frenzy of the seer and the bard. But while a comparatively small number of religious poets reach this intense realization of Deity, it is approached just in proportion to the flexibility and objectiveness of the poet's imagination. Now, Mrs. Sigourney's mind being didactic rather than lyrical, her devotional feeling rarely gushes out in pure song, with the speed of an irrepressible instinct, but approaches more the character of a steady and quiet faith, in which the soul serenely believes rather than rapturously burns, and meditates more than it imagines. The poetic faculty, therefore, most at work in her thoughtful and devotional moods, is fancy, illustrating the truth *from* nature and life, rather than imagination presenting it directly *in* nature and life.

In thus speaking of Mrs. Sigourney's poetry, as didactic, we by no means insinuate that it is prosaic, but simply that it is neither lyrical nor narrative in spirit, though much of her verse is cast in these forms. Religious thought relating to divine things, considered apart from its poetic expression, is vital or mechanical according as it directly conceives the objects of contemplation, or apprehends and applies a doctrine respecting them. In Mrs. Sigourney's book, we have illustrations of both, but more of the former than the latter. She has brooded long enough over her own experience and sympathies to give them vitality, and the poems which truly represent her own mind not only possess life, but communicate it. A healthy moral energy is diffused generally through her poems, which steals into the reader's mind through subtile avenues lying beyond his consciousness, and declares the presence of a poet gifted with the power of inspiring strength in the very heart of weakness and lassitude. This is a great poetic excellence, however limited may be the range of its exercise, and that Mrs. Sigourney possesses it cannot be denied or even contested. There are pieces in this volume which reach the religious sentiment with such sure felicity of thought and phrase, that the consciousness of the reader becomes the best criticism.

The pervading devotional tone to which we have referred, finds its finest and holiest expression in celebrating the domestic affections. The mode in which her mind acts in this province, however, illustrates what we have previously said of her mental processes. The poems entitled **"To-morrow," "Unspoken Language," "The Emigrant Mother,"** not to mention others, are full of true pathos, and reach and penetrate the heart as inevitably as any in Wordsworth; but though sufficiently tender and deep to bring moisture into the eyes even of a reviewer, we shall find, on a sharp scrutiny, that, though names are used and persons indicated, there is really nothing there but qualities. The purest types of the affections are grasped in all their firmness and delicacy, but there is no combination of them with those other human elements which, in their union, produce character. The consequence is, that we have no representations of the affections as modified by sex, age, nation, position, or character. With remarkable distinctness of conception and decision of expression, we have presented to us the type, but it is given in its simple unity, abstracted from all individuality. We assert confidently, that in this volume there is not displayed one trait of character but that of the author herself. The little poems of **"Harold and Tosti,"** and **"Bernardine du Born,"** fine as they are in sentiment, have nothing but the incidents on which they are founded to entitle them to their names. The long poem of **"Pocahontas,"** the most beautiful of all the tributes to the heroic Indian princess, is still simply a fervid expression of the impression made by the story on the mind of the writer, without any clear vision of the scenes and characters of the story as they were in themselves. (pp. 497-500)

But this peculiarity of bringing out a quality at the expense of all character, which we have indicated as a limitation of Mrs. Sigourney's genius, is probably a chief source of her influence over the hearts of her readers. She is thus enabled to stamp a deep impression of one affection, at least, on the mind; and by detaching it from the other elements of character, by making a person stand simply for an emotion, she has completely mastered one prominent source of the pathetic. (p. 500)

In taking leave of this beautiful volume, which we have subjected to a harsher analysis than we intended, the sweet and serious face that looks out from the portrait at the commencement of it seems to rebuke us for not alluding to a class of poems in the book which refer to children, and in which that elusive thing, a child's mind, is seized and represented with singular intensity of thought and stainless purity of feeling. Indeed, the relation of mother and child, in numerous pieces in the volume, is surrounded with so many holy images, and enveloped in such an atmosphere of tenderness and love, that the only proper criticism on the felicity of its treatment would be a throng of quotations for which we have no space. There is also a number of descriptive poems, displaying a fine cheerful play and interchange of fancy and sentiment, which relieve the general tone of serious thought by which the collection is characterized. In leaving a volume laden with so many pure thoughts and sacred emotions, unstained by one compromise with passion, and consecrated with such singleness of heart to the highest objects, we cannot but hope it will receive a cordial recognition wherever poetry has a welcome, affection a home, and religion a worshipper. (pp. 502-03)

"Mrs. Sigourney's Poems," in The North American Review, *Vol. LXVIII, No. 143, April, 1849, pp. 496-503.*

THE IRISH QUARTERLY REVIEW **(essay date 1855)**

[This critic, reviewing a British edition of Sigourney's poetry, identifies the qualities that make Sigourney a "first class writer."]

Mrs. Sigourney is a poetess possessing, in a remarkable degree, those qualities which entitle the possessor to the rank of a first class writer. Her vigorous comprehensiveness, lofty aspirings, brilliant fancy, philosophy, and philanthropic zeal, coupled with her sublime references to Almighty perfection, and the grand moral tendency of her poetry, unite in claiming for her an amount of admiration which enables her to hold one of the highest places among the poets of her country.

In like manner the patriotism which she has always evinced, her Spartan veneration for virtue, and scathing denunciations of crime; her deep-rooted love of nature, and the elegance, compass, and power of her language, have all had their share in accomplishing that universal success which her writings have obtained. The class of subjects she has chosen to act as the interpreters of her thoughts, are, most fortunately, the very best she could have selected, not merely for the perpetuation of her fame, but for that which is of far greater import, the extension of virtuous principles, and creation of the best incentives to every triumph of virtue. If that peculiar and most enviable capacity were more general, by whose plastic touch what has for ages appeared repulsive and difficult of accomplishment, instantaneously becomes transformed into a seductive and desiderated treasure; and what has hitherto been invested with seeming charms, and the almost irresistible delectations which luxury supposes, not alone "withers and grows dim,"—but becomes more terrible than Erinnys with her cincture of snakes; if such a gift was common even to the majority of intellectual minds, Sigourney's talents might not demand such emphatic appreciation. It is her almost total isolation in this respect, which brings her more prominently into notice, and it is only necessary to form a superficial acquaintance with her poetry to become convinced of her fearless power in advocating the cause of virtue. Truly her brilliant talents not only elevate the standard of intellectuality which dignifies her sex, but must naturally inspire its members with expectations, in which their widened influence, and far extended importance as a class, are conspicuously distinguished.

It is exceedingly questionable whether Sigourney would not gain from a comparison with her poetic sister, Felicia Hemans. Many would esteem her an equal in fancy, grace, and rhythmical beauty, while in vigor and range of comprehension she is most undoubtedly superior. **"Oriska,"** as a narrative is perfect; the beauty of the language which indeed is exquisite, the faithful embodiment of the artlessness of the heroine, the strain of wild, plaintive melody pervading the poem, which is so thoroughly in consonance with the subject, and the melancholy catastrophe it contains; the imprecation uttered by the dying mother of the heroine on her faithless husband, so figuratively beautiful! the curse of him "who knoweth where the lightnings hide," the lofty sublimity of **"Oriska"** in scorning death, and the abrupt grandeur of the conclusion, unite in constituting it a most lovely poem. (pp. 209-11)

Mrs. Sigourney has given evidence in **"Niagara,"** as well as in many other of her poems, of the possession of masculine power, and grasp of thought. How full of vigor, and lofty imagination, this line!

God hath set his rainbow on thy forehead.

As an evidence of the power of genius in investing any subject with interest, and also as an example of a well organized mind drawing sublime inferences from apparently the most trivial objects, **"The Shred of Linen"** deserves perusal. **"The Mourning Daughter"** is another instance of the forcible imagination, original conception, and exalted mind of the authoress. The tale is told with a matchless dignity, and calm simplicity, which bears us along like a majestic stream, mirroring its truth in its transparent beauty.

"Napoleon at Helena," is written in a nervous strain of lyric grandeur, evidencing great classic taste, sound judgment, and the same depth of thought, and masculine vigor, which have been already adverted to. As an exhibition of great spirit and national pride, which render it highly interesting, we shall instance **"Columbia's Ships"**—a narrative of much interest, and wearing a romantic dress. **"The Trial of the Dead,"** can hardly be read without communicating to the reader a portion of the weird and mysterious feeling, which influences its incident and language. For its length, perhaps the prettiest thing that ever was written is, **"The Death of an Infant,"** the ideas are beautiful in the extreme, and follow each other in a most natural way, which leaves an impression on the mind, of excellence not to be surpassed: it is enough to convert an Infidel, and to bring tears into the eyes of the veriest misanthrope that ever lived.

"The Rainbow" pours forth a fresh flood of her thoughtful, yet energetic, and glowing poetry: how beautifully the poet insinuates that the junction of the smile and the tear-drop, have resulted in the creation of the rainbow. It is an idea worthy of Homer, and heathen mythology has not produced any thing to surpass it. Another talisman, with power to "Ope the sympathetic source of tears," is **"The Infant's Prayer." "Harold and Tosti,"** shew the authoress to be in no wise deficient in that simple grace, dramatic power, and spirited method, so essential for the perfection of the ballad. If any other instance of the psychological beauties of Mrs. Sigourney were required, we should find one in her beautiful poem, called **"Dreams."** It is full of superb images, woven in the light of the brightest fancy, yet formed of the essence of the soundest truth: there is a most charming moral conclusion evolved from the consideration of the subject.

"Man's Three Guests," is an exquisite ballad, remarkable for its beauty, and appropriateness; it is written in an interesting, yet easily comprehended strain, which might effect more good by leading the mind to the contemplation of its more essential objects, than a thousand homilies, and all the tracts which ever yet issued from Exeter Hall. (pp. 212-13)

"The Poets of America," in The Irish Quarterly Review, *Vol. V, No. XVIII, June, 1855, pp. 193-220.*

THE NORTH AMERICAN REVIEW **(essay date 1856)**

[*This critic applauds the publication of a new edition of* Pleasant Memories of Pleasant Lands.]

It is a good sign, literary and moral, that a third edition of this book [***Pleasant Memories of Pleasant Lands***] is called for. It is more than we should have expected for a work which has absolutely nothing in it that is intense, or odd, or paradoxical, nay, which has no salient points whatever. *No salient points,* we say, and in so saying we describe what is not necessarily a merit or a fault; for the prominences thus designated may be either outcroppings of genius or forthputtings of pretentious mediocrity, while the absence of them may denote either the extreme of emptiness and platitude, or that of fulness, grace, and artistical beauty. In Mrs. Sigourney it denotes the latter. Of the numerous poems in verse and poems in prose that make up this volume, we should not know how to select one or a few for special praise, nor is there one with which we should be willing to part. The pieces taken collectively are a poet's journal of a tour in Great Britain and France, with the memorabilia of the outward and homeward passage. The successive centres of peculiar interest furnish the titles, and a portion of the material, for the successive sketches and reveries. Easy narrative, graphic description, vivid yet chastened fancy, and devotion equally mild and fervent, blend and alternate throughout, constituting a cluster of gems, each with its own individual lustre, and all of them possessing, not a superficial glitter, but a brilliancy which, like that of pure crystal, shines through the entire substance. The work is enhanced in value from its being manifestly the genuine record of heart-experiences, and that so completely that we can conceive of its being written, all of it, with no expectation of its ever leaving the writer's desk. But we are thankful that it was not left there; for her thoughts suggest reflections and kindle emotions that can hardly fail to make her readers wiser and better. (pp. 576-77)

A review of "Pleasant Memories of Pleasant Lands," in The North American Review, *Vol. LXXXII, No. 171, April, 1856, pp. 576-77.*

HOURS AT HOME (essay date 1865)

[In this excerpt from a biographical and critical sketch published shortly after Sigourney's death, an anonymous reviewer appraises her works.]

In estimating Mrs. Sigourney's literary claims, we need to refer to the faults of the age in which she lived—a period in which the desire for distinction and originality betrayed literary men into strange vagaries of language and style, and for a time threatened to barbarize the purity of our language.

Resisting the general tendency to inflation, to hard transpositions, and to rough violation of rhythmic rules, she adhered to the pure standard of our best English classics, both in rhythm, construction, and expression. Some of our modern poets will fail of wide or lasting popularity, because their involved sentences and hard renderings demand a previous *exercise in parsing,* or the dictionary, to be understood, an exercise to which the great mass of readers will not submit. In contrast to this, Mrs. Sigourney's writings never pain the ear by a foreign expression, a limping foot, a barbarous expression or missing rhythm. On the contrary, her widely circulated poems, while they charmed the common ear and heart, aided to educate the national taste, and to preserve a love for refined poetry, and a pure and classic use of our mother tongue.

The fault of her writings, to a degree, arose from her very virtues. Not only did her generous and sympathetic nature lead her to constant elegiac and funereal effusions, but she was constantly beset by mourning friends, not only among her acquaintance, but entire strangers, through the mail, entreating her to consecrate the graves of their dear ones with the flowers of her genius. How much she was thus entreated, and how difficult was the task of refusal to one so sympathizing and kind, few could realize, except those who saw her loaded mails, and the labors of love thus multiplied and generously bestowed.

That Mrs. Sigourney possessed poetic talent of a high order can not be denied. That she did not husband her pearls of thought, and string them in compact forms, her friends may regret. But in that world where love rules supreme, she may form a different estimate, and rejoice that a desire for admiration and fame was subordinated to tender sympathy and far-reaching benevolence.

And yet it must be allowed that prolixity and haste were the faults of her literary career; and that her *fifty volumes* would have been wisely reduced to half that number. (pp. 560-61)

"Mrs. Lydia H. Sigourney," in Hours at Home, *Vol. I, No. 6, October, 1865, pp. 559-65.*

THE ROUND TABLE (essay date 1866)

[This critic offers praise for Sigourney's posthumously published autobiography, Letters of Life.*]*

These letters [in ***Letters of Life***] form one of the most charming biographies that we have met with for many a day. Written with all the freedom of private correspondence, and characterized by that indescribable attractiveness of style which marks the epistolary effusions of women, they are not so verbose as to be tedious, nor so egotistical as to be disgusting. They comprise the record of seventy years, and were evidently penned hard upon the limit affixed to human life by the Psalmist. We find in these letters very few extracts from "my diary," which so often form a large portion of autobiographies and memoirs, and no records of ill-defined longings, which one is tempted to think are sometimes composed with a view of leaving a good impression of the composer upon those who may survive him or her. No suspicion of this sort can attach to this book. Moreover, the work is pervaded by a most commendable spirit. Charity for all and malice towards none might be written on the title-page. Mrs. Sigourney evidently accustomed herself to discern the good qualities of those with whom she came in contact, or, at least, to keep to herself whatever faults they might possess.

There are in these letters many charming pictures of New England life in the early part of the present century which we would like to transfer to these columns, but we have not the space. . . .

Those who have formed their opinion of Mrs. Sigourney from the fugitive rhymes bearing her name which so frequently appeared in the public press upon the death of any of her friends could not be expected to look for any humor in her mental composition. But they were mistaken. Her readiness at expressing sentiments in a rhythmical form made her the victim of countless applications for a "few lines on the death" of all sorts and conditions of men, women, and children, to accede to all of which would have been a sheer impossibility. . . .

We have only to say, in closing this brief notice of ***Letters of Life,*** that the book is a charming memento of Mrs. Lydia H. Sigourney, whose name is a household word in every Christian family in the country. Though not properly a subject for literary criticism, it is vastly more sensible and readable than most of the biographies of good people that are issued from the press, and is a conspicuous contradiction of a somewhat prevalent notion that good children never attain to old age.

A review of "Letters of Life," in The Round Table, *Vol. III, No. 27, March 10, 1866, p. 148.*

GRACE LATHROP COLLIN (essay date 1902)

[Collin evaluates Sigourney's poetry and prose, labelling her poetry imitative and attributing her prose style to the literary affectations of her era.]

It is as a poetess that Mrs. Sigourney is chiefly known, although of her fifty-six books the majority are in prose. But at the time her verse seems to have been much more popular, or at least to have been considered more of an achievement. To us there seems little originality in any of it. Its merit seems dependent rather upon that of the poem upon which Mrs. Sigourney, for the time being, modelled her style. These models were chosen from what lay convenient to her hand, even as a good housewife makes a cake from what she has in the house. Thus Mrs. Sigourney's **"Friendship with Nature"** suggests Bryant's "Thanatopsis"; **"Bell of the Wreck,"** Cowper's "Loss of the Royal George"; **"Grasmere and Rydal Water"** is after the manner of Wordsworth's "Excursion"; **"Thoughts at the Grave of Sir Walter Scott"** is in his favorite ballad metres; **"The Elm Trees"** reminds one of Hood's "I Remember. I Remember"; and **"Connecticut River,"** of Goldsmith's "Deserted Village." Her pure taste, delicate imagination, piety, and what, in our opinion, is an indispensable attribute of a true poet, her good sense, won esteem. (p. 26)

Of her prose, the examples quoted here and there illustrate the style which she considered suitable for ears polite, which is so full of absurd affectations that it is a dialect rather than the English language. And did her work stop here, with imitative verse and artificial prose, we should consider Mrs. Sigourney interesting as an author of her time, and for it, but without a link to bind her in comradeship with those who have written for all time; even as a quaintly fashioned garment has charm as epitomizing the manners and costume of a bygone day, but cannot be regarded as a pattern. But the interesting part of Mrs. Sigourney's writings lies in the fact that, although broken in upon by "graceful and elegant expressions"; cut short to make room for flowery platitudes; fragmentary at the best,—there are evidences that she had latent capabilities which, if but properly exercised, could have rendered her work as free from the popular affectations of her time as though published yesterday.

In the first place, I venture to assert that Mrs. Sigourney, when not impressed by the dignity of her vocation, had a mild sense of humor. True, at her door must be laid **"To a Shred of Linen,"** with the fatal phrase,—

> Methinks I scan
> Some idiosyncrasy, that marks thee out
> A defunct pillow-case.

But consider this informal description of a singing-school-taught choir, rendering the anthem,—

> No bolts to drive their guilty souls
> To fiercer flames below.

> Off led the treble, having the air, and expending *con spirito* upon 'fiercer,' about fourteen quavers. After us came the tenors, in a more dignified manner, bestowing their principal emphasis on 'flames.' 'No bolts, no bolts,' shrieked a sharp counter of boys, whose voices were in the transition stage. But when a heavy bass, like claps of thunder, kept repeating 'below,' and finally all parts took up the burden, till, in full diapason, 'guilty souls' and 'fiercer flames' reverberated from wall to arch, it was altogether too much for Puritanic patience.

Then there are bits of description done with a delicacy and firmness of touch, save where marred by her foibles of style, which show that she might have been one of the idyllists of New England. In [***Sketch of Connecticut Forty Years Since***], Mrs. Sigourney outlines the scene of a "warm spell" in winter, when spots of tufted green appear as the wet snow sinks into the black soil, and the air has again a sweet earthy smell. Then comes a blizzard. The elm trees are almost bent double under their heavy load of sleet and snow, the fences are drifted over, the housewalls banked, the windows and doors blockaded; and the road smooth and white till beaten again into pathways by heavy sledges, drawn by a score of oxen. With a loving but picturesque regard for detail, she recalls also the living room of Mrs. Lathrop:

> That low-browed apartment, with all its appointments, is before me. . . . I see its highly polished wainscot, crimson moreen curtains, the large brass andirons, with their silvery brightness, the clean hearth, on which not even the white ashes of the consuming hickory were suffered to rest, the rich, dark shade of the furniture, unpolluted by dust, and the closet where the open door revealed its wealth of silver cans, tankards and flagons.

Obviously, Mrs. Sigourney was mistress of two literary styles. The one, which she naïvely terms "the language of books"; the other, which she usually introduces with the phrase,—and we can imagine her coughing apologetically behind her slim hand,—"to employ the vernacular speech." It happens that she describes a New England farmhouse in each style. In the chapter on "Privileges of Age," in ***Past Meridian,*** we have it thus:

> Traits of agricultural life, divested of its rude and sordid toils, were pleasantly visible. A smooth-coated and symmetrical cow ruminated over her clover-meal. A faithful horse, submissive to the gentlest rein, protruded his honest face through the barn window. A few brooding mothers were busy with the nurture of their chickens, while the proud father of the flock told, with a clarion voice, his happiness.

Here is the other, from ***Myrtis and Other Etchings and Sketchings:***

> Cousin Jehoshaphat Jones, have a little patience. Everything in its right place. I guess you had better hear first consarning my dealings at the minister's. My business was to dig in the gardin, and to chop wood, and to take care of the dumb critters, which consisted of an old horse, quite lean in flesh, and a cow with balls at her horns, 'cause she routed down fences when she could get a chance, and a flock of hens, which it was a power of trouble to watch and scare out of the neighbors' corn.

The least fragmentary example of this honest style of hers, which ranks her with any realist in rural New England dialect and temper, is found in a few pages in [***Sketch of Connecticut Forty Years Since***]. The scene describes Farmer Larkin, who has returned as tenant to Mrs. Lathrop's farm, where he had "driv team when a leetle boy," coming to pay his respects to his landlady. Finding it impossible to approach her by keeping to the bare floor surrounding the rug, he exclaims,—

> 'I must tread on the kiverlid. . . . Your ha-ath, too, is as clean as a cheeny tea-cup, Ma'am. I hate to put my coarse huffs on it. But I ha'n't been used to seein' kiverlids spread on the floor to walk on. We are glad to get 'em to kiver us up with a nights. This looks like a boughten one. 'Tis exceedin' cur'ous. They must have had a-plenty many treadles in the loom that wove this.'

In response to Mrs. Lathrop's inquiries as to the welfare of his family, he replies,

> 'All stout and hearty, thank 'e, Ma'am, as plump as partridges, and swarmin' round like bees. Molly's the oldest on 'em and as fat as butter. She'll be fourteen years old, come the tenth of February, and that will be Sabba-day arter next. She weighs about twice as much as you do, ma'am, I guess. She's rather more stocky than her mother, and I hope will be as smart for bizness. She'll spin her run o' tow-

yarn or woollen, afore dinner; and she has wove six yards a day, of yard-wide sheetin'. She takes in weavin' when anybody will hire it done, and so buys herself her bettermost clo'es, which is a help to me. Jehoiakim, the oldest boy—he's named after his gran-daddy—and is a stout, stirrin' youngster. He'll hoe near about as much corn in an hour as I can; and cold winter days, he'll chop and sled wood through the snow, without frettin' a bit. But I s'pose 'tain't right and fittin' to brag about my children, Ma'am.

'They all go to the deestrict school, more than ha-af o' the winter; though it's nigh upon two mild from the house. In the summer time it's kept a leetle spell by a woman—and then the younger ones go, to keep 'em out o' the way o' them who are glad to work at home. I s'pose they l'arn somethin' about readin' and sewin'. But Tim, the third child, he's the boy for l'arnin'. He took a prodigious likin' to books, when he was a baby; and if you only showed him one, he'd put it rite into his mouth and stop squallin'. He ain't but eleven year old now; and when he gets a newspaper, there's no *whoa* to him, no more than to the black ox when he sees the haystack, till he's read it clear through, advertisements and all. The master says that he's the smartest of all the boys about spellin', and now he takes to cipherin' marvellously. So that I don't know but that some time or other he may be hired to keep our deestrict school. But I hope my heart ain't lifted up with pride, at sich great prospects, for I know that "God resisteth the proud, and giveth grace unto the humble."'

(pp. 27-9)

It has been said that Mrs. Sigourney's besetting sins were complacency, artificiality and vanity. In her autobiographical ***Letters of Life*** her attitude toward her own literary work is complacent only in viewing its accomplishment; and that results naturally from a sense of duty done, and expresses itself in a universal kindliness that is surely praiseworthy. Her artificiality, too, seems to be, as it were, itself artificial. Under her affectations lies an unimpeachable sincerity of character. Further, without tempering justice with mercy, we may change the reproach of vanity into the more accurate inordinate love of praise. Herein lies both the weakness of her character and the consequent weakness of her work.

From her babyhood she had been noted for her goodness. When a schoolgirl she was the monitress; when a young lady, a pattern of decorum; when married, a model helpmeet; when a writer, an authoress of whom America was proud. She was good because it was good to be good, she was good by nature, and she was good by choice; because the results of goodness brought her her dearest possession,—a meed of praise. True, she was in the main a hack writer, and the greater number of her works are potboilers. But aside from this, the star to which she hitched her wagon, in the pathless literary field which she entered as a girl of twenty and left as a woman of seventy, was approbation, popular and immediate. She did not want to obtain fame as either eccentric or strong-minded, but as a sort of literary Lady Bountiful. In her nature there was a warmth, a romanticism, an aesthetic yearning for all that is graceful and lovable, which found no other means of gratification than in being accommodating. She dreaded to be called *queer*, and she loved to be thanked and to be called *nice*, with all the feminine implication of the words. So she followed the fashion of the moment with a docility broken only in a few brief passages. And she had her reward.

But, the pity of it! True, in our lamentations over her defects, we should remember that she lived in an age characterized by production rather than by criticism, and that therefore, in spite of her occasional flashes of art, she may have been proudest of the work that we condemn; we have no reason to think that she forsook methods which she knew to be good, for those which she knew to be worthless. Whereas, we, living in an age characterized by criticism rather than by production, are judging her work by standards of whose existence she was either ignorant or oblivious, by dogmas of taste flatly contradicted since the years when Mrs. Sigourney wrote with a care "for ears polite"; and if we laugh at her unquestioning adoption of prevailing modes, in these days when the most mild mannered of our citizens joy in the clash of swords and ring of shield, we are laughing at ourselves. Yet, is there not a grim humor in the situation, of this dainty, plucky little lady of letters, capable of writing with simplicity and vividness and veracity, being thus influenced by a passing literary fashion? And has not the work of Mrs. Sigourney its significance in the literary history of our country? (pp. 29-30)

Grace Lathrop Collin, "Lydia Huntley Sigourney," in The New England Magazine, *n.s. Vol. XXVII, No. 1, September, 1902, pp. 15-30.*

GORDON S. HAIGHT (essay date 1930)

[Haight wrote what is considered the most complete account of Sigourney's life, Mrs. Sigourney: The Sweet Singer of Hartford. *In an excerpt from that work, he describes Sigourney's "gemmy," or overblown, diction, focusing on her poem "Pocahontas."]*

While it is not impossible to choose from Mrs. Hemans' poems a stanza here and there that can be matched foot by foot with one by Mrs. Sigourney, let us say . . . that "the American Hemans" *drew her inspiration* from her English prototype. The similarities Poe criticized [see excerpt dated 1836] are found throughout the "gemmiferous" school of poetry; and as Mrs. Sigourney is acknowledged the "gemmiest" of them all, the characteristics deserve to be considered at some length.

The "gemmy" poet lives in a world no ordinary mortal has ever seen, where the commonest objects bear the most elaborate names. Buildings, for example, if very small, are "mansions"; larger ones are "piles" or "domes" of various styles. "Dark domes" are prisons; "bright domes" are universities; and "holy domes" are churches. All about these buildings beneath "umbrageous" trees, grow hundreds of varieties of rather metallic flowers, gathered from the Alps and the Andes, the graves of poets and of missionaries—each with a botanical name and an adjective rarely separable from it. There one finds the "happy harebell," the "cheerful marigold," the "protean sweet-william," and the "aspiring larkspur." Many of these jewels, like the "oary-footed duck" that pursues "the people of the pool" (strange creatures resembling our bull frogs) and "the armed heel" of the small boys who "dare the frozen pool" are drawn from well-known eighteenth-century caskets.

There is a "gemmy" ocean, too, called the "storm-toss'd deep" or the "treacherous main." Here upon "sapphire waves" with "crests of snow" float two sizes of ships—the smaller ones "fragile arks," the larger, "sturdy barks." There are just three nautical parts to a bark: "bowed masts," "swelling sails," and "slippery shrouds," though a somewhat more complicated anatomy is indicated when she holds her breath in deep astonishment, or finds

her furrowing feet
Sealed to the curdling brine.

Both types of boat are navigated by a curious race of "seamen," who much prefer Bibles to rum ("Messmates! Let us do without it!") when'er they go

> To dare the whelming wave.

All day long they sit in the forecastle, telling gloomy tales of physical and moral shipwreck, and wondering how they will ever find the graves of their little children, usually girls between five and six, who are slowly dying ashore.

It is perhaps this sedentary life that makes "gemmy" sailors such a sickly lot; at least once a day the ship's bell tolls, and they file out to witness a burial at sea. The victim is, strangely enough, always one of the youngest of them, who

> oft had boldly dared the slippery shrouds
> At midnight watch.

No one knows what killed him; no one asks. While they stand gazing at the pale, hollow cheek, one remembers the blessing of his "hoary sire" and how the tears "coursed o'er his mother's cheek" when he went to sea; another seems to see the fair-haired girl who "through the woodbine of her lattice" watched "his last, far step." Still another hides in his "faithful breast"

> a bright chestnut lock, which the dead youth
> Had severed with a cold and trembling hand
> In life's extremity, and bade him bear . . .
> To his blest Mary.

At this point the seamen "bow low their sunburnt faces" and sob aloud. Then the chaplain, with whom all of Mrs. Sigourney's "barks" are supplied, reads the burial service, some of which invariably creeps into the poem; there is a plunge, and the youth goes

> Down to the floor of ocean, 'mid the beds
> Of brave and beautiful ones.

There "'neath the billows" is a region as populous as the earth, strewn with young corpses and "pale pearls" the size of crab apples. In a "dome of coral," "laved by the fathomless fountains of the deep,"

> The mermaid hath twisted her fingers cold
> With the mesh of the sea-boy's curls of gold.

The most remarkable thing about this "gemmy" world, however, is the way in which inanimate objects busy themselves with every sort of domestic activity. The "emerald isles" that "sleep" on the "breast" of the ocean are "cradled" in "robes of light." The clouds sweep round the dying sun

> With crimson banner, and golden pall
> Like a host to their chieftain's funeral.

One even reads how "winter set his frosty foot upon Spring's skirts and troubled her"; how the willow wands "hung out their curtains"; how the "rocks robed themselves in laurel, and the wild strawberry blushed as it ran to hide among the matted grass." Rivers, "dressed" in "robes of sliver," roam through the "breasts" of valleys, washing the "rich velvet of the curtaining banks." This was the style Oliver Wendell Holmes was parodying in "Evening, by a Tailor":

> Ah me! how lovely is the golden braid
> That binds the skirts of Night's descending robe! . . .
> Kind Nature, shuffling in her loose undress,
> Lays bare her shady bosom. . . .

Mrs. Sigourney's "gemminess" was not confined to her poetry. Her prose acquired the taint during the thirties, and toward the end of her life private letters and even her diary are permeated with it. To an intimate friend she writes in all seriousness that she is at the shore for her "necessary annual inhalation of saline air," apologizing for her impeccable penmanship by saying that at the hotel "the instruments of chirography are not prone to be of the best quality, or fully available to any legible purpose." Her birthday "added itself like a pearl to the necklace of life"; while such humble materials as sugar and butter become "saccarine and oleaginous matter." The perfect euphemism, however, occurs in her autobiography, where she refers to

> a quadruped member of our establishment which has not been mentioned, and is, I suppose, scarcely mentionable to ears polite. Yet I could never understand why it should be an offence to delicacy to utter the name of an animal which the Evangelists have recorded on their pages as plunging, in a dense herd, "down a steep place into the sea, and perishing in the waters."

But one looks in vain through all her fifty volumes for the three-letter word "pig." With such examples in mind, one reads with amazement contemporary reviews that commend Mrs. Sigourney's works for their "entire freedom from artificiality."

Of the many qualities for which her poems were praised the modern reader will be most likely to admit sweetness of versification. After dwelling at such length on the absurdities of her style, it is only fair to give [an example] of her poetry at its best. The [following] is from **"Pocahontas"**:

> Like fallen leaves those forest-tribes have fled:
> Deep 'neath the turf their rusted weapon lies;
> No more their harvest lifts its golden head,
> Nor from their shaft the stricken red-deer flies:
> But from the far, far west, where holds, so hoarse,
> The lonely Oregon, its rock-strewn course,
> While old Pacific's sullen surge replies,
> Are heard their exiled murmurings deep and low,
> Like one whose smitten soul departeth full of wo.

(pp. 88-92)

[**"Pocahontas"**] never reached epic proportions. In its final form it consists of fifty-four pseudo-Spenserian stanzas that follow Mrs. Hemans' "Forest Sanctuary" rather than *The Faerie Queene* or *Childe Harold,* introducing a rhymed couplet for the fifth and sixth lines and an additional rhyme for the final couplet. That Scott was not altogether neglected, however, one may judge by comparing the first line of the poem,

> Clime of the West! that, slumbering long and deep

with

> Harp of the North! that moldering long has hung,

the beginning of *The Lady of the Lake*. . . . There are indications that Mrs. Sigourney made an effort to restrain her "overgemmy" style; but though the language is sometimes less stilted, the characters portrayed are the stock figures of the religious annuals. The narrative, if it may be so called, begins with the landing of the Jamestown settlers in 1607. By the ninth stanza Mrs. Sigourney slides easily into the old formulas. The daring cavaliers sent out by the London Company are merely the old puppets, the religious pioneers.

> Yet, mid their cares, one hallow'd dome they rear'd,
> To nurse devotion's consecrated flame.

Their labors and adventures in the new country are passed over in silence for a seven-stanza description of the "Sabbath morn."

> Here, in his surplice white, the pastor stood,
> A holy man, of countenance serene

—the very same figure, indeed, who officiated at **"The Sailor's Funeral,"** and at every wedding and christening Mrs. Sigourney ever wrote about.

The dramatic scene where Pocahontas saves Captain Smith is given with more restraint than in ***Traits of the Aborigines,*** but it fails to move us.

> The sentenced captive see—his brow how white!
> Stretch'd on the turf his manly form lies low,
> The war-club poises for its fatal blow,
> The death-mist swims before his darken'd sight:
> Forth springs the child, in tearful pity bold,
> Her head on his declines, her arms his neck enfold.
>
> Know'st thou what thou hast done, thou dark-hair'd child?

inquires the bard; and in true form, answers her own question:

> As little knew the princess who descried
> A floating speck on Egypt's turbid tide,
> A bulrush-ark the matted reeds among,
> And, yielding to an infant's tearful smile,
> Drew forth Jehovah's seer, from the devouring Nile.

The next dramatic occurrence is the baptism of the Indian maid:

> The Triune Name is breathed with hallow'd power,
> The dew baptismal bathes the forest-flower.

Then Romance enters her life. Until her conversion, "nature's fervent child" had been entirely without knowledge of love, which, it seems, civilization alone can bestow. For

> love to her pure breast was but a name
> For kindling knowledge, and for taste refined,
> A guiding lamp, whose bright, mysterious flame
> Led on to loftier heights the aspiring mind.

But this is as near passion as Mrs. Sigourney ever dared come. One of the world's most romantic courtships is ignored; and Pocahontas sits studying sacred history until the next stanza brings one abruptly to her wedding.

Only familiarity with the story tells the reader that she is marrying Rolf, and not John Smith, neither of whom is named. The young bridegroom stands in the church, hailing the red men as brothers,

> While the old white-hair'd king, with eye of pride,
> Gives to his ardent hand the timid, trusting bride,

who has certainly lost all the daring with which she confronted the executioners' uplifted clubs.

The picture of the young wife is another of the "gemmy," ideal conceptions. Like all Mrs. Sigourney's characters, Pocahontas is simply an abstraction of Virtue; and except for variations in the color of their hair, and the fact that one "towers" while the other "shrinks," it is almost impossible to tell the young lady from her father. But they are soon to part. Pocahontas follows her husband to England, or rather "Albion." Here "mid the gorgeous domes of ancient days," or "mid the magic of those regal walls,"

> Stole back the scenery of her solitude:
> An aged father, in his cabin rude,
> Mix'd with her dreams a melancholy moan,
> Notching his simple calendar with pain,
> And straining his red eyes to watch the misty main
> for a daughter who will return to him nevermore.

As might be expected the poem reaches its climax with Pocahontas' death. A rather lengthy farewell address to her grieving husband is still unfinished when

> with a marble coldness on her cheek,
> And one long moan, like breathing harp-string sweet,
> She bare the unspoken lore to her Redeemer's feet.

But the end is not yet. It was a trick of the "graveyard" school of poets to revive the dead whenever it could be contrived. In this instance it is found that Pocahontas' infant son had missed the final leavetaking.

> Lo! in his nurse's arms he careless came,
> A noble creature, with his full dark eye
> And clustering curls, in nature's majesty;
> But, with a sudden shriek, his mother's name
> Burst from his lips, and, gazing on the clay,
> He stretch'd his eager arms where the cold sleeper lay.
>
> "Oh mother! mother!" Did that bitter cry
> Send a shrill echo through the realm of death?
> Look, to the trembling fringes of the eye.
> List, the sharp shudder of returning breath,
> The spirit's sob! They lay him on her breast;
> One long, long kiss on his bright brow she press'd;
> Even from heaven's gate of bliss she lingereth,
> To breathe one blessing o'er his precious head,
> And then her arm unclasps, and she is of the dead.

Griswold, who was not a gentle critic, regarded this as the best of Mrs. Sigourney's long poems, and "much the best of the many poetical compositions of which the famous daughter of Powhatan has been the subject" [see Additional Bibliography]. But it has stood the test of time as badly as all her others. (pp. 124-28)

Gordon S. Haight, in his Mrs. Sigourney: The Sweet Singer of Hartford, *Yale University Press, 1930, 201 p.*

LOUISE BOGAN (essay date 1947)

[Bogan was a distinguished American poet whose work is noted for its subtlety and restraint, evidencing her debt to the English metaphysical poets. She also served for many years as the poetry critic at the New Yorker. *In this excerpt from a 1947 essay examining the achievement of American women poets, Bogan assesses Sigourney's role as one of the first female poets in the United States.]*

The record of the verse written by women in the United States is remarkably full, for a variety of reasons. In the first place, the country became an independent republic, well equipped with printing presses and paper, during the period when American women began to write in earnest. Then, a new and eager periodical and newspaper audience, with the sort of pioneering background which holds women in high esteem, awaited bits of feminine sentiment and moralizing dressed up in meter and rhyme. Finally, the critical standard of the country remained for a long time rather lax and easygoing. A great mass of verse, good, bad, and indifferent, therefore managed to get published. Through this prolific feminine production we can trace, with much accuracy, every slight shift in American literary fashion, as well as the larger changes of an emotional and moral kind. An examination of the rise and development of female poetic talent over a period of more than one hundred and fifty years in a society which, on the whole, encouraged that talent to function freely and in the open, brings to light various truths concerning the worth and scope of women's poetic gifts. (p. 424)

We turn to the full and complete annals of American women poets hoping that we may discover facts that will lead to a new estimate of the poetic gift in women, as well as hints about its present and future direction. The first women versifiers who appear on the American scene were, it must be confessed, unendowed, grim, pious, and lachrymose. Mrs. Sigourney was provincial and naive enough to glory in two titles: the "American Hemans" and the "Sweet Singer of Hartford." She reigned, however, over a long period as the head of American female letters—from shortly after Washington's second term as president until just after the death of Lincoln, to be exact. She was fluent, industrious, and rather pushing; but she managed to put feminine verse-writing on a paying basis, and give it prestige; even Poe did not quite dare to handle her work too roughly. She gave simple men and women along the eastern seaboard and in the backwoods of the West something to be proud of; it is pleasant for a young nation to have a vocal tutelary goddess. (p. 426)

Louise Bogan, "The Heart and the Lyre," in her A Poet's Alphabet: Reflections on the Literary Art and Vocation, *edited by Robert Phelps and Ruth Limmer, McGraw-Hill Book Company, 1970, pp. 424-29.*

ANN DOUGLAS WOOD (essay date 1972)

[*Wood provides a psychosexual interpretation of Sigourney's works.*]

Most critics would agree that there was no important American poetess between Anne Bradstreet and Emily Dickinson, although there were hundreds of women offering their poetic "effusions" to the American public in the nineteenth century. Their productions, valueless and trite as they appear today, were eagerly welcomed, largely by feminine readers, and many of their authors were known throughout the United States. Consequently, their poetry, despite its esthetic insignificance, is sociologically significant as an index to the psychology and culture of nineteenth-century American women.

Mrs. Lydia Huntley Sigourney, widely hailed as "the sweet singer of Hartford," and the most popular poetess in America before the Civil War, offers a revealing case study of the wiles and ways of the feminine sentimentalist-poetic school which she headed. (pp. 163-64)

Domestically unhappy, demanding and difficult, [Mrs. Sigourney] was nonetheless touted as an exemplar of feminine virtue; born in the lower middle class, she fought her way to a position in the upper ranks of Hartford society. Yet a talent for hypocrisy does not fully explain Mrs. Sigourney, for it is too clear that she needed to deceive *herself*. The sense that her poetry, with its almost hysterical striving for bland serenity, conveys is not one of hypocrisy so much as strenuous sublimation. As she aggressively chased men and pushed her way to fame, she poured forth an endless series of tributes to feminine modesty, dependence, and shrinking sensibility. In Mrs. Sigourney's culture, this kind of schizophrenia was evidence of sense, not insanity, for sentimental effusions were the most approved way for a woman to succeed, and open competitive aggressiveness, whether sexual or career-oriented, offered only a sure road to failure.

The clearest, frankest, and most central evidence of the narrow limits placed on feminine self-expression can be found in the published views of nineteenth-century American doctors about female biology and sexuality. Mrs. Sigourney and her sister poets lived in an age when physicians had in large part anticipated Freud's supposed discoveries of penis-envy and castration-complex in women, and, like Freud, had branded these tendencies unhealthy, and even as evil. Their analysis, which may at first seem an unlikely guide to the work of a woman like Mrs. Sigourney, in actuality provides essential background for it, and even offers a paradigm for its curious tensions and patterns. The sexual repression which their theories imposed on women under the guise of biological necessity could of course foster political and social sublimation, but it could also appear as *artistic* sublimation. Mrs. Sigourney demonstrates that it not only could, but did. (p. 167)

The same doctors, in an effort to alleviate their own anxieties, liked to stress that women were all womb. Since the uterus is an organ unique to the female, to emphasize its importance in her system was to underscore her reassuring distance from the male. (pp. 168-69)

There were several attractions in this nearly complete identification of woman with her womb. For one thing, it condemned as unnatural any tendencies on her part to what one might call the clitorial sensibility—branded, in an interesting combination of ideas, as aggressive, sexual, and masculine. For another, it diminished the threat posed by woman as a possible competitor to the lord of the species, by implying that, if she was all womb, she was all disease. The womb, in contemporary medical thought, was seen as pestilential in its powers. Menstruation in itself was regarded as an illness. As Dr. Walter Taylor

Sigourney's husband Charles.

reminds his feminine readers, "every woman should look upon herself as an invalid once a month."

This conflict in feminine sexual identity between the aggressive (clitorial) and the passive (womb-derived) impulses which the mid-nineteenth-century American doctor found, or imposed, and attempted to resolve was precisely the one Mrs. Sigourney faced and which she unconsciously used her poetry to control.

Erik Erikson has argued that children use game-constructs to mirror and examine their own physiological sexuality. In a now famous experiment, he found boys building apparently phallic structures and girls building womb-like ones. His work suggests that, if an individual can use games for such purposes, he or she can probably use the highly complex game of *art* for similar ends. In a curious way, Mrs. Sigourney found in her writings a way to express, explore, and exploit the biological and sexual structures supposed to belong to her sex. As will be apparent, she took, at least for public purposes, the territory of what Erik Erikson has called "the inner space" as her imaginary world, and found her inspiration in a rather morbid spirit of sublimation. Content to sacrifice the clitoris to the womb, she wrote poetry and fiction whose *mise-en-scéne* was an enclosure, whether a convent, a grave, or simply the suffocating atmosphere of the feminine sensibility, and whose heroine was herself, but emptied of conflict, sublimated, and desexualized. In essence, she used her poetry to advertise herself as a docile and willing prisoner of the womb. The resulting poetic tableau provided a way of alleviating her own very real sexual and personal conflicts and reaping the rewards of a token profession of womanly submissiveness. And it was poetry, not life, a *game* she could play to relieve the tensions of her own existence even while it afforded her a suitable cover under which to continue her unacceptable activities of self-aggrandizement. But it also offered its own satisfactions, including an indirect release for the very aggressiveness it was pledged to exorcise.

If Mrs. Sigourney was to keep at bay her "masculine" aggressiveness, she could, in imagination, if not in life, also exclude the real thing—man. If her game-world was to be that of her own womb, she could emphasize that no male could enjoy its resources, and that its resources were essential to life. In her short story, **"The Father,"** she depicts a man, Byronic in character, tempestuous and excitable in disposition, rigid and proud in will, who spends his life alternately educating and worshipping his delicate, chaste, and subdued daughter. When she dies unexpectedly, he suffers an agony of grief, until, taut with hysteria, unable to sleep or to weep, he throws himself on her grave and apparently tries to exhume her. It is not too much to say that Mrs. Sigourney is here unconsciously dramatizing the sterility and deprivation of masculinity: the father in his unyielding and rigid despair is almost symbolic of an erection prolonged to the point of nightmare. His masculinity has become "parched and arid," a kind of sexual *rigor mortis,* and the only solace available to him is the womb, symbolized by the grave which he futilely attempts to enter.

The main efforts of Mrs. Sigourney and her sentimental peers, however, were not wasted on the agonies of the excluded male, who at best was but a guest star in their work, but instead were lavished on the tranquil charms of the figure at the center of the inner space scene which was to greet his famished eyes. The scene itself was capable of many variations, but the pattern was always the same: a small figure, usually feminine, in the center of an enclosed world. This little figure is not only weak, and often diseased, but seemingly submissive, submerged, half-hypnotized and half-automaton. Yet, like an autistic child, she is also totally self-sufficient, and exists in a state of warm satiation with the plenteous products of her own sensibility.

Frequently, this figure appeared as a stand-in for its authoress, a picture, like the illustrations printed in popular anthologies of poetesses, highly idealized and sublimated, yet hopefully advertised by its original as an authentic likeness. Mrs. Sigourney loved to write about her own literary life and poetic efforts, but always in a style that removed them from the real world of labor, deadlines, and monetary reward. Indirectly she was demonstrating that as a writer, she was an inhabitant of her own inner space and owed her inspiration solely to its resources. The backdrop and inspiration that she, with most women writers of the day, liked to claim for herself, no matter how erroneously, was the home, and she described her poetry as the effusion of a woman happily immolated on the domestic altar. Yet the home, as it existed in contemporary sentimental descriptions, if not in fact, bore striking resemblances to her own internal structure. It was depicted as the type *par excellence* of that secret and sealed recess from which the feminine sensibility was to exert its mysterious, nonaggressive, silent power. (pp. 169-72)

The backdrop of the home, however, was occasionally replaced by Mrs. Sigourney and her peers with the setting of an imaginary convent, even more satisfying than the domestic scene in its suggestions of purity and inaccessibility. Mrs. Sigourney and her literary friends, almost all busy housewives, were fond of referring to each other as though they were vestal virgins, cut off from the world. Staunch Protestants almost without exception, they apparently could pay each other no higher compliment than a comparison with a nun. . . . Mrs. Sigourney strove earnestly to create the convent atmosphere. Planning a retreat in which to write her poetry, she explained that she wished to court inspiration in a little room "with a neatly ornamented ceiling in gothic apartments . . . and a little additional gothic window of stained-glass . . . placed high up in ye gable."

Predictably, the poetic impulse, as Mrs. Sigourney liked to describe it, had no outside source: it hailed from God and sounded like another spontaneous vibration from that sensitive organ, which was believed to have such "extensive sympathies" and capacities for "influence." Mrs. Sigourney explained the visitations of her muse in her autobiography:

> Especially in my attempts at poetry was I mysterious and sensitive. It came to me from the beginning, I know not how. Waking from downy sleep, I sometimes received a few lines, and thanked with strange rapture their ethereal giver. . . .

The work she produced under this mysterious spell certainly bore no trace of any outside influences. Like the idealized, calm, timeless realm of the inner space, her imaginary world is eventless, existing in a mesmerized passivity. Mrs. Sigourney's one attempt at a novel, ***Lucy Howard's Journal,*** is fascinating in its inability to work up an incident. Lucy's religious conversion, often a source of crisis in literature as well as in life, is totally painless. In fact, as she tells her minister, she did not know it was happpening, a description which could cover the whole of her life. There is a glimmer of hope when it looks as if her lover is interested in someone else, but our heroine extinguishes it with the calm resignation that refuses to see a crisis when it stares her in the face. Lucy has but one note—one of total blandness and evenness, a tenacity of sublimation almost horrific in its strength which she calls piety:

she would be embarrassed to have more, and Mrs. Sigourney presumably shared her feeling. Monotony offered her mesmeric powers too valuable to relinquish for the pale pleasures of variety.

Mrs. Sigourney composed, according to her own account, in a state of calm hypnosis. Significantly but not surprisingly, [Dr. Frederick Hollick, author of *The Marriage Guide* (1860),] understood the ability to be hypnotized as receptivity to a sort of sublimated sexual excitement, precisely what Mrs. Sigourney's poetry offered herself and her readers. Julia Ward Howe unconsciously revealed this underlying tension when she wrote, in "The Joy of Poesy," that "Like child divine to mortal maid, / My gift is full of awe to me." Poetry was imagined by these women as a kind of immaculate conception, a creativity which excluded the male and charmed into quiescence their own sexuality. The sentimental songstress in her own fantasy life was not simply a nun: she was the Virgin Mary herself, living on the bounty of her spontaneously fertile womb.

The poetess with her sublimated, untouchable, and tranced power appeared in many guises other than her own in the work of Mrs. Sigourney and her peers. One of her most popular manifestations was that of a blind girl. Locked in vibrating darkness, the girl, like the poetess, can foreswear men and the world, and feast on her own sensibility. All her life, Mrs. Sigourney was fascinated with the blind, deaf, and dumb, who became the subjects of her poetry and the recipients of her charity. (pp. 173-75)

Mrs. Sigourney was by no means alone in her absorption with those thus handicapped. These people, cut off from the world, living in night and silence, unwillingly autistic, were almost embodiments of the inner space sensibility for its practitioners. They were like the mesmerized creator, for, as Julia Ward Howe wrote, "The poet at his song is blind." They represented in the eyes of their eulogists the totally anesthetized, sublimated creatures whose freedom from tension a normal and healthy woman could only approximate. The ladies who wrote about them repeatedly emphasized their isolation and the richness of inner experience it yielded. (pp. 175-76)

If Mrs. Sigourney was attracted by the blind girl, she was obsessed with the dying or dead girl (or child), and exploited her constantly as a stand-in, symbol, and rallying point for her own sensibility. Many of her sister poets also acted as amateur obituary-columnists. A brother of Sara C. Lippincott, who under the *nom de plume* of "Grace Greenwood" became one of the most popular writers of her day, quipped: "First the undertaker, then the minister, then Sara." But no one could rival Mrs. Sigourney's powers in this mortuary line. In looking over her poetry, one is staggered at the high proportion of elegies. ***Zinzendorff and Other Poems,*** for example, is almost solidly funerary verse, even including verses on the death of the Venerable Bede. (p. 177)

It is curious how thin is the line Mrs. Sigourney draws between the living and the dead woman. She pictures one deceased fair maiden, lying "In calm endurance, like the smitten lamb/ Wounded in flowery pastures." The dead woman is simply the one who has succeeded completely in anesthetizing herself, in sublimating her desires, in becoming the perfect expression of the suffering and receptive sensibility. There is even a conviction that a woman cannot completely fulfill her purpose *until* she is dead. Mention has already been made of the unseen, secret moral "influence" women were to exert from the home, and one discovers with a sense of shock that it exactly parallels what one writer described in "The Moral Influence of the Dead":

> From them we may confidently hope for sympathy. Of these we think and desire consolation from our thoughts; we trust in their guardian watchfulness. . . . We think of their examples, emulate them and are made better; we linger around the scenes of early association.

This echoes closely the words of a writer like Mrs. Tuthill, an etiquette expert, urging woman to exercise "the silent, resistless influence of home and the affections," and to be "sedulous" in protecting her loved ones from the hardening and searing impact of the outside world.

In her fascinated toying with death, Mrs. Sigourney reveals a willingness to project her fantasies unto real life, to play her games on a bigger scale, and to make her actual self the center of a ritual taking place in a real landscape. Yet the whole scene she created was but a larger-than-life realization of the inner-space tableau with its central sublimated feminine figure she depicted in her poetry. After her marriage in 1816, Mrs. Sigourney gave up her school, but in 1822 she began to hold reunions for her students in the woods during the summer season. From her account in the unpublished "Record of My School," we learn that their "rural festival" was celebrated in what Mrs. Sigourney loved to call "our consecrated grove," under the "sweetly shadowy trees," while her students' "forms" were to be seen "gliding among the trees, and reclining upon the green banks of the river." Significantly, the occupants of the Hartford Institute for the Blind were invited on these occasions, and, according to her account, usually came in a procession, contributing nicely to the funerary tone. The meetings themselves consisted of talks by Mrs. Sigourney, talks which focused almost exclusively on those "flowerets" who had faded during the preceding year.

Even more morbid and interesting, was Mrs. Sigourney's desire to supplant the position of the lucky dead girl of the year, and to function simultaneously as chief mourner, minister, and deceased. At the first reunion, presumably in her usual plump and ruddy good health, she nonetheless urged her listeners to go on meeting annually even if "the voice that now addresses you should be silent, the lip that has uttered prayers for your welfare should be sealed in the dust of death." In 1823, she tells her hearers that since they have last met, she has been sick, has been "(at least in thought) on the confines of the abode of spirits," and has brought back solemn words of wisdom. To have all the virtues of the dead—in other words, a sublimated femininity of the highest order—and yet still retain the life with which to boast of it was Mrs. Sigourney's idea of felicity.

In a curious way, Mrs. Sigourney achieved a version of such happiness, although she was not able to savor it. Her autobiography, ***Letters of Life,*** written in the last years of her life, was not published until after her death in 1865. She got her chance, after all, to speak from the grave, and the book presents the "sweet singer" as though already drenched in memory, sanctified and sublimated with death.-It was Mrs. Sigourney's last attempt to place her own idealized figure within an inner space landscape, and in some ways her most interesting. She pictures herself as having grown up in what she calls elsewhere the "patriarchal society." "Hermetically sealed," in her words, this simple little community is rural and preindustrial, hierarchical, and ordered. The young Lydia, growing up in happy innocence with the flowers her father tends, is nearly manic in her docility. She follows her father's commands with obsessive alacrity, and constantly produces stockings and other unsolicited tokens of her love in a kind of excess, almost sexual in its nature, of joyous servility. Indeed, she admits that ambition never moved me to transcend these limitations or to thirst after other joys." Of course she obeyed her pastor, her teacher, and her dancing-school master with equal fervor. The more imperative and fascist their tone, the more she thrilled: the choir director had the "eye of a commander," her dancing teacher was "as imperative . . . as Frederick the Great and we as much of *automatons* as his soldiers." In this tranced and narrow world in which all action has become ritual, she has totally exorcised her own aggressive will.

Finally, after transposing the rest of her life into the same monotonous and hypnotic key, the autobiography closes with Mrs. Sigourney in an enclosed garden. This garden, with its choice flowers ready to be plucked by pure feminine hands, was standard iconography in the sentimental literature of the day, and serves here as the ultimate symbol of the inner space landscape to which Mrs. Sigourney has committed herself. The book ends exactly where it began—in a garden—and that is, of course, the point. In this timeless and totally self-involved world in which "past, present and future concur like three harmonies," there can be no progress, nothing except ceremonious repetition. Progress smacks of excitement, of masculinity; a feminine ripeness is all Mrs. Sigourney desires. Furthermore, there is no one left in her imaginary world with her—no dangerous male intruders, not even a ghost from her own suppressed and aggressive sexuality. She has *denied entrance,* and she alone revels in herself. With a caressing long panning shot, the "Sweet Singer of Hartford" takes leave of her imaginary and sublimated self, a little figure getting smaller as the book nears its end, tranquilly occupied within her inner space landscape, luxuriating in her docile gratitude to her all-powerful creator, and in the "richness" of her own mellowing age. Her on-stage self-anesthetization is complete, and the sentimental saga of Mrs. Sigourney, so successfully sold to the feminine American public, is over.

Mrs. Sigourney was neither a brilliant woman, nor an unusually intelligent one. She was consciously no strategist, and her interest for the student of American culture stems from her unconscious and uncanny ability to adapt herself to the patterns laid out for the women of her day, and to exploit them. She, like her sister poets, provided middle-class American women with a manyfold example: she used poetry to gain social mobility, she used it as an advertisement for piety and as a home substitute for church ritual; but equally important, she used it as a means for a kind of militant sublimation. Her readers may not have known of the conflicts which helped to engender Mrs. Sigourney's own process of public self-mesmerism, but they knew similar ones of their own and were being pushed towards like forms of repression. Like the sweet singer of Hartford, they could hardly achieve such sublimation in actual life, and undoubtedly found its vicarious triumph in literature doubly satisfying. Mrs. Sigourney was never an outright spokeswoman for her countrywomen's rights, but she was the shining example and tireless champion of their fantasy life. (pp. 177-81)

Ann Douglas Wood, "Mrs. Sigourney and the Sensibility of the Inner Space," in The New England Quarterly, *Vol. XLV, No. 2, June, 1972, pp. 163-81.*

EMILY STIPES WATTS (essay date 1977)

[In this excerpt from her survey of American women poets, Watts offers a positive reappraisal of Sigourney's poetry, focusing on her elegies and her poems for children.]

It is true that Sigourney wrote too much too fast. Her poems need much cutting and reworking. She ran out of topics and tended to repeat herself. Especially when her family's meals depended on her pen (after 1832), her poems were padded, pedantic, and prudish. Her most satisfying poems were written before 1832; the little collection titled ***Poems*** (1834) represents her best poetry and is the volume from which I quote throughout this chapter, except as otherwise noted.

Her own preface to this edition acknowledged a debt to Coleridge; and Poe, in an 1836 review in *Southern Literary Messenger* [see excerpt above], accused her of being overly imitative of Hemans. Other authors from whom she "borrowed" include Cowper, Hannah More, Wordsworth, and Byron. She "imitated," but that is all anyone can really assert. Her "imitation" was that of an independent poet, who may have drawn thematic inspiration from the other poets, who did in fact learn prosodic techniques from the other poets, but whose thematic and image development was clearly her own.

Like nearly all poets in the nineteenth century, Sigourney wrote many poems about death. In the 1834 edition, the dead are mostly children and their mothers. . . . [Elegies] for children had been a common genre in America since Bradstreet's poetry, and dead wives and mothers had been mourned in verse so often in the eighteenth century that Benjamin Franklin's "Silence Do-Good" could even offer a "receipt" for such elegies (no. 7). With the infant and maternal death rate still high, however, it is not surprising that nineteenth-century poets, both men and women, continued to write many elegies.

And yet, if we compare the elegies of Sigourney with similar poems written by American men or by an Englishwoman like Hemans, there is a great deal of difference in concept and theme. Springing from the graveyard poetry of late-eighteenth-century England, the death poems of the American men were generally the reflective meditation established by Bryant's "Thanatopsis." Or, for Poe and others, the dead were lovely young women lost to their male lovers. Later, Whitman would write the death song of "Out of the Cradle Endlessly Rocking." Longfellow did carry "The Cross of Snow" for his wife, but, as a group, the American male poets (major and minor) since 1800 have not been interested poetically in dead children or even their dead mothers, until the twentieth century when John Crowe Ransom was astonished by the "brown study" of John Whiteside's daughter and Robert Frost examined the very different reactions of a mother and father to their child's death in "Home Burial."

Hemans wrote many poems of death, but they seldom concern dead children and mothers. Many poems deal with strange burial rituals, as in "The Sword of the Tomb," or death customs, as in "The Stranger in Louisiana." Many women do die in the section of her works called "Records of Women" (some are mothers), but they are generally famous or brave women who die for some noble cause or reason, such as "Joan of Arc" or "The Switzer's Wife." In other poems, such as "The Siege of Valencia," women do not die, but their cowardly husbands do, after the wife has acted heroically and bravely to "save the kingdom." There are only a few poems which deal in a more specific and personal sense with death, such as "The Invocation: Written After the Death of a Sister-in-Law," "The Child's First Grief," and "The Dying Girl and Flowers."

Sigourney and her followers are, in fact, legitimate heirs of the seventeenth- and eighteenth-century "native" American elegies. It is, of course, clear why the nineteenth-century male poets wished to do something quite different with the elegy, since the genre had become overworked and thus, however sincere a poem of this kind might be or however clever the poet, the genre had been fossilized by the end of the eighteenth century. Sigourney, however, reiterated this form time and again. It is too easy to explain her elegies by saying that she knew her audience, that she "catered to" her reader. If we read her poems closely, we see that she was using this form as a vehicle for several different kinds of poetic investigations.

On the most simple level, Sigourney was attempting to deal honestly and in fairly real terms with the emotions, frustrations, and tragedies of the deaths of real children and their real mothers. Unlike her contemporary Bryant, she was simply not satisfied with the general thought that we all die. Nor would she have accepted Whitman's later solution ("the low and delicious word death") because such a resolution did not really affect the problems of the survivors. Long before Whitman finally approached the problems of survivors, as in "Come Up from the Fields Father," or Dickinson asked us to "Endow the Living—with the Tears," Sigourney had declared in **"Hebrew Dirge":**

I saw an infant, marble cold,
  Borne from the pillowing breast,
And in the shroud's embracing fold
  Laid down to dreamless rest;
And moved with bitterness I sighed,
  Not for the babe that slept,
But for the mother at its side,
  Whose soul in anguish wept.

. . . . .

We live to meet a thousand foes,
  We shrink with bleeding breast,
Why shall we weakly mourn for those
  Who dwell in perfect rest?
Bound for a few sad, fleeting years
  A thorn-clad path to tread,
Oh! for the *living* spare those tears
  Ye lavish on the *dead.*

Of course, in Whitman's poem, the mourning mother simply dies from grief. For Sigourney and Dickinson, however, life, even if unpleasant, must continue.

In another poem, **"Lochleven Castle,"** Sigourney satisfied herself as to just why queens die; and she realized that biblical children were sometimes raised from the dead, as in **"The Widow of Zarephath."** Her elegies for fathers and ministers were celebrations of these good and righteous men, as in **"On the Death of Dr. Adam Clarke"** and **"Thoughts at the Funeral of a Respected Friend."**

The majority of dead children and mothers in Sigourney's poetry may be identical (just as the poems tend to follow a certain pattern), but they are identical because they are American women and children—not queens or heroines or children of nobility. If there is anything really American in the more broad philosophical sense in her poetry, it is this democratic tendency: her realization that the death of those who have "achieved" nothing or who are part of the mass (not even the humble beggar of Wordsworth's poems) is as important as the death of ministers, queens, civic leaders, heroes, or even fathers. Thus, on one level, her realization of the equalizing of death is developed parallel to Bryant's. On another and more important level, however, her concentration upon dead mothers and children is indicative of other interests for which Sigourney was poetically a pioneer.

First, Sigourney's elegies display a profound concern for the family, with each member, even the tiniest baby, as important as another, as in **"'Twas But a Babe."** Although . . . concern with infants and children was already evident in the poetry of Bradstreet and Wheatley, it was Sigourney who repeated again and again the significance of the family—and she was one of the very first poets to insist upon the importance of the family as we know it and upon each of its individual members.

In the poetry of most American women after 1800, men as fathers are almost totally absent, but in Sigourney's elegies the father is nearly always present. His voice is muted, or he feels the "poverty of speech" (**"'Twas But a Babe"**), but he is at least a presence. It is clear, however, that the father was less important to Sigourney than the mothers and children. Naturally, in a society in which woman's chief role was to bear and raise children, Sigourney tried to understand just why there were so many "failures." In early nineteenth-century middle-class American society (of which Sigourney is representative), women took little or no part in business or government; thus woman's role, her identity, was dependent upon her success as a mother. The death, therefore, of mother or child represents a kind of failure. The many dead mothers and children in Sigourney's poems are not simply reflective of historical fact, but are images of woman's limited social role. In fact, already evident in her poetry written before 1832 is Robert J. Lifton's "*total nurturing ethos:* . . . a despairing effort to achieve self-esteem and power through a mother-child relationship."

Time and again, Sigourney insisted that a mother's death would seriously cripple and deprive the children:

I wandered to a new-made grave,
  And there a matron lay,
the love of Him who died to save,
  Had been her spirit's stay,
Yet sobs burst forth of torturing pain;
  Wail ye for her who died?
No, for that timid, infant train
  Who roam without a guide.

(from **"Hebrew Dirge"**)

A father's hand your course may guide
  Amid the thorns of life,
His care protect those shrinking plants
  That dread the storms of strife;
But who, upon your infant hearts
  Shall like that mother write?
Who touch the strings that rule the soul?
  Dear, smitten flock, good night!

(spoken by the newly widowed father in **"A Father to His Motherless Children"**)

The mother as the child's spiritual guide and comforter suggests a "soul-relationship" for mother and child which the father cannot achieve. The "soul-relationship" is, in fact, the only "achievement" noted in Sigourney's poems for the dead mother. Such a situation is evidence of the disintegration of the role of woman in the early nineteenth-century. Even in the late eighteenth century, as [evident] . . . in the poetry of Margaretta Faugères, the "soul-relationship" could still be shared to some extent by the father.

Sigourney's "soul-relationship" of mother and child is extended in other poems which do not deal with death. For example, in a poem which is typical of much nineteenth-century verse in its division of city and country ("Sad I came / From weary commerce with the heartless world, / But when I felt upon my withered cheek / My mother Nature's breath''), it is not so much nature itself that salves the weary heart, but rather:

. . . a cradle at a cottage door,
Where the fair mother with her cheerful wheel
Carrolled so sweet a song, that the young bird,
Which timid near the threshold sought for seeds,
paused on his lifted foot, and raised his head,
As if to listen . . .

(from **"A Cottage Scene"**)

The innocent mother with her innocent babe thus inspires a response from both nature and the weary poet.

Woman's role, in Sigourney's view, is properly that of her own youth, that of a pre-industrial revolution, rural housewife—of a time before the machine replaced woman's own ''domestic'' industry and thus, at the same time, limited her role and excluded her from the economic world. In one of Sigourney's most anthologized poems, **"Connecticut River,"** the woman's role in the new Eden, the land of ''Freedom,'' is idyllically described:

His thrifty mate, solicitous to bear
An equal burden in the yoke of care,
With vigorous arm the flying shuttle heaves,
Or from the press the golden cheese receives;
Her pastime when the daily task is o'er,
With apron clean, to seek her neighbour's door,
Partake the friendly feast, with social glow,
Exchange the news, and make the stocking grow;
Then hale and cheerful to her home repair,
When Sol's slant ray renews her evening care,
Press the full udder for her children's meal,
Rock the tired babe—or wake the tuneful wheel.

The role of woman in this, Sigourney's most patriotic and nationalistic poem written before 1832, is as an ''equal'' bearer of burdens in a rural, preindustrial society. The machine had not yet entered the garden.

Correspondingly, Sigourney's poems which center on dead babes and their mothers emphasize their ''innocent'' natures. In **"Death of an Infant,"** the innocent babe dies, but defeats death and flies to heaven. . . . (pp. 88-9)

The invariably innocent children and mothers go to a heaven which is infinitely better than earth. For Sigourney, there is a vast difference between heaven and earth, God and humanity; and, although God may be present at all times (**"Solitude"**), there is no sense at all of mystical experience, of transcending the body or the earth in any way. Neither Sigourney nor the other woman poets of her time could have become a ''transparent eyeball,'' nor could they have hailed God as a ''Camerado.'' Religion is traditional and ritualistic, as in **"The Sabbath Bell."** On the other hand, the sense of innocence is incompatible with the traditional concept of Eve. It is possible to see Sigourney's innocent mothers and babes as a parallel to the innocent Adam of the New world. And yet these mothers and babes die much too early. Something was wrong in Eden. Thus what appears to us as morbidity and what becomes, in fact, a dull repetition of poetic genre developed into an attempt not only to justify the limited role of women in a quickly industrializing society, but also at the same time to acknowledge the existence of woman's ''failure'' and the resulting problems for the children. Sigourney's resolution of a heavenly destination may seem limited and ''nonintellectual,'' but, except for the high maternal and infant mortality rate, the conflicts which she suggested in her elegies are still present.

Sigourney, who was our first professional woman poet, was also the first woman actually to understand and express her realization that her role as a poet was in conflict with that of a housewife. In **"To a Shred of Linen,"** Sigourney uses an eighteenth-century form as a vehicle for rather revolutionary thoughts. Other women before Sigourney had shown a conscious sense of self as poets and had, further, denigrated the role of housewife. Even in Sigourney's own day, many women pleaded ''loneliness'' or a desire to ''teach friends'' as excuses for their poetry. Sigourney, however, asserted that, in fact, a role conflict does exist and, at the same time, indicated her sensitivity to the changing role of women in the early nineteenth century. (pp. 90-1)

[Not] all of Sigourney's poems feature dead women or children. She takes delight in the child for himself and yet, much like a twentieth-century mother, Sylvia Plath in ''Mary's Song,'' fears for his future:

Thou dost not dream, my little one,
  How great the change must be,
These two years, since the morning sun
  First shed his beams on thee;
Thy little hands did helpless fall,
  As with a stranger's fear,
And a faint, wailing cry, was all
  That met thy mother's ear.

But now, the dictates of thy will
  Thine active feet obey,
And pleased thy busy fingers still
  Among thy playthings stray,
And thy full eyes delighted rove
  The pictured page along

. . . . .

Fair boy! the wanderings of thy way,
  It is not mine to trace,
Through buoyant youth's exulting day,
  Or manhood's bolder race,
What discipline thy heart may need,
  What clouds may veil thy sun,
The Eye of God, alone can read,
  And let his will be done.

(from **"The Second Birth-Day"**)

The anxiety of the mother for the child who must grow up and yet the mother's acceptance of the ''buoyant youth's exulting day'' indicate another facet of Sigourney, which is not morbid or death-centered. Furthermore, it is significant that a living child is considered a perfectly legitimate subject for serious, adult poetry. Only Ann Eliza Bleecker, in the late eighteenth century, preceded Sigourney in this type of verse.

Two poems, apparently written for Sigourney's children, are the happiest and, in some ways, the most successful poetically in the 1834 edition. Although . . . American women were writing poems for children at the end of the eighteenth century, it was not until the beginning of the nineteenth century that both men and women viewed such poems as a respectable genre. Two of the most popular of all American poems for children date from this time—Sarah Josepha Hale's ''Mary Had a Little Lamb'' and Clement Moore's ''The Night before Christmas.'' Nearly every woman poet tried her pen at children's poems, a genre which affected women's ''adult'' poetry in a variety of ways. First, it encouraged the women (more than the men) to examine their own relationships with their children. Thus, in large part, form the ''children's poems'' developed the modern poetry written by such women as Plath and Sexton, who were deeply interested in the mother-child relationship. Second, it is obvious that writers of children's poems (both men and women) did not, at least at this time, employ the nineteenth-century "poetic diction" in this genre. Critics have tended to cite Robert Browning as influential in shifting use of the heightened and affected "poetic diction" to more colloquial diction in American poetry. But children's poems had employed common and simple diction for many years before Browning's poems reached America. Finally, for the women, their poetry for children was more informal, more personal, and more free in diction and meter than their other works. Often, the women made observations in poems for their children that they would not possibly have made in their poems for adults. In fact, some of the most startling and original poetry written in the second half of the nineteenth century was written by women purportedly for their children. (pp. 93-4)

Lydia Sigourney's poems for children established such an independence of spirit and diction. In **"Flora's Party,"** she not only satirizes in a light and ironic manner nineteenth-century society, but also parodies the sentimental "flower morality" so common in women's (and Poe's) poetry at this time (for example, Hale's *Flora's Interpreter; or, The American Book of Flowers and Sentiments*). Sigourney depicts a tea party to which Lady Flora extends "cards" to personified flowers, buds, and blossoms. Both males and females are gently nudged: "prudish Miss Lily" (who in the solemn moralizing of the floral anthologies is usually associated with purity or friendship) leaves the party in a huff because the Soldiers in Green "stared at her *so*"; Madame Damask complains of household chores; Ragged Ladies and Marigolds gossip; and Mr. Snowball, in a discussion of painting with Fleur de Lis, proclaims that "*all Nature's colouring was bad.*" The stilted diction, the "gemmy" words are gone. The conversational tone, the looser poetic line, the common diction dominate. Some of Sigourney's most successful lines appear in this poem as, with anapests swinging, she describes the dance of Lady-slippers, Aspens, and Sweet-briars: "And sweet 'twas to see their light footsteps advance / Like the wing of the breeze through the maze of the dance." However, the dance quickly ends:

> But the Monk's hood scowled dark, and in utterance low,
> Declared "'twas high time for good Christians to go;
> He'd heard from his parson a sermon sublime,
> Where he proved from the Vulgate—*to dance was a crime.*"
> So folding a cowl round his cynical head,
> He took from the side-board a bumper and fled.

The poem ends with Flora confessing that she "'was never so glad in her life'" that the guests had left.

"The Ark and Dove" begins with the poet's daughter asking "*'Tell me a story—please.*'" The mother's story of Noah is interrupted once "to see if her young thought / Wearied with following mine. But her blue eye / Was a glad listener." The story itself is told in diction and phrasing appropriate to a child:

> [I] told her how it rained, and rained, and rained,
> Till all the flowers were covered; and the trees
> Hid their tall heads, and where the houses stood,
> And people dwelt, a fearful deluge rolled.

Sigourney did not always write about mothers and children and home. She herself was active in a variety of charitable and other social concerns and used her poetry to encourage such causes. She considered the plight of the Indians (who she hoped would be converted to Christianity), slaves, temperance, and blind and deaf children. All of these topics, however, are treated in a passive sense; that is, the reader never feels that the poet can do much about the situation, except, as in **"Intellectual Wants of Greece,"** sending Christian books to Greece (itself, as she realized, an ironic situation).

Sigourney's prosody is as confined to eighteenth-century verse forms as was that of most of her contemporaries; in her "adult" poems, she was careless and euphemistic in diction. Her resolution of problems and many of her sentiments are traditional ones, but she opened new areas for poetic exploration and she showed a sensitivity to the roles of women in the quickly industrializing society of her time. I do not agree that she was unintelligent or that she failed to "assume her responsibilities" (as [Roy Harvey] Pearce would have it). She was not a man-hater, as were some of her feminist contemporaries; she supported the family (father, mother, and each child, as individuals) but at the same time realized that something had happened to the role of women, to their identity in nineteenth-century society. As a professional herself and as a housewife/mother, she sensed that something was wrong and expressed her knowledge through the images of dead mothers and children. We find her dull because she never developed and, later in her career, simply repeated her earlier poems. We find her poetically unsatisfying because she was sloppy and too often unaware of her craft. And yet she was a unique voice in American poetry at her time. (pp. 95-7)

Emily Stipes Watts, "1800-1850: Sigourney, Smith, and Osgood," in her The Poetry of American Women from 1632 to 1945, *University of Texas Press, 1977, pp. 83-120.*

JUDITH FETTERLEY (essay date 1985)

[Fetterley comments on Sigourney's place in literary history and offers a feminist interpretation of her short story "The Father."]

Sigourney is treated, when mentioned at all, in American literary histories or even in contemporary criticism, with almost universal contempt, but she was, like Sedgwick, a major event in the history of women and literature in nineteenth-century America. Preceding Henry Wadsworth Longfellow by a decade in the symbolic role of American poet laureate, she made poetry an acceptable and profitable profession for women. Indeed, her very success seems held against her. Certainly held against her is the identification she established between the poet, poetry, and the feminine. An intensely public figure, Sigourney made the career of poet to some degree an extension of the service role conventionally assigned to women. In ***Letters of Life*** she lists over ten pages of *samples* of the requests she received from various individuals for original poems to commemorate some event in their lives. Unable to refuse such requests, she developed an annual correspondence of over two-thousand letters. Sigourney herself was well aware of the price she paid for this vision of the role of the poet: "If there is any kitchen in Parnassus, my Muse has surely officiated there as a woman of all work, and an aproned waiter." Yet both the extent of the need readers expressed for her work and the volume of her response might suggest to us the potential significance of what susan Glaspell in "A Jury of Her Peers" refers to as "kitchen things."

Although Sigourney was not primarily a writer of fiction, **"The Father"** exhibits an imaginative power rarely found in her poetry. Indeed, this story possesses that weird and haunting quality, even the image and the act (the violated tomb, the desperate struggle to recover some lost essential self), that one associates with the work of her major male contemporary, Poe.

Given the context set by Poe's observation that a woman will never admit "a non-identity between herself and her book," Sigourney's decision to use a male narrator might well have been liberating. Released somewhat from the autobiographical presumption and freed to some degree from the conventions governing the expression of a "feminine" sensibility, Sigourney may have thus gained access to the most forceful part of her imagination. Certainly the mechanism of a male narrator enables her to express in relative safety a considerable degree of hostility to male culture, for she can present her judgment as masculine self-criticism.

In **"The Father,"** the masculine principle emerges as sterile, dependent, and ultimately impotent. Despite the apparent supremacy of masculine values, in the final context set by death, the feminine triumphs. Thus **"The Father"** is a kind of *tour de force* in that re-ordering of values which forms so large a part of the agenda of nineteenth-century women writers. The language of the opening paragraph prepares for the subsequent inversion. "I was in the full-tide of a laborious and absorbing profession," "unsparing discipline," "wealth and fame," "pursued," "determined," "distinction," "ambition's promptings," "career"—here is the world of men, its possibilities, its riches carefully catalogued. But immediately a warning note sounds; there is danger in this world, a peculiar kind of danger, the threat of becoming "indurated" (an example of Sigourney's often fatal attraction for Latin words). The overtones of this word, which means "to harden," are suggestively sexual. Indeed, as Ann Douglas points out, the father's behavior "is almost symbolic of an erection prolonged to the point of nightmare" [see excerpt dated 1972]. The only chance for release lies in the realm of "the domestic charities" wherein springs up a "fountain of living water . . . to allay thirst, and to renovate weariness." The superiority of the feminine, apparent by the second paragraph, is further conveyed, and explained, by the word "charities." Sufficient unto itself, the female world opens its doors to thirsting men as an act of kindness, a *noblesse oblige* by means of which the home becomes a sort of universal "female beneficient society" for the relief of "indurated" males.

Interestingly enough, the initial object of the narrator's fixation—his wife—plays no part in the story. Rather it is the daughter who "resembled her mother," who experiences the full weight of masculine dependency. The narrator reveals his self-delusion, confirmed by the story's ending when he discovers that his friends and not himself have acted to protect his daughter, in his pronouncements on the father/daughter relationship. Despite his claiming for this relationship a disinterest that distinguishes it from the father/son bond, the narrator describes a connection in which he is thoroughly "interested." Nameless, like her mother, the daughter exists to serve the narrator's needs. Determined to mold her and make her after his will, he seems to have accomplished his imperialist design when he can say, "It was *for my sake,* that she strove to render herself the most graceful among women,—*for my sake,* that she rejoiced in the effect of her attainments." Service takes on sexual overtones in the incident that follows this testament to his success. Trained to believe that the "husbandman who had labored, should be first partaker of the fruits," this daughter offers her fruits at home: "A form of beauty was on the sofa, by my side, but I regarded it not. Then my hand was softly clasped, breathed upon,—pressed to ruby lips. It was enough. I took my daughter in my arms, and my sorrow vanished." "Protection" is the claim of a daughter on a father, but safety from this father's demands is not to be had, even in the tomb.

The Charles Sigourney home in Hartford.

Sigourney sacrifices the daughter in order to confront the father with the limitations of his Pygmalion mythology and godlike self-concept, for though "a father's love can conquer . . . it cannot create." In his daughter's death, the father faces his own dependency, sterility, and hunger. Significantly, the bereaved father cannot cry. Cut off from the living fountain, he is himself incapable of generating a single drop of water for his own relief. As frozen as the winter landscape through whose "dreary and interminable" nights he haunts his daughter's tomb and whose "blasts . . . through the leafless boughs" mockingly echo his despair, he finally articulates the utter dead end to which his "full-tide" has carried him: *"Give it to me,—Give it to me."* No succor lies in that male world to which he returns with a vengeance after his daughters' death, for he finds it "less than nothing, and vanity," composed of "jarring competitions and perpetual strifes," "duplicity," "subterfuges," "self-conceit," "chicanery," "empty honors," and "perishable dross"—a litany that parallels, exposes, and reverses the initial catalogue of treasures.

The narrator finds relief only when he can cry, that is, when he can himself become a "woman." He becomes "feminized," in turn, only when he perceives the "feminization" of his friends. In their "tenderness," they have acted as mothers not fathers; they have sought to protect, not to violate, the daughter, and to protect her and him from the father in him. Thus the narrator's moment of revelation and awakening involves a transformation of identity. Returned to the state of a child, "as powerless as the weaned infant," he is no longer the shaper but the shaped. In the experience of subjection, he yields his imperialist imagination and pays homage to the power of the feminine whose "tenderness" accomplishes, through its "still, small voice," what "the severity of Heaven had failed to produce."

In **"The Father,"** Sigourney has written a powerful fable on the primacy of the feminine principle and the inadequacy of the masculine principle. The story's power derives from the fact that it is written, not from the relatively static point of view of the self-sustaining and self-contained female world, but rather from the point of view of the famished male outsider who frantically seeks entrance to that "tomb."

Yet, as the word "tomb" suggests, there is irony as well as energy in this choice. In a story that asserts the primacy of the feminine principle and enacts the "feminization" of men, the nameless mother and the nameless daughter never speak. Although Poe, in such stories as "The Fall of the House of Usher" and "Ligeia," could endow his women with will sufficient to burst living from the tomb to astonish, terrify, and destroy the men who have shut them living in it, Sigourney's women are thoroughly and permanently stilled. One is literally, the other symbolically, dead. Thus the assertion of female power occurs in a context that seems to deny its reality. It is difficult to determine to what degree sigourney is conscious of this irony or what she intends by it. On the one hand, one can argue that, in choosing a male narrator, she becomes complicit in a culture that defines the "most exquisite of woman's perfections" as "a knowledge both *when* to be silent, and *where* to speak," for her narrator's voice effectively silences both wife and daughter. In this reading her strategy of reordering cultural values through asserting the primacy of feminine power appears spurious at best, for only men can experience this power; actual women have none of it. On the other hand, one can argue that her decision to create a male narrator engaged in a solipsistic monologue represents a highly subversive appropriation of "that most exquisite of women's perfections," for, understanding indeed both when to be silent and where to speak, she lets the father's speech expose the arrogant egotism behind his masculine assumptions. Reversing the sexual imperialism of traditional American fiction in which male writers inhabit and speak through female characters, Sigourney implants herself in her male character and forces him to speak for her. In this reading, the form of the story itself validates the assertion of female power. Yet, however one reads **"The Father,"** one thing is certain; it provides a significant context for considering the connection between women, language, and power in early nineteenth-century American fiction. (pp. 107-10)

Judith Fetterley, "Lydia Sigourney (1791-1865): 'The Father'," in Provisions: A Reader from 19th-Century American Women, *edited by Judith Fetterley, Indiana University Press, 1985, pp. 105-16.*

SANDRA A. ZAGARELL (essay date 1987)

[*Zagarell maintains that in* Sketch of Connecticut, Forty Years Since, *Sigourney employs the genre of the village sketch in a unique way to criticize the organization and policies of the American government during the post-Revolutionary era.*]

Feminist critics have shown that antebellum American women writers had much to say about the public life of the country, but they have generally assumed that, from Sedgwick to Stowe, women's point of departure was the domestic sphere: women wanted to reform the world by making it more like the home. As literature by women continues to reemerge, however, it is becoming clear that as early as the 1820s not all writing was as directly informed by domesticity as, for example, women's fiction. In some cases, women turned a sharply analytic eye on public matters, and while they wrote from a consciously female viewpoint and drew on values of antebellum women's culture, their writing was quite directly concerned with the foundations and organization of public life. (p. 225)

In ***Sketch of Connecticut,*** Lydia Sigourney focuses on the United States at the time of its transformation into a nation. [***Sketch of Connecticut***] takes place in the early months of 1784, just as ratification of the peace treaty with the British made the country's nationhood official. Evoking in a single stroke the nation's birth and its precariousness—"The British colonies of America were numbered among the nations. The first tumults of joy subsiding, discovered a government not organized, and resting upon insecure foundations"—Sigourney poses this question: how do groups largely excluded from the formal structures of the polity—white women, Indians, and blacks of both sexes—fare within the nation's borders? Her choice of genre is audacious. Whereas other contemporary forms of narrative (novel, historical romance, frontier romance) featured (white) heroines and heroes in love and/or adventure stories and included members of marginal groups in minor roles, if at all, the village sketch's concentration on one community allows Sigourney to focus on a racially and socially diverse population. (pp. 225-26)

As [***Sketch of Connecticut***] shows, the genre could . . . both accommodate racial and ethnic tensions and generalize their significance to the country at large. Sigourney presents local life in considerable detail while casting that life in a national and explicitly political light. She portrays the Connecticut town of N— (modeled on Norwich, where she grew up) as the nation in miniature: N—'s residents include Mohegan Indians, former slaves and free blacks, an impoverished white widow with dependent children, hardy Farmer Larkin (representative of the agricultural class, which would provide the nation's official citizenry), clergymen of various stripe, children, the dying widow of a British soldier, officers and soldiers from the Revolutionary army, and the local aristocracy. As we shall see, [***Sketch of Connecticut***] suggests that the nation, as a formal, political entity, ignored the existence of many of these groups. It further suggests that all could be accommodated within a communitarian mode of life based on New Testament principles of charity and empathy, which, in Sigourney's day, were becoming identified as the particular virtues of women, and which she exemplifies in a matriarchal figure named Madam L—.

In contrast to the nation, N— (which, as [***Sketch of Connecticut***'s] title suggests, stands for all of Connecticut) has no public male figures, nor is it plagued, like the nation at large, by an absence of unifying institutions. For Madam L— presides over N—, and her policies blend values of antebellum women's culture within a hierarchically organized community to make the town a potential model for the former "British colonies of America." Herself the beneficiary of the patronage of an elite Connecticut family, Sigourney saw the wealth of Connecticut's "aristocracy" (a word she frequently uses) as a community resource acquired "through an [industriousness] which impoverished none" by those "intent . . . upon becoming illustrious in virtue." In a country still without a central government, aristocratic and compassionate Madam L— alone can develop a comprehensive public policy. She extends a "sympathy with those who mourned," propounds Christian ethics at length, disburses charity, and includes all N—'s residents in her realm. Taking up the issue of the poor, who are depicted as being dependent on private alms, she creates a plan for institutionalizing charity that will provide domicile, work, medical care, and education. One chapter describes her concept of education; two others show her managing with skill her relations with her tenant, Farmer Larkin, taking an interest in the well-being of his family and counseling him in religious tolerance. She sets an example for the nation's policy towards new immigrants by paying the road toll of a recalcitrant Irishman, and while her presence is weaker in chapters that feature blacks and Indians, the narrative voice and tone carry forward her ethic of justice and inclusiveness.

To suggest that, the model nation being communal, the ideal public leader is a woman, Sigourney amalgamates heterogeneous, culturally resonant images of leadership. She maneuvers carefully within conventional conceptions of womanhood to create a figure who, while retaining her feminine qualities, acquires public authority. Madam L— is dissociated from motherhood and domestic life, for in the second decade of the nineteenth century, thinkers like Sigourney's friend Catharine Beecher had not yet infused women's conventional roles with political resonance by giving motherhood the moral task of reforming the public sphere. The ideology of separate spheres articulated in Sarah Hale's *Lady's Magazine* in 1830 that "home *is* [women's] world" still officially restricted women's activities to a narrowly defined domestic life. Thus Sigourney prunes the kin networks within which, in her autobiography, ***Letters of Life,*** she surrounds Madam L—'s prototype and her own benefactress, Mrs. Lathrop; like Mrs. Lathrop's, the widowed, seventy-year old Madam L—'s children have predeceased her, but unlike the historical figure, Madam L— has no visible social peers and only one relative, a younger brother-in-law, Dr. L—, whose major function is to attest to her wisdom. A woman of wealth and social status, Madam L— is shown almost exclusively in the context of her public concerns, and, in contrast to Grandmother Badger, the matriarch of Stowe's *Oldtown Folks,* she is seen only in her parlor, never in the kitchen. The regal connotations of "Madam" are extended by several references to her as "the Lady," and even when she is likened to "our first mother," she is shown walking in a garden whose mixture of elegant and "personified" flowers makes it an emblem of the heterogeneous realm over which she governs. Here, unhindered by the presence of any Adam, she engages in aristocratically managerial activities: she "amuse[d] herself by removing whatever marred [the garden's] beauty, and cherish[ed] all that heightened its excellence."

If Sigourney takes pains to dissociate Madam L— from the domestic, she does anticipate Beecher, Stowe, and others in granting this character status in the one area in which women's participation in the public life was acceptable, religion. Though nominally respectful towards the clergy, [***Sketch of Connecticut***] suggests that Madam L— is a far more Christian religious leader than most clergymen. It stresses the narrow sectarianism of two religious leaders, the Congregationalist minister Dr. S*** and the Jesuit Father Paul, and attributes to both a thoughtless and sometimes destructive enthusiasm for military matters that links institutional religion with an America founded on exclusionary principles. Madam L—'s religion, on the other hand, is spiritual and all-embracing—she "looked upon the varying sects of Christians, as travellers pursuing different roads to the same eternal city"—and, in a strategy that anticipates Stowe's feminization of Christ in *Uncle Tom's Cabin,* she is explicitly identified with the savior. A description of her spiritual peace (the serenity of "one whose 'kingdom is not of this world'") draws on scriptural description of the peace of Christ. And when, alluding to her death, the narrator promises to render thanks to Madam L— "where the righteous hear the words, 'Inasmuch as ye have done good unto one of the least of these, ye have done it unto me,'" the ambiguous "me" blends the messiah with the widow.

Finally, Sigourney underscores Madam L—'s importance as an icon for public governance by associating her with the most highly respected male public figure of the day, George Washington. The connection is made in a sequence in which Madam L— is visited by a veteran soldier of the revolutionary war and two officers. The officers devote their visit to recounting a story about a brother officer, which illustrates what public leadership means for them—patriotism, honor, male camaraderie. Though they greet the disabled, impoverished veteran in a warmly military manner, all they can share with him are war memories. Only madam L—, who "felt a deep interest in those soldiers who had borne the burdens of our revolution," conceives and enacts a policy for integrating veterans into the community. "[E]xtend[ing] her unwearied friendship," she disburses medicine and food "with that judgment which accompanies a discriminating mind." These acts ally her with Washington, whose "fatherly compassion" and the principled "firmness" with which he treated his troops the officers commemorate. Because [***Sketch of Connecticut***] evokes Washington in the past tense, repressing allusions to the Constitutional Congress and federal government that he would soon head, it casts the widow as the general's political successor. [***Sketch of Connecticut***] represents the public space this heroic figure occupied as a void that only a Madam L— can fill.

Juxtaposing the nation as it really was in 1784 with this idealized, and monitory, communitarian model, [***Sketch of Connecticut***] dramatizes the economic and cultural consequences that living in the American colonies had for those among N—'s population not factored into he concept of the "national character." Sigourney exploits the openness of the sketch form to call into question the assumption that an America subsumed within so monolithic a term does, or should, exist. As she and other women developed it, the sketch frequently embraces a proto-ethnographic conception of character. Characters in [***Sketch of Connecticut***] cannot be described in terms we usually draw on for discussing fiction—"round" or "flat," psychologically or morally conceived, "protagonist" or "minor." In fact the term "characterization" scarcely seems accurate at all: [***Sketch of Connecticut***] brings to life residents of N— who in drama-based, conventionally plotted narratives would have been relegated to cameo appearances or tertiary roles, and it presents them as members of the community. It does so by destabilizing prevalent conceptions of Indians, blacks, and poor white women, juxtaposing the stereotypes through which members of these groups were conventionally perceived with portrayals that try to capture their actual experiences. Sigourney cannot, of course, transcend her cultural moment, and [***Sketch of Connecticut***] often reproduces racist and culturally biased stereotypes uncritically. But because it develops other ways to give life to the experiences of the marginalized, it also casts stereotypes as cultural constructions that overlay and obscure the actuality of those they purport to represent. Particularly with regard to the representation of the Mohegans of N—, Sigourney practices the kind of sympathetic hermeneutics prominent, in varying ways, in women like Sedgwick, Stowe, and Jewett. She scrutinizes the silences and erasures of highly regarded written sources (the Puritan histories, which were enjoying a revival in the 1820s), reading daily life as an eloquent source of information. She thus becomes at once historiographer of how whites have represented Indians and creator of a revisionary political and cultural history.

Sigourney's approach entails pushing beyond the contemporary flurry of literary interest in America's Indians that, as Richard Slotkin indicates, attended their diminishing status as a threat to American life and tended to reify them. Generally, literature in the 1820s sympathetic to Indians placed them in the past tense, often also celebrating in them qualities white civilization was thought to repress. Eulogizing Indians as a noble race swept away by the onward progress of history was a particularly common attitude, and [***Sketch of Connecticut***] is not exempt from it. Numerous passages, as well as the epigraphs that precede several chapters, invoke the "red man" "roaming" in "his" natural setting in the days before European contact; they also present the Indians as beings closer to nature than culture and naturalize their demise, in the era's favorite image, as the end of a day.

Yet [***Sketch of Connecticut***] also recuperates for the Mohegans an extended and periodicized history, which, it reveals, is inadvertently documented in the Puritan historical narratives themselves. Like a few other writers of the era, among them Irving and Sedgwick, Sigourney reverses the self-justifying intent of Puritan historians in order to reveal the Indians' actual experiences. She produces a chronology that reinstates the causes of demise erased by the natural imagery and traces the sequence of a hundred years of steady cultural and political loss. While her account never explicitly identifies the causes of the Mohegans' decline, the details on which she concentrates link this history irrevocably to the whites' formation of their nation. She connects the Puritans to America in 1784, calling them "our ancestors" and terming their narratives "our national annals," emphasizing both the Mohegans' importance to Connecticut's early settlement and the fact that the Puritans "have been careful to give us [a] reverse" picture of the reliability of the Mohegan chief Uncas. Further, she shades the information the annals contain to connect implicitly the friendship Uncas and his son Oneco display towards the whites with the Indians' loss of cultural integrity and of Power. Uncas's submission to the whites' "greater wisdom" in determining how to deal with the captured Pequod chief Miantonimoh and his modification of Indian practices for executing an enemy emerge as a precarious effort to balance white and Indian culture, while Oneco's loyalty during the War with King Philip results in what she shows to be the loss of approximately half the Mohegans' able-bodied male population. Sigourney also shows that the steady degradation of the tribe is tied to its submission to a deracinating Christianity, which Uncas, as she sympathetically reports, rejected as a rationalization of genocide. She registers the later decline of the tribe in terms of its gradual acceptance of Christianity and submission to white demands for land; after Oneco, the chiefs of the Mohegans bear Old Testament names—Joshua, Benjamin, and Samuel. The annals note the "peaceful" Joshua only for "executing deeds for the conveyance of lands to the English"; Samuel "adopted a military dress, and was fond of the customs and conversation of the whites." Her account concludes with Uncas's last descendant, Isaiah Uncas, who was educated into white ways at a Christian seminary and does not "inherit either the intellect, or enterprise, which distinguished the founder of that dynasty." The saga of cultural annihilation, ceded lands, and population decimation explains this "weakness" as the result of genocide.

[***Sketch of Connecticut***] carries this reinstatement of the repressed to the point of America's official arrival as a nation by turning its sympathetically interpretive eye to details of Indian life in N— in 1784. It reads assimilation—which a few writers, including Joel Barlow, the late eighteenth-century producer of nationalistic epic poems, had briefly entertained as the only possible protection against Indians' degeneration—as white domination and interprets the Indians' experience of Christianity as metonymic of cultural and political decline. Using a device common in village sketch literature but generally accorded only bona fide citizens, [***Sketch of Connecticut***] devotes an entire chapter to thumbnail portraits of five Indian men, distinguishing them primarily in terms of the degree to which they have accepted Christianity. The most detailed is that of John Cooper. His Anglo-Saxon first and family names symbolize an assimilationist embrace of Christianity, while his cultivation of crops, signifying his acceptance of white ways, makes him prosperous. The portrait concludes by testifying to his alienation from his tribe and the impossibility of achieving an identity that keeps the two cultures in balance. The Indians say of him, we are told, that "they 'never yet saw an Indian so eager after both worlds'."

Another proto-ethnographic technique common in village sketch literature, the reproduction of community members' interpretations of their own experience, underscores even more powerfully the alliance between white hegemony and Christianity. [***Sketch of Connecticut***] includes an extended conversation between the Mohegans' chief, Roger Ashbow, and an Indian missionary, the Reverend Samuel Occom, on the eve of the emigration of half the Mohegan tribe further west. Reflecting a Madam L—like empathy, the narrative presents the conversation—which occurs in Madam L—'s parlor—without commentary, so the Indian leaders' words stand on their own. These words reveal the Mohegan experience of Christianity to be as irredeemably problematic in 1784 as in the seventeenth century. Ashbow, who "suffered his reasoning powers to be perplexed with the faults, the crimes of Christians" despite his admiration for Christ's sacrifice for all of humanity, insists on the hypocrisy of Christian ideology. His argument takes the form of a passionate deconstruction of the self-serving character of the ideology that recalls, in its thrust, Sigourney's own earlier deconstruction of the Puritan annals: "Why are those . . . who expect an inheritance in the skies, so ready to quarrel about the earth, their mother? Why are Christians so eager to wrest from others lands, when they profess that it is *gain*, for them to leave all, and die?" (author's italics). Occom's response exemplifies the Christian minister's counseling of acceptance. He maintains that "all men, all nations of men, have sinned. In this world retribution is not perfect. It becomes not us to contend with Him, who dealeth more lightly with us than our iniquities deserve." Coming after a historical reconstruction that locates the answers to ashbow's questions in white self-justification and expansionism, such pieties expose institutional Christianity as more the handmaiden of political and cultural interests than the expression of a spiritual creed.

Far-reaching as it is, [***Sketch of Connecticut***] finally gives way under the strain of historical actuality and the limits of genre. It cannot show a transformed nation, for the historic nation did not transform itself. The characteristic ending of the village sketch (life remains unchanged, and the narrator either remains in the village and bids farewell to the reader or leaves and bids farewell to the village) would vitiate N—'s status as the microcosm of a troubled nation. Registering the irresoluble character of its own dilemmas, [***Sketch of Connecticut***] disintegrates into a hodge-podge of popular genres—captivity narrative, adventure story, the sentimental tale of the death of a young woman—as it suddenly becomes highly plotted, narrating the story of the final months of the life of Oriana, the young widow of a British soldier, with her adopted Mohegan parents, Zachary/Arrowhamet and Martha.

Yet shards of Sigourney's vision of a reconstructed nation surface. The white/Indian family stands as an alternative to assimilation *qua* annihilation, which [***Sketch of Connecticut***] had so eloquently exposed, for it entails a type of miscegenation different from, but, for an antebellum America whose ideology celebrated the family, as powerful in its way as interracial marriage. Cultural differences are honored—Zachary/Arrowhamet's double name betokes his retention of white and Indian identity, and he prays both to his native God and to the Christian one—and Sigourney's communitarianism deepens to include intense personal bonds. The three repeatedly name each other "mother," "father," and "daughter"; Oriana says she has found "joy" with her new parents; and the physical contact between the races avoided by many white writers is highlighted in the affectionate ministrations these parents perform for Oriana and the hands she extends to them as she dies. Christianity as political ideology is purged, and only a genuinely spiritual Christianity remains: Oriana, like Madam L—, embraces an inclusive religion that extends to the Indians while honoring their distinctive histories, and in a letter she leaves her minister, she urges him, too, to acknowledge their spiritual equality.

Thus, though [***Sketch of Connecticut***] replaces the nation-as-community with a purely domestic vision and preaches a change of heart rather than continuing to focus on public policy, it continues its principled exception to the temper of those actually in charge of the nation. For in 1825, President Monroe would ask Congress to plan all Indians' (non-forced) removal beyond the Mississippi because, in historian Richard Drinnon's paraphrase, "'experience has shown' the impossibility of whites and Indians becoming one people in their present state." Dismissals of Sigourney like that in the *Literary History of the United States*—though she "knew something of the humanitarian movements of the day, all . . . she did for Negroes, Indians, the poor, and the insane was to embalm them in the amber of her tears"—thus constitute a radical, if inadvertent, censorship of what the nation has meant to its writers. Perpetuating ignorance about certain modes of representing the nation, such pronouncements contribute to the sort of monolithic definitions of the national culture to which Sigourney herself so strongly took exception. (pp. 227-33)

[Sigourney mapped] out the broader contours of the literary, cultural, and political terrain that constitutes our true heritage. . . . [She stands] as testimony that, near the beginning of this country's conscious commitment to developing a national literature, women were already struggling to expand what America meant. (p. 242)

Sandra A. Zagarell, "Expanding 'America': Lydia Sigourney's 'Sketch of Connecticut', Catharine Sedgwick's 'Hope Leslie'," in Tulsa Studies in Women's Literature, *Vol. 6, No. 2, Fall, 1987, pp. 225-45.*

ADDITIONAL BIBLIOGRAPHY

Bode, Carl. "The Sentimental Muse." In his *The Anatomy of American Popular Culture: 1840-1861*, pp. 188-200. Berkeley and Los Angeles: University of California Press, 1959.

Examines the reasons for Sigourney's immense popularity in her day and offers a negative assessment of the lasting value of her work.

———, ed. "Document 34: Glorious Columbia." In *American Life in the 1840s*, pp. 279-82. Documents in American Civilization Series, edited by Hennig Cohen and John William Ward. Garden City, N.Y.: Doubleday and Co., Anchor Books, 1967.

Sigourney's "Our Country" prefaced by a discussion of the patriotic poem in its historical context.

Green, David Bonnell. "William Wordsworth and Lydia Huntley Sigourney." *The New England Quarterly* XXXVII, No. 4 (December 1964): 527-31.

An account of Sigourney's acquaintance and correspondence with Wordsworth.

Griswold, Rufus Wilmot, and Stoddard, R. H. "Lydia H. Sigourney." In their *The Female Poets of America*, pp. 91-101. 1873. Reprint. New York: Garrett Press, 1969.

An introduction to Sigourney's life and works prefixing a selection of her poetry.

Hale, Sarah Josepha. "Sigourney, Lydia Huntley." In her *Woman's Record; or, Sketches of All Distinguished Women from the Creation to A.D. 1854*, pp. 782-84. 1855. Reprint. New York: Source Book Press, 1970.

A sketch of Sigourney's life and literary career followed by extracts from her work.

Hart, John S. "Lydia H. Sigourney." In his *The Female Prose Writers of America with Portraits, Biographical Notices, and Specimens of Their Writings*, pp. 76-92. Philadelphia: E. H. Butler & Co., 1866.

A study of Sigourney's life and works with excerpts from her prose.

Hogue, William M. "The Sweet Singer of Hartford." *Historical Magazine of the Protestant Episcopal Church* XLV, No. 1 (March 1976): 57-77.

Explores Sigourney's evangelical Episcopalianism as evidenced in her poetry.

Huntington, Rev. E. B. "Lydia H. Sigourney." In *Eminent Women of the Age: Being Narratives of the Lives and Deeds of the Most Prominent Women of the Present Generation*, by James Parton, Horace Greeley, T. W. Higginson, and others, pp. 85-101. Hartford, Conn.: S. M. Betts & Co., 1869.

A biographical and critical study that emphasizes Sigourney's moral integrity.

Jordan, Philip D. "The Source of Mrs. Sigourney's 'Indian Girl's Burial'." *American Literature* 4, No. 3 (November 1932): 300-05.

Notes Sigourney's familiarity with journals published in the American West during her era.

Kramer, Aaron. *The Prophetic Tradition in American Poetry: 1835-1900*. Rutherford, N.J.: Fairleigh Dickinson University Press, 1968, 416 p.

Contains references to Sigourney's positions on secession, the slavery question, and the plight of American Indians.

Henry David Thoreau

1817-1862

(Born David Henry Thoreau) American essayist, poet, and translator.

The following entry presents criticism of Thoreau's essay "Civil Disobedience." For a discussion of Thoreau's complete career, see *NCLC,* Vol. 7.

Described by Michael Meyer as "the most famous essay in American literature," "Civil Disobedience" is the work in which Thoreau elucidated the political implications of his Transcendental philosophy, and in so doing established a defense of nonviolent dissent that came to influence the course of twentieth-century history. In this essay, Thoreau suggested that when an individual's conscience is in conflict with the laws of the state, the citizen is not only justified in disobeying such laws but morally obligated to do so. While Thoreau's immediate concern was to express his abhorrence of the proslavery policies of the American government and to encourage others to follow his example, he nevertheless generalized his advocacy of dissent to apply to all morally unacceptable state practices. The rhetorical force and eloquence of his arguments created a highly persuasive document, and "Civil Disobedience" has provided both inspiration and philosophical justification for a number of modern political and social movements.

Although biographers agree that the opinions expressed in "Civil Disobedience" were the result of lifelong reflection on Thoreau's part, the immediate inspiration for the essay was furnished by his brief incarceration in July of 1846. An ardent and outspoken opponent of slavery, Thoreau had not paid his poll tax for several years because, as he later explained in *Walden,* he "did not . . . recognize the authority of the state which buys and sells men, women, and children, like cattle at the door of its senate-house." The sheriff of Concord, Massachusetts, complying with the enforcement provisions within the tax statutes, arrested him on 23 or 24 July and confined him to the Concord jail. Within a few hours, the tax was paid by an unknown benefactor, and Thoreau was released the following morning. This experience led Thoreau to consider at length the proper relation between citizen and state, and in "Civil Disobedience" he delivered his conclusions. Little is known about the composition of the essay; Thoreau's journals of the period have been lost, and the brief account of the incarceration episode in *Walden* makes no mention of the resulting work. It was first presented to the public as a lecture entitled "The Relation of the Individual to the State," which Thoreau delivered at the Concord Lyceum on 26 January 1848; eighteen months later, it was published as "Resistance to Civil Government" in the short-lived journal *Aesthetic Papers.* The title by which the essay is commonly known today, "Civil Disobedience," was created by the editors of Thoreau's posthumously published volume *A Yankee in Canada, with Anti-Slavery and Reform Papers* and was retained in the 1894-95 edition of his collected works.

The primary argument of "Civil Disobedience" is based on the Transcendental, and ultimately Romantic, concept of natural law. Strongly influenced by the European Romantics of the early nineteenth century, Thoreau and other American Transcendentalists believed in the existence of moral absolutes or "laws" that, along with the physical laws discovered by chemists, mathematicians, and astronomers in the eighteenth century, governed the natural world. Assuming the existence of such absolutes, Thoreau begins "Civil Disobedience" with the assertion that the laws created by human societies to preserve order seldom embody principles of absolute justice. Drawing upon another Romantic idea, Thoreau suggests that each individual, by an intuitive process known as conscience, must determine what is morally right and must act accordingly regardless of civil statutes. He then laments the fact that so few people are aware of this obligation, using the powerful example of warfare: "A common and natural result of an undue respect for law is that you may see a file of soldiers, colonel, captain, privates, powder-monkeys and all, marching in admirable order over hill and dale to the wars, against their wills, aye, against their common sense and consciences. . . . They have no doubt that it is a damnable business in which they are concerned; they are peaceably inclined. Now, what are they? Men at all? or small moveable forts and magazines, at the service of some unscrupulous man in power?" After explaining his objections to the institution of slavery and his reason for choosing the poll tax as the most appropriate focus of his protest, Thoreau posits what has come to be seen as the central point of the essay: the suggestion that, by practicing similar forms of dissent, the citizen can and indeed must influence an inherently imperfect government to reflect the superior morality of natural law. In his concluding paragraph, he views such dissent not in terms of revolution, but as a necessary step in the evolution of human government from absolutism to democracy to "a still more perfect and glorious state" in which the government would "recognize the individual as a higher and independent power, from which all its own power and authority are derived."

In contrast to Thoreau's *Walden,* "Civil Disobedience" attracted very little attention in the decades following its publication. It was virtually ignored by critics and seldom mentioned in the many early biographies of Thoreau. However, in 1907 the essay came to the attention of Mohandas K. Gandhi, who was at that time engaged in the struggle to secure Indian rights in South Africa. Finding in the American institution of slavery a moral analogue to South African racial policies, Gandhi immediately adopted Thoreau's posture of passive resistance, and on 26 October 1907 he printed the text of "Civil Disobedience" in his newspaper, *Indian Opinion,* in order to disseminate Thoreau's message. Later, after he had embarked upon his campaign to free India from British rule, Gandhi told the chairman of the American Civil Liberties Union that "Civil Disobedience" "contained the essence of his political philosophy, not only as India's struggle related to the British, but as to his own view of the relation of citizens to the government." Gandhi's use of concepts taken from "Civil Disobedience" reawakened interest in Thoreau's political writings, and as the twentieth century progressed, Thoreau became an intellectual hero for many who felt politically disenfranchised.

While few commentators have questioned the eloquence and persuasive power of Thoreau's arguments in "Civil Disobedience," many have taken issue with his conclusions. Conservative critics, alarmed at the suggestion that laws should be broken according to individual inclination, have denounced Thoreau as an anarchist. Thoreau's defenders respond that Thoreau had no objection to the rule of law in general, noting that he praised the United States government as a "very admirable and rare thing" when confined to its proper role as regulator of the everyday affairs of the citizenry. Such critics point out that Thoreau demanded "not at once no government, but *at once* better government," by which he meant morally correct government. A number of critics have described Thoreau's concept of better government as paradoxical, since, as the collective will of individuals, a democratic state does theoretically embody the collective conscience of its citizens. Robert S. LaForte, who views the paradox as a serious shortcoming in Thoreau's political thought, asserts that the apparent inconsistency derives from Thoreau's tendency "to consider the state as an omnipotent individual bearing down on humanity." C. Carroll Hollis contends, however, that while Thoreau was not a distinguished logical thinker, the paradoxical statements of "Civil Disobedience" are not the result of intellectual failures, but of Thoreau's complex, mystical, and essentially correct vision of reality.

Despite continued criticism of its political and philosophical conclusions, "Civil Disobedience" remains one of the most influential works of American literature. In addition to its impact upon Gandhi and modern Indian history, Thoreau's essay has provided impetus for many of the most dramatic movements for social change in the twentieth century, including the organization of industrial labor in the thirties, the American civil rights movement of the fifties and sixties, and student protests within the United States and elsewhere, particularly those against American involvement in the Vietnam War. Writing in 1962, Martin Luther King, Jr. commented that, after reading Thoreau, he "became convinced that non-cooperation with evil is as much a moral obligation as is cooperation with good." "No other person," King continued, "has been more eloquent and passionate in getting this idea across than Henry David Thoreau. As a result of his writings and personal witness we are the heirs of a legacy of creative protest." A number of commentators have further noted that, while Thoreau's admonitions were clearly important in a time of state-supported slavery, their significance has steadily increased and will continue to do so as the influence of the state in the lives of its citizens grows stronger and more pervasive.

(See also *Dictionary of Literary Biography,* Vol. 1: *The American Renaissance in New England,* and *Concise Dictionary of Literary Biography: Colonization to the American Renaissance, 1640-1865.*)

ELISEO VIVAS (essay date 1928)

[*Vivas is a Colombian-born educator and literary critic who, in the 1930s, contributed to the theories of New Criticism, an influential movement in American criticism that also included Allen Tate, Cleanth Brooks, R. P. Blackmur, and Robert Penn Warren, and that paralleled a critical movement in England led by I. A. Richards, T. S. Eliot, and William Empson. Although the various New Critics did not subscribe to a homogeneous set of principles, all believed that a work of literature must be examined as an object in itself through a process of close analysis of symbol, image, and metaphor. Vivas has been a prolific critic, and some of his most important essays are included in the collection* Vivas as Critic: Essays in Poetics and Criticism *(1981). In the following excerpt, Vivas applauds Thoreau's anarchic politics.*]

Thoreau's anarchism is particularly interesting to the genetic student of ideas because it is not at all the result of what Santayana has called the psychology of the disinherited. It gives the lie to Neitzsche's analysis of the psychology of political radicalism. The "disinherited" denies the worth of existing institutions not so much for the evil they do him, but for the good they fail to do him; for the material benefits they fail to present him with, the sinecures they fail to offer him, which he comes subsequently to consider as evil in a sour-grapes spirit. But Thoreau was too self-sufficient to envy success and too chaste to set his price in material terms. He was an anarchist because he saw the essential uselessness of government. "The people," he tells us, "must have some complicated machinery or other, and hear its din, to satisfy the need of government they have." But government, at its best, is for him a useless contraption to which men cling because they are afraid to do without its protection. He never felt any need of it, however, because he did not possess anything he was not willing to share with any man. At its best; but where does government appear at its best? Thoreau wrote **"Civil Disobedience"** shortly after the Mexican war and the Fugitive Slave Law, when America was taking its first steps towards imperialism. What would he have to say today, after Wilson's macabre hypocrisy of the war to end war, and the development of Pan-American politics, and the ruthless suppression of liberty which has followed? What Thoreau had to say of his country is much more relevant of our own day than it was of his. "The American government," he says "—what is it but a tradition, though a recent one, endeavoring to transmit itself unimpaired to posterity, but each instant losing some of its integrity?" The notable thing about his political criticism is that it anticipated in all significant details, in all its essentials, the criticism of contemporary radicals and liberals, and in many respects it went far beyond. There are passages in **"Civil Disobedience"** and in his other political and social papers, which are much more relevant than any already quoted. It is a pity, for instance, that lily-livered, respectable liberals of today are so busy improving irremediable conditions that they have no time to read passages such as these: "Under a government which imprisons any unjustly, the true place for a just man is also a prison," or, "Those who, while they disapprove of the character and measures of a government, yield to it their allegiance and support, are undoubtedly its most conscientious supporters, and so frequently the most serious obstacles to reform. . . . Unjust laws exist: shall we be content to obey them, or shall we endeavor to amend them, or shall we transgress them at once?" But I forget that this is too strong a fare for the respectable liberalism of the sweetness-and-light liberal—it is a fare only men can digest. (pp. 6-7)

Eliseo Vivas, "Thoreau: The Paradox of Youth," in The New Student, *Vol. 7, No. 23, March 7, 1928, pp. 5-8, 15.*

HENRY SEIDEL CANBY (essay date 1939)

[Canby was a professor of English at Yale and one of the founders of the Saturday Review of Literature, *where he served as editor in chief from 1924 to 1936. He was the author of many books, including* The Short Story in English, *a history of that genre which was long considered the standard text for college students. Despite the high acclaim his writings received, Canby always considered himself primarily a teacher, whose declared aim was "to pass on sound values to the reading public." In the following discussion of "Civil Disobedience," Canby defends Thoreau against charges of anarchism.]*

[Thoreau's **"Civil Disobedience"**] was written in 1848 as a commentary upon his jailing, of which it contains an account much more extensive than the narrative in ***Walden.*** It was published in May of 1849 in Elizabeth Peabody's symposium of papers from old *Dial* contributors, called *Aesthetic Papers,* which was to be followed by others if the public responded, which they did not. **"Civil Disobedience"** attracted no attention at the time, but has since gone round the world. It was Gandhi's source-book in his Indian campaign for Civil Resistance, and has been read and pondered by thousands who hope to find some way to resist seemingly irresistible force.

The extraordinary effectiveness of Thoreau's essay on resistance to the power of the state is not due to any dramatic necessity in the cause that produced it. Here it has the Anglo-Saxon quality of understatement. No tyrant, no dictator, no Oriental despotism is even thought of by this Concord citizen of the most easy-going of republics. He assumes a democratic system. He assumes majority rule. He assumes a weak government, not a strong one. He does not exaggerate his act of rebellion, laughs at it a little, wonders if he has been too obstinate; then clamps down suddenly on the principle involved, which is good for all weathers. The most liberal government becomes a tyranny when it denies the right of the individual to be responsible for his intellectual and moral integrity. It can overrule him, yes, but he must somehow resist. If he is a crank, an opponent of order, which is essential to the state, if he is a self-centered egotist, he will suffer, and let him suffer. If, however, his integrity is based on values indispensable to a self-respecting man, then resistance is also indispensable, and will become a power unconquerable in the long run, even by force.

The political weakness of this argument is obvious. It leaves one of those wide margins that Thoreau liked in his thinking as well as in his life, and this time a wide margin of possible error. For if the individual is to determine his own rights, what authority is left to distinguish between enlightened resistance to the rulers of a state, and anarchy, which will inevitably dissolve the state itself? Thoreau would have answered that you must have faith in man, you must believe that an intuition of what is necessary for survival is a reality in human nature. And it is the only possible answer.

But this was not the lesson which thousands have learned since from **"Civil Disobedience."** The metaphysics of politics concerns them as little as it concerned Thoreau. The conflict of man against the state is real, no matter what one thinks of its rules. It wanes, it waxes—we have reached or are nearing again one of its periodical crises. There will always be those who are faced with the sacrifice either of their just rights or their security. How can those who are determined to resist oppose, with any hope of success, a régime of irresistible force? Thoreau, writing in an America soon to be in the throes of a great rebellion, was not at that time, nor for any time, thinking of mass rebellion where motives are mixed and the objective is always power.He was concerned with the individual whose power can only be his own integrity. For him he counsels passive resistance, and this is the answer which has made his essay famous:

> A very few . . . serve the state with their consciences . . . and so necessarily resist it for the most part; and they are commonly treated as enemies by it.
>
> It is not so important that many should be as good as you, as that there be some absolute goodness somewhere; for that will leaven the whole lump.
>
> A wise man will not leave the right to the mercy of chance, nor wish it to prevail through the power of the majority.
>
> It is not a man's duty, as a matter of course, to devote himself to the eradication of any, even the most enormous, wrong [so much for professional reformers]; he may still properly have other concerns to engage him; but it is his duty, at least, to wash his hands of it, and, if he gives it no thought longer, not to give it practically his support.
>
> Action from principle . . . changes things and relations; it is essentially revolutionary.
>
> If the injustice is part of the necessary friction of the machine of government, let it go, let it go: perchance it will wear smooth. . . . But if it is of such a nature that it requires you to be the agent of injustice to another, then, I say, break the law.
>
> I was not born to be forced. I will breathe after my own fashion. . . . If a plant cannot live according to its nature, it dies; and so a man.
>
> I am as desirous of being a good neighbor as I am of being a bad subject.
>
> There will never be a really free and enlightened State until the State comes to recognize the individual as a higher and independent power, from which all its own power and authority are derived, and treats him

> accordingly. I please myself with imagining a State at last which can afford to be just to all men . . . which even would not think it inconsistent with its own repose if a few were to live aloof from it, not meddling with it, nor embraced by it, who fulfilled all the duties of neighbors and fellow-men.

And until such a state arises, he is ready to resist, when necessary, brute force. While he cannot expect successfully to oppose the force itself, his resistance may be effective because it may change the minds of the men that exercise it. And therefore it is not futile quietly to declare war upon your state.

History abundantly proves that such disobedience can be effective. There is perhaps no power in the world today able to overcome aerial bombs and machine guns but intellectual and emotional resistance in Thoreau's sense, by brave men, clear of mind, and able to endure until their conviction becomes infectious.

How would the author of **"Civil Disobedience"** act if he were alive today? His revolution was a one-man revolution against a feeble state, concerned for its own prosperity. The dictatorial state, with torture at its command, and a fanaticism as strong and far less reasonable than Thoreau's, presents very different problems. His answer, I should say, to the totalitarian idea would be, that such massed individuals as support these states may for the time being be impregnable, are like avalanches, which no man can hope to resist. The citizen will have to step back and, protecting integrity by any concessions possible to it, endeavor to make the nobler moral fervor prevail. But he would disobey rather than rebel, and wrestle with weakness in himself rather than use violence against the despot in the enemy. Gandhi took such a position. He struck at the pocketbook of the state, not at its armies. He refused to conform, but did not attack his rulers. (pp. 235-38)

Henry Seidel Canby, in his Thoreau, *Houghton Mifflin Company, 1939, 508 p.*

CHARLES CHILD WALCUTT (essay date 1940)

[*Walcutt commends Thoreau's concept of civil disobedience, noting that such resistance should always take nonviolent forms.*]

Thoreau not only wrote, he lived his principles. In ***Walden*** he enunciated the doctrine that "There are nowadays professors of philosophy, but not philosophers. Yet it is admirable to profess because it was once admirable to live. To be a philosopher is not merely to have subtle thoughts, nor even to found a school, but so to love widsom as to live according to its dictates, a life of simplicity, independence, magnanimity, and trust. It is to solve some of the problems of life, not only theoretically, but practically." And this was no idle boast, for, as we have seen, he lived his principles so completely that he was a true lover of widsom. Following this policy, he refused to pay his poll tax to a state that tolerated slavery. "How does it become a man to behave toward this American government to-day? I answer, that he cannot without disgrace be associated with it. I cannot for an instant recognize that political organization as *my* government which is the *slave's* government also." On a trip to the cobbler's in Concord he was seized and thrust into jail, where he stayed until someone else paid the tax for him. To explain his action he wrote **"Civil Disobedience,"** a document which may, with the passage of time, have a profounder influence even than ***Walden.*** There he says that "It is not desirable to cultivate a respect for the law, so much as for the right. . . . Law never made men a whit more just; and, by means of their respect for it, even the well-disposed are daily made the agents of injustice." They are made the agents of injustice because they allow the law to take the place of their own moral judgments. Recognizing evil, they nevertheless acquiesce in it because, forsooth, it is legal. They recognize what is right, but they do not practice it. As Thoreau says, "There are nine hundred and ninety-nine patrons of virtue to one virtuous man." Merely voting against a patent evil, when you are in the minority, is being a patron of virtue; it is a painless way of salving your conscience. If the State is wrong, says Thoreau, why, refuse it your allegiance. But this is anarchy, you reply. Thoreau rejoins that the world is *wrong*—and who can deny it?—that a man who is right constitutes a majority of one. "A minority is powerless while it conforms to the majority; it is not even a minority then; but it is irresistible when it clogs by its whole weight. If the alternative is to keep all just men in prison, or give up war and slavery, the State will not hesitate which to choose. If a thousand men were not to pay their tax-bills this year, that would not be a violent and bloody measure, as it would be to pay them, and enable the State to commit violence and shed innocent blood. This is, in fact, the definition of a peaceable revolution, if any such is possible."

One cannot evade the truth of these sentences. "I know this well, that if one thousand, if one hundred, if ten men whom I could name,—if ten *honest* men only,—ay, if *one* HONEST man, in this State of Massachusetts, *ceasing to hold slaves,* were actually to withdraw from this copartnership, and be locked up in the county jail therefor, it would be the abolition of slavery in America. For it matters not how small the beginning may seem to be: what is once well done is done forever. But we love better to talk about it: that we say is our mission." Do we not still? In a modern totalitarian state the resistance of one individual would not accomplish a revolution; but the devout resistance of one thousand, followed by another devout thousand would soon accomplish it—even in Germany. And in America, where we still respect democracy and where the individual—though the current is flowing in the other direction with dangerous speed—is still considered important, ten respected, HONEST men in any city of thirty thousand could, by refusing to cooperate in supporting unjust laws, bring about their repeal.

Outrageous? It is not. (pp. 178-79)

The only qualification that must be made in this program is that the resistance of our honest men must be *passive,* for violence begets violence—and the violent man is, in the long run, not much better than the man he opposes. It requires courage of a sort to enlist and fight in a war to make the world safe for democracy. It requires a bit more courage to refuse when everyone is doing it—hence the fact that many pacifists join militant pacifist organizations: they need the moral support of numbers; they need, further, the comfort of activity—and so they become violently pacifistic and arouse violent opposition (which is certainly justified by their own violence) and so defeat their ends. They have contributed to the world's violence instead of counteracting it—and nothing has been gained. It requires most courage to resist quietly and passively, to refuse to contribute to current violence. This last sort of pacificism could stop any war in a short while, but it demands, unfortunately, a better sort of people than the world appears to contain. (p. 180)

Charles Child Walcutt, "Thoreau in the Twentieth Century," in South Atlantic Quarterly, *Vol. XXXIX, No. 2, April, 1940, pp. 168-84.*

CHARLES A. MADISON (essay date 1944)

[*Madison analyzes Thoreau's attitude toward the state as a feature of his "natural individualism."*]

In his quest for economic freedom Thoreau developed a profound antagonism to all authoritarianism. He was not alone, of course, in placing the individual above the state. The pioneering spirit was of necessity individualistic: the early settlers had to shift for themselves willy-nilly, and many of those who subsequently established their claims on the frontier did so to avoid the restraints of an organized society. The followers of Jefferson favored their leader's assumption that that government was best which governed least. Closer home were Abolitionists like Garrison and Wendell Phillips, who repudiated the federal and state governments as well as the Constitution for condoning the existence of slavery. Thoreau, however, exceeded even the latter in the extremity of his stand against political power. In **"Civil Disobedience"** and in various of his later writings he propounded his opposition to the state with such forceful eloquence that like-minded men the world over have acclaimed him as their spokesman ever since.

It was inevitable for Thoreau to gravitate toward the principles of philosophical anarchism. He was, according to Emerson, "a born protestant. . . . . He interrogated every custom and wished to settle all his practice on an ideal foundation." This impulsion to follow a course of action that squared with his transcendental precepts could not but accentuate his natural individualism. Emerson's conspicuous practitioner of self-reliance, he found himself again and again rebelling against the claims and conventions of society. Asking little, he wanted to give even less. To him institutions were mostly "the will of the dead" to oppress the living; he would neither respect them nor accept any part of them unless they passed his test of relevancy. Nor did he dread standing alone and apart. He recorded in his ***Journal***:

> To some men their relation to mankind is all important. I feel myself not so vitally related to my fellowmen. I impinge on them but by a point on one side. It is not a Siamese-twin ligature that binds me to them. It is unsafe to defer so much to mankind and the opinions of society, for these are always, and without exception, heathenish and barbarous, seen from the heights of philosophy.

Not that he disdained to descend from these heights in his relations with his neighbors; only he felt no need of their fellowship, and he resented any constraint put on him by either an individual or the state.

So long as he was left alone he was perfectly willing to remain a passive rebel. His civil disobedience was precipitated in 1846 by the demand of a poll tax which he believed was to further the proslavery war with Mexico. He did not object to paying taxes as such, and he was not in arrears with his highway tax; but as a strong opponent of slavery he would do nothing that favored that iniquitous institution. When he came into town one day to have a shoe mended he was put in jail and kept there overnight. The next morning his mortified family paid the tax without his knowledge and he was released.

"Civil Disobedience" grew out of his reflections upon his imprisonment. On leaving the town jail he felt the darts of antagonism—as if he were of a distinct race. Certain he was right, he regarded those who disapproved of his act of defiance as slaves to their prejudices and superstitions; for he believed that he could not as a free man have done otherwise. Basing his stand on the transcendental esteem of the individual, he reasoned that he and not the state was the best judge of right and wrong. Thus he had refused to pay church tithes and to attend religious services because he had a low opinion of the organized church. Again, since he preferred poverty and freedom to comfort and economic subjection, he insisted on living his own life in his own way. He refused to vote because he regarded the ballot as a feeble political instrument: by voting for the available candidates one merely furthered the work of the demagogues. Nor would he submit to the will of the majority in matters of principle, since he saw "but little virtue in the action of the masses of men." And, while he did not advocate fighting wrong, he certainly would not support wrong by his acquiescence. To pay the poll tax was to his mind equivalent to abetting the proslavery government in furthering the egregious evil. This he would not do. The next step was civil disobedience.

> I simply wish to refuse allegiance to the State, to withdraw and stand aloof from it effectually. . . . . In fact, I quietly declare war with the State, after my fashion, though I will still make what use and get what advantage of her I can, as is usual in such cases.

Always the practical Yankee, he saw no reason for not accepting the benefitts of government without submitting to its ignoble demands.

He did not, however, shirk the consequences of his action. If governmental iniquity, he asserted, "is of such a nature that it requires you to be the agent of injustice to another, then, I say, break the law. . . . . Law never made men a whit more just, and, by means of their respect for it, even the well-disposed are daily made the agents of injustice." He therefore submitted to incarceration rather than help strengthen slavery; cherishing his liberty as he did, he knew he would feel freer in jail with a clear conscience than at large at the price of perpetrating a wrong. This insistence on acting from principle was at the root of his ethics and motivated his entire behavior. Nor was he unaware of his radicalism.

> Action from principle, the perception and performance of right, changes things and relations; it is essentially revolutionary, and does not consist wholly with anything which was. It not only divides states and churches, it divides families; ay, it divides the individual, separating the diabolical in him from the divine.

It was his firm belief, moreover, following logically from his transcendental view of society, that if enough men who were opposed to injustice resisted passively, the government would soon be driven to capitulation. Such action on the part of a resolute minority would lead to a "bloodless revolution." "If the alternative is to keep all just men in prison, or to give up war and slavery, the State will not hesitate which to choose."

Along with Godwin, Emerson, and the extreme Abolitionists, Thoreau was not concerned with the fate of society subsequent to the collapse of government. He did not conceive of the state in the abstract; to him it was the power of government used by politicians for ends which were usually deplorable. Since its power was derived from individuals originally, their rights were of necessity superior to those conceded to the state. Man was not born to be forced; his first duty was to his conscience. If the state attempted to ride roughshod over the rights of its citizens, the latter must resist this breach of compact with all the force of uncompromising principle. The sooner the oppressive state was shorn of its power, the better. 'Government," he asserted, "is at best an expedient; but most governments are usually, and all governments are sometimes, inexpedient."

Not that Thoreau was opposed to the state as such. He knew that so long as men were subject to greed and passion they needed policing by public authority. What he objected to was the arrogation of power by the state to the detriment of its citizens. In his view this censure applied as much to the weak, liberal government under which he lived as to the most oppressive tyranny: their respective clashes with the upright individual differed in degree rather than in kind. From this standpoint "that government is best which governs not at all." Since such an ideal condition was not yet possible, he outlined the ideal state as he conceived it:

> There will never be a really free and enlightened State until the State comes to recognize the individual as a higher and independent power, from which all its own power and authority are derived, and treats him accordingly. I please myself with imagining a State at least which can afford to be just to all men, and to treat the individual with respect as a neighbor; which even would not think it inconsistent with its own repose if a few were to live aloof from it, not meddling with it, nor embraced by it, who fulfilled all the duties of neighbors and fellow-men. A State which bore this kind of fruit, and suffered it to drop off as fast as it ripened, would prepare the way for a still more perfect and glorious State, which also I have imagined, but not yet anywhere seen.

"Civil Disobedience" was written primarily to vindicate the ethical principles which led to its author's imprisonment. It is a vigorous essay, full of the sap of strong feeling, bristling with pointed epigrams and lofty rebelliousness. Nevertheless, it was a self-conscious performance: his indignation was simulated; his philosophy of idealistic anarchism was an exercise in moral contemplation. Nor was it a work of originality, the basic ideas having had political currency for nearly a century; it merely contained his considered reaction to a situation forced upon him against his will. That the essay should have become the classic statement of the ever present conflict between the individual and the state is an eloquent tribute to the great rhetorical effectiveness of Thoreau's style.

It should be stressed that the provocation in this instance was personal and relatively unimportant. A night in jail served Thoreau as an opportune springboard; being the man he was, he was bound to give expression to his anti-authoritarian views sooner or later. He therefore minimized the prison incident and dwelt mainly on the philosophical aspects of the problem. Yet as a thorough individualist he shied away from the implications of practical reform. He had a very poor opinion of both society and its institutions and preferred to live the hermit rather than try to lift men to his own lofty level. He had himself in mind when he wrote: "The true poet will ever live aloof from society, wild to it, as the finest singer is the wood thrush, a forest bird." The turmoil and turpitude of the market place was not for him. "What is called politics," he was to write in **"Life without Principle,"** "is comparatively so superficial and inhuman, that, practically, I have never fairly recognized that it concerns me at all." (pp. 113-16)

Charles A. Madison, "Henry David Thoreau: Transcendental Individualist," in Ethics, *Vol. LIV, No. 2, January, 1944, pp. 110-23.*

RAYMOND ADAMS (essay date 1945)

[In the following essay, Adams examines the sources of "Civil Disobedience": Emerson's essay "Politics," writings in the abolitionist paper the Liberator, *and William Paley's* Moral and Political Philosophy.]

Henry Thoreau shared with his mother the ability so to dramatize an act that, however imitative it may have been, it seemed original with him and bore his stamp forever after. He was not an imitater if he could help it; but neither was he entirely original in most respects. Setting himself up as natural historian for the microcosm of Concord was but doing for that town what others did for other New England towns at the same time. Whittier's uncle, described in "Snowbound," was such a one; so in Salem were Jones and Lydia Very. But it is Thoreau who is known all over the world as the American Gilbert White of Selborne. His friend and Harvard classmate Stearns Wheeler, whose early death Emerson so greatly lamented, built himself a house on the shores of Sandy Pond in Lincoln and lived there as a student, only to be forgotten. Yet Thoreau, admittedly imitating young Wheeler, built himself a house two miles to the west of Sandy Pond and made his venture and Walden Pond known to fame. Such things redounded to Thoreau's fame as if he were the first person ever to entertain such ideas. To a great degree his written records of ideas have had the same good fortune. Here the reputation is somewhat more deserved, for both ***A Week on the Concord and Merrimack Rivers*** and ***Walden: or, Life in the Woods*** were original books in the sense that no books before them had been so organized and so executed. But the matter of Thoreau's writing has its sources in spite of the original turn his independent mind gave it.

A case in point is Thoreau's **"Resistance to Civil Government."** Most editors and literary historians make perfectly clear that this essay and the jailing incident for non-payment of poll tax recorded in the essay grew out of contemporary events: the annexation of Texas in 1845, the War with Mexico in 1846, and the controversy over the obligation of Massachusetts to return fugitive slaves which came to a head in the state in 1848, the year Abolitionism forced a showdown in American politics through the Free Soil party. Thoreau wrote his essay in 1848. And in that essay he mentions specifically the Texas Annexation, the Mexican War, the returning of fugitive slaves, and the presidential election of 1848. There is no doubt about the environment of the essay. Nor is there any controversy about the night Thoreau spent in jail during July, 1846. Separating his taxes into that which indicated good neighborliness, his town tax, and that which identified him with the Commonwealth of Massachusetts as a partner in the union, his poll tax, he refused to pay the poll tax because the state was at least tacitly consenting to slavery in the United States. The state, of course, put him in jail until the tax was paid. Thus by merely balking, Thoreau felt that he had gained his point, not by taking action against the state, but by putting himself in a position where the state had to take action against him. This is the "civil disobedience" which Thoreau described and which Gandhi, for one, used so effectively many years afterward. All these circumstances out of which Thoreau's essay came are well known by now, for, with the possible exception of the "Where I Lived and What I Lived For" passage from ***Walden,*** this essay on civil disobedience is the most widely read product of Thoreau's pen. And Thoreau is commonly given credit for originating the principles enounced in the essay and for inventing the idea of non-coöperation. The essay is commonly considered as the first word of its kind, not—as may very well be the case—as the last and best word on the subject.

With the foreground so well known, there remains to be examined the background of Thoreau's essay—and it had a very clear background and rather direct sources. Curiously, discussions of the essay have examined thoroughly the environment in which it appeared; but none have sought its sources. Thoreau has been credited with more originality than he deserves, more perhaps than he desired, for he has indicated within the essay some of his readings and some of the political theorizing with which he was familiar in 1848. He did not make his theory of resistance to government out of whole cloth nor spin it of threads that arose from transcendental intuition. Neither was the essay an editorial, a comment on the current situation that confined itself to the present. It had a solid background as well as sufficient provocation at the time of its composition. It is surely not all derivative; and all of it has the rare quality of freshness with which Thoreau approached even old topics and made them his own, so that (as Lowell remarked) "everything grows fresh under his hand" [see excerpt by James Russell Lowell in *NCLC,* Vol. 7].

One source of Thoreau's thought about government is not far to seek. Emerson's essay "Politics" was published in 1844 in *Essays: Second Series,* and Thoreau was surely familiar with it. It is not necessary to prove that Thoreau read whatever Emerson published in the 1840's and 1850's; but it is especially unnecessary in this case, for a book of the year 1844 came when the friendship of the men was at its height, before their interests and their thoughts had drifted apart to any degree. Emerson's essay is on the theme of government as an expedient for the protection of persons and property, but as the product of persons and property and hence their servant rather than their master. The essay is directed against the very same evil that Thoreau aims at: the use of force by the state. Indeed, Thoreau begins his essay on that note in saying, "I heartily accept the motto, 'That government is best which governs least'; and I should like to see it acted up to more rapidly and systematically. . . . Government is at best but an expedient; but most governments are usually, and all governments are sometimes, inexpedient." But Emerson in 1844 had written in "Politics":

> Hence the less government we have the better,—the fewer laws, and the less confided power. The antidote to this abuse of formal government is the influence of private character, the growth of the Individual; the appearance of the principal to supersede the proxy; the appearance of the wise man; of whom the existing government is, it must be owned, but a shabby imitation.

The similarity of phrasing in Emerson's sentence and in the motto or text on which Thoreau's essay is based is surely striking. And Emerson in his two sentences has given the entire theme of Thoreau's essay. Thus Thoreau's general theme is the same as Emerson's and his text or motto is all but taken verbatim from Emerson, though it is likely they both were indebted to *The Democratic Review* for those words.

Throughout the two essays there are other parallels slightly less striking. Emerson's first sentence is

> In dealing with the State we ought to remember that its institutions are not aboriginal, though they existed before we were born; that they are not superior to the citizen; that every one of them was once the act of a single man; every law and usage was a man's expedient to meet a particular case; that they all are imitable, all alterable; we may make as good, we may make better.

Compare this with three sentences from Thoreau's last paragraph, where the improvability of government is declared:

> Is a democracy, such as we know it, the last improvement possible in government? Is it not possible to take a step further towards recognizing and organizing the rights of man? There will never be a really free and enlightened State until the State comes to recognize the individual as a higher and independent power, from which all its own power and authority are derived, and treats him accordingly.

Thoreau finishes his paragraph and his essay with this idealistic and unspecific thought:

> I please myself with imagining a State at last which can afford to be just to all men, and to treat the individual with respect as a neighbor; which even would not think it inconsistent with its own repose if a few were to live aloof from it, not meddling with it, nor embraced by it, who fulfilled all the duties of neighbors and fellowmen. A State which bore this kind of fruit, and suffered it to drop off as fast as it ripened, would prepare the way for a still more perfect and glorious State, which also I have imagined, but not yet anywhere seen.

Compare this fine climax of Thoreau's essay with its figure of the ripe fruit with Emerson's two statements of the ultimate goal of the state and its ultimate fruition in the wise man:

> We think our civilization near its meridian, but we are yet only at the cock-crowing and the morning star. In our barbarous society the influence of character is in its infancy. As a political power, as the rightful lord who is to tumble all rulers from their chairs, its presence is hardly yet suspected.
>
> To educate the wise man the State exists, and with the appearance of the wise man the State expires. The appearance of character makes the State unnecessary. The wise man is the State. He needs no army, fort, or navy,—he loves men too well; no bribe, or feast, or palace, to draw friends to him; no vantage ground, no favorable circumstance.

Emerson is really a bit more specific about how the perfect state shall come to pass through an application of "the power of love." There are two pertinent passages toward the close of Emerson's essay:

> The tendencies of the times favor the idea of self-government. . . . The movement in this direction has been very marked in modern history. Much has been blind and discreditable, but the nature of the revolution is not affected by the vices of the revolters; for this is a purely moral force. It was never adopted by any party in history, neither can be. It separates the individual from all party, and unites him at the same time to the race. It promises a recognition of higher rights than those of personal freedom, or the security of property. A man has a right to be employed, to be trusted, to be loved, to be revered. The power of love, as the basis of State, has never been tried.
>
> We live in a very low state of the world, and pay unwilling tribute to governments founded on force. There is not among the most religious and instructed men of the most religious and civil nations, a reliance on the moral sentiment and a sufficient belief in the unity of things, to persuade them that society can be maintained without artificial restraints, as well as the solar system; or that the private citizen might be reasonable and a good neighbor, without the hint of

> a jail or a confiscation. What is strange too, there never was in any man sufficient faith in the power of rectitude to inspire him with the broad design of renovating the State on the principle of right and love. All those who have pretended this design have been partial reformers, and have admitted in some manner the supremacy of the bad State. I do not call to mind a single human being who has steadily denied the authority of the laws, on the simple ground of his own moral nature.

Thoreau used the same word "rectitude" in the same way in the paragraph ahead of his final one. He too, as we have just seen, spoke about the "duties of neighbors and fellow-men" when he spoke of a person who had achieved such self-government that he would no longer need external government, and earlier in the essay he had spoken of his desire to be a good neighbor. The same identification of neighborliness with fairness and good citizenship is to be found in Emerson's essay:

> Whilst I do what is fit for me, and abstain from what is unfit, my neighbor and I shall often agree in our means, and work together for a time to one end. But whenever I find my dominion over myself not sufficient for me, and undertake the direction of him also, I overstep the truth, and come into false relations to him. I may have so much more strength or skill than he that he cannot express adequately his sense of wrong, but it is a lie, and hurts like a lie both him and me. Love and nature cannot maintain the assumption; it must be executed by a practical lie, namely by force. This undertaking for another is the blunder which stands in colossal ugliness in the governments of the world. It is the same thing in numbers, as in a pair, only not quite so intelligible. I can see well enough a great difference between my setting myself down to a self-control, and my going to make somebody else act after my views; but when a quarter of the human race assume to tell me what I must do, I may be too much disturbed by the circumstances to see so clearly the absurdity of their command. Therefore all public ends look vague and quixotic beside private ones.

As if commenting on this very reference to the confusing power of numbers, Thoreau too tries to see the absurdity of sheer weight:

> Again, I sometimes say to myself, When many millions of men, without heat, without ill will, without personal feelings of any kind, demand of you a few shillings only, without the possibility, such is their constitution, of retracting or altering their present demand, and without the possibility, on your side, of appeal to any other millions, why expose yourself to this overwhelming brute force? You do not resist cold and hunger, the winds and the waves, thus obstinately; you quietly submit to a thousand similar necessities. You do not put your head into the fire. But just in proportion as I regard this as not wholly a brute force, but partly a human force, and consider that I have relations to those millions as to so many millions of men, and not of mere brute or inanimate things, I see that appeal is possible, first and instantaneously, from them to the Maker of them, and, secondly, from them to themselves.

The impressive thing about Thoreau's dealing with the state is that he did not stop with theorizing but acted. He did not pay his tax under protest; he protested by not paying his tax. He not only objected to the law; he made of himself an object for the law to deal with. In other connections, Emerson expressed admiration for this quality of the concrete and specific in Thoreau, for the ability to put into action what Emerson left but a theory. He did not, however, when Thoreau went to jail, think he had acted wisely. Yet Thoreau was but putting into action Emerson's own dictum, "Every actual State is corrupt. Good men must not obey the laws too well." That is not so different from Thoreau's

> Unjust laws exist: shall we be content to obey them, or shall we endeavor to amend them, and obey them until we have succeeded, or shall we transgress them at once?

He chose to transgress them at once. And it does seem that neighbor Emerson had egged him on and given him ideas for both an essay and a dramatic brush with the law.

Thoreau's theories about governmental use of force, then, agree with those of Emerson. But how to meet this force was only hinted by Emerson, and not too pointedly. Thoreau did not need Emerson's hint. He had learned about a plan of action six years before Emerson's essay and ten years before he wrote his own **"Resistance to Civil Government."** It must be remembered that the Thoreau family, Henry's mother and his sisters especially, were among the earliest and most ardent abolitionists in Concord. Indeed, they were so early and so ardent in their abolitionism that Concord did not accept these shopkeeping Thoreaus as heartily as it might otherwise have done. And they were Garrisonian abolitionists, as later was Bronson Alcott. Thoreau himself seems not to have formally joined any of the abolitionist groups of his time; but he surely was familiar with them and could not have avoided seeing Garrison's paper, *The Liberator,* which came regularly into the home. That he saw *The Liberator* during 1838 is certain. There is no year represented in Thoreau's published letters when all of his interests center within the family home and around the lives of his parents, brother, and sisters more than in 1838. Young Thoreau was just out of college and was decidedly adrift as to occupation that year. He clung desperately to his family just then; and what interested them interested him. And Garrisonian abolitionism interested them.

It was in 1838 that Garrisonian abolitionism became non-voting abolitionism, breaking with the voting abolitionists who were led by Whittier, James G. Birney, and Elizur Wright and whose papers, the *Abolitionist* and the *Emancipator,* opposed during 1838 and 1839 the ideas which the *Liberator* advocated and which affected Thoreau. The first of these ideas which had its effect on Thoreau seems to have been the non-voting stand of abolitionists. Garrison in the *Liberator* of 1838 took his stand against any voting or participation in politics, preferring moral suasion instead. Thoreau reached voting age in 1838; he never voted. How closely this non-voting was related to the question of the use of force by the state appeared in the "Declaration of Sentiments" adopted by Garrison's Peace Convention on September 20, 1838, and printed in the *Liberator* of September 28, 1838:

> As every human government is upheld by physical strength, and its laws are enforced virtually at the point of the bayonet, we cannot hold any office which imposes upon its incumbent the obligation to compel men to do right, on pain of imprisonment or death. We therefore voluntarily exclude ourselves from every legislative and judicial body, and repudiate all human politics, worldly honors, and stations of authority. If *we* cannot occupy a seat in the legislature or on the bench, neither can we elect *others* to act as our substitutes in any such capacity.

Thoreau had one comment on voting in his essay, and he linked voting with force:

> Cast your whole vote, not a strip of paper merely, but your whole influence. A minority is powerless while it conforms to the majority; but it is irresistible when it clogs by its whole weight.

However, the "Declaration of Sentiments" of the Peace Convention and the activities of the resulting Non-Resistance Society (for the word "Peace" was soon dropped by Garrison in favor of "Non-Resistance") contained the idea of passive resistance as well as not voting. After the printing of the "Declaration" in the *Liberator,* Garrison devoted so much of that paper to the new Non-Resistance Society that the anti-slavery people began to fear that their organ was being warped over into the advocate of quite a different reform from the one in which they were chiefly interested. After the first flush of excitement, Garrison regularly devoted at least half of the fourth page to the subject of non-resistance. The pages were 16 x 23 inches, so a good deal was said altogether. In 1839, in order to clear this non-resistance propaganda from the pages of the *Liberator* and to give the New England Non-Resistance Society its own paper, Garrison and others founded the *Non-Resistant*. There is no evidence that Thoreau read this new paper; but there is every indication that he saw the non-resistance material which appeared in the *Liberator* during the latter months of 1838, when the Non-Resistance Society was forming. He was not, of course, a member of that society, as was Bronson Alcott, one of the signers of the September 20, 1838, "Declaration of Sentiments," and as was Adin Ballou, whom Thoreau heard later on the subject of non-resistance. To return to that "Declaration," it was decidedly more theological, millenial, and perfectionist than Thoreau's statement of non-resistance. Its pious tone was set in its second paragraph:

> We recognize but one KING and LAWGIVER, or JUDGE and RULER of mankind. We are bound by the laws of a kingdom which is not of this world; the subjects of which are forbidden to fight; in which MERCY and TRUTH are met together, and RIGHTEOUSNESS and PEACE have kissed each other; which has no state lines, no national partitions, no geographical boundaries; in which there is no distinction of rank, or division of caste, or inequality of sex; the officers of which are PEACE, its exactors RIGHTEOUSNESS, its walls SALVATION, and its gates PRAISE; and which is destined to break in pieces and consume all other kingdoms.

Thoreau did not accept this apocalyptic perfectionism, though it would not have been distasteful to his pious sisters at the time; but it is clear that he accepted and in 1846 practiced another passage in the "Declaration":

> But, while we shall adhere to the doctrine of non-resistance and passive submission to enemies, we purpose, in a moral and spiritual sense, to speak and act boldly in the cause of GOD; to assail iniquity, in high places and in low places; to apply our principles to all existing civil, political, legal and ecclesiastical institutions.

This passage sounds like a declaration of Thoreau's own purpose, one he applied against both the political and the ecclesiastical institutions, for in his essay on civil resistance he describes not only his submitting to being jailed but also his "signing-off" from the church.

Thoreau's awareness of this stir about Non-resistance is proved by the minutes of the Concord Lyceum, now in the Concord Free Public Library. The following are the minutes for the jfirst three lyceum meetings of 1841:

> Jan. 13, 1841.
> Lyceum discussed "Is it ever proper to offer forcible resistance?"
> Rev. B. Frost & Hon. S. Hoar—affirmative
> A. B. Alcott—negative
>
> Jan. 27, 1841.
> The Lyceum having been called to order by the President, proceeded to the discussion of the following question—
> "Is it ever proper to offer forcible resistance?"
> Mr. J. Thoreau Jr. & Mr. D. H. Thoreau, in the affirmative,
> Mr. A. B. Alcott in the negative.
> On motion of Mr. J. Thoreau Jr. Ordered, that this question lie over for farther discussion till some evening when the Lyceum is unprovided with a lecturer.
> Adjourned
> John C. Nourse, Secy.
>
> Feb. 5, 1841.
> On motion of Mr. Thoreau—Voted that, after the lecture, the Lyceum discuss the question of Non-resistance.
> A lecture was then delivered by *Rev. Mr. Ballou of Mendon* on Non-Resistance.
> This question was then discussed by Mr. Ballou, Mr. S. Hoar, Mr. Alcott, Mr. Jenkins, & the President.
> The Lyceum adjourned without taking the question.
> John C. Nourse, Secretary

Thoreau himself in 1841 seems to have landed on the affirmative side of the propriety of resistance on occasion. But this put him in the company of Samuel Hoar, who was not a non-resistant but who opposed the use of force in general, as the following passage by Adin Ballou, the speaker in Concord on February 5, 1841, will attest:

> On these occasions, especially when I had the exercises in charge, it was my custom to extend to any persons present differing from me an opportunity to state their views, and to invite questions and objections that I might answer them. This often gave much additional interest and effect to the proceedings. A memorable instance of this kind occurred at Concord, Mass., in February, 1841. I had been engaged to lecture there before the town lyceum on the subject of Non-resistance. A large audience, including many of the literary and professional elite of that community, honored me with their presence and with a respectful hearing. At the close of my regular address, the usual privilege being granted, I was plied with a goodly number of the hardest questions their sharpest critics could devise. I was favorred with a good measure of spiritual inspiration, answered their inquiries as successfully as I could, kept all in good humor, and at the close was cordially congratulated by the venerable and Honorable Samuel Hoar, father of the present Senator George F. Hoar, who, though not a Non-resistant, was an advanced International Peace man, and gave me his best wishes for the conversion of the people at large from their idolization of brute force to a more kindly and humane attitude of mind and heart.

Thoreau in his **"Resistance to Civil Government"** has one reference which indicates that he was familiar with those Garrisonian Non-resistants, and that he separated in his own mind non-resistance as a mode of protest and the foreswearing of all government. In other words, Thoreau was not one of those Perfectionists who believed that the time had already come to have done with earthly governments and to assume that divine government had long been in effect and needed only to be accepted.

> But to speak practically and as a citizen, unlike those who call themselves no-government men, I ask for, not at once no government, but *at once* a better government. Let every man make known what kind of government would command his respect, and that will be one step toward obtaining it.

His impatience of delay, revealed in the phrase he italicized, reminds one of the Garrisonian impatience over the "Gradualists" among the anti-slavery reformers and may relate to that. Thoreau here rejects Perfectionism, at least as an immediate possibility. At the very end of his essay, after "imagining a State at last which can afford to be just to all men" he goes beyond this last development of an earthly state, suggests Perfectionism, and says:

> A State which bore this kind of fruit, and suffered it to drop off as fast as it ripened, would prepare the way for a still more perfect and glorious State, which also I have imagined, but not yet anywhere seen.

A third, and perhaps the earliest source of Thoreau's thinking about government and the individual's relations and duties toward the state was the "common authority with many on moral questions," William Paley, D.D., whose *Moral and Political Philosophy* had been a textbook in Thoreau's junior year at Harvard and whose book was in Thoreau's library when he listed his books in 1840. In his 1849 essay Thoreau quotes Paley more specifically than any other source suggested in the whole essay. He gives the title of Paley's chapter, "Duty of Submission to Civil Government," a title parallel with his own title **"Resistance to Civil Government"** and even closer to the later title of Thoreau's essay, **"On the Duty of Civil Disobedience,"** though the title given Thoreau's essay more likely derives from Paley's next chapter, "Of the Duty of Civil Obedience, as Stated in the Christian Scriptures." Paley, Thoreau says, "resolves all civil obligation into expediency." Thoreau granted as much in his own essay. Then he quotes Paley directly:

> So long as the interest of the whole society requires it, that is, so long as the established government cannot be resisted or changed without public inconveniency, it is the will of God . . . that the established government be obeyed,—and no longer. This principle being admitted, the justice of every particular case of resistance is reduced to a computation of the quantity of the danger and grievance on the one side, and of the probability and expense of redressing it on the other.

His comment on this passage from Paley is to approve Paley's further remark that every man must judge for himself the merits of each particular case of resistance but to say that Paley seems not to have considered cases "to which the rule of expediency does not apply." Thoreau is perfectly clear in his own mind that the United States in 1848 was such a case.

But Paley gave Thoreau other ideas. In the chapter Thoreau quoted from there are such sentences as these:

> Resistance to the *encroachments* of the supreme magistrate may be justified upon this principle; recourse to arms, for the purpose of bringing about an amendment to the constitution, never can.

There is little here that Thoreau could not fit into the thought of his essay and that did not square with the doctrines of the Non-resistants. A few pages farther on there must have been much comfort in a little paragraph of Paley's:

> It may be as much a duty, at one time, to resist government, as it is, at another, to obey it; to wit, whenever more advantage will, in our opinion, accrue to the community from resistance than mischief.

Paley confirmed for Thoreau another cardinal principle in his stand on government. One of Thoreau's chief objections, in agreement with the general New England attitude toward the Mexican War situation, was to the maintenance by the government of a standing army. He objected to it early in his essay, and it was objected to by most Non-resistants as an anti-peace agency of the government and as the very symbol of force. Thoreau considered it the prop which held up a feeble government, one so feeble that it dared not face a resolute individual without this extra aid. How welcome to him must have been Paley's sentence: "Civil governments are now-a-days almost universally upholden by standing armies." Even the motto Thoreau chose for his essay has its countepart in Paley:

> That people, government, and constitution, is the *freest,* which makes the best provision for the enacting of expedient and salutary laws.

Thoreau preferred the motto he chose and could hardly have agreed with Paley. Yet it does seem likely that reading Paley in 1836 and afterward gave Thoreau ideas about government as a subject for speculation. It seems even to have given him ideas about how to organize his own thinking, for Paley's is a most logical presentation of political philosophy. The organization found in Paley is reflected once very definitely in Thoreau. Paley, without suggesting that one form is an improvement on another, lists "the principle forms of government" as

> I. "Despotism, or absolute MONARCHY"
>
> II. "An ARISTOCRACY"
>
> III. "A REPUBLIC, or democracy"

It is a natural order, but perhaps Thoreau had his old textbook in mind when in his own essay he wrote, "The progress from an absolute to a limited monarchy, from a limited monarchy to a democracy, is a progress toward a true respect for the individual." That was a conclusion Paley never reached.

Thoreau's use of Paley is exactly what one would expect. He took a wry delight in disagreeing with his textbook. He took a wry delight in disagreeing with any conventionality. That is what made him the individualist he was. Here, then, are three sources for his thought in **"Resistance to Civil Government."** But he did not stop with Emerson's "Politics," nor with the Non-resistants, nor yet with Paley. He took from all three and rejected much from all three, and, as we have already said, so refashioned the material and so individualized it and so intensified it or dramatized it that it has become his own. And people forget that there may have been sources, but think that a Thoreau essay written in 1848 must go no further back than 1848 in the mind of Thoreau for its ideas. (pp. 640-53)

Raymond Adams, "Thoreau's Sources for 'Resistance to Civil Government'," in Studies in Philology, *Vol. XLII, No. 3, July, 1945, pp. 640-53.*

C. CARROLL HOLLIS (essay date 1949)

[Hollis contends that, despite unresolved paradoxes, "Civil Disobedience" expresses one unassailable truth: that the perception of universal verities is a function of the individual mind and cannot be achieved by consensus.]

The famous essay **"Civil Disobedience"** is a remarkable assertion, as remarkable today as in 1849, of the relation of man to society. I use *remarkable* here as an intentionally equivocal term, for I find the essay remarkable on three distinct levels: for its literary effectiveness, for its major errors, for its essential truth.

Thoreau's literary gifts have been so generally acclaimed that I wish only to add a comment on one aspect, but a major aspect, of his language that is ignored: his use of paradox. My starting point is a hitherto unnoticed comment by Emerson [in his *Journals*] on Thoreau's style:

> Henry Thoreau sends me a paper with the old fault of unlimited contradicition. The trick of his rhetoric is soon learned; it consists in substituting for the obvious word and thought its diametrical antagonist. He praises wild mountains and winter forests for their domestic air; snow and ice for their warmth; villagers and woodchoppers for their urbanity, and the wilderness for resembling Rome and Paris. With the constant inclination to dispraise cities and civilization, he yet can find no way to know woods and woodsmen except by paralleling them with towns and townsmen. Channing declared the piece excellent: but it makes me nervous and wretched to read it, with all its merits.

Emerson is here wiser than he knows, for, although it makes him "nervous and wretched," he shrewdly and quite correctly discovers as the secret of Thoreau's style its essential foundation in paradox.

Paradox in Thoreau is the consequence of his profound awareness (which does not mean his scientific understanding) of the mystery of life. The basic paradox of existence the Hindu writers saw, the writers of the early seventeenth century saw, Blake saw, Thoreau saw. Any statement of what they saw had to be, inevitably, a paradoxical statement, no matter how simple their expression. Thoreau, then, saw paradoxes, he did not make them. Thoreau's relationship to these earlier writers is not a stylistic one merely; it is, rather, the basic similarity of a common vision. Thoreau knew intuitively, as we know through reflection, and as Emerson failed to know at all, that paradox must be taken seriously both as an essential principle of life and as an essential method of communication.

In order to reach the higher truth which Thoreau contemplated and to which he brings us through his paradoxical method, it is necessary first to disabuse ourselves of the widely current notion that **"Civil Disobedience"** is a guide to political action. From Thoreau's day, through Tolstoy, Gandhi, Emma Goldman, and others, the essay has been championed as a still current, if ideal, statement of the relation of the individual to the state. This view has highlighted the romantic heresy of which I believe Thoreau guilty.

Looked at as a political credo the essay is just wrong. In it Thoreau offends common sense and our common understanding of the need for organized society or government. The opening paragraphs exhibit this first error, his failure to recognize the primacy of the state. Most of us would admit Jefferson's dictum, "That government is best which governs least," if taken as a statement of policy in operation. But when Thoreau starts his essay with this famous remark, he leaves little doubt that he proposes the comment only in its extreme interpretation and so denies the fundamental principle that man needs the state, so needs it that he must as a rational being provide it for his own social welfare.

But Thoreau looks on government at best as but an expedient, not as an essential need with real rights and powers no matter how small the minimum exercise of these might in practice be. Even the abuse of power by a standing government does not deny its claim to *some* power; even as a standing army, to follow Thoreau's figure, may have justification despite the wrongs it perpetrates. When government activity becomes an obstacle to business or commerce, it is to be judged by its seeking the common good and not measured by Thoreau's norm of its success in letting men alone.

The second major error is the misunderstanding of democracy. In the fourth paragraph of the essay Thoreau challenges majority rule. First he claims that when power of rule is in the hands of the majority, injustice is done and violence to the conscience. A majority rules, he says, not by right or out of fairness to the minority but by physical strength. It presumes to decide right and wrong instead of dealing only with matters of expediency. In reply it might first of all be said that Thoreau fails to understand the essential characteristic of government by majority rule in a democracy such as the American state.

Democracy under the American Constitution is not like other forms of government where the majority might rule, as in an oligarchy or even monarchy upheld by an army with force or by most citizens out of sheer power of numbers. Democracy is distinct from other modes of government not in what it provides a majority but in what it promises absolutely to a minority, no matter how small.

In this way majority rule, just such as Thoreau had in mind, is a protection instead of the invasion of rights. Further, the judicial power of legitimate government necessarily deals with problems of right and wrong, and decides against even the sincere but misguided claims of *some* consciences while it vindicates those of another. Such settlement of disputes is one of the functions (because one of the common needs of men) of any government. Yet Thoreau says, "The only obligation I have a right to assume is to do at any time what I think right." In the sense in which he says this, he sets up every citizen as judge of the state. It is a testament of the Rousseauistic idea that consent on the part of the citizen constitutes the state's authority and refusal dissolves it. This is the third major error of the essay.

This, the central error of the work, concerns authority in the State. When Thoreau considers the obligation of the citizen to obey the law, he not only rejects that obligation in the light of his extreme individualism but ultimately denies authority itself. Just what does, "The only obligation I have . . . is to do . . . what I think is right," imply?

Now obligation is a correlative of right. In this case the state must have the right to impose obligation, to demand obedience. Men refusing to acknowledge such obligation denies the State the right involved, and thereby denies the authority of the State.

The last of what I call the major errors of the essay is what I consider its complete or absolute liberalism. I fancy myself as a liberal of sorts, and many of my friends are more liberal still, but I know of no one who is an absolute liberal in Thoreau's sense except Thoreau. By absolute liberalism, in the extreme and reprehensible sense in which I use the term here, I mean the exaltation of the privilege of freedom of will so as to justify its independence of authority.

In this extreme sense liberalism is the philosophy which in principle glorifies the single individual free-will until its apparent freedom isolates the person from society, releasing him from his social and civil duties. There are modified forms of liberalism wherein submission to one authority or another is denied, but absolute liberalism denies all authority. Thoreau does just this in clear and emphatic statements. He even explains his external neighborliness and outward conformance to some of his civil and social requirements as motivated by his personal preferences not by submission of his will to authority as such. He is careful to insist that he objects not to giving a dollar to the state but in giving obedience to it. In a word, although it is passive resistance he preaches, it is *active* civil disobedience of will.

The errors Thoreau makes are really errors, and as such to be denounced as vigorously as one's perception of their danger admits. Yet certainly never was there an essay in which truth so transcended its accompanying error. The paradox upon which this comment rests, and upon which Thoreau's whole essay rests, he himself explains:

> Seen from a lower point of view, the Constitution, with all its faults, is very good; the law and the courts are very respectable; even this state and this government are, in many respects very admirable, and rare things, to be thankful for, such as a great many have described them; but seen from a point of view a little higher, they are what I have described them; seen from a higher still, and the highest, who shall say what they are, or that they are worth looking at and thinking of at all?

What Thoreau does is to look at life (or in this case at one aspect of it, the State) from two and sometimes from all three of these points of view, but in the same glance. This double or complex vision occasions the paradox of his experience. Contradiction, which is the principle of paradox, arises from the opposition he perceives between these different phases of existence.

This complex vision is not contrived, but a part of Thoreau's penetrating if incomplete intuition of life. In this sense the whole fourteen volumes of his ***Journal*** are only a by-product, and what we should praise as the essential Thoreau is the man of vision. Yet this vision, because paradoxical, provides the tension in which creation works.

In Thoreau's case, and he here is in accord with an ancient tradition, creation is best manifested in short units—the sentence or the short paragraph. Every famous sentence of Thoreau's is based in some fashion or other on this three-way paradox. "Under a government which imprisons any unjustly, the true place for a just man is also a prison," from the essay under discussion. "Merely to come into the world the heir of a fortune is not to be born, but to be stillborn, rather," from **"Life Without Principle."** "The mass of men lead lives of quiet desperation," from ***Walden.*** It does not seem necessary to explain how paradox works or the kinds Thoreau uses, but it is important to note their connection with his over-all style. The three sentences quoted, like most of his paradoxes, are opening sentences of paragraphs. Once the paradox is on paper, he spends the rest of the paragraph explaining it by straight narrative or exposition.

The errors, as those noted above, come from his attempts to explain his paradoxes or from his direct presentation of a social philosophy. In either case Thoreau fails; he is not a brilliant expository writer, nor even a distinguished logical thinker. He is sometimes read as such, and often quoted, as by Emma Goldman, for purposes he would find violently ironical, yet he is no philosopher. But he is a mystic of a sort, with a true mystical vision of life. I say "of a sort" for I do not think of him as a mystic in the traditional Christian sense. A better name for him would be a mystical poet (in the sense of William Blake).

It is on this level, as a mystical poet, that Thoreau is significant for the essential truth of his utterances. What is it that a mystical poet grasps that we do not? In traditional terms I think we can say he sees the One in the Many. Not that he *reasons* to it as we do in our painful way. He sees immediately the Oneness of the universe, we see only the Many. Now Thoreau recognized his vision as the high point of man's potentialities, and "If a plant cannot live according to its nature, it dies; and so a man."

On this plane Thoreau's high individualism is not only acceptable, it is the only possible attitude to take. *We* do not and cannot have an intuitive perception of the mystery of life in the same sense that we, as a group, carry on a defensive war or any other social action. Mystical awareness is and can only be an individual experience. Thoreau is sometimes impatient with our spirutual myopia and scorns our admittedly laborious efforts to attain certainty by reason. Similarly he scorns our laborious efforts to live on the lower, physical level. His indignation at society was in large part attendant upon the State's forcing lower level responsibilities upon him and distracting him from the highest participation, some stage of mystical contemplation.

Thoreau's reaction would be like that of the Trappist whose ecstatic prayer is interrupted by a well-meant request for a donation to the March-of-Dimes Fund. Even the thought of social injustice can distract, so the social evils are to be removed. The slaves are to be freed so that they, if they wish, and Thoreau can contemplate. But even this ideal state is not the end-all, for it would "prepare the way for a still more perfect and glorious State, which also I have imagined, but not yet anywhere seen."

When Thoreau closes his essay with these words he is asserting once again for western man that our social destiny is, after all, but a part of that spiritual destiny in which our dignity as men rests. In that sense the essay is as much, indeed more important today than one hundred years ago. Then as now men of public conscience were indignant at the injustices of society, injustices that seemed perpetuated, and even created, by the State. Perhaps more in Europe than here, but certainly everywhere today, the problem of this essay—the nature and extent of obedience to the State—becomes the problem of the individual citizen whose answer defines him as anything from a martyr or prisoner to a conniver or slave. Thoreau's answer to this problem on the level of social action is, I contend, simply wrong. But on its higher level, as the classic statement of American individualism at its highest, it will become increasingly important as society becomes increasingly collective. (pp. 530-33)

C. Carroll Hollis, "Thoreau and the State," in The Commonweal, *Vol. L, No. 22, September 9, 1949, pp. 530-33.*

HEINZ EULAU (essay date 1949)

[In the following excerpt from a 1949 essay, Eulau suggests that Thoreau's ideas on civil disobedience are naive and could, if applied, yield disastrous results. Robert Palmer Saalbach has taken exception to several of Eulau's arguments; for Saalbach's comments, see the excerpt dated 1972.]

It is unfair, perhaps, to judge Thoreau's political philosophy by present-day standards. Yet, it is necessary to do so because some recent interpreters have tried, in vain I think, to make Thoreau palatable to liberalism by reading their own preferences into his writings. But even if they seek to strike a balance, the end effect of their expositions is tortuous. Max Lerner, for instance, writes inaccurately, I believe, that Thoreau's individualism should be seen as part of "a rebellion against the oversocialized New England town, in which the individual was being submerged. . . . He was not so limited as to believe that the individual could by his own action stem the heedless onrush of American life, or succeed wholly in rechanneling it" [see Additional Bibliography]. Similarly, Townsend Scudder states that "though so intense an individualist, Thoreau favored the ideal of communal living as in keeping with the spirit of America." Significantly, Lerner, Scudder as well as F. O. Matthiessen repeat, by way of evidence, a single passage from Thoreau's ***Walden***—"to act collectively is according to the spirit of our institutions." The bulk of proof is, in fact, on the other side. Even Vernon Parrington, whose progressivist bias is rarely concealed, recognized that Thoreau "could not adopt the cooperative solution." Thoreau refused to join Brook Farm because, in his own words, he "would rather keep a bachelor's hall in hell than go to board in heaven."

Thoreau does not give much comfort to those who seek to prove a point. But it should be remembered that ***Walden,*** his most famous and widely read book, does not alone represent his ideas. For an understanding of his politics, **"Civil Disobedience"** as well as the less-known and less-read essays, **"Slavery in Massachusetts"** and **"A Plea for Captain John Brown,"** are of at least equal importance. They leave little doubt that Thoreau's whole political philosophy was based on the theoretical premise of individual conscience as the only true criterion of what is politically right and just. It was the very perfection of his belief in the veracity of each man's soul and conscience as harbingers of some truth higher than human fiat that made inconsistency in his theory inevitable. Action from principle, he wrote in a prophetic sentence in **"Civil Disobedience,"** "not only divides states and churches, it divides families; ay, it divides the *individual,* separating the diabolical in him from the divine." Within the short span of ten years, Thoreau, though holding to the same premise, would draw conclusions as opposite as passive resistance and violent action. Obviously, both his personality and ideas were complex. Any attempt to reduce them to simple, and hence simpleton, propositions is futile.

While the subsequent essays are significant because they prove, better than critical argument, that "action from principle" is a politically dangerous concept, **"Civil Disobedience"** is the most complete theoretical statement of Thoreau's basic assumptions. Because it expounded a queer doctrine, unlikely to make much of an impression on his contemporaries, Thoreau apparently elaborated his political premise more fully in **"Civil Disobedience"** than in the subsequent essays.

His starting point is the half-mocking, half-serious observation that if Jefferson's motto—"that government is best which governs least"—were carried out, it would amount to "that government is best which governs not at all." Does this mean, as has been suggested, that Thoreau brought Jefferson's ideas to their logical conclusion? By no means. In placing the individual "above" the state, Jefferson attacked the autocratic state, not the democratic state which he did so much to bring about. If Thoreau went at all beyond Jefferson, it consisted in his attack on democracy. But, paradoxically, he attacked democracy not because it was strong; on the contrary, because it was weak. The American government, he wrote, "has not the vitality and force of a single living man; for a single man can bend it to his will." He refused to vote because he considered the democratic ballot an ineffective political instrument. His own contact with the government being limited to the annual *tête-a-tête* with the tax collector, his refusal to pay the poll tax loses some of its bravado. He did not really sacrifice much when he declared, somewhat grandiloquently, that he should not like to think he would ever have to rely on the protection of the state. Basically, Thoreau was the very opposite of Jefferson; he was as unpolitical as Jefferson was political. It is simply not conceivable to hear Jefferson say, as Thoreau said, "the government does not concern me much, and I shall bestow the fewest possible thoughts on it."

If Thoreau had let the matter rest at this point, his position would have been consistent. But as if he needed to test his own propositions, he would suddenly speak "practically and as a citizen, unlike those who call themselves no-government men." And as a citizen Thoreau demanded "not at once no government, but *at once* better government." Such a government would anticipate and provide for reform, cherish its "wise minority" and encourage its citizens "to be on the alert to point out its faults."

It appears that Thoreau could not fully discern that his metaphysical assumptions had to lead, almost necessarily, to ambiguous consequences when subjected to the test of practical politics. The essential weakness of the metaphysical premise is that it is absolutist as long as it deals with abstractions, just as it is relativistic when applied to unique and observable situations. Like his fellow idealists, Thoreau was incapable of recognizing those distinctions of degree which are politically decisive. He could not recognize them because he fell back, again and again, on the principle of individual conscience as the sole valid guide in political action. He realized only faintly that this principle was inherently deficient for political purposes, as when he said that while "all men recognize the right of revolution . . . , almost all say that such is not the case now." Individual conscience as a political principle was too obviously in conflict with the democratic principle of majority rule, even for Thoreau. But the rather dogmatic assertion, "there is but little virtue in the masses of men," was too hazardous in view of the manifest strength of the democratic faith of most men in his time. Thoreau's only way out was, once more, a paradox: "Any man more right than his neighbors constitutes a majority of one already."

Consequently, Thoreau had to postulate a (by democratic standards) curious distinction between law and right, with the explanation that one has to have faith in man, that each man can determine for himself what is right and just. Hence, no conflict is possible, so the argument goes, because law is law only if identical with right. Thoreau could not demonstrate, however, that there is, in case the majority is wrong, an objective criterion for assaying the correctness of an individual's or a minority's judgment.

He was content, therefore, with declaring war on the state in his own fashion:

> It is not a man's duty as a matter of course, to devote himself to the eradication of any, even the most enormous wrong; he may still properly have other concerns to engage him; but it is his duty, at least, to wash his hands of it, and, if he gives it no thought longer, not to give it practically his support.

Great as his hurry seemed in **"Civil Disobedience,"** Thoreau remained, in fact, unpolitical. Actually, he did not wish to be bothered at all with the obnoxious phenomenon of slavery. He had other affairs to attend to. "I came into this world," he concluded, "not chiefly to make this a good place to live in, but to live in it, be it good or bad." Joseph Wood Krutch has aptly described this kind of reasoning as Thoreau's "sometimes desperate casuistry."

The ideas expressed in **"Civil Disobedience"** fell into the Walden period (1845-1847) and are, to some extent, an early reaction to Thoreau's own dim sense of failure as a recluse from society. Existence at Walden Pond was an experiment for the purpose of finding reality. But subjectively real as life at Walden may have been, to judge from his famous report, it came to be unreal, apparently, when Thoreau was forced to compare it with the objective reality of the impending Mexican War which he encountered on his almost daily visits to town. There he would see his neighbors getting ready for what seemed to him a hateful and stupid enterprise. Its effect could only be the extension of the unjust institution of slavery and of the slaveholders' power. Thoreau felt a deep personal disgrace in being associated with a government which was the slaves' government also. So deeply did he feel on the issue that he was ready to warn that "this people must cease to hold slaves, and to make war on Mexico, though it cost them their existence as a people." So great seemed the evil that there was no time to change the laws except by breaking them. Refusal to pay taxes was, in Thoreau's mind, "the definition of a peaceful revolution, if any such is possible." Otherwise, he continued, the conscience is wounded: "Through this wound a man's real manhood and immortality flow out, and he bleeds to an everlasting death. I see this blood flowing now."

All his protestations about "signing off" from human institutions to the contrary, **"Civil Disobedience,"** in contrast to ***Walden,*** was a first indication of Thoreau's theoretical difficulties. It contained the seeds of its own denial, seeds which were fertilized by the untenable metaphysical premise of individual conscience as a criterion of collective action. In the very act of counseling and practicing individual resistance to and renunciation of government was implicit a growing sense of social responsibility which the hermit of Walden Pond could scarcely disclaim.

Thoreau was not, therefore, as ***Walden*** might suggest and some critics have said, an American exponent of the Rousseauist doctrine of the natural rights of man. His philosophy certainly lacked the liberating drive which Rousseau's individualism had in the eighteenth-century French context. Thoreau's individualism was, most interpreters agree, an inspired protest against the modern cult of progress, materialism and efficiency, with its deteriorating effect on the individual. But it was essentially out of date. Because it renounced industrialism rather than seeking to bring it under social control, Thoreau's individualism could not possibly find practical application. The moral and the morally real were at odds.

"Civil Disobedience" differed from ***Walden*** in another respect. ***Walden*** was the report of a highly personalized experience. And in spite of its persuasiveness, its almost egocentric individualism made communication difficult. Only the most liberal imagination can perceive it for what it was: namely, the attempt of a sensitive spirit to discover his own integrity and convey this discovery, not to be imitated literally—a mistake against which Thoreau himself explicitly warned, but to serve as a symbolic expression of man's need for finding his own integrity in whatever fashion seemed best. "I desire," he wrote, "that there be as many different persons in the world as possible; but I would have each one be very careful to find out and pursue *his own* way. . . ." As such, life at Walden Pond was a meaningful experiment, even though it was meaningless as a form of *social* living.

However, Thoreau's individualism was not simply, as Parrington remarked, "transcendental individualism translated into politics." His radicalism differed in more than degree from the innocuous, often opportunistic, politics of most Abolitionists. Their humanitarianism seemed all too sanguine to him. Were they not actually giving aid and comfort to the enemy by refusing to withdraw from political society altogether? In asking this question it must be admitted that Thoreau himself remained on a largely rhetorical level throughout his political life. Certainly, his refusal to pay the poll tax and being jailed for it was a frankly ephemeral episode. But he found it increasingly necessary to communicate his ideas in a manner which would leave no doubt where he stood. (pp. 118-23)

[In] spite of the apparent urgency of his argument in **"Civil Disobedience,"** Thoreau had experienced the Mexican War and its implications for the slavery question as a fairly remote conflict. But with the passage of the Fugitive Slave Law in 1850 it became evident, even to a political hermit like Thoreau, that continued detachment from affairs of state would not avert the threat to his personal liberty which the law implied. The state, he now discovered, "has fatally interfered with my lawful business." **"Slavery in Massachusetts"** was, therefore, as outspoken a piece of indignation as **"Civil Disobedience"** had been casual. He bade farewell to the pipedream of a state which would permit a few people, who so desired, to live aloof from it, "not meddling with it, nor embraced by it." He had never respected the government, he said, but "I had foolishly thought that I might manage to live here, minding my private affairs, and forget it." Thoreau now dropped the role of the bohemian anarchist who could wash is hands of society's "dirty institutions," as he had called them in ***Walden.*** Before, he admitted, he had dwelt in the illusion that "my life passed somewhere only *between* heaven and hell, but now I cannot persuade myself that I do not dwell *wholly* within hell."

Moreover, his rebellion was no longer a matter of denials alone. He still fulminated against majority rule, but a new line of thought occupied him. It would be too simple to say that a democratic faith emerged, but Thoreau's attack on existing institutions is certainly not that of the vociferous anti-democrat of **"Civil Disobedience."** As against judges deciding questions involving slaves, Thoreau would now "much rather trust the sentiment of the people. In their vote you would get something of value, at least, however small." It was no longer the state in the abstract, but the State of Massachusetts in the concrete which he attacked. He would recognize the possibility of a government which is worth fighting for. "Show me a free state, and a court truly of justice, and I will fight for them, if need be . . . ," he proclaimed; "it is not an era of repose. We have used up all our inherited freedom. If we would save our lives, we must fight for them."

"Slavery in Massachusetts" was not a theoretical exercise in political philosophy. It concentrated its verbal fire on an evil situation. But it is indicative of Thoreau's political immaturity that he now went so far as to join the militant abolitionists in advocating the secession of Massachusetts from the union with the slave states. He was apparently quite unaware of the possibility that the consequences of such action might accentuate the evil which he sought to remedy. That is, permit slavery to continue unopposed elsewhere. In addition, he still confused what seemed to him the iniquity of law with the legal process itself. And though he spoke of breaking the law, of boycotting proslavery newspapers, of ousting ignorant politicians and seceding from the Union, it remains unclear just what specific political means Thoreau considered appropriate to achieve his objectives. He had almost given up passive resistance, but he had not completely accepted majority rule.

With all its new affirmations, **"Slavery in Massachusetts"** did not answer the question which is central from the point of view of political theory—whether the practicality of political concepts can be assessed by any kind of objectively rational standard. It seems that Thoreau was neither willing nor able to develop such a criterion. Not even "truth" would serve that purpose. Truth, he wrote in **"Civil Disobedience,"** "is always in harmony with herself, and is not concerned chiefly to reveal the justice that may consist with wrong-doing." In other words, the consequences of an act are separable and, indeed, must be separated from its nature. Even truth is thus reduced to being a matter of individual taste. Thoreau admitted the existence of other truths, but being altogether personal and private they did not permit contact or comparison with each other. As so many of his concepts, his truth is paradoxical. His moral absolutism, being so individualized, becomes relativistic. It is not surprising to find, therefore, that Thoreau envisaged various hierarchial levels of political evaluation. "Seen from a lower point of view," he wrote, "the Constitution, with all its faults, is very good; the law and the courts are very respectable; even this State and this American government are, in many respects, very admirable, and rare things, to be thankful for, such as a great many have described them; but seen from a point of view a little higher, they are what I have described them; seen from a higher still, and the highest, who shall say what they are, or that they are worth looking at or thinking of at all?"

Paradox may serve the purpose of literary construction. In political theory it is self-defeating. Inasmuch as Thoreau's anarchism followed from the doctrine of the individual's duty to his conscience alone, it should lead to at least some mutual tolerance as an avenue to human cooperation. But Thoreau would carry the matter to absurdity. In a sentence remindful of the vicarious a-moralism of the later social Darwinians he wrote:

> I am not responsible for the successful working of the machinery of society. . . . I perceive that, when an acorn and a chestnut fall side by side, the one does not remain inert to make way for the other, but both obey their own laws, and spring and grow and flourish as best they can, till one, perchance, overshadows and destroys the other. If a plant cannot live according to its nature, it dies; and so a man.

It is quite clear that Thoreau's mind was totally closed to the democratic conception of politics as a never-ending process of compromise and adjustment. As a matter of fact, if the politics of "action from principle," with its insistence on ends, is shorn of metaphysics, it appears as little more than the old and familiar doctrine that the end justifies the means. Comparison of **"Civil Disobedience"** and **"A Plea for Captain John Brown"** underlines the fact that in Thoreau's mind both passive resistance and violent action were *right* if employed toward the accomplishment of ends whose truth is predicated on the complete assumption of responsibility by the individual for his acts.

Just as nonviolent resistance as an instrument of politics is proper if the state interferes with an individual's principles, so violence can be justified. Given Thoreau's moral intransigence, it is not surprising to find that he would round out his basic position by eulogizing an event which only the most rabid Abolitionists supported as politically justifiable. John Brown, Thoreau came to believe, was not only right in holding that a man has "a perfect right to interfere by force with the slaveholder, in order to rescue the slave"; but the doctrine that the end justifies the means was given explicit expression: "I shall not be forward to think him mistaken in his method who quickest succeeds to liberate the slave." The decisive question, Thoreau finally felt, was not "about the weapon, but the spirit in which you use it." And he would write in his ***Journals:*** "I do not wish to kill nor to be killed, but I can foresee circumstances in which both these things would be by me unavoidable."

Actually, however, **"A Plea for Captain John Brown"** was concerned with the slavery issue only indirectly. Thoreau undoubtedly felt its iniquity and the urgency of its solution most intensely, but his primary concern was again with justice and injustice, with principle and expediency, with truth and falsehood. **"A Plea for Captain John Brown"** is therefore more closely related to **"Civil Disobedience"** than to **"Slavery in Massachuesetts."** It differed, however, from his first political essay in that Thoreau had abandoned his earlier quietist position. Violence was in the air. Almost everywhere in the nation men were girding themselves for the great conflict which would soon disrupt the Union. While it may have been his intention merely to bring his disagreement with the moderate Abolitionists into sharper focus by advocating violence before the peaceful alternatives had been exhausted, the end effect of **"A Plea for Captain John Brown"** was the admission of an inveterate moralist that violence can only be combatted by violence.

It is symptomatic of his greater sense of realism that the government did not seem weak any longer as it had in **"Civil Disobedience"** ten years before. "When a government puts forth its strength on the side of injustice, as ours to maintain slavery and kill the liberators of the slave," he wrote, "it reveals itself a merely brute force, or worse, a demoniacal force. It is the head of the Plug-Uglies. It is more manifest than ever that tyranny rules. I see this government to be effectually allied with France and Austria in oppressing mankind." The government, he continued, is "a semi-human tiger or ox stalking over the earth, with its heart taken out and the top of its brain shot away."

Thoreau could no longer subscribe to the quietist doctrine of **"Civil Disobedience"** with its counsel of escape. He fiercely excoriated all those who adhered to a nonviolent solution of social conflict. "What sort of violence is that," he now asked, "which is encouraged, not by soldiers, but by peaceable citizens, not so much by laymen as by ministers of the Gospel, not so much by the fighting sects as by the Quakers, and not so much by the Quaker men as by the Quaker women?" Here Thoreau squarely faced the question of resistance by force which modern pacifism, confronted with the infamies of totalitarian terror and violence, slave labor and concentration camps, fails to answer. Here, in essence, he returned to the age-old concept of the "just war," which modern quietists refuse to acknowledge. John Brown would "never have anything to do with any war," Thoreau intimated, "unless it were a war for liberty," expressing an opinion since challenged by competent historians.

In John Brown, Thoreau had found the man of principle whom he had anticipated in **"Civil Disobedience,"** the man "who is a *Man*, and, as my neighbor says, has a bone in his back which you cannot pass your hand through!" That this abstract man of principle had changed from the passive resister envisaged in 1849 into the violent and very real actionist of 1859 suggests that Thoreau had become aware of the futility of peaceful disobedience as much as he was oblivious of the dangers inherent in the idea of "action from principle."

Thoreau's conversion to violence as a legitimate means in the social conflict cannot be attributed to a purely rational thought process. The fervor of his eulogy betrays its emotional content. He identified himself with Brown so much that he experienced the latter's ordeal after the disastrous incident at Harpers Ferry as a personal tragedy. "I put a piece of paper and a pencil under my pillow," he wrote, "and when I could not sleep I wrote in the dark." Brown had the stuff heroes are made of. "No doubt," Thoreau postulated, "you can get more in your market for a quart of milk than for a quart of blood, but that is not the market that heroes carry their blood to." As if he felt a sense of personal guilt about his own irresponsibility in days gone by, Thoreau expressed his admiration for Brown because he "did not wait till he was personally interfered with or thwarted in some harmless business before he gave his life to the cause of the oppressed." And it is more than obvious that Thoreau rationalized the a-moral consequences of his new departure when he stated that people at most criticized Brown's tactics and then added: "Though you may not approve of his method or his principles, recognize his magnanimity."

Significantly, too, the eulogy in defense of John Brown was not characterized by so transitory a feeling as that which attended the experience of his own imprisonment. On being released from jail after having refused to pay the poll tax, he had joined a huckleberry party in the highest hills, where "the State was nowhere to be seen." Many weeks after his passionate plea, he noted in his ***Journals*** that it was hard for him to see the beauty of a remarkable sunset when his mind "was filled with Captain Brown. So great a wrong as his fate implied overshadowed all beauty in the world." Bronson Alcott reported in his ***Journals*** that Thoreau had called on him because he thought that "someone from the North should see Gov. Wise, or write concerning Capt. Brown's character and motives, to influence the Governor in his favor."

It has not been my intention to disparage Thoreau's reputation as the outstanding American spokesman for those human values which the empty materialism of our culture so readily relegates to the limbo of sanctimonious oratory. Criticism of his political theory cannot possibly deprive Thoreau's words of that immortality with which his moral sincerity, his spiritual courage and his sense of genuine inquiry have endowed it. His ideas are living ideas for the very reason that he lived them, day in and day out. The acidity of his attack and the persistence of his independence are admired and emulated by thousands who grope for a way to withstand the seemingly invincible force of personal and social maladjustments. As his friend and earliest biographer F. B. Sanborn has said, "The haughtiness of his independence kept him from a thousand temptations that beset men of less courage and self-denial" [see Additional Bibliography].

But I also believe that those who neglect and even deny the ambiguities and paradoxes of Thoreau's moral intransigence misunderstand the real challenge of his politics. They overlook the essential assumptions underlying his advice of civil disobedience. Hence, they are at a loss in explaining his repudiation of his own advice and his justification of violent resistance.

Thoreau's philosophy should warn us of the dilemma into which he fell and from which he could not escape because he returned time and again, to individual conscience as the "ultimate reality." His thought was full of ambiguity and paradox, and he did not realize sufficiently how contradictory and, in fact, dangerous the moral can be. Granted, he had no fear of consequences in disregarding the law. But, as Pascal observed, "he who would act the angel acts the brute." There is no virtue in accepting the consequences of an act because the premise from which they flow might be essentially good. Thoreau's politics suggests that it is a small step, indeed, from insistence on the principle of morality to insistence on the principle of expediency. (pp. 125-30)

Heinz Eulau, "Wayside Challenger: Some Remarks on the Politics of Henry David Thoreau," in Thoreau: A Collection of Critical Essays, *edited by Sherman Paul, Prentice-Hall, Inc., 1962, pp. 117-30.*

CHARLES H. NICHOLS, JR. (essay date 1952)

[*Nichols elucidates Thoreau's concept of the ideal government.*]

Seventy-three years after the Declaration of Independence was drawn up, a man appeared who embarrassed the government by testing its actions in the light of the principles of Thomas Jefferson. For Thoreau saw that politicians and their "expedient" legislation had usurped the democratic state. Elections, parties, constitutions and laws were still in existence, but the state had lost the essential ingredient of democracy: the moral law. Therefore, he refused that government any kind of cooperation, enunciating repeatedly his allegiance to a higher law. Here was a man whose sole aim was to discover a satisfying life. "I wished to live deliberately, to front only the essential facts of life and see if I could learn what it had to teach and not, when I came to die, discover that I had not lived. I did not wish to live what was not life, living was so dear." "A poet, a mystic, a transcendentalist," he recognized at the outset that the government itself was the chief obstacle to the good life in the 1840's and 1850's. Far from restraining the materialism, the bigotry, the injustice, the exploitation of the myopic middle class, the state had set itself to defend this debauched crowd of little men. Nor was that all. The slaveholder and the merchant were able to make the most effective demands upon the state; hence, it became expedient to maintain African slavery, to engage in a vicious Mexican War, to enact a Fugitive Slave Law. The majority of the men of both North and South, "do not send men to Congress on errands of humanity," Thoreau wrote in 1854, "but, while their brothers and sisters are being scourged and hung for loving liberty . . . it is the mismanagement of wood and iron and stone and gold which concerns them." In a nation where social arrangements rested on hypocrisy, where the economy was controlled for the profit of the unscrupulous entrepreneur, where politics was a matter of expediency, a new champion of human liberty appeared.

A transcendental naturalist convinced of the infinite promise of man, Thoreau saw in nature unadorned the key to a more equitable economy. A keen thinker in whom moral and spiritual values held priority, he sought an entirely new basis for society. "The millions are awake enough for physical labor, but only one in a million is awake enough for effective intellectual exertion, only one in a hundred million to a poetic or divine life." Hence, the only defensible reason for the existence of government was to "educate the wise man," as Emerson had pointed out. But the state was itself in need of education. To show that the infinite promise of man need not be destroyed by an immoral society, Thoreau proposed to reduce living to its simplest terms. Not only was his experiment on Walden Pond part of this process, but his entire life was devoted to the discovery of a more moral basis for human relations than exploitation in economics and expediency in politics. Thus, Thoreau faced the most fundamental problem of his time. He pioneered on a spiritual frontier ever seeking to bring the society into conformity with the fundamental moral law.

Thoreau's intellectual roots were in the eighteenth century. The "natural rights" doctrine of the Enlightenment, the right of revolution, the concept of man as a noble savage debauched by immoral institutions—all these ideas he inherited. But Thoreau transmuted these political ideas into a working philosophy, essentially transcendental, optimistic, yet clear-cut and practical. His faith in the divine nature of the individual and his determined allegiance to a higher moral law are the bases of his political views. Moreover, Thoreau had the moral courage to act in terms of these convictions in dealing with a state which had committed itself to the protection of slavery.

We must consider first, then, Thoreau's conception of law. For him, ours was a moral universe directed by a law which originated not in the will of any legislature, but in the eternal power of good in the universe. Such a law had an authority, a compelling force, which would brook no interference. It was to be seen in all nature, in man, in God.

> God Himself culminates in the present moment, and will never be more divine in the lapse of all the ages. And we are able to apprehend at all what is sublime and noble only by the perpetual instilling and drenching of the reality that surrounds us. The universe constantly and obediently answers to our conceptions. . . .

Nature, then, was in tune with the fundamental law. God Himself, though in one sense the source of this law, participated in it, for it partook of His own nature. And men were free in so far as this same law was operative in their hearts, minds and actions. Any man of spiritual or moral insight was expected to test men and measures by their conformity to the fundamental law. Moreover, a man into whom God had breathed the breath of life could have no traffic with the immoral arrangements of society simply because such "laws" were set up by a legislature elected by the majority and enforced by the police power of the state. Hence, "he who lives by the highest law is in one sense lawless," for "man is superior to all laws." Such a government as had passed the Fugitive Slave Act, for example, was in direct opposition to the fundamental moral law. It was founded on expediency, on political legerdemain.

"What is called politics is comparatively something so superficial and inhuman, that practically I have never fairly recognized that it concerns me at all." Voting consisted in the adoption of the available candidate (by which the politician usually meant the candidate available for the purposes of the demagogue). To vote thus for a man or measure with no consideration of what is morally right is to participate in a series of crimes against humanity. Thus, the fundamental law requires that justice be administered no matter what the cost. "If I have unjustly wrested a plank from a drowning man, I must restore it to him though I drown muself." But as we have shown above, the state was employed to carry out the infamous schemes of the slaveholder and the merchant. Its entire foundations were rotten, for it had substituted legerdemain for the higher law.

> What have divine legislators to do with the exportation or importation of tobacco? What humane ones with the breeding of slaves? . . . What ground is there for patriotism in such a state? How can an honest man support a commerce that whitens every sea in quest of nuts and raisins, and makes slaves of its sailors for this purpose!

Our whole society, therefore, had lost its divine perspective.

> When we want culture more than potatoes and illumination more than sugar plums, then the great resources of a world are taxed and drawn out, and the result is not slaves, nor operatives, but *men*—those rare fruits called heroes, saints, poets, philosophers, and redeemers.

The conscience of the individual man is of vital importance in Thoreau's discussion of politics. If the citizens of the country were men, they would not permit slavery and exploitation of their own fellow beings. If the divine essence which dwelt in their bosoms were awakened and made active, there would be no need for the state. Surely they would support only such a government as sought to establish and maintain justice. "To speak practically and as a citizen . . . I ask for not at once no government, but at once a better government. Let every man make known what kind of government would command his respect and that will be one step toward obtaining it." Yet the moral law requires more than this. "The universe expects every man to do his duty in his parallel of latitude." And "man is the artificer of his own happiness." Hence to say that he must wait for a majority vote or public opinion, or the press or the government or the law to enact justice is to destroy the individual's sense of responsibility. Justice cannot wait. When government ceases to serve the ends of justice it is the responsibility of an ethical man to sever his connection with it.

"Show me a free state, and a court truly of justice, and I will fight for them, if need be; but show me Massachusetts and I refuse her my allegiance, and express contempt for her courts." The individual must act according to the dictates of his conscience. "Let your life be a counter friction to stop the machine."

Thoreau's comments on majority rule are illuminating, for they point up the fact that the sole basis for an equitable society is the fundamental moral law. "Can there not be a government in which majorities do not virtually decide right and wrong but conscience? . . . Must the citizen ever for a moment resign his conscience to the legislator?" And again,

> Men generally under such a government as this think that they ought to wait until they have persuaded the majority to alter them. They think that if they should resist, the remedy would be worse than the evil. But it is the fault of the government itself that the remedy is worse than the evil. *It* makes it worse. Why is it not more apt to anticipate and provide for reform? Why does it not cherish its wise minority. . . . Why does it always crucify Christ and excommunicate Copernicus and Luther and pronounce Washington and Franklin rebels?

Freedom, too, was more than the right to vote.

> America is said to be the arena on which the battle of *freedom* is to be fought, but surely it cannot be freedom in a merely political sense that is meant. Even if we grant that the American had freed himself from a political tyrant, he is still the slave of an economical and moral tyrant. . . . What is it to be free from King George and continue slaves of King Prejudice? What is it to be born free and not to live free? What is the value of political freedom but as a means to moral freedom? . . . We are provincial because we do not find at home our standards, because we do not worship truth, but the reflection of truth; because we are warped and narrowed by an exclusive devotion to trade and commerce and manufacture and agriculture and the like, which are but means and not the end.

If political freedom is a mockery in a state dominated by those who serve Mammon, freedom of speech is equally impossible where a servile press and "available" politicians are the chief spokesmen to be heard in the land. "The press is almost without exception corrupt. I believe that in this country the press exerts a greater and a more pernicious influence than the church did in its worst period." That the press was bought by the servants of Mammon to protect their own material interests was obvious.

> Probably no country was ever ruled by so mean a class of tyrants as are the editors of the periodical press of this country. And as they rule only by their servility and appealing to the worst, and not the better nature of man, the people who read them are in the condition of the dog that returns to his vomit.

Furthermore, consider how thoroughly applicable the following remarks are today:

> . . . When Simms was carried off, did it (The Boston *Herald*) not act its part well—serve its master faithfully? How could it have gone lower on its belly? . . . When I have taken up this paper with my cuffs turned up, I have heard the gurgling of the sewer through every column. I have felt that I was handling a paper picked out of the public gutters. . . .

In a state where the majority were not men of principle, where the government was bought by Mammon, where the press, debauched, "harmonized with the gospel of the Merchant's Exchange," where a thousand evils ran riot with the consent and protection of government, an honest man might well feel that only desperate measures could establish justice. Thoreau himself determined to act according to the dictates of his own conscience. He helped fugitive slaves escape northward to Canada. He refused to pay a poll tax in support of an immoral government. He spoke out vigorously for John Brown and the whole anti-slavery cause. He determined to wash his hands of this half-witted state which was as "timid as a lone woman with her silver spoons." It "did not know its friends from its foes." But he was forced again and again to take positive action. For since the state had abdicated its proper moral responsibility, the individual man must take up the cause of justice. It is this feeling that explains Thoreau's tremendous admiration for John Brown. "If private men are obliged to perform the offices of government," said Thoreau in his plea for John Brown, "to protect the weak and dispense justice then the government becomes only a hired man, or clerk to perform menial or indifferent services."

Negro slavery was, to Thoreau, merely symptomatic of a general disease in the body politic. "What we want is not mainly to colonize Nebraska with free men, but to colonize Massachusetts with free men—to be free ourselves." The men of Massachusetts were, therefore, not men at all, for not only had they allowed the slaveholder to pass the infamous Fugitive Slave Act, but they were prepared to obey the law themselves! At the time that Anthony Burns was arrested in Massachuestts and returned to slavery, Thoreau wrote, "These days it is left to one Mr. Loring to say whether a citizen of Massachusetts is a slave or not. Does anyone think that Justice or God awaits Mr. Loring's decision? Such a man's existence is as impertinent as the gnat that settles on my paper." When, some years before, Simms was returned to slavery, Thoreau explained,

> I said to myself there is such an officer, if not such a man, as the Governor of Massachusetts—what has he been about the last fortnight? Has he had as much as he could do to keep on the fence in this moral earthquake? . . . He could at least have resigned himself into fame. . . . Yet no doubt he was endeavoring to fill the gubernatorial chair all the while. He was no Governor of mine. He did not govern me. . . . What I am concerned to know is that that man's influence and authority were on the side of the slaveholder, and not of the slave—of the guilty, and not of the innocent—of injustice, not of justice.

And again,

> . . . not a soldier is offered to save a citizen of Massachusetts from being kidnapped! Is this what all these soldiers, all this training has been for these seventy-nine years past? Have they been trained merely to rob Mexico and carry back fugitive slaves to their masters?

Thoreau goes on to comment further on the irony of the situation in which the authorities of Boston celebrated Independence Day a week after they had sent an innocent man into slavery. "As if those three million revolutionary heroes had not fought for the right to be free themselves, but to hold in slavery three million others. . . . And when the sound of bells died away their liberty died away also. For in transgressing a moral law we shall have to pay the penalty for it." Such a nation as this, Thoreau predicted, would become "the laughing-stock of the world." The moral effect of making a man a slave was worse than making him a sausage, he pointed out.

> If any of them will tell me that to make a man into a sausage would be . . . any worse than to make him into a slave—than it was to enact the Fugitive Slave Law, I will accuse him of foolishness, of intellectual incapacity, of making a distinction without a difference. The one is just as reasonable a proposition as the other.

Thoreau recognized, too, the economic bases of the acquiescence of Massachusetts in the matter of slavery. Again it was Mammon and not conscience that dictated the policies of the state.

> Practically speaking, the opponents to a reform in Massachusetts are not a hundred thousand politicians at the South, but a hundred thousand merchants and farmers here, who are more interested in commerce and agriculture than they are in humanity, and are not prepared to do justice to the slave and to Mexico *cost what it may*.

To sum up, then, ideally, Thoreau's transcendental law, if operative in society, would do away with the necessity of government. The state would expire upon the appearance of the wise man. But as Thoreau looked out upon the American political scene, he was not so ingenuous as to think that the really democratic society he sought would come into being automatically. The forces of Mammon were securely in the saddle. They had taken over the government as the agent of their selfish exploitation and were using its police power to perpetuate slavery in all its forms. If a man would be free he must undertake to enact justice in defiance of the state. For "in cases of highest importance it is of no consequence whether a man breaks a human law or not." It is those men of conscience who are willing to risk their necks for the Right who will, at last, fashion a state which can afford to be just to all men. (pp. 19-24)

Charles H. Nichols, Jr., "Thoreau on the Citizen and His Government," in PHYLON: The Atlanta University Review of Race and Culture, *Vol. XIII, No. 1, first quarter (March, 1952), pp. 19-24.*

WENDELL GLICK (essay date 1952)

[*Glick regards "Civil Disobedience" as a refutation of philosopher William Paley's rule of expediency as the key to good government.*]

Henry Thoreau's **"Resistance to Civil Government,"** first published in Elizabeth Peabody's *Aesthetic Papers* in 1849 and later re-titled **"Civil Disobedience,"** has become an almost indispensable manual for those objecting to the encroachments of the state upon the domain of private behavior. And quite justifiably so. The document centers around Thoreau's protest against his own imprisonment, and it constitutes, as has been so often noted, one of the finest assertions by an extreme individualist of the superiority of private prerogatives to the authority of the state. It is, however, much more than this. A more carefully reasoned repudiation of utilitarianism does not exist in the entire canon of Thoreau's works. Considered solely as a justification for revolt against constituted authority, **"Civil Disobedience"** is a rather loosely knit attack upon federal, state, and local governments; against the legislator, soldier, and constable who formulate and enforce the law; against the system of Negro slavery which was then supported by law; and against voting and the payment of taxes which imply support of the government and which involve the private citizen in the guilt of his rulers. But these are not Thoreau's sole concerns in the essay; beneath them, and welding **"Civil Disobedience"** into a unified whole, lies Thoreau's assumption of the limitations of relativism in both individual and collective action. "What can be said," Thoreau is asking, "of the increasingly insistent claims of the utilitarians in a world which is governed by inflexible moral absolutes?" "What are the limits," he is asking, "to the use of William Paley's rule of 'expediency' as the criterion for differentiating right from wrong?"

He is not sympathetic, he hastens to make clear in the opening sentences of his essay, with those anarchists and extremists, those "no-government men," who were seeking to sweep away completely all political institutions. Such men, Thoreau believed, failed to take into consideration the then imperfect development of man the individual; not until men should be "prepared for it" would a government "which governs not at all" be practical. That time had not yet come, although Thoreau at the age of thirty or so was optimistic over the prospects. Until it did come, governments would be necessary. But, Thoreau hastened to make clear, governments were but makeshift arrangements, established temporarily to preserve order until the development of the individual should make them no longer necessary, and they should always be considered in that light. "Government is at best but an expedient," he wrote, without permanence, without absolute authority: an institution to be discarded once the need for it no longer exists. It is "an expedient by which men would fain succeed in letting one another alone," he went on, organized specifically for the purpose of preventing immature men from injuring themselves. It can have no other function.

Yet there is an ever-present danger. Governments, though organized as temporary expedients, almost inevitably attempt to establish themselves as permanent institutions, and to perpetuate themselves transgress upon provinces completely beyond their rightful pale. They encroach upon the human conscience, that faculty within men which reveals to them the "higher law"; and they attempt to set aside its dictates in favor of the dictates of expediency. They insist upon the standard "whatever will preserve order in society is right," at the expense of inalienable individual prerogatives, in order to prolong their existence. Thoreau did not object to government *per se;* what aroused his wrath was the ubiquitous tendency which he saw everywhere about him to substitute the principle of social utility for the principle of absolute right. Expedients were well and good in their place, and government was one of them; they were necessary to societies composed of immature men who, leaning too heavily upon mundane institutions, failed to keep in close touch with the moral law, but they were insidious when they came to be interpreted as having a validity equal to or exceeding that of the principles of universal morality to which both individuals and states owed unquestioning allegiance. One of Thoreau's insistences in **"Civil Disobedience"** is that government be kept "in its place"; that its inferior authority be never mistaken for more than it is; in short, that the hard line of demarcation between ultimate moral standards and the subordinate standard of expediency be scrupulously observed. "It is not desirable to cultivate a respect for the law." Thoreau observed categorically, "so much as for the right." Though government by majority rule seemed to be the best expedient under the circumstances, the will of the majority was never to be accorded the authority of absolute, moral truth. It was never to replace the human conscience, the interpreter of the moral law. Yet the American government, in the interests of perpetuating itself and extending its power over its citizens, seemed to be perpetrating just such a substitution. "Can there not be a government," Thoreau inquired, "in which majorities decide only those questions to which the rule of expediency is applicable?" That was the only sort of government which had any *raison d'être* whatsoever. Though the American government had asked its citizens to resign their consciences to the legislators, to extend the authority of the relative principle of expediency into the realm of absolute morality, Thoreau refused to substitute a secondary ethic for his primary one. His conscience was his own, and he would permit no legislator to usurp it. "The only obligation which I have a right to assume," he wrote, "is to do at any time what I think right."

An inordinate respect for the law, that is to say, for expedients, inevitably resulted, Thoreau believed, in the degeneration of the moral fiber of the individual. The process of degeneration was already far advanced. Soldiers, as a "natural result of an undue respect for law" had surrendered their manhood and had so become "mere shadow[s] and reminiscence[s] of humanity"; public servants of all kinds, in pledging their allegiance to the inferior standard of expediency represented by the government, had restricted the "free exercise" of their "moral sense" and had so "put themselves on a level with wood and earth and stones.'' Being a good citizen was a far cry from being a good man. The good citizen—the legislator, politician, lawyer or minister—rarely made any moral distinctions, but followed the expedient course prescribed for him by law; a very few ''*men* serve[d] the State with their consciences also, and so necessarily resist[ed] it,'' and consequently were ''commonly treated by it as enemies.'' Thoreau's chief purpose in **''Civil Disobedience''** was to wean men away from their adherence to an insidious relativism and to persuade them to return again to the superior standard of absolute truth.

He had no illusions as to the difficulty of the task. Proponents of expediency as the only valid moral standard had on their side a moral philosopher whose doctrines in America, from 1800 to 1850, had become increasingly influential. And for good reason. William Paley, author of *Principles of Moral and Political Philosophy* (1785), *Evidences of Christianity* (1794), and *Natural Theology* (1802), champion of relativism in morals, had been studied by every student at Yale from 1791 until 1848, the date of Thoreau's composition of **''Civil Disobedience,''** by the students at Harvard and Princeton during the greater part of these years, and by the students at nearly all of the nation's smaller colleges as well. His vogue had become enormous; dozens of editions of his books had poured from American presses. Thoreau himself had studied Paley at Harvard in 1837, but he had been far from accepting the position which Paley set forth, and was even less inclined to accept it ten years later.

Paley, Thoreau pointed out, had equated expediency with the will of God; and since governments were temporary expedients, Paley had been able to argue that governments should be accorded the same obeisance which men paid to God, whenever those governments were so well established that they could not ''be resisted or changed without public inconveniency.'' Thus ''the justice of every particular case of resistance,'' Thoreau quoted from Paley, ''is reduced to a computation of the quantity of the danger and grievance on the one side, and of the probability and expense of redressing it on the other.'' No matter how destructive a government might be of individual rights, it was the will of God that men obey it in all things, unless they could change it without disturbing the normal routine of existence. In the interest of preserving order, men were supposed to forego the dictates of their consciences and allow strong governments which chose to do so to usurp the authority of the absolute moral law. With this sort of adaptation of morality to circumstance, Thoreau would have nothing to do. ''Paley appears,'' he charged,

> never to have contemplated those cases to which the rule of expediency does not apply, in which a people, as well as an individual, must do justice, come what it may. If I have unjustly wrested a plank from a drowning man, I must restore it to him though I drown myself. This, according to Paley, would be inconvenient. But he that would save his life, in such a case, shall lose it.

However convenient it might be for the American people to hold slaves, Thoreau continued, however expedient it might be, the practice was morally wrong; however expedient it might be to make war on Mexico, the Mexican war also was immoral, and should be stopped even though withdrawal from Mexico might cost the United States its existence as a nation. Expediency could not be argued as a justification of immoral actions, either by a state or by an individual, because, and in spite of all Paley had written, in the realm of morals the rule of expediency did not apply. And the realm of morals, for Thoreau, encompassed a very broad are indeed.

Yet nations and governments, almost without exception, agreed in their practice with Paley; and in condemning them for their error, Thoreau found it necessary to devote considerable space in **''Civil Disobedience''** to an analysis of current affairs. He upbraided the state of Massachusetts, for whose integrity he was ever deeply solicitous, accusing her of conformity to the inferior standard. The merchants and farmers of the state were not prepared to ''do justice to the slave and to Mexico,'' he charged, because the cost would be too great; because, in other words, freedom for the Negro would be economically inexpedient for them. All of them knew well enough that slavery was wrong, according to absolute standards, but they preferred to follow the teachings of Paley, to be ''good citizens'' rather than ''good men,'' to avoid the uproar and inconvenience which firm adherence to the laws of absolute morality would entail. ''They hesitate, and they regret, and sometimes they petition,'' Thoreau admonished sarcastically, ''but they do nothing in earnest and with effect.''

Or, Thoreau went on, they vote. But in voting, they do nothing more than leave the issue up to the will of the majority, which has no jurisdiction in moral matters. The obligation of a decision reached by majority vote ''never exceeds that of expediency''; by voting, they give a sop to their consciences but their real allegiance to the relativism of Paley, and in actuality accomplish nothing ''*for the right.*'' ''Under the name of Order and Civil Government,'' they find themselves eventually supporting any ''meanness'' which the majority may vote acceptable. But order in society, Thoreau insisted, could be purchased at too dear a price. Even social instability, undesirable as it is, is preferable to injustice. Action from expediency may preserve the order of society, but ''action from principle,—the perception and the performance of right . . . is essentially revolutionary, and does not consist wholly with any thing which was.'' When the choice lies between the order purchased with expediency, and the disorder which often attends the firm adherence to absolute moral principle, any man worthy of the name would have no hesitancy as to which he should choose.

What specific course should the true *man* take, Thoreau asked, when government becomes an *active* opponent of absolute right and justice—when, in other words, it attempts to *compel* men to elevate the rule of expediency over the principles of right action? Then, Thoreau emphasized, first things must be put first. When injustice becomes ''part of the necessary friction of the machine of government, let it go. . . . If [government] requires you to be the agent of injustice to another, then, I say, break the law.'' When the state transgresses her limited province and intrudes upon the realm of personal morality, the wise man will not attempt, by voting, to repel the usurper, but will cast his whole vote, his ''whole influence,'' trusting in the superior strength of moral truth. He will repudiate the state's presumption to prescribe for individual morality by turning his back upon her and by asserting the primacy of his own conscience. The state had asked Thoreau to pay a tax which was to be used to purchase muskets for prosecuting the unjust war with Mexico, and to pay slave-catchers engaged in returning men to slavery. The state, in other words, had attempted to force him to be a party to immoral actions. When he had refused, it had not confronted his ''sense, intellectual or moral''; it had not reasoned with him in the interest of determining what was right by absolute moral standards; it had simply attempted to compel him to follow an expedient course by confronting him with physical force. But he had been certain of the rectitude of his stand, and he was convinced that a man who was in the right could not be forced. Inherent in the world of absolutes was a power against which the state, whose allegiance was to a temporizing expediency, could not prevail. A man's conscience, if he wished it to be so, was impregnable. "Let us see who is the strongest [sic]," he challenged. "What force has a multitude? They only can force me who obey a higher law than I." And the law of expediency was assuredly not such a law.

Lest his act of civil disobedience be misunderstood—lest it should be assumed by his neighbors that his refusal to pay his taxes had been a deed of sheer perversity rather than a deliberate, thoughtful refusal to bow to an inferior moral standard—Thoreau returned, at the conclusion of **"Civil Disobedience,"** to a reiteration of his earlier statement that he was no anarchist who possessed an irrational hate for government, but a man who, instead, subscribed to another and a superior standard. He was not spoiling for a fight; he did not wish to "split hairs"; he often detected in himself, rather, a disturbing propensity for seeking "an excuse for conforming to the laws of the land." Governments, considered simply as expedients for making decisions on questions outside the pale of morality, were necessary without question. So long as they kept within their proper province he was more than willing to respect them and honor the documents which defined their authority. "Seen from a lower point of view"—that is to say, considered as expedients rather than as arbiters in morals—"the Constitution, with all its faults, is very good; the law and the courts are very respectable; even this State and this American government are, in many respects, very admirable, and rare things." But measured against the perfection of the moral law, they were not worth thinking of at all, and when they exceeded their province and invaded the realm of morality, they invited the opposition of every honest man.

Most men, Thoreau admitted, differed with him on this issue. Statesmen and legislators would naturally disagree with him, but they were men who stood "so completely within the institution" of government that they were unable to examine it objectively. To most Americans, Daniel Webster represented the ultimate in sagacity and perspicuity, but to Thoreau, Webster was just another disciple of Paley whose ultimate allegiance was to expediency rather than to the truth, and who, like all other statesmen, was "wont to forget that the world is not governed by policy and expediency" but by the "higher law." Webster's forte was "not wisdom, but prudence," the highest virtue of the utilitarians. He determined the morality of an action by assessing its consequences, doing all that he could to maintain the status quo. To solve the moral problem of slavery he turned, not to the tribunal of absolute truth and justice, but to the Constitution, and refused to permit any issue, moral or otherwise, "to disturb the arrangement as originally made" by the founding fathers.

In allowing himself to be governed by expediency, Webster was following a wiser course, Thoreau granted, than were "politicians in general" whose decisions were based upon caprice or upon selfish interest. Though Webster's "truth [was] not Truth," it was "consistency or a consistent expediency." Despite his superiority to most statesmen, however, Webster could not be considered a fit judge of moral issues.

> They who know of no purer sources of truth, who have traced up its stream no higher, stand, and wisely stand, by the Bible and the Constitution, and drink at it there with reverence and humility; but they who behold where it comes trickling into this lake or that pool, gird up their loins once more, and continue their pilgrimage toward its fountain-head.

No man could be a genius for legislation until he had made that pilgrimage.

As a man of thirty, Thoreau could look forward to the day when governments, as well as men, would put justice above expediency, absolute right above the Constitution. The dictates of the individual conscience would then be accepted as having a validity superior to legislation, and governments themselves would admit as much. The time would then be near when governments could be dispensed with. "There will never be a really free and enlightened State," Thoreau concluded, "until the State comes to recognize the individual as a higher and independent power"; and he pleased himself with "imagining a State" which could at last "afford to be just to all men." Such a state would recognize expediency for what it was. But such a "perfect and glorious" state he could only imagine, however, for it was "not yet anywhere [to be] seen." (pp. 35-42)

Wendell Glick, "'Civil Disobedience': Thoreau's Attack upon Relativism," in Western Humanities Review, *Vol. VII, No. 1, Winter, 1952-53, pp. 35-42.*

FRANCIS B. DEDMOND (essay date 1955)

[In the following essay, Dedmond examines Thoreau's political philosophy, concluding that his insistence on the primacy of individual rights constitutes a recommendation of anarchy.]

Thoreau was not naturally political-minded, and he would have concerned himself very little with politics, politicians, and all the accouterments of government, indeed with government itself, if government had not threatened to trample underfoot the individual and if his conscience had not been an unrelenting taskmaster driving him to the defense of the individual. Thoreau agreed with Coleridge that life itself is "the principle of Individuation." Thus even the nations of the earth are inconsequential in comparison with individuals; the parts are infinitely more valuable than the whole. "Nations! What are nations? Tartars and Huns! and Chinamen! Like insects they swarm. The historian strives in vain to make them memorable. . . . It is individuals that populate the world." Being convinced of this, Thoreau argued in his ***Journal*** and in **"Civil Disobedience"** that the rights of the individual were the primary concern of the state, that mankind would never realize a free and "enlightened" state until the individual came to be recognized as a power higher than and independent from the state, and that the real power and the real authority of the state were derived from a true regard for the individual. Hence, "the effect of a good government is to make life more valuable,—of a bad government to make it less valuable." Thoreau's concept of government, therefore, to borrow a phrase from V. L. Parrington, is none other "than transcendental individualism translated into politics, with all comfortable compromises swept away" [see excerpt dated 1927 in *NCLC*, Vol. 7].

Thoreau's transcendental individualism demanded of him that he champion the rights of the individual—his rights to freedom and independence. Yet just the close attachment of an individual to the state would rob him of some of his freedom and independence. It was thus with a Canadian, Thoreau has discovered.

> It is evident that a private man is not worth so much in Canada as in the United States, and if that is the bulk of man's property, *i.e.*, the being private, and peculiar, he had better stay here. An Englishman, methinks, not to speak of other nations, habitually regards himself merely as a constituent part of the English nation; he holds a recognized place as such; he is a member of the royal regiment of Englishmen. And he is proud of his nation. But an American cares very little about such, and greater freedom and independence are possible to him. He is nearer to the primitive condition of man. Government lets him alone and he lets government alone.

Thoreau wished that government, if government there must be, would function so that a man need not be conscious of its operation. As he explained, "it appears to me that those things which most engage the attention of men, as politics, for instance, are vital functions of human society, it is true, but should [be] unconsciously performed like the vital functions of the natural body." Thoreau wished to be "healthily neglected" by the government that he might nourish and cherish his individualism. "That certainly is the best government where the inhabitants are least often reminded of the government," he noted in his ***Journal.***

Thoreau was not willing to recognize any government *per se*. He felt no compulsion to do so. "The only government that I recognize is that power that established justice in the land, never that which establishes injustice," he wrote. The strength of any government lay in its adherence to and insistence upon the principle of justice for all men. As with an individual so with a nation—neither "can ever deliberately commit the least act of injustice without having to pay the penalty for it. A government which deliberately enacts injustice, and persists in it!—it will become the laughing-stock of the world." Thoreau was no respecter of persons; the worth of the individual, of the poor and the weak as well as of the wealthy and powerful, demanded that equal justice be meted out to all men indiscriminately.

Since the *raison d'être* for government was to be found in its protection of the inalienable rights of the individual to freedom and independence and since the duty of the government toward the individual was that of insuring equal justice to all, Thoreau naturally sought that which would assure these blessings to mankind. He was, however, aware of the ineffectiveness of political action to bring about lasting good. "Politics is, as it were, the gizzard of society, full of grit and gravel, and the two political parties are its two opposite halves, which grind on each other." Thoreau's distrust of politics came early. By 1841 he had already become convinced that "the merely political aspect of the land is never very cheering. Men are degraded when considered as the members of a political organization. As a nation the people never utter one great and healthy word." Events of the succeeding years only confirmed his early opinions, and his distrust of political activities ripened to disgust as the years went by.

Arbitrary codes of law likewise offered no bulwark for man's freedom and independence nor guarantee that justice would be done. Indeed, Thoreau saw an affinity between the necessity for law and the necessity for war, "for both equally rest on force as their basis, and war is only the resource of law, either on a smaller or larger scale,—its authority asserted. . . . Men make an arbitrary code, and, because it is not right, they try to make it prevail by might. . . . It is inconsistent to decry war and maintain law, for if there were no need of war there would be no need of law." Thoreau asked, "What does the law protect? My rights? or any rights? My right, or the right? If I avail myself of it, it may help my sin; it cannot help my virtue." Nothing that found its strength in force provided what Thoreau sought. Reliance upon law, therefore, was not the answer.

Like Kant, Thoreau discovered a sure basis for government, as well as human conduct, in the moral law. Try as man would, he could never bring about any good by obeying a law which he had discovered, nor would political policy ever be effective since it was generated by expediency and was not an attempt to secure moral right. Thoreau agreed with Sir Walter Raleigh that the strength and prosperity of a commonwealth depended upon the moral condition of its constituents. Thoreau copied into his ***Literary Note-Book*** the following quotation from Raleigh's *Discourse of War:*

> And when we say we are fallen into bad times, we mean no otherwise but that we are fallen amongst a wicked generation of men. For the sun, the mediate vivifying cause of all things here below, and constant measure of time, keeps its steady course. The condition of the public grows worse, as men grow more wicked; for in all ages, as the morals of men were depraved, the vice increased, the commonwealth declined.

Thoreau looked at his own generation, and he saw men, as well as a government, that had long since forgotten the moral law. The commonwealth had not only declined but was on the toboggan, racing headlong into the Civil War. The moral law could be violated; but, Thoreau warned, "it was never infringed with impunity."

The moral law should be the criterion by which all law should be measured. It is the fundamental law; yet the most zealous of the Abolitionists and reformers were decrying, for example, the unjust slave laws because they were *unconstitutional,* not because they were a direct violation of the *moral law*. Thoreau asked, "Pray, is virtue constitutional, or vice? Is equity constitutional, or iniquity? It is as impertinent in moral and vital questions . . . to ask whether a law is constitutional or not, as to ask whether it is profitable or not." Thoreau had little reverence for the Constitution of Jefferson or Adams; but there was a Constitution—that eternal and only just Constitution which was inscribed in the inner being of man by the Creator—for which Thoreau had a profound reverence. Obedience to this Constitution alone would make operative the moral law, insure the freedom and independence of man, and establish justice. The moral law did not rely on force; its strength lay in its being part of the universal scheme of things.

Thoreau, likewise, gave much thought to the relation of the citizen to the government. The Fugitive Slave Act, perhaps, as no other one thing caused him to stop short and to look at himself in relation to the government. The Act reminded him that he was a member of the *posse comitatus* and ordered him and "all good citizens . . . to aid and assist in the prompt and efficient execution of this law, wherever their services may be required." Thoreau's reaction was violent; his whole nature revolted. Was he to become a mere tool in the hands of a government which flouted the moral law and violated the dignity of the individual? He did not have to wrestle long with this problem. As a young man he had been convinced "that conscience was not given us to no purpose, or for a hindrance." Coupled with reason, conscience provided the guide for human conduct; and as time went on, Thoreau became more and more determined not to surrender "his inalienable rights of reason and conscience"—no, not even to the government! The government must respect a man's conscience as a law transcending its statutes. A man's duty of obedience is first to the laws of his own nature and to the government only as the laws of that government are compatible with and in harmony with the laws of his nature; and, Thoreau confided to his ***Journal,*** "it is not for a man to *put himself* in such an attitude [violating the laws of his own nature], but to *maintain* himself in whatever attitude he finds himself through obedience to the laws of his being, which will never be one of opposition to a just government."

Thoreau, however, found himself a citizen of a country whose government his reason and conscience had judged and found unjust. The government had cast its strength on the side of injustice and had become nothing more than a tyrannical force—a brute force.

> We talk about a *representative* government, but what a monster of a government is that where the noblest faculties of the mind and the *whole* heart are not represented. A semihuman tiger or ox stalking over the earth, with its heart taken out and the top of its brain shot away.

Thoreau asserted the right of the individual to resist the civil authority of such a government. Treason? Men call it treason, but in his view "resistance to *tyranny* here below" inhered in the "constitution" of man himself; and unless one were willing to do violence to his own nature, no other course was offered to a man of principle but to resist. Thoreau found himself confronted with somewhat the same situation that Locke had anticipated a century and a half before, a situation in which

> the precedent and consequences seem to threaten all; and they are persuaded in their consciences, that their laws, and with them their estates, liberties, and lives are in danger . . . : how they will be hindered from resisting illegal force, used against them, I cannot tell.

But Thoreau did not counsel the use of force as Locke did. He rather wished to cast the weight of human personality and the force of men of principle against the iniquity of government, to resist passively its encroachments and abuses of power.

Much of the strength of a tyrannical government was to be found in the veneration which men attached to the various documents and concepts of that government. Thoreau, however, was little concerned with the "agreement" which his forefathers had entered into seventy years before. If the Constitution—aye, if democracy itself —had failed to safeguard man's inalienable rights and establish justice, as Thoreau was sure they had, he saw no reason why men should cling to them.

> The way in which men cling to old institutions after the life had departed out of them, and out of themselves, reminds me of those monkeys which cling by their tails,—aye, whose tails contract around the limb, even dead limbs, . . . They have not an apprehensive intellect, but merely, as it were, a prehensile tail.

It was thus that Thoreau found many of his neighbors—unconcerned about any change in government. "The weak-brained and pusillanimous farmers," he complained, "would fain abide by the institutions of their fathers. Their argument is they have not long to live, and for that little space let them not be disturbed in their slumbers." This type of reasoning did not satisfy Thoreau. "It is time we had done referring to our ancestors," he exclaimed. "We have used up all our inherited freedom, like the young bird the albumen in the egg. It is not an era of repose." Like Locke, he saw no necessity for an irrevocable form of government or one which could not undergo change and revision; and, like Locke, he insisted that the government "is morally responsible—that is, it is limited to the public good, and it is morally revocable."

There inevitably developed in Thoreau an antagonism for all authoritarianism; and in view of this antagonism, "it was inevitable," as Charles Madison had pointed out, "for Thoreau to gravitate toward the principle of philosophical anarchism" [see excerpt dated 1944]. V. L. Parrington finds the source of philosophical anarchism in "eighteenth-century liberalism with its doctrine of the minimized state—a state that must lose its coercive sovereignty in the measure that the laws of society function freely." But Thoreau's philosophical anarchism found its immediate source in his Transcendental individualism. "Thoreau began as an individual . . . [and] It was always to a defiant individualism that he returned for strength." Only the individual could stand on a sure foundation. "You can pass your hand under the largest mob, a nation in revolution even . . . ," Thoreau noted in his ***Journal.*** "But an individual standing on truth you cannot pass your hand under, for his foundations reach to the centre of the universe."

Inextricably bound up with Thoreau's philosophical anarchism, his transcendental individualism, and transcendentalism itself were the concepts of self-culture and the perfectibility of man. Without his deep faith in the individual's potentialities to develop to the point where civil government would become unnecessary, Thoreau would have had no basis on which his philosophical anarchism could rest. The "sloth and vice of man" could give way to "the purity and courage which springs from its midst," he was convinced. One of the cardinal tenets of transcendentalism was to be found in a "popular faith in the capacities of men to make states, [and] laws . . . for themselves." As a philosophy, it laid "its foundations in human nature, and placed stress on the organic capacities and endowments of the mind. . . ." "Practically it was an assertion of the inalienable worth of man." Thoreau, as a disciple of Kant, looked upon man as "a creative, re-creative force," a being who had within him latent capacities with which he could shape circumstances. However, to realize his dreams, man must, Thoreau knew, bring his will and reason into play. In a ***Journal*** entry entitled "Self-Culture," he asked:

> Who knows how incessant a surveillance a strong man may maintain over himself,—how far subject passion and appetite to reason, and lead the life his imagination paints? Well has the poet said,—
>
> 'By manly mind
> Not e'en in sleep is will resigned.'
>
> By a strong effort may he not command even his brute body in unconscious moments?

The Transcendentalists made much of the idea of "*self-culture,* the perfect unfolding of our individual nature." This perfect unfolding meant "the culture of that nobler self which includes heart, and conscience . . . , not as incidental ingredients, but as essential qualities." But Thoreau knew, as did the other Transcendentalists, that self-culture was not readily accessible or easily acquired; and with them he could insist that "of self-culture, as of all other things worth seeking, the price is a single devotion to that object,—a devotion which shall exclude all aims and ends, that do not directly or indirectly tend to promote it. . . . The only motive to engage in this work is in its inherent worth, and the sure satisfaction which accompanies the consciousness of progress, in the true direction toward the stature of a perfect man." Thoreau, we may be sure, also agreed with Emerson that "the power which is at once spring and regulator in all the efforts of reform is the conviction that there is an infinite worthiness in man, which will appear at the call of worth, and that all particular reforms are the removing of some impediment."

Once he arrived at this position, Thoreau was ready then to go one step farther and to declare, as he did in **"Civil Disobedience,"** that, when man had realized his potentialities, he no longer needed the "impediment" of government. Carried to its logical conclusion, his philosophy and concept of government demanded this position, and Thoreau dared assume it and assert it. To him, "even the best existing governments, not withstanding their apparent advantages," were no more than the ". . . abortive rudiments of nobler institutions such as distinguished man in his savage and half-civilized state." In the case of the self-cultured individual, the allegiance that he had accorded the institution of government was no longer binding upon him; he gave allegiance to a higher authority. Thus Thoreau, as V. L. Parrington has observed, "asserted the doctrine of individual compact." The individual's enlightened sense of honor and justice would prevent individualism from becoming license. Thoreau copied in his ***Literary Note-Book*** a quotation from Raleigh's *Discourse of War,* which we may take, I believe, as indicative of his attitude in regard to the moral and ethical superiority of individuals over governments, even over democracies.

> But no senate nor civil assembly can be under such natural impulses to honor and justice as single persons—. For a majority is no body when that majority is separated, and a collective body can have no synteresis, . . . which is in the mind of every man, never assenting to evil, but upbraiding and tormenting him when he does it: but the honor and conscience that lies in the majority is too thin and diffusive to be efficacious; for a number can do a great wrong, and call it right, and not one of that majority blush for it.

The idea of brotherhood, brotherhood of individuals, characterized the ideal society in which honor and conscience abounded.

Thoreau wished to live above law, above government, above restraint. He wished to be circumscribed only by the dictates of his conscience. He wished perfect freedom for himself and every man. He noted in his ***Journal*** in almost poetic language that

> he who lives according to the highest law is in one sense lawless. . . . Live free, child of the mist! He for whom the law is made, who does not obey the law but whom the law obeys, reclines on pillows of down and is wafted at will whither he pleases, for man is superior to all laws, . . . when he takes his liberty.

Thoreau was a philosophical anarchist, an advocate of no-government. He found the safeguard for his freedom and independence and that which would insure justice for all in trandscendental individualism, where reason and conscience meet in harmony and where the individual lives in harmony with his fellowmen on a plane which transcends all man-made laws and governments. (pp. 36-46)

Francis B. Dedmond, "Thoreau and the Ethical Concept of Government," in The Personalist, *Vol. XXXVI, No. 1, Winter, 1955, pp. 36-46.*

ROBERT B. DOWNS (essay date 1956)

[In the following discussion of "Civil Disobedience," Downs contends that Thoreau recommended not anarchy but a government whose laws accurately reflect the moral conscience of the people. Downs also examines Mohandas K. Gandhi's implementation of Thoreau's political philosophy.]

The name of Henry David Thoreau conjures up in the imagination a keen observer of nature, a lover of solitude and the outdoors, an exponent of the simple life, a poet and mystic, a master of English prose style.

Much less frequently is Thoreau remembered as the author of some of the most extreme radical manifestoes in American history, a spokesman, as described by one of his biographers, for "the most outspoken doctrines of resistance ever penned on this continent." Going far beyond Thomas Jefferson's "That government is best which governs least," Thoreau concluded that "That government is best which governs not at all."

These words introduce Thoreau's celebrated essay **"Civil Disobedience,"** which first appeared in an obscure, short-lived periodical—Elizabeth Peabody's *Aesthetic Papers*—in May 1849. Originally called **"Resistance to Civil Government,"** the title was later changed to **"On the Duty of Civil Disobedience,"** or merely **"Civil Disobedience."** When first published, the work attracted slight attention and few readers. During the next hundred years, it was read by thousands and affected the lives of millions.

Was Thoreau a philosophical anarchist in his beliefs? An analysis of **"Civil Disobedience,"** its setting and background, may provide an answer to that complex question. (p. 65)

Thoreau had no ambition to accumulate wealth, or to perform any work other than enough to provide him the minimum essentials for living. His consuming passion, always, was to achieve leisure time for the fundamentally important matters, as he saw them, of rambling in the Concord fields, studying nature at first hand, meditating, reading, writing—to do the things he wanted to do. His simple needs could be met without engaging in a life of drudgery, such as he observed his neighbors leading. Instead of the Biblical formula of six days of work and one day of rest, Thoreau preferred to reverse the ratios—devoting only the seventh day to labor. In short, everything he stood for was the antithesis of the teachings of Adam Smith, the maxims of Franklin's Poor Richard, and the traditional American ideals of hard work and quick riches.

To exemplify his conception of the simple life, shed of all superfluities, Thoreau spent two years at Walden Pond near Concord. There he built a hut, planted beans and potatoes, ate the plainest food (mainly rice, corn meal, potatoes, and molasses), and lived alone, withdrawn from society. It was a time of concentrated thinking and writing, out of which grew one of the greatest books in American literature: ***Walden, or Life in the Woods.***

Ostensibly, ***Walden*** is a record of Thoreau's life in his rural retreat, and is full of memorable descriptions of the seasons, the scenery, and the animal life about him. But ***Walden*** is far more than the observations of a naturalist, as Izaak Walton's *Compleat Angler* is more than a manual on fishing. Its comments on the superficialities and limitations of society and government have universal significance. Over the years, the social criticism has drawn as many readers as the portions dealing with natural history. In its way, ***Walden*** is as radical a document as the earlier published **"Civil Disobedience,"** to which it bears a close kinship.

While visiting in Concord in 1843, soon after he began his sojourn at Walden Pond, Thoreau was arrested and jailed for nonpayment of poll tax. In his refusal to pay the tax, he was following the example of Bronson Alcott, father of the "Little Women," who had been arrested two years earlier for the same offense. Both were using this means to protest against the state's support of slavery. Thoreau was imprisoned for only one night, for an aunt, contrary to his wishes, stepped in and paid the tax.

Not until several years later did Thoreau tell the story, in **"Civil Disobedience,"** of his brush with the law over the poll tax violation. Originally written as a lecture in 1848, the printed version came off the press the following year. The Mexican War of 1846-47 had but recently been concluded and slavery was a burning issue. The Fugitive Slave Law, which was to arouse Thoreau's special indignation, was soon to be enacted. These matters, plus his poll tax battle, were the inspiration for **"Civil Disobedience."**

Any war was repugnant to Thoreau's ideals, but the Mexican War particularly so, for its only purpose, he believed, was to extend the hated institution of Negro slavery into new territory. Why, he asked, should he be required to provide financial support for a government guilty of such injustices and stupidity? Here was the birth of his doctrine of civil disobedience. Anything except a politician at heart, Thoreau decided the time had come to examine the nature of the state and its government. What should be the relation of the individual to the state, and of the state to the individual? From a consideration of these questions emerged Thoreau's philosophy of personal integrity and of man's place in society.

"Government," wrote Thoreau, "is at best but an expedient; but most governments are sometimes inexpedient. The objections that have been brought against a standing army, and they are many and weighty, and deserve to prevail, may also at last be brought against a standing government."

Thoreau acknowledged that the American government was a relatively excellent one.

> Yet, this government never of itself furthered any enterprise, but by the alacrity with which it got out of its way. *It* does not keep the country free. *It* does not settle the West. *It* does not educate. The character inherent in the American people has done all that has been accomplished; and it would have done somewhat more, if the government had not sometimes got in its way. For government is an expedient by which men would fain succeed in letting one another alone; and, as has been said, when it is most expedient the governed are most let alone by it.

Almost immediately after presenting the case for no government, Thoreau recognized that man had not yet reached a state of perfectibility where a complete lack of government was feasible, and began to modify his stand.

> To speak practically and as a citizen, unlike those who call themselves no-government men, I ask for, not at once no government, but *at once* a better government. Let every man make known what kind of government would command his respect, and that will be one step toward obtaining it.

The rights of minorities and the fallacies of majority rule were emphatically stated by Thoreau. A majority rules, he argued, "not because they are most likely to be in the right, nor because this seems fairest to the minority, but because they are physically the strongest. But a government in which the majority rule in all cases cannot be based on justice, even as far as men understand it." Never, he believed, should the citizen "resign his conscience to the legislator. . . . We should be men first and subjects afterward. It is not desirable to cultivate a respect for the law, so much as for the right."

Politicians, as a class, Thoreau held in low esteem. "Most legislators, politicians, lawyers, ministers, and office holders," he remarked, "serve the state chiefly with their heads; and as they rarely make any moral distinctions, they are as likely to serve the Devil, without *intending* it, as God. A very few, as heroes, patriots, martyrs, reformers in the great sense, and *men,* serve the state with their consciences also, and so necessarily resist it for the most part; and they are commonly treated as enemies by it."

Thoreau then proceeded to attack the American government of his day. "I cannot for an instant," he declared, "recognize that political organization as *my* government which is the *slave's* government also." It was the duty of citizens to resist evil in the state even to the point of open and deliberate disobedience to its laws.

> When a sixth of the population of a nation which has undertaken to be the refuge of liberty are slaves . . . I think it is not too soon for honest men to rebel and revolutionize. . . . This people must cease to hold slaves and to make war on Mexico, though it cost them their existence as a people.

Likewise deplored by Thoreau was the citizen who felt that he had done his full duty merely by casting a ballot.

> All voting is a sort of gaming, like checkers or backgammon, with a slight moral tinge to it, a playing with right and wrong, with moral questions, and betting naturally accompanies it. The character of the voters is not staked. . . . Even voting *for the right* is *doing* nothing for it. It is only expressing to men feebly your desire that it should prevail. . . . There is but little virtue in the actions of masses of men.

The proper attitude of the citizen toward unjust laws was debated by Thoreau. Was it better to wait for majority action to change the laws, or to refuse at once to obey the laws? Thoreau's unequivocal answer was, that if the government "requires you to be the agent of injustice to another, then, I say, break the law. . . . What I have to do is to see, at any rate, that I do not lend myself to the wrong which I condemn."

It is of the very nature of government, Thoreau suggested, to oppose changes and reforms, and to mistreat its critics. "Why," he asked, "does it always crucify Christ, and excommunicate Copernicus and Luther, and pronounce Washington and Franklin rebels?"

Those who opposed slavery, Thoreau urged, "should at once effectually withdraw their support, both in person and property, from the government of Massachusetts, and not wait until they constitute a majority of one, before they suffer the right to prevail through them. I think that it is enough if they have God on their side, without waiting for that other one. Moreover, any man more right than his neighbors constitutes a majority of one already."

As a symbol of civil disobedience, a method open to every citizen, Thoreau advocated refusal to pay taxes. If a thousand or even fewer men would express their disapproval of the government in that fashion, Thoreau thought, reform would inevitably follow. Even if resistance to authority meant punishment, "Under a government which imprisons any unjustly, the true place for a just man is also a prison. . . . If the alternative is to keep all just men in prison, or give up war and slavery, the state will not hesitate which to choose." By paying taxes to an unjust government, the citizen condones wrongs committed by the state.

Thoreau saw, however, that the propertied class had too much at stake to rebel, for "the rich man—not to make any invidious comparisons—is always sold to the institution which makes him rich. Absolutely speaking, the more money, the less virtue, for money comes between a man and his objects, and obtains them for him." Not suffering the handicap of wealth, Thoreau could afford to resist. "It costs me less in every sense to incur the penalty of disobedience to the State than it would to obey. I should feel as if I were worth less in that case."

Thoreau was realistic also in seeing the weight of economic objections which held the state of Massachusetts from taking action against slavery.

> Practically speaking, the opponents to a reform in Massachusetts are not a hundred thousand politicians at the South, but a hundred thousand merchants and farmers here who are more interested in commerce and agriculture than they are in humanity, and are not prepared to do justice to slave and to Mexico, *cost what it may*.

For six years, adhering to his principles, Thoreau reported that he paid no poll tax. His short prison term left him unshaken in his convictions, but with less regard for the state.

> I saw that the State was half-witted, that it was timid as a lone woman with her silver spoons, and that it did not know its friends from its foes, and I lost all my remaining respect for it, and pitied it. Thus the State never intentionally confronts a man's sense, intellctual or moral, but only his body, his senses. It is not armed with superior wit or honesty, but with superior physical strength. I was not born to be forced. I will breathe after my own fashion.

Thoreau differentiated between taxes.He states that he "never declined paying the highway tax," nor the school tax, "beacuse I am as desirous of being a good neighbor as I am of being a bad subject." Where he drew the line was in paying general taxes to support slavery and war. "I simply wish to refuse allegiance to the State, to withdraw and stand aloof from it effectually," in these matters.

There was no desire, either, on Thoreau's part to pose as a martyr or saint.

> I do not wish to quarrel with any man or nation. I do not wish to split hairs, to make fine distinctions, or set myself up as better than my neighbors. I seek rather, I may say, even an excuse for conforming to the laws of the land. I am but too ready to conform to them. Indeed, I have reason to suspect myself on this head; and each year as the tax-gathering comes round, I find myself disposed to review the acts and position of the general and State governments, and the spirit of the people, to discover a pretext for conformity.

Furthermore, Thoreau again admitted that, though they fell far below his ideals, "The Constitution, with all its faults is very good; the law and the courts are very respectable; even this State and this American government are, in many respects, very admirable, and rare things, to be thankful for."

Despite his strictures on majority rule, too, Thoreau had some faith in popular judgment. In his view, legislators lacked ability to deal effectively with the "comparatively humble questions of taxation and finance, commerce and manufactures and agriculture. If we were left solely to the wordy wit of legislators in Congress for our guidance, uncorrected by the seasonable experience and the effectual complaints of the people, America would not long retain her rank among the nations."

Thoreau concludes **"Civil Disobedience"** with a statement of his concept of perfect government, and a resounding reaffirmation of his belief in the dignity and worth of the individual.

> To be strictly just, the authority of government . . . must have the sanction and consent of the governed. It can have no pure right over my person and property but what I concede to it. The progress from an absolute to a limited monarchy, from a limited monarchy to a democracy, is a progress toward a true respect for the individual. . . . Is a democracy, such as we know it, the last improvement possible in government? Is it not possible to take a step further towards recognizing and organizing the rights of man? There will never be a really free and enlightened State until the State comes to recognize the individual as a higher and independent power, from which all its own power and authority are derived, and treats him accordingly. I please myself with imagining a State at last which can afford to be just to all men, and to treat the individual with respect as a neighbor; which even would not think it inconsistent with its own repose if a few were to live aloof from it, not meddling with it, nor embraced by it, who fulfilled all the duties of neighbors and fellow-men. A State which bore this kind of fruit, and suffered it to drop off as fast as it ripened, would prepare the way for a still more perfect and glorious State, which also I have imagined, but not yet anywhere seen.

In essence, Thoreau's basic contention in **"Civil Disobedience"** was that the state exists for individuals, not individuals for the state. A minority should refuse to yield to a majority if moral principles must be compromised in order to do so. Further, the state has no right to offend moral liberty by forcing the citizen to support injustices. Man's conscience should always be his supreme guiding spirit.

The impact of **"Civil Disobedience"** on Thoreau's own time was negligible. References to the work in the writings of his contemporaries are almost nonexistent. With the Civil War little more than a decade ahead, it might be assumed that the essay would have struck a popular chord. Apparently it was buried under an avalanche of Abolitionist literature, and remained obscure and largely forgotten until the following century.

Now, the scene shifts to South Africa and India. In 1907, a copy of **"Civil Disobedience"** fell into the hands of a Hindu lawyer in Africa, Mohandas Karamchand Gandhi, who was already meditating upon the merits of passive resistance as a defense for his people. Here is an account of the incident, as recollected by the Mahatma, twenty-two years later, to Henry Salt, one of Thoreau's earliest biographers:

> My first introduction to Thoreau's writings was, I think, in 1907, or later, when I was in the thick of the passive resistance struggle. A friend sent me the essay on **"Civil Disobedience."** It left a deep impression upon me. I translated a portion for the readers of *Indian Opinion in South Africa,* which I was then

> editing, and I made copious extracts for the English part of that paper. The essay seemed to be so convincing and truthful that I felt the need of knowing more of Thoreau, and I came across your Life of him, his ***Walden,*** and other shorter essays, all of which I read with great pleasure and equal profit.

A slightly different version is recounted by one of Gandhi's closest associates in South Africa, Henry Polak:

> I cannot now recall, [in 1931] whether, early in 1907, Gandhi or I first came across the volume of Thoreau's Essays (published I believe in Scott's Library), but we were both of us enormously impressed by the confirmation of the rightness of the principle of passive resistance and civil disobedience . . . contained in the essay **"On the Duty of Civil Disobedience."** After consultation with Mr. Gandhi, I reproduced the essay in the columns of *Indian Opinion* and it was translated into the Gujarati language, in which, as well as in English, the paper was published, and the essay was subsequently circulated in pamphlet form. Later in the same year, *Indian Opinion* organized an essay competition on "The Ethics of Passive Resistance," with special reference to Thoreau's essay and Socrates's writings that had already come to Mr. Gandhi's attention.

Gandhi, who had been dissatisfied with the term "passive resistance," but had found no suitable substitute, at once adopted "civil disobedience" to describe his movement. Here was a statement of principle, he decided, that meant firmness without violence, and a devotion to truth and justice—a political policy completely in accord with Gandhi's philosophy. **"Civil Disobedience"** in the hands of Mahatma Gandhi became a bible of nonresistance. For his Hindu followers, Gandhi coined an equivalent, *Satyagraha,* a combination of two Sanskrit words, translated as "soul force" or "the force which is born of truth and love or nonviolence."

Thoreau's fight against slavery in the United States, says Gandhi's biographer, Krishnalal Shridharani, "imbued Gandhi with the faith that it is not the number of the resisters that counts in a Satyagraha, but the purity of the sacrificial suffering." Gandhi declared:

> Writs are impossible when they are confined to a few recalcitrants. They are troublesome when they have to be executed against many high-souled persons who have done no wrong and who refuse payment to vindicate a principle. They may not attract much notice when isolated individuals resort to this method of protest. But clean examples have a curious method of multiplying themselves. They bear publicity and the sufferers instead of incurring odium receive congratulations. Men like Thoreau brought about the abolition of slavery by their personal examples.

In this statement, Gandhi was echoing Thoreau's words on the power of a small but determined minority. Thereby, as Shridharani commented, Thoreau "not only propounded the weapon of civil disobedience which constitutes one important stratagem in Gandhi's Satyagraha, but he also pointed out the potentiality of non-co-operation, which Gandhi enlarged upon afterwards as a means to destroy a corrupt state."

Gandhi remained in South Africa through 1914, carrying on a running battle with government forces led by General Jan Smuts.The campaign was marked by persecution, violence of many descriptions, imprisonments, and all the other tools available to a powerful government attempting to suppress an unpopular minority. Gandhi's techniques of non-co-operation, nonresistance, civil disobedience, or *Satyagraha,* paid off, however, in the end, Prime Minister Smuts and his government granted every important demand of the Indians, including abolition of fingerprint legislation, repeal of a three-pound head tax, validation of Hindu and Moslem marriages, removal of restrictions on the immigration of educated Indians, and a promise to protect the legal rights of the Indian citizens.

Andrews, another Gandhi biographer, concluded that the South African campaign must stand "not only as the first but as the classic example of the use of nonresistance by organized masses of men for the redress of grievances."

According to Shridharani, Gandhi's interpretation of civil disobedience was that:

> Only those who are otherwise willing to obey the law . . . could have a right to practice civil disobedience against unjust laws. It was quite different from the behavior of outlaws, for it was to be practiced openly and after ample notice. It was not likely, therefore, to foster a habit of lawbreaking or to create an atmosphere of anarchy. And it was to be resorted to only when all other peaceful means, such as petitions and negotiations and arbitration, had failed to redress the wrong.

Early in 1915, Gandhi returned to India. There, until his death at the hands of a Hindu assassin in 1948, he led the forces that eventually won freedom for India and Pakistan. Again there were rioting, massacres, long prison terms, suppression of civil liberties, and unjust laws with which to contend. Civil disobedience was frequently used during these years and was sharpened by Gandhi into a weapon of remarkable effectiveness. The first steps were agitation, demonstrations, negotiations, and, if possible, arbitration. If these did not produce results, such economic sanctions were resorted to as strikes, picketing, general strikes, commercial boycott, and sit-down strikes. Another tactic was nonpayment of taxes.

In August, 1947, dominion status was granted by Britain to Hindu India and Moslem Pakistan.

Undoubtedly, the future will witness further use of the principles of civil disobedience, as conceived by Thoreau and perfected by Gandhi. The power of oppressed peoples everywhere, even in the ruthless dictatorships of modern times, can make itself felt through these means. A current example is the fight of the colored races of South Africa against the Strijdom government—a renewal of Gandhi's crusade.

"Even the most despotic government," said Gandhi, "cannot stand except for the consent of the governed which consent is often forcibly procured by the despot. Immediately the subject ceases to fear the despotic force, his power is gone."

Thoreau rejected authoritarianism and totalitarianism in any form. His doctrines run absolutely counter to socialism and communism, or to any other ideology that would place the state above individual rights. It must be conceded that trends of government in the mid-twentieth century show Thoreau's ideas fighting a losing battle. Nevertheless, in the world at large the problem of the citizen's relation to his government—the nature and extent of his obedience to the state—has never been more urgent. (pp. 66-75)

Robert B. Downs, "Individual Versus State, Henry David Thoreau: 'Civil Disobedience'," in his Books That Changed the World, *American Library Association, 1956, pp. 65-75.*

SHERMAN PAUL (essay date 1958)

[*In this excerpt from his highly regarded study of Thoreau,* The Shores of America: Thoreau's Inward Exploration, *Paul analyzes "Civil Disobedience" in terms of the moral and spiritual values attached to transcendentalism.*]

The years between the publishing of [***A Week on the Concord and Merrimack Rivers***] and ***Walden*** were very much like the years following Thoreau's first residence at the Emersons: there was a promise of success in the intermittent and widening demand for lectures, a few articles had been sold, but there was no real success, no self-sufficiency in these vocations. When he left the Emersons in July, 1848, he returned home to take up the family business which had begun to prosper, and which more and more, during his father's illness, needed him. He was to serve Admetus for the rest of his life, and when the call to lecture was not frequent enough, was to add to his servitude the chains of the surveyor. The failure of the ***Week,*** like the failure at Staten Island, closed the last opportunity for freedom; and this time he had no Walden Pond to go to, only a more staggering debt to pay off and increasing family responsibilities. And he was older: the bloom of life was fading; there were already indications in recurring illnesses of the slow deterioration of his vigor. In the last decade of his life the problem of vocation was nothing compared to the problem of retaining his vital heat. His heroism, now, was needed to maintain his condition as a poet, to bring about again that "marriage of the soul with Nature that makes the intellect fruitful, and gives birth to imagination."

For the harmony of relations, the organic life he had known at Walden, was behind, and breakdown before him. The unity of his life was fragmented by the necessity of laboring for other men, by the coarsening of his life and the sense of impurity, by a growing recognition in the lapse of inspiration and the feeling of the otherness of nature (which he had learned on his first visits to the Maine woods and Cape Cod), of the abyss beneath unity, and by the importunities of a society that, increasingly revealing its expediency in the Mexican war and the fugitive slave law, destroyed his felicity and drew him away from the solution of his private problems. Everything he wrote after the Walden years bore the marks of his difficulties: the satire sharpened, the tone became urgent and strident, the preaching on the absolute that began in 1848 in his letters to Harrison Blake carried over into his other writing. Like Emerson, he had not known the extent of his stake in self-reliance until he was assailed; then, however, he did not give quarter, and with an individualism which has properly become a fixed point in the American mind stood his ground to the end. In 1851 he recorded the resolve that crystallized ***Walden*** for him and that became the incentive of his remaining work:

> That way of viewing things you know of . . . take that view, adhere to that, insist on that, see all things from that point of view. . . . Do not speak for other men; speak for yourself. . . . Though you should only speak to one kindred mind in all time, though you should not speak to one, but only utter aloud, that you may the more completely realize and live in the idea which contains the reason of your life, that you may build yourself up to the height of your conceptions, that you may remember your Creator in the days of your youth and justify His ways to man, that the end of life may not be its amusement, speak—though your thought presupposes the non-existence of your hearers—thoughts that transcend life and death.

Driven back on himself, he made his individualism programmatic; the superiority that had lurked in his college essays and that had been somewhat softened in his early writing now became his last weapon, glittering in the air for the first time in the sharp logic of **"Civil Disobedience."** A champion of principle, the spokesman of conscience, he would war on expediency in any form. And he would live by his law—"I must be good as I am made to be good"—he would exploit his uniqueness to the full. Man, he said, was "not to be referred to, or classed with, any company. He is truly singular. . . ." He discovered again in trying Emerson's experiment of inverting the head that every man had a unique angle of vision and that for this reason the wisdom of his elders did not necessarily apply to his condition. "There is life," he wrote, "an experiment untried by me, and it does not avail me that you have tried it. If I have any valuable experience, I am sure to reflect that this my mentors said nothing about." And as he felt all the more the autumn of his life, he had no time to waste: he would speak for himself, and tell his valuable experiences.

One of the valuable experiences he had to tell was how he had dodged the pressures of economic life by the easy calculus of simplicity—though few who have taken this Thoreau for their ideal have seen the extent of which his repudiation of materialism was also a repudiation of expediency, and how much simplicity or poverty, as he called it, was a condition of conscience and virtue. He could utter his strong words against the state in **"Civil Disobedience"** because, as he pointed out, he had no property to protect; and he could show how wealth, rather than leading to virtue as Poor Richard claimed, leads to its sacrifice. Of course the participation in spirit and the unity of life were the most valuable experiences he had to communicate, but the means by which they were achieved, that is to say, the obstacles that had to be pushed aside to attain them, became more significant for him as he grew older. Sooner or later, in one form or another, the actual would invade his freedom; he could not set up the transcendental experiment in a vacuum, and the transcendental assumption that idea shapes circumstance would have to meet the test of society. More and more, in the various forms of servitude—at first as vocation, then in forms he could not so easily determine, reform, slavery, war—the actual bore down on him. And then he recognized that all freedom was one, that the freedom to make his life depended on a freedom from the innumerable coercions he did not seek but which nevertheless had to be faced and disposed of. He could not honestly write a manual of self-reform in ***Walden*** until he had pratically, as well as theoretically, defined the terms on which a man is free to pursue his life. Even in the ***Week,*** where he first mentioned his night in jail, he knew that to live by the law in his relation to nature required that he live by the law in all of his relations—in all those relations that were covered by tradition, institutions, and the custom of mankind.

"The Rights and Duties of the Individual in Relation to Government"—the title of the lecture that he delivered in 1848 and printed as **"Civil Disobedience"** in 1849—was a part of his larger thought on man and institutions in the ***Week***; and if the original title was not so dramatic, it was a more exact one for a statement of principles that appeared again and again, wherever Thoreau faced the general problem of society. The act of civil disobedience was not the most important thing, though it was, of course, the most vivid example of Thoreau's attempt to abide by his principles. As for so many readers, for Thoreau himself it was a courageous act that caught his imagination; and he dwelt on it in the ***Week*** and ***Walden,*** as well as in this essay, because it confirmed for him his identification with the hero. In fact, the public profession of his principles, like his pleas for John Brown before his timid neighbors, was a more significant political act than the refusal to pay his poll tax: it was a public "signing off," more forceful even than his written statement when he cut his tie with the church, a call to conscience, indeed an *act*. Civil disobedience was merely one form of conscientious objection, one way of announcing and making felt one's preference for justice. For Thoreau did not insist on passive resistance, which has been too commonly construed as passivity or passiveness. He was resisting, he was acting in the only way, or perhaps in the simplest, most available way, he could, without, as he said later, violating the laws of his own nature. Most men, he wrote in the ***Week,*** live with "'too passive a regard for the laws,'" and he even cited Krishna's advice to Arjuna in the *Bhagavad-Gita,* that "'action is preferable to inaction.'" The kind of passive resistance he had in mind—and the kind of situation in which it was to be employed—was represented for him in Antigone's adamant defense of "'the unwritten and immovable laws of the gods.'" He took his cue from her; those scenes between Antigone and Creon personalized the issue, dramatized for him the belief that government was a matter of men and conscience, and showed him the positive way in which an individual could produce a counterfriction and clog the machinery of government.

One did not rebel, however, at the expense of one's own nature. The most important thing Thoreau had to say was that the ultimate health of the state depended on conscience, that the reason it must preserve rather than destroy "the wise minority," and must even allow a few "to live aloof from it," was to keep alive the sources of virtue. Above all, there must be somewhere some repository of law; and for Thoreau, who could never find it in the *machinery* or the *association* of government, the individual alone was the "higher and independent power, from which all its own power and authority are derived. . . ." "The mass of men," he said, "serve the state . . . not as men . . . but as machines, with their bodies." They relinquished the free exercise of their moral sense—and corporations, as he had learned from Raleigh, had no conscience. But the heroes, as they were now defined in political terms, "serve the state with their consciences also, and so necessarily resist it for the most part; and they are commonly treated as enemies by it." Thoreau's view of government, of course, was of a piece with his view of reform; . . . to the do-goodism of philanthropists and governments, to the inevitable compromise and expediency of associations and majorities, he had only one reply: you must eventually rely on "the vitality and force of a single living man. . . ." By all means, then, the individual must not abdicate what for Thoreau was the only political obligation, the rightt of conscience; nor should he, in his attempt to reform the state, use any means that would violate this law of his being. No other social act was more important; indeed, he believed that by preserving the conscience, by leavening "the whole lump" of society, he was serving the state, he was giving himself entirely to his fellow men. He knew, however, that in doing this he would appear "useless and selfish," but this was the way in which he interpreted social usefulness, and it was because of this that for him, guarding and cultivating the seeds of virtue, ***Walden*** was a social book, an outright gift of the man himself.

A drawing of Concord Jail as it appeared in 1777.

Writing of Mirabeau, who said, "I reason without obeying, when obedience appears to me contrary to reason," and who took to highway robbery to test the courage of his opposition to society, Thoreau said, "A saner man would have found opportunities enough to put himself in formal opposition to the most sacred laws of society, and so test his resolution, in the natural course of events, without violating the laws of his own nature. It is not for a man to *put himself* in such an attitude to society, but to *maintain* himself in whatever attitude he finds himself through obedience to the laws of his being, which will never be one of opposition to a just government." The civil disobedience Thoreau practiced was irreproachable only when it rested on and did not violate justice, and he practiced it only because the state was unjust and because it was the least expected weapon, a weapon of incalculable spiritual force because it destroyed the assumption of absolute social right and authority. It raised the issue of conscience and justice, and thus undermined the foundations of expediency.

Thoreau had no intention of being passive; even at college he had encountered the problem of expediency and justice in Paley and Stewart, and had learned from Cicero's *De Officiis* that expediency is not law and that passivity may be a connivance with injustice. And Thoreau had no intention of not serving the state—greatness, he believed, depended on public influence. The tone of the final pages of **"Civil Disobedience"** in fact was mollifying; Thoreau declared that from "a lower point of view" the government, even the Constitution, was admirable, that he had no wish to quarrel, that he would be "but too ready to conform. . . ." He confessed that he willingly paid his highway and school taxes, that he was "desirous of being a good neighbor. . . ." But he drew the line when conformity and passivity became a connivance with injustice, and there was no inconsistency in his thought when he championed the bloody ways by which John Brown upheld the law. Blood was a price he was willing to pay: he was not speaking entirely metaphorically when he said, "But even suppose blood should flow. Is there not a sort of blood shed when a man's conscience is wounded?" A stickler for complicity, he knew that by aiding Brown he was helping him to shed it. The refusal to pay his poll tax was the least of his resistances; he had also forwarded fugitive slaves in defiance of the law; he had, in his way, contributed to Harper's Ferry. When, as Alcott complained, "How little is the social compact understood, or felt! Is it not one tissue of selfishness, fraud, and corruption?"—when the state could not purge itself, someone had to further it by the lever of resistance. And this was to act against it. Thoreau could plead for John Brown, could extol his heroism, because he felt that in his own way he had taken comparable risks. He defended Brown as a man of principle.

The justification for such action was not hard to find in a transcendental philosophy that had made Truth the absolute measure of all things. Expediency and conscience were the pivital terms of Thoreau's essay—expediency represented by Paley, conscience by Thoreau—terms which merely defined politically the larger dualism of Prudence and Spiritual Laws. Though the transcendentalist was a seeker after Truth, who, living in the flux of experience and life, knew that he could never wholly fix it; though, through this very faculty of perception, he had raised men to new dignity and enlarged the scope of democracy, he was nevertheless an absolutist; for him there was a moral law, absolute Truth, Justice, Right. "In politics," Theodore Parker said in the most brilliant clarification of the issues between the sensational philosophy and transcendentalism, "sensationalism knows nothing of absolute right, absolute justice; only of historical right, historical justice." Appealing to human history rather than human nature, the sensationalist considered absolute justice "a whim"; the only right or justice he knew was "political expediency," which, as Thoreau also said, amounted to the rule of might rather than right, and reduced all to the majority principle of the greatest good for the greatest number. And this good, Parker said, "may be obtained by sacrificing the greatest good of the lesser number,—by sacrificing any individual,—or sacrificing absolute good." Transcendentalism, on the other hand, starting from human nature, "appeals to a natural justice, natural right; absolute justice, absolute right." The source of these absolutes, Parker explained, was "the conscience of God,"—in man, the moral sense or conscience "which is our consciousness of the conscience of God." Instead of making expedient laws, of legislating pragmatically in terms of what had proved serviceable in the past, instead of seeking guidance in historical precedents and facts, the transcendentalist legislated in terms of the idea, he tried to fashion laws that were just because they were a human translation of the divine laws. To defend one's position on historical grounds, to say, as the southern spokesmen did, that slavery had always existed in the history of man, was to deny the transcendentalist's claim that idea anticipates history, that man need not surrender the future to tradition, that he was free to work toward, if not immediately realize, the ideal of justice.

The defense of minority rights, which was one of the contributions of Transcendentalism to democratic thought, was merely a part of a still greater conception of government: that government is moral, a positive agency in the furtherance of justice, that its ultimate test is not the protection of property but the extension of human rights. Everything that Randolph Bourne was later to hammer out in his study of the state was already in **"Civil Disobedience,"** and only the force of denying expediency and coercion made these individual protests appear to be anarchical statements of the theory of negative government. That government is best which governs least was not the real issue—as Thoreau's own belief in the collective spirit of our institutions and his social proposals for lyceums and natural preserves showed. Instead the issue was the end to which the *instrument* of government should be put, to the end of greed or human fulfillment, to material or spiritual uses. In behalf of this view both Parker and Thoreau cited the American Revolution, Parker claiming that "the authors of the American Revolution, as well as the fathers of New England, were transcendentalists" because they had faith in ideas rather than history. They did not yield to tradition. Reading American history in the transcendental way George Bancroft had popularized, Parker said: "The American Revolution, with American history since, is an attempt to prove by experience this transcendental proposition, to organize the transcendental idea of politics. The idea demands for its organization, a democracy—a government of all, for all, and by all [Lincoln immortalized this phrase, but also adopted the notion of "proposition," the view of American history, and the belief which followed in government as the agency of the divine law]; a government by natural justice, by legislation that is divine as much as a true astronomy is divine, legislation which enacts law representing a fact of the universe, a resolution of God."

As for the rights and duties of the individual in relation to government, they were all reduced to the single need "to be co-ordinate with justice." "Only the absolutely right is expedient for all," Thoreau said in the ***Week***; and Parker brought his logic to the same conclusion when he wrote, "Legislation must represent that [the immutable morality], or the law is not binding on any man." Man's primary allegiance—the unspecified premise of Thoreau's essay—was not to the state but to nature. For the conscience of the individual, the ideas he was to bring to bear on society, had their source in nature. As one sees in other proponents of natural rights, in Cooper's Natty Bumppo, for example, nature is opposed to the state, the individual to society—man is considered outside of society, free to leave it when it jeopardizes his integrity (free, that is, if there is still open territory in the West) or free to act on it. But he hardly acts within it. The social virtues of the eighteenth century were minimized; one did not conciliate, one reformed society in the interests of justice, and failing this, he had every right to leave it. So Parker said: "By birth man is a citizen of the universe, subject to God; no oath of allegiance, no king, no parliament, no congress, no people, can absolve him from his natural fealty thereto, and alienate a man born to the rights, born to the duties, of a citizen of God's universe. Society, government, politics come not from a social compact which men made and may unmake, but [as Natty and Thoreau attempted to demonstrate] from a social nature of God's making; a nation is to be self-ruled by justice." When man entered the state, therefore, he did so through the portal of justice, binding himself only because the laws were just. "Justice," Parker wrote, "is the point common to one man and the world of men, the balance-point." And when he extended this idea to individual ethics which, of course, underlay the social ethics, and wrote the democratic law of human relations so important to Thoreau and Whitman (and to Natty)—"I am to respect my own nature and be an individual man,—your nature and be a social man"—he said, "a scheme of morals . . . demands that you be you—I, I; balances individualism and socialism on the central point of justice . . . puts natural right, natural duty, before all institutions, all laws, all traditions."

This, of course, was a program for the American democratic sentiment. But there was this difficulty: Could one be sure that his ideas had the warrant of conscience? Did all men in their proposals for reform really act from a sense of right? Might not the transcendental politician "take his own personal whims," as Parker warned, "for oracles of human nature?" Might not the Ethan Brands, Ahabs, and Hollingsworths act rashly, "ignore the past, and scorn its lessons," and so destroy society? The danger of the position Parker had outlined was that "the transcendental moralist" might "abhor the actual rules of morality," that in his impatience with the necessity of compromise and the tardiness of social change might resort to absolutism in practice as well as in idea. Transcendental madness was the danger: to "take a transient impulse, personal and fugitive, for a universal law; follow a passion, and come to naught; surrender his manhood, his free will to his unreflecting instinct. . . ." "Men that are transcendental-mad," Parker said, "we have all seen in morals; to be transcendental-wise, sober, is another thing." There were Ahabs by the score at the Chardon Street conventions, few Captain Veres. As far as other reformers went Thoreau was aware of the danger of legislating one's dyspepsia into law, and what saved Thoreau from this predicament was his refusal to use coercion in behalf of his idea. He was not a reformer in this sense; persuasion and example were his only weapons. For him good government, like Paradise, began at home; social ethics were personal ethics, and the only valuable reform was self-reform. One could avoid the dangers of transcendental madness by limiting reform to oneself. Fortunately for the American, he wrote in ***A Yankee in Canada,*** the government still let one "*speculate* without bounds." There was still a West as close as Walden Pond, where one could experiment in new worlds, could be the true reformer and discoverer of social ideals. It was sufficient for one who would not violate his nature (or another's) to try the experiment and publish the results, letting his character and ideas leaven the lump. (pp. 237-47)

Sherman Paul, in his The Shores of America: Thoreau's Inward Exploration, *University of Illinois Press, 1958, 433 p.*

ROBERT S. LaFORTE (essay date 1959)

[*LaForte suggests that the essential paradox of "Civil Disobedience"—Thoreau's failure to recognize that in the state rests the collective will of a group of individuals—represents a grave flaw in his political thought.*]

The heart of Henry David Thoreau's political thought is best expressed in four of his writings: a review, **"Paradise (to be) Regained"**; his famous **"On Civil Disobedience"**; an essay, **"Life Without Principle"**; and a speech, **"A Plea for Captain John Brown."** Even these fall short of the metaphysical core of Thoreau's political thinking. All of his writings can be interpreted as political, since he taught an intense individualism on a second plane of abstraction differing from the first plane of immediate and obvious assumptions in that it consists of ideas drawn from consideration of the intellect, man's intuition, and the primary forces of nature.

It is difficult to comprehend many of Thoreau's meanings completely since much of his thought is couched in symbolism. A student of Oriental philosophy, he developed a Rousseauist vision of man as a "noble savage." From his second plane, he saw man as an omniscient, benevolent spirit, erudite beyond human reckoning, a Nietzschean superman transcending earthly limitations. In essence, the true Thoreau was unreal. It is therefore necessary to deal with more tangible aspects of his thought. First, he saw government as a mere expedient. He visualized American democracy as a noble adventure, as the rope Zarathustra compared to humanity reaching toward the super-end, producing the superman. Thoreau, too, saw a superman who, when ready, would slough off the coil of government.

But Thoreau was untrue to himself, for seeing this superman as an institution, that of the human free-spirit, he did not recognize his eventual man, this human free-spirit, as part of an institution. He rather spoke and wrote of man alone. He failed to comprehend that man is an interacting force combined into what practical men call society. On his second plane, society was an alien force out of which man must come. Thus, he and the Transcendentalists generally, spoke of themselves as society's "come-outers." From his lofty perch, Thoreau failed to recognize that, that which in man is composite, forms group characteristics. Nor could he see that to solidify, encourage or curb various group characteristics, governments are instituted, not in the mind of the individual, but in the minds of men.

Thus between Thoreau's low level understanding of government (as an expedient) and his highest ideals for man and his society lies an extreme paradox. C. Carroll Hollis [see essay dated 1949] explains:

> Paradox in Thoreau is the consequence of his profound awareness of the mystery of life. The basic paradox of existence that the Hindu writers saw, the writers of the Seventeenth Century saw, Blake saw, Thoreau saw. Any statement . . . had to be inevitably, a paradoxical statement, no matter how simple their expression. . . . Thoreau knew intuitively, as

> we know through reflection, . . . that paradox must be taken seriously both as an essential principle of life and as an essential method of communication.

This statement seems to allow an overabundance of wisdom to Thoreau, however difficult it is to visualize an intuitively inspired wisdom. To others, Thoreau was ". . . a great reader of books of the ancient tradition, but . . . neither a profound thinker nor a great writer . . ."

Henry Seidel Canby, one of America's leading authorities on Thoreau, simplifies the Concordian's political thought as an intense individualism, in close co-ordination with nature but in conflict with nothing. Canby concludes [in a 1949 article in the *Saturday Review of Literature*]: "It was a balance of power that he sought, where the individual, accepting the necessity of order, refused to become half-man or less . . ."

Here, Canby seems to synthesize what can be classed, for clarity, as Thoreau's first dimension thesis (that government is an expedient) and his second dimension antithesis (no government is good government). It is not the purpose of this paper to synthesize Thoreau's thought, for he gives no evidence that he felt compelled to strike a balance. It is rather that he could exist on dual planes, recognize somewhat their existence and formulate towards each.

That he did not wish to compromise is made strikingly clear in **"On Civil Disobedience":**

> The progress from an absolute to a limited monarchy, from a limited monarch to a democracy, is a progress toward a true respect for the individual. Is a democracy such as we know it, the last improvement possible in government? Is it not possible to take a step further toward recognizing and organizing the right of man? . . . I please myself with imagining a state at last which can afford to be just to all men and to that end to treat the individual with respect as a neighbor . . . A state which bore this kind of fruit, and suffered it to drop off as fast as it ripened, would prepare the way for a still more perfect and glorious state, which also I have imagined, but not yet anywhere seen.

Here Thoreau implies evolutionary movement towards the ideal order of life. Again, in regard to the assertion that Thoreau wanted a balance, Canby fails to show at what point on a continuum of Individual Power and State Power a balance would lie. All evidence seems to point to the fact that Thoreau never contemplated the balance of power. In **"Civil Disobedience"** Thoreau begins, "I heartily accept the motto, 'that government is best which governs least;' and I should like to see it acted up to more rapidly and systematically. Carried out, it finally amounts to this, which I also believe—'that government is best which governs not at all' . . ." From this, one begins to discern the strains of a Marxian evolution of political power away from the state into the arms of a classless society, without government.

Perhaps a better comprehension of Thoreau's political thought can be derived from a comparison with Marxian idealism. Thoreau may or may not have heard of Marx, but if he had he would assuredly have never agreed with him, nor realized how each sought the same end along different paths. To Marx, the class struggle would culminate in a free society. Man had nothing to say about his future, for in Marxian mechanistic history such an evolution was inevitable. Thoreau's free society would come about through the direct actions of man. Here, Thoreau and Marx are diametrically opposed. Yet their end social structure necessitates a glorified individual, one who would be operating in a no-government, or completely free civilization—if this be civilization.

On his second plane Thoreau rejected American government, as he rejected all government. He felt government was a force which restricted man from becoming completely free. Three major forces which in a large degree formed the vitriolic and caustic, yet humane Thoreau were (1) the Mexican War, (2) the slavery issue, and (3) the accelerating industrial evolution, which in his time began to make obvious impressions on American life. In each of these, government played an ignominious role, because American government has never been able to be the fully detached thing which Thoreau visualized it to be. Instead of limiting his critical comments to the society which promoted this, Thoreau added criticism of government as another force in abetting what was a distasteful business. He failed to see that once society's values were changed, so would its superstructure—government. Instead of being content with changing society, he wished for the abolition of government through an evolutionary process.

Of the three major forces influencing Thoreau, by far the most important was the industrial evolution. Like Frederich Juenger in the Twentieth Century, he saw the disillusioned masses caught in the industrial movement.

Canby writes of Thoreau's rejection and reaction, that in a time when the individual finds himself amidst an industrial movement, where the profit motive is dominant, independence is conditioned by success and success means making money. Here, he notes, the basic problem of modern civilized man is raised— ". . . man against the machine and machine-like living . . ."

Thoreau considering this same problem in **"Life Without Principle,"** laments the way life is spent and enveighs against business motives:

> This world is a place of business. What an infinite bustle! I am awakened almost every night by the panting of the locomotive. It interrupts my dreams. There is no sabbath. It would be glorious to see mankind at leisure for once. It is nothing but work, work, work. I can not easily buy a blank-book to write thoughts in; they are commonly ruled for dollars and cents. An Irishman seeing me making a minute in the fields, took it for granted that I was calculating my wages. If a man was tossed out of a window when an infant, and so made a cripple for life, or scared out of his wits by the Indians, it is regretted chiefly because he was thus incapacitated for business! I think that there is nothing, not even crime, more opposed to poetry, to philosophy, ay, to life itself, than this incessant business.

Thoreau disliked what the machine was causing under the manipulation of shrewd New England Yankees. He tied his criticism of existing government to his criticism of current business conditions by noting that government was exceedingly interested in petty economics. "Government and legislation!" he exclaimed; "These I thought were respectable professions. We have heard of heaven born Numas, Lycurguses, and Solons, in the history of the world, whose names at least may stand for ideal legislators: but think of legislating to regulate the breeding of slaves, or the exportation of tobacco." He continued to damn a government that promoted such an interest in commerce:

> A commerce that whitens every sea in quest of nuts and raisins, and makes slaves of its sailors for this purpose! . . . America sends to the old world for her bitters! Is not the sea-brine, is not shipwreck, bitter enough to make the cup of life go down here. Yet such, to a great extent, is our boasted commerce; and there are those who style themselves statesmen and philosophers who are so blind as to think that progress and civilization depend on precisely this kind of interchange and activity—the activity of flies about a molasses-hogshead. Very well, observes one, if men were oysters. And very well, answer I, if men were mosquitos.

Thoreau's case against business and the mechanical age, is unlike the usual social reformer's cries in the wilderness. It is more Christian. He had said, "Money is not required to buy one necessity of the soul." Just as an earlier reformer had harried the money changers and what they represented from His temple, Thoreau would have harried the Nineteenth Century forms from his ideal world.

Henry Beetle Hough, in his biography of Thoreau, found much of him Christlike. Hough thought his idealism had sprung directly from the pages of the New Testament. Christ was to Thoreau "the Prince of reformers and radicals." Yet as far as formalized religion was concerned, he could not accept it as an answer. He knew that perhaps his early schooling and other training had prejudiced him against the church. He felt, paradoxically, that he had come to realize the church's true value. He wrote, complaining directly against the mistakes of man in using Christ's teachings, "What are time and space to Christianity, eighteen hundred years and a new world?—that the humble life of a Jewish peasant should have force to make a New York bishop so bigoted?" When questioned by his aunt in his last moments of life "if he had made his peace with God?" Thoreau replied, "I have never quarreled with him"—"One world at a time" is all that he ever sought.

Thoreau's Walden experiment was partially evidence of his disgust with a mechanistic, business age. This does not wholly explain his march to the pond, for to Henry Thoreau this was something he desired to do. Yet what he considered false desires induced by a falsified order, brought about by the machine and emphasizing material things, did help prompt him to the exodus. His most pungent expression on the matter is expressed in his statement, "A man's life consisteth not in the abundance of the things that he possesseth."

Sinclair Lewis, almost a century later, felt that Thoreau was a one-man revolution against what he had called society's Babbitry [see excerpt dated 1937 in *NCLC*, Vol. 7]. Unable to understand the riddle of Thoreau, Lewis said the Walden experience was prompted by the George F. Babbitts of the world. This is much too negative an explanation, for Thoreau's actions always tended to be positive.

Thoreau in commenting on his two year stay at Walden pond and his reason for going there, says, "My purpose . . . was not to live cheaply or to live dearly there, but to transact some private business with the fewest obstacles. . . . My residence was more favorable, not only to thought, but to serious reading, than a university."

Slavery was the second problem that plagued Thoreau's free spirit. With the human bondage being suffered by the American Negro and with an intense abolitionism racking his native New England, he naturally became a leading opponent of the "peculiar institution."

It was not Thoreau's direct love of his fellow man that prompted this feeling, but rather his transcendental feeling toward human experience, which he thought had to be free to be full. Hough calls Thoreau a hater of mankind but not men. As indication of his feeling on the matter, Hough quotes his antisocial remark, "I have a great deal of company in my house, especially in the morning, when nobody calls . . ." Yet Thoreau seems to be neither a hater of man nor mankind. His criticism, which could possibly cause one to arrive at Hough's opinion, is that of a man unable to find men who could compare to his love for nature. Thoreau identifies himself as a "metaphysicist, transcendentalist and a natural philosopher." He exalted the simple separate person, but did not feel it was necessary to exalt the mass of simple people.

Before dealing with the heart of Thoreau's criticism of government because of the support it gave to slavery, let us consider his feelings on independence for man. A good expression of his thoughts on the subject is found in one of his poems. Here Thoreau casts off all inhibitions, and allows full scope to his willingness to wander and portray the various facets of man:

> My life more civil is and free
> Than any civil polity,
> Ye princes keep your realms
> And circumscribed power,
> Not wide as are my dreams
> Nor rich as is the hours,
> "What can ye give which I have not?
> What can ye take which I have got?"
> To all true wants time's ear is deaf,
> Penurious states lend no relief
> Out of their pelf—
> But a free soul—thank God—
> Can help itself.
> Be sure your fate
> Doth keep apart its state—
> Not linked with any band—
> Even the nobles of the land . . .

Thoreau obviously felt certain freedom in simple living. One can easily understand why he would say, "Ye princes keep your realms and circumscribed power, Not wide as are my dreams . . ." What can "Nor rich as is the hour," mean unless a free man's existence is wealth *per se*.

Recalling the jail episode in **"Civil Disobedience,"** it is often with a smirk that one thinks of the statement that in a society such as his the only freedom may be found in the confines of a jail. Looking deeper, we see how personal his idea of independence and freedom really is. Most things, which we interpret as too minute for our contemplation, were in his simplicity read into great events.

It is certain that his independence was not the economic independence that Twentieth Century man hopes to attain. He recognized a need for this type of freedom when he preached man's return to the soil. The life he praised was that of his neighbor farmer. Yet this to Thoreau was merely method. Independence in the end was a state of mind. To obtain this state of mind, man had to be, as far as possible, free upon this earth. Thus he fought for emancipation.

Thoreau never admitted that the proslavery argument had any merit. In the last few years, prior to the Civil War, Thoreau called for violent methods, which would require bloodshed, to bring about the abolition of slavery. Yet most of his life was a period of passive resistance against slavery. Thoreau personally hated Henry Clay (for his work in the Compromise of

1850) and his own senator, Daniel Webster, for his remark "because it [slavery] was a part of the original compact—let it stand." When the war became imminent and then a stark-terrible reality, Thoreau began to adjust some of his assertions regarding the pitting of man against man for the sake of others.

He was, along with Ralph Waldo Emerson, a champion of John Brown. Both men had sponsored Brown during his stay in Concord, after that mad prophet had left Kansas to establish his family. Following Brown's raid at Harper's Ferry, in the fall of 1859, Thoreau summoned his neighbors to public protest against the fanatic's arrest. Not content with stirring his Concord neighbors, he did something very unlike Thoreau, in arranging for appearances all over New England. He later decided against many meetings, because he felt little was being accomplished, but he did speak in Boston's Tremont Temple and at Worcester.

The speech which he delivered on these occasions is his **"A Plea for Captain John Brown,"** a moral argument against slavery. He knew nothing and cared nothing for the political, cultural or economic position of the South. His wisdom in choosing to defend fanatic Brown is questionable, but to people who hold second plane views on morality, moral theory is above practical consideration. (pp. 41-7)

The essence of Thoreau's disgust over the government's protection of slavery as a necessary evil comes in **"Civil Disobedience,"** when he writes, "How does it become a man to behave toward this American government today? I answer that he cannot without disgrace be associated with it. I cannot for an instant recognize that political organization as my government which is the slave's government also."

Much of Thoreau's argument against slavery was used in the Twentieth Century by another man dedicated to freeing his people. That man was Gandhi. John Haynes Holmes, discussing Gandhi, notes that he extended and deepened Thoreau's passive resistance into a potent weapon of soul-force, which achieved Indian independence. He made it not the lone protest against "tyranny of the single individual, but the massed revolt of disciplined multitudes of men. . . . the seed however was of Thoreau's planting."

The last major outside force which Thoreau argued against, and which shaped his political thought, was American intervention in the Southwest. He saw the Mexican War as a means for extending slavery; like many other New Englanders. It has been shown that war as a method to an end was not always abhorred by Thoreau, since he once signaled the end of slavery through battle. It is rather that war compelled men to do things they did not want to do. It was more of the false standard of a falsified order. He says, "Witness the present Mexican War, the work of comparatively few individuals using the standing government as their tool, for in the outset, the people would not have consented to this measure."

Thoreau did not despise America. He hated injustice and could not recognize a government "which established injustice." As Emerson described him: "No truer American existed than Thoreau. His preference of his country and condition was genuine . . . He definitely preferred American institutions, depraved as they may be, to the French or English culture."

Thoreau opposed mass government because it meant mass rights. He felt rights were of an individual nature. He argued in **"Civil Disobedience"** against mass government because it subverted the human. Thoreau, better than anyone else, summed up his thought in his journal of travels:

> As I was entering Deep Cut, the wind which was conveying a message to me from heaven, dropped it on the wires of the telegraph which it vibrated as it passed. I instantly sat down on a stone at the foot of the telegraph pole, and attended to the communication. It merely said: 'Bear in mind, child, and never for an instant forget, that there are higher planes of life than this thou art now traveling on. Know that the goal is distant, and is upward, and is worthy of all your life's efforts to attain to.' And then it ceased, and though I sat some minutes longer, I heard nothing more.

To a political scientist, who must deal with the tangibles of life, Henry David Thoreau seems highly absurd. For the most part he offends any common understanding of the need for organized society. He stands counter to the modern democratic approach to the exercise of power—that of rule by the majority. He is too mystical in his assertions of the Rousseauist idea that only what the individual considers right is right. He sidesteps or never considers that one man's rights often interfere with another's.

He speaks of the growing power of the state, and never feels that the American state is really composed of his neighbors. He seems to consider the state as an omnipotent individual bearing down on humanity.

Much of Thoreau is, however, praiseworthy. He, most of all, lived for fredom. He understood man's desire to be free, whether at the level of economic independence or at its transcendent level of uniting with nature. He spoke for individual rights and was aware, too well aware, that mass government could be as authoritarian as dictatorship. He put forth an impractical solution to the problem of majority rule, but he unknowingly emphasized a need for balance.

He raised, as has been noted, the problem of the machine age, or machine-like living. He early saw what was to become reality in the second half of the Nineteenth Century and only begin to fade after a depression in the Twentieth Century caused man to reevaluate his fate.

His most important contribution was made not to his native land, but to India. He helped to inspire and give method to the man destined to free his people. He preached independence, freedom, and, in general, the high pleasure of self-realization. He showed the need for better government and even for a better human being and human understanding. He wanted improvement of conditions in general. No man can be criticized for this. (pp. 48-50)

Robert S. LaForte, "The Political Thought of Henry D. Thoreau: A Study in Paradox," in The Educational Leader, *Vol. XXIII, No. 1, July, 1959, pp. 41-51.*

DON W. KLEINE (essay date 1960)

[In the following essay, Kleine compares the ideas expressed in "Civil Disobedience" with those expressed in Walden, *concluding that "there is significant community between the two works."]*

Thoreau's commentators in recent years have come to a juster sense of the multiplicity of their subject. Patently, the unity of this multiplicity in ***Walden*** and **"Civil Disobedience"** is to be found in these writings themselves; when suggesting the relationship of the earlier essay to ***Walden,*** modern scholars have for the most part quite properly stuck to their texts. But they have only suggested this connection, not spelled it out. Perhaps their omission is a natural one; the relationship seems obvious. Yet the link between the two is easy to acknowledge and then forget. It is a frequent strategy of Thoreau's critics to treat **"Civil Disobedience"** as a purely political manifestation of the Transcendental principles in ***Walden.*** Employed with discretion, this can be a useful tactic. But if it leads the cursory analyst to become fixated on his dichotomy of the two works at the expense of their much more important affinities it can hardly result in less than a distortion of Thoreau's thought.

The earlier essay, admittedly, might be said to declare the personal independence from communal obligation which would permit a Walden adventure. Yet this distinction is at best very limited. It refers to a difference of quantity rather than quality: ***Walden*** repeats that same manifesto, specifically with reference to the moral price we pay for tea, coffee, and meat:

> But the only true America is that country where you are at liberty to pursue such a mode of life as may enable you to do without these, and where the state does not endeavor to compel you to sustain the slavery and war and other superfluous expenses which directly or indirectly result from the use of such things.

Protest for Thoreau exists on the level of a self-liberated individual by definition opposed to a self-enslaved majority. The Walden "experiment" is, among other things, individual protest of quite the same order as the earlier refusal to pay the poll tax.

The results of the Walden sojourn were predetermined by the spirit in which it was undertaken. Thoreau already knew what were "the grossest groceries," for he had celebrated his awareness in **"Civil Disobedience":**

> You must hire or squat somewhere, and raise but a small crop, and eat that soon. You must live within yourself, and depend upon yourself always tucked up and ready for a start, and not have many affairs.

Walden Pond was not an experiment at all, but—like the night in the Concord jail—protest magnified into gesture. Going to the woods, going to prison each make formal a withdrawal from the community which has been effected long before.

The target of both gestures is the same: bondage of man to the instruments of civilization, whether machines or institutions. ***Walden*** arraigns the varieties of such bondage—to houses, clothing, fire-engines, railroads, religions, tenderloin steaks, cablegrams and governments. **"Civil Disobedience"** specifically arraigns the last of these bondages,

> If one were to tell me that this was a bad government because it taxed certain foreign commodities brought to its ports, it is most probable that I should not make an ado about it, for I can do without them. All machines have their friction; and possibly this does enough good to counterbalance the evil. At any rate, it is a great evil to make a stir about it. But when the friction comes to have its machine, and oppression and robbery are organized, I say, let us not have such a machine any longer.

The bondage and not the machine rankles Thoreau (though sometimes he found it hard to tell them apart). In fact, a machine can act as a valuable stimulant, for an overbearing state offers welcome opportunity for wholesome exercise of the free man's freedom,

> I saw that the state was half-witted, that it was timid as a lone woman with her silver spoons, and that it did not know its friends from its foes, and I lost all my remaining respect for it, and pitied it.

Indeed, the very notion of civil *disobedience* has its comic application; to disobey the impotent blusterings of this "timid" half-wit exacts rather less than the highest heroism.

But most men *are* its victims. "It is, after all, with men and not with parchment that I quarrel." Thoreau's grudge is with his neighbors, rather than the intrinsically innocent devices to which they have heedlessly consigned the best of themselves,

> But it is not the less necessary for this; for the people must have some complicated machinery or other, and hear its din, to satisfy that idea of government which they have.

Once subject, most men cannot grope out of their "complicated machinery"; quiet desperation marks how they themselves have become machines,

> The mass of men serve the state thus, not as men mainly, but as machines, with their bodies. They are the standing army, and the militia, jailors, constables, posse comitatus, etc.

The Fugitive Slave Law is a burden upon men's consciences quite as much as the barns and savings banks of ***Walden*** are upon the time of men's lives. Men must become active masters of government, not its passive victims. The concept of redemption from passivity in self-directed activity is central to ***Walden*** too:

> Do not seek so anxiously to be developed, to subject yourself to many influences to be played on; it is all dissipation.

Thoreau seeks internal action in surface passivity. He calls for strenuous husbandry, but in the right vineyard. The unreasoned diligence of the tax-gatherer in **"Civil Disobedience,"** enforcing a law which violates even his own identity, the unthinking servitude of John Field in ***Walden,*** hammering tea, butter and beef from a barren farm, are the same spendthrift sloth. The central gestures of both works involve consumer resistance—a refusal to buy either protection from prison or material superfluities at the rate which the tax-gatherer and John Field are paying. And like a buyers' strike, Thoreau's is accomplished without external violence. He *permits* the state to imprison him; he shifts noiselessly to Walden Pond on the Fourth of July.

Both abdications *seem* quite personal affairs:

> My purpose in going to Walden Pond was not to live cheaply nor to live dearly there, but to transact some private business with the fewest obstacles.

Non-cooperation in **"Civil Disobedience,"** similarly, seems to owe more to personal ethical fastidiousness than to political zeal,

> It is not a man's duty, as a matter of course, to devote himself to the eradication of any, even the most enormous wrong; he may still properly have other concerns to engage him; but it is his duty, at least, to wash his hands of it, and, if he gives it no thought longer, not to give it practically his support.

But at the same time, Thoreau's consumer resistance is highly *public*. Iconoclastic refusal to buy becomes in both ***Walden*** and **"Civil Disobedience"** dramatized public self-exile.

We have been suggesting that ***Walden*** "contains" **"Civil Disobedience"**; of course we do not mean that **"Civil Disobedience"** contains ***Walden.*** Clearly, the Transcendental vision of the latter work rests partly on Thoreau's passionate apprehension of the life of the senses: man's animality—the submergence of unique identity in sensation—is quite as fundamental as his spiritual individuality. Admittedly the ironies of this dualism are not present in **"Civil Disobedience."** We do mean to suggest, however, that on another level Walden Woods, like Concord jail, is a conscious argumentative device. Intrinsic as Thoreau's representation of nature may be to his total literary achievement, it is accidental to his achievement as a philosophical polemicist. As polemics, the Walden venture becomes not so much a return to *nature* as a return to *premises.*

We have remarked that Thoreau, in going to Walden, is trying to *prove* something, not find something out. Literally, he seeks a warrant in physical nature for exactly the bed-rock self-reliance which is the philosophical basis of **"Civil Disobedience."** Thoreau, that is, goes to the woods for additional confirmation of the victory already symbolized by his night in jail. The lake, the trees, the sky approve his gesture; the rhythms of nature orchestrate Thoreau's studied pirouette, for the instinctive world is a condition of total thrift:

> We should be blessed if we lived in the present always, and took advantage of every accident that befell us, like the grass which confesses the influence of the slightest dew that falls on it; and did not spend our time in atoning for the neglect of past opportunities, which we call doing our duty.

There is no question of primitivism here; nature teaches the social man to cut his expenses within the framework of society,

> Let us spend one day as deliberately as nature, and not be thrown off the track by every nutshell and mosquito's wing that falls on the rails. Let us rise early and fast, or break fast, gently and without perturbation; let company come and let company go, let the bells ring and the children cry—determined to make a day of it.

Nature shows the individual that he must simplify his relationship to social instruments at whatever point these instruments threaten his personal identity. Nature shows the efficacy, in other words, of precisely the simplification of Thoreau's relationship to the state involved in his secession from it:

> The proper place today, the only place which Massachusetts has provided for her freer and less desponding spirits, is in her prisons, to be put out and locked out of the state by her own act, as they have already put themselves out by their principles.

If nature offers an object lesson in simplicity, Thoreau's own attitude toward nature at the Pond offers a similar object lesson. The disciplined hedonism of Thoreau's participation in cosmic thrift forestalls sentimentality in ***Walden.*** The rapport between man and beasts is terse but friendly. It sometimes leads to such a whimsy of social fraternity as, "I called to see" Mr. Gillian Baker's cat, but "she was gone a-hunting in the woods, as was her wont," or the account of the wayward dogs,

> He did not find his hounds that night, but the next day learned that they had crossed the river and put up at a farmhouse for the night, whence, having been well fed, they took their departure early in the morning.

Thoreau relates himself to other men with quite the same candor and reserve he does to animals. The colloquy with his barn-burning jail mate significantly points this lesson of self-reliant thrift in personal relationships back to **"Civil Disobedience,"**

> He naturally wanted to know where I came from, and what had brought me there; and, when I had told him, I asked him in my turn how he came there, presuming him to be an honest man, of course; and, as the world goes, I believe he was.

Freedom, then, in both ***Walden*** and **"Civil Disobedience"** is a cheerful but inviolable solitude: "A man thinking or working is always alone, let him be where he will."

Such solitude is the sole basis of true sympathy between men. Thoreau's gregarious exile, therefore, is anti-social but not misanthropic. Lowell calls him a Stylite, and Thoreau's writings confess him exactly that: his cabin once housed thirty visitors. But if a moral of ***Walden*** is that hermitages do not make hermits, a moral of **"Civil Disobedience"** is just as surely that prisons do not make prisoners. Indeed, the prison cell in **"Civil Disobedience"** seems not the cell of a convict but of a hermit,

> The rooms were whitewashed once a month; and this one, at least, was the whitest, most simply furnished, and probably the neatest apartment in the town.

Yet like the cabin at Walden which it resembles, its austerity is deceptive. The Concord cell houses a recluse no more than the one in the woods, nor is its occupant less free. Society is a prison, for men, failing to simplify, are harshly shut from each other,

> I saw that, if there was a wall of stone between me and my townsmen, there was a still more difficult one to climb or break through before they could get to be as free as I was. I did not for a moment feel confined, and the walls seemed a great waste of stone and mortar. I felt as if I alone of all my townsmen had paid my tax.

Walden, like **"Civil Disobedience,"** declares the true nature of these barriers between men:

> What sort of space is that which separates a man from his fellows and makes him solitary? I have found that no exertion of the legs can bring two minds much nearer to one another.

In a sense, then, Walden Pond and the Concord jail are the same place. Thrift has many guises; it is just as *natural* in a prison as in a wilderness,

> Sell your clothes and keep your thoughts. God will see that you do not want society. If I were confined to a corner of a garret all my days, like a spider, the world would be just as large to me while I had my thoughts about me.

Anywhere will do for exploration of the self. Though thrift is the necessary concommitant of this exploration, place is irrelevant. It is not a journey in space, but a venture to the interior.

The Transcendentalist image of mental voyage thus figures prominently in both ***Walden*** and **"Civil Disobedience."** Thoreau's high celebration in ***Walden*** of this psychic adventure is well known:

> What was the meaning of that South-Sea Exploring Expedition, with all its parade and expense, but an indirect recognition of the fact that there are continents and seas in the moral world to which every man is an isthmus or an inlet. . . .

Less well known is the fact that **"Civil Disobedience"** also celebrates such an adventure:

> It was like traveling into a far country, such as I had never expected to behold, to lie there for one night. It seemed to me that I never had heard the town-clock strike before, nor the evening sounds of the village.

The perplexed townsmen who meet Thoreau after his release, having never traveled, are quite lost, dimly suspecting that the prisoner has somehow retrieved a prize from a distant place which, for all their "liberty," they were incomprehensibly denied:

> My neighbors did not thus salute me, but first looked at me, and then at one another, as if I had returned from a long journey.

Thoreau wants external simplification, then, so that he can thrust into this deeper complexity of voyage. The alternative is simplification of *oneself,* being oneself a mere instrument; being, like the tax-gatherer, like John Field, a ship perpetually in drydock.

Walden encompasses **"Civil Disobedience."** There is nothing "in" the latter that is not in the former (indeed, much of the prison episode is bodily incorporated into ***Walden***), though a great deal of ***Walden*** is not in the earlier essay. If either is "political" at all, ***Walden*** seems as much a politicl application of principles in **"Civil Disobedience"** as the other way around. There is significant community between the two works for, despite incongruities and vagaries, Thoreau was all of a piece. What Joseph Wood Krutch in his *Thoreau* [see excerpt dated 1948 in *NCLC,* Vol. 7] describes as "the balance and wholeness which Thoreau seems to achieve," is reflected in the unity of **"Civil Disobedience"** and ***Walden.*** There is a wholesome inevitability in the fact that by the time he stepped out of its jail, Thoreau, who traveled much in Concord, had gone a good part of the distance to ***Walden.*** (pp. 297-304)

Don W. Kleine, "'Civil Disobedience': The Way to 'Walden'," in Modern Language Notes, *Vol. LXXV, No. 4, April, 1960, pp. 297-304.*

JOHN ALDRICH CHRISTIE (essay date 1969)

[In the following excerpt, Christie elucidates Thoreau's position on resistance to civil authority.]

India has taken Thoreau with deadly seriousness as a social philosopher ever since Mahatma Gandhi first commenced offering extracts from **"Civil Disobedience"** in his revolutionary journal *Indian Opinion* on September 7, 1907. Thoreau's absence until recently from syllabi of American literature courses at the post-graduate level in Indian universities stemmed not from his exclusion from the literary pantheon but from his solid inclusion in India's more reputable one of philosophers. Not only has Indian thought taken his views on civil resistance to heart; it has had no difficulty in accommodating the whole man, accepting his views on simplification and the values of life and nature as integral parts of the specific challenge proposed in his most famous essay. Gandhi's Satyagraha, which preceded both Gandhi's and India's exposure to Thoreau's views, furnished congenial soil for the nourishment of those features of Thoreau's message most often resisted by Americans: his agrarianism, his stress upon material simplifiction, his reverence for life, his Ideal reading of nature, his emphasis upon absolute moral truths and the pre-eminence of spiritual reality, even his inclinations toward vegetarianism. (p. 5)

[Long familiar to another continent in travail, Thoreau] now enjoys a new contemporaneity on similar grounds in his own country. The fact does not, unfortunately, guarantee that either continent has done all its homework with respect to Thoreau's views on civil "disobedience." Supporters of both Gandhi and Martin Luther King, Jr., have looked to him as the American spokesman for massive non-violence, and they have been mistaken. A current contender for the American Vice-Presidency expresses the view that his civil disobedience rejects all law and order; a "free-speech" advocate at Berkeley cites him in defense of the right of the individual to any private preference; and admirers of the "professional agitator" Saul Alinsky presume his support for a national institute to train social revolutionaries; and all three are mistaken. At a moment in our history when judges, ministers, college presidents, and contenders for the highest offices of the land are defining "civil disobedience" for us with more or less tentativeness, I suggest the relevance of allowing Thoreau to speak his own position. It is not altogether as some have supposed.

One is constrained to begin with the title of Thoreau's essay and the first misunderstanding. Characteristic of so many matters attributed to writers no longer able to testify in their own behalf, a phrase made famous has been attributed to an author who did not use it. The essay which Thoreau wrote and published in 1849 in Elizabeth Peabody's *Aesthetic Papers* offers the only title Thoreau ever gave it: **"Resistance to Civil Government."** The article was essentially the lecture Thoreau delivered a year earlier on the subject **"The Relation of the Individual to the State."** The latest title, **"Civil Disobedience,"** was the invention of his posthumous editors, substituted for Thoreau's when they published the essay in 1866 in a collection titled ***Yankee in Canada, with Anti-Slavery and Reform Papers.***

The change of title was not a fortunate one, principally because it lacked the exactitude of Thoreau's own titles. Authority's rejoiner to "disobedience" is "punishment," but its response to "resistance" is simply "force"—and Thoreau knew the moral impact of the difference upon an adult conscience. Punishment implied a guilt which enforcement did not; resistance to force placed the kind of initiative and responsibility upon the "enforcer" which Thoreau intended to dramatize. "I was not born to be forced. I will breathe after my own fashion. Let us see who is the strongest. What force has a multitude? They can only force me who obey a higher law than I." Gandhi too understood the difference, although he did not appreciate the affinity he thereby shared with the essay's author. With only the substitute title of Thoreau's editors to go on, he wrote to Kodanda Rao of the Servants of India Society on September 10, 1935: "When I saw the title of Thoreau's great essay, I began to use his phrase to explain our struggle to the English readers. But I found that even **'Civil Disobedience'** failed to convey the full meaning of the struggle. I therefore adopted the phrase Civil Resistance." Even Thoreau's latest critics and biographers, while acknowledging his original title, appear to set the current pattern by settling for the editor's choice rather than the author's.

Let us turn to some features of Thoreau's view of civil resistance which would seem to need particular acknowledgement today. His concept had both conservative and radical dimensions, and a clarification of his position requires that they be recognized and to some extent distinguished.

On its conservative side, Thoreau's essay offered no clear call to anarchy. Thoreau conceived of such resistance as challenging an unjust requirement of some specific nature, a requirement that forced individual concurrence or support for an immoral end. On the occasion of his arrest in July, 1846, he resisted the government's "requirement" of his support, through its poll tax, for the waging of a foreign war in support of human slavery at home, which he regarded as profoundly immoral. Thoreau was not inclined to bog down in fine distinctions as to the exact degree of immediacy with which his taxes actually supported the invading army or the slaveholder; "I do not care to trace the course of my dollar, if I could, till it buys a man or a musket to shoot with,—the dollar is innocent,—but I am concerned to trace the effects of my allegiance." It was sufficient that the tax was the means by which the government forcibly sought his support. But while he did not qualify his resistance to this particular "requirement" of him, he went to considerable lengths to make clear that his resistance was not to the concept of law itself or to the principle of order. Although he opened his 1849 essay voicing the "ideal of no government at all (upon which the Jefferson compromise of a government that governs least was ultimately based), he disassociated himself from "those who call themselves no-government men," declaring that he spoke "as a citizen" asking not at once for no government, but *at once* a better government. Let every man make known what kind of government would command his respect, and that will be one step toward obtaining it."

It is hard to find anything in Thoreau's utterances which differs in basic principles from the ideals of government upon which his American democracy had been founded. He did not see himself as an opponent of them. He was not opposing the "authority" of the State but emphasizing that its power was empty without the consent of the governed. He did not oppose taxation (he went to pains to point out that he paid his highway tax), but only its misuse for unjust purposes. He insisted that law be the means by which an interested citizenry make certain its government act in accord with moral principles by resisting the law that did not. He could, in a later essay, turn such resistance around to reveal the bases of order it presumed, by declaring, "The law will never make men free; it is men who have got to make the law free. They are lovers of law and order who observe the law when the government breaks it." As President Harris Wofford recently reminded us, this form of civil resistance "seeks not to undermine the law, but to perfect it, 'not to abolish the law but to fulfill it.'" It actually expects a gret deal from the law, as Thoreau made clear when confronted with Massachusetts' Fugitive Slave Law: "No matter how valuable law may be to protect your property, even to keep soul and body together, if it do not keep you and humanity together." Thoreau's belief in the doctrine of a fundamental "higher law" (a belief, it should be recalled, which he shared with radicals and conservatives alike in the 1850s) presumed an exacting moral order for the maintenance of which governments and laws were originated.

Equally conservative, perhaps, was the stress which Thoreau placed so exclusively upon individual action, rather than on group or organized social action of any nature. By temperament and conviction he viewed responsibility as an individual rather than a social matter, just as he remained basically disinterested in all mechanisms and motives for manipulating people *en masse*, in groups or social entities of any shape or persuasion. The *raison* for all moral action lay with the individual alone: "It is not so important that many should be as good as you, as that there be some absolute goodness somewhere; for that will leaven the whole loaf." When twelve Massachusetts men, led by Thoreau's friend Thomas Wentworth Higginson, were arrested in Boston for interfering with the Fugitive Slave Law—they had made an abortive attempt to free the negro Anthony Burns from jail where he waited "legal" return to his Virginia owner—they were urged by the Abolitionists to plead not-guilty and seek a jury trial for better publicizing the moral case against the law. Thoreau's advice would have been otherwise: that they proudly acknowledge their action and expose the law's "power" by leaving the consequence's of the State's action against them to the conscience and determination of the State. We know that the Burns episode brought Thoreau as close as any event ever did to active support of the Abolitionist's resort to organized social protest. Even then, however, he refused to join any anti-slavery society or turn his attention to the social dimensions of his protest beyond a personal exhortation to others to look to their own individual consciences. When Concord's constable Sam Staples appealed to Thoreau for an alternative to arresting him on that famous July evening, Thoreau's only suggestion was that Staples resign his office.

When an anonymous donor paid the taxes which Thoreau had deliberately withheld, and thereby secured Thoreau's release from jail, although Thoreau appears to have resented such release, he was later to express an attitude which his more aggressive apostles today may find hard to tolerate. In the first place, he separated the integrity of his own act completely from that by another, no matter how that other person's affected the outcome of his own. And in the second place, he conceded the other person an absolute right to his own act of conscience, even though he regarded that act mistaken and even morally unsound.

> If others pay the tax which is demanded of me, from a sympathy with the State, they do but what they have already done in their own case, or rather they abet injustice to a greater extent than the State requires. If they pay the tax from a mistaken interest in the individual taxed, to save his property, or prevent his going to jail, it is because they have not considered wisely how far they let their private feelings interfere with the public good.

As neither State nor neighbor had the slightest authority over his conscience, so neither did they or he have such over his neighbor's. The power of Thoreau's posture on civil resistance stemmed from its absolute requirements for individual action, not from any call to missionary duty. This he could dramatize in a statement apt to offend both dedicated social reformer and moral zealot: "It is not a man's duty, as a matter of course, to devote himself to the eradication of any, even the most enormous wrong; he may still properly have other concerns to engage him; but it is his duty, at least, to wash his hands of it, and, if he gives it no thought longer, not to give it practically his support." Then bringing the moral test back to rest squarely where he felt it belonged, the *only* place where he felt it belonged, Thoreau concluded, "If I devote myself to other pursuits and contemplations, I must first see, at least, that I do not pursue them upon another man's shoulders. I must get off him first, that he may pursue his contemplations."

Behind the reservations of Thoreau's stress upon individual, conscionable action lay the more radical implication of its social effectiveness, of course, as Thoreau himself was quick to point out. He found "litle virtue in the action of masses of men. When the majority shall at length vote for the abolition of slavery, it will be because they are indifferent to slavery, or because there is but little slavery left to be abolished by their vote.'' At the same time, he regarded individual action from moral principle ''essentially revolutionary.''

> I know this well, that if one thousand, if one hundred, if ten men whom I could name,—if ten *honest* men only,—ay, if *one* HONEST man, in this State of Massachusetts, *ceasing to hold slaves,* were actually to withdraw from the copartnership, and be locked up in the county jail therefor, it would be the abolition of slavery in America. For it matters not how small the beginning may seem to be; what is once done well is done forever. . . . If the alternative is to keep all just men in prison, or give up war and slavery, the State will not hesitate which to choose.

It is not really possible to push Thoreau beyond this point with regard to questions of social effectiveness. He settled, rightly or wrongly, for faith in the unaided power of individual moral persuasion.

Thoreau's emphasis upon the moral premises of civil resistance dictated a further reservation regarding its practice. Such action was reserved for clear-cut issues of profound and universal moral principles, principles whose case one could not possibly assert too strongly. The discrimination was important to Thoreau. Governments, like all machines, had their ''frictions,'' most of which ''it would be a great evil to make a stir about.'' ''If the injustice is part of the necessary friction of the machine of government, let it go, let it go: perchance it will wear smooth,—certainly the machine will wear out. If the injustice has a spring, or a pulley, or a rope, or a crank, exclusively for itself, then perhaps you may consider whether the remedy will not be worse than the evil.'' The test for resistance was whether the law *required* injustice of one, whether the friction had created its own machine for producing ''oppression and robbery'': ''Then I say, break the law. Let your life be a counterfriction to stop the machine.'' For Thoreau, civil resistance was not to be practicd indiscriminately or nonchalantly. He did not advocate peering into every act of the government with a myopic moral eye, as his rejection of the issue of import tariffs confirms. As he put his reservations, ''I do not wish to quarrel with any man or nation. I do not wish to split hairs, to make fine distinctions, or set myself up as better than my neighbors. I seek, rather, I may say, even an excuse for conforming to the laws of the land.'' The moral issue prompting civil resistance from one holding a moderate and accommodating stand should speak loud and clear, so irrefutably as to warrant a virtually inevitable personal commitment.

Because of such reservations, Thoreau offers little support to those demonstrators who throw themselves into postures of civil resistance for superficial causes. He would mark the difference between the defiance of an ordinance for marching in opposition to a war and for securing later dormitory visiting hours for coeds. On the other hand, the very magnitude of the ''test'' Thoreau requires offers a more radical dimension to his stand, for it is frequently responsible for the failure of such civil resistance to meet the simple one-to-one relationship between specific law and cause which Justice Abe Fortas would make the *sine qua non* for any act of such resistance in this country. It is understandably tempting for lawyers to reduce the ''legitimacy'' of civil resistance to another step in the legal process, for on the legal level it *is* that. But for Thoreau, as one must acknowledge for a good number of our contemporary demonstrators, it was not only that. Thoreau was not ''testing'' the constitutionality of the government's right to tax him when he refused to pay his tax, any more than we can presume that all draft-card burners opposed to the Viet Nam war are resisting the government's right to draft its armed forces from a civilian population.

To the extent that a moral issue assumes dimension, it tends to transcend a particular law which only in some degree relates to it. This was reflected in Thoreau's confession that it was for no particular item in his poll tax that he refused to pay it; the whole had become symbol of the part. To the extend that the South saw the crusade of Martin Luther King as truly ''revolutionary'' (a term Thoreau uses frequently), it can be assumed it sensed the breadth and inclusiveness of King's challenge to basic inequities beyond those embodied in any single ordinance or segregation law. Particular statutes became means for ''refusing allegiance,'' as Thoreau put it, to the larger power behind them, whether that power was the local magistrate, the southern legislature, the southern white majority, or even the Federal government as it might have appeared to be an active supporter of injustice. In Thoreau's day, it should be noted, the symbol of attack eventually became the Constitution of the United States itself so long as it embodied a specific sanction of slavery. In recommending civil resistance when a government's ''tyranny or its inefficiency are great and unendurable,'' Thoreau recognized that such resistance might extend to different arms of that government's authority. Although he limited his own resistance to the poll tax, he abetted those who extended it openly to the Fugitive Slave Act and ultimately to the original slave laws of the southern states, just as he expressed support for the young men who refused to serve in the Mexican War. His test was a moral one, and only secondarily a constitutional one; but he saw such appeal as a thoroughly responsible one for a democracy, addressed to those who were the true sources of any authority properly expressed through law, an appeal ''first and instantaneously from them to the Maker of them, and secondly, from them to themselves.''

Those who whiff the smell of anarchy in Thoreau's position often trace the source to yet another cornerstone of his case: his insistence upon the individual conscience as the inviolable yardstick for judgement of the law. Certainly his view of civil resistance rests unabashedly upon the primacy of the individual conscience. The only value he saw in political freedom was its means to moral freedom, and when it came to the test of the latter, he declared he would much rather ''trust to the sentiment of the people'' than to judges or courts of law. That ''sentiment'' was indeed an individual matter with each person. But we tend to forget that Thoreau found civil resistance effective precisely to the extent that these individual ''sentiments'' accorded with very broadly accepted moral values. A distinguishing feature of the concepts of virtue which Thoreau and his mid-nineteenth-century peers held was the breadth of their intellectual base. Individual conscience was measured by universal moral laws and the ''truths'' which that conscience was expected to confirm were never less occult, parochial, or idiosyncratic. Far from resting upon the untried truth of the private inner voice, moral philosophers like Thoreau gave most of their service to the cause of testing those truths against the broadest and longest experience of the greatest number of men, testing them against the whole of western man's, and some of eastern's, intellectual heritage. A posture of civil resistance, in Thoreau's eyes, was a reaffirmation of moral values for which one could presume near unanimity on the part of all people; only the application in a particular case found some persons blind, just as the need of acting upon the obvious dictates of one's conscience found others slumbering. Today, as in the mid-nineteenth century in American history or the early twentieth in India's, it is not generally in the moral premises back of conscionable acts of civil resistance that their "radical" dimension resides.

Perhaps the most conservative feature of Thoreau's stance was his insistence on withholding civil resistance until compelled to offer it. Those who today search deliberately for such confrontations with the State find little comfort in Thoreau's position. Judge Charles E. Wyzanski, Jr., chief judge for the U.S. District Court for Massachusetts, referring to Sir Thomas More's response to Henry VIII's legal challenge to him, labels such delayed civil resistance "heroic," "the most likely to give peace of mind and to evidence moral courage" even today. Whatever one calls it, Thoreau practiced and defended it: "It is not for a man to *put himself* in such an attitude to society [of civil resistance], but to maintain himself in whatever attitude he finds himself through obedience to the laws of his being, which will never be one of opposition to a just government. Cut the leather only where the shoe pinches. Let us not have a rabid virtue that will be revenged on society,—that falls on it, not like the morning dew, but like the fervid noonday sun, to wither it." While his decision not to pay his poll tax, following the example set by his neighbor Bronson Alcott three years earlier, represented a deliberate decision on Thoreau's part to defy the State's authority, the latter's quiet avoidance of enforcing its authority saw no move on Thoreau's part to identify his gesture further or to force the State to confront him. When the State finally did, Thoreau confessed, "It is true, I might have resisted forcibly with more or less effect, might have run 'amok' against society; but I preferred that society run 'amok' against me, it being the desperate party." His resistance was required when the State "fatally interfered with my lawful business," having "not only interrupted me in my passage through Court Street on errands of trade," but having "interrupted me and every man on his onward and upward path, on which he had trusted to leave Court Street far behind." The role of civil resistance required that the State be the original initiator of the action and that such action in turn be decisive for compelling conscientious resistance. (pp. 5-9)

We recognize a wide swing of degree between Thoreau's overstated desire for accommodation in his review of the acts and spirit of the government in regard to its poll tax in 1849, and his defense of the unavoidable character of Brown's resistance to that government's military authority on the side of the slaveholder in 1859. Issues and responses had become clearer, more "just" men had faced jail, the tests of conscience had proved more immediate and conspicuous for Thoreau as well as for his neighbors in ten tears. Inevitably the stages of "relevant" resistance were advancing forward rapidly. But contrary to some who have written of Thoreau's later views of the Burns' incident and John Brown's revolt, I do not find Thoreau changing any of the basic principles of his approach. The case he makes is still that for compelled resistance dictated by individual conscience responding to a clear-cut and profoundly important moral principle, calling on other individuals to act similarly and thereby force the government's support of justice.

Readers who see a shift in Thoreau's position are apt to be responding to his changing attitude toward a subsidiary feature of his concept of civil resistance: namely, the role of violence in its expression. Here we encounter a radical dimension of Thoreau's views which has been wishfully ignored. We must note two things about it. In the first place, nowhere in Thoreau's 1849 essay, let alone in his later ones, is there any deliberate eschewal of violence as necessarily inappropriate on moral grounds in connection with civil resistance. Nowhere does Thoreau make passivism an essential concomitant of such action. He defined the prospects for a "peaceable revolution" in his 1849 essay: "If a thousand men were not to pay their tax-bills this year, that would not be a violent and bloody measure, as it would be to pay them, and enable the State to commit violence and shed innocent blood. This is, in fact, the definition of a peaceable revolution, *if any such is possible*." The italics are mine, to give warning to those who have found herein too quick support for a doctrine solely of passive resistance. For Thoreau immediately adds, "But even suppose blood should flow? Is there not a sort of blood shed when the conscience is wounded? Through this wound a man's real manhood and immortality flow out, and he bleeds to an everlasting death. I see this blood flowing now."

In the second place, we have to recognize that Thoreau's view of the degree of violence which one may be compelled to show in one's resistance, undergoes conspicuous change with the times and circumstances. We forget that he reminded us that he might have resisted "forcibly" his own arrest "with more or less effect," but chose then for good reasons not to. The Sims episode in 1851 provoked him to acknowledge greater sympathy with violent resistance, as he reaffirmed three years later with the Burns case. He now found his thoughts "murder to the State"; rather than settle for obedience to the laws of slavery until North and South were eventually "persuaded" of their injustice, he confessed he "need not say what match I would touch, what system endeavor to blow up." With the incident at Harper's Ferry and his neighbors' fearful responses to the violence of John Brown's stand, Thoreau declared outright his approval of force if such proved necessary to resist the tyranny of the majority in behalf of gross injustice. He found determining significance in the character of the violence offered, asking his countrymen to consider carefully "what sort of violence is that which is encouraged, not by soldiers, but by peaceable citizens, not so much by laymen as by ministers of the Gospel, not so much by the fighting sects as by the Quakers, and not so much by Quaker men as by Quaker women?" He concluded with as unequivocal a statement on the subject as one could ask for, one which deserves to be quoted in its entirety. It anticipated the military measures which were soon to rend North and South, and forecast his support of them. It also distinguished honestly the degree of Brown's concern from Thoreau's own, thus defining the common consistency of their respective actions on common moral grounds.

> It was his [Brown's] peculiar doctrine that a man has a perfect right to interfere by force with the slaveholder, in order to rescue the slave. I agree with him. They who are continually shocked by slavery have the same right to be shocked by the violent death of the slaveholder, but no others. Such will be more shocked by his life than his death. I shall not be forward to think him mistaken in his method who quickest succeeds to liberate the slave. I speak for the slave when I say that I prefer the philanthropy of Captain Brown to that philanthropy which neither shoots me nor liberates me. At any rate, I do not think it is quite sane for one to spend his whole life in talking and writing about this matter, unless he is continuously inspired, and I have not done so. A man may have other affairs to attend to. I do not wish to kill nor to be killed, but I can foresee circumstances in which both of these things would be by me unavoidable. We preserve the so-called peace of our community by deeds of petty violence every day. Look at the policeman's billy and handcuffs! Look at the jail! Look at the gallows! Look at the chaplain

> of the regiment! We are hoping only to live safely on the outskirts of *this* provisional army. So we defend ourselves and our hen-roosts, and maintain slavery. I know that the mass of my countrymen think that the only righteous use that can be made of Sharp's rifles and revolvers is to fight duels with them, when we are insulted by other nations, or to hunt Indians, or shoot fugitive slaves with them, or the like. I think that for once the Sharp's rifles and the revolvers were employed in a righteous cause. . . . The question is not about the weapon, but the spirit in which you use it.

The history of the impact of Thoreau's essay is that of a revolutionary document, so revolutionary that we must presume, with all its smoke, a very hot fire at its core. It is not to its implicit or explicit acceptance of resistance by force, however, that we should look for a primary source of this flame. Thoreau identified it when he reminded his readers that the moral bases for the action he recommended rendered all matters of expediency essentially irrelevant. He well recognized that herein lay an ultimate potential for power and threat in his proposed resistance. It was a posture which ruled out all those comfortable compromises with effects to which most of us are prone with respect to most of our acts most of the time, a posture fully justifying our "uneasiness" over a recourse so unmitigatingly to moral conscience. On this issue Thoreau was uncompromising: "There is no such thing as accomplishing a righteous reform by the use of expediency," he declared categorically. Taking issue with the position of William Paley, the British philosopher, in his chapter on "Duty of Submission to Civil Government" from his *Principles of Moral and Political Philosophy,* wherein all civil obligation was resolved into expediency, Thoreau ranked civil resistance under those acts where the rule of expediency did not apply, an act in which "a people, as well as an individual, must do justice, cost what it may. If I have unjustly wrested a plank from a drowning man, I must restore it to him though I drown myself. This, according to Paley, would be inconvenient. . . . The people must cease to hold slaves and to make war on Mexico, though it cost them their existence as a people."

This cardinal premise is the most radical ramrod in Thoreau's stance. The immediate "success" or "failure" of civil resistance was not to determine either its appropriateness or its essential value. Thoreau distrusted fame because "she considers not the simple heroism of an action, but only as it is connected with its apparent consequences. She praises till she is hoarse the easy exploit of the Boston tea party, but will be comparatively silent about the braver and more disinterestedly heroic attack on the Boston Courthouse, simply because it was unsuccessful." Tolstoy, who read Thoreau, wrote his letter to the desperate young Hessian candidate for conscription, demolishing the arguments he so frantically offered of loved ones dependent, of life at stake, of future service canceled, insisting uncompromisingly that the young man had no alternative but to resist and face the penalty (which both knew, in this case, to be execution) rather than betray his passivist principles. To rule out expediency was to place such resistance above legal considerations: "The lawyer's truth is not Truth," asserted Thoreau, but consistency or a consistent expediency." The same exclusion prompted Thoreau's concern for those participants in such resistance who found themselves top-heavy with material encumbrances and dependencies upon the State they wished to resist; they were bound to dread most the consequences to their properties and families of their "disobedience"; (the one time Thoreau used the term in his 1849 essay). To the extent this prompted them to weigh their actions by their losses, in a situation wherein measurement of what one had to lose was basically irrelevant, the moral ground was taken out from under their feet. Thoreau's stand was and is extremely strong advocacy, too strong for the uncommitted or the defensive. It is not a form of resistance for week-end protestors or evasive insurgents. Its winning card has always been personal cost, the strength to "take the consequences." (pp. 10-11)

John Aldrich Christie, "Thoreau on Civil Resistance," in ESQ, *No. 54, Quarter I, 1969, pp. 5-12.*

ROBERT PALMER SAALBACH (essay date 1972)

[In the following essay, Saalbach responds to Heinz Eulau's suggestion that "Civil Disobedience" fails to propose "an objective criterion for assaying the correctness of an individual's or a minority's judgment." Saalbach argues that Thoreau tacitly offers the use of reason as the most satisfactory way of determining right from wrong. For Eulau's original comments, see the excerpt dated 1949.]

In every imperfect society, including that of Thoreau and that of today, there sometimes develops a conflict between the customs, rules, and laws which society expects the individual to obey and the socially-implanted "conscience" of the individual. Today, this conflict is perhaps best expressed in the controversy over United States policy in Vietnam; in Thoreau's day, it expressed itself in controversy over Negro bondage and the Mexican War.

The conflict in Thoreau's day may be illustrated by a quotation from **"Civil Disobedience"** on the one hand and by a quotation from a later critic of that document on the other. Thoreau writes:

> [If the law] is of such a nature that it requires you to be an agent of injustice to another, then, I say, break the law.

Heinz Eulau, a critic of Thoreau, comments on this prinicple of Thoreau's as follows:

> . . . Thoreau had to postulate a (by democratic standards) curious distinction between law and right, with the explanation that one has to have faith in man, that each man can determine for himself what is right and just. Hence no conflict is possible, so the argument goes, because law is law only if identical with right. Thoreau could not demonstrate, however, that there is, in case the majority is wrong, an objective criterion for assaying the correctness of an individual's or a minority's judgment.

To persons who have been brought up on Thoreau, of course, the argument that "might makes right" is anathema. Still, in fairness to Eulau and others who defend the principle on democratic grounds, such persons should, certainly, be willing to analyze "might makes right" in order to see what, if anything, may be said in its favor. Society, by definition, is a system of mutually accepted rules of conduct limiting the behavior of individuals. Without such rules there can be only a collection of individuals none of whom has learned how he is expected to act or ought to act in reference to others. Thus the "might" enforced by such rules does make a thing "right" simply by providing a mutual structure for joint activities. Living in society, then, is a "game" which each person "plays" according to the "rules." Furthermore, the various social pressures implant in each a sense of obligation to obey the rules. Social living, like any other game, cannot be played without rules to which each player feels obligated. Through the rules people learn what specific conduct is approved and what is disapproved, and thus they learn how they are expected to act in regard to others.

In a democracy, then, as Eulau says, the principle of majority rule, functioning as it does to set up the rules of democratic society, is inviolable unless there can be "an objective criterion for assaying the correctness of an individual's or a minority's judgment." To this extent, Heinz Eulau must be adjudged to be right. What about Thoreau?

The first thing to notice about Thoreau's **"Civil Disobedience"** is that it is not always consistent. Thoreau writes in one place:

> It is not a man's duty, as a matter of course, to devote himself to the eradication of any, even the most enormous wrong. . . .

In the very first paragraph of his essay, Thoreau expresses himself as follows:

> Witness the present Mexican War, the work of comparatively a few individuals using the standing government as their tool; for, in the outset, the people would not have consented to this measure.

And, later on, he writes:

> I cannot for an instant recognize that policital organization as *my* government which is the *slave's* government also.

Certainly, however, in thus expressing strong opposition to the Mexican War and to slavery (as well as in his defense of John Brown), Thoreau does accept a duty to commit himself to "the eradication of . . . enormous wrong." Also, after saying "It costs me less in every sense to incur the penalty of disobedience to the State than it would to obey," he nevertheless calmly remarks later: " . . . the government does not concern me much, and I shall bestow the fewest possible thoughts on it."

Yet no one, surely, would feel himself obligated to disobey a directive of government if the government were really of no concern to him. To the unconcerned, an act of disobedience will not be justified on the grounds of principle.

Vernon Louis Parrington, after quoting ***Walden*** to the effect that "To be a philosopher is not merely to have subtle thoughts, nor even to found a school, but to so love wisdom as to live according to its dictates, a life of simplicity, independence, magnanimity, and trust . . . " comes to the conclusion:

> It was the reply of the arch-individualist to the tyrannous complexities of society, and it set him apart even in the world of transcendentalism.

Yet such "arch-individualism" was only one side of Thoreau, as has been seen. It is, of course, best expressed in what Heinz Eulau calls the "highly personalized experience" of ***Walden,*** "the attempt of a sensitive spirit to discover his own integrity and convey this discovery . . . as a symbolic expression of man's need for finding his own integrity in whatever fashion seemed best." Eulau then concludes:

> "I desire," [Thoreau] wrote, "that there be as many different persons in the world as possible; but I would have each one be very careful to find out and pursue *his own* way. . . ." As such, life at Walden Pond was a meaningful experiment even though it was meaningless as a form of *social* living.

"Civil Disobedience," as has been seen, is much more social in its message than is ***Walden,*** but, as has also been pointed out, the individualist experiement of living on the outskirts of society did, in some passages of **"Civil Disobedience,"** show through—and hence the social message of Thoreau, as presented in the passages on the Mexican War and on slavery, is obscured.

To go a bit deeper, one should note Thoreau's distinction between the right (as dictated by the individual consicence) and law as set down by the government. Thoreau writes:

> Can there not be a government in which majorities do not virtually decide right and wrong, but conscience?—in which majorities decide only those questions to which the rule of expediency is applicable? Must the citizen even for a moment, or in the least degree, resign his conscience to the legislator? Why has every man a consicence, then? I think that we should be men first, and subjects afterward. It is not desirable to cultivate a respect for the law, so much as for the right. The only obligation which I have a right to assume is to do at any time what I think right. It is truly enough said, that a corporation has no conscience; but a corporation of conscientious men is a corporation *with* a conscience. Law never made men a whit more just: and, by means of their respect for it, even the well-disposed are daily made the agents of injustice.

Thoreau here assumes that the law always follows expediency while conscience always follows the right. Yet Thoreau himself admits, in the latter part of this passage, that "a corporation of conscientious men is a corporation *with* a conscience"—and, if this is true, then the laws made by such a corporation (the majority in a democracy) will follow the conscience as much as expediency. Only by adopting the untenable principle that the majority are men without conscience while minorities, always defeated, are men with conscience can Thoreau justify his position. It no doubt sounds reasonable to Thoreau because he considers conscience as something innate and specific in man's makeup which tends to fade as man grows older, so that only a few (a minority) retain it. However, a person's conscience is *socially* derived. As John K. Forrest puts it [in his *Reality of Preachment*]:

> . . . because "conscience" has come to be habitually *spoken of* as if it denoted a specific capacity—"to know what is right"—we have been conditioned to accept it in this way. And as an unfortunate consequence, the real applicable sense of the term (denoting imperative feelings of obligation *toward* particular valued ends, or ultimate worths) comes to be crowded from our minds.
>
> When we deal with conscience in the real world of practice, we reasonably conceive of a man's conscience, not as a specific power but only as general feelings of obligation of two different, but interrelated kinds: (1) his feeling of internal *response* to approvals and condemnations; and (2) his feelings of *accountability* to the specific worths he holds as most crucial and imperative.

Obviously, since a person's internal response and feelings of accountability will depend on the kinds of laws and customs he has been taught to obey, his conscience will be no better than his society. Thus the distinction between law and right will not hold, and it cannot be said, as Thoreau does say, that the only obligation is to the right rather than to the law.

As has been seen, Thoreau builds here on the concept of a life on the outskirts of society, as at Walden, a life fed only by "innate" ideas offering specific guidance. And thus he sticks, in the passage here quoted, to the nonsocial (or, as Parrington puts it, the arch-individualistic side of his personality, where right belongs to the individual conscience and law to the alien society. Such a distinction, however, far from being the basis of justice through which the Mexican War and Negro bondage were to be condemned (as Thoreau believed), is really the basis for the very kind of exploitation in which these condemned activities were rooted. For if, as Thoreau says, "the only obligation which I have a right to assume is to do at any time what I think right," then, if one's socially implanted conscience tells him that it is right for him, in order to move ahead with the American dream, to exploit Negroes and take away Mexican land by force, he must do precisely that. Not even a law to the contrary would be enough to stop him. What happens, of course, is that the individual Negro or Mexican is, as a result of such exploitation, crushed into something less than human, a thing without human individuality. Hence it is true, as John Forrest has stated,

> that in actual practice, "individualism" amounts to pure egoism. It actually supports the doctrine that "all value, rights, and duties originate in individuals, and not in the social whole." . . . And thus, when "individualism" is actually practiced, it inevitably results in some men achieving *their* individuality at the expense of the individuality of *others*.

No doubt related to his distinction between "governmental law" and "individual right" is Thoreau's habit of treating government as something distinct from the individuals which make it up:

> I heartily accept the motto,—"That government is best which governs least." . . . Government is at best but an expedient, but most governments are usually, and all governments are sometimes, inexpedient. . . . This American government—what is it but a tradition, though a recent one, endeavoring to transmit itself unimpared to posterity, but each instant losing some of its integrity?

In these examples (and others may be found throughout **"Civil Disobedience"**) Thoreau speaks of government as an "it"—as something "out there" which is quite distinct from the individuals who are president, congressmen, or justices of the Supreme Court. This idea tends to reinforce Thoreau's previous choosing of "individual right" over "social law," but it is, of course, a myth. The men who make up the government are, in reality, men with socially derived consciences, which are simply their feelings of obligation toward a particular course of action. When one divorces the "rights of man" from the obligation to obey the law, he speaks for a totally untenable anarchy in which each person is a law unto himself. This fact is obscured both by treating the abstract "individual" as if he were a real person on the one hand and by treating the men who make up the government (and decide on governmental policies) as an abstract "governmental entity" on the other. As a result, philosophical anarchists, who follow Thoreau's dictum "That government is best which governs not at all," are led to call for a completely abstract freedom which lacks any specific content (actually a freedom from the dictates of society, whatever they might be), and thus they completely obscure the real claims of inidvidual persons upon those in authority for the fulfillment of their needs, including the need to grow into a mature individuality. Thoreau's position here should be quite apparent. In his "individualistic" statements, he completely overlooks the real reasons that he is opposed to the Mexican War and to Negro bondage—that they both deny the rightful claims of persons on their society for individual fulfillment.

Had Thoreau been consistent in calling for anarchical individualism, there would be no kernel of truth in **"Civil Disobedience"** to pose against Heinz Eulau's defense of a democratically-oriented "might makes right" theory. However, as is usually the case in arguments among imperfect human beings, the truth does not, by any means, lie wholly with Heinz Eulau. His article, quite critical of Thoreau for many valid reasons, nevertheless overlooks the fact that, despite his tendency to go to extremes, Thoreau did pose the "objective criterion for assaying the correctness of an individual's or a minority's judgment" for which Eulau asked.

First of all, despite his extremist statements, Thoreau did admit that there are times when one might as well obey the law:

> If the injustice is part of the necessary friction of the machine of government [Thoreau writes], let it go, let it go; perchance it will wear smooth—certainly the machine will wear out. If the injustice has a spring, or a pulley, or a rope, or a crank, exclusively for itself, then perhaps you may consider whether the remedy will not be worse than the evil. . . .

Of course it could be argued that Thoreau is talking with tongue-in-cheek; but it could be argued that, remembering the times when he went about the pursuit of his own affairs without a thought to the workings of government, Thoreau was here trying to justify a policy which falls short of complete defiance of the law.

Second, though the first two paragraphs of **"Civil Disobedience"** are pretty strong condemnations of government, including democratic government, the third paragraph is a reversal:

> But to speak practically and as a citizen, unlike those who call themselves no-government men [himself?], I ask for, not at once no government, but *at once* a better government. Let every man make known what kind of government would command his respect, and that will be one step toward obtaining it.

"Such a government," adds Heinz Eulau, "would anticipate and provide for reform, cherish its 'wise minority' and encourage its citizens 'to be on the alert to point out its faults.'

In these ways, then, Thoreau opposes the arch-individualism of which Parrington speaks. He comes, in other words, back into the political arena from the remoteness of Walden Pond, and begins "practically and as a citizen" to consider the problems of democratic government. In so doing, however, as Eulau suggests in the above quotation, Thoreau still shows greater interest in the "wise minority" than in the democratic process of "majority rule":

> After all [he writes], the practical reason why, when the power is once in the hands of the people, a majority are permitted, and for a long period continue, to rule is not because they are most likely to be in the right, nor because this seems fairest to the minority, but because they are physically the strongest. But a government in which the majority rule in all cases cannot be based on justice. . . .

Thus Thoreau is still posing an abstract justice known only to the "wise minority" over and against the power and might of majority rule. Yet he has come far enough, in these passages, to see that, as a citizen, he can not simply "wash his hands of [government]"—as he suggests in a later passage.

The crowning greatness of Thoreau, however (one which poses quite clearly the "objective criterion for assaying the correctness of an individual's or a minority's judgment" for which Heinz Eulau calls), is to be seen in the following passage:

> All men recognize the right of revolution; that is, the right to refuse allegiance to, and to resist, the government, when its tyranny or its inefficiency are great and unendurable. But almost all say that such is not the case now. But such was the case, they think, in the Revolution of '75. If one were to tell me that this was a bad government because it taxed certain foreign commodities brought into its ports, it is most probable that I should not make an ado about it, for I can do without them. All machines have their friction; and possibly this does enough good to counter-balance the evil. At any rate, it is a great evil to make a stir about it. But when the friction comes to have its machine, and oppression and robbery are organized, I say, let us have such a machine no longer. In other words, when a sixth of the population of a nation which has undertaken to be the refuge of liberty are slaves, and a whole country is unjustly overrun and conquered by a foreign army, and subjected to military law, I think that it is not too soon for honest men to rebel and revolutionize. What makes this duty the more urgent is the fact that the country so overrun is not our own, but ours is the invading army.

First of all, the statement "All machines have their friction" is reminiscent of an earlier quoted passage counseling obedience to the law, and it is here supported by a much clearer example—that of taxing certain foreign commodities. Thus Thoreau here calls for civil disobedience as the exception to the rule, rather than the rule itself, and so departs from philosophical anarchism.

This note in Thoreau has been heard by other critics, but if Heinz Eulau is to be believed, it has not been supported by reference to the above passage from **"Civil Disobedience,"** but, rather, buy a passage from ***Walden,*** one which, as Eulau notes, is quite untypical of that book:

> Some recent interpreters have tried, in vain I think, [writes Eulau] to make Thoreau palatable to liberalism by reading their own preferences into his writings. But even if they seek to strike a balance, the end effect of their expositions is tortuous. Max Lerner, for instance, writes inaccurately, I believe, that Thoreau's individualism should be seen as part of a rebellion against the oversocialized New England town, in which the individual was being submerged. . . . He was not so limited as to believe that the individual could by his own action stem the heedless onrush of American life, or succeed wholly in rechanneling it. Similarly, Townsend Scudder states that "though so intense an individualist, Thoreau favored the ideal of communal living as in keeping with the spirit of America." Significantly, Lerner, Scudder as well as F. O. Mathiessen [*sic*] repeat, by way of evidence, a single passage from Thoreau's ***Walden***—"to act collectively is according to the spirit of our institutions."

Thus Eulau dismisses the point of view of those critics who fail to recognize or try to explain away the arch-individualism of Thoreau. But evidently assuming that, if the truth is not all on one side, it must be all on the other, Eulau goes on:

> The bulk of proof is, in fact, on the other side. Even Vernon Parrington, whose progressivist bias is rarely concealed, recognized that Thoreau "could not adopt the cooperative solution." Thoreau refused to join Brook Farm because, in his own words, he "would rather keep a bachelor's hall in hell than go to board in heaven."

However, by going to an extreme here, Eulau places himself in as precarious a position as did Lerner, Scudder, and Matthiessen in the earlier passage. Every human being is complex in his makeup, not simple, and perfect consistency is a rare human trait. Thoreau, it has been shown, was not always consistent, but this very fact adds to the truth of Eulau at least the germ of what Lerner, Scudder, and Matthiessen have to say. If Thoreau was, at times, arch-individualist, he was also—as may be seen in the passage concerning the right of revolution—at other times social and democratic.

Furthermore—and of much greater importance—Thoreau does, in the passage quoted, provide the "objective criterion for assaying the correctness of an individual's or a minority's judgment," which is so necessary to the justification of an act of civil disobedience. The principle, excellently stated by Thoreau, is at the very beginning of the passage already quoted:

> All men recognize the right of revolution: that is, the right to refuse allegiance to, and to resist, the government, when its tyranny or its inefficiency are great and unendurable.

The arch-individualist, of course, might interpret this passage as endorsing the right to revolt against government whenever its acts produce some personal discomfort—as, for example, the right to refuse to stop for a red light when one is in a hurry and there is no traffic. But Thoreau, in the rest of the passage, makes abundantly clear that he is not here thinking in such terms. What he defines as great and unendurable governmental wrong is a sixth of the population being slaves and "a whole country . . . overrun and conquered by a foreign army and subjected to military law." Thus, to Thoreau as he speaks here, civil disobedience or the right to revolution is justified, not on individualistic grounds, but on social grounds. In other words, if being a slave oneself is great and unendurable wrong, then one must not make slaves of others; and, if one would object to his country's being overrun by a foreign army and subjected to military law, then he must not so enslave another country.

As was stated at the very beginning of this paper, the acceptance of the principle above enunciated is the basis of all social living. Men and women accept the rules, customs, and laws of their society as applicable to all of them in order that they may proceed with joint activities. This is the truth which Thoreau sees in this passage. There is no truth, however, in his attempt to justify this insight by individual intuition or conscience. For, if all persons had such a conscience as a birthright, they would be no more likely than Thoreau himself to live in violation of it. Such a conscience would, certainly, be instinctive, and, try as one might, one cannot violate an instinct. It is for this reason that those who do violate conscience (as Thoreau defines it) must be thought of as lacking such a conscience, and hence, in Thoreau's terms, less than human.

However, as men and women are obligated only to their fellow human beings and not to those less than human, they can scarcely agree with Thoreau's social insight as long as they agree with his concept of conscience as innate idea. In order to agree with the social insight of Thoreau, people must redefine conscience as a socially conditioned sense of right and wrong, amenable to reason. Thoreau had learned from his democratic society that what is right for one is right for all and out of this he developed a sense of obligation which he unfortunately took to be an innate idea. When, then, this sense of obligation came into conflict with the demands of government for the support of slavery and the Mexican War, Thoreau, through the exercise of reason, showed that the government was being contradictory. This was Thoreau's greatness as a man and his great contribution to mankind.

The conflict which "sometimes develops . . . between the customs, rules, and laws which society expects the individual to obey and the socially implanted conscience of the individual" is one grounded in reason rather than instinct. Through reasoning, Thoreau was able to condemn and advocate disobedience to a government that endorsed slavery and the Mexican War. Today, men and women, Americans all, can apply the same reasoning to Vietnam. (pp. 18-24)

Robert Palmer Saalbach, "Thoreau and Civil Disobedience," in Ball State University Forum, *Vol. XIII, No. 4, Autumn, 1972, pp. 18-24.*

ALFRED KAZIN (essay date 1972)

[A highly respected American literary critic, Kazin is best known for his essay collections The Inmost Leaf, Contemporaries, *and, particularly,* On Native Grounds, *a study of American prose writing since the era of William Dean Howells. Here, Kazin observes that Thoreau's insistence on freedom of individual conscience provides little pragmatic advice for oppressed individuals.]*

Nature, as we know, Thoreau could always transcendentalize. No storms or solitude or discomfort could turn him out of his fanatical control there. He felt at home in the world of savages. If he was in any sense the scientist he occasionally wanted to be, it was when he felt superior and untouched by dumb things in nature. The only object in nature that seems genuinely to have frightened him was Mount Katahdin in Maine. Describing the night he spent on the summit, he significantly confessed: "I stand in awe of my body, this matter to which I am bound has become so strange to me. I fear not spirits, ghosts, of which I am one . . . but I fear bodies, I tremble to meet them. What is this Titan that has possession of me? Talk of our life in nature—daily to be shown matter, to come in contact with it—rocks, trees, wind on our cheeks! the *solid* earth, the *actual* world! the *common sense!* Contact! *Contact!* Who are we? *where* are we?"

Still, he could always get off that mountain and return to the village of which he said, "I could write a book called Concord," and which he began to see wholly as the book he was writing in his journal. But the State, which to begin with was represented by other men he could not always ignore—this was to become the Other that he could not domesticate as he did God, Nature, and other men's books. In chapter 8 of ***Walden,*** "The Village," he describes his arrest (July, 1846) as he was on his way to the cobbler's. He was arrested for not paying the poll tax that in those days was still exacted by the state in behalf of the church. Thoreau's father had been enrolled in the church, and Thoreau's own name should not have been on the roll. He spent a peaceful, dreamy night in jail. In **"Civil Disobedience"** he reports that "the night in prison was novel and interesting enough. . . . It was like travelling into a far country, such as I had never expected to behold, to lie there for one night. . . . It was to see my native village in the light of the Middle Ages, and our Concord was turned into a Rhine stream, and visions of knights and castles passed before me." At the suggestion of the Concord selectmen, he filed a statement after he had demanded that his name be dropped from the church rolls: KNOW ALL MEN BY THESE PRESENTS THAT I, HENRY THOREAU, DO NOT WISH TO BE REGARDED AS A MEMBER OF ANY INCORPORATED SOCIETY WHICH I HAVE NOT JOINED. The experience was not a traumatic one, and on being released he "returned to the woods in season to get my dinner of huckleberries on Fair Haven Hill." But he says truly, "I was never molested by any person but those who represented the State."

In ***Walden*** Thoreau was to say of his prison experience that it showed the inability of society to stand "odd fellows" like himself. In the essay **"Civil Disobedience,"** he was to say in a most superior way that the State supposed "I was mere flesh and blood and bones, to be locked up," and since it could not recognize that his immortal spirit was free, "I saw that the State was half-witted, that it was timid as a lone woman with her silver spoons . . . and I lost all my remaining respect for it, and pitied it."

But what gives **"Civil Disobedience"** its urgency is that between 1846, when he was arrested for a tax he should have paid in 1840, and 1848, when he wrote it, the State had ceased to be his friend the Concord sheriff, Sam Staples, who so pleasantly took him off to the local hoosegow, but the United States government, which, under the leadership of imperialists like President James Polk and the Southern planters who were determined to add new land for their cotton culture, was making war on Mexico and would take away half its territory in the form of California, Texas, Arizona, and New Mexico. The Mexican war was openly one for plunder, as Lincoln and many other Americans charged. But it was the first significant shock to Thoreau's rather complacent position that the individual can be free, as free as he likes, in and for himself, though his neighbors think him odd. Oddity, however, was no longer enough to sustain total independence from society. Despite Thoreau's opposition to slavery in principle, he knew no Negroes, had never experienced the slightest social oppression. He was a radical individualist very well able to support this position in Concord; he had a share in the family's pencil business, but was not confined by it, and he was indeed as free as air—free to walk about all day long as he pleased, free to build himself a shack on Walden Pond and there prepare to write a book, free to walk home any night for supper at the family boarding house. Up until the Mexican War—and even more urgently, the Fugitive Slave Law of 1850 and finally John Brown's raid on Harpers Ferry in 1859—Thoreau's only social antagonist was the disapproval, mockery, or indifference of his neighbors in Concord. He never knew what the struggle of modern politics can mean for people who identify and associate with each other because they recognize their common condition. Thoreau was a pure idealist, living on principle—typical of New England in his condescension to the Irish immigrants, properly indignant about slavery in far-off Mississippi, but otherwise, as he wrote ***Walden*** to prove, a man who proposed to teach others to be as free of society as himself.

"Civil Disobedience" is stirring, especially today, because of the urgency of its personal morality. As is usual with Thoreau, he seems to be putting his whole soul into the protest against injustice committed by the state. He affirms the absolute right of the individual to obey his own conscience in defiance of an unknown law. But despite his usual personal heat, he tends to moralize the subject wholly and to make it not really serious. He makes a totally ridiculous object of the State, he turns its demands on him into a pure affront, and is telling it to stop being so pretentious and please to disappear. This is certainly refreshing. But anyone who thinks it is a guide to his own political action these days will have to defend the total literary anarchism that is behind it. And it is no use, in this particular, identifying Gandhi with it, for Gandhi, as a young leader of the oppressed Indians in South Africa, was looking for some political strategy by which to resist a totally oppressive racist regime. There were no laws to protect the Indians. Thoreau's essay is a noble, ringing reiteration of the highest religious individualism as a self-evident social principle. The absolute freedom of the individual like himself is his highest good, and the State is not so much the oppressor of this individual as his rival. How dare this Power get in my way? For Thoreau the problem is simply one of putting the highest possible value on the individual rather than on the state. This is urgent because we are all individuals first, and because it is sometimes necessary to obey oneself rather than the State. But for the greatest part, Thoreau is not aware that the individual's problem may be how to resist his state when he is already so much bound up with it. He can hardly just turn his back on it.

The significantly political passages in the essay have to do with what Thoreau calls slavery in Massachusetts. He of all people could not grant that property is the greatest passion and the root of most social conflicts and wars. But he insisted "that if one thousand, if one hundred, if ten men whom I could name—if ten *honest* men only—ay, if *one* Honest man, in this State of Massachusetts, *ceasing to hold slaves,* were actually to withdraw from this co-partnership, and be locked up in the county jail therefor, it would be the abolition of slavery in America." With his marvellous instinct for justice, for pure Christianity, for the deep-rooted rights of the individual soul, he said "Under a government which imprisons any unjustly, the true place for a just man is also a prison." But morally invigorating as this is, it would perhaps not have helped the fugitive slave, and the Mexican prisoner on parole, and the Indian come to plead the wrongs of his race when, as Thoreau said, they came to the prison and found the best spirits of Massachusetts there. Thoreau estimated the power of individual example beyond any other device in politics, but he did not explain how the usefulness of example could communicate itself to people who were in fact slaves, and not free. (pp. 43-7)

Alfred Kazin, "Writing in the Dark," in Henry David Thoreau: Studies and Commentaries, *Walter Harding, George Brenner, Paul A. Doyle, eds., Fairleigh Dickinson University Press, 1972, pp. 34-52.*

MICHAEL G. ERLICH (essay date 1973)

[Erlich discusses Thoreau's use of rhetorical devices in "Civil Disobedience."]

Transcendental speeches pose a unique problem for rhetorical critics. As [Irving] Rein has accurately observed [in his essay "The New England Transcendentalists: Philosophy and Rhetoric"], before 1855 their discourse violated many common expectations. The transcendentalists, for instance, ignored facts; they avoided statistics and considered personal testimony a sham. A useful approach to an analysis of **"Civil Disobedience"** is through the identification of strategies, defined as the rules, devices or patterns that were intended to bring the speaker and listener together in common accord. From a careful consideration of transcendental discourse, four strategies emerge: revelation, transcendence, salvation and omission.

Out of the search for "grand truths" grew a common transcendental strategy. For the transcendentalists, higher laws were not dependent for their authority upon any form of empirical evidence. Rather, men believed in "moral truths" because they were innate; the existence of God and the assurance of immortality, for example, were "given" in human nature. According to William Henry Channing, the result of such an intuitive faith "was a vague yet exalting conception of the godlike nature of the human spirit . . . as viewed by its disciples, . . . a pilgrimage from the idolatrous worlds of creeds and rituals to the temple of the Living God in the soul. It was putting to silence tradition and formulas, that the Sacred Oracle might be heard through intuitions of the single-eyed and pure-hearted."

The "strategy of revelation" was a means of displaying supposedly impregnable arguments and presenting them in the form of epigrams or maxims. The statement needed no conventional means of support, because it was justified by the beauty and repeatability of the phrases. Sprinkled throughout the address were Thoreau's "grand truths." In the first sentence he declared: "I HEARTILY accept the motto,—'That government is best which governs least.'" When encouraging members of the audience to oppose the pro-slavery forces in America, to obey the higher law from "within," Thoreau asserted, "For it matters not how small the beginning may seem to be; what is once well done is done forever." In turn, such a contention was "supported" as follows: "It is not desirable to cultivate a respect for the [civil] law, so much as for the right." And to individuals generally covetous of material riches Thoreau categorically, defiantly proclaimed: "Absolutely speaking, the more money, the less virtue." In many instances, then, proverbial statements were substituted for more complete arguments. The assertion and its support were contained in a pregnant phrase or catchy slogan.

Thoreau's ability to coin memorable phrases had distinct advantages. First, it was virtually impossible to frame meaningful counter-arguments. He commanded, in Rein's terms, a "thunderbolt" method of support. He could present his "grand truths," so that statistics, personal testimony, quotations or any sort of documentation would be irreleveant. For his authority, Thoreau would probably refer to the Moral Law which was written in the hearts of mankind. The typical method for criticizing statements or arguments is to attack either the premise or supporting material. Thoreau, however, gave his critics much to ponder but little to assault. His premise was so general and his evidence so scanty that they defied critical bombardment.

Thoreau's skill in the art of phraseology had a second important advantage. He may have recognized that maxims or slogans not only lessen the likelihood of refutation but have argumentative value. In *Reason and Nature* Cohen maintained that forms of language may produce certainty of conviction because they prevent the listener from being able to conceive of the other side of an issue: "so often does our psychologic certainty prevent us from even entertaining on the pursuit of truth, that it is well to reflect that the feeling of certainty is often nothing but our inability to conceive that opposite of what we happen to believe. In this sense there is no certainty as great as the initial one based on complete ignorance of countervailing considerations. Thus, men show greater certainty about the complicated and elusive questions of politics and religion than about simpler and more verifiable issues."

The tersely cogent proverb, the magical phrase, then, may be an effective means for generating belief. Thoreau did not explicitly admit that he was combining words to attract his listeners, but there seems to be little doubt that as a man of letters he had great faith in the power of words or the dazzling phrase. Always in the minority himself, Thoreau made it a tenet of his philosophy for reform that when the world was changed for the better, a minority would be instrumental in changing it. The minority might consist of only one individual who would take his stand above the mass of men. "I do not hesitate to say that those who call themselves Abolitionists should at once effectually withdraw their support, both in person and property, from the government of Massachusetts and not wait till they constitute a majority . . . I think that it is enough if they have God on their side, . . . moreover, any man more right than his neighbor constitutes a majority of one already." In unequivocal terms Thoreau revealed one of God's laws. Supported by *a priori* truth, his revelation stood forth, virtually resistant to attack.

In brief, Thoreau employed the "strategy of revelation" throughout **"Civil Disobedience."** This strategy is characterized by a display of supposedly impregnable arguments which are presented in the form of maxims or catchy phrases. Thoreau, for instance, began to lecture by quoting a popular motto. Arguments and supporting material were typically expressed in a proverbial phrase or catchy slogan; the speaker commanded a "thunderbolt" method of support. Such a reliance on form rather than on content, moreover, made it difficult to frame meaningful, counter-arguments. Finally, Thoreau's ability to coin a memorable phrase partially explains the reason for his enduring appeal. He had an extraordinary ability to capture flashes of experience, to provide the listener—or future reader—with "grand truths" in the language of a poet.

Another strategy that characterized transcendental discourse was the "strategy of transcendence," which depended on the definition of concepts rather than the pointed, intuitive statements. Essentially, the "strategy of transcendence" was a particular type of argumentative arrangement. 1) Two or more elements are defined. 2) The favored definitions are shown to be superior in various ways to the others. 3) The result is that the "inferior" definitions can be dismissed as irrelevant or as poor concepts. 4) Having nullified contradictory points of view, the speaker can proceed to expound the favored definition or concept. This strategy, moreover, was an extension of transcendental idealism. The transcendentalist believed "in the sufficiency of intuition, the ultimate authority of the soul, and the validity of *a priori* truths." He had at his disposal the universal principles of the Moral Law and occasionally bolstered his concepts with examples or anecdotes.

The "strategy of transcendence" was an identifying feature of Thoreau's speech. He argued, as Rein noted, that anarchy transcended government and that moral individualism transcended society.

In the form of rhetorical syllogisms the arguments upon which **"Civil Disobedience"** rested were as follows:

> One: The best government is the government which governs least. The government which governs not at all is the government which governs least.
>
> Therefore, The best government is the government which governs not at all.
>
> Two: The best government is a government which governs not at all. The American government is not a government which governs not at all.
>
> Therefore, The American government is not the best government.
>
> Three: The first duty of every man is to do justice. To obey the American government is not to do justice.
>
> Therefore, The first duty of every man is not to obey the American government.

Thoreau began the lecture with the first premise of the first syllogism, after which he immediately voiced the second premise. By the end of the second sentence he had stated his conclusion, "That government is best which governs not at all." He followed this argument by a series of comments on the nature of government which belittled the "American system." These remarks, bolstered by aggressive opinions and contemptuous examples, served to illuminate his first conclusion and second major premise.

> The standing army is only an arm of the standing government. The government itself, which is only the mode which the people have chosen to execute their will, is equally liable to be abused and perverted before the people can act through it. Witness the present Mexican war, the work of comparatively a few individuals using the standing government as their tool; . . . Governments show thus how successfully men can be imposed on, even impose on themselves, for their [governments] own advantage . . . government is an expedient by which men would fain succeed in letting one another alone; and, as has been said, when it is most expedient, the governed are most let alone by it.

The body of Thoreau's discourse was an elaboration of the third syllogism and demonstrated his use of the "strategy of transcendence." Defining government as an expedient, showing that justice and expediency are not to be confused, Thoreau argued that obedience to the will of the state is not to do justice. Having established to his satisfaction the validity of the third minor premise, he acknowledged the soundness of his conclusion. It is *not* the duty of every man to obey the American government. The consequences of actions based on this conclusion were then examined. The jail episode and Thoreau's personal relations—or non-relations—with the state were aspects of this exploration. By way of an analogy, Thoreau granted the government as high a place on his list of obligations as he morally could; however, he believed that when the machinery of the state exacts injustice, an individual's obligation to higher laws demands civil disobedience.

> If . . . injustice is part of the necessary friction of the machine of government, let it go, let it go: perchance it will wear smooth—certainly the machine will wear out. If the injustice has a spring, or a pulley, or a rope, or a crank, exclusively for itself, then perhaps you may consider whether the remedy will not be worse than the evil; but if it is of such a nature that it requires you to be the agent of injustice to another, then, I say, break the law. Let your life be a counter-friction to stop the machine.

In the final section of the address Thoreau pictured the kind of government he could fully obey and respect. In accordance with the major premises of syllogisms one and two, this ideal state does not govern at all but respects every man's right to do justice, thus becoming truly just itself. There will never be a really free and enlightened State, until the State comes to recognize the individual as a higher and independent power, from which all its power and authority are derived, and treats him accordingly."

In the course of the speech, Thoreau's arguments were supported by means of examples, analogies, similies, anecdotes and sarcastic comments. He villified thoughtless obedience to the state and conventional means of social reform.

Thoreau contended, for example, that voting was both ineffectual and immoral. It was tantamount to *wishing* that the "right" would prevail, and excused a citizen from taking direct action. The man who voted in accordance with the Moral Law, Thoreau asserted, had no more influence than the man who voted against it—who was usually in the majority. Voting, then, was a wholly inadequate means for making any real advance against oppression. A minority which did no more than vote was easily silenced. But a civilly disobedient minority, guided by the Moral Law, could prevail. Thoreau expressed one of his cardinal points as follows:

> All voting is a sort of gaming, like chequers or backgammon, with a slight moral tinge to it, a playing with right and wrong, with moral questions; and betting naturally accompanies it. . . . Even voting *for the right* is *doing* nothing for it. It is only expressing to men feebly your desire that it should prevail. A wise man will not leave the right to the mercy of chance, . . . When the majority shall at length vote for the abolition of slavery, it will be because they are indifferent to slavery, or because there is but little slavery left to be abolished by their vote. *They* will then be the only slaves. Only *his* vote can hasten the abolition of slavery who asserts his own freedom. . .

The sweep of Thoreau's "logic" in **"Civil Disobedience"** may have eluded many of his listeners, but they could hardly escape his goading devils.

"Civil Disobedience," in short, represented Thoreau's use of the "strategy of transcendence," a type of argumentative arrangement. Thoreau began with a proposition, "that government is best which governs least." The requirements of the strategy include examination of alternatives, then spotlighting the implication: "that government is best which governs not at all." Thoreau then considered particular abuses of government and the consequences of blind obedience to the state. Finally, he returned to a general discussion of the role of government. Such stylistic devices as examples, anecdotes, analogies and similes marked the address.

Another weapon in the transcendental arsenal included the "strategy of salvation." "The strategy was essentially a problem-solution sequence . . . the Transcendentalists attacked the opponents' hate, greed and conformity . . . The intensity of the Transcendentalists' attack created a vacuum which the Transcendentalists filled with hope for the future. All was not lost—there was a ray of hope for the sinners."

Henry Thoreau's refusal to pay his taxes was a calculated, conscientious evasion of civil responsibility; it was an act of individual defiance against a government that might have used his taxes to wage war against Mexico and that tolerated slavery. "Can there not be a government in which majorities do not virtually decide right and wrong, but conscience? . . . must the citizen ever for a moment, or in the least degree, resign his conscience to the legislator? Why has every man a conscience then?" asked Thoreau. Consistent with the "strategy of salvation," Thoreau continued his attack: "There are thousands who are *in opinion* opposed to slavery and to the war, who yet in effect do nothing to put an end to them; . . . They hesitate, and they regret, and sometimes they petition; but they do nothing in earnest and with effect. They will wait, well disposed, for others to remedy the evil, that they may no longer have it to regret. At most, they give only a cheap vote, and a feeble countenance and God-speed, to the right, as it goes by them!"

The completion of the strategy required Thoreau to provide a solution, to fill the created social "vacuum." His answer to a civil law or system of laws outrageous to his conscience was peaceful disobedience:

> I cannot for an instant recognize that political organization as *my* government which is the *slave's* government also. . . . As for adopting the ways which the State has provided for remedying the evil [unjust laws], I know not of such ways. They take too much time, and a man's life will be gone. . . . It is not my business to be petitioning the Governor or the Legislature any more than it is theirs to petition me; and if they should not hear my petition, what should I do then? . . . A minority is powerless while it conforms to the majority; it is not even a minority then; but it is irresistible when it clogs by its whole weight. If the alternative is to keep all just men in prison, or give up war and slavery, the State will not hesitate which to choose. If a thousand men were not to pay their tax bills this year, that would not be a violent and bloody measure, as it would be to pay them, and enable the State to commit violence and shed innocent blood. . . . When the subject has refused allegiance, and the officer has resigned his office, then the revolution is accomplished.

Thoreau's doctrine, however, was not totally unconciliatory, so long as matters of conscience were not involved: ". . . to speak practically and as a citizen, unlike those who call themselves no-government men, I ask for, not at once no government, but *at once* a better government. . . . I have never declined paying the highway tax, because I am as desirous of being a good neighbor as I am of being a bad subject."

The impetus for non-violent breaking of the law stems from the transcendental belief that there was a dichotomy between civil and Moral Law and that the latter was of the utmost importance. But because men respect the former, they are sometimes misled into betraying the higher law. If they discover the discrepancy, should they trust to the gradual and conventional processes of government to resolve it? Thoreau argued that if enough men who believe in the Moral Law would break the civil law—even though they were a numerical minority—they may succeed in disrupting the state to such an extent that the government would reconsider its policies and actions. Significantly, Thoreau had discovered a key to destroying the state. The man who wished to abolish the state need only cease to cooperate with it; for instance, he might refuse military induction, jury duty or the payment of taxes. The refusal to obey, in other words, was the great weapon for completely undermining the state or hastening social reform. Furthermore, as a natural extension of transcendental dogma, the Moral Law and obedience to it were determined by the consicence of the individual—to be sure, an "awakened" conscience: "It is not a man's duty, as a matter of course, to devote himself to the eradication of any, even the most enormous wrong; he may still properly have other concerns to engage him; but it is his duty, at least, to wash his hands of it, and, if he gives it no thought longer, not to give it practically his support. If I devote myuself to other pursuits and contemplations, I must first see, at least, that I do not pursue them sitting upon another man's shoulders.'' Each man, then, was his own police force, his own lawmaker, his own self-regulator.

Obedience to the Moral Law dictated that Thoreau's way of life should not become the means by which injustice could flourish; consequently, he devised his famous doctrine of civil disobedience as the solution to this moral and personal problem. While he was free from moral culpability, he was also able to pursue ''truth''—though his search might have to take place in jail. To reveal his moral imperative, Thoreau employed the ''strategy of salvation.''

A fourth strategy used by the transcendentalists to present their arguments was the ''strategy of omission.'' Since the early nineteenth century the country had been converting from an agricultural society into an urban, industrial nation. Transcendentalists, however, encouraged a return to the simple, rural, agrarian life of early America; the advance of science and industry, in their view, represented a general trend toward mechanism and conformity. Consequently, transcendental speakers did not discuss material that challenged their philosophy. The ''strategy of omission'' was designed to allow the speaker to advance his own position and to ignore conflicting doctrines or events. Such an approach allowed the transcendentalists to consider ''abstract concepts, higher law, and whirling universes.''

Thoreau used chiefly the ''strategy of omission'' when he considered participation in politics as a means of social reform. What real use was the government, asked Thoreau? Name a cowardly or an unrighteous act, and the government was probably involved.

> Some years ago, the State met me in behalf of the church, and commanded me to pay a certain sum toward the support of a clergyman whose preaching my father attended, but never I myself. ''Pay it,'' it said, ''or be locked up in the jail.'' I declined to pay. But, unfortunately, another man saw fit to pay it . . . at the request of the selectmen, I condescended to make some such statement as this in writing:—"Know all men by these presents, that I, Henry Thoreau, do not wish to be regarded as a member of any incorporated society which I have not joined.'' This I gave to the townclerk; and he has it.

Thoreau also discouraged political participation because expediency and compromise, rather than strict adherence to the Moral Law, dominated the political arena. A man such as Daniel Webster personified the corrupting nature of political participation.

> Webster never goes behind government, and so cannot speak with authroity about it. His words are wisdom to those legislators who contemplate no essential reform in the existing government; but for thinkers, and those who legislate for all time, he never once glances at the subject . . . thinking of the sanction which the Constitution gives to slavery, he says,''because it was part of the original compact,—let it stand.'' Notwithstanding his special acuteness and ability, he is unable to take a fact out of its merely political relations,and behold it as it lies absolutely to be disposed of by the intellect, . . .

Thoreau rarely made any reference to a source other than himself. When he did, it was always to his ultimate advantage. In the familiar transcendental fashion, employing abstract terms and appeals to the higher law, Thoreau concluded his indictment of men like Webster. ''They who know of no purer sources of truth, who have traced up its stream no higher, stand and wisely stand, by the Bible and the Constitution, and drink at it there with reverence and humility; but they who behold where it comes trickling into this lake or that pool, gird up their loins once more, and continue their pilgrimage toward its fountain-head.''

By employing the ''strategy of omission,'' Thoreau dismissed political activity as meaningless. ''I hear of a convention to be held at Baltimore, or elsewhere, for the selection of a candidate for the Presidency, made up chiefly of editors, and men who are politicians by profession; but I think, what is it to any independent, intelligent, and respectable man what decision they may come to, shall we not have the advantage of his wisdom and honesty, nevertheless? Can we not count upon some independent votes? Are there not many individuals in the country who do not attend conventions?'' Throughout the lecture, whether reference was made to specific events, personal examples of familiar quotations, they served to reinforce Thoreau's philosophy of obedience only to just laws. ''I was not born to be forced,'' he defiantly proclaimed. ''I will breathe after my own fashion.'' The American government, however, maintained its existence through the use of force. And compulsion, in whatever manner, was intolerable in a moral universe. Since Thoreau, furthermore, had not ''delegated'' any rights to the government, he felt he should be safe from coercion from that source also. Yet, the government had capitalized on its physical strength and had limited his protest by placing him in jail. ''The State never intentionally confronts a man's sense, intellectual or moral, but only his body, . . . It is not armed with superior wit or honesty, but with superior physical strength.'' No matter how Thoreau considered his relationship with government, participation in a corrupt, coersive system was untenable. And conventional procedures to initiate social reform could hardly prove fruitful with a government that forced compliance.

While the ''strategy of omission'' enabled Thoreau to develop his arguments on his own terms and avoid damaging material, it seems to have been designed to impress fellow transcendentalists rather than to attract new converts. As an alienated member of society, there was hardly any attempt by Thoreau to share the commonly held linguistic symbols of his audience. Rosenthal has argued that for persuasion—action consistent with the speaker's proposal—to occur, there must be a collection of linguistic symbols to which a mass audience responds in the same way. The use of numerous obscure references and abstract concepts, for example, was characteristic of Thoreau's discourse. On a typical page he might quote from a Chinese philosopher, translate from the ancient classics or quote from a metaphysical poet. He seemed to enjoy supporting his ideas by finding obscure sources or phrases and parading them before an uneducated audience. More than a declaration of independence for the immediate audience, **"Civil Disobedience"** may be more appropriately viewed as a sermon against oppression, materialism, mechanization and conformity. But only those few who already shared Thoreau's unspoiled vision of ''higher law and whirling universes'' understood his protest.

"Civil Disobedience" has been analyzed in terms of four transcendental strategies. As earlier defined, the strategy of revelation was characterized by a display of ''grand truths'' in the form of maxims, poems or catchy slogans. The strategy of transcendence was a distinguishable argumentative arrangement. The strategy of salvation consisted of attacks upon the social order, with a transcendental vision ofsociety offered in its place. And the strategy of omission involved a speaker's refusal to consider material which contradicted transcendental philosophy or to use conventional linguistic symbols.

"Civil Disobedience," in sum, was conceived by Thoreau as a reaction against a government that *demanded* allegiance and a society that had a penchant for the status quo. In all four strategies, the argument was conducted on Thoreau's terms; the emphasis was on intuition, definition, "abstract concepts, higher law, and whirling universes." Little effort was made to find areas of agreement between speaker and listener. Thoreau used almost solely those devices which bolstered his own philosophy. In the final analysis, **"Civil Disobedience"** seems to have been geared to impress other transcendentalists, such as Emerson, Alcott and Parker, rather than to attract new converts.

Had the abolition of slavery waited for a sufficient increase in the number of men and women willing to undertake it solely from principle, it might very well not have come about. Thoreau, however, served as a beacon, pointing out the road to be traveled by men awakening to the higher law. Beyond this lies organized political action, a threshold Thoreau never crossed. He made no attempt to rally the masses behind his tactic of civil disobedience as did the reformers he influenced. He formed no organization to combat military induction, for example, or the payment of taxes. For Thoreau, the radical abolitionist policy of "No Union with Slaveholders"meant *individual* dissolution of the Union.

An analysis of **"Civil Disobedience"** does more than provide an insight into the rhetorical practice of a man who spent seasons observing the life cycle of leaves or who would squat for hours in order to shake hands with a bull-frog: It increases our understanding of Thoreau's philosophy of social reform. Like John Locke, Thoreau insisted that government be limited to the common good, and consequently, that it be morally revocable. His address was a call for individuals to be more assertive, to urge each citizen to have the state recognize "the individual as a higher and independent power."

Richard Weaver has perceptively stated that "nowhere does a man's rhetoric catch up with him more completely than in the topics he chooses to win other men's assent." Nowhere was respect for the individual more pronounced than in **"Civil Disobedience."** Thoreau protested not only against slavery and a government that countenanced the "peculiar institution" but, in the name of human dignity and individuality, criticized the trends toward conformity, restrictiveness and mechanization. This criticism was perhaps Thoreau's greatest achievement and our legacy. (pp. 101-10)

Michael G. Erlich, "Thoreau's 'Civil Disobedience': Strategy for Reform," in The Connecticut Review, *Vol. VII, No. 1, October, 1973, pp. 100-10.*

CHRISTOPHER LYLE JOHNSTONE (essay date 1974)

[Johnstone views "Civil Disobedience" in the context of Transcendentalism.]

[In **"Civil Disobedience,"** Henry David Thoreau] presents a political doctrine that requires the rejection of rhetoric as a form of strategic political activity, and so, the rejection of the essay itself as an instance of such activity.

In order to appreciate fully the political philosophy embodied by the essay, we must have at least a general understanding of the larger philosophical context in which the essay appeared. Although Thoreau himself may not have been a Transcendentalist in the way that Ripley, Channing, and Parker were, his life and writings reflect the fundamental principles of Transcendentalism. Indeed, the essay on **"Civil Disobedience"** carries the spiritual principles of Transcendentalism to their socio-political conclusions. Thus, in order to place the essay in its philosophical setting, we must briefly examine the Transcendentalist doctrine itself.

Walter Harding suggests [in his introduction to *The Variorum Walden*] that "Transcendentalism was primarily a revolt against the 'cold intellectualism' of early nineteenth-century New England Unitarianism." The fundamental premise of the Transcendentalist doctrine was that the most important kind of knowledge—spiritual knowledge, moral truth, or conscience—is innate in man, and that only by turning to this divinely inspired "inner light" can the individual live a moral life. Running through the literature of Transcendentalism, therefore, is an emphasis on the sovereignty of the individual and on the superiority of moral law to civil law. The individual's first duty is to his conscience, rather than to the State. It was the chief aim of the Transcendentalists, moreover, to reawaken within each individual the inner light of moral truth, to effect the total moral rejuvenation of the individual, and to free him from the domination of any authority other than his own conscience.

As Harding has pointed out, the Transcendentalists believed that it is the "good man's obligation" to rediscover his "inner voice" of conscience, his own core of moral truth. This rediscovery ws thought to be best accomplished by withdrawing from the social realm—from the world of politics, business, and "social progress"—in order to concentrate upon the world of nature and spirit. Thus, we find that the movement was marked by a withdrawal from society, a withdrawal that was most evident in politics. The indifference toward or absolute repudiation of politics was rooted in the basic principle of Transcendentalism: if one is to be guided by God-given moral law, of what use or value is the inherently inferior civil law, or the political process through which that law is formulated? Further, the Transcendentalists' emphasis upon the individual precluded what is normally understood as political activity, since such activity involves collective rather than individual action. Finally, the Transcendentalists' repudiation of politics entailed their rejection of the validity of democracy as a form of government. It was their belief that any form of government that requires the individual to surrender to another—whether that other be king or congressman—his moral sovereignty or autonomy, or that is premised upon the concept of majority rule, could not be one of justice. Justice is not, as Thrasymachus would have it, the interest of the stronger; rather, it is action guided by principle.

It is against this background that Thoreau's political and spiritual philosophy must be understood; for, as I have indicated, the essay on **"Civil Disobedience"** represents the political conclusions of the Transcendentalist doctrine. Thoreau, more than most men, felt himself to be a child of the universe; the feeling of the transcendent unity of spirit influenced not only his solitary intellectual meanderings, but also his socio-political philosophy, and it is reflected in his books, essays, poetry and letters. "Certified as he was constantly," writes Theodore Dreiser,

> "by direct observation of all that went on about him—
> in the woods and fields, the earth, water, air and sky,
> in the actions of men and animals, birds, fishes,
> insects, flowers, the movements of winds, waters,

> suns and planets—he reached the very definite conclusion, easily to be illustrated by a thousand passages from his writings, that underlying all is a universal, artistic, constructive genius."

Thoreau, like the Transcendentalists, believed in the existence of an inner, moral truth that was superior to the laws of society as a guide to conduct. For Thoreau, the individual's first obligation is to this inner voice—his conscience—rather than to civil law. "A saner man would have found himself often enough 'in formal opposition' to what are deemed 'the most sacred laws of society,' through obedience to yet more sacred laws, and so have tested his resolution without going out of his way. It is not for a man to put himself in such an attitude to society, but to maintain himself in whatever attitude he finds himself through obedience to the laws of his being, which will never be one of opposition to a just government, if he should chance to meet with such." And how, for Thoreau, are the "laws of one's being" to be apprehended? How is one to discover, or recover, the moral truth that dwells within him? One must turn away from the superficiality and transitoriness of human affairs—from politics and commerce—in order to contemplate the eternal truths of nature and spirit.

"Let us consider the way in which we spend our lives," he writes.

> This world is a place of business. What an infinite bustle! I am awaked almost everynight by the panting of the locomotive. It interrupts my dreams. There is no sabbath. It would be glorious to see mankind at leisure for once. It is nothing but work, work, work. I cannot easily buy a blank book to write thoughts in: they are commonly ruled for dollars and cents. An Irishman, seeing me making a minute in the fields, took it for granted that I was calculating my wages. If a man was tossed out of a window when an infant, and so made a cripple for life, or scared out of his wits by the Indians, it is regretted chiefly because he was thus incapacitated for—business! I think that there is nothing, not even crime, more opposed to poetry, to philosophy, ay, to life itself, than this incessant business.

It is from this world, with its tendency to trivialize and commercialize experience, that Thoreau would have us withdraw. He suggests that we "read not the Times. Read the Eternities. Conventionalities are at length as bad as impurities. Even the facts of science may dust the mind by their dryness, unless they are in a sense effaced each morning, or rather rendered fertile by the dews of fresh and living truth. Knowledge does not come to us by details, but in flashes of light from heaven."

In addition to urging one to turn away from the realm of human affairs toward the eternal realm of nature, Thoreau also emphasizes the necessity of knowing the inner person, of knowing oneself; for "truth is such by reference to the heart of man within, not to any standard without." Thoreau puts great value on the self-sufficiency and spiritual strength gained by relying upon one's own intellectual and spiritual resources. He deplores the fact that most people know little of themselves, and thus have little of themselves to share with others.

> Just so hollow and ineffectual, for the most part, is our ordinary conversation. Surface meets surface. When our life ceases to be inward and private, conversation degenerates into mere gossip. We rarely meet a man who can tell us any news which he has not read in a newspaper, or been told by his neighbor; and, for the most part, the only difference between us and our fellow is that he has seen the newspaper, or been out to tea, and we have not. In proportion as our inward life fails, we go more constantly and desperately to the post-office. You may depend on it, that the poor fellow who walks away with the greatest number of letters, proud of his extensive correspondence, has not heard from himself this long while.

Allied to his advocacy of withdrawal from the social realm in general, and like the Transcendentalist philosophy that his writings reflect, was Thoreau's repudiation of political activity. This repudiation was based upon a deep distrust of politics. Thoreau wrote that "what is called politics is comparatively something so superficial and inhuman, that practically I have never fairly recognized that it concerns me at all." Further, he found politics at best an expedient, for "what is the value of any political freedom, but as a means to moral freedom?" Finally, the State, which is both the product and the protector of the political process, is necessarily subordinate to the moral authority of the individual. "There will never be a really free and enlightened State," he writes, "until the State comes to recognize the individual as a higher and independent power, from which all its own power and authority are derived, and treats him accordingly." "Must the citizen," he writes elsewhere, "ever for a moment, or in the least degree, resign his conscience to the legislator? What has every man a conscience, then? I think that we should be men first, and subjects afterward. It is not desirable to cultivate a respect for the law, so much as for the right. The only obligation which I have a right to assume is to do at any time what I think right."

Note particularly that it is the politics of democracy that Thoreau rejects. He rejects democratic government, first because it is liable to be inefficient and even detrimental to the good of the just man; and second, because he rejects the principle of popular government, that is, of majority rule. "The government itself, which is only the mode which the people have chosen to execute their will, is equally liable to be abused and perverted before the people can act through it." With respect to the concept of majority rule, Thoreau observes that "there is but little virtue in the action of masses of men." "After all," he writes, "the practical reason why, when the power is once in the hands of the people, a majority are permitted, and for a long period continue, to rule is not because they are most likely to be in the right, nor because this seems fairest to the minority, but because they are physically the strongest. But a government in which the majority rule in all cases cannot be based on justice, even as far as men understand it. Can there not be a government in which majorities do not virtually decide right and wrong, but conscience?—in which majorities decide only those questions to which the rule of expediency is applicable?" He adds elsewhere that "any many more right than his neighbors constitutes a majority of one already."

Because democracy is based upon the principle of popular consent, social or political change can be effected in any of several ways in a democratic society: voting, organizing people in an effort to create a majority, attempting to influence legislators, running for office, etc. However, these and other options are closed to the individual who rejects the democratic form of organization and control, and who places the individual's conscience above the authority of the State. For him, the number of alternatives is narrowed sharply; narrowed, if he is to avoid violent tactics, to a single alternative. And it is this alternative, this single acceptable option, that Thoreau advocates in his essay. By rejecting the vote, by rejecting attempts to marshall public opinion or public support for some policy, by rejecting other forms of political action that prevail in a democratic society, Thoreau ultimately limits his range of choices to one: individual, direct action in the form of civil disobedience.

That civil disobedience is the *duty* of the conscientious individual is made clear in the essay when Thoreau writes that "unjust laws exist: shall we be content to obey them, or shall we endeavor to amend them, and obey them until we have succeeded, or shall we transgress them at once? Men generally, under such a government as this, think that they ought to wait until they have persuaded a majority to alter them. They think that, if they should resist, the remedy would be worse than the evil. But it is the fault of the government itself that the remedy *is* worse than the evil. *It* makes it worse." Because an individual lives in a political society, he acts in ways that will have political consequences; and he must have some means for deciding, in many cases, how to act, for determining what will be the right action. In a society governed by law, it is the law that serves to guide action. However, for the Transcendentalists generally, and for Thoreau in particular, there is a guide to action that stands above the law, and that can—and in an unjust society often does—conflict with civil law: moral law or conscience. Accordingly, one is bound by his observance of the higher law of conscience to disobey unjust civil laws. Disobedience, then, is first an act of conscience—a duty—rather than a strategy for effecting political change. For the Transcendentalists, it might be solely such an act. For Thoreau, however, civil disobedience has an additional function: it is the only acceptable vehicle for achieving his political aim—the creation of a society based upon justice.

As the essay develops, the concept of civil disobedience evolves beyond the point of duty, to the point of political strategy. This evolution represents Thoreau's shift away from the mainstream of Transcendentalist thinking, and is based upon his rejection of other forms of political action. In refining his only weapon against the tyranny of the State, Thoreau suggests that "all men recognize the right of revolution; that is, the right to refuse allegiance to, and to resist, the government, when its tyranny or its inefficiency are great and unendurable." If the injustice of a law "is of such a nature that it requires you to be the agent of injustice to another, then, I say, break the law. Let your life be a counter-friction to stop the machine. What I have to do is to see, at any rate, that I do not lend myself to the wrong which I condemn." Here we see a clue about the new role of civil disobedience. Not only is it a duty that is dictated by one's observance of the superiority of moral to civil law; it now emerges as a strategy by which one can revolutionize society. Civil disobedience is no longer only a moral obligation; it is the means by which the *individual* can act in the political realm, by using his life to undermine the authority of the State, by using his resistance to that authority as an instrument of political change, by providing the "counter friction to stop the machine." Thoreau transforms a moral obligation into a form of revolutionary political action that is compatible with, that indeed grows out of, Transcendentalist principles. It is the just man resisting the unjust State who will, by his action, alter that State; for "all machines have their friction; and possibly this does enough good to counter-balance the evil. . . . But when the friction comes to have its machine, and oppression and robbery are organized, I say, let us not have such a machine any longer. In other words, when a sixth of the population of a nation which has undertaken to be the refuge of liberty are slaves, and a whole country is unjustly overrun and conquered by a foreign army, and subjected to military law, I think that it is not too soon for honest men to rebel and revolutionize."

Civil disobedience can effect radical political change for two reasons: first, it will, as we have seen, "clog the machine," for "a minority is powerless while it conforms to the majority; it is not even a minority then; but it is irresistable when it clogs by its whole weight. If the alternative is to keep all just men in prison, or give up war and slavery, the State will not hesitate which to choose. If a thousand men were not to pay their tax-bills this year, that would not be a violent and bloody measure, as it would be to pay them, and enable the State to commit violence and shed innocent blood. This is, in fact, the definition of a peaceable revolution, if any such is possible." Second, it will nurture the growth of a just society by altering the consciousness of the individual who employs it: "Action from principle, the perception and the performance of right, changes things and relations; it is essentially revolutionary, and does not consist wholly with anything which was. It not only divides States and churches, it divides families; ay, it divides the *individual*, separating the diabolical in him from the divine." Hence, we find that civil disobedience is, for Thoreau, both a political weapon and an instrument of moral liberation. It serves to facilitate the "moral rejuvenation" of the individual that was the Transcendentalists' principal objective, and so, to facilitate the growth of a society based upon justice, upon "the perception and performance of right."

If it is true that the act of civil disobedience is the only acceptable form of political activity by which one can attempt to alter the nature of society, then what is the proper place of rhetorical discourse in its political functions? What must be concluded, I think, is that rhetoric as a political tool has no place in Thoreau's doctrine. Anything less than personal disobedience of civil law, including, as we have seen, attempting to create or change public support for a policy through discourse, is inadequate from both a moral and a political standpoint. To conceive of civil disobedience as a duty, as Thoreau does, requires this conclusion. It is implicit in his rejection of the politics of democracy; for democracy requires that political disputes be resolved through discussion and persuasion, rather than through force. Democracy rests upon the use of discourse as an instrument of political change. Thus, in advocating the doctrine of civil disobedience, the essay solicits—indeed, requires—from its auditor a rejection of the democratic process, and consequently of the propriety of suasory discourse as an instrument of social change. Such discourse has no place in Thoreau's scheme, and his reader is asked, implicitly, to reject its validity as a form of political activity.

We may now ask, in the light of this implication of the essay's argument, what sorts of restrictions or limitations are imposed upon the form of the essay by the nature of its implied purposes. What are the demands that the essay, as a rhetorical act, makes of its reader? It is at this point that we find a conflict between the commitment that is solicited from the auditor by the substance of the argument, and the very existence of the essay itself. For, most fundamentally, the essay is a form of political activity. It represents a way of responding to a political situation. It is an effort to influence political behavior. It advocates a political doctrine. It is, indeed, rhetorical discourse functioning as an instrument of political change. But it is this very function of discourse—as a form of political activity—that the essay requires the reader to repudiate. The essay asks the reader to reject rhetoric as a mode of political action—including, it must be assumed, rhetorical transactions in which the individual is the target rather than the instigator of the action—while it asks him, implicitly, to accept the validity of the essay itself as a form of political activity. It asks him, in other words, to accept a doctrine that requires him to reject the validity of the very attempt to win his acceptance for that doctrine. Hence, we find the essay, owing to the limitations implicitly imposed upon it by its aims, in the rather paradoxical position of being a self-retracting act of communication—an utterance that obligates itself to deny its own validity, that is required by the very act of saying to "unsay itself."

This circumstance presents the auditor with an interesting dilemma: how is he to respond to the essay? It calls upon him, implicitly, to accept what it is asking him to reject. What is one to do with such discourse, accept it or reject it? It would seem that the only real option open to the auditor in such a situation lies outside acceptance and rejection: he must ignore the discourse. But are we to ignore Thoreau's statement of the principle of civil disobedience? The essay is too important from a political standpoint, and two eloquent, to be ignored; yet this seems to be the response it ultimately solicits from its auditor.

Clearly, in Thoreau's essay we have found a rather mystifying rhetorical problem. It is not a problem, however, that is limited to the essay. It will appear, in varying degrees, whenever the aims of a discourse are somehow incompatible with the form of the discourse. It will appear in its most extreme form—as the paradox inherent in Thoreau's essay—whenever discourse advocates what is essentially an anarchist position. For the foundation of such a position is, as it is for Thoreau's doctrine, that the individual is the only qualified judge in matters of morality, politics, and action generally, and that the ground for his judgment is wholly personal, unaccountable to any external standard or authority. Such a position requires that one resist the attempts of others to influence one's judgment; that is, it requires one to reject attempts to persuade him. In that kind of situation, what is to prevent the auditor from similarly rejecting the discourse that asks him to reject discourse? In order to honor the request, he must not honor the request. At this point we are reminded by the force of our own bewilderment that it is very difficult—perhaps impossible—to make sense of such discourse. It is discourse that begs to be ignored.

It would be easy for us, indeed, to ignore such discourse; or for us to ignore the paradox on the ground that few actual auditors will ever perceive it. My response to this second point is that my concern, as a critic, is with the ways in which discourse functions, with the way discourse works. I am interested in what discourse can do as much as in what it actually does; in the possible consequences of ways of communicating as much as in their actual outcomes; in the inherent properties of discourse as much as in its effects. Thus, I don't believe that the critic can ignore the paradox and still complete his critical task. My response to the first point is that we cannot ignore such discourse or dismiss it as nonsense. Thoreau's attempt to liberate his reader from the tyranny of the State, and to bring him under the authority of his own conscience, is a noble one. Moreover, any discourse that attempts the radical, or complete, liberation of its auditor may require that he resist such attempts, and consequently, may subject him to the frustration that accompanies efforts to make sense of the paradox. Perhaps the paradox, and the frustrations in auditors to which it can give rise, is a necessary characteristic of what we might call the "rhetoric of liberation." It is rhetoric that seeks, in the end, to undermine its own credibility, to bring its auditor to the realization that he is ultimately responsible for what he does, for the choices and decisions he makes, and for whom he becomes. Perhaps this realization or insight is the outcome of the auditor's attempt to deal with the dilemma with which the discourse confronts him. How does the auditor resolve the dilemma? How does he reduce the psychological tension and frustration to which it gives rise? Perhaps the solution to the paradox is to transcend it, to move to a level of consciousness where there is no longer any paradox. In the moment of transcendence, of "consciousness-raising," may come the flash of insight that constitutes the "awakening of the inner light" that it is Transcendentalism's, and Thoreau's, aim to accomplish. Perhaps it is in trying to decide what to do with the discourse, how to respond to it, how to resolve the contradiction, that the individual realizes that he need not decide, that he need only do what his spirit tells him to do. I am reminded of the process of enlightenment in Zen Buddhism: the master, employing a logical paradox, pushes the student's thinking to the point of utter frustration; the student struggles, without success, to "make sense" of the paradox according to traditional ways of thinking and reasoning. He finally resolves the paradox by seeing it in a new way, in a way radically different from traditional patterns of thought. The paradox disappears, and at that moment the student reaches enlightenment or "satori."

Might we have in Thoreau a similar process? Might we have a discourse, in the essay, that is intended to produce this paradox? Might not the conflict between form and substance serve the process of liberation? Perhaps being required to experience this paradox in one's responses, perhaps being forced by a discourse to confront and deal with this confusion, is essential to the liberation of the auditor, as to the enlightenment of the Zen monk. It is beyond the scope of the present essay to carry such speculation to its conclusion. It is my hope that it will suggest further speculation. In any event, it is a purpose of this essay to invite the systematic inquiry of the critic and theorist of rhetoric into the rhetorical paradox herein described. Such inquiry is the principal commitment that the present discourse solicits from its readers. (pp. 315-22)

Christopher Lyle Johnstone, "Thoreau and Civil Disobedience: A Rhetorical Paradox," in The Quarterly Journal of Speech, *Vol. LX, No. 3, October, 1974, pp. 313-22.*

BARRY WOOD (essay date 1981)

[In the following study of "Civil Disobedience" as a work of literature, Wood examines Thoreau's manipulation of actual events to form a symbolic narrative. Wood's remarks were originally published in the Winter, 1981, issue of Philological Quarterly.*]*

Over thirty years ago Stanley Edgar Hyman wrote an essay called "Henry Thoreau in Our Time" [see excerpt dated 1946 in *NCLC*, Vol. 7] which has since become a landmark study. "The first thing we should insist on," he wrote "is that Thoreau was a writer. . . . At his best Thoreau wrote the only really first-rate prose ever written by an American, with the possible exception of Abraham Lincoln. . . . [Thoreau was] a writer in the great stream of the American tradition, the mythic and nonrealist writers, Hawthorne and Melville, Twain and James, and, in our day . . . Hemingway and Faulkner." Along with F. O. Matthiessen's *American Renaissance* [see excerpt dated 1941 in *NCLC*, Vol. 7] with its similar stress on Thoreau as artist and writer, Hyman's essay provided the direction for criticism in the following three decades: first in the study of ***Walden*** but more recently with the early excursions and ***A Week on the Concord and Merrimack Rivers,*** Hyman also pointed to Thoreau's most famous political essay to stress the literary

Thoreau and made a crucial but largely ignored distinction: "As a political warrior, Thoreau was a comic little figure with a receding chin, and not enough high style to carry off a gesture. As a political writer, he was the most ringing and magnificent polemicist America has ever produced. Three years later he made an essay called **"Civil Disobedience"** out of his prison experience, fusing the soft coal of his night in jail into solid diamond." No one has applied this emphasis on Thoreau's literary art to **"Civil Disobedience"**; at the same time, the exaggerated efforts to find a workable plan of political action from it have not met with more than temporary approval. As Lawrence Bowling has said, writing about his social criticism: "Most of Thoreau's critics have advanced only as far as the discovery that he was not a great thinker and have not arrived at the realization that he made his major contribution in the realm of art."

The enormous influence of **"Civil Disobedience,"** not only on thinkers like Tolstoy and Gandhi but also on the British Labor Movement and American life generally, is well known. Combined with a few other Thoreau essays—**"Slavery in Massachusetts," "A Plea for Captain John Brown,"** and perhaps the "Economy" chapter of ***Walden***—it has inspired commentary so extensive that a recent book appeared devoted solely to "Thoreau's political reputation in America." Yet the single-minded emphasis in commentary on **"Civil Disobedience"** to the political rather than the artistic suggests a virtual blind spot even among the most sensitive critics, while at the same time revealing more about the shifting political attitudes in our time than Thoreau's. The fact is that Thoreau's reputation (in other areas too, not simply political) is out of all proportion to the ideas he sets forth, or even to the experiences upon which these ideas are hung. He was not the first to live in a cabin by a pond near Concord, nor the first to travel in New Hampshire, Cape Code, or the Maine Woods, nor even the first to climb Wachusett, Saddleback, or Ktaadn. Before Thoreau withheld his poll tax Bronson Alcott had done the same. Even the ideas of **"Civil Disobedience"** had important forerunners: Emerson's "Politics" and Paley's *Moral and Political Philosophy* for instance. What accounts for Thoreau's influence, lies elsewhere—in the artistic power of his work and the sense of drama running through all his writings. In the major works this sense of drama approaches what Hyman calls "a vast rebirth ritual," but everywhere we find the use of a sustained narrative thread which leads the reader forward in anticipation of discovery. The speaking "I" is always present, as Thoreau himself notes with no apologies on the first page of ***Walden,*** and this leads to a mode of writing which demonstrates discovery, the achievement of perspective, the awakening of vision, and spiritual renewal. Whatever ideas appear are enfolded in a story, so much so that the narrative structure is often the key to the ideas.

If the narrative elements of Thoreau's writings have not been stressed, neither have they been missed. The relations between the works and specific events, excursions, or sojourns in Thoreau's life are well known. But these facts are often passed over as a biographical element less interesting than the presumed "message" being developed. Such an omission ignores what the narrative ordering of the work actually *accomplishes* in the unfolding and development of the ideas. In the case of **"Civil Disobedience"** it has not yet been shown how narrative order operates as a synthesizing device for the reconciliation of the two realms of experience—the real and the transcendent. I image that Thoreau is more generally linked with Emerson than Melville among writers of his time, but some perspective is gained by comparing him with both. Emerson typically engineered his transcendental philosophy through symbolism by using nature as a "vehicle of thought" or a "symbol of spirit"; that is, he demonstrated that man lives simultaneously in two worlds which are joined in moments of "exhiliration" or, at times of creativity, when the scholar becomes Man Thinking or the poet becomes a "liberating god." Melville accomplished the same linkage of two worlds through his voyages during which his Tajis and Ishmaels find themselves literally travelling across the boundary from the real world into the transcendental. Symbol in Emerson and narrative in Melville both have a synthesizing capacity. Thoreau stands, as it were, midway: we find in him the same duality of worlds and we find him using both symbolism and narrative journeys to give a single account a double reference.

In **"Civil Disobedience"** there appear to be two rather different centers of interest. One derives from the political ideas set forth about which so much has been written. The other focuses on the story of Thoreau's night in jail, probably July 23 or 24, 1846. Reference to this story is made obliquely in ***A Week,*** but the version occurring later, in ***Walden,*** provides a fuller account:

> One afternoon, near the end of the first summer, when I went to the village to get a shoe from the cobbler's, I was seized and put into jail, because, as I have elsewhere related, I did not pay a tax to, or recognize the authority of, the state which buys and sells men, women, and children, like cattle at the door of its senate-house. I had gone down to the woods for other purposes. But, wherever a man goes, men will pursue and paw him with their dirty institutions, and, if they can, constrain him to belong to their desperate odd-fellow society. It is true, I might have resisted forcibly with more or less effect, might have run "amok" against society; but I preferred that society should run "amok" against me, it being the desperate party. However, I was released the next day, obtained my mended shoe, and returned to the woods in season to get my dinner of huckleberries on Fair-Haven Hill.

In **"Civil Disobedience"** this rather undramatic event is given considerable narrative scope, especially in the central paragraphs which are properly separated and set in reduced type in authoritative editions. This narrative effectively divides the essay into three parts. There is, in the two flanking sections, an important tonal difference, suggesting that the central narrative is operating as a bridge between the two sections of philosophical argument.

Thoreau says of his night in jail that "it was like travelling into a far country, such as I had never expected to behold, to lie there for one night. . . . It was to see my native village in the light of the middle ages, and our Concord [River] was turned into a Rhine stream, and visions of knights and castles passed before me." This vision of "a far country" and "a long journey," with imagery from Europe and the middle ages, is completed, as in the ***Walden*** account, by Thoreau's retreat from the village and ascent of "one of our highest hills, two miles off." Embedded in this account is a series of contrasts: most obviously, the village world of Concord and the natural world beyond it where the narrative begins and ends; the darkness of the night spent in jail and the sunlight of the days preceding and following it; the "medieval" quality of the Concord scene and the immediacy and spontaneity of the huckleberrying party moving up the high hill. The narrative movement—from the natural world into the village and back to the natural—sets forth in dramatic terms the dialectical progress of the larger essay: contrasts in the narrative suggest the contrasting views of the State set forth in the first and third sections; and the movement through the narrative middle, like Thoreau's own movement through the night in the Concord jail, provides a "before" and "after" polarity basic to the political idea of the essay. What *is* is seen against what *could be*. Indeed, if the Transcendentalist is understood as attemping to see *this* world in terms of *another,* the *real* as against the *ideal,* then the narrative center of **"Civil Disobedience"** can be seen as a powerful rhetorical strategy for linking the two views of the State. The narrative journey from one view to another, from one realm to another, makes possible a synthesis of the two in a higher third.

That Thoreau is operating within a polar view of things is everywhere apparent; it is part of his Transcendentalist heritage. In the first part of the essay his criticism of "standing government" links the ruling mechanism in America with "tradition . . . endeavoring to transmit itself unimpaired to posterity"; this is contrasted with the "vitality and force of a single living man." Here again is the Emersonian dilemma posed in the opening lines of *Nature*—the "retrospective" quality of American life with men desperately in need of their own "original relation to the universe"—recast in political terms. Repeatedly this dichotomy is observed: government is opposed by "character"; legislators with their tariff restrictions are contrasted with the"bounce" of a trade and commerce made of India rubber (a good example of what Bowling calls "social criticism as poetry"); government by "majority" is opposed by government by "conscience"; law is contrasted with "right"; machines are balanced by "men"; and the persistence of slavery in "a nation which has undertaken to be the refuge of liberty" is cited as grounds for "honest men to rebel and revolutionize." In Thoreau's view, the ideal possibilities of democracy are not realized because of "the opponents to a reform . . . who are more interested in commerce and agriculture than they are in humanity."

As Thoreau describes it, American life is full of contradictions and American policy is inconsistent with its stated values. Moreover, no *political* solution can eliminate these problems. At best a democratic society resorts to the vote—an artificial procedure for deciding who shall have their say by reducing right to might. The divisive tensions of society are thus left unresolved, precisely because "voting *for the right* is *doing* nothing for it." Doing *something* means, for Thoreau, resolving the polarities through action which carries dichotomies to a new level where they can be synthesized in a higher unity. "Action from principle,—the perception and the performance of right,—changes things and relations; it is essentially revolutionary." *Revolutionary:* the word is perfectly chosen, for it suggests that real action transfers political contradictions from the social world of stalemate to the cyclical, organic world of new creation. Here natural law, or what Thoreau terms "higher law," functions to resolve contradictions. Exactly this kind of organic resolution appears in Thoreau's final remarks before he describes his night in jail:

> I perceive that, when an acorn and a chestnut fall side by side, the one does not remain inert to make way for the other, but both obey their own laws, and spring and grow and flourish as best they can, till one, perchance, overshadows and destroys the other. If a plant cannot live according to its nature, it dies; and so a man.

The first long section of **"Civil Disobedience"** thus describes in symptomatic terms the basic problems of American political life, and sets a course for their solution. Tensions and polarities, Thoreau feels, may be overcome by "action from principle"; and the notion of *action* thus leads directly into Thoreau's account of his own actions. His narrative, then, is clearly the beginning of a process which will lead from the problematic politics described to the idealized vision at the end of the essay. Thoreau's action, of course, was that of not paying his poll tax, an act of resistance to civil government.

What the central narrative accomplishes is a transformation of the basic political dichotomies into a more dramatic form. The true nature of these dichotomies is rooted out, for Thoreau's actions force the State to make clear its generally unstated view of the truly self-reliant man. As Thoreau details his night in jail it becomes clear that physical incarceration is, short of capital punishment, the closest thing to death that the State can manage. Thoreau sees that the State's answer to opposition is tantamount to murder, as his imagery reveals. Thus, while he is literally put *in* jail, figuratively he is put well *below* the realm of ordinary society in a place of wood, stone, and iron where he says the window gratings "strained the light." The night spent in the dark cell, described as a journey into a far country, parallels Dante's night spent in a dark wood in canto 1 of *The Inferno* which was figuratively *his* journey into the far country of hell. Thoreau's night, like Dante's, is followed by an emergence at dawn and a renewed vision of the world. The night in prison is thus cast as a kind of mythic descent: Thoreau's remarks about the shedding and flowing of blood through the Mexican War—"I see this blood flowing now"—recall Dante's imagery of Phlegethon; and the view from his cell, leading him to "a closer view of my native town. I was fairly inside of it," suggests a descent into the belly of Leviathan so prominent in medieval mythology and iconography. Here indeed is Piers Plowman's harrowing of hell transferred to New England soil. Thoreau's descent, symbolically cast as a journey into death and hell, gives rise to a vision of his native town and the Concord River as locked in a kind of hellish death—ossified in a Massachusetts version of the middle ages, yet as unsubstantial as the old world "Rhine stream" into which it seems to turn as he looks on. This vision of death is followed by a symbolic rebirth at dawn when Thoreau is released from prison. Not only does he experience "a change" in his vision but he comes out of the darkness of his cell to ascend a hill, paralleling again Dante's ascent of Mount Purgatory in his climb toward the final haven of the *Paradiso*. That the hill Thoreau climbs is not only "one of our highest" but also named Fair-Haven completes the pattern of spiritual rebirth.

The narrative center of **"Civil Disobedience,"** then, is more than a piece of biography thrown in the midst of a primarily political essay. It is instead the key to the dual vision of the essay. The entire section of the essay preceding the narrative middle is an expansion of that night's vision of death. From this very low level, symbolically entombed, the individual is bound to experience life in the State as a series of contradictions whose precise meaning is death for the moral and spiritual man. The journey through death followed by emergence and ascent effects a narrative synthesis: political contradictions are metaphorically carried up Fair-Haven Hill from which point a new perspective is gained, leading to the resolution of these contradictions in a "higher" view.

The third part of **"Civil Disobedience,"** like the first, may be seen as an expansion of the central narrative, this time of his changed vision from Fair-Haven Hill. In place of the polarized world of the present (and past) America, Thoreau sets forth the "really free and enlightened State" he imagines for the future: a fusion of the individual and the State into mutual service. Here the individual will not be powerless, dominated by the "overwhelming brute force" of millions; instead the State will come to "recognize the individual as a higher and independent power, from which all its own power and authority are derived." Thoreau's vision here parallels Emerson's reconciliation of "society" and "solitude" whereby the greatest individual self-reliance derives from the fullest assimilation of society by the individual soul and the ideal society is constructed from completely self-reliant men. Thus, if "the last improvement possible in government"—considered without reference to the individual—is democracy with its domination of the man by the majority, "is it not possible to take a step further towards recognizing and organizing the rights of man?" This "step further" is metaphorically a step upward:

> Seen from a lower point of view, the Constitution, with all its faults, is very good . . . but seen from a point of view a little higher, they [this State and this American government] are what I have described them; seen from a higher still, and the highest, who shall say what they are, or that they are worth looking at or thinking of at all?

Significantly, the essay rises and ends on a note of heavenly vision: "a still more perfect and glorious State, which also I have imagined, but not yet anywhere seen."

If we approach **"Civil Disobedience"** primarily as a political essay as thousands of readers have done, the two flanking views of the State inevitably receive a horizontal reading, the second functioning as a solution to problems presented in the first. Some dozens of commentators who find Thoreau politically naive or his strategies for reform unclear have obviously assumed this kind of structure. The central narrative suggests, however, something akin to renewed vision or imaginative rebirth for which a programmatic reading is inadequate. In the upward passage from night to day, bondage to freedom, Concord jail to Fair-Haven Hill, Thoreau builds a vertical narrative order which transcends political categories—which moves from the realm of understanding to the realm of imagination. We are reminded of a relevant remark about this in ***Walden***: "When one man has reduced a fact of the imagination to be a fact to his understanding, I foresee that all men will at length establish their lives on that basis."

What Thoreau displays is a typically romantic perspective: a desire for a genuine metamorphosis in which the existing State is to die and an ideal state born in its place. From this standpoint, however, the ideal does not simply succeed or replace the real but is rather synthesized from it, as blossoming new life is synthesized from the materials of death. Thoreau's transcendental picture of the perfect State evolves from his death-vision of the present state and is in fact impossible without that death-vision. The narrative center of **"Civil Disobedience"** is therefore the vehicle for an imaginative synthesis, providing a mythic layering to his entry into and emergency from jail at dawn such that the reconciliation of opposites in this passage is a version of heroic triumph. Those commentators who have noted the considerable differences between the idealized account Thoreau gives and the event as reported by others are exactly right: it is precisely this displacement of the real event to the level of heroic narrative that validates the idealized vision of the essay. This is the essence of the artistry of **"Civil Disobedience"** and it is integral to interpretation.

This reading of the essay as narrative emphasizes its obvious similarities with Thoreau's other writings, especially ***Walden.*** Thoreau's passage from Concord jail to Fair-Haven Hill had already occurred in less dramatic form the previous summer (1845) with his move to Walden Pond, and his changed vision of Concord in the essay underlines the focus in the later book on renewal and rebirth. Like **"Civil Disobedience,"** with its discussion of the contradictions in the existing State, ***Walden*** begins with a long discussion of economic contradictions—the development of industry that leads to waste, the abundance of things that crushes human freedom, the poverty of wealth, the institutional life of civilization that submerges the self-reliant soul. Like the essay with its vision at dawn, ***Walden*** is full of morning visions, culminating in the rebirth ritual of spring. Such images of metamorphosis in ***Walden*** as the bank of thawing clay on later winter morning or the resurrection of a "beautiful bug" from an old apple-wood table enhance and validate the archetype of death and rebirth at the center of the **"Civil Disobedience"** narrative.

In Thoreau's major excursions and books, it appears that he designed his art around a series of journeys which thus became passages from the real to the transcendent—symbolized in the frontier regions west of Concord (**"Walking"**), the upper reaches of the Merrimack (***A Week***), the heights of mountains (**"A Walk to Wachusett"**), the primitive depths of the forest (***The Maine Woods***), or the tranquil waters of the pond (***Walden***). "I went to the woods," he wrote in ***Walden,*** "because I wished to live deliberately." In **"Civil Disobedience"** we discover a similar passage, perhaps the only one that Thoreau did not deliberately plan: a walk to the cobbler's store to get a shoe interrupted, redirected, stalled for a dozen hours by a night in jail, then resumed the next morning. It is not surprising that the artistic account took on the shape of all the other passages in his works with their ascending movements toward morning, spring, hills, mountains, and the sun. (pp. 173-81)

Barry Wood, "Thoreau's Narrative Art in 'Civil Disobedience'," in Henry David Thoreau, *edited by Harold Bloom, Chelsea House Publishers, 1987, pp. 173-81.*

ADDITIONAL BIBLIOGRAPHY

Adams, Raymond. "'Civil Disobedience' Gets Printed." *The Thoreau Society Bulletin*, No. 28 (July 1949): 1-3.

Discusses the circumstances surrounding the initial publication of "Civil Disobedience."

Anastaplo, George. "On Civil Disobedience: Thoreau and Socrates." *Southwest Review* LIV, No. 2 (Spring 1969): 203-14.

Suggests that Thoreau's concept of the relation between the individual and the state was naive. Anastaplo offers Plato's *Crito* as a more astute analysis.

Broderick, John C. "Thoreau, Alcott, and the Poll Tax." *Studies in Philology* LIII, No. 4 (October 1956): 612-26.

Provides background information concerning the Massachusetts poll tax and the tradition of refusing to pay it as a gesture of dissent.

Buranelli, Vincent. "The Case Against Thoreau." *Ethics* LXVII, No. 4 (July 1957): 257-68.

An analysis of Thoreau's philosophical viewpoint. Buranelli maintains that Thoreau's ideas were distorted by idiosyncratic thinking frequently taken to extremes, concluding that "admiration of Thoreau is justified only if tempered and delimited by a frank awareness of his contemptible side."

Combellack, C. R. B. "Two Critics of Society." *The Pacific Spectator* III, No. 4 (Autumn 1949): 440-45.
Compares Thoreau's social and economic ideas with those of Karl Marx, noting that while Thoreau's oeuvre is clearly limited, his impact on the twentieth century has been nearly as great as that of Marx.

Condry, William. *Thoreau.* London: H. F. & G. Witherby, 1954, 114 p.
A noncritical biography.

Doudna, Martin K. "Echoes of Milton, Donne, and Carlyle in 'Civil Disobedience'." *Thoreau Journal Quarterly* XII, No. 3 (July 1980): 5-7.
Identifies some possible sources for the phraseology in "Civil Disobedience" in John Milton's *Areopagitica,* John Donne's "Satire III," and Thomas Carlyle's *On Heroes and Hero-Worship.*

Drinnon, Richard. "Thoreau's Politics of the Upright Man." *The Massachusetts Review, Special Issue: Thoreau, a Centenary Gathering* IV, No. 1 (Autumn 1962): 126-38.
Examines the anarchic implications of "Civil Disobedience."

Foerster, Norman. "The Intellectual Heritage of Thoreau." *The Texas Review* II, No. 3 (January 1917): 192-212.
Discusses the writings and intellectual trends that most influenced Thoreau. Foerster notes significant gaps in Thoreau's reading and contends that his ideas clearly reflect his preference for classical and Elizabethan literature.

Harding, Walter. *The Days of Henry Thoreau.* New York: Alfred A. Knopf, 1967, 472 p.
A comprehensive critical biography.

———, ed. *Thoreau: Man of Concord.* New York: Holt, Rinehart, and Winston, 1960, 251 p.
Reprints contemporary accounts of Thoreau's personality and selections from his writings.

———, ed. *The Thoreau Centennial.* Albany: State University of New York Press, 1964, 119 p.
A collection of papers originally delivered at the Thoreau Centennial in New York in 1962. Essays include "The Last Days of Henry Thoreau," by Harding, "The Day Thoreau Didn't Die," by Raymond Adams, and "Thoreau and Human Nature," by Howard Mumford Jones.

Hendrick, George. "The Influence of Thoreau's 'Civil Disobedience' on Gandhi's *Satyagraha.*" *The New England Quarterly* XXIX, No. 4 (December 1956): 462-71.
Examines passages from "Civil Disobedience" quoted in Gandhi's journal, *Indian Opinion,* between 1907 and 1914.

Herr, William A. "Thoreau: A Civil Disobedient?" *Ethics* 85, No. 1 (October 1974): 87-91.
Contends that Thoreau's views on civil disobedience have been misunderstood, arguing that "Thoreau's position actually seems much closer to conscientious objection than to civil disobedience."

Lebeaux, Richard. *Young Man Thoreau.* Amherst: University of Massachusetts Press, 1977, 262 p.

———. *Thoreau's Seasons.* Amherst: University of Massachusetts Press, 1984, 410 p.
A two-volume biography. Lebeaux examines Thoreau's life in terms of Erik Erikson's psychodynamic theory of personality, which views human life as a continuing series of profound psychological challenges. With regard to "Civil Disobedience," Lebeaux remarks that the essay may in fact have been a denunciation of the political timidity of Ralph Waldo Emerson, with whom Thoreau had become disillusioned.

Lerner, Max. "Thoreau: No Hermit." In his *Ideas Are Weapons: The History and Uses of Ideas,* pp. 45-7. New York: Viking Press, 1939.
Applauds Thoreau's opposition to "every dominant aspect of American life in its first flush of industrial advance—the factory system, the corporations, business enterprise, acquisitiveness, the vandalism of natural resources, the cry for expansion, the clannishness and theocratic smugness of New England society, the herd-mindedness of the people, the unthinking civic allegiance they paid to an opportunist and imperialist government."

Lynd, Staughton. *Intellectual Origins of American Radicalism.* New York: Pantheon Books, 1968, 184 p.
Scattered references to "Civil Disobedience," which Lynd considers a significant document in the history of American dissent.

Meyer, Michael. *Several More Lives to Live: Thoreau's Political Reputation in America.* Westport, Conn.: Greenwood Press, 1977, 216 p.
Studies the evolution of Thoreau's political reputation in the United States from the 1920s to the 1970s. Meyer argues that the growing sympathy for Thoreau's point of view reflects a proportionate increase in the sophistication of the American view of government.

———. Introduction to *Walden and Civil Disobedience,* by Henry David Thoreau, pp. 7-36. Harmondsworth, England: Penguin, 1983.
Provides an overview of Thoreau's writings. Meyer judges "Civil Disobedience" "the most famous essay in American literature."

Miller, Henry. Preface to *Life without Principles: Three Essays by Henry David Thoreau,* pp. i-viii. Stanford, Calif.: James Ladd Delkin, 1946.
A tribute to Thoreau's politics of individualism. Miller suggests that postwar America could profit greatly from adherence to Thoreau's dictum.

Nelson, Truman. "Thoreau and John Brown." In *Thoreau in Our Season,* edited by John H. Hicks, pp. 134-53. Amherst: University of Massachusetts Press, 1966.
Discusses "Civil Disobedience" in the context of Thoreau's other antislavery writings.

Sanborn, F. B. *The Life of Henry David Thoreau.* Boston: Houghton Mifflin Co., 1917, 542 p.
An early, sympathetic biography. F. H. Allen has noted that Sanborn "occupied a unique position as the only one of Thoreau's biographers who had personal acquaintance with him, and who was at the same time an active and energetic seeker for information about his life and writings."

Schiffman, Joseph. "*Walden* and 'Civil Disobedience': Critical Analyses." *Emerson Society Quarterly,* No. 56 (Summer 1969): 57-60.
A brief analysis of "Civil Disobedience." Schiffman notes that "unfortunately, Thoreau's doctrine of conscience—so appealing on the surface—suffers from a dangerous glibness."

Stoller, Leo. "'Civil Disobedience': Principle and Politics." *The Massachusetts Review, Special Issue: Thoreau, a Centenary Gathering* IV, No. 1 (Autumn 1962): 85-8.
Identifies the premises underlying "Civil Disobedience" as Thoreau's belief that "his own imagination could map out an ideal humanity" and his conviction that "American society as it stood in the mid-forties gave no hint of ever becoming better."

Tatalovich, Raymond. "Thoreau on Civil Disobedience: A Defense of Morality or Anarchy?" *The Southern Quarterly* XI, No. 2 (January 1973): 107-13.
Extrapolates from "Civil Disobedience" Thoreau's "prerequisites for . . . obedience to law."

Ivan (Sergeyevich) Turgenev

1818-1883

(Also transliterated as Iván and Iwan; also Sergeyevitch, Sergheïevitch, Serguéivitch, Serguevitch, Serguiéiévitch, and Sergyéevitch; also Toorgenef, Tourghenief, Tourguénief, Turgeneff, Turgenieff, and Turgéniew) Russian novelist, novella, short story, and sketch writer, dramatist, poet, and essayist.

The first Russian author to achieve widespread international fame, Turgenev was accounted his country's premier novelist by nineteenth-century Westerners and is today linked with Fedor Mikhailovich Dostoevsky and Leo Tolstoy as one of the triumvirate of great Russian novelists of the nineteenth century. Turgenev's achievement is twofold. As a writer deeply concerned with the politics of his homeland, he gave to history vivid testimonials of the tumultuous political environment in Russia from the 1840s to the 1870s. Simultaneously, as a literary artist, he created works noted for their psychological truth, descriptive beauty, and haunting pathos.

Turgenev was born in the city of Orel into a family of wealthy gentry. His father, by all accounts a charming but ineffectual cavalry officer, paid little attention to Turgenev, whose childhood on the family estate of Spasskoye was dominated by his eccentric and capricious mother, Varvara Petrovna. Her treatment of her favorite son Ivan alternated between excessive affection and mental and physical cruelty; she ruled Spasskoye and its 5000 serfs with the same arbitrary power. Biographers have cited his mother's influence to explain much about the development of Turgenev's personality—particularly his horror of violence and hatred of injustice—and his fiction, populated as it is by strong women and well-meaning but weak-willed men. During Turgenev's early childhood, French was the primary language spoken in his household; though his mother later permitted the use of Russian, it is likely that Turgenev's first lessons in the vernacular came from the Spasskoye serfs. When Turgenev was nine, the family left the country for Moscow, where he attended boarding schools before entering Moscow University in 1833. At the university, he earned the nickname "the American" for his interest in the United States and his democratic inclinations. In 1834, Turgenev transferred to the University of St. Petersburg. Upon graduation, he decided that the completion of his education required study abroad. In 1838, therefore, he went to Germany, enrolling at the University of Berlin. During the next several years he studied philosophy, never, however, finishing his degree. He returned to Russia in 1841, but for the rest of his life divided his time between his homeland and western Europe.

Although Turgenev had begun writing poetry as a student in St. Petersburg, publishing his first verses in 1838, biographers generally cite the narrative poem *Parasha,* published in 1843, as the beginning of his literary career. This work attracted little attention from his contemporaries, however, and more important for his subsequent life and literary development were the friendships he made in the mid-1840s, including those with Pauline Viardot and Vissarion Grigoryevich Belinsky. Viardot was a successful opera singer and a married woman when Turgenev met her in 1843. The precise nature of their relationship is uncertain. While Turgenev's letters to her seem to indicate a grand passion, at least on his side, there is no evidence that the two were ever lovers. At any rate, their relationship endured for the rest of Turgenev's life; he frequently followed Viardot to wherever her career took her and was on excellent terms with her husband and the rest of her family. Belinsky, an extremely influential literary critic who believed that literature must both mirror life and promote social reform, was a political liberal and an ardent Westernizer who sought to bring Russia's culture and political system nearer to that of Europe. Belinsky was closely associated with the radical periodical *Sovremennik* (the *Contemporary*), edited by Nikolay Alekseevich Nekrasov, and it was in this journal that Turgenev published his first prose work, the short story "Khor i Kalinych" ("Khor and Kalinych"). Although Turgenev continued to write poetry and tried his hand at drama, he had found his niche and his audience in narrative prose. "Khor and Kalinych" was followed by a series of related pieces between the years 1847 and 1852, all first published in the *Contemporary* and later collected and published in book form as *Zapiski okhotnika* (*A Sportsman's Sketches*). In these sketches, which range from brief slices of life to fully realized short stories, Turgenev adopted the persona of a hunter in the country, drawing on his experiences at Spasskoye and expressing his love for the land and people of rural Russia. Common to the sketches is the theme of the injustice of Russian serfdom. Because of this omnipresent concern, *A Sportsman's Sketches* is frequently compared with Harriet Beecher Stowe's contemporaneous antislavery novel *Uncle Tom's Cabin,* published in 1852. Unlike the American novel, however, Turgenev's work is understated, his moral message implied rather than overt. At their first publication, Turgenev's stories were enormously popular with almost everyone but government officials. In fact, when Turgenev wrote an admiring obituary of Nikolay Gogol in 1852, he was arrested, ostensibly for excessive approval of a suspect writer but more likely because he was himself suspect as the author of *A Sportsman's Sketches*. After a month in jail, Turgenev was confined to Spasskoye, where he remained under house arrest for nearly two years. When the serfs were finally freed in 1861, there were many who credited *A Sportsman's Sketches* with having helped to effect their emancipation.

Turgenev's first novel, *Rudin,* which was published in 1856, introduced several character types and themes that appear in his subsequent fiction. The title character is a political idealist who combines a genius for words with an inability to act on them. Such "Russian Hamlets" recur frequently in Turgenev's work and were regarded by his contemporaries as insightful personifications of a national malaise of irresolution and indecision. Like Turgenev's later novels, *Rudin* is a love story. But while Nathalie, one of Turgenev's typically strong heroines, is willing to risk all for love, Rudin gives her up at the first sign of parental opposition: he is as ineffectual and passive in love as in politics, sounding early Turgenev's common themes of fatalism and frustration. *Rudin* was followed by *Dvoryanskoe gnezdo (A House of Gentlefolk),* whose hero Lavretsky is as helpless to control destiny as Rudin. The heroine Liza shows her strength not in action but in renunciation, nobly retiring to a convent when Lavretsky's unfaithful wife, believed dead, reappears on the scene. Elena, the heroine of Turgenev's next novel, *Nakanune (On the Eve),* possesses strength of a more active sort. Longing to dedicate her life to a worthwhile cause, Elena is confronted with a choice of suitors. Rejecting this novel's "Hamlet," she chooses Insarov, a man of resolution and action and, significantly, a Bulgarian rather than a Russian. Turgenev's contemporaries, attuned to the political significance of his characters, understood the novel to mean that Russia had not yet produced men of dedication and action, patriots willing, as are Insarov and Elena, to sacrifice themselves for the sake of a political ideal.

The Russia of the nineteenth century was indeed a divided and politically troubled country, unsure of its future political course. Tension existed not only between conservatives and liberals but also, in the latter camp, between the radicals, who called for immediate change and economic communism, and the moderates, who favored slow, peaceful reform and free enterprise. Turgenev managed to draw the enmity of nearly every Russian ideologue, from reactionary to revolutionary, with his next and most famous novel, *Ottsy i deti (Fathers and Sons)*. Bazarov, the protagonist of the book, is considered Turgenev's most successful and most ambiguous character (alternately attractive and repellent, he aroused ambivalent feelings even in his creator), as well as an intriguing portrayal of a political type just then coming into existence in Russia: the nihilist. While Turgenev did not invent the term nihilist, his depiction of Bazarov in *Fathers and Sons* brought it into general usage. Bazarov rejects every aspect of Russian political, social, and cultural life, believing in nothing save empirical science. As with all Turgenev's fiction, the plot is slight; most of the action consists of Bazarov's debates with his friend's uncle, Pavel, who symbolizes the older generation of Russian liberals. *Fathers and Sons* was denounced on every side: blasted by conservatives as a favorable portrayal of a dangerous radical, it was attacked by liberals as a damning caricature of radicalism.

Distressed by this unfavorable reaction, Turgenev spent more and more time abroad, and he counted among his friends some of the most illustrious authors of his era, including Gustave Flaubert, Henry James, Émile Zola, Guy de Maupassant, and George Sand. His absence from Russia left him vulnerable to charges, leveled at his subsequent novels, that he was out of touch and out of sympathy with his native land. Indeed, his next novel, *Dym (Smoke),* was considered Turgenev's most bitter work, one that pilloried conservatives and liberals alike and that, in the disapproving eyes of many Russian commentators, depicted Russia's plight as a hopeless one. Pessimistic also is Turgenev's last novel, *Nov' (Virgin Soil),* which deals with the inability of Nezhdanov, another ineffectual character, to put into practice his Populist principles by living and working with the common people. As a study of the Russian Populist movement of the 1870s, the book was considered inadequate by Russian readers. Following the publication of *Virgin Soil,* Turgenev, now virtually self-exiled from his homeland, no longer attempted to depict the Russian political scene. His remaining works—prose poems and stories—are described by critics as nostalgic, philosophical, and frequently pessimistic, and are often concerned with the occult. After a long and debilitating illness, Turgenev died at Bougival, near Paris, with Pauline Viardot at his side. His body was returned to Russia by train. There, notwithstanding the unfavorable reception of his later works and the efforts of the Russian government to restrict memorial congregations, Turgenev was widely mourned by his compatriots.

Because of the highly political content of most of Turgenev's works, the earliest Russian commentators tended to praise or damn his writings along partisan lines. Similarly, foreign critics of the nineteenth century were interested in Turgenev's books for the light they shed on the volatile sociopolitical situation in Russia. Turgenev's novels and many of his novellas and short stories were quickly translated into French, German, and English. English and American readers considered Turgenev the most accessible Russian writer, and they—particularly American critics—took a lively, generally appreciative interest in his career beginning with the publication of *A Sportsman's Sketches*. Early Russian and English-language critics by no means neglected the aesthetic qualities of Turgenev's works, however, recognizing from the start that his fiction was more than simply the literal portrayal of the people and concerns of a particular country at a given historical moment.

Turgenev's literary reputation has remained generally stable over the years, with twentieth-century commentators echoing and amplifying the conclusions reached by their nineteenth-century counterparts. Critics agree that Turgenev's work is distinguished by solid literary craftsmanship, especially in the areas of description and characterization. Keenly observant, he infused his work with precise, realistic detail, bringing a natural scene or character into focus through the evocative power of his words. Given Turgenev's slight plots, interest in the novels centers largely on the characters. Readers note that his characters—recognized both as unique individuals and as representatives of universal human qualities—are drawn with a psychological penetration all the more effective for being suggested rather than overtly stated: the minds and personalities of his characters are revealed through their own words and actions, not through direct exposition by the narrator. Turgenev was particularly adept, critics contend, at portraying women in love and at creating an atmosphere of pathos but not sentimentality in his unhappy love stories. Fatalism and thwarted desires are hallmarks of the novelist's work: his characters are generally unable to control their destiny, either because of their own flaws or through the arbitrariness of fate. Scholars suggest that Turgenev's fiction reveals his own sense of the futility of life, but add that he tempered his essentially pessimistic outlook with an appreciation of life's beauty. As the author himself remarked, "Everything human is dear to me."

Turgenev is thus renowned for his dual role as social chronicler and literary artisan. In his stories and novels he described the political temper of a turbulent era, at the same time creating works of great literary merit. As Joseph Conrad wrote: "Turgenev's Russia is but a canvas on which the incomparable artist of humanity lays his colours and his forms in the great light and the free air of the world."

*PRINCIPAL WORKS

Parasha (poetry) 1843
Dnevnik lishnego cheloveka (short story) 1850
["The Diary of a Superfluous Man" published in *Mumu and The Diary of a Superfluous Man,* 1884]
"Mumu" (short story) 1852; published in periodical *Sovremennik*
["Mumu" published in *Mumu and The Diary of a Superfluous Man,* 1884]
Zapiski okhotnika (sketches and short stories) 1852
[*Russian Life in the Interior; or, The Experiences of a Sportsman,* 1855; also published as *A Sportsman's Sketches* in *The Novels of Ivan Turgenev,* 1895]
Rudin (novel) 1856; also published as *Rudin* [enlarged edition], 1860
[*Dimitri Roudine,* 1873; also published as *Rudin* in *The Novels of Ivan Turgenev,* 1894]
Asya (novella) 1858
[*Annouchka,* 1884; also published as *Asya* in *The Novels and Stories of Iván Turgénieff,* 1904]
Dvoryanskoe gnezdo (novel) 1859
[*Liza,* 1869; also published as *A House of Gentlefolk* in *The Novels of Ivan Turgenev,* 1894, and *A Nobleman's Nest* in *The Novels and Stories of Iván Turgénieff,* 1903]
"Gamlet i Don Kikhot" (criticism) 1860; published in periodical *Sovremennik*
["Hamlet and Don Quixote" published in periodical *Poet Lore,* 1892]
Nakanune (novel) 1860
[*On the Eve,* 1871]
Pervaya lyubov' (novella) 1860
[*First Love* published in *First Love, and Punin and Baburin,* 1884]
Ottsy i deti (novel) 1862
[*Fathers and Sons,* 1867; also published as *Fathers and Children* in *The Novels of Ivan Turgenev,* 1899]
Dym (novel) 1867
[*Smoke,* 1868]
Stepnoi Korol' Lir (short story) 1870
["A King Lear of the Steppes" published in *The Novels and Stories of Iván Turgénieff,* 1903]
***Mesyats v derevne* (drama) 1872
[*A Month in the Country* published in *The Plays of Ivan S. Turgenev,* 1924]
Veshnie vody (novella) 1872
[*The Torrents of Spring* published in *The Novels of Ivan Turgenev,* 1897]
Nov' (novel) 1877
[*Virgin Soil,* 1877]
Stikhotvoreniya v proze (poetry) 1882
[*Poems in Prose,* 1883; also published as *Senilia,* 1890]
Polnoe sobranie sochinenii. 10 vols. (novels, novellas, short stories, dramas, poetry, criticism, and letters) 1891
The Novels of Ivan Turgenev. 15 vols. (novels, novellas, short stories, and poetry) 1894-99
The Novels and Stories of Iván Turgénieff. 16 vols. (novels, novellas, and short stories) 1903-04
The Plays of Ivan S. Turgenev (dramas) 1924
Polnoe sobranie sochinenii i pisem. 28 vols. (novels, novellas, short stories, dramas, poetry, criticism, and letters) 1960-68
Turgenev's Letters (letters) 1983

*Most of Turgenev's works were originally published in periodicals.

**This work was written in 1850.

V. G. BELINSKY (essay date 1848)

[Belinsky is considered the most influential Russian literary critic of the nineteenth century. He initiated a new trend in critical thought by combining literary appreciation with an exposition of progressive philosophical and political theory. His most memorable contributions to Russian literature were produced during the latter part of his career when, as chief critic for the progressive review Otechestvennye Zapiski (Notes of the Fatherland) *and later, for the* Contemporary, *he embraced a form of humanitarian socialism and became the primary spokesperson in the Russian intelligentsia's campaign against serfdom, autocracy, and orthodox religion. His insistence that literature both mirror life and promote social reform established the theoretical basis of the Natural school in Russian literature and paved the way from romanticism to realism. Belinsky and Turgenev became friends in the mid-1840s and the latter published his works in the* Contemporary *until he broke with the periodical after Belinsky's death in 1848. Here, in an excerpt from an essay written in 1848, Belinsky surveys Turgenev's career to date, determining that while Turgenev lacks original creativity, he excels in the faithful rendition of his observations of life. Accordingly, Belinsky disparages Turgenev's poetry but praises* A Sportsman's Sketches.]

Mr. Turgenev began his literary career by writing lyrical poetry; among his shorter verses are three or four noteworthy plays, as for instance **"The Old Landowner," "A Ballad," "Fedya,"** and **"A Man Like Many Others."** However, he came off well with these plays because they either do not contain anything lyrical or their principal feature is not lyricism but hints at Russian life. Mr. Turgenev's lyrical verses proper reveal a complete absence of independent lyrical talent. He has written several poems. When ***Parasha,*** the first of them, appeared, it was noted by the public for its facile verse, its gay irony, and faithful Russian landscapes, but chiefly for its felicitous physiological sketches depicting in detail the life and manners of the landowners. The poem, however, failed to achieve a lasting success, because when he penned it the author was concerned not with writing a physiological sketch but a poem of the kind for which he possessed no independent talent. Hence its best features shone forth in sort of casual, haphazard flashes. Next he wrote a poem, **"A Conversation."** Its verses are powerful and resonant and contain much feeling, thought, and intellect; since, however, this thought is borrowed and not his own, the poem, though it might even please at a first reading, evokes no desire for a second reading. Mr. Turgenev's third poem, **"Andrei,"** contains much that is good, for it has many faithful sketches of Russian life, but as a whole the poem was a failure, because it is a story of love, the portrayal of which does not lie within the scope of the author's talent. The heroine's letter to the hero is long and prolix, and it contains more sentimentality than pathos. Generally speaking, these efforts of Mr. Turgenev reveal talent, but a talent that is sort of irresolute and indefinite.

He also tried his hand at the narrative; his **"Andrei Kolossov"** contains many splendid sketches of characters and Russian life, but as a story, this work as a whole was so queer, inconsequential, and clumsy that very few people noticed the good points it really contained. It was then obvious that Mr. Turgenev was seeking a path of his own and had not yet found it, for this is not a thing that anybody can always easily or quickly find. Finally Mr. Turgenev wrote a story in verse, **"The Landowner,"** not a poem, but a physiological sketch of the life of the landowning class, a joke if you will, but a joke that somehow turned out to be much superior than any of the author's poems. Its racy epigrammatical verse, its gay irony, the faithfulness of its pictures, and at the same time an integrity sustained throughout the work—all tend to prove that Mr. Turgenev has discovered the real genre of his talent, has found his own element, and that there are no reasons why he should give up verses entirely. At the same time there appeared his story in prose, **"Three Portraits,"** which reveals that Mr. Turgenev had found his real road in prose as well. Finally his story **"Khor and Kalinich"** appeared in the first issue of the *Contemporary* of last year. The success of this short story, which had been published in the "Miscellany" column, was unexpected for the author, and induced him to continue his hunter's sketches. Here his talent was fully displayed.

Evidently he does not possess a talent for pure creative genius; he cannot create characters and place them in such mutual relationships in which they form themselves of their own accord into novels or stories. He can depict scenes of reality that he has observed or studied; he can, if you wish, create, but only out of material that is ready at hand, provided by actual life. This is not simply copying from real life; the latter does not provide the author with ideas but, as it were, suggests them to him, puts him in their way. He reworks the ready-made substance according to his ideal and gives us a scene, more alive, more eloquent and full of meaning than the actual incident that prompted him to write the scene; this sort of thing requires a certain measure of poetical talent. True, his entire ability sometimes consists only in faithfully describing a familiar person or an event of which he was a witness, since in actual life there are sometimes phenomena which, when faithfully put on paper, have all the features of artistic fiction. This, too, requires talent, and talents of this kind have their degrees. In both cases Mr. Turgenev possesses a highly remarkable talent. The chief characteristic feature of his talent lies in the fact that he would hardly be able faithfully to portray a character whose likeness he had not met in actual life. He must always keep his feet on the soil of reality. For that kind of art he has been endowed by nature with ample means: the gift of observation, the ability swiftly and faithfully to grasp and appreciate any phenomenon, instinctively to divine its causes and effects, and thus through surmise and reflection to complement the store of information that he needs, when mere inquiries explain little.

It is no wonder that the short piece **"Khor and Kalinich"** met with such success. In it the author approached the people from an angle from which no one had ever approached them before. Khor, with his practical sense and practical nature, his crude but strong and clear mind, his profound contempt for womenfolk and his deep-rooted aversion to cleanliness and neatness, is a type of Russian peasant who has been able to create for himself a position of significance under extremely adverse circumstances. Kalinich, however, is a fresher and fuller type of the Russian peasant; he is a poetical nature in common folk. With what sympathy and kindliness the author describes his heroes, and how he succeeds in making the readers love them with all their hearts! In all, seven sportsman's stories were published last year in the *Contemporary*. In them the author aquaints his readers with various aspects of provincial life, with people of diverse rank and condition. Not all his stories are of equal merit; some are better, others are worse, but there is not one that is not in some way interesting, entertaining, and instructive. So far, **"Khor and Kalinich"** remains the finest of all these sportsman's tales; next comes **"The Steward"** and then **"The Freeholder Ovsyanikov"** and **"The Counting-House."** One can only wish that Mr. Turgenev will write at least entire volumes of such stories.

Although Turgenev's story **"Pyotr Petrovich Karataev,"** which appeared in the second issue of the *Contemporary* for last year, does not belong to his hunting tales, this work is just as masterly a physiological sketch of the purely Russian character, and with a Moscow flavor at that. In this story, the author's talent is as fully expressed as in the finest of his hunting tales.

We cannot but mention Mr. Turgenev's extraordinary skill in describing scenes of Russian nature. He loves nature not as a dilettante but as an artist, and therefore he never tries to present it only in its poetical aspects, but takes it exactly as it appears to him. His pictures are always true, and you never fail to recognize our Russian landscapes in them. (pp. 66-9)

V. G. Belinsky, "A Survey of Russian Literature in 1847: Part Two," in Belinsky, Chernyshevsky, and Dobrolyubov: Selected Criticism, *edited by Ralph E. Matlaw, E. P. Dutton & Co., Inc., 1962, pp. 33-82.*

FRASER'S MAGAZINE FOR TOWN AND COUNTRY (essay date 1854)

[*In a review of a French edition of* A Sportsman's Sketches, *the anonymous critic praises the artless verisimilitude of the work.*]

It might be said, without much exaggeration, that we know as little of the interior life of Russia as of that of Dahomey or Timbuctoo. (p. 209)

We propose in this article to supply, as far as our space allows, a few materials for a . . . correct conception of the true character of Russian interior life, more especially in the provinces. They are derived from a work published some two years since at Moscow, in the Russian language, by a Russian gentleman of the class of the nobles, himself a landed proprietor, but, as far as may be inferred from his book, singularly exempt from prejudice. Not that he professes any liberal ideas; quite the contrary—he seeks to avoid self-obtrusion throughout, and limits himself to reproducing, with an instinctive fidelity, what he has heard and seen. M. Ivan Tourghenief's 'photographs' are the more interesting, inasmuch as he is not a professed writer; he has not sought 'effects,' but has transferred to paper, with the vividness of a daguerreotype, the impressions produced upon him by the various personages and scenes he describes. Nature has given him a fine perception of the beauties of scenery, and of the peculiarities of the human character: he paints them with the simplicity and ardour of a lover, and he is none the less an artist because a practised eye will detect the absence or even the want of art. Of all descriptive works, those which are produced by men of this stamp are the most valuable and the most lasting, because they are necessarily stamped with the fidelity of truth.

Mr. Tourghenief is possessed with a love of sport, which with him amounts to a passion. With his gun and his dog, and generally with an attendant of congenial taste, lent him by some friend at whose territory he stops in his rambles, he constantly follows his favourite pursuit. He is not, however, a mere sportsman, but also a keen observer of human nature and character; and as his passion leads him into all kinds of out-of-the-way places, and among all varieties of people, from the highest to the lowest, he has had ample scope for observation and amusement. What led him to write we know not; but a few fragmentary descriptive pieces, which appeared in an unconnected form in a literary review at Moscow, having attracted universal attention from the extraordinary fidelity and gracefulness with which they depicted the manners of the people, he was induced to proceed, and ultimately to publish the work of which we speak. In the original, it is entitled the ***Journal of a Sportsman;*** but such a name would very imperfectly express the peculiar character of the work, in which sporting adventures are a mere thread on which are hung the charming pictures of life, manners, and scenery of which the book is full. The author of a French translation, which has just appeared, has, with good judgment, changed the title into *Mémoires d'un Seigneur Russe,* which better indicates the value of the book, as containing the view taken by a Russian aristocrat of many of the customs and social institutions of his country.

If there are those who seek the artificial stimulus of horrors, who like to hear with the mind's ear the fall of the knout on the back of the suffering serf, or who desire that the simpler pictures of slave life shall be set in a connected narrative of refined cruelty and pain, as in the work of Mrs. Stowe, they will not find their appetite satisfied. . . . The pictures of Mr. Tourghenief are . . . 'Photographs;' there is in them always something of still life. But, at the same time, they are eminently suggestive, the more so from the utter absence of all effort, egoism, or self-display on the part of the writer. They might have been made more 'artistic,' but then they would lose a certain smack of rough reality, which inspires an almost absolute confidence in the reader. The author does not moralize in words, but in examples. He does not spare his own class, but he lets the facts speak for themselves; and as his sufferers are not angels, but Russians habituated to serfdom and its evils, you are able to look at that institution somewhat more philosophically than if your moral indignation were perpetually excited by artificial means. The bright side is given, as well as the dark one, and yet the result of the whole is a profound conviction of the iniquity of serfdom as an institution, and of its degrading effects on the subject as well as on the master. The book is a Russian *Uncle Tom's Cabin,* without its blood and gunpowder.

Serfdom, however, furnishes only episodes in these sketches, which embrace almost every conceivable social variety. (pp. 210-11)

[In one] chapter we have an amusing portrait of a lady-proprietor who from conscientious motives has remained single; she conceives it to be her duty to keep her serfs in the same state, and not a man or a woman of them is permitted to marry. In another, a beautiful girl has been brought to the capital by a fine-lady mistress, her owner, who, to keep her about her person as maid, refuses her the permission to marry a fellow-servant. The result is that the poor lovers commit themselves; the youth is sent off as a recruit, and the girl sells herself in marriage to a miller, for whom she has no love, on condition that he purchases her freedom. The poor loveless wife literally pines away before your eyes, in the author's simple narrative. Two little episodes, the **"Village Doctor,"** and the **"Village Lovers,"** are charming as idyls, irrespective of their value as pictures of manners; and the **"Russian Hamlet"** has a peculiar humour of its own, thoroughly national. . . . The Dwarf *Kaciane* is, in a literary point of view, a new character; and there is a chapter in which some boys, watching horses, recount, round a night-fire in the steppes, the various superstitions of the country, that is full of poetry and racy with nationality. Scattered through the book, too, there are portraits of individuals, each representing a class . . . ; and thus, on arriving at the close, the reader has become insensibly possessed with almost every phase of Russian life. (p. 222)

"Photographs from Russian Life," in Fraser's Magazine for Town and Country, *Vol. L, August, 1854, pp. 209-22.*

N. G. CHERNYSHEVSKY (essay date 1858?)

[Chernyshevsky was a Russian man of letters and a younger contemporary of Turgenev. As a literary critic, he held that literature must have a progressive social aim to justify its existence. In this excerpt from a review of Turgenev's novella Asya, *he sees the work's protagonist as indicative of a national malaise of irresolution. More radical politically than Turgenev, Chernyshevsky later castigated the older author for failing to call for revolution in his works. Chernyshevsky's remarks were probably first published in 1858.]*

"Straightforward, accusatory stories leave a painful impression on the reader. Therefore, while recognizing their usefulness and noble aims, I am not altogether happy with the fact that our literature has taken such a gloomy direction so exclusively." This is the way many people who are apparently not stupid speak, or rather this is the way they spoke until the time when the peasant question became the sole subject of all thought and of all conversation. I don't know whether what they say is fair or not. But I was under the influence of the same idea when I began to read practically the only good new story [Turgenev's ***Asya***] from which one could expect a different inspiration, content of an entirely different kind than that found in straightforward stories from the very first pages. Here was neither chicanery, with violence and bribery, nor filthy rogues or official villains who explain in elegant language that they are society's benefactors, nor peasants and petty officials tormented by all these horrible and disgusting people. The action takes place abroad, far from all the base circumstances of our home life. All its characters come from the best among us, are very cultured, humane, and imbued with the most noble manner of thoughts. The tale has a purely poetic, ideal direction, and does not touch on a single one of the so-called dark sides of life. "Now, then," I thought, "I'll be able to rest and refresh myself." And I really did refresh myself with these poetic ideals until the tale came to the decisive moment. But the last pages do not resemble the first, and after reading the tale one is left with an even more disconsolate impression than that created by stories about nasty bribetakers and their cynical thefts. They do evil, but then each of us recognizes them as evil people; we do not expect the amelioration of life from them. We believe that there are forces in society that will put an end to their harmful influence, that will change our life through their noble character. That illusion is destroyed in the cruelest way in this tale, whose opening pages raised the most hopeful expectations.

Here is a man whose heart is open to all the highest feelings, whose honesty is unshakable, whose mind has appropriated everything that has given our era the designation of the era of noble intentions. But what does that man do? He creates a scene the worst bribetaker would be ashamed of. He feels the strongest and purest feeling for a girl who loves him. He cannot live an hour without seeing her. All day and all night his mind traces her beautiful likeness for him, and one would think that the time had come when his heart would drown in bliss. We see a Romeo and Juliet whose happiness no one opposes, and the minute approaches when their fate will be decided forever—all Romeo has to do is to say, "I love you; do you love me?" for her to whisper, "Yes."

And what does our Romeo do—we shall call the hero of the story Romeo, for the author does not give his name—when he appears at the assignation with his Juliet? Juliet awaits her Romeo with a shudder of expectation. She must hear from him that he loves her—that word had not been pronounced between them; now it will be spoken by him and they will be united forever. Bliss awaits them, such an exalted and pure bliss that the ardent desire for it makes the triumphant moment of decision almost unbearable for a mortal being. People would die of lesser joys. She sits like a frightened bird, shading her face from the sun of love that appears before her; she breathes rapidly, she shudders. She lowers her eyes in greater trepidation when he enters and calls her by name. She wants to look at him and cannot. He takes her hand—that hand is cold and lies death-like in his; she wants to smile, but her pale lips cannot smile. She wants to talk with him but her voice breaks. For a long time both are silent; in him too, as he himself says, his heart has melted. Now Romeo finally speaks to his Juliet. And what does he say to her? He says: "You are guilty toward me; you've placed me in unpleasant circumstances; I am dissatisfied with you; you are compromising me and I must break off my relationship with you. It is very unpleasant for me to part from you, but please go as far away from here as possible." What is this supposed to mean? How is she guilty? In that she considered him an honorable man? Did she compromise his reputation by coming to him at an assignation? That's fantastic! Every feature of her pale face says she awaits the determination of her fate from his words, that she has irrevocably given him her whole soul and now only awaits his saying that he accepts her soul, her life—and he reprimands her for compromising him! What kind of stupid cruelty is that? What kind of base coarseness? And the man who acted so meanly has seemed noble until then! He fooled us, fooled the author. Yet, the poet made too gross a mistake when he imagined that he was writing about a respectable man. That man is more trashy than an out-and-out rascal.

Such was the impression the completely unexpected turn in the relationship of our Romeo to his Juliet produced on many readers. Many people have said that the story is completely spoiled by that shocking scene, that the character of the main figure is not maintained, that if that figure really was what he is presented as being in the first half, then he would not be able to act with such base coarseness, and if he could so act, then he should have been presented to us as a trashy person from the first.

It would be comforting to think that the author really made a mistake, yet the sad merit of his tale lies precisely in that the character of his hero accurately reflects society. Perhaps the tale would have gained in its idealistic-poetic aspect if the character was such as those people who are dissatisfied with his coarseness at the assignation would like him to be, if he had not been afraid to give himself up to the love that possessed him. After the enthusiasm of the first meeting, there would have followed several other highly poetic moments; the quiet splendor of the tale's first half would have been raised to an inspired enchantment in the second; and instead of the first act of *Romeo and Juliet* with an ending à la Pechorin, we should really have had something like *Romeo and Juliet,* or at least something similar to one of George Sand's novels. Whoever seeks a poetically unified impression from the tale must really condemn the author, who after attracting the reader with heightened, delightful expectations, suddenly showed him the vulgarly stupid vanity of trivially timid egoism, beginning like Max Piccolomini and ending like some Zakhar Sidorych who plays patience for pennies.

Yet was the author actually mistaken in his hero? If he was, then it wasn't the first time he committed that mistake. In all the stories he has written that lead to a similar situation, his heroes extricate themselves from the situation every time by becoming completely disconcerted before our eyes. (pp. 108-11)

Yet perhaps that pitiful trait in the heroes' characters is a particularity of Mr. Turgenev's stories? Perhaps the nature of his special talent leads him to depict such figures? Not at all; it seems to us that the nature of a talent does not mean anything here. Think of any good story, true to life, by anyone you wish among today's poets, and if his story contains an ideal side, you may be sure that the representative of that ideal side behaves precisely as Mr. Turgenev's figures do. (p. 112)

Everywhere, whatever the poet's character may be, whatever his personal views of his hero's actions, the hero acts just as other respectable people do, introduced, like him, by other poets: the hero is very daring so long as there is no question of action and one need merely occupy spare time, fill an empty head or empty heart with conversation and dreams; but when the time comes to express one's feelings and desires directly and precisely, the majority of heroes begin to waver, and are stricken dumb. A few, the bravest, manage to collect all their strength and to stammer something that gives a hazy notion of their thoughts. But let someone take up their desires, and say, "You want such-and-such very well. Begin to act. We will support you." At that reply half of the bravest heroes would faint; the other half would begin to reproach you coarsely for placing them in an uncomfortable position, to say that they did not expect such proposals from you, that they are completely dumfounded, and that they can conceive nothing, because, "How could it occur so quickly?" Moreover, they are "honorable people," and not only honorable but very peaceful, and do not want to subject you to unpleasantness; and in general, can one really fuss about everything one says merely for lack of anything to do? The best thing of all is not to undertake anything, because everything is connected with fussing and inconvenience, and nothing good can come for the time being because, as was already said, they "didn't expect and desire it at all," and so on.

That is what our "best people" are like; they are all similar to our Romeo. Whether Asya is greatly harmed by Mr. N's not knowing what to do with her and by his actual vexation when daring decision was demanded of him—whether Asya is greatly harmed thereby we cannot say. At first one thinks that she is harmed very little. On the contrary, thank heaven our Romeo's trashy weakness of character repelled the girl before it was too late. Asya will grieve for several weeks or several months, and then will forget everything and be able to give herself up to a new feeling, whose object will be more worthy of her. This is true. But the trouble is that she is not likely to find a more worthy person. That's where the sad comicality of our Romeo's relationship to Asya lies, in that our Romeo really is one of the best people of our society and that we hardly have anyone better than he.

Asya will be satisfied with her relationship to people only when she, like everyone else, learns to limit herself to beautiful discussions until the opportunity to put these discussions into action comes. As soon as that opportunity arrives, one must bite one's tongue and fold one's hands the way everyone else does. Only then will others be satisfied with her. But now, at the beginning, people will say that the girl is very nice, has a noble soul, remarkable strength of character, and is in general a girl one cannot help loving, whom one cannot help worshiping. But all that will be said only as long as Asya's character is expressed merely in words, as long as it is only assumed that she is capable of noble and decisive action. But as soon as she takes any step that justifies the expectations inspired by her character, hundreds of voices will immediately cry out:

"For heaven's sake, how can she? It's madness! To grant a young man a *rendez-vous!* Surely she's ruining herself, ruining herself completely uselessly. Surely nothing can come of that, absolutely nothing, except that she will lose her reputation! Can one risk oneself so insanely?"

"Risk one's self? That's not the worst of it," others will add. "Let her do what she likes with herself, but why subject others to unpleasantness? What sort of position did she place that poor young man in? Did he think that she would lead him that far? What can he do now when confronted with her irrationality? If he marries her, he will ruin himself; if he refuses, he'll be called a coward and he will despise himself. I don't know that it's honorable to put people who apparently have given no special cause for such absurd behavior into such unpleasant circumstances. No, that's not honorable at all. And what of the poor brother? What is his role like? What a hard pill to swallow his sister gave him! That pill won't go down all his life! She's really given him a treat, the dear sister. I won't argue that that's all very well as talk-noble intentions and self-sacrifice and God knows what other splendid things, but I'll say one thing: I wouldn't want to be Asya's brother. I'll say more: If I were in her brother's place, I'd lock her up in her room for a half a year. She must be locked up for her own good. She permits herself to be carried away by elevated feelings, don't you see? But how will others swallow what she's concocted? No, I shall not call her action noble; I shall not call her character noble because I do not call those who carelessly and boldly harm others noble."

Thus rational people will explain their opinions in a general outcry. In part we are ashamed to admit it, but it must be admitted that these opinions seem to us to be well founded. Asya really harms not only herself but also everyone who has the misfortune to be close to her through birth or circumstance; and we cannot help condemning those who do harm to all those near them for their own satisfaction.

While condemning Asya, we acquit our Romeo. What has he really done? Has he given her occasion to act irrationally? Has he incited her to an action one cannot approve? Didn't he have the right to tell her that she placed him in unpleasant circumstances in vain? You are troubled by the fact that his words are harsh; you call them coarse. But the truth is always harsh, and who would condemn me even if I let a coarse word slip out when I am mixed up in an unpleasant affair through no fault of mine and am, moreover, asked to enjoy the difficulty into which I have been dragged? (pp. 112-14)

It would . . . have been far pleasanter for Romeo to enjoy the reciprocal pleasures of happy love than to be left holding the bag and to berate himself cruelly for his vulgar coarseness with Asya. From the fact that the cruel unpleasantness to which Asya is subjected makes him ashamed of himself, rather than bringing him pleasure or utility, and that it brings upon him the bitterest of moral vexations—from that fact we see that he did not commit a crime but was the subject of a misfortune. His base behavior would have been duplicated by very many of the so-called respectable people or better people of our society. Consequently it is nothing other than a symptom of the epidemic disease rooted in our society.

The symptom of a disease is not the disease itself. And if it were only a matter of several or, better, of almost all of the "better" people offending a girl when she has greater nobility or less experience than they, then, we admit, this would have interested us very little. Forget about them, those erotic questions! They are not for a reader of our time, occupied with problems of administrative and judiciary improvements, of financial reforms, of the emancipation of the serfs. But the scene our Romeo plays with Asya, as we noted, is only the symptom of a disease that will spoil all our affairs in precisely the same base way, and we need only examine why our Romeo had this misfortune to see what all of us, so similar to him, should expect from ourselves and for ourselves in all other affairs as well.

Let us begin with the fact that the poor young man completely fails to understand the affair he is participating in. The business is perfectly clear, but he is overcome by such dull-wittedness that he cannot comprehend the most obvious facts. (p. 120)

It seems that a man who understands women well could understand what is going on in Asya's heart. But when she writes him that she loves him, her note takes him completely by surprise; he had never, don't you see? guessed it. Fine. It doesn't matter whether he had guessed that Asya loved him or not. Now he knows perfectly clearly that Asya loves him. He sees it now. Well, what does he feel toward Asya? He positively doesn't know how to answer that question. The poor thing! At the age of thirty, because he is so young, he should have a tutor to tell him when to blow his nose, when to go to sleep, how many cups of tea to drink. In view of such stupid inability to understand things it may seem to you that you see a child or an idiot before you. Neither one nor the other is the case. Our Romeo is a very intelligent man who is, as we have said, under thirty, has experienced a great deal in life, has a rich store of observations upon himself and others. Where does his incredible dull-wittedness come from? Two circumstances are responsible for it, one of which really stems from the other, so that it is all reduced to one. He is not used to understanding anything large and living because his life was too petty and spiritless, because all the relationships and affairs he conducted were too petty and spiritless. That's the first. The second is that he becomes shy, he retreats feebly from everything that requires broad determination and noble risk, again because life has taught him only pale pettiness in everything. He is like a man who played whist for pennies all his life. Set this skillful player in a rubber where gains and losses run to thousands of rubles rather than to change, and you will see that he will be completely nonplused, that all his experience will disappear, all his skill will fail him. He will make the stupidest plays; perhaps he will not even be able to hold his cards properly. He is like a sailor who has journeyed all his life from Petersburg to Kronstadt and very skillfully sailed his little boat along a path indicated by buoys, between innumerable shallows in the flats. What if this sailor experienced in his glass of water were suddenly to find himself in the ocean? Good God! Why are we analyzing our hero so harshly? In what way is he worse than the rest of us? When we go into society we see around us people in dress coats or dress uniforms; these people are five and a half or six feet tall, and some even taller; they either shave their cheeks, upper lip, and chin or let the hair grow. And we think that we see men before us. That is a complete mistake, an optical illusion, a hallucination, and no more. Without acquiring the habit of independent participation in civic affairs, without acquiring the sense of citizenship, a male child will become a male creature of middle age and later of old age, but he will not become a man, or at least he will not become a man of noble character.

It is better not to raise a man than to raise him without the influence of ideas on civic affairs, without the influence of that sense that rouses participation in them. If ideas and impulses that have social utility as their goal are excluded from the sphere of my observations and of the activities in which I indulge, that is, if civic motives are excluded, what will be left for me to observe? There will remain the troubled bustling of separate individuals with their personal narrow worries about their own pocketbook, their own bellies, or their own distractions. If I observe people as they are when the feeling of participation in civic activity has been removed from them, what kind of ideas will I form about people and about life. (pp. 122-23)

Think what conversation becomes in any society when it ceases to deal with civic affairs. No matter how intelligent and noble the conversationalists may be, they begin to gossip and prattle if they do not talk about civic matters. Backbiting baseness or lewd baseness, in either case senseless vulgarity, is the character a conversation that parts from civic interests necessarily assumes. One can judge the conversationalists by the nature of the conversation. If even those people who have attained the highest notions fall into empty and filthy vulgarity as soon as their thoughts turn from civic interests, then it is easy to imagine what a society that lives in complete indifference to such interests must be. (pp. 123-24)

Someone once wrote a fable about a healthy man who came to the kingdom of the crippled and blind. The fable goes on to relate that he was attacked by everyone because his legs and eyes were unharmed. The fable lies, since it did not tell the whole truth. The newcomer was attacked only at the beginning; but when he had become accustomed to the new place he began to close one eye and to limp himself—it already seemed to him more comfortable to look and walk that way, or at least it seemed the decent thing to do, and soon he even forgot that strictly speaking he wasn't crippled or blinded at all. If you are a fancier of sad effects, one can add that when our traveler had occasion to walk firmly and see with both eyes he could no longer do so. It turned out that the closed eye would no longer open; the crooked leg would no longer straighten itself out. From their extended constraint the nerves and muscles of the poor distorted joints lost their capacity for acting in the correct manner.

Whoever touches coal will get dirty, to his own punishment if he did so willingly, to his misfortune if unwillingly. He who lives in a pothouse cannot help smelling drunken fumes even though he doesn't drink a single glass himself. He who lives in a society that has no interests except petty day-to-day calculations cannot help being imbued with a pettiness of will. Involuntary timidity at the thought that perhaps the time will come to take a firm stand, to take a daring step that is a long cry from the daily constitutional—such timidity will creep into his heart. That is why you try to convince yourself that the time for such an unusual action has not yet come; you will try to convince yourself until the last fatal minute that everything that varies from the customary triviality is merely a temptation. The child who is afraid of the bogeyman shuts his eyes and shouts as loud as he can that there is no bogeyman, that the bogeyman is nonsense—that is the way he encourages himself, don't you see? We are so smart that we try to convince ourselves that we fear everything that we do only because we have no strength for anything exalted; we try to convince ourselves that that's all nonsense, that in reality there is nothing like that and will not be anything like it. But if there is? Well, then the same thing will happen to us that happened to our Romeo in Mr. Turgenev's tale. He too did not foresee anything and did not want to foresee it. He too closed both his eyes and drew back, and when the time came—well, your elbow is near but you can't bite it.

And how brief was the moment when both his fate and Asya's were being decided—only a few minutes altogether, and upon them depended a whole life, and having let them go by, nothing could any longer correct the mistake. No sooner had he entered the room, no sooner had he managed to pronounce several unprepared, almost unconsciously heedless words, than everything was already settled: they went parted forever, and there was no return. We don't feel sorry for Asya at all. It would have been hard for her to hear the harsh words of a refusal, but it was probably better for her that a heedless man brought her to a parting. If she had remained connected with him, it would naturally have been a great joy for him. But we do not think it would have been good for her to live in close association with such a man; whoever sympathizes with Asya must be glad that the difficult, disturbing scene took place. Whoever sympathizes with Asya is completely right: he chose a dependent being, an offended being as the object of his sympathy.

Yet we must admit, to our shame, that we take an interest in our hero's fate. We do not have the honor of being his relation; there is even enmity between our families, because his family despised everyone like us. Yet we still cannot overcome the prejudices that have been beaten into our heads by the false books and lessons we were raised on and which ruined our youth; we cannot overcome the trivial concepts inculcated in us by society around us. It constantly seemed to us (a vain dream, but nevertheless an irresistible one for us) that he might render our society some service, since he is a representative of our enlightenment, since he is the best among us, since without him we should be even worse. But the feeling that this is a vain dream about him constantly increases in us; we feel that we shall not stay under its influence very much longer; that there are better people than he, to wit, those he offends; that it would be better for us to live without him—but at the moment we have not yet come to terms sufficiently with that idea; we have not sufficiently torn ourselves away from the dreams on which we were raised.

Therefore we still wish well to our hero and those like him. While we find that the decisive moment that will determine their fate forever is approaching in reality, we still do not want to say to ourselves: They are incapable of understanding their situation at present; they are incapable of acting intelligently and at the same time magnanimously at present—only their children and grandchildren, raised on other habits and concepts will be able to act like intelligent citizens, and they are now inadequate to the role that is given to them. We still do not want to apply to them the prophet's words that "seeing they see not and hearing they hear not, for their heart is waxed gross and their ears are dull of hearing and their eyes have closed." No; we still want to assume them capable of understanding what is going on around them and above them; we want to think that they are capable of following a wise admonishment from someone who wishes to save them; and therefore we want to give people who do not know how, the ability to evaluate their position in time and to use the advantages the fleeting moment offers. Against our will our hope for the acuity and energy of people whom we beg to understand the importance of real circumstances and to act in accordance with common sense decreases from day to day—but let them at least not say that they did not hear intelligent counsel nor that their situation was not explained to them.

Among you, gentlemen (let us turn our speech to those worthy people), there are many literate people; they know how happiness was depicted in ancient mythology: it was presented as a woman with a long braid unfurled before her by the wind that is driving her. It is easy to catch her when she is flying up to you, but if you lose her from view for a moment she will fly past and you will try to catch her in vain: once you've been left behind, you cannot catch her. The happy moment cannot be brought back. You can wait forever for the favorable concatenation of circumstance to repeat itself, just as the configuration of heavenly bodies that occurs at the moment will not be repeated. Not to let the propitious moment go by—that is the highest condition of life's wisdom. There are happy circumstances for each of us, but not everyone knows how to use them, and in that art the difference between those people whose life moves successfully and those whose lives don't lies almost exclusively. And although you may not have deserved it, circumstances have formed in such a propitious way that at the decisive moment your fate depends entirely upon you. The question of eternal happiness or unhappiness then depends upon whether or not you will understand the demands of the moment, whether you will be able to use those conditions into which you are then placed. (pp. 124-27)

N. G. Chernyshevsky, "The Russian at the 'Rendezvous': Reflections upon Reading Mr. Turgenev's 'Asya'," translated by Ralph E. Matlaw, in Belinsky, Chernyshevsky, and Dobrolyubov: Selected Criticism, *edited by Ralph E. Matlaw, E. P. Dutton & Co., Inc., 1962, pp. 108-29.*

N. A. DOBROLYUBOV (essay date 1860)

[One of the most influential Russian literary critics of the nineteenth century, Dobrolyubov is noted for his contribution to the philosophy of Russian revolutionary socialism. Along with Vissarion Belinsky and Nikolai Chernyshevsky, he helped to redirect Russian critical thought by integrating revolutionary political theory into his literary criticism. Using a radical, anti-aestheticist approach, he emphasized the utilitarian aspects of literature and stressed the critic's responsibility for calling attention to the inequalities of the class system in Russian society. In his most notorious essay, "Chto takoye Oblomvschina?" ("What Is Oblomovism?"), *a review of Ivan Goncharov's novel* Oblomov, *Dobrolyubov attacked the self-absorption of Russian liberals and predicted that their ineffectuality would lead to revolution. Critics cite Dobrolyubov as a precursor of the theories of Soviet realism. In the following excerpt from a review of* On the Eve *that was first published in 1860, Dobrolyubov reads the novel as a picture of the contemporary Russian scene, concentrating on the question of when a socially and politically committed individual like Insarov will arise in Russian society.]*

Aesthetic criticism has now become the hobby of sentimental young ladies. In conversation with them the devotees of pure art may hear many subtle and true observations, and then they can sit down and write a review in the following style: "Here is the content of Mr. Turgenev's new novel" (follows a summary of the story). "This pale sketch is enough to show how much life and poetry, of the freshest and most fragrant kind, is to be found in this novel. But only by reading the novel itself can one obtain a true idea of that feeling for the most subtle poetical shades of life, of that keen psychological analysis, of that profound understanding of the hidden streams and currents of public thought, and of that friendly and yet bold attitude toward reality that constitute the distinguishing features of Mr. Turgenev's talent. See, for example, how subtly he has noted these psychological features" (then comes a repetition of a part of the summary, followed by an excerpt from the novel); "read this wonderful scene that is depicted with such grace and charm" (excerpt); "recall this poetical living picture" (excerpt), "or this lofty and bold delineation" (excerpt). "Does not this penetrate to the depths of your soul, compel your heart to beat faster, animate and embellish your life, exalt before you human dignity and the great, eternal significance of the sacred ideas of truth, goodness, and beauty! *Comme c'est joli, comme c'est délicieux!*"

We are unable to write pleasant and harmless reviews of this sort because we are little acquainted with sentimental young ladies. Openly confessing this, and disclaiming the role of "cultivator of the aesthetic tastes of the public," we have chosen for ourselves a different task, one more modest and more commensurate with our abilities. We simply wish to sum up the data that are scattered throughout the author's work, which we accept as accomplished facts, as phenomena of life that confront us. This is not a complicated task, but it is one that must be undertaken because, what with the multiplicity of their occupations and the need for relaxation, people are rarely willing to go into all the details of a literary production, to analyze, verify and put in their proper places all the figures that combine to make this intricate report on one of the aspects of our social life and then to ponder over the result, over what it promises, and what obligations it imposes upon us. But such verification and reflection will be very useful in the case of Mr. Turgenev's new novel [***On the Eve***].

We know that the devotees of pure aesthetics will at once accuse us of wanting to thrust our own views upon the author and to set tasks for his talent. We shall therefore make the following reservation, tedious though it may be to do so. No, we have no wish to thrust anything upon the author; we say at the very outset that we do not know what object the author had in view, or what views prompted him to write the story that constitutes the contents of the novel ***On the Eve.*** The important thing for us is not so much what the author *wanted* to say, as what he *said,* even unintentionally, simply in the process of truthfully reproducing the facts of life. (pp. 176-77)

The reader perceives that we regard as important precisely those productions in which life is expressed as it is and not according to a program previously drawn up by the author. We did not discuss *A Thousand Souls,* for example, because, in our opinion, the whole social side of this novel was forcibly adjusted to a preconceived idea. Hence, there is nothing to discuss here except the degree of skill the author displayed in composing his work. It is impossible to rely on the truth and living reality of the facts delineated by the author because his inner attitude toward these facts is not simple and truthful. We see an entirely different attitude of an author toward his subject in Mr. Turgenev's new novel, as indeed we see in most of his novels. In ***On the Eve*** we see the inescapable influence of the natural course of social life and thought, to which the author's own thoughts and imagination were involuntarily adjusted.

In expressing the view that the main task of the literary critic is to explain the phenomena of reality that called a given artistic production into being, we must add that in the case of Mr. Turgenev's novels this task acquires a special meaning. Mr. Turgenev may be rightly described as the painter and bard of the morality and philosophy that have reigned among the educated section of our society during the past twenty years. He very soon divined the new requirements, the new ideas that were permeating the public mind, and in his works he, as a rule, devoted (as much as circumstances would permit) attention to the question that was about to come up next and that was already beginning vaguely to stir society.

We hope to trace the whole of Mr. Turgenev's literary activity on a future occasion, and so we shall not deal with it at length now; we shall only say that it is to this sensitiveness that the author displays toward the living strings of society, to this ability of his to respond forthwith to every noble thought and honest sentiment which is only just beginning to penetrate the minds of the best people, that we largely ascribe the success Mr. Turgenev has always enjoyed among the Russian public.

It goes without saying that his literary talent too has contributed a great deal to this success, but our readers know that Mr. Turgenev's talent is not of the titanic kind, which by sheer poetic expression alone captivates you, thrills you, and compels you to sympathize with a phenomenon, or an idea, with which you were not in the least inclined to sympathize. Not a turbulent and impulsive power but, on the contrary, gentleness and a kind of poetic moderation are the characteristic features of his talent. That is why we believe that he could not have roused the general sympathy of the public had he dealt with questions and requirements that were totally alien to his readers or that had not yet arisen in society. Some readers would have noted the charm of the poetical descriptions in his novels, the subtlety and profundity with which he portrayed different individuals and situations; but there can be no doubt that this alone would not have been enough to make the author's success and fame permanent. . . . A certain profound critic once rebuked Mr. Turgenev for having in his works so strongly reflected "all the vacillations of public thought." We, on the contrary, regard this as the most vital feature of Mr. Turgenev's talent; and we believe that it is this feature of his talent that explains the sympathy, almost enthusiasm, with which all his productions have been received up till now.

Thus, we may boldly assert that if Mr. Turgenev touches upon any question in a story of his, if he has depicted any new aspect of social relationships, it can be taken as a guarantee that this question is rising, or soon will rise, in the mind of the educated section of society; that this new aspect is beginning to make itself felt and will soon stand out sharply and clearly before the eyes of all. That is why, every time a story by Mr. Turgenev appears, our curiosity is roused and we ask: What sides of life are depicted in it? What questions does it touch upon?

This question arises now, and in relation to Mr. Turgenev's new novel it is more interesting than ever. Up to now Mr. Turgenev's path, in conformity with the path of our society's development, has proceeded in one, fairly clearly defined, direction. He started out from the sphere of lofty ideas and theoretical strivings and proceeded to introduce these ideas and strivings into coarse and banal reality, which had digressed very much from them. The hero's preparations for the struggle, his sufferings, his eagerness to see the triumph of his principles, and his fall in face of the overwhelming power of human banality have usually been the centers of interest in Mr. Turgenev's stories.

It goes without saying that the background of this struggle, that is to say, the ideas and aspirations, was different in each story, or was expressed more definitely and sharply with the progress of time and change of circumstances. Thus, the unwanted man's place was taken by Pasynkov; Pasynkov's place was taken by Rudin; Rudin's place was taken by Lavretsky. Each of these persons was bolder and more perfect than his predecessor, but the substance, the basis of their characters and their entire existence was the same. They introduced new ideas into a certain circle; they were educators and propagandists—even though it was for one woman's soul, but propagandists nevertheless. (pp. 178-81)

Lately, however, demands entirely different from those which Rudin and all his fraternity roused have made themselves heard fairly distinctly in our society. A radical change has taken place in the conceptions of the majority of educated people in relation to these personages. (p. 181)

Nobody among respectable people now expresses astonishment and admiration on meeting a man who belongs to the so-called progressive trend; nobody looks into his eyes with mute awe; nobody shakes hands with him mysteriously and gives him a whispered invitation to meet a close circle of the chosen in his home to discuss the point that injustice and slavery are fatal for the state. On the contrary, anybody who reveals a lack of sympathy for publicity, unselfishness, emancipation, and so forth, arouses instinctive astonishment and contempt. Today even those who dislike progressive ideas must pretend to like them in order to gain admission to decent society. Clearly, under such circumstances, the former sowers of the seeds of good, people of the *Rudin* type, lose a considerable part of their former credit. They are respected as old teachers, but rarely is anybody with an independent mind disposed to listen again to those lessons that were learned so eagerly in the past, in the period of childhood and initial development. Now something different is needed; it is necessary to go further. (p. 182)

"What will Mr. Turgenev create now?" we asked ourselves, and we sat down to read ***On the Eve*** with the utmost curiosity.

On this occasion too the author's feeling for reality did not fail him. Realizing that the former heroes had already done their work and could no longer win the sympathies of the best section of our society as they had done in the past, he decided to abandon them, and sensing in several fragmentary manifestations the spirit of the new demands on life, he stepped onto the road along which the progressive movement is proceeding at the present time. . . .

In Mr. Turgenev's new novel we meet with situations and types that differ from those we have been accustomed to finding in his previous works. The social demand for action, for real action, incipient contempt for dead, abstract principles and passive virtue are expressed in the whole structure of the new novel. (pp. 185-86)

The heroine of the story is a girl of a serious turn of mind, possessing an energetic will and a heart filled with humane strivings. (p. 186)

Clearly, she is still beset by vague doubts about herself; she has not yet determined her role. She has realized what she does not need, and remains proud and independent amidst the habitual circumstances of her life; but she does not yet know what she needs, and above all she does not understand what she must do to achieve what she needs, and that is why her whole being is strained, uneven, and impulsive. She is waiting, living on the eve of something. . . . She is ready for vigorous, energetic activity, but she is unable to set to work by herself, alone.

This timidity, this virtual passivity of the heroine combined with her abundance of inner strength and her tormenting thirst for activity astonishes us and makes us think that there is something unfinished about Helena's personality, her lack of activity reveals precisely the living connection between Mr. Turgenev's heroine and the whole of the educated section of our society. In the way Helena's character is conceived, at bottom, it is an exceptional one, and if she were indeed presented everywhere as expressing her views and strivings she would have been alien to Russian society and would not have had that intimate meaning for us that she has now. She would have been a fictitious character, a plant unskillfully transplanted to our soil from some foreign land. But Mr. Turgenev's true sense of reality did not permit him to make the practical activities of his heroine fully coincide with her theoretical concepts and the inner promptings of her soul. Our public life does not yet provide an author with the materials for this. At present we observe throughout our society only an awakening desire to get down to real work, a realization of the banality of the various beautiful toys, of the lofty phrases and inert forms with which we have amused and fooled ourselves for so long. But we have not yet emerged from the sphere in which we were able to sleep so peacefully, and we do not yet know very well where the exit is; if anybody does know, he is still afraid to open the door. (pp. 189-90)

Strictly speaking, there is nothing extraordinary about Insarov. Bersenev and Shubin, Helena, and even the author of the novel himself, describe him in negative terms: he never tells lies, he never breaks a promise, he does not borrow money, he is not fond of talking about his achievements, he never puts off the execution of a decision once adopted, his deeds never contradict his words, and so forth. In short, he has none of the features for which any man with claims to respectability should bitterly reproach himself. But in addition to this, he is a Bulgarian whose soul is filled with a passionate desire to liberate his country, and to this idea he devotes himself entirely, openly and confidently; it represents the ultimate goal of his life. He does not think that his personal happiness can come into collision with his life's object; such an idea, so natural for the Russian nobleman-scholar Bersenev, would never enter the head of this simple Bulgarian. On the contrary, he is striving for the liberation of his country because to him it means ensuring his own peace of mind, the happiness of his whole life; if he could have found satisfaction in anything else he would not have concerned himself about his enslaved country. But he cannot conceive of himself separately from his country. . . . Thus, he pursues his cherished cause quite naturally, without posing, without any fanfare, as naturally as eating and drinking. (pp. 198-99)

Is it necessary to relate the story of how Helena and Insarov were drawn together, the story of their love? We think not. Our readers probably remember this story well, and besides it cannot really be told. We are afraid to touch this tender poetical creation with our cold rough hands; in fact, we are afraid to offend our readers' feelings, which, undoubtedly, have been stirred by the poetry of Turgenev's narrative, with our dry and unfeeling account of it. Mr. Turgenev, the bard of pure and ideal feminine love, peers so deeply into the young virgin soul, understands it so fully and depicts its finest moments with such inspired emotion, with such an ardor of love, that we actually feel in this story the quiver of her maidenly breast, her tender sighs, her moist glance, every throb of her agitated heart, so that our own hearts melt and stop beating from deep emotion, tears of happiness rise to our eyes more than once, and something bursts from our breasts as if we were sitting beside an old friend after a long separation, or had returned home to our native land after a sojourn in foreign parts. This feeling is both sad and joyful: it conjures up bright recollections of childhood, gone never to return; the proud and joyous hopes of youth, the ideal, harmonious dreams of a pure and mighty imagination as yet untamed or degraded by the trials of mundane experience. All this has passed never to return; but the man is not yet lost who can return to these bright dreams if only in recollection, to this pure and youthful intoxication with life, to these grand and ideal plans, and then shiver at the sight of the sordidness, banality, and pettiness in which his present life is passing. And blessed is the one who can rouse such recollections in others, who can awaken such sentiments in another's soul. . . . (pp. 200-01)

We shall leave our readers to enjoy the recollection of the entire development of the story while we return to Insarov's character, or rather to the relationship in which he stands to the Russian society around him. . . . [He] does almost nothing to achieve his principal aim; only once do we see him go off on a journey of sixty versts to Troitsky Posad, to reconcile his compatriots who had quarreled among themselves, and at the end of his stay in Moscow it is mentioned that he traveled all over the city clandestinely visiting various personages. But it goes without saying that he has nothing to do while living in Moscow. To do anything real he must go to Bulgaria. And he does go, but death intercepts him on the road, and so we see no activity on his part in the story. From this it is evident that the purpose of the story is not to depict for us an example of civic, that is, public heroism, as some critics try to assure us. Here there is no reproach aimed at the Russian young generation, no indication as to what a civic hero should be. Had this been the author's object, he should have brought his hero face to face with his cause—with parties, with the people, with the alien government, with those who share his views, with the enemy force. . . . But the author did not wish and, as far as we are able to judge from his previous works, was unable to write a heroic epic. His object was entirely different: from all the Iliads and Odysseys he borrowed only the story of

Ulysses' sojourn on the island of Calypsos, and further than that he does not go. After making us understand and feel what Insarov is, and in what environment he finds himself, Mr. Turgenev devotes himself entirely to describing how Insarov is loved, and what came of this love. At the point where love must at last make way for real civic activity he cuts the life of his hero short and ends his tale.

What then is the significance of the *Bulgarian's* appearance in this story? Why a Bulgarian and not a Russian? Are there no such characters among Russians? Are Russians incapable of loving passionately and persistently, incapable of recklessly marrying for love? Or is this only a whim of the author's imagination, and it is useless seeking any particular meaning in it? As much as to say: "Well, he went and took a Bulgarian, and that's all there is to it. He might just as well have taken a gypsy, or a Chinese, perhaps. . . ."

The answers to these questions depend upon one's views concerning the entire meaning of the story. We think that the Bulgarian's place here could indeed have been taken by a man of some other nationality, by a Serb, a Czech, an Italian or a Hungarian, but not by a Pole or a Russian. Not a Pole, because a Pole is entirely out of the question. But why not a Russian? That is the question at issue, and we shall try to answer it to the best of our ability.

The point is that the principal personage in ***On the Eve*** is Helena, and it is in relation to her that we must examine the other personages in the story. She expresses that vague longing for something, that almost unconscious but irresistible desire for a new way of life, for a new type of people, which the whole of Russian society, and not only its so-called educated section, now feels. Helena so vividly expresses the finest strivings of our present society. . . . We have the "desire actively to do good," and we have the strength to do it; but fear, lack of confidence in our strength and, lastly, our ignorance of what is to be done, constantly check us and, without knowing why, we suddenly find ourselves outside social life, cold and alien to its interests, exactly like Helena and all those around her. And yet the *desire* still seethes in everybody's breast (we mean in the breasts of those who do not strive artificially to suppress it), and we are all seeking, thirsting, waiting . . . waiting for someone to tell us what is to be done. (pp. 202-04)

Russian society has been longing and waiting like this for quite a long time; and how many times have we, like Helena, erred in thinking that the one we had been waiting for had arrived, and then cooled off? Helena became passionately attached to Anna Vassilyevna, but Anna Vassilyevna turned out to be a spineless nonentity. . . . At one time Helena felt well disposed toward Shubin in the same way as our society at one time became enthusiastic about art, but it turned out that Shubin lacked real content; there were only sparkle and whims about him; and absorbed in her searching, Helena could not stop to admire trinkets. For a moment she was interested in serious learning, in the person of Bersenev, but serious learning turned out to be modest, beset by doubt, learning that was waiting for a Number One to lead him. What Helena needed was a man without a number, a man who was not waiting for a lead, an independent man, who irresistibly strove toward his goal and carried others with him. At last such a man appeared in the person of Insarov, and in him Helena found her ideal; in him she found the man who could tell her how to do good.

But why could not Insarov have been a Russian? After all, he does nothing in the story; he merely intends to do something; this much a Russian could have done. Insarov's character could have been encased in a Russian skin, particularly in the way it expresses itself in the story. In the story his character expresses itself in that he loves strongly and resolutely; but is it impossible for a Russian to love in this way?

All this is true; nevertheless the sympathies of Helena, of the girl as we understand her, could not turn toward a Russian with the same justification and with the same naturalness as they turned toward this Bulgarian. All Insarov's charm lies in the grandeur and sacredness of the idea that permeates his whole being. Thirsting to do good, but not knowing how, Helena is instantly and profoundly captivated by the mere relation of his aims, even before she has seen him. (pp. 204-05)

We can fully understand her position; and we are sure that the whole of Russian society, even if it is not yet carried away by the personality of Insarov as she is, will understand that Helena's feelings are real and natural.

We say that society will not be carried away, and we base this statement on the assumption that *this* man Insarov is, after all, an alien to us. Mr. Turgenev himself, who has so thoroughly studied the finest part of our society, did not find it possible to make him *our man*. Not only did he bring him from Bulgaria but he also refrained from making his hero sufficiently endearing to us even as a man. This, if you look at it even from the literary standpoint, is the main artistic defect in the novel. We know one of the principal reasons for this, one over which the author had no control, and therefore we are not blaming Mr. Turgenev for this. Nevertheless, the pale sketch of Insarov affects the impression we obtain from the story. (p. 206)

As a living image, as a real personality, Insarov is extremely remote from us, and this explains why ***On the Eve*** produces upon the public such a faint and partly even unfavorable impression compared with Mr. Turgenev's previous stories, which portray characters whom the author had studied down to the minutest detail, and for whom he had felt such a lively sympathy. We realize that Insarov must be a good man and that Helena must love him with all the ardor of her soul because she sees him in real life and not in a story. But he is near and dear to us only as a representative of an idea, which attracts us, as it did Helena, like a flash of light and lights up the gloom of our existence. That is why we understand how natural are Helena's feelings toward Insarov; that is why we ourselves, pleased with his indomitable loyalty to an idea, fail to realize at first that he is depicted for us only in pale and general outline.

And yet some want him to be a Russian! "No, he could not be a Russian!" exclaims Helena herself in answer to a regret that had arisen in her own heart that he was not a Russian. Indeed, there are no such Russians; there should not and cannot be such, at all events at the present time. We do not know how the new generations are developing and will develop, but those that we see in action today have not by any means developed in such a way as to resemble Insarov. (p. 207)

In short, Insarov imbibed hatred for enslavers and discontent with the present state of things with his mother's milk. There was no need for him to exert himself, to resort to a long series of syllogisms to be able to determine the direction of his activities. Since he is not lazy, and no coward, he knows what to do and how to behave. There is no need for him to take up many tasks at once. And besides, his task is so *easily understood*, as Shubin says: "All you have to do is to kick the Turks out—that's not much!" Moreover, Insarov knows that he is doing right not only in his own conscience but also before the court of humanity: his idea will meet with the sympathy of every decent man. Try to picture something like this in Russian society. It is inconceivable. . . .

Is it clear now why a Russian could not have taken the place of Insarov? Characters like his are of course born in Russia in no small number, but they cannot develop as freely and express themselves as frankly as Insarov does. A contemporary Russian Insarov will always remain timid and dual-natured; he will lie low, express himself with various reservations and equivocations . . . and it is this that reduces confidence in him. (p. 209)

True, minor heroes appear among us who somewhat resemble Insarov in courage and in sympathy for the oppressed. But in our society they are ludicrous Don Quixotes. The distinguishing feature of a Don Quixote is that he does not know what he is fighting for or what will come of his efforts, and these minor heroes display this feature to a remarkable degree. For example, they may suddenly take it into their heads that it is necessary to save the peasants from the tyranny of the squires and simply refuse to believe that there is no tyranny here at all, that the rights of the squires are strictly defined by the law, and must remain inviolable as long as these laws exist; that to rouse the peasants against this tyranny means not liberating them from the squires, but making them, in addition, liable to a penalty under the law. Or, for example, they may set themselves the task of protecting the innocent from miscarriages of justice, as if the judges in this country administer the law according to their own arbitrary will.

Everybody knows that in this country everything is done according to the law, and that to interpret the law one way or another it is not heroism that is needed, but skill in legal quibbling. And so our Don Quixotes simply beat the air. . . . (pp. 209-10)

The Russian . . . , belonging, as a rule, to the educated section of society, are themselves vitally connected with what must be overthrown. They are in a position that a son of a Turkish Aga, for example, would be in if he took it into his head to liberate Bulgaria from the Turks. (pp. 210-11)

It is not much easier for a Russian to be a hero. This explains why likable and energetic characters in this country content themselves with petty and unnecessary bravado and fail to rise to real and serious heroism, that is, renouncing the entire complex of concepts and practical relationships that bind them to their social milieu. Their timidity in face of the host of enemy forces is reflected even in their theoretical development; they are afraid, or are unable, to delve down to the roots, and setting out, for example, to punish evil, they merely attack some minor manifestation of it and wear themselves out frightfully before they have time even to look for the source of this evil. (p. 211)

Incidentally, even of such heroes there are very few in this country, and most of these do not hold out to the end. Far more numerous among the educated section of our society is another category of men—those who indulge in reflection. Among these there are also many who, although able to reflect, understand nothing, but of these we shall not speak. We wish to point only to those men who really have bright minds, men who after a long period of doubt and searching attained the integrity and clarity of ideas Insarov attained without exceptional effort. These people know where the root of evil lies and they know what must be done to put a stop to evil; they are deeply and sincerely imbued with the idea they attained at last. But they no longer possess the strength for practical activity; they have strained themselves to such an extent that their characters seem to have sagged and become enfeebled. They welcome the approach of the new way of life, but they cannot go out to meet it, and they cannot satisfy the fresh sentiments of a man who is thirsting to do good and is looking for a leader. (p. 214)

Insarov, being consciously and completely engrossed by a great idea of liberating his country and being ready to play an active part in this, could not develop and reveal his talents in present-day Russian society. Even Helena, who was able to love him so fully and merge herself completely with his ideas, could not remain in Russian society, even among her near and dear ones. And so, there is no room among us for great ideas and great sentiments? . . . All heroic and active people must fly from us if they do not wish to die of idleness, or perish in vain? Is that not so? Is this not the idea that runs through the novel that we have reviewed?

We think not. True, we lack an open field for wide activity; true, our life is spent in petty affairs, in scheming, intriguing, scandalmongering, and meanness; true, our civic leaders are hardhearted and often thickheaded; our wiseacres will not do a thing to achieve the triumph of their convictions; our liberals and reformers base their schemes on legal subtleties and not on the groans and cries of their unhappy fellow men. All this is true, and all this is seen to some extent in ***On the Eve,*** as well as in dozens of other novels that have appeared recently. Nevertheless we think that *today* there is already room for great ideas and sentiments in our society and that the time is not far distant when it will be possible to put these ideas into practice.

The point is that, bad as our present way of life is, the appearance of types like Helena has proved to be possible. And not only have such characters become possible in life; they have already been grasped by the artists' mind; they have been introduced into literature; they have been elevated to a type. Helena is an ideal personage, but her features are familiar to us; we understand and sympathize with her. What does this show? It shows that the basis of her character—love for the suffering and the oppressed and a desire to do good, and weary search for the one who could show how good can be done—all this is at last being felt in the best section of our society. And this feeling is so strong and so near to realization that it is no longer, as before, dazzled either by brilliant but sterile minds and talents, by conscientious but abstract learning, by official virtues, or even by kind, generous, but passive hearts. To satisfy our feeling, our thirst, something more is needed; we need a man like Insarov—but a Russian Insarov.

What do we need him for? We ourselves said above that we do not need liberating heroes, that we were a nation of rulers, not of slaves. . . .

Yes, we are safeguarded against outside dangers; even if we were obliged to wage an external struggle we need not worry about it. We have always had sufficient heroes to perform deeds of valor on the battlefield, and the raptures that even at the present day our young ladies go into at the sight of an officer's uniform and mustaches is irrefutable proof that our society knows how to appreciate these heroes. But have we not many internal enemies? Is it not necessary to wage a struggle against them? And is not heroism needed for such a struggle? But where are the men among us who are capable of action? Where are the men of integrity who have been from childhood imbued with a single idea, who have merged themselves with that idea so thoroughly that they must either achieve this triumph or perish in the attempt? There are no such men among us, because up to now our social environment has been unfavorable for their development. It is from this environment, from its banality and pettiness, that we must be liberated by the new men whose appearance is so impatiently and eagerly awaited by all that is best, all that is fresh in our society. (pp. 223-25)

Is this possible? When will it be possible? Of these two questions a categorical answer can be given only to the first. Yes, it is possible, and for the following reasons. We said above that our social environment suppresses the development of personalities like Insarov. But now we may add the following: this environment has now reached the stage when it itself can facilitate the appearance of such a man. Eternal banality, pettiness, and apathy cannot be the lawful lot of man, and the people who constitute our social environment and who are fettered by its conditions have long ago realized the harshness and absurdity of these conditions. Some are dying of ennui; others are striving with all their might to go away, to escape from this oppression. Various ways of escape have been invented; various means have been employed to infuse some animation into the deadliness and rottenness of our lives, but they have all proved to be feeble and ineffective. Now, at last, concepts and demands are appearing, such as those that we saw in the case of Helena; these demands meet with sympathy in society; nay, more, efforts are being made to put them into effect. This shows that the old social routine is passing away. A little more vacillation, a few more powerful words and favorable factors, and active men will appear. (pp. 225-26)

Everywhere, and in all things, we observe the growth of self-realization; everywhere the unsoundness of the old order of things is understood; everybody is waiting for reform and rectification, and nobody now lulls his children to sleep with songs about the inconceivable perfection of the present state of things in every corner of Russia. On the contrary, today everybody is waiting, everybody is hoping, and children are now growing up imbued with hopes and dreams of a brighter future, and are not forcibly tied to the corpse of the obsolete past. When their turn comes to set to work, they will put into it the energy, consistency and harmony of heart and mind of which we could scarcely obtain even a theoretical conception.

Then a full, sharp, and vividly depicted image of a Russian Insarov will appear in literature. We shall not have to wait long for him; the feverishly painful impatience with which we are expecting his appearance in real life is the guarantee of this. We need him; without him our lives seem to be wasted, and every day means nothing in itself, but is only the eve of another day. That day will come at last! At all events, the eve is never far from the next day; only a matter of one night separates them. (p. 226)

N. A. Dobrolyubov, "When Will the Real Day Come?" translated by J. Fineberg, in Belinsky, Chernyshevsky, and Dobrolyubov: Selected Criticism, *edited by Ralph E. Matlaw, E. P. Dutton & Co., Inc., 1962, pp. 176-226.*

The Turgenev estate at Spasskoye.

A. I. HERZEN (letter date 1862)

[*A Russian expatriate and man of letters, Herzen operated the periodical* Kolokol *(the* Bell) *from England, calling for progressive reform in Russia. Herzen was highly influential in the formation of both the Russian Populist movement and the Socialist Revolutionary Party. In this excerpt from a letter to Turgenev, he records his impressions of Bazarov in* Fathers and Sons. *Turgenev responds to Herzen's criticism in a letter dated 28 April 1862 (see excerpt below).*]

You grew very angry at Bazarov, out of vexation lampooned him, made him say various stupidities, wanted to finish him off "with lead"—finished him off with typhus, but nevertheless he crushed that empty man with fragrant mustache and that watery gruel of a father and that blancmange Arkady. Behind Bazarov the characters of the doctor and his wife are sketched masterfully—they are completely alive and live not in order to support your polemic but because they were born. Those are real people. It seems to me that, like an amiable rowdy, you stopped at the insolent, airy, bilious exterior, at the plebeian-bourgeois turn, and taking that as an insult, went further. But where is the explanation for his young soul's turning callous on the outside, stiff, irritable? What turned away everything tender, expansive in him? Was it Büchner's book?

In general it seems to me that you are unfair toward serious, realistic experienced opinion and confound it with some sort of coarse, bragging materialism. . . .

The Requiem at the end, with the further moving toward the immortality of the soul is good, but dangerous: you'll slip into mysticism that way.

There for the moment are some of the impressions I've gathered on the wing. I do not think that the great strength of your talent lies in *Tendezschriften*. In addition, if you had forgotten about all the Chernyshevskys in the world while you were writing it would have been better for Bazarov.

A. I. Herzen, in a letter to Ivan Turgenev on April 21, 1862, in "Fathers and Sons" by Ivan Turgenev: The Author on the Novel, Contemporary Reactions, Essays in Criticism, *edited and translated by Ralph E. Matlaw, W. W. Norton & Company, Inc., 1966, p. 187.*

IVAN TURGENEV (letter date 1862)

[*Turgenev answers Herzen's letter of 21 April 1862 (see excerpt above), explaining his central difficulty in creating Bazarov: "to make him a wolf and justify him just the same."*]

I reply to your letter immediately—not in order to defend myself, but to thank you, and at the same time to declare that in creating Bazarov I was not only not angry with him, but felt "an attraction, a sort of disease" toward him, so that Katkov [Turgenev's publisher] was at first horrified and saw in him the apotheosis of *The Contemporary* and as a result convinced me to delete not a few traits that would have mellowed him, which I now regret. Of course he crushes "the man with the fragrant mustache" and others! That is the triumph of democracy over the aristocracy. With hand on heart I feel no guilt toward Bazarov and could not give him an unnecessary sweetness. If he is disliked as he is, with all his ugliness, it means that *I* am at fault and was not able to cope with the figure I chose. It wouldn't take much to present him as an ideal; but to make him a wolf and justify him just the same—that was difficult. And in that I probably did not succeed; but I only want to fend off the reproach that I was exasperated with him. It seems to me, on the contrary, that the feeling opposite to exasperation appears in everything, in his death, etc. But *basta cosí*—we'll talk more when we see each other. (pp. 187-88)

Ivan Turgenev, in a letter to A. I. Herzen on April 28, 1862, in "Fathers and Sons" by Ivan Turgenev: The Author on the Novel, Contemporary Reactions, Essays in Criticism, *edited and translated by Ralph E. Matlaw, W. W. Norton & Company, Inc., 1966, pp. 187-88.*

LEV TOLSTOY (letter date 1862)

[*Tolstoy is regarded as one of the greatest novelists in the history of world literature. His* Voina i mir (War and Peace) *and* Anna Karenina *are almost universally considered all-encompassing documents of human existence and supreme examples of the realistic novel. Critics of these novels frequently mention Tolstoy's feat of successfully animating his fiction with the immediacy and variousness of life. Particularly esteemed are his insightful examinations of psychology and society, along with the religious and philosophical issues which occupied him later in his career. The friendship between Tolstoy and Turgenev was unstable; though each generally admired the other's work, their personal clashes led to frequent quarrels and estrangements. In the following excerpt from a letter to P. A. Pletnyov, Tolstoy faults* Fathers and Sons *for coldness.*]

Turgenev's novel [***Fathers and Sons***] interested me very much, but I liked it much less than I expected. My main reproach is that it is cold . . . cold—something which doesn't suit Turgenev's talent. Everything is clever, everything is refined, everything is artistic . . . and much of it is edifying and just, but there isn't a single page which is written with a stroke of the pen and with a palpitating heart, and therefore there isn't a single page which grips the soul.

Lev Tolstoy, in an extract from a letter to P. A. Pletnyov on May 1, 1862, in his Tolstoy's Letters: 1828-1879, Vol. I, *edited and translated by R. F. Christian, Charles Scribner's Sons, 1978, p. 157.*

GUSTAVE FLAUBERT (letter date 1863)

[*The most influential French novelist of the nineteenth century, Flaubert is remembered primarily for the stylistic precision and dispassionate rendering of psychological detail found in his masterpiece,* Madame Bovary. *Although his strict objectivity is often associated with the realist and naturalist movements, he objected to this classification, and his artistry indeed defies such easy characterization. Flaubert struggled throughout his career to overcome a natural romantic tendency toward lyricism, fantastic imaginings, and love of the exotic past. A meticulous craftsman, his aim was to achieve a prose style "as rhythmical as verse and as precise as the language of science." Here, in a letter to Turgenev, Flaubert expresses the pleasure he has derived from his friend's writing.*]

Dear Mr Turgenev,

How grateful I am for the gift you sent me! I have just read your two volumes [containing ***Sportsman's Sketches, Rudin,*** **"Diary of a Superfluous Man,"** and **"Three Encounters"**], and really must tell you that I am delighted with them.

I have considered you a master for a long time. But the more I study you, the more your skill leaves me gaping. I admire the vehement yet restrained quality of your writing, the fellow feeling that extends to the lowest of human creatures and brings landscapes to life. One perceives and one dreams.

Just as when I read *Don Quixote* I feel like going on horseback along a white and dusty road, like eating olives and raw onions in the shade of a cliff face, your ***Scenes from Russian Life*** make me want to be shaken alone in a telega through snow-covered fields, to the sound of wolves howling. Your work has a bittersweet flavour, a sadness that is delightful and penetrates to the very depths of my soul.

What an artist! What a mixture of emotion, irony, observation and colour! And how it is all blended together! How you achieve your effects! What mastery!

You manage to encompass general points while writing about the specific. How many things that I have felt and experienced myself have I found in your work! In **"Three Encounters"** amongst others, and especially in ***Jacob Pasynkov,*** in the **"Diary of a Superfluous Man,"** etc., everywhere.

But what has not received enough praise in your work is the heart, that is, a sustained emotion, an indefinable deep and secret sensibility. (pp. 38-9)

Gustave Flaubert, in a letter to Ivan Turgenev on March 16, 1863, in Flaubert and Turgenev, a Friendship in Letters: The Complete Correspondence, *edited and translated by Barbara Beaumont, The Athlone Press, 1985, pp. 38-9.*

THE NATION, NEW YORK (essay date 1867)

[*This critic favorably assesses* Fathers and Sons, *focusing on Turgenev's adroit characterization.*]

What a novel should have this novel [***Fathers and Sons***] does not lack. Rather it possesses, in large measure, several of the requisites of a really excellent novel, and we feel sure of its taking an honorable place among the more valued contemporary works of fiction. . . . [It] is a great deal to say nowadays for a novel of any length, but, after beginning ***Fathers and Sons,*** it will be found easier to go on to the end than to stop. And if it be the end of novels that they be readable, as of comedies, according to Dr. Johnson, that they make people laugh—and certainly a tale that cannot be told seems to want the main thing—then this that we have already said is praise enough. But ***Fathers and Sons*** is not wholly dependent for its interest upon its plot, upon its freshness of incident, the strangeness of the manners depicted, the rapidity of movement, the dramatic situations, the careful and sometimes poetical painting of natural scenery, the humor, the pathos—though these are among its characteristics; still less is it wholly dependent upon the glimpses it gives us of the working of various social forces which are now operating upon Russia—though these also it offers us. The author is successful in the novelist's highest labor—in conceiving and delineating his characters. He does not paint with elaboration, but he sketches with a vigorous and accurate pencil; and in Bazarof, Arcadi, Paul Petrovitch, Nicholas Petrovitch, Katia, best of all in poor old Vasili Ivanovitch and his wife, he has given us real men and real women.

The central figure is Eugene Bazarof, the nihilist. "You, then, believe in science only?" Paul Petrovitch says to him; and for answer to the aristocratic elderly ex-dandy, the doctor's son says, as brutally as he can: "I have already had the honor of telling you that I believe in nothing." Not only that; but he is not so much a questioner of old authority as a hater of all authority; it is not that he searches after truth with dispassionate mind, but he revolts against the shadow of a curb and seeks the mastery for himself. Religion, filial piety, the tenderness due to age, the respect given to woman, the consideration owed to weakness, he scoffs at. He is by nature a materialist; all that which he calls "the romantic," as love, poetry, justice between man and man, offends him, and without well knowing what is meant by the ideal and the spiritual, he gibes at them bitterly. What he is in politics may be imagined; there are, perhaps, more like him in Siberia, bad a republican as he would make, than in any other part of the empire; but the author is discreetly silent on political questions, and that Russia has an autocrat, a political, social, and religious life in which "nihilism" must grow rank, one would not discover from reading this book. Bazarof's self-conceit, ambition, and courage are boundless, his intellect powerful, his passions not weak. (pp. 470-71)

This young man his friend Arcadi, who, like most other friends of Bazarof, is the nihilist's disciple, takes down into the country to the house where his father Nicholas and his uncle Paul are residing. Arcadi is an ordinary youth of good intentions, easily influenced, naturally a little sentimental. His father and his uncle stand as representatives of the old order of things in Russia. The time of the story is in the year 1858; the serfs are in the transition state between serfdom and freedom. Nicholas Petrovitch, whose estates are large, who is a kind-hearted, unassuming man, somewhat scholarly, a little dreamy, accepts the new ideas without fully understanding them and without being at all able to carry them into practical effect. Ill-health and sorrow have made him old before his time. Paul Petrovitch, bred a soldier, and in his youth gay and dissipated, after rising to the grade of captain, left the service. He was infatuated with a lady of high rank, of frivolous life and not of irreproachable behavior, who yet had in her character enough that was beyond the comprehension of the captain in the guards to keep him her slave till she died. Then, with polished manners, with aristocratic habits of mind, without any mental resources of importance, prematurely old, he retires to the country and lives there with his brother, brooding over his past life, never escaping from his memories of the woman, taking no part in the management of the farm business, reading French novels and English reviews. With these gentlemen Mr. Bazarof does not get on in the very best manner possible. They do not and cannot understand him wholly, nor do they like at all what they do understand; and as for him, he is constitutionally incapable of understanding what is best in them. What is not best is patent and gets no mercy from him.

When the story first leaves the country house of the two brothers it departs from the strict line of its development. ***Fathers and Sons*** ceases to be an appropriate title; it is no longer occupied with the contrast between two generations of Russians, the conflict between opposing ideas. We have a long episode, in which, to be sure, we get an amusing sketch or two of some Russian progressives, of poor Sitnikof, of silly little Madame Kukshin, who is illuminated to a high degree, and refers among other foreign authors to Proudhon, Bunsen, Macaulay, Cooper, and Emerson; but in all this part of the book the author has pretty effectually lost sight of his theory, and really has given us in a most dramatic episode Bazarof in love. A characteristic sort of love it is. He succumbs to Madame Odintsof, "a very fine woman," as the English say, an able woman, and a personage whose character is portrayed with perhaps greater carefulness than that bestowed on any other of the author's figures. Neither Bazarof nor Arcadi is man enough to be master of her, though the nihilist makes a great impression at first, and though what she takes to be the devotion of young Arcadi seems at the last to have touched her more than she had thought. But both are too raw, and she is an experienced woman of the world. The scenes at Nikolskoia, however, though fine, are episodical, and without delaying we go on to see our ***Fathers and Sons*** again, to see the young men at the little farm of Bazarof's father and mother—a dove-cot, or rather a rabbit-hutch, which our young bird of prey wonderfully flutters, first with joy, afterwards with grief, and again with the deepest grief. (p. 471)

But it is not our intention to tell the story. No one, we will say in conclusion, need take it up with the expectation of finding it a work of art without obvious imperfections, nor with the expectation of finding in it more about Russia than will just whet his curiosity to learn more. It must be remembered that the book was written for Russians, and it must be remembered, too, that a Russian novelist writes, as you may say, in chains. But it is a very good novel indeed. . . . (p. 472)

"A Novel from Russia," in The Nation, *New York, Vol. IV, No. 102, June 13, 1867, pp. 470-72.*

FYODOR DOSTOEVSKY (letter date 1867)

[*The author of* Prestuplenye i nakazanye (Crime and Punishment) *and* Brat'ya Karamozovy (The Brothers Karamazov), *Dostoevsky is considered one of the most outstanding and influential writers of modern literature. His greatness as a fiction writer lies in the depth and range of his vision, his acute psychological insight, his profound philosophical thought, and his brilliant prose style. Dostoevsky and Turgenev disliked one another personally and were also at odds in their sociopolitical views. In the following excerpt from a letter to a friend, Dostoevsky describes an acrimonious visit with Turgenev and offers a contemptuous opinion of* Smoke. *Dostoevsky later wrote his anti-nihilism novel* Besy (The Possessed) *in refutation of* Fathers and Sons, *including in the work a parody of Turgenev's pomposity in the minor character Karmazinov.*]

I kept putting off my visit to [Turgenev]—still, eventually I had to call. I went about noon, and found him at breakfast. I'll tell you frankly—I never really liked that man. The worst of it is that since 1857, at Wiesbaden, I've owed him 50 dollars (which even to-day I haven't yet paid back!). I can't stand the aristocratic and pharisaical sort of way he embraces one, and offers his cheek to be kissed. He puts on monstrous airs; but my bitterest complaint against him is his book ***Smoke.*** He told me himself that the leading idea, the point at issue, in that book, is this: "If Russia were destroyed by an earthquake and vanished from the globe, it would mean no loss to humanity—it would not even be noticed." He declared to me that that was his fundamental view of Russia. I found him in irritable mood; it was on account of the failure of ***Smoke.*** I must tell you that at the time the full details of that failure were unknown to me. I *had* heard by letter of Strachov's article in the *O.Z.*, but I didn't know that they had torn him to pieces in all the other papers as well, and that in Moscow, at a club, I believe, people had collected signatures to a protest against ***Smoke.*** He told me that himself. Frankly, I never could have imagined that anyone could so naïvely and clumsily display all the wounds in his vanity, as Turgenev did that day; and these people go about boasting that they are atheists. He told me that he was an uncompromising atheist. My God! It is to Deism that we owe the Saviour—that is to say, the conception of a man so noble that one cannot grasp it without a sense of awe—a conception of which one cannot doubt that it represents the undying ideal of mankind. And what do we owe to these gentry—Turgenev, Herzen, Utin, Tchernychevsky? In place of that loftiest divine beauty on which they spit, we behold in them such ugly vanity, such unashamed susceptibility, such ludicrous arrogance, that it is simply impossible to guess what it is that they hope for, and who shall take them as guides. He frightfully abused Russia and the Russians. But I have noticed this: all those Liberals and Progressives who derive chiefly from Bielinsky's school, find their pleasure and satisfaction in abusing Russia. The difference is that the adherents of Tchernychevsky merely abuse, and in so many words desire that Russia should disappear from the face of the earth (*that,* first of all!). But the others declare, in the same breath, that *they love Russia.* And yet they hate everything that is native to the soil, they delight in caricaturing it, and were one to oppose them with some fact that they could not explain away or caricature,—any fact with which they were obliged to reckon—they would, I believe, be profoundly unhappy, annoyed, even distraught. And I've noticed that Turgenev—and for that matter all who live long abroad—have no conception of the true facts (though they do read the newspapers), and have so utterly lost all affection and understanding for Russia that even those quite ordinary matters which in Russia the very Nihilists no longer deny, but only as it were caricature after their manner—*these* fellows cannot so much as grasp. Amongst other things he told me that we are bound to crawl in the dust before the Germans, that there is but one universal and irrefutable way—that of civilization, and that all attempts to create an independent Russian culture are but folly and pigheadedness. He said that he was writing a long article against the Russophils and Slavophils. I advised him to order a telescope from Paris for his better convenience. "What do you mean?" he asked. "The distance is somewhat great," I replied; "direct the telescope on Russia, and then you will be able to observe us; otherwise you can't really see anything at all." He flew into a rage. When I saw him so angry, I said with well-simulated naïveté: "Really I should never have supposed that all the articles derogatory to your new novel could have discomposed you to this extent; by God, the thing's not worth getting so angry about. Come, spit upon it all!" "I'm not in the least discomposed. What are you thinking of?" he answered, getting red.

I interrupted him, and turned the talk to personal and domestic matters. Before going away, I brought forth, as if quite casually and without any particular object, all the hatred that these three months have accumulated in me against the Germans. "Do you know what swindlers and rogues they are here? Verily, the common people are much more evil and dishonest here than they are with us; and that they are stupider there can be no doubt. You are always talking of civilization; with what has your 'civilization' endowed the Germans, and wherein do they surpass us?" He turned pale (it is no exaggeration), and said: "In speaking thus, you insult me personally. You know quite well that I have definitely settled here, that I consider myself a German and not a Russian, and am proud of it." I answered: "Although I have read your ***Smoke,*** and have just talked with you for a whole hour, I could never have imagined that you would say such a thing. Forgive me, therefore, if I *have* insulted you."

Then we took leave of one another very politely, and I promised myself that I would never again cross Turgenev's threshold. . . . The animosity with which I speak of Turgenev, and the insults we offered one another, will perhaps strike you unpleasantly. But by God, I can no other; he offended me too deeply with his amazing views. Personally, I really feel little affected, though his uppish manners are quite disagreeable enough in themselves; but I simply can't stand by and listen when a traitor who, if he chose, could be of service to his country, abuses Russia in the way he does. His tail-wagging to the Germans, and his hatred for the Russians, I had noticed already—four years ago. But his present rage and fury against Russia arises solely, *solely,* from the failure of ***Smoke,*** and from the fact that Russia has dared refuse to hail him as a genius. It is nothing but vanity, and therefore all the more repulsive. (pp. 120-24)

Fyodor Dostoevsky, in an extract from a letter to Appollon Nikolayevitch Maikov on August 16, 1867, in his Letters of Fyodor Michailovitch Dostoevsky to His Family and Friends, *translated by Ethel Colburn Mayne, Horizon Press, 1961, pp. 113-26.*

THE ATHENAEUM (essay date 1868)

[*The critic favorably reviews* Smoke, *commending Turgenev's acute and unerring depiction of character.*]

The effects produced by ***Smoke*** in Russian society are another illustration of the case of that veteran cudgel-player who "let no one beat him but his own son." On no other principle can we account for the already great and ever-increasing popularity, among its very victims, of a book which dissects every foible of the Russian character with a power which unites the skill of the surgeon with the vigour of the executioner.

M. Turgenieff's long residence abroad has blunted his sympathies while enlarging his scope of observation; and the marked difference between the tone of his early works and that of the one now before us bears full testimony to the magnitude of the change. Then he corrected like a father; now he smites like a destroyer. The placing of the scene at Baden-Baden, with its many-twinkling concourse of Eastern and Western nations, its ever-varying programme of amusements, and light rippling surface of fashionable frivolity tinged with a darker hue by the resistless under-current of high play, has opened a wide field for the exercise of his peculiar talent—the rapid successive survey of a number of characters, seizing the salient feature of each, and in a few bitter and well-chosen words branding his victims ineffaceably. The actual novel commences with the second chapter, the first being merely a gallery of brilliant and malicious photographs, in poses of studied distortion. . . .

The plot is sufficiently simple, serving (as is usual with M. Turgenieff) to develop the characters rather than to be developed by them. (p. 789)

The character of Irena alone, with its stormy passions, its strangely-mixed display of deep womanly tenderness and cool systematic cruelty, and the subtle aroma of feminine grace and beauty artfully cast around it, would of itself be sufficient to attract universal attention. Over every phase of her career lowers a tragic grandeur hitherto wanting in M. Turgenieff's heroines; and it is not without a touch of pity that we take leave of the proud and beautiful woman in her joyless home at St. Petersburg, with the tinsel of second-rate luxury for her consolation, the aimless whirl of fashionable dissipation for her employment, and the innuendoes of toothless scandal-mongers for her epitaph. Nor are the minor personages less ably drawn. Voroshiloff, the brilliant, superficial talker, dabbler in all sciences and master of none,—Bambareff, the Russian Harold Skimpole, always in debt, always smiling, and always in ecstasies about something,—Gubareff, the Jupiter of a small coterie, enthroned on his own toy Olympus, and listening delightedly to his own minor-theatre thunder,—form a matchless group. Capitolina Schestoff, the aunt of Litvinoff's betrothed, is the very picture of a cheery, garrulous, fussy old lady. The description of the Ocinin household at Moscow, "with a mosaic pavement before their door and green lions over the gate, and hardly making both ends meet by running in debt to the grocer and sitting without candle or fire in January," reminds us of some of the best passages in Thackeray, whom, indeed, M. Turgenieff strongly resembles, both in style and personal appearance. But it is in the character of Potougin, Litvinoff's friend and counsellor, that the author's peculiar views find most appropriate vent. The calm, self-possessed, admonitory cynic, trampling on social vices and absurdities with a grand and massive contempt which at times rises almost to the dignity of prophecy, stands before us a living impersonation of the long series of works which record the protest of the greatest of Russian novelists against the system from which he has exiled himself. (p. 790)

A review of "Smoke: A Novel," in The Athenaeum, *No. 2119, June 6, 1868, pp. 789-90.*

IVAN TURGENEV (essay date 1868-69)

[Distressed by the controversy engendered by Fathers and Sons, *Turgenev wrote an essay in 1868-69 to defend himself against detractors. In the following excerpt from this essay, he explains how and why he came to write the novel, insists that authors must present the truth as they see it, and reveals his own ambivalent attitude toward Bazarov. In general, Turgenev's defense did not conciliate his critics. He protests his good intentions further in a letter to I. P. Borisov dated 5 January 1870 (see excerpt below).]*

I was sea-bathing at Ventnor, a small town on the Isle of Wight—it was in August, 1860—when the first idea occurred to me of ***Fathers and Sons,*** the novel which deprived me, forever I believe, of the good opinion of the Russian younger generation. I have heard it said and read it in critical articles not once but many times that in my works I always "started with an idea" or "developed an idea." Some people praised me for it, others, on the contrary, censured me; for my part, I must confess that I never attempted to "create a character" unless I had for my departing point not an idea but a living person to whom the appropriate elements were later on gradually attached and added. Not possessing a great amount of free inventive powers, I always felt the need of some firm ground on which I could plant my feet. The same thing happened with ***Fathers and Sons;*** at the basis of its chief character, Bazarov, lay the personality of a young provincial doctor I had been greatly struck by. (He died shortly before 1860.) In that remarkable man I could watch the embodiment of that principle which had scarcely come to life but was just beginning to stir at the time, the principle which later received the name of nihilism. Though very powerful, the impression that man left on me was still rather vague. At first I could not quite make him out myself, and I kept observing and listening intently to everything around me, as though wishing to check the truth of my own impressions. I was worried by the following fact: not in one work of our literature did I ever find as much as a hint at what I seemed to see everywhere; I could not help wondering whether I was not chasing after a phantom. On the Isle of Wight, I remember, there lived with me at the time a Russian who was endowed with excellent taste and a remarkable "nose" for everything which the late Apollon Grigoryev called "the ideas" of an epoch. I told him what I was thinking of and what interested me so much and was astonished to hear the following remark: "Haven't you created such a character already in—Rudin?" I said nothing. Rudin and Bazarov—one and the same character!

Those words produced such an effect on me that for several weeks I tried not to think of the work I had in mind. However, on my return to Paris I sat down to it again—the *plot* gradually matured in my head; in the course of the winter I wrote the first chapters, but I finished the novel in Russia, on my estate, in July [1861]. In the autumn I read it to a few friends, revised something, added something, and in March, 1862, ***Fathers and Sons*** was published in *The Russian Herald.*

I shall not enlarge on the impression this novel has created. I shall merely say that when I returned to Petersburg, on the very day of the notorious fires in the Apraksin Palace, the word "nihilist" had been caught up by thousands of people, and the first exclamation that escaped from the lips of the first acquaintance I met on Nevsky Avenue was: "Look what *your* nihilists are doing! They are setting Petersburg on fire!" My impressions at that time, though different in kind, were equally painful. I became conscious of a coldness bordering on indignation among many friends whose ideas I shared; I received congratulations, and almost kisses, from people belonging to a camp I loathed, from enemies. It embarrassed and—grieved me. But my conscience was clear; I knew very well that my attitude towards the character I had created was honest and that far from being prejudiced against him, I even sympathised with him. I have too great a respect for the vocation of an artist, a writer, to act against my conscience in such a matter. The word "respect" is hardly the right one here; I simply could not, and knew not how to, work otherwise; and, after all, there was no reason why I should do that. (pp. 193-95)

The critics, generally speaking, have not got quite the right idea of what is taking place in the mind of an author or of what exactly his joys and sorrows, his aims, successess and failures are. They do not, for instance, even suspect the pleasure which Gogol mentions and which consists of castigating oneself and one's faults in the imaginary characters one depicts; they are quite sure that all an author does is to "develop his ideas"; they refuse to believe that to reproduce truth and the reality of life correctly and powerfully is the greatest happiness for an author, even if this truth does not coincide with his own sympathies. . . . In depicting Bazarov's personality, I excluded everything artistic from the range of his sympathies, I made him express himself in harsh and unceremonious tones, not out of an absurd desire to insult the younger generation (!!!), but simply as a result of my observations of my acquaintance, Dr. D., and people like him. "Life happened to be *like that,*" my experience told me once more, perhaps mistakenly, but, I repeat, not dishonestly. There was no need for me to be too clever about it; I just had to depict his character *like that.* My personal predilections had nothing to do with it. But I expect many of my readers will be surprised if I tell them that with the exception of Bazarov's views on art, I share almost all his convictions. And I am assured that I am on the side of the "Fathers"—I, who in the person of Pavel Kirsanov have even "sinned" against artistic truth and gone too far, to the point of caricaturing his faults and making him look ridiculous!

The cause of all the misunderstandings, the whole, so to speak "trouble," arose from the fact that the Bazarov type created by me has not yet had time to go through the gradual phases through which literary types usually go. Unlike Onegin and Pechorin, he had not been through a period of idealisation and sympathetic, starry-eyed adoration. At the very moment the *new* man—Bazarov—appeared, the author took up a critical, objective attitude towards him. That confused many people and—who knows?—that was, if not a mistake, an injustice. The Bazarov type had at least as much right to be idealized as the literary types that preceded it. I have just said that the author's attitude towards the character he had created confused the reader: the reader always feels ill at ease, he is easily bewildered and even aggrieved if an author treats his imaginary character like a living person, that is to say, if he sees and displays his good as well as his bad sides, and, above all, if he does not show unmistakable signs of sympathy or antipathy for his own child. The reader feels like getting angry: he is asked not to follow a well-beaten path, but to tread his own path. "Why should I take the trouble," he can't help thinking. "Books exist for entertainment and not for racking one's brains. And, besides, would it have been too much to ask the author to tell me what to think of such and such a character or what he thinks of him himself?" But it is even worse if the author's attitude towards that character is itself rather vague and undefined, if the author himself does not know whether or not he loves the character he has created (as it happened to me in my attitude towards Bazarov, for "the involuntary attraction" I mentioned in my diary is not love). The reader is ready to ascribe to the author all sorts of non-existent sympathies or antipathies, provided he can escape from the feeling of unpleasant "vagueness."

"Neither fathers nor sons," said a witty lady to me after reading my book, "that should be the real title of your novel and—you are yourself a nihilist." A similar view was expressed with even greater force on the publication of ***Smoke.*** I am afraid I do not feel like raising objections: perhaps, that lady was right. In the business of fiction writing everyone (I am judging by myself) does what he can and not what he wants, and—as much as he can. I suppose that a work of fiction has to be judged *en gros* and while insisting on conscientiousness on the part of the author, the other *sides* of his activity must be regarded, I would not say, with indifference, but with calm. And, much as I should like to please my critics, I cannot plead guilty to any absence of conscientiousness on my part.

I have a very curious collection of letters and other documents in connection with ***Fathers and Sons.*** It is rather interesting to compare them. While some of my correspondents accuse me of insulting the younger generation, of being behind the times and a reactionary, and inform me that they "are burning my photographs with a contemptuous laugh," others, on the contrary, reproach me with pandering to the same younger generation. "You are crawling at the feet of Bazarov!" one correspondent exlaims. "You are just pretending to condemn him; in effect, you are fawning upon him and waiting as a favour for one casual smile from him!" One critic, I remember, addressing me directly in strong and eloquent words, depicted Mr. Katkov [Turgenev's publisher] and me as two conspirators who in the peaceful atmosphere of my secluded study, are hatching our despicable plot, our libellous attack, against the young Russian forces. . . . It made an effective picture! Actually, that is how this *plot* came about. When Mr. Katkov received my manuscript of ***Fathers and Sons,*** of whose contents he had not even a rough idea, he was utterly bewildered. The Bazarov type seemed to him "almost an apotheosis of *The Contemporary Review,*" and I should not have been surprised if he had refused to publish my novel in his journal. *"Et voilà comme on ècrit l'histoire!"* one could have exclaimed, but—is it permissible to give such a high-sounding name to such small matters?

On the other hand, I quite understand the reasons for the anger aroused by my book among the members of a certain party. They are not entirely groundless and I accept—without false humility—part of the reproaches levelled against me. The word "nihilist" I had used in my novel was taken advantage of by a great many people who were only waiting for an excuse, a pretext, to put a stop to the movement which had taken possession of Russian society. But I never used that word as a pejorative term or with any offensive aim, but as an exact and appropriate expression of a fact, an historic fact, that had made its appearance among us; it was transformed into a means of denunciation, unhesitating condemnation and almost a brand of infamy. Certain unfortunate events that occurred at that time increased the suspicions that were just beginning to arise and seemed to confirm the widespread misgivings and justified the worries and efforts of the "saviours of our motherland," for in Russia such "saviours of the motherland" had made their appearance just then. The tide of public opinion, which is still so indeterminate in our country, turned back. . . . But a shadow fell over my name. I do not deceive myself; I know that that shadow will not disappear. But why did not others—people before whom I feel so deeply my own insignificance—utter the great words: *Périssent nos noms, pourvu que la chose publique soit sauvée* . . . i.e. may our names perish so long as the general cause is saved! Following them, I too can console myself with the thought that my book has been of some benefit. This thought compensates me for the unpleasantness of undeserved reproaches. And, indeed, what does it matter? Who twenty or thirty years hence will remember all these storms in a teacup? Or my name—with or without a shadow over it. (pp. 196-201)

Ivan Turgenev, "Apropos of 'Fathers and Sons'," in his Literary Reminiscences and Autobiographical Fragments, *translated by David Magarshack, Farrar, Straus and Cudahy, 1958, pp. 193-204.*

[C. E. TURNER] (essay date 1869)

[Turner's essay is an early survey of Turgenev's writing and philosophy. In this excerpt, he appraises Turgenev's strengths as a literary artist—noting especially his poetic genius—before studying the novels as they relate to Russian social and political progress.]

[Tourgéneff] may justly be termed the historian and painter of the moral and philosophical movements that have successively agitated the civilized society of Russia during the last twenty years. With all the quickness of a sympathising and tolerant genius, he has divined the wants and necessities of his epoch, comprehended the nature of its aspirations, and made his novels serve to illustrate and solve the particular questions occupying the minds of his countrymen at the time of the composition of his works. In this capacity for seizing on and depicting the ever-varying light and shade, which play on the stream of social life, and which constitute the spirit of the age, he is unrivalled; and his works, if only read for something more than the story they have to tell, cannot fail to afford rich materials to the student of public opinion in Russia. Much that strikes a foreigner as rash and contradictory in the tendency of contemporary Russian thought, and much that seems to be unhealthy in the tone and manners of Russian social life, assume a different aspect after we have followed, under the guidance of a wise and keen observer, the gradual course and development of those ideas on which that life is based. (p. 424)

The genius of Tourgéneff is essentially a poetical one. His every page betrays the born artist,—an artist, moreover, who is almost femininely sensitive to all that is romantic. There is in his works none of that pure and stern realism under the influence of which the large majority of contemporary Russian novels have been written. He cannot, as Goúcharoff has done in *A Common Story,* give us merely the actualities of a worldly career, apart from any idealism, without any attempt to colour or adorn the narrative. Still less can he, like Gógol, in his marvellous tale, *The Nevsky Prospect,* bring us face to face with the corruptions of city life, and by the very sternness with which he paints it in all its vileness and all its ugliness, give a moral tone to that which in itself is immoral. The life that Tourgéneff sketches is our life, but it is idealised; the characters he portrays are human, but they are raised above common humanity; the incidents on which his stories are founded are not impossible, but they are fanciful and exceptional. But in the most romantic of his tales, belief is constrained, in spite of all our experience and worldly sense, by the rare psychological skill with which the motives and general disposition of the leading personages are analysed; and however extraordinary may be the event which forms its centreplot, there is an undercurrent of poetical truth that gives it an ideal probability. At times, indeed, the story he has to tell is one of shameless guilt, but there is always the suggestion of some redeeming quality to extenuate if not to justify it, and the most vicious life is represented as being not altogether and hopelessly degraded. A tone of pity pervades such narratives; the author is evidently unwilling to admit even to himself the real extent to which modern society is corrupted; he listens to the promptings of his heart rather than to the cruel lessons of experience, and is never false to his ideal even when obliged to sketch the darker side of humanity. Thus, if a Zinaida [in ***First Love***], crushing the pure love she feels for Vladimir Petróvitch, feigns a passion for Vladimir's father, and sells her love to one who values it at the best but as a toy to be rejected when the novelty is worn off, it is to relieve her mother from the debts with which she is burdened, and a spirit of self-sacrifice redeems the harsher traits of Zinaida's character. 'Let us hope,' is the mournful commentary with which Vladimir concludes the history of his ***First Love,*** 'that our children at least may be able to relate a different story of their youth, and that their experience may be unlike ours.'

We have said that the extenuating circumstances are suggested; and this suggestiveness is a special characteristic of Tourgéneff's genius. There is with him a kind of poetic reserve, strangely at variance with the rude and coarse colouring to which sensational novelists have of late accustomed us. His characters are never fully portrayed, the minuter details of a story are only implied, even the outlines of the picture are drawn with a light and delicate touch, and the fancy of the reader is called into play to fill in the missing strokes. (pp. 424-26)

It is, accordingly, to our subtler and finer feelings that Tourgéneff appeals. He is not one of those writers who take possession of our heart by storm; he makes his approach to it by gentle and almost imperceptible steps; there is no violence or effort in his attempts to arouse our sympathy and interest; nor do we recognise the powerful hold he has obtained over us till we are completely under his sway. He never indulges in false eloquence; and, in the most dramatic of his scenes, is content to trust to the pathos of the incident, and to that alone. No style can be purer, or more simple and unaffected. However vehement may be the passion he is delineating, however tragic the position in which his characters are placed, he does not relax the strict and jealous restraint he invariably exercises over himself. We cannot call to mind a single passage in any one of his novels that can be charged with being inflated or pompous. In all that he writes we may perceive the quiet dreamer, to whom violence, whether in speech or in action, is unnatural and repugnant. The experience of life may indeed at times have rudely broken his dreams, but for him they still possess their ancient charm, and the 'tender grace of days that are gone,' is still present to inspire and delight. Hence it is the softer passions he likes best to sketch, and he is happiest when tracing the gradual awakening of a first love. It would be difficult to cite another novelist whose power of analysing each separate phase in such a passion is at once so delicate and pure. With what a keen insight into the workings of a young girl's mind is the love of Lisa for Lavrétsky drawn in the story entitled [***A Nest of Gentlefolk***]; and how thoroughly true to woman's nature is the readiness of Ellen (in his later novel, ***On the Eve***) to sacrifice all to her fond worship of Insároff, in whose patriotic devotion to the cause of his oppressed country she finds her ideal of the heroic man. The love, which in the end obtains so complete a possession of them, is born unconsciously within them; its growth into strength is so slow that it is all but unmarked; and they become its helpless slaves before they are well aware of its existence. The same fineness of touch characterises his satire. With the exception of certain scenes in ***Smoke*** (and it is not difficult, as we shall presently show, to explain this departure from his ordinary tone) the satire is neither venomous nor spiteful, but breathes a geniality that induces us to listen the more readily to his kindly exposures of social follies and human weaknesses. (pp. 426-27)

The poetical side of Tourgéneff's genius is further shown in its relation to nature. There is a freshness in his sympathy with her softer and gentler manifestations that reminds us of the love of a child for its mother. To others she may seem cold and harsh; but his own unspoilt and uncorrupted heart supplies her with a voice, and makes her respond to his feelings. As one of his characters has well expressed it, 'she awakens in us a need, but is unable of herself to supply that need. . . . It is we ourselves who must give a tongue to her, since she is 'dumb.' A harmony is thus preserved between man and nature; and in the description of a landscape, we note the full and complete reflection of the feelings of the central figure. (pp. 427-28)

All Tourgéneff's novels, with perhaps the exception of his last, have met with an immediate success. The publication of a new tale by Tourgéneff is an event in the world of Russian letters. One reason of this popularity, without doubt, is the poetic tone which pervades them, the strength of their appeal to our better nature, and the naturalness with which their characters are made to speak and act. But this alone does not explain the sympathy with which they are read by all classes of his countrymen. It is because of their subject-matter that these fictions are so eagerly welcomed and so earnestly criticised. They treat of questions in which every Russian is warmly interested—they attempt to solve the more important problems of contemporary Russian politics. They are essentially books of the day, and their heroes change with the changes that come over Russian society. In one of his earlier works, we have the portrait of 'The Superfluous Man,' which is subsequently transformed into the person of Pásinkoff; Pásinkoff in his turn becomes Roudíne; and, finally, Roudíne is developed into Lavrétsky. Each new type has a boldness and a fulness that we do not remark in those preceding it; but the fundamental traits of character are essentially the same. They are the champions of new ideas, the preachers of progress; but their propagandism is confined to a narrow circle, and they are never more than theorists. They are satisfied if they can be only propagandists, even though there be but one woman to listen to their tirades. Nor must we ridicule them for their love of theorising, or judge them by the standard of a later day. . . . A mere schoolboy or half-instructed seminarist would now express, as ordinary common-places, those ideas which, when first enounced by a Pásinkoff or a Roudíne, were received open-mouthed by the disciples of progress as words of oracular wisdom. The age of the talkers is past; something more than paper-constitutions is required; the spirit of the times demands what is practical and not simply theoretical. Roudíne, in one word, must become Insároff or Bazároff. What this change implies, and how thoroughly it corresponds with the stages through which Russian public life has passed during the last thirty years, can be best made apparent by reviewing in detail the more important of Tourgéneff's later novels, commencing with ***A Gentleman's Seat,*** the action of which is supposed to take place in the year 1842.

In its chief character, Lavrétsky, there is the same absence of activity, to which Tourgéneff's earlier heroes have accustomed us. But in the story of his life, the struggle is not against his weakness, but against a fate too strong for the strongest of men. Married and separated from his wife, he falls in love with a pure and noble-minded girl, to whom love for one who is married is a crime inconceivable. (pp. 428-29)

Our interest throughout is almost exclusively centred on the story of Lavrétsky's love. We cannot pardon the passiveness with which he from the first surrendered himself to it, but, at the same time, we cannot help feeling pity for him. As in most of Tourgéneff's novels, the woman proves stronger than the man, and not only has a keener sense of duty, but a readier courage to fulfil its requirements and laws. And if we remember the low estimation in which woman, not so long ago, was held in Russian society, and contrast it with the healthier and more natural place she now occupies, we shall not fail to attribute much of the change that has taken place in the general recognition of woman's true rank, to the generous efforts of Tourgéneff to exalt and rehabilitate her in the opinion of his countrymen. In this respect, the novel we have been reviewing cannot be too highly estimated.

But we must pass on to Tourgéneff's next work, ***On the Eve,*** in which we have situations, types, and characters of an order different from those of his earlier productions. If we remember the time at which it was written, immediately after the conclusion of the Crimean war, and that the action of the story is laid in the year 1853, we shall have no difficulty in understanding the reason of this change. The fall of Sevastopol, however wounding to its military pride, had given a healthy shock to the country at large; a new spirit of activity began to animate every class of society; the old dull routine system had been put on its trial and found wanting; something more than abstract principles and negatively virtuous theories of life was felt to be necessary to give stability to national institutions; and Russia, profiting by the experience of the other nations of Europe, became convinced that, to hold her place among the Great Powers, she must abandon her long, sluggish adherence to an ancient and worn-out system, for an honest and practical sympathy with the wants and requirements of a progressive age. In this novel we accordingly escape from simple theorists, who would be out of place in a picture of contemporary life, and in their stead we have Insaroff, the devoted patriot, and Ellen, with her longings to promote the welfare and happiness of others. To do good is their aim, and they are not, like Lavrétsky or Roudíne, content with only knowing what is good. (pp. 432-33)

And yet, it must be confessed . . . , the novel leaves an unsatisfactory and painful impression on our minds. Insároff, be it noted, is a Bulgarian, not a Russian; Ellen, after his death, remains abroad, refusing to return to her country, and asking, 'What have I to do in Russia?' It would seem as if the author despaired of his native land, as if there no great work could be accomplished, as if among her sons and daughters no practical and earnest heroism could be expected, as if they needed the presence and support of foreigners to develop and bring out into action feelings so simple as that of patriotism.

But we shall be better able to see how strong our author's distrust in the present is, and how little he sympathises with that movement in which liberal thinkers find a promise of healthy national development, if we proceed to notice his next work, ***Fathers and Children.*** . . . One peculiarity of the romance is, that it has no plot in the real signification of the word, no gradual unfolding of a story previously thought out in the mind of the writer: we are presented with a series of types and characters, drawn with all that artistic delicacy of which Tourgéneff is so consummate a master, and a succession of pictures and scenes remarkable for their minute truthfulness; but they are disconnected, and only serve to express the author's verdict on some of the more important phases in Russian contemporary life. It is the summing up into one clear and definite charge of those uneasy suspicions and distrust of the rising generation, hinted at but never so openly avowed in his earlier productions; and which are natural to a representative of the past, who observes with regret the scant reverence that is now shown to ideas once regarded as sacred and unassailable, and who, habituated to the aristocratic ease and indifference of an age, which, however near to us in time, is removed centuries from us in the radical changes the national mind has undergone, is unable to sympathise with that spirit of doubt, inquiry, and speculation which animates Young Russia, in common with the youth of every other nation. The novel, as might be expected, has in certain quarters been severely criticised as false and calumnious; but we think a wiser and more judicious estimate has been formed by writers like M. Paésareff, himself a distinguished champion of positive principles, who accepts Tourgéneff's hero as an unexaggerated type, who, in spite of the author, wins our sympathy, because he contains within himself those mental and moral qualities by which alone can be inaugurated a new epoch in Russian civilization. In this sense, the novel claims a far higher rank than could be given to it were it merely a novel, and few studies can be at once more important and more interesting than an analysis of the character of Bazároff, its hero. The youth of Bazároff is but slightly sketched, and we are told only that he is the son of a provincial doctor, and that during his university career he was industrious and economical. His favourite studies were the natural sciences, and it was his devotedness to these pursuits which gave him that negative tendency of thought, in obedience to which he rejected whatever could not be proved, and exhibited the utmost contempt for all that was not useful. Experiment was for him the sole criterion of truth, and everything else he ignored in a spirit of cold scepticism and critical indifference. (pp. 439-41)

In this way, then, Bazároff acknowledged only that which he could touch with his hands, see with his eyes, taste with his tongue; in a word, only that which is cognisable to one or other of the five senses. The rest of our feelings he attributed to the action of our nervous system, to be conquered and repressed rather than cultivated and encouraged. He was consequently unable to find any pleasure in mere views of nature, in the harmony of music, the colouring of the painter, the sweet rhyme of the poet, or the bewitching charm of woman's beauty: for him there was no ideal above and beyond the real: the aspirations of others towards something purer than what the earthly can of itself afford were to him romantic and sentimental; human, he never looked beyond the human, or busied himself with those dreams and visions of the spiritual, wherein so many find their best and surest consolation. Without these extraneous aids he was, however, thoroughly honourable in his dealings with his neighbours, not from any high motive, but simply because he had so schooled himself that it was more in harmony with his personal predilections to be honest than dishonest. He was virtuous by calculation, because he could by the practice of virtue secure greater comfort and quiet to himself, and because his judgment and practical experience of the world told him that it would in the long run pay better than being vicious. At all times and in everything he acted exactly as he believed would prove most profitable to himself. His only rule was calculation, his only guide was individual taste. Outside himself he acknowledged no authority, no law of morality; he had no lofty aim in life, but his reason, unfettered by the vagaries of a heated imagination, had given him a strength of purpose and a resolution in conduct which no temptation could undermine, no adversity of fortune could subdue. His was essentially a kind character. But when that character is thus boldly catalogued and put before us, it may seem impossible, we do not say to love, but even to tolerate or respect him. But, in truth, the more we study his nature, the better we become acquainted with the stern sincerity of his life, the less strong does our aversion to him grow. He may displease and irritate us, we may wish that he was less cold and less calculating—for after all, our love is more readily given to the erring than to the perfect man—but we can never despise him. (pp. 441-42)

From what has been previously said, our readers will easily perceive how antagonistic such a character must be to the poetical and softly romantic temperament of Tourgéneff. We need not, therefore, be surprised if in places the portrait is touched in with harsh and unpleasing colours. (p. 442)

To strengthen this dislike and distrust, Tourgéneff has given Bazároff and his followers an ugly and a damning name. He calls them nihilists. (p. 443)

Bazároff, . . . if he is to be called a nihilist, should profess exclusively negative and abolitionary doctrines, whereas he is represented in the novel as endowed with positive qualities and as advocating positive principles. Call him a rationalist, and he is intelligible; baptise him as a nihilist, and he is inconsistent and contradictory; for his negativism is confined to criticising the social and political institutions of his country. Moreover, absolute denial is scarcely ever to be found in an individual; it never can be the characteristic of a noble generation. In those identical points where Bazároff seems to be most negative, he is really positive. Does he deny art? By that denial he affirms the inferiority of art to nature. Does he deny the existence of love when it is bound by guarantees and conditions? By that denial he affirms the purity of love, inasmuch as the union of two ideas so opposed as love and bargaining is inconvenient and degrading. Does he deny that nature is a temple? By that denial he affirms work in nature's workshop to be the only worship worthy of man. Nor must we charge him with the follies and extravagances of those who profess to be his followers. There will always be Sietinkóffs and Koushkínes, who echo the cry of the hour, but in whose voice we can easily detect the ring of falsehood, who dress themselves up in borrowed robes, but in whose every step we see the strut and gait of men that are playing a part. No matter what the character they assume—the sentimentalist, misanthrope, or the philosopher—they never lose their natural vileness. The wise man will not confound them with the real workers, and even when the doctrines they preach are the most lofty, will feel the barrenness of utterances that are repeated with all the ignorant glibness of a well-trained parrot. He will act towards them as did Bazároff, who at Sietinkóff's invitation goes to Koushkíne's lunches, drinks champagne, pays no attention to Sietinkóff's frantic efforts to be brilliant and striking, refuses to be caught in the trap laid for him by Koushkíne, who is perpetually starting some theme on which Bazároff is expected to dilate, and at length, wearied and disgusted, leaves them, without even saying good bye to the hostess. (pp. 444-45)

The object of Tourgéneff in writing this novel was undoubtedly to show the worthlessness of a Bazároff; but, in fact, he has proved him to be the natural and healthy product of our age. He wished to convince us that the road on which the rising generation have entered leads nowhere; but we rise from the perusal of his book, persuaded that in these Bazároffs is one hope and promise of future progress. Even scepticism may have some part to play in the destruction of falsehoods and the counteraction of dogmatic superstitions. Tourgéneff cannot be untrue to art, and is too profound a student of human nature to represent his characters in a false light because they are repugnant to his own temperament. If at the commencement of his work he makes Bazároff a self-sufficient pedant, dead to all the softer feelings, and taking pride in the severity of his speech and in the hardness of his judgment—and such is the estimate we should naturally form of him, till we come to know him well—later on, he suggests the reason of that severity, and thereby obtains for Bazároff our respect and esteem. He is brought into contact with Olintsóva, a woman endowed with the highest intellectual qualities; her curiosity is aroused, and she wishes to find out the real character of this self-reliant and self-concentred realist. The nihilist, on his side, soon learns to look upon her with a sympathising interest, and is tempted to those tenderer instincts of his heart which no schooling has been able altogether to suppress. But the love he would proffer, unfettered by false guarantees and free from selfish motives, cannot be accepted, cannot even be given, without the sacrifice of that which is the end and aim of his whole life. The temptation is strong, but he will not yield: the happiness almost within his grasp is rejected, and with a violent effort, of which none but those who had previously well learned the lesson of self-discipline were capable, returns to his work, cold and passionless as before. From this point in the story of his life, the novelist abandons that position of hostility to Bazároffism, which had hitherto inspired him. And nowhere is this more strongly shown than in the scene . . . of Bazároff's death. We do not accept the realistic truth of the quiet confidence and hopeful submission with which such a nihilist quits life, even though it may reveal to us the nobility of the man's nature. Such men may at times fall into excesses, but in their wildest extravagance there is a certain strength and resolution the freshness and vigour of which no excess can destroy. They have trained themselves 'to look at everything from a critical point of view,' and have thus attained a calmness of judgment and an empire over passion, that sometimes emulates the faith of the Christian. It is at least the calmness of the noble brute when he lies down to die, the confidence of the pious Buddhist when he enters *Nirvana*. (pp. 445-46)

[We] can only devote a few hurried sentences to Tourgéneff's last novel, ***Smoke,*** in which he continues his war against the nihilists. But there is a bitter vehemence in the attack and a querulousness in the tone strongly at variance with the delicate satire and latent irony of his earlier productions. No attempt is made to soften the blows; there are no fine thrusts, but all is hard, downright hitting. The scenes in which the advocates and champions of progress are made to figure, such as the picnic at Baden, the evening party at Ratmíeroff's, or the assembly at Goubáreff's, are consequently exaggerated. Even when our mirth is most provoked, we feel instinctively that the characters are not true to nature, and that they have been sketched, either by a bitter and unscrupulous partisan, or by one who is not thoroughly acquainted with the real nature of the principles he is assailing. The book would seem to have been written under the influence of a feeling to which, at one period or another in their literary career, most writers have been subject. They are possessed with some all-mastering conviction, they cannot keep silent, nor can they content themselves with half or timid utterances, but are compelled to speak out plainly and without stint. The spirit that pervades every page of ***Smoke*** is one of discontent, and it may be questioned whether Bazároff himself, in his bitterest mood, could be more negative or more destructive than its writer. One of the characters, Potoógine, who plays the part of a Greek chorus, and into whose mouth are put the author's own sentiments, in a violent diatribe against modern Russia, declares that 'if a nation were suddenly to disappear from the face of the earth, and if at the same time everything which this nation had invented were to disappear from this palace,'—that is, the Crystal Palace in London,—'our good little mother, orthodox Russia, might depart to the infernal regions without loosening a single nail, without deranging a single pin: all would remain peaceably in its place, because the samovar, the peasant's shoes, and the knout, our most important productions, were not even invented by ourselves.' Is not this wilfully to ignore one of the best characteristics of contemporary Russian opinion, the belief that Russia has copied and imitated more than enough of common life, and that it is high time she began to cultivate a national and independent life of her own: that the age of Occidentalists, or Západniks, as the Russians term the admirers of all that is foreign, is over, and that in the pursuit of Russian industry and Russian art must be sought the vitality that can alone give power and independence to a people. But there are passages in the work that would lead us to infer that it is not of Russian progress only, but of progress in general, that Tourgéneff despairs, believing, apparently, that all our efforts are in vain, that we can make no step forward, and that all our seeming triumphs of civilization are but illusions and cheats. 'Smoke, smoke!' he repeated many times, and forthwith everything seemed to him to be nothing but smoke—his own life, Russian life, *everything human*, especially everything Russian. (pp. 446-47)

But we must not part from Tourgéneff in ill-humour. Rather let us hope that from this conflict of ideas, this opposition of parties, the one worshipping the past, and the other chafing beneath its bondage, and eager for any change that shall free them from its prescriptive rule, there may arise up a healthier and more vigorous spirit, to inspire those who believe their country is destined to play a dominant and noble part in the new phase of modern civilization on which we are now only entering. (p. 447)

[C. E. Turner], in a review of "The Works of Ivan Sérguevitch Tourgéneff," "Fathers and Children," and "Smoke," in The British Quarterly Review, *Vol. L, October 1, 1869, pp. 423-47.*

IVAN TURGENEV (letter date 1870)

[Turgenev's explanation of his intentions in Fathers and Sons *(see excerpt dated 1868-69) did little to pacify his outraged critics. Here, in an excerpt from a letter to I. P. Borisov, he emphasizes his sincerity and comments further on his own confused feelings toward Bazarov.]*

It seems that my little article on ***Fathers and Sons*** has satisfied no one. Just think I will disown my fame, like Rostopchin did the burning of Moscow. Annenkov has even scolded me roundly. And yet every word in it is the sacred truth, at least in my judgment. It seems that an author doesn't always know himself what he is creating. My feelings toward Bazarov—my own personal feelings—were of a confused nature (God only knows whether I loved him or hated him), nevertheless the figure came out so specific that it immediately entered life and started acting by itself, in its own manner. In the final analysis what does it matter what the author himself thinks about his work. He is one thing and the work is another; but I repeat, my article was as sincere as a confession.

Ivan Turgenev, in a letter to I. P. Borisov on January 5, 1870, in "Fathers and Sons" by Ivan Turgenev: The Author on the Novel, Contemporary Reactions, Essays in Criticism, *edited and translated by Ralph E. Matlaw, W. W. Norton & Company, Inc., 1966, p. 190.*

[T. S. PERRY] (essay date 1871)

[In this excerpt from an appreciative review of On the Eve, *Perry focuses on Turgenev's characterization and realism.]*

[***On the Eve***] does not require for its appreciation any knowledge of the materialistic philosophy, or of the social changes wrought by the freeing of the serfs, as did ***Fathers and Sons.*** All it demands is a willingness to be delighted. It can be enjoyed as well in South America as on the banks of the Neva, for it is a love-story, pure and simple. If that were its only merit, it might very well be left to take its chances with the three or four hundred other novels of the year, most of which may be classed in the same category. But the interest of the story, the vivid drawing of the characters, and the poetical charm of the work, call for more serious notice. . . .

An analysis of the story . . . would be unfair both to the writer and to the reader, whom we hope to send to the book itself. Turgeneff's way of telling it cannot be improved. It is a way so delicate, so poetical, and so rare, that the fascination of the reader is immediate and complete. Every character is drawn with a thousand nice touches, so that it represents to us not a type merely, but an individual, and one whom we know. In the book that we have before us, with what infinite vividness is Shoubine represented from the first chapter to the very last page! The author does not content himself with saying, like our duller workmen in fiction, that Shoubine was a merry-making, intelligent, cynical young fellow with artistic tastes, but he really does what many more people are praised for doing than have ever done it—he lets Shoubine appear to us as men do in life; we really find out for ourselves what sort of a man he is. On the other hand, he is very far from using the method, which, in their anxiety to avoid writing "horse" under their picture, too many of our clever writers have adopted: he does not dissect his horse, nor go into a chemical analysis of the component parts of what should be a living organism. His is an accurate and most sympathetic comprehension, and a most skilful representation of things as they really appear. But comprehension and representation are vague terms. In regard to Turgeneff, they mean in the first place a patient observation, with all the keenness of a humorist, but with a reserve, a coolness, that save him from the common faults of the humorist—sentimentality and exaggeration—and a power of description that is almost inscrutably lifelike, so wonderful is its air of reality. Indeed, we know no author whose realism is so extraordinary, who, by so few touches, can so vividly represent whatever he wishes to say. If, for instance, we compare him with Balzac, we notice with what an apparent barrenness of means he more than accomplishes the same results. Balzac uses a ponderous machinery, describing a house, for example, from the lowest stone of the foundation to the topmost brick of the chimney; in the human face, not a line escapes his eye; but this is a microscopic accuracy, a scientific accuracy compared with that of Turgeneff, whose artistic eye judges as well as sees, who catches what to another might appear to be a useless trifle, and sets it where it has more importance than would the most thorough inventory. As in our lives the memory of a tragic event will be connected with some trifle, a flower, a stain on a carpet, a hole in an umbrella, so it is with these touches of Turgeneff, delicate and true as life. He has the same mysterious power of choice that memory has. His tales are full of incidents which, at first sight, appear to be only wilful examples of his powers of observation; later, we find that they have a bearing upon the story. For instance, there is the waiting maid in the beer-garden in the story of Annonchka. Before the hero is in love, he happens to see the poor girl bemoaning the departure of her lover for the army; afterwards, when he is desperately enamored, and is leaving the town in search of Annonchka, he sees the maid flirting contentedly with another man. A simple enough incident, yet one that would hardly be noticed at the first reading. He is an artist in his realism.

We spoke of Shoubine above. What is true of him is true of all the other characters. We only mention him more particularly because, from the fact that he is so admirably drawn while he is not the hero of the book, we can see so well the care and power of our author. The heroine, Helena, is one of the most charming figures of fiction; in fact, Turgeneff draws his women with the same skill that he does his men. Those who are already familiar with his works need only be reminded of Helena herself, of Natalie in ***Dmitri Roudine,*** of Annonchka in the little story of that name, and of Marie in ***The Correspondence.*** Each leaves upon us a complete and individual impression; they are only alike in so far as they are women, and women in love.

From this same realism it naturally follows that none of Turgeneff's heroes are faultless creatures, pinks of every perfection, ideals of every virtue. They are simply human beings, with faults and foibles as well as whatever virtues there may be. Many realists see the stains upon their characters as vividly, and paint them as large as they do the virtues. With Turgeneff, however, none of the qualities are unduly magnified. He is always a narrator, never an advocate. The charming girl will fall in love with the stupid man; the intelligent or able man is too timid or too dull of perception to fall in love with the right woman. Turgeneff does not stray from the truth to bring about a happy termination. Justice is shown, too, in the construction of the story. Often this gives an unhappy ending, but this unhappy ending is an accurate one, as far removed from a wilful rending of the feelings as from the ordinary tinkle of the marriage-bells at the end of the volume, intended to suggest "happiness ever after."

Whether there is the same impartiality in his view of life that we see in the method of his stories, is another question. While with each story we might be contented to accept the sadness of its conclusion, it might still be asked whether a writer who saw life uniformly in such sombre hues were not limited in his field. There is tragedy in life, but is life all tragedy? Are the good never rewarded? Does the dullard get all the prizes? After all, optimism is much more a matter of feeling than the result of reflection; but are not the greatest poets those who have left cherry, strengthening works alongside of the deepest tragedies? And why are they the greatest, unless it be that they are the truest? Not that Turgeneff is all gloom and despair. In ***On the Eve*** we see the love of Helena outlasting everything, and, in spite of its unhappy termination, the reader is left at last in presence of the sublimity of a woman's love, rather than weighed down by an unnecessarily painful reminder of the truth that man is mortal. (p. 340)

[T. S. Perry], "Ivan Turgeneff," in The Nation, *New York, Vol. XII, No. 307, May 18, 1871, pp. 340-41.*

[W. D. HOWELLS] (essay date 1873)

[Howells was the chief progenitor of American realism and an influential American literary critic during the late nineteenth and early twentieth centuries. Although few of his nearly three dozen novels are read today, he stands as one of the major literary figures of his era; having successfully weaned American literature from the sentimental romanticism of its infancy, he earned the popular sobriquet "the Dean of American Letters." In his commentary on A House of Gentlefolk *(here called* Liza*), Howells remarks Turgenev's ability to draw the reader into the world of the novel.]*

[***Liza***] is—life; nothing more, nothing less; and though life altogether foreign to our own, yet unmistakably real. Everything is unaffected and unstrained. Here is not so much of the artificer as even his style: this author never calls on you to admire how well he does a thing; he only makes you wonder at the truth and value of the thing when it is done. He seems the most self-forgetful of the story-telling tribe, and he is no more enamored of his creations than of himself; he pets none of them; he upbraids none; you like them or hate them for what they are; it does not seem to be his affair. It is hard to reconcile the sense of this artistic impartiality with one's sense of the deep moral earnestness of the author's books: he is profoundly serious in behalf of what is just and good, even when he appears most impassive in respect to his characters; one feels the presence, not only of a great genius, but a clear conscience in his work. His earnestness scarcely permits him the play of humor; his wit is pitiless irony or cutting sarcasm. (p. 239)

The action scarcely begins till the story is two thirds told; all that precedes is devoted to the work of accounting for the characters and placing them and their ancestors and kindred, by a series of scenes, anecdotes, and descriptions, fully before you. In the mean time you come to know also a great deal of Russian life in general, though apparently no study of it has been made for your instruction: you Russianize, as you read, till you wish to address your acquaintances by their Christian names and patronymics. But suddenly, at a certain point, the threads which seemed to lie so loose in the author's hand are drawn closer and closer, till the interest is of the most intense degree. Everything that went before, tells: the effect of character, passion, situation, deepens and deepens; as the climax approaches, the light touches with which the tragedy is darkened are added one after one, till it appears impossible that you should bear more; then the whole work stands complete before you in its transcendent, hopeless pathos. It is sorrow that commands your reverence as well as your pity; Liza is so good, Lavretsky so worthy of happiness, that you can make their grief your own without losing your self-respect. (p. 240)

[*W. D. Howells*], *in a review of "Liza," in* The Atlantic Monthly, *Vol. XXXI, No. CLXXXIV, February, 1873, pp. 239-41.*

[W. D. HOWELLS] (essay date 1873)

[*Reviewing an early translation of* Rudin, *Howells suggests that the novel is primarily a character analysis of its protagonist.*]

[***Dimitri Roudine***] is mainly the study of one man's character, but a character so complex that there is little to ask of the author in the way of a story. In fact Dimitri Roudine is himself sufficient plot; and the reader is occupied from the moment of his introduction with the skilful development of his various traits, to the exclusion of the other incidents and interests. (p. 369)

We almost forget, in following this tender yet keen analysis of a pathetic character, that there is really something of a story in the book. Roudine imagines that he loves Natalie, and he wins her brave, inexperienced heart; but when their love is prematurely discovered to her mother, and Natalie comes to him ready to fly with him, to be his at any cost, he is paralyzed at the thought of Daria's opposition. "We must submit," he says. The scene that follows, with Natalie's amazement, wounded faith, and rising contempt, and Roudine's shame and anguish, is terrible,—the one intensely dramatic passage in the book, and a masterpiece of literary art which we commend to all students and lovers of that art.

We are not quite sure whether we like or dislike the carefulness with which Roudine's whole character is kept from us, so that we pass from admiration to despite before we come finally to half-respectful compassion; and yet is this not the way it would be in life? Perhaps, also, if we fully understood him at first, his relations to the others would not so much interest us. But do we wholly understand him at last? This may be doubted, though in the mean time we are taught a merciful distrust of our own judgments, and we take Leschnieff's forgiving and remorseful attitude towards him. It may be safely surmised that this was the chief effect that Turgénieff desired to produce in us; certainly he treats the story involved in the portrayal of Roudine's character with almost contemptuous indifference, letting three epilogues limp in after the first rambling narrative has spent itself, and seeming to care for these only as they further reveal the hero's traits. But for all this looseness of construction, it is a very great novel,—as much greater than the novel of incident as *Hamlet* is greater than *Richard III*. It is of the kind of novel which can alone keep the art of fiction from being the weariness and derision of mature readers; and if it is most deeply melancholy, it is also as lenient and thoughtful as a just man's experience of men. (p. 370)

[*W. D. Howells*], *in a review of "Dimitri Roudine," in* The Atlantic Monthly, *Vol. XXXII, No. CXCI, September, 1873, pp. 369-70.*

HENRY JAMES, JR. (essay date 1874)

[*James was an American-born English novelist, short story writer, critic, and essayist of the late nineteenth and early twentieth centuries. He is regarded as one of the greatest novelists of the English language and is also admired as a lucid and insightful critic. His criticism is informed by his sensitivity to European culture, particularly English and French literature of the late nineteenth century. Here, he accords general praise to such aspects of Turgenev's work as his minute observation, characterization, and sensitivity before surveying the author's career. Turgenev and James met in Paris the year after this article was published. The two became good friends and James always wrote and spoke admiringly of the Russian writer.*]

We know of several excellent critics who to the question Who is the first novelist of the day? would reply, without hesitation, Iwan Turgéniew. (p. 326)

He belongs to the limited class of very careful writers. It is to be admitted at the outset that he is a zealous genius, rather than an abundant one. His line is narrow observation. He has not the faculty of rapid, passionate, almost reckless improvisation,—that of Walter Scott, of Dickens, of George Sand. This is an immense charm in a story-teller; on the whole, to our sense, the greatest. Turgéniew lacks it; he charms us in other ways. To describe him in the fewest terms, he is a story-teller who has taken notes. This must have been a life-long habit. His tales are a magazine of small facts, of anecdotes, of descriptive traits, taken, as the phrase is, *sur le vif*. If we are not mistaken, he notes down an idiosyncracy of character, a fragment of talk, an attitude, a feature, a gesture, and keeps it, if need be, for twenty years, till just the moment for using it comes, just the spot for placing it. . . . He has a passion for distinctness, for bringing his characterization to a point, for giving you an example of his meaning. He often, indeed, strikes us as loving details for their own sake, as a bibliomaniac loves the books he never reads. His figures are all portraits; they have each something special, something peculiar, something that none of their neighbors have, and that rescues them from the limbo of the gracefully general. We remember, in one of his stories, a gentleman who makes a momentary appearance as host at a dinner-party, and after being described as having such and such a face, clothes, and manners, has our impression of his personality completed by the statement that the soup at his table was filled with little paste figures, representing hearts, triangles, and trumpets. In the author's conception, there is a secret affinity between the character of this worthy man and the contortions of his vermicelli. This habit of specializing people by vivid oddities was the gulf over which Dickens danced the tight-rope with such agility. But Dickens, as we say, was an improviser; the practice for him was a kind of lawless revel of the imagination. Turgéniew, on the other hand, always proceeds by book. (pp. 326-27)

This is a cold manner, many readers will say, and certainly it has a cold side; but when the character is one over which the author's imagination really kindles, it is an admirable vehicle for touching effects. Few stories leave on the mind a more richly poetic impression than ***Hélène*** [***On the Eve***]; all the tenderness of our credulity goes forth to the heroine. Yet this exquisite image of idealized devotion swims before the author's vision in no misty moonlight of romance; she is as solidly fair as a Greek statue; his dominant desire has been to understand her, and he retails small facts about her appearance and habits with the impartiality of a judicial, or even a medical, summing up. The same may be said of his treatment of all his heroines, and said in evidence of the refinement of his art; for if there are no heroines we see more distinctly, there are none we love more ardently. It would be difficult to point, in the blooming fields of fiction, to a group of young girls more radiant with maidenly charm than M. Turgéniew's Hélène, his Lisa, his Katia, his Tatiana, and his Gemma. For the truth is that, taken as a whole, he regains on another side what he loses by his apparent want of joyous invention. If his manner is that of a searching realist, his temper is that of a devoutly attentive observer, and the result of this temper is to make him take a view of the great spectacle of human life more general, more impartial, more unreservedly intelligent, than that of any novelist we know. Even on this line he proceeds with his characteristic precision of method; one thinks of him as having divided his subject-matter into categories, and as moving from one to the other,—with none of the magniloquent pretensions of Balzac, indeed, to be the great showman of the human comedy,—but with a deeply intellectual impulse toward universal appreciation. He seems to us to care for more things in life, to be solicited on more sides, than any novelist save George Eliot. . . . Every class of society, every type of character, every degree of fortune, every phase of manners, passes through his hands; his imagination claims its property equally, in town and country, among rich and poor, among wise people and idiots, *dilettanti* and peasants, the tragic and the joyous, the probable and the grotesque. He has an eye for all our passions, and a deeply sympathetic sense of the wonderful complexity of our souls. He relates in **"Mumu"** the history of a deaf-and-dumb serf and a lap-dog, and he portrays in **"A Strange Story"** an extraordinary case of religious fanaticism. He has a passion for shifting his point of view, but his object is constantly the same,—that of finding an incident, a person, a situation, *morally* interesting. This is his great merit, and the underlying harmony of the mosaic fashion in which he works. He believes in the intrinsic value of "subject" in art; he holds that there are trivial subjects and serious ones, that the latter are much the best, and that their superiority resides in their giving us absolutely a greater amount of information about the human mind. Deep into the mind he is always attempting to look, though he often applies his eye at very dusky apertures. . . . All rigid critical formulas are more or less unjust, and it is not a complete description of our author—it would be a complete description of no real master of fiction—to say that he is simply a searching observer. M. Turgéniew's imagination is always lending a hand and doing work on its own account. Some of this work is exquisite; nothing could have more of the simple magic of picturesqueness than such tales as **"The Dog," "The Jew," "Visions," "The Adventure of Lieutenant Jergounow," "Three Meetings,"** a dozen episodes in the ***Memoirs of a Sportsman.*** Imagination guides his hand and modulates his touch, and makes the artist worthy of the observer. In a word, he is universally sensitive. In susceptibility to the sensuous impressions of life,—to colors and odors and forms, and the myriad ineffable refinements and enticements of beauty,—he equals, and even surpasses, the most accomplished representatives of the French school of story-telling; and yet he has, on the other hand, an apprehension of man's religious impulses, of the *ascetic* passion, the capacity of becoming dead to colors and odors and beauty, never dreamed of in the philosophy of Balzac and Flaubert, Octave Feuillet and Gustave Droz. He gives us Lisa in ***A Nest of Noblemen,*** and Madame Polosow in ***Spring-Torrents.*** This marks his range. (pp. 329-32)

Writers associated with the Contemporary. *Seated from left to right are Iván Goncharóv, Turgenev, Aleksándr Druzhínin, and Aleksándr Ostróvsky; Leo Tolstoy and Dmítry Grigoróvich are standing.*

M. Turgéniew's themes are all Russian; here and there the scene of a tale is laid in another country, but the actors are genuine Muscovites. It is the Russian type of human nature that he depicts; this perplexes, fascinates, inspires him. His works savor strongly of his native soil, like those of all great novelists, and give one who has read them all a strange sense of having had a prolonged experience of Russia. We seem to have travelled there in dreams, to have dwelt there in another state of being. M. Turgéniew gives us a peculiar sense of being out of harmony with his native land,—of his having what one may call a poet's quarrel with it. He loves the old, and he is unable to see where the new is drifting. American readers will peculiarly appreciate this state of mind; if they had a native novelist of a large pattern, it would probably be, in a degree, his own. Our author *feels* the Russian character intensely, and cherishes, in fancy, all its old manifestations,—the unemancipated peasants, the ignorant, absolute, half-barbarous proprietors, the quaint provincial society, the local types and customs of every kind. But Russian society, like our own, is in process of formation, the Russian character is in solution, in a sea of change, and the modified, modernized Russian, with his old limitations and his new pretensions, is not, to an imagination fond of caressing the old fixed contours, an especially grateful phenomenon. A satirist at all points, as we shall have occasion to say, M. Turgéniew is particularly unsparing of the new intellectual fashions prevailing among his countrymen.

The express purpose of one of his novels, ***Fathers and Sons,*** is to contrast them with the old; and in most of his recent works, notably ***Smoke,*** they have been embodied in various grotesque figures.

It was not, however, in satire, but in thoroughly genial, poetical portraiture, that our author first made his mark. ***The Memoirs of a Sportsman*** were published in 1852, and were considered, says one of the two French translators of the work, much the same sort of contribution to the question of Russian serfdom as Mrs. Stowe's famous novel to that of American slavery. This, perhaps, is forcing a point, for M. Turgéniew's group of tales strikes us much less as a passionate *pièce de circonstance* than as a disinterested work of art. But circumstances helped it, of course, and it made a great impression,—an impression which testifies to no small culture on the part of Russian readers. For never, surely, was a work with a polemic bearing more consistently low in tone, as painters say. The author treats us to such a scanty dose of flagrant horrors that the moral of the book is obvious only to attentive readers. No single episode pleads conclusively against the "peculiar institution" of Russia; the lesson is in the cumulative testimony of a multitude of fine touches,—in an after-sense of sadness which sets wise readers thinking. It would be difficult to name a work which contains better instruction for those heated spirits who are fond of taking sides on the question of "art for art." It offers a capital example of moral meaning giving a sense to form, and form giving relief to moral meaning. Indeed, all the author's characteristic merits are to be found in the ***Memoirs,*** with a certain amateurish looseness of texture which will charm many persons who find his later works too frugal, as it were, in shape. Of all his productions, this is indeed the most purely delightful. (pp. 332-34)

The story of ***Rudin,*** which followed soon after, is perhaps the most striking example of his preference for a theme which takes its starting-point in character,—if need be, in morbid character. We have had no recent opportunity to refresh our memory of the tale, but we have not forgotten the fine quality of its interest,—its air of psychological truth, unencumbered with the usual psychological apparatus. The theme is one which would mean little enough to a coarse imagination,—the exhibition of a character peculiarly unrounded, unmoulded, unfinished, inapt for the regular romantic attitudes. Dmitri Rudin is a moral failure, like many of the author's heroes,—one of those fatally complex natures who cost their friends so many pleasures and pains; who might, and yet, evidently, might not, do great things; natures strong in impulse, in talk, in responsive emotion, but weak in will, in action, in the power to feel and do singly. Madame Sand's "Horace" is a broad, free study of this type of person, always so interesting to imaginative and so intolerable to rational people; Mr. Turgéniew's hero is an elaborate miniature-portrait. Without reading Rudin we should not know just how fine a point he can give to his pencil. But M. Turgéniew, with his incisive psychology, like Madame Sand, with her expansive synthesis, might often be a vain demonstrator and a very dull novelist if he were not so constantly careful to be a dramatist. Everything, with him, takes the dramatic form; he is apparently unable to conceive of anything out of it, he has no recognition of unembodied ideas; an idea, with him, is such and such an individual, with such and such a nose and chin, such and such a hat and waistcoat, bearing the same relation to it as the look of a printed word does to its meaning. Abstract possibilities immediately become, to his vision, concrete situations, as elaborately defined and localized as an interior by Meissonier. In this way, as we read, we are always looking and listening; and we seem, indeed, at moments, for want of a running thread of explanation, to see rather more than we understand.

It is, however, in ***Hélène*** that the author's closely commingled realism and idealism have obtained their greatest triumph. The tale is at once a homely chronicle and a miniature epic. The scene, the figures, are as present to us as if we saw them ordered and moving on a lamp-lit stage; and yet, as we recall it, the drama seems all pervaded and colored by the light of the moral world. There are many things in ***Hélène,*** and it is difficult to speak of them in order. It is both so simple and so various, it proceeds with such an earnest tread to its dark termination, and yet it entertains and beguiles us so unceasingly as it goes, that we lose sight of its simple beauty in its confounding, entrancing reality. But we prize it, as we prize all the very best things, according to our meditative after-sense of it. Then we see its lovely unity, melting its brilliant parts into a single harmonious tone. The story is all in the portrait of the heroine, who is a heroine in the literal sense of the word; a young girl of a will so calmly ardent and intense that she needs nothing but opportunity to become one of the figures about whom admiring legend clusters. She is a really elevated conception; and if, as we shall complain, there is bitterness in M. Turgéniew's imagination, there is certainly sweetness as well. (pp. 335-36)

The husband, the wife, and the lover,—the wife, the husband, and the woman loved,—these are combinations in which modern fiction has been prolific; but M. Turgéniew's treatment [in ***A Nest of Noblemen***] renews the youth of the well-worn fable. He has found its moral interest, if we may make the distinction, deeper than its sentimental one; a pair of lovers accepting adversity seem to him more eloquent than a pair of lovers grasping at happiness. The moral of his tale, as we are free to gather it, is that there is no effective plotting for happiness, that we must take what we can get, that adversity is a capable mill-stream, and that our ingenuity must go toward making it grind our corn. Certain it is that there is something very exquisite in Lawretzky's history, and that M. Turgéniew has drawn from a theme associated with all manner of uncleanness a story embalmed in a lovely aroma of purity. This purity, indeed, is but a pervasive emanation from the character of Lisaweta Michailowna. American readers of Turgéniew have been struck with certain points of resemblance between American and Russian life. The resemblance is generally superficial; but it does not seem to us altogether fanciful to say that Russian young girls, as represented by Lisa, Tatiana, Maria Alexandrowna, have to our sense a touch of the faintly acrid perfume of the New England temperament,—a hint of Puritan angularity. It is the women and young girls in our author's tales who mainly represent strength of will,—the power to resist, to wait, to attain. (pp. 339-40)

Lawretzky, sorely tried as he is, is perhaps the happiest of our author's heroes. He suffers great pain, but he has not the intolerable sense of having inflicted it on others. This is the lot, both of the hero of ***Smoke*** and of the fatally passive youth whose adventures we follow in the author's latest work. On ***Smoke*** we are unable to linger, as its theme is almost identical with that of ***Spring-Torrents,*** and the latter will be a novelty to a greater number of our readers. ***Smoke,*** with its powerful and painful interest, lacks, to our mind, the underlying sweetness of most of its companions. It has all their talent, but it has less of their spirit. It treats of a dangerous beauty who robs the loveliest girl in Russia of her plighted lover, and the story duly absorbs us; but we find that, for our own part, there is always a certain languor in our intellectual acceptance of the grand coquettes of fiction. It is obviously a hard picture to paint; we always seem to see the lady pushing about her train before the foot-lights, or glancing at the orchestra stalls during her victim's agony. In the portrait of Irene, however, there are very fine intentions, and the reader is charmed forward very much as poor Litwinof was. The figure of Tatiana, however, is full of the wholesome perfume of nature. ***Smoke*** was preceded by ***Fathers and Sons,*** which dates from ten years ago, and was the first of M. Turgéniew's tales to be translated in America. In none of them is the subject of wider scope or capable of having more of the author's insidious melancholy expressed from it; for the figures with which he has filled his foreground are, with their personal interests and adventures, but the symbols of the shadowy forces which are fighting forever a larger battle,—the battle of the old and the new, the past and the future, the ideas that arrive with the ideas that linger. Half the tragedies in human history are born of this conflict; and in all that poets and philosophers tell us of it, the clearest fact is still its perpetual necessity. The opposing forces in M. Turgéniew's novel are an elder and a younger generation: the drama can indeed never have a more poignant interest than when we see the young world, as it grows to a sense of its strength and its desires, turning to smite the old world which has brought it forth with a mother's tears and a mother's hopes. The young world, in ***Fathers and Sons,*** is the fiercer combatant; and the old world in fact is simply forever the *victa causa,* which even stoics pity. And yet with M. Turgéniew, characteristically, the gaining cause itself is purely relative, and victors and vanquished are commingled in a common assent to fate. Here, as always, his rare discretion serves him, and rescues him from the danger of exaggerating his representative types. Few figures in his pages are more intelligibly human than Pawel Petrowitsch and Eugene Bazarow,—human each of them in his indefeasible weakness, the one in spite of his small allowances, the other in spite of his brutal claims. In Kirsanow (the farmer) the author has imaged certain things he instinctively values,—the hundred fading traditions of which the now vulgarized idea of the "gentleman" is the epitome. He loves him, of course, as a romancer must, but he has done the most impartial justice to the ridiculous aspect of his position. Bazarow is a so-called "nihilist,"—a red-handed radical, fresh from the shambles of criticism, with Büchner's *Stoff und Kraft* as a text-book, and everything in nature and history for his prey. He is young, strong, and clever, and strides about, rejoicing in his scepticism, sparing nothing, human or divine, and proposing to have demolished the universe before he runs his course. But he finds there is something stronger, cleverer, longer-lived than himself, and that death is a fiercer nihilist than even Büchner. . . . Exquisitely imagined is the whole attitude and demeanor of Pawel Petrowitsch, Arcadi's uncle, and a peculiarly happy invention the duel which this perfumed conservative considers it his manifest duty to fight in behalf of gentlemanly ideas. The deeper interest of the tale, however, begins when the young Büchnerite repairs to his own provincial home, and turns to a pinch of dust the tender superstitions of the poor old parental couple who live only in their pride in their great learned son, and have not even a genteel prejudice, of any consequence, to oppose to his terrible positivism. M. Turgéniew has written nothing finer than this last half of his story; every touch is masterly, every detail is eloquent. . . . [***Spring-Torrents***] strikes us at first as a *réchauffé* of old material, the subject being identical with that of ***Smoke,*** and very similar to that of the short masterpiece called ***A Correspondence.*** The subject is one of the saddest in the world, and we shall have to reproach M. Turgéniew with delighting in sadness. But ***Spring-Torrents*** has a narrative charm which sweetens its bitter waters, and we may add that, from the writer's point of view, the theme does differ by several shades from that of the tales we have mentioned. These treat of the fatal weakness of will, which M. Turgéniew apparently considers the peculiar vice of the new generation in Russia; ***Spring-Torrents*** illustrates, more generally, the element of folly which mingles, in a certain measure, in all youthful spontaneity, and makes us grow to wisdom by the infliction of suffering. The youthful folly of Dmitri Ssanin has been great, the memory of it haunts him for years, and lays on him at last such an icy grip that his heart will break unless he can repair it. (pp. 341-45)

To give a picture of the immeasurable blindness of youth, of its eagerness of desire, its freshness of impression, its mingled rawness and ripeness, the swarming, shifting possibilities of its springtime, and to interfuse his picture with something of the softening poetizing harmony of retrospect,—this has been but half the author's purpose. He has designed beside to paint the natural conflict between soul and sense, and to make the struggle less complex than the one he has described in ***Smoke,*** and less brutal, as it were, than the fatal victory of sense in ***A Correspondence.*** "When will it all come to an end?" Ssanin asks, as he stares helpless at Maria Nikolaiewna, and feels himself ignobly paralyzed. "Weak men," says the author, "never themselves make an end,—they always wait for the end." Ssanin's history is charged with the moral that salvation lies in being able, at a given moment, to bring one's *will* down like a hammer. If M. Turgéniew pays his tribute to the magic of sense, he leaves us also eloquently reminded that soul in the long run claims her own. (pp. 348-49)

An imaginative preference for dusky subjects is a perfectly legitimate element of the artistic temperament; our own Hawthorne is a signal case of its being innocently exercised; innocently, because with that delightfully unconscious genius it remained imaginative, sportive, inconclusive, to the end. When external circumstances, however, contribute to confirm it, and reality lays her groaning stores of misery at its feet, it will take a rarely elastic genius altogether to elude the charge of being morbid. M. Turgéniew's pessimism seems to us of two sorts,—a spontaneous melancholy and a wanton melancholy. Sometimes, in a sad story, it is the problem, the question, the idea, that strikes him; sometimes it is simply the picture. Under the first influences he has produced his masterpieces; we admit that they are intensely sad, but we consent to be moved, as we consent to sit silent in a death-chamber. In the other case he has done but his second best; we strike a bargain over our tears, and insist that when it comes out being simply entertained, wooing and wedding are better than death and burial. **"The Antchar," "The Forsaken," "A Superfluous Man," "A Village Lear," "Toc . . . toc . . . toc,"** all seem to us to be gloomier by several shades than they need have been; for we hold to the good old belief that the presumption, in life, is in favor of the brighter side, and we deem it, in art, an indispensable condition of our interest in a depressed observer that he should have at least tried his best to be cheerful. The truth, we take it, lies for the pathetic in poetry and romance very much where it lies for the "immoral." Morbid pathos is reflective pathos, ingenious pathos, pathos not freshly born of the occasion; noxious immorality is superficial immorality, immorality without natural roots in the subject. We value most the "realists" who have an ideal of delicacy, and the elegiasts who have an ideal of joy.

"Picturesque gloom, possibly," a thick and thin admirer of M. Turgéniew may say to us, "at least you will admit that it *is* picturesque." This we heartily concede, and, recalled to a sense of our author's brilliant diversity and ingenuity, we bring our restrictions to a close. To the broadly generous side of his imagination it is impossible to pay exaggerated homage, or, indeed, for that matter, to its simple intensity and fecundity. No romancer has created a greater number of the figures that breathe and move and speak, in their habits, as they might have lived; none, on the whole, seems to us to have had such a masterly touch in portraiture, none has mingled so much ideal beauty with so much unsparing reality. His sadness has its element of errors, but it has also its larger element of wisdom. Life *is*, in fact, a battle. On this point optimists and pessimists agree. Evil is insolent and strong; beauty, enchanting but rare, goodness, very apt to be weak; folly, very apt to be defiant; wickedness, to carry the day; imbeciles to be in great places, people of sense in small; and mankind, generally, unhappy. But the world, as it stands, is no illusion, no phantasm, no evil dream of a night; we wake up to it again for ever and ever; we can neither forget it, nor deny it, nor dispense with it. We can welcome experience as it comes, and give it what it demands in exchange for something which it is idle to pause to call much or little, so long as it contributes to swell the volume of consciousness. In this there is mingled pain and delight, but over the mysterious mixture there hovers a visible rule, which bids us learn to will and seek to understand. So much as this we seem to decipher between the lines of M. Turgéniew's minutely written chronicle. He himself has sought to understand as zealously as his most eminent competitors. He gives, at least, no meagre account of life, and he has done liberal justice to its infinite variety. This is his great merit; his great defect, roughly stated, is a tendency to the abuse of irony. He remains, nevertheless, to our sense, a very welcome mediator between the world and our curiosity. If we had space, we should like to set forth that he is by no means our ideal story-teller,—this honorable genius possessing, attributively, a rarer skill than the finest required for producing an artful *réchauffé* of the actual. But even for better romancers we must wait for a better world. Whether the world in its highest state of perfection will occasionally offer color to scandal, we hesitate to pronounce; but we are prone to conceive of the ultimate novelist as a personage altogether purged of sarcasm. The imaginative force now expended in this direction, he will devote to describing cities of gold and heavens of sapphire. But, for the present, we gratefully accept M. Turgéniew, and reflect that his manner suits the most moods of the most readers. If he were a dogmatic optimist, we suspect that, as things go, we should long ago have ceased to miss him from our library. The personal optimism of most of us no romancer can confirm or dissipate, and our personal troubles, generally, place fictions of all kinds in an impertinent light. To our usual working mood the world is apt to seem M. Turgéniew's hard world, and when, at moments, the strain and the pressure deepen, the ironical element figures not a little in our form of address to those short-sighted friends who have whispered that it is an easy one. (pp. 354-56)

Henry James, Jr., in a review of "Frühlingsfluthen: Ein König Lear des Dorfes," in The North American Review, *Vol. CXVIII, No. CCXLIII, April, 1874, pp. 326-56.*

THE ATHENAEUM (essay date 1877)

[The critic discusses Turgenev's portrayal of the young Russian revolutionaries in Virgin Soil, *claiming that, with all their faults, these characters are "the representatives of the highest state of morality."]*

The subject of the new romance of M. Tourguénief cannot fail to interest, not only readers who seek artistic beauty and finish of details, but also those who are fond of studying society in the types which he introduces. It is the revolutionary youth of Russia which figures in the new novel of the most eminent of Russian writers of fiction. It is a new society, struggling into existence amid the fermentation of enthusiasm and doubt, that the author portrays in the several characters that figure in the romance. ***Nov'***,—for such is the title that M. Tourguénief gives to his romance—refers to the social virgin soil, and the pioneers who turn it up and water it with their tears represent the social struggle going on in Russia.

No one who knows the author and his antecedents can suppose for a single moment that M. Tourguénief is a demagogue, or that he has any sympathy with bloody and violent disturbances of social order. It is in the spirit of an artist that he has grasped the characteristic features of contemporary Russian society. In his novels he has left altogether untouched a number of points of view belonging to the subjects he treats of, and has contented himself with certain living types, which draw down upon him the abuse of some and the sympathy of others. He has given to the world many striking and touching scenes which remain a permanent addition to literature. We may instance, in ***Nov'***, the description of the quarrel and reconciliation of the two rivals in chap. xxi.; two scenes of the most perfect psychological delicacy between the hero and the heroine of the story, in chaps. xxviii. and xxxiii.; also the scene of the suicide, in chaps. xxxvi.-xxxvii., to say nothing of that between the two women, in chap. xxvi., and the entire portrait of the Liberal dignitary, with his brilliant discourses and patriotic activity, everywhere, in fact, avowing the most elevated principles, but finishing with denunciations to the police, under the pretence of "the duty of a citizen." He has also produced pictures of nature such as very few contemporary authors are capable of painting. In all these respects, the former works of M. Tourguénief have furnished abundant evidence of the ability of the writer, and the present by no means falls short of any of his previous romances. . . . Great importance is to be attached to this new work as a description of the social movement in Russia during the last few years.

The predominant impression which this novel makes on the reader is, that the keen-sighted and artistic observer has been forcibly impressed with the importance of the revolutionary ferment amongst the youth of Russia. The central group in the book, and that which will attract the sympathies of the reader, is a group of young people, whose sincere convictions have rendered them hostile to the state of things existing in Russia. They live by their labour; they are proud of their poverty; it is not a professional career that they are pursuing or their own personal happiness; their desire is to "serve" the people trodden down by the dominant classes, to lead them on to liberty, in the true sense of that word, to make them revolt against the existing state of things. The types of the revolutionists drawn by M. Tourguénief are of various kinds. There is the revolutionist with a fixed idea, the enthusiast Markelof, bilious and of contracted views, who reposes confidence in people who betray him, who is seized and delivered up to the authorities by the very peasants for whom he is ready to give his blood and his life. There is the midwife, Mashurin, resolute and angular, and sparing of words, who goes like a soldier to execute the orders she receives, whether they be to deliver a letter or to take part in an *émeute*. There is the young and rapt enthusiast, Marianne, the heroine of the romance, who abandons everything "to serve the people," who is thirsting for the revolution, and longs to be a martyr for the good cause. There is Salomin, the calm revolutionist, who knows the actual weakness of the party, and the impossibility of attaining their ends as quickly as his confederates desire and expect, and who knows likewise that "there is no other way" open to them by which the Russian people can arrive at a better future. So, little by little, he acquires a decisive influence amongst them; he is able to control his friends by his sympathetic nature, and his enemies, and those that are indifferent, by his superior intelligence. Evidently on this character all the sympathies of the author are centred. Finally, there is the revolutionist who has mistaken his vocation, Neshdanof, a student of philology, and the illegitimate son of a great noble, the inheritor of artistic and sceptical leanings which prevent him from sympathizing thoroughly with the party. At heart he believes neither in the movement nor in his own exertions in the cause, yet he is ashamed of his scepticism and stifles it. He throws himself into the revolutionary intrigues with all the more energy and fanaticism, inasmuch as this enables him to stifle the doubt and aversion which torment him. At last the moment arrives when he can no longer conceal from himself his moral deficiency, and nothing remains for him but suicide. This is the central figure in the romance, a new modification of the type of useless people, of those intelligent Russians thrown out of their true sphere, examples of whom are to be found in all M. Tourguénief's novels and romances.

The characters of this central group differ still more from each other by their talents and their ability; but there is one feature which characterizes them all, which separates them distinctly from the other groups, and makes us admire and esteem them, notwithstanding their defects and the evident faults they commit, in spite of the absence of sense in some of them, and the ridicule they occasionally excite by their manner. The reason is, they are the representatives of the highest state of morality; not of conventional morality, but of that innate morality which destroys all egotism, all personal desire, which makes men sincere, and ready to sacrifice everything for the sake of an unfortunate class deprived of its heritage, and for the hope of a better social state. M. Tourguénief, in this novel, has scarcely fathomed the theoretical part of the revolutionary ideas prevalent in Russia, either because he was unacquainted with them, or on account of the censorship of the press, or for some other reason; but on the other hand the morality of the Russian revolutionists, so calumniated by novelists of the school of M. Katkaff, is presented here under an aspect which will enable the mass of readers to comprehend, for the first time, the importance of the contemporary movement in Russia and the sources of its power,—a movement which depends on such a small number of persons, and of which the material resources are so insufficient. Witness those two rivals (chap. xxi.), one of whom is tormented by a devouring jealousy, whilst the other has received a flagrant insult, but who nevertheless, for the sake of the common cause, shake hands and become friends. Witness that young and passionate man to whom a charming woman, whom he fancies he loves, says (chap. xxviii.), "If thou lovest me with a real love, take me; I am thine," and who dares not take her because in his heart he owns that no real love exists between them, and that he is unworthy of her. Witness those two women face to face (chap. xxvi.): the wife who has never committed "a fault," though she has driven lovers to commit suicide by her coquetry; and the young girl who says to the man whom she follows without thinking of marriage, "Take me, if you really love me." See them when the young girl says to the "spotless" wife, "I consider myself more honest than you," and the reader will be compelled to acknowledge that she is right. Among the whole of this group of social reformers, we breathe an atmosphere of honesty, of sincerity, and of self-denial for the good of others; mixed with respect for honourable labour. When we see them weighed down, and the majority succumbing under a load of oppression, we are ready to repeat the motto of the author, "The virgin soil ought to be turned up with a strong plough, and not merely its surface scraped with a *sokha*." We say to ourselves, Yes, it will never be the Markelofs, the Neshdanofs, and the Mashurins who will incite the Russian peasantry to rebellion. Such men as Salomin are all very well for preparing the ground, but it will not be they even who will rouse the peasantry to action. *If* the author is right, *if* at this moment there exists in the Russian revolutionary camp only such types as he has sketched, the Russian revolution is still far distant.

But the question remains—Is there not some gap in the observations of the artist? In this party of revolution are there not other types to be found much better adapted to bring about a speedy movement? Those who have enjoyed a more intimate acquaintance with the Russian revolutionary youth will probably be inclined to give an affirmative answer. Whether they be wrong or right however, whether the triumph of the revolution be far distant, close at hand, or impossible, the reader of M. Tourguénief's novel must acknowledge that, amongst the groups which the author places before him, it is the only group which possesses a moral force, the only one which aims not at selfish, sensual enjoyments, which is free from personal ambition, and is willing to labour with enthusiasm and self denial for the future of the Russian people, the only one from whose ranks the friends of real social progress can come.

In contrast to this group the author places, on the one hand, the representatives of revolutionary routine; on the other, those of governmental liberalism and the retrograde party of hungry proprietors (we leave out of consideration a couple of representatives of the old school, who contribute an episode which appears to us to be entirely out of place). We have Paklin, a braggart, who slanders everything, who is utterly incapable of making himself useful, is ready to accept any compromise, and only draws down contempt upon himself from every side, after making his friends the victims of his inconsistencies. We have Kissliakof, the revolutionary corespondent *à vapeur*, galloping without rhyme or reason from one end of Russia to the other, sending off heaps of letters, a nobody entirely taken up with himself. We have Golushkin, the vain merchant, speculating in revolutionary ideas, and denying everything and everybody in the moment of danger. In the background, for he does not actually appear on the scene, we have the despotic figure of the revolutionary chief, Vasili Nikolaevich (the author evidently intends to describe Netshaief), giving impracticable orders, and sending his adherents to join in impossible revolts. It is the dirt and dust of an old and demoralized society which clogs the new machines, and is wearing them out before they are able to produce their due effect. On the other hand, we have Sipiaguin, the Liberal orator and future minister, and Kalomeitzef, the defender of property and religion. These men talk of nothing but liberty and great Conservative principles; their discourse is of the State and patriotism, and they finish by acting the part of informers and of police spies. By the side of them we have Madame Sipiaguin, the spotless wife, a beauty with honeyed words and small intense hates, urging her husband by the gentlest means possible to the most shameful deeds.

These are the representatives of the dominant classes, who have inherited from their fathers—the slaves of despotism—corruption of heart, without having acquired by their contact with the European world anything but hypocrisy and the big words with which they conceal their inward rottenness. If "order" in Russia has really no better representatives than such persons as the Sipiaguins and the Kalomeitzefs, it is worse than the vilest disorder; the aspirations of the revolutionary party in that case are amply justified, and the continuance of the present state of things is really a national misfortune, because it is the triumph of moral rottenness. (pp. 217-18)

A review of "Nov'," in The Athenaeum, *No. 2573, February 17, 1877, pp. 217-18.*

P. V. ANNENKOV (essay date 1880)

[A literary critic, Annenkov was acquainted with many of the leading literary figures of nineteenth-century Russia. In the following excerpt from his book of literary memoirs, first published in 1880, he describes how the young Turgenev's eager, eclectic approach to life and experience influenced and enriched his writing, making him the ideal chronicler of his age and nation.]

Turgenev's young years were filled with examples of . . . turnings aside from ventures started, which always had the effect of surprising and infuriating his friends, but it should be said that these deviations of his consistently emanated from the same source. Turgenev could not persist then for long in any one decision or set of feelings—out of fear of getting waylaid and missing out on life, which speeds past and waits for no one. He was beset with a kind of nervous anxiety whenever he found himself obliged to listen to the sounds of life from afar. He constantly rushed off to the various centers where life was most intense and burned with the desire to come in contact with as large a number as possible of the characters and types engendered by life, of whatever sort they might be. He offered many a sacrifice to this impulse in his nature, sometimes associating with people of rather paltry ambitions and continuing to share the same road with them for lengthy periods of time, just as if it were his own road and one particularly to his liking. He never shared the distaste of the majority of the people in his circle that prevented them from approaching characters and personalities belonging to a certain sphere of ideas and tenor of life—and, thereby, deprived them of a considerable share of instructive observations and conclusions. Moreover, an awareness of the variety of means to achieve success given him by his education and nature still tended to overshadow aims in life for Turgenev. During these years of young manhood and its enthusiasms, it seemed to him that he could try all possible kinds of existence and combine in himself solid qualities as writer and artist with qualities necessary for acquiring the reputation of victor at all the marketplaces, tournaments, and arenas of the world such as any, even slightly developed, society makes available for its idle energies and its vanity. All these ambitions soon abated as much under the influence of the passage of years as of his effort at self-mastery, especially under the influence of his finally recognizing his literary calling; but his former colleagues still remember them and certain of these people remember them even with the aim of making of these long extinguished ambitions the basic features of his biography. That is why I decided to devote space here to my remembrances about the real heart of this matter—in the hope that they, these remembrances, will perhaps help in making judgments about him with a moderation and circumspection not always maintained by the contemporaries of our poet-novelist.

Even then it was already apparent, if one paid any attention, that Turgenev's true sympathies were completely clear and defined, despite his uniformly appreciative attitude toward the most qualitatively disparate elements of society, and that his true allegiances and preferences not only had reasoned bases but were also capable of being sustained at length. Afterward, all this was clearly evinced, but our circles, having become accustomed, as a general rule, to hold themselves strictly within their own limits, to regard with alarm and suspicion anything lying beyond them and adjacent to them, could not reconcile themselves with Turgenev's prodigality with regard to connections and acquaintances. The independence of all Turgenev's moves, his crossing over at will from one camp to another opposed to it, from one sphere of ideas to another inimical to it and, also, his radical revisions of his way of life, of his choice of the occupations and interest that alternated in riveting his attention—all this was a puzzle for his inflexible friends and made him subject, in their midst, to an undeserved reputation for frivolousness and lack of moral fiber. But there has been no one among us who had more often deceived the prophecies and definitions of his critics, no one who had so successfully reversed the verdicts of the public in his own favor, as had Turgenev. While the literary world was seething with eccentric anecdotes about him supposedly testifying to his propensity to rely, for the sake of securing himself an honorable place in society, more on the effect of words and actions than on their content and merit, Turgenev had nothing else in mind than to analyze the phenomena he came in possession of via experience and observation and to convert them into his mental capital—and in this work of analysis he brought to light qualities as thinker, poet, and psychologist that stunned his premature biographers. Thus, among other things, from close and friendly contact with a variety of social strata, not excluding those listed on the "index" of our circle as being strata of outcasts unworthy of attention, a certain, I dare so express myself, *need for fair play* arose in Turgenev with regard to people and with it, as its essential coloring, an attitude of goodwill toward them which forged for him another, and this time, truer reputation—the reputation of a man of extreme sympathy, benevolence, and *wide understanding* in our Russian world.

Very soon Turgenev became the favorite, for a whole literary period, of that very complex Russian world which recognized in him its agent and entrusted him with the task of representing it in all its affairs. And all those affairs were affairs of a nonmaterial character, consisting primarily in bringing to light the rights to sympathy to which the Russian world's moral and intellectual conceptions were entitled. Turgenev proved not inadequate to this task. Almost from the very beginning of his literary career he succeeded in discovering in the simple people a whole series of remarkable conceptions and a special moral code of their own, all of which was particularly valuable inasmuch as the matter concerned a timid and unassuming class of society without any skill in or the slightest fondness for talking about itself and for itself. Turning this same searching analysis on other classes of society, Turgenev became the chronicler and historian in Russia of the intellectual and spiritual torments of his entire age in the matter of its solving the urgent problems presented by an aroused consciousness of ideas and an awakened mind and heart which did not as yet know how to find an outlet for themselves and what to do with themselves.

In fact, all Turgenev's literary activity can be defined as a long, detailed, and poetically annotated catalog of ideas that circulated in the Russian land among the diverse strata of its educated and semi-educated population over the course of thirty years amid the usual setting of life and the harsh conditions of existence in which it revolved. Turgenev discovered a special kind of creativity in Russia, a creativity in the realm of ideals, and no matter how chimerical, immature, and sad these ideals might have appeared to be, and despite the character of a private, homemade affair, of uncoordinated, separate, and distinct strivings of mind and feeling that they might have borne—their instructive side consisted in their disparity with what Russian life had then been particularly proud of and what it had usually produced. But the inner meaning of ideals, even the most modest ones, exerts so strong an attraction and possesses such a power to arouse attention and sympathy that sometimes even minds well on their way up the ladder of scientific and civic development stop and dwell on it. Ideals in general are the family property of all educated mankind, and, this being so, it often happens that some insignificant thing becomes precious by virtue of the recollections and thoughts associated with it. That is why the unanimous, almost enraptured approval with which Turgenev's stories were received in the West is to be explained—aside from the narrative mastery peculiar to Turgenev, which amazed the sophisticated artistic taste of Europe, and aside from the curiosity aroused by pictures of an unknown and idiosyncratic culture—also by the fact that these stories lifted the edge of a curtain behind which one could glimpse the mystery of spiritual and universal-human productivity among a new, alien people and the work of their consciousness and of their tormented thought. (pp. 198-201)

Turgenev did got go against the qualities of his artistry even when, later on, he brought before the public types and images of a daring, negativistic character: these cold-blooded personages, too, still showed glowing traces of the passage over them, in time past, of the same agitations, catastrophes and failures that had been caused by the idealistic strivings of the people of the preceding epoch in general. There is every justification for calling Turgenev a searcher of spiritual *treasures* hidden in the recesses of the Russian world, and a searcher in possession of unerring tokens whereby they might be procured: he dug around in a great many different kinds of existence with the aim of obtaining the concrete evidence of the idea, the *idée fixe,* that fostered them and served as their lodestar in life, and he never went away from his work empty-handed, carrying out with him, if not whole, precious psychological revelations, at least the rudiments and assays of idealistic conceptions. It was all this that made him the interpreter of his age and, at the same time, a first-class writer in his homeland and abroad. (pp. 201-02)

P. V. Annenkov, "Chapter XXXIV," in his The Extraordinary Decade: Literary Memoirs, *edited by Arthur P. Mendel, translated by Irwin R. Titunik, The University of Michigan Press, 1968, pp. 196-206.*

PROSPER MERIMEE (essay date 1880)

[*A French man of letters, Merimee wrote short stories noted for their irony, objectivity, and concision. In the following excerpt from his preface to an 1880 French edition of* Smoke, *he stresses the aesthetic and moral truthfulness of Turgenev's work.*]

The name of Ivan Turgenev is popular in France to-day. Each of his works is awaited with the same impatience and read with the same pleasure in Paris as in St. Petersburg. He is called one of the leaders of the realistic school. I do not know whether this is criticism or praise, but I believe that he belongs to no school. He follows his own inspiration. Like all good novelists, he has devoted himself to the study of the human heart, a source which, though long explored, is inexhaustible. An acute observer, accurate down to the minutest detail, in the creation of his characters he is both painter and poet. He is equally familiar with their passions and their physical traits. He knows their habits and gestures; he listens to them talk and stenographically transcribes their conversation. The art with which he constructs with all the parts a physical and moral ensemble is such that the reader sees a portrait rather than an imaginary picture. Thanks to his ability to condense, as it were, his observations and give them a precise form, Turgenev shocks us no more than does nature when it presents some extraordinary and abnormal case. In his novel, ***Fathers and Sons,*** he shows us a young girl who has large hands and small feet. Ordinarily, there is a certain symmetry between arms and legs in the human body, but exceptions are less rare in nature than in novels. Why does this charming Katia have big hands? The author saw her that way and, because of his love of truth, was indiscreet enough to say so.

He who studies nature is involuntarily obsessed by memories and associations of ideas for which he cannot account. In his creative writing Turgenev embraces at a single glance a host of details unified by some mysterious bond which he feels but which he cannot perhaps explain. (pp. 38-9)

Turgenev is no more flattering than a photographer and has none of the weaknesses which novelists usually feel for their brain-children. He creates them with their defects, even their absurdities, leaving it to the reader to assess the good and the bad and to draw conclusions accordingly. Even less does he seek to offer us his characters as types illustrating a specific passion or representing a specific idea, as has been the practice of writers in all periods. With his subtle methods of analysis he does not see general types; he knows only individuals. Indeed, does there exist in nature a human being with but a single passion, who follows a single idea without deviation? Such an individual would certainly be far more formidable than the *man of a single book,* whom Terence feared.

This impartiality, this love of truth, the outstanding feature of Turgenev's talent, never forsakes him. Nowadays, when we write a novel in which the characters are our contemporaries, it is difficult to avoid dealing with some of the big questions agitating our modern society, or at least expressing our opinion on the revolution in manners that is taking place. Yet one cannot say whether Turgenev regrets the society of the period of Tsar Alexander I or prefers that of Alexander II. In his novel, ***Fathers and Sons,*** he aroused the anger of the young and old alike. Both groups maintained that they had been slandered. He was only being impartial, and that was what both sides could not forgive. Let me add that one must not take Bazarov as the representative of progressive youth, or Paul Kirsanov as the perfect model of the *ancien régime.* They are two figures we have seen somewhere. They undoubtedly exist, but they are not personifications of the younger and older generation of this century. It would be very fine if all the young people had as much intelligence as Bazarov, and all the old men sentiments as noble as those of Paul Kirsanov.

Turgenev keeps big crimes out of his books. You must not look for scenes of tragedy in them. There are few events in his novels. Their plots are quite simple, very much like ordinary life; and that too is one of the results of his love of truth. The progress of civilization has tended to make violence disappear from our modern society, but it has not been able to change the passions hidden in the human heart. The form they take is softened or, if you will, worn down, like coins that have long been in circulation. It is in "intimate dramas," as they are now called, that Turgenev's talent excels and is most at home.

His first work, ***A Sportsman's Sketches,*** a collection of short stories full of originality, was to us a kind of revelation of Russian customs. (pp. 40-2)

We know that all artists who have excelled in painting the human face have been, when they have wanted to be, great landscapists. Hence it is not surprising to find in Turgenev, profound observer of the human heart, a talent for describing the scenes and effects of nature. Always simple and accurate, he often rises to the level of poetry. This he does without apparent effort by the liveliness of his impressions and the art of his description. (pp. 43-4)

Some time ago, I tried to show how the admirable richness of the Russian language was a shoal for writers using it; nor has Turgenev always avoided this shoal. At times he is a little too fond of his descriptions. They are undoubtedly very authentic but they could be shortened. He is fond of noting delicate nuances. I do not underestimate the merit or the difficulties of this achievement, but it is one in which he runs the risk of slowing down an interesting action. Actors, some of them very great actors, often have the defect of paying too much attention to the words of their role and not enough to the characters they are portraying. That is called, I believe, *over-acting,* and it never fails to please an audience, which quickly responds to the way in which an actor varies the inflections of his voice. But by over-acting I fear that the dramatist's intentions are distorted and sentiments attributed to him that were not in his mind.

I must hasten to add that the criticisms I have made of Turgenev refer to his first books rather than to his latest works. I have already mentioned Turgenev's talent in bringing his characters to life as people. After reading ***Smoke*** you feel that you have seen Irene and that you would recognize her in any drawing-room. . . . Although no one captures and depicts with more sharpness the foibles, vices, and absurdities of his times, it cannot be said that Turgenev writes satires. He does not feel that malicious pleasure which certain critics enjoy in uncovering human weaknesses and clichés. Those gentlemen assiduously point out the ugly aspects of the world in which we live. Turgenev is just as thorough in looking for the good wherever it may be hidden. Without prejudice, without feigning banal philanthropy, he is the defender of the weak and the disinherited. Even in the basest natures he loves to uncover some traits which uplift them. Often he reminds me of Shakespeare. He has the latter's love of truth, and like the English poet, he can create characters of astonishing reality. But despite the art with which the author hides behind the people of his invention, one nevertheless senses his own personality. And that is perhaps not the least claim he has to our affection. (pp. 44-6)

Prosper Merimee, in an excerpt, translated by Joseph M. Bernstein, in First Love: Three Short Novels *by Ivan Turgenev, Lear Publishers, 1948, pp. 38-46.*

THE SATURDAY REVIEW, LONDON (essay date 1883)

[*This reviewer, writing on the day of Turgenev's death, regrets the loss of a major novelist. The critic also compares Turgenev with Anthony Trollope, distinguishing the Englishman's straightforward presentation of events and personalities from the Russian's less clearly defined and more suggestive approach.*]

A very distinct gap is made in the ranks of European novelists by the death of Ivan Turgénieff. Few instances could be adduced to parallel the popularity and fame enjoyed by a master of fiction who wrote in a tongue so strange to the vast majority of well-educated English-speaking people that they knew and admired his works through the medium of French, English, or, as perhaps in most cases, American, translations. Yet he was almost as well known and popular, and had almost as much influence upon other writers, as well as upon his readers, as Heine, who wrote in a language far more understood at large. In great measure he was and is, indeed, to one generation or even to two, the first really representative Russian master of imaginative literature. Pouschkine, the poet, we have all heard of, and most of us can quote commonplaces about him to some extent; but for one Englishman or American who has read anything of Pouschkine, there are probably fifty or a hundred who have read a good deal of Turgénieff. . . . The Russian novelist had the gifts of clearness, smoothness, picturesque power—never degenerating into the abominable thing called "word-painting"—truth, and pathos.

These are in themselves strong equipments for a writer of fiction; but there is yet one other thing wanted to make up the necessary list—a thing, as a great French actor once said, "no bigger than my finger-nail, but the most important of all"—that thing being instruction. This Turgénieff had in a marked degree. The ease of his writing is no more a matter of chance than was the case as to that of Anthony Trollope; and in both cases numberless fine details go to make up a singularly living presentment of character, whether in the principal or in the subordinate personages introduced. There was a difference of method, and a considerable difference—which may be appreciated by comparing the treatment of any of Trollope's stories that discourse of unruly passions with Turgénieff's treatment of a like complication in the loves of Litvinof, Irene, and Tatiana in ***Smoke.*** The Russian was far more reticent than a Frenchman, even if that Frenchman were Mérimée whose style he affected, would have been; but he was less reticent than the Englishman. There was no offence, in the true sense of the word, in anything that he ever wrote; but he probably wrote more freely on such subjects, and it may be thought equally probable that what was hailed with delight as the work of a Russian might have raised doubt or disapproval if it had been the work of an Englishman. It may be worth while to add, lest we should be in any way misunderstood as to this matter, that in Turgénieff's method there was never the slightest cause for honest disapproval. Only to take one instance, one may imagine that if he had taken charge of the relations between Montagu and the American lady in *The Way We Live Now,* he would have left them a little, but only a little, less vague, than they were left by Trollope. For the rest, both writers had an extraordinarily keen eye for the manners and the cast of thought of all classes of men, and an unusually graphic power of hitting them off in writing in which there was no semblance of effort.

Of the novel they held, it would seem, very different views. Turgénieff, like Mérimée, was often content to leave the conclusion of the complications with which he had dealt unsettled. Trollope, so far as we remember, never did this. To him a story which he once undertook was a thing which had to be carried out to the very end. . . . But, for illustration of this radical difference, the short stories of both writers are perhaps more convenient than the longer novels; and for such a purpose one may perhaps contrast Turgénieff's **"Three Meetings"** with Trollope's "La Mère Bauche," a story which in a compressed form gives an indication of how much more tragical and imaginative power Trollope possessed than he cared as a rule to put forward in his longer novels. In "La Mère Bauche" every character, down to the wretched, weak-minded young man who is practically the pivot of the story, is a living reality. The stern mother, the detestable and strictly conscientious wooden-legged Captain, the girl who is driven to death by their machinations, are all actual people, people that we should recognize at once if we met them after reading about them. And one knows all that one can possibly want to know about them after the catastrophe. In **"Three Meetings"** also we know, or think that we know, the characters of the people concerned thoroughly enough. The narrator, the mysterious lady, her sister, the sleepy *starosta,* the sullen care-taker Loukianitch, even the scarce-seen high-bred rascal to whom a mystery attaches—all these are living persons, and, as in the other case, persons whom we should at once know if we met them. But in the one case, that of Turgénieff, suggestion; in the other, that of Trollope, information, is used to bring about this result. The English novelist knocks in his nail; the Russian merely calls your attention to the fact that the nail is there inviting your notice; and the Russian gives no end to his story. It begins mysteriously, it ends mysteriously. "I went home," says the narrator after his third meeting and his first interview face to face with the mysterious lady. "Since then I have met my unknown no more." Like a vision I first saw her, like a vision she passed before me, to vanish for ever." What happened at Sorrento, what was the association with the Italian ballad *Passa quei colli,* what were the relations between the lady and "the tall handsome man with the moustaches," we never learn. It is the writer's art to make us as interested in these people of whose unravelled fortunes he shows us three slight episodes, as we are in the fortunes of people whose literary creator seems to know all about them. Both methods are, in their way, in first-rate hands, equally good; and it may depend upon the reader's or student's mood whether he prefers the one or the other. There is, perhaps, more scope for imagination, both on the writer's and the reader's part, in Turgénieff's way than in Trollope's; but it does not follow that the one was necessarily more or less imaginative than the other. But in the one case the old saw of "decipit exemplar vitiis imitabile" is certainly more clearly instanced than in the other. Turgénieff's method was undoubtedly less conventional than that of our best-esteemed English novelists of the day. The want of conclusion was in his hands striking, not irritating. In the hands of his imitators it is irritating, and by no means striking. His minute treatment of detail was masterly; it all contributed to a general effect. His imitators have all the minuteness, nothing of the effect. They want, to use a common and expressive phrase, backbone. One feels in reading Turgénieff that he knows his characters, however lightly they may be touched in writing, thoroughly, and that he imparts this knowledge to the reader. One certainly cannot always feel this in reading Mr. Henry James, good as some of his work is. Turgénieff was capable of a long flight as well as of a short one. Mr. James's best work—and that is of its kind first-rate—has been in short stories. To put it shortly, Turgénieff overtopped, mentally as well as physically, most contemporary writers of fiction. His loss to the public is the greater, because he has left behind him, so to speak, a school without an instructor. His loss to his friends and acquaintances, who knew in the man the same sincerity, humour, and unostentatious purpose which were found in the writer, is inestimable.

"Ivan Turgénieff," in The Saturday Review, *London, Vol. 56, No. 1454, September 8, 1883, p. 306.*

GEORG BRANDES (essay date 1889)

[Brandes, a Danish literary critic and biographer, was the principal leader of the intellectual movement that helped to bring an end to Scandinavian cultural isolation. Brandes believed that literature reflects the spirit and problems of its time and that it must be understood within its social and aesthetic context. His major critical work, Hovedstrymninger i det 19de aarhundredes litteratur (Main Currents in Nineteenth-Century Literature), *won him admiration for his ability to view literary movements within the broader context of all European literature. In the following excerpt, Brandes praises Turgenev's work, emphasizing both his bond with and detachment from Russian culture, as well as his melancholy.]*

No earlier Russian author has been read in Europe like Iván Sergeyevitch Turgenief; he is to be regarded rather as a cosmopolitan than as a Russian author.

He opened up to the European public a new world of subjects, but he did not need the collateral interest which his work gained for him thereby; for it is the artist and not the describer of culture which Europe has admired in him. Although he has hardly been read out of his own country in his own language, he has everywhere, even in those countries which possess the most taste, been placed on a level with the best authors of the land. He has been read everywhere in translations, which necessarily distort or diminish the impression of his superiority; but the perfection of his originality asserted itself so strongly in the various more or less happy forms in which his books were cast that any want of delicacy and clearness was overlooked. Great authors, as a rule, work most effectively through their style, because by this they come into personal contact with the reader. Turgenief made a very deep impression, although the reader who was not a Russian could appreciate only the coarser qualities of his style, and could scarcely imagine with what elegance he was wont to express himself, and would be just as far from understanding his allusions as from being able to compare his interpretation and description of persons and ways of thinking in Russia with the reality from which they were taken. Turgenief conquered in the artistic race, although he was heavily handicapped; he was triumphant in the great arena, although he wielded a sword without a point.

For the cultured people of Western Europe, he has peopled the great empire of the East with human beings of the present time. Thanks to him, we know the spiritual characteristics of its men and women. Although in the vigor of his age he left Russia, never again to dwell in his native land, he has never described anything else than the inhabitants of this country, and Germans and Frenchmen only as half Russianized or even only in contact with Russians. He only presents to us beings with whose peculiarities he was familiar from his youth. That gradually, during his long exile and the estrangement which existed between the Slavophile and European Russians, it came to be regarded as proper, in certain Russian circles, to depreciate his knowledge of his fatherland, and treat him as a kind of Western European, was natural. But, if he had been a degree less cosmopolitan, he certainly would never have made his way into the whole civilized world as he has done.

He has given pictures from the forest and the steppes, from spring and autumn, from all ranks and classes of society, and all grades of culture, in Russia. He has drawn the serf and the princess, the peasant and the proprietor, and the student; the young girl who is pure soul, endowed with the finest Slavic charms, and the cold, beautiful, egotistical coquette, who in his hands seems to be more irresponsible in her heartlessness than anywhere else. He has given a rich psychology of a whole human race, and has given it with a mind greatly excited, but yet so that his mental agitations do not in any way disturb the transparent clearness of the descriptions.

Of all the prose writers of Russia, Turgenief is the greatest artist. Possibly, it depends upon the fact that he is the one of those who has lived most in foreign lands; for if his long residence in France has not increased the stock of poetry which he brought with him from his home, yet he has plainly learned there the art of setting his pictures in frame and glass.

A broad, deep wave of melancholy flows through Turgenief's thoughts, and therefore also through his books. However sober and impersonal his style is, and although he hardly ever inserts poems in his novels and romances, still his general narrative makes a lyrical impression. There is so much feeling condensed in them, and this feeling is invariably sadness,—a peculiar, wonderful sadness without a touch of sentimentality. Turgenief never expresses himself wholly emotionally; he works with restrained emotion; but no Western European is sad as he is. The great melancholy authors of the Latin races, like Leopardi or Flaubert, have harsh, firm outlines in their style; the German sadness is glaringly humorous or pathetic or sentimental. The melancholy of Turgenief is, in its general form, that of the Slavic races in their weakness and sorrow, which comes in a direct line from the melancholy in the Slavic popular ballads.

All the later Russian poets of rank are melancholy. But with Turgenief it is the melancholy of the thinker who has understood that all the ideals of the human race—justice, reason, supreme goodness, happiness—are a matter of indifference to nature, and never assert themselves by their own spiritual power. (pp. 271-74)

When Gogol is melancholy, it is because he is indignant; when Dostoyevski is so, it depends upon the fact that he is dissolved in sympathy with the ignorant and the obscure, with the saint-like, noble, and pure of heart, and almost even more with sinners both male and female; Tolstoi's melancholy has its root in his religious fatalism. Turgenief alone is a philosopher. (p. 274)

Only for Turgenief, with his quiet contemplation, even religious enthusiasm is a theme like any other, although he, too, in **"Clara Militch"** and **"The Love Song of the Conquering Lovers,"** pays his tribute to the mystical. He treats religious enthusiasm without losing his equilibrium. We recall, for instance, his Sophie Vladimirovna from **"A Strange Story,"** the young girl of good family, who accompanies a wandering saint out into the wide world.

His melancholy, therefore, is less religious than philosophical; but it is that of the patriot who has become a pessimist. In spite of all his seeming cosmopolitanism, he was a patriot, but a patriot who mourned over his fatherland and despaired of it. (p. 275)

What makes Turgenief's vein so rich and peculiar is that he is at once a pessimist and a philanthropist; that he loved the race of which he thought so poorly and esteemed so lightly.

But he had seen altogether too much go wrong and miscarry in Russia to be able to narrate any other incidents than those with unhappy or sad results. To him, a love story is not genuine Russian if it does not have an unhappy issue in consequence of the inconstancy of the man or the coldness of the woman. An undertaking does not seem to him to be genuine Russian unless it is beyond the capacity of him who attempts it, and falls through in consequence of the insusceptibility of those for whose sake it was to be carried through. But still he cannot refrain from dwelling again and again on vacillating love and fruitless struggles in Russia. For him, the land of Russia, where everything comes to grief, is a land of general shipwreck. And his chief emotion is one which awakens and is mingled with pain in the spectator of a shipwreck, in which the latter must give the sufferers themselves the greatest part of the blame. There is a strong and quiet emotion which is always softened in its expression. It is seldom that a great and productive author has made so little noise as he. (pp. 278-79)

It is diffucult to say briefly and precisely what it is which makes Turgenief an artist of the first rank. We might almost say that it is because his style is so genuine. But even this word needs an explanation. The fact that he possesses in the highest degree the quality of a true poet, of being able to create men who live, is not all. What makes his artistic superiority so perceptible is the harmony which the reader traces between the author's conception of the person who is described, his opinion of him, and also the impression which is made upon him as well as upon the reader by that person.

The point is here. The relation of the author to his own creations is such that every weakness which he has as an artist or as a man must be exposed to the light. The author may have many and rare gifts, but if he calls upon us to admire that which is not worthy of admiration, or if he would extort from us admiration for a man, or sympathy with a woman, or enthusiasm for an act, without our feeling that there is any occasion for those sentiments, then he has injured and weakened himself. When the author of a novel, whose company we have kept for a long time with pleasure, suddenly shows himself less critical or more emotional or morally more lax than we are, then his descriptions lose their point for us. If he allows a person to appear as irresistibly winning, without our finding him fascinating; if he draws a man as more gifted or even more witty than he seems to us to be; if he explains his conduct by a magnanimity we have never met with, and in this case do not believe in; if he defies us by arbitrary, immature judgments, or disturbs us by coldness, or irritates us by moralizing: then there steals in upon the reader more and more a feeling of disappointing art. It is as if you heard a false note; and even if the music is afterwards correct, the disagreeable impression lingers in the mind. What reader of Balzac, or Dickens, or Auerbach—to speak only of the great dead—has not experienced this disagreeable impression! When Balzac becomes enthusiastic over vulgarity, or Dickens childishly pathetic, or Auerbach affectedly simple, the reader feels that he is in the presence of the untrue, the abortive, and is taken aback. Nothing abortive is ever met with in Turgenief.

The subjects he has selected are all the most difficult. He refuses to be interested in romantic characters and marvellous adventures, and he no less refuses the attractions of impurity. There seldom or never happens anything unusual in his books—a catastrophe like the falling-down of a house at the close of the **"King Lear of the Steppe"** is purely exceptional—and although he does not go out of his way on account of low and vile characters, or of incidents which no English novelist would relate, yet he does not dwell upon the obscene, as those authors who once for all have disregarded conventionality are so often tempted to do. As an artist he was a decided realist, but a modest realist.

His chief domain as a narrator is the poor, the weak, the inconstant and untrustworthy, the superfluous and the abandoned.

He does not, like Dostoyevski, describe the misfortune which is externally palpable, nor the poverty, the roughness, the corruption, the crime, nor, above all, the misfortune, which can be seen at a distance. He describes the misfortune which avoids publicity, and he is especially the author for those who have submitted to their fate. He has pictured the inner life of reticent sorrow,—the still-life of the unfortunate, so to speak. (pp. 279-81)

Georg Brandes, "Chapter V," in his Impressions of Russia, *translated by Samuel C. Eastman, Thomas Y. Crowell & Co., 1889, pp. 271-300.*

A. P. CHEKHOV (letter date 1893)

[A Russian dramatist and short story writer, Chekhov is considered one of the greatest authors of the late nineteenth and early twentieth centuries. Central to his fiction are intellectual but irresolute and fatalistic characters—frequently of the upper class—whose apathy and psychological impotence render their lives meaningless. Here, in an excerpt from a letter to A. S. Suvorin, Chekhov applauds Fathers and Sons *and briefly judges Turgenev's other works, noting in particular the author's portrayal of female characters.]*

My God! What a magnificent thing ***Fathers and Sons*** is! It simply makes you desperate. Bazarov's illness is so powerfully done that I turned weak and had a feeling as if I had been infected by him. And Bazarov's death? And the old people? And Kukshin? God knows how he does it. It is sheer genius. I don't like ***On the Eve*** except Helen's father and the ending. That ending is full of tragedy. **"The Dog"** is very good; its language is amazing. Please read it if you've forgotten it. ***Asya*** is very nice, **"The Quiet Spot"** is crumpled and doesn't satisfy. I don't like ***Smoke*** at all. ***A Nest of Noblemen*** is weaker than ***Fathers and Sons,*** but the ending is almost a marvel. Besides the old woman in Bazarov, that is, Evgeny's mother and mothers in general, particularly the fashionable ladies, who all resemble each other, by the way (Liza's mother, Helen's mother), and Lavretsky's mother, the former serf, and in addition the simple women, all of Turgenev's women and young ladies are unbearable with their artificiality and, forgive me, falseness. Liza, Helen—these aren't Russian young ladies but some sort of Pithians, with their pronouncements, their excessive pretensions. Irina in ***Smoke,*** Odintsov in ***Fathers and Sons,*** in general the lionesses, ardent, appetizing, insatiable, seeking something—they're all nonsense. When you think of Tolstoy's Anna Karenin, all these young ladies of Turgenev's with their tempting shoulders vanish. Women of the negative sort, where Turgenev lightly caricatures them (Kukshin), or makes merry with (the description of balls), and wonderfully drawn and so successfully come off in him that, as the saying goes, you can't find a flaw in it. The descriptions of nature are good, but—I feel that we are already becoming disaccustomed to that kind of description and that something else is needed. (pp. 283-84)

A. P. Chekhov, in a letter to A. S. Suvorin on February 24, 1893, in "Fathers and Sons" by Ivan Turgenev: The Author on the Novel, Contemporary Reactions, Essays in Criticism, *edited and translated by Ralph E. Matlaw, W. W. Norton & Company, Inc., 1966, pp. 283-84.*

JOSEPH CONRAD (letter date 1895)

[Conrad is considered an innovator of novel structure as well as one of the finest stylists of modern English literature. His novels are complex moral and psychological examinations of the ambiguities of good and evil. In this excerpt from a letter to Edward Garnett, the editor of an English-language edition of Turgenev's novels, Conrad extols the Russian's "essential humanity."]

Turgenev's creative activity covers about thirty years. Since it came to an end the social and political events in Russia have moved at an accelerated pace, but the deep origins of them, in the moral and intellectual unrest of the souls, are recorded in the whole body of his work with the unerring lucidity of a great national writer. The first stirrings, the first gleams of the great forces can be seen almost in every page of the novels, of the short stories and of ***A Sportsman's Sketches***—those marvellous landscapes peopled by unforgettable figures.

Those will never grow old. Fashions in monsters do change, but the truth of humanity goes on for ever, unchangeable and inexhaustible in the variety of its disclosures. Whether Turgenev's art, which has captured it with such mastery and such gentleness, is for "all time" it is hard to say. Since, as you say yourself, he brings all his problems and characters to the test of love we may hope that it will endure at least till the infinite emotions of love are replaced by the exact simplicity of perfected Eugenics. But even by then, I think, women would not have changed much; and the women of Turgenev who understood them so tenderly, so reverently and so passionately—they, at least, are certainly for all time.

Women are, one may say, the foundation of his art. They are Russian of course. Never was a writer so profoundly, so wholesouledly national. But for non-Russian readers, Turgenev's Russia is but a canvas on which the incomparable artist of humanity lays his colours and his forms in the great light and the free air of the world. Had he invented them all and also every stick and stone, brook and hill and field in which they move, his personages would have been just as true and as poignant in their perplexed lives. They are his own and also universal. Any one can accept them with no more question than one accepts the Italians of Shakespeare.

In the large, non-Russian view, what should make Turgenev sympathetic and welcome to the English-speaking world, is his essential humanity. All his creations, fortunate and unfortunate, oppressed and oppressors are human beings, not strange beasts in a menagerie or damned souls knocking themselves about in the stuffy darkness of mystical contradictions. They are human beings, fit to live, fit to suffer, fit to struggle, fit to win, fit to lose, in the endless and inspiring game of pursuing from day to day the ever-receding future. (pp. 34-6)

Joseph Conrad, in a letter to Edward Garnett in 1895, in First Love: Three Short Novels *by Ivan Turgenev, Lear Publishers, 1948, pp. 33-7.*

GEORGE MOORE (essay date 1903)

[An Irish author, Moore is commonly credited with importing the themes and techniques of French naturalism into English literature. In his critical writings he advocated the aesthetic doctrine of pure form, and in his own fiction he attempted to give precedence to artistic design over statements about the world or the lives of his characters. In the following excerpt, Moore commends Turgenev's special insight into the human condition, frequently comparing his writing to the paintings of Jean-Baptiste-Camille Corot.]

Balzac was without point of view, and his great empire is held together by intensity and energy of mind rather than by a single perception of life. But his vitality is sufficient. There is more vitality in a house described by Balzac than there is in many an English novel. He never wearies of describing chimney-piece ornaments, clock and candelabra, and in every description they live with extraordinary intensity. His mind vitalized brick and mortar—his mind was the mortar with which he built. He was interested in the whole of life, in the body as well as in the soul. He was interested in the clothes the body wore. He was interested in hats and neckties, in the watch in the fob, and in the rings on the fingers. He was interested in the buckles on a lady's shoes and in the coat of arms on her carriage. He is the only writer in whom we find everything, and he seems to have exhausted the possibility of fiction, for the writers that have succeeded him have done no more than to lead us into some unexplored corner of his genius. Sometimes the light that leads is a lamp, sometimes a taper. Flaubert and Huysmans tried to write more perfectly, and they produced wonderfully carven images, but Turgenieff was alone as human as Balzac. Balzac is the whole of man, whereas Turgenieff is the heart, the ceaseless throb of the heart that knows no change. He seems to have seen clearly from the beginning that life as we see it is full of folly and evil, that morality is a myth, an academic discussion, that beauty is a reality, and that it is wiser to follow beauty; that the artist can only teach by giving the world images of beauty to admire. He was passionately interested in the emancipation of the serfs, but he only advocated their emancipation indirectly. He limited his advocacy to describing their lives, their patient sufferings. In ***The Memoirs of a Nihilist*** he never once mentioned what were the acts that caused the man to be condemned to solitary confinement. He described his sufferings, his life between the four walls of his cell. Turgenieff was aware from the first that there is nothing vainer than preaching. As I have said, Turgenieff seems to have understood from the beginning, and as if by instinct, that life as we see it is full of folly and evil. When I say life as we see it I mean the surface of life; for few look below the surface into the calm, eternal instincts. The instincts may be compared to the moveless depths of the sea whose gray-green twilights are the same as they were yesterday and yesterday the same as they were three hundred thousand years ago. The surface of life is agitated like the surface of the sea, it is full of strange and cruel life, ever at war, creatures preying on each other; but in the immortal instincts there is twilight and peace just as in the depths of the sea. Our instincts are almost as unknown to us as the green sea's depths, but Turgenieff was a plunger in the depths, the shadowy depths where nothing is seen but a shadowy rock, and in the rock a shadowy design, and Tugenieff's tales are but the reading of these shadowy designs.

Someone has said that a tale by Turgenieff is the most beautiful thing that art has given since antiquity, and this is the truth. Balzac is more astonishing and complete, and Michael Angelo is more astonishing and more complete than Phidias, but he is not so beautiful, he is not so perfect; and in the same way Turgenieff, though not so astonishing or so complete as Balzac, is always more beautiful and more perfect. Everything we say about Turgenieff we can say with equal truth about Phidias. Neither will ever be as much admired as Michael Angelo, nor will Beethoven ever be as much admired as Wagner, nor will Corot ever be as much admired as Duprez or Diaz, for art as it approaches the zenith sheds those outward signs of life by which the multitude recognize life. The circumstantial and the ephemeral alone interest the multitude, and the moment we begin a tale by Turgenieff we are amid the immemorial instincts, and the moment we look at a picture by Corot we are amid immemorial nature.

Everyone who will read this article has seen a picture by Corot, and will therefore understand what I mean by Corot's color mind. Those delicate grays which we find in his skies however blue they may be, that we find in the darkest shadows of his rocks however brown they may be, that gentle gray was the color of his mind, and the same gray was the color of Turgenieff's mind; and the illusive and intense souls that fill his pages appear and disappear enveloped in illusive grays. The temptation glides out of the mist like a phantom and the man follows, or maybe it is a woman that follows. And every tale is the same tale, and every tale is told with the same perfection. There are tales that he calls "Dream Tales," but all his tales were dream tales. In one of the "Dream Tales" a man wakes in the middle of the night hearing a sound, the sound of a harp-string, and a voice tells him to go next evening to the blasted oak by the edge of the common. He goes and meets a phantom, and the phantom tells him not to be afraid; and they fly over the world and see many things. We are taken in this tale nearer to the verge of life than the harps of "Tristan" may take us, and they take us very near to it; we feel that the great secret is going to be revealed, and the moment is an intense one.

Only the greatest writers tell the same tale. The story of Liza in ***The House of Gentle Folk*** is the same. A man has made an unfortunate marriage, his wife has lovers, he leaves her; years pass and he hears she is dead; he believes her dead; and meeting a girl who loves him and whom he loves, it is agreed that they shall marry. But the wife returns, the girl tells the man that he must go back to his wife, the girl goes into a convent, and I believe he sees her once in the convent. That is all, and yet this is one of the most beautiful things ever written, and in its beauty very like Greek sculpture. Lavretsky comes back after many years and finds a new generation growing up. The garden is changed; trees have grown, and he sits on the seat where he sat with Liza. The young people want to play hide-and-seek, but the melancholy man intimidates them. . . . He begs of them to go and play, and he says, "We old people have a resource which you don't know yet, and which is better than any amusement—recollection."

These pages are as monumental as a landscape by Corot, and they are suffused with the same intense gray; they breathe an emotion as intense as any music breathes, whether we choose Schumann or Wagner or Chopin.

In ***On the Eve*** he tells of another young girl, and she the same age as Liza. Her parents are thinking of her marriage. Young men come to the house,—artists, politicians, and professors. A professor speaks to her about Goethe; the artist laughs at him. Helen says, "Why not?" At that moment we begin to know her. That "Why not?" is as extraordinary as any one of the motives in the *Ring*. An hour later we see her sitting by her window facing the summer night. She feels something holy half rising out of, half falling into, her heart, and we know her to be the eternal maiden, she who looked at the stars ten thousand years ago, she who will look at them ten thousand years hence. The professor has stirred her heart, but he is not her predestined lover. The predestined lover is a Bulgarian, the professor's friend. But I am not interested to tell the story that Turgenieff tells; I love it well enough to refrain. It is many years since I have read this book, and were I to turn to it now I should lose the first impression. Memory is shadowy and incomplete, but I love my memory of this book, perhaps better than the book; in any case the new love would be different from the old. Like Lavretsky, I indulge in recollection. None will ever tell the tale of love's delight as well again. Helen holds happiness to her breast amid a Venetian spring, and happiness passes from her as the season passes. Her fate affects us as no personal misfortune can affect us, for when her lover dies she goes we know not whither, but we hear her cry in the wilderness and we see her lonely as Hagar amid the rose granite rocks of Arabia under a lowering sky. This mention of Hagar will seem an irrelevancy; for me it is not one, for whenever I think of a tale by Turgenieff I think of a picture by Corot, and whenever I see a picture by Corot I think of a tale by Turgenieff.

Turgenieff wrote a story called ***Spring Floods.*** In it a man is about to marry a beautiful girl, but he meets the temptation that haunts all Turgenieff's stories and wastes his life following her. The story is as beautiful as any other he ever wrote, though Turgenieff himself thought it not sufficiently perfect in outline. He perfected the outline in a novel entitled ***Smoke,*** and he lost some of the fresh color of the earlier tale. (pp. 483-86)

I remember, as everyone remembers who has read it, the story of a man who hears a woman singing in Sorrento. He is in the street, and the windows of a house are open, and a beautiful voice singing some melody of Schubert or Schumann floats out into the night air. He hears the voice again in the Steppes in Russia. The windows of a lonely house are open, and he meets her again in a ballroom in Moscow. I remember no other fact, but I remember the emotion.

I remember no other fact. I only remember the emotion, the evocation of an immortal yearning by a voice heard in the streets of Sorrento, heard afterwards in the Steppes in Russia. There is in the story some mysterious correspondence between her appearance in Sorrento and her reappearance in the Steppes. What it is I do not remember, nor is it necessary that I should. The mystery of these hauntings is implicit in their mysterious reoccurrence; the same temptation occurring again amid other circumstances leads to a belief in an eternal return, in a fate from which we cannot fly, it being part of ourselves. In ancient Greece and Rome men met it in the woods; wandering in the woods they spied a glittering breast between the leaves and were forever after unable to love mortal woman. (p. 486)

Whitman spoke of Turgenieff as "the noble and melancholy Turgenieff," and no words could describe him better. He also spoke of Turgenieff as "a most wonderful tale-teller," and the choice of the word proves Whitman to have been an artist even in his casual talk. The choice of the word proves that he understood Turgenieff as well as I understand Corot, and when I wrote my first article about Turgenieff many years ago I said, "These tales came from the East; he told tales, and we only write psychological novels." I expressed myself badly, for I then only had an inkling of the beauty I have learnt and that I am still learning to understand. Many things I have failed to understand, but two things I have understood—a tale by Turgenieff and a landscape by Corot.

Balzac and Wagner have exalted me; I have joined in their processional crowds and have carried a blowing banner. My life would have been poor without them, but neither has been as much to me as Turgenieff and Corot. Turgenieff and Corot have been the sacred places where I have rested and where I have dreamed; together they have revealed to me all that I needed. All things are contained in them. He who has seen Corot has seen all the universe, for what could we find in the furthest star more beautiful than evanescent cloud and a nymph gathering summer blooms by the edge of a lake. A cloud floats and goes out, and the blossoming wood is reflected in the lake, and lo! he has told us the tale of a spring morning. All the outward externalities of nature which Rousseau sought vainly to render Corot knew how to put aside. He knew that they were but passing things, just as Turgenieff knew that all the trivial disputes of the day are not worthy substances out of which to make art. These twin souls, the most beautiful ever born of woman, lived in the depths where all is still and quiet, where the larch bends and the lake mirrors a pellucid sky, where a man longs for a woman that has been taken from him, where a woman holds her desire to her breast for a moment, loses it, and is heard of in Bulgaria as a nurse or is heard of as a Sister of Charity, but about whom nothing certain is known. (pp. 487-88)

George Moore, "Avowals: Being the Second of a New Series of 'Confessions of a Young Man'," in Lippincott's Monthly Magazine: A Popular Journal of General Literature, Science, and Politics, *Vol. LXXII, October, 1903, pp. 481-88.*

PRINCE KROPOTKIN (essay date 1905)

[*Kropotkin was a Russian sociologist, philosopher, geographer, essayist, and critic. Born of an aristocratic family, Kropotkin became an anarchist in the 1870s and later fled to Europe, where he composed several of his best-known works. Chief among these is his* Memoirs of a Revolutionist, *which is considered a monumental autobiographical treatment of the revolutionary movement in Russia. Kropotkin also composed several literary histories, including* Russian Literature, *later published as* Ideals and Realities in Russian Literature. *In the following excerpt from this book, Kropotkin describes Turgenev's artistry, arguing that he was the greatest novelist of the nineteenth century.*]

Púshkin, Lérmontoff, and Gógol were the real creators of Russian literature; but to Western Europe they remained nearly total strangers. It was only Turguéneff and Tolstóy—the two greatest novelists of Russia, if not of their century altogether—and, to some extent, Dostoyévskiy, who broke down the barrier of language which had kept Russian writers unknown to West Europeans. They have made Russian literature familiar and popular outside Russia; they have exercised and still exercise their share of influence upon West-European thought and art; and owing to them, we may be sure that henceforward the best productions of the Russian mind will be part of the general intellectual belongings of civilised mankind.

For the artistic construction, the finish and the beauty of his novels, Turguéneff was very probably the greatest novel-writer of his century. However, the chief characteristic of his poetical genius lay not only in that sense of the beautiful which he possessed to so high a degree, but also in the highly *intellectual* contents of his creations. His novels are not mere stories dealing at random with this or that type of men, or with some particular current of life, or accident happening to fall under the author's observation. They are intimately connected with each other, and they give the succession of the leading intellectual types of Russia which have impressed their own stamp upon each successive generation. The novels of Turguéneff, of which the first appeared in 1845, cover a period of more than thirty years, and during these three decades Russian society underwent one of the deepest and the most rapid modifications ever witnessed in European history. The leading types of the educated classes went through successive changes with a rapidity which was only possible in a society suddenly awakening from a long slumber, casting away an institution which hitherto had permeated its whole existence (I mean serfdom), and rushing towards a new life. And this succession of "history-making" types was represented by Turguéneff with a depth of conception, a fulness of philosophical and humanitarian understanding, and an artistic insight, almost equal to foresight, which are found in none of the modern writers to the same extent and in that happy combination.

Not that he would follow a preconceived plan. "All these discussions about 'tendency' and 'unconsciousness' in art," he wrote, "are nothing but a debased coin of rhetorics. . . . Those only who cannot do better will submit to a preconceived programme, because a truly talented writer is the condensed expression of life itself, and he cannot write either a panegyric or a pamphlet: either would be too mean for him." But as soon as a new leading type of men or women appeared amidst the educated classes of Russia, it took possession of Turguéneff. He was haunted by it, and haunted until he had succeeded in representing it to the best of his understanding in a work of art, just as for years Murillo was haunted by the image of a Virgin in the ecstasy of purest love, until he finally succeeded in rendering on the canvas his full conception.

When some human problem had thus taken possession of Turguéneff's mind, he evidently could not discuss it in terms of logic—this would have been the manner of the political writer—he conceived it in the shape of images and scenes. Even in his conversation, when he intended to give you an idea of some problem which worried his mind, he used to do it by describing a scene so vividly that it would for ever engrave itself in the memory. This was also a marked trait in his writings. His novels are a succession of scenes—some of them of the most exquisite beauty—each of which helps him further to characterise his heroes. Therefore all his novels are short, and need no plot to sustain the reader's attention. Those who have been perverted by sensational novel-reading may, of course, be disappointed with a want of sensational episode; but the ordinary intelligent reader feels from the very first pages that he has *real* and interesting men and women before him, with really human hearts throbbing in them, and he cannot part with the book before he has reached the end and grasped the characters in full. Simplicity of means for accomplishing far-reaching ends—that chief feature of truly good art—is felt in everything Turguéneff wrote. (pp. 89-91)

Be it a small novel, or a large one, the proportion of the parts is wonderfully held; not a single episode of a merely "ethnographical" character comes in to disturb or to slacken the development of the inner human drama; not one feature, and certainly not one single scene, can be omitted without destroying the impression of the whole; and the final accord, which seals the usually touching general impression, is always worked out with wonderful finish. [The critic adds in a footnote: The only exception to be made is the scene with the two old people in ***Virgin Soil.*** It is useless and out of place. To have introduced it was simply a literary whim.]

And then the beauty of the chief scenes. Every one of them could be made the subject of a most artistic and telling picture. Take, for instance, the final scenes of Helen and Insároff in Venice: their visit to the picture gallery, which made the keeper exclaim, as he looked at them, *Poveretti!* or the scene in the theatre, where in response to the imitated cough of the actress (who played Violetta in *Traviata*) resounded the deep, real cough of the dying Insároff. The actress herself, with her poor dress and bony shoulders, who yet took possession of the audience by the warmth and reality of her feeling, and created a storm of enthusiasm by her cry of dying joy on the return of Alfred; nay, I should even say, the dark harbour where one sees the gull drop from rosy light into the deep blackness of the night—each of these scenes comes to the imagination on canvas. In his lecture, **"Hamlet and Don Quixote,"** where he speaks of Shakespeare and Cervantes being contemporaries, and mentions that the romance of Cervantes was translated into English in Shakespeare's lifetime, so that he might have read it, Turguéneff exclaims: "What a picture, worthy of the brush of a thoughtful painter: Shakespeare reading Don Quixote!" It would seem as if in these lines he betrayed the secret of the wonderful beauty—the pictorial beauty—of such a number of his scenes. He must have imagined them, not only with the music of the feeling that speaks in them, but also as *pictures,* full of the deepest psychological meaning and in which all the surroundings of the main figures—the Russian birch wood, or the German town on the Rhine, or the harbour of Venice—are in harmony with the feeling.

Turguéneff knew the human heart deeply, especially the heart of a young, thoroughly honest, and reasoning girl when she awakes to higher feelings and ideas, and that awakening takes, without her realising it, the shape of love. In the description of that moment of life Turguéneff stands quite unrivalled. On the whole, love is the leading motive of all his novels; and the moment of its full development is the moment when his hero—he may be a political agitator or a modest squire—appears in full light. The great poet knew that a human type cannot be characterised by the daily work in which such a man is engaged—however important that work may be—and still less by a flow of words. Consequently, when he draws, for instance, the picture of an agitator in ***Dmitri Rúdin,*** he does not report his fiery speeches—for the simple reason that the agitator's words would not have characterised him. Many have pronounced the same appeals to Equality and Liberty before him, and many more will pronounce them after his death. But that special type of apostle of equality and liberty—the "man of the word, and of no action" which he intended to represent in Rúdin—is characterised by the hero's relations to different persons, and particularly, above all, by his love. By his love—because it is in love that the human being appears in full, with its individual features. (pp. 92-3)

Prince Kropotkin, "Turguéneff—Tolstóy," in his Ideals and Realities in Russian Literature, *1905. Reprint by Alfred A. Knopf, 1915, pp. 88-150.*

MAURICE BARING (essay date 1915)

[During the early twentieth century, Baring—along with G. K. Chesterton and Hilaire Belloc—was considered one of the most important Catholic apologists in England. He was proficient in a number of different genres, but is remembered mainly as a novelist. He also wrote several acclaimed books on Russian and French literature and introduced English readers to the works of Anton Chekhov, Leo Tolstoy, and other prominent Russian authors. Here, he assesses Turgenev's strengths and weaknesses as a literary artist.]

Turgenev did for Russian literature what Byron did for English literature; he led the genius of Russia on a pilgrimage throughout all Europe. And in Europe his work reaped a glorious harvest of praise. Flaubert was astounded by him, George Sand looked up to him as to a Master, Taine spoke of his work as being the finest artistic production since Sophocles. In Turgenev's work, Europe not only discovered Turgenev, but it discovered Russia, the simplicity and the naturalness of the

Russian character; and this came as a revelation. For the first time, Europe came across the Russian woman whom Pushkin was the first to paint; for the first time Europe came into contact with the Russian soul; and it was the sharpness of this revelation which accounts for the fact of Turgenev having received in the West an even greater meed of praise than he was perhaps entitled to. (p. 162)

[There is] something in common between Tennyson and Turgenev. They both have something mid-Victorian in them. They are both idyllic, and both of them landscape-lovers and lords of language. They neither of them had any very striking message to preach; they both of them seem to halt, except on rare occasions, on the threshold of passion; they both of them have a rare stamp of nobility; and in both of them there is an element of banality. They both seem to a certain extent to be shut off from the world by the trees of old parks, where cultivated people are enjoying the air and the flowers and the shade, and where between the tall trees you get glimpses of silvery landscapes and limpid waters, and soft music comes from the gliding boat. Of course, there is more than this in Turgenev, but this is the main impression.

Pathos he has, of the finest, and passion he describes beautifully from the outside, making you feel its existence, but not convincing you that he felt it himself; but on the other hand what an artist he is! How beautifully his pictures are painted; and how rich he is in poetic feeling!

Turgenev is above all things a poet. He carried on the work of Pushkin, and he did for Russian prose what Pushkin did for Russian poetry; he created imperishable models of style. His language has the same limpidity and absence of any blur that we find in Pushkin's work. His women have the same crystal radiance, transparent simplicity, and unaffected strength; his pictures of peasant life, and his country episodes have the same truth to nature; as an artist he had a severe sense of proportion, a perfect purity of outline, and an absolute harmony between the thought and the expression. . . . He was a great novelist besides being a great poet. Certainly he never surpassed his early ***Sportsman's Sketches*** in freshness of inspiration and the perfection of artistic execution.

His **"Bezhin Meadow,"** where the children tell each other bogey stories in the evening, is a gem with which no other European literature has anything to compare. **"The Singers," "Death,"** and many others are likewise incomparable. ***The Nest of Gentlefolk,*** to which Turgenev owed his great popularity, is quite perfect of its kind, with its gallery of portraits going back to the eighteenth century and to the period of Alexander I; its lovable, human hero Lavretsky, and Liza, a fit descendant of Pushkin's Tatiana, radiant as a star. All Turgenev's characters are alive; but, with the exception of his women and the hero of ***Fathers and Sons,*** they are alive in bookland rather than in real life.

George Meredith's characters, for instance, are alive, but they belong to a land or rather a planet of his own making, and we should never recognize Sir Willoughby Patterne in the street, but we do meet women sometimes who remind us of Clara Middleton and Carinthia Jane. The same is true with regard to Turgenev, although it is not another planet he created, but a special atmosphere and epoch to which his books exclusively belong, and which some critics say never existed at all. That is of no consequence. It exists for us in his work.

But perhaps what gave rise to accusations of unreality and caricature against Turgenev's characters, apart from the intenser reality of Tolstoy's creations, by comparison with which Turgenev's suffered, was that Turgenev, while professing to describe the present, and while believing that he was describing the present, was in reality painting an epoch that was already dead. ***Rudin, Smoke,*** and ***On the Eve*** have suffered more from the passage of time. ***Rudin*** is a pathetic picture of the type that Turgenev was so fond of depicting, the *génie sans porte-feuille,* a latter-day Hamlet who can only unpack his heart with words, and with his eloquence persuade others to believe in him, and succeed even in persuading himself to believe in himself, until the moment for action comes, when he breaks down. The subjects of ***Smoke*** and [***The Torrents of Spring***] are almost identical; but, whereas [***The Torrents of Spring***] is one of the most poetical of Turgenev's achievements, ***Smoke*** seems today the most banal, and almost to deserve Tolstoy's criticism: "In ***Smoke*** there is hardly any love of anything, and very little pity; there is only love of light and playful adultery; and therefore the poetry of that novel is repulsive." ***On the Eve,*** which tells of a Bulgarian on the eve of the liberation of his country, suffers from being written at a time when real Russians were hard at work at that very task; and it was on this account that the novel found little favour in Russia, as the fiction paled beside the reality.

It was followed by Turgenev's masterpiece, for which time can only heighten one's admiration. ***Fathers and Sons*** is as beautifully constructed as a drama of Sophocles; the events move inevitably to a tragic close. There is not a touch of banality from beginning to end, and not an unnecessary word; the portraits of the old father and mother, the young Kirsanov, and all the minor characters are pefect; and amidst the trivial crowd, Bazarov stands out like Lucifer, the strongest—the only strong character—that Turgenev created, the first Nihilist—for if Turgenev was not the first to invent the word, he was the first to apply it in this sense.

Bazarov is the incarnation of the Lucifer type that recurs again and again in Russian history and fiction, in sharp contrast to the meek humble type of Ivan Durak. Lermontov's Pechorin was in some respects an anticipation of Bazarov; so were the many Russian rebels. He is the man who denies, to whom art is a silly toy, who detests abstractions, knowledge, and the love of Nature; he believes in nothing; he bows to nothing; he can break, but he cannot bend; he does break, and that is the tragedy, but, breaking, he retains his invincible pride, and

> not cowardly he puts off his helmet,

and he dies "valiantly vanquished."

In the pages which describe his death Turgenev reaches the high-water mark of his art, his moving quality, his power, his reserve. For manly pathos they rank among the greatest scenes in literature, stronger than the death of Colonel Newcome and the best of Thackeray. Among English novelists it is, perhaps, only Meredith who has struck such strong, piercing chords, nobler than anything in Daudet or Maupassant, more reserved than anything in Victor Hugo, and worthy of the great poets, of the tragic pathos of Goethe and Dante. The character of Bazarov . . . created a sensation and endless controversy. The revolutionaries thought him a caricature and a libel, the reactionaries a scandalous glorification of the Devil; and impartial men such as Dostoyevsky, who knew the revolutionaries at first hand, thought the type unreal. It is possible that Bazarov was not like the Nihilists of the sixties; but in any case as a figure in fiction, whatever the fact may be, he lives and will continue to live.

In *Virgin Soil,* Turgenev attempted to paint the underground revolutionary movement; here, in the opinion of all Russian judges, he failed. The revolutionaries considered their portraits here more unreal than that of Bazarov; the Conservatives were grossly caricatured; the hero Nezhdanov was a type of a past world, another Rudin, and not in the least like—so those who knew them tell us—the revolutionaries of the day. Solomin, the energetic character in the book, was considered as unreal as Nezhdanov. The wife of the reactionary Sipyagin is a *pastiche* of the female characters of that type in his other books; cleverly drawn, but a completely conventional book character. The redeeming feature in the book is Mariana, the heroine, one of Turgenev's finest ideal women; and it is full, of course, of gems of descriptive writing. The book was a complete failure, and after this Turgenev went back to writing short stories. The result was a great disappointment to Turgenev, who had thought that, by writing a novel dealing with actual life, he would please and reconcile all parties. To this later epoch belong his matchless ***Poems in Prose,*** one of the latest melodies he sounded, a melody played on one string of the lyre, but whose sweetness contained the essence of all his music.

Turgenev's work has a historic as well as an artistic value. He painted the Russian gentry, and the type of gentry that was disappearing, as no one else has done. His landscape painting has been dwelt on; one ought, perhaps, to add that, beautiful as it is, it still belongs to the region of conventional landscape painting; his landscape is the orthodox Russian landscape, and is that of the age of Pushkin, in which no bird except a nightingale is mentioned, no flower except a rose. This convention was not really broken in prose until the advent of Gorky.

Reviewing Turgenev's work as a whole, any one who goes back to his books after a time, and after a course of more modern and rougher, stormier literature, will, I think, be surprised at its excellence and perhaps be inclined to heave a deep sigh of relief. Some of it will appear conventional; he will notice a faint atmosphere of rose-water; he will feel, if he has been reading the moderns, as a traveller feels who, after an exciting but painful journey, through dangerous ways and unpleasant surroundings, suddenly enters a cool garden, where fountains sob between dark cypresses, and swans float majestically on artificial lakes. There is an aroma of syringa in the air; the pleasaunce is artistically laid out, and full of fragrant flowers. But he will not despise that garden for its elegance and its tranquil seclusion, for its trees cast large shadows; the nightingale sings in its thickets, the moon silvers the calm statues, and the sound of music on the waters goes to the heart. Turgenev reminds one of a certain kind of music, beautiful in form, not too passionate and yet full of emotion, Schumann's music, for instance; if Pushkin is the Mozart of Russian literature, Turgenev is the Schumann; not amongst the very greatest, but still a poet, full of inspired lyrical feeling; and a great, a classic artist, the prose Virgil of Russian literature. (pp. 166-75)

Maurice Baring, "The Epoch of Reform," in his An Outline of Russian Literature, *Henry Holt and Company, 1915, pp. 159-95.*

EDWARD GARNETT (essay date 1917)

[Garnett was a prominent editor for several London publishing houses, and discovered or greatly influenced the work of many important English writers, including Joseph Conrad, John Galsworthy, and D. H. Lawrence. He also published several volumes of criticism. In the following excerpt, Garnett offers a chronological survey and appraisal of Turgenev's short stories.]

In addition to his six great novels Turgenev published, between 1846 and his death in 1883, about forty tales which reflect as intimately social atmospheres of the 'thirties, 'forties and 'fifties as do Tchehov's stories atmospheres of the 'eighties and 'nineties. Several of these tales, as ***The Torrents of Spring,*** are of considerable length, but their comparatively simple structure places them definitely in the class of the *conte*. While their form is generally free and straightforward, the narrative, put often in the mouth of a character who by his comments and asides exchanges at will his active rôle for that of a spectator, is capable of the most subtle modulations. An examination of the chronological order of the tales shows how very delicately Turgenev's art is poised between realism and romanticism. In his finest examples, such as **"The Brigadier"** and **"A Lear of the Steppes,"** the two elements fuse perfectly, like the meeting of wave and wind in sea foam. "Nature placed Turgenev between poetry and prose," says Henry James; and if one hazards a definition we should prefer to term Turgenev *a poetic realist*. (pp. 163-64)

[In 1846] appeared **"The Jew,"** a close study, based on a family anecdote, of Semitic double-dealing and family feeling: also **"Three Portraits,"** a more or less faithful ancestral chronicle. This latter tale, though the hero is of the proud, bad, "Satanic" order of the romantic school, is firmly objective, as is also **"Pyetushkov,"** whose lively, instinctive realism is so bold and intimate as to contradict the compliment that the French have paid themselves—that Turgenev ever had need to dress his art by the aid of French mirrors.

Although **"Pyetushkov"** shows us, by a certain open *naïveté* of style, that a youthful hand is at work, it is the hand of a young master carrying out Gogol's satiric realism with finer point, to find a perfect equilibrium free from bias or caricature. The essential strength of the realistic method is developed in **"Pyetushkov"** to its just limits, and note it is the Russian realism carrying the warmth of life into the written page, which warmth the French so often lose in clarifying their impressions and crystallizing them in art. Observe how the reader is transported bodily into Pyetushkov's stuffy room, how the Major fairly boils out of the two pages he lives in, and how Onisim and Vassilissa and the aunt walk and chatter around the stupid Pyetushkov, and laugh at him behind his back in a manner that exhales the vulgar warmth of these people's lower-class world. One sees that the latter holds few secrets for Turgenev. . . . [In 1844] had appeared **"Andrei Kolosov,"** a sincere diagnosis of youth's sentimental expectations, raptures and remorse, in presence of the other sex, in this case a girl who is eager for a suitor. The sketch is characteristically Russian in its analytic honesty, but Turgenev's charm is here lessened by his over-literal exactitude. And passing to **"The Diary of a Superfluous Man,"** we must remark that this famous study of a type of a petty provincial Hamlet reveals a streak of suffused sentimentalism in Turgenev's nature, one which comes to the surface the more subjective is the handling of his theme, and the less his great technical skill in *modelling* his subject is called for. The last-named story belongs to a group with which we must place ***Faust, Yakov Pasinkov, A Correspondence*** and even the tender and charming ***Acia,*** all of which stories, though rich in emotional shades and in beautiful descriptions, are lacking in fine chiselling. The melancholy yearning of the heroes and heroines through failure or misunderstanding, though no doubt true to life, seems to-day too imbued with emotional hues of the Byronic romanticism of the period, and in this small group of stories Turgenev's art is seen definitely dated, even old-fashioned.

In **"The Country Inn,"** we are back on the firm ground of an objective study of village types, with clear, precise outlines, a detailed drawing from nature, strong yet subtle; as is also **"Mumu,"** one based on a household episode that passed before Turgenev's youthful eyes, in which the deaf-mute Gerassim, a house serf, is defrauded first of the girl he loves, and then of his little dog, Mumu, whom he is forced to drown, stifling his pent-up affection, at the caprice of his tyrannical old mistress. The story is a classic example of Turgenev's tender insight and beauty of feeling. As delicate, but more varied in execution is **"The Backwater,"** with its fresh, charming picture of youth's *insouciance* and readiness to take a wrong turning, a story which in its atmospheric freshness and emotional colouring may be compared with Tchehov's studies of youth in *The Seagull*, a play in which the neurotic spiritual descendants of Marie and Nadejda, Veretieff and Steltchinsky, appear and pass into the shadows. This note of the fleetingness of youth and happiness reappears in **"A Tour of the Forest,"** where Turgenev's acute sense of man's ephemeral life in face of the eternity of nature finds full expression. The description, here, of the vast, gloomy, murmuring pine forest, with its cold, dim solitudes, is finely contrasted with the passing outlook of the peasants, Yegor, Kondrat, and the wild Efrem.

The rich colour and perfume of Turgenev's delineation of romantic passion are disclosed when we turn to ***First Love***, which details the fervent adoration of Woldemar, a boy of sixteen, for the fascinating Zinaida, an exquisite creation, who, by her mutability and caressing, mocking caprice keeps her bevy of eager suitors in suspense till at length she yields herself in her passion to Woldemar's father. . . . Here we tremble on the magic borderline between prose and poetry, and the fragrance of blossoming love instincts is felt pervading all the fluctuating impulses of grief, tenderness, pity and regret which combine in the tragic close. The profoundly haunting apostrophe to youth is indeed a pure lyric. Passing to **"Phantoms,"** . . . the truth of Turgenev's confession that spiritually and sensuously he was saturated with the love of woman and ever inspired by it, is confirmed. In his description of Alice, the winged phantom-woman, who gradually casts her spell over the sick hero, luring him to fly with her night after night over the vast expanse of earth, Turgenev has in a mysterious manner, all his own, concentrated the very essence of woman's possessive love. Alice's hungry yearning for self-completion, her pleading arts, her sad submissiveness, her rapture in her hesitating lover's embrace, are artistically a sublimation of all the impressions and instincts by which woman fascinates, and fulfils her purpose of creation. The projection of this shadowy woman's love-hunger on the mighty screen of the night earth, and the merging of her power in men's restless energies, felt and divined through the sweeping tides of nature's incalculable forces, is an inspiration which, in its lesser fashion, invites comparison with Shakespeare's creative vision of nature and the supernatural.

A portrait of Pauline Viardot.

In his treatment of the supernatural Turgenev, however, sometimes missed his mark. **"The Dog"** is of a coarser and indeed of an ordinary texture. With the latter story may be classed **"The Dream,"** curiously Byronic in imagery and atmosphere, and artistically not convincing. Far more sincere, psychologically, is **"Clara Militch,"** a penetrating study of a passionate temperament, a story based on a tragedy of Parisian life. In our opinion **"The Song of Triumphant Love,"** though exquisite in its jewelled mediaeval details, has been overrated by the French, and Turgenev's genius is here seen contorted and cramped by the *genre*.

To return to the tales of the 'sixties. **"Lieutenant Yergunov's Story,"** though its strange atmosphere is cunningly painted, is not of the highest quality, comparing unfavourably with **"The Brigadier,"** the story of the ruined nobleman, Vassily Guskov, with its tender, sub-ironical studies of odd characters, Narkiz and Cucumber. **"The Brigadier"** has a peculiarly fascinating poignancy, and must be prized as one of the rarest of Turgenev's high achievements, even as the connoisseur prizes the original beauty of a fine Meryon etching. The tale is a microcosm of Turgenev's own nature; his love of Nature, his sympathy with all humble, ragged, eccentric, despised human creatures, his unfaltering, keen gaze into character, his perfect eye for relative values in life, all mingle in **"The Brigadier"** to create for us a sense of the vicissitudes of life, of how a generation of human seed springs and flourishes awhile on earth and soon withers away under the menacing gaze of the advancing years.

A complete contrast to **"The Brigadier"** is the sombre and savagely tragic piece of realism, **"An Unhappy Girl."** As a study of a coarse and rapacious nature the portrait of Mr. Ratsch, the Germanized Czech, is a revelation of the depths of human swinishness. Coarse malignancy is here "the power of darkness" which closes, as with a vice, round the figure of the proud, helpless, exquisite girl, Susanna. There is, alas, no exaggeration in this unrelenting, painful story. The scene of Susanna's playing of the Beethoven sonata (chapter xiii.) demonstrates how there can be no truce between a vile animal nature and pure and beautiful instincts, and a faint suggestion symbolic of the national "dark forces" at work in Russian history deepens the impression. The worldly power of greed, lust and envy, ravaging, whether in war or peace, which seize on the defenceless and innocent, as their prey, here triumphs over Susanna, the victim of Mr. Ratsch's violence. The last chapter, the banquet scene, satirizes "the dark forest" of the heart when greed and baseness find their allies in the inertness, sloth or indifference of the ordinary man.

"A Strange Story" has special psychological interest for the English mind in that it gives clues to some fundamental distinctions between the Russian and the Western soul. Sophie's words, "You spoke of the will—that's what must be broken," seems strange to English thought. To be lowly, to be suffering, despised, to *be* unworthy, this desire implies that the Slav character is apt to be lacking in *will,* that it finds it easier to resign itself than to make the effort to be triumphant or powerful. The Russian people's attitude, historically, may, indeed, be compared to a bowl which catches and sustains what life brings it; and the Western people's to a bowl inverted to ward off what fate drops from the impassive skies. The mental attitude of the Russian peasant indeed implies that in blood he is nearer akin to the Asiatics than the Russian ethnologists wish to allow. Certainly in the inner life, intellectually, morally and emotionally, the Russian is a half-way house between the Western and Eastern races, just as geographically he spreads over the two continents.

Brilliant also is **"Knock-Knock-Knock,"** a psychological study, of "a man fated," a Byronic type of hero, dear to the heart of the writers of the romantic period. Sub-Lieutenant Teglev, the melancholy, self-centered hero, whose prepossession of a tragic end nothing can shake, so that he ends by throwing himself into the arms of death, this portrait is most cunningly fortified by the wonderfully life-like atmosphere of the river fog in which the suicide is consummated. Turgenev's range of mood is disclosed in **"Punin and Baburin,"** a leisurely reminiscence of his mother's household; but the delicious blending of irony and kindness in the treatment of both Punin and Baburin atones for the lengthy conclusion. . . . In considering **"A Lear of the Steppes,"** ***The Torrents of Spring*** and **"A Living Relic,"** we shall sum up here our brief survey of Turgenev's achievement in the field of the *conte.*

In ***The Torrents of Spring*** the charm, the grace, the power of Turgenev's vision are seen bathing his subject, revealing all its delicate lineaments in a light as fresh and tender as that of a day of April sunlight in Italy. *Torrents* of Spring, not Spring Floods, be it remarked, is the true significance of the Russian, telling of a moment of the year when all the forces of Nature are leaping forth impetuously, the mounting sap, the hill streams, the mating birds, the blood in the veins of youth. The opening perhaps is a little over-leisurely, this description of the Italian confectioner's family, and its fortunes in Frankfort, but how delightful is the contrast in racial spirit between the pedantic German shop-manager, Herr Klüber and Pantaleone, and the lovely Gemma. But the long opening prelude serves as a foil to heighten the significant story of the seduction of the youthful Sanin by Maria Nikolaevna, that clear-eyed "huntress of men"; one of the most triumphant feminine portraits in the whole range of fiction. The spectator feels that this woman in her ruthless charm is the incarnation of a cruel principle in Nature, while we watch her preparing to strike her talons into her fascinated, struggling prey. Her spirit's essence, in all its hard, merciless joy of conquest, is disclosed by Turgenev in his rapid, yet exhaustive glances at her disdainful treatment of her many lovers, and of her cynical log of a husband. The extraordinarily clear light in the narrative, that of spring mountain air, waxes stronger towards the climax, and the artistic effort of the whole is that of some exquisite Greek cameo, with figures of centaurs and fleeing nymphs and youthful shepherds; though the post-script indeed is an excrescence which detracts from the main impression of pure, classic outlines.

Not less perfect as art though far slighter in scope is the exquisite **"A Living Relic,"** one of the last of ***A Sportsman's Sketches.*** Along with the narrator we pass, in a step, from the clear sunlight and freshness of early morning, "when the larks' songs seemed steeped in dew," into the "little wattled shanty with its burden of a woman's suffering," poor Lukerya's, who lies, summer after summer, resigned to her living death. . . . (pp. 164-75)

Lukerya tells her story. How one night she could not sleep, and, thinking of her lover, rose to listen to a nightingale in the garden; how half-dreaming she fell from the top stairs—and now she lives on, a little shrivelled mummy. Something is broken inside her body, and the doctors all shake their heads over her case. Her lover, Polyakov, has married another girl, a good sweet woman. "He couldn't stay a bachelor all his life, and they have children."

And Lukerya? All is not blackness in her wasted life. She is grateful for people's kindness to her. . . . She can hear everything, see everything that comes near her shed—the nesting swallows, the bees, the doves cooing on the roof. Lying alone in the long hours she can smell every scent from the garden, the flowering buckwheat, the lime tree. The priest, the peasant girls, sometimes a pilgrim woman, come and talk to her, and a little girl, a pretty, fair little thing, waits on her. She has her religion, her strange dreams, and sometimes, in her poor, struggling little voice that wavers like a thread of smoke, she tries to sing, as of old. But she is waiting for merciful death—which now is nigh her.

Infinitely tender in the depth of understanding is this gem of art, and **"A Living Relic's"** perfection is determined by Turgenev's scrutiny of the warp and woof of life, in which the impassive forces of Nature, indifferent alike to human pain or human happiness, pursue their implacable way, weaving unwittingly the mesh of joy, anguish, resignation, in the breast of all sentient creation. It is in the *spiritual perspective* of the picture, in the vision that sees the whole in the part, and the part in the whole, that Turgenev so far surpasses all his European rivals.

To those critics, Russian and English, who naïvely slur over the aesthetic qualities of a masterpiece, such as **"A Lear of the Steppes,"** or fail to recognize all that aesthetic perfection implies, we address these concluding remarks. **"A Lear of the Steppes"** is great in art, because it is a living organic whole, springing from the deep roots of life itself; and the innumerable works of art that are fabricated and pasted together from an ingenious plan—works that do not grow from the inevitability of things—appear at once insignificant or false in comparison.

In examining the art, the artist will note Turgenev's method of introducing his story. Harlov, the Lear of the story, is brought forward with such force on the threshold that all eyes resting on his figure cannot but follow his after-movements. And absolute conviction gained, all the artist's artful after-devices and subtle presentations and sidelights on the story are not apparent under the straightforward ease and the seeming carelessness with which the narrator describes his boyish memories. Then the inmates of Harlov's household, his two daughters, and a crowd of minor characters, are brought before us as persons in the tragedy, and we see that all these people are living each from the innate laws of his being, apparently independently of the author's scheme. This conviction, that the author has no prearranged plan, convinces us that in the story we are living a piece of life: here we are verily plunging into life itself.

And the story goes on flowing easily and naturally till the people of the neighbourhood, the peasants, the woods and fields around, are known by us as intimately as is any neighbourhood in life. Suddenly a break—the tragedy is upon us. Suddenly the terrific forces that underlie human life, even the meanest of human lives, burst on us astonished and breathless, precisely as a tragedy comes up to the surface and bursts on us in real life: everybody runs about dazed, annoyed, futile; we watch other people sustaining their own individuality inadequately in the face of the monstrous new events which go their fatal way logically, events which leave the people huddled and useless and gasping. And destruction having burst out of life, life slowly returns to its old grooves—with a difference to us, the difference in the relation of people one to another that a death or a tragedy always leaves to the survivors. Marvellous in its truth is Turgenev's analysis of the situation after Harlov's death, marvellous is the simple description of the neighbourhood's attitude to the Harlov family, and marvellous is the lifting of the scene on the after-life of Harlov's daughters. In the pages . . . on these women, Turgenev flashes into the reader's mind an extraordinary sense of the inevitability of these women's natures, of their innate growth fashioning their after-lives as logically as a beech puts out beech-leaves and an oak oak-leaves. Through Turgenev's single glimpse at their fortunes one knows the whole intervening fifteen years; he has carried us into a new world; yet it is the old world; one needs to know no more. It is life arbitrary but inevitable, life so clarified by art that it is absolutely interpreted; but life with all the sense of mystery that nature breathes around it in its ceaseless growth.

This sense of inevitability and of the mystery of life which Turgenev gives us in **"A Lear of the Steppes"** is the highest demand we can make from art. If we contrast with it two examples of Turgenev's more "romantic" manner, ***Acia,*** though it gives us a sense of mystery, is not inevitable: the end is *faked* to suit the artist's purpose, and thus, as in other ways, it is far inferior to **"Lear."** ***Faust*** has consummate charm in its strange atmosphere of the supernatural mingling with things earthly, but it is not, as is **"A Lear of the Steppes,"** life seen from the surface to the revealed depths; it is a revelation of the strange forces in life, presented beautifully; but it is rather an idea, a problem to be worked out by certain characters, than a piece of life inevitable and growing. When an artist creates in us the sense of inevitability, then his work is at its highest, and is obeying Nature's law of growth, unfolding from out itself as inevitably as a tree or a flower or a human being unfolds from out itself. Turgenev at his highest never quits Nature, yet he always uses the surface, and what is apparent, to disclose her most secret principles, her deepest potentialities, her inmost laws of being, and whatever he presents he presents clearly and simply. This combination of powers marks only the few supreme artists. Even great masters often fail in perfect *naturalness:* Tolstoy's *The Death of Ivan Ilytch,* for instance, one of the most powerful stories ever written, has too little of what is typical of the whole of life, too much that is strained towards the general purpose of the story, to be perfectly *natural.* Turgenev's special feat in fiction is that his characters reveal themselves by the most ordinary details of their everyday life; and while these details are always giving us the whole life of the people, and their inner life as well, the novel's significance is being built up simply out of these details, built up by the same process, in fact, as Nature creates for us a single strong impression out of a multitude of little details.

Again, Turgenev's power as a poet comes in, whenever he draws a commonplace figure, to make it bring with it a sense of the mystery of its existence. In ***Lear*** the steward Kvitsinsky plays a subsidiary part; he has apparently no significance in the story, and very little is told about him. But who does not perceive that Turgenev looks at and presents the figure of this man in a manner totally different from the way any clever novelist of the second rank would look at and use him? Kvitsinsky, in Turgenev's hands, is an individual with all the individual's mystery in his glance, his coming and going, his way of taking things; but he is a part of the household's breath, of its very existence; he breathes the atmosphere naturally and creates an atmosphere of his own.

It is, then, in his marvellous sense of the growth of life that Turgenev is superior to most of his rivals. Not only did he observe life minutely and comprehensively, but he reproduced it as a constantly growing phenomenon, growing naturally, not accidentally or arbitrarily. For example, in ***A House of Gentlefolk,*** take Lavretsky's and Liza's changes of mood when they are falling in love with one another; it is Nature herself in them changing very delicately and insensibly; we feel that the whole picture is alive, not an effect cut out from life, and cut off from it at the same time, like a bunch of cut flowers, an effect which many clever novelists often give us. And in **"Lear"** we feel that the life in Harlov's village is still going on, growing yonder, still growing with all its mysterious sameness and changes, when, in Turgenev's last words, "The storyteller ceased, and we talked a little longer, and then parted, each to his home." (pp.176-83)

Edward Garnett, in his Turgenev: A Study, *W. Collins Sons & Co., Ltd., 1917, 206 p.*

PRINCE D. S. MIRSKY (essay date 1927)

[Mirsky was a Russian prince who fled his country after the Bolshevik Revolution and settled in London. While in England, he wrote two important histories of Russian literature, Contemporary Russian Literature, *published in 1926, and* A History of Russian Literature, *which appeared the following year. These works were later combined and portions were published in 1949 as* A History of Russian Literature. *In 1932, having reconciled himself to the Soviet regime, Mirsky returned to the U.S.S.R. He continued to write literary criticism, but his work eventually ran afoul of Soviet censors and he was exiled to Siberia. He disappeared in 1937. In the following excerpt, first published in Mirsky's 1927 study, he traces Turgenev's career as a writer and assesses his place in Russian literature.]*

Turgénev's first attempt at prose fiction was in the wake of Lérmontov, from whom he derived the romantic halo round his first Pechórin-like heroes (**"Andréy Kólosov," "The Duelist," "Three Portraits"**) and the method of the intensified anecdote (**"The Jew"**). In ***A Sportsman's Sketches,*** begun in 1847, he was to free himself from the romantic conventions of these early stories by abandoning all narrative skeleton and limiting himself to "slices of life." But even for some time after that date he remained unable in his more distinctly narrative work to hit on what was to become his true manner.

Thus, for instance, **"Three Meetings"** is a story of pure atmosphere woven round a very slender theme, saturated in its descriptions of moonlit nights, with an excess of romantic and "poetical" poetry. **"The Diary of a Superfluous Man"** is reminiscent of Gógol and of the young Dostoyévsky, developing as it does tthe Dostoyevskian theme of humiliated human dignity and of morbid delight in humiliation, but aspiring to a Gógol-like and very un-Turgenevian verbal intensity. (The phrase "a superfluous man" had an extraordinary fortune and is still applied by literary and social historians to the type of ineffective idealist portrayed so often by Turgénev and his contemporaries.) At last **"Mumú,"** the well-known story of the deaf serf and his favorite dog, and of how his mistress ordered it to be destroyed, is a "philanthropic" story in the tradition of *The Greatcoat* and of *Poor Folk,* where an intense sensation of pity is arrived at by methods that strike the modern reader as illegitimate, working on the nerves rather than on the imagination.

A Sportsman's Sketches, on the other hand, written in 1847-51, belongs to the highest, most lasting, and least questionable achievement of Turgénev and of Russian realism. The book describes the casual and various meetings of the narrator during his wanderings with a gun and a dog in his native district of Bólkhov and in the surrounding country. The sketches are arranged in a random order and have no narrative skeleton, containing nothing but accounts of what the narrator saw and heard. Some of them are purely descriptive, of scenery or character; others consist of conversation, addressed to the narrator or overheard. At times there is a dramatic *motive,* but the development is only hinted at by the successive glimpses the narrator gets of his personages. This absolute matter-of-factness and studious avoidance of everything artificial and made-up were the most prominent characteristics of the book when it appeared—it was a new genre. The peasants are described from the outside, as seen (or overseen) by the narrator, not in their intimate, unoverlooked life. As I have said, they are drawn with obviously greater sympathy than the upper classes. The squires are represented as either vulgar, or cruel, or ineffective. In the peasants, Turgénev emphasized their humanity, their imaginativeness, their poetical and artistic giftedness, their sense of dignity, their intelligence. It was in this quiet and unobtrusive way that the book struck the readers with the injustice and ineptitude of serfdom. Now, when the issue of serfdom is a thing of the past, the ***Sketches*** seem once more as harmless and as innocent as a book can be, and it requires a certain degree of historical imagination to reconstruct the atmosphere in which they had the effect of a mild bombshell.

Judged as literature, the ***Sketches*** are frequently, if not always, above praise. In the representation of rural scenery and peasant character, Turgénev never surpassed such masterpieces as **"The Singers"** and **"Bézhin Meadow." "The Singers"** especially, even after ***First Love*** and ***Fathers and Sons,*** may claim to be his crowning achievement and the quintessence of all the most characteristic qualities of his art. It is the description of a singing-match at a village pub between the peasant Yáshka Túrok and a tradesman from Zhízdra. The story is representative of Turgénev's manner of painting his peasants; he does not one-sidedly idealize them; the impression produced by the match, with its revelation of the singers' high sense of artistic values, is qualified by the drunken orgy the artists lapse into after the match is over and the publican treats Yáshka to the fruit of his victory. **"The Singers"** may also be taken as giving Turgénev's prose at its highest and most characteristic. It is careful and in a sense artificial, but the impression of absolute ease and simplicity is exhaled from every word and turn of phrase. It is a carefully *selected* language, rich, but curiously avoiding words and phrases, crude or journalese, that might jar on the reader. The beauty of the landscape painting is due chiefly to the choice of exact and delicately suggestive and descriptive words. There is no ornamental imagery after the manner of Gógol, no rhetorical rhythm, no splendid cadences. But the sometime poet's and poets' disciple's hand is evident in the careful, varied, and unobtrusively perfect balance of the phrases.

The first thing Turgénev wrote after the ***Sketches*** and **"Mumú"** was **"The Inn."** Like **"Mumú"** it turns on the unjust and callous treatment of serfs by their masters, but the sentimental, "philanthropic" element is replaced for the first time in his work by the characteristic Turgenevian atmosphere of tragic necessity. **"The Inn"** was followed in 1853-61 by a succession of masterpieces. They were divided by the author himself into two categories: novels and *nouvelles* (in Russian, *romány* and *póvesti*). The difference between the two forms in the case of Turgénev is not so much one of size or scope as that the novels aim at social significance and at the statement of social problems, while the *nouvelles* are pure and simple stories of emotional incident, free from civic preoccupations. Each novel includes a narrative kernel similar in subject and bulk to that of a *nouvelle,* but it is expanded into an answer to some burning problem of the day. The novels of this period are ***Rúdin, A Nest of Gentlefolk, On the Eve,*** and ***Fathers and Sons;*** the *nouvelles,* ***Two Friends, A Quiet Spot, Yákov Pásynkov, A Correspondence, Faust, Ásya,*** and ***First Love.*** It will be noticed that the civic novels belong chiefly to the age of reform (1856-61), while the purely private *nouvelles* predominate in the reactionary years that precede it. But even "on the eve" of the Emancipation, Turgénev could be sufficiently detached from civic issues to write the perfectly uncivic ***First Love.***

The novels of Turgénev are, thus, those of his stories in which he, voluntarily, submitted to the obligation of writing works of social significance. This significance is arrived at in the first place by the nature of the characters, who are made to be representative of phases successively traversed by the Russian intellectual. Rúdin is the progressive idealist of the forties; Lavrétsky, the more Slavophil idealist of the same generation; Eléna, in ***On the Eve,*** personifies the vaguely generous and active fermentation of the generation immediately preceding the reforms; Bazárov, the militant materialism of the generation of 1860. Secondly, the social significance is served by the insertion of numerous *conversations* between the characters on topics of current interest (Slavophilism and Westernism, the ability of the educated Russian to act, the place in life of art and science, and so on). These conversations are what especially distinguished Turgénev's novels from his *nouvelles.* They have little relation to the action, and not always much more to the character of the representative hero. They were what the civic critics seized upon for comment, but they are certainly the least permanent and most dating part of the novels. There frequently occur characters who are introduced with no other motive but to do the talking, and whom one would have rather wished away. But the central, representative characters—the heroes—are in most cases not only representative, but alive. Rúdin, the first in date, is one of the masterpieces of nineteenth-century character drawing. An eminent French novelist (who is old-fashioned enough still to prefer Turgénev to Tolstóy, Dostoyévsky, and Chékhov) has pointed out to me the wonderfully delicate mastery with which the impression produced by Rúdin on the other characters and on the reader is made gradually to change from the first appearance in the glamour of superiority to the bankruptcy of his pusillanimous breach with Natália, then to the gloomy glimpse of the undone and degenerate man, and to the redeeming flash of his heroic and ineffective death on the barricades of the faubourg St. Antoine. The French writer thought this delicate change of attitude unique in fiction. Had he known more Russian, he would have realized that Turgénev had merely been a highly intelligent and creative pupil of Púshkin's. Like Púshkin in *Evgény Onégin,* Turgénev does not analyze and dissect his heroes, as Tolstóy and Dostoyévsky would have done; he does not uncover their souls; he only conveys their atmosphere, partly by showing how they are reflected in others, partly by an exceedingly delicate and thinly woven aura of suggestive accompaniment—a method that at once betrays its origin in a *poetic* novel. Where Turgénev attempts to show us the *inner* life of his heroes by other methods, he always fails—the description of Eléna's feelings for Insárov in ***On the Eve*** is distinctly painful reading. Turgénev had to use all the power of self-criticism and self-restraint to avoid the pitfall of false poetry and false beauty.

Still, the characters, constructed though they are by means of suggestion, not dissection, are the vivifying principle of Turgénev's stories. Like most Russian novelists he makes character predominate over plot, and it is the characters that we remember. The population of Turgénev's novels (apart from the peasant stories) may be classified under several heads. First comes the division into the Philistines and the elect. The Philistines are the direct descendants of Gógol's characters—heroes of *póshlost,* self-satisfied inferiority. Of course there is not a trace in them of Gógol's exuberant and grotesque caricature; the irony of Turgénev is fine, delicate, unobtrusive, hardly at all aided by any obvious comical devices. On the other side are the elect, the men and women with a sense of values, superior to those of vegetable enjoyment and social position. The men, again, are very different from the women. The fair sex comes out distinctly more advantageously from the hands of Turgénev. The strong, pure, passionate, and virtuous woman, opposed to the weak, potentially generous, but ineffective and ultimately shallow man, was introduced into literature by Púshkin, and recurs again and again in the work of the realists, but nowhere more insistently than in Turgénev's. His heroines are famous all the world over and have done much to spread a high reputation of Russian womanhood. Moral force and courage are the keynote to Turgénev's heroine—the power to sacrifice all worldly considerations to passion (Natália in ***Rúdin***), or all happiness to duty (Líza in ***A Nest of Gentlefolk***). But what goes home to the general reader in these women is not so much the height of their moral beauty as the extraordinary *poetical* beauty woven round them by the delicate and perfect art of their begetter. Turgénev reaches his highest perfection in this, his own and unique art, in two of the shorter stories, ***A Quiet Spot*** and ***First Love.*** In the first, the purely Turgenevian, tragic, poetic, and rural atmosphere reaches its maximum of concentration, and the richness of suggestion that conditions the characters surpasses all he ever wrote. It transcends mere fiction and rises into poetry, not by the beauty of the single words and parts, but by sheer force of suggestion and saturated significance. ***First Love*** stands somewhat apart from the rest of Turgénev's work. Its atmosphere is cooler and clearer, more reminiscent of the rarefied air of Lérmontov. The heroes—Zinaída and the narrator's father (who is traditionally supposed to portray the author's own father)—are more *animal* and vital than Turgénev usually allows his heroes to be. Their passions are tense and clear-cut, free from vagueness and idealistic haze, selfish, but with a selfishness that is redeemed by self-justifying vitality. Unique in the whole of his work, ***First Love*** is the least relaxing of Turgénev's stories. But, characteristically, the story is told from the point of view of the boy admirer of Zinaída and of his pangs of adolescent jealousy for his rival and father. (pp. 188-93)

The best of the novels and ultimately the most important of Turgénev's works is ***Fathers and Sons,*** one of the greatest novels of the nineteenth century. Here Turgénev triumphantly solved two tasks that he had been attempting to solve: to create a living masculine character not based on introspection, and to overcome the contradiction between the imaginative and the social theme. ***Fathers and Sons*** is Turgenev's only novel where the social problem is distilled without residue into art, and leaves no bits of undigested journalism sticking out. Here the delicate and poetic narrative art of Turgénev reaches its perfection, and Bazárov is the only one of Turgénev's men who is worthy to stand by the side of his women. But nowhere perhaps does the essential debility and feminineness of his genius come out more clearly than in this, the best of his novels. Bazárov is a strong man, but he is painted with admiration and wonder by one to whom a strong man is something abnormal. Turgénev is incapable of making his hero triumph, and to spare him the inadequate treatment that would have been his lot in the case of success, he lets him die, not from any natural development of the nature of the subject, but by the blind decree of fate. For fate, blind chance, crass casualty, presides over Turgénev's universe as it does over Hardy's, but Turgénev's people submit to it with passive resignation. Even the heroic Bazárov dies as resigned as a flower in the field, with silent courage but without protest.

It would be wrong to affirm that after ***Fathers and Sons*** Turgénev's genius began to decline, but at any rate it ceased to grow. What was more important for his contemporaries, he lost touch with Russian life and thus ceased to count as a *contemporary* writer, though he remained a permanent classic. His attempts again to tackle the problems of the day in ***Smoke*** and in ***Virgin Soil*** only emphasized his loss of touch with the new age. ***Smoke*** is the worst-constructed of his novels: it contains a beautiful love story, which is interrupted and interlarded with conversations that have no relation to its characters and are just dialogued journalism on the thesis that all intellectual and educated Russia was nothing but smoke. ***Virgin Soil*** is a complete failure, and was immediately recognized as such. Though it contains much that is in the best manner of Turgénev (the characters of the bureaucratic-aristocratic Sipyágin family are among his best satirical drawings), the whole novel is disqualified by an entirely uninformed and necessarily false conception of what he was writing about. His presentation of the revolutionaries of the seventies is like an account of a foreign country by one who had never seen it.

But while Turgénev had lost the power of writing for the times, he had not lost the genius of creating those wonderful love stories which are his most personal contribution to the world's literature. Pruned of its conversations, ***Smoke*** is a beautiful *nouvelle,* comparable to the best he wrote in the fifties, and so is ***The Torrents of Spring.*** Both are on the same subject: a young man loves a pure and sweet young girl but forsakes her for a mature and lascivious woman of thirty, who is loved by many and for whom he is the plaything of a fleeting passion. The characters of Irína, the older woman in ***Smoke,*** and of Gemma, the Italian girl in ***The Torrents of Spring,*** are among the most beautiful in the whole of his gallery. ***The Torrents of Spring*** is given a retrospective setting, and in most of the other stories of this last period the scene is set in the old times of pre-Reform Russia. Some of these stories are purely objective little tragedies (one of the best is **"A Lear of the Steppes"**); others are non-narrative fragments from reminiscences, partly continuing the manner and theme of ***A Sportsman's Sketches.*** There are also the purely biographical reminiscences, including interesting accounts of the author's acquaintance with Púshkin and Belínsky and the remarkable account of **"The Execution of Troppmann,"** which in its fascinated objectivity is one of the most terrible descriptions ever made of an execution.

There had always been in Turgénev a poetic or romantic vein, as opposed to the prevailing realistic atmosphere of his principal work. His attitude to nature had always been lyrical, and he had always had a lurking desire to transcend the limits imposed on the Russian novelist by the dogma of realism. Not only did he begin his career as a lyrical poet and end it with his ***Poems in Prose,*** but even in his most realistic and civic novels the construction and atmosphere are mainly lyrical. ***A Sportsman's Sketches*** includes many purely lyrical pages of natural description, and to the period of his highest maturity belongs that remarkable piece **"A Tour in the Forest,"** where for the first time Turgénev's conception of indifferent and eternal nature opposed to transient man found expression in a sober and simple prose that attains poetry by the simplest means of unaided suggestion. His last period begins with the purely lyrical prose poem **"Enough"** and culminates in the ***Poems in Prose.*** At the same time the fantastic element asserts itself. In some stories (**"The Dog," "Knock! Knock! Knock!"** and **"The Story of Father Alexis"**) it appears only in the form of a suggestion of mysterious presences in an ordinary realistic setting. The most important of these stories is his last, **"Clara Mílich,"** written under the influence of spiritualistic readings and musings. It is as good as most of his stories of purely human love, but the mysterious element is somewhat difficult to appreciate quite whole-heartedly today. It has all the inevitable flatness of Victorian spiritualism. In a few stories Turgénev freed himself from the conventions of realistic form and wrote such things as the purely visionary **"Phantoms"** and **"The Song of Triumphant Love,"** written in the style of an Italian *novella* of the sixteenth century. There can be no greater contrast than between these and such stories of Dostoyévsky as *The Double* or *Mr. Prokhárchin.* Dostoyévsky, with the material of sordid reality, succeeds in building fabrics of weird fantasy. Turgénev, in spite of all the paraphernalia introduced, never succeeded in freeing himself from the second-rate atmosphere of the medium's consulting room. **"The Song of Triumphant Love"** shows up his limitation of another kind—the inadequacy of his language for treating subjects of insufficient reality. This limitation Turgénev shared with all his contemporaries (except Tolstóy and Leskóv). They did not have a sufficient feeling of words, of language as language (as Púshkin and Gógol had had), to make it serve them in unfamiliar fields. Words for them were only signs of familiar things and familiar feelings. Language had entered with them on a strictly limited engagement—it would serve only in so far as it had not to leave the everyday realities of the nineteenth century.

The same stylistic limitation is apparent in Turgénev's last and most purely lyrical work, ***Poems in Prose.*** (Turgénev originally entitled them ***Senilia***; the present title was given them with the author's silent approval by the editor of the *Messenger of Europe,* where they first appeared.) They are a series of short prose fragments, most of them gathered round some more or less narrative kernel. They are comparable in construction to the objectivated lyrics of the French Parnassians, who used visual symbols to express their subjective experience. Sometimes they verge on the fable and the apologue. In these "poems" is to be found the final and most hopeless expression of Turgénev's agnostic pessimism, of his awe of unresponsive nature and necessity, and of his pitying contempt for human futility. The best of the "poems" are those where these feelings are given an ironic garb. The more purely poetical ones have suffered from time, and date too distinctly from about 1880—a date that can hardly add beauty to anything connected with it. The one that closes the series, **"The Russian Language,"** has suffered particularly—not from time only, but from excessive handling. It displays in a condensed form all the weakness and ineffectiveness of Turgénev's style when it was divorced from concrete and familiar *things.* The art of eloquence had been lost.

Turgénev was the first Russian writer to charm the Western reader. There are still retarded Victorians who consider him the only Russian writer who is not disgusting. But for most lovers of Russian he has been replaced by spicier food. Turgénev was very nineteenth century, perhaps the most representative man of its latter part, whether in Russia or west of it. He was a Victorian, a man of compromise, more Victorian than any one of his Russian contemporaries. This made him so acceptable to Europe, and this has now made him lose so much of his reputation there. Turgénev struck the West at first as something new, something typically Russian. But it is hardly necessary to insist today on the fact that he is not in any sense representative of Russia as a whole. He was representative only of his class—the idealistically educated middle gentry, tending already to become a non-class intelligentsia—and of his generation, which failed to gain real touch with Russian realities, which failed to find itself a place in life and which, ineffective in the sphere of action, produced one of the most beautiful literary growths of the nineteenth century. In his day Turgénev was regarded as a leader of opinion on social problems; now this seems strange and unintelligible. Long since, the issues that he fought out have ceased to be of any actual interest. Unlike Tolstóy or Dostoyévsky, unlike Griboyédov, Púshkin, Lérmontov, and Gógol, unlike Chaadáyev, Grigóriev, and Herzen—Turgénev is no longer a teacher or even a ferment. His work has become pure art—and perhaps it has won more from this transformation than it has lost. It has taken a permanent place in the Russian tradition, a place that stands above the changes of taste or the revolutions of time. We do not seek for wisdom or guidance in it, but it is impossible to imagine a time when **"The Singers,"** ***A Quiet Spot, First Love,*** or ***Fathers and Sons*** will cease to be among the most cherished of joys to Russian readers. (pp. 194-98)

Prince D. S. Mirsky, "The Age of Realism: The Novelists (I)," in his A History of Russian Literature Comprising "A History of Russian Literature" and "Contemporary Russian Literature," *edited by Francis J. Whitfield, Alfred A. Knopf, 1949, pp. 169-204.*

ANDRÉ MAUROIS (essay date 1931)

[Maurois was a French man of letters whose versatility is reflected in the broad scope of his work. However, it was as a biographer that he made his most significant contribution to literature. Following the tradition of Lytton Strachey's "new" biography, Maurois believed that a biography should adhere to historical facts regardless of possibly tarnishing the images or legends of biographical subjects. Most of Maurois's works have been translated into English and many of his biographies were widely read in America, including Ariel: The Life of Shelley *and* Proust: A Biography. *Here, Maurois acknowledges the limitations of Tur-*

genev's fictional world but discovers poetic truth in his blend of realism and pure art. Maurois's remarks were first published in French in 1931.]

Literary quarrels are one of those violent and futile games without which, it seems, men find their brief existence too long to be endured. There is no good reason why two different writers should be thought to compete for the favours of the reader, nor why their books should be regarded as waging an internecine war. But, just as in the seventeenth century the admirers of Racine behaved like jealous lovers intent on purging their mistresses' minds of every trace or hint of Corneille, so, too, in our own age has Russian literature aroused in Western Europe strange and guileless passions. Those who give to Dostoievsky a fanatical devotion (very natural and very proper) seem to think that they must, therefore, turn their backs on Tolstoy, and, more particularly, on Turgenev. (p. 295)

To blame Turgenev for not writing like Dostoievsky is about as sensible as to feel resentment because an apple tree does not produce peaches.

But surely we may be allowed to classify fruits in an order of preference? Obviously we cannot expect to find peaches on a bramble bush: but are we not entitled to say that in the general scale of fruit values, the peach is superior, in our opinion, to the blackberry? If, say the ardent followers of Dostoievsky or Tolstoy, one compares the worlds created by the three great Russian novelists, there can be no denying that Turgenev's is perfectly consistent with the man, that it is, in fact, the most Turgenevian of all possible worlds. Admittedly it has a certain charm and elegance: up to a certain point it is even true. That we must all agree. But, granted its merits, it remains a very small world. The reader can very soon make its complete circuit. After reading two of the novels he will know the typical Turgenev "setting" like the back of his hand. It is unvaryingly, or almost unvaryingly, a Russian country house belonging to aristocrats of moderate means, containing the "old familiar round-bellied chests-of-drawers with their brass fittings, the white painted chairs with their oval backs, the chandeliers with their crystal lustres"—and, we might add, the narrow beds with their old-fashioned striped curtains, the bedside table with its icons, the shabby carpets spotted with wax-droppings. The landscapes also run true to form: the steppe in the administrative area of Oriol, the copses of birch and aspen, the eternal mists. One knows, too, his human types: the Russian Hamlet—Bazarov and Rudin: the old gentleman who is a relic of the eighteenth century: the young civil servant, contented and ambitious: the talkative and ineffectual revolutionary. The same is true of the women. They can be divided into two or three recognizable groups: the sweet young girl, all perfection and frequently pious: Tatiana in ***Smoke,*** Lisa in ***A House of Gentlefolk;*** the temperamental woman, dangerous and misunderstood: Irene, in ***Smoke***; finally, the Marianne of ***Virgin Soil,*** physically strong, unmarried, with grey eyes, a straight nose and thin lips which seem to express a deep-seated need for struggle and devotion. These garrulous men, infirm of purpose, these passionate and generous-hearted women make up a tiny, shut-in universe. How far removed, we tell ourselves, from those serried ranks of human beings to whom Dostoievsky and Tolstoy could give life and movement.

True, no doubt. But I cannot, for the life of me, see why an artist's world should be found lacking on the mere score of its being small. The quality of a work of art is not to be measured in terms of size, any more than it is to be judged by the importance of the object represented. We might just as well complain of the triviality of a piece of still-life. We might just as well say that Vermeer was not a great painter because he painted only small interiors, or that Chardin is a lesser artist than Cormon because he drew his models from one social level only (the hard-working lower middle class of Paris). The truth seems to lie all in the other direction, that it is often an excellent thing for the artist to work within a strictly limited field. It is impossible to know everything well, and a small picture painted with close attention to detail may teach us more about human beings than a "vast and sprawling fresco". . . . It matters little to me that in ***A Sportsman's Sketches,*** Turgenev gives us nothing but the portraits of a few peasants living round Spasskoïe. In doing so he tells me more about the Russia of 1830 than I could learn from any number of long books about Russian history.

Besides, though the types with which Turgenev works belong to a fairly small social species, within that species there are numerous and well-defined variants. In every Turgenev novel, so it is said, you will find the temperamental woman and the Russian Hamlet. Perhaps, but these different Hamlets are none of them really alike. Bazarov is not the same man as Rudin. Bazarov is as silent as Rudin is talkative. He is misanthropic, desperate and moody. He is capable of love, whereas the other is not. Lavretzky, in ***A House of Gentlefolk,*** is another Hamlet type, but less complex, more simple-minded. Nejdanov, in ***Virgin Soil,*** is a Hamlet with something in him of Julien Sorel, but an aristocratic Julien, which makes of him quite a different character. The same can be said of the peasants in ***A Sportsman's Sketches.*** They have certain features in common, as is only natural, but they are thoroughly individualized. One might, perhaps, with more reason complain of the monotony of Turgenev's women, but the same defect is to be found in other great novelists. Most men are obsessed by a certain type of woman, and find it difficult not to run after her. (pp. 296-99)

Another complaint is that Turgenev was deficient in creative genius.

We must be quite clear about the meaning of that word, creative. Is a novelist to produce his characters from some unimaginable void, or should he, more simply, try to paint nature as he has seen it? . . . [We] know what Turgenev's own answer would be. "I have never", he said, "been able to create anything simply from my imagination. All my characters have to be modelled on real people." (p. 299)

Artistic creation is not creation *ex nihilo*. It is a re-grouping of elements taken from the real world. It would be easy enough to show that even the strangest tales, those which seem to us to be furthest from actual observation, such as *Gulliver's Travels,* Poe's *Tales,* the *Divine Comedy* and Jarry's *Ubu-roi,* owed much to memories, just as Leonardo's monsters and the devils carved on the capitals of cathedral pillars were constructed with the help of the features of human beings and of animals, or as a mechanical invention is not a creation of matter, but a new assemblage of parts already known. (p. 301)

But though creation *ex nihilo* is impossible, it remains true that the novelist may keep, more or less, close to nature. "I am a realist," said Turgenev, and maintained that the sole duty of the artist is to paint honestly what he sees. But the problem is more complex than that. (pp. 301-02)

If we are to judge works of art it is essential for us to understand that the two ideas of realism and poetry are not contradictory (and that is all that Turgenev's doctrine amounted to). A novel does not resemble life—common sense tells us that. It is limited in scope, it is organized, it is composed. But the ordered whole must be made up of details which are true to life, and it must, in itself, be convincing. A Shakespearean tragedy is not a "slice of life", though the characters in it are living beings. Polonius is a genuine courtier, Hamlet a real young man. A novelist must no more attempt to paint without a model than a dramatist. In the novels of Turgenev you will never find a character who gives the impression that he is playing a part in a melodrama. The sportsmen are "real" sportsmen who see things with the eye of a sportsman. The peasants talk like peasants and do not react to nature as a painter would. The women are feminine. I said, a while back, that Turgenev's world is small. But, precisely because he had the courage to limit his universe to what he could himself observe, he is one of those rare novelists who almost never lie.

But if Turgenev is a realist because his details are true to life, it is by the choice he makes of them that he proves himself to be an artist. . . . It was always by the evocation of . . . details that Turgenev handled his descriptions. Here are two examples, taken at random. The first is from **"A Lear of the Steppes":**

> So profound was the silence that one could hear at a distance of more than a hundred paces, a squirrel skipping across the dead leaves which already lay thick on the ground, or the faint crack of a dead branch breaking off from the top of a tree and rebounding from other branches in its fall until it reached the ground, where it lay in the withered grass, never to move again.

And this, from ***A House of Gentlefolk:***

> Peace had descended on the salon, where nothing was to be heard but the faint spitting of the wax candles, the sound of a hand striking the card table, an exclamation, a voice adding up the score.
>
> Through the windows came great waves of the cool night air, bringing with them the challenging song of the nightingale, clear-toned and ardent.

These examples, which it would be very interesting to compare with similar passages in Flaubert, are sufficient to give us an understanding of Turgenev's habitual method of procedure. He lets the vision buried within him rise again into consciousness, and notes which detail it is that first solicits his awareness. He then makes of that the key element of the required scene, round which the others gather like a retinue.

To hold tight to the essential detail, to suggest rather than demonstrate, those are the rules and methods of a certain form of art which combines delicacy with strength. Turgenev's art has frequently been compared to Greek art, and the comparison is accurate, because in both a complex whole is evoked by means of a few perfectly chosen details.

No novelist has ever employed so great an economy of means. It comes as something of a surprise to those of us who are, to some extent, familiar with the technique of novel-writing, that Turgenev should have been able, in books so short, to give an impression of solidity and abundance. An analysis of the method shows a skill in construction which is carried to perfection but is never obtrusive. A Meredith, a George Eliot delight in following their heroes from childhood to maturity. Tolstoy takes his point of departure somewhere well removed from the central episode of his story. Turgenev, on the other hand, almost always plunges straight into the main action. ***Fathers and Children*** covers only a few weeks, as, also, does ***First Love. A House of Gentlefolk*** opens with the return of Lavretzky, ***Smoke*** at the moment of the meeting with Irene. It is only later, when the reader's emotions have already been engaged, that the author turns back into the few paths which he considers it necessary to explore. When reading Turgenev one is almost inevitably reminded of that unity of time which is so marked a feature in the classic French tragedies. He is, indeed, a great classic. He even shares with the great classical writers their contempt for "plot". Like Molière, who made use of the most hackneyed subjects and the most familiar *dénouements* for his plays, Turgenev was primarily concerned to portray certain characters and to bring into a clear focus certain emotional shades. . . . Like Molière, too, he was satisfied with an almost archaic symmetry. With the *femme fatale* (Varvara, Irene) he contrasts the pure woman (Lisa, Tatiana): the artist with the practical man: children with their fathers. His construction is a great deal more ingenuous and primitive than that of either Tolstoy or Dostoievsky.

There is a similar economy of means in the portraying of character. As in his descriptive passages, a few well-chosen details are given the task of suggesting the rest. For instance, in ***A House of Gentlefolk,*** Lavretzky has left a flirtatious wife who has been false to him. He thinks that she is dead. She suddenly turns up again in his own house, and not unnaturally he receives her with some degree of severity. She shows him his little daughter in an attempt to work on his feelings. . . . (pp. 302-06)

There is an unforgettable note of callousness about the scene. Varvara Pavlovna's lack of heart, the egotism of a pretty woman who is completely sure of herself, her husband's weakness—all this we see in a single short page, as we should do in life were we in the presence of those particular characters. Yet nothing has been said by the author. We have been given no elaborate analysis of the workings of Varvara Pavlovna's mind. But, after the painful scene with her husband, the only thing she bothers about is the beauty of her hands. She asks for the gloves she wears to bed. That is enough. We know her through and through.

But as I have already pointed out, it is not enough in describing Turgenev's art to use the word "realist". It is essential to add that his realism is "poetic". What, exactly, does that mean? Poetry is one of the worst defined words in the language. We should never lose sight of the fact that, in the etymological sense, the poet is "he who makes". Poetry is the art of remaking, of re-creating the world for man, of imposing upon it a form and, above all, a rhythm. To reconstruct this mysterious unity, to establish a relationship between Nature and the human emotions, to set the individual adventure within the vast rhythmic movement of clouds and sunlight, spring and winter, youth and age, that is what being a poet and, at the same time, a novelist means.

It is impossible to think of Turgenev's books without being conscious of those great phenomena of nature which, in some way, associate it with human passions. In ***Smoke*** we watch the white clouds slowly drifting over the countryside. The garden in ***First Love*** is unforgetable, the night in **"Bèjine's Meadow,"** the lake beside which Dmitri Rudin has his last meeting with the girl he is about to desert.

A poetic realist knows that men's lives are not filled only with humdrum details, but that they also have their great moments, their periods of restlessness, mystery and noble illusions. To dream is a part of reality. If we overlook that or deliberately try to avoid it, we impoverish reality and take from it all that makes it human. (pp. 307-08)

He had most certainly been in love, or at least, halfway to being in love. He had known romantic passion. In his attitude to Pauline Viardot there had been a touch of the chivalrous. But whether what he felt had been friendship or love, there can be no doubt that he had experienced at first hand those warm and durable feelings which free from all meanness of mind and heart those whom they have touched, and impart to their spirit the distinctive "colouring" which we recognize at once, whether in a statesman or a businessman, by reason of a sort of noble serenity, so that we feel convinced that they have known true love. Much of the quality of Turgenev's books comes from that. (p. 309)

The characteristics in Turgenev to which I have drawn attention (the desire to paint only what he knew well from his own experience, the prevalence in his work of those great emotions which he himself had felt) might lead us to expect a highly subjective art. He maintained, on the contrary, that a novelist must be *objective*, and "disappear from view behind the people in his books". (p. 310)

The truth is, I think, that no writer, however objective he may want to be, can ever wholly prevent his personality from showing in his work. A man is marked by a certain number of preoccupations, and they will come to light whether he likes it or not. . . . [In] Turgenev's novels we get a very clear impression of what he was like—languid, sentimental, honest and for ever searching in vain for some strong woman who might arouse his passion. It is this, what we might call congenital, monotony that gives life to a writer's work. A novelist can cut the umbilical cord which binds his characters to the imagination which gave them birth: what he cannot do is to keep them from having a recognizable resemblance to their creator, and to one another.

Besides, Turgenev was very far from refusing to indulge in introspection. He thought that an artist should be willing to accept everything and everybody, including himself, as a possible object of observation. (p. 311)

It seems clear, then, that he was both subjective and objective. As a matter of fact, he had little liking for systems and classifications. He held that liberty is necessary for the artist. (p. 312)

About one thing only was he intransigent. He believed that no novelist should ever consciously set out to prove a thesis. The artist and the moralist are two essentially different persons. Art is a way of escape, not a demonstration. A novelist can be as much interested in ideas as anybody else. The expression of ideas, like the expression of feelings, is part and parcel of that human life which he is trying to paint, but ideas should figure in his work as belonging to his characters. They should spring from, not mould, them. They should provide moments of dramatic tension, and leave us free to choose between them. Turgenev made no effort to "understand life". He had no system of morality to preach, no metaphysics, no philosophy. That was not his job. He confined himself to telling a story, to introducing his readers to human beings. For some time now there has been a great deal of talk in France about pure poetry. Turgenev provides us with one of the best examples of the pure novel. (pp. 312-13)

André Maurois, "The Art of Turgenev," in his The Art of Writing, *translated by Gerard Hopkins, E. P. Dutton & Co., Inc., 1960, pp. 295-315.*

HARRY HERSHKOWITZ (essay date 1932)

[Hershkowitz explicates Bazarov's philosophy, describing the character as a representative of "the spirit of youth in the late fifties": the spirit of reform.]

The chief meaning of [***Fathers and Sons***] lay in the struggle for supremacy of the views of two social strata, represented by the radical and by the conservative element. We must have a restandardization of values, according to Bazarov. Just like Ibsen's heroes in a later day he insists that no notion, no matter how sacred and time-honored, has the force of an axiomatic truth. We must take nothing on authority. Conservative classes were naturally opposed to such views. Bazarov discards all that is not of a utilitarian nature. . . . But he is not merely the Spirit of Denial. In the novel he is placed far above the aristocratic dandy, Pavel Kirsanov "whose nails one could send to the exposition." He has little use for Nicolay Kirsanov's reading poetry—he would do better to learn more about farming! The romantic side of life offends him, for it destroys the equilibrium in a person's make-up. "Astonishing phenomenon these elderly romanticists! They develop their nervous system to the point of exasperation . . . and then the equilibrium is destroyed." For this very reason he considers Nicolay Petrovich behind the times, one whose "song is sung." (pp. 66-7)

In this attitude of Bazarov we see the trend of the times, in the sixties. Pisarov, the great critic of the day, is glad to note the decline of poetry. If the poet cannot produce anything of utilitarian value he advises him to sew boots instead. A work must have definite ideas that will enrich our mind. Pushkin ought to be shelved, as he does not fit into an era of analysis and investigation.

We are told that Bazarov was fond of women and of feminine beauty, but love in the ideal romantic sense he considered as unpardonable folly. He regarded chivalrous sentiments as a sort of deformity. He was too individualistic to want to submit to love for woman without a struggle, as every form of affection for another does of necessity imply a curtailment in the freedom of controlling one's actions, at least where the object of affection is involved. . . . Bazarov did not succeed, however, in getting beyond the mere outward signs of control. Inwardly he remained a prey to his affections and was perfectly "human."

The Bazarovs are the active people in a democracy where no idlers are tolerated, where there is no room for society lions, self-nominated guardians of the sacred laws of propriety. "The idea of my coddling these rural aristocrats! It's nothing but self-conceit." Pavel Kirsanov justifies his aristocratic habits by reference to a sense of duty, of respect for one's individuality: "I respect the man in myself." To which Bazarov replies: "Here you are respecting yourself, and sitting with folded hands: What is the good of that for the *bien public?* You would do the same thing, even if you did not respect yourself." All that the aristocrats feed on is high-sounding words and phrases: "Aristocracy, liberalism, progress, principles . . . when you come to think of it, how many foreign and useless words! The Russian man does not need them, even as gift."

That the work is directed against the representatives of the nobility, one can hardly doubt. That reform is to come from below, from the people, is Turgenev's opinion, which he puts into Bazarov's mouth. . . . Bazarov is not a socialist or a populist. He is far from glorifying anything coming from "the people." He will go against them, when he sees them in the wrong. . . . Sometimes he despises the peasant, for he deserves to be despised. There are occasions when he hates this peasant for whom he is to toil and moil and who will not even thank him for it.

Bazarov is an individualist who accentuates his personal "I." Does he care much about people's opinions? "A genuine man ought not to worry about that." Nevertheless, he is a torch-bearer of democracy, championing the cause of the people. His "I" is the "I" of the people, of the lowest and the unrecognized. The law must adopt measures that do not deprive the lower strata of the full benefit of society's good. These people felt that Bazarov is one from amongst their midst. The servants became attached to him, although he jeered at them: they felt that, in spite of that, he was their brother, not a lordly master. "Ask any one of your peasants, in which of us—in you or in me—he would the more readily recognize a fellow countryman. You do not even know how to talk with him," he says to Pavel.

We are told at the very beginning of our acquaintance with Bazarov that he possessed a special faculty for inspiring the lower classes with confidence in him, "although he never indulged them, and treated them carelessly." (pp. 67-9)

Bazarov comes from the lower strata, yet he not only claims equality with the nobles, but even asserts his superiority. His intellectual guides are the materialistic philosophers and naturalists, whereas the ideals of the previous generation were Hegel, Schelling, and Pushkin. Hence, he admits sensations, but denies principles: "In general, there are no principles, but there are sensations. Everything depends upon them. Why do I like chemistry? Why do you like apples? By virtue of sensations. Deeper than that, men will not penetrate."

Naturally there was going to be a clash between the men of the sixties and the men of the forties. The new man does not recognize the refinements of an idealistic spirit. Science before art; use before beauty. "A respectable chemist is twenty times more useful than any poet," Bazarov maintains. In his opinion, Raphael isn't worth a copper farthing. He admires the Germans for their progress in the natural sciences and because "they are a practical race." He believes only in facts. Everything must be tested as to its validity by reference to the senses and must be subject to experiment. The world is to him a workshop and man the master in it. A reëcho of this spirit is felt in Dostoyevsky's *Byesy* (*Possessed*), when we are told that Stepan Trofimovich was hooted out of the lecture hall for daring to maintain that Pushkin is above boots.

This utilitarian philosophy found naturally strong opposition in the older generation of the forties who were fed up on idealism. This opposition was shown strongly in the criticism of the day. Dostoyevsky could not refrain from satirizing the radical leaders in his *Possessed*, in the person of Peter Verkhovensky. Bazarov is a student. That most of Turgenev's outstanding characters are students, is significant. For a long while, the literate element of Russia formed but a small percentage of the total population, and of those who could read and write only a small portion could lay claim to being considered cultivated.

There was very little of what one might call "home atmosphere" to set up ideals for the growing youth. Fathers who wished to have their children obtain an education somewhat similar to the Western type, had to send them to Moscow or St. Petersburg, or else depend upon foreign tutors. Young men of a varying bent of mind were thrown together at the large universities. Upon their return they became sensitive to the difference between culture and the brutal surroundings of Russia. No wonder they felt that the future of Russia depended upon them as an intellectual force. The students were filled early with the conviction that upon them fell the task of regenerating their country. They are the Rudins, the Insarovs, the Bazarovs. To them belonged the future, they believed.

If any of them, like Rudin, did not figure as actors in the drama, they, nevertheless, succeeded in firing others with enthusiasm, and so their life was not lived in vain. What characterized the intellectual class was a superabundance of youthful enthusiasm. They were not daunted by struggles against society, government, even against their fathers. These protests became chronical and culminated in complete negation of everything—the mood we find Bazarov in, a mood representative of the spirit of youth in the late fifties.

The nihilist type springs up then. Bazarov is a typical nihilist. Turgenev offers an explanation of the meaning of the term. It comes from the latin "nihil"—"nothing"; consequently the word designates a man who recognizes nothing. According to him there is not a single institution of contemporary existence, either domestic or social, which does not challenge total rejection. He does not believe the family has any solid foundation, nor in the necessity of the legalization of marriage. (pp. 70-1)

Does he believe in religion? Religion, too, has to stand the test of efficacy, if one is to find a place for it. He holds firm to his stand, even when on his death-bed. "Both thou and mother must now profit by the fact that religion is strong in you; here's your chance to put it to the proof," he remarks to the heart-broken father. Society must be reformed and must rid itself of all nonsensical notions. "Moral ailments proceed from a bad education, from all sorts of nonsense with which people's heads are stuffed—in a word, reform society, and there will be no disease."

Bazarov believes in constructive measures. But before one can start the building-up process, the place must first be cleared. And so, he will demolish! He and his followers are a force—of that he is convinced. And if there are many millions who will not permit the minority to trample under foot their most sacred beliefs, and who will try to crush that minority, Bazarov is ready to submit to fate! Yet he reminds Pavel that ". . . we are not so few in number as you suppose: Furthermore, Moscow was burned to the ground by a penny candle."

Those who count are the doers, not the talkers. Among the active "doers" he would not consider the noblemen. If reforms are to be brought about, they will not come through efforts on their part. They do not know how to go about things in a business-like manner. All they do is preach and deal out learned talk. As to the nihilists, they take a different stand. (p. 72)

Nicolay Kirsanov feels that the sons know better how to go about things than their fathers. They have less of the sluggishness of "noble" blood in their veins. . . .

Pavel, too, realizes that not in the mere being "an aristocrat" lies a person's merit. Duty to others is far above that sentiment. "I am beginning to think that Bazarov was right when he reproached me with being aristocratic," says he to Nicolay. "No, my dear brother, it is time for us to cease putting on airs, and think of the world; it is time for us to lay aside all vanity. We will fulfill our duty and will receive happiness into the bargain."

Fenichka may be of low birth, but she is a true aristocrat in the nobility and sincerity of her sentiments. Nicolay is advised to give legal status to his marriage with her. It dawns upon him that "There is no room for castes in the 19th century."

What attitude do we find toward the peasant? All along we can note sympathetic touches and feel a caressing tone in the very humor that Turgenev sometimes resorts to. That humor makes these people so much more endearing to us. (p. 73)

In the attitude of the progressive type of landowners one notes signs of the coming peasant-reforms. . . . Still these ideas of coming progress found their way very slowly into many houses. Few appreciated their significance: the peasants themselves hardly realized their benefit. The young Bazarov saw all that. He felt that the cultural level of the peasant had to be raised before he could set the proper value on the coming reforms. So ingrown had become the peasant's habit of feeling himself subjugated that it was a question whether he would consider the new responsibilities of freedom thrown upon him more desirable than serfdom, which meant subjection, indeed, but also security. The question arose, whether all that colossal brutish strength let loose, would not do more harm than good.

We see in Bazarov what must have been going on in the minds of hundreds of leaders who were ready to lay down their lives, if needs must be, for the general good, but who were tormented by misgivings, as to whether the *good* will be in a form they intended it to be. So long had the peasant-serf's mind been kept in beliefs planted there for generations, that at best it was by a very slow process that one could awaken his intellect to realize things in their true light. A complete reform must have for its program the education of the lowly, the training of the coming generation. Nicolay Kirsanov, we are told in the epilogue, was traveling among the peasant folk, making long speeches, in hope that by exhausting their listening powers through repetition of the same set of words to succeed in teaching the new Gospel to them.

Fathers and Children was published in the spring of 1862 in Katkov's paper, *Russkiy Vyestnik*. The novel provoked a stormy controversy. (pp. 74-5)

Bazarov's character was apparently misunderstood. The Reactionist viewed him as a boor, as an unsocial type whose antisocial notions were intended to be an exaggeration of ideas that were beginning to circulate among the younger generation. . . . Equally strong was the reluctance of the younger generation to identify themselves with Bazarov, who, they insisted, was a caricature and not a true representative of theirs. This misunderstanding of the character by both camps is partly explained by Turgenev's technique in developing the character. One does not get the feeling, while reading the early portion of the book, that the author's sympathy is with his hero.

The fact is that the uncritical mind links its sympathies readily with a hero who is an "Idealization," rather than a "Realization." Bazarov is *real*. His actions are brusque, indeed, but they would be exactly the kind one would expect of a man who is inspired with a great idea, who is seething with desire to act in the direction in which he sees Social Salvation, but who finds contradictions and obstacles at the very start. The very people for whom he would lay down his life unhesitatingly, refuse to understand him and to consider his coin as "true." There is, consequently, a deal of bitterness in Bazarov's mind against the very people for whose happiness he fights. The environment about Bazarov is of a provoking kind and he is excited to the *n*th degree by it.

Some critics saw in Bazarov nothing but the personification of Destructive Criticism. There is reason to believe that Turgenev's purpose was to make him stand for Science and its application to Social Organization. Bazarov is first and foremost a scientist—he who collects, dissects, and observes. These characteristics are definitely alluded to in order to suggest the scientific spirit that pervades his nature. The cold logic of scientific investigation is then applied to society as he finds it. Of course, before new theories can be advanced, old hypotheses have to be discarded. So he discards, he denies; he will accept nothing on faith. No scientist can. It is the very essence of science to take nothing on faith. Superstitions, and confused notions of the past must be done away with! Sentimentalism of the Present must be held in check. So his first duty is that of the Destroying Angel. Only then can one get at the Truth. It is this attitude that explains his aversion to Art and Poetry; they appeal to sentiment and foster sentimentality. Sentimentality must not be permitted to blind the intellect. Hence, nothing of the past is sacred to him except in so far as it can find application to a new universal order of things. Customs of the past are to him ridiculous. The Law of the Past has held the mind chained in its grasp.

Only by looking upon Bazarov as the emblem of the Scientific spirit can we understand those actions of his which fail to invite our sympathy, such as his apparent harshness toward his parents. Ties of love or of family must not be permitted to hinder the advancing steps of the strong leader. There is no room for poetic sentimentality in his soul. These do not strengthen; they weaken action.

He will only succumb to the stronger Law of Nature that renders man powerless. He dies grappling with nature, but his influence has remained, and so he still lives on. Bazarov's notions can be traced in the social movement of today, in the scientific spirit of the age, in the subjection of everything to minute analysis; in beliefs of such figures as Ibsen in Norway, Hauptmann and Wassermann in Germany, Brieux in France, Shaw in England.

The man of Bazarov's stamp, like the famous Stockman in Ibsen's *Enemy of the People*, prefers to stand alone. He is not in search of honors; the laurels of public success do not lure him: public opinion is a matter of indifference to him. Even love itself must not come between him and his cause. It is only Death, the Arch Destroyer, that can and *does* cut his career short. Bazarov knows his own powers, he feels them waning—he knows that he is a Guiding Lamp to others, a lamp whose flame flickers. "Blow upon the dying lamp" he says to Odintzova," feeling that consciousness will soon leave him. He remains after his death a Guiding Lamp.

That ***Fathers and Children*** has Reform as its dominant keynote, there seems to be very little doubt. That theory becomes more apparent upon the analysis of Bazarov's character. Viewed in proper prospective, Bazarov appears mainly as the Reformer. All other characters are used either to place Bazarov's into stronger relief or merely to bring his notions to the front. Indeed, he stands like a giant among pigmies. Every one is made to feel his superiority. Everything is made to center about him. The older Kirsanovs face him as emblems of the past cult of Aristocracy and Traditions of Birth. Arkady represents Sentimental Youth of the Present, whose energy spends itself in admiration and emotional effusion. The Family hearth is represented in the persons of Bazarov's father and mother. All these are forces that the reformer has to reckon with. Each one has its noble tale to tell, but is a hindrance to the reformer.

He stands upon a height and looks into the distance where he sees bigger things in comparison with which these play but a very insignificant rôle. He is the most dominating of Turgenev's creations (pp. 76-8)

Fathers and Children shows Turgenev in the very midst of social life, recording the political and social movements of his time, giving voice and artistic interpretation to the foremost ideas of the society he lived in. Several generations owe him a part of their intellectual inheritance, as their growth was and is, perhaps, still going on under the unchanging powerful influence of the psychic impulses which are diffused in his works. Along with the charm of intimate human feelings he taught them the value of a free personality, of liberty in the broadest sense. One is reminded, in this connection, of Rudin's words to Basistov: "Liberty is one of man's most precious possessions, and happy is he on whom heaven has bestowed a morsel of bread, who is not compelled to be indebted for it to any one!" His figures embody forces in which his fatherland is poor, which the soil needs for enrichment, which the race is urged to develop. Viewed from this point of view Turgenev becomes the sympathetic Father of his country which he regards as a sick patient, for whose ills he tries to suggest remedies.

One might consider him in the double rôle of psychologist of individuals as well as of classes that compose the Russian nation. Drawing in broad lines, he cannot, therefore, center his best energies in some one character, where human nature would be studied in so far as it reveals differentiation of the species. He feels he has a mission. His chief characters are, therefore, universal characters and embrace whole classes. His method is that of creating an individual and then endowing him with qualities that make him a representative of a class, a type. Frequently he clothes the character with attributes that he should like to see universalized. He endeavors to depict this character with all the power, all the colors at his command. He arouses in the reader deep admiration for his character. He awakens a desire to act as the character acts. He appeals to our wills. Hence his greatness as a reformer. He gives his character a purpose, an aim in life. Thousands of young men and young girls have taken up this or that character and made it their model.

Not only did Turgenev show himself a great reformer but an artist of the first make. As such, he understood that straightforward discussion can appeal only to readers who are trained to a reflective type of literature. The more effective way is to make an appeal to the emotions by means of the story form. Although the tendency of his novels is to carry a social message, that artist never loses sight of the fact that he is not there to preach. The reader is in a current of real human life with all its complications. There are very few works that can compare with Turgenev's in this respect. They scrutinize to the very bottom the economic and social conditions and reproduce with remarkable vividness the spiritual struggles of men and women in their onward march to national progress. (pp. 79-81)

Harry Hershkowitz, in his Democratic Ideas in Turgenev's Works, *Columbia University Press, 1932, 131 p.*

VIRGINIA WOOLF (essay date 1933)

[A British novelist, essayist, and short story writer, Woolf is one of the most prominent literary figures of the twentieth century. Like her contemporary James Joyce, with whom she is often compared, Woolf is remembered as one of the most innovative of the stream of consciousness novelists. She was concerned primarily with depicting the life of the mind, and she revolted against traditional narrative techniques and developed her own highly individualized style. Woolf's works, noted for their subjective explorations of characters' inner lives and their delicate poetic quality, have had a lasting effect on the art of the novel. She is also considered a discerning and influential essayist. Her critical writings, termed "creative, appreciative, and subjective" by Barbara Currier Bell and Carol Ohmann, cover almost the entire range of literature and contain some of her finest prose. In the following excerpt from an essay written in 1933, Woolf describes the hallmarks of Turgenev's novels, citing his ability to combine accurate observation of reality with the selective interpretation of facts. Woolf also discusses the emotional symmetry of the author's works.]

At first, Turgenev's novels seem to us a little thin, slight and sketchlike in texture. Take ***Rudin***, for instance—the reader will place it among the French school, among the copies rather than the originals, with the feeling that the writer has set himself an admirable model, but in following it has sacrificed something of his own character and force. But the superficial impression deepens and sharpens itself as the pages are turned. The scene has a size out of all proportion to its length. It expands in the mind and lies there giving off fresh ideas, emotions, and pictures much as a moment in real life will sometimes only yield its meaning long after it has passed. We notice that though the people talk in the most natural speaking voices, what they say is always unexpected; the meaning goes on after the sound has stopped. Moreover, they do not have to speak in order to make us feel their presence; "Volintsev started and raised his head, as though he had just waked up"—we had felt him there though he had not spoken. And when in some pause we look out of the window, the emotion is returned to us, deepened, because it is given through another medium, by the trees or the clouds, by the barking of a dog, or the song of a nightingale. Thus we are surrounded on all sides—by the talk, by the silence, by the look of things. The scene is extraordinarily complete.

It is easy to say that in order to gain a simplicity so complex Turgenev has gone through a long struggle of elimination beforehand. He knows all about his people, so that when he writes he chooses only what is most salient without apparent effort. But when we have finished ***Rudin, Fathers and Children, Smoke, On the Eve*** and the others many questions suggest themselves to which it is not so easy to find an answer. They are so short and yet they hold so much. The emotion is so intense and yet so calm. The form is in one sense so perfect, in another so broken. They are about Russia in the fifties and sixties of the last century, and yet they are about ourselves at the present moment. Can we then find out from Turgenev himself what principles guided him—had he, for all his seeming ease and lightness, some drastic theory of art? (pp. 53-5)

[The novelist] has to observe facts impartially, yet he must also interpret them. Many novelists do the one; many do the other—we have the photograph and the poem. But few combine the fact and the vision; and the rare quality that we find in Turgenev is the result of this double process. For in these short chapters he is doing two very different things at the same time. With his infallible eye he observes everything accurately.

Solomin picks up a pair of gloves; they were "white chamois-leather gloves, recently washed, every finger of which had stretched at the tip and looked like a finger-biscuit." But he stops when he has shown us the glove exactly; the interpreter is at his elbow to insist that even a glove must be relevant to the character, or to the idea. But the idea alone is not enough; the interpreter is never allowed to mount unchecked into the realms of imagination; again the observer pulls him back and reminds him of the other truth, the truth of fact. Even Bazarov, the heroic, packed his best trousers at the top of his bag when he wanted to impress a lady. The two partners work in closest alliance. We look at the same thing from different angles, and that is one reason why the short chapters hold so much; they contain so many contrasts. On one and the same page we have irony and passion; the poetic and the commonplace; a tap drips and a nightingale sings. And yet, though the scene is made up of contrasts, it remains the same scene; our impressions are all relevant to each other.

Such a balance, of course, between two very different faculties is extremely rare, especially in English fiction, and demands some sacrifices. The great characters, with whom we are so familiar in our literature, the Micawbers, the Pecksniffs, the Becky Sharps, will not flourish under such supervision; they need, it seems, more licence; they must be allowed to dominate and perhaps to destroy other competitors. With the possible exception of Bazarov and of Harlov in **"A Lear of the Steppes"** no one character in Turgenev's novels stands out above and beyond the rest so that we remember him apart from the book. The Rudins, the Lavretskys, the Litvinovs, the Elenas, the Lisas, the Mariannas shade off into each other, making, with all their variations, one subtle and profound type rather than several distinct and highly individualized men and women. Then, again, the poet novelists like Emily Brontë, Hardy, or Melville, to whom facts are symbols, certainly give us a more overwhelming and passionate experience in *Wuthering Heights* or *The Return of the Native* or *Moby Dick* than any that Turgenev offers us. And yet what Turgenev offers us not only often affects us as poetry, but his books are perhaps more completely satisfying than the others. They are curiously of our own time, undecayed, and complete in themselves.

For the other quality that Turgenev possesses in so great a degree is the rare gift of symmetry, of balance. He gives us, in comparison with other novelists, a generalized and harmonized picture of life. And this is not only because his scope is wide—he shows us different societies, the peasant's, the intellectual's, the aristocrat's, the merchant's—but we are conscious of some further control and order. Yet such symmetry, as we are reminded, perhaps, by reading ***A House of Gentlefolk,*** is not the result of a supreme gift for storytelling. Turgenev, on the contrary, often tells a story very badly. There are loops and circumlocutions in his narrative—". . . we must ask the reader's permission to break off the thread of our story for a time," he will say. And then for fifty pages or so we are involved in great-grandfathers and great-grandmothers, much to our confusion, until we are back with Lavretsky at O— "where we parted from him, and whither we will now ask the indulgent reader to return with us." The good storyteller, who sees his book as a succession of events, would never have suffered that interruption. But Turgenev did not see his books as a succession of events; he saw them as a succession of emotions radiating from some character at the centre. A Bazarov, a Harlov seen in the flesh, perhaps, once in the corner of a railway carriage, becomes of paramount importance and acts as a magnet which has the power to draw things mysteriously belonging, though apparently incongruous, together. The connexion is not of events but of emotions, and if at the end of the book we feel a sense of completeness, it must be that in spite of his defects as a storyteller Turgenev's ear for emotion was so fine that even if he uses an abrupt contrast, or passes away from his people to a description of the sky or of the forest, all is held together by the truth of his insight. He never distracts us with the real incongruity—the introduction of an emotion that is false, or a transition that is arbitrary.

It is for this reason that his novels are not merely symmetrical but make us feel so intensely. His heroes and heroines are among the few fictitious characters of whose love we are convinced. It is a passion of extraordinary purity and intensity. The love of Elena for Insarov, her anguish when he fails to come, her despair when she seeks refuge in the chapel in the rain; the death of Bazarov and the sorrow of his old father and mother remain in the mind like actual experiences. And yet, strangely enough, the individual never dominates; many other things seem to be going on at the same time. We hear the hum of life in the fields; a horse champs his bit; a butterfly circles and settles. And as we notice, without seeming to notice, life going on, we feel more intensely for the men and women themselves because they are not the whole of life, but only part of the whole. Something of this, of course, is due to the fact that Turgenev's people are profoundly conscious of their relation to things outside themselves. "What is my youth for, what am I living for, why have I a soul, what is it all for?" Elena asks in her diary. The question is always on their lips.

It lends a profundity to talk that is otherwise light, amusing, full of exact observation. Turgenev is never, as in England he might have been, merely the brilliant historian of manners. But not only do they question the aim of their own lives but they brood over the question of Russia. The intellectuals are always working for Russia; they sit up arguing about the future of Russia till the dawn rises over the eternal samovar. "They worry and worry away at that unlucky subject, as children chew away at a bit of india-rubber," Potugin remarks in ***Smoke.*** Turgenev, exiled in body, cannot absent himself from Russia—he has the almost morbid sensibility that comes from a feeling of inferiority and suppression. And yet he never allows himself to become a partisan, a mouthpiece. Irony never deserts him; there is always the other side, the contrast. In the midst of political ardour we are shown Fomushka and Fimushka, "chubby, spruce little things, a perfect pair of little poll-parrots," who manage to exist very happily singing glees in spite of their country. Also it is a difficult business, he reminds us, to know the peasants, not merely to study them. "I could not *simplify* myself," wrote Nezhdanov, the intellectual, before he killed himself. Moreover though Turgenev could have said with Marianna ". . . I suffer for all the oppressed, the poor, the wretched in Russia," it was for the good of the cause, just as it was for the good of his art, not to expatiate, not to explain. . . . He compelled himself to stand outside; he laughed at the intellectuals; he showed up the windiness of their arguments, the sublime folly of their attempts. But his emotion, and their failure, affect us all the more powerfully now because of that aloofness. Yet if this method was partly the result of discipline and theory, no theory, as Turgenev's novels abundantly prove, is able to go to the root of the matter and eliminate the artist himself; his temperament remains ineradicable. Nobody, we say over and over again as we read him, even in a translation, could have written this except Turgenev. His birth, his race, the impressions of his childhood, pervade everything that he wrote.

But, though temperament is fated and inevitable, the writer has a choice, and a very important one, in the use he makes of it. "I" he must be; but there are many different "I's" in the same person. Shall he be the "I" who has suffered this slight, that injury, who desires to impose his own personality, to win popularity and power for himself and his views; or shall he suppress that "I" in favour of the one who sees as far as he can impartially and honestly, without wishing to plead a cause or to justify himself? Turgenev had no doubt about his choice; he refused to write "élégamment et chaudement ce que vous ressentez à l'aspect de cette chose ou de cet homme." He used the other self, the self which has been so rid of superfluities that it is almost impersonal in its intense individuality; the self which he defines in speaking of the actress Violetta;—

> She had thrown aside everything subsidiary, everything superfluous, and *found herself*; a rare, a lofty delight for an artist! She had suddenly crossed the limit, which it is impossible to define, beyond which is the abiding place of beauty.

That is why his novels are still so much of our own time; no hot and personal emotion has made them local and transitory; the man who speaks is not a prophet clothed with thunder but a seer who tries to understand. Of course there are weaknesses; one grows old and lazy as he said; sometimes his books are slight, confused, and perhaps sentimental. But they dwell in "the abiding place of beauty" because he chose to write with the most fundamental part of his being as a writer; nor, for all his irony and aloofness, do we ever doubt the depth of his feeling. (pp. 56-61)

Virginia Woolf, "The Novels of Turgenev," in her "The Captain's Death Bed" and Other Essays, *Harcourt Brace Jovanovich, Inc., 1950, pp. 53-61.*

HENRY TEN EYCK PERRY (essay date 1939)

[*Perry examines the plots, themes, characters, and artistic effectiveness of Turgenev's plays.*]

Turgenev wrote ten plays in all, the greater part of his dramatic work being composed in the three years from 1847 to 1850. One of the ten pieces is ***Lack of Caution,*** a tragedy of intrigue with a Spanish setting. Two of them are mere sketches which do not pretend to do more than outline a situation. ***A Conversation on the Highway*** contrasts a decadent young landowner, who has lost all his money, and a simple old coachman, who is devoted to his master from habit rather than from conviction; the difference between the cynicism of the one and the superstition of the other is used to illustrate the chasm separating social classes, in morality as well as in economics. ***Lack of Funds*** pictures another impecunious young aristocrat, who is living beyond his means in St. Petersburg and whose faithful old servant urges him in vain to return to the country home of his mother.

Lunch with the Marshal of the Nobility portrays the inefficiency of rural magistrates; ***A Provincial Lady*** hints at venal corruption in higher governmental cirles. In this latter piece the wife of a poor official in a small town is trying to get her husband a more important position in St. Petersburg by flirting with a count, who is an influential old admirer of hers. The wife has just got the count to promise that her husband shall secure the coveted post when the husband returns unexpectedly and finds the count on his knees before the wife. The count is chagrined and feels that he has been duped, but he nobly agrees to carry out his promise. How far the wife has been playing with him is the crucial point of this comedy. After the discovery she continues to hint that her affection for him may be real. "A comedy can be played well only where one feels what he is saying," she maintains, and that statement contains the heart of Turgenev's comic theory. ***A Provincial Lady*** is partly a comedy of social situation, hinging upon the desire of the lady and her husband to live in the metropolis, and partly a comedy of sentiment, with the lady's feelings perhaps more involved than she has been willing to admit, even to herself.

The same sort of ambiguity created by a conflict between sentiment and comedy pervades Turgenev's two-act drama, ***The Parasite.*** The heartlessness of an aristocratic husband and the sympathetic nature of his well-to-do wife are brought into opposition when the parasite who has been a hanger-on of the family asserts publicly in a moment of drunkenness that he is the wife's father. The husband refuses to believe the story and succeeds, as he thinks, in buying off the parasite's claims, but the wife feels that the poor man has told the truth and arranges to see him again without her husband's knowledge. The comedy ends with the dramatic irony of a misunderstanding between husband and wife which permits both of them to think that they are in the right. The background of ***The Parasite*** is a picture of life on a large country estate. As in the work of Gogol, the tendency toward realism fuses to a certain extent the satirical and emotional factors which are in conflict beneath the surface of Turgenev's art.

Another of his longer plays, in which the same fundamental contrast occurs, is ***The Bachelor,*** a detailed analysis of various kinds of love. The main subject of this drama is the struggle in the heart of an old bachelor between paternal and sexual love for his young protégée. To this principal theme several subsidiary ones are closely related. The heroine's young fiancé is torn between ambition and affection for the girl, whom he considers beneath him in social position; she is attracted at the same time to both her lover and her protector. The girl is so much the most interesting character in the piece that Turgenev might well have developed her part at greater length. He is always extremely successful with his portraits of young women uncertain of their own feelings. The heroine of ***The Bachelor*** is not a comic figure like her fiancé, who gives her up for worldly considerations, nor a sentimental one like her self-sacrificing guardian, but somewhere between the two extremes. Soon after she loses her young lover, she tells the old bachelor that some day later on she may consent to become his wife.

Turgenev handles with exceptional delicacy love affairs to which there is some obstacle, such as social position, age, or temperament. In ***An Evening in Sorrento*** he shows how a woman of thirty loses a man of twenty-eight, with whom she is in love, to a young girl of eighteen. In ***Where It Is Thin, There It Breaks*** the heroine agrees to marry a dull, phlegmatic man whom she does not love when the volatile and artistic one to whom she is attracted does not propose to her. ***Where It Is Thin, There It Breaks*** is the most effective of Turgenev's minor works for the theater. Of them all it most closely resembles his dramatic masterpiece, ***A Month in the Country,*** particularly in respect to the background against which the principal intrigue develops. The love affair in the slighter play takes place on a country estate, presided over by a flighty but not altogether impractical woman of the upper middle class. Her complicated household is composed of such diverse characters as an elderly female relative, who hates being compelled to accept the bread of charity, a French governess, who is always sewing and sighing for Paris, and a ruined ex-captain, who looks like a bully but is really a servile flatterer. They drift on and off the stage, exchanging random observations which have little to do with the plot and which intensify the air of casualness that envelops the entire proceedings. These characters are depicted, with a candor that seems almost brutal to an Anglo-Saxon, as futile creatures who discuss eating candy and mushrooms, who play at pool or preference, and who, when it begins to rain, have not the faintest idea of how to amuse themselves. With their cultivation and their incompetence, they are striking examples of the leisureliness and aimlessness of one stratum of social life in Russia during the middle of the nineteenth century.

This same atmosphere of apparent tranquillity and concealed uneasiness pervades Turgenev's one superlative comedy, ***A Month in the Country.*** The owner of the rural estate on which this play takes place is a stupid, well-intentioned man who cannot become reconciled to the fact that, although the Russian peasants are intelligent, they refuse to work consistently. He knows that they have no patience, but he respects them nevertheless. His establishment consists of his wife, his ten-year-old son, his elderly mother, his mother's companion, his son's two tutors, and a young girl dependent on the family. The life of the mother, her companion, and the German tutor is desultory, unmotivated, and only enlivened by games of preference. At the end of the play they are just where they were when it began, except that the coquettish companion is about to leave to marry a country doctor, who has analyzed for her, with extraordinary detachment, his own assets and liabilities as a husband. This doctor serves as a sardonic chorus throughout the comedy. He describes himself as a jolly but satiric person, not a very good doctor but a successful, self-made man. He is a curious mixture of brutality and honesty, shrewdness and naïve complacency.

The doctor comments slyly on the principal characters in the play, but he does not take an active part in the plot beyond acting as an amateur marriage broker for a rich middle-aged neighbor, who wants to marry Vera, the young girl of seventeen, dependent on the family. Vera finally agrees to marry the shy but kind neighbor after she has discovered that she cannot marry Belyayev, one of the tutors, with whom she has fallen in love during the month that he has been on the country estate. The character of Vera, which Turgenev himself did not consider of first importance, is one of the most finely drawn in the whole piece. The gradual unfolding of her love for Belyayev is indicated with great tenderness. She is so much of an unformed girl that she does not admit her love even to herself, until the avowal is drawn from her by the apparent sympathy of Natalya, the landowner's wife. When Vera has come to understand her own feelings, she also suddenly realizes that Natalya is her successful rival with the tutor, and she finds it hard to forgive the older woman's treachery. Vera is a girl with a straightforward emotional nature, which gradually comes to dominate her and which teaches her the harsh realities of Turgenev's comic world.

Belyayev is a much less fused and admirable human being. A simple young man, neglected by his father, he has managed to get an education and is now supporting himself by being a tutor. Though he is drawn to Vera, who reminds him of his sister, he is much more fascinated by the older and more accomplished Natalya. When he realizes that Natalya loves him, he is flattered and believes for a moment that he loves her, but he soon realizes the absurdity of his position. He falls under the influence of Rakitin, an older man, who is also in love with Natalya and who tells the young tutor with deep sincerity what a painful thing it is to be in love. Rakitin is motivated partly by jealousy and partly by a consideration for Natalya's true welfare. He himself leaves the estate to save her honor, taking the burden of her love affair with Belyayev upon his own shoulders. Rakitin cares for Natalya profoundly, but by disillusioning the young tutor he brings about the temporary unhappiness of the woman to whom both of them are devoted.

Natalya is the central figure of ***A Month in the Country.*** Turgenev admits that he was most interested in her, and hers is an effective part, although a somewhat theatrical one. Her character is not altogether persuasive, in spite of the fact that her actions can be partially explained by the lack of a sufficient outlet for her average intelligence and her more than average emotional energy. Turgenev tells us a good deal about Natalya's past history, as if he wished to suggest that her psychology may be largely accounted for by her early environment. She had a stern father, to whom she had always been slavishly obedient and whom she feared even after he became old and blind. Her childhood was a constant series of repressions; she had little real youth of her own. Now that she is a married woman and has reached the dangerous age of twenty-nine she is eager to try to recapture at second hand some of the normal sensations which she had never experienced in her girlhood. She is slow to appreciate the state of her feelings for Belyayev, but when she once does so she is ruthless in attempting to gratify them. After the tutor's departure, she is for the moment completely heartbroken, but one suspects that Rakitin's solution of the difficulty was the best one for her ultimate happiness. Natalya will sooner or later recover from her painful experience. She will be fortunate if, later on, she does not meet another attractive young man, with no Rakitin to give him mature counsel.

A Month in the Country ends without having reached a very decisive conclusion. Natalya, her husband, her husband's mother, her son, and her son's German tutor will continue living on the estate. Life will go on in much the same way as it has done heretofore, and Natalya will no doubt continue to be restless and dissatisfied. She and Belyayev seem to be badly coördinated people by comparison with Rakitin and Vera, both of whom have secured emotional tranquillity at the cost of immediate happiness. No one of the four principle characters in this play has an agreeable prospect for the future. Only Natalya's stupid husband thinks that everything has come out in the best possible way for himself and all the others.

Turgenev's constant preoccupation seems to be with the idea that love is a capricious and unpredictable emotion, strong enough to upset any sensitive human being's equilibrium but not powerful enough to cause him to direct his complete energies into a single concentrated channel. All of the people in ***A Month in the Country*** have more or less violent passions, but no one of them is able to satisfy his impulses. There is some inhibiting force within them all which makes it impossible for them to express themselves as they would like to do. The practical circumstances of their lives have too much influence over them. They lack the strength of character that they should have if they are to be the masters of their own fates. This weakness provides excellent material for a highly individualized and original type of comedy. A sense of humor becomes identified with a perception of what man would be in contrast to what the innumerable details of life have made him become. A makeshift arrangement is the best outcome that can be hoped for in matters of the heart, which have to be organized according to man-made conventions, of marriage, of property, and of class distinctions. Unless there should be a radical shift of attitude towards these human institutions, there is no possibility that a healthy balance can be established in the unsteady society which is pictured in the comedies of Turgenev. (pp. 326-31)

Henry Ten Eyck Perry, "Crosscurrents in Russia: Gogol, Turgenev, and Chekhov," in his Masters of Dramatic Comedy and Their Social Themes, *Cambridge, Mass.: Harvard University Press, 1939, pp. 314-58.*

MARC SLONIM (essay date 1950)

[*Slonim was a Russian-born American critic who wrote extensively on Russian literature. The following excerpt is taken from Slonim's comprehensive survey of Russian literature. Here, he seeks to illuminate Turgenev's philosophy of life and its effect on his writings.*]

Turgenev called himself a Realist, and defined his artistic aim as the truthful and dispassionate portrayal of life. He often pointed out his own objectivity: being a Westernizer did not prevent him from presenting the Westernizer Panshin (in ***A Nest of Gentlefolk***) unfavorably and making him come off second-best in the argument with the Slavophile Lavretsky; being an anti-Nihilist did not deter him from bringing out all the good points and even virtues of Bazarov; being an atheist did not affect his sympathetic comprehension of Liza's religious feelings.

Belinsky praised Turgenev's precise observation, his capacity for grasping the essence and the peculiarities of each character, and his superb artistry in revealing the causes and effects of human actions and in describing nature [see excerpt dated 1848]. Although he is justly considered one of the world's greatest storytellers, the story itself never attracted Turgenev: the plots of his novels and tales are so simple as to appear slight, and always hinge on the reversal of a love affair. The main thing for him is to show men and women, their relations and their emotions and ideas, without ever attempting a thorough psychological analysis—he always leaves such an analysis to the reader. The latter, however, it put on the right path by hints, allusions, and the mood created by landscapes and the rhythm of the language. The actual work of psychological penetration is done behind the scenes of the novel, by the highly intelligent author who allows only the utlimate results of his exploration to appear in his writings.

This method is responsible for the kind of psychological impressionism or imagism we always find in Turgenev's novels and stories. Turgenev has stated that he wrote not because certain incidents or adventures had occurred to him, but because he had in mind the representation of a certain person, whom he tried to conceive with factual and psychological completeness (he even wrote, for his own use, preliminary biographies of all his main characters). (p. 263)

This concreteness assumes the form of absolute compactness and economy of words. Turgenev's art is very different from Goncharov's factual thoroughness, Dostoevsky's metaphysical depth, or Tolstoy's universality. Turgenev limited himself in the scope and range of his writings, as well as in his ways of expression. His novels are short; the action unfolds without digressions or parallel plots and usually takes place in a brief span of time; the protagonists are reduced to a minimum: the author does not indulge in any analysis of their feelings or their behavior, always employing the method of indirect allusions and understatements.

When he wants to clarify a detail, however—to demonstrate Insarov's strength, for instance, or Bazarov's skeptical attitude toward accepted authorities—he does not beat around the bush but comes straight to the point. The dialogue—adroitly individualized and functional in psychological portrayal—also serves for the exposition of ideas. His protagonists not only talk, but also discuss facts and abstract concepts. Rudin and Lezhnev deliver long speeches on various subjects; Lavretsky and his friend Mikhalevich discuss the men and trends of the 'forties; Bazarov and Paul Kirsanov have arguments over love, science, and esthetics; Potughin and Litvinov exchange lengthy opinions on Europe and Russia's destinies. In general, Turgenev's heroes are defined more by what they say than by what they do.

It can be said of all his novels that they had the definite purpose of representing the aristocracy and the intelligentsia in their intellectual and social metamorphosis and that they form a gallery of Russian types as they actually existed between 1840 and 1870. His short stories, more concerned with the love episodes in the life of aristocrats, mostly Superfluous Men, are a sort of poetic accompaniment to the novels, although esthetically they are the best part of his literary bequest. But, if most of Turgenev's writings were social novels, what was their message? And, if there was none, what constituted their central theme, and what did they convey, and continue to convey, to their readers?

Turgenev did not see in life only material for his imagination. He looked for topics and people that corresponded to his personal inclinations. All the works of this objective realist were highly subjective and unraveled many inner conflicts that had tormented him since his early youth. He possessed a great gift for understanding contradictions, for picturing with an equal persuasiveness an idle aristocrat, a Nihilist, a dreamer, or a practical man. Was it objectivity or ambivalence? It certainly could not be explained, as some critics have attempted to do, only by his insight and tolerance.

There was another reason for Turgenev's noncommittal attitude. A rational atheist, he did not believe in God and showed little enthusiasm for humanity. He kept to the middle of the road in politics, went along with the gradual reformers, was on friendly terms with radicals, but never committed himself to any definite group. In art he defended the objective representation of reality, praised harmony and balance as the main principles of an aimless estheticism, and took pride in the fact (contested by the critics) that his novels, both long and short, neither proved anything nor attempted to do so. He certainly appreciated freedom, human dignity, education, culture, and progress, but he never displayed any ardor in proclaiming those values.

As a matter of fact, there was very little positive affirmation in his work. The friends of his youth, such as Belinsky, Bakunin, and Herzen, had been enthusiastic about philosophy, anarchism, or Socialism; his contemporaries, such as Gogol, Dostoevsky, Tolstoy, struggled for religion, God, or morality—but Turgenev did not identify himself with any doctrine or intense belief. Here, again, he kept to the middle of the road, like an intelligent onlooker who enjoys the show but will never take part in it as an actor. He lacked religiosity, which some people believe to be a Russian national trait, and was hardly interested in the quest of all-embracing, all-absorbing concepts or systems of ideas. (pp. 264-65)

Whoever will read several of Turgenev's novels and tales in succession will not fail to notice that they all have unhappy endings. Rudin, Insarov, Bazarov, Nezhdanov, Chertopkhanov, Pasynkov—all meet sudden and, for the most part, violent deaths. Liza dies for the world's sake; Lavretsky continues to vegetate in a sort of deadly atonement. All the love stories also end with failure or death (***Spring Freshets, First Love, Asya,*** **"Clara Milich", "Phantom",** ***Faust,*** and so on). In general, in Turgenev's tales something always happens on the threshold of fulfilment: accidents or catastrophes meet his men and women at the very door of happiness.

This is not accidental. Turgenev, like his hero Litvinov in ***Smoke,*** felt the vanity of human illusions and the absurdity of life. The idea of eternity terrified him; he speaks of it time and again, like a man who has a long and involved account to settle with it. His ***Senilia***—the most complete and frank expression of his true self—repeatedly deals with the fear of death. **"A Conversation," "The Dog," "The Hag," "The End of The World,"** and a number of other poems in prose revolve around the one topic—the inevitability of annihilation. The mysterious female vampire Ellis in **"Phantoms"** (written in 1863) reflects his own qualms: 'Why do I shudder in such anguish at the mere thought of annihilation?' For merciless and aloof Nature the existence of man is no more important than that of a flea (**"Nature"**). From the summits of the Alps, for the Jungfrau and the Finsteraarhorn, centuries pass like seconds, and to them the humans in the valley look like ants who will disappear one day, leaving immaculate the white eternity of their snow (**"An Alpimalyan Dialogue"**). A blind woman of gigantic proportions pushes on a bony, stalwart female who holds the hand of a small, bright-eyed girl, the child struggles in vain, but is driven along—and these three figures are Fate, Force, and Freedom. Men are imprisoned within a circle of fatality—and there is nothing beyond its bounds except 'the clangorous barking from the thousand throats of death,' 'darkness, eternal darkness,' the interminable void of destruction. This fundamental pessimism overshadows not only the tales of Turgenev's old age but his earlier works, such as **"Andrei Kolossov,"** ***Faust,*** **"A Backwater," "Journey to Polessie,"**—all written in his thirties.

In one of his letters to Pauline Viardot he writes: 'I cannot stand the empty skies, but I adore life, its reality, its whims, its accidents, its rites, its swiftly passing beauty.' It was not an easy love. He fled from the 'empty skies' into the palpable reality of human affairs, he sought oblivion in the activity of others, in love and illusions. Eternity is madness, death is a nightmare, and Turgenev forgets them only when he meets some spontaneous manifestation of life, in beauty, action, or thought.

The charm of a momentary pleasure moves him to tears, for he always realizes how short and transitory it is bound to be. A green branch on a spring day fills him with tremulous delight: it is the very image of beauty, of the sweet joy of being. In his lecture, **"Hamlet and Don Quixote,"** he gave preference to the Knight of La Mancha, since the Spaniard's illusions overcame his fear of death; his love of action liberated him from the burden of reflection, which dissects and kills the spontaneity of existence.

As a friend and disciple of philosophers, Turgenev, of course, was much closer to the Prince of Denmark than to the ecstatic Spanish hidalgo. In picturing the superfluous men he was in part making self-portraits, particularly when he showed how the self-analysis and self-criticism of his heroes destroyed their ability for action. But he admired the Don Quixotes, and he also loved men like Bazarov, Solomin, and Insarov, who were the very antithesis of himself.

Another curious aspect is his interest in political and social struggles. He was always excited by men's most spectacular activity—that of social transformation—because he was a patriot and sincerely loved his country and also because in this activity he found another affirmation of life, another evidence of 'whims and accidents,' which helped him to forget 'the toothless Ancient.' He was not energetic or particularly active by nature, but the others' expenditure of energy gave him a sense of security and heartened him, in the way the love of other people inspired him with joy and admiration, not unmixed with melancholy. Beauty was another, though momentary, victory over annihilation; contemplation of it brought a rapture enhanced by the consciousness of its evanescence. His tears of ecstasy were mingled with tears of regret.

Well aware of his inner conflict, he dreamt of harmony and the simple, natural life. In ***Faust,*** and in the **"Journey to Polessie,"** he came to the conclusion that 'the quiet and slow animation, the unhurried restraint of sensations and impulses, the equilibrium of health in every individual being, are the prerequisites of happiness.' The only lasting happiness lies in the serenity of a somewhat monotonous existence based upon instinct and resignation. The same law applies to art: a good work of art must possess the same equilibrium, the same poise, even when dealing with anxiety or madness. He praised highly 'the tranquility in passion' of the great tragic actress Rachel, citing her as an example of the highest esthetic achievement.

Here again his duality was patent. Although he was denied the romantic vision of happiness, all his heroes aspire to its bliss. This aspiration is an irresistible human need, a manifestation of the life instinct—and it is doomed to failure and annihilation. With incomparable poetry he describes this wistful expectation of soul and flesh, this flowering of desire and love, this hope of triumphing over the ruthless domination of time. The best pages of Turgenev are devoted to this promise of happiness that reaches its height in the awakening of love and in the springtime of nature. In **"Three Encounters"** the image of the tense, almost painful, silence of a magnificent summer night filled with scents and susurrations and cravings, with the languor and yearnings of mind and body, with a strange sensation of happiness—a promise and a recollection—is one of the most lyrical passages in the European prose of the nineteenth century; and as a parallel to these pages, there are the chapters describing Liza's love for Lavretzky in ***A Nest of Gentlefolk.***

Turgenev never pictured the fulfilment of love, the satisfaction of the senses and of the heart. For him the apex had been reached before—in the highest and most intense moment of a dream that can never come true. (pp. 266-68)

Certain severe critics contend that Turgenev's search for beauty often turned into prettiness, while his art became arty. It is true that his softness and gentleness have at times a cloying aftertaste. He makes life and nature appear rather tame, he avoids mentioning the seamy side of reality or plunging too deeply beneath its surface, for fear of encountering the monsters of depravity, hatred, or abnormality. He takes great care not to pain or shock his readers, and his prose is decorous and seemly, suave and well-bred. His voice is never raised or altered; there are no surprises in his narrative, no breaks in his sentences. Whatever one may feel about this kind of literature, its craftsmanship is undeniable: Turgenev was an extraordinary artist.

This refined and intelligent writer whose irony—and there is far more irony in his works than is usually acknowledged—

Manuscript title page of A House of Gentlefolk.

underscored his sadness, this accomplished stylist who believed that 'such a great, mighty, and free language' as Russian must have been given to a great people, this esthete who wrote social novels, this partrician who described the peasants, this democrat who sang requiems over the nobility, this realist who was so elegiac, this poet who was so precise, is one of the most beloved writers in Russia.

Widely read and enjoyed today, he will probably continue to be one of the most popular writers for many years to come—as long as his languor, his melancholic grief, combined with the exaltation in love and beauty, and his conception of art as an orderly arrangement of emotional values, still stir the poetic and esthetic senses of Russian readers. . . . (pp. 270-71)

Marc Slonim, "Turgenev," in his The Epic of Russian Literature: From Its Origins through Tolstoy, *Oxford University Press, 1950, pp. 250-71.*

JOHN GASSNER (essay date 1951)

[*Gassner, a Hungarian-born American scholar, was a great promoter of American theater, particularly the work of Tennessee Williams and Arthur Miller. He edited numerous collections of modern drama and wrote two important dramatic surveys,* Masters of the Drama *and* Theater in Our Times. *In the following excerpt from a revised edition of the former study first published in 1951, Gassner discusses Turgenev's plays, noting their psychological acuity and their adherence to the nineteenth-century Russian dramatic method of using characterization to illustrate the human condition.*]

Turgenev was a true realist—an inner realist; explaining himself, he said, "What do I care whether a woman sweats in the middle of her back or under her arms? I do not care how or where she sweats; I want to know how she thinks."

Nor did he remove himself from the social scene while observing the inner man. In his novels ***Rudin*** and ***Virgin Soil*** he exposed the failure of the intelligentsia to overcome its natural sloth and waywardness. The most famous novel ***Fathers and Sons,*** as well as ***On the Eve*** and ***Virgin Soil,*** sketched a new and vigorous generation that would grapple with the old order by means of scientific intelligence, revolutionary action, or reform. His picture of his times was consequently comprehensive and provocative.

Turgenev's outlook in his plays is, regrettably, narrower because he had no confidence in his dramatic talent. At most he hoped that the plays "though not entirely satisfactory for the stage, may afford an interest in reading"—a judgment that was reversed years later on both sides of the Atlantic when the Moscow Art Theatre and the Theatre Guild of New York produced ***A Month in the Country.*** The larger issues of his novels appear at least in solution, although they are easily overshadowed by his insight into the realities of character.

A delightful satire on the shiftless upper class is the one-acter ***Broke,*** in which the young squire Zhazikov hides from his creditors and seriously thinks of returning to the country only to forget his resolve the moment a friend lends him two hundred rubles. A typical detail occurs after a dunning shoemaker is sent away by Matvei, the old servant. Turning to the latter, Zhazikov declares: "Matvei, I want to order a livery for you. . . . I want to order a livery of the very latest style for you, a purple-gray, with blue shoulder knots. . . ." Hardly has he uttered the thought than he has to hide behind a screen when another creditor rings the bell. Turgenev's remarkable ability to describe commoners is also present here, as it was in his famous short stories in the ***Sportsman's Sketches.*** The patiently disapproving Matvei is excellently delineated, and it would be hard to equal his conversation with a persistent merchant anywhere except in the Irish theatre. ***A Conversation on the Highway*** is another authentic picture of Russian society compressed into nothing more than a spat in an old coach rolling along a country road. A quarrel between country squires over a piece of land in ***An Amicable Settlement*** also suffices to reveal a facet of Russian society.

In another one-acter ***Where It Is Thin, There It Breaks*** Turgenev's social and the individual analysis meet most effectively. Gorski is a typical Turgenev hero—introspective, complex and irresolute; and Viera is one of this author's typical heroines—a sensitive but sensible and resolute girl. Gorski loses her to a friend whom he himself introduced into the family. His hesitant wooing of her, caused by congenital irresoluteness, strains her long forbearance and insults her so deeply that she throws herself into the friend's arms. Gorski, in short, is one of Turgenev's Russian Hamlets.

The Bachelor, a full-length work, is a delicate and touching comedy about the middle-aged "collegiate assessor" Moshkin who tries to marry his nineteen-year-old ward Maria to a weak-willed young subordinate but wins her himself on the rebound when the latter abandons her. A characteristic Russian touch is the fact that Moshkin adopted her after an accidental and slight acquaintance with her mother because the girl had nowhere to go. Petrusha, the fiancé, is another well-drawn character; this weakling deserts Maria when a pedantic Russified German tells him that she isn't "cultured" enough. And as usual Turgenev is most successful when he draws his heroine;

Maria is a masterly portrait of a sensitive but courageous and practical girl. In order to avoid misunderstandings after her rejection by Petrusha, she is ready to leave Moshkin's house and is willing to brave poverty in the home of a poor aunt. Moshkin wants only to protect her by marriage, having no illusions about his attractiveness to a young girl. But Maria is grateful and sensible enough to want to give him her love, and she is unassuming enough to be as good as her word.

This play is inferior only to Turgenev's masterpiece, ***A Month in the Country,*** which possesses greater scope and complexity. A youthful and energetic tutor Bieliaev attracts the mistress of the estate Natalia, who pays scant attention to her industrious husband Islaev. Her young ward also falls in love with him while the object of so much adoration is quite unconscious of attracting either woman. Natalia becomes jealous of the young girl and tries to marry her off to a stupid and absurd neighbor, deceiving herself into believing that she is only helping her ward. The latter, however, senses that Natalia is her rival and confesses her love to the tutor, and Natalia follows suit. Her husband discovers her weeping on the shoulder of Rakitin, her platonic admirer and confidant, because of her frustrated love. Rakitin, in an embittered mood, confesses to him that he loves Natalia and prepares to leave. Finally Bieliaev also departs. The girl, who now hates Natalia decides to marry the fatuous neighbor as a means of escape, and Natalia remains alone and frustrated. The play thus ends in a stalemate with the characters fading out and their frustration deepening.

In these works one already finds intimations of Chekhov's art. They are distinguished by the same kind of psychological penetration and sensitivity, as well as by the same sense of an unhappy life seething beneath the quiet surface. Finally, they possess the same fugitive quality, for which one may borrow a term from the English critic and translator George Calderon. The ordinary Western play, Calderon declared, is "centripetal"; that is, the attention of the spectator is drawn to the group of people immediately before him in the play. The characteristic Russian drama of the nineteenth century is, on the contrary, "centrifugal"; that is, the group of characters who are on the stage draw attention to humanity at large. (pp. 500-02)

John Gassner, "Chekhov and the Russian Realists," in his Masters of the Drama, *third revised edition, Dover Publications, Inc., 1954, pp. 495-525.*

JANKO LAVRIN (essay date 1954)

[Lavrin is an Austrian-born British critic, essayist, and biographer. He is best known for his studies of nineteenth- and twentieth-century Russian literature. In such works as An Introduction to the Russian Novel, *Lavrin employed an approach that combines literary criticism with an exploration into the psychological and philosophical background of an author. Here, Lavrin focuses on Turgenev's omnipresent concern with the "superfluous" man.]*

Ivan Turgenev was the first Russian author to become generally known and admired beyond the boundaries of his own country. It was through him that Russian fiction began to penetrate into Europe as one of the major literary influences. And for good reason, since he always knew how to combine his "Russianness" with impeccable literary manners and with a technique perfect enough to challenge comparison with any great prose-writer of the West. He loses only if compared with such cyclopic geniuses as Dostoevsky and Tolstoy who can afford to be a law unto themselves. Similarly in the world of music, Mozart seems to lose if compared with Beethoven, for example: but while Beethoven may be a greater genius, Mozart remains a greater artist.

Turgenev belongs to what might be called the well-ordered Mozartian—or, for that matter, Pushkinian—type of creators. Whatever subject he took on, he handled it first of all as a perfect artist. External reality, including its most topical aspects and problems, was for him but raw material which he distilled into works of beauty. Keenly interested in the political, social and cultural struggles of the day, he had his own definite convictions, sympathies, antipathies; yet he never let them interfere with the aesthetic side of his writings. This did not exclude, of course, that unconscious interference which determines beforehand as it were one's choice of certain themes and characters in preference to others. In this respect Turgenev remained a descendant of the old "nests of gentlefolk" at the very height of the intelligentsia period of Russian culture and literature. Although himself a member of the intelligentsia and a sincere liberal with a Western outlook, he yet remained a Russian nobleman with the ancestral country-house not only in his memory but in his very blood. In contrast to the more radical intellectuals who came from the "commoners" and looked only towards the future, Turgenev the artist could not help being rooted in the past even when fighting it in the light of the vital problems of the day. The company of the impetuous "commoners," so conspicuous in the ranks of the intelligentsia during the 'sixties, hardly made him feel quite at ease. At any rate, when at the beginning of that momentous decade a split between the "gentlemen" and the "commoners" took place within the precincts of *The Contemporary* itself (the principal organ of the advanced intelligentsia), Turgenev was one of those who walked out of the editorial premises.

After that split, the "commoners"—under the leadership of Dobrolyubov and Chernyshevsky—practically monopolized the journalistic and pamphleteering activities, whereas the "gentlemen" concentrated more on literature proper. With the exception of Dostoevsky and Leskov, both of whom were of mixed origin, the principal authors of the 'fifties, 'sixties and 'seventies, dealt mostly with the country-house and the village. This applies above all to Turgenev, whose work can perhaps be defined as the swan-song of a class which had a past but could no longer look forward with confidence to a future. It is against the background of this class, with its prevalent moods, that we can best see Turgenev's life and work in their right perspective. (pp. 116-17)

In Turgenev's novels one encounters again and again the effete gentry people, unable to cope with the task of adjusting themselves to the conditions and the age in which they live. The Childe Harold-Onegin-Pechorin tradition of the "superfluous man" therefore plays in them a conspicuous part. As early as 1851 Turgenev wrote his excellent **"Diary of a Superfluous Man,"** and from that time on this unheroic hero remained one of his ever-recurring figures. Rudin, his first full-size portrait in the novel bearing the same name, is actually one of Turgenev's amazing feats of characterization. We are introduced to Rudin in the drawing-room of an "up-to-date" country-house, where he impresses everybody by his intelligence and idealism (in the style of the period). Then, to our surprise we learn that this brilliant talker is a parasite and a sponger. Soon we are compelled to revise this opinion also. After a number of contradictory features quickly following one another, he is subjected to a crucial test—in his love for the hostess's daughter Natasha. But here he shows his lack of backbone and even of ordinary courage. The author makes us alternately waver between spite, pity and affection, and each new feature of Rudin perplexes us as if it could not belong to the man we know already. Yet after a while all the contradictions adjust themselves, and we have before us an intensely real character whom, for all his strangeness, we seem to like. Full of the best impulses and intentions, but as helpless in practice as a child, this uprooted *déclassé* is unable to find an active contact with life. He does not belong anywhere. So he is doomed to remain a victim of his own dreams, and his brilliant intelligence remains sterile, however good the material out of which he is made.

If Rudin is a restless descendant of Onegin gone to seed, Natasha has affinities with Pushkin's Tatyana. Like Tatyana, she too is much stronger than the man she loves, and after her initial disappointment, finds her place in life. The whole existence of Rudin, however, is only one long series of escapes—from life as well as from himself. He embodies the woolly rootless idealism which was so often to be found among the gentry intellectuals of the 'forties, and it is almost with a kind of relief that we learn of his death on the barricades in Paris, during the Revolution of 1848.

The note of frustration is no less strong in Turgenev's next novel, ***A Nest of Gentlefolk.*** Here, too, we have a picture of gentry life against the background of which the Rudin-Natasha (i.e. Onegin-Tatyana) motif assumes, in the love between Lavretsky and Liza, a rather tragic turn. Lavretsky, a disillusioned married man whose lewd wife is enjoying herself on the French Riviera, is in essence as "superfluous" as Rudin but more purposeful. . . . Unable to disentangle himself from the grip of his depraved wife, Lavretsky surrenders to his fate without a struggle, while Liza buries her own life in a convent. Here, after a considerable lapse of time, the two once happy lovers meet again in a scene which might have become melodramatic but for Turgenev's supreme artistic tact and restraint. For not a single word is exchanged, and the two pass each other by like two pathetic ghosts.

Delicate on account of its pitfalls, the subject-matter is worked out in a symphonic manner—with numerous secondary motifs, episodes, and characters held together by the basic theme. The contrasted and mutually complementary characters; the background, the "atmosphere," and the plot itself are so well blended that here the truth of life is not only distilled but also deepened and intensified by the truth of art. Even Turgenev's mood of gentle fatalism, which pervades the book, is so well sublimated as to cease to be personal: it becomes part and parcel of the "atmosphere" itself. And so does his admiration for Liza. She may be idealized, but this does not prevent her from being alive and real—a thing which can be said, perhaps, with less emphasis of Helena, the heroine of ***On the Eve.***

In this novel Turgenev portrayed the generation of the 'fifties, that is of the years which saw the Crimean Campaign, the death of Nicholas I, and anticipated the great reforms that were to come during the next decade—the years of expectations. But were the Russian intellectuals equal to the tasks ahead? Turgenev's answer was in the negative; at least with regard to men if not to women. The heroine of this novel is represented (on the very eve of the Crimean Campaign) as the new active woman, capable of a heroic task without any heroic pose or self-admiration. Surrounded by charming and intelligently talkative Rudins, she falls in love not with a member of her own class or even of her own nation, but with the rather angular Insarov, a Bulgarian fanatically devoted to the idea of freeing his country from the Turkish yoke. But if Helena remains convincing, Insarov is overdrawn, too much of a one-track mind, to be entirely alive. One admires his firmness rather than his personality, but in the end it is his one-sided firmness which makes one feel somewhat dismayed. It is worth noting that even this novel, in which Turgenev was so anxious to portray a strong man, has an unhappy ending: Insarov dies in Venice, while on his way to foment a rising in his own country.

It was only in his next and greatest novel, ***Fathers and Children,*** that Turgenev succeeded in giving a convincing portrait of the strong new man—this time a Russian—the age was clamoring for. And since he was doubtful of the members of his own class, he had to look for him among the "commoners." He found him in the person of the nihilist Bazarov, whose prototype was a Russian doctor Turgenev had actually met in 1860, in Germany. It was not without malice that he transferred Bazarov to a "nest of gentlefolk," confronting him with the rather fossilized representatives of the 'forties. Devoid of any respect for traditions, canonized ideas or class-distinctions, Bazarov is frankness itself: always matter-of-fact, inconsiderate, even aggressive, but at the same time hard-working and full of guts. One can well imagine that the rôle he plays in the genteel "Victorian" country-house of his hosts is none too pleasant for either party. Various conflicts, hidden and open arise almost at once. They are caused not so much by the differences in opinions as by those imponderable unconscious attitudes towards certain things in life which are often a much more formidable class-barrier than rank or wealth. Turgenev surpasses himself in the fineness of touch and delicate humor when dealing with such imponderables. On the other hand, he may admire Bazarov, but does not really like him and feels more at home with the "gentlefolk." Yet he realizes that the future is with Bazarov and not with Bazarov's hosts, whom the "nihilist" cannot quite stomach. Bazarov was in fact the "commoner" who emerged among the leading figures in the intelligentsia of the 'sixties, and with whom the "gentlemen" had to put up whether they liked him or not. A "gentleman" himself, Turgenev gave in Bazarov one of the great portraits in the nineteenth century literature.

From a purely formal standpoint, ***Fathers and Children*** is as perfect as ***A Nest of Gentlefolk,*** but its texture is richer, while the interplay of the characters is considerably deeper. The "tame" Arkady (with whom Turgenev himself must have had quite a lot in common), Arkady's father and immaculate uncle, Bazarov's pathetically simple parents, the shy Fenitchka, the self-possessed (and undersexed) Mme Odintsova, her gentle sister Katya—they all fit perfectly into the pattern devised by the author and are alive even in their most casual words and movements. The finale is again a tragic one. Yet the scene of Bazarov's death is one of the most powerful ever described by an author; powerful precisely on account of its reserve. The contrast between Bazarov's manly stoicism and the frantic state of his parents—so anxious to conceal their despair from their dying son—is one of those marvels of art which are more real than reality itself. Although the novel is full of the atmosphere of the early 'sixties, it is easy to perceive behind it the eternal tragi-comedy of human relations in general: those between parents and their grown-up children; between men and women; aristocrats and "commoners"; dreamers and realists; leaders and followers. It is again a case of the truth of life being deepened and enriched by the truth of art.

The impatient younger generation of the 'sixties repudiated ***Fathers and Children.*** The storm raised by the novel brought so much disgust to its author that, for a while, he intended to give up literature altogether, as one can gather from his autobiographic sketch, **"Enough."** Turgenev's irritation at the Russian life of the period came out with a great deal of bitterness in his next novel, ***Smoke.*** As if feeling that he himself was now becoming more and more "superfluous," he preferred to live abroad. . . . (pp. 121-27)

Still, he was less out of touch with what was going on in Russia than many of his critics thought. Turgenev the artist may have been above parties, but as a citizen he was keenly interested in the political and social life of his country. Even after his differences with the "commoners" in *The Contemporary*, his outlook remained that of a liberal Westerner, for which the patriotic Slavophil Dostoevsky lampooned him (so mercilessly) in the figure of the author Karmazinov in *The Possessed*. The controversy between the two factions found an echo in ***Smoke***—a novel in which biting personal indignation and political satire, directed against all the factions of Russian life, often loom large even at the expense of the finely worked out romance, or the unsuccessful renewal of an old romance, between Litvinov (another "superfluous man") and Irina. (pp. 127-28)

With all its occasional flaws, ***Smoke*** is one of Turgenev's masterpieces. His last novel, ***Virgin Soil,*** on the other hand, can more aptly be called a brilliant failure. Here the author obviously wanted to prove that, in spite of his stay abroad, he was able to understand and to interpret the aspirations of the advanced currents in his native country. In this case he tackled the current prevalent in the 'seventies—the "populism" which aimed at bridging the gap between the intelligentsia and the people and caused a number of enthusiastic youths and girls to sacrifice everything in order to help the masses and prepare them for the hoped-for revolution. In ***Virgin Soil*** we can follow the activities of a whole group of such enthusiasts up to their complete disappointment. Anxious to blend the social-political theme with the artistic side of the novel, the author nearly succeeded—nearly but not entirely. His weakness comes out first of all in the portrait of the principal character: the "strong man" Solomin. For instead of producing a new counterpart of Bazarov, Turgenev gave here something like an abstraction of a sober, reliable, practical idealist. Solomin is too much of a "perfect" dummy to be credible as a human being. The other characters of the novels are, however, convincing and alive: the actively generous Marianna (almost a twin-sister of Helena in ***On the Eve***), for example; the "superfluous" revolutionary Hamlet—Nezhdanov; or the pompous opportunist (this time of a "liberal" brand) Sipyagin. The love between Nezhdanov and Marianna is, of course, a new variation of the Rudin-Natasha motif. The general tenor of the book is rather pessimistic about the populist movement, and Turgenev's own conclusions seem to tally with the allegorical poem by one of his heroes, **"A Dream."** . . . (pp. 128-29)

Turgenev described the various aspects of Russian life at a time when the sleeper, rubbing his eyes, was preparing to have his own say at last. What that say would be like remained a puzzle even for Turgenev. Russia's riddle and destiny were much too intricate for him to find an adequate formula, let alone a solution.

In spite of all the changes in literary fashions, Turgenev still remains one of the great artists in Russian as well as European fiction. Apart from his mellow style, his polish, his delicate irony, and his sense of construction, one admires in him that indefinable intimacy with which he impresses his characters upon us even before we are aware of it. However strange they may appear at first, we soon move among them as among personal friends whose misfortunes often agitate us as much as our own. He excels in particular as psychologist and poet of love. And whatever theme or plot he may choose, he always knows how to treat it in perspective as something deeper and more permanent than the passing show of a period. The variety of his characters, too, is surprisingly big. This is true also of his women portraits, despite his predilection for the Tatyana-type. Take the hysterically exalted girl in **"A Strange Story";** his gallery of old maids; his worldly cocottes (Mme. Lavretsky in ***A Nest of Gentlefolk,*** or Mme. Polozova in the largely autobiographic [***The Torrents of Spring***]); his blue-stockings; his enchantingly sensuous Irina in ***Smoke.*** Turgenev's weakness for Mme. Viardot-Garcia may have been responsible for the large number of weak men in his novels and stories; yet his weaklings are more interesting, more complex, and certainly more successfully worked out than his strong men. The futility of his own love is further reflected in his "atmosphere," reminiscent of a melancholy autumn afternoon, with gentle fatalism permeating the air.

The same kind of mood can be felt in his stories which are deservedly among the best in European literature. A master of impressionism in ***A Sportsman's Sketches,*** and a superb storyteller in such narratives as ***First Love, Asya,*** **"A King Lear of the Steppes",** ***The Spring Torrents,*** and many others, he can stand comparison with any famous artist of the word. Most of his stories resemble well-organized reminiscences, told in the first person (his favorite device is that of setting a story within a story) and vibrating with that vague nostalgia for the past which was typical of Turgenev himself. As a "superfluous" member of an already "superfluous" class, he felt so homeless in the rapidly changing world that the atmosphere of doom eventually seemed to emanate from his very personality. Mme. Herzen once compared him with an uninhabitated room: "Its walls are damp, and their dampness gets into your bones; you are afraid to sit down, afraid to touch anything, and you only wish to get out of it as quickly as possible." (pp. 129-31)

Turgenev the man died in 1883. But Turgenev the author continues to live as a world classic, belonging not to one, but to all ages and countries. (p. 131)

Janko Lavrin, "Ivan Turgenev," in his Russian Writers: Their Lives and Literature, *D. Van Nostrand Company, Inc., 1954, pp. 116-31.*

ALFRED KAZIN (essay date 1955)

[A highly respected American literary critic, Kazin is best known for his essay collections The Inmost Leaf, Contemporaries, *and, particularly,* On Native Grounds, *a study of American prose writing since the era of William Dean Howells. Proclaiming Turgenev the least Russian of Russian novelists, Kazin views the "fatality of love" as the most significant aspect of his novels.]*

Ivan Turgenev was the first Russian writer to be widely read outside his country, and it was through him that Europe discovered there was a Russian literature—which was promptly identified with his exquisite and elegiac art. Today, ironically, he seems of all the great Russian writers the least characteristic: a superb artist, one of the finest in the history of the novel, but hardly one who reminds us of the fierce involvement in the whole human situation, the overwhelming naturalness, that keep Dostoevsky and Tolstoy at the center of our thinking about the world we now live in. . . .

Turgenev, unlike Tolstoy or Dostoevsky or Chekhov, does not write about Russia, as if it were the world itself; he does not take it for granted as the great arena of human existence. Though he loved Russia, he preferred to do so from a distance. (p. 89)

Like Henry James, Turgenev could look at his own country from both sides at once, could even be bored by it. But while it has been traditional for American writers to be bored by America, or to abuse or to escape it, one can hardly think of many Russian writers who were so bored by Russia, who were so easily disillusioned with it. And it is this quality in Turgenev that perhaps explains why, though the center of his art is always firm, and often very beautiful indeed, there is felt all through his work an atmosphere of tepid resignation, of lyric sadness, of disenchantment, of some irrevocable disillusionment with men and affairs, and Russia itself. (p. 90)

Today Turgenev's "civilized" and "European" art seems no longer in the forefront of Russian literature, but behind it. Even Chekhov, the Russian writer most superficially like Turgenev in tone, insisted that the frustration of his characters came out of the inertia and backwardness of Russia in the nineteenth century. Chekhov's characters are frustrated by the world they live in; Turgenev's by themselves—their special mark is always the sad autonomy of human love, its final impossibility in a country that afflicts them, but which they do not recognize as their destiny. Russia is a background to their quiet ordeal; it is not, to their conscious mind, of the ordeal itself. If it had been, Turgenev's art would not have been quite so exquisite, so closed off by its own perfection, so resigned—so much, in a word, the kind of art Henry James found it natural to admire.

Turgenev is the great poet of the doomed love affair—doomed, because the characters sacrifice everything in life to love, and yet know from the beginning that it is unnatural; that seeking everything from love alone, they will never get anything from their love itself. Even ***Fathers and Sons,*** with its famous nihilist hero, Bazarov, the arrogant young doctor from whom a whole generation of Russian intellectuals formed its idea of emancipation, now seems curiously unrelated to the intellectual and political battles of a century ago. It emerges simply as an elegy on all human frustration. Bazarov's many speeches in defense of positivism, his naïve worship of science, his opposition to "poetry"—all now have an effect of parody.

It is as if Turgenev, in forecasting this new type of Russian hero, had actually rendered him absurd at the same time, for Turgenev cannot take Bazarov's ideas, or any ideas, very seriously. But Bazarov's hopeless quest of Madame Odinstova, his unvoiced despair at ever being able to win her, his unconscious suicide, when he allows himself to be infected by a patient dying of typhoid—these make the real story, these are closest to Turgenev's heart, as it is this hopelessness that creates the marvelous effect of a slow irrevocable curve, from life into death, with which the story draws to a close.

Similarly, one might define Turgenev's subject as the fatality of love. Something always goes wrong; the lovers know in advance that it will, and nevertheless they persist. Perhaps it is the idea of fatality they are in love with. In ***Smoke,*** Litvinov's hopeless love for Irena—the usual Turgenev *femme fatale,* with her trance-like astonishment at being unable to love anyone in return—is genuinely felt in a way that Turgenev's heavy satire against the Russian fops and pretentious "liberals" at Baden-Baden is not. In ***Rudin,*** a devastating portrait of the young Russian intellectual of the period, it is Rudin's inability to love that makes the story so harshly effective. In ***On the Eve,*** Turgenev's most admired heroine, Yelena, actually finds love with Insarov, but of course he dies as promptly as possible.

Still, it is precisely in this conviction of slow, inevitable frustration, of aimless drift and passage in human affairs—the "smoke" Litvinov saw from his railway carriage, symbolizing the impermanence and ennui of human affairs—that Turgenev finds the extraordinarily precise yet lyric details with which he describes the Russian countryside. Stroke by stroke, the Russian woods and streams emerge with incomparable beauty as that inner world his characters hope to win, and cannot. For they never realize how little they are committed to it as theirs; how much, beyond all their frustration, it still speaks for what is enduring—in their love itself. (pp. 90-2)

Alfred Kazin, "Turgenev and the Non-Russians," in his The Inmost Leaf: A Selection of Essays, *Harcourt Brace Jovanovich, Inc., 1955, pp. 89-92.*

RALPH E. MATLAW (essay date 1957)

[*Matlaw argues that political content is inadequately integrated, indeed, superfluous, in Turgenev's novels, with the exception of* Fathers and Sons. *The critic distinguishes Turgenev's novels from his short stories and novellas in this respect, claiming that the shorter works, with less political material, are more unified and artistically successful.*]

It may seem far-fetched, if not deliberately perverse, to state that although Turgenev was a superlative writer of fiction, he was not a successful novelist. Such a statment is not designed to characterize the achievements of his novels, but rather to comment on the insufficient integration of social background and characters appearing against this background. More simply, Turgenev was hampered by the longer literary forms. . . . (p. 249)

Turgenev did not consider himself the chronicler of his time when he wrote his works. This is a task a lesser writer, someone like Prince Boborykin, might specifically set himself. Nevertheless, because Turgenev's novels do deal in greater detail than the shorter works with social questions, and would therefore interest nineteenth century Russian publicists more, much of the critical literature on Turgenev has concentrated on his novels and their social meaning and significance. Criticism dealing with the social and political background (beginning with the famous essays by Černyševskij, Dobroljubov [see excerpts dated 1858? and 1860], and Pisarev, and culminating in H. Granjard's recent voluminously documented study [*Ivan Tourguénev et les courants politiques et sociaux de son temps*]), despite many incidental insights into Turgenev's work, presents a rather distorted picture of his development and artistic achievement.

Comparatively little has been written from a literary, formal point of view to balance such criticism. But what has been done indicates Turgenev's predominant concern with aesthetics rather than politics. . . . In this study, without attempting to fix the exact percentage of Turgenev's political and aesthetic interests, an attempt will be made to examine Turgenev's creative method and to assess the effect of social responsibility on his work, particularly on his novels.

In the preface to his novels. Turgenev states that the true artist never resigns himself to convey a program, or to write on a proposed theme; that he never serves incidental, foreign aims. "Life around him gives him the matter—he creates its *concentrated reflection.*" The question should then really be asked: what is the life around him? How does he view it? What in particular appeals to him? This can be answered much more easily for the man than for the writer. We know that he was keenly interested in the latest moral and political questions; that he had about him something like the temperament and zeal of a conscientious reporter; that he was always aware of the latest cultural and intellectual events. But to what degree this sense of immediacy or contemporaneousness impelled him to literary expression remains a moot question. Apart from several stories in the ***Sketches,*** the novels, **"Punin and Baburin,"** and perhaps one or two other stories, politics and social considerations do not enter the work. Indeed, it may profitably be compared to the work of Jane Austen. Although Turgenev lacked her trenchant, unsentimental mind, he resembles her in many ways, not the least of which is a disregard for historical setting. The men in *Pride and Prejudice* go off to the Napoleonic Wars, though this cannot be determined from the book, since the war is never mentioned. Most of Turgenev's work has just this self-contained, self-sufficient quality, and can be read with practically no knowledge of nineteenth-century Russia. On the other hand, it is impossible to appreciate fully the situations and characters Turgenev presents in his novels without considering the intellectual and social milieu in which they purportedly exist. But such knowledge does not materially affect appreciation of his work's merit, and in the final analysis applies only to that part of the work which has dated most quickly and is least valuable. (pp. 250-52)

It is generally agreed that the most dated part of Turgenev's novels are the political discussions and talks, which have lost their vitality and significance, and may be excised with profit. In ***Smoke,*** although there may be a tenuous connection between Potugin's diatribes and the Russians depicted, these sections could be eliminated with little loss to the novel: the resulting (mutilated) product would then be ***Spring Torrents*** told in realistic rather than sentimental terms. Similarly, the brief argument between Lavrekij and Panšin in ***Nest of Noblemen,*** Insarov's melodramatic revolutionary and nationalistic pronouncements in ***On the Eve,*** Solomin's and Paklin's speeches in ***Virgin Soil,*** and several great scenes of pseudo prophecy or aspiration could also be eliminated without great loss to the works.

It is possible to edit the novels so drastically because there is no real integration between the character and the political position; or because the political has little function in the novel. On the other hand, in Turgenev's most successful and profound novel, ***Fathers and Sons,*** such excision is impossible, for Turgenev has fused the character and his social or political view. Insarov's ideals tell us next to nothing about him. Pavel Kirsanov's, or any other person's views in ***Father and Sons,*** *are* that person, and present not a statement or argument about a topical question, but rather use the statement to characterize the person uttering it. Bazarov himself, although a fully rounded literary depiction, is essentially a temperament that expresses itself in everything he says and does. In ***Fathers and Sons*** even political dialogue serves to dramatize personality and conflict. In most of the other works it does not. The *reductio ad absurdum* of Turgenev's inability to dramatize the political within an artistic conception is found in the prose-poems, where ex-cathedra statements on politics and life are prettified rather than artistically concentrated. In the prose-poems Turgenev merely expresses ideas rhetorically, and their triteness is necessarily striking. Similarly, political pronouncements in the novels have, by and large, little further meaning than their immediate content: they add little to the artifact.

Yet Turgenev felt compelled to insert these dialogues, since they deal with an important part of the life he was depicting. His lack of success in doing so may indicate that politics was alien to his artistic vision, that his private dichotomy between politics and aesthetics affected his ability to integrate them artistically. Moreover, such conversations are frequently anachronistic: ***Rudin,*** due to confused chronology, reflects philosophical concepts rampant in the early 1830's, though the novel is set in the late 1830's or early 1840's. ***Fathers and Sons*** and ***Virgin Soil*** are, to put the kindest construction on the matter, almost prophetic, for they disclose political types and movements that came into being only later. It does not much matter that Turgenev may anticipate or reconstruct eras as much as fifteen years removed from the time of writing. But it is significant that he claims political and historical accuracy. Even if ***Rudin*** did depict correctly life in the 1840's, what social purpose is achieved by depicting this age in 1855? Clearly it could not have been Turgenev's intention to make a political statement in ***Rudin*** and, in fact, the motivating impulse is not politics, but Rudin's prototype, Bakunin.

In retrospect, however, the presence of political matter must have been important to Turgenev when he separated the novels from his other works, since "apolitical" stories like ***Spring Torrents*** or **"The Unfortunate" ("Nesčastnaja")** were not called novels, though they approximate them in length. The novels, then, have a more obviously expressed political orientation. . . . There is a technical distinction to be made as well. All the novels use the third-person, omniscient narrator, unlike the stories and novellas, twenty-six of which are framed or unframed *Icherzählungen*. It may therefore also be said that the novels are apparently the most impersonal and objective of his work. It should be stated again, however, that this distinction on Turgenev's part is arbitrary: it elevates, retrospectively, certain works to a more impressive category and bunches together, as it were, all the social message.

It does not suffice to maintain that political background does not contribute value to the novels in proportion to the space it occupies or the disruptive effect it creates. It may be shown that the use of political matter, almost compulsory in the nineteenth-century Russian novel, is little suited to Turgenev's literary abilities; and indeed, that the longer form does not permit him to exercise his special skills. The best way to do so is to examine his process of composition.

It is abundantly clear from his manuscripts and working notes that the core for any Turgenev work of reasonably large dimension is a characterization or a biographical event. He begins with a character sketch, usually based on a live model, and tries to see the character more and more clearly. Eventually he gathers a little group of characters, and then it is only necessary to put them into movement to find a plot that will utilize them adequately. For the purpose of analysis, characterization and description will be distinguished from action and plot, although they are, of course, interdependent. "Action" names that process which reveals character or theme; "plot" (which Turgenev called *fabula*) indicates the temporal sequence of events leading to "action."

Turgenev's biggest weakness is his inability to weave a plot. . . . Character . . . is at the center of Turgenev's work, and his interest in and use of plot is minimal ***(Rudin, Smoke).*** Plot is strikingly absent from ***Fathers and Sons,*** a novel illustrating that the only requirement for Turgenev's purpose is a series of scenes each of which reveals character in a different way, illuminates it from a different angle or perspective, or demonstrates still another facet of its personality. The sociological or political aspect of the novels, which must necessarily be expressed in terms of plot rather than action, may therefore be shown as even less germane to the novels than it at first appears to be.

It may further be stated as a formal principle (rather than as an impressionistic commentary) that there is only one action in the novels—love. The inception, incubation, development, declaration, withering, or evanescence of love provides a convenient touchstone for gauging and exposing character, but also creates new problems for the critic. Women frequently assume the initiative morally as well as amatorily, thereby usurping a role more properly that of the male, and then they proceed to dominate and control him. It is tempting—but not altogether necessary—to connect this with Turgenev's own personality. Whatever the personal motivation for such displacement may be, it is curious to observe that male inadequacy, expressed through hesitation, confusion, indirection, avoidance, and resignation, does not find its complementary qualities satisfactorily united in the opposing female. For Turgenev divides his female characters into two groups: the "predatory" or *diabolique* (in Barbey d'Aurévilly's sense), and those whom some commentators, apparently without facetious intent, label "passionate virgins." The first group, which includes Turgenev's most successful creations (Irina in ***Smoke,*** Polozova in ***Spring Torrents,*** Varvara Petrovna in ***A Nest of Noblemen),*** comes in conflict with the second, which seems to represent some moral, religious, or psychological standard, albeit of a dubious artistic quality (Tanja, Džemma, and Liza in these respective works). The love relationships are usually abortive because the males are unable to live up to the high goals of the females, or destructive because the men sacrifice all—career, position, reputation, money—to meet the demands of excessive passion. This theme reappears, with appropriate variations, beginning with the narrative poem **"Andrej"** and ending in **"Klara Milič."** Love, for Turgenev, is an absolute, and its issue is destruction. This is even more evident in the novels than in the rest of the works, for the political protagonists attempt to relegate love to an inferior position, and thereby impair both their private and public utility. The question should also be raised whether Turgenev does not, against his better wishes, betray his own cause. The morally upright figures frequently cede first place in artistic perfection to the vacillating male, the obviously superficial but memorably portrayed secondary figure, or the woman of the world.

Despite Turgenev's handling of the action involved in love, he hardly uses it to show personality development. Indeed, Turgenev's characters are static—he only deals with the finished product, not with the mainspring of the action. Such treatment or conception is not necessarily in itself a handicap to the novelist, but it is of crucial importance in explaining his creations. It is, for example, highly significant that Nataša in *War and Peace* seemed to Turgenev not completely successful, and, conversely, that Elena of ***On the Eve,*** one of Turgenev's best conceived sentimental temperaments, seemed to Tolstoj "wretchedly done." Neither procedure involves a false conception of character, but the view it represents leads to a different kind of literary product. . . . At his best, Turgenev transmits character without really indicating its formation or progress. In the attempt to portray such development, in a ***Nest of Noblemen*** or ***Virgin Soil*** (at least the first of which may be viewed as a *Bildungsroman),* he is almost always unsuccessful. He accounts for his character's past in factual digressions which are frequently too perfunctory, too close to superficial "reality," too empirical. They betray a limited imagination and a limited conception of character. By restricting his portraits to observable phenomena, by ignoring that dimension which permits the exploration of the mind and its working (and by criticizing others', specifically Dostoevskij's and Tolstoj's, depictions of these alien realms), his characters emerge somewhat foreshortened and in at least one sense superficial. Turgenev's literary works offer a unique insight into the vacillating personality or the attempt to overstep personality limitations. It is disconcerting, however, in reading his manuscripts, to note that he never attempts to find the motivation behind his characters, that he is concerned exclusively with surface phenomena. And while we gratefully accept depiction of surface phenomena when it is done with as sure a touch and with such telling effect as it is by Turgenev, it is difficult to see how such a method is really effective in presenting social or political views. A reader can be perfectly sure that Pierre Bezukhov will become a Decembrist, and that Nikolaj Rostov will not, for these political views are logical and necessary extensions of their respective personalities. It is less easy, if not impossible, to find a dynamic relation between Turgenev's characters and their political views, unless one accepts the view that portraiture and *paysage* are the static part of his novels, while love intrigue and the social idea provide its dynamics. The dichotomy itself, however, indicates insufficient integration.

Another kind of dichotomy, indicated above in touching on Turgenev's female characters, is the fundamental tenet of his characterization. In his essay **"Hamlet and Don Quixote"** . . . , which constitutes the most important body of psychological generalizations made by Turgenev, he divides all men into two categories: the Don Quixotes—idealists, self-effacing fighters for truth, unconcerned with personal risk and aggrandizement, doers, not thinkers; and Hamlets—egotists, doubters, beset by self-analysis which leads to inaction. This kind of polarization permeates Turgenev's works and particularly the novels, where "Hamlet" types are opposed to "Don Quixotes." In the essay he has greater regard for Don Quixote, though he has considerable sympathy for Hamlet; his artistic success is clearly greater with his "Hamlet" types. And again it should be noted that particularly in Turgenev's terms, Hamlets are not and cannot be political forces; they may only be political and personal failures.

Given Turgenev's theory of character and characterization, and reading his work, one is ineluctably led to a paradox, for it is in the stories and novellas, and not in the novels, that one sees a modicum of character development. It is significant that the main action in the novels always spans a brief period, usually a summer in the country, but sometimes only two weeks ***(Smoke),*** while the remaining works are not so restricted. Parenthetically, political novels in general, and to a lesser extent sociological novels, usually have an urban setting. But among Turgenev's novels only ***Virgin Soil*** gives city life any importance. Even Bazarov, as one critic has pointed out, is a fish out of water: his natural habitat is the city. So that again values of greater significance to Turgenev than politics—the countryside, hunting, leisure—tend to dominate the novels and make it difficult to introduce and subordinate political issues properly. The novels catch a personality at a vital moment and expose it to us. Some of the novellas, particularly those in the first person, span the life of a character, although even they focus on a particularly important episode or related episodes in his life.

Of course, within the novels, flashbacks, digressions, and the final summation inform the reader about the characters' past and future, and here Turgenev sometimes achieves fine effects. Thus in ***Rudin,*** technically his most striking though not best realized novel, Turgenev divulges information about the protagonist piecemeal, from different points of view, and at an appropriate time to balance and qualify some immediate judgment of Rudin. Ležnev takes a dim view of Rudin while others lionize him, but he later tries to raise Rudin's stature by noting his real virtues when the other characters have condemned him. Turgenev never returned to this striking form of narration. In his next novel, ***A Nest of Noblemen,*** he uses the single long digression on the Lavreckij family. At first this seems to have an unnecessarily disruptive effect. However, by recapitulating the history of the Lavreckijs for four generations, Turgenev indicates the patriarchic and outmoded nature of Lavreckij's family and life, and he is further justified in his method since he must cope with the problem of presenting and characterizing an inarticulate mediocrity. Turgenev constantly has recourse to others in order to formulate Lavreckij's thoughts (Liza, Lemm, Mikhalevič) and to make the portrait and theme clear. In subsequent novels the procedure is refined: the flashbacks are shorter, not nearly so detailed, and in the main concentrate on features necessary to the progress of the narrative. ***Smoke*** refines the technique of ***A Nest of Noblemen*** in recapitulating the early affair of Litvinov and Irina; a comparison of Elena's diary ***(On the Eve)*** with Neždanov's letters to Silin ***(Virgin Soil)*** marks the increased skill and impact Turgenev achieves by interspersing Neždanov's attempts at self-knowledge among episodes which reveal his inability to cope with reality. In ***Fathers and Sons,*** quite appropriately, almost no biographical information is given about Bazarov, since he lives exclusively in the present.

Because the novellas are more restricted in scope, they confront the reader less frequently with these digressions or set pieces and impinge less on the illusion of reality created by Turgenev. Even when these set pieces appear, they can be integrated much more easily into the structure as the narrator's realistic observations. In ***First Love,*** for example, everything is described through the eyes of the sixteen-year-old boy, or rather a sixteen-year-old boy once removed—that is, as he remembers the events twenty-five years later. The boy's observations are limited both physically and artistically: unlike an omniscient author, he sees only what is immediately before him; and because of his age and circumstance, he does not interpret his information correctly or sufficiently. The achievement of this story lies in that it is not merely a perfect rendition of "first love," but that it also simultaneously paints and characterizes the middle-aged bachelor who is the narrator. The narrator now understands many things beyond his comprehension then. But in the very process of narration he also indicates the profound and lasting effect of this experience and how it shaped him into the personality he now is.

Technically what has happened here (and in other stories like ***Spring Torrents*** and **"Diary of a Superfluous Man"**) is a rapid shift from the *nouvelle enficellée* to a Jamesian "point of view." One should not press this idea too far: Turgenev did not master the technique nor did he perhaps consciously use it. But an interesting study could be written about Turgenev's technique in a story like ***First Love*** or ***Spring Torrents,*** where he and the narrator have much in common. Since they are not identical, however, the mode of narration characterizes the narrator-protagonist, and what he recounts cannot be accepted at face value but must be corrected to account for the narrator's view or distortion. In any case, Turgenev's limited use of the technique occurs only in his shorter works, but significantly enough, in those which are his most successful. This again suggests an incompatibility between Turgenev's natural inclinations and those things he felt should be presented in the novels. For the "point of view" is in essence inimical if not altogether inappropriate to the social or political novel. It may observe and comment on social and political situations, but its proper technical use necessarily focuses on the individual and psychological or moral personality.

Turgenev frequently uses phrases, half-sentences, incompleted speech, and punctuation indicating ellipsis. He thereby suggests many intangible thoughts and emotional movements, and permits the reader to penetrate a little more deeply into the mind of the characters. This lack of concreteness or, from the other point of view, this suggestiveness, was noted and deftly generalized by George Moore when he stated that Turgenev's "special power seems to be in his skill in instantly laying bare not the body but rather the nerve of an emotion or passion, in indicating that which is most individual and constitutional in a character." In direct contrast, political views like those of the *raisonneurs* Potugin ***(Smoke)*** and Paklin ***(Virgin Soil)*** differ even stylistically and in details of punctuation from those passages utilizing Turgenev's best talents.

The incompatibility of Turgenev's interest and method with the social and political ideas he attempted to incorporate in his novels is evident. These works clearly contain many pages that interest the cultural historian; but these are not the same pages that appeal to the literary critic, whose rewards lie in explaining Turgenev's mastery in presenting those things closest to him: not the analysis of emotion, but its impact and manifestation; nature, which is the great mirror of emotion; and art, through whose magic and skill these may be expressed. (pp. 253-62)

Ralph E. Matlaw, "Turgenev's Novels: Civic Responsibility and Literary Predilection," in Harvard Slavic Studies: Russian Thought and Politics, *Vol. IV, 1957, pp. 249-62.*

EDMUND WILSON (essay date 1958)

[Wilson is generally considered the foremost twentieth-century American man of letters. A prolific reviewer, creative writer, and social and literary critic endowed with formidable intellectual powers, he exercised his greatest literary influence as the author of Axel's Castle, *a seminal study of literary symbolism, and as the author of widely read reviews and essays in which he introduced the best works of modern literature to the reading public. Wilson's criticism displays a fundamental concern for the historical and psychological implications of literary works. Alert to literature's significance as "an attempt to give meaning to our experience" and its value for the improvement of humanity, he also believed that "the real elements . . . of any work of fiction are the elements of the author's personality: his imagination embodies . . . the fundamental conflicts of his nature." Related to this is Wilson's theory, formulated in* The Wound and the Bow, *that artistic ability is a compensation for a psychological wound. In the following excerpt, Wilson examines the themes of evil and morbidity in Turgenev's shorter works, frequently relating the tales to circumstances of the author's life.]*

The work of Turgenev has, of course, no scope that is comparable to Tolstoy's or Dostoevsky's, but the ten volumes collected by him for his edition of 1883 (he omitted his early poems) represent a literary achievement of the concentratedly "artistic" kind that has few equals in nineteenth-century fiction. There are moments, to be sure, in Turgenev novels—***On the Eve*** and ***Virgin Soil***—when they become a little thin or unreal, but none can be called a failure, and one cannot find a single weak piece, unless one becomes impatient with

"Enough," in the whole four volumes of stories. No fiction writer can be read through with a steadier admiration. Greater novelists are more uneven: they betray our belief with extravagances; they bore or they fall into bathos; they combine poetic vision with rubbish. But Turgenev hardly even skirts these failings, and he is never mediocre; his texture is as distinguished as his temperament.

This texture barely survives in translation. Turgenev is a master of language; he is interested in words in a way that the other great nineteenth-century Russian novelists—with the exception of Gogol—are not. His writing is dense and substantial, yet it never marks time, always moves. . . . But this language will not reach the foreigner. How to render the tight little work of art that Turgenev has made of **"The Dog,"** narrated by an ex-hussar, with his colloquialisms, his pungent sayings, his terseness and his droll turns? And the problems of translating Turgenev are to some extent the problems of translating poetry. There is a passage in ***The Torrents of Spring***—a tour de force of onomatopoeia—that imitates in a single sentence the whispering of leaves, the buzzing of bees and the droning of a solitary dove. This is probably a conscious attempt to rival the well-known passage in Virgil's First Eclogue and Tennyson's imitation of it:

> The moan of doves in immemorial elms,
> And murmuring of innumerable bees.

But it would take another master to reproduce Turgenev's effects, just as it took a Tennyson to reproduce those of Virgil, and a Turgenev to compete with these.

Since I am going to go on . . . to call attention to the principal themes that run all through Turgenev's work and to relate them to his personal experience, I must emphasize here the solidity and the range of Turgenev's writings. It is only in the later stories which deal with the supernatural that these underlying themes emerge as obsessions or hallucinations. They are otherwise usually embodied in narratives, objectively presented, in which the backgrounds are always varied and in which even the individuals who belong to a constantly recurring type are always studied in a special context and differentiated from one another. Turgenev is not one of the great inventors, as his two colleagues and Dickens are, but in his tighter, more deliberate art he is perhaps the most satisfactory of the company to which he belongs, for he never oppresses, as Flaubert does, by his monotony and his flattening of human feeling, or fatigues, as Henry James sometimes does when his wheels of abstraction are grinding, or makes us nervous, as Conrad may do, through his effortfulness and occasional awkwardness in working in a language not native to him with materials that are sometimes alien. The material of Turgenev is all his own, and his handling of it is masterly. The detail is always amusing, always characteristic; every word, every reference, every touch of description has naturalness as well as point; the minor characters, the landscapes, the milieux are all given a full succulent flavor. The genre pictures—the funeral supper at the end of **"An Unhappy Girl,"** the transference of the property in **"A Lear of the Steppes"**—are wonderfully organized and set in motion, though such exhilaration of movement as Tolstoy is able to generate in such episodes as the hunt in *War and Peace* and the races in *Anna Karenina* is quite beyond Turgenev's powers, as is the cumulative fun and excitement of the town celebration in Dostoevsky's *The Devils*. But neither can fill in a surface, can fit language to subject like Turgenev. The weather is never the same; the descriptions of the countryside are quite concrete, and full, like Tennyson's, of exact observation of how cloud and sunlight and snow and rain, trees, flowers, insects, birds and wild animals, dogs, horses and cats behave, yet they are also stained by the mood of the person who is made to perceive them. There are moments, though not very many, when the affinity between natural phenomena and the emotion of the character exposed to them is allowed to become a little melodramatic in the old-fashioned romantic way—the volcanic sunset in *Faust* when the heroine is herself on the verge of eruption—but in general Turgenev is protected from the dangers of the "romantic fallacy" by his realistic habit of mind.

Let me here, also, call attention to a story that seems to me a masterpiece and that sounds a different note from those I shall discuss later: **"The History of Lieutenant Ergunov,"** of 1867. This Lieutenant is a heavy and clumsy and extremely naïve young man who is highly susceptible to women and who regards himself as something of a dandy. Stationed in a provincial town, he becomes involved with a household that purports to consist of an elderly woman living with two nieces. They are of mongrel and dubious origins; one of them, who calls herself Colibri, is semi-Oriental, exotic. The Lieutenant never discovers that the two girls are prostitutes and that their bully is lurking in the background. His suspicions are not even aroused when he has dropped off to sleep on a couch one day and been awakened by the efforts of one of the girls—he is carrying government money—to detach from his belt his wallet. He becomes so fascinated by Colibri that it is no trouble at all for her to drug him. They rob him, bash in his head and, assuming he is safely dead, throw his body down a ravine. It is only his exceptional vigor that enables him in time to recover from this. The thieves have, of course, made their getaway, but he presently receives a long letter from the girl who tried to steal his wallet, in which she tells him that though she has "a bad morality" and is "flighty," she is not really "a villainess." She is terribly sorry about the whole thing; the others had induced her to lend herself to luring him to the house and then sent her away for the day. "The old villainess *was not* my aunt." She begs him to answer, but he never does. Ergunov all the rest of his life tells the story at least once a month.

It is typical of Turgenev's art that the anecdote in itself, as I have sketched it, cannot convey Turgenev's point. Nothing could be more different than a story, say, by Maupassant. There are no tricks of the professional raconteur, no sudden surprise at the end. We follow a steady narrative, built up with convincing detail. It closes calmly enough with Ergunov's shaking his head and sighing "That's what it is to be young," and displaying his terrible scar, which reaches from ear to ear. And it is only when we have finished the story that we grasp the whole implication of the triumph of good faith and respect for the innocent over the brutal violation of human relations. Ergunov is the side of Turgenev himself that never could believe at first that the people who exploited him were not honest. It is a question in **"Lieutenant Ergunov"** not of one of the author's obsessive themes but of a feeling that, for all his demons, all his ogresses and their helpless victims, continues to assert itself almost to the end of his work—Gemma's letter of forgiveness to Sanin, in the later ***Torrents of Spring,*** reversing the roles of the sexes in **"Ergunov,"** embodies the same moral—and a feeling that he shares with the creator of Myshkin as well as with the creator of Pierre. This instinct sets the standards for Turgenev's mind, and it is the basis of his peculiar nobility. It is the essence of the life-giving drop that he has rescued from the cave of the reptiles.

But this story is almost unique. The positive force of honesty, even the survival of innocence—though they sometimes occur in the novels: Solomin in ***Virgin Soil,*** Tatyana and her aunt in ***Smoke***—are excessively rare in these tales. There are examples of religious dedication—**"A Living Relic"** in ***A Sportsman's Sketches,*** **"A Strange Story,"** **"A Desperate Character"**—but, especially in the last two of these, you feel that they are simply cases, included with the other cases, of the unhealthiness of Russian life. In general, the ogresses and devils continue to have the best of it, and the timid and snobbish young men continue to disappoint the proud women. . . . [In] 1857, ten years before **"Lieutenant Ergunov"**—this has happened to the heroine of ***Asya*** and to Gemma of ***The Torrents of Spring,*** and is to happen to the heroine of **"An Unhappy Girl"** (two of these the illegitimate daughters of gentlemen and one the daughter of an Italian confectioner). It is only in ***First Love*** that the girl under a social shadow is allowed to have a passionate love affair, and I am sure that it is partly to this, the exceptional element of sex interest, that the story owes its especial popularity—along with, for the same reason, ***The Torrents of Spring***—among Turgenev's shorter fictions. Yet note that it is not the young boy but his father who enjoys Zinaida's love, and that Turgenev explained that the story was based on an experience of his own youth. The figure of Turgenev's father plays no such role in his work as that of Varvara Petrovna, but the aloof and dashing father of the narrator of ***First Love,*** who fascinates Zinaida and slashes her arm with his riding crop, evidently has something to do with the diabolic brother of **"The Song of Triumphant Love,"** who mesmerizes and rapes his sister-in-law. If the heroes in Turgenev are inhibited from going to bed with the women and do so only, still with inhibitions, when—as in ***Smoke*** or ***The Torrents of Spring***—they, the men, are themselves seduced, the man who prevails over women is likely to treat them with violence and to become an embodiment of the Evil Force.

In the meantime, Varvara Petrovna is reappearing in **"Her Ladyship's Private Office"** . . ., and in **"Punin and Baburin,"** and the Lutovinova grandmother who killed the little serf boy turns up as a variation of the Varvara Petrovna character in Agrippina Ivanovna of **"The Brigadier."** The masculine Force of Evil, after lying in abeyance since **"The Wayside Inn"** of 1852, reappears five years later in **"A Tour in the Forest,"** and it is here for the first time invested—at least in the minds of the peasants of the story—with supernatural implications. This piece was added by Turgenev to a new edition of *A Sportsman's Sketches* published in 1860, but afterwards presented by the author—in his collected edition of 1865—in its chronological place. For it does not belong with the ***Sketches***—it is more philosophical and more complex; it shows the development of Turgenev's art. I agree with Dmitri Mirsky in his admiration for **"A Tour in the Forest"** [see excerpt dated 1927]—with its wonderful descriptions of pine forests, its feeling for the non-human life of trees that both embraces and isolates human beings, that oppresses at the same time it calms. And in the forest the demon is found—Efrem, a bad peasant who fears nobody, who stops at nothing and whom his neighbors can do nothing about. (pp. 48-54)

In reading **"A Tour in the Forest,"** it occurs to one that this indigenous demon, against whom the people of the forest feel themselves utterly helpless, against whom they can have no redress, represents a constant factor in Russian life, an ever-recurring phenomenon of history: the bad master whom one cannot resist, Ivan the Terrible, Peter the Great, Stalin. The masculine Force of Evil reappears in **"An Unhappy Girl"** as Susanna's horrible stepfather, and in **"A Lear of the Steppes"** you have one male and two female villains, all more or less unaccounted for. In **"Lear,"** the two daughters of old Kharlov, who destroy him, no doubt dominate the son-in-law, but there is nothing to explain why both of them should have risen to such positions of power save the example of Varvara Petrovna, on whose character they present variations. Maria Nikolaevna in ***The Torrents of Spring***—another strong and cunning peasant—is a still further variation. And thereafter, as Turgenev nears sixty, both the female and the male evil powers not only cease to wear the aspect of noxious products of the social system or even of elements of animal nature; they become supernatural beings, who prey upon and take possession, who swoop in on us from outside our known world. This development on Turgenev's part synchronizes—despite the fact that during the seventies he wrote, in ***Virgin Soil,*** his most ambitious social novel—with a haunting and growing sense of the nullity of human life and the futility of his own endeavors. . . . In the late ***Poems in Prose,*** this despondency has reached its nadir. You have, for example, the devastating dialogue between the Jungfrau and the Finsteraarhorn, which, waking or drowsing in the course of their millennia, see the human race, far below them, come to life, stir about for a little, and eventually die out like vermin. And at the same time the Force of Evil seems to rush in to fill this vacuum. These ***Senilia,*** as he calls them, are full of nightmares—the nightmare of the giant insect that fatally stings the young man, the nightmare of the end of the world, in which people in a country house are surrounded and swallowed up by a raging and icy sea.

These nightmares have begun in **"Phantoms"** of 1863, and this is followed, thirteen years later, by **"The Dream."** The element of the supernatural first appears in **"The Dog"** of 1866. This very curious story associates itself with **"Knock! . . . Knock! . . . Knock! . . . ,"** which follows it in 1870. Both deal with mysterious destinies, one fortunate, the other unfortunate—a suggestion of which is also to be found in ***The Torrents of Spring*** of 1871. In **"The Dog,"** the Force of Evil wears the aspect of the gigantic mad dog which persistently attacks the hero and from which he is only saved by his heaven-sent protector: a setter which has come to him first as an invisible but audible presence. The canine guardian angel is again, like the Lieutenant's innocence, a form of the life-giving drop. But this angel in the subsequent stories grows weaker and at last gives way before the Demon of Evil: the diabolic baron of **"The Dream"**; the priest's son, possessed by the Devil, of **"Father Alexey's Story"**; the sinister Renaissance sorcerer of **"The Song of Triumphant Love."** I do not agree with Mirsky that the realistic setting of these stories prevents them from being successful. They *are* certainly less compelling than the diabolic tales of Gogol, from which they may partly derive, for the reason that the world of Gogol, being always distorted and turbid, is more favorable for this kind of horror, but they are nonetheless creepy enough and can hold their own with any such fantasies. The fault that one would find with them is rather that they are not merely horrible but hopeless. The forces that battle with the goblins are too feeble; they do not have a chance of success. Compare Gogol's vampire story *Viy* with Turgenev's **"Clara Milich,"** which fundamentally it somewhat resembles. It is not only that the rude village church in which the young student of Gogol keeps his terrible vigil with the girl in the coffin is closer to peasant folklore than the "small wooden house" in Moscow where Turgenev's student lives with his aunt and has his rendezvous with the dead Clara; Gogol's hero arouses more sympathy, puts up a better fight than Turgenev's, who is actually, like Sanin in ***The Torrents,*** more attracted than frightened by the vampire.

This story—of 1882, the last that Turgenev published—is, in any case, the culmination of the whole morbid side of his work. (pp. 55-8)

Edmund Wilson, "Turgenev and the Life-Giving Drop," in Literary Reminiscences and Autobiographical Fragments *by Ivan Turgenev, translated by David Magarshack, Farrar, Straus and Cudahy, 1958, pp. 3-64.*

AVRAHM YARMOLINSKY (essay date 1959)

[Yarmolinsky was a Russian-born American translator, biographer, social historian, and critic who wrote extensively on Russian literature and edited numerous anthologies as well as works by Fedor Dostoevsky, Anton Chekhov, and Alexander Pushkin. The following excerpt is from Yarmolinsky's frequently cited study of Turgenev. Here, he discusses On the Eve, *Turgenev's essay "Hamlet and Don Quixote," and* Fathers and Sons, *focusing on the theme of the irresolute man versus the man of action.]*

While the atmosphere of ***Rudin*** is one of futility and frustration, and nostalgia pervades ***A Nest of Gentlefolk,*** a buoyant spirit of expectancy and promise informs ***On the Eve.*** The action takes place in 1853, one of the last years of the reign of that iron autocrat, Nicholas I. It was a time of darkness, but the title is not alone in intimating that the darkness is soon to lift.

"My tale," said Turgenev, "is based on the idea that we must have *consciously* heroic natures in order to move forward." He was calling for tough-minded, dedicated individuals, devoted body and soul to a public cause. As he watched the social scene, sitting, not quite at ease, in his fauteuil, he looked in vain for such a man among his compatriots; the type had not yet emerged. Accordingly, he took for his protagonist a Bulgarian. This Insarov, a merchant's son, is an ardent patriot, preparing to take part in an insurrectionist movement against Turkey. The purpose to which he is vowed has the backing of the entire nation, which is ripe for revolt against the foreign tyranny. This gives him unfaltering firmness and strength. Turgenev, characteristically, has him carried off by consumption before he can strike a blow for the liberation of his people. Moreover, the author fails to interest the reader in this excellent and wooden creature. He is obviously contrived, a lay figure draped in the then fairly fashionable garments of militant nationalism.

Projected against a familiar Russian background, the story revolves less about Insarov's plotting than about his love affair with Yelena, the daughter of a family of Russian gentlefolk. It is she who is the central figure of the novel; to her it owes its force and meaning. Endowed with an intense, passionate nature and moved, in Turgenev's words, by "a vague, yet strong aspiration toward freedom," she is capable of making a brave choice and holding to it. She joins her lot to Insarov's without flinching from the hardships and dangers it involves. When, shortly after their marriage, he dies, she remains faithful to his memory by going on with the work to which he had been pledged. "Why return to Russia?" she asks in a farewell note to her mother. "What is there to do in Russia?" She deserts her country, this torpid land that can produce only self-centered dilettantes, well-meaning idealists capable of action, conscientious, cold-hearted officials.

The book is in a sense an impeachment of an age and a generation that have failed to breed a fit mate for such a woman. "There is no one as yet among us, there are no men, look where you will," soliloquizes Shubin, one of the heroine's unsuccessful suitors. He goes on to say that the country has brought forth only dark, grubbing souls, phrasemongers, self-consuming little Hamlets who keep feeling the pulse of their thoughts and sensations. "When will our time come? When will men be born among us?" he asks Uvar Ivanovich, another secondary figure, and that vast, gluttonous sphinx of a man replies: "Give us time. They will come." At the very end of the postscript to the novel, which deals with events separated from the main action by five years, Uvar Ivanovich, asked the same question in a letter, twiddles his fingers vaguely and fixes his enigmatic gaze on the distance. Was this intended to suggest that the author wondered whether in Russia, where the situation was a complex one and the foe not a foreign oppressor but an internal enemy, men of Insarov's kind would arise? In any event, the skeptical note is too faint to mar the hopeful tone of the book. (pp. 171-72)

Simultaneously with ***On the Eve*** Turgenev published an essay of broad sweep, **"Hamlet and Don Quixote,"** which formulates a suggestive view of the patterns of personality. Mankind, he contends, can be divided into Hamlets and Don Quixotes, though in the fewest individuals is the type pure. The prince of Denmark is the skeptic, spoiled for action by too much thought, and wryly cherishing his own ego, for he finds nothing in the world he can cling to whole-heartedly. The knight of la Mancha embodies boundless faith in and selfless devotion to an ideal. He values life only as a means of assuring the triumph of truth and justice. A man of action, possessed of an indomitable will, his blind single-mindedness may make him ludicrous and is sure to make him great. The one is the complete ironist, the other the complete enthusiast. Don Quixote discovers, Hamlet elaborates. The former is belabored by the shepherds; the latter flagellates himself. The hidalgo is truly humble; Hamlet's self-abasement is mixed with a sense of superiority to others. Despising himself, he thrives on that contempt. The masses cannot look to him for leadership; they will see Don Quixote's failings as clearly as Sancho does, yet follow him through fire and water. The knight refuses to believe his eyes when Dulcinea appears to him in the guise of a slattern; Hamlet is cynical or rhetorical in his attitude toward Ophelia, being himself incapable of love. Don Quixote may fight windmills and mistakes a barber's tin basin for a magical golden helmet, but who knows exactly, asks the author, where reality ceases and fantasy begins? "It seems to me, therefore, that the principal thing is the sincerity and strength of our convictions; the result lies in the hands of the Fates . . . Our business is to arm ourselves and fight." If there are to be no more Don Quixotes, he concludes, "let the book of history be closed: there will be nothing in it worth reading." The death of either hero is moving, but Don Quixote's "unutterably" so. In his last moments the knight lays aside all his pride, declaring that, as in the old days, he is simply "Alonzo the Good." The essayist comments that "everything shall crumble to dust, but good deeds shall not vanish like smoke"; and he paraphrases the Apostle: "All things shall pass, love alone shall endure."

Turgenev, himself much the Hamlet, does not fail to sympathize with the Dane's predicament. He finds eternal values in the prince's nay-saying. The latter's skepticism is not to be mistaken for chilly indifference; he is as much an enemy of sham and other evils as his counterpart. Yet this essay, as, less explicitly, ***On the Eve,*** attests Turgenev's admiration for the knight errant, a type foreign to his own nature. (pp. 173-74)

In ***Fathers and Children*** the novelist put Bazarov through his paces by taking this brusque commoner on a visit to a house of gentlefolk; by leading him into arguments with his two middle-aged, cultivated hosts; by making him fall hopelessly in love with a beautiful lady, indolent and undersexed; by involving him in a stupid, almost comical duel with one of his hosts; by engaging him in talk with his earnest, apish, pliant disciple; by sending him home to see his pathetic old parents; by bringing upon him an untimely death, the result of an infection contracted at a rural post-mortem. (p. 196)

From the moment when we first see Bazarov taking his time about offering his bare red hand to his host, and turning down the collar of his nondescript coat to show his long, thin face, with its sandy side-whiskers and cool green eyes, to the moment, a few months later, when the dying atheist raises one eyelid in horror as the priest administers the last sacrament, we are in the presence of a figure that dwarfs all around him and carries the whole weight of the story. It is also a figure that shows the fullest measure of Turgenev's powers of characterization. He believed that a novelist must be "objective," concerned to represent the world about him rather than his response to it, that his art required an interest in and a cumulative knowledge of other people's lives, as well as an understanding of the forces that shaped them. Bazarov, the tough-minded, hard-fisted medic, with his brutal honesty, his faith in a crudely empirical science that he uses as a cudgel wherewith to hit out at the genteel culture he abominates, this professed "Nihilist," is an example of what the objective method can achieve. In some respects, he is perhaps fashioned after an image at the back of Turgenev's mind, the image of the man he admired and could not be. (pp. 196-97)

Turgenev's conscious attitude toward his protagonist was ambiguous. . . . Unquestionably the admiration the author felt for his hero went hand in hand with a desire to preserve the values that this iconoclast rejected. (pp. 198-99)

One of Bazarov's sentiments was undoubtedly shared by his creator—dislike of the nobility. Turgenev's treatment of it in this novel afforded him the satisfaction of the flagellant. . . . How well he knew these people—their good intentions, their feeble achievements, their tender sensibilities, so readily touched by a line of verse, a point of honor, enchanted memories of a dead love, the glow of a setting sun which makes the aspens look like pines! But the knowledge that made for contempt fed his sympathy, too, and Nikolay Kirsanov, at least, is a lovable fellow.

Throughout, his craftsmanship is at its best. Even the minor characters are deftly sketched in. The description of Bazarov's illness gave Chekhov, himself a physician, the sensation of having "caught the infection from him." Bathed in an atmosphere of tenderness and pathos, the passages about Bazarov's parents are among the most moving in literature. As he wrote the last lines, in which the old couple are shown visiting the grave of their only son, Turgenev had to turn away his head, so that his tears would not blot the manuscript, and even in such a dry-eyed age as ours, there must be readers who do not finish the paragraph without blinking.

True, the comings and goings crowded into the few weeks during which the action unfolds seem somewhat contrived. The structure of the novel lacks the formal beauty of ***A Nest of Gentlefolk*** and ***On the Eve.*** The touching passage at the close is flawed by the last few lines, with their suggestion of a half-hearted piety. These blemishes are negligible, however, in a work of such wide validity. ***Fathers and Children*** is a novel to which Turgenev gave his full powers: his intuitions, his insights, the fruit of his contacts with a variety of men and women, his reflections on experience, his sense of the pathos of the human condition. Rudin and Lavretzky can each be fully understood only in the context of his age and his country. Bazarov, while unmistakably Russian, is a universal and a profoundly attractive figure. (pp. 199-200)

[The] core of the novel is not so much the conflict of generations as the theme touched upon obliquely in ***On the Eve:*** revolution. The promise held out in the latter novel is to some degree fulfilled in ***Fathers and Children***. . . .

"We mean to fight," Bazarov declares. But he has no more of a chance to carry out his intention than Insarov does. The author metes out a premature death to both. The Bulgarian's demise is wholly unmotivated; Bazarov, we are told, perishes because he was born too soon. One suspects, however, that this protagonist was killed off in obedience not solely to the logic of his situation but also to the law of the author's nature. Somehow he could not quite bring himself to grant his characters a sense of accomplishment which he himself seems never to have tasted fully. (p. 202)

Avrahm Yarmolinsky, in his Turgenev: The Man, His Art and His Age, *revised edition, 1959. Reprint by Octagon Books, 1977, 384 p.*

RICHARD FREEBORN (essay date 1960)

[*Freeborn is a Welsh critic, educator, and translator who has written and edited numerous studies of Russian history, literature, and literary figures. Here, he discusses the characteristics of Turgenev's realism and the structure of his novels.*]

In terms of artistic form there is a monolithic quality about the development of Turgenev's novels. They all appear to be constructed of the same elements, the same literary properties, which are suitably rearranged and reassembled to suit the changed requirements of each novel but which are never noticeably altered. Perhaps . . . he can be 'blamed' for this undue orthodoxy. He was not eager for experiment, nor was he out to impress by employing sensational literary devices. The truth is that his was an age when craftsmanship was more essential to success than the gimmick, and he was more aware of the need for tradition than the need to break with it.

The two aims which Turgenev had always before him—that of depicting 'the body and pressure of time' and the rapidly changing face of cultured Russian society—unite in the primary artistic consideration of his novels: the fact that they are 'realistic'. Turgenev's realism is to be defined, firstly, in common human terms. His novels give us pictures of real life which are true to life and acceptable in terms of a reality that every man can experience. Secondly, his novels are realistic in the sense that they are 'social-psychological' representations of epochs in the development of Russian society. The two definitions are complementary: the reality of the artistically transformed experience must necessarily complement the reality of the particular social-psychological problem which Turgenev sets out to identify and depict. One is wary of pinning any label of 'realism' too firmly to Turgenev's novels for the simple reason that it is a hackneyed, blanket term, too often ill-used—as anyone who knows anything about Socialist Realism will readily acknowledge—and open to multifarious shades of meaning and doctrinaire interpretation. It is nevertheless the quality of the real which is so unmistakable a characteristic of Turgenev's novels and which lends them the universality of inference that must be a primary consideration, social significance apart, for it is here that Turgenev's claim to fame resides.

It is instinctive to Turgenev to hide himself. His attitude towards his fiction is one of sympathetic detachment, almost—though never quite—indifference. His aim is to be dispassionate, leaving the axes to grind themselves. There is here much artfulness as well as craftsmanship, but it is essentially his knowledge of his craft that is supreme. For he knew that no writer could ever hope to divorce himself wholly from his work and he did not labour the pretence of objectivity to the point of denying himself, as author, any role in his fiction. He appears in his novels as narrator, story-teller or observer of the human scene and he is never a false narrator, story-teller or observer, parading in the guise of some fictional 'I' or 'We' who may have opinions that run contrary to those of the author himself. When Turgenev addresses himself to the reader, it is Turgenev who is addressing us and we need never have any doubts about his role. . . . There are certainly instances when Turgenev's comments tend to violate the pictorial realism of his fiction, but it is equally remarkable how little this disturbs the balance of the composition. He is generally extremely frugal and apt in his personal comments, while his role as author of the fiction is always kept within strict bounds of artistic propriety.

In the greatest of his novels—***Rudin, A Nest of the Gentry, On the Eve,*** and ***Fathers and Children***—this objective detachment is to be seen at its best. Here Turgenev does not intrude into his fiction unnecessarily, either in the guise of narrator or as omniscient author. There are instances, admittedly, when Turgenev's personal sympathies and antipathies (more often the latter) colour the manner of description, but in no case can it be said that these novels acquire anything like the over-all bias which is, in a sense, the distinction and, more strictly, the weakness of his fifth novel, ***Smoke.*** In these first four novels the aim has been to allow the fiction to exist in its own right, to allow the story to tell itself, to let the reality of the portrait grow of its own accord. This is the essence of the realism in the Turgenevan novel. One is left with the impression that there is a reality in these novels not of Turgenev's making, which indeed surprises Turgenev as much as it may surprise and delight the reader, leaving one with a sense of having witnessed an incident in life that—as Turgenev puts it at the end of ***A Nest of the Gentry***—'one can but point to—and pass on'. Here is the secret. Turgenev, in his artfulness, is the craftsman who likes to leave the impression that he has merely indicated with an elegant gesture of the hand the humour, pity, and tragedy of human life, whereas the elegant simplicity of the gesture only conceals an absorbing knowledge of his craft.

It is the objectivity of Turgenev's attitude that is the primary characteristic of his realism and it is for this purpose that he hides himself. But, accepting this, what are the constituent elements of Turgenev's realism? How does he succeed in giving the reader a picture of reality that is universally acceptable? There is obviously no one answer to such a question, but if we are to choose any primary constituent of Turgenev's realism that is both essential to his fiction, especially his novels, and universal in inference, then we must point to the importance of nature in his work. Nature in Turgenev's novels is both the natural scene that so often supplies the backcloth and human nature that occupies the foreground. The natural scene both reflects and contrasts with the human emotions of the heroes and heroines in the foreground: it reflects their moods and their hopes and their feelings and it sets in relief their tragedies. Correspondingly, the heroes and heroines only discover the full extent of their emotional attachment or incompatibility by acknowledging their human frailty in the face of nature's unchanging, ironic, Giaconda-like smile. The important thing is that nature is always the same, ever-present, ever demanding its rights, ever highlighting the ephemerality and accidental quality of human life and happiness. It is in Turgenev's poetic ability to understand and evoke the natural scene that his artistic mastery, which might be tempted so easily into the bathetic and meretricious, is astonishing for its delicacy of proportion and subtlety of feeling.

Compare, for instance, the way in which the scene is set in Chapter VII of ***Rudin*** for the first occasion when Rudin meets Natal'ya alone and the way in which the scene is set in Chapter IX on the occasion of their last meeting. On the first occasion the day is radiant, the grass after the brief rainfall begins to flow with emerald and gold, the sky has cleared and the garden where the hero and heroine are to meet is filled with freshness and quietness. On the second occasion, when Rudin is to fail to meet the challenge offered him by Natal'ya, the description emphasises the unnaturalness and barrenness of the environs of Avdyukhin pond, while its symbolic significance, with its associations of crime and mystery in peasant legend, is doubly emphasised by the fact that 'grey skeletons of massive trees towered here and there like mournful spectres over the low bushy undergrowth'—which is in striking contrast to the symbol of the apple-tree that has broken down under the weight of its own fruit (the true symbol of genius, in Rudin's opinion) or the strong oak-tree with its new leaves breaking through which Rudin had used previously (during his conversation with Natal'ya in Chapter VI) as a symbolic means of expressing his idea of love. Here the natural scene sets the mood for what is to follow or is symbolic of the feelings of one or another of the protagonists. (pp. 47-50)

These descriptive passages are not introduced by Turgenev purely 'for effect'. They are all integral to the story or the demands of characterization, serving to evoke moods, to 'orchestrate' the feelings and thoughts of his protagonists, to introduce scenes and illustrate the psychological state of a person at a particular moment. Again, for instance, in ***On the Eve*** the scene in which Yelena and Insarov are to confess their love for each other (Chapter XVIII) is dramatically introduced by the description of the thunderstorm or, later in the novel, the concluding episode of their life together is foreshadowed by the incomparable description of Venice in the spring (Chapter XXXIII). (p. 51)

The selectivity of the detail, the contrast of far and near, the immaculate water-colour sense which informs such descriptions—each sentence a significant stroke in the composition of the picture—naturally mirrors the balance and the careful assemblage of different facets which compose his novels as a whole. But the brilliance of the technical achievement still must not hide from us the fact that nature in Turgenev's novels remains ironically beautiful and impassive; it can reflect human emotions only when the emotions are projected into it. (p. 52)

At all other times nature is strikingly indifferent, though for Turgenev's purposes it has a formal function in his fiction as backcloth and mirror of the human problems which occupy the foreground. It is the staple element in that poetic atmosphere with which all Turgenev's novels are invested. Perhaps, in the twentieth century, the idea that nature can be the complement of human emotion smacks of sentimentality; it is a preciosity that 'good' writers might wish to avoid; but it presumes a classical attitude to nature to which Turgenev avowedly adhered, which made sense to him and which was an integral component of his realism. It is to be emphasized that Turgenev's realism is not of the *tranche de vie* variety. His realism subsumes artistic tenets of form and manner which Zola-esque naturalism, stream-of-consciousness, the thraldom to Hemingway or—as in the Soviet Union—thraldom to extra-literary standards of value, have tended to force into the background, though such tenets have an importance in their own right which cannot be rejected out of hand. They are the rational disciplines of the writer-classicist as opposed to the anti-rational 'freedoms' of the writer-romantic. Both are expressions of attitudes of mind and artistic temperament that have an equal claim to be called realistic.

To this extent all Turgenev's novels have a distinct pattern to their internal construction. It is best explained on the analogy of the theatre, though it is achieved through a process of contrast which is only applicable in terms of the novel.

In the first place, there is a theatrical quality—not stagey or artificial but theatrical in the best sense—about the way in which Turgenev 'mounts' his novels. He gives each novel a location, a situation, in some cases only a house, as Dar'ya Lasunskaya's residence in ***Rudin,*** or a particular place, as Baden-Baden in ***Smoke,*** or a region with several different though mutually connected foci of interest, as in ***Fathers and Children*** and ***Virgin Soil,*** and such a location or situation serves to unify each novel, both physically and temporally. Indeed, the temporal unity is almost as important as the unity of place or location—so many of his novels are 'months in the country'—because it also serves to concentrate and limit the development of the fiction. This is the setting of the novel which circumscribes the action of the major participants as if they were performers upon a stage. Turgenev lets the reader know all the salient facts about those characters—in the shape of biographical excerpts and introductions—who are integral to each location or situation, to each 'place' in the novel, for they almost have the function of stage properties, characters of a particular place, conditioned by it and typical of it, who rarely if ever step out of the special place assigned to them. In this way his novels give the appearance of being tableaux of a theatrical variety with just the required formal rigidity, the required attitudinizing; each episode in the action is like one scene upon a stage, neatly set and neatly accomplished; but such rigidity of form is purely an artistic tenet and does not offend against life. The impression created as a result of this method is not that life has been formalized to suit the tastes and designs of the author but that life itself seems simply to have imposed its own natural scheme upon the way in which the fiction is presented to us.

In the second place, again on the theatrical analogy, there is the arrival of the stranger, the unknown or only partly known quantity, whether hero or heroine, who steps into the fiction and at once provides the element of newness and contrast. All Turgenev's heroes are strangers to the situations of their respective novels: Rudin, Lavretsky, Insarov, Bazarov, Litvinov, Nezhdanov, while his heroines are integral parts of their novels' 'place', although they may still enter the fiction as unknown or only partly known quantities. It is in the relationship between the hero who enters from outside and the heroine who embodies the most characteristic or typical features of the 'place' of the novel that the contrast becomes apparent. It is always a contrast on two planes—that of the social or ideological, on the one hand, and that of the psychological or individual, on the other. Both planes of contrast are complementary and form unities, just as the natural scene of the background complements the human nature in the foreground and serves as a unifying principle in the novels. The contrast afforded by the presence of the stranger-hero in the 'place' of the fiction is usually, firstly, that between the new and the old, between the modern and the traditional, between the younger and the older generation, between experience and innocence, because the hero usually (the only real exception to this is ***Virgin Soil***) personifies a new ideological attitude which is strange and alluring to the heroine of the 'place'. Rudin, for instance, is a fount of new ideas for Natal'ya; Lavretsky offers a new vision of the world to Liza; Insarov is an inspiration to Yelena; Bazarov is intriguing and strange to Odintsova; Litvinov offers hope of renewal to Irina—and in each case it is the ideas proffered by the hero that seem to have the major appeal to the heroine. For these ideas are the product of a different social experience, a different education, a different conditioning, and the heroine is attracted to the newness of these ideas as if they were guarantees of new and nobler psychological or individual characteristics in the hero. It is then, secondly, a disparity in psychological attitude which also affords the contrast. The love-stories in Turgenev are never between *similar types* of person; just as the heroes and heroines are typical of different types of social experience, education or conditioning, so they differ in psychological type. Yet to this extent they complement each other and reflect each other, set in relief their finer or their inferior qualities and become, perhaps even despite themselves, involved in that process of contrast which is the primary element in the love-relationship between hero and heroine in Turgenev's novels.

It is here that peripeteia has its part to play. The contrast of types afforded by the love-relationship follows a smooth course only once in Turgenev's novels (the Yelena-Insarov relationship in ***On the Eve***) and even then it is doomed. In all other cases the process of contrast is brought to a head at one vital moment when the promise of mutual happiness, previously an underlying assumption of the relationship, is irrevocably destroyed. In no novel is the cause exactly similar, but in each case it is due to the revelation of some incompatibility between hero and heroine, whether of personality or circumstance, that clearly prevents any further development in their relationship. It is at this moment that the hero's or the heroine's true nature, delineated during the process of contrast in which both of them have been involved, is finally revealed in its weakness or its nobility. All the subsequent action of the fiction is influenced by this decisive moment of climax and takes the form of a protracted conclusion or epilogue.

A theatrical analogy, therefore, supplies the clue to the internal construction of the Turgenevan novel. It provides the skeletal design which is the basic form of Turgenev's realism in his novels in the sense that they are 'staged' in some realistic setting and have a common pattern discernible in their internal development. These are the formal properties of his novels that make them distinctive as realistic novels. But however important these aids to form, these constructional elements in the novel, may be, they are clearly not the sum total of Turgenev's art.

To argue that Turgenev understood the art that conceals art would be to understate the case. He understood supremely well that the novel had to have a 'story' and for it to have a story it had to be properly constructed. He chose as his metier the love story in its simplest form, a straightforward hero-heroine relationship, unencumbered by such niceties as the eternal triangle, the problem of divorce or inversion, but concentrating on the directness of the relationship itself and the extent to which it could serve as a means of revealing the individual characteristics of the two participants. It is the way Turgenev handles his love-stories that betrays his artistry, but it is here that he also conceals his art. For his love-story is never the *only* thing in his fiction, meaning that it is never the totality of his fiction to which all else is subordinated. The love-story is usually no more than the vehicle for supplying the contrast that is so essential for the characterization. Turgenev's novels are really elaborate portraits of one or another hero or heroine, whose features are shaded in with the gradations of contrast in the surrounding scene. All the subtle facets of his novels—the descriptive material, the subsidiary characters, the ideological problems, the psychological nuances, the contrasts of light and shade, the concise and pertinent dialogue, the persuasive and poetic style—are united in the single aim of painting a portrait and embellishing it with significant detail. The figures so portrayed dominate the novels, unify them, give them life, suffuse them with their own feelings. It is their lives and destinies that engage the reader's attention and make him feel the enchantment of involvement in new worlds and new ways of living. This is the enduring feature of Turgenev's art as a novelist. His heroes and heroines transcend the fictional matter of which they are composed and acquire living traits of personality to which the reader can immediately respond; and no matter how distant the epoch in which they lived, their lives still have reference to the present day. (pp. 52-6)

Richard Freeborn, in his Turgenev: The Novelist's Novelist, A Study, *Oxford University Press, London, 1960, 201 p.*

V. S. PRITCHETT (essay date 1964)

[Pritchett, a modern British writer, is respected for his mastery of the short story and for what critics describe as his judicious, reliable, and insightful literary criticism. He writes in the conversational tone of the familiar essay, approaching literature from the viewpoint of an informed but not overly scholarly reader. In his criticism, Pritchett stresses his own experience, judgment, and sense of literary art, rather than following a codified critical doctrine derived from a school of psychological or philosophical theory. In the following excerpt, he examines Turgenev's artistry, stressing the author's realistic method.]

What is it that attracts us to the Russian novelists of the nineteenth century? The aristocratic culture made more vivid by its twilight? The feeling, so readily understood by English readers, for ennui? No. The real attraction of that censored literature is its freedom—the freedom from our kind of didacticism and our plots. The characters of our novels, from Fielding to Forster, get up in the morning, wash, dress and are then drilled for their roles. They are propelled to some practical issue in morality, psychology or Fortune before the book is done. In nineteenth-century Russia, under the simpler feudal division of society, there is more room to breathe, to let the will drift, and the disparate impulses have their ancient solitary reign. In all those Russian novels we seem to hear a voice saying: "The meaning of life? One day that will be revealed to us—probably on a Thursday." And the day, not the insistence of the plot or purpose, is the melodic bar. We see life again, as we indeed know it, as something written in days; its dramas not directed by the superior foreknowledge of the writer, but seeming to ebb and flow among the climaxes, the anti-climaxes, the yawnings of the hours. (p. 383)

Yet the use of the eventless day could not alone give the Russian novel its curious power; indeed, it can be its weakness. No novelists are easier to parody than the Russians. These people picking their noses at the windows or trying on their boots while they go through passion and remorse! The day is a convention like any other. What gives those novels their power, and these persons their gift of moving us, is something which comes from a profound sense of a presence haunting the day. There lies on those persons, even on the most trivial, the shadow of a fate more richly definitive than the fate of any individual human being. Their feet stand in time and in history. Their fate is corporate. It is the fate of Russia itself, a fate so often adjured with eloquence and nostalgia, oftener still with that medieval humility which has been unknown to us since the Renaissance, and which the Russians sometimes mystically identify with the fate of humanity itself.

I have been reading Turgenev again. . . . It was a great advantage to the Russian novelists that they were obliged to react to the Russian question; a great advantage, too, that the Russian question was to become a universal one: the question of the rise of the masses. The consequence is that Turgenev's political novels—especially ***Rudin*** and even ***Fathers and Sons***—are less dated outside of Russia than they are inside it, for we can afford to ignore the detail of their historical context. I first read ***Rudin*** during the Spanish Civil War and, when he died on his foreign barricade, Rudin seemed to me (and still does seem) one of "the heroes of our own time." At the end of all Turgenev's political stories one may detect the invisible words "And yet . . ." left there by his hesitant and tentative genius. He is so close to the ripple of life's process of becoming, that at the very moments of decision, departure, farewell, he seems to revise and rejuvenate. The leaf falls, but the new bud is disclosed beneath the broken stalk. (pp. 384-85)

A Sportsman's Sketches, A Nest of Gentlefolk, Fathers and Sons—those are the perfect books. Turgenev is the poet of spring who eludes the exhausting decisions and fulfillments of summer and finds in the autumn a second and safer spring. He is the novelist of the moments after meetings and of the moments before partings. He watches the young heart rise the first time. He watches it fall, winged, to the common distorted lot. The young and the old are his fullest characters: the homecoming and death of Bazarov and the mourning of his parents are among the truest and most moving things in literature. To this tenderness, this capacity to observe the growth of characters and the changes of the heart, as the slow days of the steppe change into the years that rattle by in Petersburg or Baden, there is . . . a shrewd, hard-headed counterpart, the experienced shot:

> In the general the good nature innate in all Russians was intensified by that special kind of geniality which is peculiar to all people who have done something disgraceful.
>
> (p. 386)

Looking back over the novels, one cannot remember any falsified character. One is taken from the dusty carriage to the great house, one meets the landowners and the servants, and then one watches life produce its surprises as the day goes by. Turgenev has the perfect discretion. He refrains from knowing in advance. In ***Rudin*** we are impressed by the bellows of the local Dr. Johnson; enter Rudin, and the brilliant young man demolishes the doctor, like a young Shelley; only himself to suffer exposure as the next day shows us more of his character. His people expose themselves, as in life people expose themselves, fitfully and with contradiction. The art is directed by a sense which the English novel has never had—unless Jane Austen had something of it—the sense of a man's character and life being divisible into subjects. Career, love, religion, money, politics, illness and the phases of the years are in turn isolated in a spirit which is both poetic and scientific. There is no muddle in Turgenev. Romantic as he may be, there is always clarity, order and economy. He writes novels as if he were not a storyteller, but a biographer. (p. 387)

But the method has one serious weakness. It almost certainly involved drawing directly from life, and especially it meant that Turgenev was (or thought he was) stimulated to write by an interest in living persons for their own sakes. Turgenev knew his own lack of invention, his reliance on personal experience, and he studied character with the zeal of a botanist watching a flower; but, in fact, the study of character, for a novelist, means the selection or abstraction of character. What is selected is inevitably less than what is there, and since Turgenev was (as he said) governed by the actual life story which he saw, he does not add to or transform his people. They have the clarity of something a little less than life. What is missing from them is that from which he personally recoiled—fulfillment. There are spring and autumn—there is no summer. If success is described, it is by hearsay. Marriage, for Turgenev, is either scandal or rather embarrassing domesticity, something for a fond, indulgent smile, but a quick getaway. Strangely enough, it is his objectivity which leads to his limpness.

There are two qualifications to add to this criticism. One is suggested by ***A Sportsman's Sketches.*** His people derive a certain fullness from their part in the scene of the steppe, which none described better than he. In this book, his scrupulous habit or necessity of stopping short at what he saw and heard gave his portraits a laconic power and a terrible beauty. There the Russian day brings people to life in their random moments. The shapelessness of these pieces is the powerful shapelessness of time itself. The other qualification is the one I have indicated at the beginning of this essay. If his people lack the power to realize themselves because Turgenev himself lacked it in his own life, they have their roots in the fate of Russia. You localize them in a destiny which is beyond their own—tragic, comic, whatever they are—in the destiny of their society. They may fail, Russia goes on. One remembers that startling chapter at the end of ***A Nest of Gentlefolk,*** where, after the bitter end of Liza's love, the novelist returns to the house. One expects the last obligatory chords of romantic sorrow, but instead, there is the cruel perennial shock of spring:

> Marfa Dmitrievna's house seemed to have grown younger; its freshly painted walls gave a bright welcome; and the panes of its open windows were crimson, shining in the setting sun; from these windows the light merry sound of ringing young voices and continual laughter floated into the street.

The new generation had grown up. It is the most tragic moment of his writing, the one most burdened with the mystery of time as it flows through the empty light of our daily life. (pp. 388-89)

V. S. Pritchett, "The Russian Day," in his The Living Novel & Later Appreciations, *revised edition, 1964. Reprint by Vintage Books, 1967, pp. 383-89.*

RENÉ WELLEK (essay date 1965)

[Wellek's A History of Modern Criticism *is a major, comprehensive study of the literary critics of the last three centuries. Wellek's critical method, as demonstrated in* A History *and outlined in his* Theory of Literature, *is one of describing, analyzing, and evaluating a work solely in terms of problems it poses for itself and how the writer solves them. For Wellek, biographical, historical, and psychological information are incidental. Although many of Wellek's critical methods are reflected in the work of the New Critics, he was not a member of that group and rejected their more formalistic tendencies. In the following excerpt from an essay first published in 1965, Wellek discusses* Fathers and Sons, *examining the ways in which Bazarov is "defeated" by his own nature.]*

Fathers and Sons stands out among Turgenev's novels for many good reasons. It is free from the sentimentality and vague melancholy of several of the other books. Unobtrusively it achieves a balanced composition, while some of the later books seem to fall apart. It shows Turgenev's power of characterization at its best. He not only draws men and women vividly but he presents an ideological conflict in human terms, succeeding in that most difficult task of dramatizing ideas and social issues, while avoiding didacticism, preaching, and treatise-writing—succeeding, in short, in making a work of art.

In Russia ***Fathers and Sons*** stirred up an immense and acrimonious debate which centered around the figure of Bazarov, the nihilist who is the hero of the novel. (p. 258)

The book is neither an anti-nihilist novel nor a glorification of the coming revolution. Its beauty is in the detachment, the objectivity, and even the ambivalence with which Turgenev treats his hero and his opinions and presents the conflict between his crude, arrogant, youthful nihilism and the conservative romanticism of his elders. We can delight in the delicate balance which Turgenev keeps and can admire the concrete social picture he presents: the very ancient provincials, father and mother Bazarov, devout, superstitious, kindhearted, intellectually belonging to a dead world; the finicky, aristocratic Pavel Kirsanov and his weak brother Nikolay, who represent the romantic 1840's; the sloppy, name-dropping, cigarette-smoking emancipated woman, Mme. Kukshin; and the elegant, frigid, landowning widow Mme. Odintsov.

Though the eternal conflict between the old and young is one of the main themes of the book, ***Fathers and Sons*** is not exhaustively described by the title. Even the preoccupation with nihilism is deceptive. The book goes beyond the temporal issues and enacts a far greater drama: man's deliverance to fate and chance, the defeat of man's calculating reason by the greater powers of love, honor, and death. It seems peculiarly imperceptive of some critics to dismiss Bazarov's death by complaining that Turgenev got weary of his hero. His accidental death is the necessary and logical conclusion: Bazarov, the man of reason, the man of hope, is defeated throughout the book. His pupil Arkady becomes unfaithful and reveals his commonplace mind. Bazarov had dismissed love as a matter of mere physiology, but fell in love himself. He is furiously angry at himself when he discovers what he feels to be an inexplicable weakness; he becomes depressed, tries to forget his love by work, and almost commits suicide when he neglects his wound. Bazarov is defeated even in the duel with Pavel, though he was the victor; he had jeered at chivalry as out of date and considered hatred irrational, but he did fight the duel after all. It was ridiculous and even grotesque, but he could not suffer humiliation or stand the charge of cowardice. He did love his parents, though he was embarrassed by their old-fashioned ways. He even consented to receive extreme unction. When death came, he took it as a cruel jest which he had to bear with Stoic endurance. He died like a man, though he knew that it made no difference to anyone how he died. He was not needed, as no individual is needed. We may feel that the moving deathbed scene is slightly marred by the rhetoric of his request to Mme. Odintsov, "Breathe on the dying lamp," and surely the very last paragraph of the book contradicts or tones down its main theme. Turgenev's reference to the "flowers" on the grave (when Bazarov himself had spoken of "weeds" before) and to "eternal reconciliation and life without end" seems a concession to the public, a gesture of vague piety which is refuted by all his other writings. Turgenev puts here "indifferent nature" in quotation marks, but as early as in ***Sportsman's Sketches*** he had said: "From the depths of the age-old forests, from the everlasting bosom of waters the same voice is heard: 'You are no concern of mine,' says nature to man." In the remarkable scene with Arkady on the haystack—the two friends almost come to blows—Bazarov had pronounced his disgust with "man's pettiness and insignificance beside the eternity where he had not been and will not be." There is no personal immortality, no God who cares for man; nature is indifferent, fate is blind and cruel, love is an affliction, even a disease beyond reason—this seems the message Turgenev wants to convey.

But ***Fathers and Sons*** is not a mere lesson or fable. It is a narrative, which with very simple means allows the author to move quietly from one location to the other—from the decaying farm of the Kirsanovs, to the provincial town, to the elegant estate of Mme. Odintsov, and from there to the small estate of the old Bazarovs, and back again—firmly situating each scene in its appropriate setting, building up each character by simple gestures, actions, or dialogue so clearly and vividly that we cannot forget him. Only rarely do we feel some lapse into satire as in Mme. Kukshin's silly conversation. But on the whole, with little comment from the author, a unity of tone is achieved which links the Russian of 1859 with the eternally human and thus vindicates the universalizing power of all great art. (pp. 259-61)

> *René Wellek, "Fathers and Sons," in* "Fathers and Sons" by Ivan Turgenev: The Author on the Novel, Contemporary Reactions, Essays in Criticism, *edited and translated by Ralph E. Matlaw, W. W. Norton & Company, Inc., 1966, pp. 257-61.*

RUTH DAVIES (essay date 1968)

[Davies closely analyzes Bazarov, assessing his importance to Turgenev and his place in Russian literature.]

After the publication of the three novels, ***Rudin, A House of Gentlefolk,*** and ***On the Eve,*** Turgenev's critics accused him of writing about a time and about character types already out of date. That this was at least in part true is attested by the repetitiousness of theme and character. Moreover, events in Russia were moving too fast to be chronicled accurately by one who spent most of his time on foreign soil. The same criticism could not be made, however, about ***Fathers and Sons.*** This extraordinary document reveals many aspects of the evolutionary temper. Towering above everything else Turgenev wrote, it is distinguished by all his best qualities of style as well as by significance of content. Most striking, it frames a character, Bazarov, who looms like a giant above all other characters this author created. Studying the personality and career of Turgenev evokes the feeling again that when he conceived Bazarov he was an involuntary instrument. The author himself did not seem quite able to understand where Bazarov came from. This book reveals the Russia of the emancipation year (1861) and immediately afterward in a state of turbulence that demanded some kind of resolution. It records the emergence of a character and an attitude which were to serve as catalysts in producing a new element in the national consciousness.

The young doctor, Bazarov, trained in the tradition of the German universities, had become a disciple of the natural sciences. He called himself a Nihilist, one who believes in nothing. Turgenev did not coin this term, but he might well have done so. From the time of the publication of the book, it became a leading word in the Russian vocabulary and a major concept in the Russian mind.

The iconoclasm of Bazarov the scientist is especially pointed in contrast to the pastoral setting and the agreeable civility of the other characters of the novel. Bazarov came with his devoted school friend and follower, Arkady Kirsanov, to visit at the latter's country home. There he was thrown into relief first by the naïve indecisiveness of Arkady and then by the personalities of the country gentlemen and landowning aristocrats, Arkady's father Nikolai and his uncle Pavel. From the first Bazarov was antagonistic to these two men. They represented to him the conditions of privilege—idleness, softness, tradition, parasitism, and culture borrowed from the West—which he believed must be eliminated from Russia. (pp. 82-3)

Nikolai tried to understand the young man in spite of his vulgarity and rudeness, but Pavel could see him as nothing but a brash upstart. Every encounter between the two ended in mutual baiting. "You don't acknowledge art, then, I suppose?" Pavel once inquired, to which Bazarov replied, "The art of making money or of advertising pills!" And to the question, "Then you believe in science only?" he answered, "I have already explained to you that I don't believe in anything."

Bazarov would not permit himself the luxury of having positive reasons for negation. He explained his attitude as a matter of biology:

> Why, I, for instance, take up a negative attitude, by virtue of my sensations; I like to deny—my brain's made on that plan, and that's all about it! Why do I like chemistry? Why do you like apples?—by virtue of our sensations. It's all the same thing.

That the negation in which Bazarov found satisfaction was in fact prompted by constructive motives, even though the young idol breaker was not willing to acknowledge them, is illustrated by his response to a question as to what possible use there could be in Nihilists:

> We suspected that talk, perpetual talk, and nothing but talk, about our social diseases, was not worth while, that it all led to nothing but superficiality and pedantry; we saw that our leading men, so-called advanced people and reformers, are no good; that we busy ourselves over foolery, talk rubbish about art, **unconscious creativeness, parliamentarism, trial by** jury, and the deuce knows what all; while, all the while, it's a question of getting bread to eat, while we're stifling under the grossest superstition, while all our enterprises come to grief, simply because there aren't honest men enough to carry them on.

Bazarov's self-analysis was consistent, but he himself was not. The many and intricate contradictions of his character make impossible a formula that fits. Whereas he asserted that he believed in nothing, actually he believed passionately in disbelief—and in humanity. Although he pretended to distrust even science and would not admit to any particular curiosity, in truth he was a devotee of the scientific spirit, for which he died. He professed a hatred of people ("I felt such a hatred for this poorest peasant"), yet he knew how to get close to them, and many—especially simple people—were drawn to him. Despising sentiment, he fell in love abjectly, like the gawkiest schoolboy, being released from his turmoil only by the coldness of the woman. He scorned conventionality and was contemptuous of established concepts of propriety, but he fought a duel to satisfy another man's idea of honor, behaving toward him with whimsical magnanimity. He was vulgar, boorish and insulting. His treatment of his parents was an outrage. And yet behind all this behavior—prompted by sincerity on a grand scale and a hatred of pretence—his fundamental integrity was admirable.

His contradictions extended even to his egotism. In spite of almost insufferable arrogance, he recognized his own limitations. Determined not to appear other than what he was, paradoxically he appeared worse than he was. One is reminded of the young Cordelia at the court of King Lear, baited by her father to give an accounting of her love for him. This she could not and would not do, but her refusal in no way diminished that love. With strengths and weaknesses inextricably blended, Cordelia set the stage for her downfall. Likewise Bazarov, though he spoke in vehement rejection, lived by the faith he professed and died in majestic acquiescence. The man who did "protest too much" in life left in his dying a sense of real loss. He was a big man, not because he tried to be, but because he was. He supplied the answer to the artist's (Turgenev's) question in ***On the Eve:*** "When will men be born among us?"

Why did he have to die? Was it because Turgenev did not really believe in life, did not believe in anything but failure and resignation? Or did the author feel he had gone too far in the creation of Bazarov and must check the advance? Was he terrified by premonitions of what was to come? Did he fear to give offense? Or was he genuinely confused and unable to see the future of his country with such men as Bazarov in command? Perhaps Bazarov was stronger than his creator, and only by killing him could the creator retain his power. Whatever the reason, Bazarov's death was ironical. It was as if Turgenev wanted to say: "There *will* be men in Russia, but there will be no certain future for them. Their weaknesses will cancel their strengths. Because of their contradictions, their tragedy will be inherent within them." (pp. 84-6)

With his Nihilist, Turgenev joined Gogol and Goncharov in the creation of a type immediately a source of universal concern in Russia. It is worthy of note that although at first most of the young radicals felt they had been maligned by the book (they considered Bazarov something of a grotesque and certain of his views and actions unworthy of their own "enlightened" attitudes), some of them—led by the young critic Pisarev—tried to emulate or go beyond Bazarov. Bazarov's view of himself was as ambivalent as the reactions to him. "I was needed in Russia," he said as he was dying, and then, "No, it's clear, I wasn't needed." This was his final contradiction. But needed or not, he was there. Unhappily, the best of Bazarov died with him. What remained was too often the callow, vociferous, and disorganized zealotry of those who found stimulation in destruction. Almost all were earnest; some were honest—with a lopsided honesty; some were genuinely humanitarian; all were completely humorless. Rejecting everything intangible, aesthetic, or traditional, as disciples of the practical they worshiped at the shrine of science. Although idolizing science, they were not scientists, for they lacked objectivity. Although professing rationality, they were not rational. Dedicated they certainly were, but to what? They talked a great deal about solving social problems, and in truth the problems needed solution. But what were their real aims? What would be the inevitable result of their sterility of spirit? It is small wonder that Turgenev was disturbed by the implications of these questions—and not Turgenev alone. The answers were provided by Dostoevsky.

Fathers and Sons is a reminder that the Nihilists emerged when the autocrats still held the winning hand. The people, coming to consciousness, had at last begun to have hopes of ridding themselves of the incubus of aristocracy and autocracy. But their leaders and spokesmen—the Nihilists and revolutionaries—could not even begin to help them realize their hopes except as they acted in defiance of the existing order. The problem was where this defiance would end and what its real purpose was. Turgenev's Bazarov cast a long shadow before him. How long, the world does not know even yet. (pp. 89-90)

[It] was in the creation of Bazarov, the Nihilist, that Turgenev's real stature as historian and prophet became evident—Bazarov—whom Turgenev himself admitted he did not know whether to love or to hate. (p. 100)

Ruth Davies, "Turgenev: The Nihilists and Virgin Soil," in her The Great Books of Russia, *University of Oklahoma Press, 1968, pp. 64-100.*

DALE E. PETERSON **(essay date 1975)**

[*Peterson explicates* First Love.]

The intense lyricism of ***First Love*** springs from an unpromising source. The "frame" narrative deftly sketches the stale atmosphere of a gentlemanly postmidnight private "smoker." An entertainment is proposed to lift the late night ennui; the married host and his two "not so young" bachelor friends will regale each other with their exploits in "first love." But foggy memories and lives of dull routine take their deadly toll until a certain Vladimir Petrovich modestly concedes that his experience was "not entirely usual." Not being good at "storytelling," he volunteers to recount his experience in a notebook. What follows, ***First Love*** proper, is the formal written reminiscence of a reticent middle-aged bachelor who has found himself lingering after hours in other people's sedate homes.

The reader suddenly is revisiting (in the past tense) the landscape of a boy's sixteenth summer. It is a landscape which betrays the hand of a master storyteller named Ivan Turgenev. We first learn that young Volodya was living with his indulgent, respectable parents in a suburban Moscow cottage located *protiv Neskuchnogo;* topographically, Volodya is situated "opposite the Neskuchny Park" which, he will soon discover, is invitingly lush and dark. For a young adolescent, it is a precarious location; but there is another sense in which he is living opposite the park. Volodya is also situated, through a verbal omen, in an environment which is "against the not dull"—*skuchnyi* being the Russian adjective for tedious and boring. As Volodya will also discover, the suburban freedom granted him by his permissive parents does not extend any license to break social or cultural proprieties. Yet he is at that "dangerous age" when, despite the storybook flowering of childish and chaste dreams of knighthood, he is suddenly susceptible to "the joyous feelings of effervescent young life." In terms of physical and biological placement, Volodya is uncomfortably situated; he is painfully wedged between powerful constraints and latencies. Meanwhile, in one wing of the summer house he inhabits there is a wallpaper factory where boys of Volodya's age press out gay patterns with the full weight of their fragile bodies. Beautiful designs are being produced, despite abject circumstances of virtual servitude. Thus, in the opening vignette of Volodya's situation we see a precariously sheltered adolescent barely separated, externally or internally, from an efflorescence of organic energy. In the background, we hear the sounds of boys at hard labor, engaged in a rudimentary aesthetic process. The landscape itself forecasts the initiations it contains.

Like so many of Turgenev's narrators, Volodya first enters the scene of an important incident as a hunter. His favorite sport is sniping at crows, birds he hates for being "cautious, predatory, and sly." Initially, the boy's hunting takes the curious form of a private vendetta; he feels morally offended by the elusive and ravenous birds. One evening, while tracking these cunning creatures of appetite, Volodya accidentally encounters the remarkable Princess Zinaida. He catches her in the act of casting explosive gray flowers at the foreheads of some young admirers; quite literally, Zinaida enters the scene with a burst of beauty in the minds of men. Himself astonished, Volodya drops his gun. Later, in the fifth chapter, Zinaida will let fall a book upon first sighting Volodya's physically imposing father. These parallel episodes rather dramatically signal the "real events" occurring within scenes of casual meetings; some readers may object to the obtrusive symbolic gestures Turgenev has planted in these moments. But the "melodrama" points up more than the existence of a love triangle; it makes emphatic the important point that both Volodya and Zinaida are capable of experiencing awkward "off guard" moments. No matter how seemingly opposite one another, Volodya and Zinaida are both innocents abroad in a world of startling erotic force. Each shall have to learn to accommodate mature experience: one by abandoning a simplistic moralism easily disarmed; the other by putting aside a bookish romanticism easily tattered.

In Volodya's reckoning with experience, we can observe a central tension between an ethical and an aesthetic sensibility. Irresistibly attracted by Zinaida's beauty, it is his fate to cross over a symbolic threshold into his first love's native environment. Zinaida's mother and her mode of life repeatedly offend the boy as *neopryatnyi* or *neblagoobraznyi*; unfortunately, the seductive vitality of the young girl has been fostered by just such an "untidy" atmosphere which is decidedly "not in good form." It is in this unnerving milieu that Volodya's shy fastidiousness is put to its first test. While carding wool, Zinaida contrives to bind the boy's hands; she then begins to interrogate her would-be suitor. Her line of questioning is significant. Cautiously, she samples the elasticity of Volodya's moral imagination. "No doubt, you have prejudged me?" she inquires. Next, in the wake of Volodya's bewildered stammerings, she appeals to the adolescent to revert to the experiential honesty of children, who speak their feelings openly. It is soon after this that Volodya fails his first ordeal. When he indirectly lies about his age, Zinaida gently raps his hands. This slight reprimand subtly initiates a major theme in ***First Love:*** the "blow" of fate which inevitably avenges any human failure to face one's actual experience. During a game of forfeits in the seventh chapter, Volodya's reticence prevents him from whispering his "secret" into Zinaida's ear. In response, she smiles slyly; then, at the first opportunity, she metes out a sharp public blow on his fingers. Throughout Turgenev's tale, there is a steady escalation in the punishments dealt for circumventing the inner truth of experience. In the ninth chapter, the infatuated Doctor Lushin attempts to exorcize Zinaida's charm by covering himself in the protective mantle of cynicism. But when he attempts to dismiss her as a coquette and actress, he goes too far. Penitent, he permits Zinaida to prick his self-righteousness by literally sticking a pin in his hand. The climax of this symbolic sadism is reached in the twenty-first chapter. There, it is Zinaida who is on the receiving end. The whipping administered by Volodya's father strikes immediately after Zinaida voices a hopelessly self-deluding command: *"Vous devez vous séparer de cette [femme]."* The ultimate "blow" in the text is the "stroke" which carries off the father on the very day he pretentiously advises his son to "fear the love of woman . . . that poison." There is, then, a symbolic sequence of escalating reprimands that punctuates Turgenev's text. Whenever moral timidity prompts a conscious evasion of actual experience, the text administers a blow of fate *(udar sud'by)* to demonstrate the inescapable revenge taken by the suppressed natural impulses.

Although ***First Love*** testifies that the lessons of experience are regularly imparted only through violence and trauma, that is but half the story. The process of initiation also involves an expanding awareness of life's energies that, within Volodya and Zinaida, is an aesthetic revelation. The fall from innocence is couched in a poetry of perception. For instance, Volodya's communion with the "sparrow's night" after his failure to utter his secret is a singularly lovely premonition of his bleak life experience. The ghostly beauty of the remote storm with its mute lightning and temperate flashes corresponds to the eerie calm of the mature bachelor's exile from love's realm. "That silent lightning, those restrained glints of light, seemed to respond to the muted, secret eruptions which flamed up in me also." Likewise, Zinaida's improvised poem in the eleventh chapter is a precocious intimation of her mature fate. This vision of a virgin adrift, borne by a relentless current toward a procession of bacchantes, and her half-voluntary abduction into the woods is a poetic forecast of Zinaida's ambivalent but somnambulistic attraction to the animal magnetism of Volodya's sensual father.

The experience of first love takes on a special texture as Turgenev sculpts its contours. The child's plunge into adult sexuality is captured in lines that emphasize the brutal outrushing of pent-up sado-masochistic impulses, and yet it is also frozen in postures that convey the artist's ultimate equanimity. Volodya's actual "fall" is prefigured comically in his recurrent stumblings onto his knees. Then, in the pivotal twelfth chapter, at Zinaida's whimsical beckoning Volodya suddenly plummets himself down from a conservatory wall; he falls into the dust at her feet, is caressed, and arises only to hand his Princess her umbrella. The entire scene is drenched in a capricious cruelty. But it is also a parodic enactment of a painful quixotic theme: the sudden transformation of chaste courtly lover into the abased servitor of an earthly passion. In one brief moment Volodya is demoted from the rank of knight to that of page of *amour*. Zinaida's fall, her loss of virginity, is similarly painted in mixed colors. The crucial chapter in her life is the fifteenth. On the pretext of illness she has been avoiding company; but one night Volodya inadvertently witnesses his Princess in a paroxysm of frustrated passion. At her window, she wrings her fingers, violently shakes her curls, and finally makes a decisive affirmative nod with her head. Three days later, an unknowing Volodya unwittingly extracts the truth about her agony:

> "Are you still unwell?" I asked her.
>
> "No, now it's all past," she answered as she plucked a small red rose.

> "I'm a bit tired, but that, too, will pass."
>
> "And now will you be the same as before?" I asked.
>
> Zinaida raised the rose to her face—and it looked to me as if the reflection of the bright petals had struck her cheeks.

At the end of this amusing interview, Zinaida offers the red rose to Volodya and it is taken. Volodya's innocent acceptance of the beautiful carnal rose is a charming anticipation of his later conscious reconciliation with errant life in a victory of his aesthetic sense over his moral sensitivity.

Through Volodya's eyes Zinaida has come to image vitality, life itself in all its intensity and contrariety. In a key meditative passage in the ninth chapter, the aggrieved adolescent, "like a beetle pinioned by its leg," keeps circling in body and mind around a favorite spot; despite the keen resentment of his wounding, Volodya is emotionally ambushed by "a nameless sensation that included all feelings." Lovingly, he gives to this rich pansensorium of all vital feelings the name "Zinaida." For Volodya (and, one suspects, for Turgenev), the vivid and exuberant alternating currents of Zinaida's nature have come to exemplify that maelstrom of possibility that experience contains. And, interestingly, neither Volodya nor Zinaida can withhold admiration for the boy's father, who, though insufferably callous and cruel at times, is also the only person who can gracefully ride the horse, Electric. The torment of first love has brought both Volodya and Zinaida to an awesome perception of the powerful protean flux of organic forces. Turgenev's tale interweaves two threads of initiation thereby assuring that all spectators will finally face up to the full tangle of knotted desires. ***First Love*** is designed to make readers come up against life's virtually criminal erotic vitality. Is there an implicit response to the burden of such an awareness? In the aftermath of what "first love" reveals, how might one sanely live? Neither in anger, nor in despair, but in a mood of alert reconciliation, keeping an outlook for each new upwelling of unsolicited beauty—such would seem to be the implicit strategy of the adult narrator of ***First Love.***

Volodya is, in the course of his initiation, proffered three modes of seeing life through. His father, a man of physical strength and strong impulse, advises: "Belong to yourself: that is the whole art of life . . . know how to desire, and then you will be free, and you will command." Dr. Lushin, the self-protective cynic, warns: "No matter where the wave carries you, it is always bad," so be "capable of getting out in time, of breaking the net." But the boy's ultimate revelation (the one that enables him to become the clement-spirited memoirist of his own entrapment in amoral "first love") recommends neither assault upon nor recoil from the seductions life contains. Volodya's deepest illumination occurs at the deathbed of an old hag, a wretched creature who has grappled all her life with the antipoetic specters of disease and deprivation. The boy observes with fascination that only after the last glimmer of *consciousness* had fled from her eyes did the crone lose the terror of death written upon her countenance. Turgenev's cruel tale of first love dramatically concludes with a coda which intones, Dylan-Thomas-like, a reverence for the stark, inhumane vitality of organic energies; having seen "the last wave by," even the wretched of the earth "do not go gentle into that good night." In the powerful, even worshipful, conclusion to ***First Love,*** Ivan Turgenev is not significantly distanced from his semiautobiographical narrator. The very telling of the tale has realized a vitalistic aesthetic, a cultivation of appreciative sight for forces gracefully deployed, for motions gracefully executed amidst the fecund and amoral energies at play in life. (pp. 124-29)

Dale E. Peterson, "What James and Turgenev Knew: The Clement Vision of Experience," in his The Clement Vision: Poetic Realism in Turgenev and James, *Kennikat Press, 1975, pp. 119-35.*

EVA KAGAN-KANS (essay date 1975)

[*Kagan-Kans investigates the linking of love and death in Turgenev's work, examining also the role of faith in the author's philosophy.*]

In Turgenev's view of the world there is a close identification of love with death. The forces of death and of life triumph over man, and so man fears both. Tolstoj's Kitty "knew" death and birth instinctively, and therefore, Tolstoj implies, neither frightened her. But for Turgenev, love comes on like a hurricane, and death, too, seizes its prey unawares (for example, the *Poem in Prose* **"The Insect"**). Often the same imagery and symbolism are used to express these two themes. Turgenev's favorite image to represent the onrush of an overpowering emotion is the whirlwind; the same image is applied to the death of a beloved person: "Oh what sorrow that was for me, it swooped down upon me like a cruel whirlwind". Death, like love, is an elemental force and man is powerless before both. Even more interesting, the image of wings, which may represent spontaneity, will, and natural exuberance, is equally easily associated with death; in **"Phantoms"**, in particular, the ominous, amorphous figure that embodies mortality approaches with a slow beating of her wings and strikes the hearts of Ellis and the narrator with dread. Death and passion represent the tragic and inevitable forces which are omnipresent for Turgenev's heroes:

> All there was between us flashed by in an instant, like lightning, and like lightning, brought death and ruin.

Passion is as destructive as death, and love compels death itself to retreat.

The theme of love and death inextricably interwoven occurs as early as ***A Sportsman's Sketches,*** in the story **"The Country Doctor".** The hero is literally compelled to respond to the force of an emotional breakthrough; for the patient, who finds a new meaning in life when faced with death, a return to health would also mean a return to meaningless, humdrum, and complacent vegetation (*pošlost'*). This experience for the protagonist is the only humanizing and meaningful event in his drab life. The choice Turgenev presents is made quite explicit here: love and death, or a grey existence.

The theme of a fatal passion which leads to death is central in such stories as ***A Quiet Spot, Faust,*** **"The Unfortunate Girl",** and **"Klara Milič".** But even earlier, in **"Three Meetings",** the symbolism of the first dream points to the tragic conclusion of the love affair, although nothing is made explicit at the end. In his dream, the narrator sees the heroine as a winged creature, turning into a cloud and devoured by the golden rays of the sun; the rays are suddenly transformed into a web spun by a gleaming spider, and in the web the heroine perishes.

There is an unexpected ending to ***First Love,*** the story of Zinaida's passion and the first awakening of erotic feeling in the adolescent narrator. Death intrudes into this romantic story not primarily in the form of the understated deaths of both Zinaida and the father, but in the gruesome details of the miserable end of a wretched old woman, the "difficult and heavy" death of a creature who has known nothing but misery and misfortune all her life.

The irrationality which is associated with passion is also present in Turgenev's conception of death. In general, Turgenev's heroes die stupidly, aimlessly, suddenly, without having accomplished either their personal or their social missions.

Just as the "reality" of passion is called into question, the "reality" of death becomes ambiguous and is surrounded by the same aura of mystery as is passion.

The motif of "incomplete" or false death recurs in **"The Song of Triumphant Love"** and **"The Dream".** The baron in the last story is killed twice, and the terror of the narrator intensifies as he imagines he sees the drowned corpse "chuckling" at him and then disappearing. In **"The Song of Triumphant Love"** the same mysterious ambiance surrounds the death of Mucij after Fabij's attack, for the magic incantations and spells of the Malayan servant seem to revive Mucij's corpse. Indeed, the reality of Mucij's life is called into question when he first appears in the story. Even there he acts and speaks mechanically, strangely, like a thing manipulated by a secret power—the power exercised by the mysterious Malayan servant.

Perhaps the ring given to Pavel Kirsanov (***Fathers and Sons***) by his beloved could stand as the perfect emblem of Turgenev's views. This object, on which are engraved the images of a sphinx and a cross, may represent the eternal mystery and the cross of love and death.

The symbol of the ring appears in Turgenev's works under fantastic or overtly erotic circumstances. To mark Sanin's bondage, Polozova gives him an iron ring, similar to the ones worn by her other lovers. The ring appears in **"The Dream"** to mark both the sensual and the fantastic elements; after the rape of the mother, the Baron removes the wedding ring from her hand, and after finding his corpse on the beach, the son, in his turn, removes the ring from the Baron's finger and returns it to his mother. Yet, as we learn, the body disappears and the reader is never completely convinced that the Baron really has died. The return of the ring thus symbolizes her release from the bondage of her memories. It is significant that the most supernatural of Turgenev's characters, the vampire-ghost Ellis, whose whole body is ephemeral, wears something as concrete as a narrow gold wedding band. All the elements referred to above merge in her relationship with the hero. He is the prey of a phantomlike yet predatory woman who demands his surrender (he must say "take me") and brings about his destruction and his death.

Fearing life, fearing love, Turgenev constantly proclaimed the power of death. "I have now become a creature who, like the pendulum of a clock, oscillates between two hideous feelings: Disgust with life and fear of death". Yet while fearing death, he asserted the magic of love and life. . . . In his ambivalence, at times he would acknowledge that death swept everything away; at others, he would affirm that love is stronger than death. "Well, what then? If I must die, let me die. . . . Death has no terror for me now. After all, it cannot destroy [me]. On the contrary, only *thus* and *there* can I be happy . . . as I have never been happy in life", says Aratov.

A fatal principle seems to be embodied in the concept of a love which contains death and which inevitably carries man to his death. This is precisely what Elcova (***Faust***) means in her warning to her daughter: "You are like ice, until you melt you are as strong as a stone". The whole story of Klara Milič, like **"The Country Doctor",** is based upon the underlying kinship of love and death. Yet this vision of love beyond the grave is anything but heavenly and blissful. It is awesome, overpowering, and independent of man's own volition. (pp. 75-7)

To have loved is to have lived, and love imparts a meaning to an otherwise worthless life. And yet to love is to assert life, and Turgenev's protagonists cringe at that and plead guilty: "But what if this is punishment", meditates Elena (***On the Eve***), "what if we have to pay the full price for our guilt? Is it possible that you who have created this night, these heavens, will wish to punish us because we have loved?" In ***A Nest of Gentlefolk,*** Liza's conviction that the return of Lavreckij's wife is a divine retribution for their transgression—the desire to love—attests to the same concept; it is as if a Jehovah-like, merciless God avenges himself on those who commit the sin of happiness.

It is not possible to explain away Turgenev's inconsistent solutions in terms of the chronology of his works, since we find an affirmation of the love-death identity in both an early story (**"A Country Doctor"**) and the final one (**"Klara Milič"**). The ***Poems in Prose*** are equally ambiguous, for **"The Sparrow"** makes a sharp contrast, in its optimism, with the total loss of vigor and hope in **"The Old Woman"** and **"Skulls".**

Turgenev's whole life and creative output can, in a sense, be seen in terms of a death wish: "The most interesting thing in life is death." And yet the tragic paradox in his thinking is that while affirming love he also affirms death, which alone seems to him to offer a possibility of reconciliation. When he speaks of "eternal reconciliation and of life everlasting . . .", his punctuation (. . .) significantly reveals the inconclusive nature of the assertion. Yet whether he rebels against it or accepts it through his heroes, it seems to him to possess the majesty of eternal truth: "the coming of death . . . its majesty, its gravity, and its truthfulness". And again: "Death had laid upon her its imprint of eternal silence and resignation". If Turgenev considers passion the one real value in human existence, how is it that his fictional characters never reach the heights of Romeo and Juliet, Francesca and Paolo, or Tristan and Isolde? His tales seem to negate everything, for they are tales of fatal love which lead to love-in-death, death-in-love, and the death of love itself. (p. 77)

Haunted by the fear of death . . . , he frequently painted pictures of death and depicted it in sinister sculptural forms. Although

Turgenev's funeral cortege.

the images in which death is embodied vary, they are always startling. In one story it is a man in white sitting on a bear (**"Certopxanov and Nedopjuskin"**), in another a black mare (**"King Lear of the Steppes"**), or else a hideous old woman with one eye ; (**"Old Portraits"**). Perhaps the most dreadful images are those which are vague, amorphous, elusive, and apocalyptic, like the mysterious figure in **"Phantoms"** or the glacial wave in the *Poem in Prose* **"The End of the World"**. In any case, there is no escape from death; the vision of a deadly insect which stings the person who least expects it reflects the essence of the human situation.

Significantly enough, some of the more repulsive images take the shape of an old hag whose toothless mouth is distorted by mockery. Turgenev's own obsession with, and fear of, cholera led him to portray the disease as a "rotting greenish-yellow stinking old hag". Thus, death often parallels and even extends the larger theme of woman as destruction.

Unlike Tolstoj, who focuses on the moment of death and the question "What am I going to be thinking when I am dying?", Turgenev is not interested in the process of dying or the moment of death, but in death as the beginning of non-Being. Death is a force from which there is no escape ("The force to which there is no resistance"), which is everywhere, and "always inevitable"; it is inevitable and all the more dreadful because it is amorphous and cannot even be defined except as something which causes fear and terror. Even nature is not immune to a fear of death, Turgenev seems to say; Xarlov (**"King Lear of the Steppes"**), who is the incarnation of the invincible, mute, elemental forces, nevertheless fears death. Nor is Ellis, whoever she may be—a human soul, a poetic dream, the vampire-muse, or Lamia—exempt from the anguish of absolute destruction; she too is only a moment in the eternity of incomprehensible non-being. (p. 78)

Turgenev's intense desire for faith (which subsumes love) offered . . . some degree of comfort. The romantic Don Quixote in him tried to overthrow the skeptical Hamlet and to find surcease from reflection. If this is medication for the disease, and the disease itself is life (which is incurable), we can surely state that the antidote of desperate faith was effective until the last day of Turgenev's life.

Religion as a complete integration of the individual with God aroused Turgenev's wonder . . . and desperate, especially in his later years, Turgenev could never bring himself to accept Russian Christianity, which his reason rejected (unlike Tolstoj and Dostoevskij, whose hearts and minds fought a constant battle between a fervent desire for some surcease from their torments and their own analytical powers). Yet it is curious to note that one of the most vivid images of the ideal Christian heroine in Russian literature (Liza Kalitina) was endowed by this artist with a positivistic world view. For Liza's resignation to the blows that destiny has raised on her is accepted in the true Christian feeling of forgiveness. Another character imbued with a similar mildness of spirit is Akim in **"The Inn"**. In both him and Liza, religious fervor motivates a lack of resistance against the circumstances.

In the light of his preference for "revolt and individuality", it is understandable why Turgenev colors Liza's religion with retribution and guilt, for Liza has always been filled with a sense of foreboding and awe. Her religion cannot allow for any personal happiness. In this sense, Turgenev's understanding of the Christian God places him in the same category as the mysterious and often malevolent forces of fate. . . . Thus, the solutions offered by both Lavreckij and Liza are the same: a denial of all personal hope and a devotion to duty.

Faith is simply a weapon designed to make life bearable. "The person who has faith—has everything and cannot lose anything; and he who doesn't have it, doesn't have anything. And I feel this all the more strongly because I belong to the havenots", Turgenev wrote on one occasion. But faith cannot be forced, as he acknowledged: ". . . but religion itself has to become a natural need for man, and the man who does not have it—well, all that is left for him is to turn away his eyes lightheartedly or stoically".

Turgenev saw this faith also in its more active manifestations. Whether it is the ardent love which wells up in Asja and Gemma or the desire for self-sacrifice in Elena, the dedication of Insarov to his oppressed land, Marianna's longing to help the people or Sof'ja's religious enthusiasm and devotion to Vasilij, all of them are possessed by passion or the ideal. Here faith in religion or in an ideal is the enemy of introspection, and it propels those who possess this fervor to action.

"Only to go somewhere far, toward prayer, toward some difficult deed", Asja exclaims, and finally she expresses this longing in love. In ***On the Eve***, Bersenev differentiates between the egotistic happiness that isolates man and concepts like fatherland, science, liberty, justice, and love (love as self-sacrifice, not love as pleasure) which unite him with the rest of mankind. However, Asja's words reveal the common denominator of all these yearnings. It is immaterial where this faith turns; in the face of death and the futility of life man cannot live by reason alone, and the act of faith, *de bonne foi*, enables him to transcend the horrors around and beyond him.The mystique of faith interested Turgenev so much that he made a series of studies of sectarians (Kas'jan, Akim, Liza's nurse Agaf'ja, Luker'ja, Sof'ja, Evlampija). It is significant that he demonstrated the same respect for the revolutionaries as for the heroine of **"A Strange Story"**, since it was the psychological side of their exaltation that he wished to penetrate: "I did not understand Sofi's act; but I did not condemn her, just as I did not later on condemn the other young girls who had sacrificed everything, in the same way, for that which *they* believed to be the truth, for that in which *they* saw their calling". Turgenev treasured not the content but the form of spiritual existence, not the efforts but the psychological result of the offering. He judged people not according to the loftiness of the idea or the subject to which they dedicated themselves, but according to the intensity of their dedication, which alone could surmount the void that existed in a divided soul.

Much has been written about the parallel solutions that both Turgenev and Schopenhauer found in compassion and love; and critics have asserted that it was in Schopenhauer's philosophy that Turgenev discovered this sovereign remedy. For Schopenhauer, pure disinterested love makes it possible to identify one's own self with others and thus help achieve complete freedom from individuality and the denial of the will to love in which he saw the source of man's misery. In effect, examples like Luker'ja and some of the ***Poems in Prose*** would tend to corroborate this view. Turgenev's alternations between "passive" and "active" states of faith (an arbitrary definition, obviously) has already been noted, and it seems plausible to consider the "active" state as being equally strong for Turgenev as the "passive". Turgenev sought a faith that could impart a positive meaning to life, however much man is wearied and degraded by suffering, agony, and questioning.

What distinguishes man, "the thinking reed", from the animals is precisely his ability to "reflect", and the ultimate result of "reflection", according to both Schopenhauer and Turgenev, is the tormenting awareness that death is all-devouring and inevitable. The only way out for Schopenhauer "is through exalted resignation, annihilating the will and resulting in complete passivity. Turgenev's Luker'ja is frequently identified as the exemplar of Schopenhauerian resignation. Indeed, she does anticipate death as a joyful event, although she knows she should be frightened. It appears in the guise of a splendid majestic woman taller than any other; the one feature that reveals the element of cruelty are her falcon-like eyes: "yellow, large and pale, oh so pale". Yet this figure does not inspire any fear in the peasant woman who is in tune with nature: "Instead of being frightened, it was quite the other way. I was as pleased as could be". Unlike Schopenhauer and Tolstoj, however, Turgenev does not negate intellectual activity, and he does not grant the comfort of a peaceful death uniquely to the peasant who in his unconscious state is nearer to nature. The student Avenir (**"Death"**) and the aristocratic lady (**"Old Portraits"**) accept their fate as easily as do Maksim and the miller. The old lady awaits her death peacefully and even prepares a ruble for the priest to read the prayers for the dying. Thus, civilization does not necessarily lead to man's separation from the mainstream of existence. Turgenev's conclusion—"Yes, the Russians die in a wonderful way"—might possibly induce us to give this statement a Tolstoyan interpretation. In "The Death of Ivan Il'ič", the peasant Gerasim is able to comfort and teach his master, simply because he is a peasant and hence a custodian of the truth. Yet is not Aratov's acceptance of his death as tranquil as the peasants'? The clue, then, is not in the protagonist's social class, nor in his intellectual acumen, but in the meaning that he can impart to his life or death. Admittedly, in ***A Sportsman's Sketches*** emphasis is given to "non-thinking" and an unquestioning submission to fate. But the lives of Telegina (**"Old Portraits"**) and Aratov have acquired a significance only through their love, and in each case they accept death freely as the end to an existence in which love is no longer possible.

We have already seen that passion brings death, and that it is the woman who embodies the principle of passion. Turgenev seems to perceive death as a return to the maternal embrace or womb. Ernest Jones emphasizes the underlying wish of the organism to return to the mother; mother means birth and birth equals death. Freud also claims that in the condition of sleep we see a likeness, both in its physical and mental aspects, of "the blissful isolation of the intrauterine existence", that prototype of the state of peace, to which, in accordance with the death instinct, it seems to be the aim of the organism to return.

In Freud's dream interpretation, a boat suggests an unconscious memory of the happiness of the cradle. The night before Aratov's death, the night of Klara's first kiss which reveals to him an unknown bliss, Aratov dreams of being in a little golden boat with a wizened little creature. On the eve of Insarov's death, Elena (***On the Eve***) dreams of a little boat which changes into a sleigh in which a wizened creature is sitting. And the image of water is also an invitation to death: "contempler l'eau, c'est s'écouler, c'est se dissoudre, c'est mourir."

From time immemorial, man has perceived the transition to the other world as a passage across water; the bark of Charon ferried dead souls to Hades. If we accept the cradle as a symbol of the return to the maternal arms, then the union of the symbols "l'eau bercée", mother, and death gives us the equation necessary to comprehend Turgenev's longing for and fear of the inevitable destruction. (pp. 78-81)

Eva Kagan-Kans, in her Hamlet and Don Quixote: Turgenev's Ambivalent Vision, *Mouton, 1975, 161 p.*

LEONARD SCHAPIRO (essay date 1978)

[In this excerpt from his biography of Turgenev, Schapiro reviews the themes and merits of Poems in Prose.*]*

A form of writing which belongs distinctively to the last years of Turgenev's life was that exemplified by the ***Prose Poems.*** Sixty-nine out of the total eighty-three of these miniature pieces were written in the years from 1877 to 1879, though much revised later in the process of recopying. . . . Although uneven in quality, the ***Prose Poems*** include examples of Turgenev's art at its best, and detailed study of them has shown the extent to which they reflect his literary experience and vast reading of a lifetime. A glance at the main themes dealt with in the ***Poems*** reveals Turgenev's private preoccupations between 1877 and 1879 (between the ages of fifty-nine to sixty-one), since at that date he certainly had no intention of publishing these fragments. A large number of the poems are concerned with death, usually his own, and his lost youth—twenty-seven out of the sixty-nine. Two very moving pieces of great simplicity are obviously addressed to Pauline. One extols the beauty which she expresses and personifies, thereby achieving the only immortality which it is possible to achieve: the other implores her not to visit his grave, but to read a favourite passage from one of the books which they once read together, and think of him—'Oh, thou, my only friend, oh thou whom I love so deeply and so tenderly!' In some cases the purpose of the story related is to underline the long-suffering submission of the Russian peasant in the face of disaster—a favourite theme of Turgenev. An example of this is the sketch entitled **"Masha",** which was based on experience, because Turgenev had related the facts to Goncourt some years before. It is a very simple and touching account of a conversation with a peasant cab driver whose much loved wife had been carried off by cholera some months before. Another is a shattering story of the war in 1805, told in a couple of pages. The narrator's military servant is accused of robbing a woman, who complains to the general who happens to be passing. The servant, who is in fact innocent, is so overcome with fear at the sight of the general that he cannot utter a word when asked what he has to say in his defence, and is ordered to be hanged. The woman is now frantic with remorse, as the stolen hens have been found. She begs all and sundry to spare the wretched servant, but the general has departed and the military machine rolls on inexorably. Just before he is hanged the servant turns to the narrator, his officer, and says: 'Tell her not to distress herself, your excellency. . . . After all, I have forgiven her.'

Some of the poems record personal events and emotions such as taking leave of the dying Nekrasov; or the tribute to the memory of Baroness Vrevskaia. There are bitter satires, little paeans of hatred—one might not have guessed that Turgenev could hate so fervently. The satire on a pharisee (**"The Egoist"**) is written with particular venom: the entry of 'Viardot' in brackets in the manuscript (not in the published version), if really intended to signify what it appears to convey, reveals sentiments towards Louis which one would not otherwise have suspected Turgenev of harbouring. There are some poems which deal with revolutionary themes, such as the conversation between two workers who, on hearing that a revolutionary is to be hanged, are concerned solely to obtain a piece of the hangman's rope which brings luck; or the famous **"Threshold"** which Stasiulevich would not publish in 1882 without alterations which Turgenev refused to make. Following Lavrov, **"Threshold"** was widely believed by the revolutionaries to have been inspired by the hanging of one of the assassins of Alexander II, Sophie Perovskaia in 1881. But since Turgenev dated it May 1878 it seems likely that it was prompted by the trial of Vera Zasulich. . . . A young girl is being examined on joining the revolutionaries—is she prepared for all the forms of hardship and suffering which her life will bring? She is. 'Are you prepared to commit a crime?' The girl drops her head. 'I am prepared for that too.' As she steps over the threshold one voice cries 'Fool!' and another 'Saint!'

This was typical of Turgenev's romantic mood at that date. Saint? The assassin who threw the first bomb at Alexander II on 1 March 1881 missed, and killed a small boy who was standing by. The Emperor left his carriage to attend to the child, and was mortally wounded by the assassin's second bomb. Who was the 'Saint'?

Finally, there are poems which deal with two of Turgenev's favourite themes: the blind, impersonal force of nature, which pursues its own ends of ensuring procreation and survival and is quite indifferent to men's aspirations; and the overriding importance of love in human relations. For example, a sketch of a terrified sparrow defending its fledgling which has fallen from the nest against Tresor (one of Turgenev's gun dogs) ends with the words, 'Love, I thought, is stronger than death and the fear of death. Only by it, by love, does life persist and move forward.' The ***Prose Poems*** are uneven in quality and some are of little merit. At their best they are among Turgenev's most exquisite and most conscious artefacts. (pp. 286-88)

Leonard Schapiro, in his Turgenev: His Life and Times, *Random House, 1978, 382 p.*

VICTOR RIPP (essay date 1980)

[*In the following excerpt from his study of Turgenev's works through* Fathers and Sons, *Ripp examines standards of judgment as they are depicted in* Rudin.]

Dmitri Rudin is an impoverished nobleman and a passionate exponent of German Romantic philosophy. When he finds himself unexpectedly at the manor house of Daria Lasunskaia, he immediately gives vent to enthusiastic, if vague, pronouncements about the need for social change. Especially impressed is Lasunskaia's daughter Natalia. Indeed, during Rudin's stay at the manor house, Natalia becomes progressively more infatuated by his intellectual energy, finally reaching the point of suggesting elopement. But at the critical moment, Rudin hesitates, citing the need to observe properties. Rudin's inability to match his grand pronouncements with action turns the plot to its conclusion. Rudin leaves the manor house in disgrace, Natalia marries the uninteresting but good man who has been courting her, life resumes the placid course that Rudin's arrival had interrupted.

Turgenev prepares us for the denouement by introducing in the opening chapters several characters who resist Rudin's enthusiasm: Pigasov, the cynical hanger-on who disbelieves all extravagant statements; Volyntsev, Natalia's rather simple-minded suitor, who relies exclusively on common sense and his aristocratic intuitions; and, most important of all, Lezhnev, who in various ways is the conscience of the book. Lezhnev knows Rudin from their student days in Moscow, when both were members of the same intellectual circle (which Turgenev bases on the famous Stankevich Circle); and as a result of that acquaintance, Lezhnev as much as predicts Rudin's failure of nerve. He is quite sure he can see Rudin's moral failings, the reprehensible inability to translate thought to action.

Rudin, therefore, repeats one of the most vexing questions of Russian intellectual life: what is the connection between abstract ideals and purposeful activity? But Turgenev has very significantly altered the usual perspective on this question. He forces us to consider those who ask it as well as the object of their curiosity. Thus, although by the end of the book Rudin stands condemned, his guilt is not absolute. He is no simple poseur; he has at least groped toward an ideal. Those who condemn him, on the other hand, only sit smugly by. Much of the time, ***Rudin*** breathes a sanctimonious air. In a world of fools and idlers, the man who most energetically tries to integrate value and action is most harshly judged. That is to call into doubt the concept of judgment. Indeed, the movement of the book, from Rudin's first public success when he arrives unexpectedly at Lasunskaia's to his public exile into the world beyond the manor house, emphasizes the theme of collective judgment. Once it becomes clear that Rudin is not exactly the man he claims to be, all the other characters pursue the secret of his personality so fervently that all other concerns virtually vanish. The book's title is doubly appropriate: it names both the hero and the main preoccupation of all the other characters.

There are two major pieces of evidence to support Rudin's eventual condemnation, and both reveal as much about the mode of judgment that is invoked as about Rudin. The first is Rudin's interview with Natalia by Avdiukhin Pond. Rudin is much to blame for what passes here; his lack of will, his invidious ability to absorb all events into a bewildering system of his own interpretations, makes disaster almost a foregone conclusion. But only "almost," for Natalia also must bear some responsibility. Though Natalia comes to Avdiukhin Pond intent on proclaiming her readiness to unite her future to Rudin's—indeed she passionately offers herself to him—her actions during the interview work to narrow drastically the acceptable basis for cooperation.

Throughout the first part of the rendezvous Natalia remains remarkably and purposefully noncommittal, dryly reporting the awful news that her mother has learned of their love, but not indicating her own reactions to this new obstacle. Natalia in effect tests Rudin, and the test is explicitly twofold: Will Rudin unequivocally reassert his love in the face of difficulty and, correlatively, will he comprehend that Natalia is the sort of person who will welcome such a declaration despite the certain hardships the lovers will have to face? In other words, will Rudin instantaneously reveal who he is and recognize who she is? Rudin fails on both counts. As Natalia says, "Yes, you did expect this, you did not know me." As a result, they must part, at once and forever. Since Natalia has invoked standards that measure individuals for what they are in their essence, there is no discussion of any mitigating circumstances in the past, nor any contemplation of adjustments for the future.

Natalia's abruptness appears fully justified. Rudin has worked, aggressively and cunningly, to make Natalia believe he possesses a capacity for action that he only wishes for. Moreover, Natalia's proposal to elope is one that no genuinely feeling man would decline. Rudin is a phrasemonger, who makes enthusiastic gestures but lacks the will to bring any project to fruition. When Rudin hesitates while answering her offer, it is reasonable that Natalia's love should turn to scorn; but it is also true that she has herself set obstacles to their mutual happiness. By withholding any expression of her feelings and by narrowing to an instant the time when Rudin could express his, she has manipulated the rendezvous so that it becomes a test of personality instead of an occasion for mutual declarations of love.

It is a test, moreover, that is based on a rigorous conception of what personality implies. To Natalia, character is fixed. What a man does, what he expresses in an unguarded instant, is a sign of what he always is. She sees no need for a discussion that would permit Rudin to modify his ideas and propensities to meet her expectations. Instead, Natalia forces the rendezvous into a form of revelation. Her abrupt termination of the conversation and withdrawal to her mother's house, leaving Rudin to shout his justifications to the empty air, is a fitting conclusion to the episode: it gives dramatic shape to her belief that an essentially unchanging self is the standard of value, and if an encounter does not instantaneously produce a sympathetic connection between individuals, nothing can narrow the gap.

Natalia represents an extreme position, which seems to foreclose the possibilities of understanding even before they have a chance to develop. But Turgenev insists on the point. He introduces another episode that projects the same standards as those invoked by Natalia. The central character in this episode is Lezhnev. For much of the beginning of the book, he has remained in the background, hinting darkly at special knowledge he possesses about Rudin's character. Only in chapter 6 does he finally tell his tale about Rudin, after much hesitation and only at Lipina's insistence, not only because it is against his code to gossip but because he is sure of the dreadful condemnatory power of what he will relate.

In fact, his charge proves highly ambiguous. While studying in Moscow years before, Lezhnev had fallen in love, and had told his secret to his older friend, Rudin, who had responded by going into raptures—a response that Lezhnev found proper. Beyond that, however, Rudin took it upon himself to explain to the lovers the importance of what they had hit upon. Such interference certainly shows poor taste; but on the other hand, Lezhnev remarks that he had "practically insisted" on introducing Rudin to his love. Considering how directly the affair proceeded under the auspices of Romantic philosophy, Rudin's behavior appears justifiable: in a period when true love was construed as a means of achieving unity with the cosmos, interest in specific instances of the emotion indicated not idle curiosity but metaphysical concern. Lezhnev makes clear that he had fully accepted Romanticism, having gone so far as to write a play modeled on Byron's *Manfred*. He has now recanted, but can he blame Rudin merely for believing in what he himself once did?

Though the charge against Rudin goes on for several more pages, listing several more putative transgressions, much of what Lezhnev reports is contradictory and unfocused, an indictment so full of charges that there is no room for proofs. Lezhnev's only unambiguous complaint is that in the emotional turmoil at the end of the love affair, Rudin stayed calm. While Lezhnev fell into a condition where "lies seemed truth," Rudin was "like a swallow flying above a pond," aware but not passionately involved. Rudin's reprehensible fastidiousness could have had little to do with correct action—indeed, Lezhnev had been arguing that Rudin too often interfered in matters that did not concern him. Lezhnev apparently guessed Rudin's thoughts, and did not like what he perceived. Lezhnev breaks off his story with melodramatic abruptness, not permitting Lipina to question him: "But enough of him. Perhaps all will end well." His manner underscores his inability to show Rudin's guilt in terms of concrete infractions, and also insinuates his belief that he does not have to.

At first glance, Lezhnev's role appears redundant. He repeats the condemnation of Rudin which Natalia makes more forcefully, and he uses the same standards of judgment that she does. But he puts the case against Rudin in an especially chilling form. Natalia exposes the flaws she intuitively believed were in him, she makes his inner weakness manifest. Lezhnev needs not a shred of evidence to confirm him in his opinion of Rudin. His confused and intricate tale blurs all lines of causality; he presents a picture that has no moment when Rudin could have done something to swing judgment in his favor. Most remarkably, Lezhnev goes on to comment that his lengthy diatribe does not even include the real reason for his animosity, that his break with Rudin actually "occurred later, when we met abroad." It is as if the critical event in the relationship between Lezhnev and Rudin has been made to regress ever further until it slips from sight altogether, and judgment comes to rest entirely on intuition.

The mode of judgment employed against Rudin is not only extreme but final. Stung by his failure at Avdiukhin Pond, he writes letters to Natalia and to Natalia's suitor Volyntsev, trying to explain his motives. The letters are a departure from Rudin's usual style: he admits his errors and seeks only a measure of understanding from those he has hurt. But everyone who learns of the letters dismisses them as the strategy of an insincere man who is trying to salvage his pride. The mode of judgment that prevails in the community constituted by Lasunskaia's and Lezhnev's manor houses permits no explanations or qualifications; explanations and qualifications are aspects of the manifest behavior it is wiser to ignore when evaluating a man's essential being.

Turgenev seems to endorse the way that the community judges Rudin, but he also questions it. He shows that the same standards that are invoked in condemning Rudin can be turned back upon the judges. In the very first chapter, Turgenev begins to prepare us for a picture of a community where judgment is out of control, where intuition runs rampant. The encounter between Lipina and Lezhnev seems a nonchalant flirtation, but the implicit attitudes of the two signal a moral crisis. Lezhnev says:

> "I am happy to meet you."
>
> "And why?"
>
> "What a question! As if it is not always pleasant to meet you. Today you are as fresh and nice as the morning."
>
> Alexandra Pavlovna laughed again.
>
> "Why are you laughing?"
>
> "What do you mean, why?" If you could see with what an apathetic and cold expression you uttered your compliment. I am surprised you did not yawn at the last word."

Lezhnev's words are treated suspiciously and then discounted altogether, even as he will deal with Rudin; and his remonstrances, like Rudin's, are rejected out of hand. The tone of the scene is light and playful, but it marks an unbridgeable distance that separates all the characters. Life in the enclave proves to be full of barbed and brittle encounters, and the larger gatherings suggest not real community but a precarious equilibrium of diverse tendencies. The characters are shown rubbing up against one another, occasionally flaring up from the friction, and then withdrawing unchanged into themselves.

Even the most positive moment in the book is made problematical by the way that members of the community habitually regard each other. Lezhnev and Lipina, now married, sit on their veranda, luxuriating in the comfort of pleasant surroundings and a company of acquaintances. Though happy, however, they lack intensity or passion. During their courtship they were never more than affectionate, and the marriage seems only a declared willingness to accept the other for what he or she is without trying to effect great change or make intimate contact. Lezhnev says to his wife, "Here we love each other and are happy, aren't we?" His polite and quizzical tone, his sense that love requires confirmation, measures the distance separating the characters in ***Rudin*** even when they are happiest. The decorous setting on the veranda, it becomes clear, is not so much a sign of harmony as a symbol of the care and restraint that is necessary to forestall an always threatening discord.

Altogether, the prevailing mixture of uncertain emotions, petty malice, and abrupt anger in ***Rudin*** makes for a noisome brew, and it is not a pleasant book to read. (pp. 127-33)

Men like Rudin, with their shifting commitment to action, had to be exposed; but the process of exposure, Turgenev's novel shows, could have its own debilitating effects. (p. 134)

Using as the only standard what man *is* rather than what he *does* makes unity either instantaneously achievable or hardly achievable at all. If a negative judgment is rendered, there is no way to appeal it, since no act is acceptable evidence. Even in the rare instances when the original judgment is changed voluntarily, the result is of dubious value. Lezhnev does finally excuse Rudin his flaws, but significantly, his change of heart occurs in the same scene in which he discounts all Rudin's practical efforts in the interval since they last met. Rudin's work on a canal, as an agronomist, and as a teacher mean nothing to Lezhnev. He changes his opinion not because of anything Rudin has done, but because he feels a surge of sympathy. His benign judgment is like a bestowal of grace, and as such is something to be thankful for but not something that can lead to real understanding. The scene ends with Rudin declining Lezhnev's invitation to visit his estate and going off to a solitary destiny. The novel thus endorses the culture's form of judgment and also questions it: in making the inner self the standard of value, men like Lezhnev help to establish a purity of motive among the members of a community, but they also put the very idea of community into jeopardy. (pp. 134-35)

Victor Ripp, in his Turgenev's Russia: From "Notes of a Hunter" to "Fathers and Sons", *Cornell University Press, 1980, 218 p.*

EDGAR L. FROST (essay date 1987)

[Frost explores the themes of love and isolation in "Mumu," suggesting as well that the story is an indictment of Russian serfdom.]

There is only one instance in his story **"Mumu"** where Turgenev directly and uncompromisingly tells the reader that love exists, and those involved are Mumu and Gerasim. Mumu, we are told, "loved Gerasim alone," while for his part "Gerasim . . . loved her to distraction." In no other scene is the reader shown unquestionable, directly attested mutual love, and it is this simple fact which Turgenev plays upon to structure the entire story and to characterize those who act it out. He does so, for the most part, by focusing on the absence of love rather than its presence. Such an approach is not surprising, since love in Turgenev's oeuvre is usually illusory or short-lived. The only two characters that love each other and show their love are the dog and her master, and, while the depths of this relationship are shown, the lone instance of such love is outweighed by all the manifestations of its absence elsewhere. (p. 171)

The first part of the story develops the ill-fated affair between Gerasim and Tat'jana; when it is finished, the stage is ready for his next love. In like manner, when the second object of his affection no longer exists, the action is again ready for a shift, and Gerasim leaves almost immediately, though he is first seen briefly by another of the serfs. The story develops by moving from one love episode to another, or, more precisely, from zero on the love scale, to fairly high, to the top of the scale, and then back down to zero. The episode with Tat'jana is a step up and a preparation for the greater love the hero finds with Mumu. The love element, in its presence, its absence, and its degrees, dominates the narrative. For it to loom so large in the plot it must be a symbol for something very important in the lives of Gerasim and others—something, perhaps, more than just love itself. I would suggest that this something was the human dignity of which the serfs were deprived. . . .

[Whether] love stands for freedom, happiness, or something else, one can surmise that in the story it represents much that is denied Gerasim. He is a serf, and therefore his life is made incomplete. In the final section, Gerasim is home again, but he remains alone, loveless. He has no family, and the reader is told that he has no dog and sees no women. He is in familiar surroundings, but the story remains pathetic precisely because he has been cut off from the two beings that gave his life a deeper meaning through love, whether real or imagined. (p. 172)

[There] is much evidence to link Tat'jana and Mumu. Both fill a void in the life of the hero, thus illustrating his otherwise empty fate at the hands of his mistress. One can scarcely help noticing the link between Tat'jana and Mumu, because of the way Turgenev structures the tale. As Tat'jana is about to leave for the remote country, to accompany her worthless husband, Gerasim comes out of his room and presents her with a red kerchief, an obvious sign of his affection for her. She responds by crying and by kissing him three times, and although the kisses are described as being "in the Christian manner," they nevertheless convey feeling for him. A few moments later, she is gone, but no sooner has the cart bearing her lurched out of his view than Gerasim turns off along the river and notices the as-yet-unnamed Mumu wriggling helplessly in the mud there, trying to extract herself.

It is, of course, quite a coincidence for Gerasim to stumble onto a new and greater love almost before the one he has lost is out of sight. The suddenness of the transition from Tat'jana to Mumu is such that it draws attention to the obvious and invites comparisons of the two objects of Gerasim's love. The precipitousness of the break also makes one mindful of the structure of the story, conveying the notion that something new and important is about to happen and thus setting up the ascendancy of the Mumu-Gerasim relationship.

The similarities between Tat'jana and Mumu make the work a Freudian delight—beginning with the fact that Mumu is a female and shares Gerasim's bed: "[She] immediately leapt onto the bed with a satisfied air." What is important, however, is not sex, but love and all that it stands for in the tale. And in that connection the links between Tat'jana and Mumu are instructive. Both are orphans of vague or unknown ancestry. . . . Both characters have known hardship. The dog has been left to die in the river, and the woman has been oppressed since her early years. Furthermore, the two resemble each other physically. (pp. 172-73)

Tat'jana is a cowering type who trembles at the mention of her mistress's name and never talks to anyone if she can avoid it. Her only interest is in finishing her work on time. Turgenev's direct words about her are, "She was of an extremely mild, or, it would be better to say, timorous disposition," and, he adds, she "was deathly afraid of others." There is a clear connection between the frightened woman and the intimidated dog that refuses to be enticed by the *barynja* and her servants. (p. 174)

The accumulation of such evidence would seem to make it difficult to deny that Turgenev had reason for equating the two—as, indeed, he had. And the reason was that he wanted to call attention to their desperate loneliness, isolation, and need of love, as well as their relationships with Gerasim. In a work so devoid of love, theirs is an eloquent connection, both with each other and with the hero. It is a deft touch in the Tat'jana-Mumu relationship that the connection . . . combines the ideas of love and a fawning, cringing attitude, two of the essential ingredients of the tale. And though the work is one of love and its absence, it is also one of the frightful cruelties perpetrated upon human beings and symbolized by the equal tyranny over a dumb beast and her dumb master. Within this scheme, too, Tat'jana serves as a link between Mumu and Gerasim, for she is of the dog's nature and the man's kind.

An avenue by which Turgenev airs the theme of nonlove is, certainly, the corollary of isolation. He begins by focusing on the solitary figure of the dictatorial old *barynja* and concludes by sketching the hero in his lonely hut, without family, with no romantic interest, and with no dog. In between, the author shows us the abandoned mongrel and the timid, then banished and isolated, Tat'jana. The work . . . is partially organized around the theme of isolation.

The opening words of the story are, "In *one* [my italics—E. F.] of the remote streets of Moscow," and forms of the word *odin* appear twice more in the first eighteen lines, thus quickly linking the two lonely figures of the *barynja* and Gerasim. *Odin,* of course, means not only 'one' in Russian, but also 'alone', and it is the aloneness of the pair that manifests itself early on. They are alone in different ways, to be sure, but ironically enough they share equally the fate of being isolated from their fellow beings. Being thus isolated, they cannot love and be loved, a common bond of loneliness between the two.

For her part, the old woman has been cast off by others because of her age and her disposition, foul and surly. (pp. 174-75)

Gerasim is just as alone, but for very different reasons. First, he is alone because the cruel old woman has brought him to Moscow, where he plainly does not fit. . . . His size and strength are of a singular nature and cause him to stand apart from others, emphasizing his isolation, his loneliness, and, ultimately, his separation from love. This is the case even among his fellow serfs, and both they and Gerasim seem to realize it. His fellow workers keep their distance, and Gerasim "didn't like people to come to see him." The repelling, rather than attracting, qualities of Gerasim become evident when one reads, "Not everyone was willing to jeer . . . at Gerasim: he didn't like jokes." . . . For Turgenev, isolation is terrible because it is a state in which one can neither give nor receive love, as we see through Gerasim's plight and through that of the *barynja*.

The difference, to an extent, between the *barynja* and Gerasim lies in his being deaf and dumb. His proportions and strength serve to make him heroic, and we are told that if it were not for his ailments, any lass in the village would be happy to link her life with his. But his physical handicaps isolate him completely, for they lend to his towering, imposing physique a frightening aspect that causes others to shun and fear him. (pp. 175-76)

Ironically, though, it is what he does to the one he loves most of all that best illustrates the terrible side of Gerasim—he drowns Mumu. There is a sense of fulfillment in the act, for he rescues the dog from a watery grave at one point, only to plunge her into one at another. Russia's serfs were often doomed to unhappiness, and this sequence of events serves to bring home the hopelessness of the existence of Gerasim. "Why bother to save the dog in the first place, if you're going to have to end her life later?" runs the implied question. It is, of course, a terribly poignant device to have the hero destroy the creature he loves. But why have him drown her? Perhaps precisely because it is a painful death, and not a quick one. Turgenev thus manages to elicit more sympathy from his readers—Gerasim has said he will kill the dog, and he does. He could do it another way, but no other way would fit quite so well in this particular tale. It demonstrates the blind, mute fury of a downtrodden people, the unthinking savagery of which they were capable. Yet, at the same time, it demonstrates their sometimes unbending honesty and straightforwardness. The act simultaneously attracts and repels.

In the story there is another dog, an old watchdog named Volčok, which is never taken off its chain. It lies about the yard day and night, firmly fastened to its place. But the most interesting thing about it is that it does not try to leave. Volčok, in Turgenev's words, "didn't demand freedom at all." This freedom—freedom to live and love—is also a central concern of the narrative. What better symbol of the situation of the serfs? Here we have an old dog, beaten down by age and experience, which has accepted its fate to the point of not even trying to change it. It barks quite halfheartedly, merely going through the motions. Obviously, Volčok will never lose his chains.

Mumu stands in the starkest of contrasts to his acceptance of one's fate. Until discovered by the old woman, she runs freely about the property and the city with her master. She enters his room, hops onto the furniture, and is familiar to the owners of the restaurant where Gerasim takes her for her last meal. She is, furthermore, a fighter, a creature with spirit. Even though weak, she is struggling for her life when Gerasim first chances upon her in the mud. Cornered by the *barynja* and her servants, she backs up against a wall and bares her teeth at the old woman. Stolen from her owner, she breaks free and returns to him. Moreover, in contrast to Volčok, she has a purpose in life, which is brought out in her barking. A good watchdog, she makes it known if there really is an intruder or something suspicious about. One may contrast this with the way Volčok lies curled up in his house, aimlessly emitting, from time to time, a hoarse, almost *silent* sound, "as if sensing all its futility himself." Mutatis mutandis, the Russian people lie silently and submissively in their hovels, living out their days, making no effort to attain freedom. Like Volčok, they bark hoarsely, almost silently, only now and then, and to no real purpose.

Gerasim, linked closely with the freedom-loving Mumu, is restless, and he finally gains some individual freedom by leaving Moscow for his native region. But, being a serf, he also shares some of Volčok's heritage. He, like Volčok, has almost no voice and is capable of making only one sound, an indistinct one at that. The Russian people had no voice in their own affairs, and Gerasim's dumbness—he cannot declare his love—symbolizes their total dependence on their owners. (pp. 177-78)

Mumu, the supreme symbol of unselfish, loyal love in the story, values Gerasim highly, and she is the force which changes his life. A willing sacrifice offered up by her master's hands, she becomes the symbol for the coming emancipation of the serfs in Russia. Simply put, she replaces Volčok in Gerasim's (i.e., the people's) life. Not indefinitely would the mužiki lie passively chained to the land owned by their masters. Gerasim remains a symbol of potential energy waiting to be unleashed, rather than one of a force roaming unchecked over the land, but he is a powerful symbol whose explosiveness is hinted at in his terrible strength and in the fear and respect he inspires in others. (p. 179)

[The] dog and the dumb peasant are brought ever closer together in a demonstration of real love, before it is shattered by the cruelty of the aged tyrant. (p. 182)

As the final severing of the relationship draws ever nearer, another connection suggests itself. After Gerasim has been deceived with regard to Tat'jana's drinking, we read of Tat'jana and Kapiton that "that same evening they . . . set out for the *barynja*'s with geese under their arms, and a week later they got married." If we compare this with the wording of a passage a few pages later, we find a strange echo pertaining to Mumu and Gerasim: stopping on the way to the boat, Gerasim "carried off two bricks . . . under his arm." The bricks will serve Gerasim's purpose, and the words "pod myškoj," repeated from the earlier instance, seem oddly coincidental. In other words, they suggest a "wedding" between Gerasim and Mumu, foreshadowed by the actual but meaningless one between Kapiton and Tat'jana. It is another "couple," but what is borne under the arm this time is not geese, but bricks. Yet the parallel is tempting, for we see two twosomes formalizing their relationships. Neither pair constitutes a normal "couple"; yet each is setting out, clearly embarking on the process of linking themselves more closely, and the parallelism is reinforced by the repetition of "pod myškoj" at key points. It is, furthermore, confirmed by what follows. Gerasim has put on his festive *kaftan* as befits a groom, and Mumu's coat "shone splendidly," as one would expect of a bride's garment. At an earlier stage, Gerasim has been seen partaking of *šči*, and now he offers Mumu the same fare, "salting" what he gives her with one of his own tears, which falls into the bowl she is eating politely from. Finally, just before he straightens up and drops Mumu into the water, Gerasim remains motionless, as if in prayer, "having crossed his mighty hands on her back." It is appropriate for him to form a cross on her with his hands, for he is playing a dual role, betrothed and priest, the former as indicated above and the latter because it is he who conducts the sacrifice of which she becomes the victim.

When Gerasim opens his hands and Mumu disappears beneath the surface of the water, the "ceremony" ends. Indeed, the whole scene and the preparations for it are carried out ritualistically, as is appropriate for both a wedding and a funeral, which are equally represented. Great love is manifested throughout by both parties: Gerasim displays extreme solemnity and sadness, and Mumu shows complete trust in him, even as he holds her above the waves. The depiction of the love between the two is, of course, what makes the scene so terrible when it has ended, because they are then irreparably separated. The level of love has been brought back to zero, where it was at the outset of the story. (pp. 182-83)

Gerasim, let it be said, had found no love in his earlier life, a point the introductory material on him makes amply clear. He lived in those days "apart from his brethren," though, as already mentioned, he might have had his pick of the village lasses but for his dual physical afflictions. The key is not merely that he is loveless at beginning and end, but rather that there is a difference because of what has happened in between. There is a finality about his lovelessness in the end that is not there at the outset, and this is a very large and vital difference. What is significant is that his chances for love are taken away by his owner. But for the heartless old woman, he might have found a Tat'jana or a Mumu in the countryside—and his hut might not have been so empty. He might have shared it with a woman or a dog, perhaps both. But, as the author tells us in conclusion, "he has completely quit associating with women, doesn't even glance at them, and doesn't keep a single dog at his place."

The stress in the last paragraph of the story is on the apparent sameness of circumstances surrounding the hero. Three times Turgenev uses the phrase "as before"—first, in reference to Gerasim's strength, which is as great as ever; second, to let us know that Gerasim still does the work of four men, just as he used to; third, to indicate that his staid and sedate nature has remained the same as before. It seems clear that the reason for the emphasis on all this sameness is to set up a distinct contrast between it and the one aspect that is not the same: the protagonist's opportunity to love and be loved. Without this opportunity, Gerasim remains less than a man, which is exactly Turgenev's point. Much more than a lachrymose dog story, **"Mumu"** was at the time of its publication—and remains today—an eloquent statement on the deprivations suffered by the Russian peasants, and its major device was the careful removal of love from Gerasim's sadly limited little world. (p. 184)

Edgar L. Frost, "Turgenev's 'Mumu' and the Absence of Love," in Slavic and East-European Journal, *Vol. 31, No. 2, Summer, 1987, pp. 171-86.*

ADDITIONAL BIBLIOGRAPHY

Åhnebrink, Lars. "The Influence of Turgenev." In his *The Beginnings of Naturalism in American Fiction: A Study of the Works of Hamlin Garland, Stephen Crane, and Frank Norris with Special Reference to Some European Influences, 1891-1903*, pp. 315-42. Essays and Studies on American Language and Literature, edited by S. B. Liljegren, vol. IX. Upsala, Sweden: A.-B. Lundequistska Bokhandeln, 1950.

Traces Turgenev's influence on the American writers Hamlin Garland, Stephen Crane, and Frank Norris.

Baring, Maurice. "Tolstoy and Tourgeniev" and "The Place of Tourgeniev." In his *Landmarks in Russian Literature*, pp. 50-73, 74-9. 1910. Reprint. London: Methuen, 1960.

Two essays. The first, a reprint of an article that was originally published in the *Quarterly Review*, examines Turgenev's oeuvre, allowing the writer moderate praise but claiming that "his vision was weak and narrow compared with that of Tolstoy, and his understanding was cold and shallow compared with that of Dostoievsky." The second essay answers criticism of the first. Baring explains that his intention was not to denigrate the achievements of Turgenev, but merely to argue that he has been overrated.

Brodiansky, Nina. "Turgenev's Short Stories: A Revaluation." *Slavonic and East European Review* XXXII, No. 78 (December 1953): 70-91.
Offers interpretations of Turgenev's short fiction.

Cecil, David. "Turgenev." In his *Poets and Story-Tellers: A Book of Critical Essays*, pp. 123-38. London: Constable, 1949.
Describes Turgenev's unique achievements as a novelist. Among the several aspects of the novelist's art Cecil examines are Turgenev's realism, spirituality, and commitment to aestheticism.

Fitzlyon, April. *The Price of Genius: A Life of Pauline Viardot*. New York: Appleton-Century, 1964, 520 p.
Contains frequent references to Turgenev's life and writings as they pertain to his relationship with Pauline Viardot.

Ford, Ford Madox. "Turgenev: The Beautiful Genius." In his *Portraits from Life*, pp. 143-63. Boston: Houghton Mifflin Co., 1937.
Records Ford's personal impressions of Turgenev.

Galsworthy, John. "Six Novelists in Profile: An Address." In his *Candelabra: Selected Essays and Addresses*, pp. 133-56. New York: Charles Scribner's Sons, 1933.
Notes Turgenev's influence in the West and the endurance of his work.

Gettmann, Royal A. *Turgenev in England and America*. Urbana: University of Illinois Press, 1941, 196 p.
A useful reference guide to Turgenev's critical reception in England and America from 1855 to 1937.

Gifford, Henry. "The Road to the Vyborg Side" and "In Search of the New Man." In his *The Hero of His Time: A Theme in Russian Literature*, pp. 133-53, 154-76. London: Edward Arnold & Co., 1950.
Examines the protagonists of Turgenev's major novels.

Hare, Richard. "Ivan Turgenev." In his *Portraits of Russian Personalities between Reform and Revolution*, pp. 68-103. London: Oxford University Press, 1959.
A comprehensive biographical and critical survey of Turgenev and his works.

Howe, Irving. "Turgenev: The Politics of Hesitation." In his *Politics and the Novel*, pp. 114-38. New York: Horizon Press, 1957.
Discusses the "balancing tensions" of Turgenev's work, stressing his themes of sexual frustration and intellectual indecision.

James, Henry. "Ivan Turgénieff." *The Atlantic Monthly* LIII, No. CCCXV (January 1884): 42-55.
James's fond personal reminiscences of his friend Turgenev.

Lavrin, Janko. "From Gogol to Turgenev." In his *An Introduction to the Russian Novel*, 3rd ed., pp. 53-66. London: Methuen & Co., 1945.
Surveys Turgenev's writing career, remarking that the author "paved the way to the triumph of Russian literature as a European power."

Lord, Robert. "Prose." In his *Russian Literature: An Introduction*, pp. 86-182. New York: Taplinger Publishing Co., 1980.
Contains general remarks on the qualities of Turgenev's novels and short stories.

Lowe, David. *Turgenev's "Fathers and Sons"*. Ann Arbor, Mich.: Ardis, 1983, 165 p.
An in-depth study of various aspects of *Fathers and Sons*, including structure, characterization, and cultural background.

Lubbock, Percy. "VIII." In his *The Craft of Fiction*, pp. 110-23. 1931. Reprint. New York: Peter Smith, 1947.
Debates the relative merits of "pictorial" and "dramatic" presentations in the novel genre. Lubbock faults Turgenev for adhering too closely to the former method, arguing that his authorial omniscience lessens the effectiveness of his narratives.

Magarshack, David. *Turgenev: A Life*. London: Faber and Faber, 1954, 328 p.
Discusses Turgenev's works in the context of his life.

Matlaw, Ralph E. "Turgenev's Art in *Spring Torrents*." *Slavonic and East European Review* 35 (December 1956): 157-71.
Explicates *The Torrents of Spring*, frequently comparing the work with *Smoke*.

Moore, George. "Turgueneff." In his *Impressions and Opinions*, pp. 65-97. 1891. Reprint. New York: Benjamin Blom, 1972.
Characterizes Turgenev as a writer of thought rather than action, subtlety rather than delineation, and keen observation rather than imaginative power.

Moser, Charles A. *Ivan Turgenev*. New York: Columbia University Press, 1972, 48 p.
A biographical and critical monograph. The author writes that "to study Turgenev carefully is to gain a fuller appreciation of life."

"Nihilism in Russia as It Appears in the Novels of Ivan Turgénieff." *New Englander* 37, No. CXLV (July 1878): 553-72.
Examines Turgenev's portrayal of nihilistic characters and philosophy in *Fathers and Sons* and *Virgin Soil*.

Phelps, William Lyon. "Turgenev." In his *Essays on Russian Novelists*, pp. 62-129. New York: Macmillan Co., 1917.
General, appreciative remarks on Turgenev, "perhaps the greatest novelist in history."

Powys, John Cowper. "Turgeniev: *Virgin Soil, A Sportsman's Sketches*." In his *One Hundred Best Books, with Commentary and an Essay on Books and Reading*, pp. 36-7. New York: G. Arnold Shaw, 1916.
Succinctly characterizes Turgenev's work, concluding that "the pensive detachment of a sensitive and yet not altogether unworldly spirit seems to be the final impression evoked by his books."

Pritchett, V. S. *The Gentle Barbarian: The Life and Work of Turgenev*. New York: Random House, 1977, 243 p.
A biographical and literary study. Pritchett writes: "My chief concern has been to enlarge the understanding of [Turgenev's] superb short stories and novels and to explore the interplay of what is known about his life with his art. He was a deeply autobiographical writer."

Saintsbury, George. "Turgenev, Dostoievsky, and Tolstoy." In *Russian Literature and Modern English Fiction: A Collection of Critical Essays*, edited by Donald Davie, pp. 23-30. Chicago: University of Chicago Press, 1965.
A reprint of a 1907 essay in which Saintsbury cites Turgenev as the "greatest novelist of Russia," in part because his work is largely free from Russian pessimism.

Schefski, Harold K. "Novelle Structure in Turgenev's *Spring Torrents*." *Studies in Short Fiction* 22, No. 4 (Fall 1985): 431-35.
Shows that *The Torrents of Spring* adheres to the structural devices of the German novella, particularly in its emphasis on the unfolding of a single plot.

Smyrniw, Walter. "Turgenev's Emancipated Women." *The Modern Language Review* 80, No. 1 (January 1985): 97-105.
Examines emancipated female characters in Turgenev's fiction.

Terras, Victor. "Turgenev's Aesthetic and Western Realism." *Comparative Literature* XXII, No. 1 (Winter 1970): 19-35.
Assesses Turgenev's aesthetic theories in relation to those of several prominent authors of the era, including Gustave Flaubert, Guy de Maupassant, Émile Zola, and Henry James.

Waliszewski, K. "Lermontov, Gogol, and Tourgueniev." In his *A History of Russian Literature*, pp. 227-98. 1927. Reprint. Port Washington, N.Y.: Kennikat Press, 1969.
An overview of Turgenev's life and career.

Willcocks, M. P. "Turgenev." *English Review* XXXIII (September 1921): 175-89.

Sees in Turgenev's work—particularly in Bazarov of *Fathers and Sons*—an early statement of the intellectual and political ideas of Willcocks's own time.

Yachnin, Rissa, and Stam, David H. *Turgenev in English: A Checklist of Works by and about Him*. New York: New York Public Library, 1962, 55 p.

A list of English translations of Turgenev's works—both those published separately and those appearing in anthologies and periodicals—and a secondary bibliography.

Zhitova, Mme. V. *The Turgenev Family*. Translated by A. S. Mills. New York: Roy Publishers, n.d., 179 p.

Contemporary reminiscences of Turgenev and his immediate family by an intimate of the Turgenevs.

Acknowledgments

The following is a listing of the copyright holders who have granted us permission to reprint material in this volume of *NCLC*. Every effort has been made to trace copyright, but if omissions have been made, please let us know.

THE COPYRIGHTED EXCERPTS IN NCLC, VOLUME 21, WERE REPRINTED FROM THE FOLLOWING BOOKS:

The Antioch Review, v. IX, Winter, 1949-50. Copyright 1950, renewed 1977 by the Antioch Review Inc. Reprinted by permission of the Editors.

Ball State University Forum, v. XIII, Autumn, 1972. © 1972 Ball State University. Reprinted by permission of the publisher.

The Commonweal, v. L, September 9, 1949. Copyright 1949, renewed 1977 Commonweal Publishing Co., Inc. Reprinted by permission of Commonweal Foundation.

The Connecticut Review, v. VII, October, 1973 for "Thoreau's 'Civil Disobedience': Strategy for Reform" by Michael G. Erlich. © Board of Trustees for the Connecticut State Colleges, 1973. Reprinted by permission of the author.

Criticism, v. V, Winter, 1963 for "Emily Dickinson's White Robes" by John Wheatcroft. Copyright, 1963, Wayne State University Press. Reprinted by permission of the publisher and the author.

ESQ, n. 54, Quarter I, 1969. Reprinted by permission of the publisher.

French Forum, v. 8, May, 1983. Copyright 1983 by French Forum, Inc. Reprinted by permission of the publisher.

The French Review, v. XLIX, February, 1976. Copyright 1976 by the American Association of Teachers of French. Reprinted by permission of the publisher.

Michigan Quarterly Review, v. XXII, Fall, 1983 for "A Conversation About Dostoevsky" by Czeslaw Milosz and Carl R. Proffer. Copyright © The University of Michigan, 1983. Reprinted by permission of the authors.

Modern Language Notes, v. LXXV, April, 1960. © copyright 1960 by The Johns Hopkins University Press. All rights reserved. Reprinted by permission of the publisher.

Mosaic: A Journal for the Interdisciplinary Study of Literature, v. VI, Summer, 1973. © *Mosaic* 1973. Acknowledgment of previous publication is herewith made.

The New England Quarterly, v. XLV, June, 1972 for "Mrs. Sigourney and the Sensibility of the Inner Space" by Ann Douglas Wood. Copyright 1972 by *The New England Quarterly*. Reprinted by permission of the publisher and the Literary Estate of István Sötér.

The New Hungarian Quarterly, v. XIV, Spring, 1973 for "Sándor Petöfi: Folk Poet and Revolutionary" by István Sötér. © *The New Hungarian Quarterly*, 1973. Reprinted by permission of the author.

The New York Times Book Review, September 11, 1932. Copyright 1932 by The New York Times Company. Reprinted by permission of the publisher.

Nineteenth-Century French Studies, v. V, Fall, 1976 & Winter, 1977; v. XI, Spring & Summer, 1983; v. XIII, Winter & Spring, 1985. © 1977, 1983, 1985 by T. H. Goetz. All reprinted by permission of the publisher.

Philological Quarterly, v. 60, Winter, 1981 for "Thoreau's Narrative Art in 'Civil Disobedience' " by Barry Wood. Copyright 1982 by The University of Iowa. Reprinted by permission of the publisher and the author.

The Quarterly Journal of Speech, v. LX, October, 1974 for "Thoreau and Civil Disobedience: A Rhetorical Paradox" by Christopher Lyle Johnstone. Copyright 1974 by the Speech Communication Association. Reprinted by permission of the publisher and the author.

Queen's Quarterly, v. LXVII, Autumn, 1960 for "To Be or Not to Be: The Literature of Suicide" by Charles I. Glicksberg. Copyright © 1960 by the author. Reprinted by permission of the author.

Slavic and East-European Journal, v. 31, Summer, 1987. © 1987 by AATSEEL of the U.S., Inc. Reprinted by permission of the publisher.

The Slavonic and East European Review, v. LII, April, 1974. © University of London (School of Slavonic and East European Studies) 1974. Reprinted by permission of the publisher.

Stanford French Review, v. III, Winter, 1979 for "From Cathedral to Book, from Stone to Press: Hugo's Portrait of the Artist in 'Notre-Dame de Paris' " by Stirling Haig. © 1979 by Anma Libri & Co. Reprinted by permission of the publisher and the author.

Tulsa Studies in Women's Literature, v. 6, Fall, 1987. © 1987, The University of Tulsa. Reprinted by permission of the publisher.

THE COPYRIGHTED EXCERPTS IN NCLC, VOLUME 21, WERE REPRINTED FROM THE FOLLOWING BOOKS:

Annenkov, P. V. From *The Extraordinary Decade: Literary Memoirs.* Edited by Arthur P. Mendel, translated by Irwin R. Titunik. The University of Michigan Press, 1968. Copyright © by The University of Michigan 1968. All rights reserved. Reprinted by permission of the publisher.

Auchincloss, Louis. From *Life, Law and Letters: Essays and Sketches.* Houghton Mifflin, 1979. Copyright © 1979 by Louis Auchincloss. All rights reserved. Reprinted by permission of Houghton Mifflin Company.

Bakhtin, Mikhail. From *Problems of Dostoevsky's Poetics.* Edited and translated by Caryl Emerson. University of Minnesota Press, 1984. Copyright © 1984 by the University of Minnesota. All rights reserved. Reprinted by permission of the publisher.

Basa, Enikö Molnár. From *Sándor Petöfi.* Twayne, 1980. Copyright 1980 by Twayne Publishers. All rights reserved. Reprinted with the permission of Twayne Publishers, a division of G. K. Hall & Co., Boston.

Bloom, Harold. From an introduction to *Emily Dickinson.* Edited by Harold Bloom. Chelsea House Publishers, 1985. Introduction copyright © 1985 by Harold Bloom. All rights reserved. Reprinted by permission of the author.

Bogan, Louise. From "A Mystical Poet," in *Emily Dickinson: Three Views.* By Archibald MacLeish, Louise Bogan, and Richard Wilbur. Amherst College Press, 1960. Copyright 1960 Amherst College Press. Reprinted by permission of the publisher and Ruth Limmer, Literary Executor, Estate of Louise Bogan.

Bogan, Louise. From *A Poet's Alphabet: Reflections on the Literary Art and Vocation.* Edited by Robert Phelps and Ruth Limmer. McGraw-Hill Book Company, 1970. Copyright © 1970 by Ruth Limmer as Trustee. All rights reserved. Reprinted by permission of Ruth Limmer, Literary Executor, Estate of Louise Bogan.

Brombert, Victor. From *Victor Hugo and the Visionary Novel.* Cambridge, Mass.: Harvard University Press, 1984. Copyright © 1984 by the President and Fellows of Harvard College. All rights reserved. Excerpted by permission of the publishers.

Cameron, Sharon. From *Lyric Time: Dickinson and the Limits of Genre.* Johns Hopkins University Press, 1979. Copyright © 1979 by The Johns Hopkins University Press. All rights reserved. Reprinted by permission of the publisher.

Canby, Henry Seidel. From *Thoreau.* Houghton Mifflin, 1939. Copyright, 1939, by Henry Seidel Canby. Renewed 1967 by Marion G. Canby. All rights reserved. Reprinted by permission of Houghton Mifflin Company.

Chekhov, A. P. From a letter in *"Fathers and Sons" by Ivan Turgenev: The Author on the Novel, Contemporary Reactions, Essays in Criticism.* Edited and translated by Ralph E. Matlaw. A Norton Critical Edition. Norton, 1966. Copyright © 1966 by W. W. Norton & Company, Inc. Reprinted by permission of W. W. Norton & Company, Inc.

Chernyshevsky, N. G. From "The Russian at the 'Rendez-vous': Reflections upon Reading Mr. Turgenev's 'Asya'," translated by Ralph E. Matlaw, in *Belinsky, Chernyshevsky, and Dobrolyubov: Selected Criticism.* Edited by Ralph E. Matlaw. Dutton, 1962. Copyright, ©, 1962, by E. P. Dutton & Co., Inc. All rights reserved. Reprinted by permission of the publisher, E. P. Dutton, a division of NAL Penguin Inc.

Crane, Hart. From *The Complete Poems and Selected Letters and Prose of Hart Crane.* Liveright, 1966. Copyright 1933, 1958, 1966 by Liveright Publishers, New York. Reprinted by permission of Liveright Publishing Corporation.

Davies, Ruth. From *The Great Books of Russia.* University of Oklahoma Press, 1968. Copyright 1968 by the University of Oklahoma Press. Reprinted by permission of the publisher.

Dickinson, Emily. Selections from *The Poems of Emily Dickinson,* edited by Thomas H. Johnson, and *The Letters of Emily Dickinson,* edited by Thomas H. Johnson and Theodora W. Ward. Cambridge, Mass.: The Belknap Press of Harvard University Press, 1951, 1955, 1958. Copyright 1951, 1955, 1958, renewed 1979, 1983, 1986 by The President and Fellows of Harvard College. Reprinted by permission of Harvard University Press, The Trustees of Amherst College and Houghton Mifflin Company./ Selections from *The Complete Poems of Emily Dickinson,* edited by Thomas H. Johnson. Little, Brown, 1960. Copyright 1929 by Martha Dickinson Bianchi. Copyright © renewed 1957 by Mary L. Hampson. Reprinted by permission of Little, Brown & Company.

Dostoevski, Fedor Mikhailovich. From *The Diary of a Writer, Vol. I.* Edited and translated by Boris Brasol. Charles Scribner's Sons, 1949. Translation copyright 1949 Charles Scribner's Sons. Copyright renewed © 1976 Maxwell Fassett, Executor of the Estate of Boris Brasol. Reprinted with permission of Charles Scribner's Sons, an imprint of Macmillan Publishing Company.

Dostoevski, Fedor Mikhailovich. From an extract from a letter in *Letters of Fyodor Michailovitch Dostoevsky to His Family and Friends.* Translated by Ethel Colburn Mayne. Horizon Press, 1961. Copyright © 1961 by Horizon Press.

Elliott, Brian. From an introduction to *Adam Lindsay Gordon.* By Adam Lindsay Gordon. Sun Books, 1973. Copyright © Brian Elliott, 1973. Reprinted by permission of Brian Elliott.

Fetterley, Judith. From "Lydia Sigourney (1791-1865): 'The Father'," in *Provisions: A Reader from 19th-Century American Women.* Edited by Judith Fetterley. Indiana University Press, 1985. Copyright © 1985 by Judith Fetterley. All rights reserved. Reprinted by permission of the publisher.

Flaubert, Gustave. From a letter in *Flaubert and Turgenev, a Friendship in Letters: The Complete Correspondence.* Edited and translated by Barbara Beaumont. The Athlone Press, 1985. Copyright © 1985 Barbara Beaumont. All rights reserved. Reprinted by permission of the publisher.

Ford, Thomas W. From *Heaven Beguiles the Tired: Death in the Poetry of Emily Dickinson.* University of Alabama Press, 1966. Copyright © 1966 by University of Alabama Press. Reprinted by permission of the publisher.

Franklin, H. Bruce. From *Future Perfect: American Science Fiction of the Nineteenth Century.* Revised edition. Oxford University Press, 1978. Copyright © 1966, 1968, 1978 by Oxford University Press, Inc. Copyright © 1988 by H. Bruce Franklin. Reprinted by permission of the publisher.

Freeborn, Richard. From *Turgenev: The Novelists's Novelist, a Study.* Oxford University Press, London, 1960. © Oxford University Press, 1960. Reprinted by permission of the publisher.

Frye, Northrop. From *Major Writers of America.* Harcourt Brace Jovanovich, 1962. © 1962 by Harcourt Brace Jovanovich, Inc. Reprinted by permission of the publisher.

Gassner, John. From *Masters of the Drama.* Third revised edition. Dover Publications, Inc., 1954. Copyright 1940, 1954 by Random House, Inc. Renewed 1968, 1982 by Mollie Gassner. Reprinted by permission of Random House, Inc.

Grant, Richard B. From *The Perilous Quest: Image, Myth, and Prophecy in the Narratives of Victor Hugo.* Duke University Press, 1968. Copyright © 1968 by Duke University Press, Durham, NC. Reprinted by permission of the publisher.

Green, H. M. From *A History of Australian Literature: Pure and Applied, 1789-1923, Vol. I.* Revised edition. Angus & Robertson, 1984. Copyright © Dorothy Green 1962, 1984. Reprinted by permission of Angus & Robertson Publishers.

Griffith, Clark. From *The Long Shadow: Emily Dickinson's Tragic Poetry.* Princeton University Press, 1964. Copyright © 1964 by Princeton University Press. All rights reserved. Reprinted with permission of the publisher.

Grossman, Leonid. From "The Stylistics of 'Stavrogin's Confession': A Study of the New Chapter of 'The Possessed'," translated by Katherine Tiernan O'Connor, in *Critical Essays on Dostoevsky.* Edited by Robin Feuer Miller. G. K. Hall & Co., 1986. Copyright 1986 by Robin Feuer Miller. All rights reserved. Reprinted with the permission of the publisher.

Haight, Gordon S. From *Mrs. Sigourney: The Sweet Singer of Hartford.* Yale University Press, 1930. Copyright 1930 by Yale University Press. Renewed 1957 by Gordon S. Haight. All rights reserved. Reprinted by permission of the publisher.

Herzen, A. I. From a letter in *"Fathers and Sons" by Ivan Turgenev: The Author on the Novel, Contemporary Reactions, Essays in Criticism.* Edited and translated by Ralph E. Matlaw. A Norton Critical Edition. Norton, 1966. Copyright © 1966 by W. W. Norton & Company, Inc. Reprinted by permission of W. W. Norton & Company, Inc.

Higginson, T. W. From a letter in *The Letters of Emily Dickinson, Vol. II.* Edited by Thomas H. Johnson. Cambridge, Mass.: The Belknap Press of Harvard University Press, 1958. Copyright © 1958, renewed 1986 by the President and Fellows of Harvard College. Reprinted by permission of Boston Public Library.

Hingley, Ronald. From *The Undiscovered Dostoyevsky.* Hamish Hamilton, 1962. Copyright © 1962 by Ronald Hingley. Reprinted by permission of Peters, Fraser & Dunlop Group Ltd.

Johnson, Thomas H. From *Emily Dickinson: An Interpretive Biography.* Cambridge, Mass.: The Belknap Press of Harvard University Press, 1955. Copyright © 1955 by the President and Fellows of Harvard College. Renewed 1983 by Thomas Herbert Johnson. All rights reserved. Excerpted by permission of the publishers.

Jones, D. Mervyn. From *Five Hungarian Writers.* Oxford at the Clarendon Press, 1966. © Oxford University Press, 1966. Reprinted by permission of Oxford University Press.

Jones, Malcolm V. From *Dostoyevsky: The Novel of Discord.* Barnes & Noble Books, 1976. Copyright © 1976 Malcolm V. Jones. All rights reserved. Reprinted by permission of the publisher.

Josephson, Matthew. From *Victor Hugo: A Realistic Biography of the Great Romantic.* Doubleday, Doran & Co., Inc., 1942. Copyright 1942, renewed 1969 by Matthew Josephson. All rights reserved. Reprinted by permission of Doubleday, a division of Bantam, Doubleday, Dell Publishing Group, Inc.

Kagan-Kans, Eva. From *Hamlet and Dox Quixote: Turgenev's Ambivalent Vision.* Mouton, 1975. © copyright 1975 Mouton & Co., Publishers. Reprinted by permission of Mouton de Gruyter, a Division of Walter de Gruyter & Co.

Kazin, Alfred. From "Writing in the Dark," in *Henry David Thoreau: Studies and Commentaries.* Walter Harding, George Brenner, Paul A. Doyle, eds. Fairleigh Dickinson University Press, 1972. © 1972 by Alfred Kazin. Reprinted by permission of the publisher and the author.

Kazin, Alfred. From *The Inmost Leaf: A Selection of Essays.* Harcourt Brace Jovanovich, 1955. Copyright 1947, renewed 1975 by Alfred Kazin. Reprinted by permission of Harcourt Brace Jovanovich, Inc.

Keller, Karl. From "Notes on Sleeping with Emily Dickinson," in *Feminist Critics Read Emily Dickinson.* Edited by Suzanne Juhasz. Indiana University Press, 1983. Copyright © 1983 by Indiana University Press. All rights reserved. Reprinted by permission of the publisher.

Lindberg-Seyersted, Brita. From *The Voice of the Poet: Aspects of Style in the Poetry of Emily Dickinson.* Cambridge, Mass.: Harvard University Press, 1968. © 1968 Brita Lindberg-Seyersted. Reprinted by permission of the author.

Lowell, Amy. From *Poetry and Poets: Essays*. Houghton Mifflin, 1930. Copyright, 1930, by Houghton Mifflin Company. Renewed 1958 by Harvey H. Bundy and G. D'Andelot Belin. All rights reserved. Reprinted by permission of Houghton Mifflin Company.

MacRae, C. F. From *Adam Lindsay Gordon*. Twayne, 1968. Copyright 1968 by Twayne Publishers. All rights reserved. Reprinted with the permission of Twayne Publishers, Inc., a division of G. K. Hall & Co., Boston.

Maurois, André. From *The Art of Writing*. Translated by Gerard Hopkins. E. P. Dutton & Co., Inc., 1960. English translation copyright, ©, 1960 by E. P. Dutton. All rights reserved. Reprinted by permission of the author and the author's agents, Scott Meredith Literary Agency, Inc., 845 Third Avenue, New York, NY 10022.

Mikhailovski, Nikolai. From an extract from "Criticism Before the Revolution," in *Dostoyevski in Russian Literary Criticism: 1846-1956*. By Vladimir Seduro. Columbia University Press, 1957. Copyright © 1957 Columbia University Press. Renewed 1985 by the President and Fellows of Harvard College, Harvard University.

Mochulsky, Konstantin. From *Dostoevsky: His Life and Work*. Translated by Michael A. Minihan. Princeton University Press, 1967. Copyright © 1967 by Princeton University Press. All rights reserved. Reprinted with permission of the publisher.

Moskowitz, Sam. From *Explorers of the Infinite: Shapers of Science Fiction*. World Publishing Co., 1963. Copyright © 1963, 1959, 1958, 1957 by Sam Moskowitz. Copyright © 1960 by Ziff-Davis Publishing Co. Reprinted by permission of the author.

Németh, Béla G. From "Sándor Petőfi (1823-1849)," in *A History of Hungarian Literature*. By István Nemeskürty and others, edited by Tibor Klaniczay. Corvina, 1983 © Tibor Klaniczay 1982. Reprinted by permission of the editor.

Pattee, Fred Lewis. From *The Development of the American Short Story: An Historical Survey*. Harper & Brothers, 1923. Copyright 1923 by Harper & Row, Publishers, Inc. Renewed 1951 by Fred Lewis Pattee. Reprinted by permission of Harper & Row, Publishers, Inc.

Paul, Sherman. From *The Shores of America: Thoreau's Inward Exploration*. University of Illinois Press, 1958. © 1958 by The Board of Trustees of the University of Illinois. Renewed 1986 by Sherman Paul. Reprinted by permission of the publisher and the author.

Perry, Henry Ten Eyck. From *Masters of Dramatic Comedy and Their Social Themes*. Cambridge, Mass.: Harvard University Press, 1939. Copyright 1939 by the President and Fellows of Harvard College. Renewed 1966 by Henry Ten Eyck Perry. Excerpted by permission of the publishers.

Peterson, Dale E. From *The Clement Vision: Poetic Realism in Turgenev and James*. Kennikat Press, 1975. Copyright © 1975 by Kennikat Press Corp. All rights reserved. Reprinted by permission of Gateway/Associated Faculty Press, Inc.

Porter, David T. From *The Art of Emily Dickinson's Early Poetry*. Cambridge, Mass.: Harvard University Press, 1966. Copyright © 1966 by the President and Fellows of Harvard College. All rights reserved. Excerpted by permission of the publishers.

Poulet, Georges. From *Studies in Human Time*. Translated by Elliott Coleman. Johns Hopkins Press, 1956. © 1956, The Johns Hopkins Press. Renewed 1984 by Louis D. Rubin, Jr. Reprinted by permission of the publisher.

Pritchett, V. S. From *The Living Novel & Later Appreciations*. Revised edition. Random House, 1964. Copyright © 1964, 1975 by V. S. Pritchett. All rights reserved. Reprinted by permission of Sterling Lord Literistic, Inc.

Rahv, Philip. From *Image and Idea: Fourteen Essays on Literary Themes*. New Directions, 1949. Copyright 1949 by Philip Rahv. Renewed 1976 by Betty T. Rahv. Reprinted by permission of the Literary Estate of Philip Rahv.

Rich, Adrienne. From *The Fact of a Doorframe: Poems Selected and New, 1950-1984*. Norton, 1984. Copyright © 1975, 1978 by W. W. Norton & Company, Inc. Copyright © 1981, 1984 by Adrienne Rich. Reprinted by permission of W. W. Norton & Company, Inc.

Rich, Adrienne. From *The Fact of a Doorframe: Poems Selected and New, 1950-1984*. Norton, 1984. Copyright © 1975, 1978 by W. W. Norton & Company, Inc. Copyright © 1981, 1984 by Adrienne Rich. Reprinted by permission of W. W. Norton & Company, Inc. and the author.

Ripp, Victor. From *Turgenev's Russia: From "Notes of a Hunter" to "Fathers and Sons."* Cornell University Press, 1980. Copyright © 1980 by Cornell University. All rights reserved. Used by permission of the publisher, Cornell University Press.

Rourke, Constance. From *American Humor: A Study of the National Character*. Harcourt Brace Jovanovich, 1931. Copyright 1931 by Harcourt Brace Jovanovich, Inc. Renewed 1959 by Alice D. Fore. Reprinted by permission of the publisher.

Schapiro, Leonard. From *Turgenev: His Life and Times*. Random House, 1978. Copyright © 1978 by Leonard Schapiro. All rights reserved. Reprinted by permission of Random House, Inc. In Canada by the Literary Estate of Leonard Schapiro.

Slonim, Marc. From *The Epic of Russian Literature: From Its Origins through Tolstoy*. Oxford University Press, 1950. Copyright 1950 by Oxford University Press, Inc. Renewed 1977 by Tatiana Slonim. Reprinted by permission of the publisher.

Tate, Allen. From *Reactionary Essays on Poetry and Ideas*. Charles Scribner's Sons, Ltd., 1936. Copyright, 1936, by Charles Scribner's Sons. Renewed 1964 by Allen Tate. Reprinted by permission of the Literary Estate of Allen Tate.

Todd, Mabel Loomis. From a letter in *The Years and Hours of Emily Dickinson, Vol. II*. By Jay Leyda. Yale University Press, 1960. © 1960 by Yale University Press, Inc. All rights reserved. Reprinted by permission of Loomis-Wilder Family Papers, Manuscripts and Archives, Yale University Library.

Tolstoy, Lev. From an extract from a letter in *Tolstoy's Letters: 1828-1879, Vol. I.* Edited and translated by R. F. Christian. Charles Scribner's Sons, 1978. Selection, English translation and editorial matter Copyright © 1978 R. F. Christian. All rights reserved. Reprinted with the permission of Charles Scribner's Sons, an imprint of Macmillan Publishing Company.

Tunimanov, V. A. From "The Narrator in 'The Devils'," translated by Susanne Fusso, in *Dostoevsky: New Perspectives.* Edited by Robert Louis Jackson. Prentice-Hall Inc., 1984. © 1984 by Prentice-Hall, Inc., Englewood Cliffs, NJ. All rights reserved.

Turgenev, Ivan. From a letter in *"Fathers and Sons" by Ivan Turgenev: The Author on the Novel, Contemporary Reactions, Essays in Criticism.* Edited and translated by Ralph E. Matlaw. A Norton Critical Edition. Norton, 1966. Copyright © 1966 by W. W. Norton & Company, Inc. Reprinted by permission of W. W. Norton & Company, Inc.

Turgenev, Ivan. From *Literary Reminiscences and Autobiographical Fragments.* Translated by David Magarshack. Farrar, Straus and Cudahy, 1958. Copyright © 1958 by Farrar, Straus & Cudahy, Inc. Renewal copyright © 1986 by Elsie D. Magarshack. Reprinted by permission of Farrar, Straus and Giroux, Inc.

Ward, Patricia A. From *The Medievalism of Victor Hugo.* Pennsylvania State University Press, 1975. Copyright © 1975, The Pennsylvania State University Press, University Park, PA. All rights reserved. Reprinted by permission of the publisher.

Wasiolek, Edward. From *Dostoevsky: The Major Fiction.* M.I.T. Press, 1964. Copyright © 1964 by The Massachusetts Institute of Technology. All rights reserved. Reprinted by permission of The MIT Press, Cambridge, MA.

Watts, Emily Stipes. From *The Poetry of American Women from 1632 to 1945.* University of Texas Press, 1977. Copyright © 1977 by University of Texas Press. All rights reserved. Reprinted by permission of the publisher and the author.

Wellek, René. From "Fathers and Sons," in *World Masterpieces, Vol. 2.* Edited by Maynard Mack. Revised edition. Norton, 1965. Copyright © 1965, 1956, renewed 1974 by W. W. Norton & Company, Inc. Reprinted by permission of W. W. Norton & Company, Inc.

Wilder, Thornton. From *American Characteristics and Other Essays.* Edited by Donald Gallup. Harper & Row, 1979. Copyright 1952 by Thornton Wilder. Compilation copyright © 1979 by Union Trust Company, Executor of the will of the Estate of Thornton Wilder. Reprinted by special permission of Harper & Row, Publishers, Inc. and the estate of Thornton Wilder.

Wilson, Edmund. From "Turgenev and the Life-Giving Drop," in *Literary Reminiscences and Autobiographical Fragments.* By Ivan Turgenev, translated by David Magarshack. Farrar, Straus and Cudahy, 1958. Copyright © 1957 by Edmund Wilson. Renewal copyright © 1985 by Helen Miranda Wilson. Reprinted by permission of Farrar, Straus and Giroux, Inc.

Winters, Yvor. From *In Defense of Reason.* The Swallow Press Inc., 1947. Copyright 1937 by Yvor Winters. Copyright 1938, 1943 by New Directions. Copyright renewed © 1965 by Yvor Winters. Reprinted by permission of Ohio University Press/Swallow Press.

Wright, Judith. From *Preoccupations in Australian Poetry.* Oxford University Press, Melbourne, 1965. Reprinted by kind permission of the author.

PERMISSION TO REPRINT PHOTOGRAPHS APPEARING IN NCLC, VOLUME 21, WAS RECEIVED FROM THE FOLLOWING SOURCES:

The Bettmann Archive, Inc.: p. 1

Illustration by Ferdinand Huszti Horvath: pp. 240, 251

ISBN 0-8103-5821-2